HORRIBLE HISTORIES

BLITZED
BRITS

Terry Deary Illustrated by Martin Brown & Kate Sheppard

SCHOLASTIC

This book is for the staff of the Durham Light Infantry Museum
in Durham City, with thanks.

Scholastic Children's Books,
Euston House, 24 Eversholt Street,
London NW1 1DB, UK

A division of Scholastic Ltd
London ~ New York ~ Toronto ~ Sydney ~ Auckland
Mexico City ~ New Delhi ~ Hong Kong

First published in the UK by Scholastic Ltd, 1994
This edition published 2016

ISBN 978 1407 16701 5

Printed and bound by CPI Group (UK) Ltd, Croydon, CR0 4YY

4 6 8 10 9 7 5 3

www.scholastic.co.uk

CONTENTS

Introduction

Once upon a time history lessons were all about things that happened hundreds of years ago. If you weren't dead then you weren't history. And it's pretty hard to be lively about dead people. History was BORING.

Then, in the 1980s, teachers suddenly realized that yesterday is History … and last week is practically ancient history! Parents are as interesting as Julius Caesar. History lessons changed … you couldn't interview Julius Caesar, but you could interview parents …

Of course grandparents have even older memories.

Still, they were pretty young at the time. They may have known what happened, but they didn't understand exactly why it happened as it did.

And teachers can't answer such vital questions because their teachers never told them the answers.

So, what you need is a history book that tells you the answers to the **really** important questions. How did people live? And **why** did they live like that? Then you can understand your history ... **and** your grandparents! What you need is a book called *Horrible Histories – The Blitzed Brits.*

And, by a strange chance, you just happen to have started reading it! So carry on...

Blitzed Brit timeline

27 January 1923 First meeting of the Nazi party in Germany. Leader, Adolf Hitler.

15 March 1933 Adolf Hitler and his Nazis take power in Germany. They rule by terror.

3 January 1938 Nervous. British Government fears Nazi invasion and promises to give a gas mask to every British schoolchild.

31 March 1939 British Prime Minister, Neville Chamberlain, makes a promise to Poland ... *If Germany invades you then Britain and France will help.*

1 September 1939 Germany invades Poland. The British Government, afraid of war, orders women and children in the cities to be 'evacuated' into the safe countryside.

3 September 1939 Britain declares war on Germany – World War Two begins. The air-raid sirens sound for the first time. People rush around like headless chickens looking for shelter – but it's a false alarm.

8 January 1940 It's the coldest winter for half a century. The Thames freezes. Ships bringing food to Britain are being sunk by German submarines. The Government fears a food shortage … so the first foods go on ration.

1 February 1940 A 'blackout' is ordered. No lights to be shown at night so enemy bombers can't see where to drop their bombs. Deaths on the blacked-out roads have doubled! Speed limit of 20 m.p.h. for cars at night.

10 May 1940 Germany attacks Holland and Belgium. Their armies march towards France – and the English Channel … Britain next? Winston Churchill is elected Prime Minister.

14 May 1940 Men aged 17 to 65 invited to join the Local Defence Volunteers – a million join. Later known as the Home Guard – better known as *Dad's Army*.

30 May 1940 The beaten British Army comes home from Dunkirk – they're picked up on the French beaches by hundreds of little boats from England.

31 May 1940 A new law says:
• All signposts have to be removed.
• Church bells can only be rung as a sign of invasion.
• All foreigners in the country must be locked up or made to report to the police.

18 June 1940 Winston Churchill tells the people that the battle in France is lost … *I expect that the Battle of Britain is about to begin. The whole fury and might of the enemy must soon be turned on us.*

10 July 1940 First of the large air raids. This is the real start of the Battle of Britain in the skies. Lady Reading (head of Women's Voluntary Service) appeals to families to give up their aluminium pots and pans to make aeroplanes. *We can all have the thrill of thinking, when we hear*

the news of a battle in the air, 'Perhaps it was my saucepan that made a part of that Hurricane plane.'

16 July 1940 Hitler signs order for Operation Sealion the invasion of England. Order 2a is the problem. 'The RAF must be eliminated.' Easier said than done! Sealion never happens.

13 August 1940 All-out German air raids lasting two days. Britain says that 185 enemy aircraft were shot down. (The true number was 60.)

24 August 1940 The Germans bomb London by mistake after Hitler had told them not to! So the British bomb Berlin in revenge ... so the Germans bomb London ... and so it goes on.

7 September 1940 Code word 'Cromwell' passed to home defence forces. This meant, 'Be on your guard – it's a good night for an invasion'. But some officers thought it meant, 'The invasion has started'! They blew up bridges – and themselves – and generally panicked everyone.

7 September 1940 Germany is losing too many bombers in daylight raids. They switch to night raids. This is the real start of the blitz.

14 November 1940 Air raids switch to Coventry for a while. This is where a lot of British war machinery is being made. Next morning nearly everyone claimed to know someone who'd been killed or injured in the city.

10 May 1941 Heaviest – and last – big bombing raid on London until 1944. House of Commons wrecked. Hitler 1 – Guy Fawkes 0.

1 June 1941 Clothing is rationed – but not **only** because clothes are in short supply! It was also to set clothing workers free to work in war factories.

22 June 1941 Germany invades Russia. This was a big mistake and probably lost them the War. Hitler could beat the Russian Army – he couldn't beat the Russian winter. Snow 1 – Hitler 0.

September 1941 The Government orders that most iron railings should be taken down and the metal used for the war effort – Buckingham Palace included.

December 1941 Japanese aircraft sink American ships in the Pacific Ocean so United States of America joins the war on Britain's side – at last.

February 1942 It's illegal to decorate cups, saucers and plates for sale – it's a waste of precious manufacturing time that could be spent making war items.

February 1942 Soap is put on ration – one small bar of soap had to last you four weeks. (Some scruffy kids could make it last a year!)

13 March 1942 The end of private motoring – only essential users will be allowed petrol. But, remember, only one family in ten owned a car anyway.

June 1942 It's illegal to make bedspreads and table-cloths.

2 February 1943 German soldiers

surrender in Stalingrad (Russia). The War is turning against them.

8 September 1943 Now Italy declares war on their old ally, Germany!

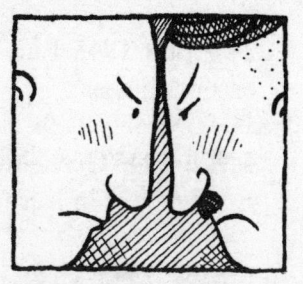

December 1943 Eighteen-year-old boys who don't join the army are made to work in coal mines. Mr Ernest Bevin thought up this law, so the young miners became known as Bevin Boys.

6 June 1944 Britain and her allies invade Europe.

IT'S NOT AS BLACK AS THE BLACKOUT

16 June 1944 The first Flying Bombs land on London. A new blitz is beginning. People nickname the V1 (Vee One) rockets 'Doodlebugs' and 'Buzz bombs'. But V1 really stands for 'Revenge Weapon 1'.

8 September 1944 The first V2 rockets arrive. Quieter and more destructive than the V1s … but the Government doesn't admit there are such things until 10 November!

14 November 1944 Home Guard abolished. The danger of invasion has passed.

WE SHOWED 'EM

24 April 1945 End of blackout except on coast.

6 May 1945 Germany surrenders – end of war in Europe.

8 May 1945 Victory in Europe (V.E. Day) – holiday and parties.

6 August 1945 The United States drops the first atomic bomb on Japan – Japan surrenders shortly after. End of World War Two.

Things they shouldn't have said

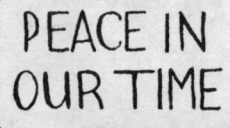

Neville Chamberlain, British Prime Minister, in 1938 after signing a peace treaty with Germany

R.H. Naylor,
astrologer in the Sunday Express

Beat the Blitz

Could you have survived an air raid? Answer these questions to see what your chances would be…

1 The air-raid sirens sound. Planes appear overhead. You are a long way from an air raid shelter. As bombs fall do you …

a) run for home (shouting 'I want my Mam!')

b) stand still (and cross your fingers)

c) lie down where you are

2 An incendiary bomb lands near your house. This sort of bomb doesn't explode. It just burns fiercely. As the fire spreads towards your house, do you …

a) pour a bucket of water over it

b) go to your nearest shelter and let it burn

c) shovel sand or soil over it

3 A bomb lands in your back garden. It sinks into the soil but does not explode – yet. Do you …

a) throw stones at it so it will go off and not catch some unsuspecting passer-by

b) tiptoe to your nearest shelter – any shelter except the one in the garden!

c) tell your local ARP Warden

15

4 As a raid starts you head for the Anderson Shelter in your garden. It is half underground and has a thick cushion of soil over the roof. You should be safer here than in the house. But you realise that the family cat is missing. Do you …

a) go out and look for it and stay out until you find it

b) stay in the shelter but leave the shelter door open so the cat can find its own way in

c) shut the shelter door

5 Do you take your gas mask with you …

a) whenever you hear the air–raid warnings sound

b) whenever you go out and have a spare hand to carry it

c) always

6 An ARP warden walks down the street spinning a rattle of the sort that football supporters used to use. You don't know what this means. Do you …

a) shout 'Up United!' and follow him to see if there's a game on

b) ask someone what it means

c) put your gas mask on

7 You wake up to the sound of bombs exploding. A raid is happening and there's been no warning! In the blackout you can see explosions coming closer and closer.

16

Do you …

a) watch to see where the next bomb will land

b) get dressed and head for the nearest shelter

c) grab your gas mask and hide under your bed

8 You want to make your shelter more comfortable. Do you …

a) take an electric cable from the house so you can have electric light and an electric fire

b) fit a wooden door to keep the draught out

c) take a candle for light and a blanket to put across the door for draughts

9 You have no shelter at home. Do you …

a) shelter upstairs in your bedroom

b) go to a public shelter

c) turn a downstairs room into a bedroom and shelter there

Answers: Mostly a) – the bad news is that you'd probably be too dead to read this. Maybe you have a death wish, maybe you haven't listened to the Government advice, maybe you panic easily … or maybe you're just a bit dim.

Anyway, if you are an a) person you probably wouldn't survive the blitz unless you were very, very lucky. It wouldn't be wise to run around the streets in a blackout, to treat bombs like big fireworks or to stand near a window during a raid – a nearby blast might **not** knock your house down but the flying glass **would** shred you!

Mostly b) – like many people in the War you knew what you were supposed to do but sometimes got a bit careless or forgetful. If you were lucky you could make a b) mistake and get away with it. On the other hand it could be the last mistake you ever made! The only good news is that you're not as thick as the people who answer a).

Mostly c) – you've followed all the Government advice. This gives you the best chance of surviving. Of course, it's easy to read this and think how clever you are. It's different actually being caught in an air raid. Even people who knew the advice could panic and make a mistake that cost them their lives.

Blitzed bomb shelters

Before the War there was a really rotten report on air raids. The Air Ministry reckoned there would be …

700 tons of bombs dropped on British cities **every** day
600,000 deaths a year

So they …

• printed a million burial forms – just to be on the safe side

• started to stockpile hundreds of cardboard coffins
No wonder the British people were worried!

(The Air Ministry was wrong! In fact 300,000 died during the six years of the war … more than half of them in London.)

The Ministry of Home Security took charge of Air Raid Precautions (ARP) and announced:

Ministry of Home Security leaflet 3 September 1940

The Government wouldn't build your shelter. The local council dumped the bits at your door and left you to get on with it.

Bomb shelter fact file

1 The Government banned people from sheltering in the London Underground train stations during an air raid. But they couldn't stop people buying a half-pence platform ticket and refusing to come up! In the end the Government dropped the ban.

2 By the end of September almost 200,000 people were using the Underground for shelter every night. They were fitted out with bunk beds and a library service was provided.

3 Some stations had closed off their toilets. If you wanted to use the toilet then you probably had to take a train to the next station. Soon 'bucket' toilets were provided. Yeuch!

4 Christmas 1940 saw the Underground stations decorated with streamers, and Christmas parties were held during the air raids.

5 If you wanted to stay in your home during the bombing then you could have a Morrison shelter. It was like a steel table with wire-mesh sides and a mattress underneath. Two adults and two small children could squeeze under – but one very fat person could get stuck!

6 In an air raid, any shelter was better than none. In a town in south-west England a young mother was caught in the street with her baby. She quickly popped the baby into a dustbin.

7 One father said, 'We don't need a shelter. Those Anderson shelters are just corrugated iron. They're no more than garden sheds. Our house is stronger.' Then he saw a house that had been flattened by a bomb. The Anderson shelter next to it had survived. He bought one the same day!

8 In Middlesbrough a popular verse gave a bit of advice:

IN A RAID, IF YOU MUST LOSE YOUR HEAD
REMEMBER THE THINGS THAT YOU HAVE READ
YOU'LL KNOW WHAT TO DO
FOR THERE'LL ONLY BE TWO
KINDS OF PEOPLE
THE QUICK AND THE DEAD

9 One of the nastiest facts about the air raids was that your house was unguarded while you went into a shelter. If your house was damaged then it could well be 'looted' – anything worthwhile was stolen. And not just by professional burglars. Neighbours might grab something of yours – so did the Air Raid Precaution Wardens, the demolition men – even the police! One family left their home when an unexploded bomb landed in their potato patch – the bomb was removed and the family returned … but there wasn't a single potato to be found!

10 Even a bombed house played its part in the war effort! The rubble was carted off to the countryside to build new runways for the Royal Air Force.

Did you know?
Sand bags were kept at the foot of lamp posts in towns. If there was a fire-bomb then you knew where to look for sand to smother it with. Good idea? Well … dogs use lamp posts as toilets. They loved the sand bags! So when you grabbed a sand bag it was always stinking

and usually mouldy – and the smelly sand often fell out of the bottom!

Barrage balloons

The blitzed Brits were especially afraid of dive-bombers. These aeroplanes swooped low to drop their bombs. To stop this sort of bombing, barrage balloons were invented.

These were huge, silvery balloons, each as big as a house. They were filled with gas and floated over towns, held down by heavy steel cables. Dive-bombers were torn apart by these cables.

Many people felt safe under the cover of these silver cigar-shaped balloons. One boy described them as 'herds of silver elephants' as they rose, glittering in the sun. But they also caused some problems …

Five fearful facts about barrage balloons
1 Sometimes the cables on a balloon snapped and the balloon floated away. They made good target practice for fighter planes.
2 Have you ever blown up a party balloon and let go of the end? If a barrage balloon got a split in it then it would charge round the sky in a similar way.
3 A balloon could catch fire – from a lightning strike or an enemy aeroplane attack. Then it could start to come down on the town below. It could be as deadly as a bomb landing on your roof!
4 A loose balloon trailed its wires. If they caught overhead power cables they could leave a town without power for several hours.

5 A trailing cable caught a Women's Royal Air Force worker (WRAF) on the back of the head. She cried with the pain and held her head in her hands. It was just as well she did … when she got to hospital her neck was found to be broken. If she hadn't held her head straight she would have died.

A blitzed ghost story

Thousands of people died in the blitz. It's not surprising that many people have stories about death and stories of the supernatural …

Megan Davies woke up suddenly. It was a nightmare that had shaken her from a peaceful sleep. She struggled to remember it. The details were faint, but the young woman knew it was something to do with her mother. There was danger in that dream. Perhaps even death.

It was still dark in the Welsh village cottage. Megan struck a match and lit the oil lamp. She dressed quickly and hurried down to breakfast.

'Penny for your thoughts,' her mother said as the young woman chewed slowly on her toast.

'What was that?'

'I said, what are you thinking about? You look worried.'

Megan looked away. 'Nothing, Mam. '

'There's something on your mind. What is it?'

Megan didn't want to tell her mother about the dream. 'I've got to get to work, Mam.'

'I want to know what's wrong – a problem shared is a problem halved.'

'I'll tell you when I get home tonight, Mam,' Megan promised. She grabbed her hat and ran for the bus.

She worked as well as she could. But the gloom of the dream dampened her day. As the bus climbed the valley towards her home that evening she prayed softly to herself. She prayed that she'd never have to tell her mother about that dream.

And, when she reached home, it seemed as if her prayer had been answered. Her mother was more worried about Megan being late than about her daughter's morning mood. 'Got a rabbit from the butcher. Nearly gone dry in the oven it has!'

'Sorry, Mam!'

'Pat's eaten hers.'

Megan smiled at the young evacuee girl. 'Rabbit pie and a safe house. You're a lucky girl.'

Pat looked back with a slight frown. 'No bomb shelter,' was all she said.

Megan sighed. 'You don't need bomb shelters in the country, Pat. Don't worry ... Mr Hitler isn't going to waste his bombs on our little village.'

Pat didn't look too sure.

And it was Pat who ran down the stairs later that night crying, 'German bomber! German bomber!'

'Just a bad dream,' Mrs Davies said.

'No!' the girl said.

Megan turned her head. There was the noise of an aircraft engine. 'Probably one of the RAF out on patrol,' she said.

'No!' Pat whined. 'I heard them every night back home! I know what they sound like!' She dived under the only shelter the house had – the piano.

Megan ran to the kitchen window. Her mother followed. There was a bright flash on the mountainside.

Seconds later came the roar of the bomb. The glass rattled in the old frames. 'He's coming up from Swansea!' she called to her mother. 'Dropping his bombs in the fields so he'll get away faster. Don't worry!'

But Megan herself was terrified. This was the dream that she'd had last night. A second flash lit the valley. Closer this time. Then a third.

Megan screamed. 'Mam! Under the piano!'

But Mrs Davies stayed in the kitchen, too terrified to move.

When the bomb hit the house she had no chance.

Megan and Pat survived thanks to the heavy piano.

When the young woman woke in hospital they told her the terrible news. Her mother had died.

Megan looked up to the ceiling. 'Oh, God,' she murmured. 'I prayed that I wouldn't have to tell Mam about that dream. Now I never will … I never can. Was that your answer to my prayer?'

Did You Know?

1 On Friday 1 September 1939 the service to the 2,000 televisions in Britain was stopped. There was no television again until 1946. Seven years without television ... today some people can't go seven minutes!

2 Men who joined the armed forces were paid just two shillings (10p) a day at the start of the War. This was increased to three shillings (15p) by the end of the War. Many families were poor and hungry as a result. Some companies and councils paid the men just the same even though they had gone off to fight in the armed forces. (Though one mean council sacked the men so they didn't have to pay them!)

3 Some men didn't have to go off to fight if they didn't want to. Their jobs in Britain were too important. One job considered too important was teaching!

4 Signposts were taken down. The idea was that if enemy soldiers entered the country (or parachuted in) they wouldn't know exactly where they were. Milestones were removed. Shop signs were painted over if they gave a clue as to where they were – 'The Bunchester Bakery' would become 'The _____ Bakery' and so on. As a result a lot of British people got lost! These rules lasted until October 1944.

5 Names of stations were removed from platforms. You didn't know where the train had stopped unless you lived there. A helpful railway poster suggested …

6 There was a shortage of beer during the War. And when there was beer to drink there sometimes weren't any glasses to drink it from. In some pubs you could only get a drink if you took your own glass!

28

7 There was a new dance invented called *The Blackout Stroll*. Take four steps forward, three short steps and a hop … then the lights go out. You change partners in the dark and then the lights come on.

8 If you had more than one dog in the house during an air raid then you were advised to shut them in separate rooms – this was to stop them biting one another in the noise and panic.

9 The Prime Minister, Winston Churchill, wanted to know why people complained about their small meat ration. He was shown a typical meat ration. 'That would be enough for me!' he said. The trouble was he thought he was looking at a day's supply of meat – but it was meant to last a week!

10 Before the War a song was banned because it was too nasty to Germany! It was called, *Even Hitler Had A Mother*. Then, even though Britain was at war, songwriters were nervous about writing anti-German songs.

The bothersome blackout

The British were told that if they showed lights at night then enemy bombers would see the light and drop bombs on them. They were ordered to cover their windows with heavy material if they wanted lights on in a building. Other blackout rules meant:

• street lights were masked to give a pinpoint of light at the base of each lamp post
• traffic lights were masked to show a small cross of colour
• cars had to drive with a mask over headlights that allowed a tiny slit of light out their bumpers had to be painted white
• torches had to be pointed down at the pavement and the glass covered with two layers of tissue
• smoking in the street was banned at first – some smokers were even fined for lighting a cigarette during an air-raid warning!
• the tops of pillar-boxes were painted green or yellow. This was so that droplets of deadly mustard gas would stain the paint and show up if there was a gas bomb attack.
• railway carriages were blacked out at first – so you could find yourself sitting on a stranger's knee!

• blacked-out buses were so dim that bus conductors couldn't tell what coins were being handed to them – bus companies found dishonest passengers had slipped them foreign coins when they checked the cash back at the depot

One railway porter found out about the bothersome blackout the hard way: *I fell off the platform last night. Clean over the edge I fell. Mind you, there was a fog at the time.*

Helpful hints for the blackout

1 In the countryside some dark-coloured cows had white lines painted on them in case they wandered on to the road!

2 Men were advised to let their white shirt tails hang out as they walked along the blacked-out roads!

3 Red velvet party cloaks for girls were made with white linings. To walk home in the dark you had to turn them inside out. (There weren't a lot of these cloaks about. More children were killed on roads in the blackout than in peace time even though there were far fewer cars.)

4 Pavements had advice painted in white. The stencil message said 'Walk on left of pavement'. Rather like driving on the left on a road, it helped avoid head-on collisions.

Blackout horrors

Bomber pilots reckoned that even a blacked-out city gave off a glow of light that you couldn't miss from the air. Still, the British people suffered the blackout with some horrible historic results …

1 In Peckham, two teenage boys used luminous paint to draw skeletons on dark clothes. In the blackout the paint glowed. Passers-by were terrified!

2 Children in a Cambridge village hid in a churchyard and jumped out on people who had to pass it.

3 Worse things lurked in the London blackout. Just as the dim Victorian streets had hidden jack the Ripper, so the darkened London streets held the Blackout Ripper. But Jack the Ripper was never caught – Jack the Ripper didn't have a gas mask! George Cummins did ... and he left it behind at the scene of a nasty attack after he was disturbed. The gas mask had his name in it, and the police traced him easily. He was tried and hanged in 1942.

4 The first planes in an air raid usually dropped firebombs. The planes that followed them saw the fires and knew where to drop their high-explosive bombs. So the job of the Air Raid Wardens was to put out these fire-bombs quickly. One string of fire-bombs fell in a London cemetery. The fire watchers rushed to put out the flames.

They did this really well. Too well. There was no fire and no light. They stumbled round the graveyard in the pitch darkness, crashed into one another and couldn't find the way out.

5 A girl was going to a dance and had to walk through the blacked-out streets. 'If a strange man talks to you then shine your torch in his eyes, kick him on the shins and run!' her mother told her. The girl set off for the dance. Bins of pig food stood on street corners waiting to be collected. As she rounded a bin a man walked towards her, muffled in a cap and scarf. She shone the torch in his face and kicked his shin. The shocked man fell neck-deep into the pig-bin. The girl ran to the dance. When she reached home her mother whispered to her, 'Your father's a bit upset. Some girl attacked him in the dark – pushed him into that pig-bin on the corner!'

Grotty gas masks

This poster appeared in 1941:

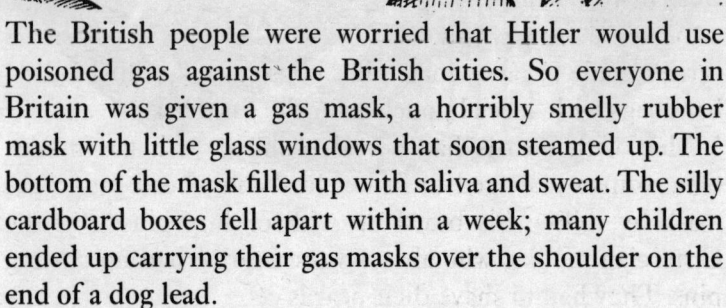

POISON GAS

1916 THE GERMANS USED POISON GAS WE DID NOT EXPECT THIS BARBARITY.

1935 THE ITALIANS USED POISON GAS.

1941 IT IS YOUR DUTY TO YOURSELF YOUR FAMILY AND YOUR COUNTRY TO BE PREPARED.

DON'T BE CAUGHT WITHOUT YOUR GAS MASK, WHEN THE WARDENS SOUND THEIR RATTLES.

DON'T BE A CASUALTY
-ALWAYS CARRY YOUR GAS MASK-

The British people were worried that Hitler would use poisoned gas against the British cities. So everyone in Britain was given a gas mask, a horribly smelly rubber mask with little glass windows that soon steamed up. The bottom of the mask filled up with saliva and sweat. The silly cardboard boxes fell apart within a week; many children ended up carrying their gas masks over the shoulder on the end of a dog lead.

Gruesome gas facts

1 There were 'gas detectors' placed at street corners. These were supposed to light up if gas was in the air. They were never used. There was never ever a gas bomb attack on Britain … yet some people reckon gas masks were one of the great successes of the war! Why? Because Adolf Hitler knew about the gas masks. He knew it would be a waste of time to bomb people with gas when the people were so well prepared – so he didn't bother!

2 Someone invented a gas-proof pram so you could take baby for a walk. It looked a bit like a coffin on wheels with a little chimney to let in gas-free air.

3 The masks made good carriers for children's bottles of school ink or the odd packet of sweets … fine, until they had an emergency gas mask practice.

4 Gas masks were usually carried in their cardboard boxes. But, if you had some spare money, you could go to a shop and buy a smart carrier made of fancy material. Shops started selling ladies' handbags with special pouches for the gas mask.

5 Men with beards had a real problem with gas masks. One woman managed to fit her husband's head into a gas mask by rolling his beard up with curling pins. But the Cistercian monks, who always wore beards, had no curling pins. They had to shave their beards off.

6 Children were persuaded to wear their masks by making them into 'fun masks'. One of the most common was the red and blue 'Mickey Mouse' mask. Children also discovered that if they wore the mask and blew very hard, the air rushed out of the side and made a very rude noise. The punishment for doing this in school was usually a whack with a cane!

WHO MADE THAT DISGUSTING NOISE?

7 Gas masks had an unusual use. Petrol was in short supply. If you needed some for business you could get it. But the special business petrol was stained with red dye – if you cheated and tried to use the red petrol for personal use then you could be caught and fined. Cheats found that if you strained the red petrol through a gas mask filter then it lost the tell-tale colour.

8 People didn't always call them gas masks. Some people called them 'Dickey-birds' (because they made you look as if you had a beak!). They were also known as 'Canaries' and 'Hitlers'. Probably the most common nickname was 'Nosebag'.

9 Some schools held gas mask tests. The children were sent to an air-raid shelter which was then filled with nasty (but not deadly) 'tear gas'. One class survived quite well except for poor little Charlie Bower. He found out the hard way that his mask had a leak – and spent the morning with tears streaming down his face!

10 The War was a time when toys were in short supply. Gas masks made a good toy! You could hold the strap and swing it round your head as a weapon. The metal gas filter could split someone's head open. The pupil with the most dents in their gas mask was seen as a champion.

CATAPULT

DOLL

GOAL POSTS

BAT

True or false: You could buy a gas mask for your dog.

Answer: True. The People's Dispensary for Sick Animals made a gas-proof kennel for dogs, but you could also buy various types of gas masks for them – the best ones were made in Germany!

Blitzed Brit kids

You may think there are boring grown-ups around today. But things haven't changed in the last 50 years. There were some pretty boring people around in the Second World War too. The following advice was given to parents ... does this sound familiar to you?

Children should:
• be sent to school at the proper times
• be encouraged to 'enjoy' their lessons
• get long hours of sleep
• be given plenty to do
• not be allowed to get over-excited
• understand that 'No' means 'No'

The good news was that the same advice said ...
Children should:
• be fed at regular hours

The unusual news was that ...
Children should:
• remember to close gates in the country
• grow to love birds and animals

(So put that cat down at once!)

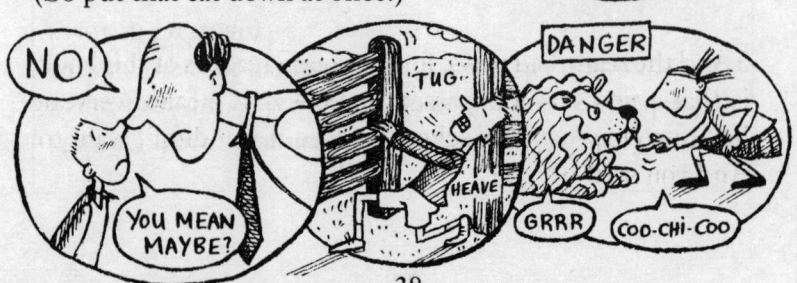

School secrets

1 The good news was that many schools were closed! Many were converted into air raid warden posts. And, of course, 20,000 male teachers went off to fight even though the law said they didn't have to! (Maybe facing enemy guns was better than facing class 3C on a Friday afternoon!)

2 So, many pupils escaped the terrors of the teachers. In January 1940 only two out of every three children had a school to go to. The bad news was that you often spent your holidays working. 'Farm Camps' were set up so that children could 'Lend a hand on the land'.

3 And the really bad news, for the young readers of this book, is that a new law was passed in 1944 that meant everyone had to go to secondary school … even if you didn't want to! And you **still** have to!

4 One school was wrecked by a bomb and 40 children died. The teacher used to take the surviving children round the streets looking for a quiet place to sit and have their lessons on a summer day. They often ended up in the local churchyard, sitting on gravestones. The pupils reckoned that this was so they could be buried quickly if another bomb hit them.

5 A school was wrecked by a land mine one night. Rescuers dug in the rubble and rescued the horrible headmaster and the cruel class teacher. The children were disappointed. But the parents were shocked. What had the headmaster and the teacher been doing alone together in the school at night? 'Fire watching,' the Head said. 'Oh, yes?' said the local people.

World War Two was a frightening time to be a child. You could be evacuated and separated from your parents; you could be sent to live with perfect strangers – strangers who didn't particularly like you in the first place; you could be separated from your brothers and sisters and your friends. You could also get a bit closer to the fighting, if you really wanted to …

The tug-boat tea boy

The British Army landed in France in 1939 and were driven back by the Germans all the way to the coast of northern France near the town of Dunkirk. There weren't enough navy ships to bring the British soldiers home. So a fleet of little private ships and fishing boats set off from England to help.

One of the little boats was a tug-boat from the River Thames. The tea boy was just 14 years old. But he offered to make the trip across the channel and the captain agreed to take him.

When the last soldier had been rescued the little boats sailed home. After 14 days at sea the boy arrived back to a hero's welcome from his proud mother. He took off his socks for the first time in two weeks. They were so stiff with sea salt and dirt that they stood up on their own like a pair of wellington boots.

What did his mother do with those socks?

1 Burn them
2 Keep them as a souvenir
3 Wash them

But staying in the towns with your family and being blitzed was just as bad as that boy's experience at Dunkirk...

Test your teacher

1 Children had to have name tabs sewn into every bit of clothing they had. Was this

a) in case the children were lost in the blackout

b) in case the clothes were stolen

c) in case a child was blown to bits by a bomb and needed to be identified by the clothing

2 How old was the youngest person killed in the war in Britain?

a) 11 hours old

b) 11 months old

c) 11 years old

3 What happened to the 250,000 school meals served each day at the beginning of the War?

a) they were abolished

b) everyone was encouraged to eat at school and they increased to nearly two million

c) they stayed the same

4 Boys had to wear short trousers to save material. When were they allowed to have long trousers?

a) when they were over 180 cm tall

b) when they were 12 years old

c) when they earned enough money to pay for the extra material

5 Because there was a shortage of hand cream something else was suggested to keep your hands smooth and soft. What was it?

a) castor sugar rubbed into wet hands

b) sandpaper to scrub off the rough bits

c) mutton fat rubbed into the hands

6 The WVS appealed for aluminium to help make fighter planes. What did they refuse to accept?

a) pots and pans

b) the artificial limbs of old soldiers from World War One

c) a set of miniature teapots given to Princess Elizabeth by the people of Wales

7 Children's groups called Cogs were formed to collect 'salvage' – materials that could be used again for war materials. What was their song?

a) 'Whale meat again' to the tune of 'We'll meet again'

b) 'It's a long way to Tip a rare pie' to the tune of 'It's a long way to Tipperary '

c) 'There'll always be a dustbin' to the tune of 'There'll always be an England'

8 To save fuel the Ministry of Fuel told you how deep to have your bath water. Was it …

a) 12.7 cm

b) 127 cm

c) 12.7 inches

SORRY SIR, BUT YOU'RE 0·5mm OVER THE REGULATION DEPTH FOR BATH WATER

ERE WHAT DO YOU THINK YOU'RE DOING?

HURRY UP DAD!

9 What was the title of a popular Christmas song in 1939?

a) 'Somewhere over the snowman'

b) 'Will Santa Claus wear a tin helmet?'

c) 'Rudolf the blacked out reindeer'

10 A cartoon character was invented to show the danger of talking to strangers and giving away secrets.
Was it …

a) Mr Chatty

b) Tell Tale Tom

c) Miss Leaky Mouth

It could have been worse 1

Teachers in Britain had to teach larger classes with fewer materials like paper and pencils. But they were better off than some German teachers. One German child broke his arm. He couldn't give the Hitler salute. The teacher told the boy he needn't bother. But one of the children in the class was a Nazi spy. The teacher was reported to the Nazi Party … and executed! (Would you report your teacher? Better not answer that one!)

45

True or false?

1 The Government urged people to save their milk-bottle tops because there were enough thrown away each year to build a Lancaster bomber.

2 The railways in Britain usually lose money. But in the War they made a lot of money by running fewer trains and cramming more people into them.

IS THERE ROOM FOR A LITTLE ONE?

3 An RAF pilot wanted seven gallons of petrol to go home in his car on leave. He was refused ... so he flew home in his Spitfire instead.

4 The readers of the comic *Hotspur* raised £700,000 to buy a warship, *HMS Hotspur*, for the navy.

5 One of the hobby clubs you could join after school taught how to keep pigs.

6 Farmers kept manure in small heaps around the edge of the fields. The manure was good for putting out fires.

7 Soldiers writing home had very little space on their cards so they used short forms like SWALK. This meant, 'Soldiers Will Always Love the King'.

8 Munitions factories (which made shells, bullets and explosives) were disguised as duck ponds so that enemy bombers couldn't pick them out.

9 Rationing finished when the War ended in 1945.

10 People who died in air raids were the responsibility of the Government's Ministry of Health.

3 True – and he used 280 gallons instead.

4 False – it was a football club that raised the money. Which club? Tottenham Hotspur, of course.

5 True – other hobby clubs taught you how to mend clothes or repair shoes.

6 True – you could keep it round the edge of the school playing fields in case your school caught fire ... then again you might have preferred to let the school burn! Manure was also used by horrible wartime children – they threw it at German Prisoners of War!

7 False – Soldiers did write home with SWALK on the envelope ... but the letters stood for 'Sealed With A Loving Kiss'.

8 True – the 'pond' was painted on. And ducks were painted swimming on it.

9 False – many things stayed on ration until 1954.

10 True – The Ministry of Health also looked after home repairs.

Blitzed books

Like everything else, paper was in short supply during World War Two. Millions of old books were turned into pulp to make new books. But the only new books to be published were ones that were sure to sell. For children, that meant books by writers like Enid Blyton.

Here's a story in old Enid's style. The only difference is that the facts in it are true ...

The Curious Case of the Kit Kat

'I say, Janet, I'm jolly hungry,' Bobby groaned. Bobby, short for Roberta, rubbed her tummy.

'I know,' Janet sighed. 'Cook dished up that awful dried egg again this morning. It's getting jolly boring!'

The girls took out their books and went to their desks. 'Gosh, Janet! What's this tin box doing on my desk?' Bobby asked.

'I don't know, Bobby. But I've got one too!' Janet cried.

'Perhaps it's a bomb from those beastly Germans!' Bobby said. Bobby always liked to make an adventure out of everything. 'Shall we open it and see?'

'No!' Janet squealed. 'Look at that label on the lid!' Bobby read it carefully. 'Do not open except in an emergency!' Bobby was a good reader. 'How odd! I wish I could look inside!'

'Miss Grant would be furious,' Janet warned her chum. 'You don't want another two hours of prep, do you? You'd miss the house hockey match!'

Bobby sighed. 'It would almost be worth it to solve the mystery.'

Just then Miss Grant marched in. Her back was straight as a poker and her thin face as sharp as a pin. The girls stood up. Miss Grant glared at them. 'Good morning, form 3A.'

'Good morning, Miss Grant,' the girls replied.

'Sit!'

The girls sat. Miss Grant pulled herself up to her full height. 'Now, girls, you're probably wondering what's inside the tin boxes on your desks.'

'Yes, Miss Grant.'

'Well, I can tell you, they are emergency rations. Your parents were asked to send them. If there's an enemy attack and our kitchens are destroyed, then the food in this box will keep you going for a day or two until help arrives,' the tall teacher explained. She looked fiercely down her thin nose at Bobby. 'You must not open these boxes. Ever! Do you understand?'

'Yes, Miss Grant,' Bobby said. Then she whispered to her pal, Janet, 'Why is she looking at me?'

'Because everyone knows what a jolly greedy little carrot you are!' Janet whispered back.

The next morning Bobby received a letter from her mother. She read it to Janet. 'Oh! I say, Janet! Mummy says she's put a bar of Kit Kat chocolate in that box. I have to have it! I'll die if I don't have a bite!'

'And you'll die if Miss Grant catches you looking in the box. Don't you jolly well dare open that box!' her friend warned her

Suddenly there was the sound of a bell clanging in the corridor outside the classroom. 'Air-raid practice!' Miss Grant said sharply. 'Let's see if we can beat last week's time of two minutes and thirty-five seconds to the shelter, shall we? And don't forget your gas masks!'

The girls stood. One row at a time they walked smartly from the room. Miss Grant looked at her watch. As they reached the end of the corridor Bobby stopped suddenly. 'Oh, lor!' she gasped. 'I've gone and forgotten my secret box! Old Grunt will kill me! She'll make me miss the hockey match for sure.'

Janet grabbed her arm. 'Don't worry. I'll go back and get it. You take mine.

'You'll cop it off Grunt!' Bobby cried.

'Don't worry, Bobs. That's what friends are for!' Janet said bravely and turned back.

As she hurried back to the classroom she saw Miss Grant standing there. In the teacher's thin hands was Bobby's box. 'Forgotten something?' Miss Grant snapped.

'Er, yes, Miss Grant. I forgot my emergency rations,' Janet said.

'I have it here,' the teacher said. 'Take it … but don't dare open it! And you can have two hours extra prep tonight.'

'I'll miss the house hockey match,' Janet pleaded.

'I know,' Miss Grant said with a wintry smile. 'And let that be a lesson to you.'

Janet nodded and turned away. Miss Grant didn't notice that the girl was smiling. Janet knew that Bobby was the best hockey player in the house. Fast as a boy and nearly as tough. So long as Bobby played the house was sure to win.

* * *

That night in the dormitory Bobby waited till after lights-out. She crept across the room to Janet's bed with the tin box clutched in her hand. 'Janet,' she whispered.

'Is that you, Bobby?' the girl asked.

'Yes. Look, Janet, how about a midnight feast to celebrate the win at hockey?'

'Oh, yes, the skipper said your five goals were

absolutely super. Well done, Bobs. But where will we get the food from?'

Bobby grinned. 'We'll eat the emergency rations!'

'Oh, no, Bobby! You'd get into terrible trouble!'

'We won't, silly! If we aren't supposed to open them then no one will ever know!'

Bobby fumbled with her torch and clicked it on. The other girls in the dorm gathered round and watched as Bobby opened the box. There was a gasp from every girl. 'Ooooh!' Janet squeaked. 'The Kit Kat! It's missing! It's been stolen!'

'Hmmm,' Bobby nodded and looked around. 'And I think I know the culprit!'

But do you? Who stole the Kit Kat? Was it …
1 Bobby herself
2 Janet, who had rescued the box from the classroom
3 one of the girls in the dormitory
4 the teacher

54

Evils of evacuation

The British expected their cities to be bombed. So, long before the war, plans were made to move the children out to foster homes in the countryside. As soon as war was declared they went by train and bus into the unknown. Very often they went together with their teachers who carried on with the same classes in a quiet country school. The two most common methods of finding a new home were ...

The Slave Market – the children stood in a group. The people who were offering homes then picked the ones they wanted. Tidy, polite little girls went first – scruffy, smelly little boys were wanted by no one.

Hunt the house – children were led around the town or village. The house-owners were asked, 'Would you like to take this one?'

Finding someone you'd be happy with was usually a matter of luck. Some evacuees were so happy they didn't want to go home after the War ... some still say their evacuation days were the happiest days of their lives. Some hosts made friendships with their guests that have lasted a lifetime.

But there were also some problems. Children born and raised in the city slums of the 1930s found the countryside as strange as you'd find living on Mars! These were the ...

Problem kids

Some of the problems the new homes had with evacuees included ...

• Home sickness – 'My name is Bobby,' the three-year old boy wept. 'I'm a big boy, and I don't cry – well, not very often!'

• Bed-wetting – some estimates say that one evacuee in three suffered from bed-wetting.

• Nits – some of the children from the poorer parts of the cities evacuated their head-lice with them.

• Dirt – some children were not used to regular baths. One pair of evacuees screamed the house down when they were stripped in the bathroom ... they thought they were going to be drowned!

• Clothing – poor city children were often 'Plastered up' for the winter. That is, they had brown paper or newspaper wrapped around their bodies to keep them warm. The paper was then held in place for the winter by a vest that was sewn up tight. When warmer weather came, next spring, the stinking vest would be cut off and the paper removed ... along with the body lice that had usually found a nice snug home in there!

• Swearing – some of the rougher evacuees shocked the foster parents in small towns who weren't used to hearing children swear. One evacuee dropped a fork and swore. 'You shouldn't use words like that,' she was told. 'I'll tell my dad about you,' she replied. 'An' he'll come an' knock your *!*!*!*! block off!'

In September 1939, as soon as war was declared, one and a half million women and children were evacuated to the country for safety. But, when the enemy bombers didn't arrive as expected, a lot went back home. By January 1940 nearly a million had returned to the towns and cities.

Some of the smaller towns were so empty for a while that they became like ghost towns. In Margate, grass grew in the streets.

Six true tales of evacuees

1 Some evacuees brought bad habits from the town to the country. Some went shopping then came back with the goods ... and the money! To the horror of the host they'd shoplifted them! Another family of evacuees pretended to dig in the garden to grow vegetables. In fact they were digging a tunnel into next-door's garden. They pinched the potatoes they found underground there. The neighbours saw the leaves of the plants still growing and didn't discover the theft until they came to pull them up in the autumn!

2 One evacuee was criticised for spilling her tea:

3 A mother went into the country to visit her little three-year-old daughter and baby son. The little girl she met was her daughter – but the baby boy was not her son! The two children had arrived two months earlier. 'It says on this paper that you have your brother with you,' one of the welcoming women had said. 'Where is he?' The little girl looked around then pointed to a toddler who was not her brother. It seemed that she didn't like her baby brother so she had picked one that she preferred!

4 A boy was sent to a huge manor house owned by a grand lady. He thought he'd escaped the bombing and the shooting. He was terrified to hear shots one day coming from inside the house! He rushed into the living-room to find the lady with a smoking shotgun pointed through an open window.

'Got him!' she said.

'A German?'

'No! A grey squirrel! I hate the things. Every time I see one in my garden I shoot the blighter!'

5 There are many stories of city evacuees being amazed at the sight of farm animals. They'd never left the city and never seen a cow or a sheep or a chicken before – except cooked and carved at the dinner table. In October 1939 the BBC News broadcast this description of a cow. It was written by a young evacuee. Could you picture a cow from this description?

The cow is a mammal. It has six sides: right, left, upper and below. At the back it has a tail on which hangs a brush. With this it sends flies away so they do not fall into the milk. The head is for the purpose of growing horns and so that the mouth can be somewhere. The horns are to butt with and the mouth is to moo with. Under the cow hangs the milk. It is arranged for milking. When people milk the milk comes and there is never an end to the supply. How the cow does it I have not realised but it makes more and more. The cow has a fine sense of smell; one can smell it far away. This is the reason for fresh air in the country. The man cow is called an ox. It is not a mammal. The cow does not eat much, but what it eats it eats twice so that it gets enough. When it is hungry it moos and when it says nothing it is because it is all full up with grass.

6 A girl evacuee loved gingerbread. Her strict hostess cooked some one day and left it to cool. While the woman was asleep the girl crept into the kitchen and nipped a bit from the side of one of the tempting pieces. This made the cake look odd, so the girl had a bright idea. If she nipped a piece from every single cake, then the hostess would not notice one odd one. It didn't work! The hostess lined up her evacuees and asked who had done it. The girl's guilty looks gave her away. Her punishment was to be locked in a cold, damp attic. Quite by chance her mother arrived on a visit later that day. She was so shocked by the treatment of her daughter that she took her straight home.

World War Three! – Hosts v Evacuees

Which was worse ... being an evacuee, or being a host in the country who had the job of living with the evacuees? There are two sides to every argument. This is what the hosts said ...

1 Host: You couldn't buy a small-tooth comb anywhere in Northallerton. They'd all been bought because a lot of the evacuees came with fleas in their hair.

2 Host's daughter: I came home from work one day and found two youths, nearly as tall as my father. They'd told mother we had to take them because we had a spare bedroom.

3 Host's daughter: There were five of us in a three-bedroom house. When we took an evacuee it meant my brother had to share my bedroom. I resented this, as I took an instant dislike to the lad who came to stay with us.

4 Host's daughter: Our evacuees arrived in shabby clothes so mother gave them new ones. They were allowed home on a visit and came back with more old clothes. Their parents had sold the new ones we'd given them!

5 Host's daughter: Our new evacuee was a terror. One day he was playing with matches and he set fire to a chair. We had to decorate after he left. The door was covered with dart holes and the walls with writing.

6 Hostess: My father used to say he never saw anything like our evacuees – they never shed a tear when their parents left for home.

7 Hostess: We had three brothers aged four to eight. They had no idea of food other than chips. They didn't know how to eat a boiled egg.

HOW TO EAT A BOILED EGG
WHICH ONE IS CORRECT?

1. POP IT INTO THE MOUTH WHOLE
2. SAW IT IN HALF FIRST
3. ATTACK WITH BLOW TORCH
4. COVER WITH BREAD AND EAT AS A SANDWHICH
5. PLACE IN SMALL DISH AND SMASH TOP IN WITH SPOON

BUT some said …

8 Host's daughter: My parents took a boy of 6. He was really a wonderful child in every way. He was brought up by my parents as one of the family. His mother came and stayed long weekends and holidays with us.

On the other hand, this is what the evacuees said…

1 Girl evacuee aged seven: The farm was three miles from the village and had only cold water which had to be pumped up into the kitchen.

2 Girl evacuee aged seven: The toilet was at the end of a long garden and was just a pit in the ground filled with ashes. It had two holes. The farmer's daughter and I always went together, particularly in the dark.

3 Girl evacuee: I remember my eleventh birthday. Mrs Spencer took me seven miles to see Tarzan of the Apes. But there was only a bus there. We had to walk back.

4 Girl evacuee aged nine: We fed the chickens each day. I thought they were pets and was heartbroken when I saw the first one killed and plucked. I once witnessed the slaughter of a pig. It was so distressing that I started having nightmares. I was firmly told that this was their way of life. I was a very silly, spoilt child who knew nothing.

5 Girl evacuee aged seven: One thing that upset me was that the only farm worker was not allowed to sit at the table with the family. He had to have his meal at a separate table.

6 Boy evacuee aged twelve: There were lots of apple and pear orchards. We thought you could just help yourself. The village kids told us we shouldn't do it. The police came to see our hosts and they put a stop to it.

7 Girl evacuee aged nine: Anything wrong in the house was always my fault because the farmer's daughters ganged together. They broke my only doll and tore my books. When mum collected me she was in tears. She could see every bone in my body.

BUT some had happy memories ...

8 Girl evacuee aged eight: We helped on the farm at weekends. I used to like watching the milking done. It was done by hand. We used to love the lambing season when we could go and see the lambs after they were born. It was all new to us. In the town we only had factories and shipyards.

Marjorie's story

I WAS SENT TO STAY WITH MRS. GRANT. ME & LITTLE KENNY

SPEAK WHEN YOU'RE SPOKEN TO OR I'LL TAKE THE STICK TO YOU

WE TRIED TO TELL OUR PARENTS, BUT MRS. GRANT JUST LIED

YES. SHE GOT THESE BRUISES PLAYING IN THE FIELD

AND LATER SHE MADE US PAY

TRYING TO GET ME INTO TROUBLE. I'LL SHOW YOU WHAT A BEATING REALLY IS.

WE WERE PRISONERS IN HER HOUSE. AFTER THREE YEARS KENNETH WENT HOME

KEN! YOU MUST MAKE MUM & DAD BELIEVE HOW CRUEL SHE IS

BUT THEY SENT MY SISTER DOREEN TO TAKE KEN'S PLACE!

DIDN'T KEN TELL THEM ABOUT HER?

HE JUST SAID HE WAS GLAD TO BE HOME

SHE WENT ON TORMENTING US.

DON'T TELL PEOPLE YOUR PARENTS LIVE IN A FLAT. ONLY CRIMINALS LIVE IN FLATS!

On 2 May 1945 evacuation was ended everywhere. Hull and London were the last places to have children returned because they were the most dangerous. Saddest of all were the children who were evacuated and never got to go back home. Some had no homes to go back to – they'd been blitzed. But some found that their parents had moved – and abandoned their children. About 38,000 children were unclaimed after the War.

Rotten rationing

Rationing was brought in by the Government to save food and materials and make sure everyone got fair shares. Everyone was given coupons. You had to have so many coupons for each rationed thing you bought. It usually worked well. But some people cheated.

1 One shop-keeper was a blind old woman. Children made their own coupons out of blotting paper. To the blind woman it felt like a coupon so she handed over the sweets!

2 If you'd run out of coupons but had plenty of money then you could buy something illegally – and hope to get away with it. The practice of selling things this way was known as 'the black market'.

3 One man called himself The Sugar Baron. His job was to send the precious sugar supplies to shops. The Government knew how much he was sent and checked that he had given it all to the shops to ration to the people. But he started giving shops short measures and holding some back. Or he 'accidentally' dropped a bag. This way he built up a private supply which he could sell for a lot of money or swap for something he needed. Even 50 years later he wasn't sorry for cheating his fellow-Britons. 'Everybody did it if they got the chance,' he said. 'Life was hard. You had to grab what You could when you could.'

4 Clothes were rationed in 1941, but by 1942 the rules for making clothes became crazy:
• men's suits could only have three pockets

• men's suits could only have three buttons on the front and none on the cuff
• fancy belts were banned
• trouser legs couldn't be wider than 19 inches (48 cm) at the bottom
• elastic waistbands were banned
• turn-ups on the bottom of trousers were banned. (You got round this one by finding a tailor who would make your trousers too long – he'd then be allowed to turn them up to make them fit. Crazy!)
• high heels on shoes were to be no more than two inches (5 cm)

5 Of course it was hard to be fair. You needed two coupons for a pair of knickers. But if a woman was fatter

than average, or preferred knickers with longer legs (bloomers), then she needed more precious elastic – she'd have to fork out **three** coupons.

6 Of course a death in the family was a very sad thing but you could always take the dead person's old clothes and use the material to make new ones for you and your family. Or, if you didn't like wearing their clothes, you might find the dear deceased person's clothing coupons and spend them quickly before the Government inspectors found out they were dead. (The law said you couldn't use your coupons after you were dead ... which seems fair enough.)

7 Petrol rationing allowed you to drive about 20 to 50 miles (32 to 80km) a week. But sharing cars saved money. If you put up a sign in your car window offering people lifts then you could get extra petrol.

ROOM FOR ANOTHER LITTLE ONE?

One way round the petrol ration was to fill a bag with household gas and adapt your car to run on it. The good news was that town gas was not rationed. The bad news was ...

THE GAS BAG WAS 3 METRES LONG 2 METRES WIDE AND OVER 1 METRE HIGH NEARLY AS BIG AS THE CAR

SO....

IT HAD TO BE CARRIED ON THE ROOF

BUT....

AS THE BAG EMPTIED IT DROOPED OVER THE WINDOWS

SO....

IT HAD TO BE HELD IN A CRATE

BUT....

THE CRATE WAS SO HEAVY IT MADE THE CAR HARD TO DRIVE

AND....

IT COST £30 TO BUY AND FIT THE GAS BAG AT A TIME WHEN A NEW CAR COST ONLY £100

YET....

ALL THAT GAS GAVE YOU AS MANY MILES AS JUST 1 GALLON OF PETROL (4·5 LITRES)

THEN....

IT TOOK 10 MINUTES TO REFILL THE GAS BAG EVERY 20 MILES (32 km) OR SO

AND....

GAS BECAME IN SHORT SUPPLY IN OCTOBER 1942

SO....

WAS IT WORTH IT?

8 After petrol for private motoring was stopped in 1942 you could claim that you needed petrol for a very

70

important journey. If you got the petrol then you had to make the journey by the shortest possible route. A business-man who went 1,200 metres out of his way to pop home for lunch was fined … and he was lucky! A writer of theatre musicals (Ivor Novello) used his car to go home every night after the show … he was given four weeks in jail!

9 Coal was rationed. Families who ran out of coal often turned on the gas oven, opened the oven door and sat round it. They even put their feet in the oven to try to get warm!

10 Cigarettes were in such short supply that shops often worked out their own rationing. They would sell just one packet to each customer. One ruthless father got his two children out of bed at 5:00 a.m. each morning and sent each to queue at a different tobacconist shop for his Winston cigarettes. That way he got double supply. But that wasn't good enough. As soon as they brought home the cigarettes he sent them out again and they swapped queues so they could each have a second packet. He got four packets a day this way! He wouldn't get away with it today – children aren't allowed to buy cigarettes!

It could have been worse 2

… you could have been living in Germany! Germany brought in rationing before the war even started. Two particularly harsh laws said:

• citizens were only allowed to take a bath on a Saturday or a Sunday
• citizens could only buy toilet paper from a 'Toilet Paper Distribution Centre' – this was to stop the precious stuff being stolen

Match the clothes to the coupons

Clothes coupons were needed according to the amount of material and the amount of work that went into making the clothes. You only had 66 coupons to last you a year – less as the War went on. If you were a government officer in charge of sharing out coupons, how many would you give for each of these items?

1 a night-dress   4 underpants

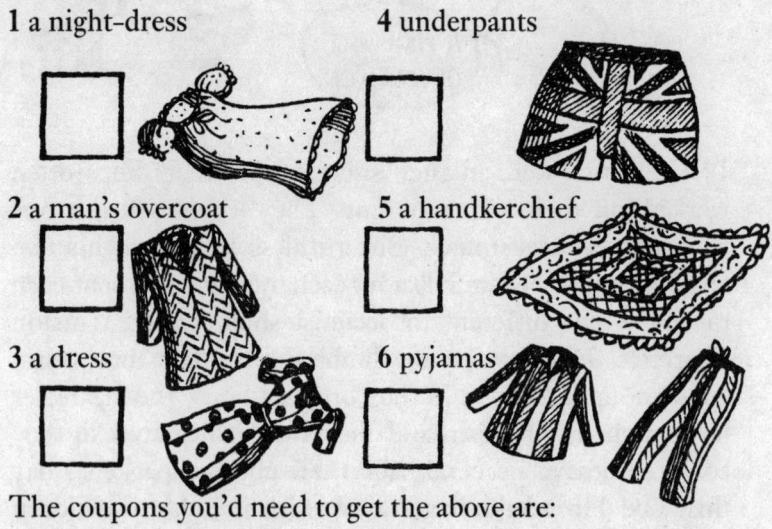

2 a man's overcoat   5 a handkerchief

3 a dress   6 pyjamas

The coupons you'd need to get the above are:
16, 11, 8, 6, 4 or a half … but which needs which?

Answer: 1) 6 coupons (so lots of people stopped wearing night-clothes during the War!) 2) 16 coupons 3) 11 coupons 4) 4 coupons 5) half a coupon 6) 8 coupons

The tale of the undressed dancer

There's a story in the Bible about a dancer called Salome. Salome wore seven thin pieces of cloth. She then did a rather rude dance in which she took off the veils one by one! King Herod was so pleased he gave her a present ... the head of John the Baptist. On a plate! (There's no accounting for taste.)

YOU SHOULDN'T HAVE....

This dance was so famous that lots of women have copied *The Dance of the Seven Veils* throughout the centuries. A dancer even performed it during the blitz to entertain soldiers. It was a bit naughty, but the police couldn't stop her.

Rationing did! As she took the veils off she threw them into the audience ... but never got them back.

And she didn't have the coupons to go out and buy new 'veils', so she had to give up the act!

73

(Yes, we know she could have bought blackout material without using her precious coupons … but *The Dance of the Seven Blackout Curtains* just isn't the same.)

Rotten war for women

The good news …
With working men fighting in the army, more women had to go out to work. They wore their trousers with pride! It showed they were part of the war effort. They had more freedom than ever before.

The bad news …
• women wore tighter clothes to save material.
• sleeveless sweaters were worn.
• pleats were banned … they wasted material and machine time.

• if a woman wanted a white wedding dress she had to make it herself … sometimes out of silk left over from making parachutes! No parachutes? Then use a satin table-cloth or a net curtain.

whoosh

Aargh!

ahhh

• After the War many women gave up the freedom they'd won in the War. They gave up the trousers and went back to fashion clothes.

• Rationing went on until 1952. The new fashions, like Dior's 'New Look', demanded lots of material. Women who couldn't afford the money or the coupons for the 'New Look' resented the women who could. In 1947 women wearing the 'New Look' had their clothes ripped off in the street by other women!

GRRR *SHRIEK* *HELP!*

Rotten rationed recipes

Any food supply that came to Britain in ships was in danger of being cut off. Enemy submarines in the Atlantic sank as many food ships as they could. They hoped to starve Britain into surrendering. The British Government had two main answers to this.

1 Make sure that no one eats more than a fair share of the food we have – give everyone a Ration Book with coupons to allow you to have so much each week and no more.

2 Persuade everyone to eat the type of food there was plenty of in Britain. Food like potatoes.

The Minister of Food was Lord Woolton. He told the British people:

THIS IS A FOOD WAR. IF WE GROW MORE POTATOES THEN WE NEED NOT IMPORT MUCH WHEAT. THE VEGETABLE GARDEN IS ALSO OUR NATIONAL MEDICINE CHEST. THE BATTLE ON THE KITCHEN FRONT CANNOT BE WON WITHOUT HELP FROM THE KITCHEN GARDEN.

How do you persuade someone to eat more potatoes?
• Well, you could try writing a jolly jingle like this one ...

THE SONG OF POTATO PETE
POTATOES NEW POTATOES OLD
POTATOES (IN A SALAD) COLD
POTATOES BAKED OR MASHED OR FRIED
POTATOES WHOLE, POTATOES PIED
ENJOY THEM ALL, INCLUDING CHIPS
REMEMBERING SPUDS DON'T COME IN SHIPS!

(If the potatoes were as bad as the poetry then you wouldn't want to eat them!)

• you could try persuading people that potatoes are the best food in the world ...

Potatoes help to protect you from illness. Potatoes give you warmth and energy. Potatoes are cheap and home-produced. So why stop at serving them just once a day? Have them twice, or even three times, for breakfast, dinner and supper.

(If you followed all this advice you'd probably end up looking like a potato! Come to think of it some people do ... well, most of us have a couple of eyes and a jacket.)

• and you could come up with scrumptious recipes that will use up those endless spuds ...

> **'FADGE'** IS HOT NOURISHING AND FILLING FOR BREAKFAST
>
> BOIL SOME WELL SCRUBBED POTATOES, THEN PEEL AND MASH THEM WHILE HOT. WHEN THE MIXTURE IS COOL ENOUGH TO HANDLE ADD SALT, AND WORK IN ENOUGH FLOUR TO MAKE A PLIABLE DOUGH. KNEAD LIGHTLY ON A WELL-FLOURED BOARD FOR ABOUT 5 MINUTES THEN ROLL INTO A LARGE CIRCLE ABOUT ¼ INCH (½ cm) THICK. CUT INTO WEDGE SHAPED PIECES AND COOK ON A HOT GRIDDLE, AN ELECTRIC HOT-PLATE OR ON THE UPPER SHELF OF A QUICK OVEN UNTIL BROWN ON BOTH SIDES. TURNING ONCE.

(Why not make this Fadge recipe … then try it on someone you don't like?)

• the Government even tried to persuade you to eat the bits you usually threw away!

THOSE WHO HAVE THE WILL TO WIN
COOK POTATOES IN THEIR SKIN
KNOWING THAT THE SIGHT OF PEELINGS
DEEPLY HURT LORD WOOTTON'S FEELINGS

SPLUTTER
SPLUTTER

(So, if you saw a man crying over a bin of pig swill it may well have been Lord Woolton!)

War time recipes you may like to try

TWO-MINUTE SOUP

INGREDIENTS

4 TABLESPOONS DRIED MILK (60 ml)
1 BEEF OR VEGETABLE STOCK CUBE
2 TABLESPOONS PARSLEY (30 ml)
A PINCH OF SALT

METHOD

1 MIX THE DRIED MILK WITH 2 TABLESPOONS OF WATER AND BEAT HARD WITH A WOODEN SPOON (OR WHISK) UNTIL IT IS SMOOTH. ADD THE REST OF THE WATER AND MIX WELL

2 PUT IN A PAN AND HEAT. BRING TO BOIL AND STIR IN THE STOCK CUBE, THE PARSLEY AND THE SALT.

3 BOIL GENTLY AND STIR FOR FIVE MINUTES SERVE WITH BREAD

COD PANCAKES

INGREDIENTS

225g COD (COOKED AND FLAKED)
15g PARSLEY (CHOPPED)
30g MIXED HERBS
175g MASHED CARROTS
PINCH OF SALT AND PEPPER
FOR THE BATTER.

25g PLAIN FLOUR
15g DRIED EGG (1 LEVEL TEASPOON)
5g BAKING POWDER (2 TEASPOONS)
HALF PINT OF WATER (800 mL)   CONT....

```
METHOD.
1. MIX TOGETHER ALL THE DRY INGREDIENTS FOR THE BATTER.
   ADD SUFFICIENT WATER TO MAKE STIFF DOUGH
2. BEAT WELL AND ADD THE REST OF THE WATER
3. MIX COD, CARROTS, PARSLEY AND HERBS WITH THE
   BATTER
4. HEAT A FRYING PAN AND ADD A LITTLE FAT.
5. PLACE THE PANCAKE MIXTURE IN THE PAN
6. COOK EACH SIDE UNTIL BROWN. SERVE WITH POTATOES
```

Ten foul food facts

1 Suggested new recipes included squirrel-tail soup and crow pie.

2 A competition for good food in the *Farmer & Stock Breeder* magazine was won with recipes for fried bullock brains and lamb's-tail broth.

3 It was an offence to give bread to birds – but birds survived. One farmer used hops from the local brewery instead of manure and spread it over his crops. The birds pinched the brewed hops – and got very drunk.

4 Rabbits made a good dinner – yes, even fluffy little pet rabbits – and the skins left over made nice warm gloves.

5 Dead horses were sold as dog food – but the flesh was dyed green to stop people selling it for beef steaks. (Luckily dogs are colour-blind!) Bones were collected in bins on the corners of streets. Meat bones were a source of nitroglycerine for high explosives, glue for aircraft, food for cattle and fertiliser for crops. Many a dog had a feast there ... hopefully it didn't explode.

6 What should you do if you saw a pretty Cabbage White butterfly during the War? Kill it! Their caterpillars eat cabbages grown for humans.

7 Shortage of meat meant that sausages often had curious things in them. One woman complained that her sausages had so much bread in them they turned to toast when they were cooked. *We didn't know whether to put mustard on them or marmalade!*

8 War children had never seen a banana. They didn't know how to eat one. There are many stories of children trying to eat them skins and all. Others peeled them correctly – then threw the inside away and ate the skin!

9 A suggestion was made for a wartime type of 'banana' – boil up turnips, then let them go cold. Mash them with sugar and you had something that tasted like banana. (You can try it – if you fancy a day off school with terminal sickness.)

10 It could have been worse. In some countries food was rationed depending on what job you had. Important people got better food. 'Nobodies' got next to nothing!

You could always go to a restaurant and eat without coupons. But it was an expensive way to eat – and the helpings were not very big ...

The Tale of the Chocolate Dog

Sammy was a sailor. Like many sailors he was very superstitious. He never walked under a ladder and never broke a mirror.

As he left his London home one morning he met a mongrel mutt called Mick. 'Hello, Mick!' the sailor said. He reached down and patted the rough, grey coat. Mick wagged his tail.

Sammy reached into his pocket and found a small piece of chocolate. He threw it in the air. Mick caught it and trotted back to the O'Malley family home chewing it happily.

'Hello, Mick,' Mrs O'Malley smiled. 'Been at the bone-bin again, have you?'

Mick just wagged his tail happily.

Sammy the sailor forgot about his gift to Mick. He set sail with a convoy into the Atlantic. The weather was calm and the crew were nervous. Enemy submarines, the dreaded U-boats, would have a clear target for their torpedoes.

After three days at sea the alarm siren sounded. Sammy grabbed a rifle and rushed to his battle station at the front of the ship. The submarine periscope was just vanishing below the water. A ripple of white foam was rushing towards the ship. A torpedo!

The captain was desperately trying to turn the ship away from the deadly missile. But it was turning too slowly and too late. The torpedo rushed towards Sammy. He knew it was the end. The sailor raised the rifle to his shoulder and tried to aim at the torpedo. If he could hit the warhead before it struck the ship then he'd be saved.

But the ship rose and fell in the water. Sammy closed his eyes. He fired.

There was a shattering explosion. A plume of white water. Spray stung Sammy's face. Then there was a curious silence. Sammy opened his eyes. The water was bubbling about fifty metres from the ship.

The crew walked towards Sammy and looked at him with wonder. 'That was the best shot I've ever seen!' the ship's cook said.

Sammy shook his head then found his voice. 'Not a good shot – just luck!'

The cook shrugged. 'Then I wish I had a piece of your rabbit's foot or your four-leaf clover, Sammy.'

Suddenly Sammy had a clear picture in his mind. 'Mick! The dog! They do say, stroke a lucky dog and the luck will rub off!'

'Then give it a pat from me,' the cook said.

'I gave it a piece of chocolate,' Sammy said.

'I've lots of chocolate in the galley. Give it the

biggest slab I can find! It's just saved all our lives!'

And so, just two weeks later, Mick the mongrel had a fortune in rare chocolate in his slobbering chops. He wagged his tail so hard you'd have thought it would fall off.

'Hello, Mick!' Mrs O'Malley said. 'What have we got here? Drop! Good boy, Mick. Drop!' She picked up the dark brown bar and wiped it on her apron.

'Well, well, well! Mr O'Malley always said you were a lucky dog! Here, I'll give you a nice old bone!'

Mick trotted off with his reward and his mistress set to work with a carving knife.

Christmas that year was a good one for John and Lucy, Tony and Arthur, the little O'Malleys. They opened their presents and almost cried with pleasure as they saw their treats.

'Oh, Ma! That was beautiful!' Lucy said as her mother tucked her into the bed under the steel table. 'How did you get all that chocolate, Ma?'

'Ask no questions and you'll be told no lies,' her mother said.

'I think it was carried here by Santa's reindeer. The clever thing carried it in his mouth,' Lucy whispered.

'And why do you think that?'

The little girl said softly, 'Because my slab of chocolate was covered in teeth marks!'

The black market

People often had money to spare – there wasn't enough food, clothing, cars, entertainment or furniture to spend it on. And of course rationing meant you could only have so much food, petrol or clothes anyway.

So, if you had something that was in short supply – and you knew someone with money who wanted it – you could sell it to them without coupons.

This was against the law, you understand. But if you could get away with it you could make a lot of illegal money. This wasn't an open market – so it was known as the black market. For some people the black market was the chance to make a little extra cash. For others it was a way of life …

Death in the Haystack – the true story of Jack Lapham.

Jack Lapham supped his pint of beer carefully. It was going to have to last him all evening. He didn't mind. It was the company in The Grey Horse that he liked.

Bill Anderson the barman leaned over the counter and murmured, 'I could top that pint up for you, Jack.'

Jack drew in his breath sharply. 'Thanks, Bill, but no thanks. We're all in this war together. If we don't share and share alike then we may as well let the Germans take over tomorrow. Besides, I'm on duty later tonight. It doesn't do to let the villagers see their Special Constable rolling round drunk, does it?'

Bill laughed. 'The amount of crime we have here in Farlington, I don't think it matters!'

The Special Constable shook his grey-haired head seriously. 'You never know, Bill. You never know.'

A chill draught swept into the bar as the door opened and a stranger hurried into the bar. The young man had dark hair that was parted in the centre and greased flat to his thin skull. He was carrying a brown paper carrier-bag under his arm.

'Good evening, sir. What can I get you?' Bill Anderson asked.

'Nuffin,' the young stranger croaked in a hoarse voice. He jabbed a grubby finger at the parcel. 'It's more a case of what I can get for you!'

'Ah, a case of whisky would come in handy.'

'Nah!' the young man scowled. He looked suspiciously at Jack Lapham and nodded for Bill to join him at the quiet corner of the bar.

Even though he spoke in that soft, croaking voice Jack Lapham could hear most of what the stranger said. 'Nice bit of beef ... fresh as a daisy ... ten shillings!'

'No coupons,' the barman shrugged.

'Nah! Don't need none. Nice bit of beef Cook it. Serve beef sandwiches to the customers, eh? Just nine shillings to you, guv!'

'Probably dog meat,' Bill sniffed.

'Hah! I'll give yer dog meat! Killed just down the road. Fresh as a daisy!' The young man's red-rimmed eyes narrowed. 'I can sell this for twice the price in London, mate!'

'Then good luck to you,' the barman sniffed and turned to polish a glass.

'Yer'll be sorry,' the stranger snapped and scuttled out of the bar.

Bill Anderson met the eyes of his old friend. 'You hear that, Jack?'

'I heard, Bill.'

'Surprised you didn't arrest him.'

'I'm not in me uniform yet … besides, I'm more interested in finding out who's supplying this meat.'

Bill rubbed his stubbled chin – new razors were hard to find these days. 'My money would be on those Wades – a shifty family if ever I saw one.'

'I'll start there,' Jack Lapham promised. He drained the last of his beer, put his cap on and set off to change into his uniform.

The blackout had begun by the time he wheeled his bicycle down the track to Farlington Marsh Farm. The slit in his front lamp gave next to no light and the thin moon was little help. The Special Constable cursed as he stumbled along the rutted track, ankle deep in mud and with overhanging brambles snatching at his hat.

The farm gate was slippery with moss as he pushed it open. There was no light at the farmhouse windows – Jack would have been upset if he'd seen any. Some of these farmers were careless about blackout. They knew the Air Raid Precaution wardens would never venture this far out.

Jack propped his bike against the farmhouse wall. He took his bike lamp and shone it into the farmhouse window. There were no shutters or curtains there. It was deserted. And as he inspected the barns he realized there was little hay or straw in there.

In the field behind the barn was a haystack with a waterproof cover. Nothing here to suggest a slaughterhouse.

He stumbled against an empty oil drum and cursed the darkness. He stopped to rub his knee. Then he realized the darkness was in fact his biggest friend. Because although he could see nothing his ears were sharpened.

There were owls in the distant woods. Odd scuttlings of rats in the barn. But there was another noise from behind the barn. Someone was sawing. Jack strained his ears and crept to the back of the barn. The soft sawing wasn't like the cutting of wood. It was the sawing of bones that he'd heard in the butcher shop.

The sawing stopped for a few moments. There was the sound of men talking, then a chopping. Jack walked along the side of the haystack and looked carefully round the corner. The wafer-thin moon lit the flat field. It was empty!

Now the sound of sawing came from behind the Special Constable. He hurried along the edge of the haystack, turned the corner and found himself looking into the deserted farmyard. For a moment Jack thought he was hearing ghosts and was ready to run for his cycle. Then he heard a loud, clear laugh from his left. From the haystack. And he realized that the sounds were coming from *inside* the stack.

Using his torch he walked carefully along the side of the stack. Bales of hay had been stacked against the side of a wooden building to disguise it. But he found the door and opened it quietly.

The light from the oil lamps was brilliant as he stepped inside from the deep purple of the night. The smell of the blood was overpowering. But most appalling were the three pairs of eyes that turned on him.

Farmer Wade held a large meat-axe and each son clutched at a dripping carving knife.

'Evening, Constable,' the farmer said. Suddenly his wooden face cracked into a smile. 'Come for your share, have you?'

'Have you a licence to slaughter and sell these animals?' Jack Lapham asked.

One of the sons stepped forward. 'Don't need one. These animals are casualties, see? Perhaps you'd like a nice steak free of charge, of course.' The knife was twisting in his hand.

'That cow couldn't walk. We had to put her down,' the second son explained.

'And those two calves?' the Special Constable said, carefully keeping his eyes on those knives.

'Motherless,' Farmer Wade said. 'Poor things had to die.'

'That looks like a pig – don't tell me the cow was his mother too!'

'No … it was old – lame. Believe me, Constable!'

'I don't believe you. We'll just see if a jury at Winchester Court believes you, shall we?'

The man's hard face turned deep red. 'One more death won't make any difference,' he growled.

'Might as well be hanged for a cop as a pig,' his son agreed and stepped towards the policeman with the knife raised. 'Nobody will ever know what happened to you!'

Jack tried to force a calm smile. He didn't feel calm. 'Bill Anderson at the pub knows where I am.'

'You're bluffing,' the farmer's son said.

'Young man, London accent, greasy black hair. Came into The Grey Horse and tried to sell some meat. Your meat. That's why I came out here. If you know the young man I'm talking about then you'll know I'm telling the truth.'

'And if we don't?'

'Then I'm a dead man,' Jack Lapham shrugged.

For half a minute the only sound was the hissing of the oil lamps and the distant owls. Finally Farmer Wade ran his thumb along the edge of the meat axe and smiled. 'Only trying to make a living, Constable. Only trying to make a living!'

What happened next?
1 The Wade family killed the Constable and he ended up in the Farlingron sausages.

2 Jack Lapham arrested the family. They went to court and were found guilty.

3 The Special Constable took a bribe. The Wades gave Jack Lapham meat and he kept quiet.

4 The Special Constable took a bribe. The Wades gave Jack Lapham meat but he reported them anyway.

> *Answer:* **2** The family claimed the animals were dead or dying so they were allowed to butcher them without a licence. However, the judge did not believe them. They were fined and imprisoned.

BUT there are many stories of less honest local policemen who took the bribe and kept quiet. Very often a whole village was involved. A pig was slaughtered and everyone got a joint – but the local constable had first choice.

Farmers had to tell the Government every time a piglet was born. But it was hard to keep a check. So, if a sow had 12 piglets then the farmer told them it was just 11!

One man was given a whole pig by his farmer-brother. It was hidden in the bath overnight. The man forgot to tell his sister that it was there. In the blackout she wandered into the bathroom. The candlelight revealed the pink, naked, bloodstained body in the bath. The woman ran out into the street screaming, 'Help! Murder! There's a body in the bath!' She woke all the neighbours and the man's guilty secret was out.

Ration fashion

If you couldn't get something during the War then you'd have to make do with something else. Women's stockings were hard to get – nylon for stockings was a fairly new invention and it was all used up to make parachutes for pilots. So, if you wanted lovely legs you would

• colour your legs

• draw a line down the back to make it look like a stocking seam

But, what would you use to stain your legs a brownish colour?

1 Gravy stock (like an Oxo cube)
2 Dye made from onion skins
3 Sun-tan lotion

Answer: All of them were used by women at some time.

Famous firsts of wartime

Lots of things were invented in wartime because they were needed to win the War. The Germans invented rocket missiles, for example. But which of the following were firsts between 1939 and 1945?

1 Dropping leaflets on an enemy town to give messages to the people (Messages like, 'Surrender now and we won't hurt you.')

2 Ball-point pens (for writing in an aeroplane)

3 Electronic computers (to calculate where a cannon shell would land)

4 Frozen food (because fresh food was hard to find)

5 Nylon (to make parachutes and nylon stockings)

6 Aeroplane ejection seats (so shot-down pilots could get out safely)

7 Radar (to warn you when enemy aircraft were coming)

8 Parachutes (to jump out of a fighter plane if you were hit)

9 Jeeps (to fight in rough countryside)

10 Women jockeys (because the men were fighting overseas)

Answers

1 No. This was done in 1806! Admiral Cochrane tied bundles of leaflets to the tails of kites. The messages were tied on with slow-burning fuses – when the fuse burnt down the leaflets dropped off! The kites were flown over the French coast. The method worked. (Perhaps you could fly messages over your house in this way. 'Have my tea ready, I'm nearly finished school!')

2 Yes. A Hungarian writer, Lasalo Biro, escaped from the Nazi invasion of his country in 1940 and took with him his idea for a ball-point pen. The British airmen were having trouble with doing navigation sums at high altitudes – fountain pens leaked and the ink wouldn't dry up there. In 1944 the British made 30,000 ball-point pens to help the war in the air. There are now more British ball-point pens than British people – and lots of people still call them Biros.

3 Yes. Mechanical computers had been invented by Charles Babbage in London between 1822 and 1871. But the first electronic one was made for the army in the United States. It began operating in 1946. It weighed 30 tons! That's 10,000 times as heavy as the computer this is being written on.

4 No. Clarence Birdseye was selling frozen food in 1930. But the first ready-cooked frozen food was made by the Birdseye company in 1939 – it was a type of chicken meal. (This gave rise to the horrible joke, 'Why did the one-eyed chicken cross the road?' Answer: 'To get to the Birdseye shop!')

5 Yes. Nylon was invented in New York (NY) and London (Lon) – hence the name, NY and Lon – Nylon! The Americans had used it for toothbrush bristles in 1938 and nylon stockings in 1940. But it wasn't made in Britain until 1941 – and the Government insisted it should be used to make parachutes, not stockings.

6 Yes. Invented by German aircraft designers in 1941. The first emergency ejection was in April 1941 when Major Schenk ejected from a test-flight and lived. The first British flier to try it was called Lynch. In 1946 he landed in the back yard of a pub ... and was later found, safe (and happy) in the bar room!

7 No. Germany had working radar in 1934 and Britain shortly after. Both used it to detect air attacks – but neither side realized at first that the other side had it! (You get the name from what it did … RAdio Detection And Ranging.)

8 No. A man called Garnerin jumped from a balloon over Paris in 1797. He didn't have a hole in the top of the parachute so it gave him a very bumpy ride. This made him the first man to be air-sick … too bad if you were underneath!

9 Yes. The United States army wanted a vehicle that would be four-wheel drive and be 'general purpose' – or GP … or jeep. (GP – jeep, get it?) The first arrived in Britain in November 1941.

10 Yes. Judy Johnson rode Lone Gallant in April 1943. She was tenth of 11 riders, beaten by 30 lengths. (That wasn't too bad – the last time Lone Gallant had been ridden by a man he'd been beaten by 400 lengths!)

The Home Front

Soldiers fighting abroad faced dangers every day. They were sometimes a bit scornful of the Local Defence Volunteers. They called them 'Dad's Army' because they were largely made up of older men who were past being called up to fight in the British Army.

Still, these brave volunteers faced dangers of their own, stumbling around in blacked-out Britain, never knowing when they might face an enemy invasion! And would it come by sea or from paratroopers?

It was a hard life and a thankless job. Here are some examples from the Durham Home Guard Accident book. The entries may seem horribly hilarious – or they could be terribly tragic ...

The dangers of Dad's Army

6 AUGUST 1940
Volunteer H.M. Wills
Collided with a marching column whilst riding motor cycle.

WE'LL SHOW 'EM

(There's no report on the injuries suffered by the marching men!)

17 August 1940
Volunteer J. E. Parker
Gunshot wounds in right arm and chest – accidentally shot by Volunteer Lumsden whilst on patrol
(Why worry about enemy paratroopers? Your own mates could shoot you!)

8 September 1940
Volunteer A. L. Mackay
Wounded in left knee. Accidental discharge of own rifle
(If the enemy didn't get you and your friends didn't get you then you could always get yourself!)

21 September 1940
Volunteer C. M. Blackmore
Gunshot wounds on left hand and right knee – accidentally shot by night-watchman at ship yard
(But if the night-watchman thought Mr Blackmore was an enemy commando, why didn't he kill him? Was he such a rotten shot that he only hit the poor bloke's hand and knee?)

And it wasn't just the fighting that was dangerous …
15 October 1940
Volunteer D. W Skellern
Fractured ankle – collapse of table while attending a lecture in Durham
(Maybe it was a booby-trapped enemy table!)

Even the floor was out to get you …
19 March 1941
J.O. Davidson
Rifle went off and splinter from
wooden floor pierced thumb

So was your uniform …
29 May 1941
J.H. Cray
Sliced top of finger whilst fixing chin strap to steel helmet

And as for hostile dogs …
14 October 1941
R. Thatcher
On duty was knocked off
cycle by a dog – damaged
knee and wrist
(Perhaps it was a German Shepherd!)

The blackout was a problem too …
26 September 1940
Injured leg run into from behind by a cyclist whilst on patrol

And simply being old and unfit was a danger …
19 August 1940
Volunteer A. C. Moody
Died after practice at Whitburn rifle range. In quest verdict:
death from heart failure brought on by the exertion on the rifle
range

Of course, the Home Guard would try to keep you fit.
All you had to do was survive the keep-fit sessions …

27 November 1940
Volunteer R. Simpson
Fell from vaulting horse – struck head. Died 30 November

And the War was not a job for men with false teeth …
28 June 1941
J. Oakenshaw Tripped over gym mat, struck face against box – damaged mouth and broke false teeth

Of course, all these dangers meant you needed first-aid training. But a teacher's life is not a happy one …

21 September 1941
Volunteer J. T. Lowell
Severed tendon in back whilst giving first-aid demonstration

In fact a teacher's life could be rotten …

25 March 1942

Private E. Fowell

Instructing recruits on rifle range received bullet wound in right thigh

(Would you shoot your teacher? Better not answer that one!)

But saddest of all were the innocent victims. The ones who had nothing to do with the War …

24 April 1943

Private Charles Stapler

Two broken toes – ran over a cat while riding a motorcycle
(There was no record of what happened to the cat.)

Home Front humour

The place where fighting happens is called the **'front'** … so British soldiers were fighting on the **European Front**. But back home people believed they were in the middle of the War too. They described the people preparing for war here as being on the **Home Front**.

(**Note:** This joke was told in a theatre as part of a comedy show. The local magistrates were asked to ban it because it was too **rude** to be told on a Sunday!)

If you didn't have an indoor toilet then you'd keep a 'chamber pot' under your bed. The common name for a chamber pot was a jerry. A nickname for a German was also a Jerry. So a particularly bad joke of World War Two went like this …

Joining the Armed Forces was usually good for a laugh …

The Government encouraged a series of touring entertainments for people in factories and theatres. The organisation was known as ENSA – Entertainments National Service Association. They performed concerts and plays. Some were serious, some funny … and some dreadful. Unkind audiences said ENSA stood for *Every Night Something Awful!*

In fact, giving new nicknames to initials was popular in wartime Britain. The Local Defence Volunteers were called the LDV for short. Many people claimed that the LDVs were a bit cowardly and said LDV stood for *Look, Duck … and Vanish!*

ARP stood for Air Raid Precautions – religious groups sent leaflets to families and said the British people should ARP *Awake! Repent! Prepare!* (to die!)

The land girls

The women of Britain were encouraged to join the Women's Land Army – the WLA. Girls from the towns were asked to volunteer to work on the land. It was usually a hard life in primitive living conditions. Some were cold in the winter because they didn't have overcoats. And in summer they got so hot they often took their trousers off and worked without any!

The farmers weren't always grateful for the land girls' help. Sometimes the farmers and the girls got on one another's nerves. One girl was sacked. Her crime? She called the farmer 'pig face'!

Another land girl, Sylvia, had a choice between working in the dairy or working as a rat-catcher. She chose rat-catching – you had to milk the cows every day, but rat-catchers always got a day off. She passed her tests and started killing rabbits, moles, crows and mice as well as rats.

Four girls in North Wales probably held the record. In 14 months they killed ...

• 7,689 rats

• 1,668 foxes

• 1,901 moles

• 35,545 rabbits

Rabbits had a hard time of it. The Ministry of Agriculture said they were pests – and had to be killed. The Ministry of Food said they made a good meal!

So no one minded rabbit poachers any more. They sold the rabbits to villagers for one shilling and eightpence (8p). If you skinned it and gave the farmer back the skin then he'd give you two-pence (1p) back – rabbit skins made good mittens!

It could have been worse – Adolf Hitler told the German people, *The lowest form of male is much, much higher than the noblest female.* So, girls, it's just as well he didn't win the War!

It could have been worse 3

Land girls had a hard life: the cold and damp caused several to suffer from arthritis at an early age. Still, it was generally a fairly healthy one. But women who chose to work in the armaments factories had a harder time. They had to make bullets, shells and high explosives. Many were killed or injured in explosions. The explosive mixture turned their skin and their hair yellow. They became known as 'Budgies'.

Oops!

Throughout the War governments and people made mistakes ... some more serious than others.

• Bombing raids had stopped. The V1 flying bombs had ceased. On 7 September 1944 the Government announced that evacuation was ended. On 8 September 1944 the first V2 rocket fell on London and they were even deadlier than the V1s!

• In 1944 King Haakon of Norway was invited to speak on BBC radio. His speech was going to be 40 seconds too short so the radio producer sent to the record library for a fanfare of trumpets. The king finished speaking, the record was played – and there were music and screams and people shouting things like, 'Try your luck on the rifles, three shots a penny' and, 'Roll up! Roll up! See the bearded lady!' The producer groaned. 'What happened to the record of the fanfare?' 'Ah ... sorry,' the assistant said. 'Thought you said funfair!'

• The British people feared the German airforce – the Luftwaffe. But the Luftwaffe lost the Battle of Britain. They also lost one or two other battles during World War Two. In February 1940, a Luftwaffe bomber sighted two warships and attacked them with cannons blazing and bombs raining down. Both ships suffered terrible damage. Unfortunately for the pilot, both ships belonged to the German navy!

• In May 1945, the war in Europe ended. To celebrate VE Day (Victory in Europe day) British warships in some ports fired their guns – it was meant to be a bit of harmless fun like November 5th bangers. A warship on the River Wear got it wrong – they used real shells instead of blanks. One shell landed on a Sunderland house two miles away. Two innocent people (who'd survived enemy bombing raids for six years) were killed!

The Royal Family

The Royal Family was particularly popular during the War. One reason was that they decided to stay in London to share the dangers of the ordinary people.

In fact Queen Elizabeth (the wife of George VI and the present Queen's Mother) was pleased when Buckingham Palace was bombed. She said she was now just the same as the poor victims of the bombing in the East End of London... This wasn't quite true since she had one or two other comfortable homes to go to when the Palace was bombed. The East-enders often lost everything! But it certainly made the Royal Family more popular than they've ever been! Queen Elizabeth must have been the only person in Britain who was pleased to be bombed!

The King during the War was George VI. Did you know ...

1 George first met Elizabeth Bowes-Lyon when he was ten and she was five. It's said that she gave him the cherry off the top of her cake!

2 George was never meant to be King. His older brother, Edward, became King. But Edward fell in love with an American woman who had been divorced. This was not on! Edward was given a choice – do you want the woman or the crown? Edward chose the woman, young George got the crown.

3 Actually, George was Albert. He used the name George as king because it was a regular royal name. But his friends and family always called him Bertie.

4 George hadn't been trained to be King. He wasn't very good at public speaking and had a stammer. His voice-trainer gave him tongue-twisters to practise on. Can you recite these? George could.
Let's go gathering healthy heather
With the gay brigade of grand dragoons
or
She sifted seven thick-stalked thistles
Through a strong thick sieve

5 When George was crowned in 1937 he had to take an oath. The bishops lost the place in the book at the last moment. The Archbishop of Canterbury held his own book for George to read from. But, George said later ... *Horror of horrors, his thumb covered the words of the oath!*

6 One of the bishops then stood on George's robe and nearly brought the new king crashing to the floor. The coronation was the first time a king had been seen live on television. This was not a great event ... there were just 2,100 sets working at that time!

7 When George and Elizabeth went on a royal visit to Paris in 1938 there was a lot of security cover for them. But, most peculiar, there were groups of stout Frenchmen leaning against some of the older trees on the route. The French were worried that the trees might fall on the royal couple!

8 The nearest the Queen came to being killed during the War was when she was attacked by a soldier ... a British soldier! He had come home to find his family had been killed in an air raid. He deserted the army and made his way to the palace. The man found his way into Elizabeth's bedroom and she woke to find him gripping her ankles! The queen didn't panic. She simply said, 'Tell me about it.' As he poured out his sad story she made her way to the bell and rang for help.

9 Britain sent its armies into Europe in June 1944. George VI wanted to go with the attacking armies. Prime Minister Winston Churchill wanted to go too. Churchill argued that if they both risked their lives and were both killed then Britain would lose its two leaders. In the end neither went!

10 Windsor Castle had a ready-made air-raid shelter for the Royal Family – the beetle-infested dungeons of the castle!

Potty poems

The Second World War was a great time for music – everyone was singing to stay cheerful. The trouble was the words were pretty awful.

The *Blackout Stroll* was a cheerful dance ... but it didn't take someone with half a dinosaur brain to come up with the chorus:

Everybody do the Blackout Stroll
Laugh and drive your cares right up the pole!

OLÉ!

Rotten rhymes

Could you have written a wartime song? Here are some classic lines – can you find the right words to complete them? Some are harder than others. The figures in brackets are the points you can score for a correct answer. Can you score ten without cheating?

1   **Run Rabbit Run**
    On the farm every Friday
    On the farm it's rabbit ___ ___
    (3)

2   **Roll Out the Barrel**
    Every time they hear that oom-pa-pa
    Everybody feels so ___ __ __
    (5)

3   I'm Gonna Get Lit Up
You'll find me on the tiles,
You will find me wreathed in smiles
I'm going to get so lit up
I'll be visible for _ _ _ _ _
(1)

4   Knees Up Mother Brown
Joe brought his concertina, and Nobby
brought the _ _ _ _
And all the little nippers swung upon
the chandelier
(2)

5   Cleanin' My Rifle
Little bit lonesome, little bit blue,
Cleanin' my rifle, dreamin' of _ _ _
(1)

6   Bless Em All
Bless 'em all, Bless 'em all
The long and the _ _ _ _ _ and the tall
(2)

7   Lilli Marlene
I knew you were waiting in the street,
I heard your _ _ _ _
But could not meet
(2)

8 In the Quartermaster's Stores
There is beer, beer, beer you can't get near
In the stores, in the stores.
There is rum, rum for the General's _ _ _
In the quartermaster's stores
(2)

9 Let the People Sing
Let the people sing, sing like any thing,
Any sort of song they choose,
Let the people sing, let the _ _ _ _ _ _ ring
Anything to kill the blues
(101)

10 ---- Me Goodnight Sergeant Major
_ _ _ _ me goodnight Sergeant Major,
Tuck me in my little wooden bed.
We all love you Sergeant Major,
When we hear you bawling 'Show a leg!'
Don't forget to wake me in the morning
And bring me round a nice hot cup of tea,
_ _ _ me goodnight Sergeant Major,
Sergeant Major be a mother to me!
(2)

Maybe the worst rhyme crime was in the song *Nursie! Nursie,* which came up with the awful rhyme ...

> *Nursie! Nursie!*
> *I'm a–getting worsie.*

Yuck!

Vile verses

The Government tried to persuade people to eat certain types of food or do things to help the war effort by writing poems they could recite and get into their heads. Would you be persuaded to do what the Government wanted if you read these verses ... ?

1 Message:

Poem:

> *The fishermen are saving lives*
> *By sweeping seas for mines.*
>
> *So, you'll not grumble, 'What, no fish?'*
> *When you have read these lines.*

(Instead you were offered whale-meat steaks – very oily and tough.)

118

2 Message:

Poem:

When fisher folk are brave enough
To face the mines and foe for you
You surely can be bold enough
To try a kind of fish that's new.

(Fish like ugly cat-fish that it spoiled your appetite just to look at)

3 Message:

Poem:

If you've news of our munitions
KEEP IT DARK
Ships or planes or troop positions
KEEP IT DARK
Lives are lost through conversation
Here's a tip for the duration
When you've private information
KEEP IT DARK!

4 Message:

WASTING FOOD IS
AGAINST THE LAW

Poem:

> *Auntie threw her rinds away.*
> *To the lock-up she was taken.*
> *There she is and there she'll stay*
> *Till she learns to save her bacon.*

The public struck back with verses of their own. The shortage of onions was mourned in one verse which ended …

> *My cupboard might as well be bare.*
> *I sadly wander everywhere*
> *And try to sniff the empty air*
> *To scent a whiff of onion.*

5 Message:

DON'T LISTEN TO BAD NEWS

STAY CHEERFUL

Poem:

> *Do not believe the tale the milkman tells;*
> *No troops have mutinied at Potters Bar.*
> *Nor are there submarines at Tunbridge Wells.*
> *The BBC will warn us when there are.*

(A bit unlikely – a submarine arriving at Hastings on the south coast of England would have to travel 30 miles (48km) to Tunbridge Wells – over land!)

6 Message:

SAVE RUBBER

BECAUSE EVERY SCRAP HAS TO BE BROUGHT ACROSS THE SUBMARINE HAUNTED SEAS

Poem:

> *R stands for rags, household Refuse and Rope.*
> *And R stands for wise reclamation.*
> *But remember that Rubber's more vital than most–*
> *And please help the whole British nation.*

> *R is for runs – and I modestly blush*
> *R is for runs in your girdle.*
> *May I suggest, if your corset's worn out,*
> *It will help us to jump the last hurdle.*
> *(This poem also had the curious line, R is for victory!)*

121

7 Message:

Poem: (from an advert for wool)

> *There's more that goes to win a war*
> *Than tanks and planes and guns!*
> *Than men prepared to do their best*
> *To overthrow the Huns **
> *The Home Front too must play its part*
> *And you can do YOUR bit*
> *To help our gallant fighting lads*
> *By starting now – to KNIT!*
> *You cannot knit too many things*
> *To keep out wet and cold;*
> *Like mittens, helmets, socks and scarves*
> *GO TO IT – young and old!*

(Pity they couldn't knit a few tanks or the odd battleship!)

8 Message:

* Hun was a name
for a German used
by the British.

Poem:

Tittle tattle
Lost the battle

9 Children were also taught rhymes to help them remember important things. It was important not to talk to strangers. Not because they might harm you, but because they might be spies and you might let secrets slip. So you were warned …

If anyone stops me to ask the way,
All I must answer is 'I can't say.'

Mr Chad

During the War a new cartoon character appeared. A fat little face peering over a wall and saying, 'Wot, no ***?'. The face appeared everywhere, scrawled on walls and drawn in exercise books at school. Mr Chad would say, 'Wot, no wellies?' one day and 'Wot, no bananas?' the next.

Billy Brown

Posters appeared on London Transport for the most unpopular cartoon character of the War … Billy Brown. Billy was a chubby little man who was meant to remind you of how to behave … a bit like a teacher. The trouble was his advice made him sound very bossy … definitely like a teacher! Billy didn't get angry about waiting in a queue for a bus …

He never jostles in the queue,
But waits and takes his turn. Do you?

123

Wartime words

Every age has its own way of talking. If you lived in the 1600s then you might say, 'S'blood, sirrah, that kind-heart is a nimenog!' *I say, mate, that dentist is a fool!*

In the early 1900s you could have gone into school dinners and said, 'Great! Scaffold poles for dinner!' And what was on your plate? chips, of course.

The Second World War brought its own slang. Can you match the slang to its meaning?

Spiffing slang

1 pit   a smuggled goods

2 kerdumf   b money

3 solid   c a teacher who joins the army

4 akka   d false teeth

5 niff–naff   e mad

6 buckshee   f face

7 pan   g mouth

8 nutty   h fuss

9 beertrap   i free

10 sardine tin   j crash

11 bolo   k chocolate

12 schooly   l stupid

13 rabbits   m bed

14 railings   n submarine

Answers:

1m) pit = bed 2i) kerdumf = crash 3l) solid = stupid 4b) akka = money 5h) niff-naff = fuss 6i) buckshee = free 7f) pan = face 8k) nutty = chocolate 9g) beertrap = mouth 10n) sardine tin = submarine 11e) bolo = mad 12c) schooly = a teacher who joins the army 13a) rabbits = smuggled goods 14d) railings = false teeth

Scare your teacher:

(Don't panic but I just found a bomb in your desk! Hah! I was just telling a big lie!)

Name that food

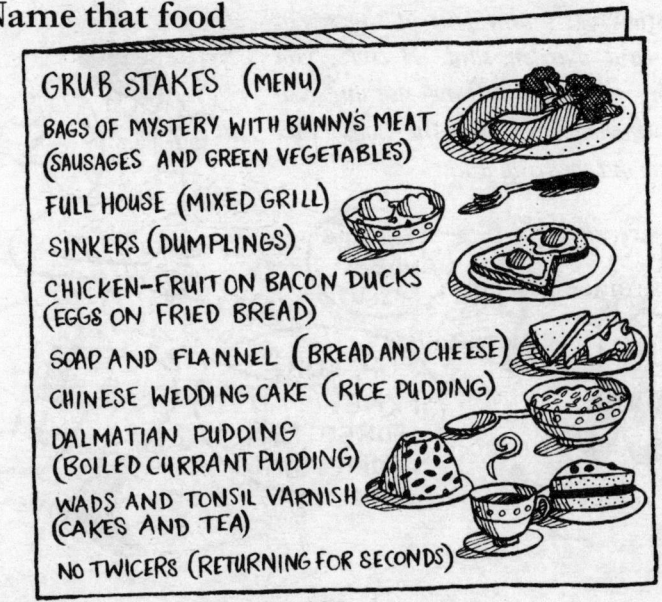

GRUB STAKES (MENU)

BAGS OF MYSTERY WITH BUNNY'S MEAT (SAUSAGES AND GREEN VEGETABLES)

FULL HOUSE (MIXED GRILL)

SINKERS (DUMPLINGS)

CHICKEN-FRUIT ON BACON DUCKS (EGGS ON FRIED BREAD)

SOAP AND FLANNEL (BREAD AND CHEESE)

CHINESE WEDDING CAKE (RICE PUDDING)

DALMATIAN PUDDING (BOILED CURRANT PUDDING)

WADS AND TONSIL VARNISH (CAKES AND TEA)

NO TWICERS (RETURNING FOR SECONDS)

Epilogue

The Second World War was different from every war the British people had ever been in before. It wasn't just soldiers who faced injury and death every day in a strange country.

It was also the women, men, children and old people who stayed at home. Their courage was tested. So was their patience, their honesty, their determination and their sense of humour.

Most people passed the tests and amazed even themselves. Some didn't even bother taking the tests – and that surprised nobody. Those few used the War to make money and to make sure they came out all right.

And not everyone showed bravery under the threat of being bombed. An old man told this story which he swore was true ...

A woman up at Tuppers Road heard the air-raid warning and panicked. She rushed out into the street wearing just a pair of stockings and a pair of shoes. An air-raid warden said, 'Aren't you going to put anything else on?' So she dashed back into the house and came out wearing a hat!

SNIGGER SNIGGER

'ERE'S YOUR 'ANDBAG MISSUS

OH, LORKS I KNEW I'D FORGOTTEN SOMETHING

She wasn't the only one to panic in the rush to a shelter. A young woman told this tale ...

YOU ROTTEN BEGGAR! WE HAVEN'T EVEN FINISHED PAYING FOR THAT HOUSE YET

A woman came flying down Dean Road in her pyjamas The buttons on the jacket were coming loose. While she was trying to do them up her trousers fall down!

The soldiers of Britain and her allies won the fighting. The people back home did their best to survive. And when the blitz was at its worst some even managed to raise a laugh or two.

In a small village in the south-west of England a German bomber swooped out of the sky, dropped a bomb and demolished the wall of a house. The woman who owned it rushed out into the road. As the plane roared off she shook her fist at it and yelled, 'You rotten beggar! We haven't even finished paying for that house yet!'

In the end, after six long years, Hitler's Nazi armies had been beaten. Britain and her allies had won on the battlefields, but nobody really won the War. The tens of millions who lost their lives were certainly the losers.

Many people still hate German people because the blitz in Britain killed so many. But as the War drew to a close, Britain blitzed the German cities too. We have to remember that the blitz on Britain cost the lives of an average of 50,000 a year. We also have to remember that a bombing raid by the Royal Air Force on the German

127

city of Dresden killed 130,000 in one night! Not soldiers or weapon-makers or Nazis … ordinary men, women and children of Dresden along with countless refugees who were sleeping in – the streets at the time.

Sometimes history can be truly horrible.

When Britain's blitz was at its worst the Britons were at their best. As Churchill said,

IF THE BRITISH EMPIRE LASTS FOR A THOUSAND YEARS, MEN WILL STILL SAY "THIS WAS THEIR FINEST HOUR"

He could well have been right.

BLITZED BRITS

BRITS

GRISLY QUIZ

**Now find out if you're a
blitzed Brits expert!**

Rotten Rules

The government introduced lots of loopy laws for the Brits in the Blitz. See if you can figure out which are true and which are tosh.

1. Church bells could only be rung when it was time for lunch.

2. Signposts were taken down because the government wanted the Germans to get lost if they invaded.

3. From 1941 everyone was given a special mask because it stopped people eating so much, which helped with rationing.

4. White lines were painted on pavements to help people find their way around in the blackout.

5. Local Defence Volunteers weren't allowed to have guns during parades – they had to use broom handles instead.

6. There was no television allowed during the war.

7. Only children were allowed chocolate.

8. It wasn't only men who were forced to join the war effort, women had to do National Service too.

9. Little boys weren't allowed to wear trousers.

10. The only meat people could eat during the war was spam.

QUICK BLITZ QUIZ

How well would you fare in London during the Blitz? Answer these questions to discover if you'd dodge death or be nobbled by the Nazis.

1. If you didn't have an air-raid shelter in your garden, where was the best place to go in London to beat the bombs? (Clue: Mind the gap!)

2. What was the best way to put out a fire from a fire bomb? (Clue: you'll need your bucket and spade)

3. How would you know when a dastardly doodlebug bomb was about to explode? (Clue: watch out for the quiet ones…)

4. How could an old saucepan help with the war effort? (Clue: frying high)

5. If you didn't have an Anderson shelter in the garden, what kind of shelter could you use in your home during an air raid? (Clue: it's a bit cagey)

6. How did the government warn people against enemy sympathisers? (Clue: careless talk costs lives)

7. Where could you shelter from an enemy dive-bomber? (Clue: silver cigars)

8. How would you know if the Germans had dropped mustard gas in your city? (Clue: it might be on a post-it note)

9. How could you avoid bumping into other people during the blackout? (Clue: White's all right)

10. How would you protect yourself against the bombs if you were an ARP warden out and about during the Blitz? (Clue: heads up)

EVACUEE EXPERIENCES

Loads of children from London and other cities were evacuated during the Blitz because their mums and dads were afraid they'd be splattered by a bomb. See if you can fill in the gaps in Little Johnny's letter to find out more about life for kids in the countryside.

Here are the missing words in the wrong order: egg, American, name tag, handkerchief, farm, chewing gum, caned, bombs, chickens, rationing

Dear Ma,

We got here OK but the train journey was long and I lost my _____(1) which made Teacher very cross. We were lined up and people got to pick which kids they wanted. I was picked last – probably because I was all dirty from the train and had forgotten my _____(2). I am staying on a _____(3), which is good. I have to feed the _____(4) and collect the _____(5). They have _____(6) here, but there's still more food than at home. I don't like my new school though. I was _____(7) for talking in class. A bunch of _____(8) soldiers

132

arrived in the village yesterday. They gave us _____(9), which was ace.

I miss you but I don't miss all the _____(10).

Lots of love, Johnny

ANSWERS

Rotten Rules

1. Tosh. Church bells could only be rung to warn that the ghastly Germans had invaded Blighty.
2. True. If the Germans had ever got as far as England there would have been hundreds of them milling about the countryside scratching their heads.
3. Tosh. The masks were in case the Germans used poisonous gas.
4. True. It didn't stop lots of pesky people pile-ups on the pavement, though.
5. True. They weren't allowed uniforms either, so they must have felt a bit daft marching up and down in civilian clothes wielding a broom. Not very threatening…
6. True. But it wasn't a terrible TV tragedy – only 2,000 people had TVs at the time.
7. Tosh. Anyone could chomp on chocolate as long as they had enough ration coupons to buy it.
8. True. From 1941 all women between the ages of 18 and 60 had to work for the war effort. Most of them didn't mind – it got them away from being housewives.
9. True. But don't worry, they didn't have to go to school in their pants (eeuww!). They had to wear shorts to save material.

10. Tosh. Some fresh meat was available but this was strictly rationed. Spam – chopped up tinned pieces of pork – was made in America and shipped to England, where it was very popular.

Quick Blitz Quiz
1. The Underground. People snuggled down on the platforms at night. It wasn't very comfortable at first, but later they put in bunks for people to sleep on! Also useful for a quick kip if your train was delayed…
2. Smother it with sand. Sand piles were everywhere in London to put out fires during the Blitz. You had to be careful of the dog poo in them, though.
3. It would go quiet. Doodlebug bombs made a loud droning sound like a big bumblebee until just before they exploded – when they went deathly silent.
4. Saucepans could be turned into Spitfires. Recycling was big in the Second World War. People donated any metal items to be melted down and used for making aeroplanes.
5. A Morrison shelter. These were like cages made of wire, which you could squeeze into to avoid the bombs. They didn't offer much protection when your house came tumbling down.
6. Posters. In January 1940 the government printed thousands of posters saying 'careless talk costs lives' that they put up all over the country, warning people about the dangers of idle chat, in case spies learned something valuable they could tell the enemy.
7. Beneath a barrage balloon. These big silver balloons floated over towns and cities and were meant to prevent dive-bombers getting close enough to drop their bombs. Even if you were safe from the enemy though, you could still be injured if a barrage balloon exploded or caught fire.

8. Look at the top of a post-box. They were painted yellow or green, which would stain if mustard gas got on it.

9. Wear a small amount of white. People were encouraged to show a little bit of white clothing that would hopefully show up in the dark. Even the cows in the countryside were painted with white stripes to avoid a cow collision.

10. Wear a tin hat. Yep – that was all the protection you got. ARP wardens were given hopeless hats made of tin while they were helping the injured and putting out fires during a raid. Not very effective when a bomb is dropped on your head.

Evacuee Experiences
1. Name tag, 2. Handkerchief, 3. Farm, 4. Chickens, 5. Eggs, 6. Rationing, 7. Caned, 8. American, 9. Chewing gum, 10. Bombs

INTERESTING INDEX

Where will you find 'fake bananas','bed-wetting',
'knickers'and 'swearing' in an index? In a Horrible Histories
book, of course!

138

Terry Deary was born at a very early age, so long ago he can't remember. But his mother, who was there at the time, says he was born in Sunderland, north-east England, in 1946 – so it's not true that he writes all *Horrible Histories* from memory. At school he was a horrible child only interested in playing football and giving teachers a hard time. His history lessons were so boring and so badly taught, that he learned to loathe the subject. *Horrible Histories* is his revenge.

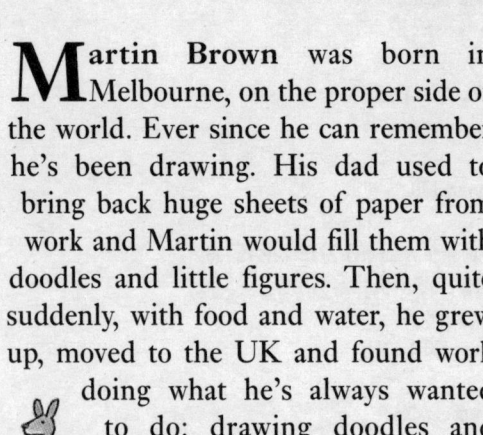

Martin Brown was born in Melbourne, on the proper side of the world. Ever since he can remember he's been drawing. His dad used to bring back huge sheets of paper from work and Martin would fill them with doodles and little figures. Then, quite suddenly, with food and water, he grew up, moved to the UK and found work doing what he's always wanted to do: drawing doodles and little figures.

H♦RRIBLE HIST♦RIES

WOEFUL SECOND
WORLD WAR

Terry Deary Illustrated by **Martin Brown**

■ SCHOLASTIC

To Stephen Shannon. With sincere thanks.

Scholastic Children's Books,
Euston House, 24 Eversholt Street,
London NW1 1DB, UK

A division of Scholastic Ltd
London ~ New York ~ Toronto ~ Sydney ~ Auckland
Mexico City ~ New Delhi ~ Hong Kong

First published in the UK by Scholastic Ltd, 1999
This edition published by Scholastic Ltd, 2016

Some of the material in this book has previously been published in
Horrible Histories: The Massive Millennium Quiz Book/Horribly Huge Quiz Book

Text © Terry Deary, 1999
Illustration © Martin Brown, 1999, 2016

All rights reserved. Moral rights asserted.

ISBN 978 1407 16391 8

Printed and bound by CPI Group (UK) Ltd, Croydon, CR0 4YY

8 10 9

The right of Terry Deary and Martin Brown to be identified as the author and illustrator of this work respectively has been asserted by them in
accordance with the Copyright, Designs and Patents Act, 1988.

www.scholastic.co.uk

CONTENTS

Introduction

History can be horrible – but some times in history are more horrible than others. . .

Of course, this is all a matter of opinion. . .

Most people seem to agree that wartimes are the *worst* of times. And wars in the twentieth century were the *most* horrible of all. Even the winners suffered terrible losses, and new weapons weren't fussy about who they exterminated – suffering schoolkids shot, peaceful pensioners pulverized and blameless babies bombed.

You might think it's easy to drop a bomb from an aeroplane because you don't have to see the suffering you cause. But war brings out the worst side of some human beings. The monsters. The few people who enjoy the pain and torture and death they are causing. . .

And it brings out the best in others – the ones who risk their own lives to fight for what they think is right. The heroes and heroines.

Most people are somewhere in between. Hopefully *you'll* never have to suffer in a war. But you will be tested from time to time. You may like to decide if you'd act like a monster or a heroine.

Any old boring history book will tell you about the battles and the dates and the facts and figures. But what you want to know is what it was really like to live through those days. How did people really behave in the Second World War? And how would you have behaved?

What you need is a horrible history of the Second World War! So read on. . .

Terrible timeline

11 November 1918 End of First World War. Germany battered and bitter. They blame their leaders, traitors at home and especially the Jews. If only they can get a strong leader they will win next time. . .

1930s

1933 German elections won by the National Socialist party – Nat–so, or Nazi party, for short. They are led by mad, bad Adolf Hitler. They begin bullying Jews and building up stocks of weapons. The Germans have enemies – especially Mr Stalin's Soviets – but they have friends like Mr Mussolini's Italy. Mr Churchill of Britain tries to warn the Brits but no one takes much notice . . . yet.

1937 In Europe two rival 'teams' are forming – the 'Allies' of Britain, France and the Soviets against the 'Axis' of Germany and Italy. The teams are spoiling for a match.

Over in Asia the Japanese attack China. So what? So their war will get mixed up with the war in Europe that is coming soon. . .

30 September 1938 Britain and France agree with Germany and Italy there'll be no more war. 'Peace in our time!' says Brit Prime Minister Neville Chamberlain. Fat chance.

5 October 1938 Adolf Hitler's Germans take over the Sudetenland in Czechoslovakia . . . peacefully. 'I am just protecting the three million Germans who live there!' he says innocently. (Rearrange the letters of 'A. Hitler' and you get 'The Liar'!)

23 August 1939 Shock! Deadly enemies unite! Mr Adolf Hitler of Germany (with a toothbrush moustache) and Mr Josef Stalin of the Soviet Union (with a yard-brush moustache) peacefully agree not to fight one another. No chance. Never trust a man with a moustache.

1 September 1939 A. Hitler (the liar) had promised not to invade Poland. Today his army invades Poland . . . and 'peacefully' shares it with the Soviets. No one asked the Poles, of course. Britain and France say they'll fight for Poland's freedom. That means war!

3 **September 1939** Britain and France declare war on Germany. Next day Mr Winston Churchill (who doesn't have a moustache or much hair at all) is made First Lord of the Admiralty. He could say, 'I told you so!'

8 **November 1939** Six people killed when a bomb explodes in a Munich beer hall. It was meant to kill Hitler – but he left fifteen minutes before it exploded. Hitler lives – millions will now die in the Second World War.

1940

9 **April** Germany invades Denmark. The Danes are so surprised they don't fight back.

10 **May** Brits make Winston Churchill their Prime Minister. 'I have nothing to offer but blood, toil, tears and sweat,' he says. And the

blood and tears of millions of others too, of course. On the same day it's the blood and tears of the Belgians and Dutch as Germany invades.

June Brit armies in France driven back to the beaches at Dunkirk. They escape. Mr Churchill says Brits will defend themselves in the streets and the hills if the Germans invade. 'We will never surrender!' Tough talk for tough times. Italians (who think they know a winner when they see one) join Germany in war against the Allies.

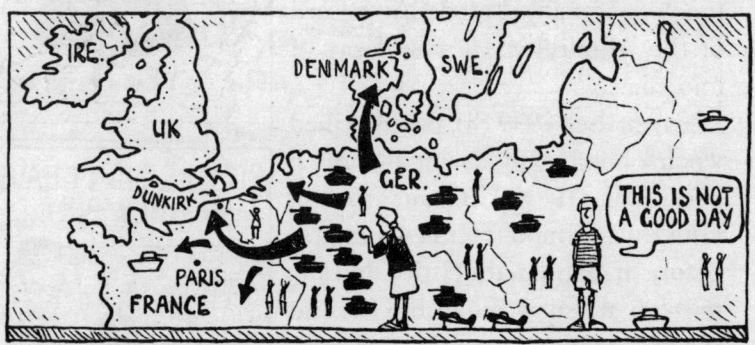

14 June Germans enter Paris. The French say, 'We gave up without too much of a fight because we didn't want our lovely city destroyed.' Germans sneer at this feeble excuse.

7 September German planes bomb London in daylight while British Royal Air Force hit dozens of

German cities. Women and children are now in the front line of war.

December Now Japan joins in the war on Germany's side. Italy invades Greece – just like the ancient Romans all over again – and Egypt. This is the start of war in the deserts of North Africa.

1941

10 May Mad Hitler's madder assistant, Rudolf Hess, pinches a plane and flies to Scotland. He wants to persuade Churchill to share the world with Hitler. The Germans say Hess is potty – and many Brits agree. The Brits lock Hess up for the rest of his long life. The next day German bombs destroy Brit House of Commons.

22 June Hitler breaks his promise to Stalin (surprise, surprise), and invades Russia. Hitler makes some

11

big mistakes but this is probably the biggest. The Soviets aren't going to give up as easily as some.

7 December Japanese warplanes bomb the US navy in Pearl Harbour, Hawaii. US goes to war with Japan in the Pacific Ocean. Then the Japanese capture the Brit colony, Malaya. Now there's a jungle war.

11 December Germany and Italy declare war on the USA. This is really becoming something you can call a World War.

1942

20 January Nastiest of all Nazi plans. German leaders meet and agree that Jews are not really human. Fit Jews will be worked to death and weak Jews will be starved or killed in death camps.

30-31 May RAF does more damage in one night raid on Cologne than 1,300 previous attacks (it says). Meanwhile, the Soviets have pushed back the German army and the US bombed the Japanese navy. The war is turning against the Nazis.

7 August In the Pacific, US marines land at Guadalcanal in the Solomon Islands. Now the war is turning against the Japanese.

4 November In the North African desert the British drive back the German tanks at the battle of El Alamein. That cheers up the Allies.

2 December A nuclear reaction is created by scientists on a Chicago squash court. If this power can be turned into a bomb it could win the war. From squash court to squashed enemies. But who'll build that nuclear bomb first? The race is on.

13

1943

February Germans finally defeated at Stalingrad, Russia. The Soviets start the long and bloody push towards Berlin.

19 April Jews in Poland rise up against the Nazi exterminators. A year ago they helped the Nazis to 'evacuate' fellow Jews to the camps because they thought it was for the Jews' own good. Now word gets back that they are, in fact, death camps. The rebels have little to lose – die fighting or die in gas chambers. But . . .

16 May Jews in Warsaw wiped out. Some prefer to die in their burning buildings or jump from the roofs rather than become Nazi prisoners. Hitler's assistant, Himmler, orders the destruction of Jewish settlements everywhere.

17 May RAF destroy German dams

14

with clever invention, a bomb that bounces on water. They wreck power supplies to German factories – and drown a lot of innocent people. Do not try this in your bath – either the bombing OR the drowning!

23 July Allies are back in Europe for the first time since Dunkirk in June 1940. They capture Palermo in Sicily and head north. It's a long way – and nearly two years – from Berlin.

25 July Italy's Benito Mussolini is thrown out of power as Italy is invaded by the Allies. Well, they have to blame someone.

1944

April In the Pacific the US are 'island hopping' towards Japan. In Europe the Soviets have reached Poland and Romania in the fightback to the north and east of Germany. Their Brit and US allies are heading

north through Italy. All they need is an attack through France to the west and, guess what…

6 June D-Day. Allies land in France and head towards Berlin. But they're still almost a year away.

12 June New German secret weapon, a flying bomb, lands on London. It's called the V1 – 'V' for Vergeltungswaffen … vengeance weapon. Within a month almost 3,000 Brits will be killed by them. Some weapon, some vengeance.

20 July Now Hitler himself is bombed – by his own German Army officers. The bomb blows Hitler's trousers off but sadly he survives.

1 August The gallant Poles rebel to throw out German invaders … again. But their Soviet and American 'friends' refuse to help them. Result? Poles poleaxed.

September First US troops set foot on German soil but the Germans fight back furiously. The end is still a long way off.

1945

27 January Soviets march in to Auschwitz concentration camp and free 5,000 prisoners, mainly Jews. But they're three weeks too late to save the last four prisoners executed for hiding explosives. All four were young girls.

14 February After two days of Allied air raids the ancient German city of Dresden is flattened. Statues, paintings and beautiful churches are destroyed . . . and a small matter of 25,000 people. Happy Valentine's Day, Dresden.

12 March A 14-year-old Jewish girl finished her diary three months ago with the words 'All people are good.' Today she dies, half starved and in a fever in Belsen concentration camp. But her diary lives on as a terrible warning to us. Thank you, Anne Frank.

28 April Italy's dictator Mussolini is tried. 'Let me live and I'll give you my empire!' he begs. Fat chance. He's shot and hanged by the heels for the people to see.

30 April Allies surround Berlin. Adolf Hitler doesn't want to end up like Mussolini. So he kills his dog, then his new wife Eva and finally himself. Guards burn the body to stop it being paraded by the conquering Soviets. Many Germans refuse to believe he's dead – many more believe it and kill themselves.

7 May New German government surrenders and the war in Europe is over. But the most fearsome drama of the war is still to be acted out.

6 August US drop first nuclear bomb on the Japanese city of Hiroshima. When a second bomb destroys Nagasaki three days later the Japanese surrender. It's hard to fight an enemy when a single bomb can kill 60,000 people in seconds. The Second World War ends five years (and 40 million corpses) after it started.

18

Home horrors

The Second World War was different to past wars because you weren't safe anywhere. Innocent young people could be lying in bed reading a comic or studying at school or sitting on the toilet one moment – and be dead the next.

Bombs could blast you, saboteurs could spifflicate you and missiles marmalize you wherever you were. A battle area was known as a 'Front'. Now countries outside the war zones had their own 'Home Fronts'.

Horrible history happened at home as well as on battle fields...

Dad's barmy army

In Britain in 1940 the people were worried about a German invasion from the sea and from the air. The brave Brits started to arm themselves with shotguns and any weapons they could lay their hands on.

The government decided it would be better to organize these fighting folk into a proper army. In 1939 Winston Churchill had wanted a Home Guard formed – when he became Prime Minister in May 1940 he got it. Churchill had hoped for 500,000. He got 250,000 in the first day and 1,500,000 by June. They were first known as the Local Defence Volunteers – the LDV.

At first these untrained men were a bit of a joke. They weren't given proper weapons, they just armed themselves with anything that could kill. One boy said:

We were sent to defend a factory with broom handles. I pinched a knife from Mum's kitchen and tied it to the top.

One 14-year-old boy took along a bow and arrow. That would have worried some German tank commander if the Germans really had invaded! Others took along a nice heavy golf club.

No wonder a popular comedian, George Formby, sang a song about them . . .

I'm guarding the home of the Home Guard,
I'm guarding the Home Guard's home.
All night long, steady and strong,
Doing what I told 'em, I can't go wrong.
One evening when on LDV,
Some German soldiers I did see.
They ran like Hell . . . but they couldn't catch me!
I'm guarding the Home Guard's home.

PLINK
PLINKA
PLINK

The government said Home Guard soldiers had to be aged between 17 and 65. But boys as young as 14 joined. Some old soldiers from the First World War lied about their age and were eighty years old. No wonder they got the nickname 'Dad's Army'.

The men in Dad's Army were keen. It was great that they felt they were doing something to help. But sometimes they were too keen and too clumsy. Then they became Dad's disasters . . .

Ten horrible Home Guard facts
1 Home Guard soldiers were worried about how to spot a German. They were warned an enemy paratrooper might be disguised as a nun, a vicar or even a woman carrying a baby. The daftest idea for uncovering a spy was to shout . . .

. . . and a German couldn't stop himself from raising his arm, clicking his heels and replying . . .

2 Home Guards were in more danger from their own weapons than from the enemy who never arrived. They

were given sticky bombs – a bit like explosive toffee apples on a stick. The idea was that they would run up to an enemy tank and slap the goo-covered bomb on to the side. But many tried to *throw* the bombs, the sticks came loose and the bombs fell at their feet. Oooops! 768 Home Guard members were accidentally killed during the Second World War and nearly six thousand more were injured.

3 And their families were also at risk. A Home Guard soldier was cleaning his rifle on the kitchen table and forgot that there was a bullet in the firing chamber. He pulled the trigger, the gun went off – and killed his wife.

4 Early in the war Home Guard soldiers seemed to believe that anyone landing by parachute must be a German. A brave RAF pilot, James Nicholson, was hit by canon fire from a German fighter. His foot was smashed and he was on fire. He stuck to his task and shot down the enemy plane before parachuting clear. As he drifted down, wounded and burning, some young Home Guards began blasting at him with shotguns. He screamed at them to stop but they were too excited to listen. Somehow he survived but was more injured by his Home Guard colleagues than by the enemy attack. (James Nicholson became the only Second World War fighter pilot to get the top medal, the Victoria Cross, for his action that day. His Home Guard attackers didn't get medals.)

5 Home Guards had to deal with reports of spies, even when those reports were a little wild. A British officer was sent to live in Winchester and was given a room in a nearby village with a vicar. The vicar's daughter immediately suspected him of being a German spy and ran to report him to the Home Guard . . .

You can tell that girl was keen to flush out spies!

And an old woman locked a man from the electricity board in her cupboard because he had a little moustache like Hitler.

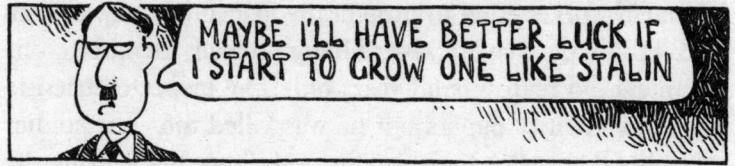

6 School children weren't safe . . . not even from their school mates. Alan Chadwick enjoyed going down to the local aircraft factory after school to watch the new planes being tested. A 17-year-old Home Guard was on patrol to stop spies. As Alan cycled by the fence the guard called him to stop. Alan ignored him. The guard called again and when Alan took no notice he fired a warning shot into the ground. But the bullet bounced off the road, hit Alan in the back and killed him. Why hadn't Alan stopped when the guard called to him? Because he was deaf.

7 Some Home Guard soldiers saw themselves as a wartime police force. They set up road blocks to stop and question everyone who came that way. One man complained he was stopped twenty times on an eight-mile journey!

Even a local milkman was sent home to get his identity papers. A Scottish man on the Air Raid Protection team was driving to Leuchars air base one night when he ignored a Home Guard road block. He was shot dead.

8 A government inspector was measuring a field one day when local villagers accused him of being a German spy. An old farm worker tried to protect the inspector and was shot and killed by a panicking Home Guard member. The harmless old man was 68 years old. The inspector tried to show his identity papers but he was killed too. The soldier who shot them went to prison for twelve months. During the Second World War 50 innocent Brits died at the hands of their own Home Guard.

9 Of course it was probably worse being a member of the Home Guard in Germany. A 59-year-old farmer, Karl Weiglein, was called to serve in the Nazi home defence army towards the end of the war. As the enemy drew near the Nazis blew up a local bridge and that annoyed the farmer. He complained to one of his neighbours, 'The people who did this are idiots and ought to be hanged.' But the Home Guard commander (the local school teacher) overheard old Karl. He arranged to have him tried and then executed. The old man was hanged from his own pear tree outside his own front door while his wife watched from the window. The body was left hanging for three days as an example to anyone else who wanted to complain.

10 The French Home Guard (The Franc-Garde or the *milice*) was set up to check on illegal food supplies. If a restaurant had more food than its ration the *milice* shared it around the poor. Sounds friendly? In fact the *milice* made themselves into an extra police force, working for the German army who were occupying France. They raided homes, spied on neighbours and betrayed freedom fighters to the enemy forces. A French survivor explained . . .

> *When you walk through French streets there are blue signs that say, 'Jacques Dupont was shot here by the Germans.' But they never say, 'Jacques was first betrayed by Frenchmen working for the Nazis.'*

The British 'Dad's Army' could be a danger to themselves and to the British people . . . but other Home Guard armies could be far more cruel.

Secret army

By 1942 the British Home Guard were given proper training and good weapons. No one knows how much use they'd have been if Britain had been invaded. But there was *another* group of fighters who would have had a good chance against invaders.

They were a secret army of highly trained commandos who were given the very best weapons and underground hide-outs. How did this special force stay secret? Was it because. . .

a) They only trained at night when everyone was asleep?
b) They trained on a deserted island off the coast of Scotland where there were only sheep to spy on them?
c) They pretended they were ordinary Home Guard soldiers?

Answer: c) Britain's secret army trained and dressed like Home Guard but were ruthless and tough. One day a farmer approached them and said, 'You don't fool me! I know your secret!' The soldiers decided they would have to kill him . . . if the Germans ever landed. 'We would have done it too,' an old soldier said.

Fighting French

In 1940 the Germans came to France and liked it so much they stayed. There were reports of German Officers shaving with champagne.[1] The Germans stayed in the north and east of France and ran it as if it were Germany – it was known as 'Occupied' France.

1. Actually they shaved with razors and just rinsed them in champagne, but you know what I mean.

They very kindly let the French run the south and west of the country from the town of Vichy – and that was known as 'Vichy' France. Of course, the French in Vichy France had to be well-behaved and act like little Germans or they'd be punished.

The Germans didn't want people from Occupied France going backwards and forwards to Vichy France, taking out secret information and bringing in weapons. The border was closed.

Oh, and there was a third bunch of French – the 'Free' French, led by General Charles de Gaulle who had escaped to England when the Germans arrived.

The German secret police (the Gestapo) made it pretty miserable in Occupied France, so secret groups began to resist German rule – they were the 'Resistance.'

Winston Churchill and the Brits decided to help the Resistance by setting up the SOE – (Special Operations Executive) – a group so secret that no one outside even knew it existed.

By 1942 they were secret agents in France to help make life tough for the Germans. While Soviet women fought in tank battles and the trenches, Western women didn't fight in the big battles of the Second World War. But they did play a brave and vital part in the Resistance.

Terrible traitors
In 1939, just before the war, there were three friends living in Paris: an Englishman, a Frenchman and a German.

There was the Nazi German, aged 50. He pretended to be a policeman on holiday, but was really there to find people who would spy for Germany when the war began.

There was the Englishman, aged 30. He had been to public school and become a newspaper reporter, but he really wanted to be a spy. When he tried to join British Military

Intelligence section 6 (MI6) they turned him down.

Lastly there was the Frenchman, aged 28. He was a brilliant pilot, and had been a trick flier in a flying circus as well as an airline pilot.

The war started and they went to their home countries (but during the war they secretly met up again in Paris).

France was soon occupied by Germany, and the German returned to France – this time to catch spies.

The Englishman took a job in SOE sending spies into France – but he didn't tell anyone about his friend, the German spycatcher.

And the Frenchman came to England and offered to work for SOE, flying spies in and out of France. He did admit he had a German spycatcher friend, but he said that would be a great help in dodging the Germans.

What would YOU do with the Frenchman? Give him a job? Or lock him away? The SOE gave him a job . . . but of course his English friend was high up in SOE.

What happened? SOE flew in spies and equipment for a year. Then suddenly the Germans swooped and arrested all of SOE's agents – 1,500 of them. They had been betrayed.

Most of those brave 1,500 agents died after they'd been

tortured. But who betrayed them? Could it have been the Frenchman? He was put on trial after the war to explain himself and he might have been found guilty but someone spoke up for him – the Englishman!

The Frenchman was set free, the Englishman got an OBE award . . . and the brave resistance fighters got a firing squad.

Terror for traitors

Germany occupied several countries and in every one they found some local people willing to help them – 'collaborators'. But not all collaborators got off as lightly as the traitors in the last example.

In Poland, a Resistance fighter described how he dealt with a collaborator . . .

A man who informed on us to the Germans lived in the village of Srednie Lany. We marked him down for execution. We went to his house at night, tied him up and made him give us the names of other Nazi informers in the surrounding villages. We also asked for the names of the people he'd betrayed. After that we called all the villagers together, read out the death sentence and carried it out on the spot. To protect the villagers against Nazi revenge I left behind a note which read: 'This is what will happen to anyone who works for the Germans.'

The Germans weren't popular in Poland. They took all the best food for themselves and the people of the occupied country went hungry. That's why they rebelled.

A Polish tax collector had the job of stapling metal tags to the ears of pigs to show they belonged to the Germans. Resistance workers entertained some villagers by grabbing the tax collector and fastening the tags through his ears. Ouch!

Women also suffered revenge attacks. A French woman fell in love with a German soldier. When the war was over the villagers came to get her . . .

> *When they came for me I thought they would break down the door. I was frog-marched into the street where men and women held me down. Their faces were twisted with hate and they called me a traitor. Then somebody grabbed a handful of hair and started hacking away with a pair of scissors. I tried to hide my fear but I almost choked when I saw the flash of a razor. It was scraped across my head painfully. The crowd were cheering and howling. They painted swastikas on my head using mud from the gutter. I have never felt so wretched in my life.*

Of course it wasn't only in France that traitors were punished by their own people. In Russia a Resistance fighter wrote . . .

> *We shot a traitor. In the evening I went to do the same to his wife. We are sorry that she leaves three children behind. But war is war!*

And murder is murder.

Fighting females

The heroes and heroines of the Resistance deserve a book of their own. These are just four examples of the work some heroines did and the things they suffered.

Name: Yvonne Cormeau

Code name: Annette

History: When her husband was killed in the London Blitz she joined SOE as a radio operator and parachuted into France. She was almost caught when agent 'Rodolph' betrayed her group. She received a bullet wound in the leg while fighting with the Resistance. She travelled through France disguised as a district nurse. When stopped at a German checkpoint her radio equipment was examined. She told the German guards it was her X-ray machine – and they believed her!

End: Survived the war. Died in January 1998, aged 88. Her blood-stained briefcase and dress with a bullet hole can be seen in the Imperial War Museum, London.

Name: Dianne Rowden

Code name: Paulette

History: An English girl who had lived with her parents in the south of France and loved the country. When the Nazis invaded she decided to try and help the French gain their freedom. She was landed in France in 1943 but didn't know that traitors had already betrayed her Resistance group. She was followed from the moment she landed, so every time she visited a contact she was accidentally betraying them! After a month the Gestapo arrested her and tortured her. She refused to talk.

End: In May 1944 the Allies were ready to invade Europe. The Nazis worried that Dianne could be freed and would tell the British who the traitors were. So she was taken to a prison camp in Germany. A doctor told her he was giving her an injection to protect her against typhus. In fact, he was injecting her with poison. Her body was 'evidence' so it was destroyed in an oven.

Name: Violette Szabo

Code name: Louise

History: Violette's husband was killed fighting with the Free French forces in North Africa. She decided to join the Resistance to avenge him. But Violette didn't want to be a radio operator – she said she wanted to 'fight with a gun in my hand.' After running into a German patrol in June 1944 her group fled but Violette twisted a weak ankle, injured in parachute practice. She held off the Germans while her companions escaped and was finally captured.

End: Violette was sent to Ravensbruck Concentration camp. She believed that being British would protect her, but in February 1945 she was taken from her cell and shot in the back of the neck. A book and a film called *Carve Her Name With Pride* were written to tell her story.

Name: Odette Sansom

Code name: Celine

History: Travelled through Vichy France carrying messages and codes for her group leader, Peter Churchill. When they were caught she tried a daring lie, saying she was married to Peter and they were related to British Prime Minister Winston Churchill. She was tortured to betray her secrets. First her toe nails were torn out one by one but she refused to talk. Then she was locked in an empty underground cell with no light and only a board to sleep on. As a child she'd been blind, so the weeks of darkness didn't frighten her either.

End: When the Germans were defeated Odette's lie about Churchill paid off. As the Allies approached the concentration camps many secret agents were executed to silence them for ever. But not Odette. The commander of her camp decided to take her to the Allied forces personally and say, 'Here is a relation of your Winston Churchill. I saved her. Take care of me.' She survived and became famous for her courage with a book and a film (both called *Odette*) about her war deeds.

Resistance dangers

Living in another country means more than simply learning to speak the language. There are dozens of ways you can give yourself away. . .

Oooops! 1 A woman SOE agent was parachuted into France from England. She arrived safely in a large town. But when she came to cross the road she looked carefully to her right . . . and was almost knocked down by a truck that was coming from her left. She simply forgot that the foolish French have the crazy habit of driving on the wrong side of the road!

The good news is the truck missed her. The bad news is that a Gestapo officer saw what she did, guessed her secret, and arrested her.

Oooops! 2 'Annette' was dropped into the Gascogne region of France. It was the custom of women there to wear jewellery in public. 'Annette' arrived with no jewellery so she stood out. She also had to learn that the locals didn't sip soup from the side of the spoon and women didn't walk with such long strides as hers.

The clumsiest mistake was to give her a cover story that said she was from Occupied France in the north and had moved to Vichy France in the south. To do that she'd have to cross the border and have her papers stamped. The stamp was missing from her false papers. Somehow 'Annette' survived the careless way she was prepared.

Oooops! 3 Secret agents were given large amounts of money to carry into France. The money was to buy weapons and other equipment and make sure the resistance groups could buy food.

Freedom fighters in the Balkans area of Europe knew that British agents would land with a money belt stuffed with cash. So some of the agents were murdered as soon as they landed. The fighters said, 'Thanks for the money, we don't need you!'

One British agent, Nigel Low, had a criminal record for stealing money from his company before the war. He was trained as an agent, given a large amount of cash and dropped in France. He simply ran off with it and was never seen again. A case of ...

THANKS FOR THE MONEY. I DON'T NEED YOU!

Polish pain

When the Nazis invaded Poland in 1939 their friends (for the moment) the Soviets marched in from the east and took areas of Poland that used to belong to them 20 years before.

The Soviets didn't want the Polish Army to fight back, so in April and May 1940 they. . .

- took all the Polish officers to the forest of Katyn where there was a large pit dug amongst the trees
- shot the Polish officers in the back of the head
- threw them into the pit and buried them ten layers deep.

The Soviets then tried to cover the graves with freshly planted trees and the tracks leading to the grave were grassed over. Still, three years later, the German army discovered the mass grave.

Who did the Soviets blame? They blamed the Nazis who'd passed that way when they invaded Russia!

IT WASN'T ME GUV, HONEST!

Stamping out trouble

The Soviets also imprisoned enemies inside Poland. Anyone who had connections around the world was an enemy. So all of the area's stamp collectors were rounded up and . . . stamped out.

When they later invaded Latvia their records show they shot a woman because. . .

She was caught singing a Latvian folk song

. . . while some Germans shot any Russian peasants who

could read and write. 'Anyone who is clever enough to read and write,' they said, 'is clever enough to cause trouble.'

The Soviet prison officers in Latvia were utterly brutal. Every prisoner who came to them was tortured. But they weren't the carefully planned tortures that the Nazis used. The Soviet jailers. . .

- beat prisoners with railings broken from fences
- crushed their fingers in the doors of their cells
- put thin books over their heads and beat them with hammers (because they wanted to cause pain, not death from a fractured skull).

One poor prisoner had his private parts wrapped in paper that was then set alight.

Whole families of Poles, Latvians, Lithuanians and Estonians were sent to Soviet prison camps in Siberia. The conditions in the trains taking them were so bad that when they stopped at stations the dead would be thrown out on to the platform.

When they arrived in Siberia things were worse. In temperatures of minus 40 degrees they had to live in holes in the ground or huts made of straw and branches. The men, women and children who survived the cold were worked to death.

When their German 'friends' invaded Russia in the summer of 1941, the Soviet jailers wiped out their prisoners in Poland with unbelievable cruelty. Sticks of dynamite were thrown in to one cell full of women prisoners. Another cell floor was found scattered with the eyes, ears and tongues of the dead prisoners.

The Soviets were as savage as their new enemies, the Nazis.

Winners and losers

For the first year of the Second World War the people outside the battle zones were hardly affected by the war. But the longer it went on the more difficult, dangerous and deadly it became, whether you were in Munich, Manchester, Milan or Moscow.

There were winners, and there were losers, as there are in times of peace.

Winners at war. . .

1 Coca Cola Coke had a 'good' war. It was supplied at a nickel a bottle to US soldiers. Coca Cola controlled 95 percent of the overseas soft drinks market. During the war, US soldiers drank ten *billion* bottles. In 1939, Coca Cola had only five overseas bottling plants. By 1945, they had 64. What made it so popular? Because the water was so disgusting. The army kept it clean by adding chlorine – so it tasted like your local swimming pool. Sometimes water was carried in old petrol tanks or oil drums just to add to the flavour. Their powdered coffee was dreadful, fruit juice was known as 'battery acid' and 'lemonade crystals' made a drink that tasted of disinfectant. Alcohol was banned in the US forces – one tank crew got their hands on an enemy supply of champagne and almost ran over a jeep . . . a jeep carrying their general.

2 Cigarette makers If you want to get on in the war then own a cinema. People who went to the cinema smoked heavily in the 1940s. One owner went around and collected the cigarette ends from the floor, took out the tobacco and turned them into new cigarettes. They were named 'RAF' – perhaps because they were 'Really Awful Fags'. The manufacturer was sent to prison for his illegal manufacture of these killer weeds but his cigarettes still kept turning up at the Front . . . so someone was still 'winning' during the war.

3 Black marketeers When food was scarce it often replaced money. It was against the law to trade food without ration books. People who did were known as racketeers and when they were caught in Germany they could be shot.

Three Nazi Ministers were suspected of being racketeers in 1944. They were investigated but their case was handled by Berlin's Chief of Police . . . one of their racketeer friends! So, were they arrested, tried and punished? Don't be daft! Of course they weren't!

A Berlin waiter ran a 'Black Market' business – he could get things for people when they were in really short supply on ration – petrol, perfume, food and drink. This man made so much money he was able to retire to a big house with an estate in the country. He was rich but had taken great risks. Even people caught hunting through bombed ruins to take valuables were dealt with savagely.

4 The German chemical industry At the start of the war a German chemical company known as I G Farben was the largest in the world. But its huge success was based on cheating. While everyone else in the world had to pay their workers, I G Farben used slave labour. The concentration camps were packed with rounded up prisoners and I G Farben was able to pay the Nazis five Reichmarks a day for each prisoner they used – the prisoner, of course, got nothing but hard work and was basically a slave. The people who ran the factories argued with the people who ran the concentration camps. . .

Of course the result was neither fed the prisoners properly and they died quickly.

When the exhausted prisoners dropped down dead they were replaced with new prisoners. The Nazis built a forced labour camp at Auschwitz to provide slave labour for I G Farben's artificial rubber plant. The prisoners were fed thin turnip soup and bread that was full of sawdust. On average, they only survived for three months.

But some prisoners' fate was even worse than slavery and starvation. Scientists and doctors were allowed to use prisoners for gruesome experiments with new drugs and chemicals and surgery. At Auschwitz, Doctor Josef Mengele was obsessed by twins, and once sewed two gypsy children together to try and create Siamese twins.

In 1942 two prisoners did escape from Auschwitz and reported the death camps to the Allies. 'Please flatten them with your bombers,' they begged. But the Allies decided it would risk too many of their pilots and crew. The deaths went on.

. . . and war's losers

1 Vienna postmen Families in Austria tried to cheer up their fighting men by sending them chocolate and soap. But the army couldn't always deliver these so they sent them through the post. Chocolate and soap were scarce and valuable so a group of 17 postmen began opening the parcels, stealing the contents and selling them. The law enforcers of Vienna were not amused. The postmen were taken to the main square in Vienna and shot in public so everyone could see what happened to such despicable thieves. That's life – Postman Pat one minute, postman splat the next.

2 A Berlin family One Berlin family were definitely war losers . . . they lost their grandfather! Here's how it happened. . .

So let that be a lesson. Wrapping wrinklies in wrugs is wrong!

3 German radio fans It was against the law to listen to foreign radio broadcasts in wartime Germany. Anyone caught would be punished.

What a silly law! How would the police know what you listen to in your own living room?

Er . . . actually there were little spies in German homes. Young people in the Hitler Youth organization were told they must report their parents if they listened to enemy radio.

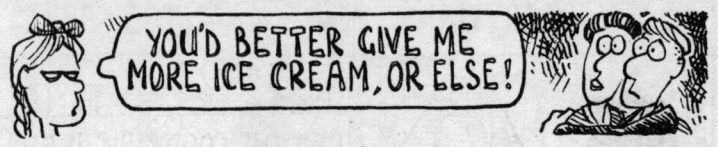

Many Hitler Youth members did just that. An Austrian ballet dancer went to prison for three years after his daughter split on him.

Would you betray your poor parents? On second thoughts . . . better not answer that!

44

It wasn't just children who betrayed family. One woman told the Gestapo to listen under her window while her husband criticized Hitler – the poor man got four years in jail. It's cheaper than a divorce.

But how's this for gratitude. . .

But it was a dangerous game, informing on others. A railway worker lied about a woman neighbour and he was proved to be lying. He was shot.

4 The people of Leningrad In the winter of 1941-42 the Germans surrounded the Soviet city of Leningrad. Hitler decided not to waste German soldiers by entering a mined and booby-trapped city. He would use the ancient tactic of 'siege'. So the Germans surrounded the city, bombed it every day, and waited for the Soviets inside to starve and freeze to death. Many did.

In January 1942 a Leningrad doctor visited a family. He described what he saw. . .

> *A horrible sight met my eyes. It was a dark room, covered with frost and puddles of water on the floor. Laid out on some chairs was the corpse of a 14 year-old boy. In a pram was the body of a tiny baby. On the bed lay the owner of the room, dead. At her side stood her eldest daughter, rubbing her with a towel to try and revive her. In one day she had lost her baby, her brother and her mother, all perished with the hunger and the cold.*

It's horribly true, but not surprising, that some of the starving people of Leningrad removed the arms and legs of the corpses and ate them. Cannibalism was the only way that some survived.

Yet the savage winter hurt the German attackers too. In time they were driven back and defeated. The starving of Leningrad may have been winners after all.

Firestorm fury

In a war you have to believe that you are fighting for the right side. When the Second World War started on 3 September 1939 the British Prime Minister, Neville Chamberlain, told his people:

> *It is evil things that we shall be fighting against – brute force, bad faith, injustice, oppression and persecution.*

In the USA in 1942 a poster showed the boxing champion Joe Louis with a rifle and neatly buttoned uniform saying:

"we'll win because we're on God's side"

The truth is that the other side believe exactly the same thing – and God doesn't usually take sides.

War is horrible but the Second World War was especially horrible because so many millions of *innocent* civilians were killed, bombed in their home towns, miles behind the battle front. Here are just ten gruesome facts about a bombing raid when the enemy destroyed a city without mercy.

Only one fact is wrong. Which one?

London – 13 February 1945

1 It was Shrove Tuesday and a carnival day. A day for children to forget the war, dress up in bright costumes and have a parade through the city streets. The circus was performing to a thousand happy families and there was no warning of what was to come.

2 First came the pathfinder planes. They found the city and dropped red marker bombs that hovered 200 metres above the city centre and marked the way for the bombers. Home Defence Fighters took off to shoot them down but the panicking gunners on the ground shot down their own planes. People who saw the flares ran for cover and the shelter of the cellars. But no air raid siren sounded.

3 The last act of the circus began and clowns rode donkeys into the ring. That's when the warnings finally rang out.

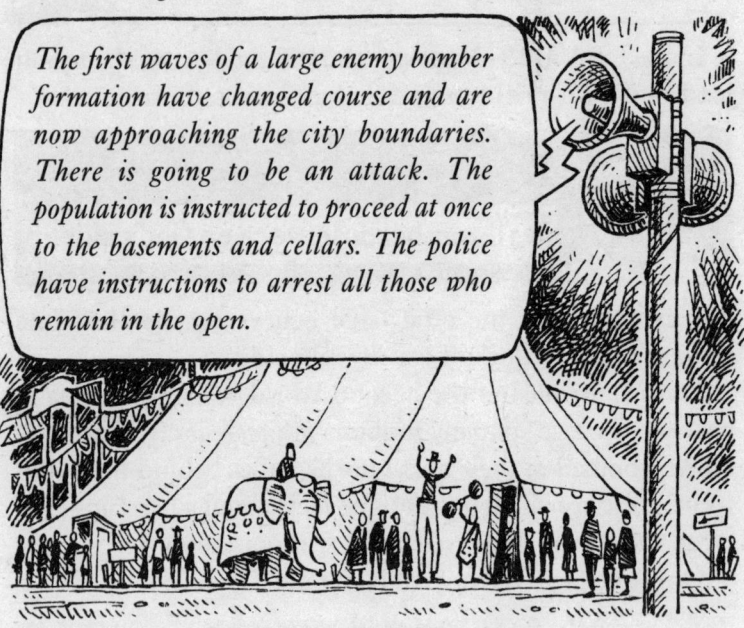

The first waves of a large enemy bomber formation have changed course and are now approaching the city boundaries. There is going to be an attack. The population is instructed to proceed at once to the basements and cellars. The police have instructions to arrest all those who remain in the open.

4 At 10:13 p.m. the first bombs fell. They were shattering high explosives that brought down buildings and trapped citizens in their shelters below the ground. But the worst was still to come. The fires, greedy for oxygen, sucked in air and winds rushed to feed them. The fires grew hotter, sucked harder, and the winds grew stronger and stronger and stronger. This was the fire storm effect the bombers wanted. It was a whirlwind of flames that uprooted trees and sucked people off their feet into the heart of the fire.

5 The next wave of bombers arrived at 1:30 a.m. They were carrying fire bombs that spread a blazing liquid over the city and turned it into a massive bonfire. They had no trouble finding the city. They could see the fires from the first wave from two hundred miles away. This time the home fighter planes stayed on the ground. No one knows why – some think the links to their aerodrome were cut. The bombers had the freedom of the skies to drop their deadly fire bombs wherever they wanted. Of the 1400 enemy aircraft that flew over the city that night only six failed to return. As the circus tent collapsed in flames the dappled grey Arab horses huddled in a frightened circle. Their glittering costumes were seen shimmering in the light of the fires.

6 Wednesday dawned. Ash Wednesday. Survivors crawled out of the rubble that was once a city centre. A three-mile cloud of yellow-brown smoke drifted over the city and carried charred debris that fell on a prisoner-of-war camp 15 miles away. Ash Wednesday. Then the third flight of bombers arrived to rain down a further 11 minutes of death. Long range enemy fighters flew low and machine-gunned anything or anyone that moved. One plane machine-gunned a children's choir.

7 Some of the people in the cellars had weakened the walls that joined their house to the ones next door. When their escape to the street was blocked they broke down the walls into other houses again and again, looking for a way out. But smoke from the fires rolled down and choked them. An army officer, home on leave, saw sixty people in a cellar, their escape barred by a fire. He tried to help them. . .

SOAK YOUR COATS IN THE FIRE BUCKETS, PUT THEM OVER YOUR HEADS, AND RUN!

CERTAINLY NOT! IT'LL RUIN MY BEST FUR COAT!

The ones who refused to take his advice died.

8 One of the main targets had been the station. That morning children's bodies were stacked there in a huge mound. Many were still wearing their bright carnival costumes. But the station wasn't destroyed. By the next day the trains were running again. So tens of thousands of people had died and the enemy had gained very little.

9 Then the job of counting the cost began. For a week after the raid the city was filled with unburied dead. Bodies were lined up on the pavement to be identified. Rescue workers were given cigarettes and brandy to mask the smell. Prisoners of war were brought in to help with the work – but the citizens attacked them. They had to take their revenge on someone.

10 Bodies were buried in mass graves but there were no coffins and no sheets. Many were simply wrapped in newspapers, some in empty paper cement bags. There were too many dead to count. Some guesses say that it was 25,000.

Answer: Terrible but true. The only 'wrong' fact is the first word of the title. For this *wasn't* London destroyed by Nazi monsters. This was Dresden in Germany, bombed by the RAF by night and the US Air Force by day – with God on their side, of course.

Frightful fighting

Most of the fighters in the Second World War hadn't chosen to be soldiers . . . they were normal people like your parents and teachers. (Well some teachers are fairly normal.) They joined the fighting forces and could be ordered to do some things they'd never have dreamed of doing in everyday life. Not just killing strangers – but killing them in some pretty nasty ways . . .

Shooting strangers

Sometimes you may be ordered to do something horrific in times of war. The trouble is you may have to spend the rest of your life with the terrible act on your conscience. Here is a true case. Imagine it happened to you.

- You are a British soldier in Burma, marching through the jungle towards the Japanese enemy.
- Your patrol captures three Burmese villagers and a ten-year-old boy who are almost certainly spying for the Japanese.

- If you let them go they will report your position to the enemy and the lives of all of your comrades will be in danger.

- The officer decides the Burmese must be shot and he selects you to be one of the firing squad.

What do you do?
a) Refuse and ask if someone else can do the shooting.
b) Agree to shoot the men but plead to let the boy live.
c) Obey. Shoot the three men and the boy.

The choice
You have *no* choice in fact.

If you a) refuse, then the officer could have you shot, and the four spies will die anyway.

The soldier in the actual story tried b), and begged the officer to let the boy live. The officer explained that if the boy escaped he would betray them all and everyone could die. The boy would have to be guarded 24 hours a day and that would be difficult.

The soldier was forced to obey c), even though the nightmare of the shooting lived with him 50 years after the event. He explained:

> *The boy faced us without a blindfold. As he was the second to be executed it meant he'd already seen his friend shot. When it came to his turn he was in a dreadful state. From close range the rifle fire made a terrible mess. It's something I've never been able to forget.*

That's war. It affects the survivors as well as the victims. Many soldiers left the war with terrible memories like this.

Quick quiz

Fighting isn't the clean and tidy adventure it looks in many war films. Fighting can be disgusting. How disgusting? Can you guess the answers to these questions?

1 The British army sailed to Italy but many were sea sick. Where did they throw up?
a) Over the side of the ship.
b) Into wet paper bags that burst.
c) They shared a big oil drum that steadily filled up.

2 On Guam Island in the Pacific there were some unusual 'winners' in the battle between the Japanese defenders and the US attackers. What were they?
a) Frogs.
b) Flies.
c) Sharks.

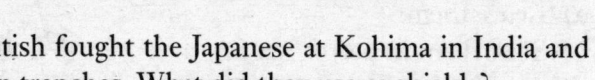

3 The British fought the Japanese at Kohima in India and sheltered in trenches. What did they use as shields?
a) Dead Japanese soldiers.
b) Dead horses.
c) Boxes of Bibles.

4 American paratroopers were safer than British because. . .
a) They had springs in the heels of their boots to make landings softer.
b) They had two parachutes.

c) They were fatter and the fat protected them from being hurt when they landed.

5 The Germans chose non-smokers to go on patrol against the Soviets in 1941. Why?
a) Because non-smokers have a better sense of smell and they could sniff out the enemy.
b) Because smokers gave away their position with lighted matches and clouds of smoke.
c) Because smoke got in the eyes of the smokers and stopped them shooting straight.

6 German soldiers needed good boots for the Russian winter. After killing 73 Soviet soldiers their commander ordered them to take their boots. But the boots were frozen to the feet of the Soviets. What did the commander order?
a) 'Leave them.'
b) 'Soak them in petrol, set fire to them and thaw them out.'
c) 'Saw the legs off.'

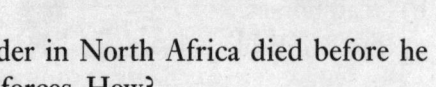

7 The Italian commander in North Africa died before he could take charge of his forces. How?
a) He fell off a camel and broke his neck.
b) His plane was shot down by his own army.
c) He was bitten on the behind by a scorpion that was sleeping on his chair.

8 Why did a Nazi torturer in Paris work dressed only in his underpants?

a) Because the water torture would spoil his clothes.

b) Because the red-hot pokers had set fire to his trousers.

c) Because the Gestapo dragged him out of bed to question a suspect and he hadn't time to get dressed.

Answers:

1c) The soldiers were kept below the decks so they couldn't throw up over the side of the ship the way your dad did on the ferry to France. During the day they had the hatches above them open, but at night the hatches were closed and the air was suffocating. That's when many men were sick. They shared a large oil drum. As the ship rolled over the waves, the vomit sloshed around in the drum. *Slop – slurp – slosh!* (Hope you're not reading this just after your delicious school dinner?) When Allied troops sailed across the English Channel to invade France the American soldiers were given seasickness pills – the Brit soldiers were given paper bags. One commando said:

The landings were a success because the men would rather face the German bullets than face going back in those boats to be seasick again.

2b) There were too many rotting Japanese corpses for the defenders to bury. The flies had a feast. On Guam there were thousands of frogs who usually fed on the flies . . . but the frogs couldn't cope! The flies simply swarmed all over the island. The US troops landed and used a strong fly repellent. It certainly kept the flies away, but the smell was so strong it led the Japanese straight to the American positions in the darkness. You had a choice – be eaten by flies or shot by the enemy.

3a) An officer wrote:

> *The place stank. The ground everywhere was ploughed up with the shell fire and human remains lay rotting as the battle raged over them. Men vomited as they dug in. In some of the trenches, rotting bodies of Japanese were used to form the parapet shield. It was almost impossible to dig anywhere without uncovering a grave or a toilet.*

4b) American soldiers jumped from their planes knowing that if their main parachute failed to open they had a spare. The Brits knew that if their parachute failed to open they would be scraped off the ground like strawberry jam. A popular paratroopers song made a joke of a parachute failure. To the tune of 'John Brown's Body' they sang:

> *He hit the ground, the sound was 'splat', the blood went spurting high,*
> *His pals were heard to say, 'Oh what a pretty way to die.'*
> *They rolled him in his parachute and poured him from his boot,*
> *And he ain't going to jump no more!*

The British Army said a second parachute would take up too much room. The truth was a second silk parachute would cost another £20 and the Army couldn't afford it. So the price of a British paratrooper's safety was less than £20.

5a) The Soviet peasant soldiers were good at hiding on the snow-covered plains – but they smelled awful. A sharp-nosed German could smell a bunch of Soviet soldiers before he saw them and had a better chance of killing them. The Soviets smelled of cheap tobacco and sweat. They also smelled of perfume that they used to kill lice in their tunics. That putrid perfume killed the lice but – if a German smelled it – it could also kill the Soviet soldier. By the way, Hitler hated tobacco and his Nazi scientists proved smoking causes cancer over 20 years before anyone else thought about it. If this Nazi science had been shared with the world then they could have saved millions of lives – which would have made a real change!

6c) Italian soldiers fighting alongside the Germans in the Russian winter had cardboard boots. The German boots weren't much better and they took Soviet army boots whenever they could get them. When they found boots frozen to dead Soviet legs their officer ordered them to saw the legs off below the knees. They carried the legs back to camp, put them in ovens for ten minutes and were able to remove the boots.

7b) Marshal Balbo flew from Italy to Libya but Italian anti-aircraft guns accidentally shot his plane down and killed him. The Italians didn't have a very happy time in the North African desert war. In September 1940 they set off in their tanks to attack the British. Unfortunately they lost their way, and drove round in a huge circle until they ran out of water and petrol. When they finally came face-to-face with the British army many Italian soldiers panicked and ran away. They were driven back into battle by their leader, General 'Electric Beard' Bergonzoli (honest, that's what they called him!). By early December they had been defeated. The Brits were surprised to find that the Italians were ready to be taken prisoner and many of them had their suitcases neatly packed and waiting to be marched off to prison. Electric Beard was shocked.

I TELL YOU WHAT JOCK, THERE'S SOME VERY STRANGE FACIAL HAIR IN THIS WAR

8a) The French Resistance radio operator, Didi Nearne, was arrested in 1944 and taken to be questioned by the Nazis. When she refused to give them the information they wanted she was sent to be tortured. The torture involved putting her in a bath of cold water and holding her head under till she began to drown. Then she was dragged upright and questioned. The torturer was stripped so he didn't get wet – but he kept his underpants on because he was embarrassed by what Didi would see if he took them off. Despite the torture she didn't betray her group. Her nasty Nazi torturer asked, 'Did you enjoy your bath?' She had the courage to smile and reply cheekily, 'Excellent!' She survived.

Funny food

One way to win a war is to starve the enemy to defeat. Cut off their food supplies. Of course, the enemy is trying to do the same to you and your people at the same time.

Britain had to bring a lot of her food from across the seas so the German submarines set out to sink the food ships. The Brits suffered. The German people suffered even worse hardships than the British.

So, if you can't eat what you want, eat whatever you can get. The US Army gave its soldiers a book with this advice. . .

THE BLUEJACKETS' HANDBOOK   Page 21

SURVIVAL

When you're far from base and your rations are low then you can stay alive by turning to Mother Nature.

Remember!

● All animals are good to eat.

● Be careful about eating poisonous snakes.

● Maggots make good food.

● Grasshoppers are tasty but pull the legs and wings off before eating them.

● Do not eat caterpillars.

Isn't history amazing? That last piece of advice is sixty years old but it's still useful today. Next time you're in a cabbage patch and feeling peckish remember *not to eat the caterpillars* – with a little digging you could find a few juicy worms.

US soldiers starving in Bataan found a rare food you don't get in burger bars. An officer said...

Would you have eaten a cute little monkey? You probably would if you'd been on the Bataan Hunger March. That was a forced march of 70,000 American and Filipino prisoners of war captured by the Japanese in the Philippines. Starting out on 9 April 1942, they were force-marched over 60 miles through the jungle. They were starved and often kicked or beaten on their way; many who fell were bayoneted. Only 54,000 reached the camp; 7,000-10,000 died on the way and the rest escaped to the jungle – where they ate monkeys or starved.

The Japanese officer who organized the march was executed after the war for his cruelty.

Hunger horror

The most famous diary from the Second World War was written by the Jewish girl who hid from the Nazis, Anne Frank. But she wasn't the only child to keep a record of her suffering.

A Dutch boy, Robert de Hoey, was living in Java with his family when the Japanese invaded in 1942. His father was sent to one prison camp while he and his mother were taken to another. For three years they suffered terrible hunger, yet survived. This is a translation from Robert's diary.

Day 1
Arrived at the camp and were told to wait for the camp's commandant. We were made to stand to attention on the football field for two hours in the baking sun. Babies cried, people fainted but no one was allowed to sit down.

Day 73
I think of food all the time. How can I stop? We play and we sleep, that helps. Day by day the rations have grown a little less. You hardly notice, then you remember how it was when we arrived. Our evening meal is usually thin vegetable soup and boiled rice. To get more food we try to grow it — carrots, onions

cabbages, tomatoes. But we have to guard
them because even the guards try to steal from
from us.

Day 236

Mama has decided that I am old enough to
help around the house. She's given me the job
of keeping the toilet clean. With all the
diarrhoea, and so many people using it, the
thing is a disgrace. There is pee down the
walls and even smears of poo. But I don't
mind. I have my own mop and it feels like
a real job.

Day 377

An important day. A food parcel has arrived
from the Red Cross. This is good because we
ate all the cats and dogs months ago. And it
is no use hunting rats. Food is so scarce here
even the rats have moved out. We shared a
can of Spam between five people, I had ten
raisins, three dried figs, a cigarette and a
piece of chocolate the size of a postage stamp.
I swapped my cigarette for another ten
raisins.

Day 580

It is hard. Every day I see my fellow prisoners with bleeding gums holding broken teeth. Hair only grows in tufts, our stomachs are bloated from hunger and disease. Some have boils the size of table-tennis balls and others have raw ulcers weeping on their legs. No one has the material to spare to make bandages.

Day 701

They say the war is ending. Some brave women have smuggled radio parts into the camp. They'd be executed if they were ever caught. But the news is that Japan is facing defeat by the Americans. Every day we wait for the end. I can't remember what it was like being free and having enough to eat.

Day 727 (last day)

Word went around last night that we should meet on the field. But we are never allowed out after dark. We'd be shot.

I could see no guards. But in the moonlight
I could see the camp gates swinging open.
None of us left. We didn't know where to go.
Then, this morning, English officers marched
in. We began to bow to them the way our
Japanese guards had trained us. The English
made us stop.

Freedom Day 3
This afternoon my father came through
the camp gate. Mama said he was
coming. I hadn't seen him for three and
a half years. I didn't recognize him. He
hardly knew me or Mama. But we are
together.
The nightmare is over.

War game

It's all very well reading history books about the war, but you're safe and warm in your cosy classroom, with your friendly history teacher to help with the long words. You even sit on super-comfortable chairs. You have no *idea* what some people went through during the war.

Of course, you could get your local army camp to put you on a firing range and use you for target practice, but don't expect them to give you a gun to fire back.

So how do you get a real feel for the war? A US soldier at Guadalcanal in the Pacific fought in the trenches in torrential rain and suggested we should all try the following game:

Dig a hole in your back garden while it is raining. Sit in the hole while the water climbs up round your ankles. Pour cold mud down your shirt collar. Sit there for 48 hours and, so there is no danger of your dozing off, imagine that a guy is sneaking around waiting for a chance to club you on the head or set fire to your house. Get out of the hole, fill a suitcase full of rocks, pick it up, put a shotgun in your other hand and walk on the muddiest road you can find. Fall flat on your face every few minutes.

> *Snoop round until you find a bull. Try to sneak around him. When he sees you run like hell all the way back to your hole in the back garden. If you repeat this every three days for several months you may begin to understand.*

I-spy

Spies have been around for thousands of years but they become really useful in wartime. In the Third World War (due to start in the year 2023 when Martians invade) you may like to be prepared with one or two Second World War tricks.

Spycatchers were always looking for secret messages being passed to the enemy. The Germans had a hugely complex machine made to make unbreakable codes – but the Brits got a copy of the machine and cracked thousands of top secret messages.

You don't always need clever machines for complicated codes. Two people beat the spycatchers with simple ideas. Next time you need to send that secret message to a friend try one of these genuine Second World War systems. . .

Comma code

Flight Sergeant Graham Hall was a terrible writer. He never used punctuation in his writing. He once joked to his wife, Vera, 'If I am ever taken prisoner and I send a letter with punctuation, then you should underline the next word. It will be a coded message.'

In June 1940 his bomber was shot down and the crew were taken to one of the famous Stalag Luft Prisoner of War (POW) camps for airmen, in north-eastern Germany. Sergeant Hall wondered if his wife remembered their joke and he tried it. It worked so well that the British secret service used him to send and receive messages from the camp – news about German weapons and troop movements, requests for help with escapes and for equipment.

You can try it. Here's an example of how it might have worked . . .

Dear Vera

I am alive and well. Escape from plane was dangerous. Planned to celebrate my birthday, night after we crashed. 22nd birthday if you remember. September in the garden is lovely and I'll miss it. Send my love to sis, ma, pa, N.D Jones and my other friends at the pub, local. Money I owe them will have to wait.

Love
Graham

Someone as clever as you does not need to have the message worked out, do you?[1]

The prisoners of war were allowed to receive parcels and letters from home through the Red Cross organization. They also received games like Monopoly and chess to pass the time. What the Germans didn't know was the games were specially altered to send in secret supplies – silk maps in the monopoly board, radio valves in chess pieces and hacksaw blades hidden inside a pencil. A pack of cards was actually a map in 52 pieces.

Lemon aid

One of the great secrets of the war was the Nazi concentration camps. Even German people believed that Jews were just being sent to work for the Nazi war effort. The real horror was hidden from them. Letters from the camp were destroyed if they hinted at the dreadful conditions.

But some clever prisoners managed to smuggle out the truth using the old spy trick, invisible ink.

Try it yourself. Write a postcard with a simple message, then add the real message in invisible ink.

1. But for the dumb or the lazy reader, the message says, 'Escape planned night 22nd September send map and local money.' An escaper would need 'local money' once they were outside the camp and a map to find their way to the coast.

Lemon Spy!

YOU NEED THE JUICE OF A LEMON, A THIN PAINTBRUSH AND A PIECE OF PAPER

DIP YOUR PAINTBRUSH IN THE LEMON JUICE AND WRITE YOUR MESSAGE. PUT MORE LEMON JUICE ON THE PAINT BRUSH AFTER EVERY LETTER.

LEAVE THE MESSAGE TO DRY THEN SEND IT

WHEN YOUR FRIEND WANTS TO READ YOUR MESSAGE THEY JUST PUT IT FACE DOWN IN THE OVEN. (THE OVEN SHOULD BE HEATED TO 175°C OR GAS MARK 4). IT SHOULD TAKE ABOUT 10 MINUTES

THIS WORKS BECAUSE THE HEAT OF THE OVEN BURNS THE LEMON JUICE BUT NOT THE PAPER. BURNING CHANGES THE LEMON JUICE AND MAKES IT GO BROWN

Concentration camp prisoners would probably not have lemons so they would have to use sweat, saliva or pee as invisible ink. They aren't so healthy – stick to lemon juice.

The postcards with secret messages were meant to be read and destroyed, but some survived. One was put on display in 1997. The card was a simple message:

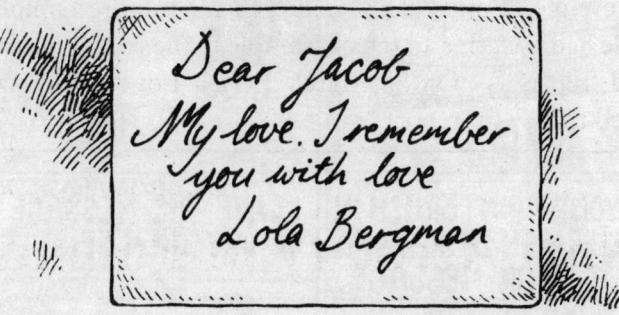

*Dear Jacob
My love. I remember
you with love
Lola Bergman*

But when the invisible message was read it gave a glimpse of the horrifying truth . . .

DEATH CAMP. THE REST
IS A LIE. HUNGER,
STARVATION, DOG FOOD,
OAT PORRIDGE. AN
EPIDEMIC. TORTURE.
TORTURE CHAMBER.
HUMILIATION. VIOLENCE
TERROR. FRIGHT
KILLING BY GAS.
EXECUTION. GALLOWS.
MURDER. INCINERATOR.
AGONIZING HELL.
OTTO.

It is believed that 'Otto' was Otto Haas, an Austrian who ended up in the death camp because he opposed Hitler.

Ruthless reprisals

Not all Germans were Nazis and not all Nazis were nasty. But there were times in the Second World War when the Nazis behaved as nastily as anyone in the history of the world.

One thing which seemed to bring out their viciousness was revenge. If one Nazi was hurt then a hundred innocent people had to suffer, to set an example to the rest. They were called 'reprisals'. On 22 March 1941 a London magazine carried this awful report . . .

The London Magazine

Nazi Atrocity in Poland

Following the death of a German soldier, one hundred Polish men were rounded up – most of them Jews – and marched through the streets with their hands tied behind their heads. They were ordered to dig their own graves and, to satisfy the barbaric cruelty of the soldiers, forced to perform a 'dance of Death' at the point of a bayonet for the Germans' amusement. There were various methods of execution, some shot, some hanged and others tied to posts and stoned to death.

Nazi violence wasn't only directed at the Jews. In Czechoslovakia in 1942 there was a similar act of cruelty . . .

Czechoslovakia Today

1 June 1942

Massacre at Lidice

Hitler's henchman, Reinhard Heydrich, was killed by a freedom fighter's bomb in the Czech capital Prague two weeks ago.

Heydrich – killed

Yesterday the German SS exacted their revenge on the small Czech town of Lidice.

They rounded up most of the 450 townspeople and shot 172 men. Seven women were shot as they were trying to escape and the rest were transported to a concentration camp at Ravensbruck. The 90 children were given new names and sent to Germany to be raised as Germans.

Today the SS will dynamite the town and the rubble will be levelled so that not a trace remains.

Of the women sent to the concentration camp, 52 died at Ravensbruck – seven of them exterminated by poison gas.

Two years later, in a French village, not even the women and children were spared . . .

FRENCH UNDERGROUND NEWS

Terror attack at Oradour-sur-Glane

Nazis may call their actions at the little village of Oradour 'revenge' – the rest of the world will call it bloody murder. The German forces massacred everyone they could find in the town and some 642 people were killed.

The Nazis marched into the town demanding to see identity papers and searched for explosives. The recent capture of an SS officer by the French Resistance fighters in the region had infuriated the Germans. Witnesses say the Germans herded the men into the barns and barred the women and children in the church.

Then the killings began. The 190 men were shot first and then smoke was seen rising from the farm houses as the SS bullies burned them. Finally the church was set on fire; women who tried to escape were machine gunned through the church windows and grenades thrown into the screaming masses killed many more. 207 women and children died.

Somehow ten lucky people survived by pretending to be dead till the SS left.

When the war was over a search was made for the Nazis responsible. In 1953 twenty were found guilty of a war crime at Oradour. Five were sent to prison – two were executed.

The abandoned village has been left in ruins as a memorial to the victims, with a single English word at the entrance of the village: Remember.

What made this tragedy even more horrible is that the Nazis had wiped out the *wrong* village. The German officer had been killed in Oradour-sur-Vayres, south of Limoges. The avengers killed the people of Oradour-sur-Glane, to the north of Limoges.

Test your teacher

It's amazing how much you don't know. And teachers, who look as though they lived through the Second World War probably know even less because their memories have begun to fade. (There arc three things that happen to a person when they start to get old. First their memories go . . . and I've forgotten the other two.)

Anyway, torment a teacher or grill a granny with this quick quiz. All they have to do is answer 'true' or 'false'.

1 British and Allied troops coloured everything khaki brown as camouflage. They even had khaki toilet rolls!

2 Japanese soldiers collected the skulls of US soldiers, cleaned and polished them and sent them home as souvenirs.

3 Some spies in Germany were executed by guillotine.

4 British soldiers in Italy were given winter clothes and died of the heat.

5 In November 1940 a man called Lloyd was arrested in Britain for lighting a bonfire in his back garden.

6 Soldiers who had skived off school when they were kids were more likely to skive off from the army and run away from battles.

7 Old people's homes in Germany were closed because all the wrinkly residents had been called up to fight in the army.

8 Blind people in Germany were not allowed to marry.

9 If you were late for work in a German factory you lost all of that day's pay.

10 Italian leader Mussolini was said to look like Oliver Hardy of the Laurel and Hardy films.

Answers:

1 True. At first Brit soldiers had white knickers and hankies. But a quick flash of white could give them away to a sharp-eyed enemy. Everything was coloured muddy, khaki brown, even toilet paper . . . and pipe cleaners! United States Marines kept white vests, though, and they saved their lives at Guadalcanal in the South Pacific. The trapped men signalled to rescue planes by spelling out 'H-E-L-P' on the ground with their vests.

2 False. But what is gruesomely true is that US soldiers *did* collect dead Japanese soldiers' skulls. In September 1942 the US Commander of the Pacific Fleet ordered: 'No part of the enemy's body may be used as a souvenir.' The order was ignored. One US sailor sent a polished rib from a Japanese airman home to his sister. She'd begged him for it. Plundering gold teeth from their Japanese enemies was another charming hobby – and the victims weren't always dead. A burned Japanese head (still wearing its helmet) was paraded on a US tank at Guadalcanal – and you thought displaying enemy heads died out with the Celts fifteen hundred years before?

3 True. In August 1942 German spycatchers uncovered a team of 46 spies. They were sending radio messages to Soviet enemy agents. The Germans named the spy group the 'Red Orchestra' and soon put a stop to their playing. The male spies were taken away and hanged. But the females were executed using the French system of the guillotine.

4 False. The opposite was true. The army planners believed it would be very hot in Italy. But it was wet and cold. In the mountains it was freezing and many British soldiers in lightweight uniforms suffered terribly from the cold; some died. When the mud dried out, the roads and tracks turned to dust. Allied tanks raised great clouds of the stuff as they rolled forward . . . and made clear targets for German guns. Cold or hot the Brits couldn't win!

5 True. Mr Lloyd liked the way Hitler did things and generally supported the Nazi party. He'd been thrown out of the army for his views. The bonfire was not a signal for enemy bombers but it was a gesture to show the Brits weren't going to tell him what to do. The magistrate gave Lloyd a prison sentence – Lloyd gave the magistrate a Nazi salute. If he'd had any sense he'd have said:

BUT IT WAS BONFIRE NIGHT!

6 True. At least it was true in the US army which did a survey. The Americans didn't like to call their men 'deserters', so those who ran away were said to be 'AWOLs' – short for 'Absent With-Out Leave'. Private Slovik was the only US soldier to be shot by his own army for deserting during the Second World War. The Germans, on the other hand, executed over 10,000 of their own men in the Second World War – and there were always plenty of volunteers to serve on the firing squads. (They executed 11 ordinary people in one day in 1942 for breaking the black-out rules!)

7 False. But this *was* a popular German joke! As the war went on and the fit men were killed or captured the German Army called for older men and younger boys to join. 65-year-olds were called to serve in the German Home Guard and that gave rise to another German joke. . .

THEY SAY WE CAN GET OUT OF IT IF WE CAN PROVE OUR FATHERS ARE FIGHTING AT THE FRONT!

8 True. The Nazis were very harsh on people with handicaps. Deaf and blind people were not allowed to marry in case they produced deaf or blind children. And the mentally ill were exterminated. Hospitals found an extra 100,000 beds for wounded soldiers by 'helping' mentally ill patients to die. This began in September 1939 (under cover of war). The plan was given the codename 'T4'. The aim of this 'mercy killing' of mentally or physically handicapped adults or children was to ensure racial purity – Germany in the future would be free of sick people. The handicapped were secretly taken from homes and hospitals and murdered. Parents and families were simply told that their relative had 'suddenly died'. Rumours spread and in 1941, the Roman Catholic Archbishop of Munster exposed the Nazi murders in a sermon. Surprisingly, it was halted.

9 False. It was much, much worse. If you were late for work then you could be sentenced to three months in prison. (And you thought an hour's detention for being late to school was cruel!) By 1944 workers were having to work 60 hours a week (or 72 hours a week in aircraft factories). If you were asked to do overtime then you had a choice . . . do it, or go to prison for 12 months.

I SUPPOSE A THREE WEEK HOLIDAY IS OUT OF THE QUESTION?

10 True. Mussolini was short and fat. When he started to go bald he had his head completely shaved. When he became ruler of Italy he wore a dark suit and a bowler hat. Somebody told him he looked just like Oliver Hardy – a comic idiot – so he began dressing in military uniforms instead. Mussolini rarely smiled or laughed – especially at Laurel and Hardy films.

Murderous mines

The Soviet Union joined the war on the side of the Allies in 1941 and its people fought as brutally as anyone in history. The Soviet Union lost an unbelievable number of its people – some Soviet historians say 43 to 47 million Soviet people died, if you include the effects of war like starvation and homelessness – that's as many people as there were in the whole of Britain at the time.

The Soviets weren't too fussy about how they fought or who died, so long as they won. The USA shot only one of their 19,000 deserters in the whole of the war, but the Soviets weren't so caring. Men who committed crimes, or ran away from the battle, were sent to punishment battalions and given suicidal jobs . . .

The good news is that a Soviet soldier who was wounded in one of these clearances would be forgiven. (Of course, he'd also be forgiven if he stepped on a mine and died. All hundred pieces of him would be forgiven.)

Angel of the minefield
The Brits in North Africa had a different way of getting across a minefield, it seems. In 1943 a soldier told this story . . .

North Africa
July 1943

Dear Elsie

I know you worry about me, out here in the desert, but I think I'm going to be all right. It seems we have some sort of guardian angel watching over us. Yes, I know I've never been religious, but after what I saw yesterday I'm not so sure.

We'd just laid a minefield in the desert to stop the German tanks advancing. We were supposed to lay tapes to show a safe, zig-zag path through the mines but the German shells began to fall before we could do it. We had to retreat to our defences.

Behind the rampart we found a young, blond-haired officer, his helmet blown off and a shell splinter deep in his chest. He was propped up against a fence post, dead. Before we could bury him we heard an engine from out in the minefield.

When we looked over the top of our rampart we saw an amazing sight. A British truck was driving over the minefield towards us. It should have been blown to pieces but it started weaving slowly, left and right and found the safe zig-zag path even though there were no markers!

When the truck driver finally reached us I asked him, 'How did you find your way across?'

'It was that young officer!' he said. 'The one with fair hair. He walked across in front of us.'

I stepped to one side and let him see

the corpse propped up against the fence post. 'Is that him?' I asked.

I thought the driver was going to faint, he went that pale. 'Yeah. That's him! What's he doing there?'

'He died quarter of an hour ago,' I said. 'It wasn't him that guided you to safety.'

~~'Then it must have been his ghost,' the~~ driver moaned. He crashed the gears of his lorry and drove off. I've never seen him again.

We buried the officer, of course. But it's strange we all have this feeling he's out there somewhere watching over us. So don't worry, Elsie, I know that I'll get home safe. Love Bill

Wild weapons

In wartime the side with the best weapons has an advantage. Potty profs and brainy boffins raced to create new ways of battering buildings, chewing up children, walloping women, splattering soldiers and pulverising pensioners.

The Brits invented Pykrete – a mixture of sawdust and water that was frozen to make a material tougher than concrete. Ships built of Pykrete would be unsinkable and win the war. The war ended before they could be built. Sounds daft – but it's terribly true.

Here are some of the Second World War's brightest brainwaves, all believed to be in existence. Some were just rotten rumours – while others were terribly true. Can you tell which are which?

1 The Molotov cocktail

2 The airblast gun

3 The swimming tank

4 The superfast rocket

5 The submarine aircraft carrier

6 Exploding dogs

Answers:

1 The Molotov cocktail. It may seem a stupid idea to attack a tank with a bottle of paraffin . . . but terribly true! Vyacheslav Mikhaylovich Molotov served in the Soviet war cabinet and they were desperate for weapons to stop the German tanks advancing. Molotov ordered the manufacture of millions of these simple bombs and they are still made by terrorists today – and still called Molotov cocktails.

Some of them worked. It isn't nearly as safe inside a tank as you'd imagine. In north-west Europe mud and ice were the enemies of UK tanks. In mud, it was known for tanks to churn themselves in until only the turret remained visible.

IF I'D WANTED TO BE IN SUBMARINES I'D HAVE JOINED THE NAVY

On ice, Churchill tanks and others which were not equipped with rubber-plated tracks (unlike the US Sherman tanks) became giant uncontrollable toboggans.

To be trapped in a tank on fire was fatal. The hatches were too small for a quick escape. A US officer described a tank fire. . .

A tank that is hit belches forth long searing tongues of orange flame from every hatch. As ammunition explodes in the interior, the hull is racked by violent convulsions and sparks erupt from the spout of the barrel like the fireballs of a Roman candle. Silver rivulets of molten aluminium pour from the engine like tears.

Germans called Brit soldiers Tommies and they nicknamed their tanks 'Tommy cookers'. US soldiers called them 'Ronson lighters' because of Ronson's advert that said their lighters 'light first time.'

So Molotov cocktails were simple, but deadly – if you could get close enough to a tank to throw it without being shot!

2 The airblast gun. A brilliant idea! Sadly it was just a rotten rumour spread around Germany. But it's such a good idea perhaps you could try it in your own classroom.

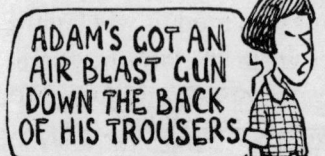

ADAM'S GOT AN AIR BLAST GUN DOWN THE BACK OF HIS TROUSERS

PTHRRRP

3 The swimming tank. Another daft idea – but terribly true! On D-Day, British 'DD Tanks' (Dual Drive) were launched from landing craft to 'swim' to the beach. Each tank had a canvas skirt and propeller. They were designed for a short journey over calm, shallow waters. 32 were set off. But the sea was rough and they were launched too far out because naval crews were too scared to go any closer to the beach. 27 sank like stones, drowning all the crews.

4 The superfast rocket. Another rotten rumour from the Germans – who seemed to believe it. You can see why. A really fast rocket could easily travel as fast as a speeding bullet. But . . . if the rocket is travelling at (say) 1000 miles an hour then the bullets in its guns are also travelling at 1000 miles an hour before they are even fired. Fire those bullets at (say) 500 m.p.h. and they're then travelling at 1,500 m.p.h., aren't they? Er . . . I think that's right. Never mind. The idea of a missile firing bullets is daft enough.

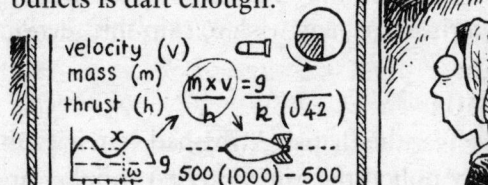 

5 The submarine aircraft carrier. An absolutely crazy Japanese idea . . . but it was terribly true. And it worked! The Americans had bombed Tokyo so the Japanese made this plan to get revenge. On 9 September 1942 Japanese submarine I25 surfaced and the pilot, Nobuo Fujita, was sent off to drop fire bombs on the forests of Oregon. The idea was the fires would spread to the west coast US cities and create panic. Only one of his four bombs went off and the small fire was easily put out by the forest rangers. Nice try Nobuo, the only man to drop bombs on mainland USA.

6 Exploding dogs. A sick, sorry and stupid idea, but terribly true, and it worked . . . sort of. It was a Soviet idea. The dogs were trained and taken on to the battlefield where the Soviets faced the Germans. Each dog had a mine strapped to its back. They were released and ran straight under the tanks. Unfortunately . . . the dogs had been trained using Soviet tanks so, of course, they ran under the Soviet tanks. The tanks were blown apart and the dogs didn't look too healthy either.

Awesome animals

Animals don't start wars but they certainly suffer in them. Vegetarians and veterinarians may wish to skip this section.

Cruel for creatures?

1 In the First World War the British Army had won with the help of horses – they pulled the guns, carried supplies and made a tasty meal when food was hard to find. But by the Second World War horses had no chance. In September 1939, Polish Cavalry charged the German Panzer tanks. A German soldier said:

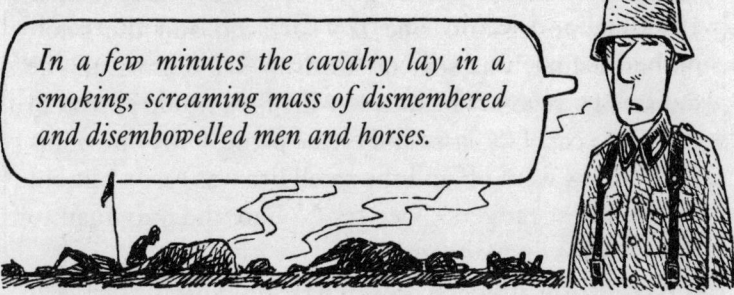

In a few minutes the cavalry lay in a smoking, screaming mass of dismembered and disembowelled men and horses.

2 Animals provided sport for bored soldiers. Horse racing was impossible but US soldiers who invaded Italy enjoyed gambling on beetle races instead.

- Each man had his own beetle and painted his 'racing colours' on the insect's back.
- A two metre circle was drawn on the ground.
- The beetles were placed under a glass jar in the centre of the circle.
- The jar was lifted.
- The first beetle to crawl out of the circle was the winner.

Top class racing beetles were bought and sold, a lot of money was won and lost gambling on the races.

3 As the war ended, and the Soviet army closed in on Berlin, the German defenders drew back to defend Tiergarten Park. In the park was a zoo. On the morning of 2 May 1945 soldiers began to surrender to the sound of starving and wounded animals. But a Russian remembered the saddest sound was an old zoo keeper – the last one left – weeping over the body of a huge hippopotamus. It had been killed by a Soviet shell.

4 When Dresden was bombed in 1945, 48 circus horses were killed and left by the river Elbe. The same raid had smashed the zoo cages. The vultures escaped and found the dead horses. Six weeks after the bombing people were still reporting seeing escaped monkeys and even a lion.

5 Adolf Hitler liked dogs. While he was fighting in the First World War he had a little pet dog called Fuschl and he trained it to run up and down ladders. (Somebody pinched the dog and he never saw it again – unless it was served up to him in a pie.) Then Hitler had Alsatian dogs as pets and his wartime pet was called Blondi. When Hitler's friends decided to kill themselves in 1945 old Hitler offered to test the cyanide poison to see if it worked. He fed it to Blondi. It worked quickly and fairly painlessly.

6 Hitler was a vegetarian and hated to see creatures suffer. Lobsters are best cooked by dropping them into boiling water, alive. Hitler hated to hear the screaming sound that they made when dropped into the water and passed a law saying they had to be killed with kinder methods. So it was a good war for lobsters as well as for foxes and deer because Hitler also banned hunting animals with dogs. Of course, it was fine for his Nazis to hunt down and murder humans!

7 Hitler's chief mass murderer, Heinrich Himmler, was keen to have non-Germans put into concentration camps, tortured, experimented upon, gassed, shot, beaten or simply worked to death. Yet Himmler said. . .

Shooting birds and animals is not sport. It is pure murder. We Germans have always had a respect for animals.

He even considered his SS killers[1] should wear bells at night so any little creatures would hear them coming, run away and

1. The SS (short for Schutzstaffel) were Hitler's personal bodyguard – by the end of the war there were 50,000 of them! Just how much body did the madman have to guard? They wore smart black uniforms and were taught to be ruthless and hard-hearted. This was the organization that executed people in concentration camps.

not be trodden on by accident. Himmler also said that he liked the medieval German custom of putting rats on trial and giving them a chance to behave themselves, rather than be exterminated. Some Nazi regions banned experiments on live animals – vivisection – while allowing experiments on live human victims in the concentration camps.

8 Soviet prisoners in Germany were always hungry. It was a real treat for them to catch a stray dog and eat it. The dogs were hard to catch . . . they didn't want to end up as dog meat. The starving Soviets begged their German guards to shoot the dogs for them. The guards didn't mind because they thought the dogs were pests and they made good target practice. When a dog was hit the hungry prisoners went crazy. A guard remembered. . .

> *When a dog fell the prisoners would fall on it and tear it apart with their bare hands, before it was quite dead. They'd stuff the heart, liver and lungs into their pockets to be eaten later. Then they'd light a fire and skewer pieces of dog meat on splinters of wood and roast it. There were always fights over the largest pieces.*

Tails of the unexpected

The Second World War produced lots of strange animal tales too.

Miaow did she do that?

The miracle mouser of London's St Augustine's Church has amazed her owner, Rector Ross. Yesterday he climbed from the rubble of his church to tell of the white cat's purr-fect prediction.

'Faith has been with us for three years,' he told our reporter. 'She kept her kittens on the top floor of the church house. But three days ago she carried them all down to the basement and tucked them into a corner. Every time I carried them back up she took them down again. Then, last night we had a direct hit. The top floor was demolished. But I found Faith and the kittens safe in the basement corner.'

The People's Dispensary For Sick Animals plans to give heroine Faith their silver medal. Even the Bishop of London admitted, 'It certainly makes us paws for thought!'

9 September 1940

Germans quackers for Freda

A Swiss visitor to London has told of a new secret weapon that the German townsfolk of Friedburg have to warn them of Brave Brit air raids. And it's not a marvellous machine – it's a feathered fowl.

The panicking poultry, a duck called Freda, rushed through the streets quacking loudly. The Friedburgers were so scared they took to their shelters – just in time! Because our brave boys in blue battered them with bombs a few moments later.

'The duck saved hundreds of lives!' the visiting Swiss watchmaker told our paper. 'The frightened Friedburgers are so grateful they plan to erect a statue to Freda.'

Of course, we Brits all know what Freda was quacking as she ran through the streets, don't we? 'The British are coming! Duck!'

30 March 1943

Dog-tired hero   12 November 1940

A British Army company in Egypt has its mascot back. The desert troops called the loveable mongrel dog Sandy (of course) but thought they'd seen the last of the mutt. The truck he travelled in after the battle at El Alamein was captured. The men were taken prisoner but the beastly Boche threw sad Sandy out to die in the heat of the desert days and the freezing nights.

Somehow the big-hearted hound walked 140 miles back to Alexandria. He even found his way through the maze of streets back to the company barracks.   PTO

'It may look like a mangy mongrel but it's got the guts of a British Bulldog!' the Company Sergeant Major said proudly.

No one could accuse super Sandy of being bone idle!

Coo! What a bird!

Yesterday the best of British pigeons, Mary of Exeter, was awarded the Dickin Medal for outstanding courage.

Mary carried secret service messages from Europe back to Britain and on her first mission arrived back with a slashed breast following an attack by a German hawk. These feathered fiends are specially trained by the Boche to bash our brave birds.

Did Mary give up? Is Adolf Hitler sane? No! Two months later the daring dove was back in action and this time returned with pellets in her body and part of her wing blown off. But the vital message got through.

Back home in Exeter her pigeon loft was blasted by bombs but somehow marvellous Mary lived to fly another day.

Her handler, Robert Tregowan, said, 'The last time we found her in a field close to home, wounded all over her body and nearly dead with exhaustion. I think she'd have walked home if she'd had to.' She's one weary warrior who's really earned her corn!

27 February 1945

Mutt medal misery

When the Allied armies landed in Sicily (10 July 1943) an American dog called Chips really earned his dog food by attacking a concrete machine-gun installation. In spite of being wounded, Chips dragged an Italian machine gunner out by the arm and three others surrendered. Soldiers have sometimes captured these strongholds single-handedly, but Chips did it with no hands!

Later the same day he rounded up another ten Italians.

When news of the daring doggy deeds got back to the USA Chips was awarded a Distinguished Service Cross, a Silver Star medal and a Purple Heart medal – even though it was against army rules to give animals awards.

A commander argued:

Brave men shouldn't have to share their awards with a dog.

So Chips lost his medals. He'd probably have been happier with a bone anyway.

Lousy liars

The first victim in war is the truth. It is killed stone dead. People tell all sorts of lies if they think it will help them survive or win the war.

The Polish plot

German troops marched into Poland in September 1939 and that was the start of the Second World War.

But Adolf Hitler didn't want anyone to blame him and his Nazis for starting the war! So Hitler's Secret Service chief, Reinhard Heydrich, came up with a big lie. . .

THE POLISH ARMY STARTED IT! THEY ATTACKED US FIRST!

Heydrich's plan was given the secret code name 'Canned Goods' and this was how it worked . . .

TOP SECRET   Canned Goods

1. Take German prisoners and shoot them dead.
2. Dress the corpses in Polish army uniforms.
3. Scatter the bodies near the German radio station on the border with Poland.
4. Invite the world's newspaper reporters to the site.

SEE! WE HAD TO DEFEND OURSELVES. THEY ATTACKED US AND HERE ARE THE BODIES TO PROVE IT!

It's hard to know if anyone was daft enough to believe this pathetic plot.

Rotten rumours

Want to know what really happened in the Second World War? Then *don't* ask someone who was there at the time! Everyone talked about the war – but there were so many lies that people began to believe them.

Tall tales

In war all sorts of superstitions are believed. Some Germans believed that whenever one of their houses was bombed then the wall where Hitler's portrait hung would remain standing!

SO WHY DIDN'T THEY STICK HIS PICTURE ON ALL THE WALLS AND CEILINGS?

Here are some of the Allies' stories that went around during the Second World War. How many of these are true?

1 British soldiers must pay for weapons and equipment they've lost in the defeat at Dunkirk

2 Japanese spies have planted broken glass in American bandages!

3 All women volunteers for the US Women's Army must take off their clothes and be inspected by male officers before they can join.

4 British soldiers fighting in North Africa know they are safe when relaxing with a game of football. Germans don't shoot footballers, even enemy footballers.

5 The Germans are short of meat and eating so many vegetables they're turning green!

6 A dog in Hawaii is barking messages to a Japanese submarine in morse code.

7 The Ford Motor Company will give a new car to the first 100 US Marines to land in Japan.

8 The British Army in the Sahara desert has ordered a million sandbags. But they arrived already filled with sand.

9 Every time the Germans launch a V1 flying bomb they have six men killed by the take-off blast.

10 Scottish soldiers will be going home after the war in ships with tartan funnels!

Answer: *All* of the stories were repeated and believed by many. None of them is true.

Many US soldiers believed they'd get a free Ford car when the war was over – what in fact they each got was a free paperback book. (Not quite the same thing.)

Who started these stories? Sometimes a government decided to upset the enemy by spreading the rumours. For example the 'British Political Warfare Executive' invented them and passed them to travellers or foreign newspapers. They also spread 'good news rumours' in Britain. This one was believed by a lot of Brits. . .

1. The truth is that experiments with blazing petrol did take place but luckily the idea was never needed.

Did you know. . . ?

Even after the war strange rumours circulated. Many refused to believe Hitler killed himself in his Berlin bunker. There were hundreds of stories about him being alive and well. Some of the strangest said Hitler was . . .

- living as a hermit in an Italian cave
- living as a shepherd in Switzerland
- working in a gambling casino in France
- working as a fisherman in Ireland
- still at sea, having escaped on a U-boat
- living in an underground hideout in Sweden with enough tinned food for years
- running a laundry in Germany
- working as a waiter in a Dutch coffee bar.

The last reported sighting of Hitler was in 1992.[1]

True lies

The US Government also had a 'Department of Liars' (called the Morale Operations Section). They spread a story that a terrible catastrophe would happen in Japan in August 1945. No

1. It's all nonsense – along with the reports that he became a London traffic warden. The truth is he escaped to become an English teacher in the north of England. I know. He taught me.

one told the 'Department of Liars' about the secret atomic bombs. On 6 August the first atomic bomb landed on Hiroshima. A lousy lie had strangely become the terrible truth.

It helps the war effort if you can learn to really hate the enemy – make them seem like savages who have to be defeated at all costs. A common US story concerned a US soldier who wrote home from a Japanese POW camp. . .

When the mother soaked off the stamp there was another message written underneath it . . .

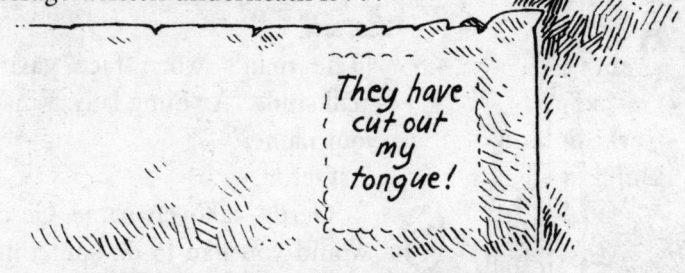

Some prisoners of war were tortured but this particular story is horrible, but untrue. How do we know? Because POW letters didn't have stamps!

Germany had its own terrible tales that were told to children. Here's a version of a cheerful bedtime story you might like to tell to a little brother or sister . . . if you really hate them that much!

Hamburg horror – a grim fairy tale

The little girl limped down the bomb-ruined road, past the hollow houses and stepped carefully round the rubble. She was as thin as the rain that fell and the soles of her shoes were thinner. She clutched a small loaf of black bread to her thin chest.

It was growing dark and she wanted to get home before night fell and the rats came out. Even if they'd been working the twisted lampposts would not be lit. She stopped. There was a soft, regular click coming from a side alley. She froze and turned her head slowly towards the noise.

A man in a heavy army coat carried a white stick and was groping his way towards her. She stepped back and a stone clattered at her feet. The man stopped, raised his white face and eyes covered by discs of dark glass. He said, 'Is someone there?'

The girl's mouth was dry. She licked her lips and spoke in a small voice. 'Yes, sir.'

The man's worn face gave a small smile. 'A young lady. What's your name?'

'Gerda, sir.'

'Gerda – a lovely name. Gerda, would you like to do something for the Fatherland? Something to help us win this war? Stop the bombs falling each night and set us free?'

Gerda stepped forward. 'Oh, yes, sir!'

'Are you a true German?'

'Yes, sir.'

'Then I can trust you with my secret,' the man said. 'I have a very secret message. It must be delivered now. But I am blind and weak. I need a nimble young person to run like the wind. Do you know Linden Street?'

'Yes, sir.'

'There is a shoe shop at number 27. Go in and tell the old cobbler that Hans sent you,' the soldier said. 'He reached into the pocket of the great grey overcoat and pulled out a crumpled envelope. 'And give him this. Whatever you do, you must not look in the envelope.'

'No, sir.'

'Good girl. Stop for no one, tell no one, trust no one. Now, run along before it gets dark!'

Gerda took the envelope, turned and ran through the empty streets past the shattered ruin of her old school and the splintered stumps of the trees in the park. The grass was mostly mud and her thin soles slipped as she sprinted across the park lawns. At the far side was the police station, an officer pulling the blackout curtains across watched her.

'Getting dark,' she panted. 'Must deliver the letter and get home before it gets dark.'

Then she stopped so suddenly her feet skidded on the cracked paving. She calmed herself, turned and walked into the police station. The weary old man behind the counter looked at her through red-rimmed eyes. 'Can I help?' he asked and though his thick grey moustache bristled fiercely his voice was kind.

Gerda told her story. The policeman nodded. 'I see,' he nodded. 'Suspicious.'

'That's what I thought!' she cried. 'I suddenly realized as I ran past here! How did he know it was getting dark if he was blind?'

The man picked up a cloak and threw it over his shoulders. 'I think I will take that note to number 27.'

It was later that night, as Gerda lay beneath a thin blanket and listened to the distant rumble of bombs that there was another rumble. Someone knocking at the door. Her mother showed the policeman into the house and Gerda sat up, wide-eyed, to listen. He told her what had happened.

'There is a cobbler shop at 27 Linden Street, run by an old man and his wife. When I went in the couple looked very nervous. Now all cobbler shops smell of sour old leather but the smell in that shop was worse. The man made an excuse and went through to the back shop. I heard the back door open then close and realized he'd escaped. So I looked around the shop and then I looked down in the cellar.'

'What was there?' Gerda asked and clutched at her mother's shawl.

'More horrors than I've seen in the whole of this terrible war,' the policeman groaned. 'There were bodies. Dead bodies. Most were cut up and wrapped like joints of meat to be sold to hungry customers.'

Gerda's mother gasped. 'I've heard of people eating human flesh.'

But Gerda had just one question. 'What was in the letter?'

The policeman passed it across to her. She unfolded the paper and read it. . .

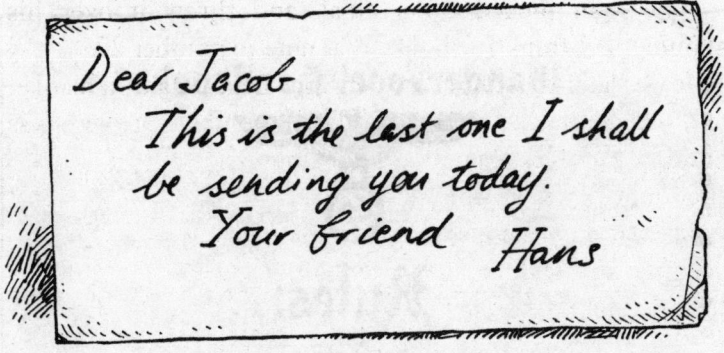

Dear Jacob
This is the last one I shall be sending you today.
Your friend Hans

Gerda felt faint and giddy. 'I was. . .'

The policeman nodded. 'You were next.'

Well? A true story? Or just a wartime version of Red Riding Hood – the girl meeting the stranger who sends her off to be eaten?

Chilling for children

The Second World War was a young people's war. British and US soldiers could be as young as 18. Anyone in the British army aged 30 or over was called 'Dad'!

Teeny terrors

How do you make proper Nazis? Take children and train them. That was the aim of the Hitler Youth movement. But Adolf Hitler and the Nazis didn't invent the idea. At the end of the 1800s Herman Hoffman created the 'Wandervogel' – the German Youth Movement.

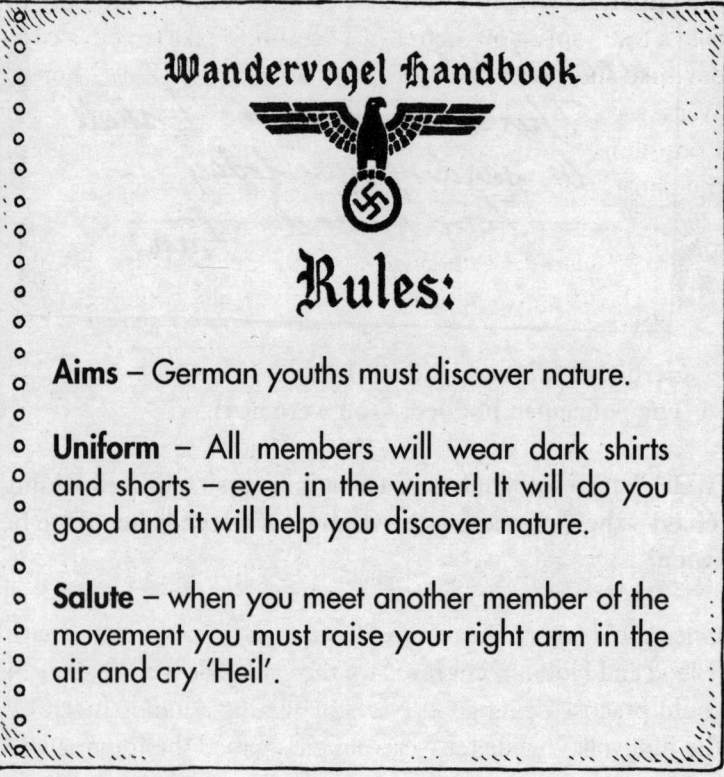

Wandervogel handbook

Rules:

Aims – German youths must discover nature.

Uniform – All members will wear dark shirts and shorts – even in the winter! It will do you good and it will help you discover nature.

Salute – when you meet another member of the movement you must raise your right arm in the air and cry 'Heil'.

In 1936 *all* German boys aged 15 to 18 had to join the Nazi Party Youth Organization – the Jugend (popularly known as the Hitler Youth). You would be called a 'Pimpf' and have to pass a test – sprint 50 metres in 12 seconds, take part in a two-day hike and recite their anthem, 'The Horst Wessel Song.' Wessel was a Nazi thug, killed in a street fight with Communists. The song cheered the Nazis by telling them the ghosts of dead Nazis were marching with them!

Once you'd passed the test you'd be given your Nazi knife with 'Blood and Honour' engraved on the blade. Boys aged 10 to 14 could practise being good Nazis by joining a junior Jugend – the Jungvolk – while ten-year-old girls joined the Jungmadel.

Gorgeous girls

The Nazis had a very clear idea of a perfect Nazi woman.

Attention Jungmadel!

Minister Joseph Goebbels has said:
'A woman has the task of being beautiful and bringing children into the world. The hen bird makes herself lovely for her mate and hatches her eggs for him.'

Will you grow to be a beautiful bird?

Remember! Good Nazi girls. . .

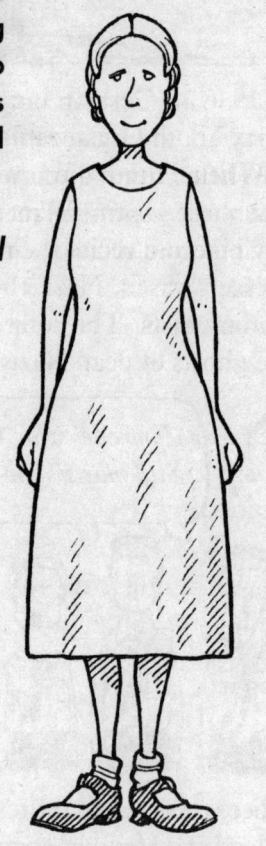

- wear their hair in a bun or plaits

- have blonde hair

- wear no make-up

- wear no lipstick

- do not smoke

- have broad hips

- and never wear trousers!

(You are also reminded that any girl under 18 caught smoking will be sentenced to two months in prison.)

Joseph Goebbels was keen on keeping girls in their place at the kitchen sink. He was Hitler's chief minister by the end of the war. He was weedy and had dark hair and skin so he was a long way from looking like the 'perfect' German he was trying to preserve.

MAYBE I SHOULD TRY A WIG

When Hitler died he left the German state to Joseph Goebbels. Goebbels knew he was surrounded by advancing Soviet forces so he poisoned his six children – Helga, Heide, Hilde, Helmut, Holde and Hedda – poisoned his wife, and then himself. But for a few hours the man known as 'The Poisoned Dwarf'[1] was the Fuhrer of Germany – or at least of the few square yards that were all that was left of Nazi Germany.

Evacuees 1

German Children were evacuated from bombed cities and sent to camps run by loyal Nazi teachers or old soldiers. Military training was more important than studying. At one camp the children were encouraged to copy from each other rather than fail the exam. You may think that's a good idea and like to see it in your school! But before you suggest it to your head teacher you should be warned – there was a bad side to this camp's rules: if there was a speck of dust found in your room you'd be whipped.

1. He was also known as 'God's Mickey Mouse' – which is extremely cruel . . . to Mickey!

Evacuees 2

British children were evacuated to private houses in the countryside. But the city children were often very rough and their new country homes sometimes very posh.

One grand country lady complained to an evacuee's mother . . .

The mother grabbed the child, smacked him and reminded him . . .

Wee war workers

What *use* were the Hitler Youth? What did they actually *do*?

As the war went on, and older men and women died, the Hitler Youth replaced them. Roughly measured, in terms of coffin-power, the jobs became more dangerous and more disgusting.

TASK	DANGERS	RATING
1939 Deliver 'call-up' papers to soldiers, hand out ration cards, collect harvest, paint kerb-stones white to help with blackout (a popular job as it was paid!).	Being knocked over while painting curb or falling into a threshing machine while harvesting.	✝
1940 Door-to-door collection of materials such as paper, scrap metals, razor-blades, bottles, brass and copper.	Cutting yourself with a razor blade.	✝
1941 Girls sent to military hospitals to help nurses, to stations to serve food to soldiers and to nurseries to care for babies.	Catching some nasty infection from a wounded soldier or being bitten by a baby.	✝
1942 Joining anti-aircraft teams to shoot at enemy bombers and operate searchlights. These tasks were meant for boys over 15 but much younger boys and girls were used.	An all-girl unit shot down a US bomber over Vienna. The next bomber hit their position and killed three of them. BOOM	✝ ✝

111

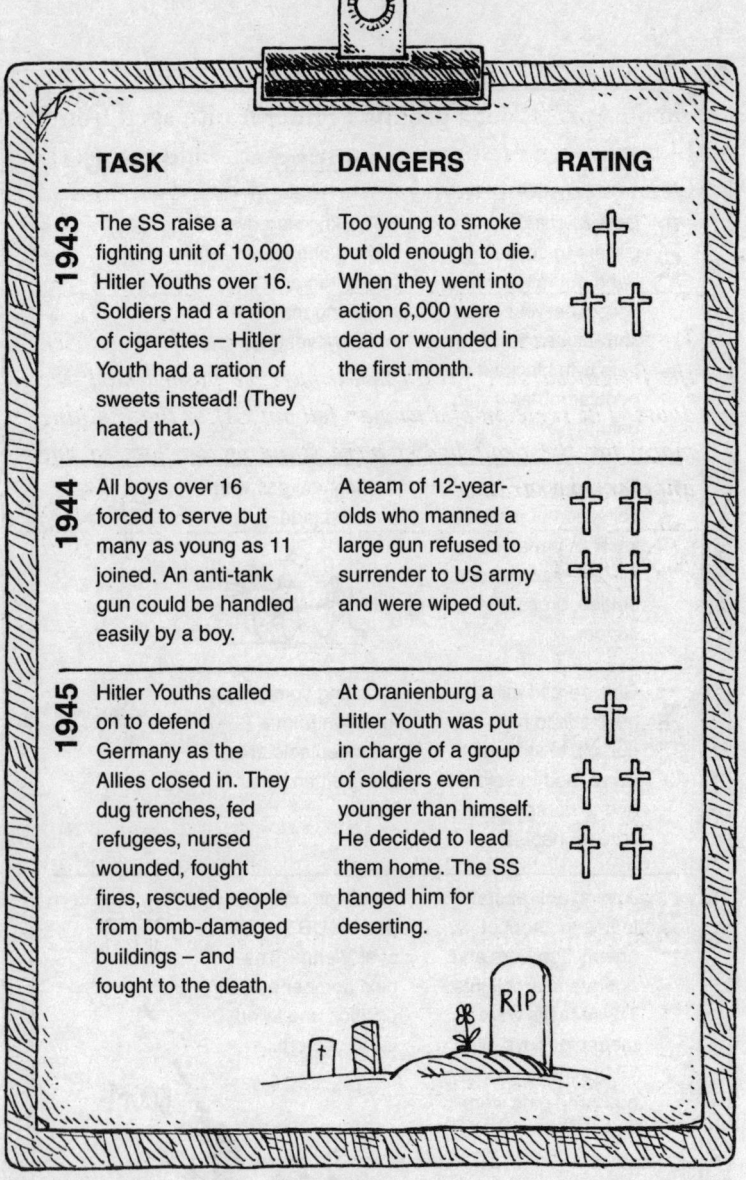

TASK	DANGERS	RATING
1943 The SS raise a fighting unit of 10,000 Hitler Youths over 16. Soldiers had a ration of cigarettes – Hitler Youth had a ration of sweets instead! (They hated that.)	Too young to smoke but old enough to die. When they went into action 6,000 were dead or wounded in the first month.	✝ ✝ ✝
1944 All boys over 16 forced to serve but many as young as 11 joined. An anti-tank gun could be handled easily by a boy.	A team of 12-year-olds who manned a large gun refused to surrender to US army and were wiped out.	✝ ✝ ✝ ✝
1945 Hitler Youths called on to defend Germany as the Allies closed in. They dug trenches, fed refugees, nursed wounded, fought fires, rescued people from bomb-damaged buildings – and fought to the death.	At Oranienburg a Hitler Youth was put in charge of a group of soldiers even younger than himself. He decided to lead them home. The SS hanged him for deserting.	✝ ✝ ✝ ✝ ✝

And when the war ended the horrors weren't over for the Hitler Youth members. They were treated by the Allies as

Nazis and made to help repair the damage of war.

On 30 April 1945, a group of Hitler Youth aged from ten to 14 were taken prisoner in Munich. US soldiers took them to Dachau concentration camp the next day. The boys were forced to help clear away the dead. One of these boys later wrote:

We were taken to a railway siding. We were ordered to open the freight cars . . . With metal bars we pushed back the doors. The skeleton of a woman fell out. After that nothing more, for the dead bodies were standing so close to one another, like sardines.

They were then taken to work in the crematorium!

Before the war the Hitler Youth movement sounded like bunches of boy scouts and gaggles of girl guides. Would you have wanted to join? And what happened to the young German people who *didn't* want to join?

Rotten for rebels

There's not a lot of information about what happened to rebels who refused to join Hitler's brutal boy scouts. There are some clues, though:

- It seemed that anyone caught enjoying themselves was guilty of wickedness. A shocked Hitler Youth report on a 'Swing Dance' (a bit like a disco today) revealed. . .

- The German SS had a section to deal with 'youths' and a special 'youth concentration camp' was set up to deal with troublemakers. (You can be sure it would be worse than the worst detention your school could give you.)
- In 1942 Helmut Hulmut was arrested in Hamburg. What was Helmut Hulmut of Hamburg's crime? He was caught listening to BBC radio programmes! He also handed out anti-Nazi leaflets. His punishment? No, not tortured by being forced to listen to BBC Radio 2 for a week non-stop. But slightly worse. He was executed.
- Jonathan Stark was called to join the army in 1943. He refused to swear an oath to Hitler because Jonathan was a Jehovah's Witness. He was sent to Sachsenhausen camp and in 1944 the young Jon was hanged.

- There were groups of misfits who hung around coffee bars and dressed in clothes the Nazis did not approve of – checked shirts and battered hats – and even wore rings. These rebels called themselves daring names like 'The Black Gang' or 'The Edelweiss Pirates'. (Since 'Edelweiss' is a flower this must be a bit like calling your class football team 'The Poppy Pirates'. *That*'ll scare the opposition!) Groups like the Edelweiss Pirates sheltered German deserters and escaped prisoners of war, and even attacked the Gestapo. The Chief of the Cologne Gestapo was killed by the Pirates in autumn 1944.

The group members were arrested all over Germany. Lucky members were sent home with their heads shaved, unlucky ones were sent to the special youth concentration camps – and the leaders were hanged in public.

- In 1942 four teenagers put up anti-Nazi posters. You could be fined for this sort of thing today . . . so don't try this at home! But in 1942 Germany they were simply executed.

- Hans and Sophie Scholl founded the White Rose movement at Munich University to oppose the Nazis. Sophie discovered the ruthless way that Nazis exterminated disabled children while Hans saw brutal actions in the war against Russia. They met up in Munich in 1942 and painted 'Down with Hitler' on university walls. Then they gave out anti-Nazi leaflets – throwing dozens from university windows. They may as well have written, 'We want to be arrested by the SS' on the walls because they had no hope of getting away with it. Both were executed by guillotine.

Fighting small-fry

As the Germans became desperate for soldiers in 1944 there were 16-year-olds fighting on the front line. By the time the Soviets moved into Berlin in 1945 boys of 12 were defending the city.

A 12-year-old German boy found himself in a group of defenders . . .

I've no rifle. What should I do?

Cheer.

Blitzed Berlin

School rules can be boring. You want to chew gum in class? The school rules won't let you. You don't like rules. But when war comes rules can disappear. People make their own. Bullies take charge. That's when you'd be glad to see some rules!

A young German boy called Claus described what happened when war came close to Berlin in 1945. Some German soldiers fled, were captured by the German army and shot. . .

A few deserters, dressed only in underclothes, were dangling on a tree quite near our home. On their chests they had placards reading 'We betrayed the Fuhrer'.

The terror of our district was a small one-legged SS officer who stumped through the streets on crutches, a machine-pistol at the ready, followed by his men. Anyone he didn't like the look of he instantly shot.

The gang went down cellars and dragged all the men outside, giving them rifles and ordering them straight to the fighting. Anyone who hesitated was shot.

The front line was only a few streets away. Everything had run out. The only water was in the cellar of a house several streets away. To get bread one had to join a queue of hundreds, grotesquely adorned with steel helmets, outside the baker's shop at 3 a.m. At 5 a.m. the Soviet guns started. The crowded mass outside the shop pressed closely against the walls but no one moved from his place. Soviet low-flying planes machine-gunned people as they stood in their queues . . . In every street dead bodies were left lying where they had fallen. Shopkeepers who had been jealously hoarding stocks not knowing how much longer they would be allowed to now began selling them. A burst of heavy shells tore to pieces hundreds of women who were waiting in the market hall.

Dead and wounded were flung on to wheelbarrows and carted away. The surviving women continued to wait. The Soviets drew nearer, they advanced with flame-throwers. Exhausted German soldiers would stumble in and beg for water. I remember one with a pale quivering face who said, 'We shall do it all right. We'll make our way to the north-west.' But his eyes belied his words. What he wanted to say was, 'Hide me. Give me shelter. I've had enough.' I should have liked to help him but neither of us dared speak. Each might have shot the other as a defeatist.

The Holocaust

The Nazis were a gang of bullies. And, like any gang of bullies, they needed victims. Adolf Hitler gave them people to hate. He told them to hate those he considered more animal than human. Who were these supposed sub-humans?

Soviets and Jews were top of the list.

The Nazis set about conquering the Soviets, taking control of their lands and using the survivors as slaves.

But the Nazis had a different plan for the Jews. Hitler's henchman, Heydrich, said:

We must exterminate the Jews wherever we find them.

This extermination became known as the 'Holocaust', which literally means wholly burnt.

'The Path to Heaven'

At first Jews were forced to dig pits, then they were shot and fell into the pits. But Hitler's head of extermination, Himmler, was worried. . .

We must have care and concern for our soldiers. Shooting Jews will upset them.

So the Nazis experimented with putting Jews into a sealed van and filling it with the exhaust gases from the van's engine. It took the victims eight minutes to die. Too slow.

At last they came up with the plan of using poisoned gas and they set up death camps to get rid of Jews at a much faster rate. One camp, Treblinka in the countryside of conquered Poland, saw the deaths of about one million people in 13 months. They were murdered by just 50 Germans with 150 Ukranian allies.

Of course the Nazis didn't tell the Jews, 'We're going to kill you.' If the Jews had known then they would have hidden or struggled or attacked the Nazis. Instead the Nazis told them lies from start to finish. They called the road to the gas chambers 'The Path to Heaven.' In fact it was the road to hell on earth.

Some Jews believed. . .   **The Nazis knew. . .**

① WE ARE BEING TAKEN FROM HOME TO TREBLINKA WORK CAMP

THEY ARE BEING TAKEN TO TREBLINKA DEATH CAMP

② AFTER THE WAR WE'LL GO TO A NEW HOMELAND FOR THE JEWS

THIS IS THE END OF THE WAR FOR THEM

③ THEY DON'T REALIZE THAT THE TRAIN IS SO CRAMPED AND AIRLESS THAT SOME PEOPLE DIE

IF THEY DIE ON THE TRAIN TO TREBLINKA THEN IT SAVES US THE TROUBLE OF KILLING THEM

120

From arriving at Treblinka station to being thrown into the burial pit would take about two hours – sometimes as little as an hour.

Escape from Hell

On 2 August 1943 the prisoners who were forced to help the exterminations in Treblinka carried out a plan to escape.

- A prisoner made a copy of the key to the gun store.
- The prisoners armed themselves.
- When they were sent to spray the wooden huts with disinfectant they put petrol in the sprayers.
- The huts were set alight.
- As the SS and the Ukranian guards fought the fire the prisoners fought their way out.
- 150 Jews escaped. Although about 100 Jews were recaptured, Treblinka was never rebuilt.

The Nazis tried to destroy the camps when they realized they were losing the war. But the site of Treblinka can still be seen to this day. The memorial stone on the spot says simply, 'Never again.'

Camp humour

One of the ways people survived the concentration camps was to turn the horror around them into humour. A popular Jewish joke in the camps went like this . . .

The Polish policeman's tale

War was an excuse for some people to act brutally. Today some football matches give hooligans a similar sort of excuse to break the rules, smash property and hurt people. But there are very few football hooligans in a crowd – and there are very few monsters even in a war.

There are more stories of individual courage than of cruelty. How would you have behaved in this situation?

1 The Germans conquered Poland in 1939, of course. But I was one who believed life was better under the Germans than the Soviets who were coming from the west. I had served in Warsaw as a policeman before the war. When the Germans arrived I kept my job and simply said:

2 The Germans gathered the Jews into one area of the city where they could keep their eye on them – the ghetto. My job was to make sure they stayed there. I never liked the Jews myself and they never liked me. From time to time we would go into the ghetto, take out the strongest and send them to the labour camps.

3 Even when I heard the stories of Jews being gassed I tried to ignore them. But we all knew that when someone went off to the camps they were never seen again. Soon there were only women and children left in the ghetto. Then one day the German military commander gave us an order.

4 It was true. The houses were like a rats' nest – corridors and stairways and cellars and tunnels where they hid when they knew we were coming. We Polish police knew them best. This raid was to be planned in secrecy. The Jews would have no time to escape. We would seal their secret routes and then drag them out. In the early hours, when they would all be sleeping, we went into the ghetto.

5 But someone had warned them. When we broke down the flimsy doors to their rooms the same sight greeted us.

6 The German Commandant ordered us to search the buildings from cellar to attic. The Commandant himself came along with me. He knew that if anyone could find the Jews it was me. We climbed through the house and I opened every secret panel and trapdoor that I knew about. Every one was empty. At last we reached the top of the house. A ladder led down from a gap in the ceiling.

7 So I took a lantern and began climbing the long ladder. The silence was so great I couldn't believe anyone could be up there in the space below the rafters. But I climbed on. At last I reached the entrance to the loft. If anyone was waiting they could have smashed my head in there and then. I looked over the lip of the hole and shone the lantern in. The light picked out the white faces and wide, dark eyes of 20 women and terrified children. The Commander called up to me.

CAN YOU SEE ANYONE?

8 The reward for taking so many Jews would be great, I knew. I'd be promoted. I'd be a loyal and trusted servant of our conquerors and I would share in their power and wealth. I turned to the Commander and called back down.

Well? What would you have done? You know you'll be sending those women and children to their deaths, but this is war. Thousands are dying every day. What's another 20? And your own wife and family must come first.

What did that Polish policeman do?

The gentle German

The war wasn't a simple matter of 'good' Allies against 'evil' Nazis. Sometimes the British were known to execute children and many Nazis were known to spare them.

A Jewish mother faced a Lithuanian soldier, working for the Nazis. The Lithuanian raised his gun and pointed it at her head. His finger tightened on the trigger. He was about to kill her for the 'crime' of being Jewish.

Suddenly a German Army officer stepped forward and rescued her. He turned to the soldier and explained:

One day history will judge us.

History *has* judged the Nazis and generally they have been found 'guilty' – but not all of them.

The woman and her three children survived the war. They lived in a hole under the floor of a barn for almost a year. The hole was about the size of a table. They were four of the 30 survivors in their town. Before the war there had been 25,000.

Epilogue

On 3 September 1939 the *Washington Post* newspaper had a headline that read:

BOTH SIDES AGREE NOT TO BOMB CIVILIANS

Six years later the United States dropped the most horrifying bombs yet invented on the towns of Hiroshima and Nagasaki in Japan.

What changed in those six years? People changed. The world had seen so many horrors that thousands of innocent civilian deaths seemed worthwhile if it meant a quick end to the war.

In 1939 most people really believed that wars were fought only by soldiers. The Second World War changed that for ever. Wars were being fought by everyone; people in the cities as well as men on the battlefields.

An American said, 'Total wars are won by the side with the biggest factories.'

MY FACTORY IS BIGGER THAN YOUR FACTORY!

In the Second World War it had become easier to kill someone when all you had to do was push a button and drop a bomb. You'd never see the suffering you caused. But the real horror of the war was that so many people were prepared to kill so many others in cold blood. A screaming child, a weeping woman or a feeble old man – the killers often showed not one drop of pity. That's what war can do to ordinary people.

They are the things that make the Second World War the most horrible history of all: the innocence of the victims, the vast numbers of them and the unbelievable cruelty of some of the fighters.

That's why truly horrible history can be so important. It helps us to look back at the horror and say the single word from the memorial at the destroyed village of Oradour-sur-Glane:

REMEMBER

WHY IS IT THAT THE ONES WHO MOST NEED TO REMEMBER ARE THE ONES MOST LIKELY TO FORGET?

WOEFUL
SECOND WORLD WAR

GRISLY QUIZ

**Now find out if you're a Woeful
Second World War expert!**

SECOND WORLD WAR WONDERS

Try this quick quiz on the Second World War. Replace the words 'Laurel and Hardy'* with one of the answers below. One of those answers is 'Laurel and Hardy'!

The missing words in the wrong order are: uniforms, 16-year-old boys, Laurel and Hardy, bonfires, nuns, toilet rolls, women, prison, parachutes, guillotines.

1. British and Allied troops coloured everything khaki brown as camouflage. They even had khaki *Laurel and Hardy*.

2. The British Home Guard were warned that an enemy paratrooper might be disguised as *Laurel and Hardy*.

3. Some spies in Germany were executed by *Laurel and Hardy*.

4. British soldiers in Italy were given summer *Laurel and Hardy* and some died of the cold.

5. In November 1940 a man called Lloyd was arrested in Britain for having *Laurel and Hardy* in his back garden.

6. US paratroopers were safer than British ones because they had two *Laurel and Hardy*.

7. The Germans sent *Laurel and Hardy* into battle when they became short of soldiers.

8. The Nazis thought ideal *Laurel and Hardy* should have broad hips.

* If you're not old enough to know who Laurel and Hardy are, then ask your teacher or a parent.

9. Workers who were late for work in a German factory ended up in *Laurel and Hardy*.

10. Italian leader Mussolini was said to look like one half of *Laurel and Hardy*.

WELL THIS WAR IS CERTAINLY KEEPING US BUSY OLLIE!

QUICK QUESTIONS

1. When the Second World War started in 1939 civilians were urged to join the Local Defence Volunteers. Comedians said LDV stood for Look, Duck and . . . what? (Clue: Vanquish? Not quite.)

2. In May 1940 Mr Hitler did something a certain Mr Fawkes failed to do. What? (Clue: remember?)

3. In 1940 a man was arrested for lighting a cigarette. Why? (Clue: night-light)

4. The British government tried to ban Londoners

sheltering in the Underground stations during bombing raids. What did the crafty Cockneys do? (Clue: train for it)

5. Car headlights were masked because of the blackout. How did farmers protect their black cattle that may have strayed on to the road? (Clue: zebra crossing?)

6. Why did parents have to label every piece of their children's clothing during the war? (Clue: bits and pieces)

7. During the war, the tops of pillar-boxes were painted green or yellow. Why? (Clue: it's a gas)

8. When the war ended in 1945 some children tried to eat bananas without peeling them. Why? (Clue: Yes! We have no bananas!)

9. In the 1940s you could eat 'chicken fruit on bacon ducks'. What was it?
a) boiled beef and carrots
b) omelette with sun dried tomatoes
c) eggs on fried bread

10. During the Second World War, US soldiers were advised to eat. . .
a) caterpillars
b) maggots
c) absolutely anything

MORE CATERPILLAR CASSEROLE PLEASE

WAR-LIKE WORDS?

At the end of the millennium, people were still bombing and killing but they'd found some new words to describe it so that it sounded less horrible. See if you can work out what these military phrases mean.

Words	Meaning
1. air support	a) human beings
2. friendly fire	b) destroy
3. neutralizing	c) planes dropping bombs
4. soft targets	d) blowing people to pieces by mistake
5. collateral damage	e) assassinating a human nuisance
6. immobilize	f) shooting soldiers on your own side

THESE DAYS YOU NEED GUNS, TANKS, SMART BOMBS AND A DICTIONARY

Answers

Second World War Wonders

1. Toilet rolls. A quick flash of white could give them away to the enemy!

2. Nuns. Or vicars or a woman carrying a baby.

3. Guillotines. In August 1942 German spy-catchers uncovered a team of 46 spies. The male spies were hanged, but for some reason the female spies were guillotined.

4. Uniforms. The army planners believed it would be very hot in Italy, but it was wet and cold and in the mountains it was freezing.

5. Bonfires. Mr Lloyd supported the Nazi party. The magistrate gave Lloyd a prison sentence – Lloyd gave the magistrate a Nazi salute.

6. Parachutes. The British Army said two parachutes took up too much room. The truth was probably that it would have been too expensive.

7. 16-year-old boys. As the war went on and the fit men were killed or captured the German Army called for older men and younger boys to join.

8. Women. The ideal Nazi woman should also have blonde hair, never wear make-up or trousers, and wear her hair in a bun or plaits.

9. Prison. You could be sentenced to three months in prison. (And you thought an hour's detention for being late to school was cruel!)

10. Laurel and Hardy. Mussolini was short and fat. When he became ruler of Italy he wore a dark suit and a bowler hat. Somebody told him he looked just like Oliver Hardy – a comic idiot – so he began dressing in military uniforms instead.

Quick Questions
1. Vanish. The LDV went on to become the Home Guard, popularly known as 'Dad's Army'.
2. His bombs flattened the Houses of Parliament.
3. He was breaking the blackout laws in force during the war.
4. They bought platform tickets so no one could stop them going down to safety.
5. They painted white stripes down their sides.
6. If the child was blown to pieces then the bits could be identified. Gruesome but true-some.
7. So that droplets of deadly mustard gas would stain the paint and show if there was a gas attack.
8. Many children had never seen a banana and didn't know what to do with it.
9. c)
10. b) A US Army handbook advised them to eat maggots and grasshoppers (with the wings and legs removed!), but advised against eating caterpillars.

War-like words
1.c) 2.f) 3.e) 4.a) 5.d) 6.b)

INTERESTING INDEX

Where will you find 'exploding dogs', 'knickers' and torn-out toe nails' in an index? In a Horrible Histories book, of course!

Terry Deary was born at a very early age, so long ago he can't remember. But his mother, who was there at the time, says he was born in Sunderland, north-east England, in 1946 – so it's not true that he writes all *Horrible Histories* from memory. At school he was a horrible child only interested in playing football and giving teachers a hard time. His history lessons were so boring and so badly taught, that he learned to loathe the subject. *Horrible Histories* is his revenge.

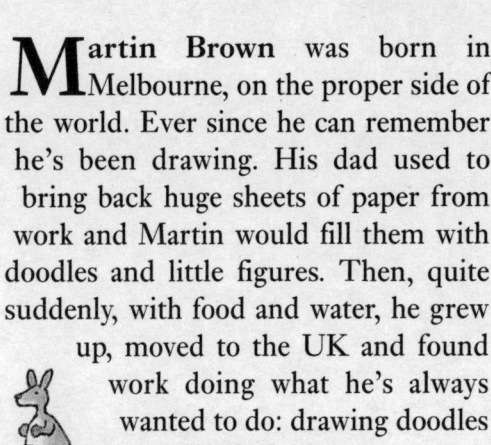

Martin Brown was born in Melbourne, on the proper side of the world. Ever since he can remember he's been drawing. His dad used to bring back huge sheets of paper from work and Martin would fill them with doodles and little figures. Then, quite suddenly, with food and water, he grew up, moved to the UK and found work doing what he's always wanted to do: drawing doodles and little figures.

HORRIBLE HISTORIES

FRIGHTFUL FIRST WORLD WAR

Terry Deary Illustrated by Martin Brown

SCHOLASTIC

To Private John Condon, Royal Irish Regiment.
Died 24 May 1915, aged 14 years old.
The youngest British soldier to die during the First World War.

Scholastic Children's Books,
Euston House, 24 Eversholt Street,
London NW1 1DB, UK

A division of Scholastic Ltd
London ~ New York ~ Toronto ~ Sydney ~ Auckland
Mexico City ~ New Delhi ~ Hong Kong

First published in the UK by Scholastic Ltd, 1998
This edition published by Scholastic Ltd, 2016

Scholastic Ltd gratefully acknowledges permission to reprint the extract from
All Quiet on the Western Front by Erich Maria Remarque,
published by The Bodley Head.

Text © Terry Deary, 1998
Illustration © Martin Brown, 1998, 2016

ISBN 978 1407 16388 8

Printed and bound by CPI Group (UK) Ltd, Croydon, CR0 4YY

8 10 9 7

The right of Terry Deary and Martin Brown to be identified as the author and illustrator of this work respectively has been asserted by them in
accordance with the Copyright, Designs and Patents Act, 1988.

www.scholastic.co.uk

CONTENTS

Introduction

History can be horrible. So horrible that some boring old fogies think young people should not be told the whole, terrible truth.

But if you never learn the truth you'll miss out on some of the most useful things in life ...

And the next time your new leather shoes hurt you, stuff them full of flowers. What happens? Nothing. The shoes stay hard and your feet get blisters.

Why couldn't your teachers tell you the truth about 'sweet pea' mixture? Either ...

a) they don't know or

b) they know ... but they are too embarrassed to say.

What you need is a book that's not too embarrassed to tell you about the awful things people used to do. You want a history of the horrible.

And it's no use telling you ...

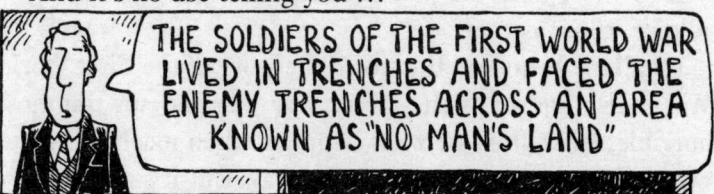

That makes it sound cosy and peaceful, doesn't it? The truth is pretty nasty, but you'll never understand how those

5

people suffered unless you read their own true memories of trenches and no man's land …

Bodies and bits of bodies, and clots of blood, and green metallic-looking slime made by the explosive gases were floating on the surface of the water. Our men lived there and died there within a few yards of the enemy. They crouched below the sandbags and burrowed into the sides of trenches. Lice crawled over them in swarms. If they dug to get deeper cover, their shovels went into the softness of dead bodies who had been their friends. Scraps of flesh, booted legs, blackened hands, eyeless heads came falling over them when the enemy fired shells at their position.

That's more like the truth because it was written by a soldier who was there.

Of all the history in the world the story of the First World War – also known as the Great War – is perhaps the most horrible. It's a story of what happens when machines go to war and human beings get in the way. But it's also a story of courage and craziness, brave people and batty people, friendships and fierce hatreds, love … and lice.

The Great War gangs

Why did the Great War start? Lots of big, thick history books have been written to answer that question. But, to put it simply, by 1914 the countries of Europe had formed themselves into two big gangs … like street gangs. The gang called the 'Central Powers' were led by the Germans and the gang we call the 'Allies' were led by the French and British.

The two gangs started collecting weapons, making threats and swapping insults, the way gangs do.

All it needed was for one gang member to throw the first stone and a huge punch–up would follow.

The Black Hand bunglers

So exactly *how* did the First World War start? It's never one of the gang leaders that starts the fight, is it? It's always one of the scruffy little kids that hangs around the edge. In this case the scruffy little kid was called Bosnia in the Allies' gang.

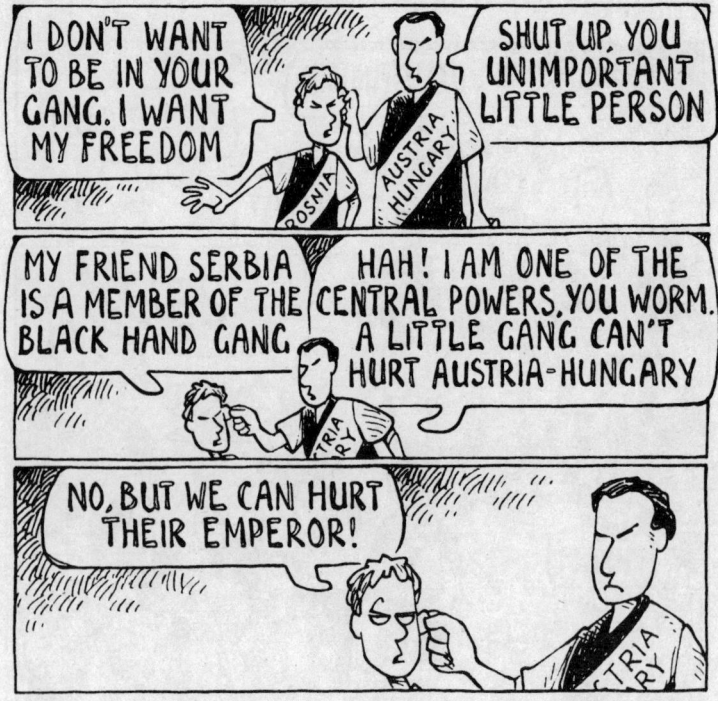

And so a Serbian gang known as the Black Hand (honest!) waited till the Emperor came to Bosnia. Gavrilo Princip was a Serbian Black Hand freedom fighter.

9

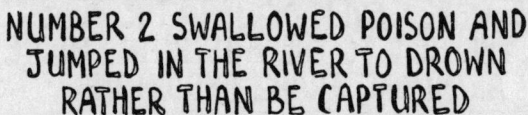
NUMBER 2 SWALLOWED POISON AND JUMPED IN THE RIVER TO DROWN RATHER THAN BE CAPTURED

BUT THE CROWD DRAGGED ME OUT OF THE RIVER AND SAVED ME ... THEN THEY NEARLY BEAT ME TO DEATH!

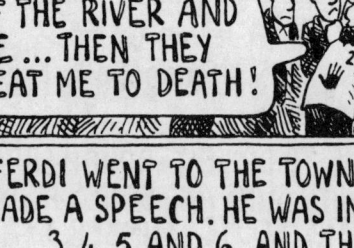
FERDI WENT TO THE TOWN HALL AND MADE A SPEECH. HE WAS IN REACH OF 3, 4, 5 AND 6. AND THEY...

ER... DID NOTHING

FERDI HEADED FOR THE HOSPITAL TO VISIT THE BOMB VICTIMS. BUT, BY AN AMAZING CHANCE, HIS DRIVER TOOK A WRONG TURNING. THIS ROAD BROUGHT HIM STRAIGHT PAST NUMBER 7...

ME! I JUMPED ON TO THE OPEN CAR AND FIRED TWO SHOTS...

I KILLED FERDI AND HIS WIFE. FERDI'S UNCLE, EMPEROR OF AUSTRIA, WAS FURIOUS. HE WANTED REVENGE AGAINST ALL OF SERBIA'S ALLIES. HE WANTED *WAR*

The first stone had been thrown. Austria declared war on Serbia, and Germany helped Austria so Russia helped Serbia so France helped Russia. Germany marched through Belgium to get to France so Britain helped Belgium.

The First World War had started. It was expected to last about four months but it lasted four frightful years.

But, before the war starts, here are two quick questions.

1 What happened to Ferdi's blood-soaked jacket after his death?

a) It was taken into battle like a flag for the Austrians to follow.

b) He was buried in it.

c) It was put in a museum, so gruesome people can go and gaze at it.

2 What happened to the assassin Gavrilo Princip?

a) He was shot by the police as he ran away.

b) He escaped and lived happily ever after.

c) He was arrested and put in prison.

Answers: **1c)** Franz Ferdinand's death was the start of the bloodiest war seen until that time. So his blood-soaked coat was an important reminder of the terrible event. It is now on display in the Austrian Historical Museum in Vienna. Go and see it … if you like that sort of thing.

2c) Gavrilo Princip was taken alive. His two shots killed millions and millions of people. Yet he was allowed to live. Just as the First World War reached an end, gunman Gavrilo died in prison, of a lung disease. Pity it didn't get him four years before!

Wacky Willie

Things may have stayed calm and the Serbian trouble could have died down. But some of the leaders of the gangs weren't too bright and weren't too pleasant. Take the German monarch …

Title: Kaiser Wilhelm

Job: Monarch of Germany

Peculiarity: Unpopular. Nobody liked poor Willy. His grandmother, Queen Victoria of Britain, couldn't stand him. His (English) mother refused to wish him a happy birthday … so he sulked for days. His father thought he would be a dangerous leader – smart dad!

Weakness: He was born with a withered left arm and it embarrassed him. When he was photographed he insisted that he hide his weak arm. People around him hid their strong left arms too.

Nasty streak: German workers went on strike and he ordered soldiers to attack the strikers. 'I expect my troops to shoot at least 500,' he said.

Most likely to say: I hate everybody.

Least likely to say: Let's talk calmly about this.

1914 - The year of the first shot

No one is surprised when a war breaks out in August 1914. Germany smashed France in the Franco–Prussian War of 1871 and it was just a matter of time before France tried to take its revenge. But people are surprised that the war is still going on by the end of 1914. The two sides are like two heavyweight boxers jumping into the ring. Each one expects a quick knockout. But they will end up slugging it out, toe to toe, till they are exhausted.

Timeline 1914

28 June Archduke Franz Ferdinand is assassinated in Bosnia. Austria is very annoyed because he was going to be their next emperor. (Franz is too dead to be annoyed.)

23 July Austria blames Serbia for the death of Ferdi because the assassins were from Serbia. Serbia grovels but apology is not accepted. This means *WAR*.

4 August German army marches through Belgium to attack France, so Britain joins the war to help 'poor little Belgium'.

23 August Meanwhile, in the east, the German army defeats the Russian army. Round one to Germany.

9 September The French stop the Germans at the Battle of the Marne. Round two to France.

ALL THOSE PEOPLE FIGHTING AND DYING OVER LITTLE OLD ME. I'M VERY TOUCHED

OI! STOP THAT!

UK

N.

BEL.

FRANCE

October Millions rush to join the armies. They're afraid it will be over before Christmas and before they can fight. It *will* be over before Christmas … 1918.

22 November The Allies and the Central Powers have battered one another to a standstill in northern France. They dig 'trenches' opposite one another … and won't move from them much for four years. No winners – only soldiers lose … their lives.

25 December Enemies stop fighting for a day or two, and even play friendly football matches. It can't last, and it won't be repeated.

Did you know …?
The first Brits to fight in the First World War fought in London! On 2 August 1914, two days before war was declared, peace marchers clashed with Londoners who wanted war.

14

True lies

When you go to war you can't fight against nice people, can you? You have to believe the enemy are real slime-balls who would murder your granny and poison your gerbil if they won. You have to learn to *hate* them.

In Germany a new national anthem was written called the 'Hymn of Hate'. And when people met a friend in the street they no longer said, '*Güten Morgen*' (good morning) they said, '*Gott strafe England*' (God punish England). These words were rubber-stamped on letters, printed on millions of postcards, and engraved on badges and brooches.

Meanwhile, in the UK, the music of German composers was banned. (Since many had died some years before the war, they won't have been too upset.)

And if your enemy *wasn't* nasty enough, what could you do? You could invent a few lies about them. So, it was widely believed that German grocers in Britain had poisoned food and that German barbers were cutting their customers' throats and secretly dumping the bodies. Here's what the enemies said about one other ... but can you spot the lies?

1 Brits believed the German soldiers were monsters ...

IN BELGIUM BRITISH NURSES ARE BEING CARVED WITH KNIVES AND LEFT TO DIE IN BURNING HOSPITALS. AND GERMAN SOLDIERS HAVE BEEN THROWING UP BABIES, CATCHING THEM ON BAYONETS, ROASTING THEM AND EATING THEM

SO WHAT DO THEY TASTE LIKE SIR?

2 And the Germans believed the British were just as bad …

3 Germans believed foreign visitors were spies …

4 And the Brits didn't even trust their allies!

5 The Brits certainly didn't trust their own businessmen …

6 While the Germans knew who was to blame for starting the war …

7 The Germans also believed the most amazing tales of heroic deeds …

8 Brits were sure the Germans were desperate for materials and especially fat …

9 They were also sure that Germany was running short of fighting men …

Every one of these stories was believed – and every one was false, of course. Some were deliberate lies but others were simple mistakes. Take the story of corpses being melted to make oil. It appeared in a German newspaper report from the Western Front in April 1917 …

We are passing the great Kadaver Exploitation Department of this Army Group. The fat that is won here is turned into lubricating oils and everything else is ground down in the bone mills into a powder which is used for mixing with pig's food – nothing can be permitted to go to waste.

Brits called corpses 'cadavers' and thought the Germans were melting *human* corpses. In German 'Kadaver' means an *animal* corpse. The corpses being melted down were horses.

The 'Fat King'

The Brits needed fat extractors too. Major Ellis – known to soldiers as the 'Fat King' – invented a 'fat extracting' plant and set it up on the French coast. This factory took waste food, dead horses and animal waste and turned it into fat. This was sent across the Channel to be made into glycerine – an important part of TNT explosives. Nine thousand tons of fat were produced by the 'Fat King's' factory.

So, a horse could be killed by a German shell (no, the army 'shells' were not like winkle shells you find on the beach. They were huge exploding bombs fired from large guns), turned into TNT and fired back at them! A perfect revenge!

WHY IS THE FAT KING LIKE A HORSE?

BECAUSE THEY BOTH ENJOY A LONG REIGN!

BOOM BOOM

Christmas crack-shots

The First World War was the first war to see aircraft used. To begin with they would fly over enemy armies and photograph their positions or bomb them. Then the defenders sent fighters to shoot down these spy planes. War in the air had begun.

Aeroplanes also meant Brits in their homes were no longer safe in a foreign war. Londoners discovered this after just four months …

FOE FLIERS FLEE

Londoners had hopes of a quiet Christmas crushed when two German planes flew up the Thames yesterday. Crowds gathered in the streets to watch as two gallant airmen from our Royal Flying Corps chased the intruders at speeds of up to 70 miles an hour!

'I could hear the gunfire quite clearly,' a resident of Chiswick told our reporter. 'What if one of those bullets landed on an innocent head?' The aircraft observers had fired rifles at one another – a common sight in the skies over France these days. No one was hurt and the horrid Huns hurried back to Germany with their tails between their legs. But the use of guns is a deadly development of war in the air. In the early days of the war observers would carry a supply of bricks and try to drop one on to the enemy.

Londoners have been ordered to dim their lights this evening in case the unwanted visitors return. It has been reported that the Germans have invented steel darts to be dropped from their aircraft. If these strike a man they will split him in half from head to foot. Is there no end to the atrocious cruelty of this enemy?

'It just makes the people of Britain all the more determined to win,' a shop assistant from Wapping told our reporter. 'I am sending my Bobby down to the recruiting office today.'

The stories of brick bombs and deadly darts were true.

Later aircraft carried machine-guns; the pilot aimed his plane at the enemy and pulled the trigger. But there was a danger that the bullets would then hit his own propeller and shatter it. In time, engineers invented a timing gear so the bullets could only fire into the gaps between the turning propeller.

But how did the first machine-guns fire forward? If you were an Allied inventor, what simple solution could you come up with?

Answer: The propellers were covered with sheets of steel. If a machine-gun bullet happened to hit the propeller it bounced off.

Great idea – and it worked. For a month or two the German airmen were terrified and puzzled by the Allied fighter planes. Finally they captured one, saw how it was done and copied it.

The trouble is there was no way of telling where the bullet would bounce off to if it hit the propeller. It could smash into the pilot's own engine, if he was unlucky – or bounce back and hit him between the eyes if he was *really, really* unlucky!

Did you know …?

In the Second World War (1939–45) there were sirens to warn people of air raids. But when air raids became common in the First World War, many defence chiefs in Britain sent out a letter saying …

B7253A/6

It has been decided that no warning of air raids will be given as it is thought this may do more harm than good.

OFFICIAL

So, you could be walking to school and the first thing you know about the air raid is when you wake up dead.

Is this a record?

On 21 December 1914, William Gilligan, aged 41, joined the West Yorkshire Regiment at Hull. The next day, he deserted at York!

1915 – The year of total war

From 1915, battles are fought from trenches dug into the ground – where these battles are fought becomes known as the Western Front. Meanwhile the war spreads around the world. It is also the year of new weapons to kill new targets … including people in their homes!

People at home can't fight back but they can take it out on foreigners living in their country (known as 'aliens', but not to be confused with little green beings from Mars!). So, in the East End of London, German shops are looted and, in one riot, German pianos are thrown from houses onto the road. A street concert is held where patriotic songs are sung. The government is forced to imprison enemy aliens for their own protection as well as to stop them spying.

In Germany anyone with 'a well-cut coat, a well-filled wallet and a notably good car' is arrested as a spy. All British people are rounded up and most are imprisoned.

Timeline 1915

19 January First Zeppelin airship raids on Britain. Women and children, cats and dogs are in this war, like it or not.

2 February Germany says it will surround Britain with submarines, sink food supply ships and starve Britain to defeat.

18 March British Government asks women to sign up for war work. Many do and they start doing it better than the men did!

22 April Nasty new weapon,

poisoned gas, first used against soldiers in the trenches.

May Allies try to sneak round the back of the German front by landing in Gallipoli, Turkey. They expect the Turks will be a pushover.

7 May German submarines sink a passenger ship, the *Lusitania* – on board are 128 Americans who are not even part of the war yet. Big mistake, Germany.

7 June Zeppelin airship shot down over Flanders, northern France. That slow-moving bag of gas makes Zeppelins easy targets.

July The Turkish state uses war as an excuse to wipe out an entire race of people, the Armenians. A step on the road to the terrors of the Second World War.

August Food getting short, especially in Germany. Prices go up and taxes go up to pay for the war – £1 million a day in Britain is needed to pay for the fighting.

September At the Battle of Loos in Flanders some brave Brits dribble a football towards enemy lines. The ball was found riddled with bullets. Like the foolhardy footballers.

12 October Nurse Edith Cavell is caught helping Brit prisoners to

escape in Belgium. She says, 'If I had to, I'd do it all over again.' Germans shoot her so she can't.

11 November Brit minister Winston Churchill gets sacked because his Gallipoli idea is a disaster. He'll be back.

20 December Allies give up on the Gallipoli attack and retreat. It was a very bloody mistake.

Pests and plagues

Soldiers had more to fear than enemy weapons. Creepy-crawlies and deadly diseases could kill you just as dead.

Fierce flies

At Gallipoli, flies in the summer of 1915 were very bad because of the number of unburied bodies. One soldier of the Australia and New Zealand Army Corps (Anzacs) wrote home about the flies …

Some of them must have tin openers on their feet, they bite so hard.

A Brit soldier complained …

In order to eat your food you had to wave your hand over it then bite suddenly, otherwise a fly came with it. Any bit of food uncovered was blotted out of sight by flies in a couple of seconds.

25

That fly had probably had a picnic on a dead donkey a few minutes before, so it's no wonder the troops suffered so much disease in Gallipoli.

Deadly doctors

Since Florence Nightingale's work in the Crimean War of 1856 it was a little safer in war hospitals. Back in Florie Nightie's day a wound could easily get infected – if the bullet didn't kill you then the germs did. But doctors could still be pretty clumsy. One soldier reported …

An Anzac soldier, Private O'Connor, was wounded in the leg and captured. He was taken to Istanbul where an Armenian doctor operated to amputate O'Connor's leg. The doctor sawed halfway through the bone, grew too tired, and snapped off the rest.

Frightful first-aid

In the middle of a battle you couldn't pop down to the local chemist shop for an aspirin or dial 999 for an ambulance. Soldiers had to look after each other and they all carried a small first-aid pack into battle. Brit soldiers also had a book, *The Field Almanac 1915*, that gave some advice.

There are some instructions you may *not* like to follow next time you are flattened in a fierce football match …

Broken limbs:
Gently put the broken limb straight after cutting off the clothes. Then fix it in this position by means of a splint made from a rifle, a roll of newspapers, bayonets, swords, pieces of wood.

A roll of newspapers! In a battle? What newspaper could be as tough as a wooden splint? The *Daily Telegraph-pole* perhaps?

By 1918, because of severe shortages in Germany, soldiers were forced to use bandages made from crêpe paper and tied on with thread.

F-f-f-f-frostbite

Frostbite is another problem you may suffer in school sports (especially during cricket matches in Britain). Again, you wouldn't want to suffer the 1915 cure ...

Frostbite:
Carry the sufferer to a room or place without a fire, remove the clothes and rub hard with a cloth soaked in water or snow.

Brrrr!

And the way of preventing frostbite was even worse ...

In the winter of 1914–15, anti-frostbite grease was supplied in two lb tins to soldiers on the Western Front. It looked like lard and it contained mostly pork fat. After 1915, whale oil was issued in rum jars. This was little used because of the terrible smell. Army orders said that, before going out on patrol in cold or wet weather, each man was to be stripped and rubbed down with whale oil by an officer. Most men refused to strip ... and most officers refused to rub!

Putrid poisons

The army listed three types of poisoning. The emergency cure for 'corrosive' poisoning looks weird ...

№ 31a   *British Army Field Almanac 1915*

Corrosive poisons:
Give scrapings from whitewashed walls or ceilings, mixed with water.

Perhaps the advice to eat walls is not so surprising. After all, Walls make great ice-cream and sausages!

Gruesome gas

A new First World War danger was gas attack. Orders went out from army headquarters ...

If you are caught in a gas attack:
1 Take out your handkerchief.
2 Urinate into the material till it is soaked.
3 Tie it round your mouth and nose and breathe through it.

fig I

The orders didn't say what you should do if you didn't feel like a pee!

Crafty cordite

Soldiers wishing to appear unwell and thus avoid duty would chew cordite, an explosive taken from their rifle bullets. Cordite gave the soldier a high temperature but the effect soon wore off.

Lovely lice

At the Gallipoli battles the soldiers were forced to wear the same clothes for weeks without even taking them off. One Australian soldier finally got to take his socks off and saw a ghastly sight ...

> And, Ma, I swear that as I dropped my socks on the floor I saw them start to move! They were a seething mass of lice!

In the trenches the soldiers found 'chatting' was a peaceful way to pass the quiet times. But 'chatting' didn't mean talking. It meant getting rid of the 'chats' or lice from the seams of their tunics.

One soldier compared lice to an army that had invaded his body ...

The Little Soldiers of the Night
Though some hundreds you may kill,
Still you'll find there's hundreds still,
For they hide beneath each other
And are smart at taking cover;
Then you have an awful bite,
They've a shocking appetite.

> *There are families in dozens,*
> *Uncles, mothers, sisters, cousins,*
> *And they have their married quarters*
> *Where they rear their sons and daughters;*
> *And they take a lot of catching*
> *Cause an awful lot of scratching.*

German soldiers described another way of dealing with their bloodsucking friends. They took the lid from a boot polish tin and held it by a piece of wire over a candle. When the lid began to glow they'd simply drop the lice on the red hot tin. The sizzle of the frying lice was a sweet sound to their ears.

Did you know ...?
British soldiers suffered from lice that were a pale fawn colour, but German soldiers had red lice. If they'd bred the two together they could have had pretty pink lice!

Seriously spooky

When your life is in danger then you start to believe in 'luck'. People in danger can be very superstitious. A few new beliefs sprang up in the First World War.

Super superstitions
Bullet-proof Bibles
Pocket-sized copies of the New Testament suddenly sold

tens of thousands of copies. They were being bought by anxious Brit mothers for their sons. There were stories of bullets being stopped by these little Bibles. There may have been one or two true cases of Bibles stopping 'spent' rifle bullets. They were not a lot of good against high explosive shells and machine-gun bullets.

God's people

Each side believed that they were in the right; that meant that God would be on their side. The Germans even went to war with a belt buckle that read, '*Gott mit uns*' (God with us). British soldiers saw the word '*uns*' and thought that proved what they knew – they were fighting the *Huns*! One very popular belief was that either God had your name and number on a bullet ... or he didn't. So, you may as well charge that machine-gun. After the war one soldier said ...

I was most amazed by the bullets that missed *me!*

But the most dangerous superstition of all was that 'Prayer can turn bullets aside'.

For the soldiers who didn't believe in God or luck there was always this common sense advice. It was a notice passed around the trenches ...

Don't worry

When you are a soldier you can be in one of two places:

> A dangerous place or a safe place.

If you're in a safe place ... don't worry.

If you're in a dangerous place you can be one of two things:

> One is wounded and the other is not.

If you're not wounded ... don't worry.

If you are wounded it can be dangerous or slight:

> If it's slight ... don't worry.

If it's dangerous then one of two things will happen:

> You'll die or you'll recover.

If you recover ... don't worry.

If you die ... you can't worry.

In these circumstances a soldier never worries.

The Third Man

NEVER LIGHT THREE CIGARETTES WITH A SINGLE MATCH

The reason for this belief was that it was a dangerous thing to do in the trenches where an enemy sniper might be watching.

First light will catch his eye, second light he'll fix his sights on the light and third light … he'll pull the trigger.

Mascots
Animals bring you luck. Regiments collected them as mascots: a bulldog mascot and the regiment is saying, 'We're tough'; a goat mascot says, 'We'll charge head-down and fearless.' What would your school mascot be?

But Bella and Bertha were an unusual choice for the Scots Guards. In late 1914, two cows were found near Ypres (pronounced 'ee-pruh' … though most Brit soldiers called it 'Wipers'), Flanders, by the regiment. They were the only survivors from a herd that had been hit by shell-fire. (Yeah, all the udders were dead.) The cows – soon named Bella and Bertha – became the battalion's mascots, providing fresh milk for the men in the trenches. After the war, the cows were taken to Scotland for retirement. When the Scots Guards marched through London on the Victory Parade, they were accompanied by Bella and Bertha.

The blasted statue
In the town of Albert, Flanders, there was a fine church with a golden statue of the Virgin Mary on top. Early in 1915 the tower was damaged and the statue toppled over

but didn't fall. For months it hung there as the war dragged on and the British defenders in Albert invented a strange superstition ...

WHEN THE STATUE FALLS THE WAR WILL END!

If the statue fell the British soldiers would be terribly discouraged, so the army set up strong cables to hold the Virgin Mary in her perilous place. For over three years the Germans failed to knock her off her perch and for three more years the war went on.

In 1918, the Germans finally captured the town and started using the top of the church tower as an observation post. From that high point they could guide their shell-fire towards the British. So it was the British who fired back and ended up demolishing the tower and brought the Virgin Mary down to Earth. The Germans were happy.

HAH! *OUR* SUPERSTITION IS THAT WHOEVER KNOCKS THE STATUE DOWN WILL *LOSE* THE WAR, BYE-BYE BRITS!

And, would you believe it? The war ended shortly after ... but with the defeat of Germany.

I TOLD YOU SO!

Funny fact: After the British knocked the statue down it disappeared – probably sent to Germany to be melted down and turned into weapons.

When the war finished, Albert and its church were rebuilt. An exact copy of the statue stands there now. But ... it was suggested that the statue should be put back in her famous wartime pose!

The people of Albert said, '*Non!*'

Ghostly tales

With so many people dying in the First World War it's not surprising that ghosts were reported. In 1916, there was a great rise in 'spiritualists' – people who said they had the power to speak to the dead.

In late 1916 (after terrible losses at the Battle of the Somme where 20,000 Brits died on the first day alone) spiritualism became very popular in the UK with mothers trying to contact lost sons. Many fake spiritualists were caught and put in prison, but still the craze continued.

Why would a spiritualist lie to a woman about her dead son and pretend that she could speak to him? For money, of course. In December 1916, during the trial of fake spiritualist Almira Brockway, it was revealed that she was receiving over £25 a week for her work. Workers in the war factories worked 48 hours each week and made just £1.

Whenever there's misery and suffering you can be sure there is someone to cash in and make a fortune out of it. But some of the spooky stories are harder to explain than frauds and fakes. They are *seriously* spooky ...

The angel army of Mons

In August 1914, British troops arrived in southern Belgium

to try and stop the German invasion. They were beaten back and slaughtered by the advancing enemy. Over 15,000 died in the early attacks. Yet some survived and reports said this was thanks to a miracle ...

WE SAW OUR ST. GEORGE LEADING A TROOP OF PHANTOM FIGHTERS ON HORSEBACK. THEY DROVE THE GERMANS BACK

OUI, MON AMI, BUT IT WAS OUR JOAN OF ARC NOT ST. GEORGE WHO CAME TO OUR RESCUE!

Arthur Machen, a journalist, turned the rumours into a short story. His story (called 'The Bowmen') said it was the English heroes of the 1415 Battle of Agincourt who had come to the rescue. (The battle was fought near by.) Machen's story was published in the *London Evening News* a few weeks after the Battle of Mons and many Brits believed it. Some of the soldiers who returned from the battle then said it was true.

THEY WAS DIRTY GREAT ANGELS WITH ROBES AND WINGS AND THINGS

Even when Machen said he'd invented the whole story there were some people who went on believing in the angels.

Explanations: Some religious people have said the phantom army was made up of the spirits of the soldiers who had just died in the battle.

Some doctors believed that the Allied soldiers had hallucinations – waking dreams – because they were stressed by fear, pain and exhaustion.

But, weirdest of all, the German spy chief, Friedrich Herzenwirth, claimed that he had created the angels. He had sent up aeroplanes with cinema projectors. These projected images of angels on to the low clouds. He did this to encourage the German soldiers who would believe God was on their side.

The Montrose ghost

In October 1917, a ghost was seen at Montrose aerodrome in Scotland. One witness said ...

> *It glided up to the door of the old aerodrome bar room and then vanished.*

It was seen several times afterwards by many officers. They were sure it was the ghost of Lieutenant Desmond Arthur who had been killed in a flying accident. Why was air-ace Arthur haunting the site of his crash?

An official enquiry had blamed the accident on Desmond Arthur himself. It said ...

> He was killed by his own foolishness.

Yet the other officers knew that Lieutenant Arthur was a good pilot. They believed that his spirit was tortured by the insulting enquiry. Arthur's friends believed the ghost would not rest until his name was cleared by a second enquiry.

When this second enquiry decided ...

> We blame the fatal accident on a badly repaired machine.

... the ghost paid one final visit to the bar room in January 1917 and then was never seen again.

Explanations: Desmond Arthur's friends were angry that he was blamed for his own death. They started the rumours of the ghost to attract the attention of the newspapers. The fascinated public then demanded to know the truth and a second enquiry was ordered.

Or ... the ghost seemed to spend a lot of time in the *bar room*. Did the 'spirits' they poured in their glasses, make the officers see 'spirits' walk through the door?

The spirit of the Somme

Soldiers in hospital enjoyed swapping stories of their experiences. Some of them were strange and mysterious ...

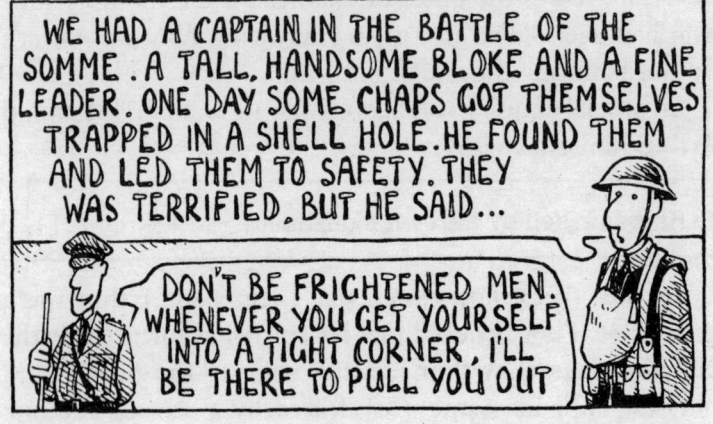

Explanations: Soldiers would be bored in hospital. They could well get into a competition to tell the most exciting story. And, if their true stories weren't exciting enough, they could make one up! After all, it's hard to prove that the storyteller was lying.

Or ... the storyteller was led to safety by an officer who

looked like the dead officer. When the storyteller lost sight of the Captain he believed he'd seen a ghost.

Or … a ghostly captain went on protecting his men even after he'd died. He became their guardian angel.

The dead poet's footsteps

One of the most famous victims of the war was the poet, Rupert Brooke. He'd written a poem about the glory of war. (This was a dumb thing to do since he'd never seen the horror of it, but the people back in Britain wanted to believe him.)

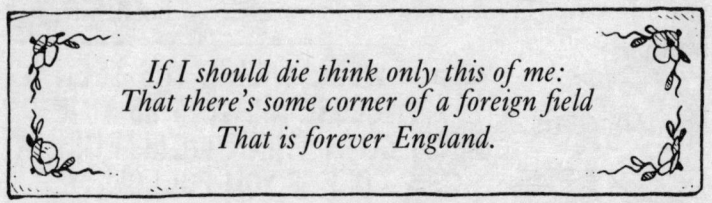

If I should die think only this of me:
That there's some corner of a foreign field
That is forever England.

Rupert used to live in Grantchester Vicarage near Cambridge, and he wrote another famous poem about it. (The poem is called 'The Old Vicarage, Grantchester' … no prizes for guessing why.)

He was sent off to fight in Gallipoli but never made it. In April 1915, he was bitten on the lip by an insect and died of blood poisoning. (It must have been a dirty insect that forgot to clean its biting teeth. This was probably *not* the glorious end Rupert imagined.) The 'corner of a foreign field that is forever England' is his grave in an olive grove on the Greek Island of Skyros, by the way.

When the war was over a doctor called Copeland moved into Rupert's old rooms in Grantchester Vicarage. One frosty evening he sat reading by the fire with his bulldog at his feet …

Suddenly the dog woke up and growled at the window. In the silence that followed I heard slow, regular footsteps coming round the house and heading for the window! I threw open the window ... and there was no one there!

GRRRR

Doctor Copeland's landlord explained that the footsteps had been heard ever since Rupert Brooke was killed four years before. (His phantom feet must have been hurting a bit by 1919!)

Explanations: The dog heard burglars.

Or ... Rupert didn't like being stuck in 'some corner of a foreign field' and wanted to come home.

Or ... the owners of Grantchester Vicarage wanted to believe that their famous lodger still remembered them. But isn't it strange that only the 'famous' Rupert Brooke came back and not some ordinary Joe Blogg?

Or ... maybe it isn't Rupert's ghost after all. Maybe it *is* Joe Blogg's ghost! This is not as silly as it sounds. In Grantchester churchyard there is a memorial for the local men who died in the First World War. There are usually flowers at the foot of the memorial, put there by poetry lovers who remember the famous Rupert. Is that fair? What

41

about the other brave men who died? Are they forgotten and do they return to haunt the Vicarage in revenge? Look carefully at the memorial and you will see half a dozen other names on there. And one of the other (forgotten) names is ... 'Joseph Blogg'.

Simple spymen

Some places were haunted long before the First World War. But the war brought them new horrors and new ghosts. Take the ancient Tower of London, for example. The war brought it back into use in a horrible historical way ...

Terror in the Tower

'Have you any last requests?' the Major asked the young man in the shabby black suit.

'I have, good sir. I would like to play my violin one last time. Before you shoot me.'

The Major nodded and opened a hatch in the steel door and called to the guard outside, 'Bring Herr Buschmann's violin from the office.' He turned back to the prisoner. 'You are honoured, young Fernando. You will be the first to be executed in the Tower of London for hundreds of years.'

The young man gave a faint smile. 'It is a greater honour to die for Germany,' he said.

'It would be better to *live*,' the Major pointed out and pulled a wooden chair to the side of the bed and sat facing the German spy.

'My wife and child will suffer back in Germany. I regret being caught ... but I do not regret spying for my country,' he said calmly.

The Major shook his head sadly. 'It was Germany that sent you here to die.'

'No, they sent me here to *spy*.'

'But they prepared you so badly we were *bound* to catch you!' the Major groaned. 'Don't you see that?'

'No,' the prisoner frowned.

The officer leaned forward and lowered his voice. 'You will die at dawn, so there is nothing to lose by telling you this, Fernando. But they trained you in the spy school at Rotterdam. The head of the spy school is Herr Flores.'

'Perhaps.'

'We *know* it is!' the Major sighed. 'And he sent you here with a passport written in his own handwriting. We recognized it at once.'

For the first time a small frown of uncertainty crossed the young German's face. The Major went on. 'He sent you to a hotel in the Strand where he sends *all* of his secret agents. He gave you a cover story – you were to say you were a salesman of cheese, bananas, safety-razors and potatoes … but you know hardly anything about those things!'

The spy lowered his head a little in an admission of defeat. 'I sent in reports the best I could,' he muttered.

'You sent in reports that said we switch on London searchlights at eight p.m. and switch them off again at 10:30 if no Zeppelins appear,' the officer said. 'That is no great secret to die for.'

'You know what messages I sent?'

'Of course! You sent the messages in code to a school-master in Holland. That schoolmaster is a *British* spy. You were an amateur, Fernando. *We* will shoot you … but it is *your* spy-masters who sent you to your death.'

There was a rap on the door and a guard handed a violin to the Major who passed it across to Fernando Buschmann. For the next three hours the sweet, mournful tones echoed round the ancient walls and stirred the ghosts of long-dead prisoners.

Slowly the sky lightened through the barred window and hobnailed footsteps clattered in the corridor outside. The prisoner played one last melody but now the notes were wavering and disconnected. 'Nice tune,' the Major said.

'By Pagliacci,' the German said. 'The music tells the story of a broken-hearted clown. Maybe that's all I was, Major.' He raised the violin to his lips and kissed it. 'Goodbye, I shall not want you any more.' He laid his precious instrument on the hard bed, straightened his back and faced the men who waited at the door. 'I am ready,' he said.

Fernando Buschmann faced an eight-man firing squad on the morning of 19 October 1915. He refused a blindfold, saying he wanted to die like a gentleman. He was one of 11 bungling, amateur German spies to die in the Tower during the First World War. A 12th was hanged at Wandsworth Prison.

On 13 November 1997 the papers connected with the case were sold at an auction in London. The saddest was the letter from his wife to his lawyer Henry Garrett that read …

> Dear Mr Garrett
>   I would be grateful if you could send me details of my husband's last moments. Was he at least allowed to keep his violin till his last hours? Had he much to suffer? Will I find his tomb in London to weep at it? My only wish is to visit and to sleep there where my beloved husband is sleeping...

There were many ways to die, and many wasted lives, in the First World War. Fernando Buschmann's was just another one.

Awful agents

In the years before the First World War Britain was overrun with German spies because they guessed this war would come one day. It wasn't till 1908 that Britain had any spy-catchers – the Secret Service Bureau.[1] Captain Vernon Kell

---

1. In 1916 this was renamed Military Department 5 – the famous MI5. By the end of the war it had 844 members.

was the only member of the Secret Service Bureau and by the start of the war in 1914 he had only nine officers. The Bureau did such a good job that they arrested 21 agents as soon as the war began.

The Bureau had a lot of help from the German spies who were not too clever. In fact, they were awful agents. They got their information from Germans working in Britain – hairdressers and pub landlords were favourites because they heard lots of gossip. And German teachers were a bit treacherous too! (Would you trust a teacher?)

Their code words included …

• eggs = foot-soldiers
• condensed milk = horse soldiers
• margarine = guns
• Dutch cheese = battleships
• tinned lobster = torpedo boats

Now that code may be hard to crack (except 'eggs' which are easy to crack) but you don't have to be James Bond to solve the following genuine German code. Match the code to the real meaning … the simple spymen left enough clues in the choice of words!

1 Floating down	a) Dartmouth Naval Base
2 Old folks at home	b) Destroyers
3 Dark melodies	c) Old battleships
4 Chattanooga Rag	d) Southampton
5 Down South	e) Submarines
6 Pirates of Penzance	f) Chatham Base

TOP SECRET

That was too easy. So try this quick quiz …

Sly spy
Which of the following statements are true?
1 MI5 agents used girl guides to carry their messages … but
the girls had to promise not to read them.

2 An American (spying for Germany) was arrested as soon
as his socks were tested. When they were soaked in water
they produced invisible ink.

3 A German spy put up a poster in Portsmouth offering £5

47

to anyone who would give him information about the warships there.

THAT'S A WARSHIP, FIVE POUNDS PLEASE

4 British spies in Germany were told, 'If someone starts taking an interest in you then you will end up having to kill him. So don't waste time. Do it.'

YOU COLLECT STAMPS, HOW INTERESTING

Answer: The above statements are all totally ridiculous. And they are all totally *true*. Girl guides *were* used to carry messages (because they proved more reliable than boy scouts!) and Brit agents in Germany really were 'licensed to kill'. In November 1997 MI5 published the secret files at last and these wacky facts came to light.

1916 – The year of the Somme

In 1914 millions of men had rushed to join their armies and fight for their countries. By 1916 they are trained and ready and are sent off to fight the biggest battle ever. The battleground is around the river Somme in northern France.

This is to be the battle that ends the war for good! All it does is end the war for the million or so captured, wounded or killed. For the rest it goes on … and on and on …

Timeline 1916

25 January 'Conscription' comes to Britain. That means fit, single men *have* to join the army whether they like it or not.

February The French and Germans begin the longest battle of the war, at the fortress of Verdun in north-eastern France. Even Big Bertha (that's a gun firing one-ton shells, not a woman) can't win it for the Germans.

BIG BERTHA SHELL   BIG BERTY SCHNELL

March German soldiers are told to have one day a week without food to save on supplies … but the officers seem to eat well *every* day!

24 April The Irish rebel against British rule and try to seize Dublin *Post Office*! Brits soon *stamp* that out!

May The only great sea battle of the war takes place at Jutland.

THINNER MEN NEED THINNER TRENCHES

Germans claim victory but never try to fight the Brit navy again.

5 June Lord Kitchener's face is on a million posters saying 'Your country needs YOU!' Today he dies when his ship hits a mine.[1]

1 July The Battle of the Somme begins. Today Brits outnumber Germans seven to one … but lose seven men to every one German. Very bloody draw.

10 August A frightful news film, *The Battle of the Somme*, is shown in Brit cinemas even though it's not over yet. It's seen by 20 million shocked Brits.

15 September New Brit super-weapon, the 'Willie', enters the war. Luckily someone has changed its name to the 'Tank', giving rise to a horrible historical joke. Question: There were two flies in an airing cupboard. Which one was in the army? Answer: The one on the tank.

October In a Brit election the 'Peace' candidate is heavily defeated by the one supporting the war. For all the bloodshed, Brits back home still don't want peace.

1. In 1930 a German spy-master said that *he* arranged to have Kitchener killed. He claimed he got Irish enemies of Britain to sneak a bomb on board Kitchener's ship, then he watched from the shore as the bomb was detonated. Don't believe him. It was a mine!

14 November End of the Battle of the Somme. Allied and German losses – over 1.3 million men. Allied gains – six miles. That's 120 men for every yard of ground won. Expensive ground.

7 December Lloyd George becomes new Brit prime minister. Old prime minister Asquith says, 'I distrust him.'

Silly (but true) story

In the great Somme advance of 1 July 1916 a soldier was given the job of taking a messenger pigeon in a basket to the front. He was told that an officer would use it to send a message when the first target was reached.

Back at headquarters they waited hours and hours for the pigeon and finally it appeared. The anxious commander cried, 'Give me the message!' and it was handed to him.

He opened it and read, 'I am absolutely fed up with carrying this bloody bird around France.'

Daft DORA

Who was DORA? DORA was Britain's Defence of the Realm Act. And DORA could be *very* fussy.

The people of Britain had to live by DORA's rules. But

which rules? Here are some strange regulations. But which are real DORA rules and which are real daft rules?

DEFENCE OF THE REALM ACT
YOU MUST NOT

1... loiter under a railway bridge
2... send a letter overseas written in invisible ink
3... buy binoculars without official permission
4... fly a kite that could be used for signalling
5... speak in a foreign language on the telephone
6... ring church bells after sundown
7... whistle in the street after 10pm for a taxi
8... travel alone in a railway carriage over the Forth Bridge
9... push a handcart through the streets at night without showing a red light at the back and a white light on the front
10... eat sweets in the classroom

One rule which upset children was the one that said, 'You must not keep fragments of Zeppelins or bombs as souvenirs'. All children hunted for these and ignored the law.

What's a Zeppelin? A huge German airship that flew over Britain and dropped bombs on cities. No one in Britain had ever suffered this sort of attack before and some people feared the dangers a bit too much.

Zeppelin Zep-panic

DORA ordered that no lights could be shown after dark. In 1916, in York, the first person fined was Jim Richardson, who was fined five shillings for lighting a cigarette in the street at night. The Zep-panicking magistrate told him that a lighted match could be seen by a Zeppelin flying 2,000 feet up.

The Rev Patrick Shaw was arrested for showing a light from his church, despite his plea that it was only a 'dim religious light'. The Zep-panicking magistrate fined him anyway.

Police also banned loud noises. In York, the Chief Constable told residents …

Do not laugh in the street, stop your dogs barking and do not bang doors because all these noises can be heard from a Zeppelin listening for its target.

The man was clearly a Yorkshire *pudding*! But was he any worse than the newspaper which had the bright idea to light a huge area of empty countryside at night to attract Zeppelins and then destroy them – like moths around a candle flame!

Foul food and worse water

If you think school dinners are bad then you should be glad you didn't live in Europe in 1914–18. It's hard to tell if the food and drink was worse at home or in the army.

Would you like a cup of tea in the trenches? Or would you prefer a drink of milk in your wartime home?

You'd like tea in the trenches? Well, the soldiers' water had chloride of lime added to kill the germs in it. The trouble was the chloride of lime made the water taste *terrible*, even when it was boiled and used to make a cup of tea. It's a bit like drinking your local swimming-bath water. Yeuchy. So, would you prefer …

Milk at home? In London, William Saxby, a milkman, was sentenced in 1917 to two months' hard labour for selling his customers milk watered down with 'foul water obtained from a public lavatory basin'. Yeuchier!

Rotten rations

British soldiers were offered a delightful tinned stew called Maconochie. A joke recipe appeared in a soldiers' newspaper. Sadly it was close to the truth!

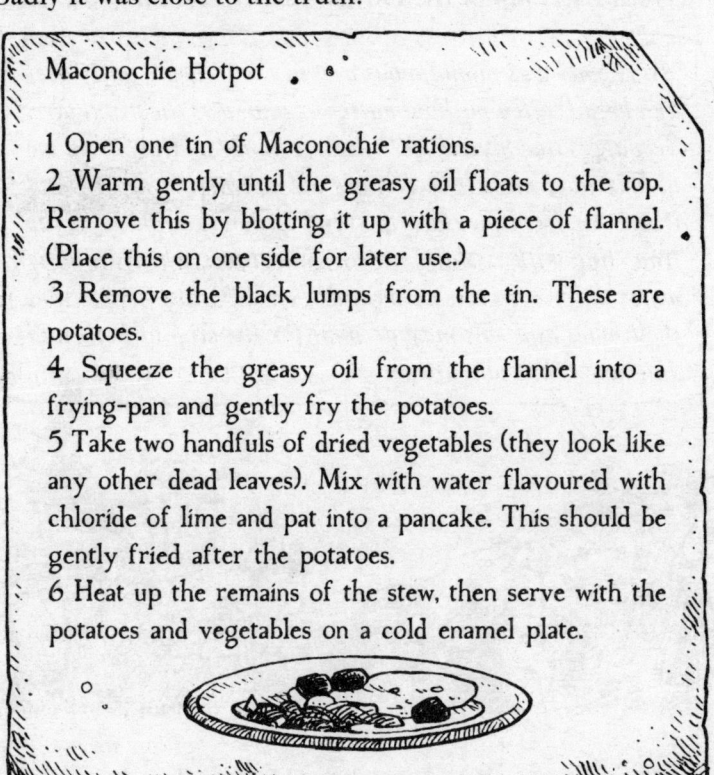

Maconochie Hotpot

1 Open one tin of Maconochie rations.
2 Warm gently until the greasy oil floats to the top. Remove this by blotting it up with a piece of flannel. (Place this on one side for later use.)
3 Remove the black lumps from the tin. These are potatoes.
4 Squeeze the greasy oil from the flannel into a frying-pan and gently fry the potatoes.
5 Take two handfuls of dried vegetables (they look like any other dead leaves). Mix with water flavoured with chloride of lime and pat into a pancake. This should be gently fried after the potatoes.
6 Heat up the remains of the stew, then serve with the potatoes and vegetables on a cold enamel plate.

Soldiers were also given bully beef (like corned beef) to which they liked to add raw onions. Sometimes they had to eat this with hard biscuits.

The French peasants who gave rooms to British soldiers were glad of these biscuits ... they made excellent firelighters!

Jam was usually plum and apple and arrived in the trenches in tins. Empty tins made useful home-made grenades!

Young soldiers suffered badly. Ernest Parker, a soldier in the 10th Battalion of the Durham Light Infantry, said …

Army food was monotonous and in the trenches bully beef and bread, often without butter or jam, was the usual fare. Teenagers like myself were always hungry. Alas, when we needed food most it sometimes did not arrive at all, and it was far from pleasant to spend 24 hours or more in the front line with nothing to eat. Sometimes when drinking water did not arrive, we were driven to boiling water from shell holes and this may account for the crop of boils and diarrhoea that plagued us.

Apart from the bully beef and the Maconochie the soldiers had two other big food complaints …

One was the cakes that friends and family sent from home! Deadlier than a German bullet some soldiers reckoned.

The other pet hate is explained in a popular poem of the time …

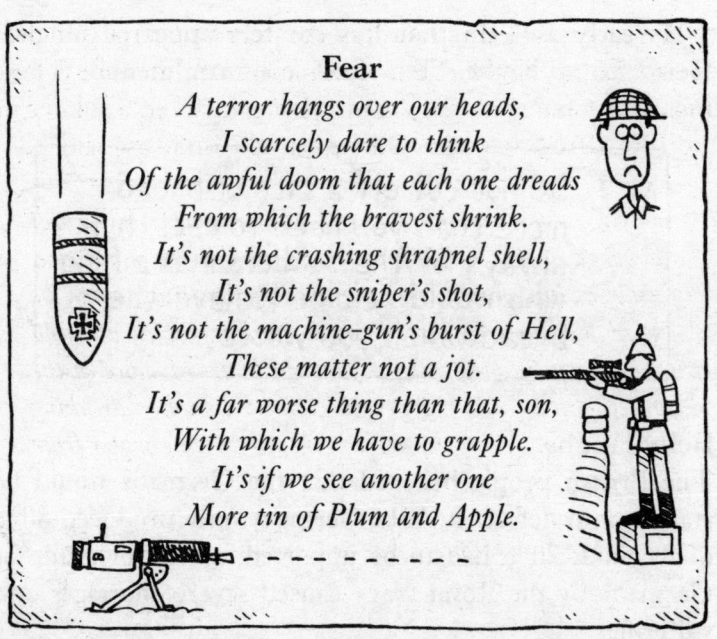

Fear

A terror hangs over our heads,
I scarcely dare to think
Of the awful doom that each one dreads
From which the bravest shrink.
It's not the crashing shrapnel shell,
It's not the sniper's shot,
It's not the machine-gun's burst of Hell,
These matter not a jot.
It's a far worse thing than that, son,
With which we have to grapple.
It's if we see another one
More tin of Plum and Apple.

Horse sense

The Allied soldiers complained but it was even worse for the German army. One tip sent to the soldiers read …

For tender roast horse flesh, you should boil it first in a little water, before you put it in the roasting pan.

But they only ate horses for the *mane* course.

Suffering civilians

British people may have gone hungry from time to time. But the people of Germany were starving for most of the First World War.

As early as 1915 'Eat less' posters appeared all over Germany with the 'Ten food commandments'. These included ...

No.7 Do not cut off a slice of bread more than you need to eat. Think always of the soldiers in the field who would rejoice to have the bread which you waste.

Belly laughs

The British people believed that the Germans would be starved into defeat. In 1914 Germany only produced 80% of its food, 20% had to be imported, so the blockade of Germany by the Royal Navy caused severe shortages and suffering.

By the end of the war Germans *were* starving, but in September 1915 they could still laugh about the British blockade. That month a Zeppelin raid on London dropped 70 bombs, killing 26 people and wounding almost 100. But the crew also dropped a ham bone attached to a parachute. On it was written, 'A gift from starved-out Germany'.

By September 1918, the German people had stopped laughing ... and they didn't have spare ham bones for jokes.

Hunger horrors

We all know what it's like to be hungry, but very few of us in Europe today know what it's like to be *really* starving, year after year.

Maybe you could try this diet for just *one day* and see how it feels. (Get your friends to sponsor you and give the money to a good cause.) Then remember this is how most Germans ate in the winter of 1916–1917 on a *good* day. It was known as the Turnip Winter because turnip was the only food that was plentiful.

The Turnip Winter diet
You need:
six slices of bread
50g of meat
two teaspoons of sugar
two teaspoons of coffee
50g of cheese
one cup of soup
vegetables (half a turnip, handful of peas, beans, mushrooms, nuts), half a cup of blackberries

Breakfast
Two slices of bread (no butter), one cup of coffee with a spoonful of sugar but no milk
Lunch
Soup with meat and turnip chopped in, peas and beans added. Cup of coffee, two slices of bread
Supper
Cheese, two slices of bread, water
Snacks
Nuts and berries

And, now, the *bad* news ...
- You would only have the mushrooms, nuts and berries if you'd gone out and picked them in the autumn. (You might have to fight the squirrels for the juicy ones!)
- The meat would probably be horse or dog. (After a day of

59

the Turnip Winter diet you may look at your pet poodle and lick your lips.) Even the kangaroos in the German zoos were killed and eaten.

- You might not even be able to get dog meat. In April 1916, all Berlin butchers were closed for five days because they had no supplies of anything. In July 1916, women demonstrated outside the Town Hall in Dusseldorf demanding more meat and potatoes. When the Mayor offered them more beans and peas, they rioted and smashed every window in the Town Hall.
- Cream was only obtainable on a doctor's prescription.
- The German newspapers tried to calm things down – one published a long article proving that overeating was the cause of baldness!
- By late 1916, women queued outside food shops all night, bringing camp stools, knitting, etc. (One woman was seen in a queue with a sewing machine to pass the time.)

Hot chestnuts

While Germans were starving, Brits were getting ready for the day when they would have to live with less food. In January 1918, this poster appeared ...

Healthy advice even today. But some of the recipes look as tasty as a can of vegetarian cat-food.

The National Food Economy League Book of War-time Recipes had this recipe that you may like to try if you really want a taste of the First World War (or if you are the sort of dustbin that would swallow anything).

Chestnut curry
You need:
one pound chestnuts; $\frac{1}{2}$ to $\frac{3}{4}$ pint curry sauce
Method:
1 Slit and boil the chestnuts for 20 minutes. Remove both outer and inner skins very carefully. (To do this, leave in the hot water and peel one by one.)
2 Place in a casserole with curry sauce (made from a tablespoon of curry powder and a tablespoon of flour in $\frac{3}{4}$ pint of water).
3 Put in a medium oven to simmer for two hours, until the chestnuts have taken up all the water and are thoroughly tender.
4 Serve with plain, boiled rice.

No wonder the Brits sang ...

My Tuesdays are meatless,
My coffee is sweetless,
Each day I get poorer and wiser.
My home it is heatless,
My trousers are seatless,
My God, but I do hate the Kaiser.

But by 1916 it wasn't only the Brits who hated the Kaiser. The Germans were beginning to turn against him. And no wonder. If food was bad in Britain it was worse in Germany …

Fake food

All Germans who lived through the First World War remembered not only the lack of food but the frightful food *substitutes* that they were forced to eat – known as 'ersatz' food. As the war dragged on, exhibitions were held all over Germany to demonstrate the huge range of ersatz food and drinks, for example …

Bread soon contained flour made from beans and peas, and often sawdust was added.

Cakes were made from clover and chestnut flour.

Meat was replaced by the rice lamb chop or the vegetable steak (pale green, made from spinach, spuds, ground nuts and eggs substitute).

Butter was 'stretched' with starch or made from a mix of curdled milk, sugar and yellow colouring.

Eggs were made from a mix of maize and potatoes.

Pepper was 'stretched' with ashes.

Fats – many attempts were made to make fats: from rats, mice, hamsters, crows, cockroaches, snails, worms, hair clippings, old leather boots and shoes. None of those was very successful.

Coffee was first made from roast nuts flavoured with coal tar – with sugar this was OK! Later came coffee-ersatz-ersatz – roasted acorns or beech nuts. Later still, when all acorns had to be fed to pigs, came coffee made from carrots and turnips.

Horrible? At least they filled the stomach. By late 1918, even ersatz foods had run out. For German soldiers struggling to fight, a meal might be turnip stew served with chunks of turnip bread.

Hungry people lose the will to fight. Germans lost that will – the Allies, who hadn't suffered nearly so much, did not lose their will. It's one of the reasons the Germans lost. It was also a reason why the Germans felt so bitter at losing. All that pain for nothing. Ten years after the First World War ended that bitterness drove them to support Adolf Hitler and a second war.

1917 – The year of the mud

The winter of 1916–17 is bitterly cold, but especially for the French. The Germans hold the north-west where most French coalmines are. One jeweller in Paris places a small lump of coal surrounded by diamonds in his window.

Houses in Paris are allowed only one electric light in each room (anyone caught with more will have their electricity cut off for three weeks!).

In Germany coal is just as short. Berlin lights are to be put out by nine p.m. Elephants from the circus are used in Berlin to pull coal carts from the railway stations – it saves wasting coal on steam trains or using horses that could be working in the army. German workers go on strike while French soldiers have their own rebellion. Everyone is desperate for peace – but the war goes on ... and on.

Timeline 1917

January A munitions factory blows up in Silvertown, East London, killing 69.

February The Russian people rebel against their leaders and Russian soldiers lend their rifles to help the revolution. Good news for Germany.

March In Britain the Women's Army Auxiliary Corps (WAAC) is founded and a new joke is born...

April The Doughboys are here! No, not bakers' men, but American soldiers as the USA joins the war.

64

Meanwhile French troops rebel against their conditions.

May UK horse-racing stopped, followed by county cricket and league football.

June Brit ban on rice being thrown at weddings and feeding birds – food is too precious.

July The war now costs Britain nearly £6 million a day. Will they run out of money or men first?

1 August Terrific rain storms as the British attack in Flanders. The mud is as deadly an enemy as the Germans.

4 September German submarines shell Scarborough. Why shell a seaside holiday town when it has a beach full of shells?

October Brit bakers allowed to add potato flour to bread while French bread has become grey, soggy stuff.

November War between Russia and Germany coming to an end as the Russian 'Bolsheviks' start to take over their country.

6 December German Giants reach London. (They're bomber aircraft, not monster men.) They're harder to catch than the old Zeppelins.

Wild Western Front

From November 1914 the two huge armies dug trenches in the ground and faced one another in a line from Belgium to Switzerland. From time to time one tried to attack and push back the other. The defenders usually won in the end ... but only after both sides had lost large numbers of men.

Lots of books have described trench life on the Western Front. The soldier's only comfort was that it was just as bad for the enemy as it was for himself. Here are six descriptions of trench life from Allied or Central Power soldiers. But which are which?

1 Which side suffered disgusting trenches?

> Lice, rats, barbed wire, fleas, shells, bombs, underground caves, corpses, blood, liquor, mice, cats, filth, bullets, fire, steel; that is what war is. It is the work of the devil.

2 Which side fought till they were exhausted skeletons?

> There were about 20 men. They walked like living plaster statues. Their faces stared at us like those of shrunken mummies, and their eyes seemed so huge that one saw nothing but eyes. Those eyes, which had not seen sleep for four days and nights showed the vision of death. Was this the dream of glory that I had when I volunteered to fight?

3 Which side fought because they thought it was their duty to God and that he was on their side?

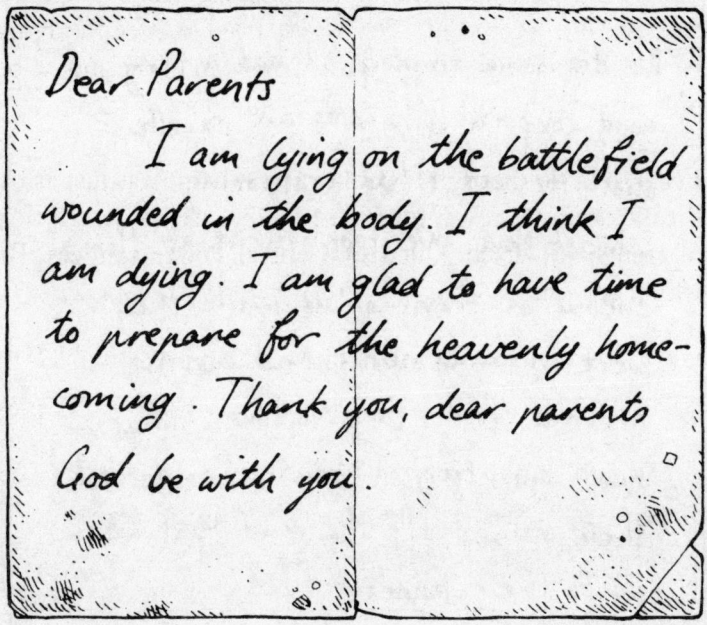

Dear Parents

I am lying on the battlefield wounded in the body. I think I am dying. I am glad to have time to prepare for the heavenly home-coming. Thank you, dear parents God be with you.

4 Which side believed that its heavy shells would destroy the enemy trenches so all they had to do was walk across no man's land and take over?

For some reason nothing seemed to happen to us at first. We strolled along as though walking in the park. Then, suddenly, we were in the midst of a storm of machine-gun bullets and I saw men beginning to twirl round and fall in all kinds of curious ways as they were hit – quite unlike the way actors do it in films.

5 Which side sometimes shot the enemy as a sport?

We did some sniping. I had a very good corporal who was an excellent shot. He and I had a shooting competition. We took turns at the enemy in front of us while they were running about and moving around from time to time. That kept our troops amused and took their minds off the mud that was up to their knees.

Terrible toilets

A German writer described the pleasures of being out of the front line. What would you do to relax? Sleep? Write letters to your family? Clean your toenails? Not Erich Maria Remarque, the author of the famous book, *All Quiet on the Western Front*, who said that ...

> *The experienced soldiers don't use the unpleasant, indoor, common toilet, where 20 men sit side by side in a line. As it is not raining, they use the individual square wooden boxes with carrying handles on the sides. They pull three into a circle and sit there in the sun all afternoon, reading, smoking, talking, playing cards.*

In the front line trenches it was different and more dangerous. There were no toilets in the Brit trenches, just buckets. If you upset the Sergeant you would be given the job of taking the buckets out after dark. Your job was to dig a hole and empty the buckets. Once you were out of the cover of the trenches you were in danger, but some soldiers still lit cigarettes to hide the smell from the buckets. Enemy snipers were just waiting to aim at the glow of a cigarette end. Emptying toilet buckets could be bad for your health.

THAT ROTTEN SNIPER HIT ME RIGHT IN THE BUCKETS

Even *going* to the toilet shed just behind the trenches was dangerous. The enemy knew men used these toilets at dawn and liked to drop a few shells among the toilet huts to catch the soldiers with their pants down!

Terrible toilet tale 1 …
A major found some deserted houses for his men. He looked at the sign at the end of the street and copied it carefully. Then he sent a message to his soldiers …

> You will find rooms in "Verbod te wateren"

Unfortunately, he couldn't read Flemish and didn't understand that the sign *wasn't* the street name. It was a warning notice that said, 'You must not pee in the street'.

Terrible toilet tale 2 …
Army boots had to be tough. The trouble was the leather was so hard it gave men blisters. Old soldiers knew the answer

You probably won't want to try this with your new school shoes. But, if you do, remember to *empty* them before you put them on!

Terrible toilet tale 3 …

In the 1917 battles in Flanders the troops didn't have properly built trenches, just shell holes protected by sandbags. And there were certainly no toilet huts. One officer complained …

> *If you wanted to do your daily job of urinating and otherwise there was an empty bully-beef tin, and you had to do that in front of all your men, and then chuck the contents (but not the bully-beef tin) out over the back.*

He forgot to mention one important thing. Find out which way the wind is blowing first!

Frightful fun and gruesome games

If you grew bored with 'chatting' you could always try one of the violent entertainments that soldiers used to pass the time …

Games you wouldn't want to play
1 Free the prisoner (Australian Rules)

To play:
• a grenade
• a German prisoner

The rules:

First find a prisoner who wants to go free. Take him to the gates of the prison and place a hand grenade in his back pocket. Pull the pin out of the grenade (which will explode in five seconds). Hold the prisoner for a count of 'One – two', then release him and tell him to run. If he gets the grenade out of his pocket in the remaining three seconds he is the winner and is free to go. If he gets the grenade out of his pocket and throws it back at you then you are the losers. But that's the risk you take.

There are reports of this happening, so it is probably true, but extremely rare.

2 Beetle racing

You need:
- two or more beetles
- a table
- sugar
- matchsticks

To play:

Each 'jockey' chooses a beetle and holds it at one end of the table. A sugar lump is placed at the other end of the table to attract the beetles. Every jockey places one matchstick on the table. On a signal, the beetles are released. The first beetle to reach the sugar wins and the winning jockey collects everyone else's matchsticks. (And the beetles get to eat the sugar.)

3 Sea swimming

You need:
- the sea

To play:

At Gallipoli the chief hobby for Anzac troops was swimming. This took a lot of courage because the Turkish army were shelling the beaches. Troops swam for fun and to keep cool (but also because there was no water for washing in the trenches). Beaches were somewhat spoilt by the sight and smell of dead horses, mules and donkeys.

IT'S STILL BETTER THAN AN ENGLISH BEACH

4 Barge boating

You need:

- a wooden box
- two shovels

In 1917, as Sergeant Ernest Parker was sitting reading at the entrance to his dugout in the banks of the Yser canal, he saw an exciting regatta …

Lustily plying two oars, a ruffian member of my band was propelling a rectangular box up and down the canal. Shovels were the oars and when rival craft were launched a naval battle began, cheered by the spectators, who were hoping that somebody would take a plunge into the black slime of the canal.

Weird words

If you were a British soldier in the First World War you would soon learn a new language – army slang. In fact, there were *two* languages to learn – one used by the officers and one by the ordinary soldiers.

Could you learn to 'sling the bat' (speak in the local language, that is) with the soldiers or the officers?

Batty bat slinging
What would you do if someone came up to you and said …

I'M HITCHY-KOO FROM THESE CHATS IN MY TEDDY-BEAR AND I WISH I WAS BACK IN MUFTI

IS THAT SO?

Of course that will all make perfect sense to you. No? Oh, well, here's an explanation …

1 I'd love some nice meat pudding followed by bread and cheese, washed down with a cup of strong tea. For afters I'd like jam on bread.

2 Now, my good man, this afternoon (p.m.) we need some tidying up before the mad army chaplain comes to inspect our sleeping-bags.

3 I received a wound that will get me sent home when a mortar bomb, a mine and another mortar bomb landed in my dugout.

4 I am itching from all the lice in my shaggy fur coat and I wish I was back in my normal street clothes.

Sometimes the soldiers cheered themselves up by making fun of official army language. Their daily ration of spirits was 'service rum, diluted' – SRD. But the sergeant who served it out tended to get to a trench and say, 'I'll have mine with you,' and pour himself a tot.

He did the same in every trench. If you were unlucky enough to be in the last trench then there was no rum and a very drunk sergeant. So what did SRD stand for? 'Seldom reaches destination'!

And the Royal Army Medical Corps (RAMC) became the 'rob all my comrades' because soldiers suspected medical staff went through the pockets of the wounded men.

The same RAMC would sometimes be unsure what was wrong with a patient so they labelled him 'not yet diagnosed' (NYD). Soldiers swore the letters stood for 'not yet dead'.

Esses Ink Gee Nuts Ack London – Toc Ack London King!
No, that isn't a secret code to *disguise* the meaning of messages. It's a way of making messages quite *clear* over a crackling phone line. So 'Harry – Edward – London – London – Oranges' is 'Hello'.

Learn the list, impress your friends and confuse your teacher with the Great War code ...

A = Ack	J = Johnnie	S = Esses
B = Beer	K = King	T = Toc
C = Charlie	L = London	U = Uncle
D = Don	M = Emma	V = Vic
E = Edward	N = Nuts	W = William
F = Freddie	O = Oranges	X = X-ray
G = Gee	P = Pip	Y = Yorker
H = Harry	Q = Queen	Z = Zebra
I = Ink	R = Robert	

Nutty names

Any names in the language of the enemy were suddenly unpopular.

France has a perfume called 'eau de Cologne' (water of Cologne), but Cologne is in Germany. They tried to change it to 'eau de Provence' because Provence is in France, but the idea never caught on.

The name changing went further in Germany. All bars, hotels and shops with English or French names were changed, causing great confusion.

In Breslau, the German military governor went to a sweet shop …

In 1915, Italy joined the war against Germany, and Berlin cafés stopped serving 'Italian salad' …

Jolly Germans

Even in the gloom of the war Germany kept its theatres open. But the plays were pretty miserable. The most popular one of 1917 was 'Maria Magdalena' about life in a small town. Well, that's not quite true … it's more about *death* in a small town!

Which character would you like to be? Can you pick the *two* that stayed alive?

1 Mrs Magdalena – a hard-working and caring mum
2 Mr Magdalena – a hard-working and caring dad
3 Maria – their daughter, a beautiful and popular girl
4 The cat – the family's faithful, furry friend
5 Fritz – Maria's lover
6 Hans – a rival for the love of Maria

Want a clue? Of the four who die, one dies in a duel, one suffers a fit on stage, one puts a bullet through their brain and (best of all) one throws themself down a well.

Answer: The mother dies of a fit on stage, Fritz is killed in a duel with Hans who commits suicide, so Maria jumps into a well. At the end only the father and the family cat are still alive!

Ropey rhymes
Poetry from the First World War is still remembered and enjoyed today by millions of people. Quite rightly.

But there were also some popular rhymes that have been forgotten. The simple poems and songs that soldiers repeated to try and stay cheerful in the bad times. The *bad* news is that most of them are too rude to be printed – even in a horrible history!

But here are a few that you may enjoy.

(Hint: Dig a hole in your back garden, flood it with water and sit there for a few hours while your family throw pots, pans or pianos out of upstairs windows on to you. This will get you in the mood.)

1 This limerick was popular around 1915 …

There was a young lady of Ypres
Who was hit in the cheek by two snipers.
The tunes that she played
Through the holes that they made
Beat the Argyll and Sutherland pipers.

2 Private Stanley Woodburn wrote his will on a postcard and carried it in his pocket. He wrote it as a poem …

My belongings I leave to my next of kin,
My purse is empty there's nothing in;
My uniform, rifle, my pack and kit,
I leave to the poor devil they will fit;
But if this war I manage to clear
I'll keep it myself for a souvenir.

Private Woodburn was killed in France in April 1918.

3 Star of silent films, Charlie Chaplin, left his home in

England in 1913. When the war started a year later he did not return to join the army. Soldiers made up a popular song ...

The moon shines bright on Charlie Chaplin,
His boots are cracking, for want of blacking.
And his little baggy trousers they want mending,
Before we send him to the Dardanelles...

Charlie didn't see the joke! 'I really thought they were coming to get me!' he said. 'It scared the daylights out of me.'

4 Many Brit soldiers had their own monthly magazines in the trenches. The poems they published were a bit of fun in the misery of the war ...

There was a young Boche at Bazentin
Who liked the first trench that he went in.
But a 15 inch 'dud'
Sent him flat in the mud
And he found that his helmet was bent in.

5 Not all of the poems were funny. There were some things that soldiers said over and over again to cheer themselves up. This simple poem in a trenches' magazine took three of the sayings as its first three lines, then added its own fourth line ...

It's a long road that has no turning,
It's never too late to mend;
The darkest hour is before the dawn
And even this *war must end.*

6 Poems were used in the hate-war against the enemy. In a children's magazine there was one to warn of the dangers of German toys which, of course, were supposed to be poisonous!

Little girls and little boys,
Never suck your German toys;
German soldiers licked will make
Darling Baby's tummy ache.
Parents, you should always try
Only British toys to buy;
Though to pieces they be picked,
British soldiers can't be licked.

7 Soldiers were fond of singing. When they couldn't find a suitable song they took a popular one and changed the words. In 1914 they were singing ...

Though your heart may ache a while
  ... never mind.
Though your face may lose its smile
  ... never mind.
For there's sunshine after rain
And then gladness follows pain,
You'll be happy once again
  ... never mind.

The words were soon replaced by more bitter ones ...

If you're hung up on barbed wire
  ... never mind.

Or …

> *If your sleeping place is damp*
> *… never mind.*
> *If you wake up with a cramp*
> *… never mind.*
> *If your trench should fall in some*
> *Fill your ears and make you dumb*
> *While the sergeant drinks your rum*
> *… never mind.*

8 Love songs became war songs …

> *If you were the only girl in the world,*
> *And I were the only boy,*
> *Nothing else would matter in the world today,*
> *We would go on loving in the same old way.*
> *A garden of Eden, just made for two …*

Became …

> *If you were the only Boche in the trench,*
> *And I had the only bomb,*
> *Nothing else would matter in the world that day,*
> *I would blow you up into eternity.*
> *A Chamber of Horrors, just made for two …*

9 Even religious songs were made fun of. *What a Friend we Have in Jesus* became ...

> *When this lousy war is over, oh how happy I will be,*
> *When I get my civvy clothes on, no more soldiering*
> *for me.*
> *No more church parades on Sunday,*
> *No more putting in for leave.*
> *I will kiss the sergeant major,*
> *How I'll miss him, how I'll grieve.*

(The word 'lousy' in the first line was often replaced by a ruder word.)

10 But the song that summed up the First World War the best was the simplest one of all. It was sung to the tune of *Auld Lang Syne* (the one drunken parents join hands to sing at New Year and embarrass you with).

> *We're here because we're here because*
> *We're here because we're here.*
> *We're here because we're here because*
> *We're here because we're here.*

Says it all really.

Horrible historical joke

The soldiers in the front line enjoyed a joke, even in the terror of the trenches. They produced their own magazines and their jokes were often about the senior officers who were miles behind the lines when the shooting started.

One popular cartoon was this one ...

Major-General (addressing the men before practising an attack in the training camp behind the lines). 'I WANT YOU TO UNDERSTAND THAT THERE IS A DIFFERENCE BETWEEN A REHEARSAL AND THE REAL THING. THERE ARE THREE ESSENTIAL DIFFERENCES. FIRST, THE ABSENCE OF THE ENEMY. NOW (turning to the Sergeant Major), WHAT IS THE SECOND DIFFERENCE?

Sergeant Major. 'THE ABSENCE OF THE GENERAL, SIR.'

Painful punishments

An army, like a school, needs discipline. Men have to learn to obey orders or else. Or else what? There were various punishments that your teachers might like to adopt for your school ... so keep this page out of their sight.

Field punishment No.1

In this notorious Brit punishment, the offender is lashed, or crucified, to a gun wheel, tied by wrists and ankles for one hour in the morning and one in the evening for up to 21 days. The intention is to humiliate the soldier. It was rumoured that soldiers were lashed to guns in action.

Toothbrush torture

The Germans had their own way of dealing with problem soldiers. Troublemakers in training were ...

- made to scrub out the Corporals' room with a toothbrush.
- made to clear the barrack square of snow with hand-brushes and dustpans.

On Sundays (the recruits' only day off) they could be ...

- forced to parade in full uniform with pack and rifle and then practise attacking and lying down in a muddy field until exhausted and filthy ...
- ... then, four hours later, made to report with every item of uniform and kit cleaned, hands bleeding and raw from the cleaning.

Once those trained men were sent to the front they were given a bunch of flowers to wear in their belts.

False fable

Many British soldiers believed that German soldiers were tied to their machine-guns to stop them from running away. In fact, German machine-gunners wore special belts with which they could carry their machine-guns and leave their hands free. If these soldiers were killed whilst carrying their gun, British soldiers would find the bodies 'tied' to the guns.

Cruel court martials

If a soldier was accused of a serious crime – like dropping his weapon and running away, or shooting himself in the foot to avoid going into battle – he'd be given a trial, known in the army as a 'court martial'.

Could you be a judge? Try these cases …

The case of Bellwarde Ridge

Private Allen and Private Burden were in the same regiment.

In June 1915 their regiment was ordered to move forward to the Bellwarde Ridge, France, which the Germans were defending furiously. Private Peter Allen didn't fancy walking towards machine-guns, so he took his rifle and shot himself in the leg. He was sent to hospital to recover and then ordered to serve two years in prison with hard labour.

Private Herbert Burden had joined up the year before. He told the recruiting officer he was 18 but he lied. He was just 16. When he was ordered to attack Bellwarde Ridge he was just 17 – the age of many schoolboys today. The attack was a

disaster and Herbert's friends died all around him. He had done his best but, in the end he turned and ran from the battlefield.

He was court-martialled and found guilty. What would you do with Herbert? Remember what had happened to Peter Allen – who didn't even get to the fight. Remember that Herbert was only a boy. And remember that he'd been under heavy fire.

a) Give him a short rest then send him back into battle.
b) Send him home because he had been too young when he joined the army.
c) Give him two years' hard labour, the same as soldiers who wounded themselves.
d) Shoot him.

The case of king's crater

Sergeant Joe Tose and his officer, Lieutenant Mundy, left the safety of their trench to patrol a huge bomb crater in no man's land known as king's crater.

As they reached the crater they were attacked by a larger patrol of German soldiers. Lieutenant Mundy was shot.

Sergeant Tose ran back to the trench and decided to warn the rest of his battalion. To slow down the German attackers he jammed his rifle across the trench and set off for the rear trenches. As he had no weapon he was charged with 'casting away his weapon in the face of the enemy'.

Everyone said that he was a good soldier. (One witness said that the Germans spoke good English and, to add to the confusion, had called out 'Retreat!') What would you do with Joseph Tose?

a) Give him a medal for his quick thinking in saving his patrol.

b) Take his sergeant's position from him and send him back to fight as a private.

c) Strap him to a gun carriage for two hours a day for 21 days as Field Punishment No. 1.

d) Shoot him.

Answers: In both cases the men were shot. Men who avoided battle by shooting themselves were not executed. Herbert Burden was one of three 17-year-olds who were shot by the British in the First World War.

Sergeant Tose was disgraced and forgotten. He did not even get his name on his village war memorial until his case was looked at 80 years later. His name was finally added in 1997.

In the First World War the British shot 268 men for deserting their posts. (These are just two examples.) The German records were destroyed but they must have had the same problems. Yet it seems they shot only 48 of their own men. The Russians gave up shooting their own soldiers and the Australians never shot one.

1918 – The year of exhaustion

The Allies and the Central Powers have been battering at one another's doors for over three years and are exhausted. The Germans have decided to have one huge attack before they starve to death.

It is like charging with a battering-ram at a rotten door. The Allies give way and are pushed back, and back and back. The Germans seem to be the winners!

But the Germans are rushing forward too quickly. Their supplies can't keep up with them and they soon run out. When the Allies stop and turn, the Germans have nothing left to give. The Allies push on and on and on. All the way to Germany. The starved and feeble Germans are the losers … and all because they had been the winners.

Timeline 1918

January Britain is forced to have two meatless days a week and no meat for breakfast. Shops with margarine are raided by desperate women!

25 February Meat, butter and margarine rationed in the south of England and the queues (and the fighting shoppers) stop.

21 March Called the 'last day of trench warfare'. The Germans break out and smash the Allies back from the trenches. Shells fall on Paris.

1 April The Royal Air Force is formed and celebrate by shooting down German ace von Richthofen – the Red Baron – three weeks later.

May The German government wants young people to marry before they are 20 to produce more children for the country (which is running short of people).

June Thirty people die in Lancashire. They had Spanish 'flu. No one has any idea how many millions it's about to kill. Far more than the war, for sure.

18 July At the Marne River the Allies stop retreating. The tide is turning back towards Germany. The Russians massacre their royal family.

8 August German General Ludendorff calls this 'the black day for the German army' as they are driven back. Still, no one expects the war to end this year.

29 September Bulgarians have had enough and ask for peace. The beginning of the end for the Central Powers.

October German sailors are ordered to make one great last voyage to destroy the Brit fleet – or be destroyed. Sailors refuse and pour water on their ships' boiler fires.

9 November Kaiser Wilhelm is thrown out of Germany. He retires to Belgium. After what he did to them four years ago it's not

surprising they don't want him! He ends up in Holland.

11 November Armistice Day and peace is agreed at last. The peace document is signed at the 11th hour of this 11th day of the 11th month.

28 December Women vote in Britain for the first time. War has changed something, anyway.

PITY IT TOOK FOUR YEARS, FOUR MONTHS AND FOUR DAYS TO GET HERE

Suffering shock

The huge shells that exploded during a battle killed and wounded millions of soldiers. But they had another effect that no one saw and few people understood in 1914–18. It was the effect of days of endless noise and dreadful fear on men's minds. Bombardments broke the minds of some men as surely as they broke the bodies of others.

The popular name for the effect was 'shell-shock' – the medical name is now 'post-traumatic stress disorder'. It doesn't matter what you call it really. Men suffered nightmares and fear of loud noises for the rest of their lives. It affected soldiers of all countries, during battles and long after them. Three survivors tell their stories …

In 1916, British Lieutenant Frederick Rees explained how shell–shock ruined a soldier's common sense …

Last night a man had an attack of nerves. He picked up a box of bombs, climbed out of the trench and threw them about in no man's land. He was lucky not to be shot. Either side would have shot him if he had come near when he still had those bombs. However, they got him back safe, poor chap.

George Bucher, a German officer in 1917, explained how the illness affected his side too. And some weren't as lucky as the man that Rees saw ...

> *After four days of the bombardment a very young soldier had had enough. He climbed out of the trench with two hand-grenades from which he had taken the safety pins. He told his comrades what he thought about the war. He was going to run towards the British rifle fire and throw his grenades at them. He threatened to throw them at his comrades if they tried to stop him. They let him go...*

Lieutenant A G May, British Army, 1917, saw how shell-shock could affect different men in different ways ...

> *The noise was impossible. Shells were bursting overhead. Near our front trench I saw a couple of our lads who had gone completely goofy. It was pitiful. One of them welcomed me like a long-lost friend and asked me to give him his baby. I picked up a tin hat from the ground and gave it to him. He cradled the hat as if it were a child, smiling and laughing without a care in the world, even though shells were falling all around us. I have no idea what happened to the poor chap but if he stayed there very long he must have been killed. A few days later I started to have uncontrollable jerking and shaking of my legs. I was quite upset because I was unable to stop it. The doctor told me I had shell-shock but I did not believe this. Later I was told to go to a special hospital for shell-shock victims.*

And, when the war had finished the nightmare of shell-shock went on and on, as a French soldier explained …

> *The noise of a slamming gate, a flaring gaslight, a train whistle, the barking of a dog or some boyish prank is enough to set off my trembling. Or, sometimes the trembling comes on without a reason. I went to a shop to do an errand for my wife. The crowd, the rustling silks, the colour of the goods – everything was a delight to look on after the misery of the trenches. I was happy and chatted merrily like a schoolboy on holiday. All of a sudden I felt my strength was leaving me. I stopped talking. I felt a shiver in my back, I felt my cheeks going hollow. I began to stare and the trembling came on again.*
>
> *In the tram I feel that people are looking at me and that gives me a terrible feeling. I feel they are looking at me with pity. Some excellent woman offers me her seat. I am deeply touched; but they look at me and say nothing; what are they thinking of me?*

'They look at me and say nothing.' That was part of the pain. No one knew how to deal with a shell-shocked man.

No one knew *what* to say.

94

Cruel for creatures

The animals that went to war didn't start the fight and didn't ask to go. But they were shot at and bombed and gassed and diseased as cruelly as their human masters. It was beastly being a beast in the First World War. If you're the sort of person who's pained by the thought of a pet with a prick in its paw, it may be better to skip this section. If you enjoy raw hamster-burgers at school dinners, read on ...

Creature cwiz

True or false?

1 In the First World War, British dogs were horses.

2 The best horses were saved for the Army priests (the chaplains).

3 German soldiers wiped out a herd of rare European bison in Poland.

4 A British regiment made a miniature steel helmet for their pet dog.

5 The German Army fitted their horses with gas masks.

6 A chick named Dick was used to detect enemy aircraft.

7 Goldfish were banned from the battle areas because water was precious.

OI! STOP THAT. WATER DOESN'T GROW ON TREES YOU KNOW

GULP

8 Horse droppings were used to make gas for heat and light.

9 Soldiers kept canaries because their song cheered everyone up.

10 The Allies won the war because they had a better supply of horses.

Answers:

1 True. The British Army supplied all the animals they needed but, to keep everything simple, they called these animals 'horses' ... even if they were guard dogs, oxen, reindeer or camels!

2 False. The chaplains were given horses at the start of the war but there was a shortage of horses for the fighting men. The chaplains had their horses taken from them and were given bicycles instead!

3 False. The herd of bison wiped out the Germans! The animals were grazing peacefully and ignoring the soldiers. Then a rifle was fired and the angry bison charged. They gored and trampled the German soldiers to death. Only 20 soldiers survived.

4 True. The dog was a stray that adopted the gunners. It became their lucky mascot. The death of the dog would have meant bad luck, so they protected it from 'stray' bullets and shells with a steel helmet.

5 True. The masks (which looked a bit like a nose-bag) didn't work very well and didn't protect the animals' eyes from the stinging gas. But at least the kindly Germans were *trying* to help their four-legged friends.

6 True. Driver David Spink rescued a half-starved chicken near St Quentin in 1918 and christened it Dick. When Allied aircraft flew over it was fine, but it dived for cover (and so did David Spink's company) when an enemy aircraft was overhead. After the war Dick travelled back to Britain in Driver Spink's haversack and enjoyed a happy retirement.

7 False. Goldfish were very useful. After a gas attack the gas helmets were rinsed with water. A goldfish was then dropped into the rinsing water. If the goldfish died then the mask was still poisoned and needed to be washed again. (Sadly, there is no record of a goldfish ever getting a medal for bravery.)

8 True. A horse produced about 14 or 15 kilograms of droppings every day. (Do you ever wonder who gets the job of measuring these things?) The British alone had 870,000 horses in action by the end of the war. That is nearly 13 million kilos of horse muck being produced *every day*! Some was buried, some

burned, some spread on fields as fertilizer. But some was heated to give off a gas that powered lamps and heaters. (Might it have been quicker just to put a lighted match to the horse's bum?)

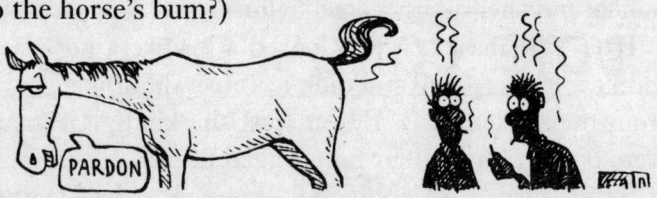

9 False. Soldiers *did* keep canaries, but they were used in underground tunnels to check for gas. (If the bird fell off its perch then there was gas down there.) Some of the bird handlers became very attached to their canaries and risked their own lives to save the birds during gas attacks. Why bother? They could always find another canary going cheap ... Cheep! Cheep!

10 True. At least that's what British General Haig said after the war. 'If the Germans had a horse service as good as the British then they would have won the war.'

Brave beasts

Men and women performed some incredibly brave acts in the face of the enemy. A German hero was covered in Iron Crosses, a British hero was covered in medals and an American hero, called Cher Ami, was covered in feathers. Because Cher Ami was a pigeon!

Duck, dove!

No, Cher Ami didn't fly over enemy forces and drop bombs on them, stupid. He carried a message from US soldiers in battle and saved dozens of lives. Imagine the sadness when he finally died ...

DOVE CONQUERS ALL

Cher Ami is dead. The pigeon that won the hearts of all true Americans, has hopped the twig and passed peacefully away to that great pigeon loft in the sky.

It was just a year ago that Cher Ami flew to fame when he joined Major Charles Whittlesey's brigade. In the Argonne Forest, eastern France, the brigade found itself surrounded by enemy forces, starving and exhausted with many dead and wounded. Then shells began to land on the American survivors – but they were American shells aimed at them by mistake. There was only one way to get a message out of the deadly circle of machine-guns: a carrier pigeon.

Whittlesey scribbled a note: 'Our own forces are dropping shells on us! For heaven's sake stop it!' He took a pigeon from its basket but the frightened bird broke loose and flew for home – the US army base camp. There was just one bird left – one last hope – a black cock called Cher Ami. Whittlesey clipped the message to the brave bird's leg and set it free. But Cher Ami

flew up to the nearest tree and began preening its feathers. The brigade threw sticks and stones but still the perverse pigeon refused to budge. Finally Whittlesey climbed the tree and shook the branch. Cher Ami took the hint and set off for home.

The enemy saw at once that it was carrying a message and turned the full firepower of the forces towards it. One shot took off part of the battered bird's leg, passed through its chest and knocked out one eye. The peppered pigeon lost height, then, amazingly, recovered and flew on to deliver the message and the brigade was saved. 'Without that bird we'd have been wiped out, that is certain,' Whittlesey said. 'The 384 men who survived owed their lives to Cher Ami's courage.'

The heroic homing pigeon was patched up and brought back to a hero's welcome in America, where he died peacefully yesterday. He will be stuffed and go on display at the Smithsonian Institute.

Feathered fighters

1 Gallant pigeons like Cher Ami had another use. If soldiers became cut off from their supplies and were starving they could always eat the birds!

2 Pigeon *pies* are very tasty, but pigeon *spies* were also valuable. Baskets full of British pigeons were dropped into

French and Belgian villages that had been captured by the Germans. Villagers could then attach messages to the pigeons who would fly back to Britain. The messages could tell the Allies what the enemy was up to. This is spying, of course, and the punishment for spying in war was to be shot. But it was even more dangerous being a pigeon. Sixteen thousand were dropped but only one in ten returned.

3 The Germans took the problem of pigeon spies seriously. They cleverly planted baskets of German pigeons in the villages. Anyone who attached a message would see the bird fly off to Germany.

4 The Germans also formed squadrons of hawks and falcons to catch any pigeon flying over the English Channel back to Britain. This was rotten luck if you were an innocent pigeon on a day trip to Paris.

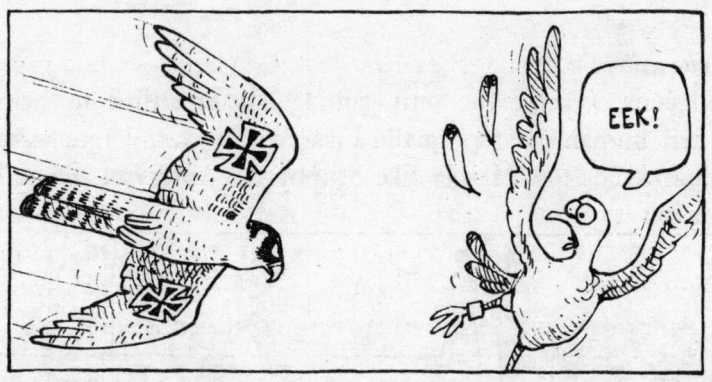

5 In the mud and rain of 1917 a group of soldiers were cut off and attached a message to a pigeon. The pigeon was too soaked to fly. It flopped into no man's land ... then started walking towards the German lines with its message! If the Germans knew the Brits were alone they would have

attacked and finished them off! The Brits had to shoot the plodding pigeon. Their other bird was just as wet. One soldier suggested drying it in the dugout oven, but in the end the soldiers dried it by blowing on its feathers. It worked.

6 A French pigeon saved hundreds of troops at Verdun in 1916. The French were being shelled by Germans but had no heavy guns of their own to fight back. They wanted to get a message out to their gunners to say, 'Here are the German gun positions. Aim at them and stop them destroying us.' A greyhound got the message through, though he was wounded. And a pigeon got through just before it died of its wounds. The pigeon was given France's highest *human* medal for bravery – the *Legion d'Honneur*. The men and women who won the *Legion d'Honneur* must have been a bit annoyed by this! It's like saying, 'Here's your medal. Wear it with pride. You are as brave as a pigeon!'

The tale of a dog

Pigeons weren't the only courageous creatures to help their human masters in the First World War. There were dog heroes too. Heroes like Stubby the American pit bull terrier …

Stubby was a poor and homeless stray when Rob Conroy found him on the streets of Hartford, Connecticut. Nothing could separate these pals, not even the First World War. When Rob went to war, Stubby went with him.

Stubby was smuggled all the way to the war zone with the gallant guys in the 102nd Infantry Battalion. But he was no pampered pet, oh no! Stubby was a priceless guard dog with sharper eyes and ears than any sentry.

No matter what the enemy threw at him, Stubby ran out on to the battlefield and found the wounded. Then he lay beside them till the stretchers reached him. They called it no man's land, but it wasn't no dog's land!

And while the tired troopers slept, Stubby watched over them. One night he warned them of a gas attack. Another night a sneaking enemy soldier slipped into the US trenches – and left with Stubby's teeth in his butt!

Stubby fought in 17 battles. There was no way they could pin all his medals on his brave little breast – so they had a special blanket made. When the proud pooch met President Woodrow Wilson he wore it.

The First World War ended, but Stubby's work went on. He toured the country with Rob Conroy to raise money for victims of the fighting. What a courageous canine! Stubby! Man's best friend ... ever!

Daring dogs

1 Dogs made useful messengers. They could be trained to run over the battlefield with messages fastened to their collars. Enemy soldiers watched for messenger dogs and tried to turn them into dead dogs.

2 Of course the Germans had dogs just as brave as Stubby. One was used to carry secret messages backwards and forwards across the trenches. The German dog was the perfect spy courier. The British tried everything to capture him – nets and traps all failed – until the Allied soldiers came up with a devious dodge. They set a female dog to attract him into their hands. One wag of her tail and the German spy-dog was caught. (Let this be a lesson to you gentlemen readers … if a young lady wags her tail at you then *paws* before you run after her!)

3 Dogs were also put in harnesses and used to drag machine-guns around the battlefield. The Italian army used them to pull supply carts over the Alps. In the summer this would have turned them into 'hot dogs', I guess.

4 Dogs also had reels of telephone cable strapped to their backs. As they ran along they left a trail of cable behind them and linked the men in the trenches to the support troops behind them. Enemy gunners were always trying to cut these links and would shoot at cable layers. Dogs were faster than men, smaller and harder to hit than men, and it didn't matter so much if a dog was killed … unless you were the dog, of course.

5 When the war started, German shepherd dogs in Britain suddenly became unpopular – just because of their name! So the name was changed to 'Alsatian' and it's stayed that way ever since. (If you want to test your teacher, tell them of the German shepherd name change then say, 'What *other* creatures changed their English name in the First World War?' The answer is … the British Royal Family. They changed their family name from the German Saxe-Coburg-Gotha to Windsor. Like the Alsatians they too are stuck with it.)

6 Some dogs went across to the enemy! No, they weren't traitors. Early in the war French and German troops were in trenches just 30 metres apart. They sent each other friendly messages, newspapers and tobacco, tied to the dog's collar. One French corporal had left his wife behind in Germany when the war started. A dog brought him a message from her saying she was quite well and sent her love; the Germans passed it on by puppy post.

7 Terriers were useful for killing rats in the trenches. A devoted soldier wrote a poem to his dog, Jim …

Jim

A tough little, rough little beggar,
And merry the eyes on him.
But no German or Turk
Can do dirtier work
With an enemy rat than Jim.

And when the light's done and night's falling,
And shadows are darkling and dim,
In my coat you will nuzzle
Your pink little muzzle
And growl in your dreams, little Jim.

There is no record of what the rats thought of little Jim.

Of course not every company in the trenches had a rat-catcher like Jim. What did these poor soldiers do? They tamed the rats and kept them as pets instead!

Rotten for rats

Rats enjoyed the First World War ... mostly. There was always plenty to eat because the soldiers brought tons of supplies with them. But most soldiers hated the robbing rodents and spent a lot of their spare time trying to massacre the creepy creatures. Apart from shooting them in the open they also tried some sneaky tricks. The following were all tried in the trenches with great success ...

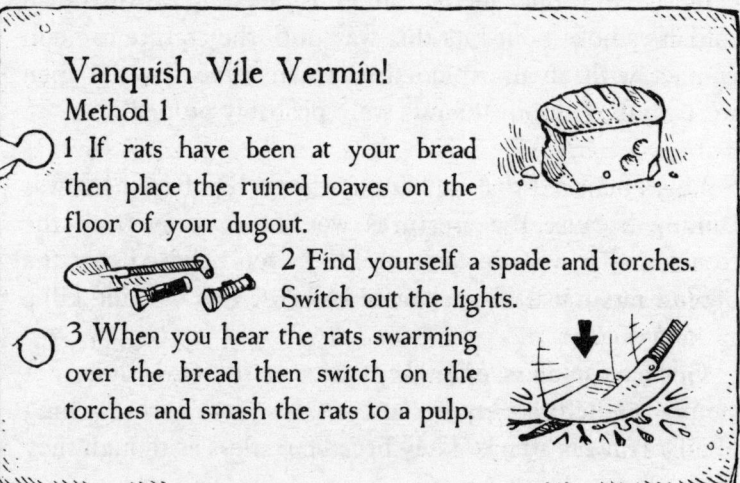

Vanquish Vile Vermin!

Method 1

1 If rats have been at your bread then place the ruined loaves on the floor of your dugout.

2 Find yourself a spade and torches. Switch out the lights.

3 When you hear the rats swarming over the bread then switch on the torches and smash the rats to a pulp.

Method 2

1 Place cordite at the entrance to rat holes and light it. The smoke will drive out the rats.

2 Wait by the exit and smash them with wooden clubs.

Method 3

1 Put a bayonet on the end of your rifle.

2 Put a piece of cheese on the end of the bayonet.

Point it towards the enemy lines.

3 When a rat begins to nibble at the cheese, pull the trigger. You can't miss!

Horrible Histories health warning: Cordite was used as an explosive to propel shells from guns. A group of Australian soldiers smoked out rats this way until the cordite came in contact with an unexploded German mine. Twenty men were injured ... but the rats were probably pulped!

Soldiers believed that rats knew when a bombardment was coming because the creatures would run away from the trenches that were in danger. They even believed that the biggest rats – usually nicknamed 'corpse rats' – could kill a cat or a dog.

German soldiers often kept cats in the front line, not simply to catch rats but because cats also gave early warning of a British gas attack. They became restless as though they could detect the poison gas in very low concentrations before the main cloud appeared.

Horrible historical joke

In June 1917 it was against British law to feed pigeons. This was part of the plan to save food. Not everyone agreed that this was a smart move.

In one of the soldiers' magazines the following joke appeared ...

> *A driver has been punished for giving his bread ration to his horse. He certainly deserved it. We are totally against cruelty to animals.*

Women and children

The First World War affected women and children more than any other war had done. Before 1914 wars had been about men fighting men; women and children had been simply victims – they got themselves massacred if they were unlucky enough to be in a battle zone. They were starved, lost husbands and children, but they didn't *give* a lot to war efforts. That was about to change.

Wicked women

In July 1915, 30,000 women paraded in London under the banner, 'We demand the right to serve'. Women slowly began to take up jobs in war-work, especially making weapons and ammunition (munitions).

The miserable men didn't want women in the factories. They thought it would give the women a taste of freedom and change them. They were right! By the end of the war

British women could …
- smoke cigarettes openly
- drink in public houses
- openly use cosmetics
- swear
- wear short skirts and bras
- wear short hair (to control the nits)
- go to the cinemas without a man
- play football (most factories started girl teams)
- Then, Land Girls, who'd taken the jobs of farm labourers, began to wear their trousers off duty!

In short, they started doing all the things men had been doing for years. (Oh, all right, you *didn't* see a lot of men in lipstick, short skirts and bras, but you know what I mean!) And women still do these shocking things today!

The German women worked just as hard but didn't earn the same sort of freedom. German men did not approve of freedom for their women. In 1917 a German politician, claimed that …

Female freedom in England has destroyed all family life there. The women are so bad that more married men than single men offered themselves as recruits for the Army. The married men, in fact, join up to escape from their wives.

In one or two cases he may have been right!

French women were allowed to drink but only very weak wine.

If it sounds fun to be a British woman, then the working women paid a high price. They worked in dangerous war jobs where ...

• 81 died in accidents
• 71 female workers died in explosions
• 61 died of poisoning

... and they were only paid half of a man's wages.

It's a fair cop
How did they get poisoned? By working with high explosives like TNT that got into their lungs and blood. The symptoms were ...

• First your nose hurt, then it bled, your eyes stung and your throat became sore.

GOOD THING WE CAN OPENLY USE MAKE-UP NOW!

• You would get pains in the chest and stomach, diarrhoea and skin rashes.

IF THE BRA'S HURTING MY CHEST AND THE TROUSERS CAUSE A RASH, CAN SWEARING GIVE ME THE RUNS?

• If you weren't treated, you'd get sickness, giddiness,

swollen hands and feet, drowsiness and finally death.

But this didn't stop the women taking risks with the TNT. In September 1917, a young munitions worker was fined for stealing TNT from the factory where she worked. She stole it because it was common for workers to use TNT powder to give their hair a chestnut colour. But a red-head could become red-hot if you struck a match near her hair!

Britain created its first policewomen during the First World War and one of their duties was to stop women workers taking explosives out of the factories, and to stop them taking cigarettes or matches into the factories. Policewoman Greta East kept a diary of her life on duty at a South Wales Munitions factory ...

10 April 1917
The girls here are troublesome about
bringing in cigarettes and matches. Last
week a woman came to the Women Police

Office and asked me to rescue her coat
from the cloakroom as she had a train to
catch. She said I'd recognize the coat
because it had her payslip in the pocket.
But, when I searched the pockets I found
them full of cigarettes. Of course the
poor wretch had to be prosecuted and
fined. She must have forgotten about
them.

A pretty dim worker, but not so dim as the underground
toilets they had to use. Greta went on to describe the
conditions …

There are no drains because the ground
is below sea level. The result is the
toilets are a horrible and smelly swamp.
There were no lights in the lavatories
and those same lavatories are often
full of rats and very dirty. The girls
are afraid to go in.

With no lights how did you find the toilet paper? Or how did you avoid reaching out for toilet paper and picking up a rat by mistake? Yeuch!

By the end of war, 30 police forces had appointed women – another First World War idea that is still with us. (Though some, like Manchester, refused.)

Warring women

Not all women were happy to 'serve' by making shells. In September 1914, French newspapers reported the story of a 28-year-old laundry woman who had been discovered fighting at the front in the uniform of a French soldier. She was sent back to her old job at the laundry but protested angrily. (Just like most people, she probably hated all the ironing.)

There is a story that a British woman also got as far as the trenches, dressed in the kilts of a Highland soldier. (This was very suitable because the Germans called the Highlanders 'ladies from Hell'.) She did it for a bet but was caught and returned to Britain. (It was probably the handbag that gave her away.)

By 1917 the Russian Army was so weak it created a women's battalion, 'The Battalion of Death', to help. Three hundred women were led by the incredible Maria Botchkareva. Maria had been married at 15 and suffered terribly at the hands of two brutal husbands. War was wonderful compared to what she endured at home! She suffered frostbite and several wounds but survived. (She probably volunteered for the pleasure of being able to shoot at men!)

Battling babes

There are many stories of boys going into army recruiting

offices to join up even though they were under age. Many army recruiting officers were willing to let them join anyway. Of course it was their duty to check on the age and reject the ones who *said* they were under age. This story is true and happened hundreds of times all over the world …

Parents were able to 'claim out' their sons if they could trace them, and the boy soldiers were sent home.

- Myer Rosenblum from London joined the London Welsh Regiment in August 1914, aged 13 years and nine months, but was 'claimed out' by his father in October 1914. He joined up again and was sent to Gallipoli where he was wounded in June 1915. His father claimed him again when he was sent back to England.
- Private James Bartaby joined the 7th East Surreys, as a volunteer, on 20 January 1915, aged 13 years and ten months. After training, he went to France in late May and was wounded and sent home in October 1915.
- In October 1915, Arthur Peyman – 'described as 19 years of age' – was in court, charged with being absent from his regiment since the end of August. During the case, his mother appeared and produced his birth certificate, showing that he was only 14 years old.

At least Arthur Peyman escaped being shot for leaving his regiment. Other boys were not so lucky.

Trench tot

It wasn't just the fighting boys who ended up in the trenches. Sometimes small children were caught up in the battlefields. In early 1916, Philip Impey was going back into the trenches near La Basse, when he found a small girl abandoned in a ditch. He couldn't take her to safety and he couldn't leave her, so Philip picked her up and carried her into the trenches.

During the week, she climbed on to the parapet in full view of the Germans, who were close by. German soldiers shouted to her, offering her sweets and chocolate.

When the soldiers left the front, they took her with them. She was eventually sent to England and survived. Sadly, Philip Impey was killed in action soon after.

Cheeky Charlies
British kids in 1917 were getting out of control. There was a huge increase in vandalism, theft and street crimes among school-aged children.

- Some people blamed the fact that their fathers were away in the army.
- Others blamed the cinema. (Nowadays they'd blame the television, so nothing much changes, does it?)
- A third excuse was weak teachers – old ladies, brought out of retirement, to take the place of the men who had gone off to fight. (Imagine that! Kids taking advantage of their tough teacher being away. You wouldn't do a thing like that, would you?)

In Germany the children had a surprise when the war started. In Berlin all English teachers were sacked! (But that was wartime so don't raise your hopes that it may happen for you!)

I DON'T KNOW. TRYING TO GET OUT OF LESSONS BY STARTING ANOTHER WORLD WAR SEEMS A LITTLE EXTREME TO ME

But by 1917 German children were so hungry they had a desperate new game … stealing any food they could find.

Wrinklies at war

- The oldest French soldier was 78 years old.
- Italy's oldest soldier was 74.
- Lieutenant Henry Webber was, at 67, the oldest British soldier killed in action at the Somme in July 1916.
- In December 1915, James White of Sowerby Bridge was sent home from the trenches when it was discovered that he had fought the Zulu War of 1878, and was 70 years old.
- In June 1918, the *Yorkshire Evening Press* told the story of a merchant sailor, William Jessop of Hull. He was 72 years old and had been torpedoed seven times.

William said …

Young men sometimes refuse to sail with me because they think I am unlucky.

OK JESSOP. ZIS TIME FOR SURE

- In 1915, Chief Gunner Israel Harding had his left leg broken when his ship was blown up in the Dardanelles, near Turkey. He was 84 years old. He had once been a trawlerman but had run away to join the Royal Navy and first saw active service in the Crimean War of 1853–56.

Frightful 'flu facts

By November 1918 the war had killed about eight-and-a-half million people. But that was nothing to what happened next. Spanish 'flu spread around the world ...

- People collapsed in the streets, at work and at home.
- It appeared to hit young, healthy people more than the old or very young.
- The deadly virus attacked the lungs, which hardened, making breathing impossible: the victim finally drowned in their own fluid.
- At the moment of death, virus-laden fluid poured out the victim's mouth and nose.
- By May 1919 Spanish 'flu had killed over 200,000 in the UK and 20 million around the world – far more in one year than the war had managed in four.
- It killed more people than the Black Death.
- No one knew where it came from or why it suddenly went away.

Some men survived four years of shells, bullets and bombs only to get home safely ... and die of the 'flu!

119

Strange but true

US soldier, Major Harry S Truman, kept his battalion guns firing till the last seconds of the First World War.

Nearly 30 years later the Major was US President Harry S Truman. He ordered the dropping of atomic bombs on Japanese towns. This brought the Second World War to an end.

In a strange way you could say the same man fired the last shots in the *two* world wars.

Test your teacher

Try this quick quiz on your teacher and watch as they strain their brain cell to the limit. If they get a question wrong you can jeer because they're a dunce – if they get it right you can jeer because they're probably old enough to remember the First World War!

1 If you lived in Britain in 1916 and wanted to know what it was like in the trenches, you could visit some. Where?
a) On the French side of the Western Front near the town of Ypres.
b) Behind the German lines, near Berlin.
c) In Blackpool.

2 A British minister in charge of food production was called what?
a) The Controller of Potatoes.
b) The Fat Controller.
c) Director of Army Food Transportation (DAFT).

3 Soldiers had an average of 20 lice crawling over their bodies. But what was the record?
a) 428.
b) 1,428.
c) 10,428.

I DON'T KNOW WHAT'S WORSE, HAVING THEM OR HAVING TO COUNT THEM

4 French newspapers of 1914 had reports that their soldiers were very comfortable in the trenches with what?
a) Wine.

BOTTOMS UP!

POP

HICK!

CHEERS!

b) Women.

c) Central heating.

5 What was a 'wibble-wobble'?
a) A soldier's name for a fat general.
b) Another name for a tank.
c) A horse with an injured leg.

6 The women who worked with TNT explosive were nicknamed 'canaries'. Why?
a) They were so happy they sang like canaries while they worked.
b) The TNT caused their hair to turn canary yellow.
c) Because the factory owners were getting 'cheep' labour.

7 The First World War changed fashions and almost killed off one fashion. What?
a) Men wearing top hats to work.
b) Women wearing knickers.
c) Children wearing wooden clogs.

8 Kaiser Wilhelm of Germany was a powerful but crazy king. What was his hobby?
a) Pulling the wings off flies.

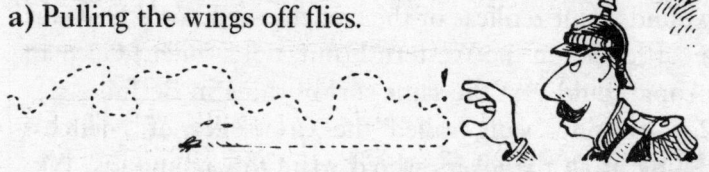

b) Throwing darts at pictures of his grandmother, Queen Victoria.

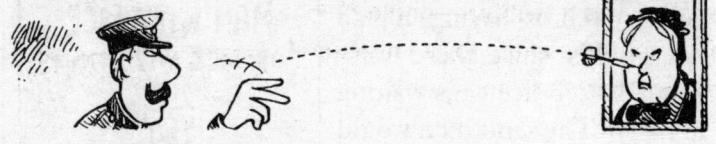

c) Chopping down trees.

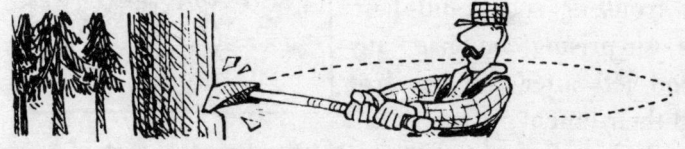

9 Brit Patrick Gara was arrested for trying to dodge joining the army. His excuse was ...
a) His mum wouldn't let him.
b) He was a coward and was afraid of getting hurt.
c) He didn't know there was a war on.

10 Brits with hard tennis courts were suspected by the police. Why?
a) Police believed they had been prepared as gun platforms for an invasion.
b) Tennis parties were a good cover for two spies to meet and swap messages hidden in tennis balls.
c) Police thought they were up to some secret racket.

Answers:

1c) That's right, Blackpool. Soldiers recovering from wounds built replicas of the trenches at Loos. (That was a battlefield on the Western Front, not a toilet.) German people could visit the same sort of thing in Berlin.

2a) Imagine being called the Controller of Potatoes! Think of all the jokers who'd write to you and say, 'My potatoes are very naughty. Can you control them for me?'

3c) As well as having 10,428 lice in his shirt there were about 10,253 lice eggs waiting to hatch. The same man would have had thousands more in his trousers, socks and hair. It's surprising he had any blood left after the lice had had their lunch!

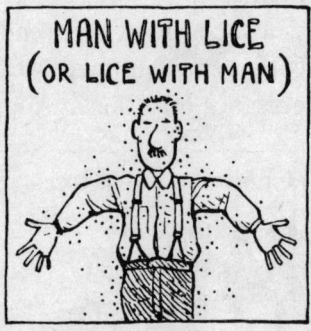

4c) The truth is the soldiers in the trenches had to be very careful about lighting fires. The smoke gave enemy gunners something to aim at. So you could light a fire and be shelled to death, or not light a fire and freeze to death!

5b) The army name for a tank was a 'landship', but they collected lots of other names too: Slug, Whale, Toad, Tortoise, Land-crab, Behemoth, Boojum. Newspapers couldn't give away the secret by showing pictures, so Brit writers described a 'long, low, dust-coloured tortoise' while French newspapers reported they were equipped in front with 'some kind of cow catcher'. But to most soldiers it looked like a water 'tank' and that name stuck.

6b) TNT caused nasty skin rashes and its fumes turned

the girls' hair bright mustard yellow – the colour of canaries. These unfortunate girls were often refused service in restaurants whose owners said, 'You are *unsightly*. Go away because you are putting the other customers off their food!'

7a) War changed British ways of life – posh people who would never have dreamed of travelling on a tram or bus before 1914, now travelled to work every day … paying their fares to 'conductorettes'. Women's fashion changed as a shortage of steel ended the wearing of tight corsets. City gents stopped wearing top hats as they were a nuisance on a bus or underground train with a low roof.

8c) Willy enjoyed felling trees at his palace at Potsdam. He was mad about stripping off the bark – which proves he was barking mad.

9b) In 1916, Patrick Gara was up before magistrates in Selby, Yorkshire, for avoiding military service. He was asked why he had not joined the army. He replied that he thought that he was safer in Selby than in the trenches! He was fined £2 and escorted to the nearest barracks. A year later, a man called Graham Whitlaw was up before the magistrates in London for not reporting for military service. His excuse was that he was a duke and a bishop

and he had been appointed Chief of the Army. He'd been appointed by King George IV (who had been dead almost 100 years). Of course Whitlaw was trying to act as if he was too mad to serve. It didn't work.

10a) Daft, but true. What use would a gun platform be in someone's back garden? You could always shell your neighbour's peas, I suppose.

Epilogue

There were lots of tragedies in the First World War. Almost every family in Britain, France, Germany and Russia lost someone. You can go to any town or village and see the names of the dead, carved on stone memorials. Many of the men who joined together died together and left their home towns desolate.

But that wasn't the *real* tragedy. The cruellest thing of all was that the First World War *didn't* solve any problems and it *didn't* bring peace. It led to the Second World War and far, far more misery, death and destruction.

Those whose names are carved on the memorials believed they were fighting for peace. Many would have given their lives gladly if they knew they had died in 'the war to end all wars'.

What went wrong? Big mistakes and small accidents. One accident so small that no one noticed it at the time. It happened in a German dugout during the Battle of the Somme. A British shell smashed into the trench and killed most of the Germans in it. But by a hideous chance one German escaped with just a shell splinter in his face.

He lived. He lived to start another war. His name was Adolf Hitler. Lucky Hitler – unlucky world.

Sometimes history is changed by great events like the First World War – sometimes it is changed by freak accidents in a fraction of a second: the arrow that hit King Harold in the eye at the Battle of Hastings ... the shell that *failed* to kill Hitler.

History can be horrible. But each of us should find our nearest war memorial, stand in front of it and read the names.

Then say, 'Never again.'

If everyone says that, and means it, then the deaths will not have been such a waste.

FRIGHTFUL
FIRST WORLD WAR
GRISLY QUIZ

**Now find out if you're a
Frightful First World War expert!**

BEASTLY BATTLES

There were lots of famous fights and crazy campaigns throughout the war. See if you can figure out which of these beastly battle facts are true and which are false.

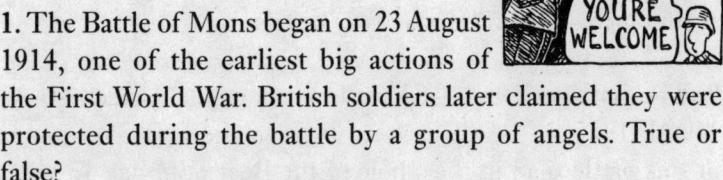

1. The Battle of Mons began on 23 August 1914, one of the earliest big actions of the First World War. British soldiers later claimed they were protected during the battle by a group of angels. True or false?

2. French soldiers were taken to the front line for the Battle of the Marne in September 1914 by taxi. True or false?

3. There were three major battles around Ypres in Belgium throughout the war. In the last battle there a young Winston Churchill – the great Second World War leader – was almost blinded in a gas attack. True or false?

4. The Battle of the Somme began on 1 July 1916 and went on until 18 November. The French and British attacked German lines. In that time the British suffered 57,470 casualties. True or false?

5. The French and British attack at Arras began on 1 October 1914. It was a failure for the Allies because they only managed to capture a single hill. True or false?

6. Verdun was the longest battle of the war, beginning in February 1916. The Germans were led by a prince. True or false?

7. The Battle of Cambrai in November 1917 was such a disaster for the British that the government ordered that church bells were not allowed to ring. True or false?

8. The Battle of Jutland in 1916 was the most famous sea battle of the war. The British won and the German fleet did not sail again for the rest of the war. True or false?

9. The Battle of Neuve-Chapelle was fought between 10–13 March 1915. More shells were fired in the first 35 minutes of this battle than in the whole of the Boer War, just 15 years earlier. True or false?

10. The Battle of the Aisne began in September 1914. It was named after a nearby town. True or false?

Terrible Trenches Quick Quiz

Take this quick quiz to find out if you would have survived life in the terrible trenches or been beaten by the Bosch.

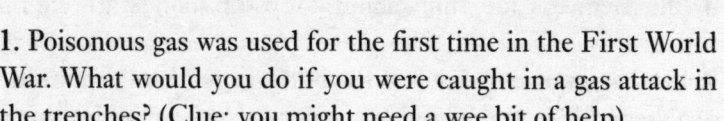

1. Poisonous gas was used for the first time in the First World War. What would you do if you were caught in a gas attack in the trenches? (Clue: you might need a wee bit of help)

2. How could you tell when an enemy bombardment was about to begin? (Clue: vile vermin)

3. Trench toilets were buckets or holes dug into the mud. With hundreds of soldiers suffering from deadly dysentery, they filled up quickly. Where could you go to poo if the foul latrines were full? (Clue: a number two in no-man's land?)

4. Things could get pretty chilly in the trenches and lots of icy infantry soldiers suffered from frostbite. How did they save their frozen feet? (Clue: you'll get snow help from me!)

5. Trench foot was caused by cold, damp and unhealthy conditions (the trenches were filled with mud and water and poo and bodies). What could you do to prevent having your feet chopped off because of this disgusting disease? (Clue: grease is the word)

6. Lice loved life in the trenches. They would live on the soldiers and make a mighty meal of them. How did the men try to get rid of the lice? (Clue: flaming lice!)

7. Many soldiers tried to give themselves a 'blighty' (a wound just serious enough to be sent home) to escape the terrible trenches, but what would happen if they were found out? (Clue: it was a deathly disaster)

8. If you were sniper, what was the best way to avoid being seen by the enemy? (Clue: think about it – you'll soon twig)

9. In an emergency, what was the best way to make a splint for a soldier with broken bones? (Clue: you're gun-na have to think of something)

10. How did the army try to reduce cases of dysentery in the trenches, caused by dirty water? (Clue: water with a twist)

NUTTY NICKNAMES

Soldiers in the First World War had nicknames for everything – their weapons, ranks and rations. See if you can understand the soldiers' slang and figure out which weird words mean what.

1. Tommy	a) Senior officers
2. Brass hats	b) Experienced soldier
3. Blighty	c) Britain
4. Coffin nails	d) Cigarettes
5. Jerry	e) British soldier
6. Old sweat	f) Jam
7. Whizz bang	g) German soldier
8. Conchie	h) Tea
9. Char	i) Conscientious objector
10. Pozzy	j) Artillery shell

ANSWERS

Beastly Battles

1. True. The British managed to beat back the Germans despite being outnumbered and they thought that God had sent a ghostly army of angels to help them. To this day no one really knows the truth about the Angels of Mons…

2. True. France ordered every taxi cab in Paris to be available to take soldiers to the frontline so they would get there in time for the big battle.

3. False. It was a young Adolf Hitler who was smothered by the ghastly gas. In the whole of the First World War horrid Hitler was awarded six medals for bravery!

4. False. The casualty figure of nearly 58,000 was for the first day alone – 1 July. This is still a record.

5. False. It was a success for the Allies because they managed to capture a single hill. That hill, known as Vimy Ridge, captured

by Canadian forces, was very important!

6. True. The Germans at the Battle of Verdun were led by Crown Prince William, son of crazy Kaiser William II.

7. False. The Battle of Cambrai was considered such a success for the British that church bells were allowed to be rung for the first time since the war began.

8. True (and false). It's true that the German fleet was so badly damaged by the British that it spent the rest of the war in dock, but no one could claim it was a great success for the British – they lost thousands of men.

9. True. Methods of warfare and weapons had changed dramatically between the end of the Boer War in 1902 and the First World War.

10. False. Like many other battles in the First World War, including the Somme and the Marne, it was named after a nearby river.

Terrible Trenches Quick Quiz

1. Pee on your hanky and then tie it over your nose and mouth. This weird wee trick really worked – the chemicals in urine kept out the gas.

2. Watch the rats. Rats were everywhere in the stinking trenches and soldiers believed that they knew instinctively when an attack was about to happen and disappeared. If you couldn't see a rotten rat then you were probably in for a beastly bombardment.

3. A shell-hole. Who needed specially dug holes when the Germans made them for you with their bombs? Just find a cosy shell hole and squat.

4. Rubbing them with snow. In fact we now know that rubbing frostbite with anything actually makes the damage worse. So

rubbing it with snow was not only parky and painful it was also pointless!

5. Cover your feet with grease made from whale oil. A single battalion in the trenches could use up to ten gallons of gooey grease every day!

6. They would burn them with a candle. This was a tricky business and more than one careless corporal set his clothes on fire in the process.

7. They would be shot. Yup – the usual punishment for soldiers who tried to cheat their way out of the war was to be sent for trial and killed.

8. Camouflage yourself as a tree. Sneaky snipers would slither into no-man's land to get closer to the enemy. To avoid being spotted they would hide under cover of a fake tree!

9. Use your rifle. Other things could be used to help soldiers with broken bones until the medics arrived – pieces of wood, bayonets, swords – but the rifle made a good sturdy splint. Not much good if you run into the enemy while your gun's tied to your lieutenant's leg, though!

10. They added chloride of lime. This was believed to purify the water supplied – but the soldiers hated it because it made the water taste disgusting!

Nutty Nicknames
1.e) 2.a) 3.c) 4.d) 5.g) 6.b) 7.j) 8.i) 9.h) 10.f)

INTERESTING INDEX

Where will you find 'beetle-racing', 'fried lice' and 'smelly whale oil' in an index? In a Horrible Histories book, of course!

137

Terry Deary was born at a very early age, so long ago he can't remember. But his mother, who was there at the time, says he was born in Sunderland, north-east England, in 1946 – so it's not true that he writes all *Horrible Histories* from memory. At school he was a horrible child only interested in playing football and giving teachers a hard time. His history lessons were so boring and so badly taught, that he learned to loathe the subject. *Horrible Histories* is his revenge.

Martin Brown was born in Melbourne, on the proper side of the world. Ever since he can remember he's been drawing. His dad used to bring back huge sheets of paper from work and Martin would fill them with doodles and little figures. Then, quite suddenly, with food and water, he grew up, moved to the UK and found work doing what he's always wanted to do: drawing doodles and little figures.

HORRIBLE HISTORIES

BARMY
BRITISH EMPIRE

Terry Deary Illustrated by Martin Brown

SCHOLASTIC

For Ronan Paterson – a star.

Scholastic Children's Books,
Euston House, 24 Eversholt Street,
London NW1 1DB, UK

A division of Scholastic Ltd
London ~ New York ~ Toronto ~ Sydney ~ Auckland
Mexico City ~ New Delhi ~ Hong Kong

First published in the UK by Scholastic Ltd, 2002
This edition published 2017

Text © Terry Deary, 2002
Illustrations © Martin Brown, 2002
All rights reserved

ISBN 978 1407 16700 8

Printed and bound by CPI Group (UK) Ltd, Croydon, CR0 4YY

4 6 8 10 9 7 5 3

The right of Terry Deary and Martin Brown to be identified as the author and illustrator of this work has been asserted by them in accordance with the Copyright, Designs and Patents Act, 1988.

www.scholastic.co.uk

CONTENTS

Introduction

What's an empire? It's a collection of countries all ruled by one emperor. You know the sort of thing – you start with one greedy little state like Rome and, before you know it, you have a Roman Empire. Everyone ruled by a super Caesar like the nutty Nero or the horrible Hadrian.

Sounds cosy, doesn't it? Well, it's not really because most of the time those countries don't *want* to be ruled by the emperor! He just sent his bully-boys in to take it over.

Imagine what that must be like! You've lived in your house all your life and enjoyed it. You're sitting at home one day when in marches a bunch of soldiers and they say...

And that's how it was with the British Empire till about 1900. The Brits just marched into somebody's country and said, 'We're in charge!' And it got worse...

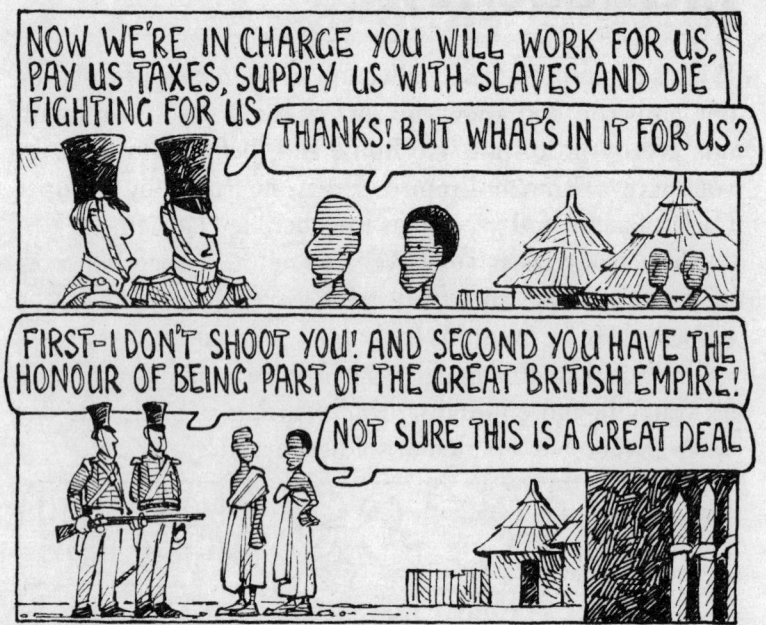

Of course, it was never quite so simple. People rebelled against the British – some succeeded and some failed. Either way, lots of people died ... horribly. In fact the history of the British Empire is full of horrible people and horrible deeds. Just the sort of stuff for a Horrible History.

And, as it happens, you're reading one now! Read on...

Terrible Timeline

Every day, somewhere in the British Empire, someone suffered. Here are just a few of the highlights – or, if you were a victim, the lowlights – of the empire up till 1900…

1562 England begins its slave trade thanks to her Terrible Tudor superior sailors. They buy people in Africa and sell them to South America.

1607 The British start to settle in America. They push the Indians out of the way and start to grow tobacco and cotton and sugar (in the West Indies). But this is hard work and the Brits don't like it! So they need even more slaves to do the work for them.

1619 The first slaves arrive in North America and the West Indies from Africa. Sugar is popular and a huge number of slaves are sent to America to grow sugar cane.

1620 The 'Pilgrim Fathers' land on the north-east coast of America and set up a colony. They will cause trouble later.

1652 The Dutch set up a colony of 'Boers' (or farmers) in South Africa. They'll cause trouble later too!

1756–63 The Seven Years War against France and Spain. The Brits

win and become the main rulers of India's incredible riches through the East India Company – a powerful trading company, backed by the British Army.

1770 Captain Cook comes across Australia. A whacking great chunk of land to add to the empire. Loads of empty space to dump convicts (from 1788). Shame the Brits taught them to play cricket.

1770 British explorer James Bruce reaches the source of the Blue Nile.

1776 The American settlers rebel against their British rulers. The Brits lose their big rich American colony so it's time to set off to take over the rest of the world! Look out world!

1789 Freed slave Olaudah Equiano publishes his life story. This helps the growing 'Abolitionist' struggle in Britain and the US to banish all slavery.

1792 There is a slave rebellion in Haiti led by Toussant L'Ouverture (1743-1803). His army of 55,000 blacks fights against the French and makes them think slavery is not such a good idea.

1795 The Brits take over the Cape Colony (South Africa) from the

Dutch – known as 'Boers' – which is a bit of a boering name. The Boers begin to move inland in search of better land and to escape British control. Those Boers will be a nuisance for the next hundred years or more.

1818 Shaka, the Zulu chief, launches the Mfecane (Wars Of Crushing And Wandering) against his black African neighbours and the white Europeans in southern Africa.

1834 Slavery is abolished in the British Empire … sort of! The slaves have to stay with their masters for four more years.

1838 768,000 slaves free at last. But many native lords in Empire countries keep slaves and the Brits can't do anything about it.

1839 The First Opium War – the Brits fight for the right to sell opium to the Chinese. Opium is making Brit drug dealers very rich … and the Chinese very dead.

1851 Gold is discovered in Australia. Hope those convicts don't pinch it!

1855 Scottish missionary David Livingstone explores the Zambezi River in Africa and names the Victoria Falls after his queen. (What a creep!)

9

1857 The Indian Mutiny. The Brits are shocked to find that the Indians do NOT like the Brits! Vicious fighting and cruelty on both sides.

1860 The Maori Wars in New Zealand. As usual the war ends in gore.

1876 Queen Victoria is crowned Empress of India. No one has asked the Indians, of course.

1879 The Zulu War. William Gladstone says: 'Ten thousand Zulus died and their only crime was to try and defend their families against the British guns.'

1899 The Second Boer War. The mighty Brit Empire struggles to beat a few farmers. It's the beginning of the end for the Empire.

Early Empire

By the 1600s British people had set out and begun to settle in America. Some were looking for freedom – they were Puritan Christians who were having a hard time at home.

When they arrived in America they found there were people already there – Native Americans. But the Christians didn't mind! The Christians believed their God had *planned* it that way! In 1625 Simon Purchas, a churchman, said…

God is wise and he made these savage countries rich so the riches will be attractive to Christians!

Kind person, the Christian God! Can you really imagine him saying . . .

LOOK, LADS, I MADE A RICH LAND AND FILLED IT WITH NATIVES. THE NATIVES DIDN'T DO A VERY GOOD JOB OF LOOKING AFTER IT. SO I'M SENDING YOU CHRISTIANS TO SHOW THEM THE WAY! THE RICHES ARE YOUR REWARD

The Christians really *believed* this. They also believed they were *better* than the Indians because they used tablecloths and the Indians didn't! Honest! In 1580 Brit explorer Martin

Frobisher came across the Inuit (Eskimos) in Canada and said...

> *These Inuit are brute people. They live in caves. They have no tables or stools or tablecloths for cleanliness!*

Er, hang on, Mr Frobisher ... if they have no *tables* then *of course* they have no tablecloths! And are you saying people who don't use tablecloths are brutes? Well, there are an awful lot of children who eat school dinners without tablecloths! Are they all brutes?

YOU REALLY WANT ME TO ANSWER THAT?

At first the Indians were friendly, so the Brit invaders decided to teach them how to be good Christians – with tablecloths. But when fighting broke out the Brits decided the Indians wouldn't make good Christians after all. Instead they treated the Indians like wild animals – to be hunted and killed. A 1622 book of rules for Brit tobacco planters in Virginia said...

> *It is easier to conquer the Indians than to teach them. For they are simple, naked people, scattered in small villages and this makes them easy to defeat. In future it will be our job to make them obey by destroying their villages and crops. They can then be chased on our horses, tracked by bloodhounds and torn to pieces with our mastiff dogs for these people are no better than wild beasts.*

For the next 300 years the Brits treated everyone else the same way – in Africa, Australia, New Zealand and Ireland for example. The rules were:

British settlers remember

1 Natives are simple people

2 It is our job to teach them how to be British and Christian

3 If they rebel then they will have to be destroyed

13

It was nonsense, but the Brits BELIEVED it. Sadly some British people in the twenty-first century *still* believe that they are better than others!

Better Brits

The Brits believed they were 'better' than the native peoples in many ways:

1 In seventeenth-century America, Brit invaders looked at the Indians with disgust because they wandered around with hardly any clothes on. But the Barmy Brits wore *too many* clothes. The ones who laughed at naked Indians were wearing hot and heavy white wigs. And in steaming eighteenth-century India, soldiers wore red woollen tunics buttoned up to the neck and felt hats. The officers wore white gloves too! One group of soldiers arrived in India wearing brass helmets under a fierce sun – this 'cooked' their heads and many died from sunstroke. And you thought school uniform was bad!

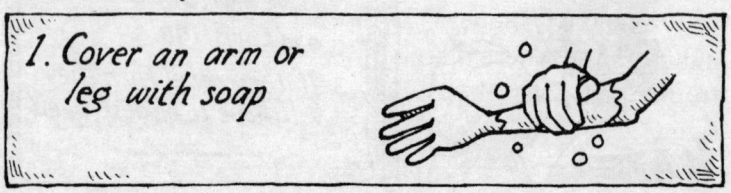

HE'S BAKING

SIZZLE

2 Over in Ireland in 1823 the Brits sneered at the 9,000 Irish people of Tullahobagly for being so poor. These 9,000 Irish had just 93 chairs between them and only 10 beds. But the Brit capital of London was no better. There was terrible poverty and the streets were full of beggars. In fact, there were so many that some of them had to cheat to get people's attention. They would…

1. Cover an arm or leg with soap

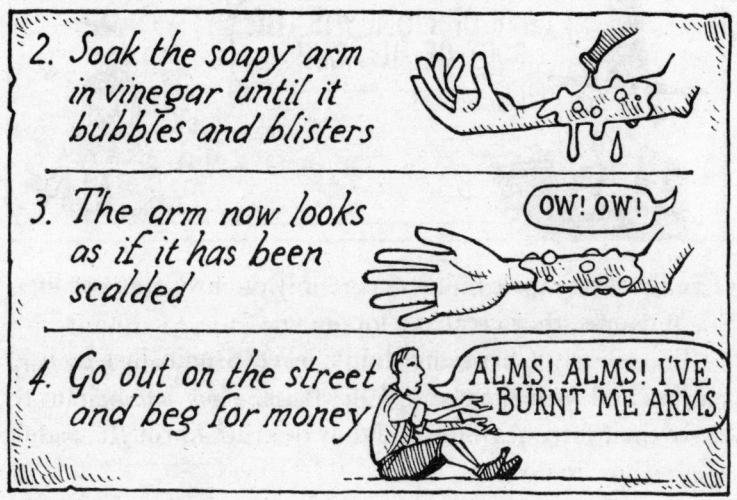

2. Soak the soapy arm in vinegar until it bubbles and blisters

3. The arm now looks as if it has been scalded

OW! OW!

4. Go out on the street and beg for money

ALMS! ALMS! I'VE BURNT ME ARMS

3 The Brits believed they were braver than foreign soldiers – even the foreign soldiers who fought with the British army. In 1883 Valentine Baker led a force of a few Brits and a few thousand Egyptians against the Dervishes of Sudan. The Brits and Egyptians had machine guns – the Dervishes had wooden clubs and knives. Baker said the Brits showed courage while the Egyptians panicked – the Egyptians fell to their knees and begged for their lives as their throats were cut. Of course the Brits (Baker said) fought bravely on … with machine guns against clubs, of course!

Making masses of money

Money, money, money. That's what the British Empire was built on. And where there's money there's greed and there's trouble. At least those Christian settlers got one thing right…

The British Empire builders certainly did love money a lot – so, of course, they created a lot of evil.

Those early Christians didn't leave Britain just to find natives and turn them into Christians. They left Britain to make their fortunes. How did they do that? Through 'trade'. Here's how to do it…

17

You can see why the British set out to find as many countries as they could to trade with. They could get tea from India, sheep from Australia and New Zealand, gold and diamonds from Africa. But a new trade grew that made even more money! The slave trade! Here's how it worked...

19

Savage slavers

Find that slave

Where did slaves come from? Mostly from Africa where African slave traders sold other Africans to the Brits. But where did *they* go to get a slave? After all, they couldn't just pop down to the local supermarket, pick up a few and flog them to the British slavers. Slave dealers in Africa either got them from tribes who had captured prisoners from other tribes in war or they simply kidnapped them.

Olaudah Equiano was captured when he was a child and sold as a slave. He is one of the few slaves who survived to write his own story. Olaudah said...

The grown-ups of our village used to go off to work in the fields. The children then gathered together to play. But whenever we played we always sent someone up a tree to watch out for the slave dealers. This was the time when slave dealers rushed into the village, snatched as many children as they could, and carried them off to the coast. There they were sold as slaves.

Imagine that! You go to play in your local park and before you know it a gang has picked you up and sold you! You'd never see your home or your family again. Cruel.

Some slave dealers even got slaves from tribes who no longer wanted them in their tribe! A tribe might sell a criminal as a slave – which is a bit like your school selling you because you let down the head teacher's car tyres. (Actually, you probably deserve it!) But they also sold people who broke the rules of the tribe. One of the saddest cases was when they sold a woman whose 'crime' was ... having twins!

Check that slave

Only fit Africans were bought as slaves, and the slaves knew that! So what would *you* do if you were going to be sold? Pretend to be sick?

Sadly this would not work.

Not all slavers picked carefully, though. Some slaves were sent to the ships even though they looked too ill to survive the journey. In 1751 ship's captain John Newton reported...

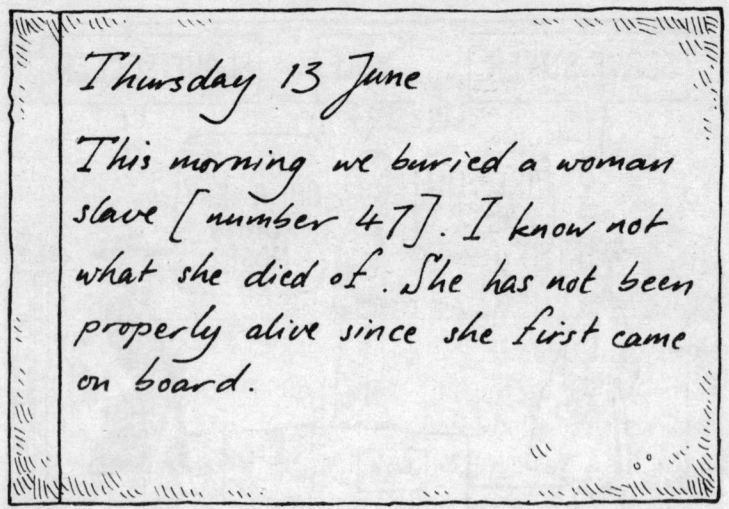

So when you died you weren't even buried with your name – just a number.

Bung that slave

Slaves were worth a lot of money but the traders didn't take very good care of them. Many died, packed into dark, stinking rooms below the decks of the ships. The sailors *did* wash them down every day, though probably by throwing a bucket of sea water over them.

A young slave described the journey of between 40 and 70 days across the Atlantic Ocean...

The stench and the heat was dreadful. The crowding meant you hardly had room to turn over. The chains rubbed some Africans raw. The filth was made worse by the lavatory bucket and many small children fell into it. One day two of my countrymen were allowed on deck. They were chained together and decided they would rather have death than such a life of misery. They jumped into the sea.

He explained how...

- the 'holds' on the ship were about 1.52 metres high and slaves were allowed just half a litre of water a day.
- the food was a vegetable mush and the slaves were told exactly how to eat: 'Pick up the food – put it in your mouth – swallow it!' (Sounds like a good idea for school dinners.)

- on long journeys food and fresh water supplies got low and the captain threw weak slaves – alive – into the ocean so the fit would survive.
- slaves who died were usually thrown over the side to feed the fishes while others arrived in America very sick.

But the traders could deal with sick slaves – sometimes in a quite disgusting way. One of the most common diseases was dysentery – which gives you very bad diarrhoea. Not many Americans would buy a slave with poo dribbling down their legs, would they? So what did the slave traders do? They cut a length of rope and stuffed it up the bum of the slave with diarrhoea and blocked it for a while. That way they could fool their customers into a sale.

Did you know…?
While the slaves were eating vegetable mush the slave-traders back in Britain had more food than they knew what to do with. In 1769 slave-trader William Beckford had a feast. Six hundred dishes were served on golden plates. It cost £10,000.

Sell that slave

You've seen New Year sales in shops, haven't you? People queue for hours to get a bargain, the doors open and the people in the queue all rush in because the first in get the best bargains. Some slave sales in the West Indies could be just like that. They were called 'scrambles'. Olaudah Equiano described one…

1 *The signal to start the scramble was the beat of a drum.*

2 *The buyers rushed into the yard where the slaves were caged and chose the ones they liked best.*

3 *The noise and the bawling, the greed on the faces of the buyers, made the Africans more terrified.*

Brand that slave

Ever had a new bike? Afraid of having it stolen? Some people have their post code stamped on the bike frame so it can be recognized. Slaves were not much different. But the 'stamp' was a red-hot 'brand' that was burned into their flesh.

A trader, William Bosman, described what happened in 1705...

When we buy slaves they are all examined by our doctors. Those who pass the examination are put to one side. Meanwhile our iron brands are heating in the fire. When we have agreed the price, our slaves are marked on the chest.

Work that slave

Have you ever taken notes while the teacher speaks? Everyone has to work at the same speed – fine if you're a fast writer, but misery if you are slow. Slaves were organized in gangs and worked a bit like that. All together. Fine if you were fit and fast – but torture if you were old, sick or slow. An 'overseer' stood behind you with a whip and lashed you if you fell behind. It wasn't unusual for a slow slave to be whipped to death. (At least your teacher doesn't do that!) And it wasn't much better for children. They had jobs too, perhaps pulling up weeds. Back-breaking, finger-aching, sweat-making, bone-wearying work, all day long – with that whip cracking behind you to keep you at it. (And you thought PE lessons were bad!)

Did you know…?
In 1700 Bristol and Liverpool were small fishing ports. Thanks to the slave trade they grew over the next 100 years and some slave-traders became enormously rich. Many of Bristol and Liverpool's fine buildings were built with the profits of slavery. As a Bristol historian put it:

Every brick in the city of Bristol is cemented with the blood of a slave.

Play like a slave
Some slaves tried to cheer themselves up by making music. They often sang songs that made fun of their white masters!

They even made their own instruments – drums, whistles, and banjos from wood and string. Here are a couple you may like to try…

Make a shaky-shekie
You need:
A piece of wood.
Two sticks.

To play:
Place the wood across your knees.
Beat the wood with the sticks.

SHACKETY-SHECKETY
SHACKETY-SHECKETY

Make a kitty-kattie
You need:
A dead pig - rip out its belly (or bladder).
A handful of dried peas.

KITTELY-KATTELY
KITTELY-KATTELY

To play:
Push the peas inside the pig's bladder.
Blow up the bladder till it is tight.
Tie the end.
Shake the kitty-kattie like a rattle.

What do you mean? You don't fancy blowing into a pig's belly? Oh, all right. Try it with a balloon instead!

Slave fight-backs

What could you *do* about being a slave? Hell, you could always *die* – of overwork or disease. In 1792 half the slaves on one Jamaica farm died in their first four years there. But if you survived you might have tried for a better life. How?

a) Run away

Difficult, because you were often forced to work in chains. And risky, because if you were caught you'd be lashed, or have your ears cut off or be executed. In 1776 in East Jamaica slave 'Jack' escaped. He was caught. The judge gave his decision…

b) Rebel

That doesn't mean you had to punch your owner on his nose. Slaves rebelled in other ways. They could simply make life difficult for their owners…

Slaves often got away with it. The owners thought these things happened because slaves were stupid and clumsy, but it was the owners who were stupid for thinking that!

One slave boy (in St Vincent, the West Indies, in 1820) wasn't worried about *what* the owners thought. He was left in charge of a large supper table while a ladies' group held a meeting. The meeting finished, the ladies arrived in the supper room … and there was nothing left but the empty dishes!

Ban that slave

Slavery was abolished in the British Empire in 1834 … but not everyone agreed that that was a good idea. A writer called Boswell said…

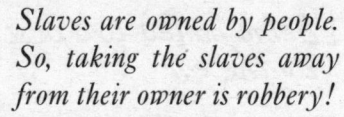

Slaves are owned by people. So, taking the slaves away from their owner is robbery!

Of course Mr Boswell *wasn't* a slave, was he? He probably would NOT have wanted to be 'owned' by anyone! The silly man went on…

There have always been slaves because God wanted it that way!

31

Maybe batty Boswell had had a chat with God and knew what God wanted … but I doubt it. But his craziest claim was…

Banning slavery is cruel to the slaves, especially the Africans. Being a slave to the British Empire has given many of them a much happier life!

HE CANNOT BE SERIOUS

Maybe brain-dead Boswell hadn't read the newspapers at that time. They listed the cruelties slaves suffered in the British West Indies:

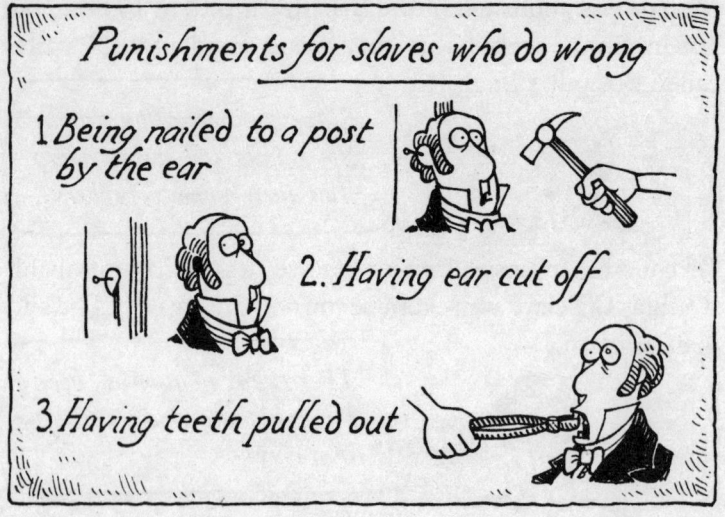

Punishments for slaves who do wrong

1 *Being nailed to a post by the ear*

2. *Having ear cut off*

3. *Having teeth pulled out*

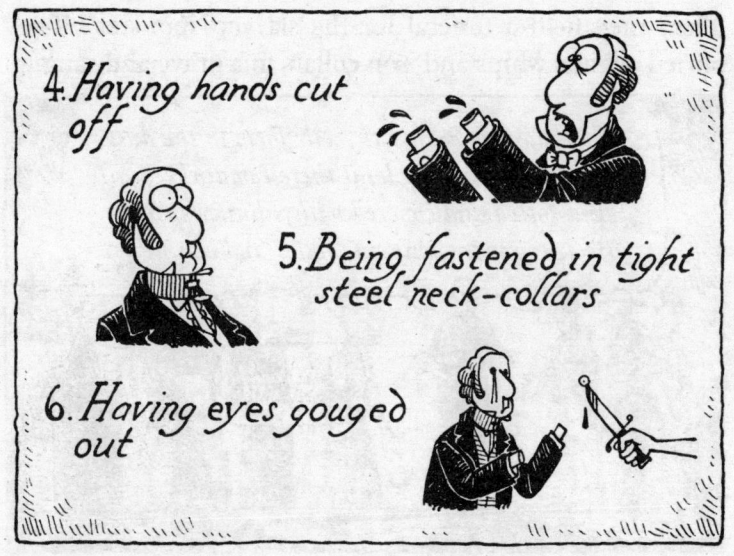

Still think slaves are 'happier', Mr Boswell?

Party time

In Falmouth the Baptist Church celebrated the end of slavery on the night of 31 July 1838. As midnight drew near the Reverend William Knibb cried…

The monster is dying!

Then as the clock struck midnight he shouted…

The monster is dead!

Then they held a funeral for the slavery 'monster'. They buried chains, whips and iron collars in a grave and sang...

> *Now slavery we lay thy vile form in the dust*
> *And buried forever let it there remain!*
> *And rotted and covered with villainy's rust*
> *Be every man-whip and fetter and chain.*

Having a funeral service for an evil thing sounds like a good way to celebrate.

HORRIBLE HISTORIES HEALTH WARNING:
The Brits abolished slavery and ever since school history books have been patting the Brits on the back for that! The books sometimes 'forget' to mention the millions of miserable slaves that made millions of pounds for brutal Brits in the 200 years before they banned it.

So, slavery was banished (almost) from the British Empire ... but the Empire only grew stronger.

After slavery

What could the British Empire do with all the free slaves? They couldn't return them to the countries where their

grandparents and great-grandparents had been kidnapped –
there was nothing there for the ex-slaves.

Someone had the bright idea of giving the freed slaves
their own country on the coast of West Africa. The Spanish
name for that country was Sierra Leone and the capital city
was named Freetown … of course.

Did you know…?
The ex-slaves came from all over and they brought their own
ways of life with them. Some of them brought some strange
superstitions and they especially hated the British redcoat
soldiers. So the superstitions about the redcoats were very
odd…

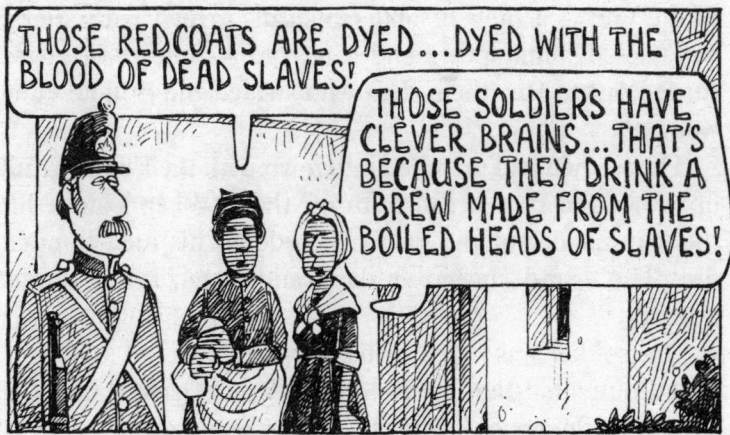

Of course this wasn't true. You will NOT pass your school
exams by drinking a brew made from the boiled head of your
history teacher!

Rotten rebels

In Jamaica the slaves were free – free to starve on the pitiful wages they could earn. By 1865 they were desperate and wrote to Queen Victoria for help. The reply (from Queen Vic's ministers, of course) was...

Riots began when a Jamaican boy was arrested for attacking a woman in his village. A mob marched on the town of Stony Gut – a mob of 500 Jamaicans armed with sticks, cutlasses, fishing spears and a few guns. The town guard turned out to face them. But who started the trouble? The women!

The women had marched into town with their baskets full of stones and they began to throw them. When a stone hit the commander of the guard he ordered his men to open fire. The crowd rushed at them and began a murderous massacre...

- One soldier was killed with a harpoon.
- A Councillor, Baron Von Ketelhodt, was hacked to death and his fingers cut off by the rioters as prizes.
- It was said that the rebels cut out the tongue of preacher the Reverend Herschell while he was still alive, then tried to skin him.
- Lieutenant Hall was pushed into a burning building to roast alive.
- A Jamaican priest (but friend of the Brits) was beaten to death and his guts ripped out.

- British Governor Edward Eyre said…

> *Many are said to have had their eyes scooped out, their heads split open and their brains taken out.*

Governor's Eyre's revenge was terrible. Here are some of his vicious punishments…

- One rebel called Wellington was shot and then had his head hacked off. The body was buried by a stream, but heavy rain swelled the stream and washed the head away. It was found and stuck on a pole – a cruel stunt from the Middle Ages.
- At Fonthill village nine men were shot then hung up in their local church – something Henry VIII had done over 300 years before to rebels in England.
- Over 600 were flogged – and the Brits often put strands of wire in the lashes to make them more painful.
- Jamaicans were hunted down and shot or hanged. Some were given trials and some weren't. A thousand homes were burned to the ground and 439 Jamaicans were killed.
- Men were lined up at a trench and shot so their bodies fell into the trench – a method the Nazis used 80 years later. The Nazis were murderers … and so was Governor Eyre. He was sacked, but he escaped real punishment. Many Brits thought he was a hero.

Painful punishments

The British didn't just move into another country and trade with the people. They liked to make sure the native people lived the British way with British law and order. But some British 'justice' was a bit horrible...

The wicked whip.

Slaves had to obey. If they were cheeky or tried to run away they were punished. Usually with the whip. The women were usually stripped naked and held down by fellow slaves while their owner or overseer ordered a black male slave-driver to flog them. An American slave song described the punishment...

O master! O master!
One Monday morning they lay me down,
And give me thirty-nine on my bare rump,
O master, O master!

The 'thirty nine' lashes were usually one for every year of the slave's life. Pity the ones that lived to seventy!

The brutal bastinado

In Beirut the Brit governor, Colonel Hugh Rose, ordered a man to be punished with the 'bastinado'. Would you like this?

The Beirut criminal's two partners got an easier punishment … they were ordered to sweep the street!

The hideous hanging

In Morant Bay, Jamaica, there was a rebellion of free slaves in 1865. Several British men and women were killed and Governor Edward Eyre decided to teach the rebels a lesson. He wrote…

> *I came up with a plan which struck terror into those wretched men FAR more than death. I made them hang each other! They begged to be shot rather than do this.*

Governor Eyre said gleefully…

> *The effect on the living was terrifying!*

Nasty. There were hundreds hanged this way – including a Jamaican priest, the Reverend G. W. Gordon. MOST of the hanged men were probably innocent!

Foul fire
In 1760 there was a West Indies slave rebellion known as 'Tacky's Revolt'. One rebel was caught and executed by 'slow burning':
- He was chained to an iron post.
- A fire was lit under his feet.
- He watched as his legs were turned to ashes.

It's said that the rebel suffered this bravely and did not cry out or even groan.

The blasting barrel
In 1832, in India, some Muslims were afraid the British would force them to become Christians. Four Muslims

plotted to massacre some Europeans in Bangalore. Their plot was discovered and their punishment was horribly messy…

- The four men were led to the place of execution by a band playing the 'Dead March'.
- They were tied to cannon barrels.
- The cannon were fired … and the men blown to little pieces.

The sweet treatment

In 1756, in Jamaica, a starving slave was caught eating the sugar cane he was supposed to be collecting. The slave owner's diary reported…

41

Incredible India

The Brits didn't have the empire idea all to themselves, of course. Spain, France and Holland wanted to grab some of this empire fortune. But the Brits found the secret of success ... a strong navy! That way they could defend all their colonies around the world – and attack the other countries!

PUSH OFF?

Young Brits joined the army to see the world and fill their pockets with loot. At that time, India was made up of many small areas, each with its own wealthy ruler. They were often at war with each other, and when the Brits fought alongside an Indian prince he would reward them well. And when they fought AGAINST an Indian prince they usually won – and took over his kingdom and wealth.

The British Empire came to India ... and robbed it.

Potted prince

In the late 1700s one of their greatest problem princes was terrible Tipu. Tipu had been fighting the Brits on and off for 20 years when he came up against them at his fortress at Seringapatam in 1799.

The Brits used two weapons to finally kill off Tipu ... What were they? Pick two from five!

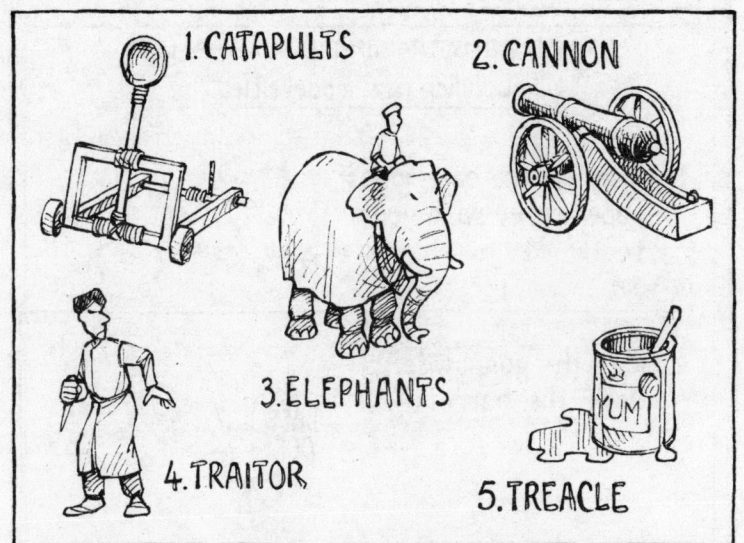

1. CATAPULTS
2. CANNON
3. ELEPHANTS
4. TRAITOR
5. TREACLE

Answer: **2** and **4**.

The cannon blasted a hole in the wall around Seringapatam while Tipu's traitor general let the Brits rush in.

Brave Tipu rushed to defend the hole in the wall. In spite of four deadly wounds he fought on till he was finally shot down. Tipu's body was found after the battle – under a pile of other bleeding corpses. Nasty!

Suffering sepoys

Indian soldiers (called 'sepoys') were brilliant fighters and the Brits used them all over the world. Yet the British managed to upset these super soldiers. In 1857 the sepoys mutinied against their Brit officers. Why?

Bullets. The Brits gave the sepoys new rifles with 'cartridges'. These cartridges had gunpowder under a paper cover. To load you had to…

Loading new model rifle

1. Tear off the cartridge's paper cover with your teeth.

2. Pour the gunpowder down the barrel.

3. Ram the cartridge with its bullet down the barrel.

4. Fire.

To make the bullet slide down (3), the cartridge was covered with grease. Of course that meant that you'd get grease in your mouth when you bit off the paper cover (1).

The sepoys were not Christians like the Brit officers. They were mostly Hindu and Muslim. The Hindus were not allowed to touch cows (because they were sacred) and the Muslims were not allowed to touch pigs (because they were filthy).

So it should have been simple for the Brits. All they had to remember was: 'Do NOT use grease made from the fat of cows OR pigs.' Easy!

What did the Brits do? They used grease made from the fat of cows and pigs!*

The sepoys rebelled, of course. Brit women and children were massacred at Kanpur and the Brit revenge was brutal.

- Muslim mutineers were sewn into PIG skins before they were hanged – a horror worse than death.
- Mutineers were forced to clean up the blood from their massacre – and if they refused they were lashed and made to lick it up.

After the Kanpur massacre the nervous Brits punished anyone on the slightest excuse. One Brit soldier boasted …

I seed two Indians talking on a cart. Soon I hear one of them say 'Kanpur'. I knowed what that meant. So I fetched Tom Walker and he heard 'em say 'Kanpur', and we knowed what that meant. So we polished them both off.

* Actually some historians say the Brits did no such thing and that the pig-fat/cow-fat story was invented by trouble-makers.

Empress's quick eastern quiz

As well as being India's great white empress, Queen Victoria also ruled over a vast Eastern Empire. Here she is, with her deceased husband, to ask you some quick questions...

47

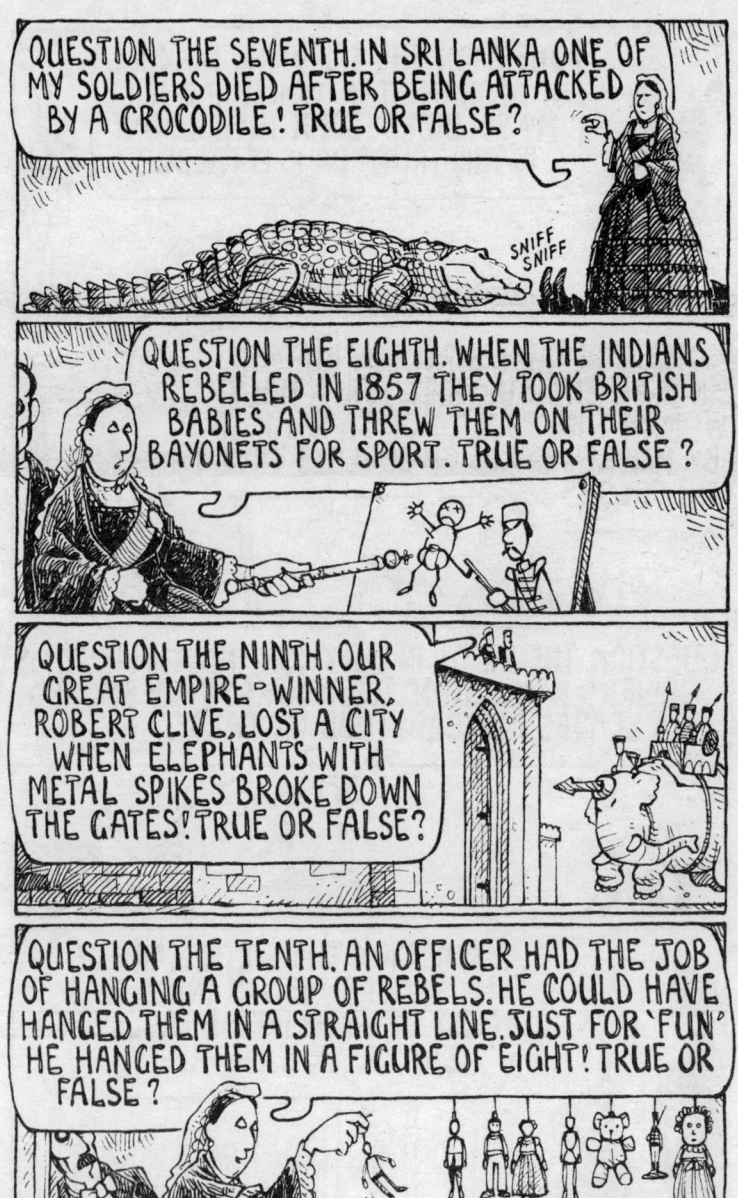

DO YOU HAVE THE ANSWERS, ALBERT?

Answers:

1 True. The Burmese had some customs that the British just didn't understand. An American visitor said in 1824 that:

The Burmese people are a simple-minded, lazy people. They are honest and polite, very generous to strangers. They like a quiet life, smoking and gossiping and sleeping through the day and listening to wild music and singing through half the night.

Does that remind you of anyone in your class at school?

2 False. The Thuggees had their own secret code and 'Pass the tobacco' actually meant 'Strangle him now!' The Thuggees got away with so many murders because they were ordinary villagers most days but ruthless killers when they joined a party of travelling strangers. Thuggees hardly ever killed British travellers though.

3 True. The Afghan Nikkuls thought John Nicholson was a god! He had great power – when an Afghan prince spat at Nicholson's feet, Nich made him lick it up! Britain never conquered the rest of the Afghans. The fierce tribesmen vanished into their mountain hide-outs. They attacked British supply columns, cut telegraph wires or picked off small patrols. They crept up to towns and attacked army families at night. As Colonel Hutchinson said calmly in the 1898 fighting:

PING! ZING! ZIP! POP!

It is extremely unpleasant, this whiz and spatter of bullets while you are at dinner or trying to enjoy a pipe round a camp fire before you go to bed!

4 False. It's what the Burmese *believed*, but in fact the holy woman was shot dead during the battle! Two British soldiers were kidnapped by the Burmese in 1824 and that gave the Brits the excuse to invade. 3,586 British troops captured Rangoon – but by 1826, the end of the war, 3,115 of those men had died in Burma. Only 150 of them died in battles – the rest died from diseases like cholera. The war cost Britain £13 million but the victory added another fat chunk to the Empire.

5 True. The Indian Mutiny broke out in 1857 when Indian soldiers in the British Army revolted. The British soldiers were trapped in the northern Indian city of Lucknow for several months (which is why they ran out of tobacco). Not a day went by without a death. The Indians dug mines under the city walls of Lucknow and blew them up – but the first one was too short and they just blew a hole in the ground outside the walls. Somebody couldn't measure! In the end more British soldiers came and rescued the trapped troops.

6 False. More died of disease than battle. But at one time the biggest killer of all was booze! The army boozer was open all day and the men could buy almost two litres of rum for 10p. An officer in India said…

There were men dying every day from drink which did more for death than fever!

HE'LL LIKE IT HERE

WHY?

HE'S AMONGST SPIRITS

Drunken soldiers were often arrested by Indian police using a neat weapon. The Indian police carried nets! They threw them over the drunk's head, knocked him off his feet and rolled him up! Then he was carted back to his army camp. Why don't teachers use that on school bullies?

7 True. A troop of British soldiers was marching by a river when a crocodile appeared and fancied a bit of Brit. The man died and his mates took their revenge by shooting any crocs they saw. (At least they weren't short of food.)

WAITER! BRING ME A CROCODILE SANDWICH—AND MAKE IT SNAPPY!

8 False … probably. When the Indian soldiers rebelled against their British rulers they massacred British women and children. British newspapers showed drawings of the Indians throwing babies on their bayonets, but these pictures were meant to stir up British horror and they aren't proof that it actually happened.

HERE'S A DRAWING OF ME KICKING THE WINNING GOAL IN LAST YEAR'S F.A. CUP FINAL

WOW! IT MUST BE TRUE

9 False. Robert Clive was a rogue who won lots of India for Britain – and made himself a fortune, of course. He captured the city of Arcot in 1751. Indian armies surrounded the city and they sent elephants with spikes on their heads to batter down the gates. Clive's defenders shot at the elephants with muskets. That didn't kill the poor jumbos – but it made them very angry! So the elephants charged *the other way* and trampled hundreds of Indians. Clive 'saved' Arcot.

IS THIS ELEPHANT WILD? WILD? HE'S LIVID!

(By the way, what is the difference between an African elephant and an Indian elephant? About 3,000 miles!)

10 True. The Brits who took revenge on Indian rebels were among the most blood-thirsty in the bloody history of Britain.

Dreadful down under

In 1788 six shiploads of convicts arrived at Port Jackson in Australia. 570 men and 160 women stepped ashore while the native Aborigine people shouted 'Warra! Warra!' at them.

Talk Aborigine

But what does 'Warra! Warra!' mean?
a) G'day! G'day!
b) Funny people! Funny people!
c) Go away! Go away!

Answer:

c) The Aborigines were not pleased to see the British convicts land. They thought they looked like bad news – and they were right!

Little terror

Of these first convicts the youngest was how old?
a) nineteen b) fifteen c) nine

Answer:

c) John Hudson was a nine-year-old chimney sweep. He must have felt a bit lost, poor kid! After all, there weren't a lot of chimneys in Australia in those days. He'd have to get a new job – kangaroo-pouch-sweep, maybe?

The oldest convict was Dorothy Handland and her job in England had been a rag dealer. Dorothy was 88 years old and it's amazing she survived that journey of 36 *weeks*! forty-eight of the other convicts had died on the journey.

Terrifying Tasmania

The Aborigines of Tasmania had lived on their island, cut off from Australia, for 12,000 years. They were Stone Age people, but they got along well enough, and up to 20,000 lived on the island when the Brits arrived in 1802. Eighty years later there were NONE.

Where did these simple (and fairly harmless) people go? They were wiped out by a Great British idea.

WHAT A GREAT PLACE TO SEND OUR CONVICTS!

Of course there were convicts at Port Jackson in Australia. But how could you punish a really rotten convict who kept breaking the laws – a sort of 'super-convict'? Why not send him (or her) to Tasmania! No need to build a prison – just dump the convicts on the island and let them wander round to live or die...

...OR KILL

These wandering criminals were known as 'bushrangers' and they brought terror to the natives of Tasmania ... the Aborigines. The bushrangers killed the Aborigines as if it were a game. Aborigine men were tied to trees and used for target practice. As one brutal bushranger said...

I'd shoot an Aborigine as easily as I'd shoot a sparrow. And at the same time I get a lot of fun from this sort of sport!

But they didn't stop there. A witness reported...

One bushranger, known as Carrots, killed an Aborigine man. Then he seized the dead man's wife. He cut off the man's head and fastened it round the wife's neck. Then he drove the weeping woman off to his den to be his slave.

55

Many Aborigine women were kept as slaves and chained in the bushranger homes till they were needed for work. One bushranger claimed…

Whenever I want her for anything I take a burning stick from the fire and press it on her skin!

But there was one cruelty that shocked even the other bushrangers. A baby was snatched from its mother and buried alive in the ground up to its neck. Believe me, you would NOT want to know what was done to the baby's head…

The savage snobs

The convicts had a small excuse for their evil behaviour…

WE CONVICTS HAVE TRAVELLED HALFWAY ROUND THE WORLD WHILE OUR FRIENDS AND FAMILIES DIED ON THE SHIPS; WE ARE FLOGGED AND STARVED. WE HAVE TO BE HARD TO SURVIVE. BUT WHAT ABOUT THE POSH FOLK? EH? WHAT ABOUT THEM?

The convicts shared the island with the governors and their families who lived as grandly as they did back in Britain. In some posh areas of Tasmania the ladies and gentlemen hunted Aborigines for 'sport'. If one of these ladies had written a letter home it may have looked like this…

Risden
Tasmania
24 July 1821

Darling Mummy,

Here we are in this awful country. I am so bored most of the time. But yesterday we had some sport. I prepared a picnic for my dear Gerald and we set off with a bunch of friends into the bush to hunt the natives. We took the hunting dogs with us to sniff them out. Usually the dogs chase the natives out of the bush and the chaps shoot them down as they run.

Yesterday the sport wasn't so good. But clever Gerald had thought of that! He'd brought with us a native woman prisoner. He set her free to run home and she made a wonderful target for the bullets!

Did I tell you, Gerald has a barrel of vinegar? Every time he kills a native he cuts off the ears and pickles them in the barrel. Clever old Gerald has almost filled the barrel!

And my Gerald is so witty! Last week he took two pistols from the house —one was loaded and one was not. He found a friendly native and showed him the pistols. Then Gerald placed the empty pistol to his own head and pulled the trigger—of course it clicked, but nothing happened. Then he gave the loaded pistol to the native and told him to do the same. The simple chap blew his brains out against a tree trunk! Laugh? I nearly wept with laughter.

Of course the natives sometimes fight back and burn the settlers' houses. But then the army go after them and destroy them. The local newspaper said, 'For every British settler they

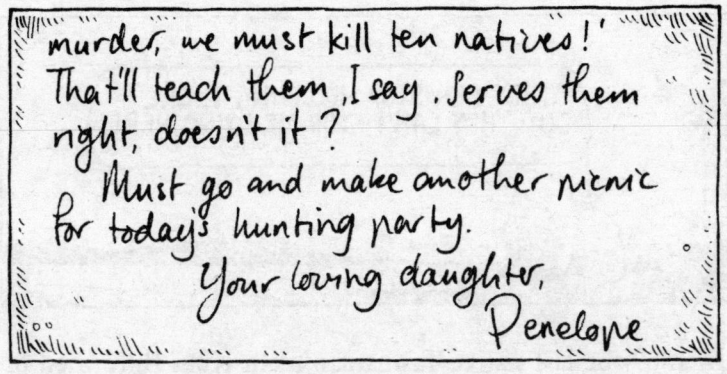

murder, we must kill ten natives!'
That'll teach them, I say. Serves them
right, doesn't it?
  Must go and make another picnic
for today's hunting party.
        Your loving daughter,
                    Penelope

This letter is made-up but the stories in it are all terribly true.

The end

The Tasmanian Aborigines were vanishing.

- More Aborigines died of diseases the British brought and the tribes shrank.
- Settlers spread across the island and the British cattle replaced the Aborigines' kangaroos so the Aborigines starved. The tribes shrank again.
- The long-suffering natives finally stopped having children altogether and that eventually made the tribes die out entirely.
- Some Aborigines even began to slaughter their own children … babies can get in the way when you are fighting to survive.

In 1832 a 'kind' British Christian had 220 Aborigines shipped off to Flinders Island where they could make themselves a nice new home – except the Island was a bleak, cold place. The Aborigines could see their old home, Tasmania, across the water but they could never return. It's said that many died of home-sickness.

In 1869 the last native Tasmanian man, King Billy, died of poisoning from drinking too much alcohol. But STILL the brutal Brits wouldn't let him rest. They wanted to study his body! So a surgeon…

- cut off his head.
- skinned the head and placed the skin on another skull.
- sent the head back to Britain.

Others cut off King Billy's hands and finally the whole body was stolen from the grave.

As you can imagine, the last woman, Truganini, was worried the same would happen to her corpse. She died in 1876, the last native Tasmanian. To save her being chopped and changed she was buried inside the walls of a prison. The plan didn't work though, and her bones ended up on display in Hobart Museum, Tasmania.

The Brutal Brits had wiped out an entire race in just 70 years. Here's how…

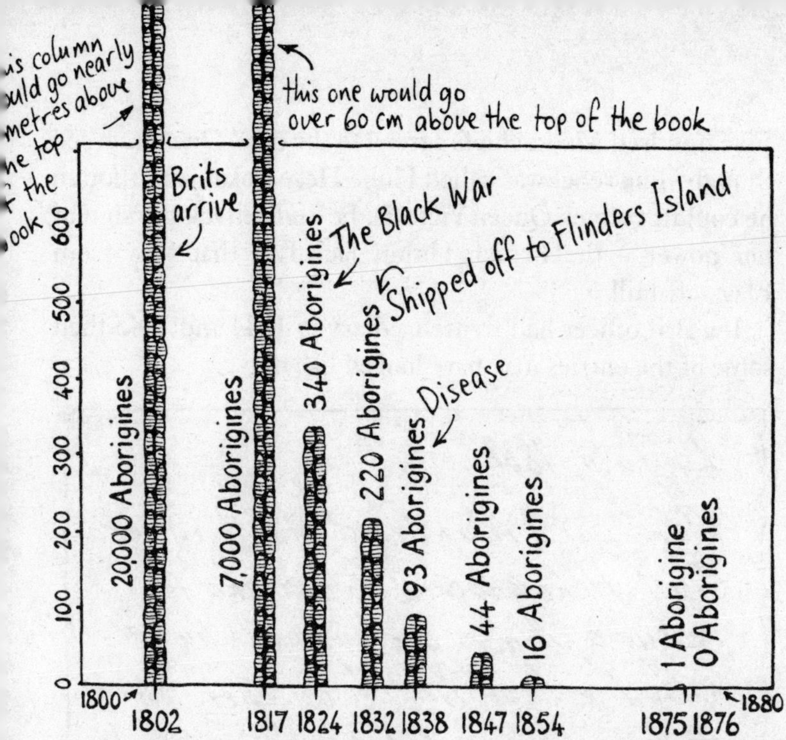

this column would go nearly metres above the top of the book

this one would go over 60 cm above the top of the book

600

500

400

300

200

100

0

Brits arrive

20,000 Aborigines

7,000 Aborigines

340 Aborigines — **The Black War**

220 Aborigines — **Shipped off to Flinders Island**

93 Aborigines — Disease

44 Aborigines

16 Aborigines

1 Aborigine

0 Aborigines

1800 1802 1817 1824 1832 1838 1847 1854 1875 1876 1880

Nasty New Zealand

Meanwhile, across in New Zealand the Brits *failed* to wipe out the natives, the Maoris.

The Brit settlers used a common trick. They made peace with the natives then got the natives to sign over the land to Queen Victoria. The Brits gave the Maoris booze and guns – the Maoris gave the Brits New Zealand. In the words of the old British proverb...

FAIR EXCHANGE IS NO ROBBERY

Five hundred Maori chiefs agreed to the deal! One disagreed though. The rebel was called Hone Heke Pokai, and though he couldn't attack Queen Victoria, he *could* attack the sign of her power – the British Union Jack flag that flew from Flagstaff Hill.

If a Brit officer had written a diary of 1844 and 1845 then some of the entries may have looked like this...

20 July 1844

There was a Maori raid on Kororareka. Chief Heke attacked Kororareka to rescue a Maori girl who was living with the local British butcher. She didn't even want to be rescued, poor girl!! She used to be one of Heke's servants and she always called Heke 'Pig's head'. No one was hurt in the raid - but oddly one of Heke's friends chopped down our flag-pole!

17 August 1844

Our new flag-pole stood proudly on Flagstaff Hill-until this morning.

Some Maoris sneaked up and chopped it down – again! It's guarded by 170 soldiers sent from Australia. We can't let sneaky Heke get away with it! Victoria's flag shall fly!

9 September 1844

New flag-pole chopped down a third time. This is beyond a joke! Britannia rules the waves and Britons never, never, never shall have their flags flattened. Captain Fitzroy has a marvellous plan to nobble the natives He is taking a huge old ship's mast – thick as a tree trunk! The Maoris can attack it, but it will take them so long to chop down we'll have the army there to stop them. The post is defended by a small fort. That's the end of horrible Heke's game!

11 March 1845

Disaster! The flag-pole is down! The men at the fort were digging ditches when Heke's men leapt on them and massacred them with their knives and coral-studded clubs. Maoris also attacked the town and set it on fire. The biggest explosion was in the gunpowder dump - not caused by the Maoris, but by a British workman with a careless spark from his pipe! I always thought smoking was bad for your health. We British retreated to the safety of a warship - six men who returned were hacked down. Final score, 19 British settlers dead and 29 wounded.

Rotten revenge

Of course the Brits sent in the army to get revenge. The band played 'Rule Britannia' as they landed. The British soldiers had the help of the friendly Maoris plus some 'pakeha' Maoris – British men who had gone to live with the natives. Men like Jackey Marmon, an ex-convict, who said he had…

- Slaughtered rival Maoris in battle and
- Eaten them at cannibal feasts!

Jackey could have been lying about noshing on natives. But

it *was* true that a dead British soldier was found with neat pieces of meat sliced off his legs. Perhaps Jackey's Maori friends *did* eat people from time to time.

The Brits finally defeated Heke but only by treachery. The Maoris had become Christians and thought Sunday was a day of peace. The Brits (who were also supposed to be Christians) attacked on a Sunday when the Maoris were praying. (Which was a bit of a cheat! A bit like taking a football penalty kick while the goalkeeper is blowing his nose.)

And that flag-pole? Heke died of a disease in 1850, six years after he started flattening flag-poles – but while he lived that flag-pole was never raised again. So who won? No one. Who lost? As usual, everyone.

Awful for animals

As they explored the world the British found plenty of new and exciting animals to kill and even sometimes exterminate. The British Empire was certainly awful to animals.

> *HORRIBLE HISTORIES HEALTH WARNING:*
> Do not read this if you are an animal lover.

Evil for elephants

African elephants had a bad time once the Brits arrived. They were simply massacred for their tusks. Why did the people of Britain need so many tusks? For something important? Oh, yeah!

They were used for...

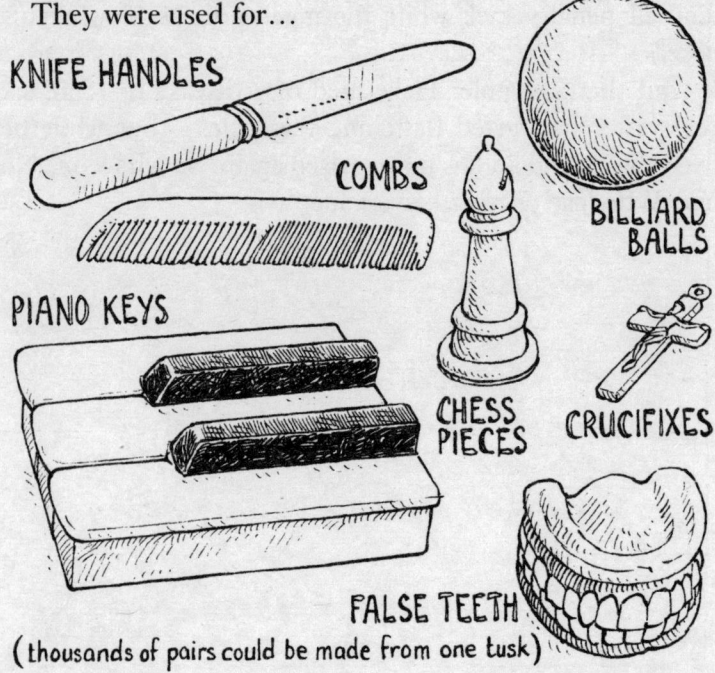

KNIFE HANDLES

COMBS

BILLIARD BALLS

PIANO KEYS

CHESS PIECES

CRUCIFIXES

FALSE TEETH

(thousands of pairs could be made from one tusk)

Some tusks were so large that they were used as door posts in houses.

Indian elephants – the ones with the smaller ears – were used by the Brits to move logs. They could be very clever, the Brits discovered. One elephant was said by an eye-witness to be especially clever…

As he passed a water pipe, feeling that he wanted a drink, he turned on the tap with the tip of his trunk and drank his fill and then went on, leaving the tap running. His owner said that it was his one bad habit. He always forgot to turn the tap off again!

Cute! But not as clever as this elephant…

A transport elephant was carrying a load of tents across a river when it got its feet into a quicksand. It immediately seized with its trunk, one after another, three natives who were walking alongside it and pushed them down under its feet to gain a foothold. This was

intelligent of it but was a thing
that wasn't done in the best
elephantine circles and the poor
thing was condemned to wear
heavy chain bracelets round each
foot for the rest of its life.

The punishment for another extraordinary elephant was
even more cruel…

Once when we had twenty elephants
in camp one of these had a grudge
against its driver and, seeing him
asleep in the midday rest time,
it put out its foot to stamp on
him but made a bad shot and
only crushed his thigh.

There was an immense hullabaloo
and the offending elephant was
taken by the other drivers and
tied to a tree. The remaining
nineteen elephants were then
formed up and told of the offence
committed by number Twenty and
were invited to give him a hiding.

> *This they did. Each elephant, taking a length of chain in its trunk, marched past in single file behind the culprit, and each, as he went by, slung the chain round with tremendous force on to his hind parts.*

Ouch!

Hideous for hippos

Life wasn't much fun for cute, cuddly hippos once the Brits arrived in Africa. The Brits liked to kill them (for fun, not because the Brits were hungry or in danger). Here's how...

- Lie by a watering-hole and watch where the hippo raises its eyes and nose.
- Aim your rifle at the spot.
- The hippo will always shove up his snout in the same spot.
- When he does it again, fire!

A hippo killed this way once made a great treat for Robert Baden-Powell's men. He described the feast they had.

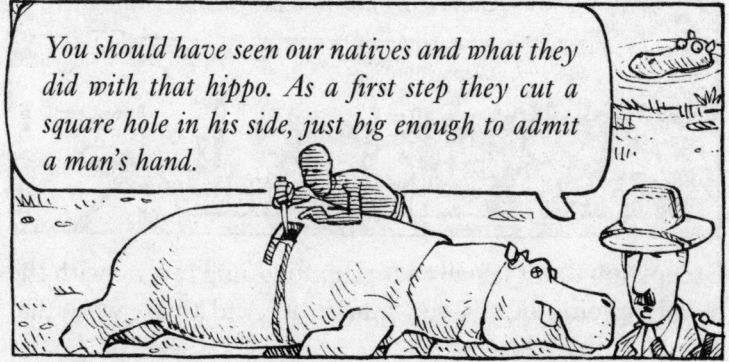

> *You should have seen our natives and what they did with that hippo. As a first step they cut a square hole in his side, just big enough to admit a man's hand.*

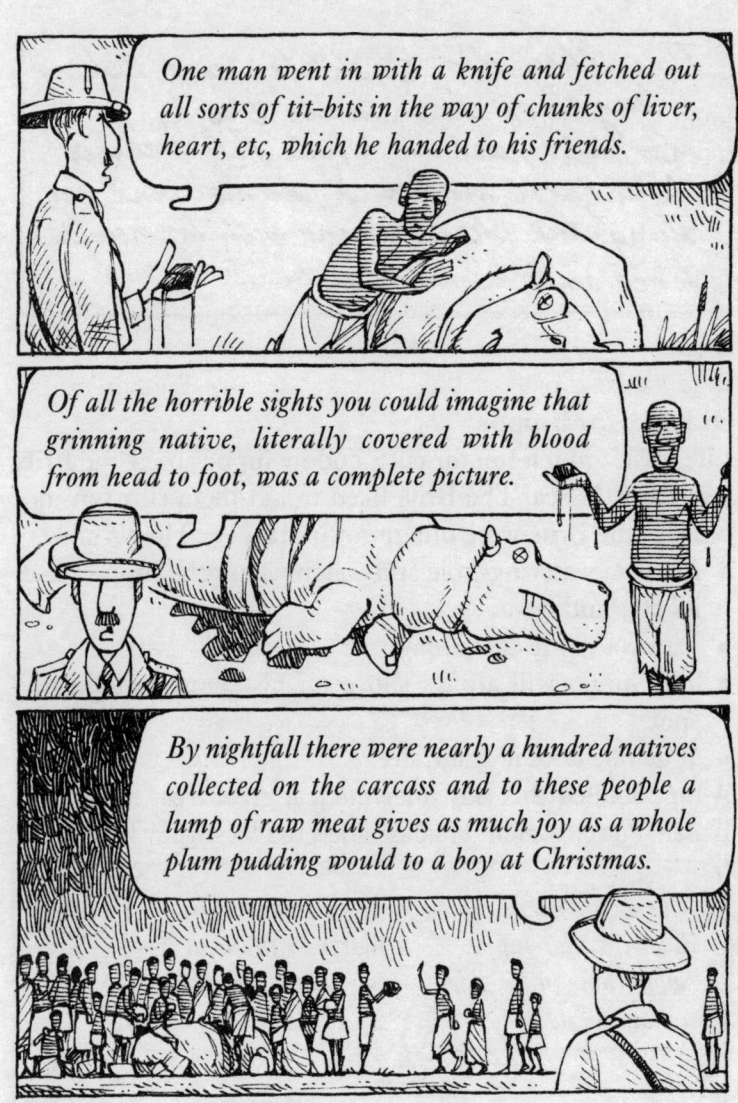

Except you don't usually eat plum pudding raw ... with the blood running out as you munch it. And that's what that group did! Yeuch!

Deadly for dogs

Wherever the British army went, dogs went with them. Some of the mad mutts seemed to 'adopt' the soldiers. Sadly this was a mistake – if they picked the losing side! Look what happened in Maiwand, Afghanistan, in 1880…

The Brits were fighting the Afghans … and losing. There were just 11 Brits left in a ruined town. They were surrounded by Afghans and the Afghans were waving knives at them … the Brits would be cruelly chopped up if they were taken alive, so they fought on. An Afghan officer described their end…

These men charged from the shelter of a garden and died with their faces to the enemy, fighting to the death. So fierce was their charge, and so brave their actions, no Afghan dared to approach to cut them down. So, standing in the open, back to back, firing steadily, every shot counting, surrounded by thousands, these British soldiers died. It was not until the last man was shot down that the Afghans dared to advance on them. The behaviour of those last eleven was the wonder of all who saw it.

Stirring stuff. But it wasn't just the soldiers who died at Maiwand. The army was a 'family' and, like most families, it had its pets – dogs. And the dogs fought and wounded any Afghans daft enough to get too close! So the dogs had to die too.

One British captain and his dog died together. The Afghans buried the man and then, as an insult, threw his dog into his grave too. But the Victorian Brits didn't see it as an insult! They saw it as two brave fighters resting in peace, side by side.

The good news is that a dog called Bobbie survived the same battle. Bobbie was a small, woolly, white dog with a brown face and brown ears on top of his flat head. His master, Sergeant Kelly, fought and fell with the Last Eleven. Bobbie fought on and was chopped with a sword.

Brave Bobbie got up and limped off to return to his home fort – 50 miles away! He survived and returned to Britain and fame.

Bobbie was dressed in a red jacket and presented to the queen. Dog-loving Vic examined his wounds and pinned the Afghan War medal on his jacket.

Happy ending? Not really. Bored Bobbie strayed from the army camp in Gosport and got run over by a cab. You can still see his stuffed body in his Royal Berkshire regiment's museum in Salisbury … if looking at dead dogs is a hobby of yours!

Did you know…?
Brit army officers in India took a pack of fox-hounds over to steaming-hot India … to hunt jackals. But India was so hot the fox-hounds all died. (The jackals probably had a bit of a party!)

Gruesome games and sick sports

The Empire let Brits try new games they hadn't imagined before. Games like hog-hunting (aka 'pig-sticking'), which is great fun … unless you happen to be a pig.

Brutal for boars
The pigs were 'wild boars' and they were hunted by wildly boring men like Robert Baden-Powell (the chap who is remembered today because he invented the Boy Scouts). This is how Lord Robert Baden-Powell described hog-hunting …

The Boar

The boar is brave and tough, as fast as a horse, and can jump where a horse cannot. He stands as high as a table, is long in the leg, and very muscular. He doesn't hesitate to swim a river, even when it is inhabited by crocodiles.

Well, that is the fellow we hunt in India on horseback with spears, and there is no sport can touch hog-hunting for excitement or valuable training.

The Hunt

Three or four riders form a 'party'. Beaters drive the pig out of his lair in the jungle, and the party then race after him, but for the first three-quarters of a mile he can generally outrun them. The honours then go to the man who can first catch and spear him. But as soon as the boar finds himself in danger of being overtaken he either 'jinks', that is, darts off sideways, or else turns round and charges his pursuer.

A spear-thrust, unless delivered in a vital spot, has little effect beyond making him more angry, and then follows a good deal of charging on both sides, and it is not always the boar that comes off second best. He has a wonderful power of quick and effective use of his tusks and many a good horse has been fatally gashed by the animal he was hunting.

Hang on, Lord Bleedin-Trowell!. The poor *horse* wasn't hunting the boar! *You* were!

Chief Scout Robert obviously had some funny ideas about 'sport' – look at his idea of killing a hyena...

Big Game

I also had a ride after a hyena with a number of Arabs, one of the most alarming games I ever took part in, for the plan was to gallop him down and surround him and for every man then to loose off his rifle at him.

As we were in a circle we were firing inwards and towards each other, but fortunately, being mounted, the guns were pointed downwards and the many bullets which missed the hyena went into the sand.

A gang of men shooting at an exhausted hyena? Call that sport? Why not just go to the fairground and shoot at ducks?

Still, it was boars that Robert was mostly interested in. And when he wasn't murdering them he was adopting them! But even his pet baby-boar ended up pretty dead.

Algernon

I was lucky enough to capture in the jungle a very young "squeaker," as young boars are called.

I took him home and kept him for a long time, and found him a delightful and interesting young friend. I got him to come to me when I called him for food.

There was an old stump of a tree in the garden around which Algernon (for that was his name) was never tired of galloping. He used to practise running a figure of eight round the stump, cutting at it with his baby tusks every time he passed, right and left alternately, thus practising for battles that were to come.

I had an old English horse loose in the field who, being a staunch pig-sticker, used to go for Algernon whenever she saw him. The little beggar loved leading her on till she tore after him, with ears back, eager to trample on him or to kick him if she could only get him.

Unfortunately one day some dogs about the place saw this chase going on and joined in and soon ran down poor little Algernon and bit and tore him so badly that he had to be killed. The killing was done with the spear as was right for his being a boar.

Never mind, Algernon would have made a good pork sausage. Why not try this recipe if your pet pig is ever attacked by dogs? It's for the Empire dish called 'Boudin'.

Recipe for Boudin

You need:
4 cups of pig blood
1 pound of pig fat
Some pig's intestines
1 cup of milk
4 onions
Mixed spices to taste
Salt and pepper

To make:
Mix the blood and milk.
Stir in the chopped pig fat, onions, spices, salt and pepper.

Mix well and stuff into the intestines.
Cook in hot water that is not quite boiling.
The sausage is cooked when it is a dark maroon colour and the filling is as thick as soft cheese.
Fry it up in butter before eating.

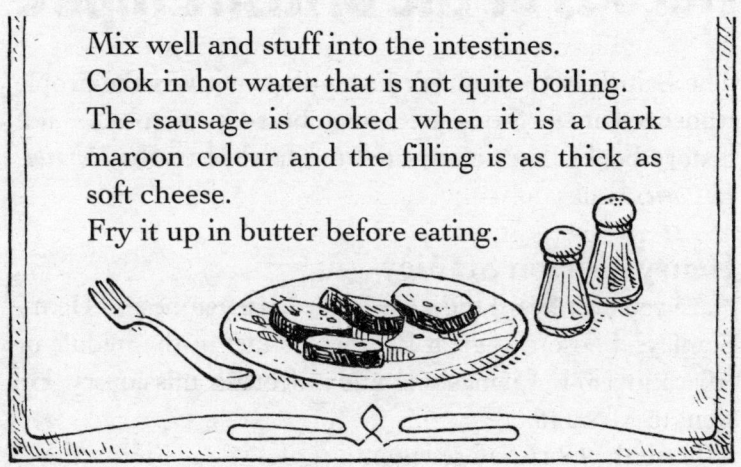

So, go on ... make a pig of yourself!

Did you know...?
In South Africa in 1879 the Brit soldiers found something they said was better than pig-sticking. A soldier described an attack by the Brits (on horses) on Zulu warriors (on foot)...

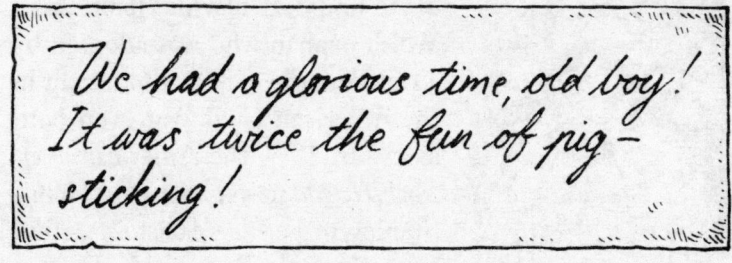

We had a glorious time, old boy! It was twice the fun of pig-sticking!

Heroes of the British Empire

The British Empire wasn't just a place – it was the people who lived in it. Some are remembered as heroes ... but history books don't always tell the terrible truth. *Horrible Histories* books do!

Henry Morton Stanley

Have you ever heard the story of Dr Livingstone and Henry Stanley? Those two great Brit heroes met in the middle of Africa in 1871. Livingstone was a Scottish missionary. He went to Africa to...

- teach the Christian religion.
- explore.
- stop African slavery.

Livingstone was the good guy. A true Brit hero. But there were no phones or faxes or e-mails in those days – just bicycle tyres and billiard balls* – so the Brit people didn't hear from Livingstone for a year or so.

That's when Henry Stanley set off to find dear David. Henry was a Welsh orphan who was adopted by a rich American, and who fought in the American Civil War – on both sides! In 1871 the American *New York Herald* newspaper paid Henry Stanley to get a great story – find Livingstone! Poor old Doctor Livingstone – he didn't even know he was lost!

* Hang on and you'll see why they became horribly historically important!

After walking hundreds of miles, through dozens of dangers, Stanley finally came across Livingstone and said those mega-cool words … four of the most famous words in Brit Empire history…

DOCTOR LIVINGSTONE, I PRESUME

Of course Doc Dave SHOULD have said…

NO! I'M A MONKEY'S UNCLE YOU BRAIN-DEAD DINGBAT!

Instead, he said that other famous word in Brit Empire history … 'Yes.'

Poor old Dave died a couple of years later. He was kneeling at his bed, as though he'd just been praying, when they found him. (But we don't know what his last prayer was. Probably, 'Please don't let me die!' or something.)

BUT … Brit history books never go on to tell you what Henry Stanley did for the rest of his life. It was so horrible, teachers wouldn't dare tell you in case you throw up over your desk and they have to mop it up! So here goes – have the sick bucket handy…

Horrible Henry
Henry Stanley was hired by King Leopold of Belgium to help Belgium conquer the Congo area of Africa (the bit in the middle).

Bicycle tyres had been invented and the world would pay a fortune for the rubber that came from trees in the Congo. The world was also keen on ivory for billiard balls that grew on elephants in the Congo . . I mean the *ivory* grew on the elephants, not the billiard balls.

Horrible Henry set about his job with true Empire spirit – and a real talent for cruelty and greed. He was also a rotten racist. Here are the top ten terrors of his visit...

1 Secret slaves. King Leopold and HH told the world they were freeing the Africans from Arab slavers. In fact, working for HH and his Belgian bosses was worse than slavery. Men, women and children had to carry huge loads for their white masters – a seven-year-old child would have to carry 10-kilo loads all day through the steaming jungles. One visitor reported...

> *I watched a file of poor devils, chained by the neck. There were about a hundred of them, trembling and fearful before the overseer, who strolled by whirling a whip. For each strong, healthy fellow there were many skeletons dried up like mummies, their skin worn out, damaged by deep scars, covered with bleeding wounds. No matter how fit they were, they all had to get on with the job. They were beasts of burden with monkey legs.*

They were fed on a handful of rice and stinking dried fish.

2 Cheerful chiquotte. The Africans of the Congo weren't slaves – they had a choice! They could produce enough rubber for Stanley's rubber farms – or face the chiquotte.

What's that? It's a specially cruel whip. If you fancy making one to try a 'Living History' lesson, with your teacher as the rubber collector, here's how...

The sharp edges meant the whip cut into the victim's skin.
- A few blows would leave you scarred for life.
- 25 lashes could knock you out.
- One hundred or more (quite common) would often kill you.

Finally the sufferer was expected to pick himself (or herself) up and give a military salute!

3 Fastened families. You don't want to work on the rubber farm? Fine ... Stanley's men would hold your wife and children prisoner until you do. Or, even nastier, those children could be thrown into the jungle and left to be eaten by the animals. Or thrown on the plains to be baked to death by the scorching sun. No food for those poor kids...

NOT EVEN A BAKED BEAN FOR THE BAKED BEING

You'll be pleased to know HH himself went hungry from time to time. On a journey through the Ituri rainforest he and his 389 men ran out of food. They survived by eating roasted ants.

4 Grim guns. Stanley's men had guns, the Africans didn't. This made fighting a bit one-sided, especially as their favourite weapon was the machine-gun. But even the ordinary rifle could be used against troublemakers in a cruel way. One of Stanley's pitiless policemen boasted...

> We surrounded the rebel camp and hid in the long grass. We watched the women as they crushed dried bananas to make flour. When we were ready I raised my rifle and shot one of the Africans clean through the chest. The game had started!

5 Handless horrors. Rebels had ears or noses sliced off. But worse was the way the police claimed their reward for capturing rebels – they chopped off an African's hand and were paid for every hand they collected. But there wasn't just an odd hand here and there – there were hundreds of hands and hundreds of bodies left to rot. At Lake Tumba, a Swedish missionary, E V Sjoblom wrote:

I saw … dead bodies floating on the lake with the right hands cut off, and the officer told me when I came back why they had been killed. It was all part of the war for rubber. When I crossed the stream I saw some dead bodies hanging down from the branches in the water. As I turned away my face at the horrible sight one of the native policemen said, 'Oh, that is nothing. A few days ago I returned from a fight, and I brought the white man 160 hands and they were thrown in the river.'

6 Terrible tricks. Stanley and his men used tricks to fool the Africans into signing over land to them.

- To make the Africans think they had magical powers, they attached batteries to their arms under their coats. When the white man grasped the black man's hand, the black man got an electric shock that nearly knocked him off his feet. (Don't try this on your grotty little brother at home!)
- Magnifying glasses were used to light cigars. The white man lied that he was a special friend of the sun, which lit his cigar. Then he threatened…

7 Pitiful prisoners. One village was captured, the people tied up and herded out. They were expected to carry heavy baskets that the soldiers gave them. The baskets contained food supplies … and some contained smoked human flesh! Prisoners had to march very quickly. One woman was dragged out with a baby in her arms; the soldiers took her baby and threw it into the grass to die. A lot of men were killed on the way and just left where they dropped.

8 Horrible heads. A British explorer who passed through Stanley Falls in 1895 reported that many African men, women and children had been brought to the Falls and their heads had been used by Captain Rom (of the Police Force) as a decoration around the flower beds in front of his house.

One of HH's men shot a native for fun and had the dead African's head packed in a box of salt and returned to London to be stuffed and mounted in a glass case.

9 Painful for pygmies. The Congo pygmies were usually a peaceful tribe, but they could be wicked. Many practised slavery and cannibalism. They went to war with anyone – even other pygmy clans – and their favourite trophy of a battle was a severed head or hand. In 1906, a pygmy from the Congo named Ota Benga was delivered to the Bronx zoo in the USA where he was actually put on display in a cage with an orang-utan. A group of African-American priests managed to get Benga released, and he stayed in the US until he killed himself ten years later.

10 Rich rewards. While Horrible Henry Stanley and King Leopold ruled the Congo half of the native people there died.

DID THE DREADFUL DUO GET WHAT THEY DESERVED?

NOT QUITE... KING LEOPOLD DIED AS THE RICHEST MAN IN THE WORLD

BUT DIDN'T THE BRITS PUNISH HORRIBLE HENRY?

NOT EXACTLY. VICTORIA KNIGHTED HIM AND MADE HIM SIR HENRY STANLEY IN 1899 AND THE BRIT PEOPLE MADE HIM A MEMBER OF PARLIAMENT FROM 1895 TO 1900

The only good news is he didn't get his dying wish – he wanted to be buried in Westminster Abbey next to the good Doctor Livingstone! In fact he was buried in Furze Hill in Surrey ... and he still is.

Cool courage...

People in Britain believed their soldiers were better and braver than any other soldiers in the world – even when they got stuffed by the enemy! The British public loved tales of terrific courage. Some famously Cool Britannia heroes included...

The Light Brigade

At the battle of Balaclava (in the Ukraine) in 1856 the Light Brigade were ordered to charge at the Russian cannons. It was suicide. They did it and they died – and the horses became a bit of a mess too! Did anyone ask the horses if they wanted to charge?

The Private of the Buffs

Even common, dirty little Brit soldiers didn't give in. Private John Moyse (who came from Scotland) joined a Brit regiment called the Buffs. In the China War of 1860 a Chinese lord captured Moyse and told him to kneel. Moyse said, 'We Brits don't kneel in front of you Chinese! Not even a poor Brit like me will bow to a posh Chinese lord like you!' The Lord had Moyse's cheeky Scottish head lopped off.

Moyse became famous when Sir Francis Hastings Doyle

wrote a poem about him – 'The Private of the Buffs'. It said he was a true Brit – standing up to bullies even though it cost him his life! You wouldn't want to read the whole thing nowadays but a sharp sample goes…

The Private of the Buffs

And thus with eyes that would not shrink,
With knee to man un-bent,
Un-faltering on its dreadful brink,
To his red grave he went.

The poem should have been about using your head not losing your head! Something like this…

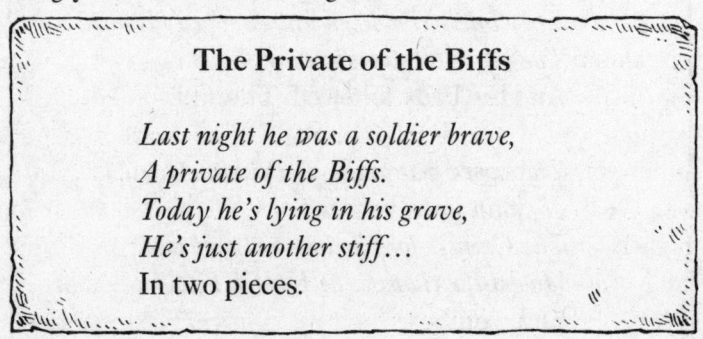

The Private of the Biffs

Last night he was a soldier brave,
A private of the Biffs.
Today he's lying in his grave,
He's just another stiff…
In two pieces.

He stood before the Chinese lord
And showed no drop of fear.
A British heart beat in his chest,
But no brain between his ears...
Or anywhere else for that matter.

'Just kneel down there!' the Chinese said
'Kneel down, I'll spare your neck!'
'I won't! Cos I'm a battling Brit!
I won't, I say, by heck!'
Oooops!

The Chinese lord he shrugged and sighed,
'You are a brain-dead Biff
To make me lop your silly head!'
The lord, you know, was miffed...
A bit put out.

So Private Moyse they took him out,
And made him dig a pit.
They knelt him down and chopped his head
The head fell straight in it...
And the body followed. Thump!

The sword was quick, so Private Moyse
No pain in his neck felt.
The Chinese lord he laughed and said,
'To get the chop ... he KNELT...
So I won!'

Moyse lost his head, his grave was red,
And don't you feel like blubbin'?
He didn't die for Britain's queen!
He died cos he was stubborn...
As a mule.

Did you know...?
The Chinese later said Private Moyse had died of drink! Perhaps mad Moyse's messy end was just a story? Private Moyse's boss, Captain Brabazon, *was* beheaded by the Chinese.

Dead brave

Dying bravely was seen as a 'British' thing to do. Yet the Brits admired their enemies who died bravely too ... so maybe it wasn't so 'British' after all! Brave enemies included...

- Tartar warriors in China who killed themselves in a Chinese temple rather than be captured alive.
- South African Zulus who fell in heaps as they ran at the Brit guns ... then stopped to pick up their dead friends and used them as shields! Would you do that to your friend? (Better not answer that!)
- Sind troops in India who attacked Brit guns with swords and were massacred, of course.

And talking of Sind, you need to know about the only Brit Empire joke ever invented! Brit General Sir Charles Napier captured Sind in February 1843. He sent a message back to Britain. It was the Latin word…

It means, 'I have sinned'. Get it? 'I have Sind!' Oh, never mind.

There are hundreds of examples of Brits mowing down native peoples – guns against spears. The Brits SAID they admired the courage of the enemy – but that didn't stop the massacres!

Popham's people

A Brit force attacked Buenos Aires in 1806 to 'free' the South American people from their rotten Spanish rulers. The Brit leader, Admiral Hope Popham, hoped to pop 'em off quickly. When the Brit soldiers attacked, Admiral Pop said…

They marched forward with all the cool courage that is the sign of the British soldier.

That was what the British soldier was supposed to be like. Cool and courageous – Old Pop should have added … and 'cruel'. Here's why…

Admiral Popham had a problem with his Spanish prisoners of war. If he kept them they'd eat the food his men needed. If he set them free they'd join the Spanish friends and fight against him. So Popham abandoned the Spanish prisoners on a rock in the middle of the Rio Plate river.

The Spanish prisoners had...
- no food.
- no fresh water.
- no shelter.

It would have been a slow death for the Spanish but for one thing ... seals. Yes! Those cute, fluffy, furry, flabby, lovable little creatures! The Spanish were so pleased to see them! They smashed the seals to death, skinned them and made water-wings from the seal skins! Forty trapped prisoners used them to swim to safety!

Did you know...?
The Brits could be pretty mean to their own soldiers. Men who stole or refused to obey an order could be whipped on

their bare back with a whip called a cat-o'-nine-tails. (It was called that because there were nine strings to the lash, not because it was made of dead cat.) The flogging could go on till the man was dead. Then, in 1829, the number of lashes was cut to just 500!

Food was usually dreadful. A soldier was paid 12 pence a day – then charged 6 pence for his food! But the most cruel charge of all was for the soldier who had to pay for his own coffin! The man fell sick when he was on duty in Australia and the doctor said he would die. The army carpenter made his coffin but then the man got better! The army still sent the soldier the bill, though! He paid it, but insisted that he keep the coffin in his room. It was fitted with shelves and held all his clothes neatly.

Nasty natives

The Brits battered people all around the world. But the natives could be pretty nasty too. They often had horrible habits that disgusted the Brits and may even disgust you! Here are a top evil eight with a disgustometer alongside…

Thuggees (India 1200-ish to 1840-ish)

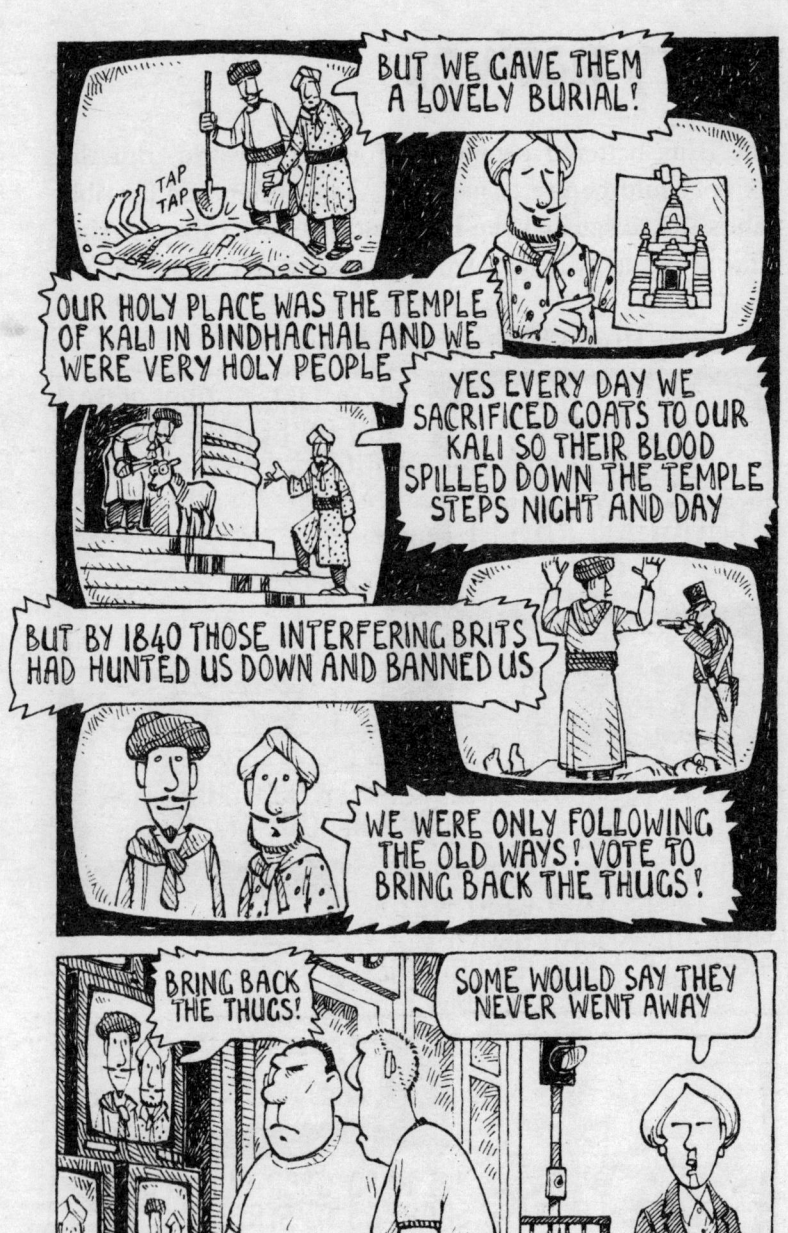

96

Nasty note:

How is it religious to go around strangling people? Well…

- It's all because of this Kool Kali that the Thuggees worshipped. Modern pictures of her show her standing on a dead body.
- She has four arms, a necklace of 50 human skulls and a belt of human arms while she is holding an axe, a severed human head, a trident and a bowl of blood! (It's handy having four arms!) Her long tongue drips with the fresh blood of her enemies.

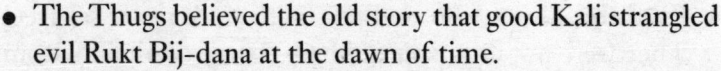

- The Thugs believed the old story that good Kali strangled evil Rukt Bij-dana at the dawn of time.
- Kali then created two humans from the sweat of her brow.
- Kali ordered the humans to worship her … but to strangle anyone who didn't worship her!

How did they manage to strangle travellers when the travellers MUST have known the dangers and been prepared? Well…

- The Thugs pretended to be travellers and mixed with them on the journey. These journeys were usually between November and May, the 'travelling season'.

- They were quick killers, using their silk scarves as a noose and attacking from behind – noose over the head, knee in the back and … Cccct! When they had time the Thuggees ate and slept among their victims' corpses.

- The Thugs cut the victims' bodies with holy gashes and then buried them – or threw them down wells, which made the water taste awful. They burned the things they didn't take with them so they left no traces: they were 'thuggee' … hidden.

How did the Brits get rid of these Kali killing, noose-knotting, goat-goring, scarf-stranglers? Well…

- In the 1830s Brits (led by a ruthless soldier, Colonel William Sleeman) managed to snatch some stranglers and offered a deal: 'Tell us who the other Thugs are and we'll spare your life.' One of Sleeman's jobs was to dig up the victims!

- Even the Thugs who told the truth were never set free! They were put in prison and had a tattoo on their bottom eyelid with the word 'Thug'.

- Thugs who didn't give up their wicked ways were hanged – but not with a nice silk scarf! By the 1840s most of the thuggery had ended. Not before time – a Thug named Buhram said he had strangled 931 people! (That must have stretched his silk scarf a bit!)

The Thugs are now gone from India but blood-dripping Kali is still one of India's most popular goddesses.

(Strange that the men we call 'thugs' today are usually football supporters … from Britain, waving scarves!)

DISGUSTOMETER RATING:

Canadian lacrosse (Canada, 1700s)

THE BUMPER BOOK OF SPORTS

No. 173: Lacrosse

You need:
A pitch about 100 metres by 60 metres.

A goal in a circle ten metres from each end of the pitch.

Two teams of ten. (Each player has a stick with a net on the end. If you haven't got lacrosse sticks then use a tadpole net.)

A ball. (Some people like to play lacrosse with a hard rubber ball about the size of a tennis ball. BUT it was said that some Canadian Indians used a human head instead of a ball. *The Bumper Book of Sports* does not advise this. A freshly chopped head will splatter blood and brains all over your strip, your face and the playing field – very slippery and dangerous. Of course you could use the head of a traffic warden – then you won't have a problem with splattered brains.)

RUBBER BALL   TENNIS BALL   DENNIS SMALL

To play:
Each team has a goalkeeper, three defenders, three midfielders and three attackers. There must always be four players in your own half and three in the enemy half.

Players can use their sticks to carry, catch or pass the ball and can kick it but not handle it.

Play four 15-minute quarters.

To score:
Pass the ball and shoot it into your opponents' net.
No tripping or hitting your opponents with your stick, but shoulder charges are allowed.

Nasty note:
The tale of the head for a ball may not be true – the Canadian Indians may have invented it to scare their enemies. But the following terrible tale *is* true. In 1763 the Brits had conquered Canada and a force of soldiers settled in Fort Michilimackinac. The Indians couldn't defeat the Brits while they sat in their fort, so they came up with a neat plan. They

said to the Brits, 'Say, you guys, would you like to come and watch us play lacrosse on the field outside the fort?' The Barmy Brits agreed. When the Indian players came close to the soldiers they threw away their lacrosse sticks and took out their tomahawks. Chop! Chop!

DISGUSTOMETER RATING:

Zulu Dingaan

From 1828 to 1838 a man called Dingaan was leader of the South African Zulu tribe – and Dingaan was not a nice man, as you'll discover in...

The *Horrible History* Zulu *Quiz*

Are you tough enough to be a Zulu chief like Dingaan? Just answer these simple questions and check your score. . .

1 How would you get to be Zulu chief in the first place?
a) Go down to the local job centre and fill in a form.

101

b) Be born a prince and wait patiently for your older brother, the king, to die.

c) Be born a prince and murder your brother, the king.

2 For most rulers, it's important to show off. How would you show the world you are a great Zulu chief?

a) Have jesters and dwarfs to entertain your guests.

b) Have lots of fat women for wives.

c) Have jesters, dwarfs AND loads of fat wives.

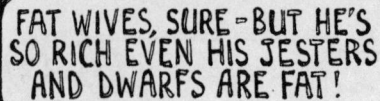

FAT WIVES, SURE – BUT HE'S SO RICH EVEN HIS JESTERS AND DWARFS ARE FAT!

3 Being top dog isn't all work and no play. How would you like to entertain yourself as Zulu chief?

a) Play football with your mates.

b) Hunt lions and other dangerous animals.

c) Have a palace glutton eat a whole goat for you.

BRAVO!

I HOPE HE DOESN'T WANT AN ENCORE

4 A friendly white Boer settler has returned 700 lost cattle to you – and cattle are a sign of wealth. How do you reward him?

a) Give him 70 cattle and two of your fat wives.

b) Spit on him and send him away with nothing.

c) Get him and his followers drunk, and kill them.

102

5 If you decide the man and his followers must die, how would you kill them?

a) Quickly and cleanly with a sharp chop of the axe while they are drunk and asleep.

b) Wait till they are awake and hang them.

c) Tie them up, take them to the Hill of Execution, bash their heads with clubs, then stick sharp wooden poles through their bodies from underneath. Let the man who helped you watch his followers die, then kill him last. Cut out his heart and liver.

6 You have 10,000 warriors. You come across a band of 460 white settlers at Blood River. What do you do to this pathetic mob of white men?

a) Spare their miserable lives.

b) Capture them and make them your slaves.

c) Attack and try to kill them all.

Answers:

Count the numbers of a), b) and c) answers. See which you have the most of.

Mostly a) – Sorry. You are a wimp. You will never be a tough cookie like Dingaan. You're more of a Dingbat. Get a soft job. Infant school teacher may suit you.

Mostly b) – You are not a very nice person. People who steal dummies from babies are nicer than you! But you still aren't tough as old Dingaan.

Mostly c) – Each c) answer is what Dingaan actually did. If you'd do the same you'd make a great Zulu leader ... just don't come near me, you nasty pastie!

But Dingaan's cruelty didn't do him any good. When his 10,000 Zulus attacked the 460 white settlers, the Zulus lost! There were 3,000 dead Zulus on the battlefield at Blood River – and just *two* dead settlers! Dingaan fled for his life and found safety in Swaziland. That's where he was murdered – by his own people. It's hard to feel sorry for him, isn't it?

DISGUSTOMETER RATING:

Zulu Shaka

If you think Dingaan was bad you would NOT like to meet the brother he killed – Shaka, who ruled from 1816 till 1828! Here are some foul facts about Shaka's life. But, *beware* – one of these facts is not true. Which one?

a) Before Shaka was born his mother said, 'The swelling in my stomach is just ishaki!' And 'ishaki' means 'a bad gut'. When the baby was born he was named ishaki (or Shaka) – so his name meant 'bad gut'.

b) Shaka and his mother were sent away from the Zulu nation. Life was hard, and they spent some time living in a cave, so Shaka grew up tough. Other boys picked on him, poor lad, because his naughty bits weren't very large. He grew up to be a big youth (though his naughty bits stayed a bit on the small side) and returned to the Zulu to lead them – so the first thing he had to do was kill the chief ... his own father. Would *you* kill your dad? (Better not answer that!)

c) Shaka was a great warrior chief – but a bit odd. For a start he was afraid of growing old and he was afraid a son would grow up to kill him. We can guess why he was worried about that! He had 1,200 wives but didn't want to be a father – so, if one of his wives got pregnant he murdered her! His 1,200 mothers-in-law must have been annoyed!

d) Shaka's mum died and he was really upset. Really REALLY upset. So he had 7,000 antelopes slaughtered for her funeral.

e) Shaka invented new weapons – a short stabbing-spear and a tough cow-skin shield. He also invented a new way of fighting. His army split into three and attacked the enemy from left, right and centre. Before Shaka invented this way of fighting, the Zulu warriors would just throw their long spears and run. Shaka made them sprint up to the enemy and stab – and it worked well in Shaka's day. Sadly it didn't seem to work so well when the Zulu came up against machine-guns 50 years later.

f) Shaka banned soldiers from wearing shoes. (Try saying 'Shaka scraps soldiers' shoes!' with a mouthful of mushrooms.) He made his army give up their sandals and toughen their feet so they could run faster – up to 50 miles a day!

g) Shaka punished any cowardly soldier with death. He also had them executed if they forgot to bring their spear to practice! (Imagine if there was death every time someone forgot their towel for school swimming lessons!) Shaka's soldiers were not allowed to have girlfriends either. The punishment? Death, of course.

WHAT HAPPENED TO HIM?

HE LEFT HIS SPEAR AT HIS GIRLFRIEND'S HOUSE

h) Between 1815 and 1828, Shaka destroyed all the tribes in southern Africa that were opposed to him. This jolly time became known as Mfecane … or 'The Terror'. He probably caused the deaths of a MILLION people – that, readers, is totally terrible terror.

i) Shaka seemed to enjoy being cruel. After he killed someone he had a little catch–phrase you may like to copy. He shouted…

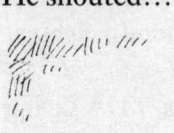

NGADLA!

You don't need me to tell you what that means! You do? Oh, all right then. It means, 'I have eaten!'

j) Shaka punished the Zulus after his mother died – he said they weren't sorry enough! His people had almost starved to death and he wasn't a popular lad any longer. Plots were plotted. But Shaka trusted his half-brothers, Dingaan and Mhlangane, and met them for a chat. They turned on him and hacked him to death. As he fell he said some great last words…

> BROTHERS! WHAT HAVE I DONE?

That's what you call a really good question. Sadly, he didn't live long enough to hear the answer. Mighty Shaka's body was thrown in an empty grain pot (corny, but true). It was then filled with stones.

Answer:

d) is not true. When Shaka's mother died he didn't slaughter thousands of antelopes – he slaughtered thousands of PEOPLE. Shaka said…

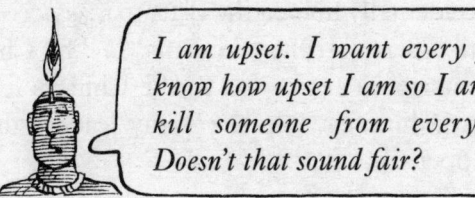

> *I am upset. I want every family to know how upset I am so I am going to kill someone from every family! Doesn't that sound fair?*

107

It's reckoned 7,000 people died because Shaka's mother died!

Smoking, choking Chinese

Through the early 1800s the Brits in India were making a fortune selling drugs to the Chinese. The drug was a pain-killer called opium, and the Chinese smoked the stuff till they became addicts. Many smoked far too much and killed themselves.

The Chinese emperor tried to ban the Brit dope dealers so the British government went to war with him. They wanted their drug dealers to carry on making money from the opium misery.

Of course the Brits had better weapons than the Chinese and were happy to massacre them! On 10 March 1842 the Chinese even accidentally helped the Brits to massacre them at Ningpo town! There were two reasons: **1)** The Chinese were superstitious about tigers and **2)** the Chinese leaders spoke Mandarin Chinese while the Army leaders didn't. This is what happened...

The order went out from the Mandarin leaders…

It was not really a good idea to attack Ningpo because the Chinese knew the Brits were ready for them. But the Chinese believed all the tigers would help them!

Unfortunately, they didn't translate the rest of the Mandarin order properly. What it really said was…

What they thought it said was…

They left their guns behind and tried to attack Brit muskets and cannon using knives. No contest. The second wave of attackers had to climb over the corpses of the first wave. A British reporter said…

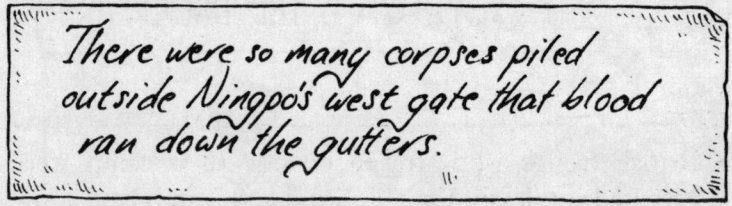

There were so many corpses piled outside Ningpo's west gate that blood ran down the gutters.

The Chinese had no more luck at Chen-hai later that year. The problem was, the Chinese commander was drugged out of his mind with smoking opium – the stuff he was fighting to stop!

So what tricks did the nasty natives get up to when they fought the Brits? The usual fairly average cruelty…

- A British opium dealer was captured and executed by being strangled.

I'M REALLY CHOKED ABOUT THIS

- British sailors were thrilled to see red boxes floating in the river. These were the boxes that posh Chinese ladies used to keep their rich fur and silk clothes in! A great present for the girlfriends back home, the sailors must have thought. They flung open the lids … and the bombs inside went off.

- British troops who strayed outside their camp were executed ruthlessly. Captain Stead let his ship land at the wrong harbour. He was taken ashore, tied to a post and skinned alive.
- Chinese defenders fought ferociously but if they looked like losing they would often slit the throats of their own wives and children to stop then becoming Brit prisoners. Then they would hang themselves from the rafters. This even sickened a tough Brit soldier who wrote...

> When the Chinese could no longer stand against us they drove their wives and children into wells or ponds, then destroyed themselves. In many houses there were eight to twelve dead bodies and I myself saw a dozen women and children drowning themselves in a small pond the day after the fight.

- A Chinese soldier cut his wife's throat with a rusty sword and threw his children down the garden well. But then he changed his mind and bandaged her up again and pulled the kids out – alive! She was not a happy woman!
- One Chinese soldier had his life spared by an Irish soldier who took him prisoner instead. The Chinese soldier was not pleased. He drew his knife and started to cut his own throat before the Irishman stopped him!

One Brit commander, Sir Hugh Gough, wrote…

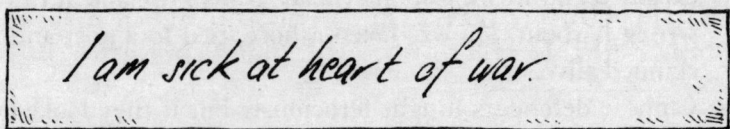

I am sick at heart of war.

In 1842 the Chinese made peace, gave the British $21 million and they also gave them Hong Kong. But the Brits went on selling opium, and the Chinese went on smoking it … and dying.

DISGUSTOMETER RATING:

Bad in Benin

The American invention, the Maxim gun, fired ten bullets every second and helped Britain rule over the Empire. Troublemakers were attacked and had no chance. As the witty wallies said at the time…

Whatever happens,
We have got
The Maxim gun …
And they have not!

The Brits used the Maxim gun like a teacher used to use the cane – to teach someone a lesson! That's what happened in Benin, West Africa, in 1897.

The Brits had been worried about Benin ever since they came across it in the early 1800s. They didn't like the way the Benin people behaved. According to the Brits, the Ju-ju religion was cruel and humans were sacrificed. One Brit witness said…

TWELVE MEN WERE TAKEN WITH 12 COWS, 12 GOATS, 12 SHEEP, AND 12 CHICKENS

THE ANIMALS WERE KILLED NEAR THE ALTAR AND THE BLOOD SPRINKLED ON THE BRASS AND IVORY ORNAMENTS

THE HUMAN PRISONERS WERE GAGGED AND EACH DRAGGED OFF BY FOUR MEN TO A WELL

AT THE WELL THEY WERE BEHEADED!

The truth is probably that the executed men were criminals and the beheading wasn't as cruel as the public hangings that were happening back in Britain at that time! The Brits also said ...

- the Benin Oba (king) was a slave trader and he had to be stopped.
- in 1886 Benin natives attacked British servants, took them to Sacrifice Island, executed them ... and then ate them.
- in 1896 Oba Overami chained criminals to a building where their ears were sliced off with a razor.
- Oba Overami also had the path to his palace littered with 40 rotting corpses, skulls and human bones to show his power.

But Oba Overami was guilty of the greatest crime of all ... he didn't want to be ruled by the Brits or be part of their empire!

In 1897 an expedition set off to chat to him about this. It was made up of a group of British traders, 250 native bearers to carry their luggage ... and a drum and pipe band! They set off on 2 January. On 12 January *The Times* newspaper reported bad news:

The Times
12 January 1897

EXPEDITION TRAGEDY

Alarming news has reached London from the West Coast of Africa. A party of British men has been captured, and possibly murdered, near Benin City.

The British police chief in West Africa was Captain Alan Boisragon. A few weeks after the newspaper report he sent a telegram to his wife. It was a one-word telegram which said...

Telegram

Saved!

from Sapelle, West Africa, to Mrs Alan Boisragon

Mrs Boisragon was probably pleased to hear that! But imagine if he'd had time to describe all the gory details in a letter! A letter like this...

My dearest wife,

Saved! It was a miracle. As you know we set off to meet Oba Overami in Benin City on 2 January. After taking a steamer and smaller boats up Gwato Creek we landed to walk the last 25 miles. All along the road we were met by friendly people with warm greetings from their king, Oba Overami.

Our revolvers were mostly locked in the luggage cases because we were expecting no trouble. By 5 January we were about halfway there when we came across a fallen tree. Behind the tree was an army of Oba Overami's men armed with muskets and hatchets. They opened fire and began a horrific massacre. As soon as our men fell they had their heads hacked off.

Robert Locke was lucky. He'd stopped to tie his bootlace and was at the back of our group. I was wounded and staggered into the thick forest where I came across Locke. We were the only two British survivors. I have heard that Kenneth Campbell was captured alive but Oba Overami had him taken to a nearby village and beheaded.

Locke and I wandered through the swamps and bush with only dew to drink and leaves to eat. Locke had a revolver and killed several natives who followed us. I was wounded again as I tried to beat them off with a stick. It was five days before we reached a friendly Beni village and then we were brought back to the British stronghold at Sapelle. They say we picked a bad time to visit Benin City. Oba Overami was slaughtering slaves that week and didn't want to be disturbed! How were we to know?

When I am fit to travel I will return home, my love. But you have not heard the last of Benin. The British Empire will not stand for this, you'll see. We will return, and next time we will have our trusty Maxim guns.

Your loving husband,

Alan

All the horrible facts in the letter are true.

Rawson's revenge

Sir Harry Rawson was given the job of leading the war of revenge. His troops marched through temperatures as high as 130° (Fahrenheit) – but there were horrors more sick-making than heat.

Alan Boisragon reported…

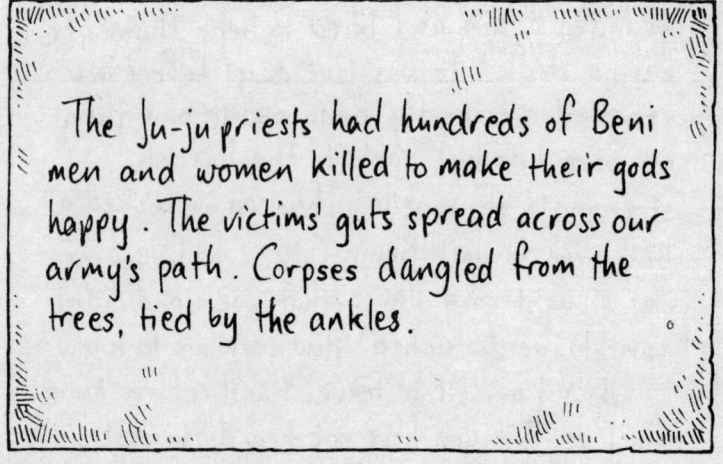

The Ju-ju priests had hundreds of Beni men and women killed to make their gods happy. The victims' guts spread across our army's path. Corpses dangled from the trees, tied by the ankles.

(This did NOT stop the enemy … so don't try it if you are being hunted down by the school bully! Try scattering banana skins instead!)

Rawson's army entered Benin City but Oba and the Ju-ju men had fled – leaving behind a town that 'smelled of human blood' (a reporter said). The Brits also found…

- two victims, crucified.
- deep holes filled with corpses.
- a field covered in a carpet of human bones.
- wells full of bodies – including one of Alan Boisragon's servants – amazingly still alive!

● Ju-ju temples with the remains of human sacrifices.

These were the horrors that Oba Overami had tried to stop Alan Boisragon's expedition from seeing. In the end the Maxim guns destroyed every Benin army it met. Oba Overami was captured and told to kneel down and eat the soil at his feet. The new British ruler said…

> *Now this is white man's country. There is only one king in this country, and that is the white man.*

Oba Overami had lost his kingdom and the Brits had added another piece of land to their empire.

DISGUSTOMETER RATING:

Suffering Sri Lanka

● The island of Sri Lanka was full of rich temples and peaceful people – the Singhalese – until the Portuguese arrived and started pinching their gold and their spices and their jewels and their women. The peaceful people fought back.

● They didn't have European guns but they were great at hiding in forests and setting traps and ambushes. Guns are great killers – but they're not much use when a Singhalese team drops a boulder on your head as you walk under a cliff!

SUCCESSFUL SINGHALESE →

SOLDIER SAUSAGE

- And, if they captured you, they could teach you a lesson you'd never forget. Fifty Portuguese prisoners were sent back to their camp with TEN eyes between them – and they'd all had their naughty bits cut off too! Ouch!

When the Brits arrived in 1795 the Singhalese had some nasty tricks up their sleeves. Because of their Buddhist religion they were not so keen on taking the life of their Brit enemies so what did they do?

a) Left them out in the rain to catch cold and die.

b) Gave them food that was a week old so they'd get food poisoning and die.

c) Laid them on the ground and got a trained elephant to trample on them.

OH, IT'S A HORRIBLE JOB. YOU'LL BE PICKING BITS OF SQUISHED BRIT FROM BETWEEN YOUR TOES FOR WEEKS!

Answer:

c) It could have been worse. They could have been made to suffer those awful elephant jokes and been bored to death. You know the sort of thing. What do you get if you cross an elephant with a whale? A huge pair of swimming trunks. (*Yawn!*) What do you get if you cross an elephant with a butterfly? A mam-moth. (*Yawn! Yawn!*) What's the difference between an elephant and a banana? Have you tried peeling an elephant? (*Hey! That's not so bad!*)

The British army tried to attack the Singhalese king in his mountain palace but were forced to make peace. The Singhalese said the Brits were free to go back to their camp on the coast … and they could leave the 149 wounded Brits in the hospital. The Singhalese promised to take care of them. They took care of them all right! Of the 149, only two lived to tell the bloody tale. One survivor, Sergeant Theon, reported…

> They mostly knocked out our soldiers' brains with clubs, then pulled the dead and dying out by the heels. They threw many down a well and many bodies were left in the streets to be eaten by dogs. But none were buried.

Sergeant Theon woke under a pile of bodies. A guard saw him and hanged him … but the rope broke and he crawled away to hide in a hut. A week later he was captured again and this time he was treated well. He then married a Singhalese woman and stayed on the island. He clearly enjoyed hanging around the place!

IF YOU CAN'T KILL ME, MARRY ME!

The army that had left him behind weren't so lucky, though. The Singhalese changed their minds and attacked the Brits before they reached the coast. Every soldier was beheaded … except for Corporal George Barnsley. His executioner chopped his neck and Barnsley fell. He was amazed to find he was still alive, so he pretended to be dead and later escaped.

Barnsley was a Brit hero – but a drunk. (He was lucky to have a neck to pour the booze down!) He was sent home to Britain and drank himself to death two years later.

DISGUSTOMETER RATING:

The awful Ashanti

The Ashanti tribe of West Africa were slave traders and head-hunters. Each warrior carried a knife to lop off the head of a dead enemy. Were the Brits worried by this? No, because the Ashanti lands were rich in ivory, gold and slaves, and the greedy, grasping Brits wanted a share, as usual.

They did good business with the Ashanti – till Britain banned slavery in the Empire. Then Brit Governor Sir Charles McCarthy tried to stop the Ashanti slavers so they cut off his head. But he was a brave enemy, so they did him a great honour ... they turned his skull into a drinking cup for great royal events!

I SAY, YOU CHAPS.THIS SLAVERY GAME'S A BIT OLD-HAT, WHAT? CALL IT A DAY AND ALL THAT?

? ? ?

One of the nastiest Ashanti tricks was to cut telegraph wires so the Brit forts were cut off from the cities, and the Brits had to use messengers to carry letters. The Ashanti would then...

- capture the Brit messengers
- hang them up by the ankles
- use the cut telegraph wire to whip their feet till they bled.

The messengers were then set free to carry the messages ... if they could!

But the Ashanti had one curious custom the Brits failed to stop. The worship of *stools*! The Ashanti believed that the ghosts of their dead friends lived inside the wooden stools of the tribal chiefs. These stools were the holiest things in the land. But one stool, held by the Ashanti king, was the holiest stool of all. It was a golden stool and was buried, they said, at the king's palace. There was one golden rule about the golden stool:

NO ONE SITS ON THE STOOL!

It may have LOOKED like a stool but it wasn't for sitting on. Think of a Christian church today. It has an altar that LOOKS like a table but you don't sit and eat your baked beans off it! But Brit Governor Fred Hodgson was too stupid and big-headed to understand this. In March 1900 he marched into the Ashanti capital and demanded the stool.

YOUR KING IS CAPTURED. SO IN FUTURE YOUR LEADER IS MIGHTY EMPRESS QUEEN VICTORIA!

FAIR ENOUGH

AS YOUR NEW LEADER, QUEEN VICTORIA MUST HAVE THAT STOOL

SHE SHOULD REALLY

And a bloody war started all because Hopeless Hodgson wanted to sit on a stool. Over a thousand Brits and countless Ashanti died. The Brits won through in the end, but that holy golden stool was never found and Queen Vic never got her fat bot on it. So was it all worth it?

Did you know...?

Using someone's skull as a drinking cup is disgusting. But don't think that it was only the Ashanti who had such horribly historical ideas!

In 1884 the nutty General Gordon went to Khartoum (Sudan) to help the British soldiers trapped there. Goofy Gordon decided to stay and got himself massacred by the enemy 'dervishes' – which probably served him right.

Gordon was followed by General Kitchener, who defeated the dervishes then ordered that the dead dervish leader should have his grave wrecked. He took the skull and had it made into a desktop decoration to hold ink-pots and pens!

A leader of his people (and Kitchener)

Queen Victoria was shocked, so he gave up the idea. But kruel Kitchener was a Brit national hero for the next 30 years!

Epilogue

Britain has always been a tiny group of islands … tiny in size, that is, though their effect on the rest of the world has been enormous. Britain created an empire which changed the world – and made herself very rich in the process. The trouble is, 'great' deeds like that cost a lot – they cost a lot of pain and suffering. The native peoples that the Brits met were conquered, broken and sometimes even wiped out.

If you had stopped a British conqueror and asked, 'Why are you doing this?' he (or she) might have said…

If you'd asked them 'How are you doing this?' then honest empire-builders would have had to answer…

Most Victorian people believed their country was the…

LAND OF HOPE AND GLORY...MOTHER OF THE FREE!

The terrible truth is that the only 'free' ones were the white natives of the British Isles (and even then life was usually miserable unless you were wealthy).

The British Empire did help to get rid of a lot of evils, like cannibalism and human sacrifice – but it taught the conquered natives some new evils instead, like how to love money and how to massacre with machines.

Throughout the twentieth century, especially after the Second World War, the native peoples were slowly given back the lands that belonged to them. Some fought and died for that freedom – some were handed it by the Brits, who started to see how the world had changed. Empires were no longer a grand and glorious thing to have – just a sign of a greedy grasping nation and an excuse to be a bully. Since the Second World War, and Mr Hitler's attempts to build an evil empire, no one puts up with bullies any more.

The British Empire is now dead but no one can quite agree on just how good – or bad – it was. Some Brits say…

THE BRITISH EMPIRE ABOLISHED SLAVERY!

But you could remind them…

126

Maybe you should ask the people who had to put up with it how much good the British Empire did them! On 15 August 1947 the Brits gave back India, Pakistan and Bangladesh to the native people. The British politician Winston Churchill said…

The Indian Empire was the finest achievement of the British people!

What did the Indians think? They celebrated 15 August 1947 and freedom by tearing down the statues of the British Generals and the British rulers that the Brits had erected over the past 200 years.

So was the British rule of India a good thing for India and for the world?

Depends on who you ask!

BARMY
BRITISH EMPIRE

GRISLY QUIZ

**Now find out if you're a
barmy British Empire expert!**

BOLD BRITISH EMPIRE QUIZ

You've probably gathered that the Brits were a selfish bunch – they wanted the world and they stopped at nothing to get it. Take this quick quiz and see how well you know those evil empire-builders.

1. Why did early empire-builders take to the seas?
a) They wanted to get rich through trade with other countries
b) They wanted to learn the ways of other people
c) They wanted to find out if the Earth was really flat

2. What was the free-for-all sale of slaves known as?
a) A scrabble
b) A "Buy one get one free"
c) A scramble

3. What happened when the slave trade ended in Britain?
a) The freed slaves were given their own country
b) The freed slaves threw a great party with fireworks and cake
c) There was a riot in which loads of slave owners were killed

4. What was a bastinado?
a) A basket used by slaves to carry cotton
b) A form of punishment for slaves who didn't do as they were told
c) A prison for bad slaves

130

5. How were Indian rebels punished?
a) They were made to eat pig fat
b) They were forced to eat a really hot curry
c) They were made to lick up the blood from the people who had been killed

6. How were the native Aborigines of Tasmania treated by the posh governors of the prison colonies?
a) They were taken in and fed cucumber sandwiches
b) They were hunted for sport like animals
c) They were kept in cages and people paid to come and see them

7. What did the Barmy Brits give the Maoris in exchange for New Zealand?
a) Alcohol and guns
b) The island of Tasmania
c) A good beating

8. What did Shaka the Zulu do to his soldiers who forgot to bring their spears to their stabbing lessons?
a) He made them write 'I must not forget my spear' 100 times in the sand
b) He made them practise with a stick
c) He had them killed

QUICK QUESTIONS

When the Beastly Brits arrived in their new territories they often set about killing the locals and generally being cruel conquerors. See if you can answer these questions about the Brits and their beastly behaviour.

1. Queen Victoria ruled over the great British Empire. She was Queen of Great Britain and Ireland, but she also had another title. What was it? (Clue: She certainly made an Empression)

2. Where did the Brits decide to send their convicts so they could keep their own country criminally clear? (Clue: Surely it's Oz–ious?)

3. What was the name of the drug that the British and the Chinese went to war over in the nineteenth century? (Clue: I 'ope you remember the answer to this!)

4. How were slaves punished by their mean masters if they tried to run away? (Clue: Has this question got you beaten?)

5. How did the Brits finally defeat the Maoris of New Zealand? (Clue: Pray don't attack on this day.)

6. How did horrible Henry Stanley punish slaves who rebelled in the Congo? (Clue: It's a handy way of cutting out the trouble)

7. What did the Zulus use as shields when facing the British spears? (Clue: There's no friend like a dead friend)

8. What did the name of the nasty Indian rebel group Thugees mean? (Clue: It has a hidden meaning)

THE SICKENING SLAVE TRADE

The 1700s were a sorry time for slaves. Caught and savagely shipped to foreign shores, they were forced to live a life of peril and punishment. But which of these sad slave stories are true and which are false?

1. African slaves were often captured by members of other African tribes and sold to traders.

2. Criminals were never sold to slave dealers as they were put to work by their own tribes.

3. Slaves were worth a lot of money, so they were well-treated on the voyage.

4. Britain was the smallest slave-trading nation in Europe, so it shouldn't be judged too harshly.

5. Many British people believed that keeping slaves was a kindness and that freeing them would be cruel.

6. One in five of the captured slaves died within the first four years of life on the plantations.

7. When slavery ended, the plantation owners were given money to make up for their lost workers (or the fact that they had to start paying them something!)

8. After they were freed, some plantation slaves earned so much money that they bought the plantations.

HORRIBLE HEROES

Many men became famous – or infamous – for their evil actions and cool crusades. Can you match the man (or woman!) with their mission?

1. Henry Morton Stanley
2. T. E. Lawrence
3. Harry Rawson
4. David Livingstone
5. Florence Nightingale
6. Robert Clive
7. Captain James Cook
8. Robert Baden-Powell

a) Went to Africa to stop the slave trade
b) Went to the Crimea to cure sick soldiers
c) Went to India to take advantage of trade
d) Went to Africa to overcome the Ottomans
e) Went to South Africa to butcher the Boers
f) Went to Africa to conquer the Congo
g) Took to the seas to take new territory
h) Went to Benin to kill the king

Bold British Empire Quiz
1a) 2c) 3a) 4b) 5c) 6b) 7a) 8c)

Quick Questions
1. Empress of India
2. Australia
3. Opium
4. They were flogged (whipped)
5. They attacked on a Sunday – a day of rest for the Maori's.
6. They had their hands cut off
7. The bodies of their comrades who had already been killed
8. It literally meant 'hidden'!

The Sickening Slave Trade
1. True. It wasn't just the slave traders who indulged in cruel kidnapping.
2. False. Criminals were among the first to be thrown to the dastardly slave dealers.
3. False. Nothing could be further from the truth – they were chained and packed in the hold like battery hens.
4. False. Not on your nelly! It might have been a small country, but Britain was the biggest slave-trading nation in Europe.
5. True. Barmy as it sounds, loads of peculiar people thought the slaves were better off in England than back in sunny Africa.
6. False. One in five? They should be so lucky! Half of them died in the first four years.

7. True. And the freed slaves got nothing!
8. False. They were paid so little that there were many rebellions.

Horrible Heroes
1f) 2d) 3h) 4a) 5b) 6c) 7g) 8e)

INTERESTING INDEX

Where will you find 'bad guts',
'eating ants' and 'smashed seals' in an index? In
a Horrible Histories book, of course!

Terry Deary was born at a very early age, so long ago he can't remember. But his mother, who was there at the time, says he was born in Sunderland, north-east England, in 1946 – so it's not true that he writes all *Horrible Histories* from memory. At school he was a horrible child only interested in playing football and giving teachers a hard time. His history lessons were so boring and so badly taught, that he learned to loathe the subject. *Horrible Histories* is his revenge.

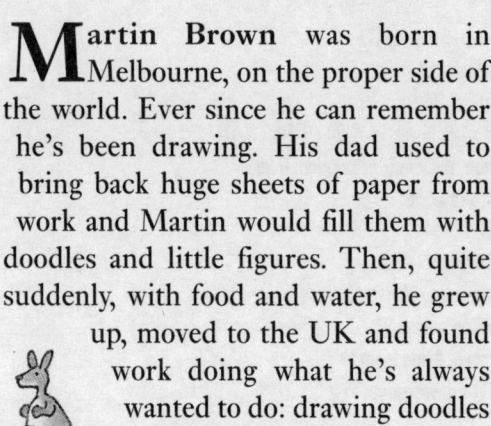

Martin Brown was born in Melbourne, on the proper side of the world. Ever since he can remember he's been drawing. His dad used to bring back huge sheets of paper from work and Martin would fill them with doodles and little figures. Then, quite suddenly, with food and water, he grew up, moved to the UK and found work doing what he's always wanted to do: drawing doodles and little figures.

HORRIBLE HISTORIES

VILLAINOUS
VICTORIANS

Terry Deary Illustrated by Martin Brown

SCHOLASTIC

For Ben and Sam Goakes – who are not villainous Victorians.
(Well, they're not Victorians.) TD

To Richard Smith, for all the no worries. MB

Scholastic Children's Books,
Euston House, 24 Eversholt Street,
London NW1 1DB, UK

A division of Scholastic Ltd
London ~ New York ~ Toronto ~ Sydney ~ Auckland
Mexico City ~ New Delhi ~ Hong Kong

First published in the UK by Scholastic Ltd, 2004
This edition published 2017

Text © Terry Deary, 2004
Illustrations © Martin Brown, 2004
All rights reserved

ISBN 978 1407 17868 4

Printed and bound by CPI Group (UK) Ltd, Croydon, CR0 4YY

4 6 8 10 9 7 5 3

The right of Terry Deary and Martin Brown to be identified as the author and illustrator of this work has been asserted by them in accordance
with the Copyright, Designs and Patents Act, 1988.

www.scholastic.co.uk

CONTENTS

4

Introduction

History is horrible. People in the past did dreadful things to one another and committed terrible crimes. They still do.

But by the 1800s the laws had become even more cruel than the crimes! If you were caught chopping down someone else's tree you could be hanged!

The laws became so cruel you could feel just as sorry for the villains as for the victims! The prisons were full of poor people who pinched pennies by picking pockets.

Posh people didn't have to mug and murder to make money. They owned the filthy factories and murky mines where the poor slaved and suffered. Many mine owners didn't mind how many died in their damp and gas-filled pits as long as they themselves made lots of money.

So, in the dark days of Queen Victoria, who were the *real* villains? The poor, pilfering people of the slums? Or the mean, miserly men in their massive mansions? And how would YOU have got on in those terrible times?

Teachers may tell you Victoria's Britain was an exciting place…

But it was also a time of cruelty and wickedness.

What you need is a book that tells you the other side of the story – the *villainous* Victorians. Now, where will you find a book like that…?

Terrible timeline 1830s-1840s

1837

In July 1837 a seriously weird artist, Robert Cocking, jumped from under a hot-air balloon to test a parachute. Robert was 61 years old in 1837 – quite a wrinklie at that time. His parachute looked like an umbrella when it's blown inside out. It was made to carry his weight – 90 kilos. Sadly Robert *forgot* to add on the weight of the parachute itself, another 110 kilos.

Robert had a drink of wine, took off his coat and climbed into the basket under the parachute. A hot-air balloon carried the whole thing 1.5 kilometres into the air over London.

He called up to the balloon pilots…

I never felt more comfortable or more delighted in my life. Well, now I think I shall leave you. Goodnight, Spencer! Goodnight, Green!

Brave Bob pulled a rope and let the parachute go. He fell towards Greenwich in London. He fell very fast. The stitching that held the parachute was a bit feeble. The basket fell off and Robert was smashed on the ground like a hedgehog on a motorway.

And it was…

GOODNIGHT, COCKING

I DON'T THINK HE CAN HEAR YOU

And crackers Cocking was crocked.

In July 1837 a seriously weird woman called Victoria became Queen of Britain. Queen Victoria became famous for saying, 'We are not amused.' But though she never said it, she did write in her diary, 'We were very much amused.'

Tubby Victoria reigned for another 63 years and – even though *she* didn't do a lot – the last 60 years of the 1800s are known as the 'Victorian' age. So her name is remembered.

'Victorian' men and women like Brave Bob went round the world, doing daring and daft things. They risked their lives so that people like you and me can live in a different world. (Well, SOMEBODY had to try things like parachutes so today's airmen can fly safely.)

But while brave (though batty) people like Robert Cocking are forgotten,[1] un-brave (though fatty) people like Victoria are remembered.

Is that fair? No. Most history books tell you about the famous and the fortunate – there are a few thousand of them. But most history books *don't* tell you about the forgotten and the failures. There are millions of them. Yet we can learn just as much from the failures as we can from the famous!

It's time someone wrote about the real people in Victoria's world. A world full of wild, wacky wonderful people like Robert Cocking as well as vile, vicious and villainous people like Jack the Ripper. So here are some of the famous and fortunate along with the forgotten failures because it takes both to make real history…

[1] Robert Cocking is buried in St Margaret's Church, Lewisham, London, if you fancy going along to say 'thank you'. Look for the grave marked: 'Robert Cocking whose parachute detached from the Great Nassau balloon in 1837'.

1838 ————————◆————————

Isambard **Brunel** builds the first steamship to cross the Atlantic, while railways take people all the way from London to Birmingham. Brits are going places fast – but with lots of choking sooty smoke. Brunel himself almost choked on a coin that he swallowed doing a children's magic show. He invented a machine to turn himself upside down and shake it out.

William **Lovett** creates the 'Charter'. The 'Chartists' want votes for all men (but not women, of course). They get a great petition together and take it to Parliament. But Parliament throws it out and Lovett ends up in prison. He came out and tried selling books but that didn't make him any money. Neither did teaching or writing school books. He died in poverty.

1842 ————————◆————————

Thomas **Arnold** dies and he was only 47. He is one of the few people ever to become famous for being a teacher. He taught at Rugby School – a school where the senior boys had been teaching the younger boys how to riot. Spoilsport Arnold

Billy **Bean** shoots at the Queen – but his gun has more paper and tobacco stuffed into it than gunpowder. Then on 29 May **John Francis** fired at Her unpopular Highness and missed. He went back the next day and fired with an

10

put a stop to that. Terrible Tom Arnold also brought in the teaching of French (foul) and mathematics (miserable). Blame him.

empty pistol (couldn't afford the powder). Neither is executed and Queen Victoria is furious. Billy and John – forgotten failures.

1843

Charles **Dickens**, the writer, is having a bad time. His latest book, *Martin Chuzzlewit*, is not a huge hit and he is running out of money. Will he have to give up writing novels and get a proper job? No, because this year he writes the best-selling blockbuster *A Christmas Carol*. Everyone is saved – Dickens, Scrooge and Tiny Tim!

Frances **Evans** is a Welsh preacher's daughter. She leads rioters into the Carmarthen workhouse, where Frances and the poor people of the town have been suffering. Soon soldiers arrive and batter them. All the rioters want is 'Better food, free tools and freedom'. Not a lot. The riot doesn't do much good.

1848

Thomas Babington **Macaulay** writes a big fat history of England – so blame him for your history tests. He says England is gradually getting better – for him maybe! He says he isn't too bothered about any mistakes in his writing. So he'd never pass his SATs tests then.

Father MacIntosh is a good Scottish priest. The Irish Famine is remembered but people forget that Scots suffered at the same time when their potatoes rotted and they starved. Lord Cranstoun at Arisaig doesn't care about his clan. Hero MacIntosh is left to help them. Many die anyway.

Cruel criminals

When Victoria was Queen the poor workers of Britain were crowded into dark, damp and filthy little houses. (Well, the houses were handy for the foul factories that belched out choking smoke; the factories that paid them a pitiful wage. So the workers suffered the slums.)

But one class of people liked the dingy streets and black back lanes – the criminals. The slums were home to Whizzers, Van-draggers and Screws.

You don't know what they did? Oh, very well, I'll tell you. Whizzers picked pockets, Van-draggers stole from the backs of horse-drawn vans and Screws burgled houses.

The really villainous ones carried squirters … no, not water pistols, you dummy. *Real* pistols!

No, no, no! A 'bogie' was a policeman.

Now here's a word you really needed to know if you were going to survive Victoria's England…

13

Gruesome garrotters

In the 1850s and 1860s a new terror hit the city streets – garrotting. A Victorian villain explained to our *Horrible Histories* reporter…

What did half of these villains do when they weren't robbing people in the alleys?

a) They were cab drivers.
b) They were teachers.
c) They were policemen.

A newspaper reported: 'London is a battlefield of raging cabmen.'

By 1863 there were 115 garrotting cases in London and other cities in Britain were starting to copy. Of course there were always 'honest' people who made money out of people's fear. In the 1860s a new type of men's clothing appeared…

SCARED OF GARROTTERS?
PROTECT YOURSELF WITH OUR NEW
LEATHER COLLAR

Wear this tough leather collar round your neck and feel safe.

NO GARROTTER CAN HARM YOU WHILE YOU WEAR THIS WONDERFUL INVENTION

Smart and comfortable too
ONLY 2 SHILLINGS EACH

Putrid punishments

Of course, the villainous Victorians couldn't be allowed to get away with their vicious crimes. When they were caught they were punished … and I mean PUNISHED.

Would you nab a 'kettle and tackle' if you could be whipped for it?

Here's a report of one beating from Leeds Jail.

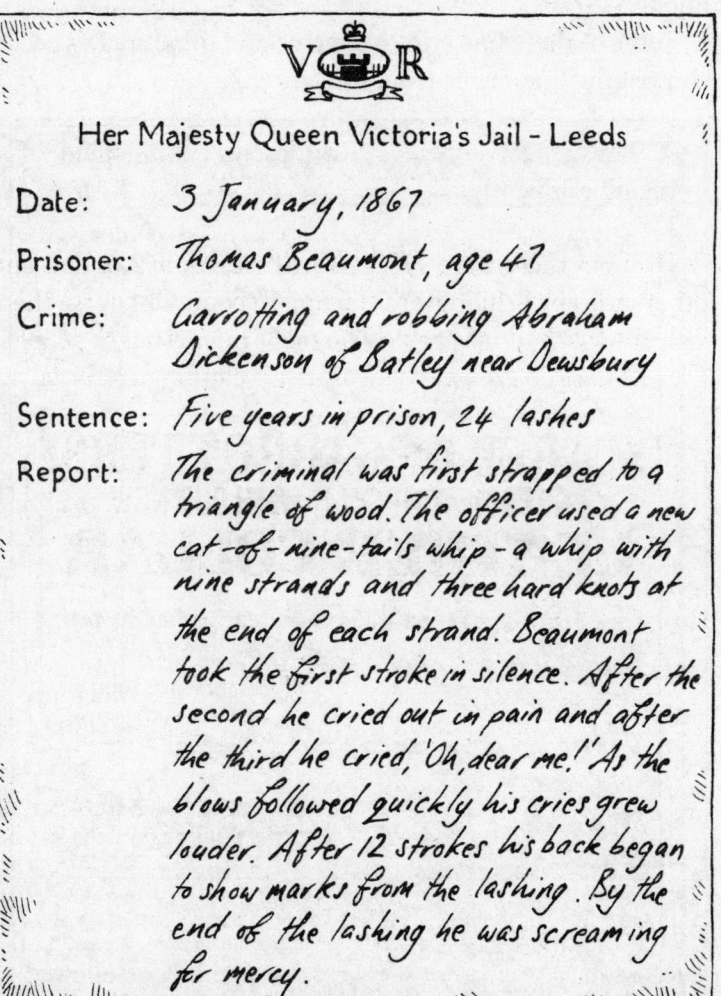

V R
Her Majesty Queen Victoria's Jail – Leeds

Date: 3 January, 1867

Prisoner: Thomas Beaumont, age 47

Crime: Garrotting and robbing Abraham Dickenson of Batley near Dewsbury

Sentence: Five years in prison, 24 lashes

Report: The criminal was first strapped to a triangle of wood. The officer used a new cat-of-nine-tails whip - a whip with nine strands and three hard knots at the end of each strand. Beaumont took the first stroke in silence. After the second he cried out in pain and after the third he cried, 'Oh, dear me!' As the blows followed quickly his cries grew louder. After 12 strokes his back began to show marks from the lashing. By the end of the lashing he was screaming for mercy.

And you thought detention was bad?

Cruel to criminals

Victorian punishments could be a bit harsh, even if the villain was a child. If you were lucky, though, you'd just be fined.

Some of these fine crimes are true and some are false. Can you tell the fine-crime from the fake…?

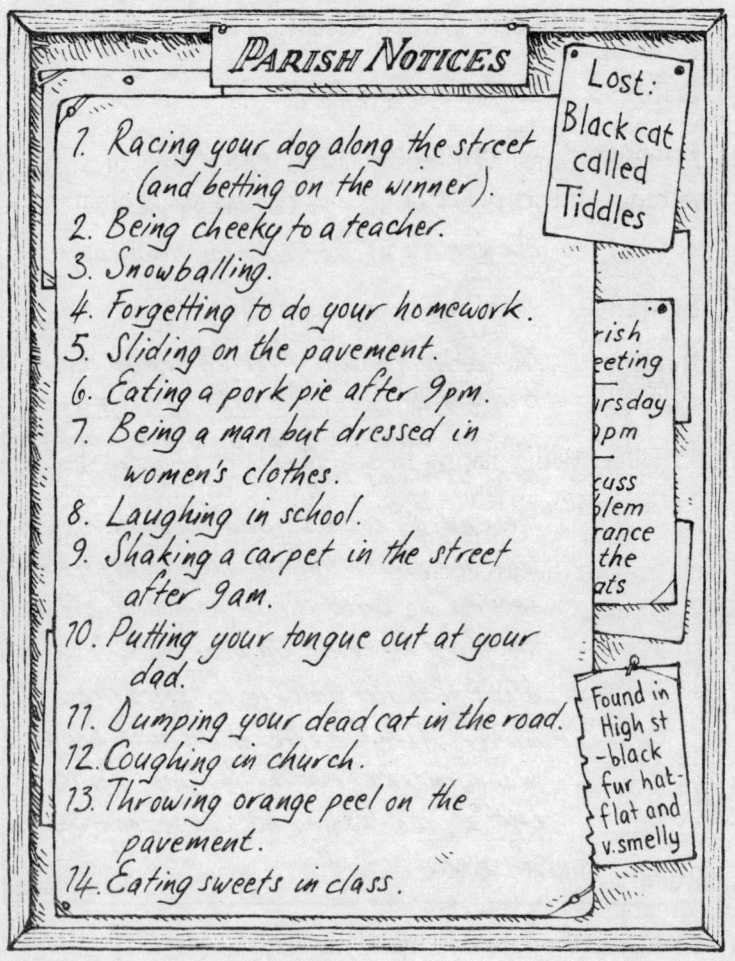

PARISH NOTICES

1. Racing your dog along the street (and betting on the winner).
2. Being cheeky to a teacher.
3. Snowballing.
4. Forgetting to do your homework.
5. Sliding on the pavement.
6. Eating a pork pie after 9pm.
7. Being a man but dressed in women's clothes.
8. Laughing in school.
9. Shaking a carpet in the street after 9am.
10. Putting your tongue out at your dad.
11. Dumping your dead cat in the road.
12. Coughing in church.
13. Throwing orange peel on the pavement.
14. Eating sweets in class.

Lost:
Black cat called Tiddles

rish
eeting
rsday
pm
uss
lem
rance
the
ts

Found in High st
-black fur hat-
flat and
v.smelly

18

Answers:

1   True. Three boys who trespassed on a man's land were each fined just one penny but racing your dogs on the road would cost you a pound.

2   False.

3   True. Snowballing really could get you a fine back in Victorian times.

4   False.

5   True.

6   False.

7   True. James Wilson got away with a fine of two shillings and six pence (12p) for dressing as a woman.

8   False. Being happy in school wasn't a crime, but being happy in the street could be! In 1873 Peter McKenna was fined £2 for whistling, singing and dancing in the street.

9   True.

10   False.

11   True. You could be fined up to £5 for dumping a dead animal, rotten meat or poo in the street.

12   False.

13   True. Throwing orange peel cost one young man a 12p fine in 1873 – and it's still a crime today. (So is being drunk in charge of a horse and cart, which cost someone £1 in the 1860s.)

14   False.

Putrid prisons

Putrid prisons were for more serious crimes. Were these punishments fair? Or foul?

- In 1846 William Cleghorn killed Michael Riley in a boxing match and went to prison for six months.
- In 1873 Thomas Clark sent a chimney sweep lad up a 30-centimetre-wide pipe where the boy suffocated to death. Clark got six months in prison.
- In 1875 Isabella Reilly went to prison for *seven* years for stealing a purse with £10 in it. Isabella was 19 years old.

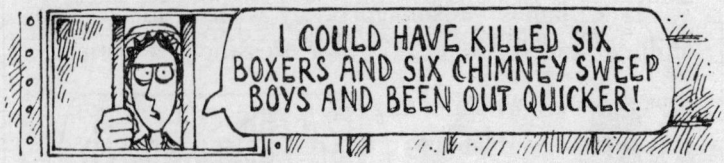

- William Lee stole a dress that had been put out to dry and got a whipping as well as two months in prison.
- Eleven–year–old Ellen Woodman was part of a girl gang caught stealing scrap metal. She was sent to prison for seven days.

Horribly hard labour

When convicts went to prison they didn't just sit around and chat. They had to work – taking thick, rough, used ships' ropes and untwisting them so the material could be used again. The work often made their fingers bleed.

But it was even tougher when the judge sent them to jail with 'hard labour'. Sometimes this meant breaking stones with a hammer. And if there weren't any stones to be broken, the prisoners were often given silly jobs just to exhaust them. Jobs like...

SHOT DRILL *Prison Life Weekly*

Our reporter has been inside Pentonville Prison to see the conditions there. He is happy to report those evil men are really suffering. If you've ever had your pocket picked or your house burgled then you'll be glad to see this, dear reader.

Here is the sort of punishment a man can expect if he is sentenced to hard labour.

1 There are three lines of men. At the end of each line is a pyramid built from cannonballs. Each ball is as heavy as a sack of coal.

2 The man on the end must lift a cannonball off the top and put it down. The next man must pick it up.

3 So each cannonball goes along the line. The last man puts it down at his end of the line.

4 This goes on until the pyramid has been built at the other end of the line. Once that has been done, they begin to move it back again.

5 This goes on and on, backwards and forwards for an hour and a quarter. By this time the men are quite worn out.

Maybe they will remember this next time they think about stealing your wallet!

A reporter said the men worked till they sweated. A few seconds' rest might be allowed but mostly the prison warders shouted and bullied the men to keep going. A warder said…

> *The hardest part is picking the cannon-ball up. There's nothing to get hold of and their hands are slippery with sweat so it's like a greasy ball. The work makes the shoulders very stiff too.*

Makes your PE lessons look easy, doesn't it?

Anyone who failed to do the 'shot drill' could be sent to work 'the crank'. That is, turning a handle on a machine – a handle that a strong man could turn once every three seconds. But in Birmingham Prison the punishment was to turn it ten *thousand* times. Even a fit man would take over eight hours to finish.

THIS IS A WIND-UP

Prison pain

Young criminals would also be set to work on the crank. If they failed they were...

- fastened into a straitjacket;
- tied, standing, to the wall of their cell for four to six hours.

If they fainted they had a bucket of cold water thrown over them.

I CAN'T WORK THE CRANK JUST NOW, I'M A BIT TIED UP

This happened to one boy called Lloyd Thomas three days in a row. Lloyd was ten years old. Another boy, Edward Andrews, refused to work the crank. He was punished for two months before he managed to hang himself. Edward was 15 years old. No one was punished for the cruelty that drove Edward to kill himself.

The crank was last used in 1898.

Fry and Fry again

One woman, Elizabeth Fry, led the fight to make 1800s prisons less cruel. In Preston Prison the treadmills were replaced with weaving looms so the prisoners could do some useful work. Good idea? Not everyone agreed.

Some people fought against her. They said prison *should* be tough.

The Reverend Sydney Smith, for example, argued that…

A PRISON SHOULD BE A PLACE OF PUNISHMENT AND IT SHOULD FILL A MAN WITH HORROR

IT SHOULD BE A PLACE OF REAL SUFFERING, PAINFUL TO REMEMBER, TERRIBLE TO IMAGINE

WORK SHOULD BE AS DULL AS POSSIBLE — PUSHING AND PULLING INSTEAD OF READING AND WRITING

FOOD SHOULD BE NO BETTER THAN WATER-GRUEL AND FLOUR PUDDINGS, FOR THIEVES ARE GREEDY PEOPLE

MRS FRY IS A PLEASANT WOMAN BUT HER WAY IS NOT THE WAY TO STOP CRIMES

But Mrs Fry slowly made changes. Thanks to her there were:

- separate prisons for men and women;
- different punishments for serious and not-so-serious crimes;
- useful work and training;
- better food, warmth and clothing for all.

PAH! THAT WOMAN OUGHT TO BE LOCKED UP?

But it's Liz Fry who is famous and remembered, while savage Syd is forgotten.

Cruel to kids

Do you ever get fed up with being treated like a kid? Want to be treated like a grown-up? Not if you were a Victorian kid you wouldn't. Because Victorian children could be *punished* like adults! One boy told his story to a reporter…

THE BEGGAR'S TALE

Our reporter met a boy of about ten as he left prison and the boy told his story. We present it here for our readers. Judge for yourselves the state of Queen Victoria's Britain.

I was born in Wisbech near Cambridge. My mother died when I was five and my father married again. My step-mother hated me so I ran away.

I lived by begging and sleeping rough and made my way to London. There I'd sleep on doorsteps or anywhere that gave a little shelter. I suffered terribly from hunger and at times I thought I'd starve. I got crusts but I can hardly tell how I lived.

One night I was sleeping under a railway bridge when a policeman came along and asked me what I was up to. I told him I had no place to go and he said I had to go with him.

The next morning he took me to court and told the judge there were always a lot of boys living under the bridge. They were young thieves and they gave a lot of trouble. I was mixing with them so I was given 14 days in prison.

I'll carry on begging and go from workhouse to workhouse to sleep. I am unhappy but I have to get used to it.

We don't know what happened to this boy. Did he ever find happiness? Did anyone care?

Some boys went pick-pocketing and were not bothered if they were caught. If they were sent to prison then at least they had food and shelter.

Child cheats
Want to make some dishonest money? Of course you don't. But if you DID, here are some tips from villainous Victorian children you must NOT try at home…

The shivering dodge

ON A COLD MORNING DRESS IN YOUR THINNEST CLOTHES AND STAND ON A STREET CORNER. START SHIVERING AND PLEADING FOR MONEY, TO BUY A WARM COAT. TAKE A WORN HANDKERCHIEF AND COUGH INTO IT AS IF YOU ARE ILL

I'M PERISHING

GET LOST, YOU LITTLE PERISHER!

The shivering dodge was a favourite of 'Shaking Jemmy'. He went on shivering so long he couldn't stop himself – even when he was in a warm house.

The lucifer dodge

You can get your little friends to gather up the matches and try it again … and again…

The tea and sugar dodge

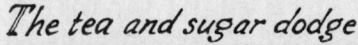

This dodge could earn up to 18 shillings in one morning when many working men didn't make ten shillings a week.

The scaldrum dodge

If looking ill doesn't help then pretend to choke on a piece of dry bread. Take money to get ale to wash the dry bread from your throat.

If everything fails then try this really disgusting one…

The bird-bread dodge

It is best if the bread is covered in maggots. Do NOT shake them off before you eat the bread – after all, they make a nice bit of meat in your sandwich.

Terrible transportation

Really serious villains were sent to America in the 1600s. But the Americans rebelled in 1776 and refused to take any more Brit criminals – after all, they had enough of their own.

About the same time as America rebelled, Captain Cook discovered Australia. A big, almost-empty place for dumping British villains. They were usually sent for 7, 10 or 14 years to suffer hard labour.

Imagine that! Sent away from your damp slum houses, your dreadful diseases, your smelly streets and your putrid water to the horrible sun and fresh air of Australia. Ugh!

The journey was a punishment in itself, though. It took four or five months in a rickety sailing ship. Out of every 100 prisoners transported one would die before they even got to Australia.

This 'transportation' to Australia lasted until the 1850s.

How bad did you have to be to be transported? It depended where you lived.

- In Yorkshire you were transported if it was your *third* crime.
- In Warwickshire and Dublin you were transported if it was your *second* crime.
- In Leeds and Manchester you could go to Australia for your *first* crime.

And age didn't matter too much. Children weren't supposed to be transported till they were 14 but younger ones were sent early in Victoria's reign...

Which of these crimes would get a child sent to Australia for seven years in the 1840s?

Stealing two loaves of bread from a baker – 11-year-old, Cheltenham

Spitting on the pavement – 13-year-old, Bath

Stealing three spoons – 11-year-old, Dublin

Stealing money – 8-year-old, London

Skiving off school – 10-year-old, Aberdeen

Answer: 1, 3 and 4 got children under 14 sent to Australia. It was theft that was really seriously taken by the judges. In 1849 Michael Walton was transported for ten years for stealing two turkeys and ten hens – that's almost a year for each bird!

Terrible transportation facts

1 Girls were hardly ever transported. Out of every eight convicts transported only one was a woman.

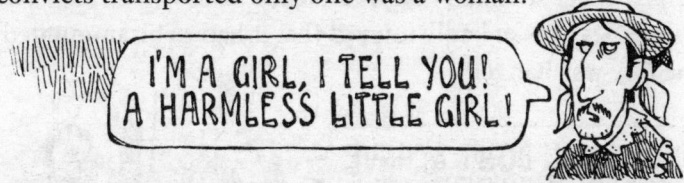

2 Young villains were taught in a school on the ship. Who was the schoolmaster? A convict, of course.

3 Transportation schools taught about an hour of English and an hour of maths each day. At the end of the week there was always a test.

4 The most terrible transportation? Probably a boy sent to Australia at the age of six. It was said he could hardly talk properly.

5 Transported villains could be punished AGAIN if they did wrong in Australia. A transported boy of 16 grew to hate his prison officer so much that he attacked him with an axe. The officer's leg was so badly injured that it had to be amputated. The boy was hanged.

Horrible hulks

When the prisons filled up, the courts had to send criminals to 'hulks'. These were old ships that were too ancient and rotten to sail. They were left in the river to rot and were filled with prisoners. They were crowded, damp and full of rats.

There was even a 'hulk' for young criminals – the *Euryalus*. The work was boring, and the kids kept themselves amused by bullying. The only escape was to fall sick and get on to the hospital hulk, the *Wye*.

How do you get on to a hospital ship? Don't try this at home…

Sometimes a friend would help you break your arm. They'd hold your arm on a bench, then let a dinner table fall on it. Ouch!

Miserable mother

A child was taken to court in Birmingham. He was a thief. The judge said to the child's mother…

IF I SET THE BOY FREE, WILL YOU TAKE HIM HOME AND MAKE SURE HE BEHAVES?

CERTAINLY NOT!

Would *your* mother rather see you in prison than take you home? (Better not ask her in case she says 'yes'.)

The judge had to send the boy to a hulk. The boy was too feeble to take it, and died. He was six years and seven months old. A young Victorian villain who got what he deserved? Villainous Victorian victim.

Little devils

In 1857 a new law was passed and it came up with a new way of punishing little criminals who committed little crimes. What was this new punishment?

a) Little devils were whipped ten times with a leather belt.

b) Little devils were sent to school.

c) Little devils were fastened in stocks and pelted with cold cabbage.

CUT OFF MY FINGERS? PHEW! FOR A MINUTE THERE I THOUGHT YOU WERE GOING TO SEND ME TO SCHOOL

d) Little devils were fastened in stocks and pelted with hot cabbage.

e) Little devils had their little fingers cut off.

The Industrial Schools Act of 1857 let judges send
children from 7 to 14 to 'industrial schools' where they
would be taught reading and writing, and learn useful skills
like sewing and woodwork.

In 1861 the law said the industrial schools should be used
for any child…
- under 14 caught begging;
- found wandering homeless;
- found with a gang of thieves;
- under 12 who has committed a crime;
- under 14 whose parents say they are out of control.

See that last one? That's probably why YOU'VE been
sentenced to school.

And industrial schools were even worse than the ones you
have to go to. Children worked from six in the morning till
seven at night.

You'd be too *tired* to go 'out of control' after that.

Trouble with trousers

What would *you* do if you were a Victorian judge? Here is a true case from Scotland. There is no doubt that the girl is guilty. She admits it. If you set her free, then the posh people of the town will have you sacked – they don't want thieves to get away with their crimes. (After all, those rich people could be next.) But how much punishment do you give this villainous Victorian girl?

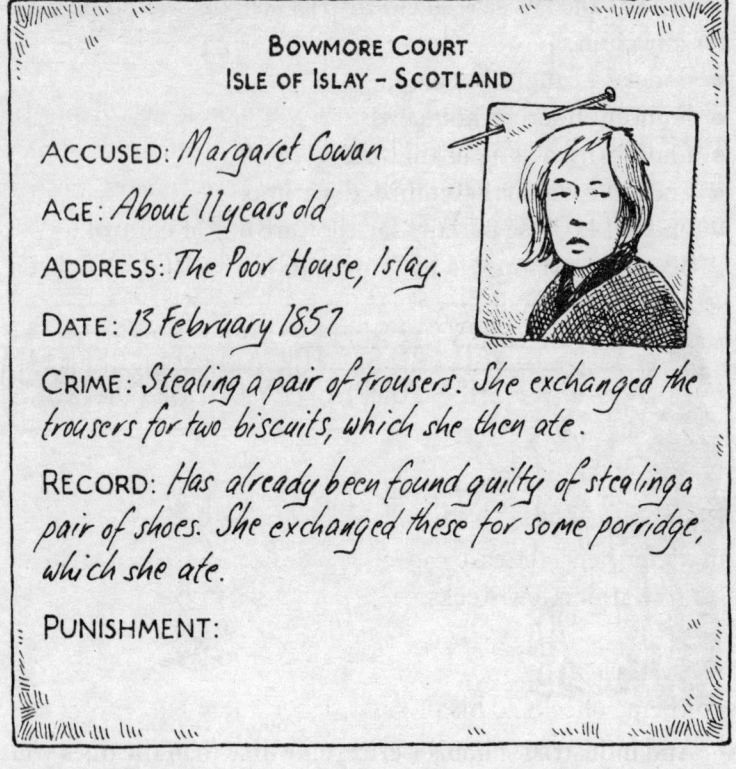

**BOWMORE COURT
ISLE OF ISLAY – SCOTLAND**

ACCUSED: *Margaret Cowan*

AGE: *About 11 years old*

ADDRESS: *The Poor House, Islay.*

DATE: *13 February 1857*

CRIME: *Stealing a pair of trousers. She exchanged the trousers for two biscuits, which she then ate.*

RECORD: *Has already been found guilty of stealing a pair of shoes. She exchanged these for some porridge, which she ate.*

PUNISHMENT:

Well, judge? You can send her to prison, send her to prison *with* hard labour, send her for transportation to Australia, or send her to a reform school, where she will learn useful work.

Answer: Margaret was sent to prison in Argyll for 40 days *and* then she was sent to reform school in Glasgow for three years. Pretty harsh for stealing a pair of trousers worth a couple of biscuits.

As Margaret Cowan didn't say…

It wasn't just Scotland that was tough on little villains. In 1875 Emily Davies (aged 13) was caught pinching apples from a rich man's garden in Ross-on-Wye (on the border between England and Wales). Like Margaret Cowan, she got prison followed by *four* years in reform school.

Emily wept as she was led off to prison. But there was good news for her. Her case caused so much protest that she was set free after a few weeks.

Did you know…?
For being cheeky to his prison teacher James Richmond was locked in a dungeon with only wooden planks to sleep on and bread and water for two days. Punishments like this, time after time, made him ill and he died in prison. James Richmond was just ten years old.

39

Crime school

In 1870 a new law said there had to be schools for everyone. This took criminal kids off the streets and into criminal classrooms instead.

The kids learned maths and English and so on but they did *not* learn speaking and listening skills like they do in British schools today. What a shame! Imagine some of the *true* stories those criminal kids could have told...

This happened in London in 1848 but could have happened almost any time, any place, in Victoria's Britain.

In 1852 this really happened. Many parents dropped unwanted babies into canals in Victorian times, but it was not so common for them to try to kill off grown boys!

Children as young as six years old were up to this trick. Sometimes they used girls to get the shopkeeper's mind off his till by talking to him. They thought shopkeepers would trust girls more than boys. Hmm.

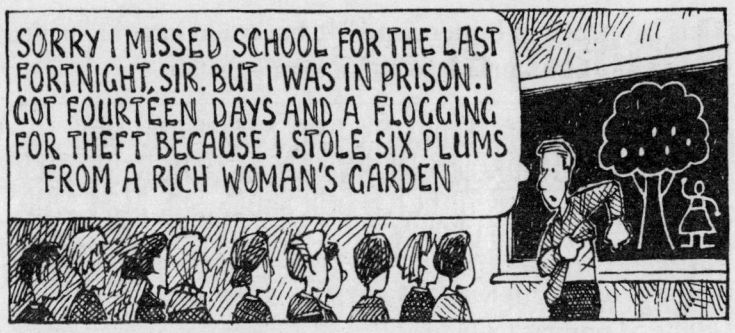

The boy was eight years old when, in 1855, he was flogged and locked in prison for stealing a few plums.

Did you know…?
There's a game that has been played ever since doors were invented. But in the 1850s it was against the law and children who were caught could go to prison…

Young people could also be locked up for throwing stones – sometimes they threw them at gas-lamps in the street. One boy threw mud and was locked up.

Hanging around

Execution in Victorian Britain was by hanging. Up to the year 1868 convicted people were hanged in public – and crowds turned up to watch. They turned it into a bit of a holiday. One of the most famous executions of Victoria's time was of Mr Frederick and Mrs Maria Manning.

The Mannings had killed Patrick O'Connor after inviting him round to their house for a meal. O'Connor was a rich moneylender and the cut-throat couple planned to rob him.

First Maria shot O'Connor and then husband Frederick beat him to finish him off. Frederick told the judge...

I NEVER LIKED HIM MUCH

Thank you, Frederick, I think we might have guessed that.

The terrible twosome buried O'Connor under their kitchen floor but were found out and sentenced to hang.

A public execution was also a chance for pickpockets to work in the crowds. One thief described the fun he had at the Mannings' hanging...

Mrs Manning was dressed beautiful when she came up. She screeched when the hangman pulled the bolt away. I made four shillings and sixpence at the hanging – I nicked two handkerchiefs and a purse with two shillings in it. It was the best purse I ever had.

Mrs Manning was 'dressed beautiful' in a black satin dress. After the hanging those dresses suddenly went out of fashion. Wonder why?

As usual, reports of the murder and the hanging sold thousands of copies at a penny a time. These reports were called 'broadsides' and some of them were written in verse...

The Manning Murders

The Mannings planned O'Connor's murder,
Nothing could the poor man save.
The dreadful weapons they prepared
And in the kitchen dug his grave.

As they fondly gave him supper
They slew him – what a dreadful sight,
First they mangled, then they robbed him,
Frederick Manning and his wife.

Old and young that do pass by,
Do not rob or take a life,
For the murder see them hang there,
Frederick Manning and his wife.

Models of the Mannings appeared in Madame Tussaud's waxwork museum in London. Visitors went along and threw coins at the wax dummies – though that probably didn't hurt as much as the hanging.

A reporter sneered...

> *George Manning is greatly improved by his appearance in Madame Tussaud's. He looks like a very clean undertaker.*

That's a bit unkind to undertakers, who are very nice people!

Charles Dickens was at the Manning execution and wrote about it with horror. It gave him nightmares – and he was a grown man. Dickens changed Mrs Manning's name to Hortense and put her into his book *Bleak House*.

Did you know...?

The Victorians may have been ruthless when it came to hanging people. But they were better than 30 years before. Before Victoria came to the throne, they hanged children.

- In 1800 a boy of ten was hanged. The judge said...

WE DON'T WANT CHILDREN THINKING THEY CAN GET AWAY WITH CRIMES

- In 1801 a boy of 13 was hanged for breaking into a house and stealing a spoon.

- In 1808 two sisters were hanged in Lynn for theft. One was aged 11. Her little sister was just eight.
- In 1831, just six years before Victoria took the throne, a nine-year-old boy was hanged at Chelmsford for setting fire to a house.

Anyone under seven was too young to be hanged. The problem was there were no birth certificates to prove your age until 1837. So how did you know if a person was too young to hang?

Scaffold school

But what about the children who went along to an execution? If adults were sickened by the horror of hanging then surely parents wouldn't take their children along to an execution?

But many did. After all, it was a lesson…

The last man to suffer hanging in public was Michael Barrett. What might a child have made of the day of his death…

It was a picnic. Thousands of men, women and children stood in the square outside Newgate Prison. They chattered and laughed, and tucked into their breakfasts. A few hundred of the richer ones sat at the upstairs windows of the houses opposite the prison. They paid good money for the view.

Outside the prison wall stood a wooden platform. There was a scaffold above it with a dangling noose and in the floor was a trapdoor with a bolt.

As eight o'clock struck on the prison clock the babble of noise dropped to a murmur. The prisoner, Michael Barrett, was led out of the prison, his hands tied.

'What are they doing with that man?' a child's voice piped through the quiet morning air.

'They're going to hang him by the neck till he's dead,' his mother murmured.

'Why are they doing that?' the child asked.

'Because he's wicked. He killed twenty people!' the woman hissed.

A gentleman beside her said, 'It was twelve people dead and about a hundred injured.'

'Twelve, then,' the woman sniffed.

'Did he shoot them?' the child asked and had pictures in his head of a dozen loaded guns.

'No, my child,' the man sighed. 'The man on the platform is Michael Barrett – an Irishman. His friends were locked away in Clerkenwell Prison and he tried to get them out.'

'How did he do that?' the child persisted.

'He took a barrel of gunpowder and put it up against the prison wall. He thought his friends were on the other side of the wall and, when it was blown down, they'd be able to escape.'

'And did they get away?' the child gasped, her round eyes blinking.

'No. The prison officers knew something was going to happen so they locked the prisoners away. The blast blew down the wall but it also wrecked a lot of houses in the street called Corporation Row nearby. A lot of people died.'

The child turned pale and looked back towards the wooden platform. The prisoner in his dark red coat and striped grey trousers was climbing to the top of the platform with a steady tread, and talking to the priest who was waiting there.

Then the door in the prison wall opened again and the crowd gasped with horror. A powerful old man with a grey beard stepped out. He wore a tight black cap and a dark cloak. He was the grimmest and ugliest man the child had ever seen. She shrank behind her mother's skirts.

'That's William Calcraft – the executioner,' the man explained. 'A butcher. His victims always die a slow and painful death. I don't know why they keep him in the job.'

'Because no one else would do it,' the woman said. She was pushed in the back as the crowd jostled and surged towards the platform to get a better look. The child was so tight against her mother's skirt that she couldn't see what was happening at the scaffold.

The girl turned to the man. 'Lift me up!' she pleaded.

'No,' he said. He took a fountain pen and a notebook from his pocket and began to scribble words.

He glanced up and saw the executioner disappear beneath the scaffold. A hush fell on the vast crowd so great that the child could hear sparrows fighting on the rooftops and the scratch of the man's pen. There was a grating sound as the bolt of the trapdoor was pulled.

There was a gasp from the crowd, then a roar and a half-hearted cheer. 'That's what the Fenians deserve!' a man cried.

'She's fainted,' a woman groaned and the girl turned to see a young woman being carried out of the tightly packed crowd.

'That's Michael Barrett's girlfriend ... poor girl,' the man sighed and scribbled some more.

'I couldn't see anything,' the girl sighed as the crowd turned away and began to thin.

The man put his pen and notebook back in his pocket. 'And you never will,' he said to the girl.

'What do you mean?'

The man tugged his dark beard. 'I mean this will stop soon ... hanging men in public will stop. It's barbaric. Something from the Middle Ages. The public have no right to see it – children should not be allowed to see it.'

The girl's mother turned an angry shade of red. 'Teach the child a lesson. That's what happens to killers.'

The man shook his head. 'The people here today didn't come to learn a lesson. They came to see an innocent man murdered with a rope.'

'Innocent?' the woman jeered. 'What do you know? A jury found him guilty. Who are you to say he didn't do it? Eh?'

The girl had never heard her mother so angry. The woman waved a finger in the man's face.

'Eh? Go on. Tell me. Who are you?' she ranted.

The man raised his hat politely and said quietly. 'My name is Dickens, madam. Charles Dickens. You may have heard of me.'

He patted the girl on the head and turned away from the mother whose mouth hung open foolishly.

'Can we go and look at the dead man now, Mum?' the girl asked.

The mother wrapped a shawl around the child's head and dragged her off down the street. 'No, child. No. Let's go home.'

Michael Barrett was a Fenian. The Fenians were Irish people who didn't want English Queen Victoria ruling them. They tried to drive the British out with bombs and killings. In 1881 the Fenians tried to blow up Salford Army Camp but only managed to kill a seven-year-old boy. The Fenians were dangerous but not very successful.

(There were eight attempts to kill Queen Victoria in 60 years – four of those were Irish attempts. In 1887 Victoria went to Parliament to celebrate her 50 years as queen. There was a Fenian plot, just like Guy Fawkes's, to blow her up with her ministers. Several ministers knew about it and were sure they could stop the attack. They did, but they let Vic take the risk anyway!)

Barrett said at his trial:

> *I have never deliberately injured a human being. I love my country and if it would help Ireland, I would willingly sacrifice my life – I will meet death without a murmur.*

Many people believed him when he said he hurt no one. They said the police bribed and bullied people to say they saw Barrett at the scene of the Clerkenwell explosion. Barrett had to die to make it look as if Victoria's police were doing their job.

Many years after Barrett's death, another Fenian admitted that he planted the bomb that exploded at Clerkenwell. Barrett was innocent. So the police were suspected of telling porkies.

Charles Dickens was so sickened by public hangings that he was one of the people who spoke out against them and had them stopped. Three days after Michael Barrett was executed the law was changed so no one was ever hanged in public again.

Terrible timeline 1850s–1860s

Famous and Fortunate   *Forgotten and Failed*

1853 ────────◆────────

Dr **John Snow** was born in 1813 in a York slum. One of the first doctors to use 'chloroform' to knock patients out before he saws off bits of their body or sticks a surgeon's knife into them. Dr J uses chloroform on Queen Vic so she can have a baby (Prince Leopold) with no pain. Vic likes it and makes slum-kid Snow rich ... till he dies this year aged just 45.

Thady **Wynne** and brother Michael kill a man and are sentenced to being 'transported' to Australia. Michael is too poorly to travel but Thady leaves his wife and seven children back in Curreentorpan. He should be famous as one of the LAST ever convicts to be sent to Australia – the Australians don't want any more! But Thady is forgotten.

I KNOCKED OUT THE QUEEN, DRUGGED PEOPLE, CUT THEM UP AND CHOPPED OFF ARMS AND LEGS

SO HOW COME *YOU'RE* NOT BEING SENT TO AUSTRALIA?

1854 ────────◆────────

Florence **Nightingale** – a posh kid who hears God calling her to do something good – leads a team of nurses to help the sick Brit soldiers dying of disease in the Crimean War in 1854. (She is

Mortimer **Grimshaw** is a leader of the Preston Cotton Mill workers' strike. They don't want a pay rise – they just want back the money the bosses have cut. The bosses close the factories and really clever at maths and it helps her do sums that will save lives.) Becomes ill and blind for so long she takes more nursing than she gave out! Sickly Flo doesn't enjoy her fame much.

try to starve the workers till they are forced to go back to work. The workers give in. So Mort Grim is a failure – though 12 years before, five Preston strikers were shot dead. So Mort was a lucky failure.

1857

David **Livingstone**, the Scottish explorer, comes back from exploring Africa a hero! He has discovered vast waterfalls and named them after Victoria – the creep! He has also shown the way for Brits to get into Africa – they will take diseases and Christianity in, and they will take wealth out. But Dave's a hero, so that's all right.

In India British troops are taking over from leaders like **Nana Sahib**. Nana leads the Indian Mutiny and holds Brit women and children prisoners. When the British attack him at Lucknow he has 200 of them hacked to pieces and the bits thrown down a well. Doesn't do him much good. Brits win – Nana vanishes and probably dies.

1865

Edward **J** **Eyre** is the governor of Jamaica when the Jamaicans rebel against Brit rule. Evil Edward had rebels shot, hanged, and even had heads hacked off and stuck on poles like a ruler from the Middle Ages. He is brought back to Britain, where a lot of people think he did a good job. He is not punished for the 400 men and women he had massacred. A nice way to get famous!

Edward **Whymper** is one of a group of four Brits to get to the top of the Matterhorn mountain in Switzerland. But only Ed came back. The others fell 1,400 metres off the mountain on to a glacier below – very careless that, and rather painful. Whymper gets home; yet it is the famous (but splattered) leader Lord Francis Douglas who is remembered. Whymper's no wimp but he is forgotten.

Massacre man   Matterhorn man

1867

Alfred **Nobel**, the Swedish inventor, shows off his new invention in Surrey. It is a high explosive called 'dynamite'. It will kill millions over the years. It will make a really good weapon for rebels! But Alf will give money for 'Peace prizes' – so he'll be remembered as a man of peace

Charles **Brett** is a poor policeman who's in the wrong place. The Irish are revolting. The leaders of the rebel group, the Fenians, are arrested. Their friends hold up the police van and order Sergeant Brett to open the door. But Brett refuses. He puts his eye to the keyhole even though he made himself rich and famous with something so deadly. Funny old world.

to see what's happening – just as a Fenian puts a bullet through the keyhole. Ouch!

1869

Dr **Joseph Lister** operates on sick people using disinfectant and only 15 per cent of his patients die from his operation – with other doctors it's 45 per cent. He has a nasty habit of doing tests by cutting up live animals. Queen Vic tries to stop him but she fails. Cat-cutting, rabbit-ripping Dr L goes on to fame and fortune. Animals are not amused. Lister later operates on Vic and she makes him 'Sir Joseph'.

Mrs **Josephine Butler** sets up ... deep breath ... 'The Ladies Association for the Repeal of the Contagious Diseases Acts'. The laws say homeless girls can be injected by police doctors whether they have diseases or not. ('Police wouldn't dare do it to me,' Mrs Butler reckons.) She wins – in 1886, after 17 years! So, not a failure, but almost forgotten – after all those years of struggle.

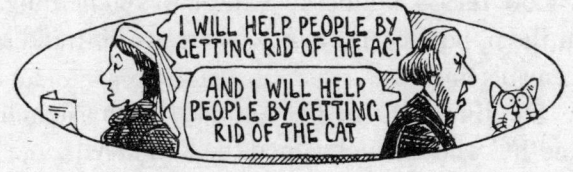

Mr Peel's pained police

Sir Robert Peel thought the nightwatchmen in London were pretty useless at stopping the villains. So he created the police force in 1829. When Victoria came to the throne police forces began to spread all over Britain – like spots on a kid with chicken pox.

They popped up everywhere. You may think people would be glad to have their local police there to protect them. But at first they weren't all that popular.

Here are 10 foul facts...

It's not very nice being called names, is it? Your teacher would *hate* to be called 'fat face' just because she has a fat face, wouldn't she? Well policemen hated the cruel names the public called them. Victoria's police were called names like...

- **Peelers** – No, NOT potato peelers. They were named after Robert Peel who invented them.
- **Peel's Bloody Gang** – Charming.
- **Raw Lobsters** – Not because there was something fishy about them, but because raw lobsters are blue and so is a policeman's uniform.
- **Blue Devils** – not to be confused with Manchester United FC who are nicknamed the Red Devils.
- **Crushers** – Well they could give your head a bit of a crushing with those truncheons.

- **Cheese** – But dairy you call a policeman that today?
- **Cops (or Coppers)** – The Romans used the word *capere*, which means to capture. That's what policemen did so they became 'caps' and then the word changed to 'cops'. Bet your history teacher didn't know that!
- **Pigs** – Some things never change.
- **Rozzers** – A word meaning 'strong man' in gypsy language (used from about 1890).
- **Noses** – Because the police stick their noses into villains' business? Who nose?
- **Slops** – Because 's-l-o-p' is 'police' spelt backwards. Almost.

2. We look stupid in these uniforms

PC Cavanagh described how he was dressed on his first day:

When I looked at myself in the mirror I wondered why on earth I had decided to become a peeler. My top hat was slipping all over my head, my boots were two sizes too large and were rubbing the skin off my heels; my thick leather neck tie was almost choking me. I would have given all I owned to get back into ordinary clothes!

Of course, the leather neck tie was to keep away garrotters.

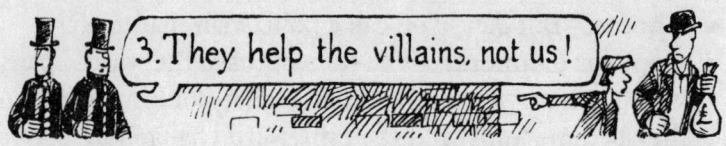

3. They help the villains, not us!

The law said you had to help a policeman if he needed it. If you refused, then you could go to jail. But the ordinary people often helped criminals by warning them. As soon as they saw a policeman in the north of England, the cry was: 'Cheese, my lads!'

In London children chanted…

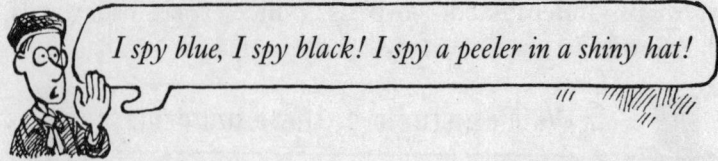

I spy blue, I spy black! I spy a peeler in a shiny hat!

(They should have been arrested for trying to rhyme 'black' and 'hat'.)

4. They lie to us

FIB FIB FIB FIB FIB

Some children were taught by their parents to lie to the police. A man was accused of being drunk. His little daughter told the police…

He couldn't have been drinking that afternoon. He was having a shave from 1 p.m. till 6 p.m.

They arrested the man anyway. The judge didn't believe the girl for some reason.

London Police Inspector Restiaux was lucky to escape with his life in November 1840. He led a group of policemen into the slums and arrested a forger. As they left the house with the forger a crowd gathered and pelted the police with stones.

The police fled with their prisoner but the mob charged. The mob leader had a knife. Restiaux wrestled with him and disarmed the man. The police escaped with the forger to the safety of the police station.

The slums were known as 'The Holy Land' – Restiaux could have ended up with a holey hand.

The rich people were forced to pay the taxes that paid for police wages. Earl Waldegrave had a real hatred of the police. Once Waldegrave paid a professional boxer to attack PC McKenzie in Piccadilly, London, while crowds of his friends watched. The boxer almost killed the policeman.

The rich sometimes told their coachmen to lash out at policemen in the streets as they drove past. Some even drove their coaches straight *at* the police.

Earl Waldegrave and a friend jumped on PC Wheatley and held him on the ground while his coach drove over him. PC Wheatley lived, but was badly hurt.

He never worked again.

Policemen worked 10 hours a day and walked about 20 miles on duty. Nearly a marathon every day. They had no days off and only one week's holiday a year ... and they didn't get paid when they were on holiday.

Birmingham had no police force in 1839. That year riots started there and the government sent for the London police.

A hundred police eventually calmed the troubles. Then 60 policemen were sent back to London – and the rioters heard that only 40 were left in Birmingham. The rioters drove the

40 police into a yard and trapped them there while they ran through the town, burning and stealing. The army had to be sent in to free the police.

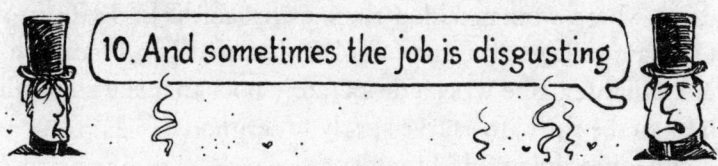

10. And sometimes the job is disgusting

The police went to the worst slums to arrest criminals. And criminals could have some very dirty habits. One policeman reported…

I entered the house and began to search it. I thought the gang had used the cupboard as a hiding place for stolen goods. I found the gang had been using the cupboard as a toilet.

Another policeman reported…

I found a wellington boot on the seashore … with a man's foot inside it.

A POLICEMAN'S LIFE IS *NOT* A HAPPY ONE!

YOU SAID IT, MATE

Awful arrests

The police sometimes had to arrest people for the saddest of crimes. For example, in Victorian times there were often cases where women killed their own babies. In 1846, in a Durham village, Margaret Stoker drowned her 14-month-old daughter. She was so desperately poor that she couldn't bear to see the baby starve slowly to death.

The policeman told his story…

WHEN I ARRESTED HER SHE SAID…

I HOPE THE JUDGE WILL GO EASY WITH ME. IT'S THE FIRST WRONG THING I'VE EVER DONE

I SEARCHED HER HOUSE. ALL I FOUND WAS HALF A PENNY, A THIMBLE AND A PIECE OF NET

AYE, THAT'S ALL I HAVE IN THE WORLD

SHE ASKED TO SEE THE BODY OF HER CHILD. SHE PICKED IT UP AND KISSED IT

MY DARLING, DARLING CHILD. WHAT MADE ME DO THIS TO YOU? WE'VE WANDERED SO MANY WEARY MILES TOGETHER

I HAD TROUBLE GETTING THE DEAD CHILD AWAY FROM HER

Margaret Stoker was sentenced to death but the judge took pity on her and let her live.

Pickpocket police

The 'dredger-men' didn't trust the police at all. Who were these 'dredger-men'? Well, they had one of the most cheerful and charming jobs in Victorian England – they went out on the river and fished out dead bodies.

They helped to keep the river clean and were paid for every body they found. But they could also rob the corpses before they handed them over.

A reporter who wrote about London said:

It is strange that no body brought in by a dredger-man ever happens to have any money about it when it is brought to shore. And the dredgers do not see anything dishonest about emptying the pockets of a dead man. They say that anyone who finds a body would do the same. And if they didn't do it then the police would!

Foul feuds

Big Victorian cities were filled with 'costers' – people who sold food or clothes or goods from barrows in the streets. (It was cheaper to buy a barrow than to buy a shop.) But the barrows could clutter up the streets and the police often removed them. Sometimes a coster thought a policeman had it in for him and plotted his revenge.

A writer called Mayhew described what happened in one case…

> The costers believe that getting revenge on a policeman is one of the bravest things a young man can do. Some men went to prison time after time for attacking the police and the costers treated them like heroes.
>
> Sometimes a coster would track an enemy policeman for months till he got a chance to attack him. One young man I spoke to waited six months for his revenge. He told me, proudly, that he rushed in and gave the policeman a savage kicking. 'When I heard he was injured for life, I was full of joy. They sent me to prison for a year but, believe me, it was worth it.'

These costers were often violent people who lived in a violent world of their own and they gave themselves odd nicknames. One woman was called 'Cast Iron Polly' because she was hit over the head with a cast-iron pan once and it didn't hurt her.

SEE? NO EFFECT. JUST HER OLD, NORMAL SELF

THAT'S NORMAL?

Here are ten coster nicknames – two have been made up … can you spot which two are the odd ones out?

Answer:
Odd ones out: Daft Darren, Smelly Sharon. If you thought 'Rotten Herrings' was a bit odd I can't blame you. The name is definitely a bit fishy. How did One-eyed Buffer get his name? No eye-dear.

Wicked for women

Women had a rotten time in Victoria's Britain. Husbands were allowed to beat their wives with sticks ... so long as the stick was no thicker than his thumb. And even if a young man was just a 'boyfriend' he treated a girl as if he owned her. One 16-year-old boy put it this way...

> *If I seed my gal talking to another chap I'd give her such a punch of the nose it would sharp put a stop to it.*

> *HORRIBLE HISTORIES* HINT TO BULLIES: Notice he doesn't hit the 'chap'. Maybe because the 'chap' would hit him back? Remember – if you want to be a bully, be a coward first.

Some men even had the nerve to say...

> *It's an odd thing but the girls axully like a feller for walloping them. As long as the bruises hurt she'll be thinking of the bloke that gave them to her.*

Sounds like a good excuse for the school bully, doesn't it? 'Actually, sir, the wimps love it when I hit them ... so that's all right, isn't it?'

And if the boyfriends didn't beat the young women then their parents could do it instead. Some girls were sent out to sell things like apples. If they came back with the apples instead of the money, there was trouble…

Anyway, you can see why Victorian women grew up tough. And some grew up wicked. Take Elizabeth Pearson, for example…

Busy Lizzie

Elizabeth Pearson was 28 years old in 1875. She lived with her husband and son in Gainford, County Durham. Her uncle and aunt lived nearby and then her aunt died…

The jury did not say, 'Show her mercy'. So she was sent to hang at Durham Prison.

At 8 a.m. on the morning of 2 August 1875 Elizabeth Pearson was taken to the gallows with two other killers, both men. All three were to hang together. Elizabeth Pearson was the calmest of the three.

Her husband and son wept, but no one else did. At 8:03 a.m. a black flag was raised over the prison to show the executions had been completed. Villainous Victorian.

Battered Bridget

The day before Elizabeth Pearson was arrested a man called John Tully was arrested just 35 miles away in Hartlepool. He was charged with killing his wife, Bridget.

Witnesses said John Tully kicked his wife in the stomach, held her tight by the hair to beat her and smashed her against the wall. He was caught when he was just about to hit her with a poker.

Tully was found guilty of beating his wife. Remember, Elizabeth Pearson had hanged for murdering her uncle. What happened to John Tully for his actions?

a) He was one of the men hanged alongside Elizabeth Pearson.

b) He was sent to prison for 20 years because the killing was accidental.

c) He was sent to prison for nine months.

So what's the message? A woman kills a man – she hangs. A man kills a woman – he goes to prison for nine months. Is that fair? Maybe not, but that's Victorian justice for you.

Pretty deadly

If Victorian Britain was tough for women, then some fought back with any weapon they could get hold of. The idea of a killer woman made a good story, and three cases in particular hit the headlines. Here are four casebooks – three really happened and one of them was invented for a novel. But can you tell which is the made-up one and which three are true?

Murdering Maddie

Name: Madeleine Smith
Aged 21 in 1857. Living in Glasgow.

Victim: Her boyfriend, Pierre Emile L'Angelier
Madeleine's mum and dad didn't like Emile and found her a better husband. Emile was furious and said he'd show the world the love letters she had written to him. They said mushy things like...

> 3 September 1855
> I live for you alone; I adore you. I could never love another as I do you. Oh dearest Emile, I wish I could clasp you to me heart right now.

The letters would wreck her marriage. Emile had to go.

Method: Poisoned by arsenic

Madeleine had bought arsenic poison at chemist shops. She said it was to put on her skin to make her look good. Emile died with at least 14 grams of arsenic inside him – enough to give an elephant gut ache.

L'Angelier

What happened? The court said 'Not Proven'. That's Scottish Law meaning, 'We know you did it but we can't prove it.' The problem was she bought the poison, he had it inside him, but no one could prove that she actually gave it to him. Madeleine went free. Villainous Victorian? Probably.

Awful Aurora

Name: Aurora Floyd

Aged 27 in 1862. Living near Doncaster.

Victim: Her ex-husband, James Conyers

Aurora married Conyers but left him because he beat her and went off with other women. She read a report that he had been killed so she thought she was free to marry John Mellish and she did. Conyers turned up and threatened to tell her new husband she was already married.

> Darling Aurora,
>
> I cannot tell you how surprised I was to hear you had married another man. As I remember, you are still married to me. But do not worry, I can keep my mouth shut. For a price. Meet me one week from tonight by the pool in the forest and bring £2,000. That is how much my silence will cost.
>
> Your loving husband (still!) JC

Conyers had to go.

Method: Shot in the back

The corpse of Conyers was found near a pool in the forest. When the police looked at his clothes they found a marriage certificate proving Aurora Floyd was married to the dead man. She was questioned and told them she had met her ex-husband in the wood and had paid him £2000 to go away. She said she had not killed him – but there was no money on the corpse.

What happened? Aurora Floyd was released without charge. A servant was later blamed for shooting Conyers and stealing the £2,000. Villainous Victorian? Not really.

Flighty Florrie

Name: Florence Bravo
Aged 30 in 1876. Living in Balham, London.

Victim: Her husband, Charles Bravo
Florence was a good 'friend' of an old doctor called James Gully but Dr James was already married. So she married Charles Bravo. Charles turned out to be a bully and a meanie. He grew worse when a mystery writer sent him a letter...

MR BRAVO

YOUR WIFE LOVES DR JAMES GULLY. NOT YOU. YOU ONLY MARRIED HER FOR HER MONEY SO YOU DESERVE IT.

SIGNED, A FRIEND

Bully Bravo had to go.

Method: Poisoned by antimony

This poison was used in the Bravo stables to kill stomach worms in horses. It has no taste. Charles Bravo drank wine at dinner and was taken ill. He died three days later.

What happened? The court said he had been murdered – but they couldn't say who did it. Florence went free – but drank herself to death two years later. Villainous Victorian? Probably.

Foul Flo

Name: Florence Maybrick

American, living in Liverpool, 1889.

Victim: Her husband, James Maybrick

James was 24 years older than Florence. Florence had a boyfriend in Liverpool but James was no angel – he had several girlfriends himself. He was also a drug addict. James had to go.

Method: Poisoned by arsenic

Arsenic was found in meat juice. Florence had bought fly-papers and soaked them to get the arsenic out of them. She said it was for her skin. But ... James was found dead with arsenic in his body. The evidence made her look guilty but no one could decide how James had died.

• Some doctors said James died of a stomach fever.

• James was always sick and took lots of poisonous stuff to try to cure himself – including arsenic.

- James's family didn't like her or trust her. When he fell ill, they banned her from his sick room.
- No one could say how the arsenic got into James – did he take it himself? Did Florence feed him it in the meat juice? Did his family feed it to him AFTER they banned her from his room?

The judge was mentally ill and he told the jury...

Florence Maybrick had a good reason to want her husband dead

What happened? Florence was found guilty and sentenced to hang. The court <u>should</u> have set Florence free. Under pressure, the government said she had only 'tried' to kill her husband, and spared her life. She served 15 years in prison. Villainous Victorian? Maybe.

So which one was *not* a true case?

Answer: It was Awful Aurora. This was the plot of the novel *Aurora Floyd* written by Mary Elizabeth Braddon. It was a huge Victorian success, especially with women readers, and it was turned into a very popular play.

Foul fun

The Victorians didn't have television. So no soaps for them ... in fact no *soap* for a lot of them either! But they did enjoy going to the theatre.

The Victorians enjoyed plays with a bit of blood and murder in them, and if they were based on a true story then they were even more popular. Top of the Victorian pops in plays was *Maria Marten – The Murder in the Red Barn*. It was the true story of Maria, who was murdered – guess where? Yes, in a red barn. Her boyfriend, William Corder, shot her and as she died she made a lovely speech...

William! I am dying! Your cruel hand has stilled the heart that beat in love for thee. Death claims me and, with my last breath, I die blessing and forgiving thee.

The crowds cheered for heroines like Maria, booed the villains like Corder and generally shouted at the actors – it was more like a football match today.

People peepers

Another way Victorians told stories was to put little puppets in a box. The viewers paid to peep through a hole and watch the puppets act out the story as one person told the tale and did all the voices. (This was cheaper than having a big stage with lots of actors, of course.)

The *Murder in the Red Barn* peep show was still popular in the 1860s, 30 years after the murder happened. It was so popular the box had to have 26 windows for people to peep.

In the 1860s a murder took place in the Red Lion pub in Berkshire, when a farm worker chopped the landlady with his reaping hook. One peep-show family group quickly changed the story of Maria Marten and added lots of red paint. What did they call the new play? *Murder in the Red Lion*, of course.

Petrifying plays

The Victorian audiences just loved villains – and they also loved amazing scenes. The following villains and amazing scenes were shown live on stage...

1 *Uncle Tom's Cabin*
Plot: Play based on the famous book about slavery in the USA.
Villain: Wicked slave owner.
Big scene: Slave girl Eliza escapes over frozen Ohio river, chased by dogs as a captured wild horse escapes.

2 *The Colleen Bawn*

Plot: An Irish story about a poor girl, Eily, with a posh husband who keeps her hidden.

Villain: Hardress Cregan – the husband

Big scene: Eily in a rowing boat with the murderous Danny, who pushes her in the lake. She is rescued by hero Myles.

3 *After Dark*

Plot: Play set in London and the Underground railway.

Villain: The criminal who drugs our hero.

Big scene: The hero is laid across the railway track and is rescued as a train rushes across the stage. The rescuer has broken through a cellar wall.

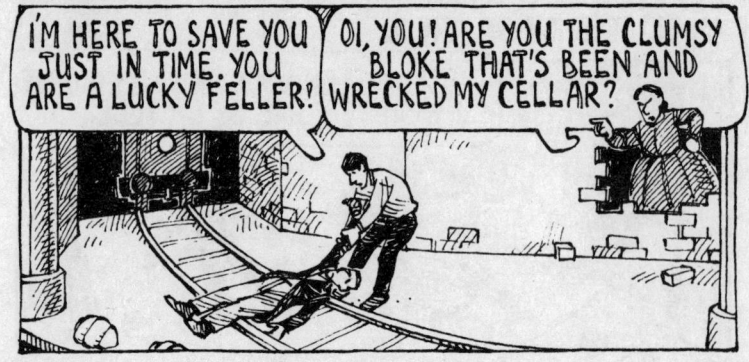

4 *The Octoroon*

Plot: A story about a slave girl (Zoë) in the USA (again).

Villain: The slave trader.

Big scene: A steamboat on the Mississippi river explodes, burns and sinks, killing Zoë.

THE GIRL STOOD ON THE BURNING DECK,
THE FIRE AROUND HER FLICKERS
A MIGHTY FLAME SHOOTS UP HER DRESS
AND SETS FIRE TO HER KNICKERS

5 *The Flying Scud*

Plot: A play about a racehorse that must win the Derby if the villains are to be defeated.

Villain: The bookmaker who drugs the jockey.

Big scene: A horse race with cardboard horses on a revolving stage – then a real horse enters at the end.

ROUND AND ROUND THE DERBY COURSE
THE HORSES GO A CHASING
BUT THESE ARE CARD, I GUESS THAT'S WHY
THEY'RE CALLING IT FLAT RACING

Did you know…?

A play called *The Derby Winner* tried to copy *The Flying Scud* and have a horse race on a turning stage. But the machine broke down on the first night. The actor had to stand in front of the curtains and say…

ER… THE HERO WON

WELL THERE'S A SURPRISE

Putrid performances

In the pathetic play *Pluck* a train crashes. As the hero goes to rescue a trapped child from the wreckage, a second train crashes into it. The stage trains didn't look too good, and one newspaper said…

'Pluck' is one of the worst plays ever to be placed on the stage of a theatre.

But that didn't stop writers and actors making bigger and dafter dramas. On Victorian stages you could see earthquakes, avalanches, shipwrecks, boat races and even waterfalls.

- In *The Streets of London* you would see a house on fire across the width of the stage. It was then attacked by firemen with a real fire engine.
- In *The Ruling Passion* a hot-air balloon took off and crash-landed in the sea, where a lifeboat came to its rescue.

- In *The White Heather* the audience watched an underwater fight between the hero and villain dressed in diving suits. Each had a knife and the fight ended when the hero cut the villain's air-line and left him to drown. The stage appeared to be underwater and there even seemed to be fish swimming around the fighting men.

Why did these plays stop? Why can't you see them today? Because of a Victorian invention – the moving picture show. After 1920 the cinema was able to show bigger and more exciting scenes (using camera tricks) than they could ever do on stage. So in the end there was the most dramatic and sudden death of all – the death of the Victorian theatre.

Grim ghosts
Poor people couldn't afford to go to the theatre. So in the dim and flickering firelight of a gloomy evening, how did they entertain themselves? With stories.

And what better than a ghost story. Especially if it was a *true* ghost story. Here is a case from Cornwall about some villainous Victorians to chill your bones colder than a tombstone in the snow...

Listen, me dears, and I'll tell you the tale of two brothers. One brother was Edmund Norway and he was a seaman. On the night of 8th February 1840 he went to bed in his cabin and fell asleep around 11 p.m. He was a thousand miles away from his home in Cornwall.

He soon had a terrible dream that made him wake up sweating and screaming. He told it to the ship's officer, Henry Wren. He said...

'I dreamed I saw my brother killed. He was riding his horse along the road from Bodmin to Wadebridge. As he rode two men attacked him, and I watched in horror as one pointed a pistol at my brother. The pistol misfired twice so they dragged him from the horse and used the pistol to club him to death before they robbed him. Then one man dragged him across the road and dropped him in a ditch. I have a terrible fear that my brother has been murdered.'

Officer Wren said, 'It was just a bad dream. Go back to sleep. We'll be home in a week and you'll see your brother is safe and sound.'

But when Edmund Norway landed there was terrible news for him. 'Your brother, Nevell, has been murdered,' they said.

The constables had made an arrest. On 13th April William Lightfoot and his brother were found guilty of murdering Nevell Norway and sentenced to hang. Before he died, William confessed.

'I met my brother at the top of Dummer Hill and we plotted to rob the next person who came along. Around 11 p.m. we saw a man riding his horse along the road from Bodmin to Wadebridge. As he rode we two attacked him. He refused to hand over his money so I pointed my pistol at him. The pistol misfired twice so we dragged him from the horse and used the pistol to club him to death before we robbed him. Then my brother dragged him across the road and dropped him in a ditch.'

How did Edmund Norway know about his brother's death a thousand miles away and sailing in an ink-black sea?

Perhaps his brother's dying spirit slipped into his dreams to say farewell? Who knows? There's nothing as mysterious as death.

So, when the night time comes, and darkness falls, go gently, my dears, and may the angels watch over you.

Wrotten writers

The Victorians loved reading books. Popular writers then were like pop stars today – and just as wild and wacky in the way they lived.

Know-it-all adults think they know everything about Victorian writers. But you can find out just how much they know by asking them which of these odd facts about Victorian writers are true and which are false?

1 H G Wells had two pens for writing – a big pen for big words and a small pen for small words.

2 Charles Dickens' house was so cold his ink froze solid.

3 Poet Alfred Tennyson amused his friends by sitting down and pretending to be someone on a toilet.

4 Playwright Dion Boucicault said, 'On my gravestone I want you to write, "Not dead, just sleeping".'

5 Author Joseph Conrad tried to shoot himself ... but missed.

6 Playwright Oscar Wilde wrote *The Ballad of Reading Gaol* in jail.

7 Joseph Kipling wrote *The Jungle Book*.

8 Poet William Wordsworth wrote about flowers (like his famous 'Daffodils' poem) because he was mad about their smell.

9 Writer Anthony Trollope stood for Parliament and won.

10 Poet Algernon Swinburne ate his pet monkey for dinner.

Answers:

1 True. In his book *The History of Mr Polly* his character says, 'Sesquippledan verboojuice!' It means 'big words'. What sort of pen did he need for that?

2 False. Dickens was poor as a child, but did well as a writer and lived comfortably.

3 True.

4 False. Boucicault said he wanted…

Boucicault wrote 150 popular plays so he deserved a break. Dying is a break too far for most people, though.

5 True. Conrad was fed up because he'd lost all his money gambling. He shot himself but missed his heart and lived.

6 False. Wilde went to jail from 1895 till 1897. But he wrote the poem about the disgusting prison life in 1898 – a year *after* he came out of jail. Not a lot of people know that.

7 True. Know-it-all adults will tell you, 'It was *Rudyard* Kipling who wrote *The Jungle Book* in 1895.' And you can have great pleasure in telling them…

8 False. It must be false because William Wordsworth had NO sense of smell.

I WANDERED LONELY AS A CLOUD AND THEN I SAW A BUNCH OF ROSES. I CAN'T SMELL THEM, NOT A WHIFF NOT IF YOU STUFFED THEM UP ME NOSES

ER... KEEP TRYING, WILL

9 False. Trollope stood for Parliament and *lost*. The writer only got 740 votes. He said going around trying to get votes…

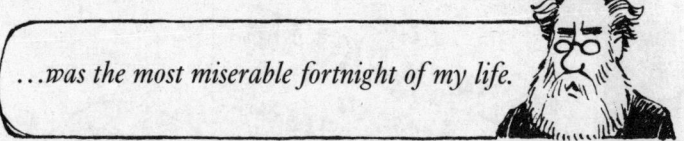

…*was the most miserable fortnight of my life.*

10 True. He used to dress the monkey as a woman and treat it like a lady. But one day the monkey became jealous of one of Swinburne's friends and tried to bite its master. The monkey was never seen again. Swinburne said he'd had it killed and grilled and eaten.

I HOPE YOU LIKED YOUR SOUP AND FISH, I HOPE YOU LIKED YOUR PEACH AND GRAPE. I KNOW YOU LIKED THAT 'CHICKEN' DISH— WELL, SORRY FOLKS, THAT WAS MY APE

Foul fairs

The Victorians could be pretty bloodthirsty and cruel when it came to their idea of 'fun'. Dogs killing rats, or men boxing without gloves till their faces were bloody pulp – that was their 'fun'. Even the fairgrounds were cruel places. In between the swings and roundabouts were 'freak shows'. In the 1860s you really could go and could see these...

the
HYDE PARK FAIR
Presents
A SPECTACULAR TO CELEBRATE
QUEEN VICTORIA'S 30 YEARS
ON THE THRONE
⟩ *SEE* ⟨
THE TALENTED PIGS.
THE WORLD'S FATTEST MAN.
THE WORLD'S SPOTTIEST BOYS.
THE PONIES THAT TELL
YOUR FORTUNE.
MISS SCOTT–
THE TWO-HEADED LADY.
YORKSHIRE JACK–
THE LIVING SKELETON.
MADAM STEVENS–
THE PIG-FACED LADY

Now you may wonder what people really saw when they paid to see Madame Stevens, the Pig-faced Lady?

They saw a *bear* that:
- had its face and paws shaved;
- had its paws laced into padded gloves;
- was strapped to a chair with a table in front of it.

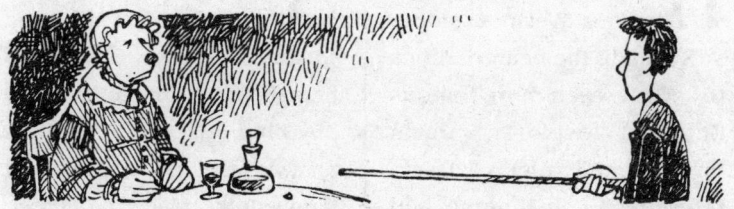

Then the performance began. The bear was asked questions. A boy prodded it with a stick after each question. The bear grunted and that seemed to be a reply...
- Are you 18 years old? (Prod – *Grunt.*)
- Is it true you were born in Preston in Lancashire? (Prod – *Grunt.*)
- Are you well and happy? (Prod – *Grunt.*)
- Are you planning to get married? (Prod – *Grunt.*)

But this was too cruel even for the Victorians and when the fair reached Clerkenwell it was banned.

Terrible timeline 1870s-1890s

Famous and Fortunate   *Forgotten and Failed*

1871

Henry Morton Stanley, famous Welsh explorer, sets off into the heart of Africa to find even-more-famous Scottish explorer David Livingstone. Sickly David refused to come home and died a couple of years later. But Stanley went on to report his adventures and became famous. His fortune came from working for the Belgian King Leopold, turning the African people into slaves with torture, whippings and chopping off bits of their bodies.

Sir Charles Dilke thinks Queen Vic is a bit of a waste of space. She shuts herself away and doesn't do anything useful. Charlie's answer? Get rid of the royal family and replace the Queen with a 'President' that everyone (well, every man) gets to vote for. Charlie wins a lot of support. But then Vic's son, Edward Prince of Wales, falls ill. People feel sorry for Vic and haven't the heart to throw her off the throne. Cheers for Charlie vanish and he is soon forgotten.

1874

Charles Kingsley wrote one of the first children's books, *The Water Babies*,

Thomas Castro, Australian butcher, turns up in England and he claims to be which made him famous. A cheerful little story about ten-year-old Tom who suffers terribly as a chimney sweep. Tom falls into a river and drowns, but that's all right because he is changed into a fishy water baby. Just don't try jumping into a river if your cruel parent makes you sweep a chimney. This year Charles falls ill and dies soon after – but does NOT change into a water baby. Shame.

the long-lost son of Lady Tichborne. He also claims the long-lost son's fortune. Lady T's family can't bear to see their fortune go to a phoney! Tom is taken to court. He loses the case and gets 14 years' hard labour. Tough! But men, women and children are still working 14 hours a day in Victorian factories – so, even out of prison, many poor people do 'hard labour'. Like Tom, they are forgotten.

1879

Joseph Swan is a clever bloke from Sunderland, north-east England. Clever Joe invents something we all use millions of times in our lives – the electric light bulb. All right, it's not a very good one and it doesn't last long but it's a Victorian first. In New York, Thomas Edison makes a light bulb too. Joe Swan says

General Hutchinson should have stuck to being a general. Instead he gets a job with the government to check that bridges are safe. He checks the Tay Rail Bridge near Dundee – the longest bridge in the world at the time. 'It's fine!' says General Hutch. But on 28 December a storm

Tom pinched his idea. Tom Edison says Joe pinched his idea. Let's call it a draw. Joe goes on to be famous – but not as famous as Tom.

wrecks it and sends a train with a hundred passengers plunging 27 metres into the freezing water. The general isn't on the train. Shame.

1881

Benjamin Disraeli dies but he has had a pretty successful life as a Prime Minister and as a writer of novels. What is the secret of his success? He was a creep. He kept telling Queen Victoria what a wonderful woman she was and she loved it – and she loved him. He came up with a super-duper idea to cheer up the miserable monarch. In 1877 he persuaded Parliament to make her 'Empress of India' as well as Queen. She was so pleased that she made Disraeli 'Lord Beaconsfield'. Fair swap.

Sir George Colley has been sent to sort out some troublesome Dutch farmers in South Africa – part of the British Empire. Sir G says the farmers (Boers) are 'feeble soldiers'. Easy job then? But at Majuba Hill these 'feeble' Boer soldiers beat his force of 1,500 'proper' soldiers. One of the Boers changes Sir G's mind. How did he do that, you ask? He puts a bullet through Sir G's forehead. And your mind doesn't get much more changed than that! Boers will cause Britain a lot of trouble for 20 years.

1888

Jack the Ripper is the most famous Victorian villain of all, yet no one knows his (or her) real name. Hundreds of clever writers have written hundreds of clever books to 'prove' dozens of suspects they think did it. But they can't all be right – unless there were dozens of Jack the Rippers working together in a team to chop up the eight victims. Some detectives think Jack was a doctor to Queen Vic, some think he was a relative of Victoria: a famous person who led a double life. As Jack might have said, 'Who nose?'

Dr Joseph Bell is a really clever feller. So clever that Joe's friend, a writer called Arthur Conan Doyle, makes him the star of a new detective book he has written. But Arthur doesn't call the detective Dr Joseph Bell. Oh, no. He gives the book detective a seriously weird name – Sherlock Holmes. Now Sherlock is the most famous detective never to have existed. Joe Bell, in the meantime, is not famous at all. Joe is very annoyed down there in his coffin. How do I know? Elementary, my dear reader.

1889

Robert Louis Stevenson retires to Samoa. This popular author is best known for his children's book, *Treasure Island*. He started by drawing a map of the imaginary island and used his friend W E Henley as the villain, Long John Silver. Would you make your friend into a villain? If you are a *Horrible Histories* reader then the answer is probably 'yes'. Anyway, Rob Lou knocked the book out in two weeks and said, 'It was to be a story for boys. Women were excluded.' Oo-er! Famous – among boys anyway.

Richard Pigott is a newspaper reporter and he wants a good story about the head of the Irish Parliament – Charles Parnell. So Richard makes one up. He says Parnell was part of the Phoenix Park Murder Plot in Dublin. And to prove it Richard has letters from Parnell ... except Richard wrote them himself. There is one problem with the forged letters – the spelling. The judges give Pigott a spelling test and the forger fails miserably. He is so bad that the judges fall about laughing. They must be teachers in their spare time.

1890

Cecil Rhodes, failed cotton grower, set up a diamond mine in South Africa and made his fortune. This year he becomes prime minister of

Joseph Carey Merrick – forgotten as Joe Merrick but, sadly, remembered as 'The Elephant Man'. At the age of five he got a disease that the Cape Colony. He wants to make Africa into a British colony and make the British rich. Queen Vic loves that idea and thinks Rhodes is a star. Rhodes tricks the African natives out of their lands, upsets the Dutch (who also want to rob Africa of its riches) and generally gets Britain into the messy Boer Wars. But Cecil is all right.

swelled his head and feet; bags of brownish skin hang from his face while one arm grows almost like a flipper. He is locked in a workhouse but escapes – to a worse fate. Instead of showing him pity, villainous Victorians put him on show in fairgrounds for people to come and leer and jeer. Dr Treves rescued Joe but Joe dies this year at the age of 27.

1896

HG Wells is a writer with a great idea. Take all this science stuff that is going on in Victorian Britain and write stories about it. Last year he wrote *The Time Machine* and now he is working on an even wackier idea – *The Invisible Man*. He is even planning a book about an alien invasion from Mars, called *War of the Worlds*. A hundred years later and none of these things have

Ellis Roberts didn't enjoy a wonderful Victorian invention. A railway up Snowdon – the highest mountain in Wales – opens on 6 April this year. But at the opening two trains run out of control and crash into each other before they tumble over the Cwmglas cliff. Two hundred people survive and no one is killed – but pub owner Ellis Roberts hurts his happened – but some people swear they have seen alien invaders. Blame Wells. He started it.

leg and it has to be cut off. Oops! The railway goes on to be a success, while Ellis and his leg are forgotten.

1899

Sir Herbert Kitchener is a British army commander. He likes to use machine guns to massacre enemies who don't have machine guns. In the Sudan (Africa) his Brit army killed 10,000 natives and lost only 28 Brits. Kitchener goes on fighting in South Africa against the Boers. He will be put in charge of the British army in the First World War. Then BOTH sides have machine guns – result? Millions dead. Thanks, Kitch.

Percy Pilcher is another of those brave Brits who has a dream of humans being able to fly. Percy has a glider, a bit like today's hang-gliders only not so strong. At Market Harborough in England a big crowd gather to watch him. If they are hoping for a disaster they get it. The tail falls off Percy's machine and he falls ten metres on to his head. Dead. Britain needed brave people like him – they died but they tried. Still, he is forgotten.

Talk like a villainous Victorian

Now you may think you're smarter than those villainous Victorian kids who never went to school (lucky kids!). And if you met one, they might struggle to understand you!

SO I TEXTED HIM ON HIS MOBILE AND TOLD HIM 'BOUT THIS WICKED ROCK GROUP ON THE BOX

But the truth is *you*, with all your schooling, would find it just as hard to understand *them*!

I'M A BIT OF A PUDDING-SNAMMER AND A SNICK FADGER, WHILE MY MUM IS MORE OF A SNOW DROPPER AND A JERRY SNEAK

OF COURSE MY DAD IS A RIVER RAT AT NIGHT AND A FOGLE HUNTER BY DAY-TILL HE BECAME AN ANABAPTIST THAT IS

REALLY?

You got that? No? Oh, well here's what those words mean…

Villainous Victorian Phrasebook

pudding-snammer	someone who steals from bakeries
snick fadger	someone who steals little coins
snow dropper	someone who steals washing hung out to dry
jerry sneak	someone who steals watches
river rat	someone who strips corpses found drowned in a river
fogle hunter	someone who steals silk handkerchiefs
Anabaptist	a thief who has been caught and thrown in a pond
back jumper	a burglar who goes through back doors
fagger	a small boy who can slip through a small window to let a burglar in
little snakesman	a fagger who slips through drains to get in a house
Tom Tug	mug or idiot
doddy	Scots for idiot
gump	Yorkshire for idiot
strut noddy	someone who doesn't know how stupid they really are
cracked the crib	broke into a house
yaffle	shout
ding on the coconut	bash on the head

twisted	killed
sturrabin	prison
pan	workhouse
staggering bob	scraps of meat
dogsbody	pease pudding
cod's head	fool
kiddy-nipped	pick-pocketed
spangle	money
wobbler	boiled leg of mutton

Getting the message

Victorian villains didn't just have their own speech. They had their own set of coded signs too.

Are you a door-to-door salesman (a 'hawker') going to call at that posh house and ask for some food or money? Better look at the sign chalked on the gatepost first. Your villainous friends have been there first and left a secret note...

Why not learn from history? Mark your teachers!

Criminal cures

Living in Victorian Britain was smelly, painful and cruel. Could you have survived even one single day?

The Victorians had some cures that would shock a modern doctor. For example, the chemical arsenic is a deadly poison – Victorian murderers loved to use it. But some people swallowed arsenic to cure their warts. (Swallow too much and you would never have to worry about your warts again!)

It cost a lot of money to visit a Victorian doctor. So parents would come up with their own (cheap) ways of treating their children.

Can you match these Victorian cases to their cures? Probably doesn't matter if you get them wrong – they wouldn't work anyway!

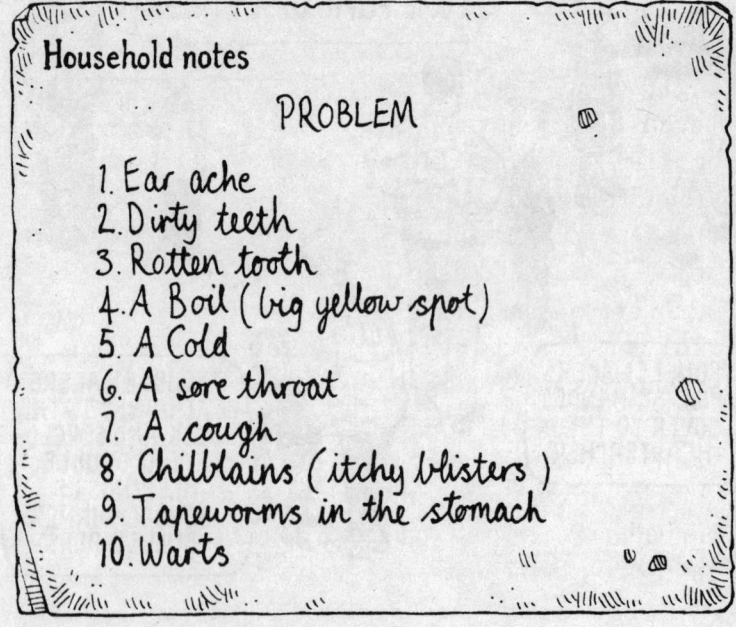

Household notes

PROBLEM

1. Ear ache
2. Dirty teeth
3. Rotten tooth
4. A Boil (big yellow spot)
5. A Cold
6. A sore throat
7. A cough
8. Chilblains (itchy blisters)
9. Tapeworms in the stomach
10. Warts

CURE

a) Fill it with rubber
b) Wrap a sweaty sock around the neck
c) Starve yourself, then fry some bacon
d) Rub with soot and salt
e) Drink a mix of beer, vinegar, black treacle and brown sugar
f) Bury string in the ground
g) Baked potato on the painful area
h) A bath in cold water every day
i) Wrap a red bandage round the neck
j) Slap on hot porridge

Answers:

1g) A potato would be baked in an oven, then wrapped in a scarf that was fastened round the head so the hot potato was against the ear. A baked onion would do if you  didn't have a potato handy. Some people said it worked!

2d) The salt works well as a tooth cleaner – not so sure about the soot. Would you want to kiss someone who'd cleaned their teeth in soot?

3a) The Victorians used a sort of rubber called 'gutta percha'. It was used for toys and golf balls. It went soft in boiling water so all you had to do was heat it, bung it in the hole in the tooth, then let it set. Useless!

4j) A cure for boils was to put on something hot, wrapped in cloth – a 'poultice'. Porridge oats would work – but you could use mashed carrots, a slice of wet bread, a cloth soaked in vinegar (if you want to smell like a chip shop) or hot beer (if you want to smell like a pub).

5b) Phew! But true. The scent of a mouldy sock was supposed to clear the head. The Victorians also put wet salt in the hand and sniffed hard. It was supposed to help with a blocked nose – but if your nose was sore it would be very painful. 'Snot nice. Better to sniff and suffer. Or you could try one of these other useless cold cures…

- Soak your feet in hot water with mustard.
- Roast a goose and scoop out the grease to rub into your back and chest.
- Drink hot whisky.

6i) For some reason the bandage had to be red. The usual material was a wool stuff called flannel. Cosy. But a cure? I think not.

7e) Boil them all together for 20 minutes, then add a small bottle of rum. Have a teaspoon of the mixture three times a day. Yeuch! Let's face it – if YOU had a cough, and someone threatened to give you a dose of that lot, you'd soon stop coughing. Perfect cure!

8h) Nice, eh? Especially in winter. If you got the dreaded chilblains on your feet, then you could slap wet bread on them. That's a bit awkward if you fancy a game of football.

9c) These jolly little worms live in your gut and feed on your food. So all you have to do is starve yourself and you starve the worm. Now comes the clever bit – fry some bacon and the smell will drive the hungry little parasite mad. It will leap out of your mouth to get at the bacon. You got him! Unless he gets the bacon first, turns round and gets you!

10f) Bury one piece of string for each wart. As the string rots then the wart rots away. That's a lot of rot. Another trick was to rub your wart with a piece of steak, put the steak in a matchbox and bury it. Don't stake your life on it working.

Quacks for the Queen

Victoria was potty about her husband, Albert. Then Albert died. She was so miserable that she refused to be seen in public for years. Victoria photographed every part of the room where Albert died to make sure nothing would change – so she could pretend he hadn't died. A jug of hot water was placed in his room each day. His dressing gown was laid on his bed each night. She even had a cast made of his hand and kept a copy so she could hold hands with him.

The doctors couldn't make her happy – so they gave her happy drugs (laudanum). Before long, Queen Vic was a drug addict.

While sad Vic swallowed her happy drugs, the poor people in Britain had no pill for their sicknesses...

Singing the blues

The disease 'cholera' was caused by drinking dirty water full of human poo and pee. In 1849, 54 people from London's slums wrote to *The Times* newspaper about their terrible toilets – or 'privies' as they called them. The cholera must have affected their spelling too, because here's what they wrote…

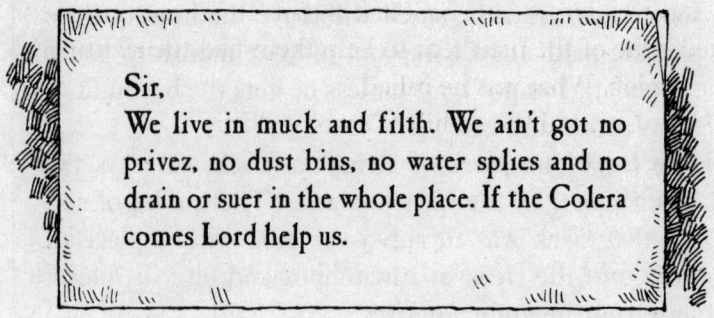

Sir,
We live in muck and filth. We ain't got no privez, no dust bins, no water splies and no drain or suer in the whole place. If the Colera comes Lord help us.

Test your teacher

Teachers are clever people. Far too clever to read a *Horrible Histories* book. So keep this one hidden in case they stumble across it and see the answers to the villainous questions you are going to ask them about the Victorian age. Here we go...

1 A potato famine hit Scotland in the 1840s and hundreds died. One of the men sent to help them had the right name for the job. What was he called?
a) Ivor Cornhill (I've a hill of corn, geddit?)
b) Pine Coffin
c) Scot Feeder

2 Sir Robert Peel created the police force, but the bobbies couldn't stop him dying in a traffic accident. How did he die?
a) He was crushed under the wheels of a carriage while crossing the road. Splat!!!
b) He was crossing a railway line when a train hit his coach. Splinter!!!
c) He fell off his horse and the horse fell on top of him. Scrunch!!!

3 In 1875 the first one was opened in London. First what?
a) Roller–skating rink
b) Ice–skating rink
c) Bottle of ink

109

4 In 1876 William Gladstone lost his job as prime minister to old enemy Benjamin Disraeli. So now he spends his time writing a book! What does he write?

a) A book on how to become a great prime minister, just like him. Boastful.

b) A fairy story for children with a man like Disraeli as the wicked wizard. Revengeful.

c) A horrible history book. Dreadful.

5 Queen Victoria's son, Edward, got married. One guest at the wedding was a three-year-old German prince. What did he do that caused a bit of trouble?

a) He was supposed to carry the 'train' at the back of the bride's dress. But he had stuffed himself with sweets and threw up all over it.

b) He was guarded by two princes because he was so naughty and he bit their legs to try to escape.

c) The archbishop, in his tall hat and fine robes, walked past and the prince stuck out a foot and tripped him up. The archbishop died and the wedding was put off.

6 How did some Victorians try to discover the name of a thief who robbed them?

a) They called in Sherlock Holmes – great brain.

b) They baked a toad in a ball of clay – great pain.
c) They went to church and prayed for God to strike the thief with lightning – not sane.

7 The Gloucester hangman liked to show off at public executions to give the crowd a laugh. What did he do?
a) He tap-danced on the scaffold while the crowd waited for the prisoner to arrive – a bit of a jig.
b) He wore a black hood over his head but put false hair on top of it – a bit of a wig.

c) He let the victim drop, then twirled the rope – a bit of a pig.

8 A train crash in Wales left 33 passengers dead. What did their train hit?
a) A couple of petrol wagons. The passengers fried – boom and sizzle.
b) The wall of a dam. The passengers drowned – bang and drizzle.
c) A lorry carrying fireworks. The passengers exploded – whoosh and fizzle.

9 In the 1860s women were wearing wide skirts called 'crinolines'. Very fashionable. One big problem. What?
a) The crinoline material could be itchy. As Victorian women wore no knickers, they spent half their lives trying not to scratch their bottoms.

b) The crinoline material was made from the skin of very rare white badgers and they became extinct by 1873 when the last one was shot.

c) The skirts were very wide at the bottom and could easily get too near a coal fire. Crinoline burned fast and furious, and several women were burned to death in accidents.

10 Top actress Sarah Bernhardt had a curious habit. What?

a) She liked to have a bath in the milk of 20 black asses.

b) She liked to sleep in a coffin each night.

c) She liked to polish her false teeth with white boot polish to make them shine.

Answers:

1b) Sir Edward Pine Coffin was given the job of making sure the extra food supplies were shared out in Scotland. Of course, the starved Scots didn't use pine coffins – they were just buried in blankets.

2c) In July 1850 Bob Peel was riding up Constitution Hill in London when he fell and his horse fell on top of him. This was not good for his health. Do not try it at home – or on Constitution Hill.

UURH, YOU'VE SAT IN SOMETHING SQUISHY

3a) Roller skates had been invented over a hundred years before but this was the first 'rink' to be built. Back in 1760 skates were worn by Joseph Merlin to a musical party. He skated into the ballroom, playing a violin. Sadly he lost control, skated into a £500 mirror, smashed it, smashed his violin and almost cut himself to shreds.

I CAN SEE MYSELF GETTING INTO TROUBLE HERE.

4c) *The Bulgarian Horrors* is about the terrible Turkish torturers that had attacked the helpless Bulgarian people. The book was a huge success, selling 200,000 copies in a week. But Gladstone went back to Parliament and became prime minister again. Well, being prime minister is easier than being an author … as any author will tell you.

5b) Little Prince Wilhelm of Germany was 'guarded' by two English princes because he was so naughty. And little Prince W did not want to be guarded, so he dropped off his seat in church, crawled along the floor and bit the legs of his guards. This charming child grew up to be Kaiser Wilhelm who led Germany into the First World War against Britain. Millions died. Shame he didn't just stick to biting legs.

CAN YOU GET RABIES FROM PRINCES?

6b) In the Middle Ages the peasants believed this old magic worked. They baked a toad in a ball of clay, then broke open the clay; they believed the toad would scratch the name of the thief before it died. Amazingly some people in Victorian England still believed this nonsense.

7c) Not only did he spin the corpse on the end of the rope, he also slapped it on the back and shook hands with it. He pretended to have a chat to it and all the while the audience were laughing.

8a) The train was travelling from Chester to Holyhead when it hit a couple of petrol tankers. The passengers were swallowed by a fireball. Horrible.

9c)

10b) Sleeping in a coffin was fine so long as nobody came along and nailed the lid down. Sarah also kept a cheetah as a pet.

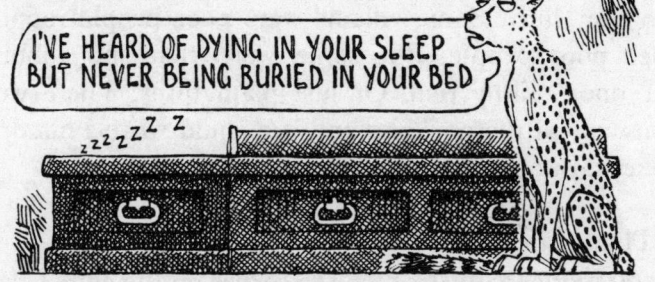

115

Top ten villainous Victorians

Victorian villains were greedy, ruthless, cruel and didn't care who they hurt. Some villains were poor people robbing other poor people. But some were rich and robbing everyone – filthy rich. Or just plain filthy. There were thousands of these villains and you could write a hundred top tens. But here is a *Horrible Histories* top ten.

10 Theophile Marzials

Charge: Murdering the English language

Theo was a poet who made hundreds of people suffer when he started reading his poems. One of the worst was the poem he called 'A Tragedy'. Next time your teacher asks you to read your favourite poem to the class, then make them all suffer with this codswallop…

Death! Plop.
The barges down the river flop.
Flop, plop!
The oozy waters that lounge and flop
On the black scrag-piles where the loose cords plop,
As the raw wind whines in the thin tree-top.
Plop, plop.
At the water that oozes up, plop and plop,
On the barges that flop
And dizzy me dead.
I might reel and drop.
Plop Dead.
Drop Dead.
Flip. Flop Plop.

Villainometer rating: 2/10

9 William Foster

Charge: Cruelty to children for over 130 years

Up until 1869 parents could send their children to school IF they wanted to – and IF there was a school in the area. Then in 1870 wicked William Foster came up with a horrific idea – school for everyone and everyone will be *forced* to go!!!

There are a hundred ways that young people learn – Will decided that packing a bunch of kids into the same room to learn the same thing at the same time is the best. And today's young people are still stuck with that wacky idea. Cruel or what?

AND WE BAN CROSS-EYED TEACHERS BECAUSE A TEACHER MUST BE ABLE TO CONTROL HIS PUPILS! EYES-PUPILS, GEDDIT? HEH! HEH!

OH, BOY! ONE HUNDRED AND THIRTY YEARS OF THIS

Villainometer rating: 3/10

8 Justice Blackborough

Crime: Using the law to make money

Justice Blackborough was a judge. He was paid well for being a judge but he was greedy. He was paid more every time someone was set free on 'bail' – when arrested, people paid him money so they didn't have to stay in jail while they waited for a trial. Every time Blackborough gave someone 'bail' he was paid two shillings and four pence – a week's wage for a poor flower-seller. So Blackborough simply had dozens of innocent people arrested, gave them bail and pocketed the money.

Villainometer rating: 4/10

7 George Hudson (the 'Railway King')
Charge: Robbing the rich.

Georgie had over a thousand miles of railways built in Britain and made the Victorian period the age of the railways. But his main aim was to make himself very rich. He lied and cheated to get money from other people – and even sold land that didn't belong to him. Neat trick. But when he was found out hundreds of people lost their money. George was the Member of Parliament for Sunderland, and he kept that job even when the world knew he was a cheat.

Villainometer rating: 6/10

6 Mr Sneyd-Kynnersley

Crime: Cruelty to children

Mr S-K was head teacher at a public school in Victorian England. One of his pupils was the artist Roger Fry who described Sneyd-Kynnersley's beatings of the boys. Roger Fry had to help the horrible headmaster with the floggings…

In the middle of Sneyd-Kynnerley's room was a large box covered in black cloth. The victim was told to take down his trousers and lean over the block while I and another boy held him down. The swishing was given with the master's full strength and it only took two or three strokes for drops of blood to form everywhere. It continued for 15 or 20 strokes by which time the wretched boy's bottom was a mass of blood. Generally the boys took it in silence but sometimes there were scenes of screaming and howling and struggling, which made me almost sick with disgust.

And that wasn't the worst. There was a wild, red-haired, Irish boy, a cruel brute himself, who was punished. Either it was deliberate or he had diarrhoea, but he let fly. The angry headmaster, instead of stopping, went on with even more fury till the ceiling and the walls of his room were covered with filth.

Villainometer rating: 6.5/10

And you thought your teacher was bad?

5 Lord MacDonald

Crime: Robbing the poor and needy

The MacDonald clan were starving in the 1848 Scottish famine, but there was cheap food for them in Liverpool. 'I will buy it!' said the Scottish chieftain, Lord Mac. He bought it – then sold it for twice as much as he'd paid. Lord MacDonald pocketed the money, while his people starved.

Villainometer rating: 7/10

4 Queen Victoria's government

Crime: Making poor people's life a misery

It was the government that made the laws. But the government was run by the rich people, so the laws they made were for the rich. (The government even started a war in China to *look after* rich British drug dealers.)

When there was suffering it was the ordinary people who suffered. The poor were punished for petty crimes – even children – and were left to rot in slums and die of disease.

And the government could be criminally useless too. They sent men off to fight in the Crimean War against Russia, but...

Villainometer rating: 7/10

3 Dr Neill Cream

Crime: Serial killing

For some reason the Victorian age was the age of the poisoner, and Neill Cream was one of the deadliest. Dr Cream went to prison in the United States for murdering three women and a man. But they released him so he could come to Britain and kill still more. (Thanks, America.)

He offered tablets to girls saying they would make them really lovely – they made them really dead instead.

He then offered to help the police to catch the killer. He seems to have had a twisted sense of humour. He emptied the posh Metropole Hotel in London by printing and sending out a notice to all the guests. It read…

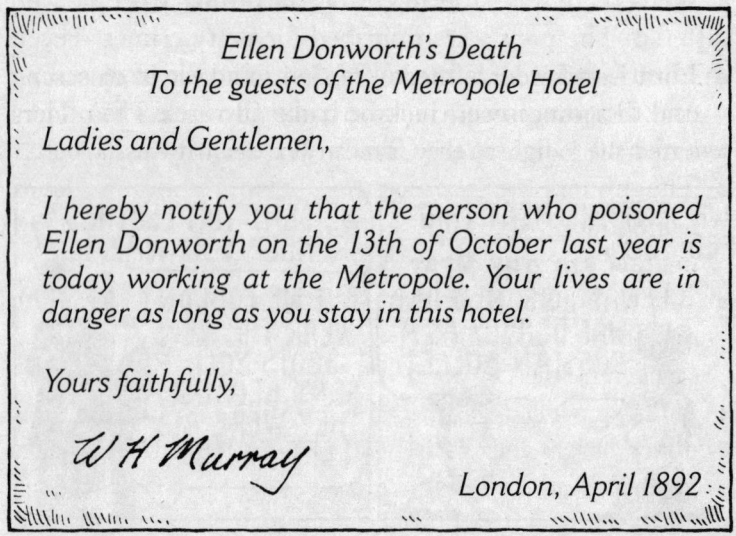

Ellen Donworth's Death
To the guests of the Metropole Hotel

Ladies and Gentlemen,

I hereby notify you that the person who poisoned Ellen Donworth on the 13th of October last year is today working at the Metropole. Your lives are in danger as long as you stay in this hotel.

Yours faithfully,

W H Murray

London, April 1892

As Cream was hanged he cried, 'I am Jack the Ripper!' However, when Jack the Ripper was killing girls in London, Neill Cream was in prison in America – so he must have used a very long knife to chop them. Still, Cream probably killed more people than the famous Ripper, and his victims died more slowly and in more pain.

Villainometer rating: 8/10

122

2 Lord Londonderry

Crime: Slavery

The Londonderry family owned lots of land in the north of England. When coal was found on their land they made a fortune selling it. But the men, women and children who did the digging and the dying to get that coal were treated like slaves.

- Lord Londonderry made £61,364 in a year from selling coal. His miners were lucky to make £8 a year. The miners hated the Londonderry family. Wonder why?
- The miners went on strike for more money. Lord Londonderry threw them out of their homes and brought in other cheap workers to keep his money coming in.
- When there was an explosion at a colliery, the mine managers blocked off the mineshaft so the coal could be saved. The men underground were left to die.
- A disaster killed 95 men in one of his pits and the poor miners' wives and children were paid just one week's wages for their dead husbands. The rest of the town raised £4265 for the families. Lord Londonderry refused to give a penny.

- A writer later turned the tale into a poem…

> *The hundred men of Haswell, all died on that same day;*
> *They all died in the same hour; all died the self-same way.*
> *'Oh you rich man of Haswell, now help us, please,' they cried.*
> *A full week's wage he paid them for every man who died.*
> *And when the wage was given, his rich chest locked up he;*
> *The iron lock clicked sharply, the women wept bitterly.*

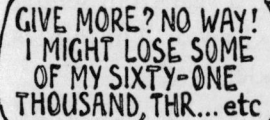

GIVE MORE? NO WAY! I MIGHT LOSE SOME OF MY SIXTY-ONE THOUSAND, THR... etc

Villainometer rating: 9/10

1 Queen Victoria

Crime: Robbery

Victoria took the throne and all the wealth that went with it. While most of her people had to work hard to earn their money, Victoria did nothing. In fact, after her dear husband died she spent 40 years hidden away from the people she was supposed to lead … but still took the money, of course.

Taking money you haven't earned? Isn't that robbery?

We were very much amused

That's all right then. She was amused, while millions of her people slaved in the mines and the factories, shivered in the slums and the workhouses, and starved with the poverty and the famines.

Villainometer rating: 10/10

Epilogue

In 1901 Queen Victoria died and her son, Edward VII, took the throne. He was 59 years old and was beginning to think the old Queen would never kick the bucket.

A lot of things changed in the 63 years she was on the throne – at the start people were hanged in public, women and children worked down mines, and doctors wore mucky black coats to operate on patients.

At the end there were motor cars, a massive British Empire and machine guns. (The last two killed millions in the 20th century, but the first is catching up fast.)

There were still slums, wars, disease and crime when Edward came to the throne. There still are...

SOME THINGS NEVER CHANGE

Victorian Prime Minister Benjamin Disraeli said Victoria did not rule over *one* nation – she ruled over *two* nations.

- Two groups of people who each didn't understand how the other one lived or thought or felt.
- Two groups of people who ate different food, had different ways and even lived under different laws.
- Two groups of people who might have been from different planets...

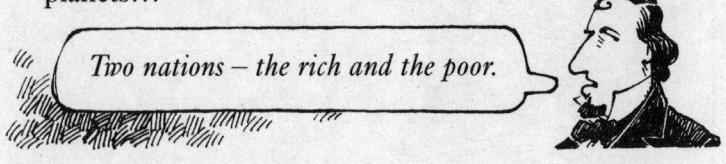

Two nations – the rich and the poor.

Many of the poor were villainous. To stay alive, they *had* to be. They robbed and rioted, grabbed and garrotted, stabbed and stole in a world of hangings and hatred, disease and easy death.

Many of the rich were villainous. They had to be to cling on to what they had. There were cheating chieftains and beating teachers who made slaves of servants and delighted in drink and drugs.

The two nations often hated one another. The writer G W Reynolds knew which was the worst. In his book, *The Sailor's Wife*, one of his characters raves…

> *There is no class in the world as heartless as the English upper class. Even when they give money to the poor they are only giving back a tiny part of the massive wealth they have made from the poor. They made it from the blood and the muscles of the wretched, slaving, starving millions.*

HEARTLESS UPPER CLASS?

I CAN'T THINK WHAT HE COULD MEAN

VILLAINOUS VICTORIANS

GRISLY QUIZ

**Now find out if you're a
Villainous Victorian expert!**

QUICK QUESTIONS

1. In 1830 the Liverpool to Manchester railway opened. How did Liverpool MP William Huskisson celebrate? (Clue: it's a knockout)

2. In 1831 the north-eastern port of Sunderland brought in a new import. What? (Clue: dis eez a horrible thing to suffer)

3. In 1842 women were banned from doing something they had been doing for hundreds of years. What? (Clue: mine, all mine!)

4. In 1844 a lady wrote that people were pleased when they smelled bad drains. Why? (Clue: red sky at night)

5. In 1846 a 16-year-old boy was charged with travelling on a train on a 12-year-old's half-price ticket. What was his excuse? (Clue: time to grow)

6. London 'toshers' waded though sewage every day – up to 1.5 metres of the stuff. Why? (Clue: a golden opportunity)

7. In 1847 the Irish were crowding on to 'coffin ships'. Why? (Clue: they've had their chips)

8. In 1848 many European countries were in revolt. The British rebels, the Chartists, had a rally in London but it was a failure. Why? (Clue: it's a wash out)

9. In 1852 in London a small room is opened for men in

Fleet Street and they are very relieved! Why? (Clue: gents still use them)

10. In 1853, Australia got stroppy and refused to take any more from Britain. What? (Clue: if they're barred from Australia they'll be barred in Britain)

11. In 1855 Florence Nightingale was nursing Brit soldiers who were fighting the Russians. What happened to their amputated limbs? (Clue: it will make you pig sick)

12. Punching opponents and gouging their eyes was banned in which sport in 1863? (Clue: players put their foot in it)

13. Irish rebels in 1866 invaded which British territory? (Clue: they mounted a successful defence)

14. In 1869 sailors were banned from wearing what? (Clue: it's a close shave)

15. When this man died in 1870 it was said he was 'exhausted by fame'. Who was he? (Clue: no more Christmas Carols)

16. In 1870 a new law forced everyone to do it, even poor little children. What? (Clue: you had to join the class war)

17. In 1879 the Tay Bridge collapsed and a train with almost 100 passengers sank. The bridge inspector had said it was safe. How many bridges had he inspected before? (Clue: not enough)

18. In 1880 the famous writer George Eliot died. What's unusual about him? (Clue: he isn't)

19. SS *Daphne* was launched on the river Clyde and the workers got a huge surprise. What? (Clue: duck!)

20. In 1888 the police named a murderer even though they never caught him (or her). Who? (Clue: and Jill?)

21. In 1890 a man died. He had been cruelly put on show to the ghoulish public because of his unusual illness. It made him look like what? (Clue: big ears)

22. Copy-cat Blackpool built a copy of the Eiffel Tower in 1894. But is the Blackpool Tower bigger or smaller than the French one? (Clue: it's one or the other!)

23. In 1896 Londoners saw 'Boxing Kangaroos' in Australia. How? (Clue: somebody shot the kangaroos)

24. In 1896 motorists were glad to see the back of a rule that slowed them down. What rule? (Clue: they weren't glad to see the back of this man)

25. In 1899 Percy Pilcher fell 10 metres and was killed. What did he fall from? (Clue: he was hanging around)

26. Queen Victoria's son-in-law, Prince Christian, lost an eye in a shooting accident. At dinner parties he entertained guests with his collection of what? (Clue: quite a sight)

BEHAVE LIKE A VICTORIAN

If a time machine dropped your dad in Victorian London would he act like a gentleman ... or a slob? Test him with these 'do' and 'don't' problems taken from a book of Gentlemen's Manners and see if he could have been accepted by polite Victorians. Just one problem ... if he makes a single mistake he could well be frowned on for the rest of his life!

Do or don't...
1. offer your hand to an older person to be shaken.
2. eat from the side of your soup spoon and not the end.
3. write to people you know on post cards.
4. remove your overcoat before you enter someone's living room.
5. use slang words.
6. bite into your bread at dinner.
7. call your servants 'girls'.
8. raise your hat to a lady in the street.
9. spit on the pavement.
10. sit with legs crossed.

Quick Questions

1. Huskisson stepped from his carriage to say hello to friends, was hit by a train and died.

2. The disease of cholera. Not only does it give you disgusting diarrhoea but victims turn blue before they die. 20,000 died in the next year.

3. Women (and boys under 10) were no longer allowed to work in mines. They lost their wages so it isn't all good news.

4. It was a sign of bad weather on the way. People were glad of the warning. Modern weather forecasts smell better.

5. 'The train's so slow, I was 12 when I got on it.' On most lines 30 mph was thought to be quite fast enough.

6. They were looking for coins and metal dropped through drains. Would you stick your hand down a toilet for your pocket money? Toshers would.

7. They were emigrating from Ireland because they were starving in the potato famine. The old ships, nicknamed coffin ships, didn't always make it. Starve or drown? Some choice.

8. It rained heavily and many people stayed at home rather than get wet.

9. It was the first flushing public toilet for men – but not women, who would have to keep their legs crossed!

10. Convicts. Australia was a dumping ground for Brit criminals and now it stopped. Brit criminals got harsher sentences at home instead and no kangaroo steaks.

11. They were dumped outside the hospital and eaten by pigs. Then the pigs were eaten by the patients ... including the patients who lost arms and legs. You could say they

ended up eating themselves! Yeuch!

12. Soccer. The new rules said that only the goalkeeper could handle the ball. It also banned fighting on the pitch. Someone should tell today's players!

13. Canada! Yes it sounds odd but with the help of US troops the Irish rebels attacked Brit troops in Canada as the first stage of attacking Brit troops in Ireland.

14. Moustaches. Sailors could be clean shaven or wear beards, but moustaches were popular with soldiers and the navy didn't want its men to look like their great rivals in the army!

15. Charles Dickens. He was only 58 but was racing around the country, reading and acting his characters. It killed him.

16. Go to school. The Education Reform Act forced everyone to suffer at school whether they liked it or not.

17. None. The inspector wasn't trained and had never inspected a bridge before. He wouldn't have known a bad bridge if it had jumped up and bitten him on the nose.

18. George Eliot was a woman, real name Mary Anne Evans. She didn't think publishers would print a book by a woman so she lied and said she was a man.

19. The ship slid into the river, rolled over and drowned 124 of them. Well, they built it, so they couldn't complain – and they didn't.

20. Jack the Ripper. He killed eight women and the mystery has never been forgotten – or solved. But Queen Victoria showed an unusual interest in the case. Hmmmm!

21. An elephant. Joseph Merrick was known as the Elephant Man and he was treated as a freak, rather than a sick person. He died aged just 27.

22. Smaller. Blackpool Tower is only half the height of the Eiffel Tower – but people falling off the top end up with

exactly the same amount of deadness.

23. The kangaroos were in the first cinema show in Britain. Now you know the answer you'll be hoppy.

24. Motorists were now allowed to drive without being led by a man with a red flag. The speed limit also went up from 4 mph to 20 mph. Scary!

25. An early hang glider.

26. Glass eyes. His favourite was a bloodshot eye which he used when he had a cold!

Behave like a Victorian

1. Don't. Wait until they have offered it to you.

2. Do. And remember you mustn't gurgle or suck in your breath while you sip your soup.

3. Don't. Write letters or nothing at all.

4. Do. Even if it's only a very short call.

5. Don't. Well, usually. There are some slang words that a gentleman may use. If you don't know what they are then avoid slang altogether.

6. Don't. Break off a piece and place it in your mouth.

7. Don't. Call them maids or servants.

8. Do. BUT ... wait till she has bowed to you first and do not wave your hat in the air the way the French do – put it straight back on to your head.

9. Don't. Or anywhere else for that matter!

10. Don't. The book admits that most men do this but says it is extremely impolite.

INTERESTING INDEX

Where will you find 'chilblains',
'pig-faced lady' and 'squirters' in an index?
In a Horrible Histories book, of course!

Terry Deary was born at a very early age, so long ago he can't remember. But his mother, who was there at the time, says he was born in Sunderland, north-east England, in 1946 – so it's not true that he writes all *Horrible Histories* from memory. At school he was a horrible child only interested in playing football and giving teachers a hard time. His history lessons were so boring and so badly taught, that he learned to loathe the subject. *Horrible Histories* is his revenge.

Martin Brown was born in Melbourne, on the proper side of the world. Ever since he can remember he's been drawing. His dad used to bring back huge sheets of paper from work and Martin would fill them with doodles and little figures. Then, quite suddenly, with food and water, he grew up, moved to the UK and found work doing what he's always wanted to do: drawing doodles and little figures.

HORRIBLE HISTORIES

VILE
VICTORIANS

Terry Deary Illustrated by Martin Brown

SCHOLASTIC

Scholastic Children's Books,
Euston House, 24 Eversholt Street,
London NW1 1DB, UK

A division of Scholastic Ltd
London ~ New York ~ Toronto ~ Sydney ~ Auckland
Mexico City ~ New Delhi ~ Hong Kong

First published in the UK by Scholastic Ltd, 1994
This edition published by Scholastic Ltd, 2016

Some of the material in this book has previously been published in
Horrible Histories: The Massive Millennium Quiz Book/Horribly Huge Quiz Book

Text © Terry Deary, 1994, 1999
Illustration © Martin Brown, 1994, 1999, 2016

All rights reserved. Moral rights asserted.

ISBN 978 1407 16387 1

Printed and bound by CPI Group (UK) Ltd, Croydon, CR0 4YY

8 10 9 7

www.scholastic.co.uk

CONTENTS

Introduction

History can be horrible! Sometimes you can have horribly clever teachers using horribly funny words . . .

But you may find that history can be horribly exciting. Stories of great and gory deeds. Even a teacher can get carried away by stirring tales of daring deeds performed by our ancestors . . .

And sometimes history can be horribly horrible. Some of the things that happened to people may seem horribly disgusting to us . . .

That's the sort of history you'll find here. Be warned! This book is not for the squeamish. If you have a weak stomach then don't read it – or, if you have to read it, then read it with your eyes closed.

You wouldn't believe some of the things the vile Victorians got up to. After you've read this book you still might not believe them. But they are true, I'm afraid. Some Victorians could be Vicious and Violent and Villainous – Vile, in fact.

When you've finished the book you'll probably know more fascinating facts about the Victorians than your teacher. You may find that History is absolutely Horrible – but learning about it is horribly fascinating.

Be warned, again! This book is not suitable for adults. Victorian adults did some pretty nasty things to children. You wouldn't want your parents or teachers to get any horrible ideas, would you?

6

Vile Victorian timelines

The good

1837 Victoria becomes queen at the age of 18.

1838 Northumberland girl, Grace Darling, rescues five survivors of a shipwreck.

1830s William Henry Fox Talbot prints his first photographs.

1840 World's first sticky postage stamp – the Penny Black – goes on sale.

1842 Law passed to ban women and children from working in mines.

1851 The Great Exhibition (of British industry) opens in the Crystal Palace.

1852 The first men's flushing public toilet opens in London – that's a relief!

1867 Joseph Lister, surgeon, uses a disinfectant, Phenol; deaths after surgery fall from 45 per cent to just 15 per cent.

1868 Wilkie Collins writes the first 'detective' story, *The Moonstone*.

7

1871 Queen Vic opens the Albert Hall, named after her husband – Albert, that is, not Hall!

1877 Mr Boot opens a chemist's shop . . . and another. (So we have the first pair of Boots).

1883 First electric railway – a shocking success.

1887 First Sherlock Holmes story published – the case called *A Study in Scarlet*.

1896 First moving pictures seen in public in Britain – films including *The Boxing Kangaroo*, *Three Skirt Dancers* and *The Epsom Derby* were shown in London.

1901 A non-league club wins the FA Cup. They call themselves Tottenham Hotspur.

The bad

1842 A report reveals that half of all children die before their fifth birthday.

1845 Famine in Ireland as the potato crop fails.

1851 The first cigarettes are sold in Britain – people have been dying for a smoke ever since.

1853 Small earthquake shakes the south of the country.

1854 British troops fight Russian in the Crimea – Florrie Nightingale patches them up.

1858 Telegraph cable laid from Britain to America – it snaps 28 days later!

1861 Prince Albert dies. Victoria goes into mourning . . . and stays there for the rest of her life!

1870 Charles Dickens dies, 'exhausted by fame' – but filthy rich.

1882 England Cricketers lose to Australia at the Oval for the first time! National disaster! British pride burnt to Ashes!

1883 *Treasure Island* written by Stevenson. 'A story for boys – women are excluded', he says. Typical.

1890 The first comic, *Comic Cuts*, is printed. As a man dodges a dart he cries, 'That was an arrow escape!' (Groan!).

1891 Education **FREE** for every child – now there's **no** excuse for not going to school.

1896 Speed Limit for cars increased 400 per cent – from 4 mph to 20 mph! Men with red flags out of a job!

9

1897 George Smith, London Taxi driver, is the first drunken driver ever.

1901 Queen Vic dies aged 81.

The ugly

1837 Robert Cocking jumps 180 metres from a balloon to test a parachute. It doesn't work. Splatt!

1846 Report says over 40,000 people are living in cramped cellars in Liverpool.

1849 Two thousand people a week die in the latest cholera epidemic – they get rotten diarrhoea, turn blue and then die.

1854 The last of London's great medieval fairs, Bartholomew Fair, is banned. People enjoy it too much!

1857 Indian rebels massacre bullying British rulers in India so British soldiers massacre Indians.

1870 An Education Act means school for everyone . . . and that means **YOU** . . . but it costs a penny a day.

1872 The empty ship, *Mary Celeste*, found adrift in the Atlantic – did the crew meet a gruesome end?

1879 The British army takes on the Zulus at Isandhlwana – the Zulus 'washed their spears' in British blood. Yeuch!

1883 Matthew Webb, who swam the English Channel in 1875, dies trying to swim rapids above Niagara Falls. Not a good idea.

1888 Jack the Ripper strikes in London – he is never caught.

1894 Blackpool Tower opens – a copy of the Eiffel Tower in Paris.

1897 Nine-year-old boy crushed by London taxi. First ever road death . . . of many.

1899 Percy Pilcher (honest, that's his name) flies in a hang glider – but not for long. Lands on head. Splatt. Dead.

Vile Victorian Queen

Victoria lost her father when she was eight months old. She lost her husband, Albert, when she was 42. The only thing she couldn't lose was her sense of humour . . . she never had one! Here are . . .

Ten things you should know about Victoria

1 Victoria's father was Edward Duke of Kent, the fourth son of George III. The playwright, Sheridan, suggested that Edward was bald because he hadn't enough brains inside his head to feed hair on the outside. What he actually said was, 'Grass does not grow upon deserts'.

2 She discovered she was heir to the throne when she was nearly eleven years old. She immediately promised, 'I will be good!' She meant, 'I will be a good little teacher's pet from now on.' Later, people twisted the meaning of these words and said she meant, 'I will be a good queen when I get my fat little bottom on the throne.'

3 Victoria could hardly wait. When the Lord Chamberlain brought her the news of William IV's death he ended by saying ' . . . you are the Queen.' No sooner had he got the word 'Queen' out of his mouth than Victoria shot out a hand for him to kiss.

THAT WAS QUICK

ZIP!

4 The Queen did not grow to five feet tall – she made up for it by being about five feet wide in later life. Funnily enough this 'shortest' British monarch ruled 'longest' of any of them.

5 Victoria fell in love with her cousin Albert at first sight. She wrote . . . *Albert is really quite charming, and so excessively handsome, such beautiful blue eyes, an exquisite nose, and such a pretty mouth with delicate moustachios and slight but very slight whiskers; a beautiful figure, broad in the shoulders and a fine waist.* Soon after, Victoria proposed to Albert.

6 Albert died in 1861. A historian, Lytton Strachey, described Victoria's agony at Albert's death . . . *She shrieked – one long wild shriek that ran through the horror-stricken castle – and understood that she had lost him forever.* She became a changed woman. She refused for many years to appear in public. Then, when she did, she insisted on wearing her black widow's bonnet and not a crown.

7 Victoria spent much of her time in Scotland where she had a devoted manservant, John Brown. Rumours said that Brown had married Victoria (not true), that Victoria stopped him from marrying one of her maids (probably true) and that he was a 'Spiritualist' – he held seances in the room where Albert died and let Victoria talk to her dead husband (almost certainly not true!). He died in 1883.

8 The Queen's favourite Prime Minister was Benjamin Disraeli. In 1876 he had the Royal Titles Bill passed which made her Empress. (She was the first, last and only British Empress of India). As Disraeli lay dying in 1881, someone suggested that the Queen should come and visit him. He replied, "She would only ask me to take a message to Albert.'

9 Victoria's least favourite Prime Minister was William Gladstone. She said he was 'half crazy and, really in many ways, a ridiculous old man.' The admiring public nicknamed him G.O.M. – Grand Old Man. Disraeli said it stood for God's Only Mistake!

10 Queen Vic survived seven attempts to assassinate her. The first three attempts took place in 1842. As the Queen rode in London's Mall with Albert, a man came out of the crowd and fired a pistol at her. He was just six or seven paces away. The gun misfired!

You would think Victoria would have learned her lesson. The very next day Victoria rode past the same spot . . . and the same man fired again! The gun only had a blank in it, but John Francis, the gunman, was still sentenced to death. He was granted a reprieve before he was executed.

LINE UP! LINE UP! HAVE A POT AT THE QUEEN, THREE SHOTS A PENNY!

In July of that same year, a youth with a pathetic face fired at Queen Victoria as she was out riding in her carriage. Luckily for Queen Vic, the youth, John Bean, had put more paper and tobacco in the pistol than gunpowder.

Ten useless bits of information about Victoria . . .

1 Victoria had bishopophobia – a fear of bishops. When she was a little girl she was scared of their wigs. Her dislike of bishops lasted all her life.

2 As a child she could be a bad-tempered little madam. Her music teacher told her she 'must' practice the piano if she wanted to learn. She slammed the piano lid and snapped,

When she was playing with a friend she once said . . .

3 Victoria's coronation was quite an event, with the lords of the land queuing up to touch her crown as part of the ceremony. Some couldn't quite manage the last four steps up to the throne, as Harriet Martineau described . . .

Lord Rolle, a large and feeble old man, had to be held up by two lords. He had nearly reached the royal footstool when he slipped through the hands of the two lords and rolled over and over down the steps, lying at the bottom coiled up in his robes. He was instantly lifted up and he tried again and again amid shouts of admiration for his bravery. It turned me very sick.

One unkind witness suggested that he got the title of Lord 'Rolle' because of his coronation trick!

The ladies were as gruesome as the old lord. Harriet described them as . . .

Old hags, with their dyed or false hair drawn to the top of the head to allow them to put on their coronets. They had their necks and arms bare and glittering with diamonds; and those necks were so brown and wrinkled as to make one sick; or dusted over with white powder which was worse than what it disguised.

4 The coronation was curious in other ways. The Archbishop placed the coronation ring on the wrong finger and Victoria suffered 'great pain' in getting it off again. She went into a chapel at the side of the abbey where the Archbishop was supposed to give her the golden Orb. He couldn't. Victoria already had it!

The Queen's Treasurer scattered gold and silver medals among the lordly congregation . . . but that caused a lot of 'turbulent scrimmaging' as they fought to pick them up! It was reported that . . .

The Aldermen of London sprawled over the floor in their furred gowns and grabbed one another by the sleeves in their rude scramble for the pieces.

tinkle
tinkle

18

5 Victoria's weight caused her adviser, Lord Melbourne, to nag her . . .

Lord Melbourne had no answer to that. Victoria didn't take up exercise. She got fat instead. The royal doctor said, 'She is more like a barrel than anything else.'

6 Queen Victoria's son-in-law, Prince Christian, was a truly vile Victorian. He lost an eye in a shooting accident. At dinner parties he would have a footman deliver his collection of glass eyes to the table. Christian would then tell the story of each eye. His favourite was the bloodshot one which he wore when he had a cold!

7 Victoria's most famous 'saying' is, 'We are not amused.' Her diaries are full of the phrase, 'I was very much amused,' but she never, ever said or wrote, 'We are not amused.' It's just a story! So there, now you know.

8 Old Victoria died in January 1901. She was buried with a picture of John Brown and a lock of his hair wrapped in tissue. The dead Queen's hair was cut off to be put into lockets for friends and family.

9 Victoria's vile son Edward became King Edward VII when she died. He was particularly fond of hunting. He once chased a deer from Harrow to Paddington where it was cornered at Paddington Station and killed as railway porters and guards watched. He shot down an elephant in Africa, hacked off its tail and jumped on its side to do a dance. But the elephant was only stunned, not dead. It rose to its feet and staggered off into the jungle . . . not wagging its tail! Edward wrote a letter home, complaining that the leeches in Africa 'climb up your legs and bight you.' He was even worse at spelling than he was at shooting elephants!

10 Victoria lived so long that Edward was an old man before he came to the throne. He complained . . .
I don't mind praying to the Eternal Father, but I must be the only man in the country plagued with an eternal mother.

Vile Victorian childhood

Vile Victorian parents – or, growing up is hard to do!

You may think your parents are pretty vile. They nag you to tidy your room, force you to eat your spinach and wear sensible clothes.

But at least you have some room, some food and some clothes! Many Victorian children weren't that lucky! When a new Victorian baby arrived, people would ask, 'Has it come to stay?' Growing up for many was like getting over an obstacle course of death.

MEET

TINY TIM®

THE NINETEENTH CENTURY ACTION BABY – THE VICTORIAN TOT WITH A LOAD OF SURVIVING TO DO!

1 An 1860s report said . . .

In the last five years, in this district alone, at least 278 infants were murdered; more than 60 were found dead in the Thames or the canals or ponds of London and many more than a hundred were found dead, under railway arches, on doorsteps, in dustholes, cellars and the like.

And those were just the ones the police **knew** about. Many more babies suffocated at birth and the doctors didn't notice the cloth, dough or mud that had been used to smother them – 'Death by natural causes,' they said.

2 Let's face it – babies are smelly, noisy and expensive to keep. Some parents decided that the best way to deal with this was to send their child to a 'Baby Farm' – no that's not a nice place in the country like a sheep farm! A baby-farmer was a woman who would offer to look after your children for you. For five pounds you need never see your child again. Of course, the baby-farmer couldn't raise a child for life on five pounds, so the babies were neglected. If the baby died then that saved money. Baby-farmer, Margaret Walters, was brought to trial for her treatment of baby Cowan, who was described as . . .

scarcely a bit of flesh on the bones. It could only be recognised by the hair. It did not cry, being much too weak for that. It was scarcely human; I mean that it looked more like a monkey than a child. It was a shadow.

Baby Cowan died. Baby-farmer Walters was hanged.

3 You may object to sharing a bedroom with a grotty little brother. But in the 1860s, James Greenwood saw . . .

. . . grown persons sleeping with their parents, bro-thers and sisters, occupying the same bed of filthy rags or straw. I have note of a locality where 48 men, 73 women and 59 children are living in 34 rooms. In one house I found a single room with one man, two women and two children; and there was the dead body of a poor girl who had died a few days before. The body was stretched out on the bare floor without a shroud or coffin.

A French visitor, Hippolyte Taine, found a London family 'whose only bed was a heap of soot; they had been sleeping on it for some months.'

4 There wasn't enough food around to fatten a scavenging cat. Hippolyte said he saw . . .

A miserable black cat, skinny, limping, half stupefied. It was watching an old woman fearfully out of one eye while sniffing and pawing through a pile of rubbish. No doubt it was right to be nervous – the old woman was watching it with a look as hungry as its own, and mumbling. It looked to me as if she were thinking there went two pounds of meat.

5 As soon as a child could crawl it could work. Making matchboxes was a boring, badly paid job, but at least children could do it from a very early age. If that was too boring then you could go on the street corners and sell the matches. You might not be able to afford shoes so you would freeze to death.

6 The young Doctor Barnardo from Dublin wanted to be a medical missionary in China. When he saw the state of the London children he decided he was more needed there. He opened homes for orphan children and educated them too. Many went to good jobs in England and abroad. Most of the girls went into service at the age of 16.

You've survived!

Getting a good job as a servant is proof that you've survived the Growing-up Game of life and death in London . . . But would you get that job? When you left Barnardo's you were placed in a division. Here are the four 'Divisions' you could be placed in at the age of 13 . . . Which one would **YOU** end up in?

First Division:

All girls who, at 16, have a good record of conduct and character. They will receive an outfit worth five pounds which they can keep if they stay in their first job 12 months. If they have a good report after 12 months they will receive a special prize.

Second Division:

Girls who have frequently given way to ill temper, disobedience, insolence, laziness or other grave faults cannot be placed in the first division, but if they make a special effort in their final year to improve then they may be placed in the second division. They will receive an outfit worth three pounds and ten shillings and if they have a good report after 12 months will also receive a prize.

26

Third Division:

Girls who up to the time of their leaving continue to show bad conduct, ill temper, self-will, disobedience or insolence can only be placed in the third division with their mistress being informed of their faults. They will receive a third class outfit, value three pounds, the whole of which must be paid for out of their own wages. A girl in the third division will not be eligible for a prize till she has been in service two years and has earned a good report.

Fourth Division:

Girls who are found to be dishonest, regularly untruthful, violent and uncontrolled in temper, vicious, or unclean in their personal habits, will not be sent out to service, nor will they have an outfit but will be dismissed from Barnardo's in disgrace or sent to a school of discipline.

So? Where would **YOU** end up? And if you ended up in the first division would you **WANT** to be a maidservant in Victorian London? Here is a typical day.

A day in the life of a parlour maid – or, is it worth going to bed?

Morning tasks

6.00 Get out of bed, wash, dress, brush hair into a bun.

6.30 Go downstairs. Put the kettle on. Pull up blinds, open windows, clean fireplaces.

7.00 Make early tea and take it to master and mistress.

7.30 Sweep the dining room and dust. Lay the table for breakfast.

28

8.00 Serve breakfast.

8.30 Go upstairs, strip the beds, open the bedroom windows, have own breakfast.

9.00 Clear breakfast table, wash up, put on clean aprón, make the beds, clean the taps, wash the baths and bathroom floors, clean the toilets, dust every bedroom.

12.00 Change dress to serve lunch; lay the lunch table, serve the lunch, clear the table, wash up all the glass and silver, put everything away in its place.

1.00 Clean the pantry sink and floor, eat own lunch.

᪳DAILY GRIND REMINDER᪳

2·00 pm – 6·00 pm

Monday: Help with laundry, wash brushes and combs, clear out pantry

Make sure to get the grease off the master's comb...

Tuesday: Clear out dining room, clean windows, clean fireplaces

after fireplace WASH HANDS before cleaning windows

Wednesday: Clear out a bedroom and a dressing room

Mistress's bedroom, keep the cat out

Thursday: Clean all the silver cutlery, plates and ornaments

Polish the Master's domino trophies v. carefully

Friday: Clean toilets, passage, stairs and hall

don't forget the fiddly bits

Saturday: Clean out servants' bedrooms

do Cook's first OR ELSE!!!
Cook

Sunday: Afternoon off

(sleep)

Evening tasks

6.00 Lay the table for dinner.

7.00 Serve dinner and wait at table.

8.30 Clear dinner table, wash up.

10.00 Eat own supper, wash up.

10.30 Go to bed.

Next day . . . start all over again. Of course, you would be paid. Paid nearly six pounds – six pounds a **YEAR** that is! And that's what you'd get for being a **GOOD** girl!

Five rules for servants

1 No followers – that is to say, no boyfriends for the maidservants. The mistress of the house didn't want strange men hanging around and she didn't want anyone getting married so she lost their services just as she had got them fully trained.

2 No dishonesty – a common trick was for the mistress to hide a coin under a carpet. If the servant didn't find the coin then she hadn't done the sweeping properly – she'd be sacked; if she **did** find the coin and kept it then, of course, she'd be sacked for dishonesty!

DON'T OVER-DO IT DEAR !

3 Wear a uniform – men had to wear dark suits or evening dress; women had to buy (or make) a cotton dress for morning wear and a black wool dress with a white cap and apron for the afternoons. (As a special treat she might be given some cloth as a Christmas present to make a new dress!)

4 Stay invisible – servants were to keep out of the way as much as possible; if a lady or gentleman of the house appeared, they had to stand aside to let them pass.

5 Stay fit – a sick servant cost money to keep fed and housed. The ill or the very old would usually be dismissed to make room for a fitter or younger person.

So, life as a servant could be hard and the hours long. But at least the work wasn't usually **dangerous**. Life in the coal mines, on the other hand, could be positively deadly – even for children . . .

The Monster of the mine

I

'Deep below the ground there's a great dark monster,' Granny Milburn mumbled through her toothless mouth.

'What does it look like?' Geordie asked.

'No one knows. They never see it, only hear its rattling roar and then its iron claws strike sparks from off the railway lines!' the old woman said and scrubbed her grandson's skinny back as he shivered in the old tin bath.

'And what does this dark monster do?'

'It eats up little boys that fall asleep below the ground,' she warned.

'But just the ones that fall asleep?'

'Yes. Just the ones that fall asleep!'

'But is this story true, Gran?' little Geordie breathed and his big grey eyes glinted fearful in the firelight.

The woman helped her grandson from the bath and rubbed him with a dry cloth. 'You had a brother, Tommy, once. He was just your age – just eight years old. One day he went off down the mine. He never came back home.'

'What happened, Gran? The monster? Did it get him?' young Geordie cried, and shuddered in his nightshirt.

'What's all this talk of monsters?' Geordie's mam asked as she came into the room. Her arms were full of cold, wet washing which she spread on some wooden rails above the fire to dry.

'Our Granny says there's monsters down the mine,' the boy said.

'Don't listen to your Gran!' his mam said wearily. 'You're eight years old – too old for fairy tales . . . we need the money that you'll get down Burnhope pit. Ten pence every week while your poor dad's laid off with coal dust in his chest.'

'I know, mam . . . and I want to work. It's just I'm scared the monster's going to get me!'

'Now get to bed!' his mother snapped and pushed him to the door. 'And don't you wake your father up or else he'll take his belt to you!'

'I won't, mam! Night Gran!'

'Good night, boy!' Granny Milburn sighed, then muttered, 'God preserve you down that mine.'

Geordie took a candle and stepped around his dad who snored upon some straw-sacks on the floor. The boy slipped between his three young sisters and his baby brother. His mother wrapped a blanket round his body and whispered, 'I'll wake you up at three o'clock tomorrow morning. Sleep well.'

As she left, the boy said, 'Mam!'

'Yes, Geordie?'

'Can I take some candles down the mine?' he begged.

The woman shook her head. 'They cost more than a penny every day! You'll spend most of your wages just on light!'

'Please mam!' Geordie asked. 'Just until I get used to the work.'

'All right! But just for one week and then no more!' she warned and blew her candle out.

II

Mister Wilson's boots clacked crisply on the cobbles while Geordie stumbled on and tried to stay in step.

'Am I to be a trapper?' Geordie panted.

'You are,' the man said briskly.

'What do trappers have to do?' the boy asked. 'Do they have to trap things?'

He stepped into the cage, crammed amongst the men, and gasped as it dropped suddenly into the blackness. The air rushed upwards, smelling hot and damp and choking Geordie. After half a minute the cage jolted to a stop. Geordie's knees were weaker than his cold tea.

He staggered out into the cave. The candles of the men sparkled in a line like a necklace of light as they set off along the tunnel.

'This is the horse-way,' Mister Wilson said.

Geordie nodded. Horses clattered past with wagons full of coal to load into the cage. 'So where do I work?' Geordie dared to ask.

'Another mile,' the tall man answered.

A mile! Geordie's little legs could never walk a mile! He trudged on after Mister Wilson. Men began to disappear down some passages that opened from the side walls of the horse-way. At last they were alone. The grey-faced overman pointed down a passage. 'Turn off down this barrow-way!'

The barrow-way was narrow and the darkest place that Geordie had ever been. Mister Wilson's candle glinted on the dark, damp walls and on the iron railway lines that ran along the floor.

At last the light shone on a wooden door. Mr Wilson turned and faced the boy. The candle shone up on his thin grey face, casting shadows in his tired red eyes. He pointed to the door.

'That's your trap!' the tall man said. 'You open it by pulling on this string. Here, try.'

Geordie pulled the string and watched the wood door open. 'It's there to keep the air out of the barrow-way. See?' the overman said.

37

'Yes,' young Geordie said, although he didn't really.

'The door has to stay closed,' the man went on. 'But of course it has to open when the trucks or barrows come along. That's your job – to open the door. And if a miner comes along and you aren't there and ready then he'll give you such a beating!' Mister Wilson warned.

'Is that what happened to our Tommy?' Geordie asked.

The man leaned forward and he peered hard in Geordie's face. 'No, lad. Tommy didn't wander off from duty. Tommy did a much worse thing!'

The young boy wondered what could be much worse. 'What was that?' he asked.

Mister Wilson spoke slowly and quite cruelly. 'What young Tommy Milburn did was simply fall asleep.'

'Fall asleep!' young Geordie squeaked. His mouth went dry. Fall asleep! The monster must have got him.

'He fell asleep. He fell asleep and fell across the line. The next time a truck came by, it . . . urrgh!' the tall man shuddered. He put his hand on Geordie's shoulder and led him to a little hole hacked in the side of the barrow-way wall. A hole no bigger than the kitchen fireplace far above in Geordie's home. 'You sit in here . . . now, take the string . . . the first truck should be down in half an hour.'

And then he left and took his candle with him. 'Mister Wilson!' Geordie called. His words just echoed off the empty walls. He had a pocket full of candles but nothing to light one with.

He sat there in the dark and he'd never felt so lonely in all his eight years.

His eyes grew used to the dark but he couldn't get used to the quietness. The odd drips of water made him jump. A steady thumping noise turned out to be his own heart. Sometimes the voices of men drifted to his door. But all the time he waited for the rattle and the roar of the great dark monster.

Geordie tried to sing a song he'd learned in Sunday school, but his dry mouth croaked a miserable sound and he gave up. He closed his tired eyes and thought about the Sunday school. The summer trips down to the river. The warm sun and the picnic food. He could smell the sweet grass and feel the cool water.

And the thoughts drifted into dreams as Geordie fell asleep! But when he'd fallen deep asleep the nightmare monster came to haunt him. He heard the rattle and the roar and then he thought he saw his Granny saying, 'Only boys who fall asleep! Only boys who fall asleep!'

He forced his tired eyes open. The rattle and the roar was real enough! His head was lying on the track and that whole track was shaking. Sparks were flying off the track and Geordie jerked his head back just in time. He hauled the string, the trap flew open and the heavy truck rushed by! 'Well done, young 'un!' a miner cried before he vanished in the black.

III

'They don't have monsters down the mine,' he told his granny as she tucked him in that night. 'They just have trucks that rush along.'

Granny Milburn nodded wisely. 'Sparking on the iron rails and rattling and a-roaring! That's what Tommy said. Just like monsters.'

'But still,' he yawned, 'that story saved my life! The nightmare woke me up in time! I'll never fall asleep again.'

Granny grinned and showed her pale pink gums. 'Yes you will,' she said. 'You'll fall asleep before the clock strikes ten!'

'I mean,' the boy began to murmur. 'I mean . . . at work. . . .'

The woman tucked his blanket in and ran her old hand through his new-washed hair. 'Sleep well,' she said.

Did you know. . . ?
In 1842 the law was changed. Children under ten years of age, and women, were no longer allowed to work in the mines.

Vile Victorian names

Victorian parents could be cruel to their children in many ways. For example, they could torture them for life by giving them a terrible name. Which of the following names were given to Victorian children?

ABISHAG?

FEATHER?

LETTUCE?

BRAINED?

SHEEPDOG?

HAM?

UZ?

CLAPHAM?

TRAM?

DESPAIR?

WATER?

KYLIE?

ENERGETIC?

MURDER?

WONDERFUL?

Answer: All are vile Victorian names except Kylie and Sheepdog.

Vile Victorian child labour . . . or, Wouldn't you rather stay at home?

Home life was not easy. With parents and elder brothers and sisters at work for most of the day, you could find yourself left at home to care for toddlers and babies. George Simms in 1881 describes a typical life of one such carer.

There she sat, in the bare squalid room, perched on a sack, erect, motionless, expressionless, on duty . . . left to guard a baby that lay asleep on the bare boards behind her, its head on its arm, the ragged remains of what had been a shawl flung over its legs.

Question: How old was this girl?
Answer: Four years old.

If you were not lucky enough to find work as a servant, or in the mines or factories, you could find other ways to earn your keep. Here are some examples. Which do you prefer?

Nail making

On average a child would earn three to four shillings a week if his nails were good quality. If not, he could expect a severe beating, or something much worse . . .

Somebody in the warehouse took him and put his head down on an iron counter and hammered a nail through his ear, and the boy has made good nails ever since.

Children's Employment Commission (1842)

42

Chimney sweeping

This was a popular job for young boys and girls, who were chosen for their size and agility.

Life was cruel and conditions were vile. Working in hot, dark and cramped conditions was very hard and tiring. Children often scraped their elbows and knees as they climbed up inside the chimneys. One sweep said . . .

No one knows the cruelty they undergo in learning. The flesh must be hardened. This is done by rubbing it, chiefly on the elbows and the knees, with the strongest brine (salt water) close by a hot fire. You must stand over them with a cane . . .

But beware! Any of you who think this job was easy, think again! If a worker was found sleeping on the job, or if by his own misfortune he became stuck in the chimney, his master would light a fire beneath him!

Ribbon making

You may think that making ribbons for the hair and the dresses of ladies was a pleasant, gentle occupation? Think again!

Three hundred boys were employed in turning hand looms. The endless whirl had such a bad effect on the head and the stomach that the little turners often suffered in the brain and the spinal chord and some died of it. In one mill near Cork six deaths and 60 mutilations have occurred in four years.

Victorian observer

Vile Victorian schools

So you have to go to school? Blame the Vile Victorians! In 1870 the Education Bill was passed. The aim was . . . *to bring education within the reach of every English home, aye, and within the reach of those children who have no homes.*

Children of the 1990s still suffer the horror of homework, the terror of teachers and the dread of school dinners. But, if you think school is bad in the 20th century, you should have gone to school in the 19th!

Here are four school sins. What punishment would you give for each one?

Make the punishment fit the crime

1 Throwing ink pellets in class, punished by . . .

a) A severe talking-to by the teacher

b) Kneeling on the floor with your hands behind your head

c) A treble helping of lumpy mashed potato at school dinner.

2 Missing Sunday church, punished by . . .

a) A severe talking-to by the priest and detention while you listen to the sermon you missed

b) A beating with a strap

c) Doing extra work for the church – polishing the candlesticks, digging a few graves, copying out the bible etc.

3 Being late for school, punished by . . .

a) Having your name written in the Punishment Book so you may not get a job when you leave school

b) Being hit over the hand with a cane

c) Both.

4 Ink blots and fingermarks on work, punished by . . .

a) Being caned (so your hands are sore and you probably make even more mess)

b) Having to do the work again

c) Death.

Answers:

1 b) Kneeling

One punishment was to kneel on the hard, rough floorboards, with your back upright and your hands placed on the back of your neck for a long period of about twenty minutes. Should you lop over, aching all over, the teacher would slap you across the head with his hand and shout sternly, 'Get upright, will you?'

Victorian boy

2 b) The strap

Every Monday morning the priest came to each class and asked us who had missed church the day before. I always had to miss Sunday because Sunday was washing day and we only had one lot of clothes. So, week by week we admitted our absence and were given the strap for it. We should have been able to explain but we were ashamed to give the real reason. Once, just once, I answered back.

'Don't you know,' the priest said, 'that God loves you and wants to see you in His house on Sundays?'

'But if he loves us, why does he want us to get the strap on Monday?' I asked.

I don't remember what the priest said, but I do know I got a double load of stripes when he'd gone.

Victorian girl

3 c) The punishment book

With no exams at the end of your school life, the chance of a good job after school depended on your final report – your reference. One boy was kept back by his father and so he was late for school . . .

46

The only boy in the school to be late. I was humiliated in front of three hundred boys by the headmaster and afterwards got six mighty slashes on the fingers with a thin cane. My God, it hurt, believe me. And something else which hurt even more. My name was inserted in the disgrace and punishment book and put on record for future reference.

Victorian boy

4 a) The cane
Some teachers chose specially thin canes because they hurt more. Many a time the cane would be broken over the hand (or bottom) of the pupil. Caning still went on in English schools more than eighty years after Victoria died. (Ask your parents!)

The terrible teachers' top ten facts

1 One of the most famous teachers in the 19th century was William Shaw. But he was famous for all the wrong reasons. Shaw was the headmaster of Bowes Academy in North Yorkshire. The writer Charles Dickens heard about Shaw when the headmaster's bad treatment landed him in court. Shaw was so cruel that two of his pupils lost their sight.

Dickens visited the school in 1837 and observed the man. He then created the villainous headmaster, Wackford Squeers, in his book *Nicholas Nickleby*. Everybody knew that Wackford Squeers was really William Shaw.

The publication of the book ruined Shaw's business. He died in 1850. Serves him right? End of story? Not quite. Some of the local people of Bowes thought that Dickens had been unfair to Shaw. They dedicated a window to Shaw in the local church after his death.

2 Some vile Victorian teachers didn't believe in talking to pupils to find out why they did something wrong. They simply punished them. Teachers had a motto . . .

For bad boys a yard of strap is worth a mile of talk.

3 Teachers could train by working in the classroom with an older teacher. Trainee teachers started at the age of 14.

4 Trainees could go to college. Some college rules were worse than school rules! At one men's college, the trainee teachers could . . .

not leave the college except at certain times
not go to the bedrooms during the day
not stay up after 10:00 p.m.
not have a light on in their bedroom
not go to any public house
not smoke
not make friends with the local people

FUN, FUN, FUN

And they had to take some form of active exercise every afternoon!

5 The Victorians believed that boys should be treated differently from girls . . . and that men were more important than women. This showed in the schools.

In 1870, women teachers were paid 58 pounds a year . . . but men were paid 94!

Boys' lessons included carpentry, farmwork, gardening, shoe making, drawing, handicrafts.

Girls' lessons included housewifery (sweeping, dusting, making beds and bathing a baby), needlework and cookery.

6 Cookery lessons were difficult in poorer schools where pupils couldn't afford the ingredients. An inspector once made a report on a class of girls who had a lesson on roasting meat. One single chop was prepared and cooked by 18 girls!

7 Lessons were often just learning things by heart, then repeating them. A typical (horrible) history lesson went like this:

8 Reading books were even worse! Children learned to read from books which had wonderful lines like . . .

Do not nod on a sod.

Can a ram sit on a sod?

Let Sam sip the sap of the red jam.

9 There were often as many as 70 or 80 pupils in one class. The teachers would have to shout or even scream to be heard above the noise of the children. One doctor had so many teachers complaining of sore throats he called it, 'Board School Laryngitis'!

10 Punishments were given in factories to get the most work possible from a child. One man, Joseph Lancaster, invented a similar system of punishments which was used in some schools. (They are quite vile, so please don't try them out on your teacher!)

'The log' A piece of wood weighing four to six pounds was tied across the shoulders of the offending child so that, when he moved, the log acted as a dead weight. It was a punishment for talking, which often didn't work, as the child would be in floods of noisy tears.

'Pillory and stocks' Unlike earlier times, children who suffered this 'pleasure' were not pelted by rotten tomatoes. They were put in the stocks, left and forgotten about.

'The cage' This was a basket suspended from the ceiling, into which the more serious offenders were put.

51

Vile Victorian schools – six of the best

Did you know . . .?

1 Many parents couldn't afford to send their children to the new Board Schools set up in the 1870s. It wasn't just the penny a week they had to pay – it was the fact that children weren't free to help their mothers with the housework, or earn the family extra money by working.

2 Some schools had special offers like, 'Three for the price of two'. If there were three children in a family at school, then the parents paid for the first two and the third could go free.

HOW MUCH FOR THIRTEEN?

3 Some parents blamed teachers for making the children go to school. One teacher wrote . . .

I well remember how, early in my career as a teacher, I had to avoid various missiles thrown at me by angry parents who would rather have the children running errands or washing up things in the home than wasting their time in school with such things as learning.

4 If a parent didn't want to send their child to school, they would say that the child was ill. A School Board Inspector would have to go to check if the 'illness' went on too long. One inspector was told that a child was dead – when he visited the house he found the 'dead' child was so well she was skipping in the middle of the living-room floor!

5 School Board Inspectors were so unpopular in some areas that they had to go around in pairs – to protect each other from angry parents!

6 School Dinners – 1885 style

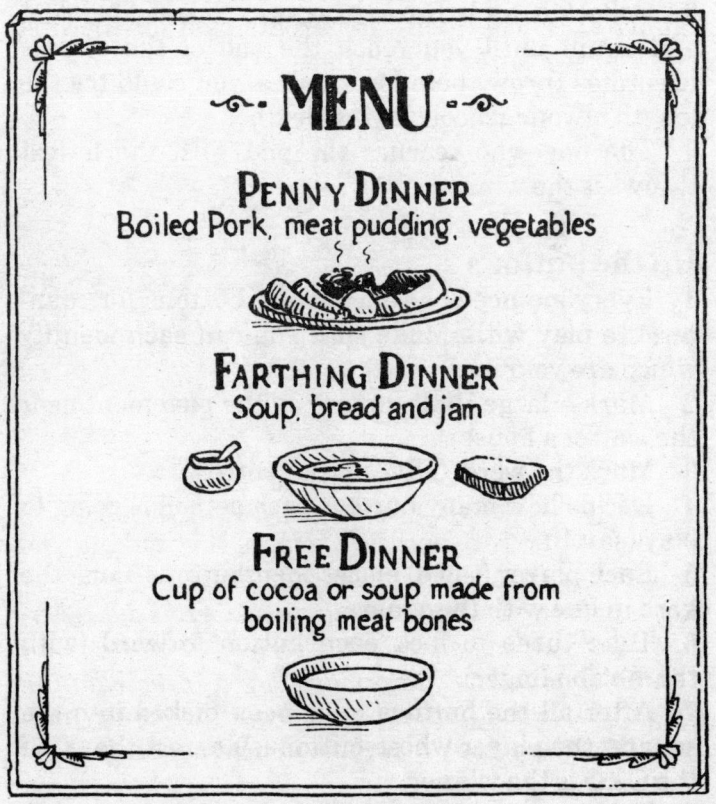

⊸• MENU •⊸

PENNY DINNER
Boiled Pork, meat pudding, vegetables

FARTHING DINNER
Soup, bread and jam

FREE DINNER
Cup of cocoa or soup made from boiling meat bones

Vile Victorian fun and games

Some games you could try

Geordie bowling

Each competitor has a ball of clay the size of a tennis ball – or a rag ball, or a bean bag if you prefer.

1 Taking turns, throw your ball as far as you can.
2 Collect it and throw it again . . . and again . . . and again until you reach the end of the course. (Geordies threw them for a mile – you could try the length of your school playing field).
3 The one who reaches the end with the fewest throws is the winner.

Up the buttons

1 Everyone needs a collection of buttons (or counters) to play with. Make sure you can each identify which are your own.
2 Mark a large chalk square on the pavement near the wall of a house.
3 Mark the word 'OXO' in the centre.
4 Decide how many buttons each person is going to play (say 10).
5 Each player (say 6) places their buttons along the kerb in line with the square.
6 Take turns to flick each button forward (with thumb and finger).
7 After all the buttons have been flicked into the square, the player whose button is nearest the 'X' of the OXO is the winner.
8 The winner gathers up all the buttons.

Vile Victorian games you must never ever try!

1 Only the very rich had proper toilets with water to wash the contents into the sewers. The poor had to make do with a small building at the bottom of the yard. There was a wooden bench with a hole in it. Underneath were ashes from the fire. Once a week the ashes would be collected by Night Soil Men and taken away on a cart to be dumped.

But . . . some vile Victorian children took sticks and dipped them in the waste. They then carried the dirty sticks to the posher streets and wiped them on the door-knockers of the houses!

2 A popular trick was to tie two door-knockers together across the street, rap on the doors, then hide and watch as the two house owners struggled against each other to open the doors!

Some sports you would find very vile

Ratting

Bets are placed on how many rats a dog can kill in a given amount of time. The fight takes place in a large rat pit.

A 19th-century visitor describes a ratting event . . .

The floor was swept and a big, flat basket produced, like those in which chickens are brought to market. Under the top can be seen a small mound of closely packed rats. This match seemed to be between the rat-pit owner and his son. The bet was a bottle of lemonade. It was strange to watch the daring manner in which the lad pushed his hand into the rat cage and fumbled about and stirred up with his fingers the living mass, picking up only the big ones, as he'd been told.

When 50 animals had been flung into the pit they gathered themselves into a mound which reached one third up the sides. They were all sewer and water-ditch rats and the smell that rose from them was like that from a hot drain.

The moment the terrier was loose he buried his nose in the mound till he brought one out in his mouth. In a short time a dozen rats were lying bleeding on the floor and the white paint of the pit became grained with blood.

In a little time the terrier had a rat hanging on to his nose which, despite his tossing, still held on. He dashed up against the sides of the pit, leaving a patch of blood as if a strawberry had been smashed there.

'Time!' called the owner. The dog was caught and held, panting, his neck stretched out like a serpent's, staring at the rats that still kept crawling about.

The lad with the rats asked, 'Would any gentleman like any rats?'

Boxing

No gloves. No real rules, except you don't kick an opponent when they're on the ground. The winner is the one left standing at the end. Women's boxing was common. Large crowds would gather when a challenge was issued . . .

'I Elizabeth Wilkinson of Clerkenwell, having had angry words with Hannah Highfield, do invite her to meet me on the stage and box for three guineas. Each woman is to hold a half-crown coin in each hand. The first woman that drops her money loses the battle'.

E Wilkinson

The reply came . . .

'I Hannah Highfield of Newgate Market, hearing the challenge of Elizabeth Wilkinson, will not fail, God willing, to give her more blows than words.'

H Highfield

Vile Victorian sportsmen

The Eighth Earl of Bridgewater was fond of shooting. But when his eyesight began to fade, he had the wings of pigeons clipped to slow them down. That way they were easier to hit! But at least the Earl loved his dogs . . .

He had soft leather boots made for them to protect their paws.

He took half a dozen of them for rides in his carriage each day.

He dined with twelve of them every night in the great hall of his house.

Each dog had a clean white napkin round its neck. Servants stood behind them, dishing out food onto the family's silver plates while the Earl chatted to the dogs politely.

And if you think he was odd, what about the Second Baron Rothschild? He had a carriage drawn by four zebras. Snakes twined themselves around the bannisters of the stairway in his house.

A tame bear had a habit of slapping lady guests on the bottom. Twelve dinner guests found they had 12 beautifully dressed partners sitting next to them – they were monkeys!

A question of Victorian sport

1 Matthew Webb was the first man to achieve a great feat in 1875. The Mayor of Dover welcomed him and announced . . .

I make so bold as to say that I don't believe, in the future history of the world, any such feat will be performed by anybody else.

He was wrong! What did Matthew Webb do?

2 Blackburn Rovers had to play a soccer match against Burnley in 1891. It had been snowing for three hours before the game. The Blackburn team weren't too keen to turn out. By half time they were three goals down. For the second half only seven players bothered to leave the warmth of the dressing room.

Ten minutes later, Lofthouse, one of the Blackburn players, smacked the face of the Burnley captain. The Burnley captain hit him back. They were both sent off. The Blackburn players followed them – except the goalkeeper, Clegg. Burnley played on and scored. The Blackburn goalkeeper claimed the goal was offside. He was right. The referee abandoned the game.

But why had the Blackburn players walked off?

3 In 1885, in Scotland, the team Bon Accord stayed on the pitch even though they were losing ten-nil at half time. After the break they got tired and gave away even more goals. The final score is the greatest ever recorded in a professional soccer match.
What was that score?

4 In 1894, a cricket record was broken in Australia – the highest number of runs scored from a single ball. The ball was hit in the air and landed in the forked branch of a tree. The batsmen started to run. Two fielders climbed the tree. A branch snapped and they fell out. The batsmen ran on. The fielding team decided to chop the tree down – they wasted a lot of time looking for an axe. The batsmen ran on. The fielding team found some guns and shot the branches off the tree. By the time the ball fell to earth, the batting team had declared and had gone for tea. But how many runs had they scored?

5 The first cyclist to take a long-distance ride ended in Glasgow, where he knocked down a little boy in the street. He was taken to court and the magistrate fined him five shillings.

But who paid the fine?

6 The Duke of Beaufort liked to play 'real' (or indoor) tennis at his stately home. He played in the picture gallery of the house but gave up. The ball was wrecking the precious oil paintings on the walls. Instead he played a similar game but replaced the ball with something else. The game had been played in India, where it was known as Poona. But Victorian people who learned to play it named the game after the Duke of Beaufort's house. We still play The Duke's game today.

But what do we call it?

Answers:

1 He swam the English Channel.
2 They were cold.
3 Arbroath 36 – Bon Accord 0.
4 286 runs.
5 The magistrate! He thought the machine was so wonderful!
6 Badminton – of course! And the tennis ball was replaced by the shuttlecock.

Vile Victorian poems, plays and songs

If the Victorians had a favourite subject, then it was Death. There was nothing they liked better than a sad story of suffering, heartbreak, tragedy and cruelty. The trouble was it was not just the subjects that were painful. The writing was pretty bad too! The Victorian ballad writers were probably the world's worst poets.

Vile Victorian love songs

No radio or television, no records or tapes. How did the Victorians entertain themselves at home? The middle classes would buy a piano, learn to play it and then sing some songs. Love songs were as popular then as they are today, but can you imagine standing by the family piano and singing this?

That is Love
See the father standing at his cottage door,
Watching the baby in the gutter rolling o'er,
Laughing at his merry pranks, but hark! A roar!
Help! Oh, help him! Gracious Heav'n above!
Dashing down the road there comes a maddened horse!
Out the father rushes with resistless force.
Saves the child . . . but he lies there, a mangled corpse.
That is love, that is love!

If that's not cheerful enough for you, then you may prefer a children's song. The moral of the song is that death's not really that bad if you've behaved yourself in this life . . .

Shall I be an Angel, Daddy?

One day a father to his little son
Told a sad story, a heart-breaking one,
He took from an album a photo, and said,
'This is your mother, but she's been long dead;
You she has left me to cherish and love,
She is an angel, my child, up above.'
The boy in an instant drew close to his side,
And these are the words that he softly replied . . .

Chorus:
Shall I be an angel, daddy?
An angel in the sky?
Will I wear the golden wings,
And rest in peace on high?
Shall I live forever and ever
With the angels fair?
If I go to heaven, oh! tell me, Daddy,
Will I see Mother there?

Are the tears running down your legs? Or do you just feel sick? Perhaps you'd be better getting out of the house and going to the theatre.

Vile Victorian plays

The theatres were very popular. So popular that they built huge ones to fit all the people in. If your seat was at the back, then you were a long way from the actors, of course. Never mind. The actors shouted all their lines and made huge gestures with their hands. In fact they over-acted like mad so that everyone got the point.

The plays were written to match this style. Simple plots and characters. Baddies were bad and goodies were good. You booed and hissed the villain and cheered for the hero. This style of theatre was known as 'Melodrama'. Songs were mixed with the action.

And the messages were simple too. In *Ten Nights in a Bar-Room*, written by William W. Pratt in 1858, the message was simply, 'Don't drink alcohol.' Here is the most touching scene – have a tissue handy to wipe away your tears . . .

SCENE: Interior of the *Sickle and Sheaf* Public House. Joe Morgan is drinking with his friends, including Simon Slade, the landlord. Little Mary Morgan is outside the door.

Mary: (Crying) Father! Father! Where is my father? (Enter Mary – she runs to Morgan)
Oh! I've found you, at last! Now won't you come home with me?

Morgan: Blessings on thee, my little one! Darkly shadowed is the sky that hangs gloomily over thy young head.

Mary: Come, father, mother has been waiting a long time, and I left her crying so sadly. Now do come home and make us all so happy.

Mary: (singing)

Father, dear father, come home with me now!
The clock in the steeple strikes one.
You promised, dear father, that you would come home
As soon as your day's work was done;
Our fire has gone out – our house is all dark –
And mother's been watching since tea,
With poor brother Benny so sick in her arms,
And no one to help her but me.

Chorus:

Come home, come home, come home,
Please father, dear father, come home.
Hear the sweet voice of the child,
Which the night winds repeat as they roam!
Oh! Who could resist this most plaintive of prayers?
Please, father, dear father, come home.

Father, dear father, come home with me now!
The clock in the steeple strikes two;
The night has grown colder and Benny is worse –
But he has been calling for you.
Indeed he is worse – Ma says he will die,
Perhaps before morning shall dawn;
And this is the message she sent me to bring:
'Come quickly or he will be gone.'

Chorus:
Come home . . .

Father, dear father, come home with me now!
The clock in the steeple strikes three;
The house is so lonely – the hours are so long
For poor weeping mother and me.
Yes, we are alone – poor Benny is dead,
And gone with the angels of light;
And these were the very last words that he said –
'I want to kiss Papa goodnight!'

Chorus:
Come home . . .

Morgan: (Suddenly realising the evil of his drinking habit)
Yes, my child, I'll go. (Kisses her) You have robbed me of my last penny, Simon Slade, but this treasure still remains. Farewell, friend Slade. (To Mary) Come, dear one, come. I'll go home. Come, come! I'll go, yes, I'll go.
(Exit Morgan and Mary)

Happy ending – except for poor Benny, of course? No chance. Later in the drama, a glass is thrown at Morgan. It misses him – and hits little Mary on the head instead. She dies while singing a hymn to her grief-stricken parents. As Morgan collapses on the couch and Mrs Morgan sobs over the body, the curtain falls.

NOW the Victorian audience could go home happy! They could also go to the pub. In London, one house in every 77 was reckoned to be a public house. In part of Newcastle, there was one pub for every 22 families.

Mr Morgan could well have drunk a lot of beer. Dishonest landlords like Slade would add salt to the beer, so the more you drank the thirstier you got! (Today they have crisps and peanuts instead!)

69

Vile Victorian books

But it wasn't just the popular writers who loved sentimental mush. The 'serious' writers were at it too. The ones your teachers call 'Classical' – people like Charles Dickens . . .

The Old Curiosity Shop

(The boy Kit has come to visit his friend Little Nell. She's as dead as a rocking-horse's hoof, but her aged father doesn't want to believe it.)

'Where is she?' demanded Kit. 'Oh tell me but that – but that, dear master!'

'She is asleep – yonder – in there.'*

'Thank God!'

'Ay! Thank God!' returned the old man. 'I have prayed to him many, and many, and many a livelong night, when she has been asleep. She is sleeping soundly,' he said; 'but no wonder. Angel hands have strewn the ground deep with snow so that the lightest footsteps may be lighter yet; and even the birds are dead so that they may not wake her.** She used to feed them. The timid things would fly from us. They never flew from her.'

Kit had no power to speak. His eyes were filled with tears.***

For she was dead.**** There upon the little bed she lay at rest.

She was dead. No sleep so beautiful and calm, so free from trace of pain, so fair to look upon.

She was dead. Dear, gentle, patient, noble Nell was dead.

Where were the traces of her early cares, her sufferings, her fatigues? All gone.

And still her former self lay there. Yes. The old fireside had smiled upon that same sweet face. At the still bedside of the dying boy there had been the same mild, lovely look. So shall we see the angels in their majesty after death.

The old man looked in agony to those who stood around as if imploring them to help her. She was dead, and past all help or need of it.

She had been dead two days.

* Being dead as a duck's toe nail she will get one heck of a shock when she tries to wake up.

** But not as dead as Little Nell!

*** He's guessed!

**** I told you so!

Vile Victorian poetry

And the most respected of Victorian poets, Alfred, Lord Tennyson, the Poet Laureate. His most popular poem was *In Memoriam*, written in memory of his dead friend, Arthur. Queen Victoria loved it! It drones on for hundreds and hundreds of verses about death. Verses like . . .

> *I sing to him that rests below,*
> *And, since the grasses round me wave,*
> *I take the grasses of the grave,*
> *And make them pipes whereon to blow.*

Can you imagine that . . . taking grass off a grave to make a pipe to play?

At least some Victorian poets could laugh at the serious ones with hilarious poems that made fun of the tragic ones . . .

Mr Jones by Harry Graham (1899)
'There's been an accident!' they said,
'Your servant's cut in half; he's dead!'
'Indeed!' said Mr Jones, 'and please
Send me the half that's got my keys.'

Vile Victorian life

The industrial revolution

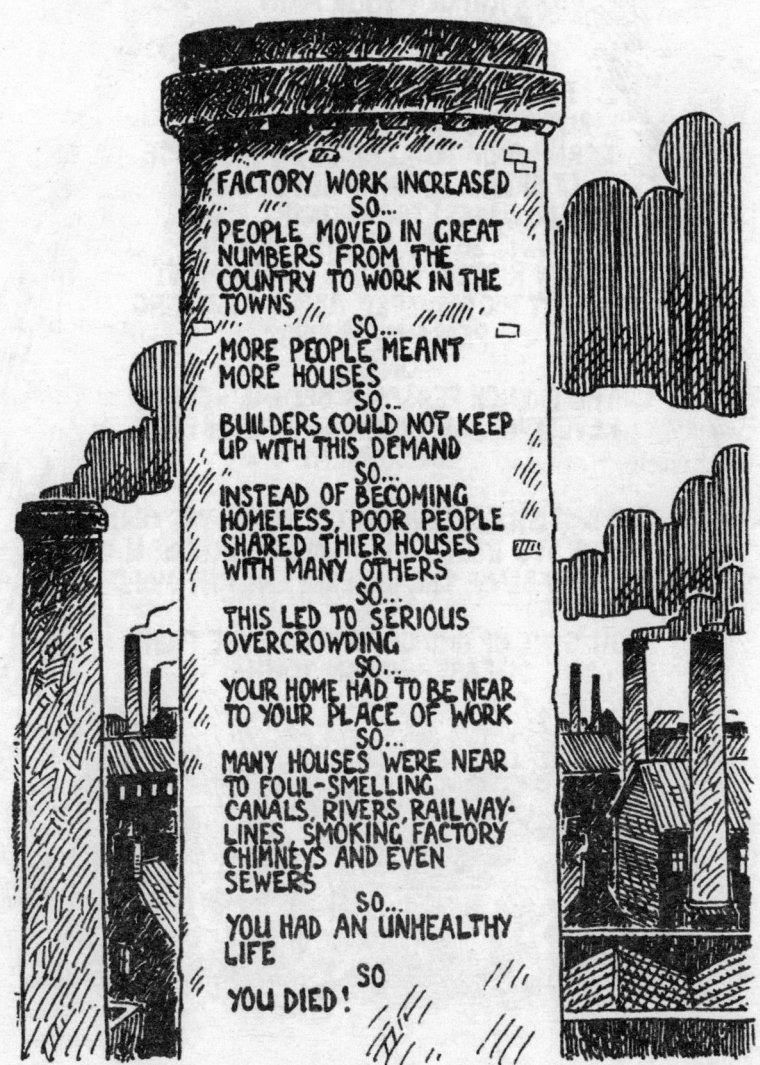

FACTORY WORK INCREASED
SO...
PEOPLE MOVED IN GREAT
NUMBERS FROM THE
COUNTRY TO WORK IN THE
TOWNS
SO...
MORE PEOPLE MEANT
MORE HOUSES
SO...
BUILDERS COULD NOT KEEP
UP WITH THIS DEMAND
SO...
INSTEAD OF BECOMING
HOMELESS, POOR PEOPLE
SHARED THIER HOUSES
WITH MANY OTHERS
SO...
THIS LED TO SERIOUS
OVERCROWDING
SO...
YOUR HOME HAD TO BE NEAR
TO YOUR PLACE OF WORK
SO...
MANY HOUSES WERE NEAR
TO FOUL-SMELLING
CANALS, RIVERS, RAILWAY-
LINES, SMOKING FACTORY
CHIMNEYS AND EVEN
SEWERS
SO...
YOU HAD AN UNHEALTHY
LIFE
SO
YOU DIED!

The Corn Law revolution

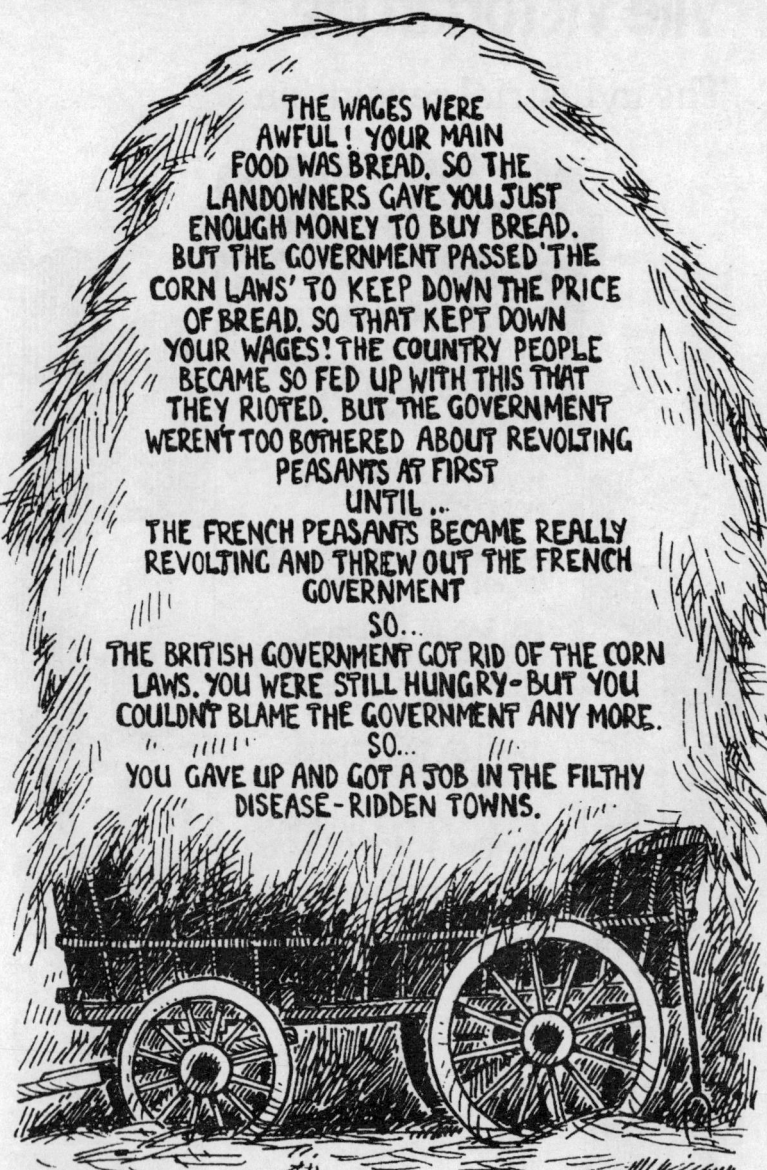

THE WAGES WERE
AWFUL! YOUR MAIN
FOOD WAS BREAD. SO THE
LANDOWNERS GAVE YOU JUST
ENOUGH MONEY TO BUY BREAD.
BUT THE GOVERNMENT PASSED 'THE
CORN LAWS' TO KEEP DOWN THE PRICE
OF BREAD. SO THAT KEPT DOWN
YOUR WAGES! THE COUNTRY PEOPLE
BECAME SO FED UP WITH THIS THAT
THEY RIOTED. BUT THE GOVERNMENT
WEREN'T TOO BOTHERED ABOUT REVOLTING
PEASANTS AT FIRST
UNTIL...
THE FRENCH PEASANTS BECAME REALLY
REVOLTING AND THREW OUT THE FRENCH
GOVERNMENT
SO...
THE BRITISH GOVERNMENT GOT RID OF THE CORN
LAWS. YOU WERE STILL HUNGRY - BUT YOU
COULDN'T BLAME THE GOVERNMENT ANY MORE.
SO...
YOU GAVE UP AND GOT A JOB IN THE FILTHY
DISEASE-RIDDEN TOWNS.

1 Carter	2 Blacksmith	3 Pedlar
4 Mower	5 Milkmaid	
6 Mole-catcher	7 Shepherd.	

Ten foul facts on vile Victorian towns

1 All the sewage of Cambridge used to flow into the river, which made it a pretty disgusting place to walk beside. In 1843, Queen Victoria was walking beside the river when she asked one of the university teachers an embarrassing question.

'WHAT ARE THOSE PIECES OF PAPER FLOATING DOWN THE RIVER ?'

'THOSE, MADAM, ARE NOTICES SAYING THAT BATHING IS FORBIDDEN'

2 In 1853 a cholera epidemic in London killed 11,500. London's drains carried sewage and germs straight into the river Thames. The river water was then used for washing clothes and even cooking! The Thames was such a stinking sewer in the hot summer of 1858 that the blinds of the Houses of Parliament had to be soaked in chloride of lime so that the MPs could meet without choking on the smell.

3 Until the mid 1860s, London relied on water pumped from the river Thames as its main source. But up to 200 sewers emptied into it! Raw sewage could be seen coming out of standpipes in the streets of London, and out of kitchen taps in the houses of the rich, the water flowed a 'healthy' brown colour! In London, an Inspector in 1847 discovered that sewage was a problem which would not go away on its own. He reported . . .

The filth was lying scattered around the rooms, vaults, cellars and yards, so thick and so deep, that it was hardly possible to move through it.

4 Some men were given the job of clearing rubbish from the river Thames . . . and for recovering dead bodies. There was a reward for finding a missing person, but the Thames body-finders had an extra reward – they stripped the body of its valuables. As Dickens said in *Our Mutual Friend* . . .

Has a dead body any use for money? Is it possible for a dead man to have money? Can a corpse own it, want it, spend it, claim it, miss it?

5 The Victorian poor were known affectionately as 'The Great Unwashed'. Why? There was very little water in the poorer areas of town. What there was had to be taken from a standpipe in the street – when it was available. What little water they had was barely enough to cook with, so to save it they went without a wash!

6 The Victorian dead were more important than the living poor! When St Pancras Station was built, the railway company had to put a line through a graveyard. They had to contact the relatives of the dead and pay the costs of doing whatever the relatives wanted. But the homes of thousands of poor people were flattened – the railway company didn't have to pay them a penny!

THE DEAD

GET LOST!

THE NOT DEAD

7 Drainage was not introduced in London until 1865. Until then, water from sinks and makeshift toilets ran down old sewers into the Thames, or drained into huge cesspools under houses.

8 The Metropolitan Underground railway line opened in 1863 – steam trains pulled open trucks at first. In 1887, R. D. Blumenfeld wrote . . .

The compartment in which I sat was filled with passengers who were smoking pipes, as is the British habit, and as the smoke and sulphur filled the tunnel, all the windows have to be closed. The atmosphere was a mixture of sulphur, coal dust and foul fumes from the oil lamp above; so that by the time we reached Moorgate Street I was near dead of asphyxiation and heat. I should think these Underground railways must soon be discontinued, for they are a menace to health.

9 A report on the Borough of Tynemouth revealed the following in 1851 . . .

Eleven persons had been living in this house for a long time with no other means than thieving. They were feeding themselves with a piece of roast beef, eggs, tea and some hot whisky. The rooms of the house were in the most filthy condition that can be imagined; it beggars description. In one of the cupboards, having occasion to search there for some stolen property, there was a deposit of human filth; there were four beds in the room, three persons to a bed; behind the beds was a hen roost with a deposit of filth; the smell from the room was most overpowering. Connecting that room with the one above was a trapdoor by which a person could escape from one room to another when pursued by the police.

10 One of Victoria's least favourite towns was Newcastle. In 1850 she went there to open the new high level railway bridge. The London to Edinburgh rail link was now complete and she could travel from London to her summer holiday palace in Scotland without a break. She ought to have been pleased.

But, the story goes, a celebration banquet for the opening of the bridge was held in the Station Hotel in Newcastle. Before Victoria left, the manager of the hotel presented her with the bill for the banquet.

The Queen was furious! She vowed never to look upon the town again. For the next 50 years she drew the curtains on her railway carriage every time she passed through.

(But she allowed Newcastle 'Town' to become a 'City' in 1882.)

And even if you escaped to the fresh air of the Victorian countryside your life could still be very vile.

Vile Victorian work

Small clothing factories were known as sweatshops.
To save money the workers were crammed into a
small room, often a basement with no light or fresh
air. To press the clothes that the women made, the
tailor heated an iron on a gas or coke fire. The room
was full of steam and the air was full of choking dust
from the cloth. The wages in the 1890s could be as
low as three shillings (15p) a week. Thomas Hood
wrote this poem in 1843 about the girls who sewed
shirts.

The Song of the Shirt

With fingers weary and worn
With eyelids heavy and red,
A woman sat in unwomanly rags
Plying her needle and thread –

Stitch! stitch! stitch!
In poverty, hunger and dirt.

Work–work–work
Till the brain begins to swim;
Work–work–work
Till the eyes are heavy and dim;
Till over the buttons I fall asleep
And sew them on in my dreams!

Oh men with sisters dear,
Oh men with mothers and wives,
It is not linen you're wearing out
But human creatures' lives
Stitch! Stitch! Stitch!
In poverty hunger and dirt,
Sewing at once with a double thread
A shroud as well as a shirt.

Thomas Hood

Vile Victorian factory work

True or false?
Rules for the factory workers were as bad as school rules. Which of the following facts were true for workers in Victorian factories?

1   There was to be no breathing between the hours of 9 a.m. and 5 p.m.
True/False

2   There was a fine for whistling or singing while you work.
True/False

3   Start work at 6 a.m. but no breakfast until 8 a.m.
True/False

4   There was a rule against losing fingers in the machinery.
True/False

5   There was a fine for talking with anyone outside your own line of work.
True/False

6 Anyone dying at work would be sacked on the spot. True/False

7 The managers would alter the clocks so you'd be late for work. Then they'd fine you for your lateness. True/False

8 No young children to be brought by parents into the factory. True/False

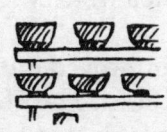

9 'Mould runners' – child workers in the Midland potteries – worked for 12 hours in temperatures of 100–120°F/35–40°C. True/False

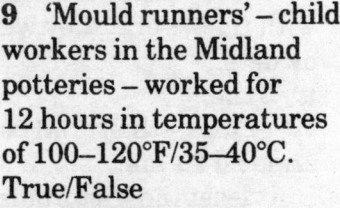

10 Boy labourers worked for chainsmiths and used huge hammers. This gave them powerful, muscular bodies. True/False

Answers:

1 False – not even the Victorians were that bad!
2 True – whistling or singing disturbed the other workers, the managers said.
3 True – 30 to 40 minutes were allowed for breakfast, one hour for lunch and 20 minutes for tea.
4 False – there was no actual rule against losing a finger, but it was one of the most common forms of accident. Less common, but still possible and even more vile, was the loss of a hand or arm; because of infection this could easily lead to death.
5 True – in some factories it was forbidden to talk to anyone at all!
6 False – but you wouldn't get much more than a minute's silence for your death; children had very little chance of getting payment for the death of a parent.
7 True – this was known to happen; there were once 95 workers locked out of a weaving mill; each one was fined three pence.
8 False – parents often took their children to help with their work; they were free labour for the factory owners.
9 True.
10 False – their frail bodies were twisted and crippled for life.

At least the Victorians improved life a little from the bad days of the early 1800s. The 1833 Factory Act cut the working day to 'only' ten hours if you were under 18 years old – and 'only' 48 hours a week if you were under 13. And the under-13s had to attend school, the law said. The trouble was there were usually no schools for them to attend!

The vile Victorian way of life and death

Life was hard and the death rate was very high. In Manchester, children and their parents were working 12 hour shifts in the factories and mills. If you were a child there was a good chance you wouldn't reach the age of 17, due to overwork, lack of food or the poisonous air which was all around you.

LIFE'S NOT SO BAD SON... IF THEY DON'T WORK YER TOO MUCH, AND A MACHINE DON'T KILL YER. AND YER DON'T STARVE, AND YER DON'T GET POISONED, OR FROZEN, OR DISEASED, OR SACKED, OR CRIPPLED OR IN DEBT, OR PUT IN PRISON, OR...

Accidents in the factories were common, but many died before they were old enough to work. In Manchester, in the 1830s, over half of the number of children who died were only five years old! An official report on the death of a woman living in one room with her husband and son, shows the suffering of those living in slums.

She lay dead beside her son upon a heap of feathers which were scattered over her naked body, there being neither sheet nor coverlet. The feathers stuck so fast over the whole body that the physician could not examine the body until it was cleansed. Even then he found it starved and scarred from bites of vermin. Part of the floor of the room was torn up and the hole used by the family as a privy (toilet).

85

Ten things you always wanted to know about a pauper's funeral:

The Victorians' obsession with death went so far that families would rather starve than miss one payment towards the cost of their burial. Those who died without burial club money would face the disgrace of . . . a pauper's funeral!

Would you fancy one?

1 They were free.

2 You'd be buried in a public graveyard . . . at the back somewhere, where you would never be found, as . . .

3 Paupers' graves didn't have headstones.

4 A headstone was 1p extra.

5 You wouldn't have a grave all to yourself.

6 You would share your grave with other dead paupers.

7 It was common for a pauper to share with more than 20 other bodies!

8 Burial grounds became so full with paupers' graves, that the bodies started to poke through the earth's surface, letting off a vile stench.

9 Grave diggers often had to jump up and down on the bodies in the mass graves, so that they could squeeze more bodies into them.

10 As for a religious funeral service . . . there wasn't one.

Perhaps you'd hope a doctor could cure you before you died? Not if it was a vile Victorian doctor like Dr Meyers of Sheffield. He invented a wonderful cure for tapeworms in the stomach – a 'Tapeworm Trap'. It was a small metal cylinder tied to a piece of string. Some food was placed in the cylinder as 'bait'. To make the tapeworm hungry the patient had to

starve himself for a few days. The trap was then swallowed. The starving tapeworm would pop its head into the cylinder where it would be caught with a metal spring. The trap would then be hauled back up with the tapeworm – in theory.

Dr Meyers had to stop selling this brilliant invention. The tapeworms weren't killed ... but the patients were!! They choked to death on the traps!

Weird Victorian superstitions

The Victorians claimed to be Christians but they had a lot of superstitions that were definitely un-Christian. Can you match each superstitious action with its consequence?

Warning – the following can be damaging to your health

1 Placing new shoes on the table
2 Rocking an empty cradle
3 Planting yellow flowers in the garden
4 Putting a garment on inside-out
5 Swallowing a spider in butter
6 Throwing the first Shrove Tuesday pancake to the hens
7 Drinking elderberry juice
8 Killing a spider
9 Turning your money over in your pocket while staring at a new moon
10 Planting a leek somewhere on the house (the porch-roof or a cranny)

OI! WATCH WHERE YOU'RE THROWING THOSE PANCAKES!

What will happen

a) Brings good luck

b) Will give you plenty of eggs for the rest of the year

c) Means the wearer will die within the year

d) Is a powerful charm against warts

e) Brings bad luck

f) Makes sure the family will be protected from witches

g) Prevents the house from catching fire

h) Will double your money

i) Is a cure for whooping cough

j) Means there is a baby on the way

Most superstitious of all was the composer Schoenberg. He was born on 13 September 1874. He believed that he would die on the 13th of a month. Since the numbers 6 and 7 add up to 13, he believed that he would die at the age of 76. He died in 1951 on Friday 13 July. Of course, that made him 76!

Vile Victorian food

Vile Victorian eating habits

Frank Buckland, a naturalist, and his father, Dr William Buckland, had a taste for trying unusual food.

True or false?

The Bucklands ate . . .

Elephant trunk	True/False
Roast giraffe	True/False
A mole	True/False
Stewed bluebottles	True/False
Alligator	True/False
Mice on toast	True/False
Squirrel pie	True/False
Mice in batter	True/False
The mummified heart of Louis XIV	True/False
Roast ostrich	True/False

Did you know . . .?

The Sanitary Commission of 1855 found . . .

STARCH AND FLOUR IN COCOA

RED LEAD AND OCHRE IN CAYENNE PEPPER

AS MUCH AS 50 PER CENT ADDED WATER IN MILK

INSECTS AND FUNGI IN SUGAR

DID YOU ENJOY YOUR LUNCH DEAR?

COPPER CONTAMINATION IN PRESERVED FRUITS

CHLORATE OF LEAD IN CONFECTIONARY

ALUM IN BREAD (SO IT WOULD HOLD WATER AND WEIGH MORE)

Vile Victorian food for you to try

Here are some recipes you might like to try. The Victorians ate them. They won't harm you and you may even like them!

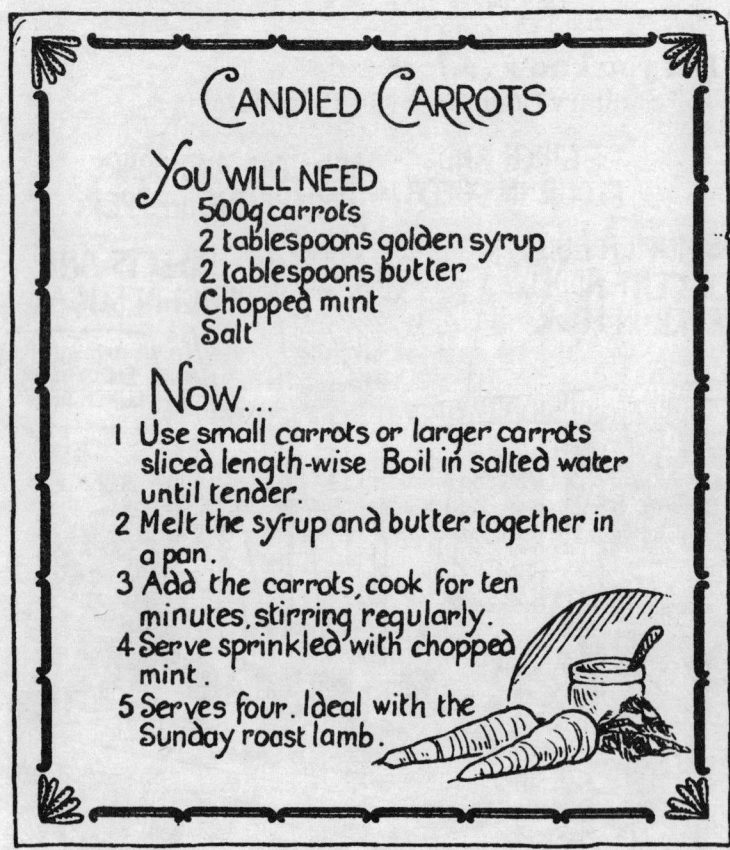

CANDIED CARROTS

YOU WILL NEED
500g carrots
2 tablespoons golden syrup
2 tablespoons butter
Chopped mint
Salt

NOW...

1 Use small carrots or larger carrots sliced length-wise Boil in salted water until tender.
2 Melt the syrup and butter together in a pan.
3 Add the carrots, cook for ten minutes, stirring regularly.
4 Serve sprinkled with chopped mint.
5 Serves four. Ideal with the Sunday roast lamb.

On the other hand, if you want to eat like a **poor** Victorian, then you might like to try this recipe from Mrs Beeton. She said it was . . .

seasonable at any time, especially during hard times, using whatever ingredients are available.

Half Pay Pudding

You WILL NEED
250g suet
125g breadcrumbs
250g flour
A handful of currants and raisins
2 tablespoons treacle
half pint of milk (minimum)

Now

1 Put the suet and flour in a mixing bowl and rub in thoroughly.
2 Add raisins and currants, and mix.
3 Slowly add the milk, stirring continuously until the mixture is thick and smooth.
4 Add treacle and stir well.
5 Place in a greased, oven-proof bowl and gently sprinkle breadcrumbs on the top.
6 Cook in a moderate oven until risen and breadcrumbs become toasted.
7 Serves all the family – but the more there are the less you get!

Vile Victorian facts

Test your teacher

1 Robert Peel (1788 - 1850) was famous for what?

a) Bringing the first oranges into the country – and that's where we get the phrase 'orange peel';

b) Founding the first police force – that's why they were called 'Peelers';

c) Being the first man to swim the English Channel blindfolded.

2 Florence Nightingale was so ill when she got back from nursing in the Crimean War (1854 - 6) that she spent the rest of life in bed. But in 1890 she managed to . . .?

a) Have tea with the Queen.

b) Take part in a charity fun run.

c) Record her voice on Edison's new machine.

3 William Schwenck Gilbert (1836 - 1911), the writer of the most popular Victorian comic operas, died at the age of 75. How did he die?

a) Drowning in his own pond trying to rescue a girl?

b) On stage during a performance of his last opera?

c) Choking on a chicken bone at a party to celebrate his latest success?

4 Who wrote the dreadful lines of poetry, describing a pond:

> *I've measured it from side to side;*
> *'Tis three feet long and two feet wide.?*

a) Famous Victorian poet, William Wordsworth (1770 - 1850);

b) Comic opera writer, W S Gilbert (1836 - 1911), in *The Pirates of Penzance*;

c) Queen Victoria in her diaries.

5 Victorians thought it was rude to use the word 'leg'. Instead they used the word:

a) Unmentionable – as in, 'We are having a lamb's unmentionable for Sunday lunch.'

b) Limb – as in, 'He's only pulling your limb, Jim.'

c) That-which-you-walk-on – as in, 'You put your right That-which-you-walk-on in, you put your left That-which-you-walk-on out, in out, in out, shake it all about.'

6 A Victorian husband had the legal right to do which of the following?

a) Lock up his wife;

b) Beat his wife;

c) Own all his wife's belongings, clothes and money.

Answers:

1b) Created the police force in 1829. Fell off his horse and died 21 years later, probably while exceeding the speed limit.

2c) The recording was made at her home on a cylinder.

3a) He was teaching the girl to swim at the time!

4a) He also wrote the famous *Daffodils* poem. He wandered round the Lake District with his sister, Dorothy, writing poems. During the French war in 1797 they were suspected of being spies, making notes for the enemy!

5b) Some Victorians even covered the legs of tables and chairs so that ladies wouldn't be shocked by the sight of a naked leg! And instead of having to say the shocking word 'trousers', some ladies preferred to call them 'the southern necessity'.

6a) b) and c): a) until 1891, b) until 1879, c) until 1882.

MY POOR POOR HUSBAND TRIPPED OVER THE UNMENTIONABLE OF THE CHAIR, HURT HIS THAT-WHICH-YOU-WALK-ON, AND PUT A RIP IN HIS SOUTHERN NECESSITIES

Mad Victorian guide to travel

The richer Victorians were very keen on travel and exploration. They travelled the world to stop themselves from becoming bored at home. They massacred African wildlife to bring back lion-skin rugs, and they robbed poor countries of their historical treasures to fill our museums. Most travellers had servants to make life abroad as comfortable as life at home. But if you were brave enough to face foreign parts alone, there were guide books to help you.

Mad Victorian scientist, Francis Galton, published a book in 1855 called *The Art of Travel.* He suggested a cure if you felt unwell as you travelled in foreign countries.

Drop a little gunpowder into a glass of warm, soapy water and drink it. It will tickle the throat, but clear the system.

Sir Francis had other good travel hints that you may like to copy. What solutions would you come up with for these problems?

1 How could you light your pipe while out riding in a strong wind?
2 How would you keep your clothes dry in a tropical storm?
3 How would you soothe blisters on your feet?
4 How would you stop your brain from overheating with hard work (like in a horrible history lesson!)?
5 How would you cure a wasp sting?

Answers:

1 Get your horse to lie down and then use it as a wind shield, of course.

2 Take them off and sit on them until the rain stops! (Why didn't you think of that, eh? Maybe Sir Francis wasn't so mad after all!)

3 Make a lather of soap bubbles to fill your socks then break a raw egg into each boot. (Okay – maybe he was a few fruit cakes short of a picnic after all.)

4 Have a hat with holes in to let the air circulate. (Sir Francis had one with shutters so he could open or close the holes whenever he needed to.)

5 Take the gunge from your pipe and rub it into the sting.

The vile Victorian Army

The vile Victorians set out to conquer the world. When they defeated another country they could take its wealth, and its natural resources (diamonds from South Africa, sugar from the West Indies, cotton from Egypt, tea from India and so on). The Victorians back in England could make even bigger fortunes by trading with the conquered countries.

To conquer these countries Victorian Britain needed an army. Queen Victoria was very proud of her army. The army was pretty proud of itself. And that's surprising, because they weren't very good.

Did you know ... or foul facts about the Victorians at war

1 Flogging of soldiers, long abolished on the continent, continued in the British army till 1881.

2 The British commander during the Crimean war was Lord Raglan. He was already rather senile at the age of 67. He had fought against the French in the Napoleonic wars about 40 years before. He insisted on calling the enemy, 'The French'. The enemy were the Russians – the French were on Raglan's side in the Crimea. No wonder he lost his Light Brigade!

3 The vile Victorian poets didn't just write about love and nature. They enjoyed writing about war too. Adam Linsay Gordon (1833 - 1870) had all the talent of a five-year-old, but published this epic on war ...

Flash! Flash! bang! bang! and we blazed away,
And the grey roof reddened and rang;
Flash! Flash! and I felt his bullet flay
The tip of my ear. Flash! bang!

4 The poets did have their uses in war, though. In 1857, during the Indian Mutiny, piles of books were used as a defence. Byron's *Complete Poems* was almost destroyed but at least it stopped a cannonball.

5 During the Second Boer War in South Africa, Queen Victoria ordered tins of chocolate to be sent to each of her 'dear, brave soldiers'. A bullet hit Private James Humphrey's tin and saved his life.

IT'S PRIVATE HUMPHEY'S IDEA SIR

6 The Second Boer War (1899 - 1902) was fought in South Africa against the Dutch settlers who thought the land was theirs. This time the British weren't fighting against natives with spears – they were fighting determined settlers armed with German guns. And they didn't do very well. The British wore red uniform jackets – this made them easy targets – but at least they didn't show the blood. One of Victoria's 'dear brave soldiers' was badly wounded in the face by a piece of shell. He had been lying for hours, wounded, on a hillside. At last he was rescued. His face was too badly torn for him to speak. He signalled for a piece of paper to write on. The nurses thought he was going to ask for something vital. But he slowly, painfully wrote just three

words. 'Did we win?' They nodded tearfully . . .
nobody had the heart to tell him the British had lost!

DOES HE MEAN THE ARMY OR TOTTENHAM HOTSPUR?

7 The British lost many men in the First Boer War against a group of farmers and boys. At the Battle of Majuba Hill the British lost 93 soldiers. 133 were wounded and 58 captured. The Boer farmers lost just one person and five were wounded. One of the British dead was their leader, General Sir George Colley. Victoria sighed, 'Poor Sir George,' when she heard he'd been shot in the head . . . shot by a twelve-year-old boy!

8 Bobbie was a little mongrel dog and a tragic hero of the Afghan war. In 1880 his master was killed and the dog escaped to the British head-quarters at Kandahar. His wounds were bandaged and he was taken back to England to be presented to Queen Victoria and receive his Afghan Medal from her. Having lived through the Afghan war it was a bit sad that he was shortly afterwards run over by a hansom cab and killed. He was stuffed and placed in a glass case (with his medal). He can be seen in the regiment's museum in Reading today.

9 The Indian Mutiny of 1857 was particularly vicious. As well as losing many lives in the mutiny, the Indians lost their nation's wealth. The British troops who captured Delhi began to loot it. One group stole a golden wine cup studded with diamonds. They decided to give it to their lieutenant. They reckoned he could sell it and use the money to but himself a promotion to captain. He sold it in London. It turned out to be one of the most valuable Indian treasures ever seen. The lieutenant sold it for £80,000 (or more than a million pounds today) and he became one of the richest men in England!

It wasn't only the vile Victorian army that got things wrong. In the American Civil War, General John Sedgwick looked over the top of his troops' defences at the battle of Spotsylvania in 1864. He scoffed at his men for hiding behind the defences. His last words were, 'They couldn't hit an elephant at this distan . . .!' Splatt! Bullseye!

The world's shortest war

But ... the British Navy wasn't quite so bad. In 1896 the British Battle fleet was sent to Zanzibar. Said Khalid was trying to take over the country and the British wanted him out.

1   Rear Admiral Rawson told Said to get out of the palace by 9:00 a.m. Said refused.

2   At 9:02 fighting broke out.

3   By 9:40 it was all over. It was one of the shortest battles in the history of the world.

4   The only Zanzibar warship, an old British steamer called *The Glasgow*, was sunk with two shells.

5   The palace was destroyed.

6   But the British navy hadn't finished making the locals suffer. They sent a bill to the people of Zanzibar, asking them to pay for the shells used to wreck the place!

Fifteen foul things that Florence found – or, Flit on cheering angel

Florence Nightingale became a legend for her nursing work during the Crimean War in Russia. She visited Scutari hospital in 1854 and reported back the terrible conditions . . .

1 The men can lie in filth for two weeks before being seen by a doctor.

2 The men are lying on unwashed floors.

3 The floors are crawling with vermin and insects.

4 One visiting priest left, covered in lice.

5 Few men have blankets or pillows . . .

6 . . . they rest their heads on their boots and use overcoats for blankets.

7 Operations are carried out in the ward in full view of everyone.

8 The screams of the men having limbs cut off is terrible.

9 I had screens put around the operations – but they couldn't shut out the sound.

10 There are 1000 men in one hospital, many with diarrhoea.

11 There are just 20 chamber pots between them.

12 The toilets overflow onto the floor.

13 Men without shoes or slippers must paddle through this.

14 Amputated limbs are dumped outside to be eaten by dogs.

15 Men are surviving the battles and being killed by the hospitals!

Did You Know . . .?
Rearrange the letters of FLIT ON CHEERING ANGEL and you get FLORENCE NIGHTINGALE!

The vilest Victorian victory . . . or, I'm dying to attack those cannon!

The Victorian Army won a few battles – somehow! But their most famous battle was at Balaclava – that's right, it was so cold they had to invent knitted helmets to keep out the cold. Balaclava helmets. (To tell the truth there was another old knit in charge of the Light Brigade – Lord Cardigan! Honest!)

Anyway, Lord Lucan was in charge of the cavalry – soldiers on horses – when they fought the famous Charge of the Light Brigade. The Queen's poet, Lord Tennyson, even wrote a popular poem telling what heroes they were. But were they brave or were they batty? Make up your own mind . . .

The charge of the Light Brigade 1854

'Forward the
Light Brigade'

Was there a man dismayed?

Someone had blundered.

Theirs not to make reply

Theirs not to reason why

Theirs but to do and die

Into the valley of Death

107

LUCAN SENT CARDIGAN, AND THE LIGHT BRIGADE ATTACKED THE WRONG GUNS

CHARGE!

Rode the six hundred.

NOLAN WAS FIRST TO BE KILLED – HIS CHEST RIPPED OPEN BY SHELL SPLINTERS

OUGH!

Cannon to right of them,
Cannon to left of them,
Cannon in front of them
Volleyed and thundered;

HORSES AGAINST GUNS – IT WAS NO CONTEST. THE LIGHT BRIGADE ATTACKED BRAVELY – AND MOST OF THE 600 DIED

Stormed at with shot and shell
While horse and hero fell,
They that had fought so well
Came through the jaws
of Death
Back from the mouth of hell,

Tennyson finished with the words . . .
When can their glory fade?
Oh, the wild charge they made!
All the world wondered.
Honour the charge they made,
Honour the Light Brigade,
Noble six hundred!
A Frenchman who watched the charge from high on a ridge had a different point of view. General Bosquet muttered the famous words . . .
It's magnificent, but it isn't war – it's stupidity!

108

Vile Victorian soldering – or, Let's have a whip round for the soldiers

Would you have liked to fight in the Victorian army? Smart red uniforms (made you a good target for the enemy!). Officers who lived like gentlemen and treated the men like servants.

RIGHT SMITH, AFTER YOU'VE POLISHED MY BOOTS, ATTACK THAT ARMY OVER THERE, AND IF YOU'RE NOT BACK IN TIME TO SERVE ME MY TEA I'LL HAVE YOU FLOGGED

And if the enemy didn't get you then your own army might! Apart from being killed by the enemy you could end up . . .

Flogged to death

Private Slim died after being punished by 50 lashes in 1867. He was lucky! In 1846 Private White died after receiving 150 lashes. In 1825 a soldier was sentenced to 1900 lashes – they stopped after he'd received 1200 and he survived. Maybe their arms got tired.

Frozen to death

At Balaclava in 1854 soldiers found something to help them survive the cold. Chocolate. But they didn't eat it!

Chocolate used to be sent out to us, this reaching us made up in shape like a big flat cheese; this chocolate we found would burn so, breaking it into pieces and piling stones around we would set fire to it, this being the only way we succeeded in staying warm for the first few months.

WHAT SHALL WE HAVE FOR SUPPER ?

HOW ABOUT A CUP OF HOT CHOCOLATE ?

Murdered

A sergeant had a soldier put in prison for gambling. He then had the man released . . . but the soldier wasn't going to forgive.

Loading his musket, he watched for the return of the sergeant and shot him through the back as he was about to enter his room.

Executed

Striking an officer could be punished by death.

One man struck the doctor while in hospital. He was shot. I saw this. It was early in the morning. Everything was so still that a pin might be heard to fall. The coffin was put on the ground. The man knelt upon his own coffin. The crack of the muskets was heard and the man fell dead.

Dying of thirst

Many soldiers died from lack of water in droughts in India. One sad case was of a soldier who helped to save the town of Lucknow. He received a deadly wound and lay dying. Some English ladies had been living in Lucknow at the time. The heat was terrible and the soldier was too ill to reach water. As the English ladies passed him, he begged the women to bring him a drop of water. They pointed to the well and said . . .

He died.

Dying of hunger

When the enemy cut off supplies (in a siege) the soldiers could starve to death. In the Boer War in South Africa, the soldiers managed to joke about their pitifully small meals. They said grace after a meal –

We thank the Lord for what we've had,
If it were more we should have been glad.
But as the times are rather bad,
We've got to be glad with what we've had.

And after all that . . .
If a soldier survived he retired.
The grateful Victorian government paid him a pension of less than 4p a day.

Vile Victorian villians

The Victorian villains were as vile as any you'd never wish to meet. The real villains would cut your throat, poison you, club you to death or shoot you just for the sake of your purse.

As if these thieves and murderers weren't bad enough in real life the Victorians made up even worse horrors in their books. Count Dracula, Frankenstein's Monster and Doctor Jekyll and Mr Hyde were all Victorian inventions.

The viler the crimes the viler the punishments. The Victorians liked nothing better than a good hanging to bring out the crowds. All in all it was a vile and violent time to live.

The real live vile Victorian villains

Jack The Ripper
For over a hundred years police, historians, writers and criminal experts have tried to work out who the dreaded 'Jack the Ripper' could have been. He was never caught. Why did he kill? Why did he stop?

Many books have been written by people who claim they can 'prove' who the killer is. But each new book proves the other writers are wrong. The writers have claimed that Jack the Ripper was the following. Which one would you choose?

A mad London doctor called Stanley
A mad Russian doctor called Pedachenko
An unnamed butcher
A lawyer called Druitt
Queen Victoria's grandson, the Duke of Clarence (Her Majesty always showed an unusual interest in the case!)

The Duke of Clarence's best friend, James Stephen (who was hit on the head by the sail of a windmill and became mad)

The Duke of Clarence's doctor, William Gull

An artist named Sickert

A bootmaker called Kaminsky

A believer in black magic called D'Onston.

Or would you go for one of the wilder ideas? Someone at some time has said it was . . .

A policeman (perhaps a senior policeman destroyed important evidence – to protect one of his officers?)

A man dressed as a woman

A cannibal

A Canadian wearing snow shoes

A woman – Jill the Ripper?

The truth is that nobody really knows who Jack the Ripper was. He (or she) killed just eight women but became a legend as the vilest Victorian of all.

If you ever find out the killer's true identity, and if you can prove it, you could sell your story for a million pounds.

Mary Ann Cotton

If the vilest criminal is the one who murders the most then Britain's worst killer of all time killed four times as many victims as Jack the Ripper. Men, women, children and little babies. And it isn't a man . . . it's a woman.

She lived in the North Eastern corner of England and not many people have heard of her. In July 1872, in West Auckland, County Durham, an inquest was held into the death of a little boy, Charles Edward Cotton. The jury had to listen to the evidence and decide how he died. Was it . . .

'Natural Causes' – he died of an illness?

'Murder' – did someone kill him deliberately? And how?

'Manslaughter' – did someone kill him accidentally?

'Suicide' – did Charles Edward kill himself?

Here is the evidence. What do you think the jury decided?

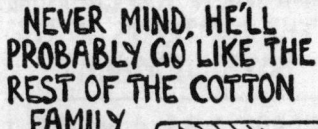

NEVER MIND, HE'LL PROBABLY GO LIKE THE REST OF THE COTTON FAMILY

YOU MEAN THIS HEALTHY LITTLE FELLOW IS GOING TO DIE?

YOU'LL SEE HE'LL NOT GROW UP

THEN ON FRIDAY SHE WAS STANDING IN HER DOORWAY AND SHE SAID TO ME...

THE BOY'S DEAD

DOCTOR KILBURN CAME AND EXAMINED THE BODY

CALL DOCTOR KILBURN!

I HAD BEED TREATING THE BOY FOR AN UPSET STOMACH.. I GAVE HIM MORPHIA FOR THE PAIN AND HYDROCYANIC ACID FOR THE FEVER

115

ISN'T HYDROCYANIC ACID A POISON?

IT WAS A VERY WEAK MIXTURE YOUR HONOUR

AND WHEN YOU EXAMINED THE CONTENTS OF THE BOY'S STOMACH?

THERE WAS A WHITE POWDER THERE - THE STOMACH WAS INFLAMED

COULD THE WHITE POWDER HAVE BEEN POISON?

IT COULD - OR IT COULD HAVE BEEN THE MORPHINE I GAVE HIM

AND THE INFLAMMATION? POISON?

OR THE BOY'S ILLNESS. I HAVEN'T HAD TIME TO TEST IT

CALL MRS MARY ANN COTTON

I GAVE MY STEP-SON ARROWROOT - AND I BOUGHT THE ARROWROOT FROM RILEY THERE! HE HATES ME BECAUSE I WON'T GO OUT WITH HIM!

ASK HER ABOUT HER HUSBAND'S DEATH, AND HER OTHER THREE CHILDREN WHO DIED SINCE SHE ARRIVED HERE!

SILENCE IN COURT! THE JURY MUST FORGET THEY EVER HEARD THAT REMARK. NOW, JURY, YOU DECIDE. DID CHARLES EDWARD DIE OF POISONING? IF SO, WHO POISONED HIM AND WAS IT DELIBERATE OR ACCIDENTAL? OR DID CHARLES EDWARD DIE NATURALLY OF A STOMACH FEVER?

If you were the jury what would you have decided?
Verdict: The West Auckland jury decided that Charles Edward died naturally of a stomach fever! Mary Ann Cotton was free.

Then the local newspapers checked her past life and found she had moved around the North of England and lost three husbands, a lover, a friend, her mother and at least a dozen children! And they had all died of stomach fevers!

Doctor Kilburn then tested the white powder in Charles Edward's stomach. It was the deadly poison, arsenic. Mary Ann Cotton was tried for murder, found guilty and hanged at Durham Jail in 1873.

The vile Victorian children made up a nasty little skipping song about her. It was sung in the streets of Durham till quite recently. It went:

Mary Ann Cotton
She's dead and she's rotten
She lies in her bed
With her eyes wide open.
Sing, sing, oh what can I sing?
Mary Ann Cotton is tied up with string.
Where? Where? Up in the air
Selling black puddings a penny a pair.

Mary Ann Cotton got away with killing at least 15 and maybe as many as 20 people because . . .

1 Poison was easy to buy. Arsenic mixed with soap was sold in chemists' shops as a killer of bed-bugs. Wash away the soap and you would be left with pure arsenic.

2 Arsenic poisoning gave the victim sickness and diarrhoea – so did gastric (or stomach) fever. Busy doctors couldn't tell the difference.

3 A cheap baby food was flour mixed with water. Mothers fed this to babies and didn't realise that it gave their babies stomach upsets. Sickness in babies was very common. A doctor would see a sick baby and not think it unusual or suspicious.

4 Death was very common in the Victorian times. In the 1880s a quarter of all people died in their first year, a half were dead by the time they were 20 and three quarters were dead by 40. Mary Ann was thought to be 'unlucky' to lose so many during her stay in West Auckland, but nobody (except Riley) thought it was unbelievable.

5 Mary Ann Cotton moved about the North East. Each time she remarried she changed her name. Nobody could know the trail of deaths she left in her wake because nobody made the connection between Mrs Robson, Mrs Ward, Mrs Robinson and Mrs Cotton, who had all lost husbands and children in different towns.

Don't worry! Police experts reckon she would not get away with it today!

The vile Victorian make-believe villains

As if Jack the Ripper and Mary Ann Cotton weren't enough for the Victorians to read about in their newspapers, they wanted to read about violent crime in their books and magazines. Popular, cheap crime papers were called *Penny Dreadfuls*. New and horrific criminals were invented to satisfy the readers. Even today there are many people who believe these villains really existed. Villains like . . .

Sweeney Todd – the Demon Barber of Fleet Street

The sailor rubbed his bristling chin. He needed a shave. He looked along Fleet Street for the familiar sign of a barber's shop: a red-and-white striped pole. He soon spotted one over the door of number 186. The name plate said, *Sweeney Todd – Barber*.

The sailor pushed open the door and entered the dim and musty room that smelled of soap. A large, red-faced man watched him from the shadows. 'Good morning, sir! A nice close shave, perhaps?'

'Ah, yes!' the customer said and squinted through the gloom. The chair in the middle of the room was dark and heavy and hard. He sat in it wearily.

'I'll just bolt the door, sir,' the barber said. 'I'll polish you off then close for lunch.'

The sailor heard the heavy bolts slide into the door with a booming that rang through the room. 'There. We won't be disturbed!'

The barber picked up a bowl and a brush and whipped up a rich, thick lather. He began to talk while the sailor closed his eyes and lay back. 'Yes, nearly time for lunch. Have you had lunch yet? No? Ah, I'm the luckiest man in London, there. I live next to the best pie shop in the city. Mrs Lovatt's meat pies are famous. People come from miles to buy them.'

The sailor grunted and Sweeney Todd the barber brushed the foaming soap gently into his bristling beard.

'You've never heard of Mrs Lovatt's pies? You do surprise me! You must be a stranger? Yes? You don't know London then? No? And no one in London knows you, I suppose.'

The only sound in the room was the soft sizzle of the soap bubbles settling. The barber took a razor from the bench and slowly sharpened it on a leather strap that hung beside the mirror. He looked at his own face in the mirror and grinned. 'It's sad to be alone in a big city, sir. No one to talk to. And no one to miss you if you disappeared . . .'

Sweeney Todd walked towards the sailor with the razor catching a chink of light that had crept through the dust-crusted windows. He brought the razor closer to the customer's trusting face. 'We'll have you finished in no time, sir!' the barber chuckled.

Something in his voice made the sailor open his eyes. He looked up into the shiny face of the barber

120

and the razor-bright eyes. He opened his mouth to
cry out.

Sweeney Todd pressed a small metal catch with
his foot and the chair rocked backwards. The floor
opened and the chair disappeared into a black hole.
There was a cry of terror, a crunch as the sailor's
head hit the stone cellar floor below. Then a sudden
silence.

The barber put his razor down carefully. He pulled
at a rope and the chair rose back into its place –
empty now. A click of the catch and it was ready for
the next customer . . . or victim.

Sweeney Todd wiped his sweating hands on his greasy apron and walked towards a door at the back of his shop. The door led to stone steps down into the cellar.

The Demon Barber of Fleet Street looked at the broken body of his latest prey and nodded happily. He crossed the floor of the cellar and came to the steps that led upwards into the shop next door. He tapped on the door and tugged it open a touch.

The warm smell of fresh-baked pies met his nostrils. 'Ah, Mrs Lovatt,' he said gently, 'One of your delicious meat pies, if you please.'

The smiling woman handed him a steaming plate and looked at him with one eyebrow raised, questioning.

Todd nodded. 'Yes, Mrs Lovatt. You'll find a nice, fresh supply of meat on the cellar floor ....'

Of course, Sweeney Todd never really existed, but a hundred years later his story is still told and has even been made into a musical play!

Ask ten sensible adults about Sweeney Todd – or ten teachers if you can't find any sensible adults. See how many think it may be a true story. But it isn't! It really isn't!

The real dead vile Victorian villains

Public executions

If the real villains of Victorian Britain were caught then they faced fearsome punishments. They could be sent to the 'hulks' – ancient ships tied up by the river. By day the villains would break stones, clear sewers or move earth for building works. By night they would return in iron chains to the filthy, crowded ships where disease killed many. In 1841, at the start of Victoria's reign, there were 3625 prisoners in these floating prisons on the Thames. By 1857 there were none. (The villains had been transported to Australia.)

But they still faced the death penalty by hanging. And hanging in public.

WE'RE NOT GOING TO HANG YOU, YOU'RE BEING TRANSPORTED TO AUSTRALIA

IS THAT GOOD?

Foul facts about public executions

In 1846 public executions were held outside Newgate Prison. Rich people paid between 20 and 50 guineas (a guinea was a bit more than a pound) to rent the houses opposite the prison to have a good view of seven pirates being executed. (That's several thousand pounds in today's values!)

Charles Dickens said . . .

I believe public execution to be a savage horror behind the time.

But he wasn't against executions going on inside the prison walls.

In 1856 a group of politicians from the House of Commons said that public executions should end. The House of Lords rejected the idea. They said that executing someone in public set an example to other people who thought about committing a crime.

The Lords' decision was popular with many people who did good business at executions . . . for example, the sellers of 'ballads' – popular poems written about the murderer. The poetry was usually awful.

Franz Muller was executed for the murder of an old man in a railway carriage in 1864 – the first ever railway murder. He tried to escape to America but was brought back to face a trial. He confessed to the murder in the final second before the gallows trap-door opened and he fell to his death. The poems written about him were crimes against the art of poetry! They included terrible lines like . . .

> *That fatal night I was determined*
> *Poor Thomas Briggs to rob and slay*
> *And in the fatal railway carriage,*
> *That night, I took his life away.*
> *His crimson gore did stain the carriage.*
> *I threw him from the train, alack!*
> *I, on the railway, left him bleeding.*
> *I robbed him of his watch and hat.*

About 50,000 people attended Muller's execution. The day after, *The Times* newspaper reported . . .

None will ever believe the open manner in which garrotting and highway robbery were carried on.

In 1868, public hangings were stopped – not because they were inhuman, but because they caused so much crime and death among the crowds that went to see them!

The man they could not hang

Not everyone was as successfully executed as Franz Muller. Twenty years after Muller's crime, a middle-aged man, John Lee, had been working for a Miss Emma Keyse who had once been a maid to Queen Victoria. After an argument she cut his wages – in return he cut her throat.

He was tried and sentenced to hang. The hangman's name was Berry. Mr Berry placed a hood over Lee's head, put the rope round his neck, then pulled the lever to open the trapdoor. Nothing happened!

Berry jumped up and down on the trapdoor. Still nothing happened. Lee was taken back to his cell to wait while the machinery was tested. It worked perfectly. Lee was brought back.

Mr Berry placed a hood over Lee's head, put the rope round his neck then pulled the lever to open the trapdoor again. Nothing happened! Again Berry tested it. Again it worked perfectly.

Third time lucky perhaps? Mr Berry placed a hood over Lee's head once more, put the rope round his neck, then pulled the lever to open the trapdoor. Nothing happened!

It was thought that wet weather had swelled the wood and Lee's weight made the trapdoor jam shut.

The local justice ordered a postponement of the execution until the government minister had been informed of the strange events. At last the reply came . . .

Don't try again. John Lee is to be imprisoned for life instead.

John Lee's neck got away with murder!

Five further facts about John Lee:

1 Lee served 22 years in prison and then was released.

2 No one knows what happened to him after he was released.

3 Some people thought he was innocent of the crime. The sticking trapdoor was God's way of making sure that justice was done.

4 A film was made about the case and called, *The Man They Could Not Hang*.

5 A pop group has called itself, *The Men They Couldn't Hang*.

Criminals

Victorians thought they could tell a criminal by his looks and general appearance! Things they looked for were:

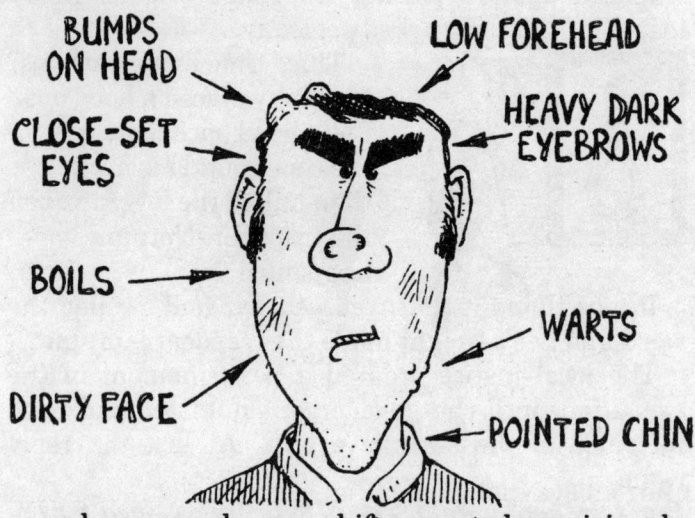

BUMPS ON HEAD

LOW FOREHEAD

CLOSE-SET EYES

HEAVY DARK EYEBROWS

BOILS

WARTS

DIRTY FACE

POINTED CHIN

... and anyone who was shifty or acted suspiciously. Most of the population were like this really!

The Victorian police . . . or, Has anything changed?

Sir Robert Peel had invented the police in London in 1829 to try and prevent the sort of crime the Victorians suffered. Perhaps they did some good but . . .

1 Early policemen were paid just one shilling (5p) a day. A shilling was called a 'bob' and policemen were called 'bobbies' (Bobby is also the nickname of someone called Robert – so they could have taken their name from Sir 'Robert' Peel).

2 Really clever people would be earning much more than a shilling at other jobs – so the police force didn't attract many really clever bobbies.

3 The police force employed practically anyone – even if the man could barely read or write.

4 The police force didn't much mind where a policeman came from or who his friends were.

5 The first police only worked in London – within five miles of Charing Cross – and patrolled on **horse**back (not pandas)!

6 It wasn't until 1856 that the rest of the country had paid policemen.

Epilogue

The Victorian age wasn't all vile, of course.

The Victorians were energetic and inventive. By the time the old Queen died we had electric lights . . . and electric chairs.

We had motor cars . . . and crashes.

We had schools . . . and teachers.

We had the very, very rich . . . and the very, very poor.

Every silver lining has a cloud, as they say.

Charles Dickens wrote brilliant novels . . . and he wrote some pretty vile stuff.

But, when he was writing well he was one of the best. He wrote a brilliant summary of France in the 1790s, after the French Revolution. He could have been writing about the Victorian age. It sums it all up pretty well.

It was the best of times, it was the worst of times, it was the age of wisdom, it was the age of foolishness, it was the season of Light, it was the season of Darkness, it was the spring of hope, it was the winter of despair, we had everything before us, we had nothing before us, we were going direct to Heaven, we were all going direct the other way.
A Tale of Two Cities

DISEASE, POVERTY, FILTH, CRUELTY, IGNORANCE, BIGOTRY, EARLY DEATH.. AH YES. THOSE WERE THE GOOD OLD DAYS.

VILE VICTORIANS

GRISLY QUIZ

**Now find out if you're a
vile Victorian expert!**

HOWZAT VICTORIA?

The English lost a cricket match against Australia for the first time in 1880. They burned a bail to ashes and have played for those Ashes ever since. 'How's that?' the cricketers cried (or 'Howzat?' in cricket language) when they thought a batsman was out. And 'Howzat?' is the question about these curious Queen Victoria facts.

1. She was the shortest and the longest reigning monarch Britain ever had! Howzat?

2. Victoria was responsible for the death of her beloved husband, Albert. Howzat?

3. The police set Victoria up as the target for a murdering gunman. Howzat?

4. Victoria was highly respectable all her life yet she caused a scandal in her coffin. Howzat?

5. Albert and Victoria were married in 1840 though he never proposed to her. Howzat?

6. The Victorians liked portrait paintings but she preferred a particular kind. Howzat?

7. Victoria was Queen of England yet the 'Queen's English' was never very good. Howzat?

MANCHESTER MISERY

Not many men in Victorian England were gentlemen – which was unfortunate because gentlemen lived longer than working men. If you were an upper class person living in Manchester in 1842 you could expect to live 38 years (on average). But, if you were in the working class what was the average you could expect to live?

a) 37 years **b)** 27 years **c)** 17 years

UMMS AND ERRS

The 1800s were the age of the melodrama. Before the days of television the century's soap operas took place in thrilling theatres where villainous Victorians battled against hapless heroes. You just know what they are going to say ... or do you?

1. East Lynne

Poor Isabel leaves her husband but sneaks back (disguised as a governess) to nurse her sickly son. He dies in her arms as Isabel cries...

Oh, Willie, my child! Dead! Dead! Dead! And never called me **errrr!**

2. Youth

A bunch of English soldiers struggle against the enemy who must be evil because they aren't English. (The Victorians could be nasty racists.) Their colonel encourages them...

Remember, Great England is looking at you! Show how her sons can fight and **errr**!

3. The Fatal Marriage

Poor Isabella loses her husband and marries a dear friend. Then her first husband returns. She tries to murder him then decides to stab herself instead. (Don't try this at home.) Isabella sobs...

When I am dead, forgive me and **errr** *me!*

4. The Harp of Altenberg

Our heroine, Innogen, is captured by the villain, Brenno. As she tries to escape he grabs hold of her and Innogen cries...

Errrr *me!*

5. Sweeney Todd or, The Barber of Fleet Street

Sweeney Todd the Barber cuts the throats of customers and drops the corpses into his cellar. There his next-door neighbour collects the bodies and chops them up to make meat pies. As Sweeney cuts a throat he cries...

I **errrr** *them off!*

6. Maria Marten or, Murder in the Red Barn

Based on a true 1827 murder. William Corder waits in the barn for sweet Maria but plans to shoot her. Corder sneers...

I now await my victim. Will she come? Yes, for women are foolish enough to do anything for the men they **errrr!**

Quick Questions

1. How old were the youngest chimney sweeps in 1804? (Clue: not infants)

2. How was Lord Nelson's body brought home after his death at Trafalgar in 1805? (Clue: not a barrel of laughs)

3. John Bellingham blamed the government for ruining his business. How did he get his revenge in 1812? (Clue: a blow to the head)

4. Napoleon lost the Battle of Waterloo in 1815. What did Brit General Lord Raglan lose? (Clue: 'armless sort of chap)

5. In 1817 Brixton prison invented a new punishment for criminals. What? (Clue: hamster toy)

6. In 1818 Mary Shelley wrote a horrific story that is still popular today. What is it called? (Clue: frankly monstrous)

7. In 1820 in Scotland a rebel weaver was the last man to be sentenced to an ancient punishment. What? (Clue: long and drawn out)

8. In 1821 Queen Caroline died. What did this odd queen put on her head to keep cool while she was out riding? (Clue: American pie)

9. In 1822 King George IV visited Scotland and wore a kilt. How did he keep his knees warm? (Clue: they weren't loose)

10. In 1823 a boy at a public school, William Webb Ellis, cheated at football and invented a new game. What? (Clue: you have to hand it to him)

11. In Edinburgh in 1828 WilliamBlake was accused of 16 murders. What did he do with the bodies? (Clue: they were a little cut up about it)

Answers

Howzat Victoria?
1) She was the shortest in height but the longest in the time she spent on the throne.
2) The dirty water from her toilet leaked into Albert's drinking water and gave him the disease that killed him.
3) The gunman tried to shoot her as she drove in her carriage in London. His gun misfired and he escaped. The police told her to drive in the same place and at the same time the next day so that he could try again. He did! They caught him.
4) She was buried with a photograph of her 'friend', her Scottish servant. In her hand was a lock of his hair. What had they been up to when she was alive, people wanted to know!
5) Victoria proposed to him!
6) Victoria (and hubby Albert) preferred the people in the pictures to have no clothes on!
7) She was from the German Hanover family so she always spoke with a German accent.

Manchester Misery

c) In London slums people would, on average, live 22 years – but average upper class people would live twice as long. The unhealthiest place to live in 1842 was Liverpool, where the average age of death was just 15 years old. Queen Victoria lived to be 81. The average age was so low because lots of children died very young.

Umms and Errs

1) **Mother**. 'On the telephone' is definitely wrong! So is 'a taxi'.
2) **Die**. 'Fight and win' would not be very English – look at the present-day cricket team.
3) **Pity**. 'Bury' makes a bit more sense, you have to admit.
4) **Unhand**. Not a word you'll hear very often but remember it next time a history teacher grabs you!
5) **Polish**. This is such a famous line your granny probably knows it. In fact she probably ate the pies!
6) **Love**. 'Get chocolates from' is not a good enough answer.

Quick Questions

1) Four years old. The sweeps weren't supposed to be under nine but employers lied about the ages of their workers.
2) Pickled in a barrel of brandy. It preserved the body – and the sailors drank the brandy afterwards!
3) He shot the Prime Minister, Spencer Perceval, dead. The only Brit PM to be assassinated. Bellingham was hanged.
4) His arm. He also almost lost his wedding ring when the arm was amputated. 'Here! Bring that arm back!' he cried

from his hospital bed.

5) The 'treadmill' – a bit like a hamster wheel, where the prisoners walk and walk and go nowhere.

6) Frankenstein. Monstrous Mary was only 18 when she dreamed up this story of a man put together like a Lego kit. Seriously weird writer.

7) Wilson was sentenced to be hanged, drawn and quartered. In fact he was hanged then beheaded. His 'crime' was to lead a march in protest against unemployment.

8) A pumpkin. She probably changed it each time she rode, which is more than she did with her stockings. She wore them till they stank.

9) Tights. He had them made the colour of his flesh because he didn't want to look like a wimp.

10) Rugby. He picked up the ball and ran with it. The game was named after his public school, Rugby, so we don't say, 'Fancy a game of Ellis?'

11) He sold them to doctors so they could experiment on them. Of course the doctors weren't punished.

INTERESTING INDEX

Where will you find 'bottom-slapping',
'fried earwigs' and 'mice on toast' in an index?
In a Horrible Histories book, of course!

Terry Deary was born at a very early age, so long ago he can't remember. But his mother, who was there at the time, says he was born in Sunderland, north-east England, in 1946 – so it's not true that he writes all *Horrible Histories* from memory. At school he was a horrible child only interested in playing football and giving teachers a hard time. His history lessons were so boring and so badly taught, that he learned to loathe the subject. *Horrible Histories* is his revenge.

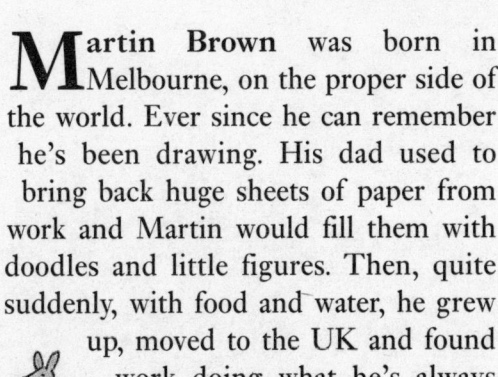

Martin Brown was born in Melbourne, on the proper side of the world. Ever since he can remember he's been drawing. His dad used to bring back huge sheets of paper from work and Martin would fill them with doodles and little figures. Then, quite suddenly, with food and water, he grew up, moved to the UK and found work doing what he's always wanted to do: drawing doodles and little figures.

HORRIBLE HISTORIES

GORGEOUS GEORGIANS

Terry Deary illustrated by Martin Brown

SCHOLASTIC

This book is for Charlotte Clare, winner of the *Horrible Histories* joke competition.
Her joke is in the picture on page 16.

Scholastic Children's Books,
Euston House, 24 Eversholt Street,
London NW1 1DB, UK

A division of Scholastic Ltd
London ~ New York ~ Toronto ~ Sydney ~ Auckland
Mexico City ~ New Delhi ~ Hong Kong

First published in the UK by Scholastic Ltd, 1998
This edition published by Scholastic Ltd, 2016

Some of the material in this book has previously been published in
Horrible Histories: The Massive Millennium Quiz Book/Horribly Huge Quiz Book

Text © Terry Deary, 1998
Illustration © Martin Brown, 1998, 2016

ISBN 978 1407 16389 5

Printed and bound by CPI Group (UK) Ltd, Croydon, CR0 4YY

8 10 9 7

The right of Terry Deary and Martin Brown to be identified as the author and illustrator of this work respectively has been asserted by them in
accordance with the Copyright, Designs and Patents Act, 1988.

www.scholastic.co.uk

CONTENTS

Introduction

History is horrible. For a start, everybody in history is dead. Some are very dead indeed.

Of course history teachers don't tell you this, do they?

And then teacher drones on about boring battles and dusty dates. What you really want to know is the really interesting stuff. How did people live ... and how did they die?

For example, teacher may tell you that in the age of King George III, Britain won the Battle of Waterloo (thanks to a man in Wellington's boots). But you really want to know about what happened *after* the battle, don't you? When people went over the battlefield looking in the mouths of the corpses for nice, shiny teeth. And, when they found them, they pulled them out.

Could you rip teeth out of a fresh corpse? Probably not. So why did the tooth collectors of Waterloo? For money!

No, stupid, they didn't put them under their pillows and wait for the tooth fairy. They sold them to people who made sets of false teeth.

Could you wear false teeth knowing they'd been picked from a variety of dead bodies?

See? The Battle of Waterloo is just an important date to remember for a history teacher. But it was a good day for business if you were a tooth collector.

There are plenty of books full of dates – they're called diaries. But if you want a bit of real live death then you need a book that tells you all about the horrible side of history.

And it just so happens you are reading one ...

Timeline

1714 Queen Anne of the Stuart family dies. George I comes from Hanover (Germany) to take the English throne. He's not popular, but the other Stuarts are Catholics and most Brits don't want that.

1715 Stuart supporters want James III to rule so they have a rebellion in support of him – these 'Jacobite' rebellions are crushed ... for now.

1727 George II comes to the throne when George I has a violent attack of diarrhoea and dies. Pooh!

1745 Bonnie Prince Charlie – the last of the Stuart family – lands in Scotland to claim the throne of Britain in another Jacobite rebellion. The Scottish clans are brutally beaten by the Brit Army.

1750 First organized police force in London – the Bow Street Runners.

1760 George III comes to the throne – and stays for 60 years in sickness and in health.

1770 Captain Cook claims Australia for Britain. He doesn't bother to ask the Aborigines if they want to be British, of course.

1775 American colonies rebel against British rule.

1788 Australia welcomes its first

British convicts. It's a good place to dump them. And only 48 die on the voyage!

1789 The French peasants revolt against their rulers. Soon they'll be slicing noble heads off with the guillotine.

1792 First gas lighting in houses, invented by some bright spark.

1793 The French have chopped their King Louis' head. Now they're looking for a fight and pick on Britain. The start of 20 years of wars – the Napoleonic Wars.

1798 Steam-powered spinning mill opens in Bradford. Bad news for spinners working from home, being replaced by machines. They'll all have to take jobs at the dangerous, dirty factories.

1801 Ireland joins Great Britain and another red cross is added to the flag to make the Union Jack.

1804 Captain Dick's Puffer starts running! The first steam railway locomotive, invented by Richard Trevithick.

1805 British Navy wins Battle of Trafalgar against the French and lose their admiral, Horatio, Lord Nelson, potted by a hot-shot.

1806 Steam-powered looms

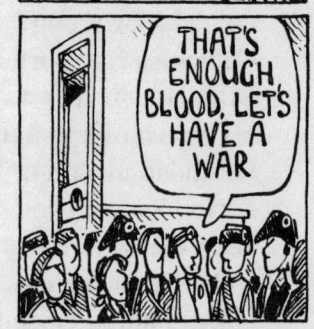

invented. Bad news for weavers.

1807 Britain bans slave trading – having made a fortune out of it for the past hundred years or so.

1811 Out of work weavers wreck the machines that put them out of work. They call themselves Luddites and male wreckers often dress as women!

1815 Britain defeats Napoleon and his French armies at Waterloo. (A village in Belgium, not a London station.)

1819 It's now against the law for children under nine to work or for older children to work more than 12 hours a day.

1820 Popular (but blind, deaf and mad) George III dies. Unpopular (fat and dishonest) George IV takes over.

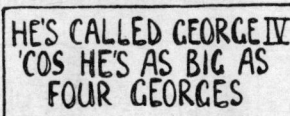

1825 First steam-driven passenger railway runs from Stockton to Darlington. Crowds turn up to watch … they are disappointed when it doesn't explode!

1830 Fat George IV dies and his brother, boring William IV, takes over. End of Georgian age.

1837 Queen Victoria comes to the throne. A right madam who will reign even longer than George III.

Gorgeous Georgians

Vicious verses and cruel cartoons

The Georgians could be very cruel to one another. They had their own way of mocking people.

Poets, like Alexander Pope (1688–1744) were especially nasty. (Lady Mary Wortley Montague called him 'the wicked asp of Twickenham'.) His poems poked fun at people but especially people who loved themselves.

Unimportant note 1: The posh word for cruel fun is satire – remember that word!

The other cruel artists were cartoonists. Men like Hogarth (1697-1764) – he made people look ridiculous in his drawings.

Unimportant note 2: The posh word for this is caricature – remember that word too!

Georgian makeover

By the 1770s some of the fashions became quite ridiculous. So here's a *satire* and a *caricature* of ladies' fashion in the age of George III. (And now you can forget those two words. Which two words? Er ... I've forgotten.)

Modern magazines offer readers a 'makeover' – they say they'll change someone's appearance from grot to hot in ten easy steps. If the Georgians did a makeover then the results would have been just as stunning ...

1. *White is beautiful, dear ladies,*
   Smear your face with paint of lead;
   Never mind the lead has made
   The men who mixed it ill ... or dead.

~ Make-up is a flat white lead paint

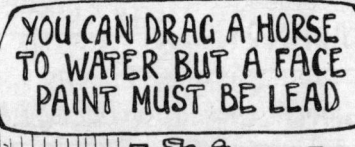

2. *Take some silk of red or black,*
   Cut a circle or a crescent;
   Stick it to your face to cover
   Smallpox scars ... it's much more pleasant.

~ Silk beauty spots are cut out and stuck on

3. *Take some plaster, dyed bright red,*
   Crush it to a ruby paste;
   Smear it on your lips, dear ladies,
   Never mind the chalky taste.

~ Red Plaster of Paris is used for lips

4. *Shave your eyebrows clean away,*
Take a trap and catch some mice;
Make false eyebrows from the mouse skin,
Stick them on to look so nice.

~ Black lead eyelashes and mouse-skin eyebrows are needed

CHEESE MADAM?

YUMMY!

YES PLEASE!

5. *Make your face look sweet and chubby,*
Pack your mouth with balls of cork;
Fit your false teeth in the middle,
Hope you don't choke when you talk.

~ Cork balls held in the cheeks improve the face

BUT MADAM, CRICKET BALLS ARE MADE OF CORK!

6. *Next you need a monster wig*
If you want to look real smashin';
When your wig has reached the ceiling
Then you'll be the height of fashion!

~ Build up the hair like a pyramid

I'M SURE MADAM'S UMBRELLA IS IN THERE SOMEWHERE

12

7. *Decorate your lovely hairpiece,*
Use the feathers of a parrot;
Add some ribbons, fruit and flowers,
From your ears then hang a carrot.

~Never wear your hair plain

8. *Wear a dress of finest satin,*
Over wide, hooped petticoats;
When you walk along the pavement
Push pedestrians in the road.

~Wide skirts and long trains are the fashion

9. *Don't forget to take your handbag,*
Fill it with the usual stuff;
Perfume and sweet vinegar.
To clear your head you'll need some snuff.

~Fashionable ladies clear their heads with snuff

13

10. *Last of all you'll need a fan*
To flutter at your favourite feller;
Now you'll look like Ugly Sister
To the pretty Cinderella!

~The finished effect should be a vision of beauty

AAARGH!

Heights of fashion

It wasn't only poets and cartoonists who made fun of ladies. A theatre director called Garrick had a character on stage dressed with every kind of vegetable and a carrot dangling from each ear. Of course real ladies never wore carrots – but they did wear the scarlet flowers of runner beans!

BZZZZZZZZZZZZZZZZZZZZ.......

In 1786 four overdressed ladies were scoffed at as they entered the theatre. Actresses stopped the play and returned wearing similarly ridiculous dress to make fun of the ladies.

In the 1780s the high hair went out of fashion. The writer Addison said …

> *I remember the time when ladies' hair shot up to a great height so that women were so much taller than men. We appeared like grasshoppers beside them. I remember ladies who were once nearly seven feet high and are now a few inches short of five feet.*

Fans were waved in front of the face to keep a lady cool in the steaming hot theatres. Some men complained that the large fans were more like windmills! They were decorated with pictures but also with verses of songs or paragraphs from popular books. (If you got bored at the opera you could always read your fan.) Ladies learned to use fan-fluttering as a signal to people watching. One flutter might mean anger while another flutter might mean love. Fans were also useful to hide a lady's mouth if she had rotten teeth. And they could wave away the foul smell if she had bad breath.

Dresses were worn over wide, hooped petticoats. These came into fashion in 1710 and went out of fashion in 1780 – but at the royal court they were still being worn over 40 years later. A writer complained that when one young lady walked down the street she took up the full width of the pavement.

In 1776 a lady made the mistake of wearing a decorated hat in the country. It was covered in fruit and vegetables which were fastened on with metal pins. As she sat down for a picnic a passing cow rushed across to eat the hat. Sadly it ate the metal pins too. One stuck in its throat and the cow died a few hours later.

Gorgeous Georgian men

It's easy to poke fun at Georgian women but the men were just as bad. They were known as *fops*, meaning *posers* (and other ruder words!).

1 From 1660 till 1760 it was the century of the slapheads. Men wore wigs – even when they weren't bald! Wigs were popular until the 1760s. They could be very expensive so they were often stolen. Thieves would ride on the back of a carriage, carefully cut a hole through the back, snatch a wig off the passenger and jump off.

2 But wigs could be nasty, filthy things. Topham Beauclark took pleasure in shaking bugs out of his wig in front of lady friends. Many men shaved their heads so the wigs would fit. If they took the wigs off in the comfort of their own home they wore a night-cap (like Wee Willie Winkie!) to keep their heads warm. Really fashionable men wore a turban!

3 Wigs were held in place with powder (made from flour, nutmeg, starch and, maybe, gold dust). Even when wigs went out of fashion a gentleman would hold his hair in place with powder. Walking behind a gentleman on a windy day could choke you! When Prime Minister Pitt put a tax on hair powder in 1795 men stopped using it.

4 Many fops became very fussy about keeping clean and had regular baths. But the clothes of some men were as bad as the dirty wigs. Chelsea pensioners took lice from their coats and bet on races between them.

5 Umbrellas came into fashion in Stuart times but were more common in gorgeous Georgian days. But men who used umbrellas were jeered at in the street. Even in 1797 they were a rare sight – in Cambridge, there was only one umbrella in the whole town. It was kept in a shop and you could hire it if you were caught in a shower.

I WAS CAUGHT IN THE RAIN, I'M SOAKED! CAN I HIRE YOUR UMBRELLA TO KEEP ME DRY?

THERE'S A FLAW IN THAT REASONING SOMEWHERE

6 Rich gentlemen could afford clothes just as gorgeous as the ladies'. Silk or velvet coats could be embroidered with silver thread and trimmed with lace. Gorgeous! But the collars and neck-cloths that became popular in the 1820s were starched and ironed till they were stiff as a board. There were reports that some stiff collars chopped off the ear lobes of the young men who wore them!

7 The three-cornered hat, famous in pictures of highwaymen and pirates, was popular in the 1700s. But towards the end of the century an amazing new fashion appeared. Tall, silk, top hats. (You'll have seen them at weddings perhaps.) But the Georgians were amazed when they first saw them. A writer said, 'Women fainted at the sight, children screamed and dogs yelped.'

8 Fashionable young men of the early 1770s were known as Macaronis. They wore thick white make-up, cheek blusher and lipstick. George IV was especially vain about his appearance. He covered his ruddy face in chalk dust and even used leeches to suck his blood to try to make him pale. George also wore a corset to make his bulging waist thinner but his friend, Beau Brummel, told him his trousers didn't fit anyway. George burst into tears.

9 Beau Brummel himself was a leader of men's fashion in Georgian Britain. He plucked or shaved his face several times every day and used three hairdressers. He refused to wear make-up and bathed regularly … unlike many of his smelly friends. When he argued with George IV he became unpopular and died mad and penniless.

10 Men changed their shape with padding worn under their clothes. They padded the calves of their legs so they didn't look skinny when they wore tight trousers and put pads on their chests to make them look mightier than Tarzan!

I THINK I'VE GOT MY PADDING ON THE WRONG WAY

Gorging Georgians

Clever cakes

You've probably heard the rhyme:

> *Pat-a-cake, pat-a-cake baker's man!*
> *Bake me a cake as fast as you can;*
> *Pat it and prick it and mark it with 'B',*
> *Put it in the oven for Baby and me.*

But do you know what 'mark it with "B"' means? No? Ask your teacher. Surprise, surprise, they don't know either.

A Georgian child could have told your teacher that a lot of people cooked over open fires and didn't have ovens. They could roast meat or boil puddings but they couldn't *bake* a cake. So a cook would mix a cake and take it to the local baker to bake in his oven. They didn't want their cake mixed up with someone else's, so they marked it with their initial … 'B' for 'baby' in this case.

If your name was Sarah Isobel Catherine King, or Benjamin Uriah Morton, or even Philip Oliver Nigel George Young, then you wouldn't want all of your initials on the cake – would you?

And cake was eaten at breakfast as well as teatime.

Clever cooks and minding manners

Here are some Georgian inventions that made life tastier.

1 Tasty toast The Georgians invented toast. A nasty Swedish visitor said the English invented toast because their houses were too chilly to spread butter on cold bread!

2 Yummy Yorkshires Ovens were improved so you could roast meat and cook a batter pudding in one at the same time. This pudding became known as a Yorkshire pudding. (Probably because it was eaten with roast Yorkshire terrier – only joking!) Yorkshire pudding was often a treat for Christmas Day.

3 Chocolate chunks Chocolate was drunk at the end of the 1600s – mixed with wine! The wine was heated and the chunk of chocolate grated into it. Sounds disgusting. Later, water was used to make hot chocolate and by the end of the 1700s you could eat chocolate bars.

4 Terrific tea Tea and coffee were also popular with the rich in Georgian times. Tea was so expensive it was kept in a tea caddy with a lock on. There was a good trade in used tea-leaves. Traders put some colour back into the old tea leaves with chemicals. These chemicals could make you ill – or even kill you – but the traders didn't mind too much. (After all, they didn't drink the stuff!)

5 Spiffing spits Some cooks still roasted meat on a spit, but a Georgian spit could be turned by a clockwork motor. Poor people still roasted meat (when they could afford it) by hanging it by a hook from the mantelpiece over the fire. This was known as a 'danglespit' – no prizes for guessing why.

6 Super sandwiches In 1760 John Montague, the fourth Earl of Sandwich, was playing cards and didn't want to stop for dinner. He ordered that his meat be slapped between two pieces of bread so he could eat it while he played. Everyone started to copy him and asked for 'A beef as-eaten-by-John-Montague-the-fourth-Earl-of-Sandwich, please.' (The Romans had this idea more than 1,000 years before, but you don't eat a jam julius caesar, a ham hadrian or a peanut butter nero. You eat a *sandwich*.)

7 Kindly cooks At the start of the Georgian age butchers used to kill their animals in some cruel ways. (You really wouldn't want to know what they did to turkeys because it would ruin Christmas for you forever.) One recipe told a

cook, 'Take a red cockerel that is not too old and beat him to death.' (Battered chicken is still popular today – but it's not quite the same thing!) By the end of the Georgian period, you'll be pleased to hear, the killing of animals for food was kinder – but the animals still ended up just as dead.

8 Trendy teatime In the early 1700s people had dinner at two or three pm. By the end of the century this had moved to six or seven pm. Of course you'd get hungry long before that so fashionable people had 'afternoon tea' at about four o'clock. Did you realize that

your four o'clock tin of beans makes you a trendy Georgian?

9 Fab fruits The Georgians started to eat raw fruit. In earlier times doctors had said that eating fruit could spread

the plague! With new 'hot houses' the Georgians could grow their own exotic fruits, like grapes, peaches and pineapples. They also grew tomatoes and cooked them, but it was another 100 years before they ate them raw.

10 Cool rules Georgians wrote down rules on how the upper classes ought to behave at meal times. (You may like to try these at school dinners.)

- Guests walk in to the dining room in order, ladies first. Ladies and gentlemen sit next to one another. (At the start of the 1700s all the women had sat at one end and the men at the other.)
- Don't eat too quickly, because it shows you are too hungry.
- Don't eat too slowly, because that might mean you don't like your food.

- Never sniff your food when it's on the fork or the cook will think it's rotten.
- Don't scratch yourself, spit, blow your nose, lean your elbows on the table or sit too far back from the table.
- Do *not* pick your teeth before the plates are removed.
- If you need to go to the toilet then go and return quietly without telling everyone where you're going. (This was a great improvement on earlier dinner arrangements where pots were kept in the dining room for people to pee in!)

I PREFERRED THE OLD WAYS. YOU COULD CONTINUE TO CHAT WITH YOUR CHUMS AT THE TABLE AND TINKLE AT THE SAME TIME

Did you know ...?
Over in the American colonies in 1748 a schoolboy copied out rules from a French book of manners. He wrote, 'Do not clean your teeth with your fork, your knife or the tablecloth.' Clean your teeth with a tablecloth? Sadly the boy who wrote that mustn't have cleaned his teeth with *anything* because he ended up with false teeth made of wood. The boy's name was George Washington and he grew up to be America's first president.

Fatten up your friends
William Verral wrote a book called *The Cook's Paradise* with recipes for cooks to try. You can invite your friends to try this fairly simple recipe and it's pretty certain that it won't kill them. They may even enjoy it and invite you to share their next school dinner with you.

Strawberry fritters

You need:

450 g large strawberries (More if you have a lot of friends)

175 g plain flour

50 g caster sugar

2 teaspoons grated nutmeg

2 eggs

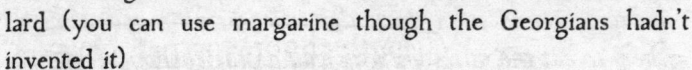

225 ml single cream

lard (you can use margarine though the Georgians hadn't invented it)

Method: Start this at least two hours before your guests arrive.

1 Dry the strawberries but leave the stalks on so you can hold them when you eat them.

2 Mix the flour, nutmeg and sugar in a bowl.

3 Beat the eggs, stir in the cream and slowly stir the mixture into the flour and sugar.

4 Leave this batter to stand for two hours.

5 Heat some lard in a frying pan. (It's best to get an adult to do this. If anyone's going to get burned it may as well be an adult rather than you. Adults are also useful for washing up your mess afterwards.)

6 Dip each strawberry in the batter – holding it by the stalk.

7 Drop a few strawberries into the hot lard and fry them gently till they are golden brown.

8 Drain them on kitchen towel and keep them warm in an oven while you cook the rest.

9 Eat the strawberries but not the stalks.

10 If you like them then share them with your friends. If you absolutely adore them then scoff the lot, describe the taste to your friends ... and tell them to cook their own.

Foul food

Not everything in the Georgian pantry was as tasty as strawberry fritters. There are a few gorgeous Georgian foods you may not like so much.

1 Daniel Defoe, the author of *Robinson Crusoe*, described his visit to Stilton, the town famous for its cheese …

> *The cheese is brought to the table with the mites or maggots round it so thick that they bring a spoon with them to eat the mites with, as you do the cheese.*

2 A doctor and writer, Tobias Smollett, complained about London bread …

> *The bread I eat in London is a harmful paste mixed with chalk and bone ashes, tasteless and bad for the health. The people know what is in it but prefer it to good corn bread because it is whiter.*

IT'S TOTALLY POISONOUS BUT VERY WHITE

I'LL TAKE TWO

Smollett died when he was just 50. Maybe he ate too much bread!

3 Writer Jonathan Swift (famous for his book *Gulliver's Travels*) came up with a cure for the problem of food shortages in Ireland …

> *I have been told that a young, healthy child of a year old is a most delicious, nourishing and wholesome food, whether it's stewed, toasted, baked or boiled. I humbly suggest that 100,000 infants may be offered for sale to rich people in the kingdom. The mothers should try to make sure that they are plump and fat and good for the table.*

I LOVE CHILDREN... BUT I COULDN'T EAT A WHOLE ONE

(He was joking, but making a serious point about how the Irish were treated.)

4 When a scientist took a close look at pepper he discovered that there was more in it than peppercorns. There was also the sweepings from the floors of the store-rooms. If there were mice and rats in the store-rooms then their droppings would be ground up with the pepper-powder. Of course, French shopkeepers ground in powdered dogs' droppings.

5 Milk was sold on the streets of cities by milk maids who carried it round the streets in open pails. The trouble was the pails collected extras on their journey. Tobias Smollett described them ...

> *Dirty water thrown from windows, spittle, snot and tobacco squirts from passersby, spatterings from coach wheels, dirt and trash chucked into it by roguish boys for the joke's sake, the spewings of infants and finally the lice that drop from the rags of the nasty drab woman that sells this precious mixture.*

Top of the class

Daniel Defoe went on a tour of Britain and described the country. He thought Manchester was the 'greatest village in England' – so he'd be pleased to know the village football team is now doing well. He wrote that Liverpool was 'one of the wonders of Britain', and this was 200 years before The Beatles!

He also saw some pretty dreadful sights, especially among the poor people. The old ways were changing and, as usual, it meant the poor got poorer and the rich got richer. One of the problems was 'Enclosure.'

'What's that?' you cry! (Or if you *don't* cry it then your teacher probably will – and expect you to write about it in your next test.) So here's N. Idiot's guide to Enclosure …

HELLO! I AM N. IDIOT. NOW, YOU CAN CALL ME AN IDIOT IF YOU LIKE...BUT THINGS WERE BETTER IN THE GOOD OLD DAYS

The GOOD old DAYS before ENCLOSURE

Peasants share Common Land and Grow Crops.

Happy Peasant with his pig.

Happy Peasant's wife spins wool in happy cottage.

Unhappy Lord in Manor House wants that common land.

Happy pig and happy sheep.

Happy Peasant's happy children helping in the fields.

ENCLOSURE ACTS AFTER 1720 GOT RID OF THE OPEN FIELDS ALL OVER BRITAIN. MORE MONEY COULD BE MADE BY LESS PEOPLE

The BAD GEORGIAN days of ENCLOSURE

Fields fenced off so one Landowner can make more money.

Unhappy Peasant has to find work in town.

Unhappy Peasant's wife has to work in miserable mill.

TOWN

Happy Lord in Manor House owns the lot.

Unhappy Peasant children have to work in seedy slums, foul factories or murky mines.

Happy pig and sheep with flocks of friends.

ENCLOSURE MADE 'BRITAIN' RICHER... AND MOST OF HER PEOPLE POORER. NOW, CALL ME AN IDIOT, BUT I WONDER IF IT WAS WORTH IT?

Daniel Defoe reckoned there were *seven* classes of people in Georgian Britain. Nothing is ever that simple, of course. But here are Defoe's seven classes. Which one would you like to have been in?

Class 7: 'The miserable, who really suffer want' In 1757 a mother and nine children in Buckinghamshire went several days without food. The mother found some money and bought the heart, liver and lungs of a calf to make a meal. Then she went off to gather fire wood. When she got back the children had eaten every scrap, gullet and all.

29

The same year a mother and two children in Cumberland had no bread and tried to survive on horse bran. They were all found dead one morning and the children had straw in their mouths.

Class 6: 'The poor, whose lives are hard' A family of seven in Derbyshire lived in a cave. The father was a lead miner and had been born in the cave, so had his five children. The cave was divided into three rooms by curtains and a hole had been dug through the roof to make a chimney. A pig and its piglets ran round the door. The miner earned about £6 a year and his wife could wash the lead ore and earn another £4 a year. Defoe wrote …

Things inside did not look as miserable as I'd expected. Everything was clean and neat and they seemed to live very pleasantly. The children looked plump and healthy, the woman was tall, clean and attractive.

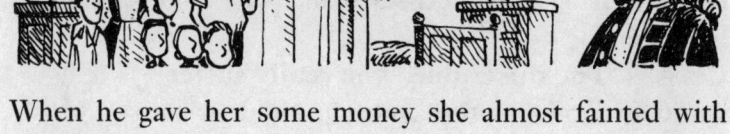

When he gave her some money she almost fainted with happiness.

Class 5: 'The country people, who manage indifferently' (not too well) The days of the peasant families with their own strips of land were finished in Georgian times. A writer said the main problem was the country people owned nothing. Before Enclosure they used

to keep a cow and a pony, a goose and a pig on the 'common' land. They'd have the odd wild rabbit, nuts and berries. But the common land was fenced off and sold to the richer farmers. The poor workers couldn't afford a large farm and there weren't any small ones. What was the point in working? A writer said …

Go to an ale house in the country and what will you find? It is full of men who could be working. They ask, 'If I work hard will I be allowed to build my own cottage? No. If I stay sober will I have land for a cow? No. If I save up can I get half an acre for potatoes? No. All you are offering me is the workhouse! Bring me another pot of ale.'

Life in the country wasn't fresh air and roses. You worked when the farmer wanted you – harvest or sowing times – and you went hungry the rest of the year.

Class 4: 'The working trades, who labour hard but feel no want' The workers worked long hours, in terrible conditions, for poor pay. Yet in the north of England from the 1790s, tens of thousands flocked to the mills in the towns to get away from the country. They crowded into dark, filthy houses so they could be near their work. With children as young as five working, a family would have enough to eat and stay warm, but it wasn't much of a life.

Spinners worked 14 hours a day in steamy temperatures up to 90°C – it had to be steamy to stop the thread snapping.

The weavers were better paid and could earn £2 to £3 a week when Defoe was writing. But within a hundred years machines were replacing them and their wages fell to 12 shillings (60p) a week.

Builders built houses in the factory towns especially for weavers. They were built over ditches so the weavers could work in a nice damp cellar. It ruined their health but at least the threads didn't snap.

Class 3: 'The middle sort, who live well' The people in the middle didn't do too badly. Priests could be poor, but some had some very good parishes and lived very comfortably. A lady went to dinner with the Rector of Aston in 1779 and described her meal ...

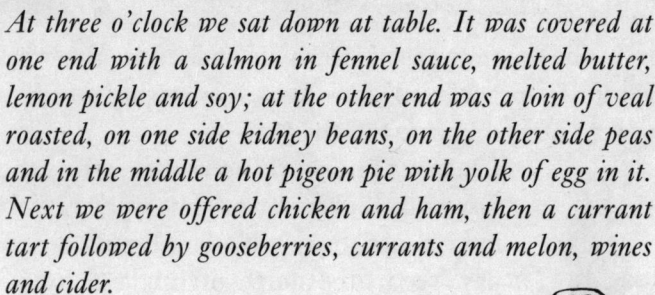

At three o'clock we sat down at table. It was covered at one end with a salmon in fennel sauce, melted butter, lemon pickle and soy; at the other end was a loin of veal roasted, on one side kidney beans, on the other side peas and in the middle a hot pigeon pie with yolk of egg in it. Next we were offered chicken and ham, then a currant tart followed by gooseberries, currants and melon, wines and cider.

Class 2: 'The rich, who live plentifully'

Some rich people thought the local village spoiled the view from their great houses ... so they knocked the village down and moved the poor somewhere else.

But other rich Georgians made their wealth by trading in people. Slavers. They captured Africans, transported them across the Atlantic Ocean like cattle and sold the ones who survived.

The slave journey wasn't the worst part of the experience. Being a slave was miserable. Nicholas Cresswell, a visitor to the West Indies in 1774, described their life ...

We went ashore and saw a cargo of slaves land. They were all naked except for a small piece of blue cloth. If they made the slightest mistake they were tied up and whipped without mercy. Some of them die under this harsh treatment.

Class 1: 'The great, who live profusely' (with a lot to spare)

Most lords managed to earn £5,000 a year – that's about £300,000 today. They enjoyed their money. Some of the great country houses you can see today were built in the Georgian period. In 1762 George III bought 'The Queen's House' in London

and turned it into Buckingham Palace. (It cost him £21,000 – the price a dog would pay for a kennel in London today.)

The Duke of Chandos had his own orchestra of 27 musicians while Sir Robert Walpole spent £1,500 a year on wine (£90,000 today) and £1 every night on candles, (the miserable could buy food, drink, fuel and shelter for five weeks for that £1).

BUT ... the 'great' needed the votes of the lower classes when it came to elections for parliament. They had to invite the farmers into their great homes! Yeuch! The Earl of Cork whinged ...

> *At election time I have to open my doors to every dirty fellow in the county who has a vote. All my best floors are spoiled by the hobnailed boots of the farmers stamping about them. Every room is a pigsty and the Chinese wallpaper in the drawing room stinks so terrible of tobacco that it would knock you down to walk into it.*

Poor Earl of Cork!

Posh politics

The posh Georgians in Britain sent people to 'Parliament' to argue with the king. Where did this Parliament thing come from? Here's a quick horrible history ...

🏛 The first big argument was in 1215 when the posh people of England (the Barons) fell out with King John. They made him sign a great charter (posh name: Magna Carta). This said he couldn ' t have everything his own way just because he was king. John sulked but he signed.

🏛 Then along came King Henry III who forgot all about the Magna Carta and started demanding money. So one of the Barons, Simon de Montfort, organized a group of Barons to talk about horrible Henry. They talked in French ('cos they was posh). French for 'to talk' is parler so a talk-shop is 'parler-ment' or Parliament. Geddit?

🏛 Simple Simon went to war with Henry. He lost at the Battle of Evesham and had his head cut off – not to mention his arms and his legs! But his Parliament idea lived on.

🏛 Members of Parliament (MPs for short) were the chief men of the towns and counties. The rich men voted for them and sent them to argue with the kings and queens. (Women, even rich, posh women, had no say at all.) Sometimes the MPs got really angry and turned nasty – in 1647 they went to war with King Charles I and ended up cutting his head off.

🏛 The last Stuart Queen, Anne, enjoyed going to Parliament and listening to them talk. But she didn't argue with them very much. The situation was desperate! Who on earth could they argue with? They began to argue with each other, and split up into two parties – one lot were nicknamed the 'Whigs' and the other lot were called the 'Tories'. These were actually very insulting names. A 'Whig' was a Scottish robber who usually murdered his victim, while a 'Tory' was an Irish cattle thief. The queen cheated a bit to make sure her favourites, the Tories, stayed in power.

That brings us to the gorgeous Georgians …

Potty parties

Disaster! King George I didn't do a lot of arguing with his Parliament because he hardly spoke any English. He gave a lot of presents and power to the Whigs and they ruled the country for him. The Tories hated George I – they only supported him because they thought he was better than the Catholic James Stuart. Even the Whigs didn't like him much!

Parliament now had the power!

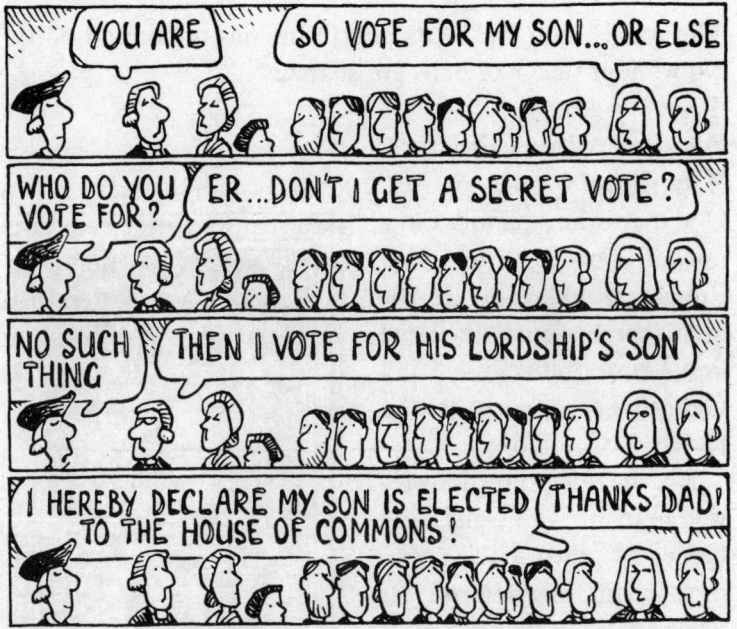

There were more Lords' sons in the House of Commons than any other group.

Did you know …?

- Some places had so few voters they could be paid to vote the way someone wanted – they were called 'rotten boroughs'.
- Some of the growing factory towns couldn't send anyone to Parliament at all.
- Some places were run by a powerful family who could send anyone to Parliament they liked – these were known as 'pocket boroughs'.
- MPs weren't paid. Only rich men could afford to be MPs. Who would they stick up for in Parliament? Their rich friends, of course.

The way Britain picked its politicians was unfair and potty. No wonder the Georgians got so many …

Peculiar prime ministers
Wily Walpole

One man whose family ran a pocket borough was Sir Robert Walpole. He is the man that historians call the first prime minister – King George I's top dog in the House of Commons.

But the title prime minister was an insult! It meant 'King George's favourite creep in parliament'. (It's a bit like someone calling you a teacher's pet!) So Robert Walpole said, 'I am NOT a prime minister.' Then he went on not being a prime minister for the next 21 years. (That's still the record, Mr Blair! Can you beat it?)

He had a good way to make sure he won every vote in parliament. He paid the MPs to vote the way he wanted.

EVERY MAN HAS HIS PRICE

This is dishonest – Britain got the laws that the rich paid for, not the laws that the poor needed – but no one seemed to mind too much.

Poorly Pitt

William Pitt (the Elder) – PM in 1757 – was dead honest. He did not believe in bribing MPs, unlike Walpole. But he did find the job a strain. He became almost mad with the strain and the cure was to lock him in a darkened room. His wife passed food through to him.

Being half mad didn't stop George III being king and it didn't stop Pitt being prime minister. They let him out of the room to speak in the House of Lords. This was a big mistake. While he was speaking he collapsed and died.

No-good North

Lord North – PM in 1770 – has been called the worst prime minister ever. He soon got bored in Parliament and would nod off to sleep. He'd ask to be woken up when the speaker got to the end. He was also the ugliest prime minister Britain has ever had.

Lord North often complained that it was a terrible strain being prime minister …

> *I'd rather be hanged than suffer the pain of running the king's business.*

So, how did he get the job? When he was a boy he was a playmate of King George III, so George gave him the PM job.

Portable Pitt

William Pitt (the Younger) – PM from 1783 – was honest like his dear departed Dad. And, like his Dad, was pretty miserable in his job. He was the youngest prime minister ever at the age of 24.

He led Britain through many of its years of war with France. He made the proud boast …

> *I can save this country, and no one else can.*

He did this by raising new taxes. He put a tax on houses with more than seven windows – some grumpy Georgians just bricked up the extra windows to dodge the tax! But as he lay ill in 1806 he heard that Napoleon had battered the Brit armies at Austerlitz and he groaned …

> *Oh, my country. How I leave my country!*

The man who'd boasted, 'I can save my country' did the most sensible thing possible. He died straight after saying those words.

He broke another record: he became the youngest prime minister ever to *die* in office when he popped his parliamentary clogs at the age of 46. It wasn't the darkened room that killed this Pitt but the bottles of port wine he swilled.

Potted Perceval

Spencer Perceval – PM in 1812 – was about as popular as the plague. A man called Bellingham was imprisoned in Russia and lost all his money. Bellingham thought the British government should give him back the money he'd lost. The government said, 'No'. Bellingham said, 'Right! I'll show you!' and he took a pistol into the House of Commons where he shot PM Perceval dead. He's the only British PM ever to be assassinated.

Crowds came out onto the street to cheer, 'Perceval is dead! Hurrah!'

Pretty soon Bellingham was dead too because he was hanged. (This was cheaper than paying him the money he wanted.)

Prime ministers have their famous last words recorded by historians for teachers to bore you with. At least PM Perceval left us with a nice short final speech:

Cheerless for children

One of the worst classes to be in was the 'children's' class.

Children were dressed as adults and often worked as adults from a very early age. The hard part was surviving childhood …

1 First you had to survive being born. One child out of three didn't live to be 15, and careless mothers cost babies' lives. There were many cases of a baby sharing a bed with mother, father, brothers or sisters and being smothered when someone rolled on top of them in their sleep.

2 Poor families could not afford too many children. There were cases of babies being left in the streets to die, or strangled and dumped on the local rubbish tip or into a drain.

3 Next you had to survive your christening. At a christening in Surrey a nurse got very drunk. She undressed the baby and went to put it in its cradle. By mistake she put it too close to a large fire which killed it in a few minutes. She told the judges who tried her that she thought the baby was a log of firewood. The judges set her free! (Georgian judges were often drunk in court. The nurse's judges must have been if they thought a baby and a log could be mistaken!

They probably said, 'She was so drunk she wooden know the difference.')

4 A child who was brought up by a paid child-minder, a 'nurse', was unlucky. Children with nurses were twice as likely to die. Nurses were well known for being drunk. Nurses of poor children often deliberately damaged the child's face or legs so the child would grow up to be a more pitiful sight. The nurse would then hire out the child to a beggar who would make more money.

5 Thomas Coram opened a hospital for unwanted children in 1741. He was flooded with so many sick and dying babies, dumped on the doorstep, that about 10,000 of the children died. But his good example led the later Georgians to look after poor children better.

6 Young girls in rich homes had to grow up to be ladies with fine figures. That meant having a narrow waist. Some were fitted with a steel cage under their clothes that pinched their stomachs in. The pinching went a little too far with Elizabeth Evelyn. She died. Elizabeth was *two* years old!

7 Orphans could have a terribly tough time. To keep large numbers of them quiet at night they'd be given a mixture called Godfrey's cordial which was full of the powerful drug

opium. It sent them to sleep all right – but give them too much and they didn't wake up … ever!

8 Children were often taken from orphanages to become servants. But Elizabeth Brownrigg treated them more like slaves. Girls were kept in filthy cellars, left in the cold with no clothes and constantly whipped. They slept on rotten straw and were given scraps to eat. Of course many girls died after this sort of treatment. Then one escaped and reported Elizabeth Brownrigg to the parish officers. They visited the Brownrigg house and found another girl on the point of death. They arrested Brownrigg and she was hanged.

9 Then you had to survive school. Some poor children went to 'dame' schools run by a local woman or to 'charity' schools, paid for by rich people in the area. But 'public' schools, where rich parents paid to send their children, were in a dreadful state in Georgian times. Teachers were violent and pupils were worse! A boy wrote home to complain about his life in the bedrooms: 'I have been woken up many times by the hot points of cigars burning holes in my face.'

MORNING, SMITHERS

10 But children *did* fight back! In 1793 there was a 'Great Rebellion' at Winchester school. The boys took over a tower at the school and refused to come down. The gentle boys threw stones at the teachers below – the not-so-gentle ones

fired pistols! At the same school in 1818 a pupil rebellion had to be dealt with by soldiers using bayonets.

NAPOLEON'S CAVALRY IS ONE THING, BUT ARMED ANGRY PUBLIC SCHOOLBOYS ARE QUITE ANOTHER

BANG   POP

Did you know …?
One of Winchester's old pupils, Thomas Arnold, went as head teacher to Rugby School and wrote the famous book *Tom Brown's School Days* about life there. But Rugby had its own problems before Arnold got the job there. In 1797 a gang of pupils used gunpowder to blow up the headmaster's door! (And you thought you were daring when you dropped a stink-bomb in school assembly?)

Wild women

Being a child wasn't fun – but it was probably worse being a woman. Men expected their wives to be quiet and to obey them. But there were times when a bit of wildness in a woman came in handy.

In Georgian times it was women who went to market to buy the corn. If the price of corn was too high then their families would go hungry. And it was the women who bullied the farmers into cutting their prices.

The wild women of Bewdley, for example, cut open sacks of wheat and told the farmers they would only pay what people were paying in nearby towns. The women won.

In Exeter, the townsmen heard that farmers were going to put up the prices of corn. They sent their women to market to argue for a lower price … or 'take it by force'! The women won again.

In Bewdley and Exeter the men were happy to stand back and send the women to battle for the food.

Of course, women were not treated so well when it came to work and pay … especially pay. Women worked as hard as men in the farmers' fields – but they were paid half as much. Then, when farm jobs were short, it was the women who got the sack.

But what was it like for Georgian women? Test your brain-power with this simple test. Which of these foul facts were true for woeful Georgian women?

1 Georgian men believed that women were not as intelligent as they were.

2 Georgian girls married when they were just 12 years old.

3 A woman who killed her husband could be burned alive as a punishment.

4 Some men would get rid of a wife by selling her at an auction.

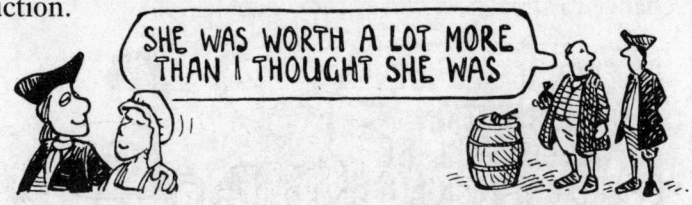

5 A husband who beat his wife would be punished.

6 Women used arsenic poison to make themselves look beautiful.

7 In the middle of the 1700s a hard-working man in industry could earn £3 a week – a maidservant in a house would earn £3 *a year*!

8 Lady Wortley Montague was famous for being the cleanest woman in Britain.

9 A woman could be divorced if she'd used make-up to trick a man into marrying her.

10 Fashionable women wore masks to keep the sun off their faces.

Answers:

1 True. That's what they believed. Of course they were wrong. Women were every bit as intelligent as men but were not given a good education and didn't have the chance to show how clever they were.

EVEN IF YOU HAD AN EDUCATION, WE WOULD STILL BE MORE INTELLIGENTER

2 False. The average age was about 24. Very few married at under 16 but there is a curious report of a Christchurch parson who married a girl of 13. He was 83 years old at the time. But he was seriously weird. He was a rich man who dressed so carelessly he was often mistaken for a tramp.

3 True. A man murdering his wife was hanged but women could be burned. In 1726, Catherine Hayes was sentenced to die at the stake. The 'kind' judges decided she would be strangled first so she didn't suffer death by burning. But the flames were lit too soon and the executioner couldn't reach her to kill her quickly. In Maidstone in 1769 Susannah Lott died at the stake before she was burned and didn't suffer so much. This law was finally changed in 1789 so women got equal rights – the right to be hanged for murder.

4 True. It was not legal but it sometimes happened. The woman was taken to market with a rope round her neck and sold to the highest bidder. Sometimes a woman would fetch a few pounds and sometimes she could be traded for an ox – better for pulling a plough, of course, but it didn't make such a good cup of tea. This uncommon sort of divorce was last heard of in 1887.

5 False. A husband was allowed to beat his wife. The stick he used must be no thicker than his thumb, so he could whip her with a cane but probably not a walking stick.

6 True. The white powder was put on the skin to make it pale and smooth and beautiful. If too much of the white poison got into your mouth you'd be pale and smooth and dead. This happened to a famous beauty, Maria Gunning in the 1750s. (She was warned!) There was also poisonous mercury and lead in some of this make-up which could make you go bald. And it was a mistake to kiss these women! There was a scandal in Italy when over 600 men died from getting too close to wives wearing arsenic make-up!

DON'T YOU THINK MY HUSBAND IS DEAD HANDSOME?

WELL, YOU'RE RIGHT ABOUT THE FIRST PART

7 True. A mirror in a great house like Holkham Hall, Norfolk, was said to have cost £500. If a £3-a-year maid broke that mirror then the owners would have to stop her wages for 166 years and eight months to pay for it.

8 False. Lady Wortley Montague was filthy. She was once told that her hands were rather dirty. She replied, 'If you think they are dirty then you ought to see my feet!'

9 True. In 1770 the British government passed a law saying a woman who tricked a man with make-up was as bad as a witch. If he married her, and found she was ugly underneath all the powder and paint, then he could be un-married any time he wanted.

10 True. A pale skin was beautiful to the Georgians. A mask in front of the face would protect the skin. Of course it was awkward trying to hold a mask up so some had a button attached to the back and the button was held between the teeth. These masks had eye cut-outs so were suntanned eyeballs all right?

Gruesome Georgians

Georgian Britain was a prime crime time. In 1700 there were about 50 crimes that could be punished by death. By 1822 they had lost count! There were at least 200 hanging crimes and some experts believe there were as many as 350! These included …

- Going armed in disguise (so the Lone Ranger would have been in trouble)
- Poaching fish (but a poached egg was fine)
- Forging bank notes (but not sick notes to teachers, so you'd have been safe)1
- Cutting down trees (with criminals rooted out by the men of Special Branch).

And, of course, murder …

The mystery of the moors

Daniel Clarke was a Yorkshire shoemaker who married a wealthy woman. The trouble was he liked to boast about his riches. 'I'm the richest man in Knaresborough! You should see my jewels!'

On 8 February 1745 he disappeared, never to be seen alive again.

Law officers found some of Clarke's jewels in the house of a man called Eugene Aram. Aram was arrested but said Clarke had given them to him before he left the county. The magistrates had to let Eugene Aram go free.

Of course, as you may have guessed, Aram had murdered Clarke and stolen the jewels. Not only did he get away with it, but he got to keep the jewels and he moved to Kings Lynn in Norfolk. He had got away with murder! Until …

1. In 1820, 46 people were hanged for forging banknotes. But after the executions, some of the notes were shown to be genuine. Oops!

Fourteen years later a labourer was digging for limestone in a cave when he came across some human bones. No one could prove that they were the bones of Daniel Clarke, but Eugene Aram was arrested anyway. He was found guilty and hanged. His body was hung in a cage by the Knaresborough road where the murder happened. As the body rotted, and the bones fell through the bars of the cage, his widow was allowed to pick them up. But one night a doctor took the skull and it's still on view in the Royal College of Surgeons' Museum in London.

Gruesome!

So here's the mystery. What sort of man would murder the shoemaker for his money? Can you guess? Was Eugene Aram ...

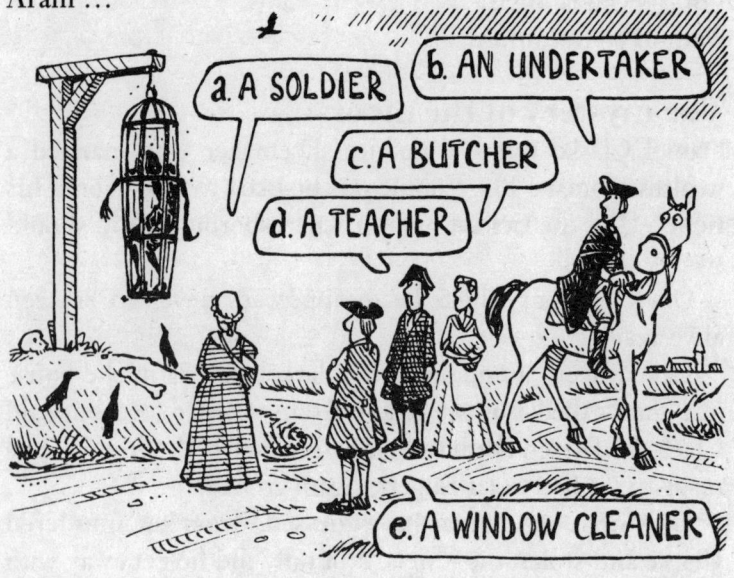

a. A SOLDIER

b. AN UNDERTAKER

c. A BUTCHER

d. A TEACHER

e. A WINDOW CLEANER

Answer: d) Eugene Aram was an English teacher. Which just goes to show ... something!

Heroes and villains

The Georgians had some pretty famous villains. The trouble is they became heroes, a bit like Robin Hood. You know the sort of thing ...

I ONLY ROB THE RICH

'COS THE POOR HAVE NOTHING WORTH PINCHING!

Take smugglers, for example. Georgian Britain was a time for smuggling. Lots of people seemed to think they were doing a good job – half the tea drunk in Britain was smuggled in to the country. Lace was smuggled in – stuffed inside geese; brandy kegs were hidden inside lobster pots; tobacco was twisted into ropes and hidden amongst the ropes used on the ships.

All good fun and part of the game called 'cheat-the-government'. Smugglers today are seen as brave outlaws. You probably know the poem by Rudyard Kipling ...

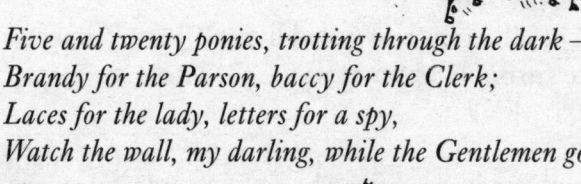

Five and twenty ponies, trotting through the dark –
Brandy for the Parson, baccy for the Clerk;
Laces for the lady, letters for a spy,
Watch the wall, my darling, while the Gentlemen go by.

The trouble was these 'gentlemen' were nasty, cruel and greedy. They'd probably cut your throat just for the fun of it and then say, 'You still think I'm a hero?'

In 1748 a man called Chater betrayed a smuggling gang and a law officer called Galley tried to arrest them. A magazine of the time described what happened next ...

They began with poor Galley, cut off his nose, broke every joint of him and after several hours of torture dispatched him. Chater they carried to a dry well, hung him by the middle to a cross beam in it, leaving him to perish with hunger and pain. But when they came, several days after, and heard him groan, they cut the rope, let him drop to the bottom and threw in logs and stones to cover him. The person who told the magistrates the story was in disguise because he feared the same would happen to him.

Some 'gentlemen' they turned out to be.

Never mind the story books and poems. Here is the terrible truth about these exciting criminals!

The highwayman
Name: Dick Turpin (also called himself John Palmer)
Claim to fame: Highwayman
Life: 1705 – 1739
The story:
• Brave and handsome hero who was a wonderful rider.
• He robbed stage coaches but was always very polite ... especially to ladies.
• He rode his gallant horse, Black Bess, all the way from

Essex to York in record time to prove he couldn't have committed a crime ... though he had.

The terrible truth:

- He was a butcher boy till he decided there was more money in stealing cattle than chopping them. He joined 'The Essex Gang' of violent house-breakers. They entered someone's home, robbed it and tortured the occupants till they handed over their money and valuables.

- When most of the Gang was arrested Turpin tried his hand at a different crime. He stopped a gentleman on the road and threatened him with a pistol. That man was Tom King, the famous highwayman. King took Turpin as a partner. They spent two years terrorizing the Essex roads. When King was caught Turpin tried to rescue him but accidentally shot his partner dead!

- Turpin was arrested for stealing sheep in Yorkshire. No one knew he was the famous highwayman until his old teacher recognized his handwriting! Turpin ended up hanged in York. He never made the famous ride on Black Bess – though another highwayman, John Nevison, may have done.

Not to be confused with: Black Beauty, Turnip Townsend, Mashed Turnip.

The outlaw

Name: Rob Roy MacGregor (also known as Red Roy or Robert the Red. When he joined the English he changed his name to Robert Campbell.)

Claim to fame: Outlaw

Life: 1671 – 1734

The story:

- Poor Rob was the Scottish Robin Hood. He was outlawed just because he was from the clan MacGregor, not because he was a criminal. For years he lived in caves and woods, often escaping the law by the skin of his teeth.

- He led his poor neighbours in their struggle against cattle thieves from the north. Rob Roy led them to freedom from the terror.

- He fought bravely for his country in their struggle against the English.

The terrible truth:

- A cattle thief by the age of 20. He fought for Scotland in the Glorious Revolution against England – but switched sides when he saw he was going to lose.

- Became a respectable cattle dealer but, when times got hard, he took his customers' money and ran off with it to the Western Isles.

- While he lived as a bandit he threatened cattle owners: 'Pay me to leave your cattle alone.' Switched sides again and fought against the English but was captured. King George pardoned him. He went home to live a quiet life.

Not to be confused with: Red Rum, Roy of the Rovers.

The pirate

Name: Blackbeard (full name Edward Teach, also known as Tache or Thatch – though he was christened Edward Drummond)

Claim to fame: Pirate

Life: Born in Bristol, date unknown, died 1718

The story:

- Blackbeard went into battle with six pistols at his waist and lighted matches under his hat to make him look frightening. (He was a bit of a hot-head.)

- He was a brave English hero who stole from the French. His treasure was buried on a desert island and no one has found it to this day.

- Blackbeard died fighting against a small army. When his body was thrown into the sea it swam round the ship three times before it sank.

The terrible truth:

- Blackbeard was a vicious bully. He went into business with the Governor of North Carolina in America. The Governor let Blackbeard attack ships – any ships, not just the French – so long as he got a share of the loot.

- The 'treasure' wasn't gold and jewels but goods like barrels of sugar. The American people (not the French) became so fed up with Blackbeard they sent a naval ship to stop him.

- In a hand-to-hand battle Lieutenant Robert Maynard shot Blackbeard dead – then cut his head off just to make sure.

Not to be confused with: Bluebeard, King Edward potatoes, teachers called Edward, Margaret Thatcher, Black Bess, Black Beauty, black pudding – and there's no truth in the story that his crew said a Teach should be nicknamed Blackboard!

And, talking about pirates ...

Pirates, parrots and eye-patches

Have you ever seen a film about pirates? They were funny old characters, and liked a good laugh and a quick chorus of 'Fifteen men on a dead man's chest, yo-ho-ho and a bottle of rum!' Then they battled bravely against huge Spanish galleons and made the cowardly captains cough up some terrific treasure.

Right?

Wrong.

Here is the terrible truth about the gorgeous Georgian pirates:

1 **Spanish treasure ships** By Georgian times there were no Francis Drake characters attacking Spanish galleons and winning gold for England and the Queen. They attacked little trading ships to steal tobacco or slaves or just spare sails and anchor cable. ('Your anchor cable or your life?' doesn't sound so gorgeous, does it?)

2 **Head-scarves** Did they really tie large, coloured handkerchiefs round their heads? Yes. (If you want to try this then use a clean hankie. 'Snot very nice otherwise.)

3 **Walking the plank** Have you ever seen the play *Peter Pan*? Cut-throat Captain Hook plans to make the Lost Boys walk the plank and drop off into crocodile-infested waters. Very dramatic. But true? No. Pirates couldn't be bothered

with that sort of play-acting. Some cruel pirates did tell their captives, 'You're free to walk home!' while they were in the middle of shark-filled seas. If they wanted to get rid of their victims then they just hacked them to death and threw them over the side. (That's a bit boring – especially for the victim, who'd be bored to death – but it saved a lot of time.)

4 Marooning Did they really leave a sailor on some desert island with a bottle of water and a gun? Yes, they did. It was a punishment usually kept for pirates who tried to desert their shipmates. The most famous marooned sailor was Alexander Selkirk whose adventures were turned into the story *Robinson Crusoe*. (Imagine being alone and lonely with no friendly human to talk to. You'd go mad. And teachers are still doing this today. They call it detention.)

5 The Jolly Roger flag Did pirates fly the black flag with a white skull and crossbones? Sometimes. Most Tudor and Stuart pirates flew a red flag – they put a story around that the flag was dyed with blood. Georgian pirates started to come up with their own designs. (What picture would you have on your flag to strike terror into the hearts of your enemies? A school and cross boys, perhaps.)

HOW DO YOU SUPPOSE THAT IS GOING TO STRIKE TERROR INTO THE HEARTS OF OUR ENEMIES?

6 Wooden legs Did pirates limp around on wooden legs? Some did. Fighting against the cannon of naval vessels was dangerous, and legs, arms and heads must have flown around like skittles in a bowling alley. Of course they didn't have doctors on board to make a neat job of a mangled arm or leg – but the ship's carpenter could carve you a neat replacement.

7 Parrots Did pirates have parrots on their shoulders? Not usually – but they often carried them in cages back to Britain from South America. They could teach them to speak during the voyage back across the Atlantic then sell them as pets in Britain.

8 Buried treasure Much more money has been spent *searching* for pirate treasure than has ever been *found*. If you won a million on the lottery would you bury it? No, you'd want to spend it. So did the pirates. Was there ever such a place as Treasure Island? The writer Robert Louis Stevenson spent a wet holiday in Scotland in 1881 and painted a map of an island for fun. He named it Skeleton Island and liked it so much he wrote the book *Treasure Island* to go with the map. Stevenson never met a pirate and he pinched the 'Dead man's chest' song from another writer's book.

9 Keel hauling A pirate found guilty of a crime against the crew would be forced to swallow cockroaches – if he was lucky! If he was unlucky he'd be *keel hauled*. A rope was tied under his arms and another to his feet. He was thrown into the sea and dragged under the bottom of the boat ('hauled' under the 'keel'). He might survive drowning but there were very rough barnacles clinging to the bottom of a wooden ship that would scrape the skin. (And, when he got back, the rotten crew didn't even give him an Elastoplast!)

10 Gold earrings Did tough pirates wear pretty gold rings in their ears? Yes! They were a superstitious lot and believed that a gold earring gave them better eye sight. (A pirate never wore glasses, because he didn't want to make a spectacle of himself.)

Painful punishments

Georgians tried to be tough on criminals. Hangings were performed in public so everyone could see what happened to naughty boys and girls.

Of course the Georgian newspapers loved crime stories as much as today's papers. Here are some genuine press cuttings ...

Fortune-telling

A local record book records a curious crime and a cruel punishment in the north of England ...

Susannah Fleming stood in the pillory at White Cross for an hour for fortune-telling. Though she was not bothered by the public she was nearly strangled either because she fainted or because her neck was held too tightly. A sailor, out of kindness, brought her down the ladder on his back in nearly a dying state.

Suicide

The Georgians thought they were wiser than the people of the Middle Ages and Tudor times. But old superstitions lingered on.

Killing yourself was against the law, so it had to be punished. How do you punish people who have killed themselves? The Georgians had no problem. *The Western Flying Post* newspaper reported the death of an old man in 1755 …

On 6 June an old man hanged himself by his handkerchief at Linkincehorn in Cornwall. The coroner decided that he had committed suicide. He was buried at Kesbrook Crossroad and a stake driven through his body.

A suicide victim could not be buried in a churchyard because, the Georgians said, he had gone against God's law. He was buried at the crossroads so the ghost would be confused about which way to go to get back home. Why a stake through his body? Because people believed this would stop the man rising from his grave and haunting the area.

STAKE NOT STEAK!

Sheep-stealing

Stealing a sheep could be punished by hanging in Georgian times – a 12 year-old boy was sentenced to death for stealing a lamb in 1802. But one sheep thief saved the law officers a rope! He stole a sheep and managed to hang himself. In 1762 the *Gloucester Journal* reported ...

On Tuesday afternoon a man was found strangled in a field. He had stolen a sheep and, to carry it away, had tied the back legs and put the cord over his head. When he rested on a gate the sheep kicked, the cord dropped over his neck and strangled him.

At least he died with a *sheepish* grin on his face. The good news is the sheep lived. The bad news is it was certainly eaten by someone else not long after.

Did you know ...?
Prison in Georgian times was not like prison today. Prisoners could keep pets. But in 1714, Newgate Prison in London banned one of the most popular pets: pigs.

WE'RE TREATED LIKE ANIMALS IN HERE!

Witchcraft

The ancient way of testing for witchcraft was to throw a suspect into water and see if they floated – a witch would float (be taken out, hanged and die) while an innocent person would sink (probably drown and die anyway).

Ruth Osborne was beaten and drowned at Tring in 1751 as a suspected witch. Twenty years later, in the same town, a man and his wife both suffered the 'water ordeal' – the woman died and the man *just* survived.

But things were changing. In 1770 a man accused a 55-year-old woman of witchcraft. She said, 'I don't think I'm a witch – but you'd better try me, just to make sure!' The *Northampton Mercury* newspaper described what happened …

A miller in the area was chosen to perform the ducking ceremony. The poor woman went to the mill where a great number of people were gathered. The miller remembered what had happened in Tring and refused to try her in front of such a large crowd. He promised he would try her, in secret, as soon as he was alone.

The crowd left. The woman survived. We can guess that the miller didn't try too hard to drown her. Wise man. Maybe the Georgians were learning some common sense after all.

Theft

Any sort of theft was punished very harshly in Georgian times. In Norwich a girl was hanged for stealing a petticoat. No one seemed to object, though the girl was just seven years old.

Bodies for sale

Wild life, wilder death

Jonathan Wild was a thief–taker. He promised to find your stolen goods for you … if you paid him a reward, of course.

People came to him from all over London. 'Can you get back my stolen property?' they asked.

'I'll leave messages in certain places,' he said. 'The thieves will leave your stolen goods where I can find them. I will leave them a reward. Everybody's happy.'

'You are wonderful, Mr Wild.'

'I know,' he said.

The truth was that Jonathan Wild had organized the robbery in the first place! No wonder he knew how to get the stolen property back. In time every thief in London was working for Wild and every victim in London came to him for help.

No thief dared to upset Wild because Wild would simply betray the thief to the law. He had 75 criminals convicted and 60 of those were hanged.

Wild grew rich and fat. By 1724 he was in complete control of London crime. But in the end Wild's wickedness was uncovered and he was hanged. Thousands gathered to pelt him with mud and stones as he was taken to the gallows.

Yet Wild still had some friends left and they did a curious thing. They smuggled his dead body away and buried it in a secret place at the dead of night. Why would they do such a thing? Because they were afraid William Cheselden would get his hands on the body. Mr Cheselden was a surgeon and he was interested in learning about the human body by cutting up dead ones. (He was also interested in cutting up live ones but they wouldn't let him!)

Where did Mr Cheselden get his dead bodies from? He

bought bodies of criminals who'd been hanged. That's what Wild's friends were afraid of.

Did Cheselden get Wild's body? Yes. The secret grave was found, the body was dug up and delivered to the surgeon. (The skeleton of Wild can still be seen today in the Hunterian Museum at the Royal College of Surgeons if you are sick-minded enough to want to look at it.)

The age of the bodysnatcher had begun!

'Better get back in your coffin, mate!' – a gorgeous Georgian tale of terror

Edward Henson was crying and the tears spilled into his ale. 'You're pathetic,' the landlord said. 'You're drunk.'

'I'm not,' Edward argued but his voice was slurred and his eyes were rolling in his leather-skinned face.

'I've seen a lot of drunks in my time and I tell you, sailor, you're drunk. You don't even know that you're crying into your beer,' the landlord sneered, wiping a greasy hand on his stained apron.

The air of the quayside tavern was smoky with

the cheap tallow candles and shadows hid the filth on the floor. 'I'm sad,' Edward moaned.

'You'll get no more ale in this tavern,' the landlord said firmly.

'No! Listen. I had a friend. The best friend a man ever had. His name was Geordie. Poor Geordie.'

Edward took a deep drink of the clouded drink and wiped his mouth on the back of his sleeve, then he wiped his nose, then he wiped his eyes. 'He's dead.'

'I'm sorry,' the landlord said. 'What did he die of?'

'Don't know. I'm not a doctor. He woke up yesterday morning and he was dead!' the sailor said.

'These things happen,' the landlord shrugged.

'I went to Geordie's funeral this afternoon. Sort of said goodbye to him. We've sailed together for ten years or more. All over the world.'

The landlord slipped onto the bench alongside the drunken sailor and lowered his voice. 'I hope he rests in peace,' he said.

'He will, he will. He'll go straight to heaven, will Geordie.'

'I'm sure his soul will go to heaven,' the landlord said. 'It's his body I'd worry about.'

'His body? It's dead. I saw it myself! I said, "You're quiet this morning Geordie," and he never replied. That's because he was dead, you know. Did I tell you he was dead?'

The landlord grabbed the sailor's arm and shook him. 'The sack-'em-up men are in this town.'

'Shack-'em who?'

'Sack-'em-up men! Bodysnatchers! In the past six weeks we've lost five bodies from the local churchyard.'

'Lost them? How can you lose a body?'

'They were dug up, put in a sack and taken to the hospital.'

'So the doctors could make them better?' Edward said cheerfully. 'Will they make my friend Geordie better?'

'No! The doctors want to cut them up. To try their experiments on. If you don't want your friend to end up on a doctor's table then you'd better go and have a look at the grave tonight. But be careful. These sack-'em-up men aren't too fussy about what they take. If they catch you interfering they'll slap a pitch plaster over your mouth to shut you up.'

'A pitch plaster? I'll suffocate!' the sailor cried.

'Then that'll save them digging up your friend,' the landlord warned. 'Most people watch their friends' graves in groups of four or five. Some people even sleep near the graves for two or three weeks.'

'Two or three weeks?'

'Till the body's too rotten to be any use to the doctors,' the landlord explained.

'My ship sails in two days,' Edward moaned.

'But tonight's the night when the sack-'em-up men will be after him.' The landlord took the sailor's ale tankard and helped him to his feet. Out of the door, turn right and climb

the hill. 'The churchyard's on your right. It's behind the high wall.'

Edward Henson looked almost sober as he said, 'Thank you. I'll go and look after Geordie.'

He staggered towards the door, crashing against tables and upsetting tankards. The night air was damp and there was a light, chill mist blurring the moon. Edward took a few deep breaths and used the wall to guide himself along the muddy lane that ran along the river front.

The mist seemed to deaden the sounds of the night. All the sailor could hear was the squish of his boots in the mud and his own creaking breathing. The pie stall at the end of Low Row was closed. Two men had been there earlier in the night with their cheerful cries of 'Chelsea buns!', 'Pies all smoking hot!' and 'Mutton pies!' Edward suddenly realized that he was hungry. He turned away from the deserted pie stall and up the hill. He passed the small stone prison cell at the foot of Crown Street and left behind the pitiful sobbing of its solitary prisoner.

After ten minutes he reached a high wall that was soft and slimy to the touch with the moss that grew on it. In the faint moonlight he saw a white shape looming ahead of him. He strained his eyes and at last made out the shape of a man. A man dressed in a white night shirt. A rope was fastened under his armpits and he was hanging over the churchyard wall by the rope.

Edward blinked. He took a few steps towards the figure then stopped. The face was ghastly but he knew it.

'Geordie!' he cried. 'It's you, Geordie!'

Geordie didn't reply.

The sailor reached out a hand and grasped the wrist of his friend. 'My, but you're cold, Geordie!' he said. 'It's not like you to be out on a chilly night like this dressed in your nightgown.'

Geordie didn't reply.

Edward Henson rubbed a hand over his eyes. 'Oh, but I was forgetting! You died yesterday! You'd better get back in your coffin, mate, before you catch your death of cold!'

Suddenly the rope went tight and a moment later the

71

corpse was whisked back over the graveyard wall. There was a muttered conversation and footsteps padding over the grass behind the wall.

Edward straightened his shoulders and seemed suddenly sober. He hurried to the house that stood at the gateway to the graveyard. He rapped on the heavy oak door. A window rattled open. 'Who's there?'

'It's me.'

'Who's me?'

'Edward Henson, from the collier ship *Cushie Butterfield*.'

'What do you want?'

'Are you in charge of this graveyard?'

'I am.'

'Well, I'm here to tell you the dead uns are getting out of the churchyard!'

There was a roar of anger from the man at the window. It slammed shut and he was down at the door a few minutes later. He ran out with a gun and vanished between the shadowy gravestones. Edward Henson heard shots and cries.

He walked wearily up the hill to his lodging house. Without bothering to undress he fell onto his straw mattress next to a snoring sailor, pulled a rough wool blanket over himself and was asleep in no time.

The next night he was drinking his ale a lot more slowly.

'So you saved your friend from the sack-'em-up men, I hear,' the landlord said. He was looking at Edward Henson with a little more respect tonight.

'I did. And I hear they found a trail of blood in the churchyard this morning,' the sailor said. 'They do say the bodysnatchers won't be back in this town for a while.'

'Then I owe you a drink, my friend,' the landlord grinned.

'I'd rather have a bite to eat.' There were no pies on sale tonight.

The landlord leaned forward, his thick hands planted heavily on the wet table. 'They do say the two pie men have vanished. A funny couple of men. Foreigners. From Scotland.'

'Ah!'

'And that pie stall was in the perfect place to watch everything that went on in the churchyard.'

'You mean ...'

'It looks like they may have been the bodysnatchers.'

Edward Henson shuddered and took a long drink of his ale. 'You say they sold the bodies to the doctors?'

'They did. They got four guineas apiece for fresh ones. The doctors can't get enough of them. Why?'

The sailor shook his head and looked into the dregs of his ale. 'I was just wondering about their tasty mutton pies...'

Would you make a good bodysnatcher?

The three leading members of a Scottish bodysnatching gang were known as The Spoon, The Mole, and Merry Andrew. Merry Andrew cheated the other two out of some bodysnatching money and they were angry. They planned their revenge. Merry Andrew's sister, Sarah, had just died and they planned to snatch her body and sell it to the doctors.

Imagine you are Merry Andrew. You guess what your partners are up to. What are you going to do about it …

a) You can report The Spoon and The Mole to the law officers. A watch will be kept on your dear sister's grave. As soon as the bodysnatching villains appear, the law officers will appear and stop them, Sarah can rest in peace and the wicked plan is ruined.

b) You can watch the graveyard. When The Mole and The Spoon appear you can go off to fetch the law officers. The bodysnatchers will be caught in the act. They will have sweated for nothing and they will probably go to jail. Poor beloved Sarah will have been disturbed, but it is worth it to see them locked away.

c) You can hide in the graveyard alone. When The Spoon and The Mole have dug up your sister you can leap out of hiding, dressed in a white sheet, pretending to be a ghost and scare them off. You can put your sister back and cover up her grave again. The villains won't be back and Sarah will be safe.

d) You can hide in the graveyard alone. When The Spoon and The Mole have dug up your sister you can leap out of hiding, dressed in a white sheet, pretending to be a ghost and scare them off. You can take your darling Sarah's body to the surgeon and sell her. The Mole and the Spoon have done the work, you collect the money ... if you can bear to sell your own sister, of course.

Which of the above would you do?
Which did Merry Andrew do?

Answer: d) Merry Andrew sold his sister's body to the surgeons. He even chased The Mole and The Spoon away from the cart they had waiting. He borrowed it to get his sister to the surgeon. He enjoyed telling the story and always had a good laugh. 'The Spoon went without his porridge that night!' he'd chuckle.

If you answered **d)**, and you have a sister, then someone should warn her about you!

75

Quaint quack doctors

The more bodies the doctors cut up the more they learned about the human body. But there was still a lot of ignorance about sickness and disease and many people still took curious cures for their problems.

Newspapers were packed with adverts for curious cures. The following advert is invented but the cures offered are all real Georgian medicines.

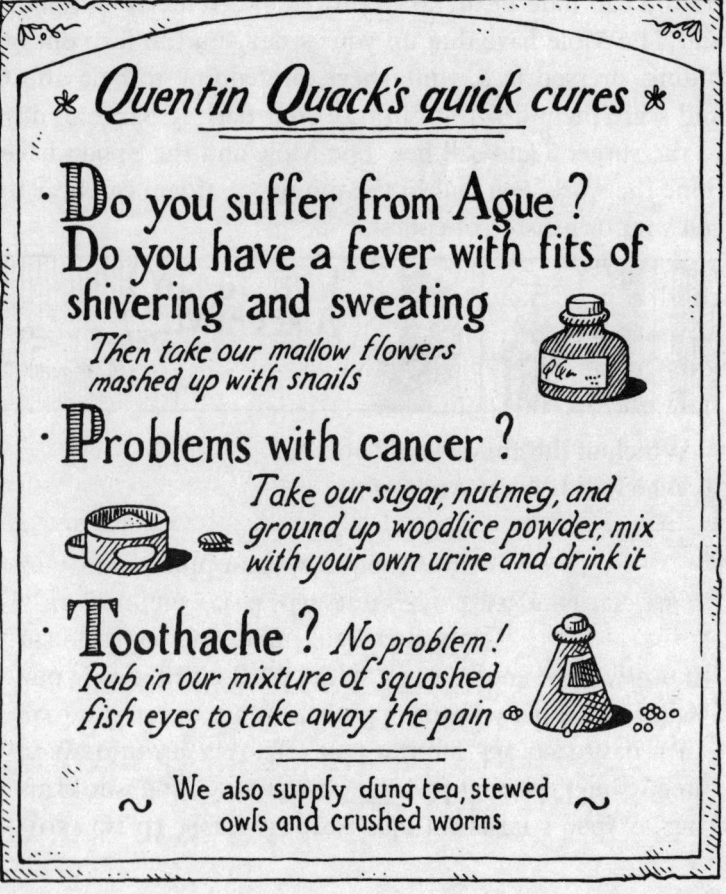

* *Quentin Quack's quick cures* *

- **D**o you suffer from Ague?
  Do you have a fever with fits of shivering and sweating
  Then take our mallow flowers mashed up with snails

- **P**roblems with cancer?
  Take our sugar, nutmeg, and ground up woodlice powder, mix with your own urine and drink it

- **T**oothache? *No problem!*
  Rub in our mixture of squashed fish eyes to take away the pain

  We also supply dung tea, stewed owls and crushed worms

Dodge the doctor

Some people didn't fancy visiting their doctor or dentist – especially the dentist. Yet the dentists were no worse than they are today.

They would invite you to lie on the floor and strap you down. Then they would kneel over you with your head between their legs, say, 'We'll have this out in no time!' and get to work. Just like your dentist, eh? What on earth is there to be afraid of?

If you were really rich then the dentist could have a poor child lying beside you. As soon as your bad tooth was whipped out (or ripped out) a good 'live' tooth would be pulled from the child and planted in the gap in your gums. (Don't worry, the child would be paid!)

Other toothless patients had false teeth made from tusks of hippopotamus or walrus or from pottery. These false teeth never fitted very well and were often taken out so the wearer could eat a meal. (Still they were better than Victorian false teeth made from rubber and celluloid. Sydney Dark fell asleep with a cigar clamped between his celluloid teeth. When the cigar burnt down it set fire to his teeth!)

But let's suppose you were a real wimp and wanted to dodge the doctor and dentist. Here are ten Georgian cures you may like to try. There's just one problem ... nine of the crazy cures were actually tried by the Georgians. One has been made up and was never used by the Georgians – or anyone else. Can you spot which is the odd one out …

1 James Woodforde had a sty on his eyelid. He heard that it would go if he rubbed it with the tail of a black cat. He tried it … and it worked!

2 Thomas Grey's friend suffered from swollen joints and heard that boiling a whole chicken and eating it with six litres of beer would cure him. He tried it … and it worked!

3 People bitten by a mad dog could catch the dog's disease, rabies. The cure was to take a hair from the dog and put it on the wound or swallow it … this never worked.

4 Toothache is easily cured. Take a poker and heat it in the fire. When it is nice and hot then burn the ear lobe with the poker and the pain in the tooth will go away.

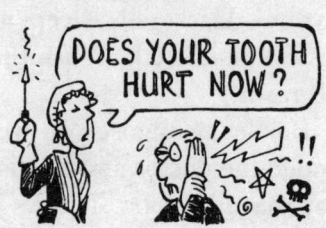

5 Lavinia Cordle found that a boil on her bottom was painful. Bursting it with a needle caused the boil to spread. Her friend said the trick was to burst it suddenly. Lavinia lifted her skirts and bent over with her back to a horse. Her friend tickled the horse's leg with a stalk of straw. When the kick of the horse landed on Lavinia's backside, the boil burst. The iron of the horse's hoof helped the sore spot to heal in half the time. Lavinia was able to sit down within a month – as soon as the bruise from the kick went away.

NOW HE HAS A SMELLY MOUTH AND SMELLY EARS

6 Bad breath caused by rotten teeth could be a problem. (You can tell if you have bad breath – friends like to chat to you from the far end of a football pitch with a megaphone.) The Georgians believed the best cure was to scrape the skin off a turnip, roast the pieces and wear them behind the ear.

7 Another Georgian cure for rabies was said to be a bath in salt water or, even better, a dunk in the sea. A man from Bristol was bitten and taken out to sea in a boat. He said, 'I'll never survive the dip in the sea!' They dipped him anyway and pulled him back into the boat, where he immediately died.

AT LEAST HE HASN'T GOT RABIES ANY MORE

8 A wasp sting inside the throat can kill you. The Georgians believed that you should swallow the juice of an onion to cure a sting like that. It may save your life. And the wasp will buzz off with its eyes full of tears. (Of course the best cure is not to go around with your mouth open.)

9 An adder sting is nasty ... and the Georgian cure was nastier! In 1821 a woman was bitten by an adder near Southampton and was a long way from a doctor. The local people took a chicken, killed it and placed its warm guts over the wound. Sounds *foul*, but they said it worked.

WHERE DID THE SNAKE BITE HER?

NEAR SOUTHAMPTON

10 Smallpox had killed many people through the ages but the Georgians found a way of preventing it – vaccination. They actually gave people a cattle sickness called cow pox. The cow pox didn't harm them but it did keep the smallpox sickness away.

Answer: 5. The other crazy cures were all really tired. And number **10**, vaccination, is a brilliant Georgian invention that has led to thousands of modern cures and saved millions of lives.

Bedlam, blood, blisters and baths

If you had problems with your mind it was a dreadful life for you in Georgian times. Mentally ill people were called 'mad' and locked away. Treatments included …

• being beaten
• being thrown into cold baths
• being made to vomit
• having blood let out of the body.

The most famous Georgian to suffer mental illness was King George III. So-called treatments included …

• fastening him to his bed

I NEED TO SCRATCH MY NOSE!

• shouting at him – after stuffing handkerchiefs in the king's mouth so he couldn't answer back

WHY CAN'T I STUFF THE HANDKERCHIEFS IN MY EARS?

- forming blisters on his head then bursting them – to let the badness out of his head

- giving him medicines that made him so sick he prayed to be cured or dead.

George's joke

George's behaviour was strange but he wasn't stupid. He was visited by a new doctor, Doctor Willis, and he hated the man on sight. The king questioned the man …

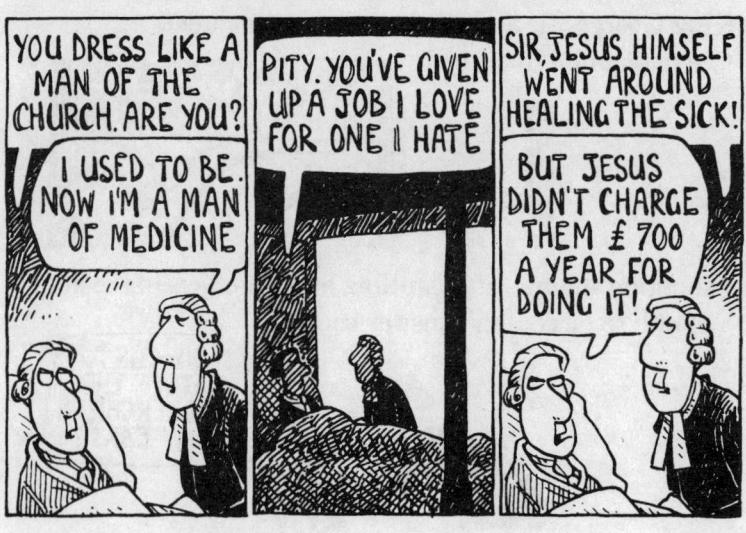

In fact Willis was later paid £10,000 (over half a million pounds at today's value) to treat mad Queen Maria of Portugal. He failed to cure her but was paid anyway.

Still, George could have been treated worse! Ordinary people in London's Bethlehem Hospital (known as Bedlam for short) were chained in their cells if they had mental problems. The porters in charge of the hospital made extra pocket money – they let the public look into the cells to 'give them cause for laughter' and charged a penny.

Gory Georgian fun and games

The people of Georgian Britain liked to enjoy themselves in great crowds. They flocked to fairs and packed into parks, thronged theatres and crowded coffee shops.

Of course Georgians didn't have televisions to amuse them. But maybe you'd swap a night's television for the fun of the Georgian fair? You could see ...

- Miller the German Giant (other 'freak shows' included 'a girl of 15 with strange moles on her backside')
- Violante the acrobat
- a conjuror
- a waxworks display
- a fire-eater
- a performing dog
- a dancing horse
- a slack-rope walker (unless he'd had a bit too much to drink, in which case he'd become a 'tight' rope walker). Slack-rope walker Madame Margaretta stood on one leg on a rope and balanced 13 full glasses on a tobacco pipe.

There were one or two horrors you might not enjoy so much, like …

- bear-baiting (the bear was chained to a post. Spectators paid a shilling each to set their dogs on the bear.)
- badger-baiting
- cock fights (often arranged in village churchyards!)
- goose-riding (a goose was hung from a tree by its feet. Riders would gallop underneath it and try to snatch its head off. This was made difficult by greasing the bird's beak.)

Any sort of cruelty to animals was enjoyed by some people. One advert announced …

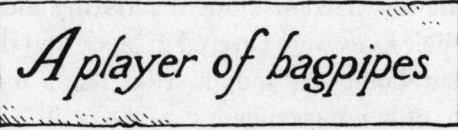

A *WILD BULL* will be turned loose with *fireworks all over him*

Not quite so bad was cruelty to humans at a fair which advertised …

A player of bagpipes

There were also fights between women. A foreign visitor called Cesar de Sassure described one ...

> *Both women wore very little clothing. One was a stout Irishwoman and the other a small Englishwoman, full of fire and very nippy. The weapons were a sort of blunt, two-handed sword. Presently the Irishwoman received a cut across the forehead and that put a stop to the first part of the fight. The Englishwoman's supporters threw money and cheered for her. During this time the wounded woman's forehead was sewn up, this being done on stage, she drank a large glass of spirits and the fight began again. The Irishwoman was wounded a second time then a third time with a long and deep wound all across her neck and throat. A few coins were thrown to her but the winner made a good income from the fight.*

In another fight two women fought a 'boxing and scratching match' till their faces were covered in blood and their clothes torn off their bodies. It sounds a bit like a girls' hockey match today, only not so violent.

In a London club a man fought three women at the same time and knocked them all out.

De Sassure went on to describe men fighting with the same weapons. The loser's ear was almost cut from his head.

A public notice appeared in Gateshead in County Durham on 22 May 1758. It read ...

*On this day
the annual ENTERTAINMENTS
at Swalwell Fair will take place
This will consist of...*

~ Dancing for ribbons

~ Women running for smocks

~ Ass races

~ Foot races for men

~ With the odd whim of a man eating a
  cockerel alive, feathers, entrails and all !!!

In Cambridge in 1770 a 16-year-old boy 'ate a whole cat smothered with onions.' But at least the cat was dead and cooked!

Sports and games you may not want to play

1 **Fighting animals** Eating a live chicken sounds cruel but cock-fighting was still a popular sport and bull-baiting was watched by huge crowds. In some places it was finally stopped when spectators were injured. The magistrates

didn't stop it because they were worried about the cruelty to the animals. Rich people, like the Duke of Cumberland, got pleasure from setting a tiger to kill a stag ... in a 1764 contest the stag won.

2 Horse racing Horse racing could be cruel. Horses raced time and again in heats as long as four miles. The exhausted horse that won the most heats was the winner.

There was also cruelty to jockeys – they were fond of barging, pushing and whipping their opponents. A writer said ...

> *I remember one jockey who used to boast of the damage he did by striking with the handle of his whip. He liked to describe the number of eyes and the teeth he had beaten out.*

A lot of money was gambled on horse races and some gamblers were bad losers. They sometimes set upon a jockey with sticks and stones and whips!

3 Soccer Football games were often organized in the street. Two sides booted a leather ball filled with air and weren't too bothered about how many windows they broke in houses and coaches. In Gloucester in 1811 the *Shrewsbury Chronicle* reported ...

An apprentice was convicted of playing football on a Sunday. He was sentenced to 14 days in prison.

Nowadays he'd be paid £10,000 a week and sentenced to play 90 minutes a week! (That's about £1.85 a second.)

4 Cricket In 1748 a court finally decided that another dreadfully dangerous game was actually legal – though people had been playing it for hundreds of years. This weird game was called 'cricket.' Teams of men (with some women players in London) threw a hard ball at some wooden pegs. The players wore no pads or gloves so broken bones, torn fingernails and bleeding injuries were common. A farmer was killed by a cricket ball in 1825. Maybe a return to Georgian cricket would liven the sport up today! Or this unusual Surrey match of 1773 ...

Last Wednesday an extraordinary match of cricket was played on Guildford Downs between a carpenter on one side and nine tailors on the other side. The prize was a quarter of lamb and a cabbage. The match was won by the Carpenter by 64 runs.

What a pity that Georgian carpenter isn't around to play for England's cricket team today. In 1997 England's cricketers lost to Matabeleland and Zimbabwe – in Britain in 1770 nobody had even heard of Matabeleland and Zimbabwe!

I WISH PEOPLE STILL HADN'T HEARD OF MATABELELAND AND ZIMBABWE!

5 Hunting The deer hunting of earlier times went out of fashion and fox-hunting became the most popular entertainment for the upper classes. Hare hunting was popular too because hares didn't run so far.1 In 1790 a hare actually escaped from the pack and the *Newcastle Chronicle* reported …

The hare fled and, with a wonderful leap, darted through a pane of glass in a window of The Globe Inn. It landed amongst a pile of legal papers since the inn was crowded with lawyers at the time. As soon as they recovered from the shock, the lawyers presented the poor hare to the cook …

You'd think the lawyers would have given it a fair hare trial, wouldn't you? But that's life. Hare today, gone tomorrow.

6 Rugby In 1823 two teams of boys were playing football at Rugby school when William Webb Ellis picked up the ball and ran with it. This new idea became quite popular (it gives your feet a rest) and the school had invented a new ball game! What should they call it? William-Webb-Ellis-Ball?

1. Popular for ladies and gentlemen, that is. Two boys who killed a hare for food were given a public whipping in Reading in 1773.

No. How about Pick-it-up-and-run-with-it-till-somebody-jumps-on-you-ball? That's better.

STRANGE... IT SEEMS TO HAVE GOT DARK

7 Ballooning In Newcastle Upon Tyne, there was a report of a new entertainment in 1786. An old history book told the story ...

Mr Lunardi, the famous aeronaut, made an attempt to ascend in an air balloon from the river bank. In filling it Mr Lunardi added the last of the acid and the hot steam became remarkably strong and thick. This gave so much alarm to those on that side of the balloon, who thought that it was on fire, that they immediately let go of their side of the net. The balloon being free on one side made a sudden stretch upwards. The balloon, set free,

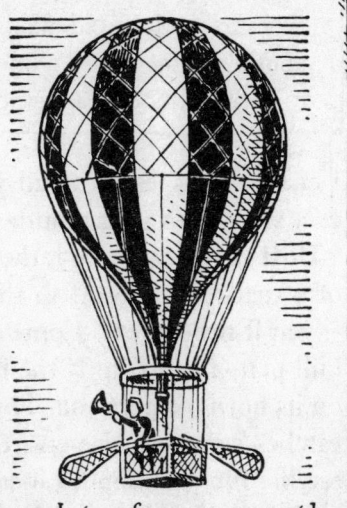

ascended rapidly and dragged with it Master Ralph Heron. The boy had one of the balloon ropes twisted round his hand and arm. When he reached a height of 500 feet the rope snapped off the balloon and he fell into a nearby garden. He died soon after.

8 Chuckstones This game involves throwing up stones and catching them on the back of the hand. It's been popular since ancient times but two Georgian boys came up with a new version in 1760. You could call it 'kill-a-wrinkly' …

In a small Devon village an old labouring man, John Wilson, was lying on a bench fast asleep. Some boys were playing at 'chuckers' and the old man's mouth being open, one of them chucked a stone directly into his mouth. This woke him, but the stone stuck in his throat and choked him before help could be brought. The man was over 90 years old and had never had any sickness.

Let that be a lesson to all you chuckstone players. Never, ever sleep with your mouth open.

9 Bull running Put a rather angry bull in a pen at the end of a road, then go off to the local tavern for a few drinks – you'll need them. Come back and open the gate of the bull pen. Then run. If the bull catches you it will toss you on its horns or gore you. This is no fun at all. But if the bull catches someone else and throws them up in the air it is terrific fun. In 1785 a Lincoln newspaper grumbled that it was a stupid and wasteful sport …

92

It is just an excuse for drunkenness and idleness. Even if a man escapes bodily hurt his family is harmed because of the money he spends.

10 Pinching matches Two people stand toe to toe and pinch one another. The one who can stand it the longest is the winner. If a player gets angry or starts to swear then he or she is the loser.

IT'S ALL RIGHT SIS, YOU CAN GO FIRST

The *Hertfordshire Mercury* reporter described a contest between a 'puny' little man and a 'stout' man …

They kept pinching each other for an hour, chiefly on the flesh parts of the arm. At the end of that time the stout man's arms fell powerless to his side and he had to give in from exhaustion and pain. The puny man offered to fight any man in England for the pinching championship.

... and games you definitely wouldn't want to play

1 A newspaper report of 1818 described this game that turned into gore ...

> On Saturday three boys were playing in a field where some cows were feeding. One of them, about 16 years of age, suggested that they tie another to the tail of a cow. But the enraged animal dragged the victim up and down the field at full speed, plunging in all directions. Before he could be rescued his life was totally extinct.

2 Apple bobbing is popular today but one Georgian invented 'silver bobbing'. A silver coin was dropped into a tub of water and players had to pick it up using their teeth. If you think apple bobbing's hard then don't try this.

3 In 1764 a bored lord in Huntingdon invented a game called 'hunting the hen'. The players had their hands muffled in thick bandages. They had to catch a hen and pull a feather out. The first to take a feather won the hen.

Did you know …?

A man called Jedediah Buxton travelled the country, entertaining people as a mathematical wonder. Jed had never been taught to read or write but he was famous for his maths skills. He was once asked to work out how many hairs' breadths (at 48 hairs to the inch) it would take to reach from Tyneside to London. He answered in less than three minutes (and without a pocket calculator) 833,310,720. And that, give or take a few curls, is about right!

WHEN ARE PEOPLE AROUND HERE GOING TO LEARN HOW TO SPELL?

A game you might like to play
A jingling match

This was a popular game played by women at fairs and can be played by a class of pupils in a school hall, yard or field.

You need:
• a bell on a string
• 12 scarves.

To play:

1 12 players are selected.

2 The rest of the class join hands to form a large circle round the 12.

3 One player – the Jingler – has the bell hung round her (or his) neck and her hands tied behind her with a scarf.

4 The other 11 players have scarves tied over their eyes.

5 The blindfolded players try to catch the Jingling player who can move anywhere in the circle to escape.

6 If the Jingler escapes for one minute then he or she wins.
7 If a blindfolded player catches the jingler then he or she wins and becomes the Jingler.

A jingling match

Prizes:
Decided by the players before the game. A new computer or a trip to the Bahamas (paid for by the teacher) would be a reasonable sort of prize.

Wacky Georgian words

The language we use is forever changing. Old words are forgotten or get new meanings and new ones are invented. Georgian Britain was no different.

Forgotten words include *odsbodikins* (a swear word) and *hock-dockies* for shoes. What a sad loss they are.

Changed words included *respectable* to mean polite. (And the Georgians tried to be polite. They used fewer swear words. No *respectable* person said *belly* or *bitch* any longer.)

The bill for food at a tavern was called the *scran*. It changed in Georgian times to mean the food itself ... and it still does.

New words came along with new fashions. A man in Georgian times could often be judged by the size of his hair-piece. So what did they call a very important man? A *bigwig* of course.

If you are going to understand the Georgians you probably need to know some of their words.

Match the following words to their meanings ...

1. A blue pigeon flier	a. is an idiot
2. A louse trap	b. is a coat
3. A sumph	c. is a horse
4. A wooden suit	d. is a gossip
5. A daisy-kicker	e. is a comb
6. A magpie	f. is a neck
7. A cover-me-queerly	g. is a thief who steals the lead off your roof
8. A sad man	h. is a coffin
9. A tattle box	i. is a trouble-maker
10. A scrag	j. is a small coin

Answers:

1g) *Blue pigeon* is lead, probably because of the colour.

2e) Obvious when you think about it. Similar to the delightful modern phrase 'nit rake'.

3a) That's a Scottish word. You can probably get away with calling your teacher this ... unless your teacher is an expert in Scottish words in which case you'll be needing a wooden suit!

4h) So don't let anyone measure you for a wooden suit! (Just say, 'It wooden suit me.')

5 c) So, if your name is Daisy then don't go near a horse.

6j) Also known as a maggie. But watch out for a maggie rab in Scotland because it's a forged coin.

7b) Actually a ragged coat. If you have a good coat then you can call it a *cover-me-decent* ... which it will.

8i) Of course if you're a troublemaker who gets caught then you'll be a sad, sad man.

9d) Just like a match box is full of matches, a lunch box is full of lunch, a tattle-box is full of tattle. So why isn't a pillar-box full of pillars?

10f) The Georgian meaning of *scragging* someone is hanging them. So, a scrag boy would hang you from the *scragging-post* till your scrag was totally *scragged*!

Rotten revolutions

Britain has always suffered from riots. The Georgians seemed to suffer more than most.

A writer said ...

> I have seen this year riots in the country about corn; riots about elections; riots about workhouses; riots of miners, riots of weavers, riots of wood-cutters; and I have seen riots of smugglers in which law officers have been murdered and the king's troops fired at.

And this was in 1769. Twenty years later the French had a terrifying revolution where the king and the nobles were executed. The Georgians feared the same could happen over here. It never did, but the British went to war with the French Emperor who replaced the headless king, Emperor Napoleon Bonaparte.

Napoleon expected the British people to support a revolution – after all, there had been all of those riots. When he sent French soldiers to help a British revolution he got a surprise ...

Mum's army

In 1797 a French force of 1,400 soldiers landed on the Welsh coast and they expected the local people to help them. They thought there would be a Welsh Revolution that would drive out the evil English. The defence of Britain rested on Lord Cawdor of Stackpole Hall.

If Lord Cawdor had written to a friend of the time he may have admitted that his victory was a great surprise – to the British defenders more than the French attackers!

February 1797

My dear Thomas,

You have probably heard the tale of the French invasion of Wales by now. But the truth is even stranger than the reports that have appeared in the newspapers. Of course they say I'm a hero, but to tell the truth I had some unexpected luck.

I was having supper at Stackpole Hall when a messenger arrived on a horse that was foaming with sweat and more dead than alive. 'Lord Cawdor!' he cried. 'The French have arrived!'

'What? Here? Now?' I asked. 'They're just in time for supper.'

'No!' he groaned. 'Thousands of them have landed at Fishguard! They're raiding every farm in the area. They're stealing every drop of wine they can find.'

'Anyone been hurt?' I asked.

'Not exactly,' the man shrugged. 'They're a bit nervous. They're shooting at anything that moves. Huw Thomas at Pencaer Farm said one of the French soldiers came into his parlour and heard a noise behind him. He turned and fired wildly.'

'Did he hit anyone?'

'No but he wrecked Huw's grandfather clock. That's what was making the noise, you see?'

I couldn't believe what I was hearing, Thomas. 'So, we have a couple of thousand scared Frenchmen shooting our clocks. And you've ridden 30 miles to tell me this? It's Colonel Knox you should be telling. He's the man in charge of the local defence force, the Fishguard Fencibles.'

'Colonel Knox was at a ball when he got the news. He said "The Fishguard Fencibles are no match for a French army." He decided to retreat.'

I can tell you, Thomas. I almost exploded with rage. 'He ran away!'

'He retreated, sir,' the miserable messenger said.

'Then the Stackpole Yeomanry will have to show him how its done,' I said.

I guess it took less than an hour for the men to come in from the surrounding villages,

gather their weapons and meet at
Stackpole Hall. Of course everyone had heard
about the invasion and my men were ready
for them. We set off for Haverfordwest the
next morning, camped there and gathered
more men, then set off for Fishguard the day
after. I suppose we had 500 men in all by the
time we spotted the French camp.

Now my men were spoiling for a fight, but
it was clear the French outnumbered us. So I
sent a message to their commander. 'My forces
are growing stronger every hour. Surrender
now or you will be wiped out.' It was a lie, of
course, but the commander's reply was the last
thing I expected.

The French commander was actually one of
those rebel American fellows. A man called
William Tate. His reply said: 'We surrender
on condition that the men you have already
captured are set free.'

I accepted his surrender and met him at
Fishguard harbour to take his men's weapons
and accept the surrender. And that's when I
told him, 'We haven't actually captured any of

your men.'

The American shook his head and pointed up the main street. 'Your British Army red-coats took 20 of our men. The rest of the French were so drunk they ran away when the red-coats attacked.'

Now I knew that the nearest red-coat army was still 40 miles away in Carmarthen. But when I looked along the harbour I saw 20 French soldiers trooping along looking very sorry for themselves. And they weren't being held by red-coats... they were being marched along by red cloaks! A little group of women were wearing their red Welsh cloaks and those tall black hats they have in this country. They were armed with pitch-forks and reaping hooks and they had the French terrified.

The woman in charge strode across to me. A huge woman – she certainly terrified me. She threw a huge salute and grinned. 'Mistress Jemima Nicholas at your service' she said.

It seems the French had made the mistake of trying to attack these women and they'd been taken prisoner instead. The rest of the

French invaders had lost heart and persuaded
Tate to surrender.
   So there you have it! They say the Stackpole
Yeomanry and I are the heroes. The truth is the
mighty Jemima Nicholas and the women of
Fishguard have saved our country from the invaders.
Her name should go down in history with heroines
like Boudicca and Queen Elizabeth.
   God save the King, and God bless you too my
friend.   yours Robert Lord Cawdor

Everybody remembers the first French invasion – they remember King Harold the hero who died with an arrow in his eye. But he was a man and a king so he's remembered even though he lost.

Sadly Jemima Nicholas and the Pembroke 'Mum's Army' have been almost forgotten. She was a woman, of course, and it doesn't seem to matter that she actually won! (You could be reading this in French if she hadn't!)

After this defeat the French never tried invading Britain again. In fact no invader has landed on Britain's shores since. (Unless you count a few German pilots shot down in World War II.)

During the Napoleonic Wars Lord Nelson and the navy protected the British from attack by sea. Then British armies crossed to the continent and finally defeated the French at the Battle of Waterloo in 1815.

A few troublemakers tried to copy the French Revolution in Britain, but they didn't get much support. George III kept his head.

The American Revolution

Of course the British had another Revolution to worry about. They had some colonies on the far side of the Atlantic Ocean in a place called America. It had been a good place to dump convicts at one time.

But in the reign of George III those American Colonists started to get stroppy. They weren't happy with being told what to do by a king and a parliament back in Britain. They wanted to make their own decisions – they wanted to be free to kill Native Americans and steal their land, free to invent hamburgers and free to play cowboys. But above all, they wanted to be free of paying tax to Britain.

Not everybody in America wanted to be a rebel, of course. But the Americans who tried to stay loyal to Britain could be given a tough time.

The diary of a rebel tells what happened to one American soldier who disagreed with his rebel friends …

8 August 1775.
  Riflemen took a man in New Milford who had called them 'damned rebels' and other insulting names. They made him walk

in front of them to Litchfield, a journey of 20 miles. He was made to carry one of his geese in his hand all the way. When they arrived there they covered him in tar and made him pluck his goose. They stuck the feathers to him, drummed him out of the rifle company, forced him to kneel down and thank them for being so merciful to him.

(The writer of the diary doesn't say what happened to the goose, but they probably cut it up, covered it in batter and fried it – another American invention: *Litchfield Fried Goose*, perhaps?)

In the end America got the freedom they wanted. Britain couldn't fight a war at a distance of 3,000 miles. They created a new country – the United States of America – and elected a president instead of a king. They picked a leading rebel fighter, George Washington, to be the first President.

Back in Britain poor old George III was the loser – he lost the American Colonies and went on to lose his marbles.

The Luddite revolts

The Industrial Revolution meant that one man and a machine could do the work of (maybe) ten men. It meant that nine men were put out of work. They were not a happy nine men. Some of the nine believed that the answer was to smash up the machine!

(This does not make a lot of sense. One horse could do the work of ten men – pulling a plough, say – but you didn't see farm workers going around beating up horses, did you?)

Trouble started in 1811 in Yorkshire and spread through Nottinghamshire and Lancashire. Machine breakers gathered in gangs and marched like an army to destroy machines. The army was called in to defend the machines with guns – the machine-wreckers armed themselves with guns. Many died in the battles that followed.

Machine owners who tried to defend themselves were murdered – the murderers were hanged – the youngest to hang was a boy of 15 and the oldest a man of nearly 70. These machine smashers were called Luddites because they were said to follow the mighty machine-breaker, Ned Ludd. 'Disobey Ned Ludd and you die!'

The very name brought fear to the hearts of the mill-owners, mothers used the name to scare their children: 'Behave yourself or Ned Ludd will get you!'

But who was this Ned Ludd? The truth is he was never a rebel leader. This is what happened …

108

The truth is the Luddites never had any leader. Each group was dealt with by the army one at a time and the Luddite riots died as quickly as they had started.

If they'd had a single, strong leader it might have been different, but they never had one. They certainly never had one called Ned Ludd – and Ned Ludd was never a Luddite.

The Peterloo massacre

The machine wreckers went quiet for a long time while the war against Napoleon came to its bloody end at the Battle of Waterloo in 1815.

But soldiers came home to a Britain where corn prices were getting higher and wages were getting lower. When that happens, of course, you get hungry ... and you get angry.

By 1819 the people of the north were particularly angry.

A huge meeting was called at Saint Peter's Fields near Manchester. Workers and their families came from all over the north to hear the famous Henry Hunt speak about the changes the workers wanted. Above all they wanted to vote for members of parliament.

Sixty thousand people packed into the fields till, someone said, 'their hats were almost touching.'

But the magistrates of the area panicked. They called in soldiers to keep the crowds in order. But, in the front line, were the part-time soldiers – local men who were not very well trained but enjoyed wearing the uniforms and swaggering around. Their regiment was called The Manchester and Salford Yeomanry Cavalry – the MYC for short.

In France the angry people turned against the nobles. But in Britain they turned against each other. That was the difference.

Workers didn't like the Prince of Wales who ruled the country while his father was mentally ill. But they really, really hated men like Tom Shelmerdine ... one of their own people who tried to stop their peaceful protest.

If Tom Shelmerdine had kept a diary then it may have looked like this. The diary is imaginary, only the sad facts are true ...

Tom Shelmerdine's diary

Workers gathering into a union to get higher wages was against the law in 1819. Many workers wanted to change the law but they couldn't gather together to protest against because it was against the law to gather together and protest!

Some tried. But Tom Shelmerdine of Manchester wasn't one of them ...

21 May 1819 Some of the men in the weaving mill are traitors. I'm sure they're planning to form one of those trade union things. Of course they don't tell me. They think I'll report them and have them arrested. They're right. I would.

For the workers who didn't want to join a union there was something else they could do ...

27 May 1819 I'll join the loyal subjects of King George and put a stop to the mill-workers' treason

111

> I'll join the yeomanry. They train in their spare time and it's a little extra pay. But best of all they are standing up to the troublemakers

The local guard regiments were amateurs. A bit like boy scouts with big swords ...

> 9 June 1819 Joined the MYC. I look very smart in the uniform though I say it myself. A nice blue with white trim. Yes, very smart. Of course I'm not very good on a horse, but none of the other lads of the MYC are either

In the summer of 1819 the workers of the north planned a peaceful protest. The leaders taught the protesters how to march in formation. They wanted this protest to look really well organized – not just a mob. But the magistrates and the law officers got the wrong idea entirely ...

> 27 June 1819 The weavers have started marching. They are practising drill like an army. The MYC lads reckon they are planning an attack. The yeomanry send their swords away to be polished every month. But this time they've sent them to be sharpened. I keep falling off my brute of a horse.

A meeting planned for 60,000 people couldn't be kept a secret from the magistrates for long, of course ...

> 13 July 1819 Major Trafford, our commander, has told us the rebel secret. They are planning a meeting. The trouble-maker Henry Hunt will

112

On the morning of 16 August 1819 the workers gathered
all over the north and began marching to St Peter's Fields
for the great meeting. Meanwhile the full time soldiers, the
Hussars, gathered in Manchester. The part-time soldiers,
the MYC, gathered in the local pubs! Giving big swords to
boy scouts is not a good idea. Giving big swords and strong
drink to boy scouts is stupid. But that's what Hugh Hornby
Birley did with the MYC …

16 August 1819 Sixty thousand traitors in
St Peter's Fields, they reckon. The MYC are in
this public house and ready. Mr Hugh Hornby
Birley is buying us as much ale as we want.
They say the rebels in St Peter's Fields are
quiet and orderly. But we think that's just a
trick. When the signal comes we'll be ready. Here
it is now! The constables are going to arrest
Henry Hunt! And the MYC, not the hussars,
have been chosen to escort them.
To horse Lads!

Of course a lot of the drunken MYC had trouble climbing
on their horses, never mind staying on them. The crowds
were packed into the field. The constables struggled to
get through to Hunt on the platform. So the gallant MYC
drew their sabres and hacked their way through. The rest is
horrible history …

17 *August 1819* It's over. It was exciting, I think, but I don't remember too much about it. I do remember we galloped onto the field and you should have seen those traitors panic! They'd have run away if they hadn't been so crowded together. They started to scream and that was a big mistake. Well, I mean, it panicked the horses and they went wild. Some of us have enough trouble with a quiet horse. Imagine how dangerous we were on scared horses. I came face to face with old Meg Willis. She recognised me, of course, because she used to nurse me as a child. 'Nay Tom Shelmerdine, thee will not hurt me, I know!' she said. Of course I wouldn't. But the horse did, the brutish animal. Still, it has to be said, if old Meg hadn't been there then she wouldn't have been killed.

Tom Shelmerdine was remembered, and hated, because of the way he rode down the old woman who used to nurse him. Other MYC riders struck out wildly with their sharp sabres. They cut their way through the crowds to get to Hunt. It was a bit like boy scouts cutting their way through a tangled wood – but it wasn't bushes they were hacking at – they were human beings.

18 *August 1819* There's a lot of bad feeling about that St. Peter's Fields business. The newspapers are mocking us for charging at unarmed men, women and children. But we

> *didn't know they were unarmed, did we? They could have been hiding pikes under their coats couldn't they? Heroes of Peterloo they are calling us. They forget, we were only doing our job.*

It was the magistrates who sent in the half-trained, half-baked, half-witted MYC when they could have sent in the Hussars. The Hussars went in later and struck people with the flat of their swords to drive them back. The MYC had used the edge of their swords to kill and wound. It's the MYC who were remembered and hated – the local men. These rebels didn't blame the government so much as the French had. They blamed the people they knew. People like Tom Shelmerdine.

So 'Peterloo' killed 11 people and wounded 500.

Peterloo foul facts
- The MYC were sent in to protect the police. But several police were trampled by the rampaging yeomanry. Special Constable Thomas Ashworth died.
- One of the men at the meeting had taken a cheese for his dinner. He stored it under his hat. It saved his life when a sabre chopped at his head!

115

- A weaver called John Lees had lived through the horror of the Battle of Waterloo and Napoleon's powerful army. But at Peterloo he was cut by a sabre, smashed by a truncheon and trampled by a horse. He died.

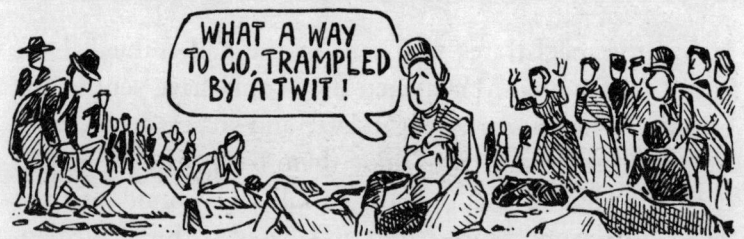

- The youngest victim was William Fildes, a baby in his mother's arms. She was walking along the street when the MYC galloped, out of control, towards St Peter's Fields. The baby was knocked to the ground and trampled. Mrs Fildes wasn't even at the meeting.
- A poet at the meeting described the charge through the crowd: 'Sabres were used to hew a way through held-up hands and defenceless heads; chopped limbs and wound-gaping skulls were seen; groans and cries were mingled with the din of that horrid confusion.'

- Hunt was arrested and taken to Lancaster Jail. On his return from Lancaster his horse, Bob, died near Preston. He was buried under a weeping willow with a headstone that read, 'Alas! Poor Bob!!!' Thousands of people went to the funeral.

- BUT ... seven years later Bob's remains were dug up and his bones turned into snuff boxes. A knee-cap was given a silver lid and presented to Hunt.

IT'S INSCRIBED 'NO NEIGH NIGH NOR NEAR... NOW NEW KNEE'

Instant 'Peterloo' quiz

The government had an enquiry into the massacre. Who got the blame ...

a) The magistrates for sending in the MYC
b) The MYC commanders for getting the men drunk
c) The MYC members for being out of control
d) Henry Hunt for arranging the meeting

Answer: d) Of course. What did you expect?

117

Test your teacher

Teachers love asking questions. They even get paid for it! It would be really boring if every pupil got every question right, so teachers learn to enjoy it when their pupils get the *wrong* answers. Now it's your chance to get your revenge. Test your teacher (or pester your parent) with this amazingly difficult quiz.

When they get a wrong answer you can mutter, 'I thought you'd have known that!'

1 What would a Georgian doctor do with a 'pelican'?
a) Train it to catch fish alive so patients could swallow them and cure swamp fever.
b) Use it to pull out a deeply rooted, rotten tooth.
c) Boil its eggs, grind them up with beetroot and make plague plasters.

2 In 1750 a gentleman bought a pound of tea from a smuggler. He didn't like the look of the tea so he fed it to the dog. What happened next?
a) The dog became a tea addict and had to be fed a saucer every day.

DOG AND BONE

DOG AND BONE CHINA

b) The dog refused to drink it until the gentleman added sugar and milk.

HOW MANY TIMES HAVE I GOT TO TELL YOU, MILK FIRST, *THEN* THE TEA!

c) The dog had a fit and died.

3 What did Robinson Cruso do for a living?
a) He made beds and auctioned furniture.
b) He was a sailor who enjoyed being shipwrecked and writing about it.
c) He was a writer whose most famous book was about a desert island.

4 Carlisle Spedding invented a steel mill – it struck sparks off a flint stone and gave light. Useful for pitmen in a coal mine. But … when it was used in a mine it could explode firedamp gas. It killed a lot of miners. But how did Spedding himself die?
a) His steel mill set fire to his wig.
b) His steel mill failed, he stumbled in the dark and fell in a river.
c) His steel mill caused an explosion of firedamp in a coal mine and killed him.

5 A gentleman in Georgian Britain would not wear what?
a) Trousers.
b) A waistcoat.
c) Stockings.

6 Tearing hares apart with hounds is an ancient sport, enjoyed by the Georgians. But when was it stopped?
a) Not until 1826 in the reign of George IV.
b) Not until 1897 in the reign of Queen Victoria.
c) Not at all. Hare hunting is still legal in Britain.

7 The Georgians spent a lot of time at war with France. They weren't too keen on any foreigners. What did they do to some foreigners on the streets of London?
a) Spat at them.

b) Threw dead cats and dogs at them.

c) Swore at them in French.

8 Sailors in Nelson's navy suffered bad food. The cheese was often too hard to eat, but they had another use for that. What?
a) They used it in mouse traps. The mice broke their teeth on the cheese and starved.

b) The sailors carved the cheese with their knives to make tough, hard wearing buttons for their coats.

c) They used the cheeses to play a game like shove-ha'penny on deck. It was called shove cheddar.

9 What useful thing did the watchmaker Andrew Cumming invent in 1775 that we still use today?

a) A stink trap.

b) Roller skates.

c) Knickers held up with elastic.

BUT AT LEAST HER KNICKERS DIDN'T FALL DOWN

IT WAS HORRIBLE, SHE ROLLER SKATED STRAIGHT INTO THE STINK TRAP

10 Highwaymen couldn't always afford pistols. In 1774 a Huntingdon highwayman held up a coach using what?

a) A bow and arrow.

IT'S ROBIN HOOD!

b) A savage dog.

HAND OVER ALL YOUR MONEY!

AND YOUR SAUSAGES

c) A candlestick.

THIS IS A CANDLESTICK-UP!

Answers:

1b) A 'pelican' was a tool for pulling out difficult teeth. When pliers failed to remove the tooth, the pelican would rip it out sideways. A careless doctor could rip out good teeth along with the bad. There were even cases of good teeth being torn out and the bad one left! The instrument got its name because it looked like a pelican's beak.

A pelican with some bad teeth

2c) The dog died and the gentleman complained to the local newspaper. Of course the gentleman couldn't complain to the law because he should not have been buying cheap tea from a smuggler. He couldn't complain to the smuggler because no one could trace him. Still, he was lucky. If he'd drunk the tea he wouldn't have complained to anybody – ever again!

3a) Robinson Cruso, a bed-maker, lived in Kings Lynn High Street. The writer Daniel Defoe visited Kings Lynn on his travels and must have seen the name Robinson Cruso outside the shop. Defoe then told the story of shipwrecked sailor Alexander Selkirk and changed his name … to Robeson Cruso. (Later publishers changed the spelling to Robinson Crusoe.) So, next time your parents tell you to 'make your bed' say, 'Who do you think I am? Robinson Crusoe?' That'll confuse them!

STRANGE CHILD

MAYBE IT'S TOO MUCH READING

4c) Carlisle Spedding's invention caused an explosion. Poor old Spedding. Spark – boom! – and Spedding is speeding up a mine-shaft!

5a) Peasants wore trousers to work in the fields and a gentleman would not be so common as to wear them. Gentlemen wore tighter fitting 'breeches' with stockings. Did you guess that? If not it was a turn-up for the books!

6c) That's right. Hare 'coursing' as it's called is still enjoyed today by many people and many packs of hounds. The hares must enjoy it too, otherwise they'd arm themselves with hare-rifles, wouldn't they?

7b) It makes you wonder where they got the dead cats and dogs from! Were they just lying around in the street for ruffians to pick up and throw when they saw a foreigner? Or did they say, 'Look! A foreigner. Let's kill a cat and throw it! Here pussy, pussy, pussy!'

8b) The biscuits were worse than the cheese. They were full of black-headed maggots. The sailors usually shut their eyes and ate them. I wonder if the maggots shut their eyes as they were about to be eaten?

9a) A 'stink trap' is a bend in the toilet pipe that stops smells coming up from the drains. Every home should have one. It's a pity no one's invented a stink trap for a team of boys who have been playing football. Phew!

10c) The candlestick may have looked like the barrel of a pistol but the guard on the coach wasn't fooled. He shot the highwayman with a blunderbuss gun and two slugs ended up in the thief's forehead. The candlestick robber was snuffed out. He probably got on the guard's wick.

Epilogue

George I could have travelled through his new kingdom, Britain, in 1714. He'd have bounced along rutted roads and moved very slowly. From his carriage he'd have seen lots of large areas of common ground divided into strips where poor people farmed their own little piece of land. He'd have seen some magnificent houses and some that were not fit for animals.

SCHÖNE AUSSICHT – SCHADE DASS DIE ARMEN LEUTE IM WEG SIND*

* NICE VIEW, SHAME ABOUT THE POOR

If his great-great-grandson George IV had made the same journey over a hundred years later he may have taken one of the new steam trains – they were sooty and noisy and cold but at least they were much faster. And they'd have crossed over those new canal things. The common ground would be mostly gone and there would be fields closed in with hedges and fences now. The poor people who used to live off the common ground would have gone too. Some would have had to go and work for one of the farmers who owned the fields. More would have gone to the towns.

That would be the biggest change. The towns had become huge and crowded; factory smoke blackened the skies and faces of the workers. The factories made Georgian Britain the richest nation on Earth … and made some lucky people very rich too. The Georgians also left behind a world that was famous for its slums and some unfortunate people who had to live and die in them.

The gorgeous Georgians changed some things for the better – they got rid of slave trading in their country and they avoided the worst horrors of revolutions.

But would *you* like to have lived in Georgian Britain? If you have money, and if you like to make yourself look gorgeous with make-up and wigs and fine clothes, then you might have enjoyed it!

But Georgian Britain is a bit like the moon; it's bright and flashy to look at from a distance … you may even like to visit it … but you wouldn't want to live there.
Would you?

GORGEOUS GEORGIANS

GRISLY QUIZ

**Now find out if you're a
Gorgeous Georgians expert!**

QUICK GEORGIAN QUESTIONS

This was the age when pirates were the scourge of the seas, highwaymen haunted the roads, a crackpot was king and the Americans were revolting... some things never change. It was also the age of thick make-up, beauty spots, monstrous wigs and padded bosoms – and that was just the men.

1. In 1700 John Asgill went to prison for writing a short book called, *A man can go from here to heaven without...* Without what? (Clue: everybody does it)

2. In Scotland in 1700 a teacher was whipped through the streets of Edinburgh (don't laugh!). What was his crime? (Clue: tough teacher)

3. In 1707 the son of the Duke of Queensberry murdered a kitchen boy. How did he dispose of the evidence? (Clue: it's in really bad taste)

4. Why did Queen Anne's doctors shave her head and cover her feet in garlic? (Clue: sick idea)

5. Queen Anne died in 1714 and she was buried in a coffin that is almost square. Why? (Clue: if the coffin fits, wear it)

6. German George I took the throne. But where was his wife Dorothea? (Clue: she flirted once too often)

7. In Banff in 1714 the town hangman had to catch stray dogs. He was paid for each dog he caught. How did he prove he'd caught a dog? (Clue: hide!)

8. In 1717 a Scottish teacher murdered two pupils in his charge. Before he was hanged he had an odd punishment. What was it? (Clue: he'd never write on a blackboard again)

9. In 1718 the dreaded pirate Blackbeard was shot and beheaded by a navy officer. Blackbeard's body was thrown over the side of the ship. What's supposed to have happened next? (Clue: maybe he crawled)

10. Many Georgian pirates wore gold earrings. Why? (Clue: go to see?)

11. In 1722 an elephant died on its way to Dundee. What did Doctor Patrick Blair do with the corpse? (Clue: jumbo scientist)

12. In 1724 murderer Maggie Dickson escaped execution. The law said she couldn't be hanged. Why? (Clue: second time lucky)

13. In 1727 George I's hated wife, Dorothea, died. He set off for the funeral but failed to get there. Why? (Clue: a second funeral delayed him)

14. Soon after George I died a raven flew in at the window of his girlfriend, the Duchess of Kendal. She looked after it better than any pet. Why? (Clue: it was something George had crowed about)

15. How can a hot poker cure toothache? (Clue: ear we go again)

16. In 1739 the famous highwayman, Dick Turpin, was

executed. His handwriting was recognized by someone who knew him at school and he was betrayed. Who betrayed Turpin? (Clue: master of treachery)

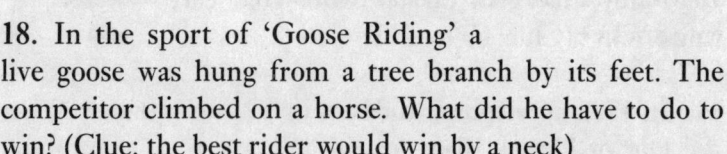

17. George II and his family ate Sunday dinner in style. What could the public buy on those Sundays? (Clue: feeding time at the zoo?)

18. In the sport of 'Goose Riding' a live goose was hung from a tree branch by its feet. The competitor climbed on a horse. What did he have to do to win? (Clue: the best rider would win by a neck)

19. In 1743 George II became the last British monarch to lead an army into battle at Dettingen, Germany. But his horse disgraced him. How? (Clue: might have made a good race horse)

20. In 1746 James Reid played his bagpipes in York. He never played them again. Why not? (Clue: the noise he made was criminal)

21. In 1747 Lord Lovat became the last person to be beheaded in the Tower of London. As he went to his death 20 other innocent people died. How? (Clue: curiosity killed the cat)

FOUL FOR FEMALES

What was it like for Georgian women? Try this simple test – answer true or false...

1. Georgian women put cork balls in their cheeks to improve their appearance.
2. The average age for women to get married was 15.
3. A woman could be burned alive for murdering her husband.
4. Georgian wives were sometimes sold by their husbands at auction.
5. Men were allowed to beat their wives with sticks.
6. Ladies used cement as make-up.
7. The average wage for a maid was £3 a month.
8. Georgian women often took snuff.
9. A group of Welsh women stopped an invasion by the French.
10. It was fashionable for women to have a sun tan.

WACKY WORDS

Can you match the following Georgian words to their meanings..?

1. grunter	a) idiot
2. hock-docky	b) hangman's noose
3. sumph	c) police constable
4. scrag	d) horse
5. bolly dog	e) shoe
6. big bug	f) eye
7. squeezer	g) shilling coin
8. sad man	h) neck
9. daisy-kicker	i) trouble-maker
10. killer	j) important man

Answers

Quick Georgian Questions

1. Dying. The booklet was burned, so we'll never know how to do this clever trick!

2. He had flogged a pupil until the pupil died. And there are still people today who want to bring back beatings for children. Avoid them.

3. He roasted the boy and ate him. Do not try this with your school dinner ladies, please.

4. They were trying to cure her illness. They also blistered her skin with hot irons and gave her medicines to make her vomit. She died – and was probably glad to go.

5. Anne was so fat she was almost square.

6. She was locked away back in Germany. This was her punishment for flirting with Count Konigsmark. It was worse for the count. He'd been murdered and secretly buried at the castle. Jolly George.

7. He collected the skins of the dogs. He was probably happy to do this because one of his other jobs was to sweep up doggy poo from the streets!

8. He had both hands chopped off.

9. It's said Blackbeard's headless corpse swam round the ship three times before finally sinking!

10. They believed it helped their eyesight.

11. He cut it open to see how an elephant's body works.

12. Because she had been hanged once and pronounced dead. As she was taken off to the graveyard in her coffin she sat up! Lucky Maggie lived another 30 years before dying a second time – for good.

13. George died on his way to the funeral. He had held up Dorothea's funeral for six months. If he'd been quicker he'd have had the pleasure of seeing her put six feet under.

14. George had said that he would visit her after his death. She believed the raven was George. Caw! Imagine that!

15. Burning a hole through the lobe of your ear was supposed to cure the pain in the tooth. Crazy! If you ever see your dentist with a hot poker you know it's time to change dentists.

16. Turpin's school master betrayed him.

17. The public could buy tickets to watch George II and the royal family dine. You could try selling tickets for your neighbours to watch you eat your beans on toast!

18. Grab the head of the goose and tear it off. This was made harder by greasing the goose's beak.

19. As soon as it heard enemy gunfire it ran away. George couldn't stop it! The fat little feller had to go back to his command on foot.

20. He was hanged. The bagpipes were declared 'an instrument of war' after the Scottish Jacobite rebellion of 1745. Happily it is now legal to play these beautiful melodic instruments.

21. Spectators crowded on to wooden stands to watch Lovat get lopped. The stands collapsed and killed 20 people. Served them right.

Foul For Females

1. True.

2. False. The average age was about 24. Very few married under 16.

3. True. But this law was changed in 1789 and the punishment was changed to hanging.

4. True. It wasn't legal but it sometimes happened – and continued to happen until 1887.

5. True. But the stick he used had to be no thicker than his thumb, so that's all right.

6. False. But they did use lead paint, arsenic powder and

plaster of Paris.

7. False. They would be paid about £3 a year.

8. True.

9. True. In 1797 a small group of women from Pembrokeshire, led by Jemima Nicholas, captured 20 men from the invading French. They were so terrifying that the French army surrendered.

10. False. A pale skin was beautiful to the Georgians and women would sometimes wear a mask in front of the face to protect the skin.

Wacky Words
1.g) 2.e) 3.a) 4.h) 5.c) 6.j) 7.b) 8.i) 9.d) 10.f)

INTERESTING INDEX

Where will you find 'pinching competitions', 'squashed fish eyes' and 'stink traps' in an index? In a Horrible Histories book, of course!

Terry Deary was born at a very early age, so long ago he can't remember. But his mother, who was there at the time, says he was born in Sunderland, north-east England, in 1946 – so it's not true that he writes all *Horrible Histories* from memory. At school he was a horrible child only interested in playing football and giving teachers a hard time. His history lessons were so boring and so badly taught, that he learned to loathe the subject. *Horrible Histories* is his revenge.

Martin Brown was born in Melbourne, on the proper side of the world. Ever since he can remember he's been drawing. His dad used to bring back huge sheets of paper from work and Martin would fill them with doodles and little figures. Then, quite suddenly, with food and water, he grew up, moved to the UK and found work doing what he's always wanted to do: drawing doodles and little figures.

HORRIBLE HISTORIES

SLIMY STUARTS

Terry Deary Illustrated by Martin Brown

SCHOLASTIC

For Fiona and Vanessa King – much nicer Kings than the historical ones.

Scholastic Children's Books,
Euston House, 24 Eversholt Street,
London NW1 1DB, UK

A division of Scholastic Ltd
London ~ New York ~ Toronto ~ Sydney ~ Auckland
Mexico City ~ New Delhi ~ Hong Kong

First published in the UK by Scholastic Ltd, 1996
This edition published 2016

Some of the material in this book has previously been published in
Horrible Histories: The Massive Millennium Quiz Book/The Horribly Huge Quiz Book

ISBN 978 1407 17405 1

Printed and bound by CPI Group (UK) Ltd, Croydon, CR0 4YY

4 6 8 10 9 7 5 3

www.scholastic.co.uk

Contents

Introduction

History can be simply horrible. This history book is simply horribly *interesting*. It will tell you things about Stuart times that not many teachers know.

James I used the power of the rack to torture Guy Fawkes. Now you can torture your teacher with ... the power of *the question!*

You can amaze your relations with terribly true tales of dreadful deeds...

Become the most popular person in your class by learning new words. Yes, even *you* can become the *dossy* with a little practice.

You'll end up knowing a bit more about life in the slimy 17th century. The funny, the foul and the fantastic. They are all here…

Slimy Stuart timeline

1603 Elizabeth I kicks the royal bucket. Last of the Tudors. James VI of Scotland comes down to be James I of England as well. First of the Stuarts.

> *Slimy Jim, snotty Jim,*
> *Slobbered when he drank*
> *his beer;*
> *Hated witches, hated ciggies.*
> *Loved to murder little deer.*

1605 A plot to blow James all the way back to Scotland is discovered – known as the Gunpowder Plot. Guy Fawkes gets the blame.

1616 Playwright, William Shakespeare, dies on his 52nd birthday. That probably spoiled the party a bit.

1621 Puritans who can't stand James settle in America. They don't bother to ask the native American Indians, of course.

1625 James I turns up his regal toes – he snuffs it. Son Charles I gets to put bum on throne.

> *Charlie One, on the run;*
> *He'd upset the Roundhead chaps.*
> *Said that God was on his side;*
> *God not there when Charlie axed!*

1629 Charles upsets Parliament in a row over who's in charge, them or him. Slimy Charlie says he can rule without them. And, to prove it, he does.

1637 Charles upsets the Scots by trying to force them to use his new Prayer Book. Charles has the nerve to call Parliament again to help him. Charlie and Parli just argue.

1642 War breaks out between Charlie (with his Cavaliers) and Parli (with their Roundheads). Brother fights brother.

1647 Charlie loses war and makes friends with the Scots and with Parliament. Sadly, Parliament is now ruled by its army under General Oliver Cromwell who makes sure…

1649 Charlie gets the chop. Royal head in un-royal bucket. England ruled without a king until…

1658 Oliver Cromwell dies and his son Richard takes over until …

1660 The 'Restoration' – the monarchy returns with Charles II. Cromwell dug up, strung up and beheaded – *very* slimy.

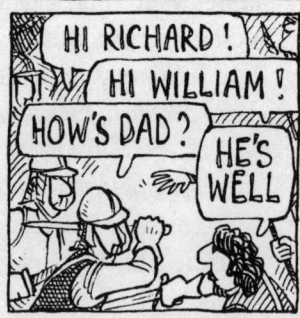

Charlie two used to woo
Lots of women, what a bloke!
Merry monarch – plague then fire,
Sent the laughter up in smoke.

1665 The Great Plague – in London alone 100,000 people die … and just as many rats.

1666 The Great Fire of London – destroys many of the filthy wooden buildings that housed the plague.

1685 King Charles II sick. Given 'Spirit of Human Skull' but dies anyway. (He apologized to his doctors for taking so long to die.) Catholic brother, James II, takes over.

King Jim, rather dim;
Made it clear he liked the Pope.
Britons told him,
'Push off, Jimmy!
Catholic Britain? Not a hope.'

1688 James thrown off throne. Even his daughter, Mary, is glad to see the back of him. She takes over with hubby, William of Orange.

Mary big, ate like pig;
Willie small like her pet eat.
Smallpox killed her; as for Willie,
His horse stumbled, he went splatt!

1702 Mary's sister, Anne takes over the throne – she doesn't share it with hubby. When you're as fat as Anne there's no room to share a throne with a pin.

> *Annie, stout; feet with gout;*
> *Food and brandy she would*
> *gorge.*
> *Children all dead, no more*
> *Stuarts;*
> *Throne passed on to German*
> *George.*

1707 England and Scotland united under one Parliament.

1714 Anne pops her clogs – just as her 17 children have before her. End of slimy Stuarts.

Slimy James I (reigned 1603-1625)

The Stuarts were a funny lot … funny-'peculiar'. *Not* so funny-'haha' if you were one of their victims. They were wheelers and dealers, always ducking and diving to keep out of trouble. You could never be quite sure what they were up to. In fact they were rather slimy characters. The slimy Stuarts.

James the slob

James was 37 when he became king of England. He had a straggling brown beard and hair, watery blue eyes and spindly legs. A French visitor described James when he was 18 years old…

He was of middle height, more fat because of his clothes than his body. His clothes always being made large and easy, the doublets quilted to be dagger-proof. His breeches were in great pleats and full stuffed. He was naturally timid, his eyes large and always rolling after any stranger came into his presence. His beard was very thin. His tongue too large for his mouth which made him drink very badly as if eating his drink which came out into the cup from each side of his mouth. His skin was soft because he never washed his hands, only rubbed his finger ends slightly with the wet end of a napkin.

And those were just his good points! Fontenay forgot to mention James was bow-legged and picked his nose. The king used his sleeve instead of a handkerchief ... though he sometimes preferred to use a finger and thumb. Maybe Fontenay didn't notice! Among James's other bad habits were swearing and drinking too much.

A famous historian called Macaulay said James was like *two* men. One was a witty scholar who argued well – the other was a 'nervous drivelling idiot'. You decide which from something that happened when he arrived in England. James complained that the people of England were forever pestering him to make a public appearance. He refused – very rudely.

A wit? Or a twit?

Killer James

James I wasn't so sure of English customs when he arrived from Scotland. On his way to be crowned in London he stopped at the town of Newark. As the crowds packed the streets to greet him a pickpocket was caught. James ordered that the pickpocket should be hanged. The obedient councillors had the man executed.

Only *then* did they quietly tell James that in England the king did not have the power to put anyone to death without trial. This was no comfort at all to the pickpocket.

On his way to London James enjoyed some hunting. To make sure the king had enough fun the English cheated. They kept hares in cages and let them out in time for the king to catch them.

Gunpowder, treason ... and lies?

Everybody knows about Guy Fawkes ... or do they? Test your teacher with these well known 'facts' about Guy Fawkes and the Gunpowder Plot. How many are true and how many false?

1 Guy Fawkes was born a Catholic.

2 Guy Fawkes was the leader of the gunpowder plot.

3 Luckily, Guy Fawkes was caught just before he blew up James and his Parliament.

4 Guy Fawkes was tortured and betrayed his friends.

5 Guy Fawkes was burned on a bonfire.

Answers: False! False! False! False! Oh, and ... false!

Here's how…

1 Guy (or Guido as he was christened) was brought up a Protestant. When he was ten his new stepfather (Denis Bainbridge) taught him to follow the Catholic religion. The Catholics had already tried to dispose of Elizabeth I (with a little help from foreign friends, Armadas and poisonous plots). James was just another Protestant monarch to be disposed of … nothing personal!

2 The leader of the Gunpowder Plot was Robert Catesby. Guy was fighting as a soldier for the Spanish army when the plot was first dreamt up. He was smuggled back into England to help – probably because he was an explosives expert.

THIS IS A BOMB

GOSH!

3 Guy was caught at least 12 hours before Parliament was due to meet the king. And it wasn't 'luck'. The soldiers who caught Guy had been tipped off and were searching for explosives when they found him there. King James had also been tipped off. He was never in any real danger from the Gunpowder Plot.

4 Guy was tortured on the rack for two days before he even gave his real name. It took another two days before he confessed to the plot then *six* more days before he named any other plotters. But, by that time, his partners had already been hunted and arrested or killed. They *had* been betrayed … but not by Guy Fawkes.

5 Guy was due to be hanged, drawn and quartered. This was the punishment for 'treason', a crime against the king. Burning was for a crime against the Church.

Slimy James

Not everybody loved James when he arrived. What James needed was to give the English a shock. He needed to say, 'You'd be worse off if I was dead!' ... then arrange an attempt on his own life. A *failed* attempt, naturally. Is that what this slimy Stuart did?

1 First find an enemy who would want James dead. The Catholics were a good choice.

2 Get spies to persuade a Catholic group to kill the king – suggest a plot to blow him up in Parliament with all his ministers.

3 Then catch them just in time.

On November 5th 1605 the king's chief minister, Robert Cecil, said...

It has pleased God to uncover a plot to kill the King, Queen, Prince and the most important men of this land, by secretly putting gunpowder into a cellar under Parliament and blowing them all up at once.

Guy Fawkes, who was caught in the cellars of the Houses of Parliament, was tortured and executed.

As an example to others, an execution for treason was super-savagely slimy. After hanging the victim for a few moments he was cut down and cut open. His guts were thrown on to a fire before he was beheaded and cut into quarters.

Guy cheated the executioner, who wanted Guy to really suffer. When the rope was placed round Guy's neck he jumped off the ladder so that his neck broke. He was dead when they cut him open – and the executioner was dead disappointed.

The English people were so shocked at the thought of losing their new king that James became more popular than ever ... and the Catholics more hated and feared. Or was that what James wanted? A Catholic visitor to England in 1605 said...

Some people are sure that this was a trap. The government tricked these men.

So, did slimy James 'set up' Guy Fawkes to be caught?

Did you know?
James spent a lot of money on rich clothes, but he had no use for the magnificent jewelled dresses of Queen Elizabeth I. The Master of the Wardrobe sold over 1,000 of them and made himself a fortune!

Curious cures

Stuart medicine was a mixture of the clever and the crazy. *Clever* William Harvey discovered that blood 'circulates' – that is to say it goes from the heart, round the body, back to the heart and off again. Harvey discovered this by cutting up corpses, of course. He was so used to dead bodies that he wasn't bothered when he saw so many victims after the battle of Edgehill. In fact he sat under a hedge and read a book to pass the time. Then he grew cold … so he pulled a corpse over him to keep warm.

Before Harvey's discovery people knew that blood moved, but they thought it went backwards and forwards like a Yo-Yo. At the same time some *crazy* doctors still believed that a good way of curing someone was to let a lot of that blood out of the body. They tried this for almost every illness known.

Similarly, people couldn't agree about the effects of smoking. Most people know about James I's hatred of smoking. He said smoking was…

… a custom loathsome to the eye, hateful to the nose, harmful to the brain, dangerous to the lungs, and in the black stinking fumes it resembles the smoke of the pit that is bottomless [Hell].

James then put large taxes on tobacco to put people off smoking. *Clever* James I. But, while the king was writing those wise words, the smokers were pointing to crazy Nicholas Culpeper's *Complete Herbal* book of 1653, where he claimed that tobacco...

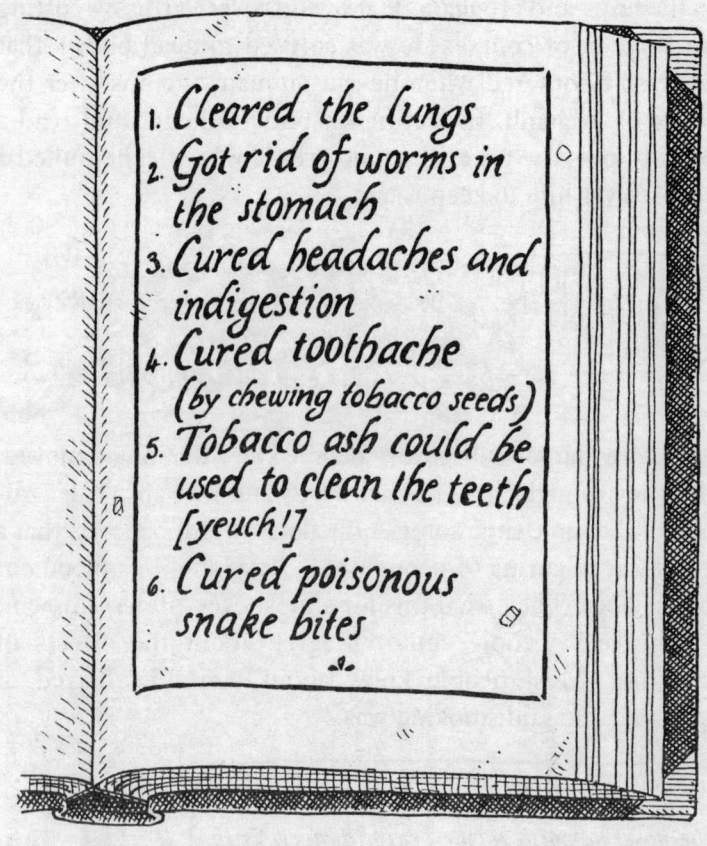

1. Cleared the lungs
2. Got rid of worms in the stomach
3. Cured headaches and indigestion
4. Cured toothache (by chewing tobacco seeds)
5. Tobacco ash could be used to clean the teeth [yeuch!]
6. Cured poisonous snake bites

He also claimed that rubbing tobacco juice into children's heads would kill lice in their hair.

Who would you rather believe? King James or Nicholas Culpeper?

Did you know?

Sir Walter Raleigh was said to have brought tobacco to Britain. In 1994, anti-smoking campaigners said Raleigh was to blame for 300 deaths a week from smoking illnesses. Queen Elizabeth II was asked to take Sir Walter's knighthood from him – even though he'd been dead nearly 400 years. The Queen refused, saying, 'He suffered enough.' That was true. James I cured Sir Walter's smoking habit for good by having his head cut off.

A sick idea

Smallpox was a common disease in Stuart times. Many died from it – 1,500 smallpox deaths in London in 1659. If you recovered from the disease then your face would probably be scarred for life with marks left by the spots.

Children recovered better than adults. So what would you do if you heard someone nearby had smallpox? Take your child to visit them in the hope that the child would catch the disease! They were probably young enough to recover and could go through life without having to worry about it.

Find the cure! Here are ten illnesses. If you were a Stuart doctor what would you prescribe? Match the cure to the illness … just don't expect them to work and *don't* try them on your friends!

Illness

1 *Accidentally swallowing a snake (!)* [Boot it out]
2 *Heavy bleeding* [This should make it all write]
3 *Stopping yourself from becoming drunk* [Make a pig of yourself]
4 *Colic (stomach pains)* [The cure shouldn't kill you stone dead]
5 *Toothache* [You'll be oak-kay after this]
6 *Consumption (lung disease)* [This should slip down nicely]
7 *Fever* [Coo—what a thought]
8 *Accidentally swallowing a horse leech in drinking water* [Make it flee]
9 *Preventing the plague from infecting you* [A rich food]
10 *Jaundice (liver disease)* [wear a clothes peg on your nose]

Cure

a Place a cold marble stone
(on which the sun has never
shone) on the stomach

b Drink a mixture of fleas and vinegar

c Eat snails boiled in milk and a few
chopped worms if you wish

d Burn the sole of an old shoe
and breath in the smoke

e Place a gold coin in the mouth

f Write the word 'Veronica' on your left
thumb

g Take two 'tench' fish, split them open
and place them on the feet. Leave for
12 hours 'even if they begin to stink,'
then put fresh ones on

h Cut a pigeon in half and place one half
on each foot

i Scratch your gum with
a new nail then drive the
nail into an oak tree

j Eat the roasted lungs of a pig first
thing in the morning

Answers:

1 d) *R. Surflet, 1600*. He reckoned snakes could creep into farmers' mouths as they slept in the fields. He also swore the cure was 'tried and approved'.

2 f) *Madam Suzannah Avery, 1688*. She actually wrote a book with many sensible cures in. This wasn't one of them.

3 j) *John Goldsmith, 1678*. Other medicines included powdered berries of ivy dissolved in vinegar. After that you probably couldn't face drinking anything else!

4 a) *Traditional cure*. Probably helped soothe the pain! If you couldn't find a piece of marble then a lump of turf was supposed to work too. (If you want to try this, shake the worms out first.)

5 i) *J. Aubrey 1670*. He said, 'This cured William Neal's son when he was so mad with pain he was ready to shoot himself.'

6 c) *Traditional cure*. Stupid Stuarts? Well, this cure was made even slimier by the American settlers who brought it from Britain – they ate a *live* snail every morning for 9 days. And they were still doing it in 1929!

7 h) *Traditional cure*. No good for the fever sufferer. Worse for the pigeon!

8 b) *R. Surflet, 1600*. If you accidentally swallow a horse leech while drinking a glass of water it's probably your eyes that need seeing to!

9 e) *John Allin, 1665*. Doctor Allin said a coin with Queen Elizabeth's head on works best.

10 g) *J. Aubrey, 1670*. Don't *eat* the used fish – bury them or the cure won't work.

Charles I (reigned 1625-1649)

Ch-ch-ch-charlie

Charles I didn't really expect to be king. His older brother, Henry, was the first in line to the throne. But Henry fell ill. Doctors suggested a remedy of pigeons pecking at the bottom of his feet! Henry died – Charles was heir to the throne.

Charles was shy and nervous but tried hard to cover this up by acting strong. He had his father's Scottish accent and a squeaky little voice with a stammer. His eyes never rested on the people he was talking to, but seemed to look through them. Charles had few friends. He listened to his father's favourite adviser, Buckingham, and really let him run the country. But Buckingham was stabbed to death by a soldier. The soldier was upset because Buckingham hadn't given him the promotion he thought he deserted.

Charles's fatal friends

When Buckingham was murdered Charles grew closer to his wife, Henrietta Maria. The British people thought this was dangerous because she was a Catholic and they never really trusted her or liked her.

Charles also asked Thomas Wentworth, nicknamed 'Black Tom', for advice. Black Tom was hated for his brutal methods.

Charles's Archbishop of Canterbury, William Laud, gave Charles bad advice as well. Laud angered the Scots *and* the

Puritans with his orders … he wanted them to pray just like those dreaded Catholics! The Puritans entered Parliament and tried to bring in new laws.

Parliament raised an army … so Charles raised an army. The King's army (the Royalists or Cavaliers) fought the army of Parliament (the Roundheads).

Slimiest acts

Slimy act 1: Parliament wanted Charlie's best pal, Black Tom, executed. Charles said he'd protect Black Tom within a week of making that promise he signed Black Tom's death warrant.

Slimy act 2: When Charles started to lose the Civil War he made a secret deal with the Scots. They would send an army to help him. The Roundhead leader, Cromwell, was furious! He said this was treason to the English people … and the punishment for treason should be death!

Charlie was one slimy Stuart who tried to be slimy once too often. He lost the war and Parliament sent him to be executed. That put a stop to his slimy games.

The execution of Charles

Charles stepped on to the scaffold and prepared to say those famous last words ... but what were they?

As he took off his jewels and handed them to the bishop beside him he said, 'Remember!' Brilliant! What a dramatic last word! But, no. Charlie had to go and spoil it.

After a few moments of silent prayer he took off the cloak and put his neck on the block. The executioner brushed Charles's hair to the side to give him a clean cut.

Charles said, 'Wait for the sign.' *What a let-down.* 'Wait for the sign.' What sort of last words are they? They could be the last words of a policeman trying to stop a steam-roller at a crossroads.

Anyway, Charles stretched out an arm, the axe fell and severed the head cleanly. The crowd surged forward and some dipped handkerchiefs in the blood.

Did you know…?
After his execution Charles's head was sewn back on to *his* body so relatives could pay their last respects before he was buried. After Cromwell's death, however, his body was dug up and hanged, then thrown in a ditch!

Slimy Stuart riddle
The Scots hated Charles I's *Church of England Prayer Book* – but Scottish priests were ordered to use it. One Scottish bishop only dared to read it to his angry congregation if he held a loaded pistol in each hand. The Scots didn't want to be Church of England – they wanted to be *Presbyterians*.

Test your teacher with this old riddle: Presbyterians are said to be the most religious people. Why? (Clue: rearrange the letters of 'Presbyterians' to make a phrase of three words with four, two and seven letters.)

Answer: 'Best in prayers'.

The Civil War

A 'civil' war is where people in one country fight among themselves. They are usually especially slimy affairs. The English Civil War was no different. It had its fair share of comical and gruesome moments...

1 In The English Civil War (1642–1649), brother fought brother and sometimes groups of soldiers switched sides. Sir Faithful Fortescue's men changed sides – but they forgot to change the sashes they wore when fighting ... so their new allies shot them!

2 Sir Arthur Aston was not a nice man. When one of his soldiers committed a crime he ordered that the man's hand should be sawn off. But a year later Sir Arthur was showing off on his horse to impress some ladies. He fell off and broke his leg. It turned septic ... and had to be sawn off.

3 But that wasn't the end of Sir Arthur's punishment for his cruelty. He had a wooden leg fitted and boasted he was as good a fighter as any man with two legs. He wasn't. In 1649 his army was defeated by Cromwell at Drogheda in Ireland. A soldier caught Sir Arthur and beat his brains out. What did the soldier use to batter him? Sir Arthur's own wooden leg, of course.

4 Prince Rupert, the Royalist leader, took his white poodle, Boy, with him everywhere – including to his battles. The Roundheads were afraid of the dog's devilish powers. They said Boy could talk several languages and make himself invisible. They thought he also gave his master the power to be weapon-proof. Then, at the battle of Marston Moor, Boy wandered on to the battlefield and was killed.

5 King Charles's army suffered from having some dimwitted generals. In 1644 Lord Byron took charge of some fresh troops from Ireland and surrounded the Roundhead town of Nantwich. No Roundhead could get out of the town because Lord Byron's troops made a circle right round Nantwich even though the town was on the edge of a river! It was icy weather. The river was frozen. Brilliant Byron's troops could cross it when they liked. Surely Nantwich would surrender? But ... *the ice melted*. The troops across the river were cut off, and Byron's two half-armies were easily defeated. Just to make things worse, bird-brain Byron's fed-up Irish troops agreed to switch sides and fight with the Roundheads.

6 Lord Byron managed to do even *worse* at the next battle – Marston Moor, in Yorkshire. He sat with his horse-soldiers (cavalry) behind a deep ditch and rows of foot-soldiers with pikes. All he had to do was wait for the order and attack the Roundheads. Then he saw the Roundheads coming towards him. They would be slowed up by the ditch and battered by the pike men.

All he had to do was *wait*. He couldn't. He charged forward. First he *flattened* his own pike soldiers, then he got his own men tangled in their own ditches where the Roundheads were able to cut them to pieces. The battle was lost and with it the whole of northern England. All because Lord Byron couldn't wait.

7 The Cavalier leader, Prince Rupert, also came face to face with the Roundheads on Marston Moor, in 1644. By the time he reached the battlefield there was just an hour of daylight left. Hardly worth starting a battle now, he thought. So he ordered his men to stop and have supper. The Roundheads couldn't believe what they were seeing. While the Cavaliers were having a bite to eat the Roundheads attacked and massacred 3,000 of them. They fought on in the moonlight and by midnight the Cavaliers had lost the battle.

8 In 1643 a group of London women surrounded the Houses of Parliament shouting, 'Peace and the King.' They were asked to leave. They refused and started beating up Members of Parliament – especially the crop-haired Puritans. In the end the army was called in to drive them out. Three women were killed and many others locked in prison.

9 The Cavalier town of Colchester, Essex, was under siege in 1648. The siege went on for three months and the inhabitants were forced to eat cats and dogs. It got worse. When they heard that Cromwell was winning the war, they gave up. The leaders expected to be treated honourably as prisoners of war. The Roundheads took them to Colchester Castle and shot them. (Maybe they were cat-lovers.)

10 The Parliament forces had problems too. Beeston Castle was left in the care of a Parliament commander whose peace-time work was selling cheese. One night a Cavalier officer and eight men climbed the rock that the castle was built upon and crept into the castle. The cheese-seller was so shocked he surrendered his 60 men … and then invited the attackers to supper and a drink of beer. When the angry Roundheads caught up with the cowardly cheese-seller, they shot him.

The spooky Stuarts

The stuffed chicken's revenge

Francis Bacon was a great statesman in the days of James I. (No jokes about his name, please.)

Then he got involved in a scandal and had to give up government work. Instead he turned his great brain to solving the problems of the world. (Sir Francis was an expert on manure, among other things.)

The problem of preserving food was one that strained his brain for a while. Then, as he was riding through London one snowy March day, he noticed that the frozen grass in the tracks was as fresh as ever. 'Aha!' he thought. 'Maybe the cold is preserving the grass. I wonder if it would preserve meat the same way?'

He ordered the coachman to stop the carriage at the nearest farm. He jumped out and bought a chicken. The coachman was ordered to kill the chicken, to pluck out most of its feathers and to clean out its insides. This he did.

Sir Francis bent down and began stuffing the chicken full of snow. He then packed it into a sack full of it.

But the cold was too much for 65-year-old Francis. He started shivering and collapsed in the snow. Within a few days he was as dead as the chicken.

Deader than the chicken, in fact. For the chicken wasn't

finished. It continues to haunt the place to this day. Half-stripped, it runs and flaps and shivers around Pond Square in London. Someone tried to catch it during World War Two but it disappeared into a brick wall. It was last reported in the 1970s. But that's not the only Stuart ghost story…

The Civil War soldier spooks

One of the Civil War battles was at Edgehill on October 23rd 1642. Charles claimed that he'd won – so did Cromwell!

Charles's nephew, Prince Rupert, led a charge of horse soldiers. It was a great success. They broke through the Roundhead lines and reached their supply wagons. But the nutty nephew didn't know what to do next. The Cavaliers spent some time plundering the supplies then decided to join the battle again. Unfortunately they were too late. Charles was already running away to Oxford.

Two months later some farm workers near Edgehill complained that they were disturbed at night by the charging of horses, the roar of cannon and the blowing of bugles. The villagers went to see what was happening … and they saw the battle of Edgehill – again. And again. And again … and again. Ghosts seemed to be acting out the battle every weekend.

Charles sent some of his officers to report and they saw the battle too. Charles's reporters had been at the original battle and recognized some of the ghostly soldiers. They saw Sir Edmund Verney who had been holding the king's flag until his hand was cut off – still holding the flagpole.

The ghostly battle can still be seen every year on October 23rd, it is said…

Chopped Charlie's last chance
Charles himself was visited by a ghost...

CHARLES DASHED TO HIS ARMY COMMANDER, PRINCE RUPERT

WHAT SHOULD I DO, RUPE?

JUST A BAD DREAM. FORGET IT

SO CHARLES FOUGHT ON... LOST THE NEXT BATTLE, AND LOST HIS HEAD OF COURSE

TOLD YOU SO!

The terror of Tedworth

One of Britain's most famous ghost stories happened in Stuart times. It concerns the *Phantom Drummer of Tedworth*.

Magistrate John Mompasson was visiting the town of Ludgershall in Wiltshire when he heard the deafening sound of a drum.

'What's that horrible racket?' he asked.

It's a beggar. He has a special licence to beg and to use that drum to attract attention,' his friend explained.

'Look, I know the magistrates round here. None of them would sign a licence like that. Fetch him here.'

So the beggar, William Drury, was brought before Mompasson and showed his licence. It was a very clumsy forgery. Drury went to prison but begged to be allowed to keep the drum. Mompasson refused. Drury escaped from the prison and the drum was sent to Mompasson's house.

IT'S SIGNED BY A 'MR MAJYSTRAIT'

For the next two years the house suffered terrible drumming noises. Then the ghost grew more violent...

• A bible was burnt.
• An unseen creature gnawed at the walls like a giant rat, purred like a cat and panted like a dog.
• Coins in a man's pocket turned black.
• Great staring eyes appeared in the darkness.
• The spirit attacked the local blacksmith with a pair of tongs

• A horse died of terror in its stable.
• Chamberpots were emptied into the children's beds.

Drury was arrested again for stealing a pig in Gloucester. He claimed it was his witch powers that were cursing Mompasson. So Drury was tried for witchcraft and sentenced to transportation overseas.

The haunting of Mompasson's house stopped. Drummer Drury was lucky. Twenty years earlier he would have been burnt at the stake as a witch.

Test your teacher

Is your teacher a historical brainbox or a hysterical bonehead? Test him/her/it with these simple true or false questions…

True or false?

1 In 1648 James II was a 14-year-old prince. His father had lost the Civil War and the young prince had to escape from England. To disguise himself he dressed as a servant with old clothes and a dirtied face.

2 Roundheads were called Roundheads because of the shape of their helmets.

3 Cavalier General, Prince Rupert, taught his dog to cock its leg every time someone said the name of the Roundhead leader, 'Pym'.

YOU SHOULD SEE WHAT HE DOES IF SOMEONE SAYS 'CROMWELL'

4 Charles I went to France to marry Henrietta.

5 The Earl of Berkshire committed suicide by shooting himself with a bow and arrow.

6 At some cattle markets men sold their wives.

7 Stuart boys wore petticoats until they were six years old.

8 In south-west England children were forbidden to smoke.

9 People believed that a dead person's tooth, worn as a necklace, prevented toothache.

10 Guy Fawkes was arrested and taken to King James's bedroom to be questioned.

Answers:

1 False. James dressed as a girl with a specially made dress. The tailor who made the dress was given James's measurements. He said he'd never known a woman that shape before - but he made it anyway and it fitted. Anne Murray, who helped him, said 'he looked very pretty in it.'

2 False. It was the shape of their crop-haired heads that gave them their name. In fact many Cavalier soldiers wore the same helmets as the Roundheads and became so confused at times that they killed their own allies.

3 True. It also jumped happily in the air when he said 'Charles'.

4 False. He didn't go *anywhere* to marry her. He sent his friend, the Duke of Buckingham, who acted as Charlie's stand-in at the wedding in Notre Dame, France.

5 False. The Earl of Berkshire *did* commit suicide but he used a cross-bow and bolt. Easier than a longbow, but equally horrible.

6 True. This did happen from time to time. One husband was so pleased with the five guineas he got for his wife that he went to Stowmarket and ordered the church bells to be rung.

7 True. At the age of six they were 'breeched' – given their first pair of trousers – in a ceremony. They were also given a small sword to wear.

8 False. Children in Somerset, Devon and Cornwall actually took their clay pipes to school. Smoking was

considered healthy then. Pupils at Eton were ordered to smoke during the plague years because it was said to help you avoid the disease. The smell could well have sent the plague-rats packing.

9 True. Some people went into graveyards to dig skeletons up and pinch their teeth.

10 True. Knowing some of James's disgusting personal habits, a visit to his bedroom could have been nastier than a visit to the torture rack.

Teach your teacher … Silly Stuart facts.

Impress your teacher and get a wonderful report at the end of term. How? Approach teacher's chair/desk/cage and say 'I was reading a jolly good history book the other day and I learned some amazing facts…' then amaze/ entertain/ sicken your teacher with these intriguing tales. (One each day for a week should do the trick).

• Here's a sad thing … Off the coast of Cornwall is the dangerous Eddystone Rock. In 1693 Henry Winstanley built a lighthouse to warn ships away. The 26-candle lighthouse was built of rock and stone. Iron bars were sunk into the rock to keep it as firm as the Eddystone Rock itself. In 1703 a storm swept the lighthouse away. Winstanley may have been disappointed for a short while – a *very* short while. He was inside it at the time and disappeared with his invention.

• Here's a weird thing … The people of Caernarvon in Wales were desperate for a ferry boat to carry them across their river. They were so desperate that they pinched the wood from Llanddwyn church to build the boat. 'God will be angry,' the villagers of Llanddwyn said. 'So what?' the boat-builders replied. So … the ferry sank in 1664 and 79 people drowned. 'Told you so,' taunted the villagers of Llanddwyn.

• Here's a curious thing … Some Stuart tramps made money by performing marriage ceremonies for couples. They called themselves Strollers' Priests. The marriage was made by the bride and groom shaking hands over the corpse of a dead horse.

These marriages were not legal, of course.

• Here's a nasty thing … During the Civil War the soldiers used simple muskets – pour the powder down the barrel, put the lead shot in, light the powder: 'Bang!' Or, sometimes, 'Bang … ouch!' Because accidents were common. As one Royalist officer said, 'We bury more toes and fingers than we do men.'

• Here's a horribly historical thing … An essential substance in gunpowder was 'saltpetre'. This was made from bird-droppings and human urine. Government officers had the right to dig these ingredients from hen-houses and toilet. In 1638 'saltpetre men' tried to get permission to go into churches to collect material because, 'women pee in their seats which causes excellent saltpetre.' (It must have been those long, long, sermons!)

Remember, remember…

Remember, remember the 30th of January! Charles I is remembered by some Church of England churches which have been named after him. Charles is remembered as a martyr who died for his religion. Charles churches can be found in Tunbridge Wells, Falmouth and Plymouth.

Remember, remember the 29th of May! It used to be Oak Apple Day and celebrations were held in remembrance of the Royal Oak … the tree that Charles II hid in to save his life. Oak Apple Day is now generally forgotten, but many towns now have a pub named after the Royal Oak – perhaps your town has.

Remember, remember the 3rd of September! On that day a small group of Oliver Cromwell supporters gather outside the Houses of Parliament. They sing a few hymns and a bugler plays a military tune of farewell, The Last Post. This marks the day of Cromwell's greatest victories (at Dunbar in 1650 and Worcester in 1651). It was also the day on which Cromwell died.

Remember, remember the 5th of November! James made this a public holiday when Guy Fawkes failed to blow up Parliament – 'Fawkes was the only man to enter the Houses of Parliament with an honest reason,' some people have said! But in 1678 there was a fear of another Catholic plot, so on November 5th people burned images of the Pope.

Sickly Stuart snacks

Would you like to have eaten like a Stuart? Like the Tudors before them, the rich people ate a lot of meat. They had servants to do the hard work of preparing it. Turning meat over an open fire was a hard job. It was usually given to a young kitchen boy whose front would be roasted by the fire, while his back would be chilled by the draught of the cool air drawn into the flames.

So the inventors of Stuart times came up with a couple of clever devices. One was a clockwork turner. The other was a sort of large 'hamster-wheel'. But instead of a hamster you popped a dog inside. As the dog walked forward, the meat turned.

The people of Stuart times not only invented new ways of cooking. They also discovered new food ideas…

The inventive Stuarts

Which of the following new food fads became popular in Stuart Britain?

1. DRINKING TEA
2. EATING SANDWICHES
3. EATING CABBAGE
4. EATING WITH FORKS
5. PINEAPPLES
SNIFF
6. DRINKING COFFEE
7. MAKING ICE-CREAM
8. BANANAS
9. DRINKING CHOCOLATE
10. EATING CHOCOLATE

Answers:

1 Yes. A Chinese legend says that Emperor Shennong learned how to make tea in 2737 BC when a few leaves from a tea plant accidentally fell into water he was boiling. A likely story. But it wasn't until the Stuart age that tea-drinking became popular in Britain. People of the 17th century thought it was quite all right to drink tea from the saucer. It took another 300 years (1920 to be exact) for someone to invent tea bags.

2 No. British politician John Montagu, fourth Earl of Sandwich (1718-1792), had a habit of eating beef between slices of toast so he could play cards without stopping to eat. But he was born *after* the Stuarts. And, though he gave his name to that type of food, the idea of eating meat between bread was first tried by the Romans over 1,000 years before.

3 No. Blame the Tudors for that. Sir Anthony Ashley of Dorset brought cabbages to Britain from Holland. (The stewed green mush you get for school dinners is not quite that old. Honest.)

4 Yes. Forks had been used on royal tables as early as the 14th century but only became popular when Thomas Coryat published a book about their use in Italy. Most people in Britain had used knives with sharp points to 'spear' their food and had spoons to scoop up the smaller pieces.

5 Yes. Oliver Cromwell was presented with a pineapple in 1657. The first in Britain. He probably didn't know whether to eat it, wear it or give it a bowl of milk.

6 Yes. Coffee was a popular Arab drink for hundreds of years before the Stuarts discovered it in the middle of the 17th Century.

7 Yes. From the early 1660s 'ice houses' with thatched roofs were built, or snow pits were dug in the ground. Winter snows were kept all year round. Sweet cream (sometimes with orange-flavoured water) was frozen for a couple of hours and then served.

THE RECIPE SAID MIX ORANGE AND CREAM THEN STAND IN ICE HOUSE FOR TWO HOURS

8 Yes. Thomas Johnson showed bananas in his London shop window in 1633.

9 Yes. The Spanish brought chocolate back from Mexico in 1519. But it became really popular in Stuart Britain. In the 17th century, 'chocolate houses' were the popular meeting places of the day, rather like the local pub today. But you probably wouldn't have enjoyed the drink; it was full of cocoa butter and rather greasy. Some dealers added soil to the cocoa paste to cheat the buyers.

10 No. The Dutch first made eating chocolate in 1828.

Eat like a Stuart

If you were invited to eat at an upper-class house then you'd eat off fine silver and gold plates … but you'd be expected to take your own spoon. Forks were not generally used until the reign of William and Mary at the end of the Stuart age.

Then Stuart people discovered how *really* useful forks could be. They found they were great for picking out bits of food that got stuck between your teeth!

And that wasn't their only habit that we'd find a bit disgusting today. They used their fingers a lot to pick up meat – and threw the bones on the floor for the dog. Everyone at the table used the same bowl to rinse their fingers in – and some people even rinsed their spoons in the same water.

One writer described a gentleman's country house in Dorset…

A house so badly kept that it shamed him and his dirty shoes. The great hall was scattered with marrow bones, it was full of hawks' perches, hounds, spaniels and terriers. The upper sides of the hall were hung with fox skins from this year's and last year's skinning. Here and there a polecat intermixed. Usually two of the great chairs in the parlour had litters of cats on them and the gentleman always had two or three accompanying him at the dinner table.

46

But some people worried about good table manners. A Stuart book gave advice on how to eat politely. Its top ten recommendations were…

If you wish to be POLITE at the DINNER TABLE

- Wipe not your greasy fingers upon the tablecloth
- Dip your food into the common salt dish before you eat it but not after you have taken a bite from it
- Bring not your cat to the dinner table
- Pick not your teeth with your fingers or your knife
- Make not a noise as you drink your soup
- Shout not at the table, 'I eat none of this, I eat none of that etc.'
- Blow not upon your soup to cool it
- Belch not at the table
- Spit not and cough not at the table
- Scratch not your head whilst you sit at the table

Fair gingerbread

People enjoyed going to fairs and eating. They didn't have candy-floss and hot dogs, though. Their favourite fair food was gingerbread. Some of the towns, like Birmingham, had Gingerbread Fairs. Want to know what gingerbread tasted like in Stuart times? Try this recipe.

Stuart Gingerbread

Ingredients
225g white breadcrumbs
5ml ground ginger
5ml cinnamon
5ml aniseed
25g sugar
150ml water

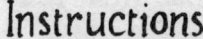

Instructions
1 Dry the breadcrumbs in an oven but don't let them turn brown
2 Mix the other ingredients in a saucepan and add the dried breadcrumbs
3 Warm gently and blend with a wooden spoon until you have a stiff dough
4 Dust a chopping board with ground ginger and cinnamon
5 Turn the dough out onto the board and roll it to about 5mm thickness
6 Cut into small circles (about 2-3 cm across)

Eat them without further cooking

Have a cup of tea (sugar but no milk) with your gingerbread for a truly Stuart snack. And, talking about eating...

Stuart food you may not want try

Stuart Christmas Pudding

Do you like Christmas Pudding? Most people do. You probably enjoy the candied peel, raisins, sugar and spices. So did the Stuarts. They were all in the Stuart pudding ... along with *chopped cow's tongue and chicken*. Fancy a spoonful?

Sweets

Decorate your table for that special occasion with sugar models. Make them into the shapes of animals and plants. Eat them to finish off the meal. Sir Hugh Platt described how to make the stuff in 1609:

> *Take violets and heat them with a little hard sugar. Steep them in rosewater and grind them into a paste. This will have the colour of the violet and smell of the violet. In the same way you may work with marigolds, cowslips, primroses or any other flower.*

Eating flowers! Whatever next? Carnations and custard? Pansy pie? Baked buttercups and tulips on toast?

Charles II (reigned 1660-1685)

Cheerful Charlie

The leader of the Roundheads, Cromwell, died in 1658. His son wasn't very keen on running the country and the British people wanted a king again. So Charles I's son, Charles II, returned to the throne.

Charles II was known as the Merry Monarch because he brought back all the games and entertainments the Puritans had banned.

He wisely agreed to work along with Parliament in future. But Members of Parliament were still worried about a Catholic take-over – Charles was married to Catherine of Breganza, a Catholic princess from Portugal! Still, Charles himself was a good Protestant ... wasn't he?

Slimiest act

Parliament wanted to pass a law which banned any Catholic from ever becoming king – this was aimed at Charles's younger brother, James, who was a Catholic. Charles II was annoyed and sent Parliament away so the law couldn't be passed. He ruled without Parliament until his death in 1685 ... then James came to the throne as the royal family had planned.

But, slimiest of all, Charles II knew he couldn't be King of England *and* a Catholic - so he *pretended* to be a Protestant. Then, as he was dying, he told a Catholic priest he wanted to die a Catholic. He was 'converted' on his death-bed.

Charlie's cheerless childhood

In 1641 Charles I was forced to sign the death warrant for his friend, the Earl of Strafford. He wondered if Parliament might like to change its mind so he sent his son Charles to ask if they'd like to change Strafford's sentence to life imprisonment … or, if they *had* to execute him, could they at least wait until Saturday, please?

Young Charles toddled off to Parliament with his dad's message … he was just ten years old. The prince soon learned what a tough life it was. Parliament refused the plea and executed Strafford the next day.

Within a year little Charlie was involved in the Civil War and trying to take on a fully armed Roundhead with his pistol at the battle of Edgehill. He shouted 'I fear them not!' as the Roundhead charged … but a Cavalier arrived just in time to save his royal bacon.

The Great Escape

In 1651, when Charles II was a prince, he was at the Battle of Worcester, fighting against the Roundheads. His army lost. He fled to a friendly house and was hunted by the Roundheads. Charles's friend, Colonel Carlis, led him to a huge oak tree. They climbed into it and the house owner took the ladder away. The king managed to sleep in the tree with a pillow he'd taken.

With the help of a haircut and a face blackened by soot, Charles escaped to Holland and safety.

Fire and plague

Londoners who lived through Charles II's reign were pretty lucky ... lucky that the plague didn't get them! And if the plague spared their lives then the Great Fire probably destroyed their houses. Would *you* have survived in Stuart London?

The plague ... read all about it!

PLAGUE WEEKLY

9th Sept 1665

ON THE SPOTS REPORTS

Only 2OP WEEKLY

BOOZY BARD BEDEVILS BURIAL BOYS

Last night the brave burial boys, who collect your old corpses, were almost scared to death themselves. A strolling singer sat up and spooked them just as they were about to pop him in the pit.

Dirty

Corpse collector Samuel Simple (34 or 37) said, 'It's a dirty job but somebody has to do it. We was going along picking up bodies off the doorsteps where their loved ones had dumped them. We came across this scruffy little feller in a doorway. The door was marked with a red cross or we wouldn't have taken him. Stuck him on the cart with the others and went off to the graveyard'.

His partner, Chris Cross (24-ish) added, 'We was just about to unload the cart when the bodies started moving, didn't they? Gave me a right turn, I can tell you. Turned out to be this singer trying to get out of the cart. What a mess. Bodies all over the place!'

Smelly

Wandering minstrel Elwiss Prestley, of no fixed abode, said 'I'd had a few jars of ale and just sat down for a nap. Woke up under this fat, smelly feller. Thought it was somebody trying to muscle in on my sleeping spot. Told him to get off, didn't I? Course he didn't reply … well, he wouldn't, him being dead like.'

Tonic

Sam and Chris were able to laugh about their grave mistake. 'We'll buy Elwiss a drink to make up for it,' Sam said. 'We can afford it – after all, business is good at the moment. They're dropping like flies.' Asked how he stays so fit and healthy Chris said he put it all down to 'Doctor Kurleus's Cureall Tonic'.

Doctor Kurleus Cures All

This is to give notice that John Kurleus, former physician to Charles I, offers a drink and pill that cures all sores, scabs, itch, scurfs, scurvies, leprosies and plagues be they ever so bad. There is no smoking or sweating or use of mercury or other dangerous and deadly substances. Doctor Kurleus sells the drink at three shillings to the quart and the pill one shilling a box. He lives at the Glass Lantern Tavern, Plough Yard in Grays Inn Lane

He gives his opinion for nothing

Plague pottiness

Doctors *said* that dogs and cats, pigs, pet rabbits and pigeons could spread the plague. The government believed them and tried to prevent the plague by killing all the dogs in the town. Dogs were banned from towns and dog-killers were appointed to round up strays.

Other doctors blamed dirty air – huge bonfires were lit in the hope that they would 'purify' it.

No one understood that the real enemy was the rats, whose fleas spread the plague. That fact wasn't discovered until 1898.

Other doctors offered miracle cures for the plague. They would also offer free treatment, as in the advert (above). There was a catch, of course. Doctor Kurleus would look at a plague victim and say, 'You need a quart of my medicine. That'll be three shillings please.'

'I thought your advert said you give your opinion for nothing!'

'I do,' the devious doctor would shrug. 'My *opinion* is free, the *drink* is three shillings.'

Sick people, afraid of dying a painful plague death, would give anything for a cure. The fake doctors grew rich and the people died anyway.

Dying to get to heaven

When there was no plague and families had time to bury their dead properly, the people of Stuart times had some curious customs. You may have thought burying corpses with money and belongings went out of fashion when Tutankhamun died. It didn't.

A 17th-century body was buried with…
• a coin (to pay St Peter at the gates of heaven)
• a candle (to light the way to heaven)
• a 10-centimetre layer of bran cereal on the bottom of the coffin (for comfort).

There was also a custom in some counties for families to hire a 'sin-eater'. This was a poor person who was given a loaf of bread to eat and a beer to drink …
while standing over the corpse. The idea was the dead person's dead sins would enter the bread and be eaten – their ghost could then get into heaven.

Graves should have a headstone with a rhyme carved on to it. For example…

HERE LIES THE CARCASS
OF HONEST JOHN PARKHURST

Awful rhyme – but difficult with some surnames. What would you rhyme with your name?

Fire from France
This is the story usually told about the fire…

1 A little boy crept into Thomas Farriner's baker's shop in Pudding Lane. He reached up to steal a loaf that was cooling by the window. The baker swung round quickly. Too quickly – he scattered ashes over the wooden floor.

OI! WHAT YOU UP TO!

2 The shop caught fire. Soon the whole street of wooden houses was burning fiercely. Burning sparks spread the fire to the next street, and the next. It seemed half of London was ablaze.

SOMEONE SHOULD WARN THE KING!

3 When Charles heard of the problem he did two things…

MY ORDERS ARE TO BLOW UP HOUSES TO STOP THE SPREAD OF THE FIRE

YAY!

4 And then the King himself set off to join the fire-fighters. He ended up blackened by smoke and soaked with water ... but won huge popularity with the people of London.

5 So did his final action…

YAY!

AND HERE IS A PURSE OF 100 GUINEAS FOR THE BRAVE FIRE-FIGHTERS!

That's the *heroic* story. Teachers never tell you the horrible historical *truth*. Did you know, for example, the people of London blamed French spies for starting the fire? Whenever they met a Frenchman in the street they would attack him.

A blacksmith met an innocent Frenchman walking down the street and struck him with an iron bar 'until the blood flowed in a plentiful stream down to his ankles.'

A crowd threw a French painter's furniture into the street then ripped his house to the ground. 'Maybe you'd like to set fire to it,' they said, 'just like you set fire to the rest of London!'

Several innocent foreigners were dragged in front of magistrates and charged with starting the fire. Then the son of a French watchmaker *confessed!* No one knows why. Farriner the baker (where the fire had started) said the watchmaker could not have got into the bakery to start the fire.

What did the magistrate do with this unfortunate Frenchman?

1 Deported him back to France.

2 Put him in jail so the mob couldn't take their revenge on him.

3 Set him free.

4 Hanged him anyway, if that's what he wanted!

Answer: 4 The man was hanged even though he could not possibly have been to blame.

59

James II (reigned 1685-1688)

Dim Jim

Charles II died without children so the crown passed to his brother, James II. But James was a *Catholic* and the people of Britain still had that fear and hatred of Catholics. The only thing that saved him was the fact that he had no son to take over after his death.

His daughter, Mary, was a good Protestant and husband William was the Dutch Protestant leader. When James died, Protestant Mary would lead the country. Things were fine ... until a 'son' suddenly and mysteriously appeared! Was this another slimy, sneaky Stuart plot?

Slimiest act - the warming-pan switch

James's wife, Mary of Modena, had five babies from 1672 till 1682 – and they all died. Then she was expecting another baby. When it arrived her doctor was miles away. Two nurses saw to the birth. To the horror of the British people it was a living boy! It would become another Catholic king! But a story went around...

- The two nurses had been paid the huge sum of £500 each – to keep them quiet?

- Mary's baby had died – but someone else's new-born baby boy was smuggled into the Queen's room!

- The baby was smuggled into the room in a warming-pan – a metal pan with a lid, usually filled with coals and used to warm a bed.

- The Queen's dead baby was smuggled out in the same pan.

Jamie's judge

Four months after James came to the throne there was a rebellion led by the Duke of Monmouth. The duke's rebel force was smashed at Sedgemoor, in Somerset, by James's troops. Monmouth was executed.

That wasn't good enough for James. He had all of Monmouth's supporters rounded up as well and sent to trial. He wanted revenge. He wanted to destroy, wipe out, annihilate, eradicate, exterminate, obliterate and mangle all opposition. He couldn't do that himself. He had to have some sort of trial – and some judge who would be as ruthless and rotten as necessary.

He chose Judge George Jeffreys. Good choice. He was described by the writer Violet Van Der Elst as follows...

Judge Jeffreys was known to have a very handsome face and at times would look almost kind and angelic. But there was no man living who had a blacker soul. Innocent men were hanged along with the guilty. There was the case of Charles Lindell. He said he had not left his shop – in fact he was arrested there. The night he was supposed to be out fighting with Monmouth he was sitting at home with his mother and sweetheart. All this he told to Judge Jeffreys. With his most kindly smile he listened and seemed to sympathize. Then his face twisted into a most horrible grimace as he turned to the poor prisoner, who had thought he had a good hearted judge. He now realized the judge was a fend, not a man. Judge Jeffreys told him he would be hanged by the neck, if not for taking part in the rebellion then for telling lies under oath. This man was only one of nearly two hundred that Judge

Jeffreys condemned to death Another eight hundred were sentenced to transportation and slavery in the colonies – a slower but equally certain form of death.

WE'RE HEADING FOR A FATE WORSE THAN DEATH

WHAT'S THAT?

AMERICA

The trials were known as 'The Bloody Assizes' – no prizes for guessing why. The angelic judge did have a little soft spot for Lady Alice Lisle – he actually let her sit down during her trial because she was 70 years old. She was accused of sheltering rebels. She was found guilty and the thoughtful judge sentenced her to be burnt.

The executed rebels had their bodies preserved in tar. The bodies were then sent around the west of England as a warning to anyone else who thought of rebelling.

BUT, there was some Stuart justice ... after James II was finally overthrown in December 1688, Jeffreys was arrested; he died in the Tower of London.

Cowardy custard James
But did Dim Jim really expect to get away with the warming-pan trick? If he did then he was disappointed. Another Catholic king was more than the British could bear. They didn't wait for the baby to grow up and take over the throne.

Parliament invited Dim Jim's daughter, Mary, to take the throne with her very Protestant husband, William.

William landed in England – James ran off to Ireland. William's take-over was known as 'The Glorious Revolution'.

In 1690 James II tried to defend Ireland against William. He lost the Battle of the Boyne and retreated safely to Dublin. He met Lady Tyrconnel, an Irish noblewoman, in Dublin and complained...

"MADAM, YOUR COUNTRYMEN HAVE RUN AWAY"

"SIRE, YOUR MAJESTY SEEMS TO HAVE WON THE RACE"

Jim slipped away to France and safety.

Jim the brave

James wasn't afraid of fighting once he got into a battle. At the Battle of Lowestoft – a sea battle against the Dutch – he spent 18 hours on deck while sailors all around were being shot down. As the famous poet *didn't* say...

> *The king stood on the burning deck*
> *Till all the Dutch were beat,*
> *The crown of England on his head...*
> *And blisters on his feet*

Slimy Stuart crime

The Stuart age was one of the classic ages of the highwayman. Stage-coach journeys had begun. 'Stand and deliver! was the famous cry and the horse ride from London to York was the amazing achievement of one man … but which one?

The great escape

But what was the great adventurer's name?

1 Dick Turnip (nicknamed Tricky Dicky)
2 William Nevison (nicknamed Swift Nicks)
3 Dick Turpin (nicknamed Dick Turpin)

Answer: 2 It was William Nevison who got away with this crime – he was so pleased with himself he boasted about his great ride from London to York.

You've probably heard the famous story about Dick Turpin riding from York to London to avoid being convicted of a robbery. Turpin *never made that ride.* A writer simply pinched the Nevison story and tacked it on to the Turpin tale.

Nevison met King Charles II, who gave him the nickname and a pardon. The Merry Monarch had a habit of doing that – even when the crime was one of the greatest in history...

Blood and the Jewels
Some people become famous because of what they do. And some become famous because of what is done to them. Talbot Edwards had that sort of fame. He lived to a good old age but never grew tired of telling people about the time he was robbed...

Old Talbot Edwards sat in the corner of the tavern and emptied his mug of ale. He ran a tongue over his toothless gums and enjoyed the flavour. Then he pushed the mug across the table to the young couple who sat opposite him. 'Another pint of ale will help my memory,' he smiled.

The young man signalled and the landlord brought a fresh jug to the table. Talbot dabbed at his watery eyes with a grubby handkerchief and reached for the ale. 'So you've heard about me, eh?'

'We have, Mr Edwards,' the young man said eagerly. 'I'm writing the story for a newspaper and wanted to hear your side of it.' .

'It's ten years since the robbery,' Talbot shrugged. 'Why now?'

'Because Blood's dead,' the young woman put in.

The old man blinked and paused with his mug half way to his lips. 'Blood? Dead? No-o. Blood's not the sort of man to die. I just don't believe it.' He shook his head slowly.

'Tell me about him,' the young man urged.

Talbot Edwards sat back on the oak bench and half closed his eyes. 'Funny little feller, Colonel Blood. Ugly face with smallpox scars, short legs and brilliant blue eyes. Lovely Irish voice. He could talk the tail off a pig. I was in charge of the Tower of London back in 1671 when he turned up on my doorstep. He was dressed like a parson, and he *told* me

68

he was a parson … so I believed him!'

'He was a soldier, though, wasn't he?' the young woman asked. 'Came to England to fight for Cromwell and the Roundheads?'

Old Talbot threw back his head and laughed. 'Bless you, no! He came to England to fight for the Cavaliers … he only switched sides to the Roundheads when he realized that King Charles was going to lose!' He chuckled and supped his beer. 'Of course he wasn't too popular when Charles the Second came back to the throne. The new government took everything Tom Blood had.'

'That's when he decided on the robbery?' the reporter asked.

'Aye. But being Colonel Blood it couldn't be any ordinary robbery, could it? No. It had to be the most daring robbery of all time. He had to go for the Crown Jewels, didn't he.'

'And it was your job to guard them?' the young woman asked.

'I was the keeper. Lived on the floor above the jewel room. Of course, my job was to show visitors the jewels – especially *respectable* visitors like 'Parson' Blood. And I never suspected a thing. He spent months setting it up, you

see. Brought his wife with him on the second visit.

I remember she took ill in the jewel room and my wife Nell looked after her. Parson Blood was so grateful he came back two days later with a pair of new gloves for Nell. After that he became a sort of friend of the family.'

'And he didn't show an unusual interest in the jewels?'

'No–o. He seemed more interested in making a match between his rich nephew and my daughter. Of course the women were keen on that!' old Talbot said.

'So how did the robbery happen?' the reporter asked.

'I'm coming to that,' the old man said and took a long drink of his ale. 'Parson Blood brought his good-looking nephew to meet Nell and Alice – that's my daughter – and he brought a couple of friends along too. "Now we don't want to be bothered with this marriage business, Talbot, do we?" Blood says. "No," I says. "Why don't we take my two friends here down for a look at the jewels while the women have a chat?" And I agreed.'

'And that's when he tried to steal the jewels?' the young woman asked.

'I'm coming to that,' Talbot Edwards said. 'Being a private visit I didn't have any of the Tower guards around, did I? So, there I was, alone in the jewel room with three villains. No sooner had I unlocked the door than Blood gave me a whack over the head with a wooden mallet. When I woke up they'd already pulled away the iron grating and were pulling out the crown, the sceptre and the orb A hundred thousand pounds' worth of jewels … what a robbery, what a man!'

'You sound as if you admired him,' the puzzled young woman said.

70

Old Talbot chuckled. 'Can't help it, can't help it. Anyway, when I woke up I found they'd tied my hands and feet. I started shouting, "Treason! Murder!" That's when Blood drew his sword and ran it through my shoulder ... lucky it missed my heart, really. Want to see the scar?' he asked and reached for the buttons on his doublet.

'No!' the young woman said quickly and turned up her small nose with a little show of disgust.

Talbot Edwards shrugged. 'That's when Blood had his one stroke of really bad luck. Like I said, it was a private visit so we shouldn't have been interrupted. They'd flattened the crown with the mallet and were stowing the jewels in a bag. Who should arrive at the Tower? My own son. On leave from the army fighting in Holland. I wasn't expecting him – and Blood certainly wasn't. He made a run for it with his nephew and his two helpers. The blood was pouring out of my chest but I managed to shout out. My son heard and came and found me.'

The old man was becoming excited now and his watery eyes were glowing in the yellow light of the candles.

'Your son raised the alarm?'

'He did. A sentry tried to stop Blood . . . so Blood shot him. The second sentry saw that and ducked. He let the robbers through the first door. There was a lot of confusion, you understand – guards were attacking each other by mistake. That let Blood reach his horse at the gate. But the Captain of the guard, a man called Beckman, saw what was happening and grabbed Blood just before he got on his horse. Blood pulled out a pistol, pulled the trigger ... and had his second bit of bad luck. The pistol misfired. Beckman wrestled him to the ground and the whole gang were arrested.'

The young woman leaned forward. 'What I don't understand is why didn't Blood hang for the crime?'

The old keeper shook his head. 'Didn't I tell you? Blood could charm milk from a bull. He insisted he had to talk to King Charles himself. In the end the king agreed to see him. Now, Blood knew the king liked an adventurous rogue. Sure enough, Charles pardoned him . . . even gave him lands in Ireland worth £500 a year to make up for what he'd lost.'

'And the king gave *you* a reward,' the reporter said.

The old man looked into his empty ale mug a little shyly. 'A good king is Charles. I'd drink his health ... if I had a drink.'

The reporter smiled and signalled for the landlord to refill the old keeper's mug. After they had drunk the health of King Charles, Talbot Edwards sighed. 'So Tom Blood is dead, you say?'

The reporter nodded. 'I'm writing his story now. You know he'd just lost a court case to the Duke of Buckingham? The court ordered Blood to pay £10,000 to the duke. He was ruined.

The old man looked up. 'So Colonel Blood came to a bad end after all,' he said.

The young woman spoke in a low voice so no one could overhear. 'There were stories that Blood had faked his death. That there was some other person's body in the coffin. The magistrates had it dug up and identified. It was Blood all right.'

Talbot Edwards looked disappointed. 'Trust Colonel Blood to cheat his enemies to the last.'

'Oh, but he didn't cheat them…' the woman began.

The old man cut in. 'He did, you know. Because he cheated them out of what they wanted most of all … what they really wanted was to see him hang!'

And in the smoky light of the tavern candles the old man chuckled so loud and long he could scarcely drink his ale.

Did you know ?

1 Colonel Blood was involved in many outrageous crimes in his lifetime. In 1660 he tried to capture Dublin Castle and hold its governor to ransom. When he failed he fled to Holland.

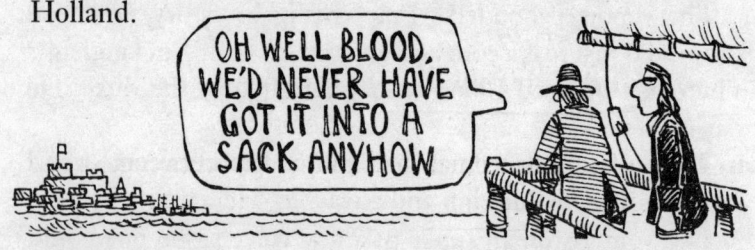

2 In 1661 one of Blood's partners in the Dublin Castle kidnap was taken to London for execution. Blood returned to England, overcame a guard of eight soldiers and rescued his friend.

3 Blood's greatest enemy was Lord Ormonde. One night Ormonde was on his way to a banquet when his coach was stopped by a band of armed men. They could have killed him on the spot but Blood wanted a more dramatic death for his enemy. He wanted him taken to Tyburn gallows and hanged like a common criminal. The coachman raised the alarm and the plot failed.

4 When Charles met Blood, the Colonel had the cheek to tell the king that the Crown Jewels weren't really worth that much. People said they were worth £100,000 – Blood said he wouldn't give £6,000 for them. Charles was amused and released the thief.

5 Not only did Blood get an Irish estate from Charles, he was also welcomed into the royal court where he was a popular figure. He was admired as the man who almost stole the Crown Jewels ... and Talbot Edwards was almost as famous as the man who almost lost them.

The teacher and the lord

Who would you rather marry, a lord or a teacher?

PERSONALLY I'D RATHER MARRY A *CHIMPANZEE* THAN A TEACHER

In 1709 a Scottish woman had the choice between Robert Lord Balfour of Burleigh and a teacher, Henry Stenhouse.

SHE CHOSE LORD BALFOUR OF COURSE

She chose the *teacher*. Lord Balfour was furious. He decided to sort Henry the teacher out. He killed him. Lord Balfour was arrested.

CRUELTY TO ANIMALS I SUPPOSE

Arrested for *murder*, found guilty and sentenced.

KILLING A TEACHER? DESERVES AN HOUR'S DETENTION AT THE MOST

Lord Balfour was sentenced to *death*. He was thrown into prison and waited to be executed. When the warders came to lead him to the scaffold they found he'd gone. Lord Balfour had swapped clothes with his sister when she came to visit. He walked free. Of course the poor woman married neither of the men.

Before Stuart times lords expected to get away with murder. James I put an end to that when he ordered the execution of Lord Maxwell for murder in 1613. Maxwell had called a peace conference with his ancient enemy, John Johnstone. When Johnstone arrived at the meeting place, Maxwell shot him. Maxwell expected James to pardon him because he was a lord. James didn't. Maxwell was beheaded ... and the other lords were a bit more careful about who they murdered in future.

The Archbishop of Canterbury, on the other hand, *did* get away with murder. He was out hunting for deer when he carelessly shot one of his gamekeepers with a crossbow. King James I was told of the tragedy. 'Ah, well,' the king sighed, 'No one but a fool or a villain could blame the Archbishop. It could happen to anyone.' The Archbishop went free.

Painful punishments

1 Sir Walter Raleigh had been a hero in the days of old Queen Elizabeth. But he'd been accused of plotting against James I and was sentenced to death on the scaffold in 1603. James decided not to execute Raleigh – he thought he'd just lock him up instead. But James had to have his little joke. First he let Raleigh grovel for his life, then he let Raleigh climb on to the scaffold. The crowd held its breath and looked forward to a bit of blood splashing around. Only *then* did James let him know his life was spared.

After 13 years in jail he was released to seek gold in America. But Raleigh had upset the Spanish king, who demanded that James should execute him. James didn't have a very good reason to execute the old man – so he dug up the old 'plot' accusation from 1603. In 1618 Raleigh's head rested on the block for a second time. If he thought James was going to have another little joke he was disappointed. This time – 15 years after he'd first put his head on the block – it hit the ground.

2 The Duke of Monmouth led a rebellion against James II in 1685 but was defeated and captured. On the scaffold he tested the edge of the axe and said he thought it was a little blunt. The Duke offered the executioner, Jack Ketch, six gold guineas to do a quick, clean job. But the Duke was cooler than Ketch, who took about five chops to get the head off. The crowd was furious and Ketch had to be protected from them as he left.

3 They didn't have that problem in Halifax. They had a machine there to execute people. It was a guillotine. The blade was released by pulling on a rope. That rope was

passed to the crowd so everyone pulled together. That way no single person was to blame for the criminal's death. If the criminal had stolen an animal then it was tied to the rope and driven away. So a cow could guillotine a man!

4 A Scottish law said that people could be sentenced to drowning in the sea if they refused to support the Scottish church. No one believed the old law would ever be used again. But it was, in 1685. Sixty-year-old Margaret McLauchlan and 18-year-old Margaret Wilson were tied to stakes at low tide. As the tide rose the sea would drown them. The old woman was placed lower in the water. The officers hoped

she would die first and the sight would persuade young Margaret to change her religion. It didn't. Old Margaret drowned and a soldier put young Margaret out of her misery by forcing her head under the water.

5 Scotland wasn't a healthy place to be at that time. In 1691 the Scots chiefs were told to take an oath to show they were loyal to King William III. But they had to take that oath before January 1st 1692. Alisdair McIain, head of the Macdonald clan, went to Fort William to take the oath. He was told to go to Inverary, 60 miles away. He battled through snow storms and arrived six days too late.

THIS IS THE WORST HOGMANAY I'VE EVER HAD

That was enough for the Scottish secretary to order the killing of all the Macdonalds. Thirty-five men and an unknown number of women and children died when the commander of the Argyll regiment, Robert Campbell, ordered his men to massacre the defenceless Macdonalds in their village at Glencoe. To this day the Macdonalds and the Campbells are said to distrust each other.

6 The Puritans brought in new laws after they had won the Civil War. Puritan punishments included:

CRIME	PURITAN PUNISHMENT
A man disagreed with the Puritan religion	Soldiers sold his furniture sent his servants to London and dug up every tree in his orchard
A woman swore [seven rude words]	Fined 12 shillings [60°]
A barber trimmed someone's beard on a Sunday	Fined
A man stole lead from a house roof	Whipped for two hours 'till his body be bloody' and sent to prison till a fine was paid
Being actors in a travelling theatre company	Whipped and sat in stocks
A maid mended a dress on Sunday	Sat in the stocks for three hours
People went to church on Christmas Day	Sent to prison

The poet Richard Brathwaite wrote…

> *One day to Banbury I came*
> *And there I saw a Puritane*
> *Hanging of his cat on Monday*
> *Cos it killed a mouse on Sunday*

(Mr Brathwaite wrote that in 1638, of course. He wouldn't have dared to write that 12 years later when the Puritans were running the country!)

No wonder the people were pleased to see Charles II return. He really seemed to be a 'Merry Monarch' – but after the Puritan reign, a game of chess with a chimpanzee would have seemed a 'merry' idea.

7 An actor called Wilson played the part of 'Bottom' in Shakespeare's *Midsummer Night's Dream*. He had to dress as an ass for part of the play. The magistrates must have had a sense of humour. While Wilson sat in the stocks he wore a label round his neck saying .

> *Good people, I have played the beast,*
> *And brought bad things to pass.*
> *I was a man, but now I've made*
> *Myself a silly ass!*

8 A man called Titus Oates was sentenced to be tied to the back of a cart as it was driven from Aldgate to Newgate. As he was dragged along he was whipped. King James ordered that the treatment should be repeated on a second day. Oates was too weak to walk – he was fastened face down on a stretcher and dragged through the streets again being whipped. And Oates was lucky ... he deserved worse! His crime was that he had dreamed up a story about a Catholic plot to murder Charles II. The country was thrown into a panic and innocent Catholics were tortured, executed or driven out of their homes by frightened Protestants. Oates claimed the Catholics had invited a French army to invade, and...

- An army was reported to have landed one night in Dorset – but in daylight the French soldiers turned out to be a hedge and their officers a few grazing horses.
- Chains were thrown across London streets to stop French cavalry charging.
- Tailors started selling 'armour' to rich men and women. It became very fashionable because it was silk armour.

9 William Prynne was a Member of Parliament and simply hated the theatre. He wrote a strong attack on plays and actors. Charles I on the other hand loved the theatre. So Charles had Prynne punished for his writing. Prynne had both ears cut off.

Five years later Prynne was writing nasty things about bishops. This time a judge said…

…*and* he pointed to a pair of stubs. These were cut off and he was branded on the cheeks.

William Prynne lived to see Charles II come to the throne – and Charles gave him a well-paid job in the Tower of London.

10 The dreadful Judge Jeffreys was especially thoughtful at Christmas time. He once sentenced a woman to be whipped but kindly added an instruction to the man with the whip, 'Pay particular attention to this lady. Beat her soundly till the blood runs down. It is Christmas, a cold time for madam to strip. See that you "warm" her shoulders thoroughly.'

11 When the Roundheads captured a Scottish Cavalier they put him in the stocks. They then held his mouth open with two sticks, pulled his tongue out to its full length and tied two sticks to it. The man couldn't pull his tongue back in. He had to stay like that for half an hour.

12 Not many people know that James I was a detective. True! A servant called Sarah Swarton said she had witnessed Lord Roos taking part in some hanky-panky with a woman who wasn't his wife. She said she'd hidden behind a window curtain in his Wimbledon home. Lady Roos went to King James to complain and have her husband punished. 'Sherlock' James went to the scene of the crime and asked the maid Sarah to stand behind the curtains. The curtains only came to her knees. She couldn't have stood there without being seen! Lord Roos was cleared – false-witness Sarah was charged with 'perjury', or lying after swearing to tell the truth. She was punished by being whipped then branded – she would probably have had the letter 'P' for perjurer burned into her cheek.

Potted punishments

Can you match the name of the Stuart punishment to its description?

NAME	DESCRIPTION *The victim...*
Branks	1. had his thumbs placed in a vice which was tightened until he talked
Repentance stool	2. was placed in a barrel with a hole in the top and bottom [For head and legs] and a hole in each side for the arms. Victim walked round street dressed in barrel
Cropping	3. had to wear an iron mask with a spike that went into the mouth. She then walked around the town wearing it. A punishment for women who nagged or talked too much

Drunkard's cloak	4. sits down in church while the priest tells everyone what a disgusting person this is
Thumbekins	5. had his head put in a pillory and his ears nailed to the wood. The ears were then cut off and often left fastened to the pillory

Answers:

Branks 3 First used in England in 1623 at Macclesfield, but Scotland had been using it for 50 years before that. Maybe it was an idea brought south by James I. **Repentence stool 4** Used mainly in Scotland. Often used for married men who were caught going off with other women. **Cropping 5** A punishment often used for authors who upset the government. Authors, of course, should never, *ever* be treated with such cruelty. **Drunkard's cloak 2** A punishment for people who drank too much. **Thumbekins 1** Brought to Scotland in 1660 by Thomas Dalyell who used to torture a man accused of trying to assassinate Charles II.

William (reigned 1689-1702) and Mary (reigned 1689-1694)

Slimy Mary

Mary had no regrets about taking the throne from her own father, James II, when he ran away to France. In fact, when she arrived at her father's palace, she was so happy she ran through the bedrooms and bounced on all the beds. (Mary was a large woman – but there is no record of the damage to the beds)

Slimy William

William had a girlfriend called Betty Villiers. Mary's father, James II, tried to stir up trouble between the couple. He said his spies had found out all about Betty Villiers – what was she going to do about it?

What she decided to do was have a very sharp word with William. But Willy used weasel words to worm his way out of it. 'I swear to you by all that is most sacred that I've done nothing wrong!' he lied.

Mary, the mug, believed him.

William sacked the spying servants ... and went on seeing Betty Villiers.

Dreadful deaths

Mary died in 1694 from smallpox. She was only 32 years old.

William died eight years later after falling off his horse. The horse stumbled on a mole hill.

He broke his collar bone and his surgeon 'set' it. He'd probably have recovered but he stupidly chose to return to Kensington Palace that evening. The coach ride was long and the Stuart roads rough. The broken bone was jerked out of place. This time it didn't heal and an infection eventually killed him. He died despite some incredible medicines ... like powdered crabs' eyes!

The supporters of James II (who wanted the old king back) were thrilled. Over the years they drank many toasts to the mole that dug that hole.

Slimy Stuart facts

Are you a mastermind or a mug? Answer these questions *without cheating and looking at the answers first!* Score five or more and you're a Stuart Mastermind.

1 What souvenir could you buy at the coronation of Charles II?
a) A slice of coronation cake.
b) A coronation mug.
c) A piece of Charles's coronation robe.

2 Samuel Pepys wrote a famous diary in the middle of the Stuart period. What did he write with?
a) A fountain pen.
b) A typewriter.
c) The feather of a mongoose.

3 What would you do with a 'lobster tail pot'?
a) Eat it.
b) Go fishing with it.
c) Wear it.

4 How much would you expect to pay a well-trained maid in the middle of the 17th century?
a) Two pounds a year.
b) Twenty pounds a year.
c) A hundred pounds a year.

5 When Queen Henrietta first saw her baby Charles (later Charles II) what were her first words?
a) 'He looks just like his father.'
b) 'He is so beautiful I am quite, quite proud of him.'
c) 'He is so ugly I am ashamed of him.'

6 What was the London speed limit for coach drivers set in 1635?

a) Thirty miles an hour.

b) Three miles an hour.

c) Twelve miles an hour.

7 A well-known cure for measles was to go to bed with…

a) A warm drink of rum.

b) A warm brick.

c) A warm sheep.

8 At the siege of Basing House the Roundheads ran out of bullets. What did they do?

a) Made new ones from lead coffins dug up from the local graveyard.

b) Made new ones from lead off the church roof.

c) They picked up Cavalier bullets and fired them back.

9 Where would rich Stuart people get false teeth from?

a) Carpenters made wooden ones.

b) Potters made china ones.

c) Poor people sold their good ones.

10 The Stuarts had some strange names for their dance tunes. Which of these is NOT a Stuart dance tune?

a) *An Old Man's A Bed Full Of Bones*

b) *Punk s Delight*

c) *My Lady's a Wild Flying Dove*

Answers:

1 b) They were the first coronation souvenirs sold in Britain.

2 a) The fountain-pen didn't work too well and most people stuck with the old quill pen for another 200 years, but Pepys did use one of the first fountain pens from time to time.

3 c) The lobster pot was the name given to the Roundheads' helmets because of their curious shape. The neck guard was like a lobster's tail.

FLAP FLAP

4 a) A manservant would earn double what a maid could earn. A steward (the head servant) who ran a large house for its owner would expect £20 and the Earl of Bedford paid his steward the huge sum of £40 a year.

YE GODS BEDFORD, THAT'S OVER THREE POUNDS A MONTH!

WHAT IF EVERYONE WANTED THAT MUCH?

YOU'LL RUIN US!

5 c) Later, Charles grew up to agree with her. 'Odds fish, I am an ugly fellow,' he claimed. He said it!

6 b) Of course there were no policemen with speed traps – but if a coach overtook a walking law-officer he could face a fine.

7 c) 'Sheep', Stuart doctors said, 'are easily infected with measles and draw the sickness to themselves, by which means some ease may happen to the sick person.'

8 a) They scattered a lot of bones around but thoughtfully chalked the names of the dead on the wall so they would not be forgotten.

9 c) 'If a gentleman has lost his teeth there are dentists who will insert into his gums teeth pulled from the jaws of poor youths.' - *Advert*, 1660

10 c) This is a 1960's pop song. A 'punk' in Stuart times was a wild woman. a) and b) are genuine Stuart dance tunes and other titles included *Petticoat Wag* and *Dusty my dear*. Scotland had the delightful, *The Lamb's Wind*.

Stuart women and children

Women have had a pretty hard time in many eras of history. But some modern historians believe that Stuart women weren't too badly off – compared to the Tudor women who lived before them or the Georgians who came after them. Stuart women had the usual problems of staying beautiful, of course…

Ten beastly ways to beauty

Stuart Superwoman April 1664

Beauty Tips
PAGE

editor

Girls! Do *you* want to look special for that man in your life? Here are the top ten tips from our Beauty Editor, Patricia Pasteface.

1 Hair flair – want to have those lovely locks glowing like gold? Then why not try washing them in rhubarb juice and white wine? If you prefer to be a red-head then dye it with radish and leaves from a privet hedge.

2 Silky skin – don't let spots spoil that special date. If you have spots then why not try rubbing in the blood of: a freshly killed cockerel or a pigeon? (But, girls, don't forget to wash the blood off before you leave the house!)

3 Pale complexion – we know men love that pale and interesting look. If you have a weather-beaten face then burn the jaw bone of a pig and grind it to a powder. Mix with poppy oil and rub it into the skin. It'll turn as pale and pink as that pig in no time. Of course every woman wears chicken-skin gloves at night to keep those fair hands soft and white.

4 Sparkling eyes – spread a cloth on the grass on any night in the month of May. In the morning it will be soaked with dew. Wring out the dew and collect it in bottles. A quick rinse will make sore red eyes as good as new. But remember, only *May* dew will do.

5 Body beautiful – soak for two or three hours in a bath that's waist deep. Fill the bath with three gallons of milk then stir in a boiled mixture of violet petals, rosemary, fennel, mallow and nettles. Step out of the bath then go to bed and sweat, being careful not to catch a cold.

6 Farewell to foul freckles – wash those ugly freckles away with water of strawberries or the juice from watercress.

7 Dental delight – take the herb rosemary and the alum flower and burn them. Clean your teeth with the ashes for that sweet, sweet smile. And remember … sleeping with your mouth open helps keep teeth white.

8 Rout the wrinkles – if your face has more creases than a cockerel's crest then wash them away with a mixture of elder flowers, irises, mallows and bean blossom.

9 In tune with the moon – wash your face in the weeks when the moon is growing smaller. Use a sponge morning and night in those two weeks and your beauty's guaranteed.

10 Teen queen – stay looking like a 15-year-old by washing in a mixture of eggs, asses milk and cinnamon spice.

These sound pretty useless treatments – but at least they were *harmless*. That's more than could be said for the gruesome Elizabethan make-up of a hundred years before. This had involved rubbing poisonous lead mixtures into the skin. And cleaning your teeth with ashes doesn't sound too tasty, but Stuart teeth were healthier than in most ages.

Of course, women were not only told they should be beautiful: they were also told how they should behave. You will notice that, as usual, it is a man who is telling them…

The English Housewife by Gevase Markham

THE NOTABLE HOUSEWIFE MUST…

· be brave · be patient

· be tireless · speak wisely…
WAAA!
A STITCH IN TIME SAVES NINE

· … but not too much · be secret in her affairs
mmmmf
– DON'T SAY I TOLD YOU THIS BUT…

Witches

As in most other ages, most of the people accused of being witches in Stuart times were women. King James I was fascinated by witches. He believed there were several black-magic plots to kill him before he came to the English throne. He even wrote a book about witchcraft.

But the English were never quite as harsh towards witches as the Scots. A horrible history story from Victorian times could well be true…

The Witch of Irongray

'In the reign of James I, or in the early years of his son Charles's reign, there is a tale of a woman burned as a witch in the parish of Irongray in Scotland. In a little mud-walled cottage lived a poor woman who earned a little money by spinning wool and weaving stockings. She lived alone and was often seen on a summer's evening, sitting on a jagged rock above the Routing Stream.

Sometimes she would gather sticks, late on a November evening, among the rowan tree roots. Lying in her window she sometimes had a black-letter bible which had two brass clasps of a grotesque design to fasten it closed. When she went to church her lips were sometimes seen to be moving. She was known to forecast showers or sunshine at certain times and her forecasts were often right.

The Bishop of Galloway was urged to punish this woman for being a witch. He was afraid he'd be reported to the king if he failed to deal with her so he ordered her to be brought before him near to the Routing Stream.

She was dragged roughly from her home. Several neighbours were called to declare the wicked things that she had done.

She was sentenced to be drowned in the Routing Stream. But the crowd insisted that she should be shut up in a tar barrel and thrown into the River Cluden. Unwillingly the bishop agreed. The wretched woman was enclosed in a barrel, fire was set to it and it was rolled in a blaze into the waters of the Cluden.'

The unlucky woman was Alice Mulholland. The English gave up hanging witches during the reign of James II and they didn't have any more witch trials after 1712. But the Scots went on persecuting witches a little longer. The last to be burned for witchcraft in Scotland was in 1722.

Women were still 'ducked' on a stool into freezing water if they nagged too much. That nasty habit went on until 1817 when Sarah Leeke was ducked. It all ended as a bit of a joke – when Sarah Leeke was ducked they couldn't get her under the water. The pool they'd chosen was too shallow!

Cheerless children

Would you like to have been a child in Stuart times? If you were the child of a strict Puritan then you could have started off life badly by being stuck with a rotten religious name. Which of the following nasty names were really given to nippers?

1. SILENCE
2. HELPLESS
3. FORSAKEN
4. MISERICORDIA
5. FIGHT-THE-GOOD-FIGHT-OF-FAITH
6. SORRY-FOR-SIN
7. GOOD-FOR-NOTHING
8. POSTHUMA
9. LAMENT
10. DISCIPLINE

Answer: All except number 7 were Stuart christening names.

The Puritans also had:
Kill-sin, Increase, Faint-not, Desire, Search-the-scriptures, Remember, Seek-wisdom, If-Christ-had-not-died-thou-hadst-been-damned, Safety on-high.

There was also a name for those of us who have normal names - it was 'Be-thankful'!

Of course, you had to survive the christening ceremony in church. Stuart superstition said it was a good sign if the baby cried at its christening. That was a sign that the evil spirits were leaving it. Just to be on the safe side, the godparent holding the baby would give it a sharp nip to make it howl.

Toothy trouble

If you survived your christening then you still had to survive growing up. Many babies died because Stuart families didn't understand about germs. For every 100 people who died in Stuart times, 40 were under two years old.

Some rich parents couldn't be bothered with wailing and whingeing babies. They sent the baby away to nurses in the country until the child was old enough to walk and talk. They visited it from time to time.

Of course when a baby starts to cut its teeth it tends to cry a lot. The nurses had an answer. In *The Queen's Chest*, published in 1664, there was a little recipe for soothing those painful gums...

Boil the head of a hare. Mix the brains with honey and butter. Rub the mixture on the gums as often as you please.

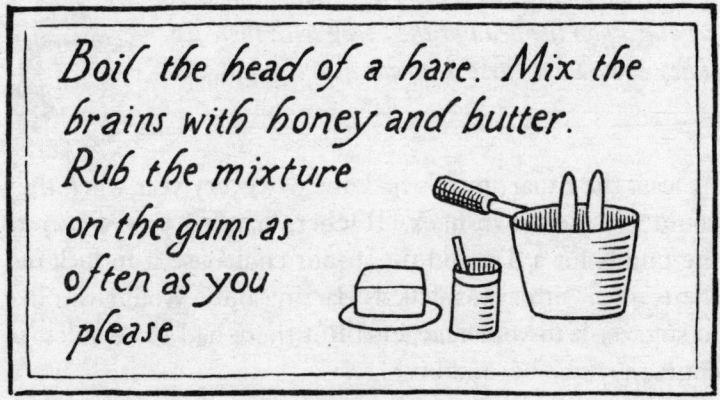

Boil the head of a hare. Mix the brains with honey and butter. Rub the mixture on the gums as often as you please

Switching schools

Would you like a school switch? Probably *not* if it was a Stuart school switch. Because a switch was a thin wooden stick and it was used to beat naughty boys ... girls didn't usually go to school.

Some people thought boys should have this thin 'switch' rather than the stiff wooden 'ferula'...

> *As for the ferula I wish it could be banned from schools. A good birch switch will not break bones or damage limbs. A good switch about the shoulders should be sufficient.*

(Charles Hoole 1660)

Isn't that kind?

The rules of Chigwell school suggested...

> *Schoolmasters should not give more than three strokes of the rod at any one time. They should not strike any scholar upon the head or the cheek with their fist. They should not curse or swear at the pupils.*

At least the Stuart pupils had one day every year when they could get their own back. Teachers handed power over to the pupils for a day and the pupils could use it to lock out the teacher – this was called 'Barring out'. Would you like to suggest it to your teachers? But there had to be rules, of course...

- The school master must know about it beforehand.
- The pupils must behave politely.
- Pupils must not use weapons to injure one another.
- Pupils must not damage the school.

Doesn't sound so much fun now, does it? In fact 'Barring-out day' sometimes got out of hand. In a Birmingham school in 1667 the governors complained...

Some of the scholars, being assisted by certain townsmen, did put into practice a violent exclusion of their master from the school. Though they deserted the school at about nine o'clock at night on the 27th November, some returned on 28th with unruly members of the town wearing masks and carrying pistols. Then they not only threatened to kill their school master but, for two hours, tried to break in. They threw stones and bricks at him through the window and broke through the walls of the school to endanger his life.

That sounds a bit more lively, doesn't it? The report went on to say...

Some governors think the master should pardon the offending scholars. But they believe the people from the town who joined the riot should be punished by the law. Any pupil who attempts to exclude the master again should be expelled.

So now you know. Getting the town toughs to attack your teacher is *not allowed*. Not even if teacher's a bit of a crook like the ones at Caistor School in 1631 where the school was *supposed* to be free and…

The schoolmasters are not to expect, demand or extract money for teaching any child, other than their wage.

But they did. The rich parents paid the school teacher *extra* money to give their children *extra* lessons. (Of course, nowadays your teachers are so well paid they wouldn't dream of taking extra money from your parents, would they?)

In 1673 Bathusa Makin opened a school for young ladies. She wrote that there would be more schools like hers but they wouldn't be popular with men. '1 expect to meet with many scoffs,' she said, 'because men would be ashamed of their ignorance.' In other words, brainy girls would show the boys up. (She could be right.)

Joyless jobs
Stuart boys would often be sent to learn a trade as an *apprentice* as soon as they left school. Their father would pay a skilled craftsman to teach his son a trade.

This was like another five to eight years of school … only *worse* in some cases. A boy called Francis was sent to a scrivener for eight years to learn how to be a clerk. After three years he was suffering so much he wrote home to his father to complain. The letter may have gone something like this…

January 1643

Dear Dad

That's it I want to come home. Three years I've suffered here with old Bootley and I've had enough. There are three apprentices here and one of them is Bootley's own son. So guess who gets all the rotten jobs? That's right. Me

It's bad enough getting the boring copying to do, But you didn't tell me I'd have to slave in the house as well! Who cleans the boots before breakfast? Me. And who empties the ashes, fills the coal bucket, sweeps the shop, and cleans that nasty long sink? Me. I'm supposed to be learning to be a clerk!

Then Mrs Bootley uses me like a manservant. I'm in the middle of writing and what happens? The kitchen maid comes and orders me to fetch Mrs Bootley a farthing's worth of mustard or a pint of vinegar. Last week she sent me for a pint of beer, didn't like the taste, and sent me back to change it.

You paid old Boot-face thirty pounds for this. AND you paid him a hundred pounds for my good behaviour. If I make trouble you lose that hundred pounds. I know. So I daren't make a fuss. Just take me away from here! Your loving son

Frances

What happened to Francis after the letter was sent?

1 Francis's father complained to Mr Bootley and things got better.

2 Francis's father complained to Mr Bootley and Mr Bootley beat Francis with a cane...

3 Francis's father took his son away from Mr Bootley and lost his £130.

Answer: 2 Francis wrote ... I was little the better for writing to my father. No sooner had I come into my master's house than he went into his cupboard and fetched out a sturdy cane. Without 'By your leave' or 'With your leave' he lifts his sword arm like a fencer and gives me a lusty thwack across the shoulders. He said, 'I'll teach you to make complaints to your father.'

Many masters *deliberately* treated their apprentices badly. They took a dozen apprentices at £50 each and made them so miserable that they ran away. The parents couldn't get the money back and the masters were hundreds of pounds richer.

Awful apprentices
The teenage apprentices often went around in gangs and were the 'problem' kids of their time. When the Puritans abolished holidays it was the London apprentices who went on strike to get them back.

In Tudor Newcastle there had been laws to stop them 'playing dice and cards, drinking, dancing and embracing 'women'. The older people thought the apprentices looked disgraceful with their silk-lined clothes, bearded faces and daggers at their belts: 'They are more like raging ruffians than decent apprentices.'

Fifty years later when James I came to the throne, nothing much had changed – except the apprentices had to find new ways to make trouble, and the old fogies had to find new ways to stop them.

A 1603 law said, 'Apprentices are forbidden to use any music by night or day in the streets. Nor shall they wear their hair long over their ears.'

Young people of today argue with their parents and their teachers about hair styles – perhaps you do! Then just be glad you didn't live in 17th-century Newcastle. Anyone found guilty of having long hair was...

• Sentenced to jail...
• *And* to having a basin put over the head and the hair chopped off along the edges!

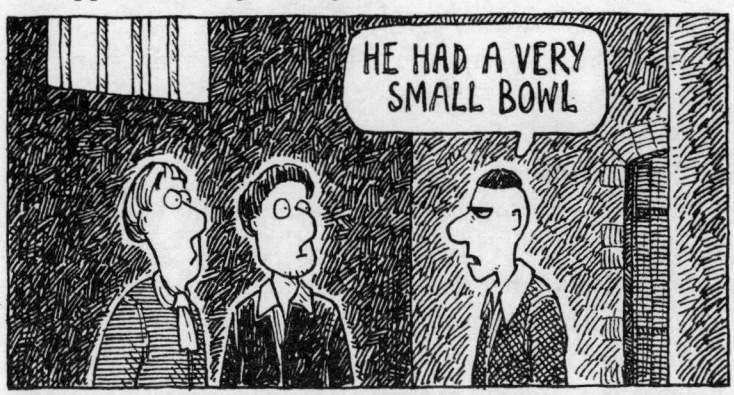

University students had the same problem. In 1636 Edmund Verney went for his final exam with the head of his college. He wrote home to Dad, 'The head spoke to me very politely as he could not find fault with my hair, because I had cut it before I went to him.'

Battered bride

There was some sort of equality for women in Stuart times. Boys were beaten with sticks … girls were beaten too!

Young Frances Coke didn't want to marry the rich John Villiers. John had occasional fits of madness when he might smash a glass in his hand and bleed all over the floor. Maybe Frances didn't fancy mopping up after him.

Her Father, Sir Edward Coke, said she *had* to marry John Villiers. There were 10,000 good reasons why she should – John was paying Sir Edward £10,000 for Frances's hand.

Frances ran away with her mother and hid. Sir Edward found the house, battered down the door and dragged the girl from the cupboard where she was hiding.

£10,000 FOR MY HAND ? I WONDER WHAT THE REST OF ME IS WORTH ?

'Marry John Villiers or else,' she was told.

'No,' she replied.

So she got the 'or else'. She was 'tied to the bedposts and whipped.'

She changed her mind – wouldn't you? – and finally agreed to marry the loathsome John Villiers.

Frances Coke was just fourteen years old at the time. Frances and John did not make a happy couple. She found a new boyfriend and ran off to live with him.

But it wasn't a happy ending. She lost her fortune to John Villiers's grasping family and she died in poverty.

Talk like a Stuart

Every age has its own slang. Are any of your schoolmates 'bagpipes' or 'barnacles?' (That's chatter boxes or hangers-on, of course.)

Do you have any 'muck in the sack of your kicks' at the moment? (That's money in the pocket of your trousers, if you hadn't guessed.)

Slimy Stuart villains

A book called *Leathermore s Advice* was published in 1666 and the writer complained…

> Towards night there come Hectors, Trepanners, Guilts, Pads, Biters, Prigs, Divers, Lifters, Kid-Nappers, Vouchers, Mill-kens, Pymen, Decoys, Shop-lifters, Foilers, Bulkers, Droppers, Famblers, Dannakers, Crosbyters… generally known as Rooks.

You might not understand what he was writing about, but you get the picture. Stuart towns were not a safe place to be at night.

Why not amaze and impress your teacher/parent/gerbil by reciting this sad tale. They will certainly say, 'Well!/ Gosh!/Eeeek!' … and then ask you to explain.

The fate of the fustilugs

There once was a fustilugs[1] slabberdegullion[2]
Who grew up quite buffle[3], not dossy[4].
He learned how to mill–ben[5], to pug[6] and to dub[7]
Then this dunaker[8] jiggled[9] a hossy[10].

But at budging[11] a beak[12] he was such a fopdoodle[13]
He was caught and sent down to the clink[14].
'Oh the cage[15] belly-timber[16] is pannam[17] and old horse[18]
And we only get water to drink.'

1 a dirty eared child
2 a slob
3 stupid
4 brainy
5 break and enter houses
6 steal
7 pick locks
8 animal thief
9 rustled
10 horse – all right, this is *not* a Stuart slang word – but *you* try

finding something to rhyme with 'dossy'
11 dodging
12 constable – later a judge
13 useless person
14 the name of a London prison
15 prison
16 food
17 bread
18 dried, salted beef

Beware the bung-napper![1]

If you wanted to survive in Stuart Britain you had to know who was out to get you. Can you match the criminals to their methods and their crimes?

THIS CRIMINAL	WOULD...	AND...
DARKMAN'S BUDGE	WAIT BY THE ROADSIDE	STEAL FROM YOUR HOUSE
SNOWDROPPER	HIDE IN YOUR HOUSE TILL DARK	ROB STAGE COACHES
SNUDGE	PLAY CARDS WITH YOU	LET A GANG INTO YOUR HOUSE
THIMBLE-RIGGER	CLIMB INTO YOUR HOUSE	STEAL YOUR WASHING
FOOTPAD	WALK PAST YOUR HEDGE	CHEAT YOU OUT OF MONEY

1 purse–snatcher

And that's not all! A *sneaksman* was the lowest sort of thief. He just sort of lurked around and pinched anything he could get his hands on. A bit like next-door's cat.

- A *foist* would dip his hand into your pocket or purse while a *nip* would use a knife to cut a purse that hung from your belt. We'd call them pickpockets today.

- A *leatherhead* or a *ding boy* would simply beat you up and take your money – a bit like the school bully. (Note: It is *not* a good idea to call the school bully either of these names!)

- A *varnisher* would give you a fake coin – smartened up with (guess what?) a coat of varnish.

- Nothing was safe! Because you may find a *buffernapper* has pinched your dog or a *bleating cull* might snaffle your sheep. (Would we call him a *ram raider* today?)

110

Aren't you just glad you live in the 20th century where all you have to worry about are hackers (who don't use a hacksaw), twockers (who don't steal twocks), muggers (who aren't after your mug), armed robbers (who have three arms … left-arm, right-arm and fire-arm) and serial killers…

Fox your friends

Say these two sentences to a friend then ask which of the two makes sense:

1. I'M NOT PLAYING MONOPOLY WITH YOU BECAUSE YOU USE A BRISTLE

2. DID YOU KNOW THE RIVER AVON RUNS THROUGH THE TOWN OF BRISTLE?

Answer: 1 A bristle was a dice that was 'loaded' to show any number the thrower wanted. It was used by slimy Stuart cheats.

Stuart fun and games

Fun at the fair

Stuart fairs were great holiday events. Lots of food … and fighting. Lots of weird and wonderful entertainments. Can you picture this rope dancer from the description in the *Daily Courant* newspaper?

the Daily Courant

DANCERS ON A ROPE

At the Great Booth will be seen the famous company of rope dancers, the greatest performers of dancing on the low–rope, and walking on the slack and sloping rope. They are said to be the only amazing wonders in the world in every thing they do.

There you will see the Italian Scarramouch dancing on a rope. He has a wheel-barrow in front of him with two children and a dog in it. He also has a duck on his head who sings to the crowd and causes much laughter.

John Evelyn described a fire eater in his diary...

He devoured glowing coals before us, chewing and swallowing them. He melted a beer glass and ate it quite up. Then he take a live coal on his tongue and put on it a raw oyster. The coal was blown with bellows until it flamed and sparkled in his mouth. There it remained until the oyster was quite boiled. Then he melted tar and wax which he drank down as it flamed; I saw it flaming in his mouth a good while.

Slimy toads

If you lived in Stuart times you'd probably look forward to the annual fair in your area. Just like today's fairs there was magic, excitement and danger . . . and special food.

But would you like to eat a slithery, slimy *live* toad? Probably not. What about if someone offered you money to swallow that toad? Probably not. Because, not only would it be disgusting, it would probably kill you.

So one of the strangest sights at a Stuart fair would be the Mountebank. (A Mountebank was a man who called himself a doctor.) Imagine him going through the fair selling miracle cures...

'Ladies and gentlemen,' the Mountebank cries. 'Do you ever suffer from problems of digestion and distempers? Why suffer when you can try Doctor Cureall's Herbal Healing Tonic? This tonic is made from herbs to a secret and ancient recipe from ancient Egypt. It includes such rare ingredients as powdered mummy from an Egyptian pharaoh.'

'Rubbish!' someone calls from the crowd around him.

'Ah! We have a disbeliever, do we? Well, sir, what must I do to prove my miracle cure? I'll tell you what I'll do ... I'll poison someone, then cure them!' the Mountebank smiles. He reaches into his black bag and pulls out a fat, warty toad. 'I have here a toad. Probably the most poisonous creature known to mankind. If anyone swallowed this then it would lead to almost certain death, would it not?'

There is a muttering amongst the crowd. They agree toads are poisonous.

'My miracle cure will defeat even the might of a toad's powerful poison. Now, can I have a volunteer to swallow this toad? Some brave person?' The Mountebank turns to the man who shouted 'Rubbish!' and offers it to him. The man turns his head away in disgust.

'Very well, I shall pay someone *six pence* if they will offer to swallow this deadly creature then be revived by my potion. No one? *Ten* pence, anyone? Very well I shall offer *one shilling* plus a free bottle of Doctor Cureall's Herbal Healing Tonic – which is worth a shilling itself. Do I have a volunteer?'

A shabby young man steps forward. 'I'll do it for a shilling,' he says.

'Ladies and gentlemen, a round of applause for this gallant young man.' The crowd claps. The noise of their clapping brings more fair visitors into the circle round the rough wooden stage. Everyone is hooked on this performance now.

Doctor Cureall pulls the stopper from a dark-blue bottle. I shall have the Herbal Healing Tonic ready to administer. But don't worry, young man, Doctor Cureall's tonic will work even if you are *dead!*'

The Mountebank passes the toad to the young man who looks at it nervously. 'One shilling,' Doctor Cureall promises, 'just for swallowing this creature.'

The scruffy young man closes his eyes, tilts back his head … and quickly pushes the toad into his gaping mouth. He gives a huge swallow. The crowd gasps, and waits.

The volunteer's face begins to crease in pain. He gives a low moan and clutches at his stomach. His eyes begin to pop with the strain. He falls to his knees and cries, 'The cure! The cure!'

The Mountebank holds the bottle in the air, well out of the reach of the cringing young man. 'Shall I give him the cure?'

Someone laughs nervously, 'Let him die. Serve him right!'

But the young man screams in agony. 'Give him the cure,' someone shouts. Others join in, 'For God's sake, give him the cure!'

By now the young man is lying on the stage, rolling in agony. Doctor Cureall slowly reaches down and forces the bottle between the lips of the dying man. He drinks it greedily. Slowly his twisting body calms and he lies still on the stage. The crowd is silent.

The young man opens one eye. Then the other eye. He raises his head from the stage. He looks at his stomach with wonder and sits up. 'It's a miracle!' he cries. 'Here, Doctor Cureall, don't give me a shilling...
just give me another bottle of that
Herbal Healing Tonic!' He jumps
to his feet and clutches at his two
free bottles as if they were liquid
gold. The Mountebank turns to
the crowd. 'Now, who else
would like a bottle – only
a shilling for a bottle of the
secret of life itself'

The crowd pushes and jostles to force money into the happy Mountebank's hand.

It is the end of the busy fair. And it is dark behind the Mountebank's stage. The doctor is counting his money when a by young man approaches. 'Have you had a good day, Doc?'

'Eight pounds and 16 shillings, my toady-eating friend. And here are your five shillings for your excellent job.'

The young man jingles the coins happily in his hand and turns to find a tavern to spend them in.

'I think you've forgotten something,' the Mountebank says sharply.

The young man grins a yellow-toothed grin. He reaches into his pocket and hands something over to Doctor Cureall.

A fat, warty toad.

Toad-eating facts

1 No one is quite sure how toad-eaters managed the trick. The young toad eater was probably a clever magician who *appeared* to eat a toad but never did.

2 When a toad is attacked it squeezes out a deadly milky poison. If the smell doesn't put off the attacker then the taste will. A dog trying to eat a toad will start foaming at the mouth and howling.

3 Even the Romans knew about toad poison. There is a record of Roman women using toad poison to kill their husbands. They threw the toad into boiling water and the poison rose to the surface. It was skimmed off and fed to the unlucky man.

4 Italian poisoners of Stuart times had learned to blend toad poison with salt.

5 Toad-eating was considered to be the lowest form of job. Clowns and jugglers at the fairs were more respected than a toad-eater.

6 A real creep will do anything for their boss, no matter how disgusting. So in Stuart times a new word was invented for creeps – 'toad-eater'.

7 Later the word changed to 'toady'. So instead of calling a pupil a teacher's pet' they would be called a 'toady' in Stuart times.

8 Some people swore they saw the toady swallow the toad. So, was it possible? There is just a chance that toad eaters really did swallow live toads … and live. How? The toads could have been 'pets' who learned to trust their trainers. He might even allow them to sit on his tongue for a while so they didn't get excited by the idea and sweat poison. Then, on the day of the fair, he popped the happy toad on his tongue – and swallowed it quickly before the toad could react.

THIS ONE'S OLIVER, THE OTHER ONE'S JAMES, AND THERE'S CHARLES. AND WILLIAM AND...

9 A young man who was fit, and who had just eaten a good meal, could probably survive a toad swallowing in this way. It could give him stomach and head pains, but he'd live.

10 A toady who wasn't fit could well die.

Next time someone offers you some sausage in a batter pudding, known as 'Toad in the Hole', you'll know what to say: 'Did I ever tell you about people who ate real toads...'

ON SECOND THOUGHTS I'M NOT HUNGRY

Eating toads wasn't the only fun you could have at a Stuart fair. There were prizes to win on the side shows and there were presents to take home for the family. Gifts to take home from the fair were known as 'fairings.' A popular fairing was a coloured ribbon.

There are many songs written about fairs. One of the most famous is 'O dear, what can the matter be?'

> *O dear, what can the matter be?*
> *Dear, dear, what can the matter be?*
> *O dear, what can the matter be?*
> *Johnny's so long at the fair.*

> *He promised to buy me a pair of sleeve buttons,*
> *A pair of new garters that cost him just tuppence,*
> *He promised he'd bring me a bunch of blue ribbons*
> *To tie up my bonny brown hair.*

But, did you know … young men would often go to the fair, drink too much beer and fall asleep. In the 1700s the navy 'Press Gang' would kidnap these sleeping young men and take them off to serve in the navy.

That could be why Johnny was so long at the fair … he'd been press-ganged!

THE FAIR'S OVER LADDY, GET UP THAT RIGGING!

Sick Stuart sport

The Tudors, like Henry VIII and Elizabeth I, were supposed to live in cruel times, while the Stuarts are often thought of as 'modern'. The terrible truth is the Stuarts could be just as vicious as the Tudors ... or the Vikings for that matter! Here's a report from the end of the Stuart age. Make up your own mind about how 'modern' the Stuarts were from this report by a foreign visitor...

June 23, 1710

Towards evening we drove to see the bull-baiting, which is held here nearly every Monday in two places. On the morning of the day the bull, or any other creature that is to be baited is led round. It takes place in a large open space or courtyard, on two sides of which high benches have been made for the spectators. First a young ox or bull was led in and fastened by a long rope to an iron ring in the middle of the yard; then about thirty dogs, two or three at a time, were let loose on him but he made short work of them, goring them and tossing them high in the air about the height of the first storey. Then amid shouts and yells the butchers to whom the dogs belonged sprang forward and caught their beasts right side up to break their fall. They had to keep hold of the dogs to hinder them from returning to the attack without barking. Several had such a grip of the bull's throat or ear that their mouths had to be forced open with poles

When the bull had stood it tolerably long, they brought out a small bear and tied him up in the same fashion. As soon as the dogs had at him he stood up on his hind legs and gave some terrific buffets; but if one of them got at his skin he rolled about in such a fashion that the dogs thought themselves lucky if they came out safe from beneath him.

But the most diverting and worst of all was a common little ass, who was brought out saddled with an ape on his back. As soon as a couple of dogs had been let loose on him he broke into a prodigious gallop - for he was free, not having been tied up like the other beasts - and he stamped and bit all around himself. The ape began to scream most terribly for fear of falling off. If the dogs came too near him, he seized them with his mouth and twirled them round shaking them so much that they howled prodigiously. Finally another bull appeared, on whom several crackers had been hung; when these were lit and several dogs let loose on him on a sudden, there was a monstrous hurly-burly. And thus was concluded this truly English sport, which vastly delights this nation but to me seemed nothing very special   Zacharius von Uffenbach

In 1760 bull-baiting was finally banned in Newcastle-upon-Tyne. A young sailor was gored in an accident. The 'sport' was banned because it was dangerous to the public, not because it was cruel to the animals!

Anne (reigned 1702-1714)

Anne was shy, stout, short-sighted and suffered from gout. In fact her gout was so painful that she had to be carried to her coronation!

She had 17 babies and 16 died. Only William survived infancy ... then *he* died at the age of 11.

Slimiest act

Would you betray your dear old dad? Anne did. Anne was Protestant and didn't want to follow her Catholic father, James II, during the 'Glorious Revolution'.

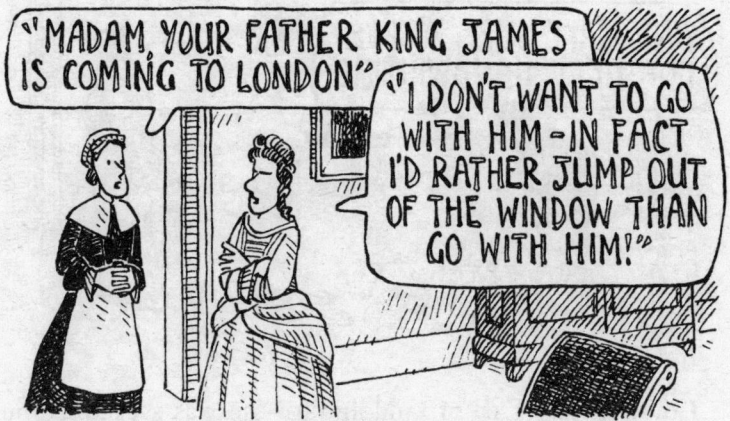

She didn't *exactly* 'jump out of the window' but she *did* make a secret escape at night down the back stairs. James went into exile and never sat on the throne again ... but Anne got her (very) fat bum on the throne 14 years later.

The Spiteful Stuart

Anne died in 1714 – she had grown so fat that when she died her coffin was almost square. Anne was the last of the Stuarts. Some said she was the *best*.

Her *friends* and *family* didn't say that.

Among the people she was spiteful towards were…

• Best friend Sarah Churchill - she was sent away when it suited the queen. Sarah was in tears, pleading for another chance. All Anne could reply was, 'Put it in writing'.

• Loyal adviser Earl of Godolphin – he was sacked. Anne didn't even tell him to his face. She just sent a message for him to snap his symbol of authority (a white staff) and get out.

• Her great army commander, Marlborough, who had won brilliant battles for her – he was sacked with a letter so nasty that he threw it into the fire and never spoke of it again.

• Her step-brother, James – Anne was quick to spread the rumour that he wasn't really her father's son; he was just a baby smuggled into the birth room in a warming pan. She then did an about-turn and tried to get baby James the throne when she died, instead of…

• Her successor George I – she knew his family would come to the throne of Britain when she died but she banned any of them from entering the country while she lived. Her main reason was simply that she disliked George.

For over 100 years her family had battled with Parliament. Anne brought peace by attending the House of Lords in person. She sat on the throne and listened to the debates – or in winter sat on a bench by the fire. When she died her doctor said, 'She welcomed death like a weary traveller welcomes sleep.'

Some Members of Parliament couldn't believe the news. 'She's not dead!' they tried to argue.

'Dead!' came the reply. 'She's as dead as Julius Caesar. '

Epilogue

Anne was as dead as Julius Caesar, but the Stuarts weren't quite as dead as a hedgehog squashed on the road. They kept trying to get that throne back. In the next 31 years the family of James II had a couple of attempts – 1715 and 1745 if you're really interested in dates.

A prince from Germany, George I, was invited to take over when Anne died. A new family sat on the throne the Hanovers. George I didn't speak English and never bothered to learn – he was especially cruel to his wife, whom he had locked up for 32 years.

IT'S A PITY SHE'S NOT AROUND

YES. AT LEAST SHE COULD TRANSLATE FOR HIM

The British people did not like George I. But they *didn't* support the Stuart attempts to get the throne back. Why not? Because they hated the slimy Stuarts *more* than the horrible Hanovers!

Kings had been overthrown (or over-throne) before in British history. They had been 'usurped' by powerful *lords*. But the Slimy Stuarts lost power to *the people*. And they didn't manage this once – they did it *twice*.

Now *that's* unpopularity for you. Quite simply, the Brits didn't want a Catholic monarch. The Stuarts kept *saying* they were Protestants – but acting like Catholics. That's sneaky and sly – slimy in fact.

Lots of innocent people died in civil war and revolutions during the reign of the Stuarts. Next time you light a firework on the fifth of November, look into the sparks and say to yourself...

> *Remember, remember the fifth of November,*
> *Gunpowder treason and plot.*
> *Was Guy Fawkes a devil, the Stuarts all saints?*
> *Are we glad that they stopped him . . . or not?*

SLIMY STUARTS

GRISLY QUIZ

**Now find out if you're a
slimy Stuarts expert!**

SUPERSTAR SHAKESPEARE

William Shakespeare used 17,677 different words in his writing. Amazingly, about 1,700 of those were new words! Can you spot the words (or phrases) first used by Shakespeare?

1. A place to stay is...
a) accommodation
b) a hotel
c) hard to find

2. If you're puzzled you say...
a) it's Greek to me
b) I don't understand
c) eh, you what?

3. If you're not mean you're...
a) kind
b) generous
c) sharing your chocolate biscuits

4. If you're unashamed you're...
a) open
b) barefaced
c) a nudist

5. To make someone go faster say...
a) quicken

b) hurry
c) little puff

6. A sudden wind is a...
a) blast
b) gust
c) little puff

7. A children's game is...
a) leapfrog
b) hopscotch
c) hopfrog

8. A reliable person is a...
a) tower of strength
b) brick
c) teacher

9. A person with no friends is...
a) lonely
b) friendless
c) smelly

10. Something that gets smaller…
a) dwindles
b) lessens
c) goes like a jumper in a hot wash

11. An lethal attack on a powerful person is…
a) murder
b) assassination
c) a bad idea

Remember, remember…

Since the Gunpowder Plot was discovered it has passed into English history and is remembered every 5 November. But how many of these funny Fawkes facts are false?

1. In January 1606 Parliament passed a new law. It said that 5 November would become a holiday of public thanksgiving.

2. Guy Fawkes hasn't always been the one on top of bonfires. At different times in history dummies of different people have been burned on 5 November.

3. It wasn't until 1920 that fireworks were added to the 5 November celebrations.

4. For many years the people of Scotton village in Yorkshire refused to celebrate 5 November with fireworks and bonfires.

5. The government decided that the cellars beneath Parliament should be patrolled night and day to prevent another Gunpowder Plot. That patrol stopped a long time ago.

QUICK QUESTIONS

1. At the Civil War battle of Edgehill the famous doctor, William Harvey, settled down with a book as soldiers fell all around him. When he grew cold he pulled what over his legs to keep warm? (Clue: the doctor was no use to them)

2. Charles I was captured by Oliver Cromwell's army and held prisoner in Newcastle. They let him out to play what game in the nearby fields? (Clue: join the club)

3. Charles I went to his execution in 1649 wearing two shirts. Why? (Clue: it was 30 January 1649)

4. Sir Arthur Aston had a wooden leg so he was easily caught in a 1649 Irish battle. He was beaten to death. With what? (Clue: did he put his foot in it?)

5. Oliver Cromwell died in 1658 and the public queued to see his mummified body. But it began to go rotten. What did the government do next? (Clue: you wooden believe it)

6. Charles's head was sewn back on so he'd look good in his coffin. But his tomb was entered many years later and the neck bone stolen. It was used at the dinner table by Henry Halford. For what? (Clue: needed on chops!)

7. In 1653 Charles Culpepper wrote that this plant clears bad chests, cures headaches, worms and indigestion, and the juice kills lice in children's hair. What is this wonder plant? (Clue: it cures nothing and has killed millions)

8. In 1660 Charles II returned and punished the men who had had his dad, Charles I, beheaded. One condemned man had his belly opened and his guts lifted out for burning. How did he shock his executioner? (Clue: you can't keep a good man down)

TEST YOUR TEACHER...

How much does your history teacher know about the 1600s? Test them with this quiz — and if they get more than half wrong, threaten them with the Stuart cure for consumption!

1. Why were Oliver Cromwell's followers called 'Roundheads'?
a) because of the shape of their helmets
b) it was an insulting name given to them by the Cavaliers
c) because of their haircuts

2. Which Stuart king was described as 'a nervous drivelling idiot'?
a) James I
b) Charles I
c) James II

3. How did Charles II describe himself?
a) 'the most handsome man in England'
b) 'the King of Elegance'
c) 'an ugly fellow'

4. Who was the leader of the Gunpowder plot?
a) Guy Fawkes
b) Robert Catesby
c) Simon Montfort

5. Prince Rupert, a Cavalier leader during the Civil War, had a dog he took with him everywhere. What breed was it?
a) a black Great Dane
b) an Irish Wolfhound
c) a white Poodle

6. When he was a prince escaping from England (because his father had lost the Civil War), James II dressed as
a) a girl
b) a servant
c) Little Red Riding Hood

7. In the 1600s, who were Stroller's Priests and what did they do?
a) tramps who performed illegal marriages for couples
b) priests who roamed the countryside doing good works
c) thieves who stole from churches

8. What was a 'bung-napper' in Stuart times?
a) a sleep-walker

134

b) a purse-snatcher
c) a dustman

9. Which of the following was a real 1600s cure for spots?
a) drinking vinegar mixed with chopped-up worms
b) washing in your own pee
c) rubbing in the blood of a freshly killed pigeon

10. Who did Londoners blame for starting the Great Fire of London in 1666?
a) French spies
b) Catholics
c) plague victims

Answers

Superstar Shakespeare
1.a) 2.a) 3.b) 4.b) 5.b) 6.b) 7.a) 8.a) 9.a) 10.a) 11.b)
Anyone who answered c) has a brain like Shakespeare's!
(Dead for 400 years.)

Remember, remember...
1. True. People lit bonfires to celebrate and threw dummies on the fire dressed as Guy Fawkes.
2. True. The first record of this was at Cliffe Hill in

London 1606 where a dummy of the Pope joined Guy Fawkes in the flames.
3. False. Within a few years of the plot people began to use fireworks on November 5.
4. True. This village was where Guy Fawkes used to live and the people didn't think it was fair that Guy should take all the blame.
5. False. A search of the cellars is still carried out before the opening of every Parliament.

Quick Questions
1. Corpses. He was used to cutting them up for experiments so he wasn't too bothered about using them as blankets.
2. Golf. A popular game with his family, and granny Mary Queen of Scots enjoyed it too.
3. Charles didn't want to shiver in the cold in case people thought he was shaking with fear.
4. With his own wooden leg.
5. They replaced the corpse with a painted wooden dummy with glass eyes.
6. As a salt cellar.
7. Tobacco. Culpepper even said tobacco ash was good for cleaning the teeth! Ugh!
8. He sat up and hit the man who was cutting him open! That took guts!

Test your teacher
1.c) 2.a) 3.c) 4.b) 5.c) 6.a) 7.a) 8.b) 9.c) 10.a)

INTERESTING INDEX

Where will you find 'bird-droppings', 'chamberpots',
'rhubarb-juice' and 'toad-eaters' in an index? In a
Horrible Histories book, of course!

138

Terry Deary was born at a very early age, so long ago he can't remember. But his mother, who was there at the time, says he was born in Sunderland, north-east England, in 1946 – so it's not true that he writes all *Horrible Histories* from memory. At school he was a horrible child only interested in playing football and giving teachers a hard time. His history lessons were so boring and so badly taught, that he learned to loathe the subject. *Horrible Histories* is his revenge.

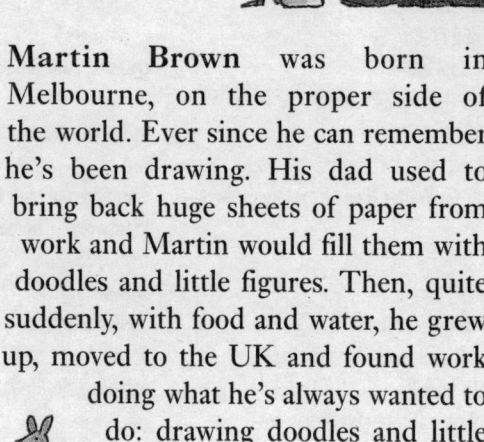

Martin Brown was born in Melbourne, on the proper side of the world. Ever since he can remember he's been drawing. His dad used to bring back huge sheets of paper from work and Martin would fill them with doodles and little figures. Then, quite suddenly, with food and water, he grew up, moved to the UK and found work doing what he's always wanted to do: drawing doodles and little figures.

HORRIBLE HISTORIES

MEASLY
MIDDLE AGES

Terry Deary Illustrated by Martin Brown

◣SCHOLASTIC

With sincere thanks to Helen Greathead.

Scholastic Children's Books,
Euston House, 24 Eversholt Street,
London NW1 1DB, UK

A division of Scholastic Ltd
London ~ New York ~ Toronto ~ Sydney ~ Auckland
Mexico City ~ New Delhi ~ Hong Kong

First published in the UK by Scholastic Ltd, 1996
This edition published by Scholastic Ltd, 2016

Some of the material in this book has previously been published in
Horrible Histories: The Massive Millennium Quiz Book/Horribly Huge Quiz Book

Text © Terry Deary, 1996, 1999
Illustration © Martin Brown, 1996, 1999, 2016

All rights reserved. Moral rights asserted.

ISBN 978 1407 16390 1

Printed and bound by CPI Group (UK) Ltd, Croydon, CR0 4YY

8 10 9 7

The right of Terry Deary and Martin Brown to be identified as the author and illustrator of this work respectively has been asserted by them in accordance with the Copyright, Designs and Patents Act, 1988.

www.scholastic.co.uk

CONTENTS

Introduction

History is horrible. Horribly confusing at times. People can't even agree what happened yesterday . . .

When events happened last year, last century or hundreds of years ago we have no chance of knowing the whole truth . . .

You see the problem? Queen Isabeau was described as a tall, short, dark, fair woman, while French peasants were starving, well-fed, smelly people who had regular baths. Historians and teachers have usually said what they thought and that's not the same as giving the facts.

Who can you believe? No one! Your school-books will probably give you one side of the story . . .

This book will give you the other side . . .

Look at the facts and make up your own mind!

Timeline

410 The Romans in Britain go home. The Early Middle Ages start – usually known as the Dark Ages.

793 First Viking attack is on a monastery where the measly murderous maniacs massacre a few monks.

851 Vikings stay for the winter in England for the first time.

871 Alfred the Great becomes King of Wessex. He rules the south and kindly lets the Danish Vikings rule the north of England.

899 Alfred dead and buried. Alfred the Great becomes Alf-in-a-crate.

1017 Vikings triumph when Knut (or Canute) becomes king of all of England.

1066 Nutty Norman Knights aren't satisfied with living in France. The fighting fellers want Britain too. They invade, and hack English King Harold to bits. Their boss, William the Conker, pinches his throne. Historians usually start the Later Middle Ages here.

1086 Measly meanie William orders a record of all his land and people – so he can tax them. That's how the 'Domesday Book' came about.

1099 European armies set off to capture Jerusalem for the Christian Church. These religious expeditions to the Holy Land are known as Crusades. Away win for Crusaders!

1215 Measly King John gets too greedy for money and power. His barons make him sign the Magna Carta and give power back to the people . . . well, the rich people.

1264 Henry III has trouble with the barons. Rebel leader Simon de Montfort captures him and takes over the country for a year. The royal forces kill Simon within a year and send his head to Lady Mortimer as a gift. (And it wasn't even Christmas!)

1291 The Crusaders are driven out of the Holy land. End of Crusading. Who can these men in cans fight next? Each other!

1303 The Baltic Sea freezes over and starts what we now see as the Little Ice Age (lasts till 1700). Shorter growing seasons –

measly food means hunger and misery for millions.

1315 Floods compared to Noah's flood in the Bible. Ruined crops. Hungrier and miserabler millions. Reports from Europe of people eating cats, dogs, pigeons' droppings and even their own children.

1337 English king Edward III says he's king of France. The French don't agree and so they fight – and fight – and fight (on and off) . . . the start of the Hundred Years War.

1349 The Black Death kills off millions in Europe.

1431 French heroine Joan of Arc is captured after stuffing the English armies in battle. She is burned as a witch.

1453 Hundred Years War ends – 116 years after it started.

1459 Now the English start to fight each other! The Wars of the Roses between the Lancaster family (the red rose) and the York family (the white rose) for the throne of England.

1485 Henry Tudor wins the Battle of Bosworth Field and takes the crown from Richard III.

He unites the red and white roses.

1492 Christopher Columbus discovers America. New World, new age, end of measly Middle Ages (though nothing is ever quite that neat!).

Nasty Normans

The bruised Brits had been battered for a thousand years. In 43 AD the Romans ruined them, in the 5th century Saxons savaged them, in the 9th century the Vikings vanquished them. These were the Dark Ages. (No jokes about them being called 'Dark' because there were a lot of 'knights' around in those days.)

But in 1066 the Normans finally nobbled them. Even teachers know that William the Conqueror landed in 1066 and won the Battle of Hastings. The Nasty Normans took over.

These Normans were Vikings who'd settled in Northern France. They wore pointy hats. And who can blame them? They'd probably heard the story of King Geoffrey of Brittany . . .

King Geoffrey was on a journey to Rome when one of his hawks attacked a chicken in a tavern yard. The inn-keeper's wife was furious. She picked up a big iron pot and threw it at Geoff. It hit the king on the head and killed him. The nasty Normans nipped in and nicked Geoff's land for themselves – wearing helmets to avoid low-flying pots, of course.

The Normans had more writers and monks to record the history of their times. We are no longer 'in the dark' so much. We've left the Dark Ages and entered the Later Middle Ages.

The measly Middle Ages when times were tough and life was hard. Measly food and a measly death by plague . . . or war . . . or torture . . . or simply overwork.

And you think homework, school dinners and history lessons are bad?

Bloodthirsty Bill
Bill the Conqueror was Norman leader in 1066. He said King Edward of England had promised him the English throne – King Harold said the same thing. It was a fight to the death for two tough fellers. The English must have hoped Harold would win because Big Bill was bloodthirsty . . .

• William of Normandy was teased because he was said to be the son of a tanner – a leather-worker. When he attacked Alençon in France in 1048 the people poked fun at him by hanging out skins and shouting, 'Plenty of work for the tanner's son.' This may not have upset *you* – but it made Big Bill furious. He attacked and took 34 prisoners. He paraded them in front of the town walls. As the people of Alençon watched he had their hands and feet cut off and lobbed over the wall. 'That's what'll happen to you if you don't surrender,' he promised. They surrendered.

- William led an army against the Count of Arques. But he marched so fast that he arrived outside Arques town with just six men. The count was waiting with 300 knights. William charged at the Count who turned and galloped for the safety of the town. The 300 knights fled after him. And the Count was William's uncle!

- William wanted Maine in France as well as England. Walter of Mantes claimed both of them, too. Willy captured Wally and his wife and locked them up at Falaise where they died. Some historians say they were poisoned!

- When Will conquered England his reign was harsh. One historian of the time wrote that 'devils had come through the land with fire and sword'. But kind William abolished the death penalty. His last law said, 'I forbid that any man be executed or hanged for any offence, but let his eyes be gouged out.' Of course when an English earl called Waltheof rebelled in 1076 William *forgot* that law. Will gave Walt a chop at Winchester. Measly.

- Some English rebels didn't know how cruel William

could be. They soon found out in the North of England. When Will and his Normans marched on York every English man and boy they met was slaughtered. The army was broken up into smaller wrecking parties. Anything of any use to a human was destroyed – houses burned to the ground, crops burned, cattle killed and farm tools broken. From York to Durham a whole generation of people were wiped out. The roads were scattered with corpses and some said the survivors turned to cannibalism to stay alive. In 1086 York was still almost deserted.

You'll be pleased to know that when Billy the bully tried to do the same to a town called Mantes his horse trod on one of the burning cinders and stumbled. The fall hurt William's great gut and he died in agony.

Family feuds
The Normans didn't like the English – in fact they didn't even like their own family! William the Conqueror's brother, Odo, looked after England while Bill popped back

14

to Normandy. What thanks did Odo get? William threw him in jail!

But Bill's sons were worse. They fought against each other and they even fought against their dear old dad.

William the Conqueror probably couldn't write – he had clerks to do that for him. But if William could have written a letter to his wife Matilda in 1079 . . .

Gerberoi Castle
Normandy
January 1079

Dearest Matilda

You won't believe what our Robert has gone and done! Only gone and beaten his dad in battle thats all! The ungrateful little swine (oops! Pardon my French.)

As you know he was rebelling against my rule so I rode up to Gerberoi with a few hundred lads to sort him out. What does he do? He locks the gates. What do I do? Well, I besiege him don't I? A few hungry weeks without his venison pasties and he'll come begging for mercy, won't he. Always been fond of his grub has our Robert.

But he doesn't! Instead he gets his forces together and comes charging out of the castle! He attacks me! I thought I was supposed to be attacking him!

Of course he's made a big mistake. No one has ever beaten your William in battle as you know. He charges straight for me. Took me by surprise, that did. Knocked me clean off my horse. (Don't worry, my love, he didn't hurt me very much).

The rest of his men began moving in for the kill when that English lad, Toki, rides up with a fresh horse and saves my life. Poor young Toki got killed, but the main thing is I survived.

Now, I don't want to worry you, my darling, but our young Will was fighting on my side and he took a bit of a knock. He's recovering nicely and he's quite a hero. I always thought he was a useless little twerp until now, as you know. But I've decided to give him the throne of England when I go to that great throne in the sky.

As for Robert, he can have Normandy... and the ungrateful little beggar is welcome to it.

Home soon, my dearest one

William
(Conqueror)

Dear William

Just wait till I see our Robert. Fancy knocking you off your horse. He needs teaching some manners. Mind, I always did say you spoilt that boy something rotten. A few whacks with the flat of your sword would have done him no harm at all.

And I suppose you needed Toki's help because you are getting too fat to get back on your horse by yourself. When you get home you are going on a diet my lad.

Do you think you could remember to bring me some of that local woollen cloth? Green if you can get it.

Hurry home. The dogs are missing you, and I'm keeping your throne warm.

Love, Matilda

P.S. Don't forget to wipe your feet before you come into the great hall. I've just had new rushes put down.

William forgave Robert enough to leave him Normandy. But when old William died, young William Rufus got England. This caused a lot of quarrels between the brothers. Each wanted what the other had! A third brother, Henry, got just 5,000 pounds of silver. Who came off best?

Henry, actually.

William Rufus was killed by an arrow when he was out hunting in the New Forest – though some historians think measly Henry might have arranged that 'accident'. Henry took William's English throne, crossed over to Normandy and defeated Robert in battle and took Normandy too.

Henry had the lot. William the Conqueror would have been proud of his murdering, fighting, ruthless son!

The fatal forest

The story about William Rufus being shot in the New Forest is quite well known. His brother, Henry, is suspected of murder because he was in the same forest at the time of William's death.

But, strangest of all is the fate of Richard. Richard who? Richard was the fourth son of William the Conqueror. In 1074 Richard was killed in a riding accident . . . guess where? That's right – in the New Forest.

Richard came to a very painful end. He was charging through the forest on his horse when he collided with a tree. (There were no driving tests for horse riders in those days. If there had been then Richard would have failed.)

Richard was carried back to Winchester, but his injuries were so bad that he died soon after.

William the Conqueror was really upset. (And the tree can't have been too happy either!)

18

Feudal fellows

The Normans brought the 'feudal system' with them. The king was at the top of the heap and peasants at the bottom. They paid for everything – they worked in his fields, worked in his castle, repaired his roads . . . all for free. The peasant then worked on a small patch of his own land in his spare time – not a lot of *that*. If the peasant made any money then he paid taxes to his lord. He paid the lord for grinding his corn, pressing his apples or baking his bread in the measly lord's oven.

The feudal system

I'M A VILLEIN. MY LORD LETS ME LIVE ON HIS LAND. IN RETURN I WORK FOR HIM. I'M A SLAVE–THE LOWEST OF THE LOW

AND I'M EVEN LOWER THAN YOU

I'M A FREE PEASANT. I FARM THE LAND OWNED BY MY LORD. IN RETURN I PAY HIM RENT. I'M POOR AND MISERABLE

I'M POOR, MISERABLE *AND* OVERWORKED

I'M A KNIGHT. I GET MY LAND FROM THE KING. IN RETURN I FIGHT FOR HIM WHEN HE NEEDS ME. NOTHING BUT FIGHT, FIGHT, FIGHT.

AND WHO HAS TO LOOK AFTER THE LANDS WHILE HE'S AWAY? POOR ME!

I'M KING. I GET MY LAND FROM GOD, IN RETURN I SAY PRAYERS, BUILD CHURCHES AND FIGHT FOR HIM. BUT THERE'S ALWAYS SOMEONE AFTER MY THRONE

AND I'M ALWAYS TRYING TO GIVE HIM SONS TO CARRY ON THE ROYAL FAMILY. WHAT A LIFE

I'M GOD. I THOUGHT I'D MADE ALL THESE CHAPS EQUAL. MAYBE MY OTHER SERVANT WILL SORT THIS OUT FOR ME ...

I'M DEATH. THEY'RE ALL EQUAL AS FAR AS I'M CONCERNED. BUT A DOSE OF PLAGUE WILL DO THEM THE WORLD OF GOOD

And the plagues of the 14th century certainly changed the world. After the Black Death there weren't so many peasants about! Peasants became rare . . . and valuable!

MY DEAR LITTLE WORKING CHAP, WORK FOR ME AND I'LL PAY YOU DOUBLE WAGES

IT'S MORE PLEASANT FOR PEASANTS AT PRESENT

THAT'S A BIT BETTER

BUT REMEMBER, I'LL BE BACK

You'd think the peasants would be better off dead – they weren't! After a peasant died the measly lord took his best possessions . . . after all they had only been 'loaned' to the peasant during his lifetime. No wonder . . .

The peasants are revolting

In the measly Middle Ages peasants had a short life, but a miserable one. If overwork didn't kill you then you could die from ordinary things like a rotten tooth. Storing food over the winter could give you a type of food poisoning. Then there were extra nice diseases to look forward to, like St Anthony's Fire – an arm or a leg would get a burning pain . . . then drop off.

When you died you'd hope to go to heaven, but stories went around that a peasant's soul didn't get to heaven – demons refused to carry it because of the horrible smell. They were *really* revolting!

While the peasants froze in the fields, died in ditches or starved in slums, the rich people had 'fun'. In the 14th century Count Robert of Artois had a very pleasant garden. It had . . .

- statues that squirted water at you as you walked past
- a trapdoor that dropped you on to a feather bed
- a hosepipe that squirted water up ladies' dresses
- a statue that squawked at you like a parrot
- a room that greeted you with a thunder storm as you opened the door

HAVE A NICE RELAXING WALK IN THE GARDEN HE SAID... HA, HA.

No wonder the peasants hated the nobles in their castles. The peasants didn't go to school but they knew one simple sum: 'There are more of US than there are of THEM!' In France in 1358 they decided to take over.

The French rebellion was known as the Jacquerie because . . .

1 Any peasant was known as a 'Jacques' (a 'John' in English) – a very common name – so it was a revolt of the 'Johns'! Or . . .

2 They wore padded, boiled-leather jackets as a sort of cheap armour and these jackets were called 'Jacques' – so it was a revolt of the padded-boiled-leather-jackets.

Take your pick. Either explanation could be right – or both could be wrong!

Of course the peasants weren't used to organizing themselves – the nobles were. At first the Jacques murdered a few surprised nobles . . .

| 22 June 1358 | *The PARIS POST* | STILL ONLY 25 CENTIMES |

PEASANTS HAVE KNIGHTS IN DAZE!

The brave battling peasant army has a new leader who is leading the jolly Jacquerie to victory. His name is Will Cale and he's just what the proud peasants need – a strong leader and an experienced soldier.

The revolt began four weeks ago when the peasants grew furious that the French king had been captured by the English and the noble knights had done nothing – except run away. Armed with axes, scythes and pitchforks a 10,000-strong army captured over a hundred castles.

Knights fled with their families – or stayed and died. There are reports of Jacques jokes like roasting a knight on a spit – then forcing his wife to eat the roasted flesh!

Amazingly, two enemies, an English knight and a French knight, joined forces to help Meaux when it suffered a Jacques attack. Captal de Buch and Gaston Phoebus said, 'When noble ladies are in danger a knight's gotta do what a knight's gotta do.'

The knights with an armed force of just 120 cut the Jacques to pieces with their weapons. 'Using swords against scythes is cheating,' Will Cale grumbled.

Now there are rumours that Charles of Navarre is leading a fightback in the east. Cool Cale says, 'Charles of Navarre? Charlie's for the chop – you'll see.'

The Paris Post supports their battling efforts.

Our Brave Boys

But Charles of Navarre used one weapon that Will Cale didn't have . . . brains!

CRUEL CALE CONQUERED

The knights are back in power – where they belong! The Paris Post proudly announces that Wicked Will Cale is dead. The Jacquerie is over! Peace has returned to our troubled towns.

Charles of Navarre's likeable lads faced Will Cale's revolting rats near Paris. Charles suggested that they should talk and Cale, the clot, arrived without a guard. Naturally, Navarre nabbed him and locked him in chains! 'That's cheating!' Cale cried but no one was listening. The leaderless louts of the Jacquerie were massacred – or ran like rabbits.

Cheerful Charles gave Cale the crown he craved – a crown of red hot iron! Then he cut off his hateful head. Now he plans to lead an army of destruction through the region. 'Peasant houses, fields and families will be destroyed!' the noble Navarre promised.

The Paris Post supports the overthrow of the sewer-scented masses and the return of our true leaders.

Champion Charlie

The English peasants were a little way behind the French when it came to rebelling. The English peasants' revolt happened 23 years later in 1381. It wasn't only the French knights who could do a bit of cheating. English King Richard II was pretty good at it too!

The peasants in southern England were so fed up with paying a Poll Tax that they marched on London to see the king. They murdered a few unpopular lords on the way and stuck their heads on long poles . . .

HOW DO I FASTEN THE HEAD ONTO THE POLE?

TRY SOME POLE TACKS!

THAT'S NOT FUNNY

But the lords were probably glad to have their noses well away from the smelly marching feet!

The head of the revolting peasants was called Wat Tyler . . . which could have been a problem . . .

WHAT'S YOUR NAME?

THAT'S RIGHT IT IS!

WHAT IS IT?

YES!

ASK A CIVIL QUESTION...

Anyway, Wat's 20,000 rebels reached London and presented their demands . . .

The lords in London promised to give in to his demands. Wat didn't believe them (what a wise Wat!). His army raised their trusty, rusty swords and marched into London, murdered a bishop, a lord or two and as many foreigners as they could get their scythes on. The 14-year-old king (Richard II) perched on a war horse promised Wat his support! Wat believed the king. (Showing he was really an unwise Wat.) The head peasant boasted . . .

In four days' time all the laws of England shall be coming from my mouth!

But Wat Tyler hadn't read his Horrible History books. He didn't learn from what had happened to Will Cale 23 years before. He agreed to meet the king and his guards at Smithfield.

Some historians say that Wat Tyler began by picking a fight with the king's squire and drew his knife. The Lord Mayor of London (William Walworth) drew his sword and killed Tyler.

The leaderless peasants gave in – just as the French peasants had after Cale's death.

Which just goes to show . . . history repeats itself . . . itself . . . itself . . . itself . . . itself . . . itself . . .

Wat's head was stuck on a lance. The head peasant had become a head-less peasant.

The Saxon streaker

William and his Normans are famous for the Domesday Book – a record of everything everyone owned in England. Once the Normans knew what people were worth then they could tax them. A lot of people forget that the poor people of England knew all about paying tax – long before the Normans arrived.

The most famous tax dodge was the deal made by a famous Saxon streaker called Lady Godiva. Roger of Wendover wrote the first report of her daring deed. Here it is in modern English. What is missing from Roger's version of this famous story?

The good Countess Godiva longed to free the town of Coventry from the misery of heavy taxes. She often begged her measly husband, Earl Leofric of Chester, to free the town of those taxes. The Earl laughed at her. 'Your request is foolish,' he said. 'Don't you see how we need that money? To cut those taxes would be to hurt me. Don't ever mention the subject again.'

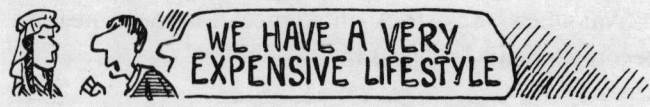

WE HAVE A VERY EXPENSIVE LIFESTYLE

But Countess Godiva had the stubbornness of a woman (a very sexist remark that Wendover would not get away with today). She would not stop pestering her husband about the matter until finally he snapped at her, 'Get on your horse, ride naked through the market place in front of all the people. If you do that I shall grant your request.'

Countess Godiva replied, 'If I am willing to do this do I have your permission?'

'You do,' he agreed.

At this the Countess loosened her hair and let it fall until it covered her body like a veil. She mounted her horse and, escorted by two knights, she rode through the market place without being seen except for her fair legs.

When she had completed the journey she happily returned to her astonished husband and was granted her request. Earl Leofric freed the town of Coventry from all taxes.

When the story was repeated a hundred years later a historian added a new character to the story. A fiendish feller called Peeping Tom. While all the other citizens of Coventry went indoors and gave the Countess some privacy, terrible Tom spied on her.

Which just goes to show – don't believe every story you read ... especially history stories!

Did you know ... ?
A knight owned his peasants – they were considered part of his wealth. If you attacked a knight then he'd probably shut himself safely away in his castle. The next best thing to do was to attack his peasants in the villages around. In 12th-century France, Thomas de Marle (nickname 'The Raging Wolf') attacked his father's peasants, cut off their feet or put out their eyes. What a measly way to go!

Dreadful disease

In 1347 Death strolled through Europe with his scythe, mowing some down and missing others. Swish! Swish! In 1349 he sailed across the Channel to the British Isles. The terrified people never knew who was going to be next. As an Italian diary recorded . . .

> *There appeared certain swellings in the groin and under the armpit, the victims spat blood, and in three days they were dead*

These swellings began to ooze with blood and pus. Purple-black blotches appeared on the skin and you smelled absolutely revolting!

Swell – Spit – Smell – Swish! You were gone.

Death's 'scythe' was the bubonic plague and the piles of bodies grew like chopped straw into a haystack. They were loaded on to carts, dropped into pits – or, in Avignon in France, thrown in the river.

Children were Death's particular favourites when it came to the swish. We now know the real reason for this: if you are an adult then you have had quite a few diseases in your lifetime and build up a 'resistance'; children have had fewer diseases and far less resistance. They die easily.

Of course, preachers said the children probably got what they deserved! One explained . . .

It may be that children suffer heaven's revenge because they miss going to church or because they despise their fathers and mothers. God kills children with the plague — as you can see every day — because, according to the old law, children who are rebels (or disobedient to their parents) are punished by death.

You can see that not much has changed.

DO WHAT I SAY... OR DIE!

SWISH

Crazy cures

The trouble was that doctors didn't know what caused the plague and they didn't know how to cure it. People mistakenly believed you could catch it by . . .

- looking at a victim
- breathing bad air
- drinking from poisoned wells.

In France they said the English did the poisoning, in Spain they blamed the Arabs. In Germany, suspected poisoners were nailed into barrels and thrown into the river. And everyone blamed lepers!

And the cures were almost as dreadful as the disease. Doctors already had some wacky cures for illnesses. They said . . .

- wear a magpie's beak around the neck to cure toothache
- cut a hole in the skull to let out the devil and cure madness.

> WELL AT LEAST HE ISN'T MAD ANY MORE

With something as deadly as the bubonic plague they had no chance! They suggested . . .

- throw sweet-smelling herbs on a fire to clean the air
- sit in a sewer so the bad air of the plague is driven off by the worse air of the drains

> PERHAPS THE PLAGUE'S NOT SO BAD AFTER ALL

- drink a medicine of ten–year–old treacle
- swallow powders of crushed emeralds (for the rich)

- eat arsenic powder (highly poisonous!)
- try letting blood out of the patient (when the patient's horoscope was right!)
- kill all the cats and dogs in the town
- shave a live chicken's bottom and strap it to the plague sore

- march from town to town flogging yourself with a whip.

The doctors checked the urine of their patients. If there was blood in it then there was no hope.

Some people who caught the plague had a natural resistance to it so they recovered. Others took the only 'cure' that worked – run away from the plague-infested towns into the countryside. The rich people, with country houses, could do this. The poor stayed at home and died.

The real cause of the plague wasn't discovered till just a hundred years ago. And people still don't understand – they think rats carried the plague. Fleas carried the plague germs. They lived on rats and their germs killed the rats.

A dead rat is not very tasty (as children who stay to school dinners will tell you) so the fleas looked for a new 'home'. If there were no rats about then the fleas would hop on to a human and spread the germs to that human. When their new human friend died they'd hop on to another human – maybe the person who'd nursed the first victim. And so it went on.

I THINK I'VE GOT FLEAS DAD

SCRATCH SCRATCH

ALL THIS PLAGUE AROUND AND YOU'RE WORRIED ABOUT A FEW FLEAS

Suffering Scots

The plague had its funny side – if you have that sort of sick sense of humour! The Scots hated the English and were delighted to see the plague destroying so many of their old enemy.

They decided 1349 would be a good time to invade – the English would be too weak to defend themselves. As their forces gathered the plague struck. Many Scots soldiers died – many more ran home to their towns and villages . . . taking the plague with them! In the wars between England and Scotland, Death didn't take sides.

Plague dogs

In Messina, on the Italian island of Sicily, people believed that plague death appeared as a large black dog. It carried a sword in its paws and smashed the ornaments and altars in their churches. Many swore they had seen it!

I ALWAYS KNEW THOSE DOGS WERE UP TO NO GOOD

34

In Scandinavia the people saw Death as a Pest Maiden. She flew out of the mouths of the dead and drifted along in the form of a flame to infect the next house. (Never give the kiss of life to a plague victim or you'd get singed lips!)

In Lithuania a similar maiden waved a red scarf through the window to let in Death. A brave man saw the waving scarf and sliced off the maiden's hand. He died but the village was saved. The scarf was kept in the local church for many years. (Of course, it could have belonged to some 'armless girl, couldn't it?)

Fantastic flagellants

Some people believed the best way to get rid of your wickedness was to beat the devil out of you. In Europe groups of 200 to 300 people called flagellants went around whipping themselves (and each other) for 33.3 days – the number of years Christ lived on Earth. Apart from the steel-tipped whips, they had to put up with . . .

No shaving
No washing
No change of clothes
No comfortable bed
No talking to women

At first the flagellants blamed the priests for the evil of the plague. But the priests fought back with threats to ban the flagellants. So the measly flagellants decided to blame an easier target – the Jewish people in towns. They rushed to the Jewish part of each town and murdered everyone they could find.

In some places, like Worms (in Germany) in 1349, the Jewish people cheated the flagellants of their sport – they set fire to themselves in their houses in a mass suicide. Six thousand died in Mainz that year and not one of the 3,000 Jewish people in Erfurt survived.

Mystic medicine

Of course the Black Death was not the only illness that doctors had to deal with in the Middle Ages.

Since ancient times doctors believed that one of the best ways to get rid of sickness was to let the bad blood out of your body. People of the Middle Ages would pop down to the local barber shop and have a vein opened. (If you wanted to save time you could have your hair cut while you waited!)

How could you spot the local barber shop? There was usually a bowl of fresh blood in the window! (In London this was considered bleeding bad taste and banned in 1307. All blood had to be thrown straight into the Thames.)

Apart from bleeding there were other 'interesting' cures in the Middle Ages. But can you match the right cure to the right illness? Try this test – it doesn't matter if you get them all wrong, actually. None of them works anyway!

37

Answers:

1f) Washing in a boy's pee might kill you so it would certainly give your ringworm a nasty shock. (Don't try this at home.)

2i) Warning! Don't try to eat the honey after you've finished with it.

3a) Plague doctors sold powdered pearls or powdered emeralds to very rich parents. This was very healthy for the doctor's wallet.

4h) In the mid-14th century a vicar was caught importing four dead (and smelly) wolves' bodies in a barrel. The idea was that the disease would 'feed' on the wolf skin instead of the human sufferer. Surgeons were furious that a vicar was pinching their job!

5b) Eating ginger for loss of memory is quite harmless. I tried it once. It may even have worked – but I can't remember.

6e) Treacle was the great cure of the 15th century. It cured practically everything – including loss of speech, spotty skin and snake bites. (It was a real star among medicines, hence the song, 'Treacle, treacle little star, how I wonder what you are.')

7d) Bacon fat should be mixed with wild boar's grease if you can get it. The trouble is you'd probably get more bruises fighting the boar. Then you'd have to go out and catch another wild boar . . . and so on! Note: An angry teacher should not be killed for his or her grease. They are wild BORES, not boars.

8j) Make sure the feathers are not still attached to the chicken when you set fire to them. The RSPCA takes a very dim view of this.

9c) 'Snot a very nice cure, this one.

10g) If you are embarrassed by a dead toad hanging round your neck, tell your friends it's the latest fashion. Alternatively you may prefer to bleed to death.

Top tip for teachers

The best way to avoid a hangover is to drink with your hat off. Doctors of the Middle Ages said this allows the harmful fumes to pass out of your head. A hat holds them in and gives you a headache. But if the drink affects your kidneys then here's a beetle brew discovered by John of Gaddesden . . .

I cut off the heads and wings of crickets and put them with beetles and oil in a pot. I covered it and left it a day and a night in a bread oven. I drew out the pot and heated it at a moderate fire. I ground it all together and rubbed the sick parts. In three days the pain disappeared.

SPOING

(**Health warning:** Make sure you use crickets, or little grasshoppers, and not cricketers in this cure. Try cutting a cricketer's head off and you may get a bat in your measly mouth.)

Arab medicine

Arab doctors were far in advance of European doctors. Their cures showed more understanding of disease and their treatments were more gentle – and usually more successful. They could scarcely believe the way doctors behaved in Europe.

Usama ibn Muniqidh told the story of an Arab doctor. He was treating a knight who had an abscess on his leg; he put a dressing on it. For a woman with a lung disease he prescribed the right sort of fresh food.

Along came a European doctor. 'You have no idea how to cure these people,' he said. First he took an axe and cut the knight's leg off. The knight died.

Then he cut a hole in the woman's skull, removed her brain and rubbed it with salt. The woman died.

'I hope you have learned something about medicine today,' the European doctor said.

'I certainly have,' the Arab doctor replied.

The first flying doctor

Australians are proud of their 'Flying Doctors' – a medical service in aeroplanes. But the Middle Ages saw Doctor Damien of Stirling in Scotland become the first doctor to take to the air.

Doctor Damien was a hopeless doctor and killed as many as he cured. Measly-brained King James IV gave him lots of money to turn ordinary metals into gold – but he failed. Then in 1504 he tried flying. A writer of the time said . . .

> *Damien took it in hand to fly with wings, so he made a pair of wings from feathers. These being fastened around him he flew from the walls of Stirling Castle, but soon fell to the ground and broke three bones. He blamed the failure on the fact that there were chicken feathers in the wings. He said, 'Chickens belong on a dung heap and not in the air.'*

Luckily King James was a pretty good doctor himself and could patch up Damien. The first flying doctor was no chicken – which is more than can be said for his wings!

Nutty knights

The Normans brought the art of castle-building to Britain. Mounds of earth with a wooden wall protected them from the beaten Brits. As they settled in, the castles became larger and were built of stone because now they were protecting themselves from each other!

Of course, castles weren't built by just any old peasant. They were built by knights. Wealthy and powerful soldiers who wore armour and fought on horse-back. These knights were big bullies who battered British peasants into doing as they were told or fought for the king and battered foreign peasants.

IF THERE'S ONE THING WORSE THAN A GROVELLING PEASANT IT'S A PEASANT WHO CAN'T GROVEL IN ENGLISH

Then knights and kings began to do something disastrous . . . they learned how to read! Now they read stories about an ancient king called Arthur of Britain. And Arthur had a strange idea: knights should be gentlemen. Knights treated ladies with respect but, weirdest of all, they treated their enemies with respect! King Edward III (ruled 1327 till 1377) even created a Round Table just like King Arthur was supposed to have.

A knightly fight now had rules. You didn't sneak up on another knight and stab him in the back, even though that saves a lot of trouble and effort. You had to challenge your opponent to a fight and agree the time and place. This may seem a bit strange to you or me – it's like saying, 'Excuse me, my dear fellow, but would you meet me next Thursday, at noon at the meadow by the river, when I will do my best to beat your brains out?'

I'M AWFULLY SORRY, I'VE GOT MY BRAINS ALL OVER YOUR NICE CLEAN ARMOUR

But, as the boy who put a drawing pin on the head-teacher's chair said, 'Rules are there to be broken.'

Forget the fairy-tales about knights in shining armour battling boldly to win glory . . . or death. In truly horrible historical fashion, the most measly knights of the Middle Ages broke the rules. They cheated.

This true 12th-century story is from Ludlow Castle on the border between England and Wales. We learn not all knights were gentlemen – not all maidens were meek and weak. And, in horrible history, not all stories have a happy ending . . .

Midnight terror (or, Terror amid knights)

'Women?' the young knight, Geoffrey, laughed and the sound echoed round the cold stone walls of the dungeon cell. 'They love me. And who can blame me. I'm handsome, strong and brave. Any woman would be proud to be my love!'

The rat twitched his whiskers and scuttled back to its

nest under the straw. 'You don't appear to believe me, Master Rat,' the young man said. 'I'll bet you a piece of stale bread that I'll be out of here within a week!'

Geoffrey turned his head sharply as he heard the rattle of keys in the lock of the cell. He brushed the straw off his jerkin, sat up straight and fixed a smile upon his face. The door swung open and the girl hurried in with a dish of gruel and a mug of ale. Her nose curled back at the smell in the filthy air and she placed the food carefully on the floor. It was the only time she would come within reach of the chained man. Suddenly his chain clattered, his hand shot out and grabbed her wrist.

'Ah!' she cried.

'Hush!' he said quickly. 'Stay just a few moments, Marian,' he went on softly.

'My father will be suspicious,' she said anxiously.

Geoffrey spoke quickly and didn't release his grip on the girl's wrist. 'Yesterday, after you'd gone, his lordship came to see me. He has given me just three days to talk. He wants me to tell him our plans for capturing Ludlow Castle. I would not betray my friends, of course.'

'And after three days?' she asked.

44

'After three days he will torture me. First he will use hot irons on my face . . .'

'No!' she gasped.

'I can bear the pain,' the young man shrugged, 'but it may spoil my looks. No maiden would marry me with those scars. Or he may gouge out my eyes . . .'

'No!' she gasped. 'His lordship's not a cruel man.'

The prisoner shrugged one shoulder. 'We'll see . . . at least *you'll* see. I won't have any eyes left to see!'

'How can you joke about such a thing?' she asked.

'True. I'd be sad to lose my eyes. I'd never be able to see a beautiful face again. A beautiful face like yours.'

The girl blushed and tore her wrist away from his grip. She hurried from the cell and closed the door. The young man smiled.

The next day she came in and knelt beside him silently. She took a small key from her belt and unfastened the chains that bound his wrists. She slipped a larger key from the ring and pressed it into his hand. 'The key to the outer door,' she muttered.

He touched her hand softly. 'Thank you, Marian. You have saved me and I owe you my life. The only way I can repay my debt is by marrying you.'

The girl looked up, startled. 'You'll take me with you?'

'Ah!' he whispered. 'Not just yet. I need time to get away. I want you to stay here, to cover for my escape as long as you can. I'll return for you a week today. Listen, here's what we'll do . . .'

That night, as the monastery bell tolled midnight, he slipped away from the moon-shadows of the castle and stole a horse from the village below. Within an hour he was ten miles from Ludlow. Within a week he was back, as he had promised.

A ladder hung from the window as he knew it would. It was made of strong leather rope and led up to a window in the west tower. A window that wasn't overlooked by the patrolling guards.

Geoffrey climbed it swiftly and felt Marian's strong hands grasp his wrists and pull him over the stone sill. A candle lit the room and glinted on the knight's excited eyes. Marian gave him a nervous smile and moved towards the window. 'Where are you going?' he asked.

'Down the ladder. Away with you,' she said.

He shook his head. 'We have one or two visitors who want to climb that ladder first,' Geoffrey grinned.

'Visitors?'

'Friends of mine. Friends who want a little revenge on your lord.'

A man's face appeared at the window ledge. Geoffrey pulled him into the room. That man in turn helped a second then a third. In five minutes the room was crowded with hard-faced, leather-jacketed men with soft boots and cruel knives.

'What are you doing?' the bewildered girl asked.

Geoffrey ignored her. Instead he turned his back on her and spoke to the men. 'Kill the guards, throw their bodies over the walls then lower the drawbridge . . .'

'My father's on duty tonight!' Marian cried.

'Kill *all* the guards,' Geoffrey said slowly. 'Our troops will ride in and finish the job.'

Marian opened her mouth but before she could scream a warning the knight had clamped a rough, gloved hand over it. He held it suffocatingly tight until the last man had left the room and closed the door. 'Women are fools,' he sneered at her.

But while he held her mouth closed he couldn't control her arms. She had carefully slipped the dagger from his belt and turned it till the point was under his ribs. With all of her strength she pushed upwards.

His lips went tense and his eyes showed more surprise than pain. There was a soft gurgle in his throat as he fell back against the wall. He remained there for half a minute, clawing helplessly at the thing in his side before he slid slowly to the floor.

Marian hurried to the door and looked out on to the battlements. There were cries of terror as men struggled in the darkness and tumbled from their posts. The drawbridge dropped with a crash and there was the sound of horses clattering into the courtyard.

One man's voice seemed to rise above the other cries. 'We've been betrayed!' the voice wailed. 'Betrayed.'

Marian turned back to the room, walked past the lifeless knight and climbed on to the window ledge. 'Oh, we've all been betrayed,' she said dully. The girl simply leaned forward and let herself drop.

In the dark chaos of the night no one heard one more small cry, one more soft crunching of bone on rock.

Did you know . . . ?

Marian wasn't the only castle-dweller to be betrayed. A robber held in Haverfordwest in Wales became friends with some young squires who were training to be knights. He fixed arrowheads for them and gave them to the boys for their bows. The boys begged that the robber be allowed out for some fresh air – in their care. He took them hostage and used them to bargain for his freedom.

And Marian wasn't the only young woman to die in a fall from a castle. Just over the Welsh border in Abergavenny a young girl fell while trying to catch her pet squirrel that had escaped.

OOPS

Jolly jesters

Castle life wasn't all dungeons, doom and draughts. There were feasts and entertainments. The chief entertainer was the jester.

A 13th-century writer described the skills a jester needed if he was going to get a job in a royal castle . . .

A jester's little joke

Jesters also had to be quick witted. At the Battle of Sluys (1340) the measly English archers fired so many arrows that the French were driven from the decks of the ships and their fleet destroyed. No one dared tell King Philip VI of France. His jester stepped forward . . .

Reports said that the fish drank so much French blood that if they could talk they would have spoken French!

A terrible tale

Jesters weren't the only entertainers in castles at the time. There were minstrels too. They had heroic tales of knights and dragons and ladies. Of course, they didn't have comics in the Middle Ages but they had cheerful little stories that would have made very good comic strips. Stories like 'Renault and the Dame of Fayel' . . .

51

Awful Angevins

King Stephen followed Henry I as the last Norman king. Henry Duke of Anjou wanted the English throne and, since he was a bit rough, no one argued with him – not even Stephen's sons.

When old Steve died, in 1154, Henry of Anjou became Henry II – the first Anjou (or Angevin) king. Henry had lots of bright ideas for improving England and one of the first things he sorted out was the law. Now . . .

- Accused people could be tried by the people of their own class – juries. (A bit like your classmates deciding if you are guilty of the crime of slopping your school-dinner custard down Alice Anderson's neck.)
- The king's judges then decided what the punishment should be for the guilty. (A bit like the teacher then deciding you have to mop the custard off her neck and pay to have her dress cleaned. Get it?)
- Townspeople took it in turns to act as 'Constable' to question and arrest suspects. (A bit like a classmate having the job of patrolling the school dining-hall to make sure you keep your custard to yourself in future.)

Cruel crimes

'Crime doesn't pay.' That was the message the law wanted to give to people thinking of a spot of murder, treason or thieving. William the Conqueror may have banned executions but they soon returned after his death.

But even executions were all too soon forgotten, so the officers of the law needed a way of reminding the public to behave itself, like . . .

Upon London Bridge I saw three or four men's heads stand upon poles. Upon Ludgate Arch the top quarter of a man is set upon a pole. Upon the other side hangeth the bottom quarter with the leg. It is a strange sight to see the hair of the heads fall off or shrivel away while the gristle of the nose is eaten away and the fingers of the hands wrinkle and wither to the bare bones. It is a sight for all young people and a warning to them that they should behave themselves.

A schoolteacher came up with this jolly piece of writing! He wrote it as an exercise for his pupils to copy out in Latin – and as more than a little hint to his pupils: 'This is what will happen to you if you don't do as you are told!'

Criminal capers

Henry II's laws were really needed by the poor people of England. While kings and barons fought each other, the bullies in the country took the law into their own hands. The Middle Ages were wild and dangerous times. But it wasn't just the poor peasants who turned to crime . . .
1 Robin Hood may have lived in the royal forests of

Sherwood in Nottinghamshire . . . or he may be an invented character and about as real as Donald Duck. But outlaw Sir Gosseline Denville did exist. After wasting his family fortune he became the terror of the north of England. Like most bullies he liked 'soft' targets and often robbed monasteries and convents. In the end he was cornered in Yorkshire by the Sheriff and 600 men. They called on Denville to give himself up. What happened next?

2 The church was no better. The monasteries owned large areas of land and rented it out. Then they employed tough gangs to collect the rent from poor peasant farmers. In 1317 a gang grabbed a traveller on the path to a monastery and held him to ransom for £200. What was unusual about this gang?

3 A Scottish priest sacrificed a man at a black magic ceremony. He had his hands and feet cut off and his eyes put out as a punishment. Kind King David of Scotland took pity on the priest and gave him shelter in his palace. In 1114 the priest thanked the king by murdering his young son – he used the iron fingers of his artificial hands to tear the child apart. David decided to tear the priest apart . . . how?

4 The de Folville brothers had a fine career in theft and ransom. But when Eustace de Folville joined the army to fight for the king he was pardoned of all his crimes.

Brother Richard was a priest. A law officer chased rich Richard till the pilfering priest ran into a church and claimed sanctuary. ('No one can touch me while I'm in the church building.') The officer ignored the sanctuary rules, dragged Richard out and beheaded him. How was the officer rewarded for his success?

5 Sir Roger Swynnerton of Staffordshire was accused of murder. There were several witnesses who said they had seen him do it. Sir Roger was set free to return to Swynnerton village where the murder had taken place. What did Sir Roger do?

6 Henry II became fed up with his Archbishop of Canterbury, Thomas à Becket, and said that he wished he were rid of him. Four knights thought they'd do Henry a favour and get rid of Becket for him. They battered Becket to death as he clutched at his altar.

Henry was horrified and felt it was his fault. As a punishment he went to the scene of the murder, walked barefoot into the Cathedral and prayed. There were several monks and priests there. How did they complete the punishment of the king?

Answers:

1 Deadly Denville's gang killed 200 before they were finally overcome.

2 The gang members were all monks! But don't be too surprised – in the 15th century there were records of parsons being arrested for poaching, highway robbery and forging coins. They also had a bad name for gambling and drinking in the local taverns. Two priests were arrested in 1453 for beating up an Oxford man – they were helped in the attack by a measly schoolteacher!

3 A wild horse was tied to each arm and leg, then they were sent off in different directions. Your local riding school will probably not allow you to try this on your teacher . . . but in the name of historical research, it's worth asking, I suppose.

WELL, AT LEAST IT'S A GOOD EXERCISE IN PHYSICS

4 The officer had broken sanctuary rules and killed a priest. The officer was punished by being beaten with rods outside all of the churches in the area!

5 The murderer was so upset by the witnesses that he forced them to pay him 50 marks as a punishment for speaking out against him.

6 They stripped him to the waist and took it in turn to give him three to five lashes from each of them. (That's more lashes than you have on your eyes!)

Painful punishments

Henry II tried to make modern laws but the punishments for breaking them were still very old-fashioned and definitely measly.

The Forger
Name — John Stubbs
Crime — He did make copies of the king's coins and used the forged coins to buy food
Punishment — John Stubbs's hand was tied to a block of wood. A meat axe was placed on his wrist and struck with a hammer till the hand was cut off

[Amputation of a hand was a rare punishment but the law was still in force in 1820]

The Thief
Name — Peter of Clarendon
Crime — Felony. He did steal a horse to the value of two shillings
Punishment — The Sheriff of Wiltshire had a pit dug and filled with water which was then blessed by a priest. The thief was thrown in. If he sank he was innocent. Peter of Clarendon floated and was therefore guilty. He was taken out and executed.

[Sheriff Ranulf Glanville of Yorkshire killed 120 men in this way]

The Beggar
Name — Martin of Cheapside
Crime — Begging for money when fit and able for work
Punishment — Three days and three nights in the stocks in the market place, fed only on bread and water. He was then thrown out of the town and ordered not to return

[The kind Tudors reduced this punishment to one day and one night in the stocks in 1504]

The Attacker

Name — Thomas of Elderfield

Crime — Fought against George of Northway and did wound him

Punishment — Sentenced to fight a duel with George. He was defeated, and the law demanded that Thomas's eyes be gouged out by George's family. [It is recorded that Thomas was nursed back to health by St Wulfstan. His eyes were miraculously restored]

The Assassin

Name — The Earl of Athol

Crime — Assassinated King James I of Scotland in 1437

Punishment — Taken to the Cross in Edinburgh where he was crowned with a red-hot iron crown and his flesh was nipped off with red-hot pincers.

The Liar

Name — John de Hackford

Crime — In 1364 he announced that 10,000 men were gathering to murder the London councillors. This caused widespread fear and panic. Punishment — He was jailed for a year. Every three months he was taken out, stood in a pillory (or Stretch-neck) with a stone round his neck and a notice "False Liar" pinned to his chest

The Hawk Finder

Name — John of Rivers

Crime — He did find his lordship's hawk on the roof of his house. He failed to report this to his lordship

Punishment — The hawk shall be fed on six ounces of flesh cut from John of Rivers' chest.

58

The Scold
Name – Ann Runcorn
Crime – She did disgrace her husband by
  scolding him in public, calling him "villain"
  and "rogue".
Punishment – Ann was fitted with a cage
over her head called a "brank". A metal rod poked into
her mouth to hold down her tongue. Ann had to sit on
a horse facing backwards, and be led through the market
where people could mock her.
[A Brank in the town of Shrewsbury was last used in 1846]

Hawking Henry

A hawk was valued more than a peasant by the lords who owned it. A 14th-century historian told a story about Henry II's nasty habit – swearing – and how God taught him a bit of a lesson . . .

In the early days of his reign Henry cast off his best falcon at a heron. The heron circled higher and higher, but the swift hawk had almost overtaken him when Henry cried out loud, 'By God's eyes or by God's gorge, that heron shall not escape – not even if God himself has decided it!' At these words the heron turned and as if by a miracle stuck his beak into the falcon's head and dashed out his brains. The heron, himself unhurt, threw the dying bird to the earth at the very feet of King Henry.

Wonder why God killed the hawk and not the offensive Henry?

Jolly John

The first Angevins were just like the first Normans. Father (Henry II) fought against sons Richard I, Geoffrey and Henry. But this time the boys had their mother, Eleanor, on their side. (Henry II tamed her treachery by locking her away for 16 years!)

Henry's favourite son was young John. When Henry found that John had joined his three brothers it broke the old king's heart. He died.

Richard took the throne. (His heart was a lion heart so it was harder to break.) Of course, Richard went off Crusading and got himself captured. John looked after the country, spent the royal money and made plans to pinch Richard's throne.

Richard forgave John ('You are just a child,' he said), then very kindly went off to another battle and got himself killed. John was king! But one of the measliest monarchs of the Middle Ages. He liked fine clothes, fine food, fine girlfriends . . . and he enjoyed upsetting people . . .

- John laughed at the long beards and national dress of the Irish princes – the Irish chieftains were upset.
- John married his cousin; the Archbishop of Canterbury objected but John got the Pope to overrule him – the Archbishop of Canterbury was upset.
- John arranged for the murder of his greatest rival, Arthur of Brittany in France – the French king (Philip II) was upset and went to war (though Arthur was too dead to be upset).
- John picked a new Archbishop of Canterbury against

the wishes of the Pope – the Pope was upset.

- John raised huge taxes from the English people and the barons to fight against France; the war went badly and the barons were upset. This, of course, led to . . .

The Magnet Carter
The Barons made John agree to give power back to them and the people; no taxes, no wars and no laws unless the people agreed . . .

Please note that this is utter nonsense of the kind you would only find in a Horrible History. Any boring teacher will tell you that Magna Carta means 'Great Charter' in Latin.

John died after pigging himself on peaches and cider. But the food in the Middle Ages was so bad he could have died just as easily from drinking a glass of water!

Foul food

In the Middle Ages the Church had rules about what you could (or could not) eat. Until the start of the 13th century adults were 'forbidden four-footed flesh-meat'. (Try saying that with a mouthful of mushy peas.) And no one was allowed meat on a Friday – only fish.

The trouble was, people cheated. If they couldn't eat 'four-footed flesh' then they ate large birds. Turkeys hadn't been discovered so they ate birds called bustards. What happened? Bustards became extinct in England!

Fancy a bit of red meat on a Friday? Then eat a beaver. Beavers used their tails for swimming, so they could be called fish ... couldn't they? (Er ... no, actually.) What happened? Beavers became extinct in Britain.

And it wasn't only bustards and beavers that had a hard time. A 1393 French recipe book advised eating hedgehog – skinned, cleaned and roasted like a chicken. Of course, catching hedgehogs was harder in those days. You didn't usually find them ready-squashed in the middle of the road. Or perhaps you did!

LOOK! MEALS ON WHEELS!

Tasty treats

It wasn't only turkey that was unknown to the Middle Age munchers. There were no potatoes either. Imagine a world with no chips or crisps!

Of course, they had the dreaded cabbage. But forget school-dinner cabbage – pale grey strips of slime flavoured with sweaty socks. Try this recipe for cabbage soup and see if the Middle Ages people had more scrumptious scran than you . . .

Cabbage soup

❡ You need:
- 600g cabbage (leaves cut into strips)
- 225g onions (peeled and chopped small)
- 225g leeks (white part sliced into thin rings)
- half-teaspoon of salt
- quarter teaspoon of coriander
- quarter teaspoon of cinnamon
- quarter teaspoon of sugar
- quarter teaspoon of saffron strands (rather expensive – can be missed out, or use half a teaspoon of turmeric powder)
- 850 ml water
- chicken stock-cube (or vegetable stock-cube if you're a vegetarian)

❡ Method:
1 Boil the water in a saucepan and crumble in the stock cube
2 Stir in the saffron, cinnamon, coriander, salt and sugar
3 Add the sliced cabbage, chopped onion and leek rings to the boiling stock
4 Cover the saucepan and boil gently for 20 minutes
5 Serve with 1 cm squares of toast or small strips of fried bacon on top

The only difference in the original recipe was that it said, 'Boil the cabbages all morning'. But cabbages in the Middle Ages were tougher and needed it. Boil modern cabbages all morning and you'll end up with school-dinner green slime.

When it came to sweet dishes the rich people ate all the sugar they could get their teeth on ... until the sugar rotted their teeth, of course. One flavour that was popular then is rare now – the flavour of roses.

Try this rose pudding and see what you think. (Cooks in the Middle Ages didn't have liquidizers, of course, but you might. Cheat a bit and use one if you have. Any greenfly you've failed to wash off the rose petals will be turned into serious hospital cases.)

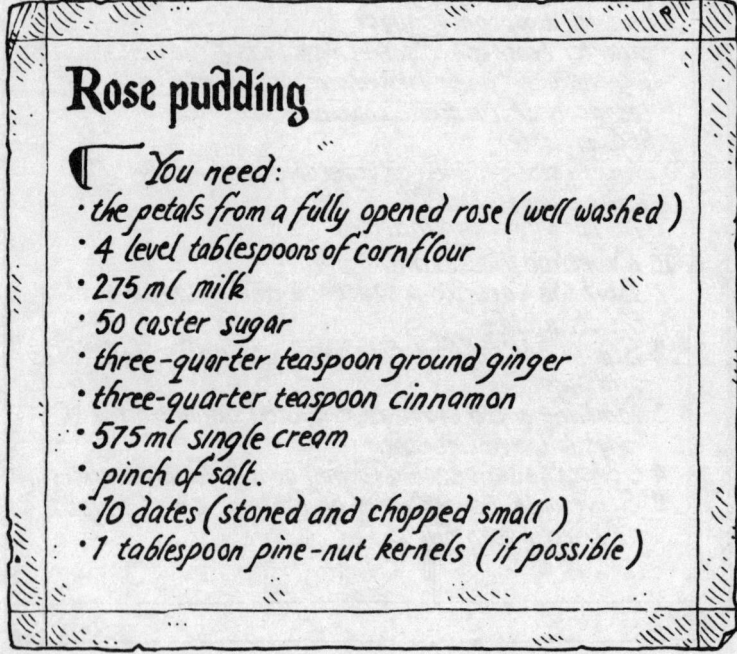

Rose pudding

You need:
- the petals from a fully opened rose (well washed)
- 4 level tablespoons of cornflour
- 275 ml milk
- 50 caster sugar
- three-quarter teaspoon ground ginger
- three-quarter teaspoon cinnamon
- 575 ml single cream
- pinch of salt
- 10 dates (stoned and chopped small)
- 1 tablespoon pine-nut kernels (if possible)

Method:

1. Boil the rose petals in water for two minutes
2. Press the petals between kitchen towels under a heavy weight
3. Put the cornflour in a saucepan and slowly add the milk, stirring all the time
4. Put the pan on to heat and warm until the mixture starts to thicken
5. Pour the mixture into a blender, add sugar, cinnamon, ginger and rose petals
6. Blend until smooth (or until the greenfly have a headache)
7. Blend in cream and salt then return the mixture to the saucepan
8. Heat and stir until the mixture is like thick cream
9. Stir in dates and pine-nut kernels and heat for further two minutes
10. Pour into glasses and leave to cool (stirring to stop a skin forming)
11. Eat this straight from the fridge and amaze your parents... just don't tell them that you pinched a prize rose from the garden

Boozing bachelors

In the Middle Ages everyone drank ale. It was safer than drinking the water in some of the filthy large towns.

Special ales were brewed for special occasions and usually *sold* to drinkers (you'd expect to get your drinks free today). So, a man would brew a 'Bride Ale' when he got married. The wedding guests all bought pots of the ale and the money went to the bride.

Imagine going to a wedding today being told, 'Raise your glasses of champagne and drink a toast to the bride – but don't forget to drop a fiver in the best man's hat!' A measly marriage if ever there was one!

Funerals were another popular occasion for a special brew. The corpse often paid for the special ale . . . usually before he died. This was especially popular with drinkers who liked their ale with a bit of body.

The Church became upset by all this drinking and tried to ban it. People enjoyed themselves too much so the Church decided, 'If you can't beat them, join them.' They brewed 'Churchyard Ales' and sold them to raise money for repairs to church buildings!

The Lord of the manor brewed an ale about three times a year; he expected his workers to buy it at a high price. It was a sort of extra tax the workers had to pay. But sometimes the bachelors of the village were given a challenging treat.

They could drink as much of the ale as they wanted, free . . . so long as they stayed on their feet. If they sat down they had to pay.

Foul food facts
1 Butchers were banned from slaughtering animals in the City of London. They'd been in the habit of dumping the guts on the pavement outside the Grey Friars' monastery. A Winchester butcher killed a cow on the pavement outside his shop, while 15th-century Coventry cooks threw chicken guts out of their kitchen windows into the street.
2 Butchers were not allowed to sell meat by candlelight. This was so the customer could see what they were getting! A man was caught trying to sell pork from a dead pig he'd found in a ditch. He was fastened in the pillory and the rotten meat burned under his nose – a common punishment for this sort of fraud.
3 Large towns had takeaway food suppliers selling delicious thrushes (at two for a penny) and tasty hot sheep's feet. They would even deliver cooked food to your home. (Could the sheep's feet maybe deliver themselves . . . simply stroll round to the customer's house?)

4 If you went to a tavern for a mug of ale you could have 'Huffcap', 'Angel's Food', 'Dragon's Milk' or 'Mad Dog Ale' (*that* had a bit of a bite to it). These were probably safer than Eleanor Rummyng's ale – she allowed her hens to

roost over the brewing vats. Their droppings fell into the ale and old Eleanor just stirred them in before she sold it.
5 Drinks could be pretty nasty with lots of 'foreign bodies' floating in them. One 13th-century writer complained that some ale was as thick as soup. 'You didn't drink it, you filtered it through your teeth.' (Of course, King Edward IV had his brother, Clarence, drowned in a barrel of wine in 1478. Now that's what you'd call a foreign body in your drink!)

IS HE DEAD YET?

NO, BUT HE'S QUITE TIPSY

6 Many towns checked the quality of bread and punished bakers who tried to cheat. Some were found guilty of adding sand to loaves and, in one disgusting case, a loaf contained cobwebs.
7 Housewives often prepared dough then took it to a baker to be cooked. Some bakers had a clever trick. They placed the housewife's dough on the counter. There was a small trapdoor in this counter with a boy underneath. While the baker kept the woman chatting, the boy opened the trapdoor and pinched a fistful of dough. The measly baker made the stolen dough into loaves which he baked and sold. The housewife paid him for baking her loaf and went home with less than she'd brought. (If he was caught then he spent a day in the pillory – there are no records of the boy-thief being caught and punished.)
8 Servants were forbidden to wear hanging sleeves like their masters. This was partly because lords hated their servants to look too grand . . . and partly because long sleeves dropped into the soup as they served it!

9 Henry VIII is famous for his Terrible Tudor feasts but in 1467 there were feasts just as fattening as those. Richard, Earl of Warwick, threw a little party to celebrate his brother becoming Archbishop of York. The 60 cooks prepared 104 oxen, 2,000 pigs, 1,000 sheep and 13,000 sweet dishes. In case this made the feasters thirsty there were 300 large barrels of ale and 100 casks of wine.

10 Peasants ate bacon because it was easy to kill and salt a pig every winter. They ate vegetables because they could grow those themselves. As a result most noblemen would never be seen eating bacon or vegetables!

Mucky manners

Young people had books to teach them table manners. Unfortunately not a lot of young people could read. It may have been better to have had illustrations to help.

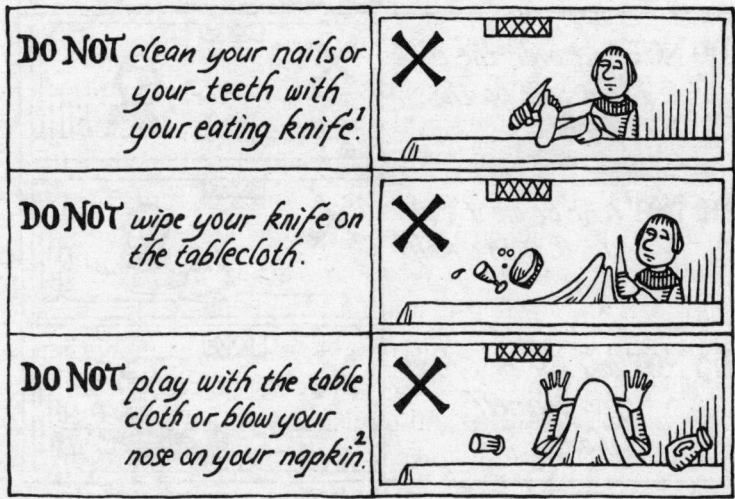

DO NOT *clean your nails or your teeth with your eating knife.*[1] ✗

DO NOT *wipe your knife on the tablecloth.* ✗

DO NOT *play with the table cloth or blow your nose on your napkin.*[2] ✗

1. Scratching your head at the table 'as if clawing at a flea' was also impolite.

2. But it was common for people to pick their noses at the table.

DO NOT *dip your bread in the soup.*

DO NOT *fill your soup spoon too full or blow on your soup.*

DO NOT *eat noisily or clean your bowl by licking it out.*

DO NOT *speak while your mouth is full of food.*[1]

DO NOT *spit over the table but spit on the floor.*

DO NOT *tear at meat but cut it with a knife first.*

DO NOT *take the best food for yourself. Share it.*[2]

1. You could burp at the table... but not too close to someone's face.
2. And you are asked not to steal food from someone else's plate.

Terrible toilets

The Middle Ages were pretty smelly times. Most rubbish ended in the streets. Butchers killed an animal, sold the meat and then threw the guts into the street. The town councils passed the odd law to clean up the streets and London had public conveniences built over the river Fleet to the west of the city.

One writer said that 'each toilet seat is filled with a buttock' so the boatmen sailing underneath had to watch out!

And it wasn't only the boatmen who had this problem. Many private toilets took a bit of controlling. The London council took Thomas Wytte and William Hockele to court in 1321 . . .

A jury decided that Ebbgate Lane used to be a right of way for all men until it was closed up by Wytte and Hockele who built toilets. These toilets projected from the walls of the houses so that human filth falls on to the heads of the passers-by.

Not everyone bothered with a toilet. They shared a room with animals and behaved like the animals. Even by 1515 a

Dutchman was complaining about the filthy English homes . . .

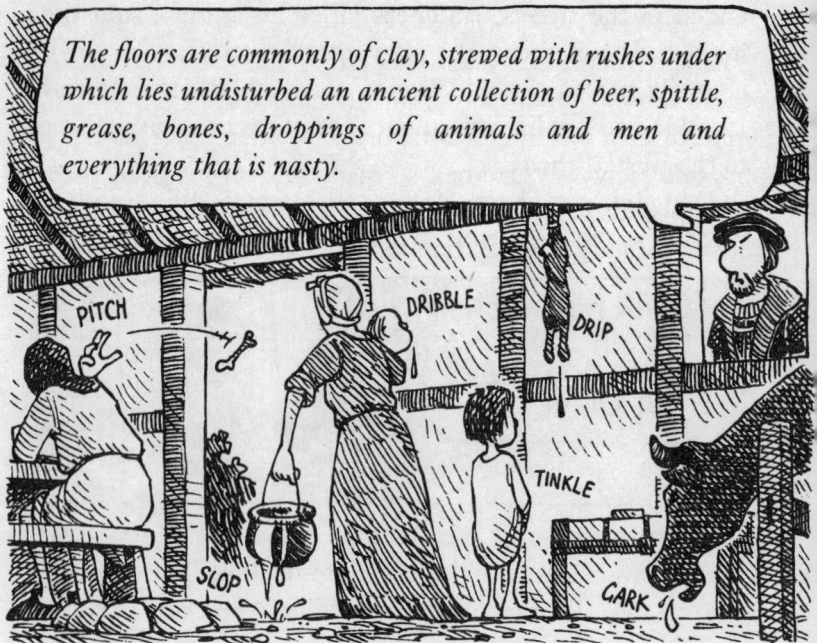

> *The floors are commonly of clay, strewed with rushes under which lies undisturbed an ancient collection of beer, spittle, grease, bones, droppings of animals and men and everything that is nasty.*

Of course, careful housewives collected the family urine because it helped with the laundry! They made their own soap by boiling wood ash with scraps of meat fat. The urine was stored until it was really strong and then added to the wash where it acted as a sort of bleach. (Note: If you fancy bleaching your hair then go to the chemist for the bleach. It will cost a bit more but at least you won't smell like a broken toilet.)

Lousy Lancastrians

The last Angevin king was Richard II. He was a poor weak thing and no one was too upset when his cousin Henry had him thrown off the throne in 1399. Henry Lancaster became Henry IV. He had so many lice on his head they reckoned his hair wouldn't grow. He was lousy . . . the first of several lousy Lancastrian kings.

A KING OR A CARTER, ONE HEAD'S AS GOOD AS ANOTHER

The trouble is his grandson, Henry VI, was another measly weak king. And weak kings were just asking for strong lords to fight for their throne. When Henry VI went mad in 1453 his Lancaster family started scrapping with the York family for power.

Each family had a rose for a badge – a red rose for Lancaster, a white rose for York. After 30 years of bloody battles, Henry 'Red Rose' Tudor defeated Richard 'White Rose' III but, cleverly, married Elizabeth 'White Rose' York. This brought the fighting to an end. Those battles became known as 'The Wars of the Roses'.

The Middle Ages began and ended with important battles . . . and there were several others in between. If those battles had been won by the losers then history would have changed.

Bloody battles

Nowadays wars are fought between machines – laser-guided missiles, tanks, submarines, bombs and aeroplanes. A fighting man can kill a million people at the push of a button and never set eyes on one of his victims.

But in the Middle Ages men fought hand to hand – or at least within arrow-shot of the enemy. There was plenty of blood, plenty of cruelty and lots of stupidity.

But in the excitement of a battle it's easy to make mistakes. Winning (or losing) was often decided by simple decisions. How would history have changed if you'd been in command? What would you have done in these famous battles of the measly Middle Ages?

1 Hastings, 14 October, 1066

Armies:

King Harold of England v. Duke William of Normandy. The first major battle in the Norman Conquest.

Battle:

- 9:00 a.m. Harold's English army are sitting on Senlac Hill, tired but happy to defend the place.
- The Normans have three lines of attack – archers, followed by foot-soldiers followed by knights on horseback.
- The first Norman attack fails – the archers are firing uphill and the English catch the arrows easily on their shields.
- The foot-soldiers advance but the English drive them back with spears and stones (but very few archers).
- The Normans turn and stumble back down the hill. Harold turns to you and asks, 'What do we do now?'

What do you tell him?

Advice:

2 Bannockburn, near Stirling, Scotland, 24 June, 1314
Armies:
Edward II of England v. Robert the Bruce of Scotland.
Battle in Scottish war of independence against England.
Battle:
- Robert Bruce's 40,000 Scots are besieging the English in
  Stirling so Edward marches 60,000 English soldiers to
  drive them off.
- When the English draw close to Stirling they see the
  Scots camped on the far side of a swampy stream, the
  Bannock Burn.
- The Scottish foot-soldiers are armed with long poles
  with axe heads and spikes on the end – weapons called
  pikes.
- They group themselves tightly so that charging knights

will face a hedgehog of metal bristles.
- Edward's 2000 knights want to charge at the pikes, but first they have to tear doors off nearby cottages to make a wooden path across the swamp.

What would you advise Edward to do?

> **A:** THE SCOTS ARE IN A STRONG DEFENSIVE POSITION. FIRST BREAK UP THOSE TIGHT GROUPS OF PIKE-MEN, POUR ARROWS INTO THEM, MAKE GAPS IN THEIR RANKS AND THEN SEND THE KNIGHTS IN TO CUT DOWN THE SURVIVORS

> **B:** THE SCOTS ARE ON FOOT BUT OUR KNIGHTS ARE ON HORSES. SEND THE KNIGHTS IN FIRST TO BATTER AT THE PIKE WALL. AS THE SCOTS PIKE-MEN BREAK DOWN AND RUN AWAY, SHOOT THEM DOWN WITH THE ARCHERS.

3 Crécy, Northern France, 26 August, 1346

Armies:

Edward III of England v. Philip VI of France. The first major battle in the Hundred Years War.

Battle:

- Edward's army of 18,000 has less than 4000 armoured knights. He faces Philip's 38,000 men including 12,000 knights.
- The English wait on a small hill. The French have to cross a stream and attack uphill (but this will be no problem for the knights.)

76

- As the two armies face one another there is a shower of rain. The English take the strings off their longbows and keep them dry. The French archers use crossbows and the soaked string makes them pretty useless.
- The sun comes out and it is straight in the eyes of the French. They can't make out the enemy forces very clearly. They can see that the English archers are at the front.
- Behind the archers the English knights are waiting on foot. The English knights cannot reach their horses in time to fight off the French knights!

What do you advise Philip to do?

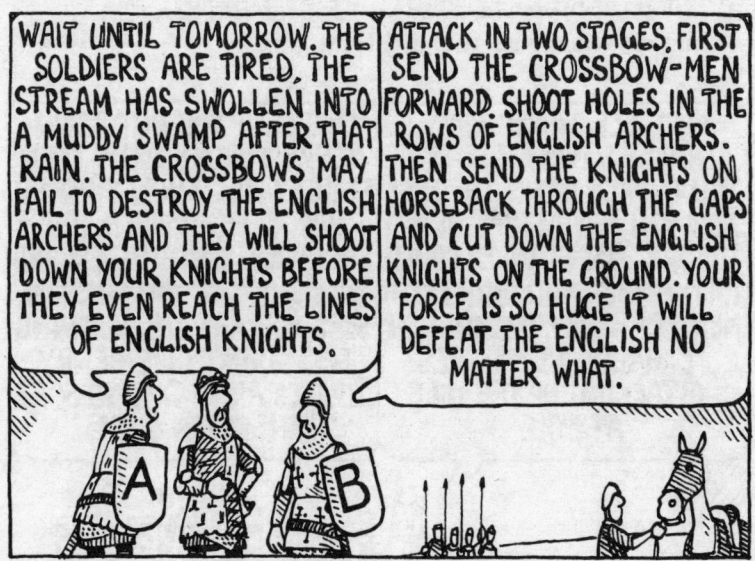

> WAIT UNTIL TOMORROW. THE SOLDIERS ARE TIRED, THE STREAM HAS SWOLLEN INTO A MUDDY SWAMP AFTER THAT RAIN. THE CROSSBOWS MAY FAIL TO DESTROY THE ENGLISH ARCHERS AND THEY WILL SHOOT DOWN YOUR KNIGHTS BEFORE THEY EVEN REACH THE LINES OF ENGLISH KNIGHTS.

> ATTACK IN TWO STAGES, FIRST SEND THE CROSSBOW-MEN FORWARD. SHOOT HOLES IN THE ROWS OF ENGLISH ARCHERS. THEN SEND THE KNIGHTS ON HORSEBACK THROUGH THE GAPS AND CUT DOWN THE ENGLISH KNIGHTS ON THE GROUND. YOUR FORCE IS SO HUGE IT WILL DEFEAT THE ENGLISH NO MATTER WHAT.

4 Bosworth Field, Leicester, England, 22 August, 1485

Armies:

King Richard III and the Yorkists v. Henry Tudor and the Lancastrians. The final battle in the Wars of the Roses.

Battle:

- Richard has won the race to get his army on higher ground; he has reached the top of Ambion Hill and waits.
- Henry's army had trouble lining up on the rough ground at the foot of the hill.
- Richard could charge at them while they sort themselves out, but he has a couple of problems: a) A third army is waiting nearby under the command of Lord Stanley. Stanley promised to fight for Richard . . . and Stanley promised to fight for Henry Tudor! b) Richard is unsure about one of his own commanders, Northumberland, who is at his back.

What do you advise Richard III to do?

WAIT. SEE WHICH WAY STANLEY'S ARMY FIGHTS. IF YOU CHARGE DOWN THE HILL NOW YOU MAY DEFEAT HENRY TUDOR... BUT STANLEY COULD THEN ATTACK YOU WITH FRESH MEN. LET HENRY TUDOR'S MEN EXHAUST THEMSELVES ATTACKING UP THE HILL AT YOU.

CHARGE. IF YOU CUT DOWN HENRY TUDOR'S ARMY THEN STANLEY WILL KNOW THAT HE HAS TO FIGHT WITH YOU. SIMILARLY, NORTHUMBERLAND WILL SUPPORT YOU WHEN HE SEES YOU ARE THE WINNING SIDE. DON'T GIVE HENRY TUDOR'S ARMY TIME TO SORT THEMSELVES OUT!

Answers:

1 Hastings Harold follows the advice from soldier 'A' . . . and loses. Once the English leave the hill the Normans turn and attack them on the flat ground. (Some historians believe the 'running away' was just a trick to get the English off the high ground.) It works. Norman archers draw fresh supplies of arrows and fire high in the air. As the English hold their shields over their heads the Norman knights charge them from the front. Harold should have listened to soldier 'B' and stayed where he was. He is wounded with an arrow in the eye then cut down by Norman knights. The Normans will go on to rule England.

2 Bannockburn Edward follows advice from soldier 'B' . . . and loses. The knights feel they are the most important soldiers there and they want the glory of charging at Robert's army first. The archers are hardly used. The knights struggle to cross the swampy ground and then find the Scots have dug pits and traps for the horses. There is no great charge but English knights stumble into Scottish pikes where they are cut down and driven back to drown in the swampy stream. Edward II runs away and his army runs after him. The Scottish people are free of the English.

3 Crécy Philip follows advice 'B' . . . and loses. The crossbow-men fire . . . and are met by deadly showers of arrows from the English longbows. They stumble back . . . and are trampled by their own knights moving forward. The powerful longbows punch holes in the French armour. Horses and knights fall, more horses and knights stumble over them. When a few knights do get through they are surrounded and pulled down by the English knights on foot. Ten thousand French fighters die, and King Philip is wounded by an arrow in the neck but escapes with his life. The English king can claim to be King of France.

4 Bosworth Field Richard follows advice from soldier 'A' . . . and loses. He misses his chance to hit Henry Tudor's army at their weakest. Henry Tudor's men use cannon and arrows to damage Richard on his hilltop. Richard's men come down from their hilltop and fight hand to hand with Henry's men. When Richard calls for Northumberland to move forward with fresh forces, Northumberland refuses. Richard leads a charge personally at Henry Tudor but Stanley decides this is the moment to join the battle – on Henry Tudor's side. Richard is cut down – the second and last English King to die in battle – and Henry Tudor takes the crown. This is the end of the Wars of the Roses. For many historians this is the end of the Middle Ages.

Did you know . . . ?
The Duke of Suffolk had been a loyal servant to Lancastrian king, Henry VI. But when he lost in battle to the French he had to go. Henry didn't want to execute his faithful friend so he sent him off into exile. The Duke of Suffolk set sail from Ipswich but didn't get very far. At Dover his enemies caught

SORRY SUFF.' YOU'RE DUFF. I'VE HAD ENOUGH. I KNOW IT'S ROUGH BUT THAT'S JUST TOUGH up with him, dragged him into a small boat and cut his head off with a rusty sword. (WARNING: Do *not* try this in your local park pond. Cutting someone's head off with a rusty sword could give them a serious case of blood poisoning.)

Sickly singers
Not everyone was horrified by war. Some enjoyed the excitement. Bertrand de Born was a troubadour – a sort of Middle Ages pop-singer. One of his biggest hits was this gory little number . . .

> *My heart swells up with happiness every time I see*
> *A mighty castle being attacked, its strong walls beaten*
>   *down,*
> *The soldiers on those broken walls being struck down*
>   *to the ground,*
> *While horses of the dead and fallen roam the field at*
>   *random.*
> *And, when battle starts to seethe, let all you noble*
>   *men*
> *Put all your will to breaking heads and arms.*
> *It's better far for you to die in battle than to lose and*
>   *live.*
> *I tell you that my greatest joy is just to hear the*
>   *shouts,*
> *'On! On!' from both sides and the screams of horses*
>   *with no riders,*
> *And the groans of, 'Help me! Help me!' from the*
>   *fallen wounded.*
> *The bliss when I see great and small fall in the ditches*
>   *and the grass*

And when I see the corpses pierced clean through by
  shafts of spears!
So, Knights, give up your castles, leave your lands or
  lose your cities,
But my lords, I beg you, never ever give up war.

Woeful women

The Church in the Middle Ages taught that men were better than women. This could have something to do with the fact that the priests were men!

Women were told they had to obey their male relatives till they married, then they had to obey their husbands. Even in the 1990s women can still choose to get married with a promise to 'love, honour and obey' their husbands.

And, if the wife decided to disobey, then the husband was encouraged to beat her. He was told not to do this if he was drunk or in a temper. Just if she 'deserved' it. As an Italian proverb said . . .

A horse, whether good or bad, needs a spur. A woman, whether good or bad, needs a lord and master – and sometimes a stick.

A priest, Robert d'Abrissel, went further when he said:

A woman is a witch, a snake, a plague, a rat, a rash, a poison, a burning flame and an assistant of the Devil.

WHO ME?

Do you get the idea that he didn't like women very much? The trouble is men listened to him, believed him and treated women badly because of his wicked words.

Women were told it was sinful to use make-up, to dye their hair or pluck their eyebrows. The priests said this was 'vanity' and women would be punished in Hell. The women did these things anyway.

Then, in the 14th century, priests became worried that men were wearing colourful, fancy clothes and becoming more like those 'snaky, ratty, poisonous' women! And the worst thing a man could do was to be like a woman. That was a sin. So the measly Church started to frown upon . . .

Foul fashions
Fashionable men gave up wearing gowns and started wearing tights. The really fashionable young men wore their tunics so short that a writer complained the tights revealed 'parts of the body that should be hidden'!

The friars, monks and priests had some savage things to say about fancy 14th-century fashions . . .

. . . and the women *did* burn their steeple hats – for a while. When measly monk Tom took himself off, the women went back to wearing their steeple hats which were . . . taller than ever!

In many countries laws were passed in the Middle Ages saying that only nobles could wear fine clothes. Peasants were not to be seen wearing rich clothes – otherwise people would mistake them for someone better!

Most of the laws were there to control women's clothes. Laws were passed to stop women wearing platform shoes, for example. Generally men used any way they could to make sure women 'obeyed' them. As Goodman of Paris told his wife . . .

Copy the behaviour of a dog which loves to obey its master; even if the master whips it, the dog follows, wagging its tail.

But, not surprisingly, women were not always as meek as Mr Goodman would have liked. Women had a difficult a life in the Middle Ages. But some fought back. A few were true . . .

Hooray heroines
Jeanne de Clisson

In 1313 Olivier de Clisson was executed on the orders of Philip the Fair, King of France. His wife, Jeanne, decided he was Philip the Un-fair and decided to get her own back. First she sold off all of her lands to raise money. Jeanne bought three warships; they were painted black and had red sails. Admiral Jeanne began destroying Philip's ships and murdering their crews . . . but she always left two or three alive to carry the story back to the king. After all, that was part of the fun!

Philip died – which could have spoilt Jeanne's fun – but she decided to continue her revenge on his sons as they took the French throne. After 13 bloody years the last son of Philip died and Jeanne retired. It was said that she enjoyed capturing ships with French noblemen on board, then personally chopping off their heads with her axe. (Some women with a fleet may have a fish and chip shop. But when Jeanne caught her enemies on a fishing ship then she would have a fishing-ship chop.)

Her grey ghost still walks the walls of Clisson Castle – don't go there if your name is Philip!

Marcia Ordelaffi

Marcia's husband, Francesco, was not an easy man to live with. In 1358 his son suggested that Francesco should surrender his fortress in Italy. Old Fran didn't like the idea much so he stabbed the lad to death.

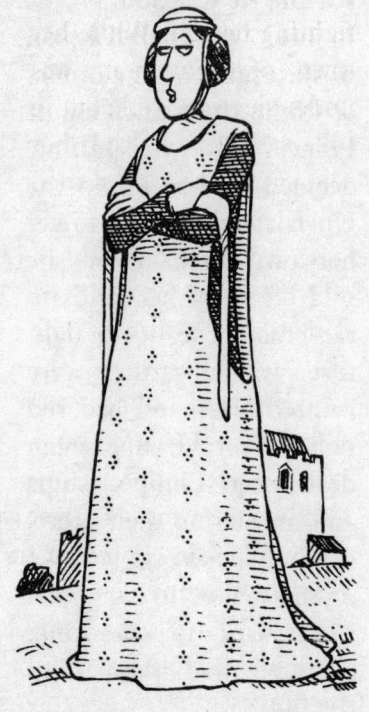

The kid killer left wife Marcia in charge of the defence of Cesena a few years later. Sensible Marcia did NOT suggest that they should surrender . . . at least, not until he had gone off to defend another city.

Marcia suspected that one of her councillors was talking to the enemy about a surrender. She had him arrested and beheaded. This was quite a good way to make sure he didn't talk to anyone ever again.

Tough-talking Marcia then talked her way out of the siege and escaped alive with her family.

Madame de Montfort

When John de Montfort was captured in a 1341 battle in Brittany, his wife took over the war effort. Apart from raising armies she liked to do a bit of fighting herself. While her town of Hennebont was under siege she rode out in full armour to lead her soldiers. Arrows rained down but she rallied the men. She told the women of Hennebont to cut their skirts short; that way they could run up to the ramparts with stones and pots of boiling tar to pour over the attackers.

When the attackers grew tired Madame de Montfort led a group of knights out of the town through a secret gate. They rode round behind the enemy and destroyed half of the army. The siege was over and Hennebont was saved.

John de Montfort escaped and hurried home to his warrior wife. What did the wimp do next? Help her? Take over as army leader? Give her a thank-you kiss? No! He died! How very inconsiderate.

Madame de Montfort carried on the war for her son. She went mad, was captured by the English and locked away for 30 years till she died.

Jeanne la Pucelle

Jeanne was a French farmer's daughter . . . probably! (Some nutty historians say she was in fact the daughter of the Queen of France!)

Jeanne heard angel voices telling her to lead French soldiers to victory against the invading English. Against all the odds this is what she did.

In spite of being wounded with a crossbow bolt she defeated the English siege of Orléans in 1429. Unfortunately she couldn't defeat France's other enemy, Burgundy. The Burgundians captured Jeanne and very sensibly sold her to the English. The English couldn't execute her as a soldier, so they said she was a witch and burned her at the stake. Her main crime? Wearing men's clothes!

The English lost the war in the end – which served them right for being so mean and measly to this 20-year-old young woman. She became known as Joan of Arc.

Isabella of England

Isabella was the daughter of King Edward III and a useful bargaining tool for old Ed. At three years old she was engaged to Pedro the Cruel of Spain – luckily for Isabella that one fell through! When she was 15, King Ed decided to marry her off to Count Louis de Male. Now King Ed had led the English at the battle of Crécy where Louis's dad had been killed. Louis said, 'No!' to the idea of marrying the English king's daughter.

His people locked him away until he agreed to marry Isabella. After a few months of prison he gave in and he was released from his prison. Louis was still closely guarded, of course, but they said 'he couldn't so much as pee without his guards knowing.' (Charming!) Just before the wedding Louis went out hawking and chased after a

heron . . . and didn't stop till he was over the border in France! He'd escaped . . . and Isabella was ditched.

But Isabella was a tough lady. Four years later she promised to marry another young man, Berard d'Albret. Just as she was about to set sail for the wedding in France she changed her mind and went home.

She'd made a monkey out of Berard. Or, rather, she made a monk out of him. Poor Berard was so upset he gave up women altogether and joined a monastery.

Did you know . . . ?

In the 14th century, Emperor Ludwig's daughter was married . . . but it was Ludwig who said, 'I will.' Why? Because his daughter was too young to talk. When she grew up dumb, people said, 'It's God's way of showing that Ludwig shouldn't have married off his baby daughter.' But why did the girl have to suffer? Why didn't God strike Ludwig dumb?

Cheerless children

If women had a hard time then how did children manage? Would you have survived to your present age? Probably not! Look at how the Middle Ages were . . .

Kruel for kids
1 Parents paid little attention to children till they were five or six. After all, they were probably going to die. Only one child in three lived to their first birthday. Only one in ten lived to their tenth. (No one made birthday-cake candles in those days. There wasn't enough business!)
2 Parents of the Middle Ages may have been measly, but at least they were a small improvement on Anglo-Saxon parents. Many of the Anglo-Saxons believed that a child born on a Friday would have a miserable life – so they spared them the unhappiness by killing them when they were born! Others 'tested' the new baby by putting it in a dangerous place – a roof-top or a tree branch. If it cried it was a wimp and was killed – if it laughed it lived. (And if it laughed so hard it fell out of the tree it died anyway!)

3 But life was still very tough for children in the Middle Ages. If the plague didn't get you then one of the other Middle Age marauders might! In 1322 Bernard de Irlaunde's baby daughter was playing in her father's shop. A passing pig wandered into the shop, bit the baby on the head and killed her. What a swine!

4 Children from rich families were cared for by nurses. The babies were wrapped in tight bands of cloth so they couldn't move – this was supposed to make their legs grow straight. In fact the lack of use made them weak for a year or two.

PERHAPS THAT'S TOO TIGHT!

5 Peasant children, on the other hand, had no clothes at all until they could walk. Before then they were kept warm by being laid in front of the fire. Curious little crawlers ended up cooked! But even the ones who lay still could have an accident. An old law said . . .

If a woman place her infant by the hearth and a man put water in the cauldron and it boileth over, and the child be scalded to death, the woman must be punished for her neglect.

If there was a law against it then there must have been a lot of cases of it happening. (Notice it's the woman who gets the blame and not the man? But that's another story!)

6 Parents didn't have the Royal Society for the Prevention of Accidents to advise them! They could be very careless about where they left their children. In Canterbury some very young children were left by the river and drowned. In another case an archer was practising his shooting and accidentally shot a child.

7 Worst of all were the beggars who broke their children's limbs so the public would give generously to the twisted, suffering little child!

8 Writers suggested that it was a mistake for parents to be too kind to their children. Children should be respectful to parents. One boy told how he would greet his father with the words . . .

My right reverent and worshipful father, I praise your good fatherhood in the most humble way possible and humbly beg your good fatherhood for your daily blessing.

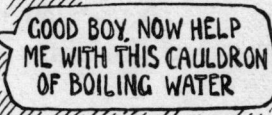

(This may well be a wise thing to say to your own father if you are planning to ask for an increase in pocket money.)

9 Don't laugh, girls. It would have been worse still for you. A book on a girl's behaviour said she mustn't laugh too loud, swear, walk too fast, yawn too wide or jerk her shoulders around. The advice on dealing with troublesome girls went . . .

If your daughters will rebel
and not bow down low,
If any of them do some wrong
then do not curse and blow.
Just take a large rod in your
hand and beat them in a row
Until they cry for mercy and
until their guilt they know.

This comes from the late-Middle Ages poem, 'How the Good Wife Taught Her Daughter', which was written by . . . a man, of course!

10 Boys who served lords had to stand perfectly still in the castle hall while their masters ate. A 15th-century book said . . .

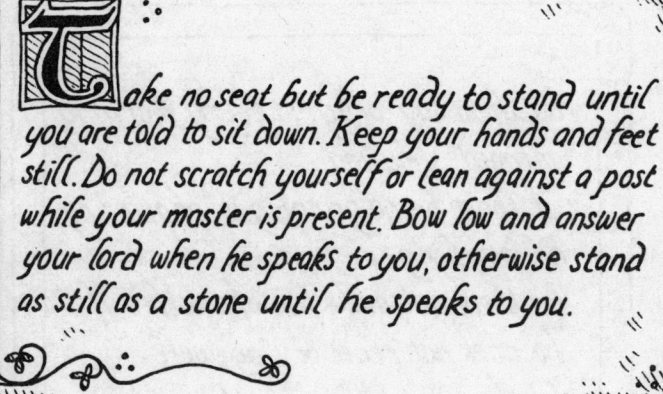

ake no seat but be ready to stand until you are told to sit down. Keep your hands and feet still. Do not scratch yourself or lean against a post while your master is present. Bow low and answer your lord when he speaks to you, otherwise stand as still as a stone until he speaks to you.

Sounds a bit like school assemblies today. And, talking about schools . . .

Schools – the good news
- You didn't have to go if you were poor . . . or a girl.
- Most boys only went to school from the ages of 7 to 14.
- There was no homework.
- There were no spelling corrections – you spelled English any way you wanted to.

Schools – the bad news
- You had no break-times – only a short stop for lunch.
- Make a mistake and you were beaten – usually with branches of a birch tree.
- You had to buy your own paper, ink and books – which were very expensive.
- And of course there were 'School Rules' . . .

School rules . . . OK?

Westminster School in the 13th century had the following rules . . .

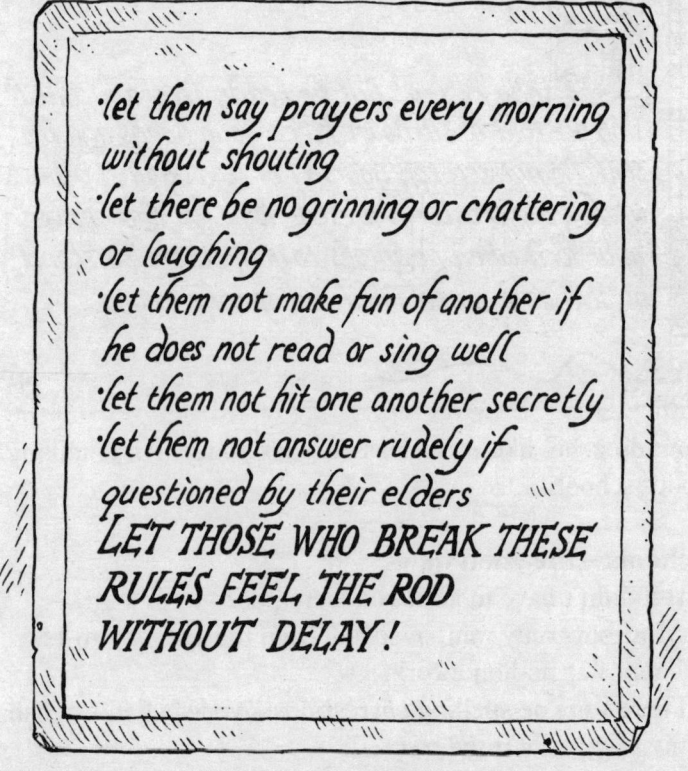

· let them say prayers every morning without shouting
· let there be no grinning or chattering or laughing
· let them not make fun of another if he does not read or sing well
· let them not hit one another secretly
· let them not answer rudely if questioned by their elders
LET THOSE WHO BREAK THESE RULES FEEL THE ROD WITHOUT DELAY!

Not too bad so far? Not much different from your own school, apart from the bit about being hit with a rod!

But if you knew Latin then you *had* to speak it. For each word of English or French that you spoke you received a stroke of the rod. Just imagine, turning to your friend and saying, 'Please can I borrow your book?' would get you six of the best. Measly!

And some of the other rules are odd. But they must have

needed these rules because someone actually did these dreadful deeds . . .

Anyone who has torn to pieces his school mate's bed or hidden the bedclothes or thrown shoes or pillow from corner to corner or thrown the school into disorder shall be severely punished in the morning.

No wonder this boy's 15th-century poem was so popular with pupils. He wrote about being late for school and giving a cheeky reply to his teacher . . .

My master looks like he is mad
'Where have you been, my sorry lad?'
'Milking ducks my mother had!'
It is no wonder that I'm sad.

My master peppered my backside with speed,
It was worse than fennel seed;
He would not stop till it did bleed,
I'm truly sorry for his deed.

I wish my master was a hare,
And all his fat books hound dogs were.
Me, the hunter, I'd not spare
Him. If he died I would not care!

Why was the boy late? You might well ask. Well, school often began at five o'clock in the morning in summer time! Wouldn't you be late?

Schools – the bad news for teachers

- Schoolteachers were not very well paid. Two hungry Huntingdon teachers were arrested for poaching in 1225.
- In 1381 a Suffolk teacher was arrested for riotous behaviour – if he was anything like my teachers then 'riotous behaviour' probably meant laughing out loud at a joke. (A rare event – teachers don't normally understand jokes.)
- In Oxford, England, one teacher's devotion to duty lead to a shocking end. If his pupils had written a diary then it might have looked like this . . .

Dear Diary, today we had a terrible tragedy. Our school teacher Master Dicken, decided to thrash us all with the birch because Peter de Vere left a dead rat on his desk (It was meant to be a gift. Peter's funny like that.) Master Dicken began thrashing the first boy on the register Thomas Abbot and the birch twigs began to split. "Copy out Psalm 34 onto your wax tablets while I collect more birch twigs,"

Master Dicken told us. We went to the window and watched him march down the school garden to the river bank. All the branches hanging over the garden were dry and brittle. It has been a dry summer. The really springy hurting branches hung over the river. We watched, amazed, as he began to climb the tree and make his way out to the branches over the river. We counted as he cut ten, eleven, twelve whippy twigs. They do say thirteen is an unlucky number. As he cut number thirteen he lost his hold and tumbled into the water. His heavy gown soaked up the water and dragged him down. We raced out of the classroom and down the garden to get a better look. Master Dicken was waving at us. Each time his head came above the surface he waved. We waved back. At last his head went under one last time. We watched for another hour but saw no more of him. "I think he's in trouble," Peter de Vere said. "Shall we go for help?" he asked. "Give it another hour — just to be sure," I told him.

The teacher died. But death wasn't the only thing faced by teachers. There was worse! Damage to precious school-books! One Middle Ages schoolteacher wrote a letter to a parent complaining of his son's greasy fingerprints and scribbled notes on his books not to mention . . .

> *In winter it is chilly, his nose runs, and he does not even bother to wipe it until it has dripped and dirtied the book.~*

Groovy games you may like to play
At least children in the Middle Ages did have toys – like dolls with their own carriages. The carriages were pulled along by mice. (It's annoying opening a Christmas present today and finding it has dead batteries. Imagine opening one and finding it has dead mice!)

Children played games that are still played today – see-saws, swings, skipping, hide-and-seek, and follow-the-leader.

They also played some very rough games that you may not enjoy so much. Their Blind Man's Buff game was known as Hoodman Blind or Hot Cockles. A child would be 'It' and turn their hood around so it covered their face. They knelt on the ground with their hands behind their back while the others ran past and swiped the hands. If the hooded child guessed who had struck them then the striker became 'It' and so it went on.

Some games were played by adults as well as children. Games like . . .

Raffle

You need:

• three dice
• a score sheet and pen

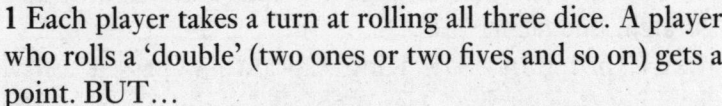

Rules:

1 Each player takes a turn at rolling all three dice. A player who rolls a 'double' (two ones or two fives and so on) gets a point. BUT…

2 If both players roll a double then the highest wins the point. (Double four beats double two, say.)

3 The first player to 10 points is the winner BUT…

4 Any player rolling three dice the same wins the whole game with that throw.

Kayles

You need:

• ten skittles (or plastic bottles of the sort used for powdered milk)
• a stick (or a 30 cm ruler)

Rules:

1 Place the skittles in a triangle with the point towards the thrower. The first row has one skittle, row two has two, row three has three and row four has four. (Even you can remember that!) The skittles should be fairly close so that if one falls it will knock over another one.

2 Agree a mark of 2 to 3 metres away from the skittles.

3 Each player throws the stick twice at the skittles.

4 The player who knocks over the most in two throws is the winner.

Note: Another arrangement is to place the skittles in a straight line facing you.

Extra note: In 1477 King Edward IV passed a law banning this game. He probably couldn't stand the thought of poor people enjoying themselves!

Gruesome games you wouldn't want to play

People enjoyed playing ghastly games. Some are still played and have hardly changed in the last 700 years . . .

Camp ball

The game was similar to football. You grabbed the ball and tried to get it into your opponent's goal a few dozen metres or a couple of miles apart. There were any number on each

side and hardly any rules. The trouble was there were no football strips – players wore their normal clothes . . . including knives! In Newcastle-Upon-Tyne in 1280, Henry de Ellington ran into David le Keu. David was wearing a knife at his belt, the knife stabbed Henry in the gut and he died. Deadly David didn't get a red card but hacked Henry probably got a very red shirt.

Stool ball

A milkmaid sat on a three-legged stool. Measly men bowled a ball at her like skittles while she tried to dodge. If they hit her then they got a prize. But beware! The prizes were not gold medals. They were cakes . . . or kisses!

Ice jousting

Ice-skating was popular but the skates were made of animal bones strapped to the feet. The skaters didn't move their feet the way modern skaters do. They pushed

themselves along with poles (like skiers). This harmless sport became deadly when savage skaters charged at each other at speed and used the poles like knights' lances. Lots of broken poles but even more broken bones. Then there was the danger of thin ice.

Archaeologists dug up the skeleton of a woman from the bed of a river. Bone skates were still attached to the skeleton bones of her feet. No prizes for guessing what happened to her.

Snowballing

This popular game was probably played by cavemen. But the people of the Middle Ages had to think of a particularly nasty use for it. They used snowballs to pelt Earl Thomas of Lancaster . . . while he was being taken to his execution!

Middle Ages mind-benders

Pester your parents or torment your teachers with these questions. After all, those wrinklies are a few years nearer to the Middle Ages than you. They have a better chance of getting them right.

1 If you go to a wedding today then you may throw confetti over the bride for luck. In the Middle Ages the guests threw . . .
a) Grains of rice.
b) Tins of rice.
c) Sawdust.

2 Universities were wild places where one rule said . . .
a) It is forbidden to stick a knife in an examiner just because he asks you a hard question.
b) Students who get a question wrong must miss a day's food.
c) Cheeky students must write out 1000 times, 'I will obey.'

3 A miller in the Middle Ages dug clay from the middle of the road to mend his house. What happened next?

a) He was arrested and forced to fill in the hole with stones from the seashore ten miles away.

b) The hole filled with water after a storm and a travelling glove-maker fell in and drowned.

c) The local people took the clay back to the road and the miller's house fell down.

4 Superstitious people in the Middle Ages believed in monsters in far-off lands. One such monster was the Sciapod. He was a one-legged giant. But how did people say the Sciapod shaded himself from the sun?

a) With an umbrella made from the skins of human beings he had eaten.

b) He ripped up an oak tree, rested it on his shoulder and used the branches as a sun shade.

c) He lay on his back, stuck his leg in the air and sheltered under the shadow of his huge foot.

THAT BIG MR SCIAPOD'LL GET TERRIBLE SUNBURN ON THE SOLE OF THAT FOOT OF HIS IF HE'S NOT TOO CAREFUL

OOOO YES

5 The Count of Armagnac argued with his wife over some property. How did he try to persuade her to sign it over?
a) Sent her a wagon-load of flowers, 20 new dresses and a barrel of perfume.
b) Broke a few of her bones and locked her away.
c) Placed a rope around his neck and threatened to jump off the castle roof.

6 In the Middle Ages many lords employed someone called a 'panter'. But what was a panter's job?
a) To look after the pantry in the castle kitchen.
b) To run through the forest (panting) and drive deer out for his lordship to shoot at.
c) To work in the tailor's shop making pants.

IT'S HIS FIRST DAY

7 The peasants' revolt was led by a soldier called Wat Tyler. How did he get the name 'Wat'?
a) His parents christened him 'Wat'.
b) His initials W.A.T. stood for Wilfred Andrew Tyler and 'Wat' became his nickname.
c) Wat was short for Walter.

8 Boys at St Paul's school had to pee into large tubs. Why?
a) Because it was more hygienic.
b) Because the school could sell the urine to local leather workers for softening leather.
c) Because it was too far to the river-side toilets and they would miss lessons.

9 How did monks in the Middle Ages keep the bald patch (tonsure) in the middle of their heads?

a) They polished it with a piece of stone.

b) They singed the hair with a wax taper then dusted the ash off with a leather glove.

c) They pulled the hair out one strand at a time with tweezers.

10 Dick Whittington died in 1423 after twice being mayor of which town?

a) Storytown (because he never really existed).

b) London.

c) Calais.

Answers:

1c) Rice is an Asian crop not grown in England. If any did reach Britain in the Middle Ages then it would be far too precious to waste on a buxom bride! ('Buxom' meant 'obedient' because that's what a Middle Ages woman promised to be.)

2a) Students in Oxford became highwaymen to pay for their classes. The townspeople of Oxford responded by attacking the students – they killed and scalped quite a few! (Punishment c) was still being given to school pupils in the 1970s – but at least they had stopped scalping by then.)

3b) The miller took so much clay that the glove-maker rode into what looked like a puddle but was really deep enough to drown him . . . and his horse!

4c) And if any other Sciapods came along to disturb him then he'd tell them to hop it! (Only joking.)

5b) He was the sort of bully who gets his own way by putting somebody's eye in a sling.

6a) He worked with the ewerer (and if you were a ewerer you were a man in charge of washing the tablecloths and napkins) and with the spit boys (who spitted meat but didn't spit spittle) and with pot boys (who didn't have pot bellies).

7c) Wat Tyler was Walter Tyler. In fact the peasants mightn't have followed him if they'd known they were being led by a Wally.

8b) The school sold the urine and put the money they made towards the school fund. Many modern schools find ways to make money for the school fund. Has your school thought of this one?

9a) They used a type of stone called pumice stone – a sort of volcanic rock that is still sold today. People now use it in the bath to smooth off rough skin on the feet. (WARNING: If you find some in your bathroom, do not practise on your dad.)

10c) Dick Whittington was a real person. Everyone knows the story of Dick and his cat and the bells that said, 'Turn again Whittington and you shall be Lord Mayor of London three times.' BUT not a lot of people know that he was also Mayor of Calais – twice! Which just goes to show, eight out of ten cats (and Calais voters) prefer Whittington!

Rotten religion

People of the Middle Ages were pretty superstitious. They believed in almost anything supernatural, including . . .

Ropey relics
Monasteries collected religious articles. They attracted visitors and were often said to perform miracles. Relics like a tooth of Saint Apollonia – the patron saint of toothache – could cure your tortured tootsie-peg. (Her teeth had been knocked out by the Romans before they burned her.) Hundreds of monasteries had a tooth from her mouth. Big mouth? No, simply another miracle, the monks explained. Henry VI of England collected a ton of them.

Why not start your own collection of saintly relics? Next time you cut your fingernails, save the clippings – that's what one group of measly monks did and said they belonged to St Edmund. Bones make very popular relics. (Your local butcher's shop may be able to help! Many travelling friars used pigs' bones to cheat people.)

Here are just ten 'relics' from churches and monasteries across Europe . . .

- a piece of St Eustace's brain (wonder what it thought about being a relic?)

- wood from the manger in which Jesus was born and the cloth that the baby Jesus was wrapped in
- the coals on which St Lawrence was roasted
- Saint John's handkerchief (complete with Saintly snot)

- one of the stones used to stone St Stephen to death (bloodstained, naturally)
- a piece of the stone on which Jesus stood as he ascended to heaven
- a piece of bread chewed by Jesus
- the head of John the Baptist (Angers and Amiens Cathedrals both had one!)

- the crown of thorns placed on Jesus' head at his crucifixion
- a piece of wood from Jesus' cross (thousands of these).

All right, so I made up the handkerchief, but the others are all genuine relics! Or genuine fakes, but the believers took them seriously. Dead seriously. The monks of Conques pinched a saint's body from another monastery!

One saintly monk was terrified to hear that a monastery was planning to kill him and boil his body down so they could have his bones as relics – he changed his mind about visiting them.

Pay as you pray
In 1303 King Philip of France argued with the Italian Pope Boniface about who people should obey – kings or popes. Philip decided the matter by kidnapping 86-year-old Boniface from Rome. The Pope never recovered from the shock and died.

OH WELL, I SUPPOSE WE CAN STILL SELL HIM IN BITS AS RELICS

The next pope was a Frenchman called Clement. Wise Clement decided to stay in France – after all, the Italians might get their own back and kidnap him if he went to Rome. (There was also a little matter of Clement's girlfriend. He wanted to stay with her in France.)

Once the Pope and his headquarters moved to France they set about cashing in on their power. If you ever become Pope then here are a few measly Middle Ages ways of making money . . .

Religious rip-offs
1 If you commit a sin (like pinching a penny or pinching the bum of the girl in front of you) then the church can

114

'pardon' you . . . if you pay.

2 If you want to be important in the church (say, a cardinal because they get to wear a red cloak and you think red suits you) then you can have the job . . . if you pay.

3 If a church owns some very holy object (like the toe-nail of a saint or the feather from an angel's wing) then you can have it . . . if you pay.

4 If you give a gift to your local church (maybe money so the church will say prayers after you are dead), the Pope will take a share.

5 The Pope may raise a tax to pay for a Crusade (to fight against the non-Christians in the Holy Land) . . . you fork out, but he won't actually spend it on a Crusade.

6 If you want to be buried in two places at once (your heart in one place and your body in another, like Richard II) then you can have permission . . . if you pay.

7 If you want to marry a close relative (like your dead husband's brother) then you can have permission . . . if you pay.

8 If you are a nun and want to keep two maids (one to do your cleaning and one to do your praying, maybe?) then you can have permission . . . if you pay.

I HAVE TO TRY TO SAVE MONEY, CAN YOU PRAY WHILE YOU CLEAN?

9 If you want to trade with those 'awful' non-Christian chaps from the East (and after all we do want their delicious spices, don't we?) then you can have permission . . . if you pay.

Potty plays

The local craftsmen formed themselves into groups called guilds. Around Easter the guilds came together to produce plays for the people – the masses. These plays were based on Bible stories: Miracle Plays and Mystery plays. That doesn't sound too measly – yet. The guilds performed the plays depending on their own mastery – so they called them mystery plays. Mastery-mystery, geddit?

At first these were performed at the altar of the church – but they became too popular and the churches were full of smelly people. So the plays were moved into the churchyards. But people began trampling on the graves to get a better view. In the end they were taken out of the churches and on to the streets.

The plays were always religious – but that didn't stop them being fun and horribly dangerous! In those days there was no one to give a 'rating' to the plays. Nowadays you know a film is a bit scary if it has a PG (Parental Guidance) rating. In the Middle Ages a lot of the plays were PG – Pretty Gruesome! Which of these horrors could be seen on stage in the Middle Ages?

1 John the Baptist having his head cut off.
2 Jesus being crucified.
3 Jesus rising from the dead and ascending into heaven (or the roof of the stage).
4 The tigers eating the hamsters on Noah's Ark.
5 The donkeys of the Three Wise Men leaving piles of dung droppings on the stage.
6 The Roman Emperor Nero slitting open his mother's stomach.
7 Adam and Eve appearing naked in the garden of Eden.
8 Judas hanging himself from a tree.

117

Answers:

1 True. At the last moment the actor was switched for a dummy. The fake neck was chopped, splitting a bag of ox blood that splashed into the audience.

2 True. The nails through the hands were faked but the suffering for the actor could still be quite nasty – he was tied up to the cross for as much as three hours . . . while the actors playing Roman soldiers spat at him! A local priest played Jesus – and almost died on the cross!

3 True. A series of weights and pulleys were used to winch the actor up on a platform.

4 False. But Noah's Ark was very popular with floods from barrels of water and great drums of stones rumbled to make the sound of thunder. Noah was often shown as drunk and nearly naked.

5 True. The 'donkeys' were actors in a donkey skin. They pushed piles of manure out from under the tail!

6 True. It was a fake stomach, of course. When the sword split the skin, a bundle of pig's guts from the butcher spilled out on to the stage.

7 False. Adam could have played the part – Eve would have had a bit of a problem since all the actors were men!

8 True. An actor playing Judas 'hanged' himself at the end of the play . . . and did it so well he almost died!

In 1326 the people of London turned against the Church because of the taxes it collected. They grabbed a bishop, cut his head off and left his naked body in the street – that was for real; no acting involved!

Batty beliefs
Medieval people believed that in faraway lands there were . . .
- forests so high they touched the clouds
- tribes of people with horns who grow old in seven years
- men with the heads of dogs and six toes
- trees that grow wool

- cyclopeans with one eye and one foot who moved faster than the wind (when told to hop it)
- 100-metre snakes with jewels for eyes.

Eerie eggs.
Got a sickly sister or a plague-spotted pal? Want to know if they'll recover? The doctor would take a hen's egg and write the letters i, so, p, q, x, s, y, s, 9, o on the side. The egg was left in the open air overnight then cracked open in the morning. If there's blood in the egg then call the undertaker!

(Of course this is *nonsense*! But it meant the doctors could say, 'See! They are fated to die. Don't blame me – blame God . . . and here's my bill.')

Miserable monks

Life was unpleasant for peasants. As the Middle Ages went on, some were able to move from the land to the towns which were starting to grow. After the Black Death the Feudal System began to fall apart. Peasants became free to sell their labour or to move.

In towns they could become craftsmen or traders. They weren't tied to the land by the old Feudal System and some grew rich as merchants. But for others the only way out of the measly miserable life on the land was to join the church. Boys and girls as young as seven could be taken on as monks or nuns.

At first the young trainee monks were called novices – a bit like learner drivers in cars today, they weren't allowed to go out on their own. But it was a very hard life . . . even harder than school today! Some of the mini-monks must have had a miserable time . . .

> Dear Mum,
> Hope you can get someone in the village to read this to you. The fact is, I want to come home. It's horrible here and I miss your rabbit pies.
> It all starts at 2 in the morning. First prayers. That awful bell wakes us up,

and I have to put on my sandals. I don't have to dress because we sleep in our robes — and they're rotten and itchy. Last night I stumbled into the back of old Brother Benedict. He whipped me with a cane. Have you ever tried praying for two hours with a burning backside?

I got back to bed at 4 and slept two hours — on my face, of course — then that bell's ringing again to call us off to Prime service at 6. Brother Benedict breaks the ice on the water trough and makes me wash. He says it will stop me falling asleep. It just freezes my cheeks. Did you know the Benedictine monks pray at least eight times a day? I asked old Benedict if God wouldn't want us to stop so he could get some sleep. He whipped me — Benedict, that is, not God.

We get breakfast at 7. It's usually porridge. Thin, cold, gritty porridge. Except this morning brother Edward stood on my toe and I cried out. We aren't allowed to make a noise at meals. I was whipped and told I'd eat bread and water for three days. I'd rather have your rabbit pies.

At 8 it's the meeting in the Chapter House — but the novices don't get a word in while the old goats groan on about money and work. It ends with prayers for the dead. But Mum... I don't know anybody that's dead. I sometimes wish I was dead though. Heaven has to be warmer than this place.

After Terce service at 9 we work. It was writing practice in the scriptorium for me. Brother Eamon makes us write on vellum — that's skins taken from the bellies of calves. I wonder why God wants us to do that? This letter's written on the belly of a calf, but I didn't kill it. I can't hold the goose-feather pen in my cold hands. I make smudges and Brother Eamon beats me.

It's High Mass at 11 then off to the fields to work. I had to dig cow muck into the soil. The smell would have made me sick, if I'd had any food in my stomach.

I'm almost glad to get indoors for the None service at 3 then it's lessons till Vespers at 6. I had to sit next to Anthony and I argued with him. He gets beaten as hard as me so I didn't feel too bad. Just hungry.

Compline at 7 and I have bread and water while the other monks eat peas with herbs. That tastes worse than bread and water. Every day. peas and herbs, peas and herbs. Sometimes I imagine I have herbs and peas for a change.

At 8 I have a little time to write this before I go to bed and it starts all over again at 2 tomorrow morning. Just let me come home, Mum, and I promise I'll be the best son you've ever had. I'll walk all the way, I'll pay back the gift that you gave to the monks when they took me in. Just let me come home Mum. I do miss your rabbit pies. Please, Mum.

Your loving son,

Arthur

Mischievous monks

The monks can't all have been saints because rules were written down to say what monks must NOT do. So somebody must have done these terrible things or they wouldn't have had to have the rules! Some of the rules look rather similar to school rules!

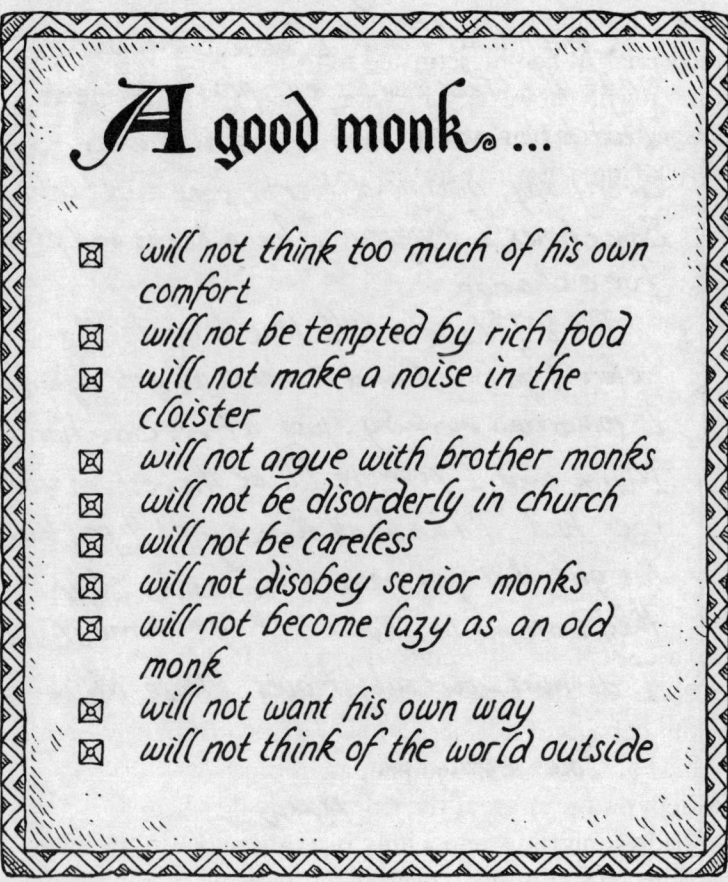

A good monk ...

- ☒ *will not think too much of his own comfort*
- ☒ *will not be tempted by rich food*
- ☒ *will not make a noise in the cloister*
- ☒ *will not argue with brother monks*
- ☒ *will not be disorderly in church*
- ☒ *will not be careless*
- ☒ *will not disobey senior monks*
- ☒ *will not become lazy as an old monk*
- ☒ *will not want his own way*
- ☒ *will not think of the world outside*

Rules for nuns were very similar. How would *you* have survived?

St Roch

People who caught the plague used to call upon the spirit of St Roch for help. Roch caught the plague when he was a young man and went to a wood to die. A dog brought him food and he recovered. When he returned to the town, however, he was suspected of being a spy and thrown into jail where he died. A strange light filled the cell as he died and his captors believed it was a miracle. They decided that if you called for his help then you'd be cured of the plague. On the other hand you may *not* be cured of the plague! This was not St Roch's fault. This was because God decided you had been too wicked.

St Charles

Charles of Blois (in France) was a saintly man. He . . .

- never washed his clothes so he was crawling with lice, put pebbles in his shoes and knotted cords tightly round his body so he suffered pain at all times.
- slept on the straw at the side of his wife's bed.
- made a pilgrimage to a holy place, barefoot in the snow. When his admirers covered the path with blankets he took another road and walked till his feet were frozen and bleeding.

125

Charles of Blois was a vicious and cruel man. He . . .

- used large catapults to hurl the heads of dead prisoners into an enemy city.
- massacred 2,000 men, women and children when he captured a town called Quimper.

Cruelty alongside saintliness. That pretty well sums up the measly Middle Ages.

Epilogue

Richard III was killed at the Battle of Bosworth Field in 1485. His body was stripped and paraded in public for two days. That was the sort of gruesome spectacle the people of the Middle Ages would have enjoyed.

But things were changing. In England Henry Tudor began a new era – that of the terrible Tudors. The English had been invaded by the Normans, and seen Matilda and Stephen fight a civil war for the crown. The barons had rebelled against King John then gone to war with Henry in another war. Then the country went into a Hundred Years War with France at the same time as it was ravaged by the terrible Black Death. No sooner had the Hundred Years War finished than the vicious Wars of the Roses tore the country apart.

At last Henry Tudor brought a new and wonderful gift to the English people. Peace. And in those peaceful few years the people were able to enjoy life a little more. They became 'civilized'. Life was never quite the same crude, rough, dangerous (and short) thing it had been.

That's why some historians draw the line at the Battle of Bosworth Field and say, 'That was the end of the Middle Ages.' Of course nothing's ever that simple or neat. But things were happening in the rest of the world that meant change was on the way. Just a few years later, in 1492, a bloke called Columbus discovered America. Then Henry Tudor's son, Henry VIII, cut England's links with the Catholic Church and the Pope in Rome.

By the time slimy Stuart king James I united England with her old enemy, Scotland, in 1603, those old days of the measly Middle Ages seemed a world away.

But a clever Frenchman called Voltaire said, 'History never repeats itself . . . humans always do.' The cruelty and stupidity and superstition of the Middle Ages should be a distant nightmare. Yet in the 20th century people can still find ways of making life miserable for others. Bullies with muscles, bullies with money or bullies with power. Just read today's newspapers.

Until they stop we are not really out of the Middle Ages. We're still living in them.

MEASLY
MIDDLE AGES

GRISLY QUIZ

**Now find out if you're a
measly Middle Ages expert!**

MIDDLE AGES MIND-BENDERS

A muddled monk wrote these facts about the Middle Ages. But he jumbled the words and he added one word to each sentence that doesn't belong there! Can you sort the words into the right order? (Clue: the odd word out is always in the same position in the sentence)

KNOW HOW YOU HARD WHEN IT'S NOT REALLY TROUT

1. Brides threw over the guests sawdust wedding cake.
2. Teachers were allowed to stab their students not Mondays.
3. A rider road and drowned his horse in a hole in the head.
4. An umbrella used his foot as a giant single snail.
5. The Count of Armagnac broke his bones in a wife's row boat.
6. A pantry looked panter after the castle crumbled.
7. Walter Tyler's proper rebel name was Wat luck.
8. Barrel boys' at St Paul's school collected a pee in the teachers hats.
9. Heads polished their stone with a monks habit.
10. Calais Dick Whittington was twice mayor of London.

CLUELESS CURES

The people of the 1300s didn't know how to cure the plague but made some weird guesses. Which of the following did they actually try?

1. Sniff scented flowers.
2. Kill all the town's cats and dogs.
3. Wear a magpie's beak around your neck.
4. Build huge bonfires in the street to burn the bad air.
5. Drill a hole in your head to let out evil spirits.
6. Don't drink from any well because it could be poisoned.
7. Sleep on your side because sleeping on your back lets foul air run into your nose.
8. Drink cream mixed with the blood from a black cat's tail.
9. Eat onions, leeks and garlic.
10. Eat ten-year-old treacle mixed with marigold flowers and powdered egg.
11. Stop having baths or shaves or a change of clothes.
12. Run away to the countryside where the air is fresh.
13. Throw sweet-smelling herbs on a fire to clean the air.
14. Sit in a sewer so the bad air of the plague is driven off by the worse air of the drains.

15. Swallow powders of crushed emeralds.
16. Eat arsenic powder.
17. Try letting blood out of your body (when your horoscope is right).
18. Shave a live chicken's bottom and strap it to the plague sore.
19. March from town to town flogging yourself with a whip to drive out devils.

WEIRD WORDS

Books began to be printed in English and people could read the horrible sufferings of the peasants – though the peasants themselves probably wouldn't have been able to read. William Langland wrote a poem about a peasant called 'Piers Ploughman' and his miserable life. Can you work out just how miserable from this part of the poem? Some of the words have been scrambled by a careless printer – well, the first book printed in English was produced in 1475, so he hadn't had a lot of practice.

The Peasant

His coat of a cloth that is NITH (1) as the East wind,
His DOHO (2) full of holes with his HARI (3) sticking through,
His clumsy HOSSE (4), knobbled and nailed over thickly,
Yet his SOTE (5) poked clean through as he trod on the ground.
Two miserable mittens made out of old GRAS (6),
The fingers worn out and the FHLIT (7) caked on them,
He waded in mud almost up to his KLANSE (8),
In front are four NOXE (9), so weary and feeble
Their BRIS (10) could be counted, so wretched they were.

132

QUICK QUESTIONS

1. In 1301 King Edward I's son, Edward, was proclaimed a prince. But he wasn't proclaimed Prince of England. Instead he was named prince of where? (Clue: not the Prince of Dolphins)

2. Edward I brought law and order to England. How did they say he dealt with a leading outlaw who was robbing travellers? (Clue: king of the road)

3. In 1314 the Scots were still fighting the new English king, Edward II. Scot James Douglas captured Roxburgh castle with a trick. What? (Clue: hide in places!)

4. In 1337 Edward III claimed to be King of France. The French disagreed and the Hundred Years War started . How long did it last? (Clue: not a hundred years!)

5. In 1376 Edward III died and ten-year-old Richard II was crowned the following year. He walked into Westminster but was carried out. Why? (Clue: zzzzz)

6. One of the curious rumours that was going around was that Richard II was born without what? (Clue: you can have sausages like this, but not humans)

7. In 1381 Richard's government charged an unpopular 'Poll Tax' of four pence for every person. A rebellion was led by a man called Tyler. What was his first name? (Clue: Yes, it is!)

8. The end of the century brought the end for Richard II.

In September 1399 he was forced to give up his throne to Henry IV. If he burst into tears then something he had invented would come in useful. What? (Clue: who nose if he really did invent it?)

9. The 1400s were just six days old when Richard II died. He had been a prisoner of the new king, Henry IV. How did Richard die? (Clue: he has no stomach for a fight)

10. Henry V took the throne in 1413 and married Catherine. Two hundred and thirty years later the writer Samuel Pepys kissed her. How? (Clue: everyone likes a kiss from their mummy)

11. Henry VI sat at the head of his parliament. But he sat where no English king has sat before or since. Where? (Clue: another kiss from mummy)

Answers

Middle Ages Mind-benders

1. Wedding guests threw sawdust over the brides. (If you go to a wedding today then you might throw confetti over the bride for luck. In the Middle Ages the guests threw sawdust.)
2. Students were not allowed to stab their teachers. (It was forbidden to knife an examiner just because he asked you a hard question!)
3. A rider and his horse drowned in a hole in the road. (A miller dug clay from the middle of the road to mend his house. The hole filled with water after a storm and a travelling glove-maker fell in and drowned – along with his horse.)

4. A giant used his single foot as an umbrella. (Superstitious people believed in monsters, such as the one-legged 'Sciapod'. He lay on his back stuck his leg in the air and sheltered under the shadow of his huge foot.)

5. The Count of Armagnac broke his wife's bones in a row. (He was trying to persuade her to sign over some land. After beating her he threw her in a dungeon. This was gentle persuasion.)

6. A panter looked after the castle pantry. (He could have been named after the place where he worked – or he could have been a panter because he had to run up and down all those castle stairs!)

7. Rebel Wat Tyler's proper name was Walter. (He could have been called a Wally.)

8. Teachers at St Paul's school collected the boys' pee in a barrel. (It was sold to leather workers to soften the leather. So if your shoes are hard and uncomfortable, you know what to do? Limp.)

9. Monks polished their heads with a stone. (It was a stone called a 'pumice'. The slaphead monks would have used sandpaper if it had been invented.)

10. Dick Whittington was twice mayor of Calais. (Dick Whittington was a real person. Everyone knows the story of Dick and his cat and the bells that said, 'Turn again Whittington and you shall be Lord Mayor of London three times.' BUT not a lot of people know that he was also mayor of Calais – twice!

Clueless Cures

1–19. ALL are true except 3 (a cure for toothache), 5 (a cure for a headache) and 8 (a cure for a cough).

Weird Words
1) Thin 2) Hood 3) Hair 4) Shoes 5) Toes 6) Rags
7) Filth 8) Ankles 9) Oxen 10) Ribs

Quick Questions
1. Prince of Wales. It's a title that has been given to an English monarch's oldest son ever since.
2. Ed rode out and took on the outlaw in a fight. He beat him and made the road safe. (This is probably not a true story, though)
3. His soldiers disguised themselves as cattle! Under the cover of the skins they got close enough to surprise the guards.
4. 116 years.
5. Richard collapsed under the strain of the excitement – and the heavy robes and crown.
6. A skin! He was supposed to have been wrapped in a goat skin to save his life! Weird.
7. Wat.
8. The Handkerchief.
9. He starved himself to death, some said. Others said he'd been starved on the orders of the king.
10. Catherine's corpse was turned into a mummy and put on show next to the coffin of Henry V. People could look at her for a couple of pennies and she stayed there for almost 300 years. Samuel Pepys kissed the mummy – weird!
11. Henry sat on him mum's knee. He was just eight months old when he took the throne. Some days he had such screaming fits that his visits to parliament had to be cancelled.

INTERESTING INDEX

Where will you find 'brewed beetles', 'bottom-shaved chickens', 'ten-year-old treacle' and 'toads' in an index? In a Horrible Histories book, of course!

Terry Deary was born at a very early age, so long ago he can't remember. But his mother, who was there at the time, says he was born in Sunderland, north-east England, in 1946 – so it's not true that he writes all *Horrible Histories* from memory. At school he was a horrible child only interested in playing football and giving teachers a hard time. His history lessons were so boring and so badly taught, that he learned to loathe the subject. *Horrible Histories* is his revenge.

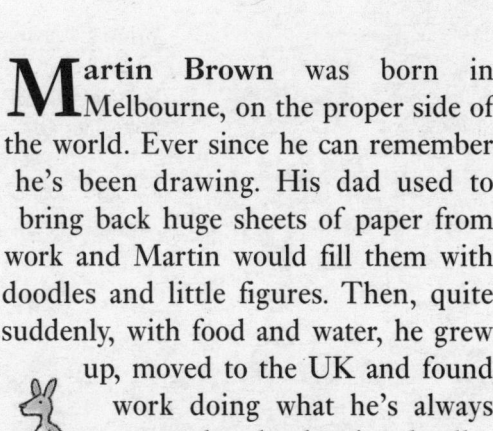

Martin Brown was born in Melbourne, on the proper side of the world. Ever since he can remember he's been drawing. His dad used to bring back huge sheets of paper from work and Martin would fill them with doodles and little figures. Then, quite suddenly, with food and water, he grew up, moved to the UK and found work doing what he's always wanted to do: drawing doodles and little figures.

HORRIBLE HISTORIES

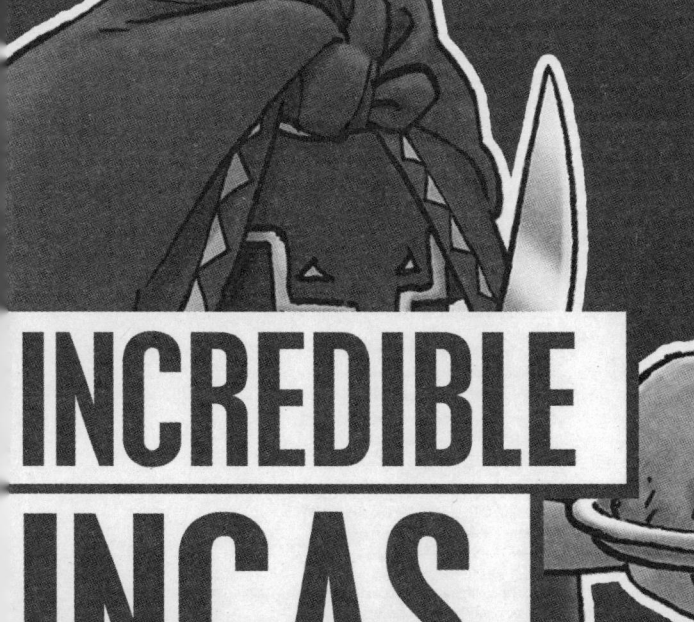

INCREDIBLE
INCAS

Terry Deary Illustrated by **Martin Brown & Philip Reeve**

SCHOLASTIC

To Virginia Garrard-Burnett, who proposed this book and researched it.
Sincere thanks.

Scholastic Children's Books,
Euston House, 24 Eversholt Street,
London NW1 1DB, UK

A division of Scholastic Ltd
London ~ New York ~ Toronto ~ Sydney ~ Auckland
Mexico City ~ New Delhi ~ Hong Kong

First published in the UK by Scholastic Ltd, 2000
This edition published 2017

Text © Terry Deary, 2000
Cover illustration © Martin Brown, 2008
Inside illustrations © Philip Reeve, 2000

ISBN 978 1407 17866 0

Printed and bound by CPI Group (UK) Ltd, Croydon, CR0 4YY

4 6 8 10 9 7 5 3

The right of Terry Deary, Martin Brown and Philip Reeve to be identified as the author and illustrators of this work has been asserted by them in accordance with the Copyright, Designs and Patents Act, 1988.

www.scholastic.co.uk

CONTENTS

Introduction

History can be horrible because history, like school, can be full of bullies ...

You'll be having a nice, peaceful life when along comes a bully and changes all that...

Who do you feel sorry for? The victim, of course!

But history is never that simple. Sooner or later the bully will meet up with an even more scary bully – usually one with better weapons...

Who do you feel sorry for now?

And what does the bully do when s/he's bullied? Give in and become a slave? Or stand up to the new bully?

The Incas were a bit like that. They came along and bullied the people of Peru into handing over their wealth. Then along came the Spanish invaders (the 'conquistadors') and turned the Incas into slaves.

So who do you feel sorry for?

To be honest there are no easy answers. That's why history is so horrible.

Of course school history books like questions with easy answers!

Question: 'When did the Spanish arrive in Peru?'

Answer: '1532.'

B-O-R-I-N-G!

But this is a horrible history and it will look at the questions that really matter. So trash that textbook and find out the terrible truth about the Incas ...

Timeline

Early Incan timeline

11,000 BC The first people settle in the area we now call Peru.

1250 BC Tribes of people begin to form in the Andes. They're called things like Chavin and Chimu, Nazca and Tiahuanaco.

AD 600 For a couple of hundred years the people from the Huari region will boss the western Andes. With them comes the spread of mummy burial. (That's corpses wrapped in cloth, not burying your mother.)

900 The Huari have gone (in a bit of a Huari) and the people split into tribes again. Most of these little states are no bigger than a single valley.

1105 Around this time the first Incan lord, Sinchi Roca, begins to rule his tribe, but his people are not very powerful … yet.

1370 The Chimu people are the biggest bullying bosses in Peru. They're led by Nancen Pinco who lives in Chan Chan. It seems as if these Chimu built a new palace for each new ruler and kept the old palaces going after the rulers died.

1438 The little Incan tribe starts to grow quickly and that means trouble. Over the next fifty years the incredible Incas will conquer all the other tribes and rule them.

Incan Empire timeline

1100 The Incas start to spread out and conquer other people. Maybe a few years of dry weather left them low on food so they had to go out and pinch it.

1438 The Chanca people attack the Incas. They're defeated but the invasion starts the Incas fighting amongst themselves.

1492 Chris Columbus stumbles across America. He'll soon be followed by Spanish conquistadors who'll conquer the South American peoples. They haven't reached the Incan lands yet ... but give them time.

1525 A terrible plague sweeps through the Incan homeland – probably a disease like measles or smallpox brought from Europe. The Spanish aren't in Peru yet but their germs are!

Later we'll see what happens when the Spanish arrive...

Legendary lords

Where do humans come from? People have wondered this since they had two brain cells to think with.

Scientists say . . .

They could be right.

Christians say…

They could be right. The Bible reckons God made us in his image and some of us are very god-like, aren't we?

But the Incas came up with an even more sensible idea…

A bit like worms!

Lord number 1: Mighty Manco

There are three caves at Paqari–tampu where (they say) the first Incan leader first saw the light of day. His name was Manco Capac and he popped out of one of the caves with his three brothers and four sisters. Ten groups of people appeared from the other caves, but naturally the Incas were the leaders. Then they set off on a great journey through the Andes...

THEY LOOKED FOR GOOD SOIL TO FARM AND GROW CROPS. MANCO HAD A BRIGHT IDEA...

MY BROTHERS EAT TOO MUCH! THERE'LL BE MORE FOOD FOR THE REST OF US IF I KILL THEM!

THAT'S WHAT HE DID. ONE WAS SEALED IN A CAVE AND TWO WERE TURNED TO STONE. THEN HE DID SOMETHING VERY STRANGE...

I NEED A WIFE. I CAN'T MARRY ONE OF THE COMMON PEOPLE. I'LL MARRY MY SISTER, MAMA OCLLO!

HELP!

IN TIME THEY HAD CHILDREN...

LET'S CALL THIS LITTLE CHAP SINCHI ROCA

AT LAST THE INCAS ARRIVED AT CUZCO.

SEEMS LIKE A NICE PLACE!

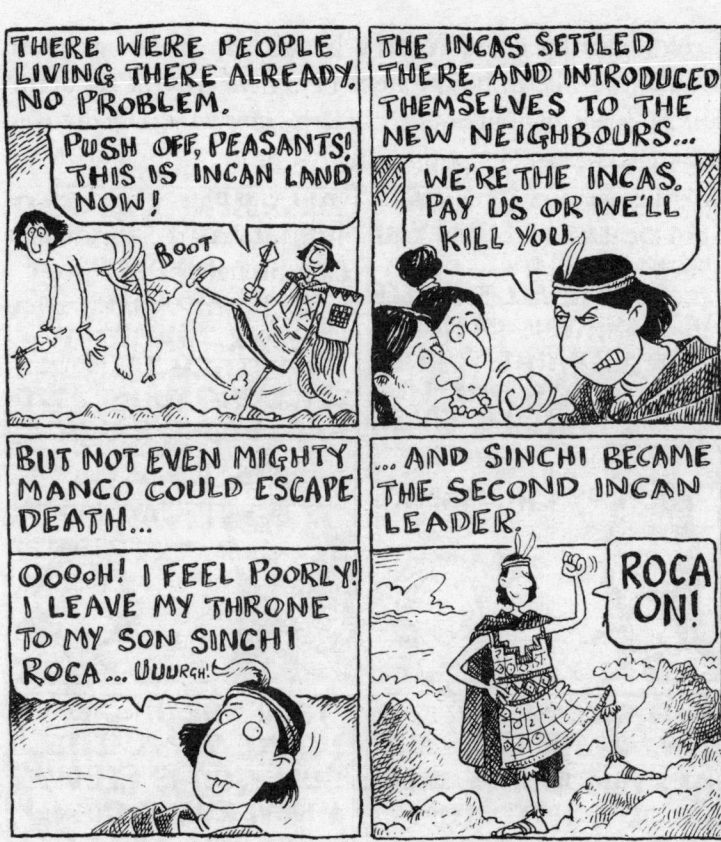

Incan legends say Manco was the first of eight Lords of Cuzco – their valley in the Andes. No one is sure how true the stories about the eight lords are. The important thing is that most Incas *believed* these stories.

Lord number 2: Super Sinchi

Another story says that when Manco Capac died there were lots of his children who could have taken his place. The people all wanted Sinchi Roca… but Sinchi was NOT expected to take the throne ahead of his brothers.

11

How did he do it? With a bit of help from his mum! Would you like to be the next Prime Minister/President/King/Queen of your country? Here's how Mama Ocllo fixed it for Sinchi…

HI THERE KIDS! TODAY I'M GOING TO SHOW YOU HOW TO MAKE A MONARCH! ALL YOU NEED IS A FORTUNE IN GOLD AND A BRIGHT YOUNG KID. HERE'S ONE I MADE EARLIER, SINCHI ROCA.

HI MAMA!

FIRST, BEAT YOUR GOLD INTO A THIN SHEET AND CUT OUT HUNDREDS OF CIRCLES ABOUT THE SIZE OF YOUR THUMBNAIL. NOW STITCH THEM ON TO A LONG TUNIC AND DRESS YOUR KID IN IT.

PHEW—IT'S HEAVY MAMA!

NOW TAKE THE KID TO A CAVE IN THE HILLS AND GET HIM TO HIDE THERE UNTIL YOU TELL HIM IT'S TIME TO COME OUT.

'BYE, MAMA

TELL THE INCAN PEOPLE THAT THE SUN GOD IS SENDING A NEW RULER DOWN TO EARTH AND HE'LL BE APPEARING FROM A CAVE, JUST LIKE THE FIRST INCA DID!

The trick seemed to work and Sinchi Roca was made the new Lord of Cuzco.

Stylish Sinchi

Sinchi was much more peaceful than dead old Manco. He spent less time murdering people and more time inventing things. What was his greatest invention? It was something that would show all the people who the royal family were, at a glance.

What did super Sinchi invent?

a) golden crowns **b)** purple robes **c)** fringe hairstyles

Answer: **c)** Yes, Sinchi Roca said that the Incan rulers would have their hair cut straight across the forehead.

Did you know…?
Sinchi Roca started another new trend after he died! He was the first of the Incan lords to be turned into a mummy. The corpse was kept so well it was put on show in Cuzco two hundred years after he died.

Lord number 3: Lovely Lloque

Third emperor (Lloque Yupanqui) was a pretty peaceful bloke compared to Manco. Even though he didn't go around flattening farmers, looting lands and ruling ruthlessly he was still remembered as . . .

Surprisingly enough, Lloque was called 'left-handed' because… he was left-handed.

Unforgettable? Well anyone who looked at Lloque would never forget him. That face would haunt your dreams for ever. He was simply the *ugliest* man anyone had ever seen! His sad story is soon told…

- People who saw him ran away.
- His chief wife couldn't stand the sight of him.
- He had no children with his chief wife.
- He was advised to take the daughter of a neighbouring chief for a wife – she couldn't stand the sight of him either.
- Her father forced her to marry Lloque and she gave birth to Mayta Capac.

Unforgettably ugly – do you know anyone like that?

Lord number 4: Mighty Mayta Capac

The fourth Lord of Cuzco, Mayta Capac, was big trouble from the moment he was born.

- Legend said that he was born six months before he was due.
- As a newborn baby he was strong and had all his teeth.
- By the time he was a year old he was as big as an eight-year-old. (Imagine the size of his nappies!)

Mayta ruled in the 1300s and began invading the tribes next to Cuzco valley. What was it that made Mayta such a nasty neighbour? The weather!

... AND DRY WEATHER IS FORECAST FOR THE NEXT FEW YEARS. CROPS WILL BE POOR, PEOPLE WILL STARVE AND WATER WILL BECOME PRECIOUS. OH, AND DON'T FORGET YOUR FACTOR 99 SUN CREAM IF YOU'RE GOING OUTSIDE! GOODNIGHT!

Mayta wasn't going to go hungry. He was simply going to train his people to fight and go out and pinch the food and water from other tribes. He was going to be the biggest bully since Manco Capac.

It's not surprising, really. Stories say Mayta had grown up as a big, bad boy, picking fights with any boys he came across. (You probably know someone like that.) He wasn't afraid to fight with bigger boys and the legends say he 'beat them badly'.

While he was still a boy he picked a fight with some peasants near Cuzco and killed them. This started a revolt by their tribe and his dad had trouble keeping it under control...

So mighty Mayta Capac was the perfect emperor to start conquering his next-door neighbours and making them hand over their hard-earned food supplies.

It was soon time to make Mayta a man. He had to go through the correct Incan ceremony...

Bye-bye boyhood
Do you know anyone who is growing into a man? Then instead of a birthday party or a school-leaver's do, why not give them a special treat? An Incan initiation! Follow these simple Incan rules to see your pal safely into the adult world...

MAKING IT INTO MANHOOD
(How to turn a boy into a man.)

You need: a llama, a sharp knife, a whip, a running track, a sling, a shield, a hard wooden club (called a 'mace'), a hole punch, a breechcloth (like a big boy's nappy) – and don't forget the boy!

1. First sacrifice your llama. (Sneak up behind the llama with your club. Club it to death, skin it and roast the meat.)

2. Offer the meat to the god of the sun.

YUM!

3. Strip the boy to the waist, give him the whip and let him whip himself to drive out his boyhood.

OW!
AGH! OUCH!
HOP IT, BOYHOOD!

4 Arrange a foot race around a running track so the new man can show his speed against the other men.

PUFF!
PANT!

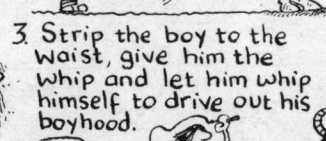

5. Give the new man his weapons – a sling, a shield and a club.

OOH, TA!

(Wipe the llama's blood off the club before you present it.)

6. Pierce the new man's ears so everyone can see at a glance he is no longer a boy.

OW! ME EARS!

7. Give him his new name and his breech-cloth.

Lord number 5: Conquering Capac

Mayta Capac made his son, Capac Yupanqui, Lord of Cuzco… then Mayta died. Most lords named their oldest son to be the next ruler. Young Capac Yupanqui *wasn't* Mayta Capac's oldest son. What was wrong with Capac Yupanqui's older brother?

a) he was too thick

b) he was too ugly

c) he was too kind and gentle

Answer: **b)** Yes, the poor lad took after his grandfather, Lloque, and was considered too ugly to be the Lord of the Incas. (Not like royals today! It seems they *have* to be ugly to get the job!)

Capac Yupanqui was the first Incan lord to capture lands outside the Cuzco Valley where the Incas started. But he only got about 12 miles from Cuzco. He wasn't exactly Julius Caesar or Alexander the Great, you understand.

Did you know . . .?
Capac Yupanqui was known as the 'Unforgettable King' ... unfortunately we know very little about his reign. It seems that everyone has forgotten!

Lord number 6: Roca on – again!

Capac Yupanqui's son, Inca Roca, conquered a bit more to the south-east of Cuzco but the Incas weren't the greatest warriors, as the following story shows...

Lord number 7: Huacac whack, whack!

Yahuar Huacac couldn't have hated his Ayarmaca captivity that much. He married an Ayarmaca girl! But then he also married other wives. Not a very healthy thing to do. Today, in most countries, marrying two women will get you punished. But in Incan times it was more deadly.

Yahuar Huacac announced…

And, would you believe it, the second wife arranged for the second son of the first wife to be murdered.

This was followed shortly after by the emperor's own death…

Lord number 8: Vicious Viracocha

Viracocha probably ruled around the early 1400s. He wasn't satisfied with being a 'lord' – he called himself 'Creator God'. (This is a bit like your head teacher calling themselves Minister of Education. A teeny bit over the top.)

Before Vile Vira came on the scene the Incas had attacked other tribes, conquered them, then gone home. Now Vira decided it was time they stayed there and ruled. First they decided to take over the Ayarmaca people who lived to the south of the Incas' Cuzco valley. So what did they do?

Wrong! The Incas were smarter than you – that's why they got to rule Peru, which is more than you'll ever do. No, the Incas attacked the Urubamba! This was a valley beyond the Ayarmaca.

It worked. Whichever way the Ayarmaca faced they'd be stabbed in the back.

Evil emperors

The eight Incan lords had so far ruled only little Cuzco ... and if that had been the end of the story you'd probably never have heard of them. But then they became more and more greedy. They wanted more land, more wealth, more people to push around. They weren't happy with a valley, or even a country. They wanted a whole empire. And, it was the next Incan lord, a lad called Pachacuti, who was the man for the job.

Did you know...?
Pachacuti got his name after a great battle victory. 'Pachacuti' means 'cataclysm' – or 'he who shakes the Earth'.

Pachacuti's date with fate: 1438

The Incas didn't get all their own way in bossing the Andes. Another people, the Chancas, to the west of the Incas, were getting pretty powerful. In 1438 the Chancas attacked first!

The Lord of Cuzco's son, Pachacuti Inca Yupanqui, defended their Cuzco home while his dad, Viracocha, went off with his other son, Urcon, to a safer fort near Calca. Now there were *two* Inca states – Pachacuti's and Viracocha's. But not for long. First Viracocha died.

Then Viracocha's other son Urcon got into a fight with Pachacuti's forces and was killed.

It left Pachacuti in charge.

Pach's pinching

Pachacuti defeated the Chanca attack thanks to a bit of luck. The Chancas took an image of their god into battle and Pach's warriors managed to capture it. The Chancas panicked and began to run away. They were massacred. Pach made the most of this victory and told a bit of a fib to make it sound more magical...

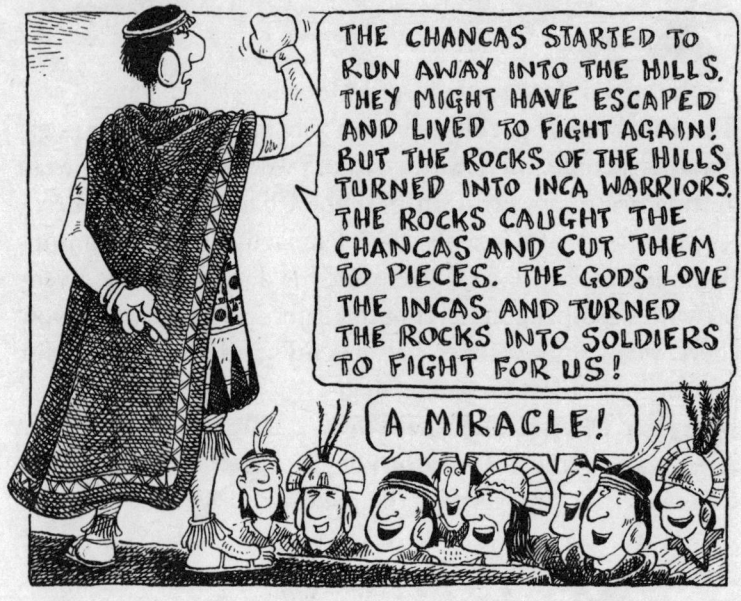

The truth? As the Chancas ran away hundreds of Inca supporters, living in the hills, ran down and attacked them. Yes – the Chancas were massacred in the hills. But, no – the attackers weren't rocks!

Terror tactics

Pachacuti's big fib was widely believed. Enemies of the Incas were scared and the Incan warriors made the most of that fear. This is what they did…

1 Incan armies started to carry platforms into battle. On these platforms were piles of sacred stones.

Future enemies took one look at the pile of Incan rocks and gave up without a fight!

2 To add to the fear-factor the Incas took the defeated Chanca leaders and stuffed their skins with straw and ashes. The scarecrow corpses were taken to a special burial ground and seated on stone benches. The stuffed arms were bent so

that when the wind blew the dead fingers beat the stretched skin on their bellies like drums! The message was clear...

3 The Incan warriors went into battle with war songs that were grisly and gruesome. Want to try one? Next time your history teacher gives you a dreadful detention then fight back with this ancient Incan chant...

We'll drink chicha from your skull
From your teeth we'll make a necklace
From your bones we'll make our flutes
From your skin we'll make a drum

Of course you couldn't *really* drink chicha from your teacher's skull because chicha is beer. You wouldn't want to get into trouble for under-age drinking, would you? Probably best if you just drink cocoa from the teacher's skull and stay out of trouble. (And no playing those bone flutes and skin drums when people are trying to get to sleep!)

Brotherly love
Pachacuti's warriors seemed unbeatable. The trouble was that Pach's younger brother, Capac Yupanqui, was having a great time invading neighbours and becoming a rich, powerful, popular general. Pach was worried.

What did he do? Well, if the Incas had a motto it would be, 'When in doubt, snuff them out!' So of course, Pachacuti had his brother murdered. Being the brother of an Incan emperor was a job for life – but sadly that life was often very short.

Pachacuti's sons went north and south conquering their neighbours and making the Incan Empire safe – safe for the Incas, that is.

Now Pachacuti could stop the fighting and enjoy a bit of ruling.

Pach's patch and Top Cat Topa

Pachacuti decided it was time for some changes and he had the power to make them. He had only taken over as emperor from his father after a lot of fighting and he didn't want that to happen when he died, so he made his son Topa Inca Yupanqui the next emperor, then retired.

Topa was topa the pops when it came to ruling and he and his dad made some nice new rules. If the Incas had been able to write, their laws may have read something like this…

THE TEN INCA COMMANDMENTS

1. Cuzco will be the capital of the Incan Empire. The fortress of Sacsahuaman in Cuzco will be the strongest in the world.

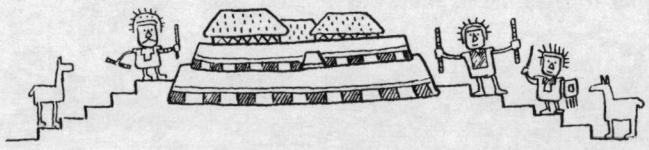

2. The people will work on improving the Cuzco valley farms – levelling the earth and moving the river – so it will be the greatest food producer ever.

3. A dead emperor's lands will be shared out amongst his family. Each new emperor must conquer new lands of his own.

4. Conquered peoples will be scattered round other parts of the Incan Empire to work for the Incas – that will also stop them gathering together to revolt.

5. Girls of conquered tribes may become Chosen Women (Quechua Aclla Cuna) to serve in the Incan temples or be married off to great Incan soldiers.

6. A number of conquered men will be chosen to serve in the Incan Army.

7. Everyone will worship the Incan god, Viracocha. There will be priests, prayers and temples. All conquered peoples must worship Viracocha, and pay his priests with food and work. (But they can keep their old religion too.)

8. The emperor may marry his sister, but no other men may marry their sisters.

9. The emperor may marry as many women as he wishes, but no other man may. A chief minister may have 50 wives, an ordinary minister just 30 and the lower your class the fewer wives you may have.

10. If anyone wishes to speak to the emperor then he or she must take off their sandals and place a small load on their back as a sign of respect.

Imagine that in your country! First you're invaded and then you're…

- Split from your friends – all those mates who share the same jokes and support the same football team.
- Split from your sisters who are sent off to work in some distant temple or forced to marry some great national hero … like Prince Charles!
- Forced to work to pay for food that mostly goes to your enemy … like a vegetarian working in a butcher shop.

- Shipped off to another part of the invader's world where you don't know the language and live in a strange house. It could be anywhere … like Bournemouth, Blackpool or Buckie!
- Taught a new religion with new prayers and forced to worship a new god. It's a bit like being forced to support a new football team … like Bournemouth or Blackpool or Buckie Thistle!

The only good news is that the Incas will allow you to worship your old gods – as well as the new Incan ones.

Cheerless Chosen Women

Would you like to be an Incan 'Chosen Woman'? Sounds a bit special, doesn't it? If the Incas had advertised for Chosen Women they might have done it like this:

GIRLS!

THE CHANCE OF A LIFETIME!

Why don't YOU apply to be a

QUECHUA ACLLA CUNA

— that's right, a **CHOSEN WOMAN!**

GET TO LIVE IN THE TEMPLE!

NO MEN TO BOTHER YOU!

SIMPLE TASKS INCLUDE:
☽ **COOK THE HOLY FOOD.** ☉ **KEEP THE SACRED FIRE GOING.**
☉ **WEAVE THE EMPEROR'S TEMPLE CLOTHES.**

ALL YOU NEED IS TO BE BEAUTIFUL AND CLEVER AND AGED BETWEEN 8 AND 10 YEARS!

STAY SHUT UP FOR AT LEAST SIX HAPPY YEARS!

THE LUCKY ONES WILL LEAVE TO MARRY LORDS! *

Apply to the matron (Mama Cuna) of your local temple or the High Priestess (Coya Pasca) — the wife of the Sun god himself!

*The really lucky ones will end up as a temple sacrifice, of course.

By the 1500s there were several thousand of these Chosen Women. Would you apply?

31

Apart from ending up as a temple sacrifice there was another danger in being a Chosen Woman ... You must never *ever* become pregnant. The punishment was pretty horrible...

Amazingly there *was* one way that a Chosen Woman could avoid this terrible treatment. All she had to do was say ...

... and she would be free!

Rotten royal roads

Another thing the Incas could do with conquered peoples was force them to work on building the Incan 'Royal Roads'.

Four roads led from the four quarters of the Incan kingdom and they met in the middle of Cuzco. The Incas called their empire 'Tahuantinsuyu' – which, as you know, means 'The Four Quarters of the World'. The four Royal Roads were important.

So what? you ask! So *you* try building a path down your back garden without…

- iron (for tools like shovels and pick-axes).
- written words (for making plans and organizing work).
- wheels (so everything had to be dragged).
- money (so paying workers and supplying them with food was tricky over big distances).

The Incas had none of these things!

The roads were useful for a fast messenger service across the empire and to move Incan armies quickly when trouble broke out. The Spanish conquistador Pedro de Cieza de Leon described one road…

> *In human memory no highway is as great as this. It is laid through deep valleys and over high mountains, through snow banks and swamps, through live rock and along raging rivers. In some places smooth and paved, in others tunnelled through cliffs, skirting gorges, linking snow peaks with stairways and rest stops, everywhere clean-swept and litter-free, with taverns, storehouses, and temples of the sun.*

The mountain roads had walls along the edge to stop you falling off the mountain. Very thoughtful, but a huge task to build hundreds of miles of walls. And doesn't it make you wonder who got the job of sweeping up the litter?

Marvellous messengers

The Incas had no way of writing things down (although they did have a clever recording system by tying knots in coloured string). Instead stories and messages were remembered.

There was no Postman Pat to carry letters around the Empire. Instead there was a relay-team of runners – the *chasqui*.

- These young men ran about a kilometre each to the next post and carried a message in their head. They then went back to their post and waited for the next message.

The chasqui chain were able to carry messages hundreds of miles across the Empire very quickly.

- The skill wasn't just in the running, but in the remembering. They had to get the messages exactly right, word for word. One word wrong and they would be punished – a bit like a history exam.
- The runners worked 15 days before they had some time off.

- They carried a badge to show they were servants of the emperor. They also carried a sling and a star-headed mace to defend themselves against wild animals.
- Messages were carried at around 150 miles a day – that's London to Cardiff if you want to look it up on a map.
- Messengers didn't just carry messages – they could be asked to carry food.

One emperor loved sea food and had it brought by messenger from the coast every day. If the fish wasn't fresh then the messenger was executed!

Did you know...?
The Incan armies marched north, south, east and west but they stopped at the edge of the Amazon rainforest. That rainforest was occupied by lowland tribes and many of them were head-hunters.

Wonder why they stopped there?

Horrible Huayna

Emperor Topa followed the trend of all the Incan emperors and died. (Around 1493 if you're interested in dates. Some people are, especially the sort you get in cakes.) He named son Huayna as next emperor ... but then just before he died he said...

Huayna was a bit upset and his supporters murdered the guardian of young emperor Huari. Huayna got the throne he was supposed to have in the first place, so that was all right – unless you were Huari's guardian who got the chop, of course.

Remember, Incan emperors didn't get all their father's lands, which were shared out. A new emperor like Huayna had to go out and conquer more new land for himself. Huayna picked on the country we now call Ecuador, to the north.

He spent most of his reign battering Ecuador. In fact he liked it so much he thought he'd have a second capital city up there in Tumi Bamba. The lords back in Cuzco must have been shocked and horrified at the thought of a rival capital.

But before the Cuzco lords could revolt Huayna did a daft and deadly thing...

THEN A MESSAGE ARRIVED FROM CUZCO.

TELL ME YOUR MESSAGE WHILE I WIPE THESE LAST FEW REVOLTING PEOPLE OUT...

OH, DON'T MIND US...

DEAR EMPEROR HUAYNA,

HOPE THIS MESSAGE FINDS YOU WELL AND YOU ARE ENJOYING YOUR LITTLE BREAK UP THERE. I'M SURE YOU'RE DOING LOTS OF BLOOD-LETTING AND BUTCHERY TO KEEP THE PEASANTS IN THEIR PLACE.

ANYWAY, THINGS BACK HOME IN CUZCO ARE QUIET. VERY QUIET. NOW, DON'T GET TOO UPSET OR WORRIED, BUT THE REASON WHY THINGS ARE SO QUIET IS THE PEOPLE ARE DEAD OR DYING IN THEIR THOUSANDS. AND YOU DON'T GET MUCH QUIETER THAN A DEAD INCA.

IT SEEMS TO BE SOME SORT OF PLAGUE SWEEPING THE COUNTRY. IT'S COME FROM BOLIVIA. THE PEOPLE GO ALL FEVERISH AND SPOTTY AND DIE. LOTS OF THE WORKERS IN THE VALLEY ARE TURNING UP THEIR TOES AND HOPPING THE TWIG. IT'S JUST A MATTER OF TIME BEFORE THE PLAGUE REACHES

THE CITY AND I HATE TO THINK WHAT WILL HAPPEN THEN!

OF COURSE THE STUPID PEOPLE ARE PANICKING. THEY WANT TO SHUT THE CITY GATES AND KEEP THE PLAGUE OUT. THE TROUBLE IS, IF WE SHUT THE CITY GATES THEN WE KEEP THE FOOD OUT AND WE STARVE TO DEATH. AWKWARD, I'M SURE YOU'LL AGREE.

AS I SAY, IT'S NOT A HUGE PROBLEM AT THE MOMENT, BUT I THOUGHT YOU MIGHT LIKE TO KNOW. IF YOUR MIGHTY MIND CAN THINK OF AN ANSWER THEN PERHAPS YOU COULD LET US KNOW PRETTY DARN QUICK.

YOUR HUMBLE SERVANT,

GENERAL YASCA

TIPPY TOE

Yes, it's tough at the top. You get the throne but you also get the problems. What could unhappy Huayna do? What would you do? Only an idiot Inca would rush back to Cuzco, catch the plague and die! But that's what Huayna did! He died so quickly he didn't name the next emperor ... so that started another Incan punch-up for the throne. Nothing new there then.

Did you know…?

Huayna's son died a few days after his dad from the same plague. That meant two half-brothers (Huascar and Atahuallpa) were left to fight one another for the throne. While they were fighting, the Incan Empire was divided – just as Spanish invaders arrived. That's what made it so easy for the Spanish to defeat them.

You could say the Spanish plague was the first attack which helped the conquistadors to win. Maybe as many as eight million of the twelve million Incas died before the Spanish arrived. Invisible germs were the best weapons the Spanish could ever have had! Which just goes to show, 'Coughs and sneezes spread diseases … and spread Spanish empires with eases!'

Top of the class

Incan people were told what they should be doing at each age and what they should be wearing ... just like school. Only Incas never got to leave school the way you do.

Dire dress

Everyone had to wear what they were told. Each tribe had its own head-dress – and you were not allowed to pretend you were from another tribe by wearing their head-dress instead! You also had to dress the right way for your class – you couldn't be a peasant and dress too posh!

Peasant dress-sense

If you want to look like an Incan peasant here's how...

MEN   **WOMEN**

A LARGE CLOAK OVER THE SHOULDERS, TIED IN THE FRONT. (THE FINER THE CLOTH AND EMBROIDERY, THE HIGHER YOUR CLASS.)

A SLEEVELESS TUNIC

A BREECH-CLOTH

A SHOULDER MANTLE

A WRAPAROUND SKIRT THAT REACHED FROM BENEATH THE ARMS TO THE ANKLES, WITH THE TOP EDGES DRAWN OVER THE SHOULDERS AND FASTENED WITH STRAIGHT PINS.

A DECORATED SASH

Wee women

Girls! Now that you look like an Incan woman you need to dress your hair like the Incas. Here's how to do it…

1 Collect pee in a bucket. (Your family and friends can all chip in and help you fill that bucket fast.)

2 Leave the pee for a week to brew (the way beer is left to brew – except your pee won't end up tasting like brown ale).

3 Wash your hair by soaking it in the bucket of brewed pee. (This will get rid of the grease and leave your hair lovely and shiny – honest!)

4 When your hair is dry you can start making it into braids. To hold the hair in place wet it with some of that pee. (Hair spray hasn't been invented. Sorry.)

5 Find your Prince Charming and say…

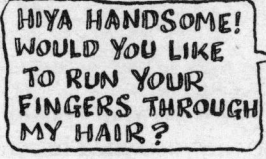

Then hope that your Prince Charming likes a Cinderella who smells like a toilet!

Weather wizardry

The Incan family groups were called 'ayllu' and the head of a large family was called a 'curaca'. A curaca had power over everyone in the family … but you'd have to be crackers if you wanted to be one of the curacas. Curacas took the complaints from the family and went to the gods for help…

WE COULD DO WITH A BIT OF RAIN. HOW ABOUT IF I SACRIFICE THIS LLAMA TO YOU?

When it worked the curaca was a hero … but he also got the *blame* when things went wrong. What would you do if your garden was ruined by a drought?

A Spaniard described what happened to one clumsy curaca…

> *A powerful curaca called Fempellec was the ruler of his village. This lord moved the statue of a god from the temple. The villagers said that this made the gods angry and they sent a terrible drought. His people died. The priests then took Fempellec and drowned him.*

If there was a drought then how could they drown him? The Spaniard didn't explain. Maybe they drowned him in a dried-up river?

Would you kill your dad for a dried-up garden? (On second thoughts you'd better not answer that!)

Mister masters
Men ruled Tahuantinsuyu. Women worked and had children but had no power. A man, though, could increase his power

by having children. It was almost like a supermarket loyalty card – the more points you had the richer you were ... except instead of points you had children and wives.

THE TUZCO BONUS OFFER

MEN! TAKE THE INCA TRAIL TO POWER!
It's so simple!

JUST COLLECT THOSE KIDS AND WIN TERRIFIC TITLES

5 CUTE KIDS AND YOU'LL BE NAMED 'LITTLE OVERSEER'

FOR JUST 10 CHARMING CHILDREN WE'LL NAME YOU 'OVERSEER'
BUT GO FOR THE JACKPOT!

A MAN WITH A FABULOUS FAMILY OF 50 CAN BE LORD OF HIS OWN VILLAGE!

Yes! You too can be a cool Curaca. Start right now collecting the wonderful wives that will take you to the Tuzco Top!

Remember our motto:
THE MORE THE MERRIER!

More children meant more workers to produce more food and more power ... for the men.

Keeping in class

Now you are ready to live like an Inca. What you *did* each day depended on your age. The Incan laws told you exactly what you should be doing. They divided their people into 12 classes. If the Incas could have written their rules down they'd probably have looked something like this...

1 **Babies** (in arms) and 2 **Infants** (up to one year): In the care of their parents.

3 **Children** (aged 1–9): Children aged 1–5 may play. Children aged 5–9 must help parents in small tasks. Girls must help mind the babies, cart water and animal feed, weed, and help the women make beer. At age 5 girls must start to learn how

to weave. Girls planning to be servants will be sent away to be trained.

4 **Youths** (aged 9–16): Boys to be trained as *llamamechecs* (llama herders of the llama herds). Girls aged 9–12 will gather flowers and herbs for the dyeing of textiles and for medicinal use. Girls aged 12–16 will work at home, keeping house and

producing textiles (though some may serve as *llamamechecs*). Girls are allowed to marry at 14, although most will wait until they are 18.

5 **Young men** (aged 16–20) and 6 **Prime men** (aged 20–25): Will work as post-runners, as senior llama herdsmen to the *llamamechecs*, and as servants to military officers.

7 **Young women** (aged 18–30): Women are considered full adults at 18 (unlike men who will not become adults until 25.) At this age they should be wives and mothers.

8 **Puric** (men 25–50): This age group of men should be married. At 25, they will be heads of households. They must learn to farm their given piece of land and pay taxes and serve in the army if they are called to. They might also be sent out to some remote part of the empire to pioneer it and to keep an eye on any hostile or disloyal natives in the area. Some men in this class are also called on to work in the state's mines.

9 **Unmarried women and widows** (women 30–50):They will make pottery and cloth, and work as house servants.

10 **Old men** (aged 50–60): These men are semi-retired and have no state or army duties. They are expected to help out from time to time during harvest and planting seasons, or to do light work as public officers, clerks, and storekeepers.

11 **Elders** (aged 60–80): Both men and women will eat, sleep, and may do light work if they are up to it, such as tending guinea pigs. They are pensioners and are tended to by the state.

12 **Invalids** (sick and disabled): They are expected to work as their disabilities allow, but are otherwise in the care of the state.

You'll notice there is no class at all for people over 80, so it seems not too many Incas made it that long! Imagine having your whole life planned for you by the government like this! Still, there was always death to look forward to.

Stinging school

You will also notice there's no school in there for you peasants. But if you were a lord's child then you would get four years of lessons…

INCAN SCHOOL TIMETABLE
YEAR 1: THE INCAN LANGUAGE (QUECHUA)
YEAR 2: RELIGION
YEAR 3: KNOTTED STRING (QUIPUS)
YEAR 4: HISTORY

Imagine! A whole year doing history! Horrible!

Of course you could make it more fun by messing about in lessons, but be warned! The punishment was pretty nasty…

The Incan teacher-training manual

THE CUZCO CANING

1. Take a thin cane.

2. Have the older boys grip the victim by his ankles.

3. Have them lift the victim's feet into the air.

4. Cane the victim across the soles of his feet.

Please note: Do not give more than ten strokes of the cane and do not give a Cuzco Caning more than once a day.

And you thought being sent to do sums outside your head-teacher's door was nasty!

Shake, rattle and stroll

Of course the festivals would give you a few days off school. There would be a parade of men playing drums, tambourines, flutes and pototoes ... no, not *potatoes*, dummy! The pototo was a large shell (called a conch) that was blown like a trumpet.

ONE POTOTO, TWO POTOTO, THREE POTOTO, FOUR...

When you went to the parade you could join the dancing and wear 'shaker bracelets' on your wrists and ankles. What would you use to make your rattling bracelets?

a) glass beads
b) small seashells
c) dried llamas' toenails

Answer: c) Dried llamas' toenails, of course. Pop along to your local llama sacrifice with a pair of pliers and rip the toenails out before the rest of the animal is burned as a sacrifice. Dry them in the sun, drill a hole in each one and thread them on to a string. You're ready to rattle!

The pulverizing Puric

You can see from the Incan class list that the men who went off to serve in the emperor's army were expected to be married at that age. This meant that the men had to leave their wives behind.

An old Incan legend, passed on by word of mouth, tells of the dramatic result of this on one family…

Once upon a time there was a young man, a Puric, who was sent for to serve as a soldier. He had to leave his young son and his wife.

'I will miss you both,' he sniffed.

'I'll miss you too,' his wife snivelled.

'And I'll mith you motht of all!' the little boy lithpt … I mean *lisped*.

When the Puric had left, his wife wept over her weaving and cried over her cooking and sobbed over her sewing. 'Don't cwy, Mummy!' the little boy said.

Suddenly a breeze blew a white butterfly through the window. 'It's a signal from my husband,' the woman whispered. 'So long as the butterfly visits I will know he is safe!'

'What dat?' her son said and pointed a podgy finger at the butterfly.

His mother sighed, 'It's my lover!'

And so they lived happily till the Puric returned. As it happened the little boy was pulling weeds in the garden so he was the first to see his father marching down the road. He ran on to the road and the Puric swept the boy up into his strong arms. 'My son! How have you been?'

'Gweat!' the little boy laughed.

The man stopped and put him down. 'Weren't you upset? Weren't you and Mummy lonely?' he gasped.

'No!' the little boy laughed. 'Mummy's lover came to thee her everwee day!'

The man picked up his mighty club, raced into the house and smashed his wife till she was a crushed corpse.

The little boy came in and saw the butterfly flutter round the head of his panting father. 'Look, Daddy!' he cried. 'Here is Mummy's lover, come to thee her!'

Live like a lord

It seems to have been much more fun to be an Incan emperor. Why not try it and find out what it was like? If you want to be Incan emperor (Sapa Inca) of your class then here's a quick guide…

You looking at me, mate?

The Sapa Inca is descended from the sun – a sort of sun son. No one can look at the sun, so no one can look at *you* directly. Wherever you go your subjects must look down … or else. When the lower classes want to speak to you they must turn their backs and bow to show respect. (Though someone turning and bowing may show their backside, which hardly shows respect!) At court the Sapa Inca often sat behind a screen.

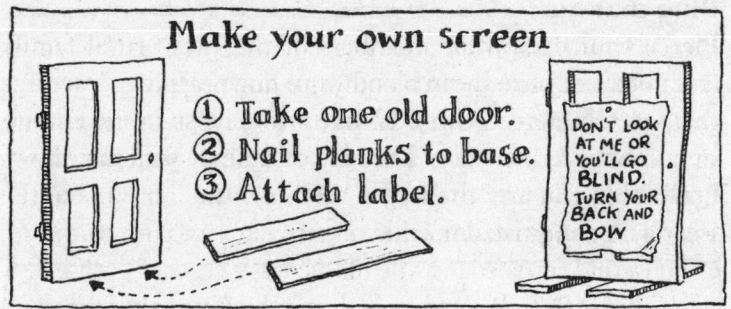

Make your own screen

① Take one old door.
② Nail planks to base.
③ Attach label.

DON'T LOOK AT ME OR YOU'LL GO BLIND. TURN YOUR BACK AND BOW

Atahuallpa spoke from behind a screen to his brother who passed on the messages like a walking cordless telephone.

Tassel hassle

It's no use being an emperor if you don't let people know you're in charge. As Sapa Inca you wear a special fringe *not* a crown. On your head-dress you wear a fringe of red, woollen tassels hung from little gold tubes.

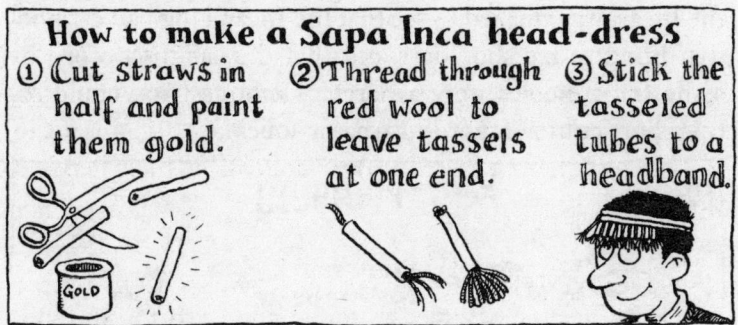

How to make a Sapa Inca head-dress

① Cut straws in half and paint them gold.

② Thread through red wool to leave tassels at one end.

③ Stick the tasseled tubes to a headband.

GOLD

Tinge that fringe

Pick your heir – the favourite son of yours who will take the throne when you die or decide to retire. Your heir wears his hair under a fringe that's tinged bright yellow. (Try saying that with a mouthful of mushy peas!) He also has a stick with a feather on it that sticks out 10 cm from his forehead.

Plug that lug

Pierce your ears. Male members of the Incan royal family and nobles of pure Incan blood wore huge earplugs (earrings that stretch pierced ears). Unlike anyone else in the empire they cropped their hair. The size of hole in your ear shows how noble you are; the larger the hole, the more noble the wearer. A conquistador said...

> *He who had the largest ears was held to be the finest gentleman.*

Francisco Pizarro, the Spaniard who came and conquered the Incas, was amazed to see that the Incan king had earlobes that hung to his shoulders and that the ear discs worn by some Incan nobles were as large as oranges. You could try this short cut to emporer-sized ear-lobes...

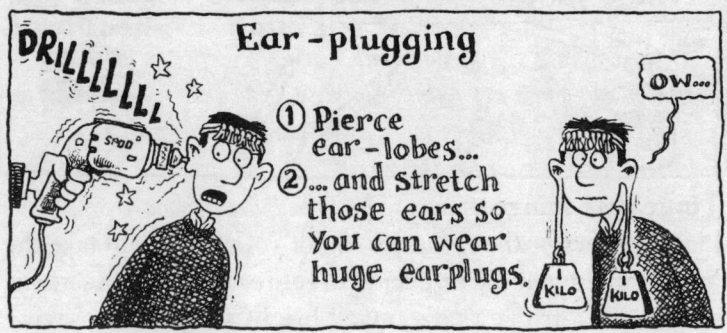

Ear-plugging

DRILLLLLLL

① Pierce ear-lobes...
②...and stretch those ears so you can wear huge earplugs.

OW...

Perhaps the strangest custom of all was for the royal family to fit earplugs ... to their llamas!

Nibble your nosh

The Incas didn't have tables. They ate off cloths on the floor. But you are an emperor! We can't have that.

- First, sit on your throne – a curved piece of wood about 20 cm high.
- Send everyone else out of the room – because a Sapa Inca always eats alone.
- Now clap your hands and your serving women will bring in your food – they will stand there, holding the plates while you eat from them.

Throne alone

(School dinner ladies)

But there is one Sapa Inca habit you probably shouldn't try at home – or in your school dinner hall. A conquistador said …

If the emperor coughed or spat, a woman held out her hand and he spat into her palm. And any hairs that fell from his head on to his clothes were picked up by the women and eaten. The reason for these customs is known; the spitting was a royal thing to do; the hairs because he was afraid of being bewitched.

Yeuch!

Pick up that litter

As Sapa Inca you are too grand to walk. You will be carried everywhere in a 'litter'.

The holes in the side let the air in and let the emperor see out, but peasants can't see in. Why not train 20 strong and steady litter-carriers and go for a quick run down the motorway? Your wives and your treasure can follow on in hammock-litters.

Live like an Inca

Crime time

There was very little crime in Tahuantinsuyu because everyone shared what they owned so there was no point in stealing. But what would happen to a man who murdered his wife? Well, for a start, he would NOT be locked in prison.

There were three main crimes to be punished: murder, insulting the emperor, and insulting the gods. The punishment for these was death and the Incas had a nice simple way to execute someone. What was it?

a) They would cut the criminal to pieces and feed them to the guinea pigs.
b) They would drown the criminal in Lake Titicaca.
c) They would throw the criminal off a cliff.

Answer: c) Which would you prefer?

A rare, but really serious crime was to have one of the emperor's wives as a girlfriend. The punishment was to be stripped naked, tied to a wall and left to starve to death.

Smaller crimes had lesser punishments – nice little things like having hands or feet chopped off or eyes gouged out! (The criminal could see the point of the punishment ... but then not much else!)

Particular punishments

We have 'set' punishments for some crimes today. So a motorist who drives 10 miles an hour above the speed limit will be fined a set amount and have 'penalty points' put on his or her driving licence. The Incas didn't have money so they didn't have fines and they didn't have driving licences ... possibly because they had no paper. But they did have 'set' punishments for certain crimes.

Could you be a law enforcer in Tahuantinsuyu? Match the crime to the powerful punishment ...

FOR THE CRIME OF...

1. BEING A WITCH OR WIZARD
2. KILLING AN ASSISTANT (IF YOU'RE A GOVERNMENT WORKER)
3. REBELLION AGAINST THE STATE
4. GOING AGAINST THE LAWS OF THE GODS
5. TREASON AGAINST THE EMPEROR

THE PUNISHMENT WAS TO BE...

a) GIVEN A SLOW AND AGONIZING DEATH AND THEIR BONES TURNED INTO MUSICAL INSTRUMENTS

b) BEATEN TO DEATH AND THE BODY LEFT TO BE EATEN BY GIANT BIRDS CALLED CONDORS

c) BURNED ALIVE, HAVING HIS HOUSE BURNED TO THE GROUND, THE TREES UPROOTED AND THE CROPS DESTROYED

d) PLACED IN A CAVE FULL OF DANGEROUS ANIMALS FOR TWO DAYS

e) LAID FACE DOWN ON THE GROUND AND A STONE DROPPED FROM A METRE HIGH ONTO THE BACK

In the cave of Sancay, prisoners convicted of treason were placed in a cavern full of wild animals, toxic toads, and venomous reptiles. If a convict survived two days in these surroundings he was pardoned and released, since his survival seemed to signal that he was obviously under the protection of the gods.

5d) A conquistador described this punishment…

4c) Seems a bit cruel to punish the trees! Maybe they just picked ash trees to match the ash owner!

3a) It's nice to think that, after you are dead, your bones will give people so much pleasure, isn't it?

2e) This sometimes killed the prisoner. If it didn't then he was left with severe injuries for the rest of his life.

Answers: 1b) … witch is not very pleasant.

Foul food

Beastly beer

When the Incas had a festival they enjoyed large amounts of their 'chicha' beer. It's probably more fun to watch llamas being slaughtered when you've had a few pints!

Do you have a school assembly you have to go to? Need a cup or two of chicha to give you strength? Then follow these simple (but disgusting) Incan instructions…

On the other hand you may prefer to stick to lemonade –
without the spit.

Tasty tatties
The Incas ate lots of potatoes. One of their words for these
vegetables was 'papa' which Spanish invaders changed a
little to give us the modern word 'potato'. But the Incas
and the tribes they conquered had over 200 other words for
potatoes! (I wonder who counted them?)

We only have about a dozen …

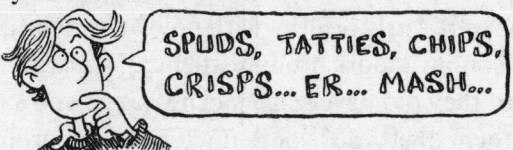

SPUDS, TATTIES, CHIPS, CRISPS... ER... MASH...

The Incas even had dried potatoes long before they appeared in your local supermarket. They picked their potatoes in the autumn when the Andes days were warm and the nights fell below freezing. Then they'd…

- spread the potatoes on the ground overnight to freeze
- let them thaw the next morning
- gather them into large piles in the afternoon
- trample them under their bare feet to squeeze out the water
- spread out the pulp to dry
- store it over the winter months
- add water whenever they fancied some spuds – just like today's packets of dried potato.

The potato crop, like the rest of the Incan farm food, was divided into three equal parts…

- one for the village
- one for the stores in case of famine
- one for the priests to burn as a gift to the gods.

Wood was scarce in some parts of the Andes so how did you roast your potatoes? Over a fire of dried llama droppings, of course! (Well, you enjoy Smoky Bacon crisps – why not Roast Llama Dropping flavour?)

SCRUNCH SCRUNCH SCRUNCH YECH!

ACTUALLY THE LLAMA DROPPINGS TASTE BETTER!

Terrible treatments

The Incas were fairly healthy with no plague-type diseases – until the conquistadors brought them as a special gift from Spain! But they did have some sicknesses … and some ways to treat them that your local doctor would probably not advise today…

Cuzco Cures

Reliable remedies for ill Incas

Wicked wounds: Got a nasty llama bite? Been stabbed or stoned by an enemy warrior? Simply take the bark from a pepper tree, boil it in water and slap it on the wound. It's hot stuff for curing wounds is the pepper tree.

Dreadful diarrhoea: Take the leaves from the coca plant and chew them. These wonderful leaves also help lessen your hunger and stop you feeling sick when you climb those high mountains.

Awful aches: Take a glass knife and gouge a hole between your eyes. This will cure your headache in no time! Or if the pain is in your arm then let out arm blood – you'll see that there's no 'arm in it!

Hot tots: If baby has a fever then collect the family pee in a pot and wash baby in the lovely liquid. If that doesn't work then give it to baby to drink! Yummy drink from Mummy!

Ill infants: All sensible mothers cut their baby's umbilical cord when it's born then dry it and store it. When the child falls sick just give it the umbilical cord to suck on and it will suck the pain and evil spirits from its body!

Horrible headaches: Draw an oval on the skull then drill holes along it about a quarter centimetre each. Lift out the bone and let out the evil spirits from the head. Another way is to saw two lines at right angles. Of course the patient would like plenty of coca leaves to drug them while you do this! There's nothing like a hole in the head to drain the pain!

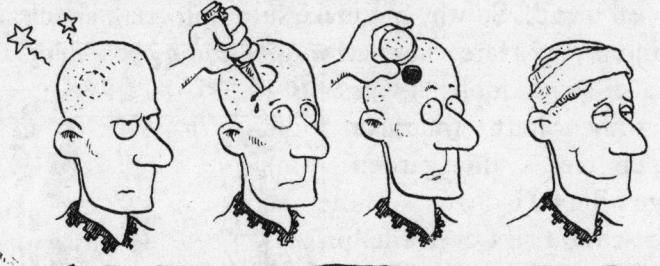

It seems that the hole-in-the-head treatment worked. Archaeologists have found skulls with these pieces removed and it is clear the wound healed and the patient survived.

Did you know…?

Village healers also used a special trick to make sick people believe they were cured. First they fed the patient black and white corn flour then hypnotized them into a trance. While the family watched, the healer pretended to open up the

patient's stomach with a knife. He would then appear to pull out a nasty collection of snakes, toads and other objects. (Naturally this was a conjuring trick.) They then cleaned the blood off the body and said, 'Look! The wound is healed and all this poison inside you is gone!'

The patient would feel better because they really *believed* they'd been cured.

Brush up your appearance

Boys! There's nothing a girl hates more than rotten teeth and bad breath. So why not make sure your teeth are clean the Incan way? Here's how …

1 Take some molle twigs (from the South American pepper tree – the garden hedge will NOT do).

2 Roast the twigs over a hot fire till the ends are smoking.

3 Place the hot roast twig against your gums.

A conquistador described what happened next…

> *The twigs scald the gums, the burnt flesh falls off to reveal new flesh underneath. This new flesh is very red and healthy!*

Now, lads, go out and find your dream girl. With luck she will be a cannibal who enjoys kissing a lad who tastes of roasted human flesh.

HORRIBLE HISTORIES HEALTH WARNING
Do not try this! A baboon's bum is red and healthy but you wouldn't want it in your mouth! Remember, smoking can damage your health … and so can putting a smoking twig into your mouth.

Funny money

The Incas didn't use money. They exchanged their work for what they wanted. Good idea for school…

CLEAN THE BLACKBOARD AND YOU GET A BAR OF CHOCOLATE!

WHAT DO I GET IF I CLEAN THE TOILET?

SMELLY HANDS

They also used materials and clothing as a sort of money. Not such a good idea...

It isn't as if a sort of money hadn't been invented. The Sican people (conquered by the Incas) used copper axe-heads as coins. You can make these yourself and be the richest Sican in your class. All you need is half a tonne of sheets of copper and a big hammer. Cut and hammer the copper into axe-head shapes. Each one is about 5 cm long by 3 cm wide.

Rich Sican lords were buried with up to 500 kg of these axe-heads, stacked up in piles of 500 around them. Sican lords were also buried with up to twenty human sacrifices.

The Incas never copied the idea of copper-axe money, which may not be a bad thing. After all, the Bible says the love of money is the root of all evil. So maybe the Incas simply decided the copper axe–coins were just axing for trouble!

Funnier money

Another reason the Incas had no money may be to do with the way they *thought*. So, you and your parents and the people in your country *think*...

A RICH PERSON IS SOMEONE WITH A LOT OF MONEY...

... but an Inca would think...

A RICH PERSON IS SOMEONE WITH LOTS OF FOLLOWERS...

The conquistadors never really understood this. An Incan lord would have lots of wives so he could have lots of children and grandchildren – that would make him 'rich'. The Spanish were horrified and wanted to hang an Incan lord, Don Juan, because he had lots of wives.

Don Juan tried to save his life in two ways...

1 Don Juan gave a fortune in buried treasure to the Spanish officer who wanted him executed. It was valuable to the Spaniard, but not to Don Juan.

2 The Spanish officer said, 'Send your extra wives to the home of a good Christian woman to learn Christianity.' Don Juan sent the Incan women ... but cheated and kept his favourite extra wife at home. He sent another woman in her place.

Sadly the Spanish discovered the bribery and the trickery. Don Juan was very quickly hanged ... for doing what his ancestors had always done.

Inca Inquisition

Have you noticed how teachers like to ask you questions? Why do they bother when they probably know the answers?

It's time to turn the tables and torment your teacher with this simple quiz. If they get less than 5 out of 10 they are probably ready for early retirement. If they get more than 5 out of 10 then they were probably around in Incan times and are ready for retirement anyway! Answer true or false...

1 When an Inca became too old to work they were turned into a mummy and buried ... even if they weren't dead!

THIS IS NO WAY TO TREAT YOUR MUMMY!

2 Old people were given the job of collecting lice.

3 Inca Huaca was released by the people who captured him because he cried.

4 Atahuallpa's leading general, Chalcuchinma, had his legs burned to a crisp to get him to reveal Incan treasure stores.

5 Emperor Atahuallpa's chair carriers gave up when the Spanish chopped off their hands.

6 Modern Peruvian men have mock sling fights in memory of their Incan ancestors, but no one gets hurt.

7 The Incan warriors were expert archers.

8 The Incas enjoyed popcorn.

9 The Incas ate dogs.

10 The Incas rode on llamas.

Answers:

1 False. The Incas were among the first people to look after their old people. They had the first old age pensions – food supplies not money, of course. Some of the emperor's wealth was set aside for widows, orphans, old people and the disabled. The emperor's collectors took more food and materials than they needed, then they stored it in case there was a drought or a famine. (A bit like the way you save in a piggy bank. But, being from the Andes they probably had guinea-piggy banks!) The blind were given the task of picking seeds out of cotton plants and were paid with food and shelter.

2 True. When you were too old to farm you went to the Incan food store and you collected your old-age food pension. This was usually at the age of fifty. (Nowadays you get a bus pass at sixty and that's all – and they taste terrible.) But the old were expected to make themselves useful. Collecting firewood … and collecting lice. You then took your collection of lice to the leader of your family group.

LICE TO MEET YOU.

3 True. But Huaca had an incredible talent … he cried tears of blood! His captors were so amazed they set him free. (Don't try it yourself or you'll make a right mess of this book.)

4 True. But don't feel too sorry for the general. His favourite sport was drinking from the skulls of dead enemies. He survived the charred legs to go on and poison the emperor who took Atahuallpa's place. Not a nice man.

GRRR!

5 False. It is TRUE that they had their hands chopped off … but they did NOT give up their work, carrying Atahuallpa around the country! They carried the covered chair (litter) on their shoulders until they bled to death. (Maybe they carried on because they were devoted servants – or maybe because the Incas had a law against dropping their litter!)

6 False. The men from rival regions fight one another like knights fighting for the love of beautiful girls. These are mock fights yet every year several men get themselves killed.

7 False. The warriors preferred to use stones fired from slings. They didn't use bows and arrows because good wood for bows doesn't grow in the Andes.

8 True. Corn was their main food and they ate it toasted, boiled or ground into flour and baked. They also heated it till it 'popped'. Pity they didn't invent the cinema to go with the popcorn.

9 False. The Incas conquered the Huanca tribe and the Huanca loved to eat dog as a special treat. The Incas were a bit disgusted by this. They much preferred to eat guinea pigs (roasted or in a stew). The little furry friends ran around the house like pets till they were wanted for dinner. The Incas also ate llama meat (tastes a bit like mutton) but generally not much meat at all.

HERE FLUFFY! DINNER TIME!

?

10 False. Llamas were used like donkeys to carry loads but the Incas never rode them. Probably because the llamas have a nasty habit of stopping and sitting down for hours on end if they are overloaded or upset! The Incas were also wary of the llamas' greatest skill – spitting a long way, with a great aim, at anything (or anyone).

The cruel conquest

By 1532 the Incas had conquered dozens of states and ruled over 12 million people who spoke at least 20 different languages. Their empire stretched 2,000 miles from north to south and 500 miles east to west.

But the Spanish had discovered America thanks to Christopher Columbus. They smashed the Aztecs in Central America then they began to march south, looking for treasure. The Incas were attacked by Spanish invaders – all 250 of them! (Oh, all right, 198 soldiers and 62 horsemen if you want to be picky.)

So the Incas outnumbered the Spanish about 60,000 to 1. No contest?

Timeline

1526 Francisco Pizarro from Spain lands on the coast of Peru and is welcomed by the rich Incas. He is given lots of gold – he'll be back for more, of course. Next time he'll have an army!

1527 Emperor Huascar, one of Huayna's sons, takes the throne. His half-brother, Lord Atahuallpa, decides to fight him for it. Atahuallpa wins and captures Huascar.

1532 Pizarro and his little army arrive back in Peru and meet the young emperor Atahuallpa. The Spanish kidnap Atahuallpa and hold him to ransom. Many Incas believe

71

the Spanish could be fair-skinned gods. They don't fight.

1533 The Incas pay Atahuallpa's ransom, but the Spanish execute him anyway. That is a very sneaky thing to do. End of Incan Empire and the start of Peru's suffering.

1537 Incan rebel Manco Capac II sets up a new Incan kingdom at Vilcabamba. It can't last.

1541 Pizarro is assassinated ... not by the Incas though. This is a seriously unpopular bloke.

1572 The last Incan rebel stronghold is captured and emperor Tupac Amaru, son of Manco, is beheaded. Without a head the new Incan Empire is finished – and without a head Tupac Amaru isn't too grand either!

1600 For every hundred Incas alive when the Spanish arrived there are now only ten. Slavery and diseases from Europe have almost wiped them out in seventy years.

1782 Tupac Amaru II, descendant of last Incan emperor, leads a revolution against Spanish rule ... and fails. The Spanish make him watch the executions of his wife and sons, then they hang, draw and quarter him. (And you thought the Incas were cruel?)

1808 South American countries begin to rebel against Spanish rule. **1824** The Spanish are defeated and new countries are formed. In the old Incan homeland the country of Peru is set up.

Peculiar Peru

The Incas said they lived in Tahuantinsuyu. So, how come the Spanish arrived and called it Peru? Here's how…

The Spanish landed on the east coast of America. In 1511 the Spanish conquistador, Balboa, was weighing some gold when a young Amerindian chieftain struck the scales with his fist and said…

Then the Spanish heard stories of 'The Golden Man' – a South American king who was so wealthy he covered himself in gold dust every morning before he took a bath in his holy lake.

The Incas were doomed from that moment. It took the Spanish twenty years to find 'Peru'. But once conquistador Pizarro arrived the Incas had had their chips. (Pizza and chips have always gone well together.)

Powerful Pizarro

The leading conquistador in Tahuantinsuyu was the Spaniard Francisco Pizarro (or Franny to you and me). With his 260 men he conquered millions of Incas. Who was this Pizarro? Some sort of Superman? Here are some terrible truths...

Franny's fantastic facts

1 Franny grew up in Spain as a poor boy whose job was to look after the pigs. That's where he first learned to bring home the bacon.

2 It is said that his parents ran away and left him. He survived because he was brought up by a sow!

3 Franny never learned how to write (the sow never taught him). He couldn't even write his own name and it was needed on the official documents. So what did Franny do? He had a stencil made of his name and coloured it in when he needed to sign a paper!

4 Franny joined the explorer Nunez de Balboa when he crossed Panama and discovered the Pacific Ocean in 1513. Balboa was beheaded by the king's trusted general, Pedrarias Davila. Franny wasn't daft and he became a follower of Davila and kept his head.

5 Franny then joined up with the soldier Diego de Almagro and they set off to conquer lands south of Panama. The people of Panama couldn't believe anyone could take such a risk – they nicknamed Almagro and Pizarro's little army 'the band of lunatics'. The Panama people were right; Franny came back with just a little gold – and left behind a lot of dead soldiers.

6 On his next expedition into South America Franny was wounded by arrows seven times but carried on.

Franny and 250 Spanish soldiers retreated to the safety of an island where he made a famous speech. He drew a line in the sand and said …

Gentlemen, this line is work, hunger, thirst, weariness and sickness. If you wish to join me in facing these perils then cross the line and stand beside me like true friends. No matter how few there are, I know that we will be victorious.

Would you cross the line? How many of those 250 gallant Spanish men crossed Franny's line? Was it …
a) 13?
b) 113?
c) 213?

Answer: **a)** Just 13 swallowed this brave talk and joined him. He must have felt a bit of a twit!

7 Like all great leaders Franny had a lot of luck. One of his 'Glorious Thirteen' was a giant of a man called Pedro de Candia. This man offered to explore the trail ahead alone. He said …

If I'm killed you will only have lost one man which is not important. But if I succeed your glory will be great!

De Candia carried a metre-long wooden cross and marched towards the Incan town of Tumbez. It's said the Tumbez councillors released the Emperor's lion and tiger on to the path. The creatures weren't hungry and lay down at de Candia's feet. He patted them on the head and the people of Tumbez were gobsmacked. Or god-smacked. They were sure de Candia had come from the sun god and worshipped him.

8 Peru was peppered with Pizarros. Franny's three brothers helped him to conquer the country. None of the brothers lived happily ever after. One, Hernando, went back to Spain and was locked in prison for 20 years for his great work! He was released and died at the age of 100 in terrible poverty.

Plotting Pizarro
The Spanish arrived in Tahuantinsuyu looking for gold. The King of Spain had given them ships and paid the Spanish soldiers. In return he wanted South American gold. Lots of it. Lots and lots and lots of it.

Exam time for teacher. Ask your history teacher, 'Can you answer each of these questions in just two words...?' (Of course they'll fail! Teachers can never use two words when two hundred will do!)

Franny Pizarro may not have been able to read and write ... but at least he could answer these horrible historical challenges. Could you?

Question 1: How did a handful of Spanish conquistadors defeat the vast numbers of Incan warriors?

Answer: They cheated.

Pizarro led his men into the city of Cajamarca – the Incas thought this might have been a visit from some wandering gods and didn't try to resist.

Then Pizarro sent a message to Emperor Atahuallpa…

Pizarro then had his cannon hidden covering the square and horsemen in the side streets. The Incas had never seen a cannon or a horse before. When Atahuallpa's bodyguard marched into the square the cannon opened fire and the horsemen rode in to finish them off. Up to seven thousand were butchered and Atahuallpa was taken prisoner. It makes those Spanish soldiers sound like brave but heartless killers. Yet Pedro Pizarro, who was there, said …

While they waited for the signal many Spaniards wet their pants from terror without noticing it.

Pizarro may sound like a ruthless and cruel villain. But then Atahuallpa's plan had been to capture the Spanish, sacrifice some of them to the gods and turn the others to slaves ... after cutting off their naughty bits. Pizarro just got his attack in first!

Question 2: How did Pizarro get the Incan wealth from all corners of the 2,000 mile empire?

EASY PEASY!

Answer: Ransom Atahuallpa.

That way you get the Incan people to bring their treasure to you! Pizarro had Emperor Atahuallpa locked in a cell. He simply said ...

> IF YOU WANT YOUR EMPEROR BACK, THEN I WANT THE CELL FILLED WITH GOLD!

The Incas, incredibly, agreed. They brought 13,265 pounds of gold (6,017 kilos, give or take a nugget). They also brought 26 pounds (12 kilos) of silver. I guess that was their small change. It took the Incas eight months to bring all the treasure to the city.

Question 3: How did Pizarro make sure Atahuallpa didn't destroy him once the ransom was paid?

Answer: Kill Atahuallpa.

Oh, yes, I know the Incas imagined their Emperor would be set free once the ransom was paid. But Pizarro wasn't daft. He never planned to let Atahuallpa go.

He said to Atahuallpa, 'We will burn you to death!'

That upset the Emperor a bit because he wanted his body to be turned into a mummy after death ... and it's a bit hard to make anything out of ashes (unless it's an ashtray, of course).

Pizarro made a deal. 'Tell you what, Atty, old man. If you agree to become a Christian then I'll be really kind to you and have you strangled instead!'

Atahuallpa agreed.

The Emperor was tied to a stake, a cord was placed round his throat and tightened by twisting a stick until he was strangled – a cheerful little execution method called the garrotte.

IT'S NO CHOKING MATTER!

Of course Atahuallpa didn't mind too much … he was sure he'd be reborn again! Emperors didn't die, they just found a new body!

The Incan armies were lost without their leader and the small group of conquistadors easily took control. Pizarro had just one problem … and it wasn't with the Incas…

Awful Almagro

The trouble with being a great success is that some people will get jealous and hate you. If you want to be popular then be a failure and everyone will love you! The man who hated Franny Pizarro more than anyone was fellow Spanish conquistador, Diego de Almagro.

- Almagro and Pizarro conquered Tahuantinsuyu between them but Pizarro was the Spanish King's pet and Almagro got jealous.
- Almagro was sent south to help conquer Chile. Not only did he fail, but the Incas in Cuzco rebelled while he was away.
- When Almagro returned to fight the rebels he turned to Pizarro's brothers for help … but they refused to obey his orders during the fighting.
- Almagro put the brothers in prison and Pizarro was not a happy bunny.

- Spaniard fought Spaniard as Pizarro attacked Almagro. When Pizarro captured his old friend he showed Almagro the same mercy he'd shown to Atahuallpa. He had him strangled in the same way – then had his head cut off just to make sure!

YOU CAN'T BE TOO CAREFUL!

Getting it In-ca neck

Almagro's expedition to Chile was a disaster because he made some daft mistakes. For a start he set off over the mountains in winter. Even the tough Incan helpers froze to death. Almagro set out with 12,000 Incas and 10,000 died in that first winter.

The Incas were chained together in long lines with iron collars around their necks …

When an Inca fell sick it would take a long time, with frozen fingers and cold keys, to unfasten that collar. Almagro came up with a quick way of removing the Inca from the neck collar so the march wasn't held up for long. What was Almagro's short cut?

Answer: He chopped off the Inca's head.

82

Did you know…?

Almagro wasn't the only conquistador to fail in Chile. The next conquistador to return to Chile, Pedro de Valdivia, who tried to take over the region in the 1550s, died when the Indians poured molten gold down his throat, saying,

You came for gold, now we give you all the gold you can use.

Franny's finale

Franny was killed by Almagro's son and his Spanish friends in the end, not by the Incas. He had built himself a palace in Lima and that's where they got him. But he went down fighting. He killed two of his attackers and then they came up with a wonderful plan – they threw one of their mates at Pizarro's sword! (Nice friendly thing to do!) As Pizarro tried to pull his sword out of this third corpse they stabbed him in the throat.

   Franny died a Christian. He dipped a finger in the blood from his throat and made the sign of a cross on the floor. He kissed the bloody cross … then the last blows rained down on him. Plenty of people went to the funeral but no one cried. The leader of the assassins, Almagro's son, got the chop a year later.

Awesome Atahuallpa

It's easy to say, 'Aw! Poor Atahuallpa! Tricked and murdered. It's not fair!' But the truth is Atahuallpa took the throne from his half-brother with trickery and murder ... so perhaps he got what he deserved!

Atahuallpa ruled in the north – Atahuallpa had been his dad's favourite so Dad gave him a region of his own before he died. But that made the new Emperor (Atahuallpa's brother Huascar) nervous. First Atahuallpa promised to obey the Emperor...

I WILL SEND YOU SERVANTS FROM MY REGION TO DO YOU HONOUR!

He sent the best soldiers he had, armed to the teeth! By the time Huascar realized this was actually an invading army it was too late. He was captured and his guards slaughtered in front of his eyes.

Atahuallpa wasn't finished ...

I WANT ALL OF HUASCAR'S MINISTERS AND CAPTAINS TO GATHER TOGETHER TO MAKE NEW LAWS! THEY WILL BE SAFE!

When they arrived he had them all put to death! That left the main danger lying in Atahuallpa's royal family – his 200 or so brothers and cousins.

I WANT THEM SACRIFICED! I WANT THEM HANGED, OR THROWN INTO A LAKE WITH STONES AROUND THEIR NECKS, OR THROWN FROM A CLIFF... AND YOU CAN LET HUASCAR WATCH THE FUN!

That should do it, eh? No. The women and children of the royal family had to go next. They were starved and then hung by the neck or the waist and left to die. (A Spanish writer said they were hung 'in ways too disgusting to mention' ... so we won't mention them.)

CENSORED!!

Yuk!

Enough, Atahuallpa? Nope! The servants and water-carriers and gardeners and cooks were massacred too. In some cities just one man remained for every ten women.

Now he was safe from his half-brother. The trouble was he had weakened his fighting men when the threat came from the Spanish invaders.

Awfully big mistake, Atahuallpa!

The men with soft swords
Atahuallpa had defeated Huascar when he heard about the strangers who had arrived. He also heard about their guns, swords and horses – the things that would defeat him.

But the Incan generals didn't want to scare Atahuallpa so they told him a few little fibs…

THEY HAVE THESE THINGS CALLED 'GUNS' – BUT THEY CAN ONLY STRIKE TWICE AND THEN THEY'RE FINISHED!

THEY HAVE THESE STICKS CALLED 'SWORDS' – BUT THEY ARE AS SOFT AND HARMLESS AS A WOMAN'S WEAVING STICK!

THEY HAVE THESE CREATURES CALLED 'HORSES' – BUT THEY ARE POWERLESS TO MOVE AT NIGHT!

NOTHING TO FEAR THEN, CHAPS! LET'S MEET THEM AT SUNSET AND WE'LL BE FINE!

?

They did … and they weren't! When Atahuallpa arrived a priest explained the Christian religion to the Emperor … in Latin! He handed Atahuallpa a Bible … but the Emperor didn't even know what a book was! Not surprisingly, Atahuallpa was bored with the sermon and threw the Bible down. That was when the hidden conquistadors struck. A Spaniard wrote …

It was a wonderful thing to see. To see so great a lord as Atahuallpa, who came with such power, taken prisoner in so short a time.

86

The writer also enjoyed the fact that while thousands of Incas were killed, not one conquistador died.

While Atahuallpa was imprisoned he didn't forget his brother Huascar. He sent out secret orders to have Huascar killed!

Silvery suffering

The Incan peasants had worked for their leaders and in return their leaders had cared for them. But the Spanish conquistadors made the Incan peasants work with just enough to keep them alive.

The greatest suffering was in the silver mines. The Spanish back in Spain were desperate for money (to pay soldiers to fight wars). The silver mine at Potosi was discovered and the Spanish worked the Incas to death to get its treasures.

Yet it wasn't the Spanish who discovered the mine. It was a llama herder. The story goes like this …

The shaking mountain was probably a small earthquake.

That old story of angry gods didn't bother the Spanish when they heard it. In 1571 they started mining for the silver and paid the workers with what?

a) pieces of the silver
b) pieces of farmland
c) pieces of cloth

Answer: c) The Spanish gave cloth to the chiefs who shared it out among the Incan mine workers. Imagine your teachers being paid in cloth!

So many Incas suffered in those mines they must have wished that herder had kept his mouth shut.

Working woes

The Spanish found new ways to make money from the Incas and brought them new ways to die...

- In the silver mines the workers would sweat to fill their cloaks with rocks then drag them to the surface. When they reached the cold air at the top of the mine they were chilled and many caught pneumonia and died.
- In the mercury mines the mercury could be breathed in with the dust and could poison the miners. It gave them raw throats, fever and a slow death.
- In the sugar-cane factories the Spanish brought in heavy machines to crush the sugar cane. They often ended up with crushed Incan peasants as well.

Routed rebels

Of course the Incas tried to rebel against Spanish rule from time to time. Not very successfully. They not only failed but suffered terribly.

During Manco Capac's Easter Uprising, in 1536, Spanish soldiers came towards the city to put down the uprising, and the Incan fighters taunted the Europeans by lifting their bare legs at them! (The insult is still used in the Andes.) Insulting, perhaps – but not very effective!

THIS'LL SHOW 'EM!

The battle raged for over a month. The Spanish tried terror tactics: they chopped up Indian women and cut off the right hands of captive warriors to toss them out of their fortress for the Indians to find.

After the Cuzco uprising, Pizarro first tried to befriend Manco Capac. That failed, so the Conquistador had Manco's sister-wife...

- stripped
- tied to a tree
- whipped with rods
- shot to death with arrows.

Then her corpse was put in a basket and floated downstream into the Incan camp.

Pizarro also burned alive Manco's best general and 15 other important Incan captains.

Manco thought he'd made friends with a Spanish ally of Almagro, but the Spaniard stabbed him to death. Some friend.

Terrific temples

When the conquistadors arrived in Cuzco they could scarcely believe their eyes. In fact conquistador Pedro de Cieza de Leon said …

If I wrote down everything I saw then no one would believe me!

But in his book *Chronicle of Peru* he wrote down enough to give a glittering glimpse into the strange world where they came, they saw and they robbed.

We reached their Coricancha, the Incan House of the Sun. Around the wall, half-way up, was a band of gold, two palms wide and four fingers thick. The many doorways and the doors were covered in gold and inside the walls were four houses. The houses were not very large but each was covered with plates of gold on the outside and the inside.

No wonder the greedy Spanish eyes popped out!

But the Incas didn't just cover their Sun Temple with gold. They were also great artists and filled the palace with golden models. Imagine Madame Tussaud's where everything is made of gold instead of wax!

In one of the temple houses was the figure of the sun, large and made of gold. It was cleverly made and studded with precious stones.

They also had a garden, but the soil was made from golden nuggets, and solid golden corn grew there. There were twenty llamas with their lambs, shepherds guarding them with slings and crooks – every single thing made of gold.

There were huge numbers of jars and pots and vases, all made of gold or silver and studded with emeralds.

And, in the Incan world every scrap of gold belonged to just one man: the Emperor. The Spanish planned to change that completely … and for ever. They stripped off the gold, melted down the statues and shipped the lot back to Spain!

Savage sacrifices

What did the Incas actually *do* in their Sun Temple? They made sacrifices to their sun god. If you can build a gold-plated palace, 100 metres long and 30 metres wide, then you can try this for yourself…

HOLY SMOKE

You too can be a perfect priest if you follow these simple instructions!

Sacrifice of the Day

First you need to make sure our Lord Sun appears each day, don't you? Then you'd better do the corn sacrifice each and every day … or else it's goodnight to daylight!

First light a nice hot fire.

Then scatter corn on the fire and toast it.

As the corn toasts, chant,

EAT THIS, LORD SUN, SO YOU WILL KNOW WE ARE YOUR CHILDREN!

Then step outside and watch the Sun come up.

No one knows why this works but it does … every time!

Sacrifice of the Month

On the first day of each month, take a hundred pure white llamas.

Lead your llamas round to the images of the gods.

Divide the llamas among the thirty priests of the temple (one priest for each day of the month).

Massacre the llamas, throw chunks of their flesh on to the fire, then grind their bones into powder for use in your services.

Yes, those cute little bundles of fur, guinea pigs, were turned into guinea pork as sacrifices. But don't cringe too much. There are worse things than roasting pets, as you're about to find out. But first …

Did you know …?
When an emperor died the Incas would often pluck out *his eyebrows* and throw them to the wind as a gift to the gods. Goodness knows what the gods would do with them! Maybe make eyebrow wigs of their own?

OH GREAT. MORE EYE-BROWS. JUST WHAT I NEEDED...

Killing kids
If the Incas were in desperate trouble – defeat in battle, famine or plague – only *human* blood was good enough to bribe the gods. And the purest blood was a child's blood. The Incas believed their gods preferred a nice sweet kid!

Cold graves
The Incas made their human sacrifices up in the mountains. Germs don't like the thin mountain air – they can't afford oxygen masks – and the constant cold is like a fridge. So the

child sacrifices haven't rotted away. They are still there to be found after 500 years.

A newspaper report in April 1999 described one find, an Incan sacrifice in Argentina ...

She was found 22,000 feet up on the summit of the Lullaillaco volcano in the north-west Argentine Andes. The 500-year-old girl's face looks peaceful in spite of the way she died. They got her drunk on beer and she was numb with the cold before she was wrapped in blankets and brightly coloured cloth. Then she was buried alive.

The little Incan girl's face is the best preserved of any ever found. She and another boy and girl were naturally mummified by the extreme cold and lack of oxygen.

Scans have shown that their organs are not damaged, there appears to be frozen blood in their veins and the remains of their last meals are still in their bowels. The girl, whose face can be seen poking through the dusty rags, was about 14. Her cheeks are swollen but she looks like one of the dark-skinned children who play in the streets of Salta today, in the shadow of the mountain their ancestors worshipped.

Happy gods mean sunny days

It sounds incredibly cruel to take a child to the top of a mountain then bury them alive. But the Incas believed they were doing the right thing. If you asked an Incan priest they would have given you reasons …

So children went to a gruesome death to keep a god happy. Very often the sacrifices were made as a way of saying 'Thank you!' to a god for a great victory in battle.

Terror for teenies

The journey to the top of the mountain took days, with stops every night in bare stone shelters.

Did the children know that death was waiting for them at the top of that mountain? In spite of the beer they had to dope them, the children must have been terrified.

An archaeologist described one find …

> The crown of the boy's skull is as bare as an eggshell. His adult teeth are just coming through. There is a crack caused by a heavy blow that killed him. Through the crack you can see his shrunken brain. But he still has a face and it looks twisted with what looks like fear.

Was it fear? Or was that just the imagination of the archaeologist?

Grave robbers

The child sacrifices were buried with a small supply of food, so they'd have something to eat on the journey to the next world. They were also buried with sea shells and gold figures of men, women and llamas.

The Spanish conquered Tahuantinsuyu in order to steal Incan gold, and treasure-hunters *still* wreck old graves to steal the golden images. They don't care about the history they are destroying and they certainly don't have any respect for the poor dead children. An archaeologist came across one grave that had been blown apart with dynamite...

THERE WAS A MUMMY FROZEN IN A BLOCK OF ICE AND WE HADN'T THE EQUIPMENT TO GET IT OUT. WE RETURNED A MONTH LATER BUT TREASURE-HUNTERS HAD BEATEN US TO IT. THEY HAD BLASTED THE ICE APART. WE FOUND ONE OF THE MUMMY'S EARS BURIED IN AN OLD INCAN WALL BY THE FORCE OF THE DYNAMITE. WE DIDN'T FIND MUCH ELSE.

WALLS HAVE EARS!

The statues are often sold to rich collectors so they can't be seen in museums where the rest of us can study them. It isn't only the Incas and the conquistadors who are ruthless, greedy and selfish.

Pointy heads
Some of the child victims have been found with strange-shaped heads. It seems that they had wood strapped to their heads from the moment they were born so the infant heads were forced to grow to a point. The head took on the shape of the mountain on which they'd be sacrificed!

What if the mountain had twin peaks? Then the Incan parents managed to bind the children's heads in such a way that the skull grew into two peaks! Horrible but true!

And, after all that effort, they killed them.

Modern mummy murders

Archaeologists who visit the sites to examine sacrificed mummies make a gruesome claim …

SOME PEOPLE STILL MAKE SACRIFICES TO THE MOUNTAIN GODS TO THIS DAY… PEOPLE ARE IN JAIL TO PROVE IT. THERE HAVE BEEN ARRESTS!

Another visitor to the Incan lands that are now in Argentina said …

COUNTRY PEOPLE STILL CLIMB THE MOUNTAINS TO LEAVE GIFTS OF GRAIN. ONE OLD MAN SWORE THAT LOCAL SUGAR PLANTATION BOSSES KILL AND EAT ONE OF THEIR WORKERS EVERY YEAR TO MAKE SURE THEY HAVE A GOOD CROP.

Which is a bit like a head-teacher killing and eating a pupil every year to make sure they have good exam results! Let's hope no head-teacher reads this book.

Did you know…?
You may think the Incas were bloodthirsty, but some of the other tribes in Tahuantinsuyu were worse. The Spanish Friar Valverde, who baptized Atahuallpa, tried to flee when Francisco Pizarro was assassinated. He got to Ecuador, but was captured by Indians in Puná, who killed him … then ate him. (They probably sold him at a Friar Tuck shop.)

Llucky llama

In April each year the Incas had a ceremony in honour of Napa – the white llama. A white llama was dressed in a red shirt and had gold ear ornaments attached. He drank chicha beer and chewed coca leaves, the same as the priests.

NOT BAD… I WONDER IF THEY'VE GOT ANY CRISPS?

Then he made a chicha sacrifice to the gods. How on earth can a llama make a sacrifice? Pots of chicha were laid out in the temple and the llama was sent in to kick them over! (Bet you wouldn't have thought of that!) And the biggest treat for the llama wasn't the beer … it was the fact that the priests let him live. The Napa llama was never sacrificed!

Other llamas weren't so lucky…

- two 'red' llamas were always sacrificed at a wedding
- 100 llamas were sacrificed every month at the Sun Temple
- thousands of llamas were sacrificed to the gods before a big battle

What if there were a drought or a famine? What would the people do?

SACRIFICE A LLAMA?

GOT IT IN ONE!

That's an awful llot of llama.

And you really wouldn't want to know how the priests went about sacrificing a llama, would you? You would? Oh, very well, they slit their throats. (And that makes a right mess on a white llama's coat.)

And you really wouldn't want to know what the priests did with the blood, would you? You would? You *are* sick! If you must know the priest drank some of the blood and scattered the rest on the ground.

Did you know…?
Modern visitors to the ancient sacrifice site at Mount Sara Sara can stock up with food for the journey. In the villages at the foot of the mountain you can buy dried frogs. This is to make that popular dish, frog soup. If that's what you enjoy then hop over to Peru!

Groovy gods

Who were these gods who had to be kept supplied with fresh meat? The Incan gods could be grim and gruesome – like a lot of gods in a lot of countries. Here are a few for you to worship if you feel like it.

Viracocha
Job: Creator of Earth, humans and animals.
You may like to use one of his other names…

- Lord Instructor of the World (Sounds like he was a head-teacher!)
- The Ancient One (Yes … definitely a head-teacher!)
- The Old Man of the Sky.

Tall tales: Viracocha not only made humans – he also destroyed them, made them again out of stone, then scattered them around the world. After teaching humans how to survive he took his cloak, made it into a boat and sailed off into the Pacific Ocean.

Some Incas said that was a silly story …

HE DID **NOT** MAKE HIS CLOAK INTO A BOAT! THE TRUTH IS, HE WALKED ON THE WATER!

OH YEAH, MUCH MORE LIKELY!

Viracocha was a good friend to the Incas. When Emperor Pachacuti was under attack by the Chanca, Viracocha appeared to him in a dream and encouraged the Emperor on to victory. Pachacuti made a temple to Viracocha in Cuzco to say 'Thanks'. Appearance: Pachacuti had the god's image made in gold. This figure was about the size of a 10-year-old child. Was Viracocha a small god? Or was Pachacuti just a bit mean with the gold?

Inti

Job: Sun god.
He is named after an Incan emperor called Inti, which means 'My Father', because Inti was thought to be the parent of the Incan lords.
Appearance: A human face on a golden disc with sun-rays around the edge.

Mama-Kilya

Job: Moon mother and wife of Inti
Tall tales: The Incas believed that when Mama Moon cried her tears fell as silver. (A very handy mama to have if you need some extra pocket money! Chop an onion under her nose and get enough to buy a new computer game!)

Apu Illapu

Job: Rain-giver and god of thunder.
This was the god the common people prayed to mostly because rain was so important to them.
Terrible tales: Temples to Apu were usually in high places. When the people needed rain they climbed up to the temple and made a sacrifice. This was often a human sacrifice. It was a sort of straight swap – a human life for a shower of rain.

(If your grandad's cabbage patch needs some rain then you may like to sacrifice a history teacher to Apu and see if it works.)

Appearance: You can't see Apu but you can see his shadow – it's the band of stars we call the Milky Way. The Incas believed Apu took his water from the Milky Way. (That's daft, of course, because it would rain Milky Rain if it was true. The streets would be covered in butter!)

Pray-time

The Incas had priests and temples in every corner of their empire and a chief priest in Cuzco who was nearly as powerful as the Emperor.

As well as a temple you could pray at a 'huaca' – that's a holy place. But this holy place could be...

- a mountain
- a bridge
- a mummy (especially the mummy of a dead emperor)
- a cairn (a pile of stones by the side of a road – add a stone and the gods will grant you a safe journey).

Mummy magic

Going into battle? Then you need the help of the dead Incan emperors. Here's how to get it ...

1 Take out their mummies and parade them in front of the warriors. (There was no mummy of the first emperor, Manco Capac, who turned to stone when he died.)

2 Get a military band to play music on bone flutes (made from human shin-bones) and tambourines.

3 Have poets recite long epic poems about the dead emperors. You may want to try this when your school next does battle with a rival school in soccer, hockey, netball or tiddlywinks. Parade your mummies while the school orchestra plays and recite an Incan epic. If you don't know any Incan epics then make one up, something like this ...

HERE'S OUR MUMMY, SINCHI ROCA,
TRY TO STOP US AND WE'LL CHOKE YER!
AND THE MUMMY OF OUR LLOQUE,
WE CAN'T LOSE WITH THIS GREAT BLOKE!
MAYTA IS THE NEXT IN LINE,
WE WILL BEAT YOU EVERY TIME.
FOLLOWED BY THE GREAT YUPANQUI,
WE WILL STOP YOUR HANKY PANKY!
INCA ROCA IS THE NEXT,
WHEN WE BEAT YOU, YOU'LL BE VEXED!
SEE THE FAMOUS LORD HUACAC,
HE'LL BE WITH US IN ATTACK!
VIRACOCHA, MIGHTY LORD,
HE'LL CHEER WHEN WE'VE SCORED!

Scary! No wonder the Incas won most of their battles!

Make that mummy

The emperor mummies were different to the sacrifice mummies that are found frozen on the mountain tops today. The emperor mummies were prepared more like Egyptian mummies. Their insides were taken out and they were stuffed with herbs. The eyes were then taken out (nice job for someone) and replaced with shells that were made to look like eyes.

The emperor's mummy was then stored carefully and well looked after by a team of servants. They made sure their mummy-monarch had...

- regular changes of clothes
- a cloth laid with his favourite food each day
- a special treat ... visits from the most beautiful of the Chosen Women from the temple.

It was never boring being an emperor's mummy. As well as getting out and about in parades he would also be visited by the royal family who wanted advice. All in all it was a hectic and tiring life being dead.

Horrible horoscopes

The Incas believed that life was controlled by the gods and you had to check with them before you did anything. With the help of the priests you could…

- discover a criminal
- tell who would win a battle
- find the cure for a sickness.

The best place to chat to a god was at an 'oracle', a place where the god would make himself known. The oracle at the Huaca-chaca bridge must have looked a bit weird. A conquistador described it like this …

THE ORACLE WAS A WOODEN POLE AS THICK AS A FAT MAN. IT HAD A GOLDEN BELT AROUND THE WAIST AND TWO GOLDEN MOUNDS LIKE A WOMAN'S BREASTS!

A SORT OF TREASURE CHEST, THEN?

The Incas spoke to the oracle and the spirit of the river spoke back to them. (A pole as thick as a fat man could have

WHAT MUST I DO, OH GREAT ORACLE?

HOP IT, I'M STARVING!

held a priest as fat as a thin man inside, couldn't it? The priest could answer the question – then get to eat the sacrifice when the Incas had gone.) This may sound very artistic and charming. It wasn't. Spanish visitors reported that these 'oracles' were spattered with blood from sacrifices – often human blood.

Here are some other ways to find out about the future…

Faking firemen
It wasn't just priests at oracles who could cheat. There were
men called *yacarca* who would speak to the spirits in a fire
and answer your questions. They blew through a tube to
make the fire glow red hot. The fire spirits then 'spoke' to
anyone who wanted an answer to a question. But a clever-
clogs conquistador spotted that the *yacarca* was actually a
'ventriloquist' – speaking the fire-spirit answers without
moving his lips!

Coca crawlers
Another way to tell the future was to look at a dish of
leaves picked from the coca plant. (A bit like reading the
future by looking at tea leaves
in a cup as some people still
do today.) You could also take a
powerful drugged drink called
ayahuasca and see the future in
the wild dreams it gave you. But
strangest of all was to watch the
way a spider wandered across
the floor. That would tell you
everything you wanted to know!

Llama lungs

Watching spiders not strange enough for you? Then try this ...

Remember, it must be a *white llama*. Next-door's cat is just not good enough.

Strange signs

An ancient Incan story said that one day strangers would land in Peru and destroy both the Incas and their religion. Emperor Huayna was worried, but especially when in 1532 he received more 'signs' from the gods...

- At the Feast of the Sun an eagle appeared, chased by a flock of buzzards, and fell at the Emperor's feet. The priests fed and cared for it but the eagle died. What was the meaning? If the king of birds could be destroyed then so could an emperor?

- There were an unusual number of earthquakes. Great rocks shattered, mountains crumbled and tidal waves swamped the shores. What was the meaning? If a mountain could fall then so could an emperor?

- Comets filled the sky and the moon appeared to have three rings of light around it – one blood-red, one greenish-black and one smoky-grey. Of course the moon was believed to be the Emperor's mother. What was the meaning? A priest explained to the Emperor …

THE BLOOD-RED RING AROUND YOUR 'MOTHER' MEANS THAT WHEN YOU DIE A CRUEL WAR WILL BREAK OUT AMONGST YOUR PEOPLE. BLOOD WILL BE SHED IN STREAMS. THE BLACK RING MEANS THAT NOTHING WILL SURVIVE OF OUR RELIGION. EVERYTHING WILL VANISH IN SMOKE – THAT IS THE THIRD RING!

Three years later Huayna died, the Spanish had arrived with a new religion and the priest's words came true. Amazing! (Bet you wish that predicting-priest was around today. He could tell you next Saturday's lottery numbers!)

So how did the Incas think they might avoid their dreadful fate? By keeping the gods happy with lots of sacrifices: when Huayna died the Incas killed four *thousand* people to be buried with him. (And a fat lot of good it did them.) All because of a dead bird, a few earthquakes and a ring round the moon.

Fossil fuel

Who was the most important member of an Incan family?
Dad? No. Mum? No. Mummy? Yes!

The ancient founder of a family – like your great-great …
grandad – would have been turned into a mummy and was
the family's most valuable member. In fact if another family
kidnapped your mummy it could be held to ransom!

The Spanish arrived and were shocked at the way the Incas
worshipped their ancestors. What did the conquistadors do
with the mummies?

a) gave them a Christian burial
b) burned them
c) turned the mummies into shop-window dummies

Answer: **b)** Don't try this with your grandad …
especially if he's not dead yet.

Good God

Once the Incan emperors had been defeated the Incas squabbled
among themselves. Some rebelled and some made friends with
the Spanish invaders. Inca killed Inca and Spaniard killed
Spaniard as they fought over land and gold and religion.

The Spanish tried to make the Incas worship the Christian
God, rather than Incan gods and mummies. But just when

112

the plan seemed to be working a Spanish priest made a horrifying discovery. He told the governor the shocking news. His letter may have read something like this …

Parinacochas Village
Peru
21 June 1564

Your Grace,

The whole of Peru is in terrible danger. I discovered the truth here in my own parish. Send help at once. Send soldiers. Send arms.

I had noticed that the Indian men in my village disappeared every night to a large meeting hut. They wouldn't let me in! Me! Their priest! But I waited till they were all inside and listened at the door.

First they began to pray, and I realized they were praying to their old Incan gods. If that wasn't bad enough, one of their leaders (Curacas as they called them) stood up and began to scream at them. I remember his evil words now.

'The Christians have one God, they say. But we Incas have many more powerful ones. We also have hundreds and thousands of ancestors who care

PTO ➤

for us. They have told us that the Incan gods are going to rise up and destroy the Christian God! Floods will be sent to wash away all traces of the Spanish. We can start again. The Spanish will die. So will any Incas who follow them. If we Incas want to survive we must stop worshipping the Christian God and we must stop obeying the Spanish. Our gods are hungry and thirsty because Incas have stopped giving them Chicha beer and sacrifices. We must start again!'

The Incas say their gods are coming down from the hills and taking over their bodies. Some of these 'possessed' people shake, tremble and fall, or dance insanely.

After their meeting I took one of the weaker villagers and said I would burn him if he didn't tell me everything. It seems this rebel movement is spreading across Peru. We must destroy their holy places and burn their mummies. If we don't we will all die. In God's name, send help! Send help!

Your devoted servant,
Father Luis de Olivera

The Spanish sent investigators and discovered the rebellion was spreading fast. It took them three years to destroy all the holy places (huacas) they could find. They also destroyed 8,000 Incan rebels. The rebellion failed. Their mummies had let them down!

114

Purify that priest

The Incas found it painful to rebel against the Spanish Christians. Rebel Incas went on doing it in secret. These Incas thought Spanish priests made the Tahuantinsuyu ground impure by walking on it. So, after the priests had gone, they used a horribly historical way of cleaning their pathways...

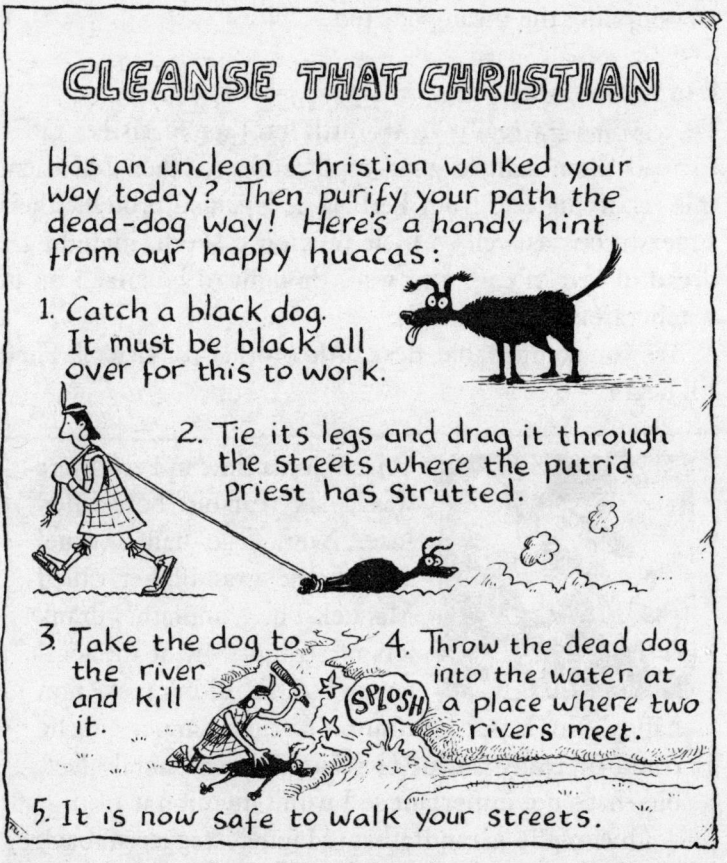

CLEANSE THAT CHRISTIAN

Has an unclean Christian walked your way today? Then purify your path the dead-dog way! Here's a handy hint from our happy huacas:

1. Catch a black dog. It must be black all over for this to work.

2. Tie its legs and drag it through the streets where the putrid priest has strutted.

3. Take the dog to the river and kill it.

SPLOSH

4. Throw the dead dog into the water at a place where two rivers meet.

5. It is now safe to walk your streets.

Don't try this at home! Dead dogs in rivers can pollute the water, kill the fish and make drinking water dreadful.

A 1613 revolt against the Catholic Church was crushed by the Spanish and the leaders arrested. These Incan leaders were so upset they poisoned themselves rather than become Christians.

And when one Incan leader (a Curaca) failed to support his people they poisoned him. But that sort of violence was rare. Most Incas pretended to be Christians but went on worshipping the Incan gods too.

Terrible tales

Do you have a really grotty little brother or sister? Offer to read them a little good-night story ... then tell them this terrifying tale from Peru. The Spanish brought their superstitions as well as their religion to Peru, including a dreadful fear of cats who were thought to be mixed up in witchcraft and black magic.

Are you comfortable, dear little brother (or sister)? Then I'll begin.

Once upon a time in Peru there was a six-year-old boy called Jose. Now, Jose had a cruel and wicked grandfather called Manuel. The grandfather drank lots of strong wine at the local tavern but that didn't make him happy! No, it put him into a terrible temper and he could be really nasty. (He also had very smelly feet, but that's not important so I won't mention it.)

One night Grandfather Manuel staggered back from the local tavern in a terrible rage.

116

'I'm in a terrible rage!' he roared.

'W-w-w-why?' Jose asked.

Grandfather Manuel frowned and his ugly face twisted in disgust. It was as if someone had stuck his smelly feet under his nose. 'Don't ask stupid questions!' he roared. 'Ooooh! Me chest!' he gasped.

The old man's eyes popped, his knees flopped, his tongue swelled, his feet smelled and he fell forward, flat on his ugly face, dead!

'Ooooh! What a shame!' the people of the village wailed on the streets.

'Yippee!' the people of the village cheered when they were alone in their homes.

That was until they heard about the strange will he had written before he died. Grandmother Consuela read it to little Jose (who was a bit too young to read).

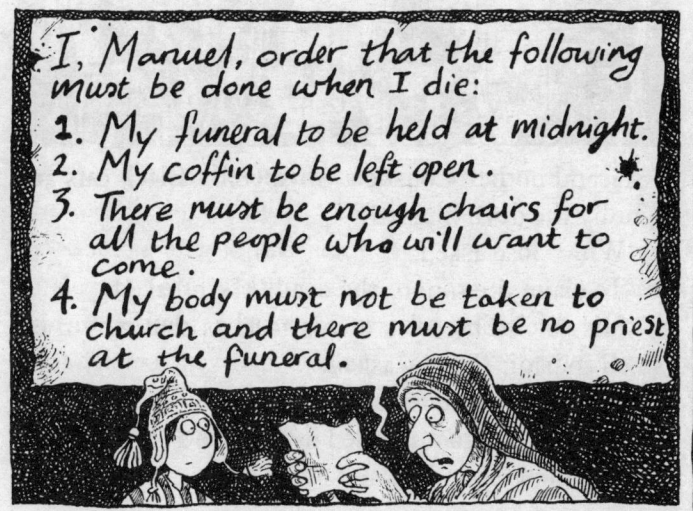

I, Manuel, order that the following must be done when I die:
1. My funeral to be held at midnight.
2. My coffin to be left open.
3. There must be enough chairs for all the people who will want to come.
4. My body must not be taken to church and there must be no priest at the funeral.

Grandmother Consuela quivered and Jose shivered. 'I can smell the fires of Hell in this!' the old woman wailed.

'I thought it was the smell of his feet,' her grandson sighed.

The evil smell filled the room where the coffin lay. No one came to visit the corpse – who can blame them?

At midnight a distant church bell rang. In the trembling silence a black cat stalked into the room. It had eyes as red as the coals of Hell. It was followed by a second cat, then a third and more. Soon every chair in the room was filled by a black cat with red eyes.

Grandmother Consuela whispered, 'Black cats are sent by the devil himself!'

'Why?' Jose asked.

'To claim the soul of the dead!' she croaked.

'His sole? The soles of his feet? Is that why they smell so bad?' the boy asked.

Before she could reply a cat started to wail and soon every cat in the room joined in to make a fearful noise like a school violin lesson.

The candles flickered and there was a soft creaking of the coffin. Grandfather Manuel sat up. His eyes were lifeless as ever but his body moved. First one smelly foot, then the other, was swung over the side of the coffin and the corpse stood on stiff legs.

The black cats marched from the room, tails held high, and the corpse shuffled out behind them.

'Where's Grandfather Manuel going?' little Jose asked.

Grandmother Consuela chewed her knuckles and mumbled. (You'd mumble too if you had a mouthful of knuckle.) 'He was an evil man in life, now his punishment is to have no peace in death. The devil has made Grandfather a *condenando* ... he must wander the earth for ever more, never sleep and never rest!'

'Ooooh! That's horrible,' Jose sighed.

Grandmother Consuela jabbed a bony finger at the boy. 'And that's what'll happen to you if you are wicked or cruel to your big brother (or sister)! The black cats will come to get you!'

When you've finished the story your really grotty little brother or sister will have learned an important lesson from Spanish Peru. If they ever dare to upset you again all you have to say (as they say to nasty nippers in Peru to this day) is, 'Is that a black cat I see over there?'

Inca mystery quiz

An Inca would look at you and think, 'Goodness me! These 21st century people are strange! They kill one another with metal machines called "cars"! Children play games with moving pictures where they learn to massacre hundreds of people on machines called "computers"! They have delicious meat but mash it up and fry it till it tastes like a dung-beetle's birthday cake and they call it a "burger"!'

There's nothing odd about Incan life – it's just that it looks that way to you. So here is a perfectly sensible Inca quiz...

1 The Incan people liked to keep their dead kings happy. How?
a) They fed them lots of beer so they could be Incan drinkas.
b) They put the latest books in the grave so they could be Incan thinkas.
c) They changed the shoes on the kingly corpses every week because they didn't want them to be Incan stinkas.

2 We call everyone who lived in the Empire 'Incas' today. But in those days 'Inca' was a word that was used for what?
a) Only the men (because women didn't matter)?
b) Only the people of Cuzco (because conquered people didn't matter).
c) Only the royal family (because no one else mattered).

3 The Incan Empire of Pachacuti stretched from the Amazon rainforest in the east almost to the Pacific Coast in the west. Why did the Incas not settle on the west coast?

a) Because it was too wet.

b) Because it was too dry.

c) Because they were afraid that sea monsters would jump out and eat them.

4 An Incan emperor wore a 'poncho' coat just once. What happened to each of these ponchos once he'd finished with it for the day?

a) They were given to the poor to keep them warm.

b) They were sacrificed to the gods.

c) They were stored in a special poncho palace.

5 Cuzco, like much of the Incan homelands, was 4,000 metres above sea level where the air is thin and most humans would struggle to breathe. How did the Incas manage?

a) They had really big strong hearts for pumping what little oxygen there was around their bodies.

b) They had big noses and big mouths so they could gulp down more air than most people.

c) They had big air tanks like aqualungs (made from llama skin) that they filled each day with lowland air and carried home to breathe.

6 How did the Incan men get rid of their facial hair?

a) They smothered their whiskers in honey and put their face in an anthill. The ants chewed off the honey and the hair. (That's a sweet idea.)

b) They shaved using razors made from sharp sea shells. (Shore is a good idea.)

c) They pulled their whiskers out one at a time using bronze tweezers. (They needed to be pretty plucky!)

7 When an Inca killed an enemy what could he use the dead man's skin for?

a) To cover a drum … so the enemy will be beaten twice! (Boom! Boom!)

b) To wrap some sandwiches for the journey home.

c) To scrape thin enough to let light through and use as a window in the family home.

8 An Incan princess died accidentally on a hunting trip. Her heartbroken Incan love, Illi Yunqui, buried his dead princess in the Lake of the Incas, high in the Andes. It is said that the water changed colour as her corpse splashed in and it's still that colour today. What colour?

a) Red, from her blood.

b) Green, the colour of her eyes.

c) Gold, the colour of the jewellery buried with her.

9 What nickname did the Spanish conquistadors give to the Incas when they first met them?
a) Big Ears.
b) Noddies.
c) Mr Plods.

10 A conquistador rode up to Emperor Atahuallpa and stopped just short of trampling him – it was meant to show how powerful the Spanish were. Atahuallpa didn't so much as blink … but some of his warriors did. How did Atahuallpa reward the warriors who had shown so much fear for their Emperor?
a) He gave them each their weight in gold for being so loyal.
b) He gave them a painful death for being cowards.
c) He gave them a llama to practise trick-riding like the Spanish.

Answers:

1a) The Incan lords made some peasants produce extra grain to brew into beer. This beer was then 'fed' to the mummies of the dead kings who probably became dead drunk as a result.

2c) Only the royal family were 'Incas' in Incan times. The Lord of Cuzco himself had the title 'Sapa' Inca – meaning 'King'. There were never more than 1,800 pure-blood Incas of the royal family. But, when they

---

ran short of a royal to rule they could 'adopt' a trusted outsider. These 'adopted' Incan royals were called 'Hahua' Incas.

3b) The shoreline of the Pacific was dry and not suitable for growing crops. It's said that anyone living there might see a shower of rain once or twice *in their lifetime*! The Incas probably could have conquered it if they'd really wanted.

4b) The poncho was taken to a temple where it was burned as a sacrifice to the gods. You may like to try this with your dad's smelly socks.

5a) Incan hearts could carry 60% more blood round the body than the average human. And blood carries oxygen to the brain and the muscles that need it. The air was thin but the Incan people got more of it. (And put on a dunce's cap and go to the bottom of the class if you answered **c)**.) The Incas also seemed to survive the cold better. A Spanish monk, Barnabe Cobos said …

I'm amazed at how warm the Incas are in the coldest weather, and how they can sleep on snow a palm's width deep. They lie on it as if it was a feather bed. I believe the reason is they have stomachs as tough as an ostrich's!

Uh?

6c) Incan men plucked their facial hair out with bronze tweezers. These tweezers were so valuable to them they were buried with their owners. That's a good idea and it must work because you never see an Incan mummy with a beard!

7a) The Incas went into battle playing drums and tambourines made with the skin of dead enemies.

8b) The lake is green, said to be the colour of her eyes. (No one has trawled the lake for her corpse to find out if she really did have green eyes. Anyway the fish have probably scoffed them.) It is said that on still winter nights you can still hear the moans of her heartbroken love. (More likely to be some tourist moaning, 'My God, it's cold up here! I wish I'd worn me thermal knickers!')

9a) They called them Big Ears because of the way the Incas stretched their ear lobes to wear big ornaments.

10b) An example of how Atahuallpa's soldiers were treated very strictly. They always did what they were told. So, when Atahuallpa told them not to harm the conquistadors they didn't. They didn't fight back when the conquistadors began to massacre them! Atahuallpa's ruthless rule backfired on him.

Epilogue

No one says the Incan emperors were kind rulers. But the Incan people suffered far, far more under the Spanish conquistadors.

The Incan way of life had some good ideas. They said that everyone should help everyone else with everything. The government tried to make sure that this happened. Life would be so much easier if that happened today!

The Incas also had some pretty dodgy ideas. They believed in Heaven and Hell like their Spanish conquerors, but they were a little different. Heaven was the sun where the good people went for warmth and food – Hell was inside the Earth where the bad suffered cold and hunger. So children, who were too young to be evil, would go to Heaven and happiness ... and by burying a child sacrifice alive you were doing the child a favour!

But they lived in a harsh world where earthquakes and landslides could destroy all they'd spent years building, where it could take days to walk just a few miles and where survival depended on the warmth and the kindness of the sun. It was a brutal world so it's not surprising there could be brutal people in it.

Pachacuti was one of the greatest ever native Americans. As he lay dying he managed to be quite poetic about his fate ...

Like a lily in the garden I was born,
Like a lily I grew up.
Years passed, I grew old.
I withered and died.

He could have been writing about the tribes who inhabited the Andes before the Incas. He could have been writing about the Incan nation itself. He could have been writing about the conquistadors.

All a bunch of lilies.

A bitter Incan survivor of the conquest wrote a poem to his gods about the fate of the Incas ...

You are lying spirits,
You are cruel and devilish enemies.
You are the cause of my misery and my failure!
I have adored you with all my power,
I have worshipped you with great sacrifices,
With human sacrifices.
You are just greedy robbers
And cruel enemies of my soldiers.
You shall be cursed for what you have done.
None of my children will worship you,
Not even the tiniest girl-child,
And not my royal grandchildren,
I curse you for ever.

All those men, women, children and llamas were sacrificed to the gods. In return they asked the gods to protect them and care for them.

The gods let them down.

INCREDIBLE INCAS

GRISLY QUIZ

**Now find out if you're a
incredible Inca expert!**

CRAZY CUSTOMS

The Incans had some batty beliefs and puzzling practices, from harming llamas to making their heads pointy, but which of the following curious customs do you think are true and which are false?

1. The emperor Pachacuti would only eat from golden plates.

2. Inca men were allowed to marry their sisters.

3. The Inca believed that the smaller your earlobes the more important you were.

4. The Incas treated childhood fevers by bathing the baby in wee.

5. The money used by the Incas was made of copper.

6. The Incas' preferred method of transport was the llama.

7. Incans believed it was a great honour to sacrifice their kids to the gods.

8. The Incas cremated their dead after three days.

RUTHLESS RULERS

The early Inca rulers were a crazy, cut-throat, conquering bunch. Can you match these loopy lords with their claim to fame?

1. Manco Capac
2. Sinchi Roca
3. Lloque Yupanqui
4. Mayta Capac
5. Capac Yupanqui
6. Inca Roca
7. Yahuar Huacac
8. Viracocha

a) Being the ugliest Inca lord ever
b) Being a woeful warrior in the war against the Ayarmarca
c) Being the first Inca lord to be mummified
d) Being a 'Creator God'
e) Being the first Inca lord to capture lands outside the Cuzco Valley
f) Being the first Inca lord
g) Being a beastly bigamist (having a number of wives)
h) Being the biggest, baddest Inca bully

PAINFUL FOR PERUVIANS

Life was tough in the Inca Empire – rituals were rough, work was worrisome and if you broke the law or upset the emperor punishments were very painful indeed. Find out what life was like for the incredible Incas with this quick quiz.

1. What did Inca emperor Pachacuti do to his brother when he grew too powerful and popular among the people?
a) Banished him to become a llama farmer
b) Murdered him
c) Had him locked up for the rest of his life

2. Which of the following was not part of the Inca manhood initiation ceremony?
a) Having to whip yourself
b) Having your ears pierced
c) Eating a llama's heart

3. What punishment did Chosen Women suffer if they got pregnant?
a) They and their families were hanged
b) They were buried alive
c) They were forced to sacrifice the child to the gods

4. How were naughty schoolchildren punished?
a) They were caned across the soles of the feet
b) They were given 12 lashes on the back
c) They were made to sleep with the llamas for a week

5. What was the punishment for murder in Inca society?
a) Being thrown off a cliff
b) Being trampled by llamas
c) Hanging

6. What was the punishment for cuddling the emperor's wives?
a) Having your feet chopped off and your eyes gouged out
b) Being fed to the llamas
c) Being stripped naked, tied to a wall and starved to death

7. What did the Incans do with the bones of people executed as witches or wizards?
a) They made them into musical instruments
b) They made them into spoons
c) They were given to the llamas to gnaw on

8. How did the Incans treat a headache?
a) By drinking a mixture made of bark from the pepper tree
b) By gouging out a hole in their head
c) With two aspirin and an early night

LIVE LIKE AN INCA

Everyone had roles and responsibilities in Inca villages and towns, even the llamas. How much have you learned about the day-to-day life in the Inca Empire?

1. What was the *chasqui* chain? (Clue: Get the message?)

2. What did Inca women over 50 do? (Clue: *We'ave* covered this already…)

3. What did Inca women use to hold their hair in place instead of hairspray? (Clue: A strange kind of toiletry)

4. What were Incas over the age of 80 expected to do? (Clue: Oh come on – it's dead easy!)

5. What did the Incas use to make fire when there wasn't any wood? (Clue: An a-llama-ing habit)

133

6. Which part of the emperor did the Incans offer to the gods after he had died? (Clue: Eye-eye)

7. What did the lucky white llama get to drink in the ceremony to honour Napa? (Clue: Can you *beer* to find out?)

8. Who was the Incan sun-god? (Clue: His name means 'my father')

Crazy Customs

1. True. Crazy Pach believed he was related to the sun god Inti and demanded the greatest luxuries.

2. False. Only the Inca emperor was allowed to marry his sister – it was meant to keep the royal blood pure.

3. False. They believed the BIGGER your ears were the more important you were – and they'd wear huge ear-plugs to stretch their ears.

4. True. They also made the baby drink the wee (would you want to knock back a glass of your little brother's widdle?)

5. False. The Incas didn't use money – they would work for anything they wanted.

6. False. They never rode on the llamas (which were hopeless as horses).

7. True. They thought killing the kids was a fair exchange for the sun and the rain that the gods provided.

8. False. The Incas preferred mummification and burial to cremation. That way they would make it to the afterlife.

Ruthless Rulers
1f; 2c; 3a; 4h; 5e; 6b; 7g; 8d

Painful for Peruvians
1b; 2c; 3b; 4a; 5a; 6c; 7a; 8b

Live like an Inca

1. The relay runners who carried messages across the Inca empire

2. They wove cloth to make clothes

3. Their own wee

4. Nothing – no one lived that long
5. Llama droppings (those llamas came in very handy!)
6. His eyebrows!
7. The Incan beer called chichi

8. Inti (father ... sun ... geddit?!)

INTERESTING INDEX

Where will you find 'frog soup', 'llama droppings'
and 'showing backsides' in an index? In a Horrible
Histories book, of course!

137

Terry Deary was born at a very early age, so long ago he can't remember. But his mother, who was there at the time, says he was born in Sunderland, north-east England, in 1946 – so it's not true that he writes all *Horrible Histories* from memory. At school he was a horrible child only interested in playing football and giving teachers a hard time. His history lessons were so boring and so badly taught, that he learned to loathe the subject. *Horrible Histories* is his revenge.

TERRIBLE
TUDORS

HORRIBLE HISTORIES

TERRIBLE
TUDORS

Terry Deary & Neil Tonge Illustrated by **Martin Brown**

■SCHOLASTIC

For Stephen.

Scholastic Children's Books,
Euston House, 24 Eversholt Street,
London NW1 1DB, UK

A division of Scholastic Ltd
London ~ New York ~ Toronto ~ Sydney ~ Auckland
Mexico City ~ New Delhi ~ Hong Kong

First published in the UK by Scholastic Ltd, 1993
This edition published 2017

Some of the material in this book has previously been published in
Horrible Histories: The Massive Millennium Quiz Book/The Horribly Huge Quiz Book

Text © Terry Deary and Neil Tonge, 1993, 1999
Illustrations © Martin Brown, 1993, 1999
All rights reserved

ISBN 978 1407 17867 7

Printed and bound by CPI Group (UK) Ltd, Croydon, CR0 4YY

4 6 8 10 9 7 5

The right of Terry Deary, Neil Tonge and Martin Brown to be identified as the authors and illustrator of this work has been asserted by them in
accordance with the Copyright, Designs and Patents Act, 1988.

www.scholastic.co.uk

CONTENTS

Introduction

If you think history is horrible then this is the book for you!

Sometimes history lessons in school can be **horribly** boring . . .

Sometimes it can be **horribly** confusing . . .

And sometimes history can be **horribly** unfair . . .

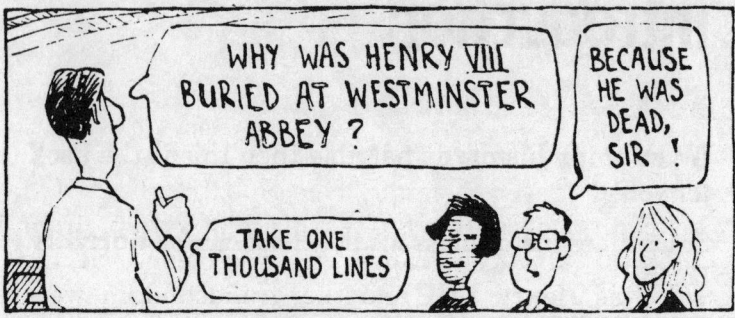

But this book is about **really horrible** history. It's full of the sort of facts that teachers never bother to tell you. Not just the bits about the kings and the queens and the battles and the endless lists of dates – it's also about the ordinary people who lived in Tudor times. People like you and me. Commoners! (Well, I'm dead common, I don't know about you!)

And what made them laugh and cry, what made them suffer and die. **That's what this book will try to help you understand**. You might learn some things your teachers don't even know! (Believe it or not, **teachers do not know everything!**)

There are one or two activities you can try. That's about the best way to find out what it was like to be a common Tudor.

There are some stories that are as chilling as the chilliest horror stories in your library. (You may have to read them with the light turned off in case you are scared of the shadows!) The facts and the stories should amaze you and teach you and amuse you, and sometimes make you sad.

Hopefully you'll find them all **horribly interesting**.

The terrible Tudors

What is a terrible Tudor?

What your teacher will tell you . . .

The Tudors were a family who ruled England, and poked their noses into the rest of Great Britain, from 1485 till 1603. The grandfather was Henry VII, his son was Henry VIII and the grandchildren were Edward VI, Mary I and Elizabeth I.

Five rulers and 118 years that changed the lives of the English people.

Who's who?

HENRY VII

Henry VII (Henry Tudor of Lancaster) King from 1485 to 1509

Defeated King Richard III at the Battle of Bosworth and took his crown. Married Elizabeth of York to stop their two families whingeing and scrapping over the crown.

HENRY VIII

Henry VIII King from 1509 to 1547

Son of Henry VII. Wanted a son to keep the Tudor line going – and he didn't care how many wives he had till he got one.

When he got rid of his first wife by divorcing her, the head of the Catholic Church (the Pope) didn't approve of it . . . so Henry made his own church (the Church of England), with himself as the head.

Henry got rid of the Catholic monasteries with their monks and nuns. (The money he got for their riches came in very handy!) But he still worshipped as a Catholic, and chopped off the heads of those who didn't.

~ HENRY VIII's WIVES ~

GOOD WIFE GUIDE

CHILDREN	WHAT HAPPENED
⚲ GIRL ♂ BOY	🦵 DIVORCED ✝ DIED
😠 NO CHILDREN	🪓 BEHEADED 👑 SURVIVED

CATHERINE OF ARAGON
QUEEN · Apr 1506 to Apr 1533   ⚲ Mary I   🦵

ANNE BOLEYN
QUEEN · Jan 1533 to May 1536   ⚲ Elizabeth I   🪓

JANE SEYMOUR
QUEEN · May 1536 to Oct 1537   ♂ Edward VI   ✝

ANNE OF CLEVES
QUEEN · Jan 1540 to July 1540   😠   🦵

CATHERINE HOWARD
QUEEN · July 1540 to Feb 1541   😠   🪓

CATHERINE PARR
QUEEN · July 1543 to Jan 1547   😠   👑

Anne Boleyn's last words before she had her head chopped off were **not**, "I'll just go for a walk around the block!"

Edward became king first, even though he was the youngest. That's because a male child always took the throne before a female child. The same rule still applies in England.

EDWARD VI

Edward VI King of England from 1547 to 1553
Was too young to rule, so had a Protector, the Duke of Somerset, to "help" him out. King Edward was engaged to Mary Queen of Scots, but this fell through. Just as well, really, as Edward was a Protestant and Mary a Catholic, which would have caused big problems. The Duke of Northumberland, made Edward get rid of Somerset. Northumberland became the next Protector – what a surprise! Poor Edward was a sickly lad and died of tuberculosis at the age of 16.

Lady Jane Grey Queen of England in 1553
Put on the throne by Northumberland, who had persuaded Edward to make her his heir because she was a Protestant, and was great-grand-daughter of Henry VII. She was also Northumberland's daughter-in-law! Lady Jane sat on the throne for nine days then Mary Tudor raised an army and walloped Northumberland. So Lady Jane was pushed off her throne and her head was pushed on the block.

LADY JANE GREY

Mary I (Mary Tudor) Queen of England 1553 to 1558

Was a devout Catholic, so she made the Pope head of the English church again. Married King Philip of Spain, also a Catholic. People were frightened of Philip's power, and the marriage led to Wyatt's rebellion, which was crushed by Mary's army. Philip, never short of an idea or two, persuaded Mary to fight the French. The English lost. Mary was getting more unpopular by the minute, but was probably too insane to care. Ended up with the nickname 'Bloody Mary', owing to regular head-choppings and burnings of Protestants.

MARY I
(MARY TUDOR)

ELIZABETH I

Elizabeth I Queen of England from 1558 to 1603

Had pretended to be a Catholic while Mary Tudor was Queen, just to keep her happy. But changed both herself and England into Protestants when she came to the throne. Locked up Mary Queen of Scots and chopped off her head because she was a Catholic, and because Catholic Europe thought that Mary should be Queen of England. Elizabeth never married, because she said that she was married to England! But she had a definite soft spot for the Earl of Essex, which didn't stop her from having **his** head chopped off as well.

13

Terrible Tudor Limericks

Confused? You may be, but try learning these limericks, and you'll easily remember . . .

Henry VII
Henry Tudor beat Richard the Thirder
When the battle turned into pure murder.
Henry pinched Richard's crown
For the ride back to town.
He was top man! He could go no furder.

Henry VIII
King Henry was fat as a boar
He had six wives and still wanted more.
Anne and Kate said,
"By heck! He's a pain in the neck!"
As their heads landed smack on the floor.

Edward VI
At nine years the little King Eddie
Had a grip on the throne quite unsteady.
He was all skin and bone,
Grown men fought for his throne
And by sixteen young Eddie was deadie.

Mary I

Bloody Mary, they say, was quite mad.
And the nastiest taste that she had
Was for protestant burning –
Seems she had a yearning
To kill even more than her dad.

Elizabeth I

A truly great queen was old Lizzie,
She went charging around being busy.
She thought herself beaut,
But her teeth looked like soot
And her hair it was all red and frizzy.

Terrible Tudor times

1485 – reign of Henry VII

Henry Tudor beat King Richard III at the Battle of Bosworth Field and became the first Tudor king. The Wars of the Roses ended – they had been dividing the country for over 30 years.

1487 A boy called Lambert Simnel claims to be king. His revolt fails. Is given a job in the palace kitchens!

1492 Christopher Columbus lands in America – the world is never the same again!

1497 Perkin Warbeck tries to take the English throne. Warbeck hanged in **1499**. England settles down under Henry VII and becomes richer and more peaceful than in the past.

1509 – reign of Henry VIII

1516 Mary I born – daughter of Henry VIII's Catholic first wife, Catherine of Aragon.

1517 First real Protestant revolt against the Catholic Church begins in Germany.

16

1520 Henry VIII appears at the Field of the Cloth of Gold – a ceremonious meeting between Henry and Francis I of France.

1533 Elizabeth I born, daughter of Henry's second wife, Anne Boleyn.

1534 Henry takes over as head of the Church in England.

1535 Henry begins to execute Catholics who object to his Church takeover.

1536 Anne Boleyn, (Elizabeth I's mother) executed and Henry begins to close down monasteries.

1537 Edward VI born – but his mother dies shortly afterwards. Edward always a weak child.

1547 – reign of Edward VI

1547 Edward VI just nine years old when he takes the throne.

The Duke of Somerset runs the country for the boy. His title is 'Protector'.

1549 Kett's rebellion in Norfolk against the new Protestant king.

1550 The Duke of Somerset executed and replaced by Duke of Northumberland as the new Protector.

1553 Edward is ill. He is persuaded to name Lady Jane Grey as the next Queen – this is partly to stop the Catholic Mary getting her hands on the throne . . . but the plan doesn't work. Young Ed dies.

1553 – reign of Mary I

Mary tries to return England to the Catholic faith. She has over 300 Protestants burned.

1556 Thomas Cranmer, Henry VIII and Edward VI's Protestant Archbishop of Canterbury, burned at the stake for opposing Mary.

1558 The English lose Calais (in France) to the French people. Mary unpopular for this and for her marriage to the Catholic Philip II of Spain. Luckily she dies before she is overthrown!

1558 – reign of Elizabeth I

1564 William Shakespeare born.

1567 Mary Queen of Scots thrown off her throne. She flees to England a year later.

1568 England and Spain begin to argue over control of the oceans.

1577 Francis Drake begins his voyage round the world – returns in 1580.

1587 Mary Queen of Scots executed.

1588 The Spanish Armada tries to invade England but is defeated.

1601 The Earl of Essex rebels against Elizabeth and is executed.

1603

End of Terrible Tudors – in come the Slimy Stuarts.

Kett's Rebellion

In Norfolk, 1549, the problem was too many sheep and too few jobs. The grumbles grew into a revolt. The revolting Norfolk men were led by the most revolting Robert Kett – a local landowner. But Robert's rebels grew hungry and weak. Edward VI sent the Earl of Warwick to deal with them. The Earl cut the rebels to pieces . . . but they weren't as cut up as Robert Kett might have been. He was sentenced to . . .

. . . be dragged to Tyburn, where he is to be hung and whilst still alive his entrails taken out and burned before him, his head cut off and his body cut into four pieces.

As it happened, Robert was taken to Norfolk Castle and hung in chains over the battlements.

Terrible Tudor life and death

Life begins at 40

Would **you** like to have lived in Tudor times? A 1980 school history book said . . . *All in all the Elizabethan Age was an extremely exciting time to be alive.* But this is a *Horrible History* book. You make up your own mind about how "exciting" it was when you have the real facts. For example . . . You probably know a lot of people who are 40 years old, or older. But would you have known as many in Tudor times?

Imagine that ten children were born on a particular day in a Tudor town. How many do you think would still be alive to celebrate their 40th birthdays?

a) 6   b) 9   c) 1   d) 4

Answer: c. On average, only one person in ten lived to the age of 40. Many died in childhood – the first year was the most dangerous of your life.

Why were Tudor times so unhealthy? Perhaps these will help you understand . . .

Half a dozen filthy facts

1 Open sewers ran through the streets and carried diseases.
2 Toilets were little more than a hole in the ground outside the back door.

3 Water came from village pumps. These often took the water from a local river, and that river was full of the filth from the town.

4 Country people made their own medicines from herbs, or went to an "apothecary". People still use herbal cures today . . . but would you take one from a Tudor apothecary who didn't know the importance of washing their hands before handling your medicine?

5 A popular cure for illness was "blood-letting". Most people believed that too much blood made you ill. All you had to do was lose some and you'd feel better. Where could you go to lose some blood? The local barber. (He had a part-time job as a surgeon when he wasn't cutting hair!) Sometimes the barber would make a deep cut, other times a scratch was made, followed by a heated cup over the wound to "suck" the blood out.

6 Some doctors used slimy, blood-sucking creatures called leeches to suck blood out of the patient. (And some doctors today still use leeches to cure certain blood diseases!)

Doctor, doctor. . . !

If you were a doctor in Tudor times, what cures would you suggest for illnesses?

Here are ten illnesses – and ten Tudor cures. Match the cure to the illness . . .

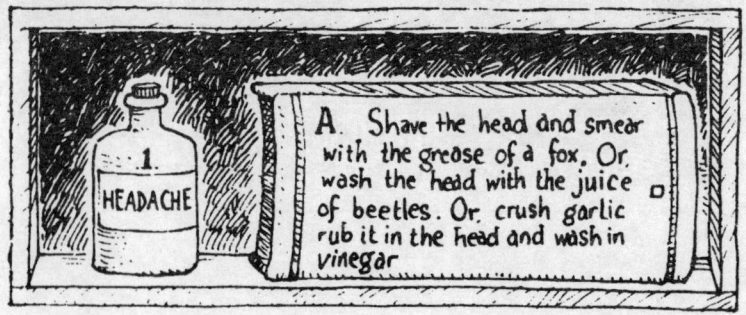

1. HEADACHE

A. Shave the head and smear with the grease of a fox. Or. wash the head with the juice of beetles. Or. crush garlic rub it in the head and wash in vinegar

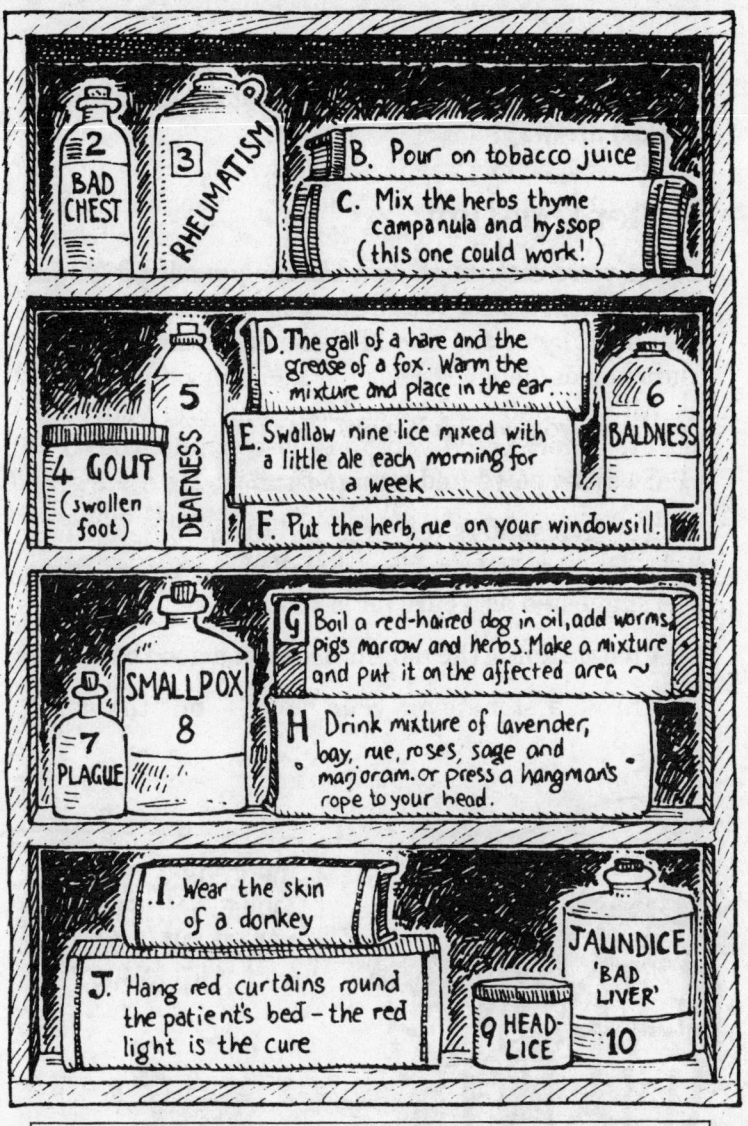

2 **BAD CHEST**

3 **RHEUMATISM**

B. Pour on tobacco juice

C. Mix the herbs thyme campanula and hyssop (this one could work!)

D. The gall of a hare and the grease of a fox. Warm the mixture and place in the ear....

E. Swallow nine lice mixed with a little ale each morning for a week

F. Put the herb, rue on your windowsill.

4 **GOUT** (swollen foot)

5 **DEAFNESS**

6 **BALDNESS**

G. Boil a red-haired dog in oil, add worms, pigs marrow and herbs. Make a mixture and put it on the affected area ~

H. Drink mixture of lavender, bay, rue, roses, sage and marjoram. or press a hangman's rope to your head.

7 **PLAGUE**

SMALLPOX 8

I. Wear the skin of a donkey

J. Hang red curtains round the patient's bed – the red light is the cure

9 **HEAD-LICE**

JAUNDICE 'BAD LIVER' 10

Answers: 1 = H 2 = C 3 = I 4 = G 5 = D
6 = A 7 = F 8 = J 9 = B 10 = E

How did you do, Doctor? It wouldn't really matter if you got them all wrong. Most of them wouldn't have worked anyway!

Patient, patient . . .!

If you were sick in those extremely exciting Tudor times, which would you rather do?
Feel sick . . . or try one of these extremely exciting Tudor cures?

Ten cures you wouldn't want to try . . .

1 Swallow powdered human skull.

2 Eat live spiders (covered in butter to help them slide down a little easier). Swallowing young frogs was suggested as a cure for asthma.

3 Fustigation – the patient is given a good beating.

4 Throw a stone over your house – but the stone

OF COURSE IT'S BIG..
HAVE YOU EVER
SEEN THE SIZE OF
A SHE-BEAR?

must first have killed a man, a wild boar or a she-bear.

5 Eat the scrapings from the skull of an executed criminal.

6 Eat bone-marrow mixed with sweat.

7 Sniff sneezing-powder to clear the head.

8 Have burning hot plasters placed on the body to raise blisters.

9 Mix the blood from a black cat's tail with cream, then drink it.

10 Place half a newly-killed pigeon on plague sores.

Nowadays we know that the dreadful plagues were carried by fleas. The Tudors didn't know about the disease they carried. Still, they weren't keen on fleas because they bit and made you itch. They had a cure you might like to try if you ever have them in your bedroom . . .

First, to gather all the fleas of thy chamber into one place, cover a staff with the grease of a fox or a hedgehog. Lay the staff in thy chamber and it shall gather all the fleas to it. Also, fill a dish with goat's blood and put it by the bed and all the fleas will come to it.

DON'T SLURP!

Fleas love to bite humans to get at their blood. They might well dash off to a whole dish of goat's blood!

25

Terrible Tudor schools

Parents, grandparents, teachers and other old fogeys . . . they all do it. They all talk about "The Good Old Days". Then they go on to talk about how terrible it was in school. They say things like . . . "When I was a young lad/lass/goldfish just knee high to a grasshopper/grass hut/grass skirt schools were schools. You kids have it easy these days. We used to get a caning/whipping/sweet if we as much as opened our mouth/eyes/door. We had 6/12/25 hours of homework every night and we were kept in detention/prison/vinegar until we did it. They were the best days of our lives!"

If they think **their** schools were tough it's as well they didn't go to school in Tudor times. (Or maybe they did and they're lying when they tell you they're only 39.) If they had they would know that . . .

1 Most village children didn't go to school. A few might attend a "Dame" school run by a local dame (woman).

2 Children rarely had books. They may have had "Horn" books, though. These were pieces of wood the shape and size of a table-tennis bat. On one side was a printed page with the alphabet and perhaps, the Lord's Prayer. The other side was blank and could be used to practise writing.

'HORN' BOOK FOR SHORTSIGHTED PUPILS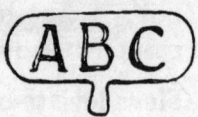

3 Richer children could be sent away to school. At first, the monks in the monasteries ran most of the schools, known as choir schools. Henry VIII closed the monasteries because they were run by the Catholic Church. He started a new church, the

Church of England, but he lost the schools in the process, and was left with only a handful of grammar schools. He had to encourage new ones to be set up, but in fact only 20 more grammar schools were established during his reign. So much for education!

How does your school compare with a Tudor school? Check out these Tudor school rules and decide . . .

What to expect at school

Timetable

School lessons went on from dawn till sunset with a break for school dinners.

(If you lived a long way from school, you'd have to get up in the dark to allow time for walking. The roads were muddy, cold and dangerous on the short winter days.)

~ SCHOOL RULES ~

No scholar shall wear a dagger or any other weapon. They shall not bring to school any stick or bat, only their meat knife.

Manchester Grammar School 1528
It is ordered that for every oath or rude word spoken, in the school or elsewhere, the scholar shall have three strokes of the cane.

Oundle School 1566
Scholars shall not go to taverns or ale-houses and must not play unlawful games such as cards, dice or the like.

Hawkshead School 1585
Punishment for losing your school cap . . . a beating
Punishment for making fun of another pupil . . . a beating.

School swots

Working hard at school was not always popular with the upper-class parent.

One father said, *I'd rather see my son hanged than be a bookworm. It is a gentleman's life to hunt and to hawk. A gentleman should leave learning to clodhoppers.*

~ SCHOOL MEALS ~

Breakfast
Bread and butter and a little fruit

Lunch
Rye bread, salted meat and ale

Tea
Bread with dried fruit and nuts – fresh fruit in summer

Rules at meal times
1 Wear a cap to keep your hair out of your food.
2 Don't wipe your mouth with your hand or sleeve.
3 Don't let your sleeve drag in your food.
4 Don't lean on the table.
5 Don't pick your teeth with your pen-knife or your fork.

Punishment for breaking a rule ... a beating.

WHERE'S MY CAP?

School teachers
Their job (in Westminster School at least) was to see that their pupils:
behave themselves properly in church and school as well as in games, that their faces and hands are washed, their heads combed, their hair and nails cut, their clothes and shoes kept clean so that no lice or dirt may infect themselves or their companions.

School punishments
Schoolmasters would often beat their pupils. Henry Peachum wrote,
I know one who in winter would, on a cold morning, whip his boys for no other reason than to warm himself up. Another beat them for swearing, and all the while he swore himself with horrible oaths.
But they weren't all so bad. The headmaster of Eton in 1531 was Nicholas Udall. He wrote the first English play that wasn't religious, and it was also the first comedy play.

School holidays
No long holidays. Schools would close for 16 days at Christmas and 12 days at Easter, but there were no summer holidays.

Lessons
A class might have as many as 60 pupils. Many hours were spent learning long passages from textbooks by heart. This not only kept them all quiet – it also saved having to buy books! Main subjects: Latin, Arithmetic, Divinity (Religious Study), English Literature.

School sports

A Shrove Tuesday custom was to take money to school, and with it the schoolmaster would buy a fighting cock. The master put a long string on the cock and tied it to a post. Boys would then take turns at throwing a stick at the cock. If a boy hit then the cock became his – if every boy hit then the cock belonged to the schoolmaster.

School equipment

Pupils had to write with quill pens made from feathers. These would have to be sharpened with a knife nearly every day. The small knife used was called a pen-knife – and we can still buy "pen-knives" today . . . even if we don't sharpen our ballpoints with them.

If you'd really like to know what it was like to write with a quill pen then you could try making one.

You need

1 A strong feather – goose quill is best, but turkey or any other strong feather will do.
2 A pen-knife – if you haven't a pen-knife then a Stanley knife will be just as good.
3 Tweezers.
4 Ink.
And an adult to make sure you don't get chopped fingers on the table!

How to make it

1 Shorten the feather to about 20cm.
2 Strip off all the barbs (the feathery part) from the shaft.
(Yes, I know! In all the pictures you've seen the writers appear to be writing with feathers. They hardly ever did – they only used the shaft and threw the rest away. Honest!)
3 Cut the bottom of the shaft off with your pen-knife (Figure 1).

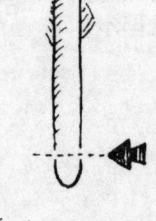

4 Shape the bottom of the shaft as in Figure 2. Take out the core with tweezers.

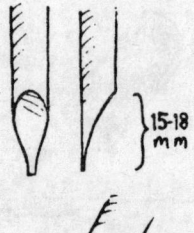

15-18 mm

5 Make a slit at the end of the nib about 5mm long (Figure 3).
6 Trim the end of the shaft again, this time at an angle. (Figure 4 shows the angle for a right-handed writer)
7 Dip the quill in ink. Try writing an alphabet.

ABCDE ᴸᴸ Gh 👁 JK l m

Test your teacher on Tudors

Here are a couple of facts your teacher (or parents or friends) may **think** they know. Perhaps you'll catch them out if you ask . . .

1 The first post

You: Please, Miss! (or Sir, or Fatface) Who had the first postal service in this country?

Teacher: I'm glad you asked me that . . .

(Teachers are always glad when you ask them something – it makes them think you are interested.)

            . . . Of course, everybody knows that the famous Victorian, Rowland Hill, invented the postal service.

You: (with a sigh) But my book on the Terrible Tudors says the first postal service was invented in the reign of Elizabeth the First!

Then go on to quote these facts . . .

Rowland Hill created the Penny Post and postage stamps, not the postal service. Tudor Guilds and universities had private postal services. The government was worried about spies sending messages out of the country this way. So they insisted that a service under The Master of Posts should carry all letters sent outside England – that way they could read them if they suspected something!

2 A miss is as good as a mile

You: Please, Sir! (or Miss, or Fairy-features) If you asked Henry VIII how many yards there are in a mile, what would he say?

Teacher: I'm glad you asked me that . . . He would say 1,760 yards, of course.

You: That's not what my book on the Terrible Tudors says. It says that if you asked Henry VIII how many yards there are in a mile he would say, "It depends where you are."

Teacher: Eh!?!

You: (Explain) It wasn't till Queen Elizabeth's reign that a mile was fixed at 1,760 yards. Before that it depended on where you lived.

LONDON MILE = 5,000 yards
ENGLISH MILE = 6,610 yards
WELSH MILE - about 4 modern miles
IRISH MILE = 2,240 yards
SCOTTISH MILE = 1,976 yards

I THOUGHT YOU MIGHT HAVE KNOWN THAT, MISS!

Then count your lucky stars that you aren't in school in Tudor times!

Tudor crimes ... and terrible punishments

In Britain in 1992 crime was the fourth largest "business" in the country – people on both sides of the law made 14 billion pounds. In Tudor times it must have been as bad, with more than 10,000 homeless beggars on the city streets. Many were simply rogues who tricked, cheated and stole from kindhearted people who thought they were helping the poor. Yes, there were more crimes in those days, ... and more punishments. Some of them seem incredible today.

35

Thieving

Humphrey Lisle's story – Newcastle, 1528

Humphrey Lisle must have been worried. Dead worried.

He knew the English laws of 1528: steal up to eleven pence and you went to prison. Steal twelve pence (one shilling) or more . . . and you could be hanged. Humphrey had been one of a gang of Scottish raiders who'd stolen much more than twelve pence. One of the charges against Humphrey said that he . . .

at Gosforth, a mile from Newcastle, took prisoner twenty-seven people passing by in the High Street, from whom he took 26 shillings and 8 pence. He ransomed all but seven whom he kept for a while as slaves in Scotland.

Stealing twenty-seven shillings! Kidnapping! Slavery! Humphrey and the gang had been caught and locked up in Newcastle jail. The gang were the worst villains in the North and now they were safely in chains in prison.

They were still in chains when they went to court. One by one the judge sentenced them to death. Humphrey's father was sentenced to death first. Then it was Humphrey's turn.

"You admit to all the charges against you?" the judge asked.

"Aye, sir," Humphrey answered.

"But I am not going to sentence you to death," the judge went on.

A gasp of surprise went around the court. They had been looking forward to seeing Humphrey's head stuck on a pole on the town walls. It was just what he deserved, wasn't it? The Newcastle people couldn't understand why the judge spared Humphrey's life.

Can you give a reason for the judge sparing Humphrey's life?

Was it because . . .

1 Humphrey had friends outside who threatened to have the judge killed?

2 Humphrey was very rich and offered the judge a lot of money?

3 Humphrey was the youngest in the gang and the judge wanted to give him a second chance?

4 Humphrey was Scottish and so was the judge?

Answer: 3. Humphrey Lisle was just **twelve years old** when he joined the gang that stole, burned, murdered and kidnapped its way through the North. The judge took pity on him. Within a few years Humphrey Lisle was working for the English . . . helping to catch Scottish raiders!

Believing is a crime

Tudor people were very concerned with religion. It was important to the kings and queens, to the people and to the law. Catholicism was the religion of England and most European countries until the 16th century.

But the invention of the printing press in the 15th century meant that more and more people had access to the Bible. and were beginning to question the wisdom of priests. Ordinary folk were expected to believe all sorts of things, and were encouraged to buy "relics". These were things like bits of old bone and hair that some priests said belonged to saints. Yuk! Anyway, all this led to people wanting change within the Church.

And some kings and queens, who wanted absolute power without interference from Catholic leaders, were only too happy to encourage this change, which was known as the Reformation. The "reformists" were generally known as Protestants. There was a lot of hatred between the Catholics and the Protestants.

Catholics wanted . . .
The Pope as head of the church – services in Latin – churches decorated with paintings and statues.

Protestants wanted . . .
No Pope – services in English – plain churches.

Often, the hatred between them was terribly deadly . . .

Margaret Clitheroe's story – York, 1586

Margaret Clitheroe was a Catholic. In the days of Elizabeth I that was not a safe thing to be. But a lot of Catholics kept their religion and stayed secure by playing safe. They went to the Church of England services as the law said they had to. They kept their Catholic beliefs quietly to themselves.

But Margaret Clitheroe was not that sort of woman. She was a "recusant" – she refused to go to a protestant church.

Her husband, John, was a rich butcher in the city of York. "Margaret," he sighed, "the officers of the law cannot ignore you any longer. They will take you to court and fine you. Come to church with me today. It can't do you any harm!"

But Margaret was stubborn. "No, John." He shook his head and left for church. He walked by Micklegate Bar, one of the main gates of York. The remains of executed Catholics were still hanging there, more grisly than anything on his butcher's stall. He shuddered and wished his wife would learn some sense.

He'd have been still more worried had he known that Margaret was doing more than just missing church. She was also hiding Catholic priests in their house. But not for much longer.

The officers had started questioning people who knew Margaret Clitheroe. They were trying to make a case against her. When they captured a young servant, that case was complete. They threatened him with a beating, so he told them everything they wanted to know – and more. He told them about hiding Catholic priests. He showed them the hiding places.

On Monday 10 March 1586 they came for Margaret. She stood silent before Judge Clinch. "Have you anything to say, Margaret Clitheroe?" the judge asked.

Margaret said nothing. She knew that if she answered the charges then the law would call witnesses against her. The best witnesses would be her own children. If the children didn't want to talk then they would be tortured until they betrayed their mother.

The judge nodded. "Of course, the punishment for refusing to stand trial is Death By Crushing, do you know that, Mrs Clitheroe?"

Margaret knew. She had heard about "death by crushing". The accused was laid on the ground, face up. A sharp stone, about the size of a man's fist, was placed under the back. The face was covered with a handkerchief. A heavy door was laid on the accused. Large stones were placed on the door until the accused was crushed to death.

Margaret had to choose. Did she . . .

1 Remain silent and face death by crushing?
2 Stand trial and have her children as witnesses against her?

The good – the Justice of the Peace

Which would you rather do:
1 live by the laws of the Tudor land?
2 break the laws of Tudor times?
3 have the job of enforcing Tudor laws?

The people who had the job of enforcing the laws were usually Justices of the Peace. (We still have them today but they don't have so much power.)

If you were a Justice of the Peace you would have to . . .

RIOTS ?
ROADS ?
WORKERS ?
REPORTS ?
WHIPPING ?
CHECKING ?
OH DEAR

1 stop riots
2 look after the building of roads, bridges, jails and poor-houses
3 decide how much local workers could be paid
4 report people who didn't go to church
5 be in charge of the whipping of beggars
6 check on the local alehouses.

But your main job would be to judge cases in your local court. Would you know all of the curious laws? Try to match the law to the crime first . . .

LAW	CRIME
1 Archery	A. More than 3 people making trouble together.
2 Unlawful games	B. Quarrelling
3 Rescue	C. Playing bowls, cards or dice on a holy day.
4 Barratry	D. Stirring up trouble for the king or queen.
5 Inmate	E. Refusing to go to church.
6 Riot	F Not going to regular weapons practices.
7 Recusance	G. Taking a person or an animal by force.
8 Sedition	H Letting part of your house to someone without a job.

Answers: 1 = F   2 = C   3 = G   4 = B
5 = H   6 = A   7 = E   8 = D

Now test your teacher! Bet they can't get more than 5!

Try your own court case
Now that you know the laws you can try a few cases. If you were a judge you'd have a lot of different punishments you could deal out. On the right is a list of the punishments – on the left is a list of crimes. Can you match the punishment to the crime?

41

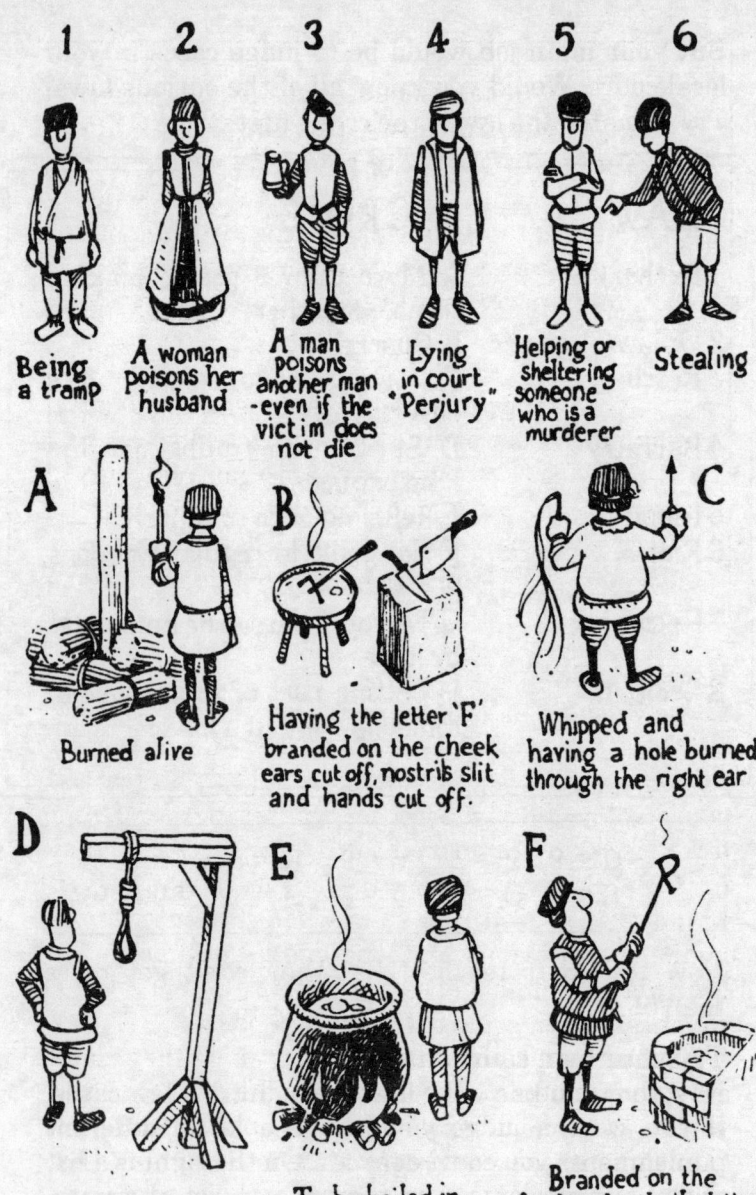

1 Being a tramp

2 A woman poisons her husband

3 A man poisons another man – even if the victim does not die

4 Lying in court "Perjury"

5 Helping or sheltering someone who is a murderer

6 Stealing

A Burned alive

B Having the letter 'F' branded on the cheek ears cut off, nostrils slit and hands cut off.

C Whipped and having a hole burned through the right ear

D Death by hanging

E To be boiled in water or lead

F Branded on the forehead with the letter 'P' using a hot iron

42

Answers: 1 = C Be found guilty a second time of "vagrancy" (being a tramp) and you'd have a hole burned through your other ear – a third time and you were executed.

2 = A Alice Arden was burned for arranging to have her husband murdered in 1551.

3 = E

4 = F

5 = D George Bradshaw was executed for helping Alice Arden murder her husband (2) – even though the guilty people all swore he had nothing whatever to do with it!

6 = B This happened to a man called Maynard in Exeter. The court was being kind to him . . . they could have ordered his execution!

Rotten rules

There wasn't a lot of freedom in Tudor times. Henry VIII passed a law telling people how much money they could earn . . . a craftsman could make just six pence a day in 1514. For that you had to work from five o'clock in the morning till six o'clock at night from March to September. In the winter months you would just(!) work from sunrise till sunset with one hour for breakfast and one-and-a-half hours for lunch. A servant could earn 160 pence a year – but a woman-servant could only earn 120 pence!

Elizabeth I passed a law telling people they could only wear clothes the queen thought suitable. And you had to wear a woollen hat on Sunday – or else! (That was so the English wool trade could make big profits and pay lots of lovely taxes to the queen!)

Even if you stayed out of trouble with the Justices

of the Peace, you still had to worry about work. Most workers belonged to a Guild – a sort of union for their trade. There were guilds for goldsmiths and weavers and carpenters and shoemakers and so on. And every guild had its own laws. Heaven help you if you broke a guild law! It was worst for the young people who joined the guilds for the first time – the "Apprentices". Here are just a few of the rules they had to obey . . .

Apprentices must not use any music by night or day in the streets. Neither shall they wear their hair long, nor hair at their ears like ruffians (1603).

And the punishment for long hair? A basin was put over the boy's head and the hair chopped off in a straight line. He was then sent to prison for ten days! (We still call a straight-cut fringe a pudding-basin cut.)

ANY CHANCE OF TAKING THE PUDDING OUT FIRST NEXT TIME

Apprentices were in trouble in 1554 for *playing cards, drinking, dancing and embracing women*, and their appearance was so grand and flashy they were banned from wearing silk-lined clothes, from having beards or from carrying daggers.

In a Weaver's Guild meeting (1527) you had to behave or . . .

Any brother misbehaving at meetings to be fined six pounds of wax.

(Wax was valuable, as it was needed for candles)

. . . but worse, such was the hatred between the Scots and the English, that

Any brother calling another "Scot" to be fined six shillings and eight pence.

. . . that's twelve weeks' wages!

The Tudor law

The rich nobles had been a "law unto themselves" – the Tudors put a stop to that. They were no longer allowed to keep private armies.

Bribing of judges and juries had been common – the Tudors stopped that . . . well, *mostly*!

The rich had been able to dodge the law – now rich lawbreakers could be taken before the Tudor kings' "Star Chamber". Punishments usually took the form of big fines.

Terrible Tudor detectives

The Tudors had no policemen. They did take it in turns to be "constables" and check on some of the laws. They also had local "detectives" called "cunning men", or "wizards". The village Cunning Man might use good magic to cure illnesses and tell fortunes. But he also had a use as a detective.

One of his methods of finding out a guilty person was to make a list of all the "suspects". Each suspect's name was written on a piece of paper. Each piece of paper was wrapped in a clay ball. The clay balls were dropped into a bucket of water. The one that unrolled first had the name of the guilty person on it! That's if the water didn't wash the ink off first!

The bad – the criminals

If you weren't afraid of being caught – or if you were very desperate for money and food to stay alive – you might become a criminal.

What sort would you like to be? A prigger of prancers? A dummerer? Or, maybe a ruffler?

What do you mean, you don't understand? If you're going to become a Tudor criminal you need to learn the language.

~ROGUES~
DICTIONARY

beak – magistrate
boozing ken - ale house
a bung – a purse
chats - gallows
a cony – an easy victim
cove – man
couch a hogshead –
  go to sleep
draw – pick a pocket
filchman – strong pole for
  walking or hitting
a foist – a pickpocket
glaziers – eyes
greenman's – fields

ken – house
lift – rob a shop
mort – woman
nab – head
peck – food
prancer – horse
prig – steal
a snap – a share of loot
stamps – legs
stow you – shut up
three trees with a ladder
  – gallows
walking mort – woman
  tramp

THAT HISTORY TEACHER'S A WALKING MORT. I WISH SHE'D STOW HER SO I CAN COUCH A HOGSHEAD. IN FACT IF YOU KEEP YOUR GLAZIERS ON HER I MAY JUST PRIG A NAP!

Become a terrible criminal!

Learn some of the language yourself – add new words of your own – and baffle everyone around you! Once you've grasped the language, you are almost ready to learn some tricks of the trade. But first you'll need a name – to protect your true identity. You need to change your name.

In Tudor times a few villains' nick-names were . . .
Olli Compoli,
Dimber Damber,
Black Will,
Shagbag.

Women were . . .
the White Ewe,
the Lamb, and so on.

What would you call yourself? You can make up your own name.

The Wickedness – the crimes

What villainy would you like to be involved in? You could try being one of these . . .

An Autem Mort – a woman who steals clothes off washing lines.

A Hooker (or Angler) – a thief who uses a long pole with a hook on the end to "lift" other people's property.

HOOKER

DUMMERER

I SAID CAN YOU PASS ME THE KNICKERS!

AUTEM MORT

They carry with them a staff five or six feet long, in which, within one inch of the top, is a little hole bored. In this hole they put an iron hook. With the same they will pluck unto them anything that they may reach. The hook, in the daytime, they hide and is never taken out until they come to the place where they do their stealing. They will lean upon their staff to hide the hole while they talk to you.

A Prigger of Prancers – a horse stealer.

A Ruffler – a beggar who tries to squeeze money out of you with a sad story about how he fought and was wounded in the wars.

A Dummerer – a beggar who tries to win sympathy by acting both deaf and dumb.

An Abram Man – a beggar who pretends to be mad, wears ragged clothes, dances around and talks nonsense ... Try saying, "Please let me have some of your sheep's feathers to make a bed!"

Highway Robber – seems to be a beggar when he stops you on a quiet road, but when you take your purse out he snatches it and may throw you off your horse and take that too.

DO-BE-DO LA LA GOLDFISH

ABRAM MAN

PRIGGER OF PRANCERS

FUNNY I THOUGHT I WAS A HORSE

Palliard – a beggar with dreadful sores. Could be genuine disease, but (more often) they'd be faked.

They take crowfoot, spearwort and salt and lay them upon the part of the body they desire to make sore. The skin by this means being irritated, they first clasp to a linen cloth till it sticks fast. When the cloth is plucked off the raw flesh has rat poison thrown upon it to make it look ugly. They then cast over that a cloth which is always bloody and filthy. They do this so often that in the end they feel no pain, nor do they want to have it healed. They travel from fair to fair and from market to market. They are able to live by begging and sometimes have about them five or six pounds altogether.

A Doxy (or walking Mort) – a woman tramp.
On her back she carries a great pack in which she has all the things she steals. Her skill sometimes is to tell fortunes or to help cure the diseases of women and children. As she walks she knits and wears in her hat a needle with a thread in it. If any poultry be near she feeds them with bread on the hook and has the thread tied to the hook. The chicken, swallowing this, is choked and hidden under the cloak. Chickens, clothing or anything that is worth the catching comes into her net.

WOW! THEM'S GREAT SORES!

PALLIARD

CUTPURSE

IF I TELL YOU YOU'RE BEING ROBBED, WILL YOU LET ME GO?

DOXY

A *Cutpurse* – purses were small coin-bags hanging from the belt. If you couldn't "foist" the purse (dip in and pick the money out) then you would have to "nip" it (cut the purse off).

A good foist must have three qualities that a good surgeon should have and they are an eagle's eye (to spy out where the bung lies) a lady's hand (to be little and nimble) and a lion's heart.

Terrible Shakespeare

Terrible Shakespeare has been torturing school pupils for hundreds of years!

It isn't his fault, though. Teachers were taught by teachers who were taught by teachers who were taught, "Shakespeare is the greatest poet and playwright ever. You are going to listen to him even if it bores the knickers off you! Now, sit still and stop yawning!"

In fact, Shakespeare didn't write for school pupils to read his plays and study every last word. He wrote the plays to be **acted** and **enjoyed** . . . so **act** them and **enjoy** them.

You can start by practising a few Terrible Shakespeare insults. Go up to the nearest nasty teacher (or policeman or parent or priest) and try one of these insults on them. Then, just before they mince you into hamster food, say, "Oh, but Sir (or Miss or Constable or Your Holiness), I was just practising my Shakespeare. He's the greatest poet and playwright ever." Smile sweetly and add, "And you do want me to study Shakespeare, don't you?"

Here goes . . .

(Never mind what they mean . . . just enjoy saying them aloud!) Feeling really brave now, are you? Then try . . .

Feeling suicidal? Then go up to the man with the biggest ears you can find and say Shakespeare's nastiest insult . . .

53

The Tudor Theatre

Being an actor in Tudor times was just a little different from today. For a start there were no actresses in Tudor theatre. All the women's parts were played by boys. Often the women in Shakespeare's plays disguised themselves as boys, so you'd have a boy pretending to be a woman pretending to be a boy. Nowadays women play the women's parts so you have women pretending to be boys pretending to be women pretending to be boys!

Get it? Oh, never mind.

Shakespeare's theatres were all open air stages. The audience would sit around three sides of the stage – if you were poor you would have to stand . . . and Shakespeare's play, *Hamlet*, went on for over three hours!

His plays are often performed on Elizabethan-style stages today. You can see them in Shakespeare's birthplace, Stratford-upon-Avon.

Most of the audience couldn't read so it was no use putting up posters. The signal that a play was going to start was a cannon fired from the top of the theatre roof. Unfortunately, one such cannon shot set fire to the thatched roof of one of Shakespeare's theatres and burned it to the ground.

Dramatic facts about William Shakespeare

1 Shakespeare was born on St. George's Day (23 April) in 1564. He died in 1616 . . . on 23 April, St. George's day! That must have put a bit of a damper on his 52nd birthday party.

2 Shakespeare chose the epitaph for his own gravestone. It says:

WILLIAM
~ SHAKESPEARE ~
1564 - 1616

BLEST BE THE MAN THAT
SPARES THESE STONES
AND CURST BE HE THAT
MOVES MY BONES

Some people think there may be new and priceless Shakespeare plays buried in the tomb . . . but no one has risked the curse of digging it up.

3 In his will he left his wife his *second-best bed, with the furniture.*

4 Some people have tried to rewrite Shakespeare's plays. In the eighteenth century, a man called Nahum Tate rewrote many. He took the sad and gory tragedies (like *Macbeth*) and gave them happy endings just because people prefer them!

5 Actors are very superstitious people. Their greatest superstition is that *Macbeth* is an unlucky play. Never, never say a line from the play (unless you are acting, it of course). Don't even say the title . . . call it "The Scottish Play" if you have to call it anything. And if you do act in it then watch out . . . the

"Macbeth Curse" may get you. This is the terrible bad luck that seems to happen to every production – accident, illness and even death. Many actors will swear that it's true because it's happened to someone they know.

6 The most dramatic fact of all? Perhaps William Shakespeare didn't write William Shakespeare's plays! Some very serious teachers believe that the man called Shakespeare could not have written plays. Why not? Because . . .

a William Shakespeare's father could not read or write, nor could Shakespeare's children

b the few signatures of Shakespeare that remain show a very poor scrawl

c William Shakespeare was known in Stratford as a businessman, not a writer

d there are no manuscripts of Shakespeare's plays in the man's own handwriting – there are lots from other writers of the time

e he left no manuscripts in his will and no copies of his plays are mentioned as being in his house

f a monument put up in Stratford church 15 years after he died show his hands resting on a sack (a sign of a tradesman) not a pen

g there is no evidence, apart from the name, to link the Stratford actor/businessman with the play-wright.

7 Professor Calvin Hoffman has studied the language used by writers. If you look at the way a writer uses words of a certain number of letters then you can recognise his writing. Every writer is different – just as everyone has different fingerprints. Yet Shakespeare's writing "fingerprint" is identical to that of another leading Elizabethan playwright, Christopher Marlowe.

So, did Marlowe write the plays and put William Shakespeare's name on them? Is it possible? No. Because, six months before Shakespeare's first publication, Christopher Marlowe is said to have been murdered.

Or was he . . .

Terrible Tudor mystery

The murder of Christopher Marlowe?

The murderer's story

Date: Wednesday 30 May 1593
Place: Eleanor Bull's Tavern, Deptford, London

Mrs Bull mopped at the spilt ale on the table with a dirty cloth. It dribbled onto the sawdust on the floor. Suddenly, three men clattered down the stairs and fell into the room. Three of the men she'd let the upstairs room to.

"Mrs Bull! Oh, Mrs Bull!" the skinny Ingram Frizer gasped as he clutched at his head.

"What's wrong?" the woman snapped. Frizer was a well-known trickster who'd tried to cheat her more than once.

The man took his hand away from his head. It was soaked in blood. "Murder!" he said hoarsely.

"Sit down," she said briskly. Frizer's two friends, Skeres and Poley, helped him to a bench. The woman mopped at the head wounds with her ale cloth and sniffed. "Not murder, Mr Frizer, just a couple of two inch cuts. You'll not die. Who did it?"

"Marlowe," the man moaned, "Christopher Marlowe."

The woman looked at the stairs and snatched a bread knife from the bar. "Roaming around stabbing people, is he?"

The wounded man shook his head slowly. "Not any more, he's not."

Mrs Bull relaxed. "You overpowered him, then?"

Frizer's voice dropped to a whisper. "I killed him!"

The landlady grabbed the man by the collar and marched him towards the stairs. "Let's have a look at poor Mr Marlowe, shall we?" she demanded. Frizer couldn't argue. Skeres and Poley lurked behind as she threw open the door.

The body lay on the floor. One lifeless eye stared at the ceiling. The other was covered in blood from a neat wound just above it.

"I knew you were trouble, you three," the woman moaned. "That Mr Marlowe seemed such a nice young man. What happened?" She looked closely at the body and shook her head. "Doesn't look a bad enough wound to kill a man that quick," she muttered.

Frizer swayed and let himself fall onto the bed.

"He was lying here, on this bed. We had our backs to him, didn't we Poley?"

Poley nodded. The local men said Poley made his money from spying. "Our backs to him," he said.

"Suddenly he jumped up from the bed, snatched my dagger and started stabbing at my head!" Frizer groaned. "I had Skeres on one side of me and Poley on the other. I couldn't get out of the way, could I?"

"He couldn't!" Skeres agreed. Everybody knew that Skeres was a cutpurse and a robber.

"If he attacked you from behind he could have killed you easily, not just scratched your scalp, Mr Frizer," the landlady argued.

"I moved," the man said lamely.

"Then he stabbed himself in the eye, did he?" Mrs Bull asked with a sneer.

"No!" Poley cried. "I managed to get the dagger

59

60

from him. We struggled. It went into his eye by accident."

"A strange sort of accident. Doesn't look the sort of wound you'd get from a scuffle. Looks more like he was lying on his back when the knife went in," the woman said carefully.

The three men looked at each other nervously.

"Just one of those things," Poley mumbled.

"So what were you arguing about?" the landlady asked. "I didn't hear any argument."

"About the bill," Frizer said quickly.

"And why didn't your two friends help?" she asked suspiciously.

"It wasn't our argument," Skeres shrugged.

"You'll hang for this, Mr Frizer," Mrs Bull said contentedly.

Frizer looked up slowly from the bed. A curious smile came over his face. "Oh no I won't, Mrs Bull. Oh, no I won't."

And he didn't.

A strange sort of accident indeed. But the jury decided that was just what it was. You might have decided the same if you'd been on the jury. But looking back over 400 years you have a few more facts to go on. Here they are . . .

The powerful and important Sir Thomas Walsingham was a friend of all of the men and could have helped them get away with a plan such as this. Christopher Marlowe was certainly his closest friend.

Marlowe was in deep trouble at the time of his "death". His friend, Thomas Kyd, had just been arrested for having writings which said that Jesus was not the Son of God. The punishment for this was death. Kyd said the writings belonged to Christopher Marlowe! (It did Kyd no good – he died after being "put to torture" in prison a year later.)

Frizer went back to work for Walsingham after he had been tried for the murder of Marlowe.

So what happened in Mrs Bull's tavern that day? If you don't believe Frizer's story, here are two other stories that fit the facts . . .

The execution theory

Marlowe had been careless. He'd left those writings in Kyd's room. Marlowe would be arrested and executed. Marlowe was as good as dead.

Kyd had accused Marlowe. But if Marlowe went to court he might have brought Sir Thomas Walsingham into all this. That would never have done.

Sir Thomas called his three loyal cut-throats to him. He gave them their orders, "Kill Marlowe and I will reward you well. Make it look like an accident and I'll use all my power to make sure the court lets you go free."

The three agreed to meet Marlowe in the tavern. As the playwright lay drunk on the bed, Skeres and Poley held him down while Frizer pushed the knife into his eye. Skeres or Poley then gave Frizer a couple of cuts on the head to back up their story of a fight.

Or . . .

The escape theory

Sir Thomas Walsingham was a great friend of Christopher Marlowe. He heard that Marlowe was about to be arrested for a crime that could lead to his execution. Sir Thomas wanted to protect his friend.

He called the four men to his house and told them

of his plan. Marlowe must leave the country as soon as possible. As soon as he was safe abroad the other three must take a stranger to Mrs Bull's tavern and kill him.

After the murder, Frizer must confess. Say it was a fight and that "Marlowe" had been killed. When a man owns up to murder, the constables are interested in establishing the *killer* – not the identity of the *victim*. The stranger was buried in a grave named "Christopher Marlowe" and the real Marlowe was safe.

Of course, the real Marlowe was a successful playwright. Imagine Marlowe wants to go on writing plays. So he does. He sends them to Walsingham. Walsingham gives them to an actor. An ambitious young man who happily signs his own name to Marlowe's plays.

He signs them, "William Shakespeare".

Possible? What do you think? Remember, history is not always simple or straightforward. In cases like this historians make up their own minds from the facts that they have. So, you can be an historical "police officer". In cases like this, what **you** think is as good as what another historian might think.

Terrible Tudor kings and queens

Things they try to teach you

Henry VII
Henry Tudor became King Henry VII after defeating Richard III at the Battle of Bosworth Field.

True, but Henry had a lot of help from other lords, including one (Stanley) who might have fought for Richard. When he chose to fight for Henry he won the battle for him and changed the course of English history!

Richard III was a grotesque man – he was hunch-backed and cruel.

Richard was no crueller than most rulers of the time. The stories of his twisted body were added to by Henry Tudor's history writers. England was full of cruel lords – only the cruellest of all could hope to control them – and that was Henry Tudor!

Richard III died in battle crying, 'A horse, A horse! My kingdom for a horse!'

That's extremely unlikely! The lines were written by William Shakespeare 100 years after the battle in his play *Richard III*.

When Richard was killed in the Battle of Bosworth, his crown was found hanging from a thorn-bush and Henry was handed it on the battlefield.

It's a nice image, but not necessarily true.

64

Henry was fighting Richard III in the so-called 'Wars of the Roses'. Richard was fighting under the White Rose of the York Family emblem and Henry Tudor under the Red Rose of the Lancaster Family emblem.

In fact Richard fought under the banner of a Boar, while Henry Tudor battled under the Dragon symbol of his native Wales. The white-rose/red-rose idea was thought up by Henry Tudor years later.

 Henry VII was a clever man and a wise ruler.

True – but he was also a man of the Middle Ages with some strange ideas. The story goes that he'd heard that the Mastiff type of dog was the only one brave enough to attack a lion. But the symbol on the English flag was a lion – so he ordered all the Mastiff dogs in England to be destroyed! (Richard was just as super- stitious. Freak weather conditions meant that there appeared to be two suns shining in the sky before the battle of Bosworth Field. Richard took this as a sign that he was going to lose . . . and he did.)

 Henry VII made England a wealthy country by care- fully handling its money.

True – but Henry was **so** careful with money most people would call him very, very mean! And he wan- ted lots of money so that he didn't have to beg Parliament for it – which meant that he didn't have to take any notice of what Parliament said.

 All the money Henry VII saved for England was spent by his son, Henry VIII . . .

True!

Things you could try to teach them!

Henry VIII

● Henry is famous for his six wives. But, did you know that in just one year (1536) his first wife (Catherine) died, his second (Anne Boleyn) was beheaded and he married his third (Jane Seymour).

● Henry was fond of cock-fighting so he had his own cock-fighting pit built at Whitehall in London. There are different battles fought on the site today – it is number 10 Downing Street, the home of the Prime Minister!

● Henry was famous for his love of music. He composed many pieces and was a keen singer. He owned ten trombones, 14 trumpets, five bagpipes, 76 recorders and 78 flutes. It is said he composed the tune, *Greensleeves*.

● Henry was a show-off. He organised a great tournament near Calais in France, known as the *Field of the Cloth of Gold*. It seemed mainly a chance for him to display his own sporting talents. He is said to have tired out six horses while performing a thousand jumps . . . *to the delight of everyone.*

● Henry was an expert archer. He used to have competitions with a hundred of his guards and often did well. At the *Field of the Cloth of Gold* in 1520 he amazed people by hitting the bulls-eye repeatedly at a distance of 220 metres.

● Henry fancied himself as a wrestler. At a wrestling contest at the *Field of the Cloth of Gold* he created a stir by challenging King Francis I of France with the words . . . *Brother we will wrestle.* Francis couldn't refuse even though Henry was taller and heavier. Francis used a French-style trip and won – the English thought this was cheating; the French probably thought it served big Henry right.

● Henry liked to play an indoor tennis game called "Paume". He didn't go to see his wife, Anne Boleyn, executed. He was playing tennis while she had her head chopped off. As soon as he was brought the news of Anne's death, he rushed off to see his next love, Jane Seymour.

● Even hard Henry VIII had a heart. He needed a son to carry on the Tudor royal name. He was so furious when Anne Boleyn produced baby Elizabeth that he refused to go to the christening!

● Henry wanted to get rid of Anne Boleyn for giving him only a female child. Her other babies died. One of the things he accused her of was being a witch. He had some support from the Tudor people in this. Anne had been born with a sign of the devil on her . . . she had six fingers on her left hand!

● Only his third wife, Jane Seymour, gave him the son he wanted – then she died a few days later. Of his six wives it was Jane Seymour he asked to be buried next to when he died.

● Henry agreed to marry Anne of Cleves after he was shown a picture of her. She turned out to be a bit uglier than the picture. Henry was so upset he accused the Dutch of sending him a horse instead of a princess. He called her the Flanders Mare and divorced her after just six months.

Elizabeth I – what they said about her

It's difficult to know what Elizabeth looked like because although there are a lot of portraits of her, she didn't pose for many of them. And if a picture displeased her then she would have it destroyed.

Many painters have done portraits of the queen but none has sufficiently shown her looks or charms. Therefore her majesty commands all manner of persons to stop doing portraits of her until a clever painter has finished one which all other painters can copy. Her majesty, in the meantime, forbids the showing of any portraits which are ugly until they are improved. Lord Cecil

So, will we ever know exactly what she looked like? Only from what people wrote about her. Could you draw her from the descriptions?

She is now about twenty-one years old; her figure and face are very handsome; she has such an air of dignified majesty that no one could ever doubt that she is a queen.

VENETIAN AMBASSADOR

She is now twenty-three years old; although her face is comely rather than handsome, she is tall and well-formed, with a good skin, although swarthy; she has fine eyes and, above all, a beautiful hand with which she makes display.

ANOTHER VENETIAN AMBASSADOR

70

> Her hair was more reddish than yellow, curled naturally in appearance.

SCOTTISH AMBASSADOR 1564

> In her sixty-fifth year her face is oblong, fair, but wrinkled; her eyes small, yet black and pleasant; her nose a little hooked; her teeth black (a fault the English seem to suffer from because of their great use of sugar); she wore false hair, and that red; her hands were small, her fingers long and her height neither tall nor short; her air was stately, her manner of speaking mild and good-natured.

GERMAN VISITOR 1598

> When anyone speaks of her beauty she says she was never beautiful. Nevertheless, she speaks of her beauty as often as she can.

de MAISSE FRENCH VISITOR 1597

Elizabeth did not want to have her rotten teeth removed. Perhaps she was afraid. To show her how easy and painless it was, the brave Bishop of London had one of his own teeth taken out while she watched.

What Elizabeth I said about herself

I know I have the body of a weak and feeble woman, but I have the heart and stomach of a king, and a king of England too. I think foul scorn that any prince of Europe shall dare to invade the borders of my realm.

SHE WOULDN'T WANT THE STOMACH OF HENRY VIII

Her speech to her troops as the Spanish Armada approached

A weak and feeble woman? That's not what writers of her time said. Elizabeth had a temper which everyone feared. William Davison, her unfortunate secretary, was just one who suffered:

She punched and kicked him and told him to get out of her sight.

And . . .

She threw a slipper at Walsingham (her secretary) and hit him in the face, which is not an unusual thing for her to do as she is always behaving in such a rude manner as this.

And . . .

Once she sent a letter to the Earl of Essex which was so fierce that he fainted. He became so swelled up that all the buttons on his doublet broke away as though they had been cut with a knife.

What can we do about Mary?

In 1568 Mary Queen of Scots had to leave Scotland in a great hurry. She was suspected of being mixed up in the murder of her husband, and she was a Catholic. She also had a claim to the throne of England. She was a threat to Elizabeth, so what could Elizabeth do?

Elizabeth kept Mary in prison for a few years while she made up her mind. (It was 16 years in all – Elizabeth could sometimes take a long time to make up her mind!) Then, in 1587, Mary was proved to be plotting against Elizabeth. The English Queen had to act quickly. If you were Elizabeth I what would you do? You could . . .

1 help poor Mary to get her Scottish throne back: after all she is related to you through Henry VII – but this would upset the Scottish Protestants and may cause a war with Scotland if the plan failed.

2 let her go abroad to Catholic France or Spain – but Mary might get those countries to join her in a war to take the English throne. The English Catholics would certainly support her.

3 hand Mary back to the Scots for trial and possible execution – but Mary is a relative.

4 execute her – but English Catholics might rebel with help from Spain and France. And could you be so cruel as to do this to a woman who came to you for help?

5 sign an order for Mary to be executed. Wait for the execution to be carried out, then try to cancel the order. When the cancellation arrives too late say, "Oh, dear! I did sign the execution order – but I

73

never really meant it to be delivered! It's the messenger's fault! Put him in the Tower of London!" But nobody would swallow that, and Spain or France may still attack.

6 keep Mary in prison – but English, French or Spanish Catholics may try to free her.

What did Elizabeth decide? Number 5.

The Queen's mind was greatly troubled. She signed a death warrant for Mary and gave it to Davison, her secretary. The next day she changed her mind but it was too late. The warrant was delivered and Mary was executed. William Davison was fined heavily and put in the Tower of London.

According to one account, Mary was beheaded by a clumsy executioner who took at least three blows of the axe and a bit of sawing to finish the job. This eyewitness described it . . .

The executioners desired her to forgive them for her death. She answered, "I forgive you with all my heart for now, I hope, you shall make an end to all my troubles."

74

Kneeling down upon a cushion, without any fear of death, she spoke a psalm. Then she laid down her head, putting her chin on the block. Lying very still on the block she suffered two strokes with the axe, making very little noise or none at all. And so the executioner cut off her head, sawing one little gristle. He then lifted up her head to the view of all the assembly and cried, "God save the Queen!"

Elizabeth did apologise to Mary's son, James . . . *My dearest brother, I want you to know the huge grief I feel for something which I did not want to happen and that I am innocent in the matter.*

So that was all right!

But the Spanish didn't believe in Elizabeth's innocence – they didn't want to. King Philip II of Spain was sick of English ships raiding his own, laden with treasure from his overseas territories. Philip was a Catholic, like Mary. So he used her execution as an excuse to send a huge invasion fleet, The Armada, to take revenge for these English crimes. But that's another story . . .

Mary's Secret Message

Did Mary Queen of Scots deserve to die? Elizabeth had sheltered her when she fled from Scotland. How did she repay Elizabeth? By plotting with Elizabeth's enemies, especially English Catholics, to kill her. Of course Mary didn't go shouting it from the rooftops. It was a secret plot between her and the English conspirators. The leader of these treacherous plotters was a rich young Derbyshire man called Anthony Babbington.

So, if it was secret, how did Elizabeth find out about it? She found out because she had a very

75

clever spy in her service, Sir Francis Walsingham. First, Walsingham sent servants to Mary's prison who pretended to work for Mary . . . in fact they were spying on her.

Every time Mary sent a letter to Babbington the servants took it to Walsingham first. Mary tried writing in code. But she had sent the code to Babbington first. Walsingham had a copy. This is Mary's code . . .

A B C D E F G H I J K L M

N O P Q R S T U V W X Y Z

OF THE NOT FROM YOU

And this is part of the message that Walsingham read and passed on to Queen Elizabeth – the part that led to Mary's execution. Use the code to read it.

You could try writing your own messages in this code.

Elizabeth I's sharp and cruel tongue

It was said that if someone tall disagreed with her she would promise . . .

I will make you shorter by a head.

She seemed to have a thing about height. She asked a Scot how tall Mary Queen of Scots was. The man replied that Mary was taller than Elizabeth. Elizabeth said . . . *She is too tall, then; for I myself am neither too tall nor too short.* And, of course, Elizabeth then went on to make Mary Queen of Scots "shorter by a head"!

Elizabeth also made her favourite the Earl of Essex "shorter by a head" when he tried to lead a rebellion against her in February 1601. She was so fond of him that she wore his ring for the rest of her life. It must have upset her to order his execution . . . though not as much as it upset Essex.

Elizabeth's "wedding" ring

Elizabeth was the last Tudor because she never married and had children. Some people dared to hint that she should marry. Her reply was:

I have already joined myself in marriage to a husband, namely the kingdom of England.

77

Then she would show her coronation ring. She went on:

Do not blame me for the miserable lack of children; for everyone of you are children of mine.

But, when Elizabeth grew old and fat, the ring began to cut into her finger. She had to have it sawn off in January 1603. The superstitious Tudors saw this as a sign that her "marriage" to the country was ended.

Two months later she was dead.

Not a lot of people know that ...

... Elizabeth was one of the cleanest women in England. She was proud of the fact that she took a bath once every three months. One person was amazed and reported that she had four baths a year *whether she needed it or not!* (Even 100 years later King Louis XIV of France only had three baths in his whole life!)

... Elizabeth was a fan of an early sort of five-a-side tennis ...

About three o'clock, ten men hung up lines in a square grass court in front of her majesty's windows.

They squared out the form of the court making a cross line in the middle. Then in this square (having taken off their doublets) they played five on each side, with a small ball, to the great liking of her highness.

... Queen Elizabeth owned the first wristwatch in the world. Perhaps she lost it, because her dying words were ...
All my possessions for a moment of time.

Terrible Tudor joke ...
The Tudors were Henry VII, Henry VIII, Edward VI and Mary ... but who came after Mary?

Answer: Her Little Lamb.

Terrible Tudor witches

Black cats and broomsticks

Witches casting magic spells then flying off on their broomsticks. They make great stories. But few people believe them today. The Tudors, though, thought that witches were capable of anything. And unfortunately for the so-called witches, the Tudors believed the best way to deal with a witch was to burn him or her. (Seven out of every ten people accused of being witches were women.) Some "witches" believed they would be spared if they admitted they were witches. In 1565 Elizabeth Francis confessed . . .

I learnt this art of witchcraft at the age of twelve years from my grandmother. She told me to renounce God and his word and to give my blood to Satan. She gave me Satan in the form of a white spotted cat. She taught me to feed the cat with bread and milk and to call it by the name of Satan.

When I first had the cat Satan I asked it to make me rich. He promised me I should and asked what I would like (for the cat spoke to me in a strange, hollow voice.) I said, "Sheep," and this cat at once brought 18 sheep to my pasture, black and white. They stayed with me for a time, but in the end did all vanish away. I know not how.

I then asked for a husband, this Francis whom I now have, and the cat promised that I should have him. We were married and had a child but we did not live as quietly as I'd hoped. So I willed Satan to kill my six-month old child and he did.

When I still could not find a quiet life I asked it to make my husband lame. It did it in this way. It came one morning to Francis' shoe, lying in it like a toad. As he put on the shoe he touched it with his foot and he was taken with a lameness that will not heal.

Elizabeth said that she gave the cat to her friend Agnes Waterhouse. Agnes claimed that the cat . . .
*killed a pig
killed three of a priest's pigs
drowned a cow
drowned geese
killed a neighbour
killed her husband.*

Elizabeth Francis went to prison for a year – by confessing to her witchcraft she saved her life. Agnes Waterhouse was hanged.

The Truth about Margaret

If you were Margaret Harkett's judge you might decide . . .

1 William Goodwin hated the old woman because she was a beggar and a nuisance.

2 Goodwin's lamb must have been sick because healthy lambs aren't brought into the kitchen.

3 The lamb dying at the same time as Margaret's visit was just bad luck – coincidence.

You might also decide . . .

1 Mrs Frynde was upset and bitter at the death of her husband and wanted to blame someone.

2 Frynde's fall from the pear tree was bad luck.

3 It was odd that Frynde never mentioned the curse until he was dying.

4 Frynde died of one of the many illnesses of those times or as a result of the fall.

Do you judge Margaret Harkett "Guilty" or "Not Guilty"? What did her judge do in 1585?

Margaret was executed. So were hundreds of other old women who were simply blamed for any accidents or illnesses in the area. They were usually alone – they had no one to stand up for them. They were usually too weak to stand up to their bullying neighbours.

Which is witch?

The Tudors had a way of testing a person for witchcraft. They would put the suspected witch into a sack and throw them into a nearby pond or stream. If s/he floated then s/he was a witch and would be taken out and executed. If s/he sank then s/he was innocent . . . but probably dead from drowning.

Another test was to have the accused witch recite the *Lord's Prayer* without one mistake – could you do that, knowing that the first slip and you would die?

Witch fact . . .

In the sixteenth and seventeenth centuries about 100,000 people in Europe were accused of being witches and were killed.

Witchcraft laws

Witchcraft wasn't seen as particularly serious until 1542, when it became punishable by death if it was used for . . .

. . . discovering treasure

. . . injuring others

. . . unlawful love

In 1569 a list of magical practices that were banned included . . .

. . . curing men or beasts

. . . summoning wicked spirits

. . . telling where things were lost

Tudor superstitions

The death rate from disease was very high in Tudor times. Babies were especially likely to die from an illness. With so much death around the Tudors tried their own type of "witchcraft" to keep death and bad luck away. They didn't call their actions "witchcraft" – they called it "superstition". Some of the things they believed may seem odd to us today. They believed . . .

. . . when a baby was born they must ring church bells to frighten away evil spirits. Sometimes evil fairies stole the child and left a wicked fairy child in its place (a changeling).

. . . it was unlucky to wrap a new-born baby in new clothes, so it spent the first few hours of its life wrapped in an old cloth or in the clothes of older brothers or sisters. The baby had to be carried upstairs before it was carried downstairs.

. . . the twelfth night after Christmas was another time when evil spirits were flying around – protect yourself by chalking a cross on the beams of your house.

. . . it was unlucky if a hare ran in front of you – **hares**, they thought, were one of the shapes that a witch took to get around the country quickly! (Witches also disguised themselves as cats, dogs, rats, toads, wasps or butterflies. They would be fed with milk, bread and blood sucked from the witch.)

THAT'S NO REGULAR BUTTERFLY !!

. . . it was unlucky to leave empty eggshells lying about – they could become a witch's boat.

. . . in an ancient way to tell your fortune. You had to jump over a lighted candle. If the candle stayed lit then good luck was coming . . . but if the candle went out then bad luck was sure to follow. Which nursery rhyme describes this fortune-telling method?

Answer: *Jack be nimble, Jack be quick, Jack jump over the candlestick.*

Witch ghosts

In Buxted, Sussex, there is a lane called Nan Tuck's Lane. Nan Tuck had been accused of being a witch and the villagers tried to drown her. Nan escaped but was later found hanging in a nearby wood. Her ghost can be still seen running to the safety of the church, along Nan Tuck's Lane.

It is said that the screams of witches tortured by the witch-finder general can be heard in the dead of night at Seafield Bay in Suffolk.

Anne Chattox, the head of a group of Lancashire witches, was accused of digging up three skulls from a churchyard to use in a spell. She was hanged.

Father Ambrose Barlow's skull can be seen not far away, at Wardley Hall in Lancashire. He was a Catholic priest who died for his faith. The legend goes that this skull must not be disturbed in any way ... or else it will give the most blood-chilling scream you ever heard!

Terrible Tudor food

Foul facts on food

Tudor women, men and children in England drank beer, wine, sherry (or "sack"), mead and cider. This was not because they were drunkards. It was because the water was not fit to drink unless boiled.

The rich could buy or hunt for a wide range of meats. The poor had very little meat. Their main food was bread. Sometimes they caught rabbits, hares or fish to go with their turnips, beans and cabbage.

Tudor people were keen on spices. Most of the food was heavily salted to stop it going bad, so spices helped to disguise the salty taste. It also disguised the taste of rotten meat! Cinnamon, cloves, garlic and vinegar were all used.

Sugar was a rare luxury but, when they could get some, they used it on most of their food . . . including meat! Their other means of sweetening food was with honey.

Hot cross buns were made at Easter – but not always eaten – they were kept as luck charms instead!

Sailors had too much salt meat and not enough fresh vegetables on their long sea journeys. As a result they developed a disease called scurvy. Their gums began to rot, their breath to smell and their teeth began to drop out. Henry VIII's ship, the *Mary Rose*, was sunk in 1545 but recovered in 1982. The sailors had drowned, but modern-day tests show that many were already dying of scurvy.

People who went to see a play would usually eat while they watched. The actors could be really put off by people cracking nuts or trampling on the shells while they tried to act!

Four-and-twenty blackbirds baked in a pie? Not so daft a rhyme. Tudors and Stuarts loved eating birds – favourites were peacocks, larks and seagulls. And not just dead birds. This incredible recipe was included in a cookery book . . .

TO MAKE PIES THAT THE BIRDS MAY BE ALIVE IN THEM AND FLY OUT WHEN IT IS CUT UP

Make the piecrust of a great pie.
Fill it full of flour and bake it.
Being baked, open a hole at the bottom and take out the flour.
Then having a real pie the size of the hole, put it inside the piecrust. Put under the piecrust, around the real pie, as many small live birds as the empty piecrust will hold.
This to be done before such a time as you send the pie to the table and set it before the guests
Uncovering, or cutting up the great lid of the pie, all the birds will fly out, which is a delight and a pleasure to the guests.
So that they may not be hungry, you shall cut open the small pie.

ye woman's weekly pg 76

90

Got that? A big, **fake** piecrust covers a small, **real** pie **and** a flock of birds, yes? But the recipe doesn't explain what the birds are doing to the small pie – or what they are doing **on** the small pie – while they are waiting to be released.

Tudor foods you may want to eat

EGGS IN MUSTARD SAUCE

Ingredients :
Eggs- one for each person
& for each egg -
25 g butter
5 ml mustard (1 teaspoon)
5 ml vinegar (1 teaspoon)
A pinch of salt

Cooking :
Boil the eggs for 5 to 6 minutes.
While the eggs are boiling put the butter in a small saucepan and heat it.
When the butter has melted and begins to turn brown, take it off the heat.
Stir in the salt, mustard and vinegar.
When the eggs are ready remove the shells, cut them into quarters and put them on a warm dish.
Heat up the sauce again and pour it over the eggs.

ye womans weekly pg 77

JUMBLES (KNOTTED BISCUITS)
Ingredients:
2 eggs   15 ml aniseed or caraway (3 teasp)
100 sugar   175g plain flour
Cooking:
Beat the eggs. Add the sugar and aniseed (or caraway) and beat again. Stir in the flour to make a thick dough. Knead the dough on a floured board. Make the dough into rolls 1cm wide by 10cm long. Tie the strips into a single knot. Drop the knotted dough (6 at a time) into a pan of boiling water. They will sink to the bottom so use a spoon after a minute to help them float to the top. When the knots have floated for a minute and swelled, take them out of the water and let them drain on a wire rack. Put the knots on buttered baking sheets and bake for 15 minutes at Gas Mark 4 (or 350 degrees F. or 180 degrees C.). Turn them over and bake for another 10 minutes until they are golden brown.

A Tudor guide to table manners

Do you ever get nagged for your behaviour at the dinner table? So did Tudor children. These complaints may sound familiar. A 1577 Tudor book suggested . . .

At the table you must . . .
not make faces
Scratch not thy head with thy fingers when thou art at meat.
not shout
Fill not thy mouth too full, lest thou perhaps must speak.
not gulp down drink too fast
Pick not thy teeth with thy knife nor with thy finger end.
not shuffle feet
not blow on food to cool it
Nor blow out thy crumbs when thou dost eat.
not take all the best food for yourself
Foul not the place with spitting where thou dost sit.

Terrible Tudor greed

The rich would eat much more than the poor. One feast for Henry VIII at Greenwich Palace lasted seven hours. Breakfast for the poor would be boringly the same every day – bread and ale; sometimes porridge made with peas or beans.

The tables of the rich would be laid with the usual salt, bread, napkins, spoons and cups. But each guest used his or her own knife.

And where were the plates? They used large slabs of bread called "trenchers" instead. The food was served straight onto that.

Every type of fish, meat and pastry was eaten, along with 20 types of jelly. The jellies were made into the shapes of castles and animals of various descriptions.

In November 1531, Henry had five banquets at which he and his guests ate . . .

24 *beefs*
100 *fat muttons*
51 *great veals*
34 *porks*
91 *pigs*
over 700 cocks and hens
444 *pigeons*
168 *swans*
over 4000 larks.

YOU SHOULD HAVE SEEN YESTERDAY'S BREAKFAST

Many dishes were more for show than eating. A peacock would be skinned, roasted, then put back into its skin for serving. A "cockatrice" would be made by sewing the front half of a cockerel onto the back half of a baby pig before roasting.

Terrible Tudor fun and games

Blood sports

In the Middle Ages people worked long hours, but they had as much as one day in three as a holy day (a saint's day usually) or holiday. What did they do?

And what did they do on those long dark winter nights? No television or radio or records or cinema. They played sports, played games and watched sports. Some are quite similar to today's. Others are very, very different!

Animal torture

In Southwark, London, there are two bear gardens with bears, bulls and other beasts to be baited in a plot of ground for the beholders to stand safe.

A 1599 report described this "sport" . . .
Every Sunday and Wednesday in London there are bear baitings. The bear pit is circular with stands around the top for spectators. The ground space down below is empty.

Here a large bear on a rope was tied to a stake. Then a number of great English Mastiff dogs were brought in and shown to the bear.

After this they baited the bear, one after the other. Although the dogs were struck and mauled by the bear they did not give in. They had to be pulled off by sheer force and their mouths forced open with long sticks. The bear's teeth were not sharp and they could not injure the dogs; they have them broken short.

When the first mastiffs tired, fresh ones were brought in to bait the bear. When the bear was tired a powerful white bull was then brought in. One dog at a time was set on him. He speared these with his horns and tossed them so they could not get the better of him. And, as the dogs fell to the floor again, several men held sticks under them to break their fall. Lastly they brought in an old, blind bear which boys hit with canes and sticks. But he knew how to untie his lead, and he ran back to his stall.

The audience might bet on which one would win.

In Congleton, Cheshire, the town had its own bear. The bear died in 1601. There is a story that the Corporation wanted a new one but didn't have the money . . . so they ordered the town bible to be sold to pay for it!

Football

Rules:

The pitch – could be the land between one village and the next – even if it is several miles.

The ball – a pig's bladder or a ball of rags.

Scoring – the team that gets the ball back to their village is the winner.

Referee – none.

Playing rules – none. Get the ball any way you can.

Match Commentary . . .

Doesn't every player in a football game lie in wait for his opponent, seeking to knock him down or punch him on the nose? Sometimes the players' necks are broken, sometimes their backs, sometimes their arms and legs are thrust out of joint, and sometimes their noses gush with blood.

Hunting for fish

The rich used to hunt for small animals using trained hawks. But there was also a sport of using birds to hunt for fish. First a cormorant, a diving sea bird, was trained to come back to its owner. When it was trained its head was covered with a mask and it was taken to the sea. At the sea shore it was unmasked and allowed to fly over the sea with a leather band around its neck. When it caught a fish it would return to the owner . . . but the poor bird couldn't swallow the fish because the leather band was fastened too tight. The owner simply took the fish from the poor cormorant's beak!

Public executions

Very popular. The person to be executed would always dress in their finest clothes and make a speech so the spectators felt they had been to a good "show".

Play it yourself

Stoolball (Tudor Cricket)

1 Pitch two posts about four metres apart.
2 Use a bundle of rags for a ball.
3 Use a stick as a bat.

The bowler tries to stand at one post and hit the other post with the ball, while the batter tries to hit the ball. If the bowler hits the post then the batter is "out" and the next member of the team has a turn. If the batter hits the ball to a fielder he can be caught out.

The batter scores by hitting the ball and running from post to post and back again. The team that scores the most runs is the winner.

Loggats

Plant a stick in the ground, a "stake". Each player takes turns in throwing smaller sticks, "loggats". The player whose "loggat" finishes nearest the "stake" is the winner. You can invent your own scoring system.

Tame games

Table games

Dice, cards, dominoes, backgammon, chess and draughts were popular in Tudor times as they are today.

Here are some Tudor games you can try for yourself . . .

Hazard

You need two dice and any number of players.
1 Everyone throws two dice. The highest scorer is the "Caster".
2 The Caster throws until s/he gets 5, 6, 7, 8 or 9. The number s/he gets is the "Main Point".
3 The Caster throws again until s/he gets a number 4, 5, 6, 7, 8, 9 or 10. This is the "Chance Point". The "Chance Point" cannot be the same as the "Main Point".

4 The Caster throws again and tries to get the Chance Point – if s/he does then s/he is the winner.

5 If the Caster throws the "Main Point" before s/he manages to throw another "Chance Point" then s/he loses.

6 Use matchsticks to gamble with. If the Caster wins, s/he takes one matchstick from each player. If the Caster loses then s/he pays out a matchstick to each other player.

7 Once the Caster loses s/he passes the dice to the next player who throws for a new "Main Point" and a new "Chance Point".

Trump

You need a pack of playing cards and two or more players.

1 Place a pack of cards on the table face down.

2 Turn one card over. That number card is the "Trump".

3 Each person, one at a time, will turn the other cards over.

4 Every time one matches the "Trump", all the players hit the table with the left hand and shout "Trump!" Whoever is the last to shout and hit the table is out.

Merelles

You need a board marked like the one on page 101. Draw it onto a large piece of card.

You need ten counters, or coins, and two players.

1 Each player takes turns to place a counter on a dot.

2 The aim is to place three counters in a row.

3 If all the counters are on the board and there are no rows of three then the players can begin to move their counters.

4 A player can only move to an open dot and only one space each turn.

5 The first to get a row of three is the winner.

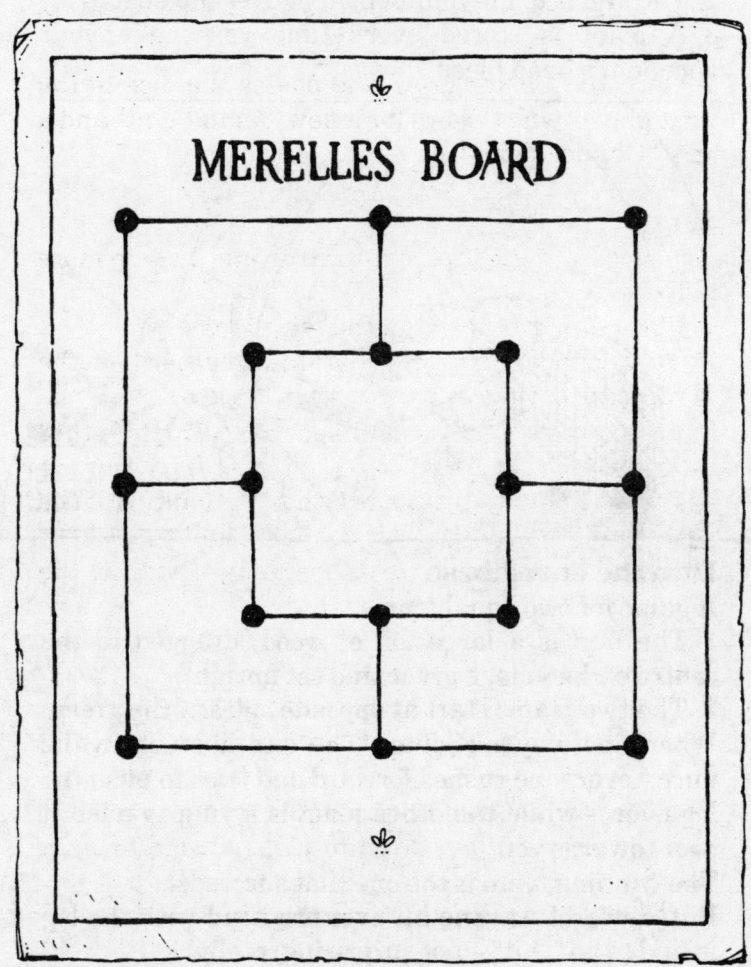

MERELLES BOARD

Some Tudor games you shouldn't play

Cudgelling
A game for two players.

1 Each is armed with a short stick.

2 The aim is to hit your opponent over the head.

3 A point is scored every time you make your opponent's head bleed!

NEXT TIME I GET THE BIG STICK!

Dun the cart-horse
A game for two equal teams.

1 The dun is a large log of wood, dragged to the centre of the village green and set upright.

2 The two teams start at opposite sides of the green. When one player shouts, "The dun is stuck in the mire," everyone rushes forward and tries to push the log over – while the other team is trying to push it over towards you.

The winning team is the one that succeeds.

But, beware! Anyone hit over the head with the log is said to be "Out" – not surprising, really!

102

Hurling

A game for two teams of 15 to 30 players.

1 A wooden ball is boiled in candle-grease to make it more slippery.

2 The aim is to pick up the ball and run through the other team's "goal".

3 If a player with the ball is tackled, he must pass the ball but he can only pass it backwards.

4 If your team don't have the ball then your aim is to stop the other team scoring – stop them any way you can!

Tudor sports reports

The Prior of Bicester Abbey has been paying money to players who play football on holidays. They are England's first professional footballers.

1491. Golf has been banned in Scotland by law because it's a wasteful pastime.
In no place in the country shall there be football, golf or other such unprofitable sports.

1513. King Henry VIII is so keen on bowling at Skittles that he took a portable bowling alley with him on a trip to France.

Terrible Tudor sailors

The sailors of Tudor Times are legendary for their daring exploits – trips around the earth in little leaking boats, fighting the mighty Spanish, French and Dutch navies, roaming the oceans with piratical plots.

Sir Francis Drake was the scourge of the oceans. He raided the coasts of the Caribbean and South America, sucking the wealth from these Spanish territories. As Drake filled Queen Elizabeth's coffers with plundered gold, she gave him more and more little jobs to do, such as helping to defeat the great Spanish Armada in 1588. It is of no surprise that many legends have been woven round Drake's cunning exploits. And wherever there are legends there are lies. Could you sort out the historical from the hysterical?

Hearing and believing

Drake's Drum

From 1577 till 1580 Sir Francis Drake sailed around the world in the service of Elizabeth I. At last, in the West Indies in 1596, he lay dying. He sent for his drum, an instrument that his men believed had magical powers. He ordered that it be sent back to England. He swore that he would return to defend his homeland if anyone beat the drum when England was in danger.

The drum was taken back to Buckland Abbey near Plymouth, where it remains to this day. The legend has changed a little over the years. The drum beats out its own warning when the country is in danger.

The drum is said to have rattled when Napoleon Bonaparte was brought to Plymouth after the battle of Waterloo. It seemed to know that the great enemy of England was nearby.

Then it has been heard three times this century. It sounded in 1914 when the first World War started; it sounded towards the end of that war when it had been taken on board the Royal Navy flagship, *The Royal Oak*.

When it sounded on *The Royal Oak*, the German fleet were approaching. They were heading towards the British fleet in order to surrender . . . perhaps it was giving a "Victory" salute.

Men were sent twice to find out where the noise of the drum was coming from – and twice they returned with no answer. The commander searched the ship for himself . . . and found nothing. Every sailor was at battle-stations in the ship. No one could have played the drum. The *Royal Oak* dropped anchor.

The drum-roll stopped as mysteriously as it had started.

The last time the drum was heard was in the darkest hours of World War Two. The British forces had crossed the channel to attack Hitler's German army. They were being driven back to the beaches. The German army was closing in, ready to massacre them. A miracle was needed.

The drum was heard sounding – the miracle occurred! A fleet of little British boats set off from the fishing ports and coastal towns of Eastern England. Somehow they crossed the channel, rescued huge numbers of men, then brought them safely home.

Was Sir Francis Drake watching over this feat of sea bravery, which was surely as great as his own trip round the world?

The Spanish Armada – Who won? Who lost?

The Spanish Armada, its special date
Is fifteen hundred and eighty-eight.

King Philip II of Spain was fed up with the English. His wife had been Mary I, Queen of England. He reckoned that he should be king, now that she was dead. But Elizabeth had grabbed the throne.

Also, English sailors were roaming the high seas and attacking the Spanish ships and colonies for their riches.

 Why was the Spanish Armada so expensive to run?

Because they only got 20 miles to the galleon.

Worse, Philip was Catholic and Elizabeth I was a Protestant, chopping off Catholic heads. In 1587 she had Mary Queen of Scots executed. This was the last straw as far as Philip was concerned.

So, in 1588 he decided it was time to teach the English a lesson once and for all. He assembled a huge fleet, an "Armada" of 130 galleons, and sent his armies off to invade England. They failed. This is what happened . . .

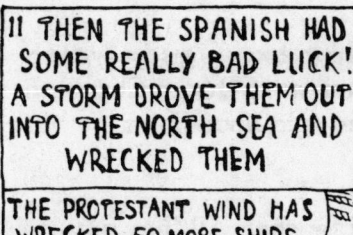

11 THEN THE SPANISH HAD SOME REALLY BAD LUCK! A STORM DROVE THEM OUT INTO THE NORTH SEA AND WRECKED THEM

THE PROTESTANT WIND HAS WRECKED 50 MORE SHIPS

AND IT'S MADE ME AS SEA-SICK AS A PARROT!

12 THE ENGLISH HAD SUNK 16 SPANISH SHIPS – THE STORM HAD SUNK 60 THAT'S WHY THE ARMADA MEDAL THAT WAS AWARDED TO THE ENGLISH SAILORS SAID:

GOD BREATHED AND THEY WERE SCATTERED

Of 130 galleons that left Spain in the summer of 1588, only about 50 returned in late September. As many as 19,000 Spaniards are thought to have died – it took them so long to sail back to Spain that many who didn't drown starved instead.

But the English sailors had their problems, too. In August 1588 the English Admiral, Lord Howard, wrote . . .

The sailors cry out for money and know not when they are to be paid. I have given them my word and honour that I will see them paid. If I had not done so they would have run away from Plymouth in their thousands.

But worse was to follow. Just the next day, Howard was writing . . .

Sickness and death begin to wonderfully grow among us. It is a most pitiful sight to see, here at Margate, how the men, having no place to go, die in the streets. It would grieve any man's heart to see them that have served so bravely to die so miserably.

So, Elizabeth won – she kept her throne. But who really lost? The English sailors? The Spanish sailors? Or both?

109

Sir Walter Raleigh

Sir Walter Raleigh was a sailor, too . . . **and** a writer, **and** explorer. He was a favourite of Queen Elizabeth I. A lot of stories have been told about him . . . but are they all true?

Try these questions on your teacher. All they have to answer is "True" or "False".

1 Walter Raleigh once spread his cloak in the mud for Queen Elizabeth to walk over.
True or False?

2 Walter Raleigh was the first man to bring potatoes to England.
True or False?

3 Walter Raleigh was the first man to bring tobacco to England.
True or False?

> **Answer:**
> All are false!

110

The Truth About Walter

1 Most people have heard the story of Sir Walter Raleigh and the cloak. It was supposed to have happened when Raleigh was a young man. The queen was passing through crowds of her people when she reached a muddy puddle in the road. She stopped. After all, she didn't want to spoil her fine shoes.

Quick-thinking Walter Raleigh pulled off his new cloak and covered the puddle so she could step over without walking through mud. The queen smiled. Walter's act was to make him a rich and powerful favourite of the queen.

A great story. But a true story? No. It originated with Thomas Fuller who was a historian of the 17th century who liked to "dress up" boring history with lively little incidents like the story of Raleigh's cloak . . . even if they didn't really happen!

2 Walter Raleigh's potatoes? For hundreds of years Walter Raleigh teachers have taught that Raleigh brought the first potatoes to England when he returned from a voyage to America in 1586. **But** there is **no** evidence from Tudor times to say this happened. A book called *Herball* (written by John Gerard in 1597) talks about someone called Clusius who had grown potatoes in Italy in 1585. The vegetable became very popular and was grown everywhere in Europe within ten years.

3 Walter Raleigh's tobacco? Again there are records of tobacco being used in France in 1560 – 26 years before Raleigh's ships returned from Virginia. It was brought there by John Nicot (whose name gives us "Nicotine"). It must have crossed the English Channel long before Raleigh's ships even set off.

In 1573 William Harrison wrote . . .

In these days the taking in of the Indian herb called "Tobacco" is greatly taken up in England. It is used against rheums and other diseases of the lungs with great effect.

But not everyone agreed. In 1614, Barnaby Rich was writing . . .

They say tobacco is good for a cold, rheums, for aches, for dropsies and for all manner of diseases. But I see the ones who smoke most are as affected by those diseases as much as the ones who don't. It is now sold in every tavern, inn and ale-house as much as beer.

Oddly enough, the man who hated tobacco-smoking the most was King James I. He wrote that smoking was . . .

A custom loathsome to the eye, hateful to the nose, harmful to the brain and dangerous to the lungs.

(If Raleigh really **did** smoke and James I was the first anti-smoking campaigner, then James was a great success. In 1618 he cured Raleigh's "loathsome" habit for good. James had Raleigh's head cut off for treason!)

What is it?
Drake found some new foods on his journey round the world. But what were they?

1 *We found a plant with a fruit as big as a man's head. Having taken off the back (which is full of string) you shall come to a hard shell which holds a pint of sweet liquid. Within that shell you will find a white, hard substance as sweet as almonds and half an inch thick.*

2 *We found a store of great fowl which could not fly, the bigness of geese, whereof we killed 3000 in less than one day.*

Terrible Tudor clothes

Did you know?

It was during the Tudor period that English clothes for the rich became exciting and different. Merchants were in touch with countries as far away as Russia and America. While the Tudor poor still wore rough woollen clothes, the Tudor rich were better dressed than ever before with velvets and satins from Italy, lace from France and starch from Holland. And starch meant they could make those stiff collars, "Ruffs", that were so popular in Elizabeth's time. But . . .

Ten things you probably didn't know . . .

1 Sometimes the stiff ruffs were so wide that ladies couldn't reach their mouths to eat! Silversmiths had to make extra-long spoons for them.

2 Ruffs were usually white but could be another colour. Yellow ruffs were popular for a while. Then a famous murderess, Mrs Turner, was hanged wearing one. They suddenly went out of fashion!

114

3 A puritan, Philip Stubbes, claimed . . .
The devil invented these great ruffs. But if it happen that a shower of rain catch them, then their great ruffs fall, as dishcloths fluttering in the wind.

4 Henry VIII looks very fat in his portraits. But as well as having an over-fed body, his clothes were thick with padding – at least it kept him warm in his draughty castles.

5 The Elizabethan ladies' fashion was for tiny waists. To help them squeeze into smart dresses, the ladies (and even the girls) wore iron corsets.

6 Girls showed that they were unmarried by wearing no hat in public.

7 Elizabethan men wore short trousers called "hose". They had to pad them so they wouldn't show any creases. They weren't too fussy what they padded them with – horsehair (itchy!), rags or even bran (horsefood)! If the "hose" split the bran would run out.

8 Poor country girls often wore shoes with iron rings under them. Sometimes they had thick wooden soles. This was to keep their skirts out of the deep mud and rubbish in the streets and market places.

  EARLY PLATFORMS

9 In 1571, Elizabeth's parliament made a law forcing all married women to wear white knitted caps, and all men (over the age of six) to wear woollen hats. The caps and hats had to be knitted in England using English wool. Elizabeth got a lot of taxes from the wool trade – English wool was in great demand from other countries, too.

10 Aprons were quite a new idea in Tudor times. You could often tell a man's occupation from the design of his apron . . .

millers and cooks   – white
barbers   – checked
builders and blacksmiths – leather

Terrible Tudor trousers

If you'd like to act like a Tudor, feel like a Tudor, or if you're off to a fancy dress party, you may like to try making these Tudor "hose".

1 Wear a pair of tights or tight trousers first.

2 Take a pair of old, baggy trousers. Cut them off at the knee. Slit them as shown.

3 Put the baggy trousers on over the tights. Tie them at the knee with ribbon or a scarf.

4 Stuff the baggy trousers with material of a different colour so it shows through the slits.

5 Wear a loose shirt and ruff and a belt with a sword or dagger – wooden, of course.

6 Go around saying, *To be or not to be*, or *Alas, poor Yorick*. (They're famous lines from William Shakespeare plays – adults and teachers will be totally impressed.)

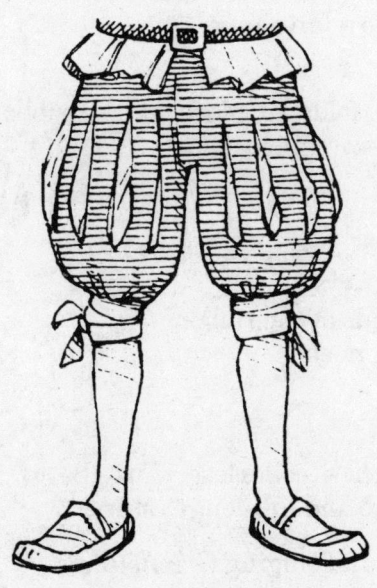

A ruff idea

1 Take seven 24 cm doilies (lacey paper table decorations, usually used at parties).

2 Cut them in half.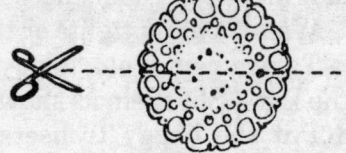

Use sticky tape to attach them to a 4 m strip of ribbon, allowing enough ribbon to tie at the back.

3 Make 2 cm folds in the doilies folding each one into a fan shape.

4 Keep the folds in place at the ribbon end with small stitches or sticky tape.

5 Tie the ends of the ribbon around your neck.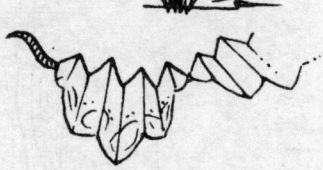

6 Wear with a collarless shirt (boys). Girls, wear with a blouse and full-length skirt.

7 Stroll around singing *Greensleeves*.

Terrible Tudor life for women

A woman's life is hard in ten terrible ways . . .

1 Girls could marry at 12 (boys at 14). This was usually arranged by their parents. They would still live with their parents at this age, though.

2 Many upper-class girls were married by 15. At the age of 16 they could live with their husbands.

3 It wasn't usually considered worth the money to send a girl to school. Her mother could teach her all the household crafts she would need to be a useful wife.

4 If a girl didn't marry there wasn't much she could do. The convents had been abolished by Henry VIII – so she couldn't become a nun. Very often, unmarried girls would have to stay at home with their parents and spin. That's why they became known as "spinsters" – a word we still use.

JUST BECAUSE I DIDN'T GET MARRIED WHEN I WAS STILL PLAYING WITH MY TEDDY MEANS I'VE GOT TO SIT AND SPIN FOR THE REST OF MY LIFE

5 One farmer described a good wife's behaviour. He said she should . . .

pray when first getting out of bed, then clean the house, lay the table, milk the cows, dress her children, cook meals for the household, brew and bake when needed, send corn to the mill, make butter and cheese, look after the swine and collect the eggs.

6 Anthony Fitzherbert added to that list and said she should . . .

shear corn and in time of need help her husband to fill the dung cart, drive the plough, load hay and go to market to sell butter, cheese, milk, eggs, chickens, pigs, geese and all manner of corn.

(What did he expect her to do in her spare time?!)

7 But English women were better off than those in other countries – at least, that's what the men said! Thomas Platter said that . . .

the womenfolk of England have more freedom than in any other land. The men must put up with such ways and may not punish them for it. Indeed, the good wives often beat the men.

8 Girls were expected to help in the house by collecting fine feathers (down) for mattresses, making candles, spinning, weaving and embroidering. Once every three months, the household tablecloths and bed-clothes were washed; the girls were expected to help with this.

9 Women could be punished for nagging or "scolding". A court record from 1592 says . . .

The wife of Walter Hycocks and the wife of Peter Phillips are common scolds. Therefore it is ordered that they shall be told in church to stop their scolding. But, if their neighbours complain a second time, they shall be punished by the ducking stool.

And "the ducking stool" meant being tied to a chair and lowered into a nearby river.

10 If the ducking stool didn't work then there was the "branks" – an iron mask that clamped onto the head with a metal bar going into the woman's mouth to hold her tongue down. Wearing the branks, a woman would be paraded round the town to show other women what might happen to them.

121

Miss World – Tudor style

The Elizabethans had a clear idea of what a beautiful woman should look like. Here's a shopping list . . .

1 extremely white skin
2 blue eyes
3 ruby-red lips
4 fair hair

You don't fit the description? Never mind, you can always change if you want.

Dark hair can be bleached with a mixture of sulphur and lead. This will, unfortunately, make it fall out in time. Never mind, as an Elizabethan said, Elizabethan girls are . . .

not simply content with their own hair, but buy other hair either of horse, mare or any other strange beast.

Skin too dark? A deadly mixture of lead and vinegar can be plastered on. (This has the same effect as making an Egyptian mummy.)

Lips too pale? Lipstick could be made from egg whites and cochineal – what is "cochineal"? It's a dye made from crushed cochineal beetles.

THREE SIMPLE STEPS TO A MORE BEAUTIFUL YOU!

Eyes don't sparkle enough? Drop in some belladonna (which means, "beautiful lady"!) to make them look larger. Keep it away from your lips, though. Belladonna is a poisonous drug made from deadly-nightshade.

If a mother wanted her daughter to grow up beautiful she was advised to bathe her in milk to give her a pale skin. Unwanted freckles? (Definitely out of fashion.) Treat with "brimstone" (sulphur).

Smelly? **Don't** have a bath! (Baths aren't considered "healthy"!) Just cover up the smell with perfume.

So . . .

Would you like to have been a Tudor woman or girl? In fact, would you have liked to live in the Terrible Tudor times at all? The "Golden Age" of Good Queen Bess and Jolly Old Henry VIII?

Every age has its problems. But, as a historian once said . . .

In reviewing the past I think that we of the present day have much to be thankful for.

You've reviewed some of the Tudor past in this book. So, are you "thankful" that you didn't live then? Or do you agree with the history book that said it was an *extremely exciting time to be alive*?

Epilogue

Old Elizabeth died and the last of the terrible Tudors was gone. Mary Queen of Scots was dead too . . . but her son, James VI of Scotland, was very much alive. The first of the sinister Stuarts.

The Stuart family in Scotland had a history every bit as bloody and violent as the Tudors in England.

● James I was murdered in a toilet in 1437 while he was trying to defend himself with a pair of fire tongs

● James II was killed by an exploding cannon in the seige of Roxburgh in 1460

● James III was murdered by his nobles in 1486

● James IV was killed at the Battle of Flodden in 1513

● James V died of despair shortly after his defeat at the battle of Solway Floss in 1542.

● Mary Queen of Scots, as we already know, murdered her husband then fled to England to avoid the chop. Elizabeth gave it to her instead

● James VI became the first James of England . . . and the first lucky Stuart to come from Scotland. He came south and added the English throne to his collection.

Of course, not everyone was happy with James. Not everyone wanted a king with such disgusting habits! For a start, he picked his nose!

TERRIBLE TUDORS

GRISLY QUIZ

Now find out if you're a terrible Tudor expert!

HORRIBLE HENRY

Henry VIII was one of Britain's cruellest monarchs ever. Here's a quick quiz to test your brains. Get one wrong and your head goes on the block. . .

THAT'S WHAT YOU GET WHEN YOU TAKE ON A TUDOR!

1. When wife no. 1, Catherine of Aragon, died Henry had a...?
a) ball
b) fight
c) cup of tea

2. Wife no. 2, Anne Boleyn, needed the toilet a lot during her coronation. Her ladies-in-waiting kept her potty handy...?
a) under the table
b) in a room close by
c) on the throne

3. When Anne gave birth to a daughter, Henry...?
a) sulked
b) cheered
c) fell out of his pram

4. While Anne was being beheaded, Henry was playing...?
a) tennis
b) music
c) the fool

5. Henry divorced wife no. 4, Anne of Cleves, because she was...?
a) ugly
b) stupid
c) vegetarian

6. Wife no. 5, Catherine Howard, was sentenced to death for

having lovers. She begged for mercy but Heartless Henry locked the door and left her...?
a) to wail
b) in jail
c) looking pale

7. Henry had his old friend Thomas More executed and his head stuck...?
a) over London Bridge
b) under London Bridge
c) in a fridge

8. Henry had Cardinal Fisher beheaded and showed disrespect by leaving the headless body...?
a) naked for a day
b) on the main highway
c) in a window display

INGENIOUS INSULTS

Can you match the words in these columns to come up with ten insults that Shakespeare put into his plays? WARNING: Do NOT call your teacher any of these names.

1.	taffeta	a)	lump
2.	scurvy	b)	ape
3.	red–tailed	c)	chuff
4.	threadbare	d)	bumble-bee
5.	mad–headed	e)	punk
6.	fat	f)	juggler
7.	false	g)	crookback
8.	bloodsucker of	h)	caterpillars
9.	scolding	i)	sleeping men
10.	deformed	j)	lord

QUICK QUESTIONS - MEAN QUEENS

1. Catholic Mary came to the throne in 1553, and the Protestants showed what they thought of her by leaving something on her bed. What? (Clue: hounding her out of the palace?)

2. Mary married Spanish Prince Philip in 1554. He hated something that came from her nose. What? (Clue: 'snot what you think)

3. Philip left Mary and went to fight in Europe. She tried to tempt him back with what? (Clue: the way to a man's heart is through his stomach, they say)

4. Mary had a lot of Protestant 'heretics' burned. Her chief helper was Reginald Pole who chose really odd 'heretics' to burn. What was odd about them? (Clue: they never felt a thing)

5. Mary sent Archbishop Cranmer to the stake in 1556. He had written an apology then changed his mind. When he saw the fire he did a strange thing. What? (Clue: he went to his death single-handed)

6. Mary died and the news was taken to half-sister Elizabeth, the new queen. They say Elizabeth was reading in the garden when the news came, but that's unlikely. Why? (Clue: remember, remember when Mary died)

7. Elizabeth had a new tax created which only men could pay. It was a tax on what? (Clue: it might grow on you)

8. Elizabeth I's godson, Sir John Harrington, disgraced himself by making rude remarks to her ladies-in-waiting. She banished

him. He went off and invented something that was so useful she forgave him. What? (Clue: flushed with success?)

9. In 1576 the explorer Martin Frobisher returned to England with a load of 'black earth'. What use did he think it would be? (Clue: he thinks the soil is rich)

10. Eloye Mestrell invented the first machine in England for making coins for the government. Yet in 1578 he was arrested and executed. What was his crime? (Clue: double your money)

11. Mary Queen of Scots had Sir John Huntly beheaded but then discovered he had to be tried properly and found guilty if she was to get his fortune. What did she do? (Clue: head on over to the courtroom)

12. Mary Queen of Scots became unpopular in Scotland, and fled to England to ask cousin Elizabeth I for protection. How did Liz protect Mary? (Clue: no one can get in to get her)

13. James Douglas of Scotland invented the 'Maiden' machine. In 1581 the Maiden killed him. What was it? (Clue: a chip off the old block)

14. Mary Queen of Scots had lots of troubles. She finally met a man and thanked him for, 'making an end to all my troubles'. What was this man's job? (Clue: not an agony aunt!)

15. When Mary Queen of Scots was beheaded in 1587 her head was supposed to have been lifted high in the air by the executioner to prove she was dead. But he dropped it. Why? (Clue: hair today, gone tomorrow)

Would you believe it?

Queen Elizabeth I ruled from 1558 to 1603. There are lots of stories about this famous queen, but which of these tall tales are true and which false…?

1. She threatened to pass a law banning her courtiers from wearing long cloaks.
2. She died because of a rotten tooth.
3. Elizabeth was overjoyed when her sister, Mary, died.
4. She liked to read her horoscope.
5. Elizabeth ate a chessboard.
6. She had regular baths.
7. Elizabeth never even considered getting married.
8. Elizabeth had beautiful red hair.
9. She was always true to her Protestant faith.
10. She punched and kicked her secretary.

Answers

Horrible Henry
1–8. All answers are (a). Anyone answering (c) should give up quizzes … now.

Ingenious insults
1.e) 2.j) 3.d) 4.f) 5.b) 6.c) 7.h) 8.i) 9.g) 10.a)

Quick Questions – Mean Queens
1. A dead dog. The head was shaved, the ears cropped and

a noose put around its neck. The message was clear: 'This is what we do to Catholics.'

2. Philip hated Mary's foul breath. It was an illness she had and not her fault. But it put him off, and he left her broken hearted.

3. His favourite meat pies. She had them sent across the English Channel to him. He ate all the pies but didn't go home for more.

4. They were dead. Reggie dug them up and burned them anyway. Funny feller.

5. He stuck his writing hand in the flames to punish it for writing the apology. (No jokes about second-hand shops, please.)

6. It was November. Not many people are daft enough to sit in the garden in an English winter.

7. Beards.

8. A flushing toilet. It took him six years to invent it but Liz loved his loo.

9. He believed it contained a fortune in gold. It didn't. He was just a clueless captain.

10. Eloye made a second, secret, machine and forged money for himself. Usually forgers had a hand chopped off but Eloye was hanged.

11. Huntly's head was sewn back on and his corpse was put on trial.

12. Elizabeth locked Mary in prison. She left her there for years before deciding to execute her.

13. The Maiden was a type of guillotine. He was executed on it.

14. He was her executioner. Actually he made a messy end to her troubles, taking three chops and a bit of sawing to get the head off.

15. Mary was wearing a wig. When he grabbed it, the head slipped out and bounced on to the floor.

Would you believe it?
1. True. She was terrified of being killed and wanted her courtiers' swords uncovered and ready.
2. False. Elizabeth is famous for having rotten teeth, but that didn't kill her. She caught a cold and never recovered.
3. True. She said, 'This is the Lord's doing and it is marvellous in our eyes.'
4. True. A mathematician (and magician!) called John Dee used to read Liz's horoscope and foretell the future for her.
5. True. Of course, it was made of marzipan.
6. True. Elizabeth did bathe regularly ... once every three months!
7. False. Liz had a few close calls when it came to marriage, including Lord Dudley and the French Duke of Anjou.
8. True and False. She did at first, but she ended up bald with a collection of 80 wigs!
9. False. While Catholic Mary Tudor was queen, Elizabeth said she was a Catholic too.
10. True. Secretary William Davison was just one of the unfortunate palace workers who suffered Liz's temper tantrums.

INTERESTING INDEX

Where will you find 'blood-sucking fleas', 'smelly breath', 'swearing' and 'sewers' in an index? In a Horrible Histories book, of course!

Terry Deary was born at a very early age, so long ago he can't remember. But his mother, who was there at the time, says he was born in Sunderland, north-east England, in 1946 – so it's not true that he writes all *Horrible Histories* from memory. At school he was a horrible child only interested in playing football and giving teachers a hard time. His history lessons were so boring and so badly taught, that he learned to loathe the subject. *Horrible Histories* is his revenge.

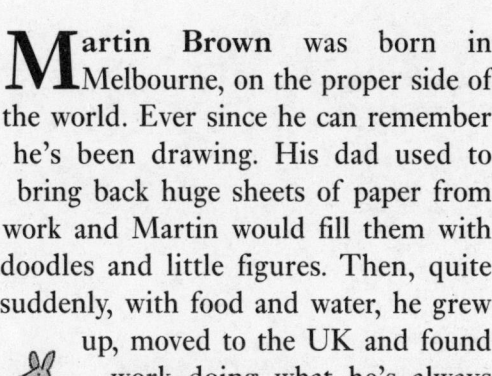

Martin Brown was born in Melbourne, on the proper side of the world. Ever since he can remember he's been drawing. His dad used to bring back huge sheets of paper from work and Martin would fill them with doodles and little figures. Then, quite suddenly, with food and water, he grew up, moved to the UK and found work doing what he's always wanted to do: drawing doodles and little figures.

HORRIBLE HISTORIES

ANGRY
AZTECS

Terry Deary Illustrated by **Martin Brown**

SCHOLASTIC

For Aidan Doyle.

Scholastic Children's Books,
Euston House, 24 Eversholt Street,
London NW1 1DB, UK

A division of Scholastic Ltd
London ~ New York ~ Toronto ~ Sydney ~ Auckland
Mexico City ~ New Delhi ~ Hong Kong

First published in the UK by Scholastic Ltd, 1997
This edition published 2016

Text © Terry Deary, 1997
Illustrations © Martin Brown, 1997
All rights reserved

ISBN 978 1407 16699 5

Printed and bound by CPI Group (UK) Ltd, Croydon, CR0 4YY

4 6 8 10 9 7 5 3

The right of Terry Deary and Martin Brown to be identified as the author and illustrator of this work has been asserted by them in accordance with the Copyright, Designs and Patents Act, 1988.

www.scholastic.co.uk

CONTENTS

Introduction

History can be horrible. Horribly foul facts and fouler figures, dusty dates and dustier dead people, lousy laws and lousier wars.

Now's the time for a revolution - not the French Revolution, the American Revolution, or even the rotten Russian Revolution but ... the Classroom Revolution!

Of course, a revolution needs weapons. So here is a classified secret. A secret so terrible that it is only whispered in staffrooms around the world. It is the answer to every pupil's question...

What is the weapon that every teacher fears more than anything in the world?

No! It's not the smell of Billy Brown's socks!

No! It's not the taste of school-dinner skunk-burgers!

No! It's not the head teacher finding the brandy in the book cupboard!

It is … a question!

It is … the question 'Why?'

Try it for yourself … but only use the 'Why Weapon' against a nasty teacher who deserves it. And keep on using it till they break down and admit they do not know the answer!

Here is an example…

See? Not only do you get revenge on your horrible history teacher … you also start to explore the really, really interesting thing about history. The question, 'Why did people behave the way they did?'

If you can answer that then you can begin to understand the question, 'Why do people behave the way they do now?' And, in the end you answer the only question that matters in life: 'Why do I behave the way I do?'

Hopefully this Horrible History book will help you to understand a little bit about history ... but an awful lot about PEOPLE!

Terrible timeline

The good news is that the world won't end tomorrow.

The bad news is that it is going to end on 22 December 2012. (So I hope you're a fast reader, otherwise you'll be seriously dead before you finish reading this book and you'll have wasted your money.)

In case you are interested in how you are going to die I can tell you that there will be disastrous earthquakes. If the cracks in the earth don't swallow you up then the terrible shaking that your brain cells get will give you a fatal headache. (It might be a good idea to stock up on aspirin now!)

How do we know this cheerful bit of information? Because an ancient people called the Maya worked it out. They could read the stars like you can read the Sun (newspaper that is). And the stars say that's when the world will end.

These Mayan people were just one bunch of some remarkable old South American nations who were a bit like hedgehogs on a motorway – they didn't have wheels (they never got around to it) and were flattened by people who did.

The other interesting Central American Indians are called Aztecs and they lived in an area we call Mexico today. They moved in as next-door neighbours to the Maya (in Yucatan) and naturally learned quite a lot from them.

The Aztecs were the neighbours from Hell. Within a few hundred years they had made themselves the top tribe in Mexico. Nobody argued with an Aztec. Arguing with Aztecs made them angry. And an angry Aztec was awful and far from 'armless. In fact you'd be the arm-less one as they bit into your biceps.

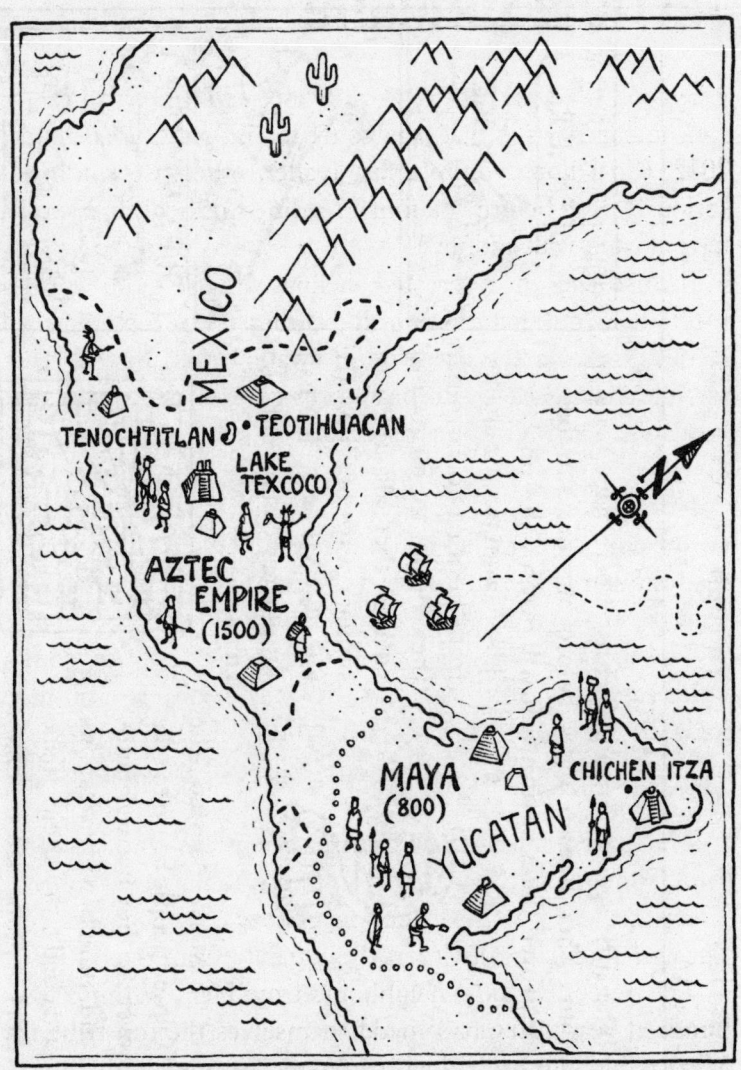

Time was very important to the Maya – their gods controlled time, which in turn controlled the lives of humans. Here's how time ran out for the Indian nations…

Date	Mexico	Yucaten
3114 BC	The fifth age of humans begins. There have been four other human races before but the sun has destroyed them in turn as it will destroy this one!	
1500 BC		The Mayan people change from hunting to farming; they begin to form into villages that all follow a similar way of life. (A bit like Millwall football supporters but not so vicious.)
1200 BC	In Eastern Mexico the Olmec people begin to take over ... they use war clubs and punch with weapons attached to their fists. Sort of stone-age knuckle-	

300 BC — dusters! They sacrifice humans by clubbing them on the head.
Olmecs disappear! They leave behind pyramids and stone carvings and the calendar.

200 BC — City of Teotihuacan is built in Mexico with pyramids and a main road known as the 'Avenue of the Dead'. It's at least two miles long. That's a lot of dead!

Mayan cities begin to grow with priests and kings having the power of life and death over the farming peasants.

AD 150 — Start of the great age for Mexico. In Teotihuacan they offer human hearts to the gods. In 1,000 years the Aztecs will copy this idea!

The Maya begin to build temples which will grow bigger and richer in time.

Date	Mexico	Yucaten
AD 300		Start of the great period of the Mayan people. Lots of great pyramid building and cruel ceremonies.
AD 600	Teotihuacan is destroyed. No one is sure why or who dunnit! Mexico filled with lots of tribes and cities.	
AD 850	Toltecs arrive in Mexico – great artists and builders. Pyramids as big as the ones in Egypt, and metal. End of Stone Age in Central America, but still they don't have the wheel!	The Mayan cities are abandoned. Why? Like the disappearance of dinosaurs, it's anybody's guess.

12

WHAT'S SO SIMPLE ABOUT FARMING?

SORRY WE'RE LATE

HOME SWAMP HOME

AD 1200	Now it's the turn of the Toltecs to be destroyed. They fall and their Tula City is ruined. Tribes from the north move into Mexico…	The Maya live on in small villages with a simple farming lifestyle.

AD 1300	One of the last tribes to arrive are the Aztecs. They are fine fighters. Aztecs work as slaves for the people of Colhuacan, but murder the princess (in the hope that she'll become a war goddess). They are driven out and squeezed on to an island in a swamp … but not for long.	

Date	Mexico	Yucaten
1345	The Aztecs build a new capital, Tenochtitlan (now Mexico City).	
1367	Aztecs fight for the Tepanec kingdom and go on to conquer the valley for them.	
1375	Aztecs decide it's time to elect a king to lead them.	
1427	Aztecs getting too powerful. Tepanec lords try to destroy them but the Aztecs fight back and become rulers of the valley.	
1492	Christopher Columbus lands in America. For Aztecs life will never be the same again. It will be worse.	

1519	Spanish conquistador Hernan Cortés lands in Mexico and Aztec King Motecuhzoma welcomes him as a god. But by ... Hernan Cortés has conquered the Aztecs. It takes him just 2 years.	First Spanish trips into Mayan lands looking for gold. They don't find it, and Mayan warriors kill Spanish leaders ... but they'll be back!
1521		
1542		Spanish conquer most of the Maya, but tribes in the jungle will give trouble for centuries.
1696		Some of last free Mayan tribes meet Christian missionaries ... and sacrifice them!
1901		Mexicans conquer the last free Mayan group. The Maya live on as peasants in the lands they used to rule.

15

The mysterious Maya

Nations come and nations go. They can be a bit like balloons … they get bigger and bigger and bigger until suddenly … pop! They disappear quite suddenly.

The first great group of people in Central America were probably the Olmecs[1] - they started a lot of the ideas that the copy-cat Maya and Aztecs would take up later … courts for the fast and furious 'ball game', statues of gods and kings, pyramid temples … oh, and the nasty little habit of killing and eating people. (Well, nobody's perfect.) Then the Olmecs disappeared. Pop! (It would be nice to think they ate each other all up … but they probably didn't.)

The Maya in Southern Mexico picked up where the Olmecs left off and built even bigger pyramids to sacrifice even more people. For over a thousand years they were the cleverest, most powerful people in the area. Then, in AD 900, their great cities with huge pyramids were abandoned. They were swallowed up for a hundred or more years by steamy jungle. Pop! At least, the cities went 'Pop!'. The Mayan people lived on as village farmers.

1. A few archaeologists are quite sure that the Maya came before the Olmecs. Some day they may prove it. But, even if the Maya did come first, it doesn't alter our story too much.

Further north in Mexico some of the strange Olmec and Mayan ways were being copied by the people of Teotihuacan (who went 'Pop!') then by the Toltecs (who went 'Pop!').

THERE GOES ANOTHER BUNCH OF MEXICANS

POP!!

At last the Aztecs moved into the area, picked up a lot of Toltec ideas and habits and formed the last great people of Ancient Mexico. So, you see, if you want to understand the Aztecs you need to know a little about the Maya.

(And, by the way, the Aztecs didn't go mysteriously 'Pop!'. They were 'discovered' by people from Europe who came along and conquered them. But more of that later...)

The mystery of the Maya -1

There are two mysteries. Where did the Maya come from? And where did the Maya go?

Where did they come from? They came from Asia, across to Alaska (when it was joined by a frozen sea) and down through what is now North America.[1]

Like their cave-cousins in Asia they made flint weapons and hunted animals. Then they began to settle down and grow food and build villages about 3,500 years ago.

They would pray to their gods that the rains would come and the crops would grow. After a few hundred years they

1. This happened 50,000 years ago or just 12,000 years ago depending on which archaeologists you believe! For you and me it doesn't matter.

found some people were better at praying than others. They made these people priests – which was nice for them because they didn't have to do all that hard work in the fields. While farmers farmed, the priests prayed and worked out a fantastic calendar so everyone would know when to sow their seeds and when to expect the rain.

This was a great success. If the rains came then the priests said, 'We told you we were good!' If the rains didn't come the priests said, 'You people must have been bad - the gods are annoyed - don't blame us!' Anyway the priests became very popular and the farmers would take time off to build the priests bigger and better temples. They decided they'd be nearer heaven if they built them on high platforms.

In time (around 1,700 years ago) these platform temples became huge pyramids – then they built new pyramids round the old pyramids till they were as close to heaven as a pigeon on a pogo stick. The pyramids are deserted now but they are still there if you want to go and see them, trample over them and vandalize them the way tourists have for the past hundred years.

Hunters to farmers to priests. Simple, yes?

No.

Because some clever people came along, looked at the pyramids, looked at the native farmers and said, 'These simple farmers could never have built those pyramids!'

'So who did?' they asked themselves. (Clever people spend a lot of time talking to themselves.)

'The Egyptians built pyramids!' they answered themselves. 'The Egyptians must have sailed across the Atlantic Ocean 2,000 years before Columbus and settled in Mexico!'

Sensible historians said, 'This is all nonsense. Forget it. The Egyptians did not cross to South America.'

But on 1 September 1996 a sensational story appeared in the newspapers...

were the PHAROHS DRUG PUSHERS?

Traces of cocaine and tobacco have been found in Egyptian mummies. The discovery is a mystery that is baffling scientists: how did the pharaohs know about the drugs 3,000 years before they were discovered in the Americas?

The experiments suggest that the Egyptians had trading links with America long before Columbus crossed the Atlantic. This is the first evidence that they

Smoked tobacco or chewed coca leaves – the source of cocaine.

German scientist Svelta Balabanova did not believe the results when she tested the mummies from British and German museums. 'The results were a shock. I was sure it was a mistake,' she said. But she was convinced after repeating the tests.

The Keeper of Egyptology at Manchester Museum said, 'we have always said there is no evidence of links between Egypt and the Americas – but there is never any evidence until it appears.'

The discovery of silk in the hair of 3000-year-old mummies supports the claim that the pharaohs had trade links around the world. Cocaine has only been found in the coca plant in South America.

So there you are! A real mystery. There is just a chance that the Maya were Egyptians after all!

But before you get too excited look at the differences:

• Egyptian pyramids are carefully engineered and built from solid stone so they cover a tomb inside. They were graves, and took an incredible amount of brain-power to build.

• Mayan pyramids are piles of sand and rubble, covered with a stone face and an altar on the top. They were temple-platforms, and you didn't need to be a genius to build them.

Other writers have said the Mayan people were . . .

• Irish – the Irish are famous for their love of potatoes which originally grew in South America! Maybe they were early potato hunters who found their beloved vegetables and stayed there?

• Vikings – who, most historians agree, probably sailed to the north of America long before Columbus.
• Survivors from Noah's Ark – because Noah's Ark was built in America, some people say.

Y'ALL GO CHECK ON THEM THAR VARMITS Y'HEAR

• Survivors from the Greek defeat of Troy – who floated over the Atlantic on the wooden horse, perhaps?

YOU CAN LEAD A HORSE TO WATER BUT YOU CANNOT MAKE IT SINK

• Alexander the Great's Greek sailors – who turned right at the Mediterranean instead of left and became a little lost?
• Chinese – who turned left at Japan instead of right and crossed the Pacific by mistake?

There is, of course, one other explanation you might like to consider. In the 1960s a Swiss writer came up with a new theory. The beings who planned the Mayan pyramids weren't human. They were aliens from outer space! The pyramid platforms would make landing pads for their flying saucers! This may sound wacky and fantastic to you. But remember … he sold an awful lot of books!

Horrible habits

Whether the Maya came from the Mediterranean or Mars, the important question is, 'Would they be the sort of people you'd take home to meet your mum for tea?'

Here are some of their curious little habits…

Miserable Mayan children

Children in Mayan cities had a hard time. Maybe you'd prefer to be a Mayan rather than a modern?

1 In a Mayan city there were two wells. (Well, well!) One was for drinking and the other was for speaking to the gods. At dawn a girl would be thrown into the water almost 20 metres below. At noon she was brought out and asked, 'What did the gods say to you?' Whatever she replied the Maya would believe. (Of course there was a good chance that she'd have drowned. In that case she would not be saying very much. Oh, well.)

2 When a Mayan baby was born the child and its mother had to be ignored for three days. This was so evil spirits didn't notice there was a new body around to attack. The mother would tie cords around the baby's wrists and ankles to stop its soul escaping. Tied up and ignored – even a teacher shouldn't be treated like that …well, not tied up, anyway.

3 The Maya had broad heads. Broad heads were common

and the Mayan lords didn't want their children to look common. They wanted to give their children narrow heads. How do you narrow a child's head? Strap boards to either side as soon as the baby is born and keep them bound like that for at least two days. The poor babies would have to lie strapped in their cradles – board out of their minds.

4 Other heads were bound so that they were egg-shaped with the point at the back. Archaeologists have found these strange skulls and wonder how the owners could think straight. But they seemed to manage and the priests were clearly very clever people – real egg-heads in fact.

5 Cross-eyed kids are cute. Who says? The Maya. How do you make someone cross-eyed? Fasten a ball of wax to one of their head-boards (or to the hair on their forehead) and let it dangle in front of their noses. (If my parents did that to me then I'd be cross-eyed and how cross I'd be.)

6 The children were sent out to collect the nests of mud wasps. The nests were full of the maggots that would grow to become wasps. The mud nests were heated up until the sweating maggots wriggled out. As soon as they did, the Maya would pop them into their mouths as a nice warm snack. (Try it some time. They'll give you more of a buzz than a packet of crisps.)

7 Boys would be taught to fish as soon as they were old enough. But the Maya cheated. They blocked off a stream with a dam then threw drugs into the water to knock out the fish. When the doped fish floated to the surface the Maya picked them out.

8 If a Mayan child died then its mother would cut the end off one of her own fingers and have it buried with the child! Pity the poor woman who lost ten children – still, she'd save on nail files.

9 Children were taught the importance of giving blood to the gods. If they couldn't sacrifice an enemy warrior then they could at least give some of their own blood. Blood was let out with the spines from a stingray's tail. In an important festival a Maya would give blood from the ears, the elbows and (if you were a boy) from your naughty bits! Oooof! Girls could instead pull a rope of thorns through a hole in their tongues. Owwww!

10 When a child was still very young it had its ears, its nose and its lips pierced so ornaments could be hung from them when it grew older. The wind must have whistled through all those holes like a bagpipe!

THAT SOUNDS LIKE SOMEONE'S TRYING TO PIERCE THE EARS OF A MAYAN *CAT!*

THANKYOU

It was a terrible crime for a Mayan man to run off with someone else's wife. If he was caught then the angry husband was allowed to kill the wife-stealer. He had to do this by dropping a rock on the victim's head!

Mayan lyin'

In the Ancient Mayan city of Chichen Itza there is a stone track over half a mile long. The track ends in a huge pit, 20 metres deep and filled with water.

A temple stands on the edge of the pit and owls are carved on the side of the temple. It is known as the Temple of the Owls (even your teacher could guess why).

There was an ancient story that said young girls were thrown to their deaths in the underground lake as sacrifices to the planet Venus. Nasty!

But when scientists dragged up dozens of human skeletons and examined them they found more than half were the bones of old people. (But don't get any ideas about throwing granny in the local swimming pool.)

So the story of sacrificing young girls was exaggerated. You can't believe everything you read … unless you read it in a Horrible Histories book, of course.

Did you know…?
The story of the sacrifices at the Temple of the Owls was told on a wall painting at the temple. But tourists had a

stupid sport of throwing bottles at the ancient painting. It is practically destroyed now. It's just a shame no one thought of throwing the tourists into the pit before they ruined the priceless painting for the rest of us!

April, Maya, June

The Maya created an incredible calendar that most of the nations of Central America copied for over a thousand years. They also had a form of picture writing (which other nations seemed to forget) and a system of numbers:

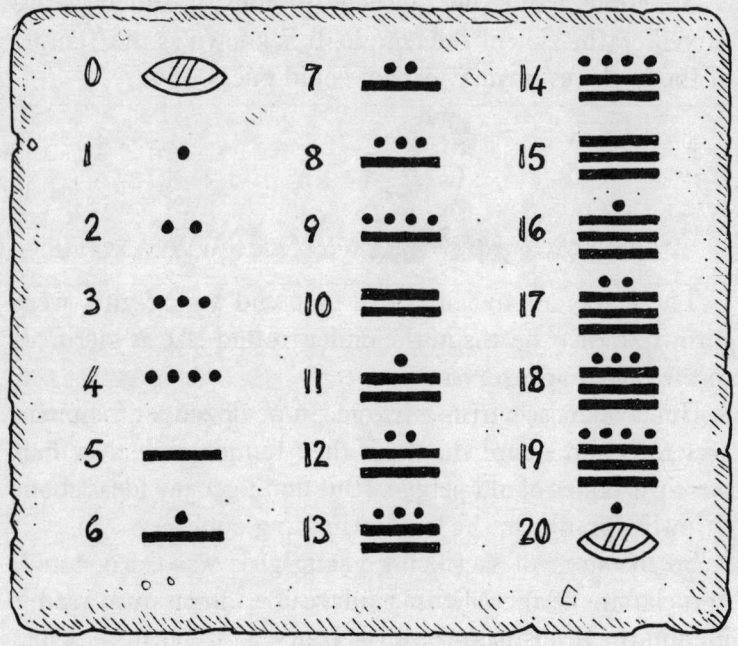

Amaze your friends by learning this system. It's easy really. The dot is one and the dash is five. So four dots is four, three dashes are fifteen. A dot and two dashes is eleven and so on. The sign for '0' is a shell.

Now you are a Mayan mathematician, can you spot which of the following sums is wrong?

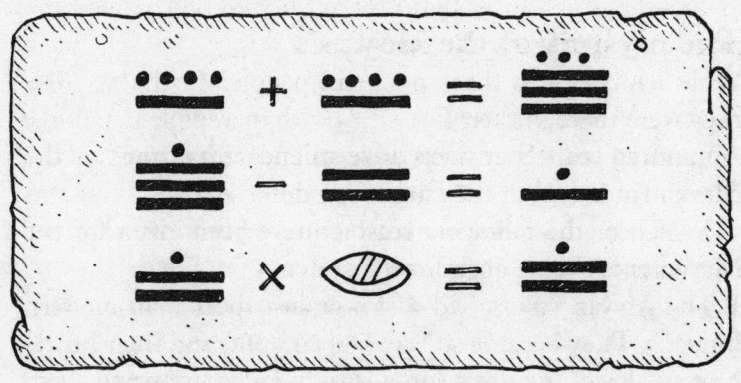

Answer: Did you spot the wrong answer? The third sum is wrong, so if you worked that out then you are right. $9 + 9 = 18$; $16 - 10 = 6$; $11 \times 0 = 11$ ... which is wrong, of course, because $11 \times 0 = 0$.

Years later the Aztecs were still using the bars and dot numbers to count how much people owed them! Why not use the system to claim a rise in pocket money? After all, it usually worked for the Aztecs (with a little help from a sacrificial altar, of course!).

Did you know...?
The climate of the Mayan land is very damp and warm. Even in the dry season the air is heavy with moisture. This can be wonderful for plants to grow in but very tiring for visitors from Europe. And it can also cause other problems. An archaeologist working on a Mayan city site had continual problems with his ear. At last he reached a doctor

...and the doctor pulled out several tiny mushrooms that had taken root deep inside his ear!

The mystery of the Maya - 2

What happened to these powerful people? In the AD 900s they were there in their fine cities with incredible pyramids. A hundred years later there were still peasant farmers in the Mayan lands ... but the cities were deserted.

Which of the following reasons have been given for the Mayan cities being abandoned?

1 The Mayan rulers had a slower heartbeat than modern humans. They became so lazy and content, and their hearts beat so slowly the great lords simply faded away and died. With no leaders the people of the cities couldn't work together. The working farmers always worked harder and were fitter, so the peasants kept going.

2 The Maya didn't know about fertilizer. Their fields became too poor to grow the food the cities needed. The lack of food caused the city people to move away and find new land to farm.

3 There was a terrible earthquake. The people thought this was a punishment from the gods and fled from the danger of falling buildings. They never returned.

4 There was an invasion from northern Mexican tribes. The invaders robbed the rich and executed them or turned them into slaves.

5 The peasant farmers became fed up with the priests. The priests did no work but took large amounts of food as taxes. The farmers attacked the cities, wiped out the ruling classes and then returned to their fields.

6 There was a terrible plague. In Europe the Black Death left cities empty as people fled to find safety in the cleaner air of the countryside. Perhaps the Maya did the same but never returned.

Answer: All of these ideas have been put forward. But they all could be wrong.
Perhaps the rulers really were aliens who one day got homesick and flew back to Alpha Centuri. The simple natives couldn't run the cities without their alien lords! The truth is, no one really knows the answer. It's yet another mystery.

The Mayan gift

Whatever happened to the Ancient Maya it was probably what they deserved. Because they brought to Central America the horrible historical practice of human sacrifice. In order to keep the gods happy they would kill their prisoners of war. The peasant prisoners would be turned into slaves, but the lives of enemy leaders would make wonderful prezzies to the gods. (Imagine our dear Royal Family being the victims of an enemy sacrifice! You would miss them … wouldn't you?)

The sacrifice could be made anywhere but usually at a

temple pyramid and usually at a platform on the top of the pyramid.

The victims would be kept in cages while they waited to be sacrificed – some wall paintings in Mayan cities show these prisoners being tortured by having their fingernails torn out!

After ripping open the victim's chest and tearing the heart out, the victim was thrown down the side of the pyramid where priests were waiting to take the skin off and wear it to dance in.

Then bits of the victim were eaten. This was so that some of the spirit of the dead person could enter into the killers.

Imagine if this is true! Next time you eat a beefburger you could well become a real bull-y! If your mother feeds you pork chops then she can't complain if your room is like a pigsty. Chicken nuggets will turn you into a real bird brain, while fish and chips could help you win the next school swimming gala! Of course it sounds nonsense – 'Baa! Humbug!' as Mr Scrooge said when he finished his roast lamb with mint.

So, you see, the braver and more noble the victim, the braver and more noble the sacrificers became!

This Mayan religion was copied throughout Mexico and hundreds of thousands of people died. As late as 1696 the last free Mayan tribe disposed of some visiting missionaries by making them a ritual sacrifice.

Sort of, friar today, fried tomorrow.

Suffering slaves
Of course being a peasant prisoner wasn't much fun either. If you worked for an important person then there was a chance you'd be killed and buried so you could still serve

your lord in the afterlife.

Long after the Mayan cities were abandoned, the idea of sending servants to the afterlife was still being copied.

Take the terrible Tarascans, for example. The Aztecs didn't conquer everyone in Central America. They didn't beat the tough Tarascan people for a start. The Tarascans were well organized and built strong fortresses that kept out the Aztec attackers.

They were also just as ruthless as the Aztecs. When their king died he was sent to the next life with all the people he'd need to run his palace there. The Tarascans executed and buried the following servants with the king…

BLEED

ARE SURE YOU'VE GOT THE RIGHT JUG?

• the palace cook – she got the chop
• the king's wine bearer – she needed bottle for that job
• the keeper of the king's urinal who must have wet herself when the king died
• the keeper of the king's gold-and-turquoise lip-ornaments – who had a gilt complex
• 40 men-servants … including the doctor who failed to cure the king's last illness (the other 39 probably thought murdering the doctor was fair enough).

Dreadful dentists

Next time you have to go to the dentist you should be happy. It could be worse. You could have had a Mayan toothache. If you did then here's the cure...

For a Broken Tooth

Crumble the soot that clings to cooking stones and wrap it in cotton wool. Place it on the tooth and the pain will stop. Or take the tooth of a crocodile and use it to grate the skin of a fish. Wrap the grated fish skin in cotton wool and place on the tooth. The pain will stop.

To Remove a Tooth

There is an iguana lizard that is yellow beneath the throat. Tie it up and burn it on a flat plate till it is reduced to ashes. Rub the ashes on the tooth, take your pincers and you can pull out your tooth without pain. Try this first on a dog's tooth before you pull your own tooth

The superstitious Maya believed that even dreaming about a broken tooth was a terrible curse – someone in the family would be sure to die.

They also believed that starting any job on a Tuesday or a Friday was unlucky ... but the best time to plant seeds, get married or gamble was a Monday or a Saturday.

And the doctors weren't much better. They said that anyone who sneezes till their joints hurt will die within a day ... unless you take a handful of orange leaves, boil them, rub the liquid into the feet and then all over the body! (Next time you sneeze you could try soaking your feet in orange squash. But don't pour it away and waste it. Take it to school the next day and give it to your worst enemy!)

Mayan medicine
Would you like to try any of the following tasty treats ... even If you were dying?

1. EATING BIRD FAT

2. SMOKING TOBACCO (TO CURE SNAKE BITE!)

3. SWALLOWING RED WORMS

4. EATING BAT'S WINGS

5. DRINKING A WHOLE BAT DISSOLVED IN HONEY WINE

6. DRINKING A LIVE TOAD DISSOLVED IN WINE

7. SWALLOWING A WOODPECKER'S BEAK

8. EATING DRIED TAPIR DROPPINGS

9. EATING SHREDDED COCKEREL FEATHERS

'If all else fails,' one Mayan medical book says, 'have the sick person remove one sandal, unnate in it and drink it.'

The Maya did all of these things. So swallow your cod liver oil and stop complaining

Did you know…?
The Maya lived in an area to the south east of Mexico that we call Yucatan.

But how did the place get its name? This is the true story!

The modern Maya

Since the destruction of the Mayan cities around AD 900, the Mayan people have survived in the south-east of Mexico. And they have had to survive some terrible tragedies in a horrible history.

When terrorists moved in to Mayan villages in the 1970s the poor villagers had to give them food and shelter. When the government fought back it was the Maya who received the worst of the punishments. Almost 200,000 were killed or 'disappeared'. Others fled and were forced to live in refugee camps in Mexico.

Mayan groups who stayed have seen their peasant farms destroyed and converted to huge cattle ranches to supply the Americans with beef for their hamburgers.

Maya who wanted to follow the old religions have been converted to Christianity … and, anyway, they can't go back to worship their old temples because they are swamped with tourists!

Still, the Maya are increasing in numbers and are hopeful. A new king will awaken in the ancient city of Chichen Itza, they say. He will rise along with thousands of warriors who have been frozen in time. A stone serpent with feathers will come to life and lead them all in a great war.

Perhaps those tourists had better take their cameras and run!

The awful Aztecs

The Aztecs (who called themselves the Mexica at first) probably lived in the north of Mexico until they decided to move south some time in the AD 1200s.

They said that they ate some fruit from the tree of a god. The god was so angry that he made the Aztecs wander through Central America. They must have arrived in the rich valley of Mexico in the early 1300s where the people living there called them 'the people whose face nobody knows'.

The wandering, homeless Aztecs were defeated and almost exterminated by the Lord of Culhuacan city. The surviving Aztecs became slaves. But even as slaves those Aztecs were a nuisance, so the Lord of Culhuacan sent them off to fight a powerful enemy who would finish them off … at least that's what he thought.

The Aztecs actually returned. The surprised Lord of Culhuacan said, 'You must have run away, you cowards!'

But the Aztec warriors opened sacks and poured out mountains of human ears over the lord's feet! 'These are from the enemy you sent us out to fight. We beat them!'

The story of the wandering is probably true – but what happened in the wanderings is most likely just Aztec legend. But there is something awfully, terribly possibly about the legend of the Princess of Culhuacan…

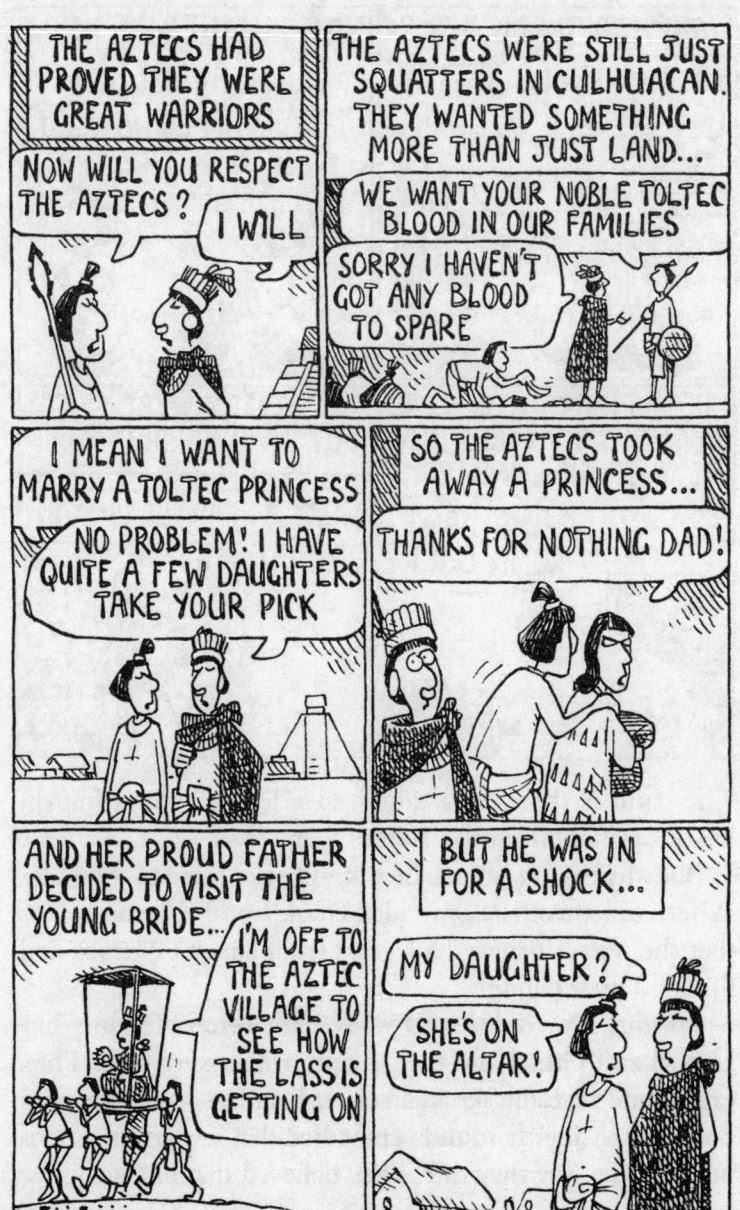

The truth is the Aztecs would have learned about human heart sacrifices from the Toltecs themselves.

But why cut out human hearts and offer them to the gods? Where did this gruesome idea come from? The answer is that the Aztecs believed a legend from ancient Mexico and followed its teaching.

Imagine if we did that! If we actually believed a story like Hansel and Gretel and then acted as if it were true. Then every time we came across an old lady at her oven door we'd push her inside! It sounds crazy but that's why the Aztecs behaved the way they did. They believed that old story.

What was the story? Well, I'll tell you if you promise not to believe it and follow its lesson. Are you sitting comfortably? Then here it is…

The truly terrible tale

Once upon a time there were humans on the earth. And the humans ate maize and they grew into giants. (Now, cornflakes are made from maize. So, when your mother says, 'Eat up your cornflakes and you'll grow into a big strong person,' then you know she is telling the truth.)

But even these giants weren't tall enough to keep their heads above water when a great flood came. It swallowed the sun and ended the first age of the earth after 4,008 years. Almost every giant on earth was drowned and turned into a fish. That's where fish come from. (Remember that when you next eat fish fingers. You are really eating dead giants' fingers.)

Still, two humans survived by climbing into a tree. They were called Nene and Tata and they started the human race off all over again in the second age. But, after 4,010 years, what do you think happened? No, it wasn't another flood. This time there was a great wind that came along and blew out the sun.

The wind blew so hard that humans had to cling to the trees with their hands and feet and even grew tails. They all turned into monkeys. That explains why the chimp in the local zoo looks so much like your Uncle Dave – they were both humans at one time … at least the chimp was.

Again, two humans survived by standing on a rock. They started the human race off all over again in the third age. But, after 4,081 years, what do you think happened? No it wasn't a flood and it wasn't a wind, it was a great fire that carne along and destroyed the earth.

Of course, someone survived and started the fourth age and, of course, the humans of the fourth age were wiped out by rain of blood and fire. Nothing could grow and humans starved.

And that brings us to the fifth age – the one we're in now and the one that will end with earthquakes on 22 December 2012. (The Aztecs didn't have Christmas so they didn't realize how this will ruin everyone's Christmas in AD 2012. On the other hand you will be able to save money because there's no point in buying presents that will never get opened.)

At the start of the fifth age the gods met in Teotihuacan. That's a Mexican name that means 'The place where the gods are born'.

And it was dark. (Well, it would be, since the sun of the fourth age had been destroyed by the rain of blood and fire.) As you may know, there is only one way to make a sun, and that is for a god to set fire to himself.

Nobody wanted the job. Would you?

At last the boastful Tecuciztecatl said he was the greatest god and he really should be the new sun. No one agreed because no one really liked him. Still they built a huge bonfire and invited Tecuciztecatl to jump in.

The god looked at the fire and suddenly remembered he

was far too busy to become the sun today. Tecuciztecatl was Tecucizte-totally-chicken. That's when the wise and popular Nanahuatzin took a long run, a hop, a step and a jump and landed in the fire. Pow! The earth had a sun.

Tecuciztecatl was so ashamed of himself he too took a long run, a jump, a step and a hop and followed Nanahuatzin. Pow! The earth had another great ball of light in the sky - Tecuciztecatl had become the moon.

The gods were feeling pretty pleased with themselves when one of them pointed to the sun in the sky and said, 'It isn't moving!'

And it was true. Nanahuatzin had given his life to make the sun, now he wanted the other gods to give their lives before he would set off across the sky.

Of course they grumbled a bit at first. 'I wish he'd said that before he jumped in the fire,' one of them muttered.

'Well, it's done now,' another one said reasonably. 'I'll give my heart if you'll give yours!'

So, one by one, the gods came to the feathered snake god, Quetzalcoatl, and had their living hearts torn out of their bodies. When the sacrifices had been made the sun began to move across the sky as it has done ever since.

It was said giants built the pyramids of the sun and of the moon in Teotihuacan and the first leaders were buried inside them. The ruins of the pyramids still stood in Teotihuacan when the first Aztecs arrived in Mexico. The simple Aztecs looked at the pyramids, were sure they could only have been built by giants and they really believed the tale of the gods.

BUT … the Aztecs said, 'If the gods had to give their hearts to keep the sun moving in the sky then we humans should do the same. We must make sure the sun is properly fed with regular supplies of heart.'

And that's why the Aztecs began sacrificing humans to the gods.

It's silly and it's savage and thousands of people died horrible deaths, all because of a story.

Did you know…?
A Spanish priest called Siguenza came to Mexico in the 1500s. He didn't believe the story about the gods of Teotihuacan. But he didn't believe that normal humans had built those great pyramids in the deserted city either. He had a different theory about the people who built the pyramids. He said some incredible people had arrived in Mexico from a huge island called Atlantis before it sank into the sea. And even to this day some people believe that's where the ancient Mexican rulers came from.

Swamp serpent soup

The greatest Aztec legend says they were led to their new land by a prophet called Tenoch. If the first settlers had written letters back to their old homeland then they may have looked something like this…

Dear Mum

Here we are in our new home and it's really smashing. Lots to eat. As you know, Tenoch the prophet led us down here from Aztlan and kept going on about a snake and an eagle and a cactus. He'd had a dream. Well, we all have dreams but we don't go rushing off with half the tribe to make the dreams come true, do we? Personally, Mum, I thought he was potty. But we pushed on until we reached this swampy lake. A horrible place, but the land around the lake was fine.

Of course the trouble was - you've guessed it - some other tribes already live on this land. Now I'm a warrior, as you know, Mum, but their warriors were bigger than me and there were more of them. "What do we do, Tenoch?" we asked.

"We talk," he said. "We ask them to give us some land."

If I thought Tenoch was a nutter <u>before</u> then I was <u>sure</u> he was a few bricks short of an adobe then! Ask! For land!

Anyway, we asked. The five tribes were ready with an answer. They had smug little grins on

43

their ugly little faces as they pointed at the lake. Because there, in the middle of the lake, was an island. They even offered Tenoch a boat to go and have a look at it. So off he paddled and came back a while later. "The snake, the eagle and the cactus!" he cried. "It is my dream! I saw an eagle, perched on a cactus tearing at a snake it had caught!"

"Oh, yes, didn't we tell you?" the enemy chief said. "The island is full of snakes! Poisonous snakes!" he chuckled. That's when I saw their sneaky little plan! They wanted rid of us so they sent us across to a snake-infested island so the serpents could kill us off.

They don't know the Aztecs! We jumped into the boats and paddled there as fast as the weeds would let us!

We jumped ashore and were met by the snakes. Lovely, long fat things. And they'd never seen many humans before. They just looked at us with their cute little faces and licked their poisonous fangs with their pretty purple tongues. There was a funny sort of surprised expression on their faces as their heads hit the ground.

The snakes were as simple as the tribes-folk. They didn't know that a favourite Aztec meal is snake meat!

'**S**o I can't wait for you to come and join us, Mum. Snake soup, snake stew, roast snake steak, minced snake burgers and spicy snake fry. I'm working on a new recipe myself. I call it snake and kidney pie.

So we've named our new home Tenochtitlan, after the prophet. Still, I have a feeling we won't be staying here for long. Those smug little tribes had better watch out. We weren't killed off by the snakes. We are warriors and we'll be looking for someone to war against very soon.

Your loving son,

Mex

The Aztecs soon turned the shallow lake into *chinampas* gardens made by piling up mud from the bottom of the lake. They built bridges and canals for transport and soon became a great trading centre. They also set about seizing power from the surrounding tribes.

The Aztecs proved to be fierce and fearless fighters.

By 1520 the Aztec emperor Motecuhzoma II ruled over a great empire in Central America. Little did he know that the Spanish were coming and the mighty Aztecs were going to fall a lot quicker than they had risen.

It's easy to think the Aztecs arrived with their special way of life and they forced the rest of Mexico to follow them. But things don't work like that. The Aztecs took control of the Toltec lands – but the Toltec religion took control of the Aztec minds!

And the Toltecs had been very bloodthirsty people. Very, very. In fact you could say very very, VERY!

The good gore guide

You know that the sun is a star ... a large celestial body composed of gravitationally contained hot gases emitting electromagnetic radiation, especially light, as a result of nuclear reactions inside the star. (No, I don't understand what it means either but it sounds good if you say it quickly.)

Anyway the Toltecs believed it was actually a god. A superhuman being who has power over human life.

Now these god people can be very tricky. If you upset them then they'll make you suffer – shine too hot on your crops, shrivel them up and starve you, or send a plague of locusts to eat all your food. The thing to do is keep your god (or gods) happy.

Some people think their god will be happy with a bit of praise and a few hymns and prayers. Other people believe they have to give prezzies to their god.

The terrible Toltecs believed you had to give a life to their god – a sacrifice.

But the awful aztecs took it to extremes. They believed they had to give their sun god human lives – thousands of them. And, not only that, they had to be sacrificed in a gruesomely gory way.

HEALTH WARNING: Readers who are sickened at the sight of a squashed rabbit on the road should NOT read this section.

The Aztecs didn't sacrifice the odd human on special occasions like the king's birthday or Bank Holiday Mondays. They did it all the time. They...
• sacrificed 50,000 a year (that's a thousand a week, six an hour or one every ten minutes!)
• sacrificed 20,000 in a single party when they opened the temple at Tenochtitlan
• had an army specially organized to keep the priests supplied with victims
• stirred up trouble among the conquered tribes so they had an excuse to go in and take prisoners who became sacrifice victims.

A Spanish history book said that when the Great Temple was opened in 1487 there were 80,000 victims sacrificed in one ceremony. But don't believe everything you read in history books! Because sacrificing 80,000 would have been just about impossible! The Aztecs would have needed machine guns and bombs to massacre that many. (In fact it's only in the past hundred years that humans have learned to kill each other at that rate – but modern people call it war and that makes it all right.)

What a way to go…

The Aztecs preferred sacrificing enemy warriors. The braver the enemy then the better the sacrifice. If an Aztec captured an enemy he would say, 'Here is my well-beloved son.' The victim would reply, 'Here is my dearest father.' You might say this sort of thing when you're asking for more pocket money! You'd better hope 'dearest' father doesn't then go on to sacrifice you.

The Aztecs had five main ways of sacrificing their victims – some more cruel than others. Which would you choose? Here's a rough guide. How would you score the methods?

1 Lie the victim on their back over the sacrificial stone, open the chest with a knife, pull out the heart and offer it to the gods in a carved stone vessel.

Score: ☆ ☆ ☆ ☆ ☆
Not bad so long as the stone isn't too cold!

- -

2 Cut off the head. This was usually the fate of female victims who'd spent some time acting the role of a goddess.

Score: ☆ ☆ ☆ ☆
A quick way to go and you'd have had a lot of fun: being treated as a goddess.

3 Tie the victim to a large rock and give him a sword club to defend himself He then fights against an Aztec warrior whose sword club has a knife edge.

Score: ☆ ☆ ☆

You'd go down fighting but you wouldn't last long!

- -

4 Tie the victim to poles and fill him full of darts or arrows. Mark his heart with a white spot, but don't aim at that spot with the first few dozen arrows. The blood from the wounds makes the earth richer for growing crops ... or so the Aztecs believed.

Score: ☆ ☆

You wouldn't enjoy being a human pin-cushion.

- -

5 Throw the victim into a fire then pull him out, repeat a few times. When he's lightly baked, do the heart sacrifice.

Score: ☆

Nasty!

Monster mother

In 1803 Baron Friedrich Heinrich Alexander von Humboldt visited Mexico to study Aztec history. He uncovered a 3-metre high statue that weighed 12 tons. It had been carved out of a single block of volcanic stone and It was horrible. In fact it was so shocking that he buried it again!

It was a statue of the goddess Coatlicue. Victims were sacrificed in front of Coatlicue ... and after seeing her ugliness they might have died of the shock before the priests got them!

Cuddly Coatlicue was roughly human in shape but had...
• a double head of two snakes facing one another
• snakes for arms
• a cloak of snakes twisted in the wings of a vulture
• feet of a jaguar (the big cat, not the car, stupid)
• a necklace of hearts, skulls and severed hands strung together with guts.

Do you ever get bored in your school art lessons? Why not ask teacher if you can make a model of Coatlicue from modelling clay? (You don't get ideas like this on *Blue Peter*.)

When it's finished you can rip out the living heart of a jelly baby as a sacrifice. (Use a spoon for this because we wouldn't want you to cut yourself, would we?)

There is every chance that if you follow these instructions you will be expelled from your school, for being sick and disgusting. So that's another reason for doing it!

Here is cool, cute and blood-curdling Coatlicue.

SSSSSS

Remind you of anyone?

Coatlicue's story is as gruesome as her statue. Coatlicue was a goddess and was expecting the baby who would grow up to be the sun. But before the baby was born Coatlicue was murdered by her daughter, the goddess of the moon, and her 400 sons who were the stars. They cut off Coatlicue's head – and the snakes from the neck are an image of the blood gushing out.

But the baby was born anyway and he avenged his mother's death by throwing the moon goddess off a mountain and defeating his 400 brothers. (What a baby!)

Every dawn the sun drives the moon and stars from the sky – provided he gets his regular supply of sacrifice blood, of course.

It's certain that some sacrifices ended with some bits of some victims being cooked and eaten. (The arms and the thighs were the only bits the priests allowed people to eat.) In the 1980s clever professors reckoned that the Aztecs had huge cannibal feasts – all that meat gave them the strength to fight and capture even more victims.

In the 1990s even cleverer professors say this idea is potty.

In fact the Aztecs had plenty to eat without picnicking on people ...

Eat like an Aztec

Funny food

It's hard to imagine modern food without the plants discovered in Mexico 500 years ago. For example, the Maya gave us chicle – for chewing gum. And the Aztecs had other treats. What would your life be like without…

• spices … like chilli pepper for curry
• corn … to make your cornflakes
• pumpkin … so Cinderella could get to the ball and you can have a hallowe'en lantern
• tomatoes … for the sauce in your baked beans
• turkeys … for your Christmas dinner.

The Aztecs had chocolate beans but they were so precious they were used as money. They grew peanuts that traders brought from South America. Imagine the cinema without the Aztecs – no popcorn or peanuts or chocolates.

Of course, the Mexicans didn't have cooking fat before the Spanish arrived with pigs from Europe. The Aztecs had never tasted fried food. So a great invention like chips needed potatoes (which originally came from South America) to get together with European frying before it could be enjoyed.

Ten tasty treats you wouldn't want to eat…

The people of Mexico have always had interesting food. 10,000 years ago they were driving mammoths into swamps and killing them with stone knives and spears. They would make real jumbo meals.

We can enjoy a lot of pleasant food thanks to the people of Mexico. But there are some things they used to eat that you may not be so keen to taste. Things like…

1 Monkeys – the spider monkey and the howler monkey were enjoyed by the Aztecs and are still eaten by the native inhabitants today! The howler monkey gets its name from its roar that can be heard at least 3 km (2 miles) away. If we could understand them they'd probably be howling, 'Look out! The Aztecs are coming to eat you!'

2 Toads – archaeologists found bones from marine toads in many early Mexican villages. Since the skins of these toads are poisonous they guess that they were used as a sort of drug, but too much could kill you. Wart a way to go!

3 Frogs – are safer than toads and very tasty – ask any French chef. And the Aztecs could crack awful jokes like:

4 Cactus – the maguey cactus was amazingly useful. The Aztecs used it to make needles (and the spikes) and thread, and as fuel, from paper, rope, cloth, mats and as thatching for their house roofs. The plant was boiled to give a sweet syrup and the syrup could be used to make a sort of cactus wine. The trouble was there was an Aztec law against getting drunk and the punishment was death.

5 Dogs – that's right. You wouldn't want pet pie, baked beagles on toast, Yorkshire terrier pudding or a boxer chocolate would you? Would you wolf hound after you whippet out of the oven? Surely not. The Aztecs would.

6 Lake scum – yes, the green stuff you see floating on top of the park pond. The Aztecs in Teotihuacan would collect it from the edge of the lake, press it into cakes and eat it. The trouble was the lake became polluted with chemicals used to make whitewash for the houses. Some of this scum could make an Aztec sick as a Panama parrot.

7 Lizards – tricky to catch but a very tasty bit of meat on the creatures. Nothing better than a lizard in your gizzard … it's wizard!

8 Ants - people in Europe are used to being eaten by ants when they try to picnic in a field. But the Aztecs had a better idea … they ate the ants. Lovely crunchy little snacks! Would you eat one? Perhaps one crawled into your picnic sandwich when you weren't looking! Perhaps you've already become an Aztec ant-eater!

9 Tadpoles – ask your parents about sago. It's a sort of rice-pudding dish but with clear globules that look like frogspawn. It was served regularly for school dinners – and refused regularly by children. The Aztecs would have enjoyed it because they ate tadpoles.

10 Larvae – you know what they are? Insects before they grow up. So fly larvae are known as maggots and butterfly larvae are caterpillars while beetle larvae are known as grubs.

THOSE AZTECS CERTAINLY KNOW HOW TO ENJOY THEIR GRUB!

Something you wouldn't want to drink...

The Mayans learned to make strong alcohol from the runny honey of their bees. But the honey needed bacteria (germs) to make it turn into alcohol. How did they put the germs into the honey?

Answer: Girls took the honey into their mouths, swished it around and they spat it out into a large bowl. After a few days it began to froth and bubble and turn into alcohol. But don't try this at home ... all that honey-swishing will make your teeth rot!

... and what the Aztecs didn't want to eat

Surprisingly, they didn't want to eat chocolate. The Aztecs had cacao beans from which we now make chocolate. They

58

knew how to grind up these beans, boil them to a froth with water and sweeten the drink with vanilla and honey.

So why didn't the Aztecs drink this tasty stuff?

Because the cacao beans were too precious. For an Aztec, making a cup of chocolate would be like you eating a five-pound note sandwich … a waste of money.

Of course rich people liked to show off by drinking chocolate. They could afford it.

Food you might like to eat
Tortillas
The main food of the Aztecs would be maize which they ate with almost everything. They would make very thin maize 'pancakes', called tortillas, and use them to scoop up food from a dish or to make a parcel around some filling.

Maize flour is not common outside Mexico but ordinary flour would do. You can make about 6 tortillas with 150g of plain flour, 25g of lard and 90ml of warm water. Mix it into a dough and roll it so thin you can see the board underneath. Then heat a 20–25cm circle of dough on a flat-bottomed frying pan for about 40 seconds. It should bubble if the temperature is right. (Well, you'd bubble if you were thrown into a hot pan, wouldn't you?) Turn it over and cook the other side for about 30 seconds.

Best of all is to buy your tortillas ready-made from a supermarket!

Quesadillas

Heat a heavy frying pan till sprinkled water sizzles on it. Drop a tortilla on to the hot pan. Cover the tortilla with about 25g of grated cheese then some thin slices of onion. Lastly pop another tortilla on top. After about a minute or two the cheese begins to melt. Turn the whole thing over and heat for another minute. Eat!

You can add strips of sliced green chilli if you want a flavour of the Aztecs' favourite spice.

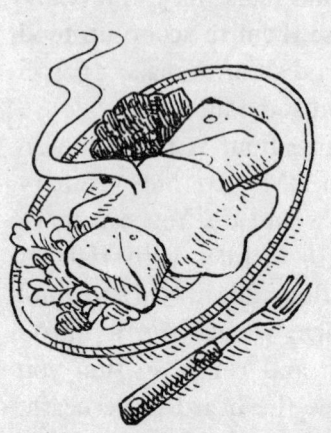

Burritos

The people of the USA call tortilla snacks 'burritos'. That means 'little donkeys' … but don't worry, they don't have to take nuggets of Neddy from the knackers' yard. There is no donkey-meat in this at all. They are fillings of whatever you fancy wrapped in tortilla parcels.

It's a dog's life

Mexican dogs probably had very happy lives. They would not have been so happy if they knew what was going to happen to them! Luckily dogs can't see into their future. So, if you have a dog, be kind to it – don't tell it about Aztec dogs and don't leave this book lying around where Rover can read it. Because...

• The Aztecs bred small dogs for food. These dogs were practically hairless because it was so warm in Mexico ... in fact they were dogs with no ruff at all. These dogs were pot-bellied little things and Mexican potters were so fond of them they made clay models of the cute curs.

• The Maya bred dogs that didn't bark! That would give them a bit of peace and quiet at night ... but how did the poor mutts talk to one another?

• Some natives of Mexico believed a dog could help its owner to cross over into the afterlife when they died. The trouble was the dog had to be dead at the time. Whenever an owner died then the dog would be killed and buried with them. Sort of 'Spot!' Splatt!

Aztec days

Disgusting Diary

The Aztecs had a calendar of 365 days – like us but without the leap years. This calendar, and the movement of the stars and the sun, gave them a disgusting diary for the years.

The city of Tenochtitlan was massive and the twin pyramids of the Great Temple looked down on the streets. Twin pyramids to the gods – the gods of life and the gods of death ... but mainly death for the people who were conquered by the Aztec warriors.

And the streets below weren't filled with filth and rotting rubbish like the streets of Europe at that time. They were kept clean by thousands of sweepers every day. Rubbish was collected, loaded on to barges and shipped away to be dumped.

The sweepers were usually captives from other tribes who were forced to serve the Aztecs. If one of those sweepers had kept a diary then it would have been gruesome.

It may have looked something like this...

① NOVEMBER – ⑳ NOVEMBER: DAYS OF THE PRECIOUS FEATHER

① NOVEMBER New Year. And how do the warriors celebrate? They fast – starve themselves for days on end. I'm glad I'm not a warrior who has to fast … it's bad enough being a slave. I've had my breakfast, but I'm still so hungry I could eat three dogs and still find room for a rattlesnake.

---

⑤ NOVEMBER Today the Aztecs remember the dead warriors. Well, the older warriors remember them. I would have remembered them but I forgot. Great hunting with prizes for the best hunters. Because this is the time of the hunter they take their prisoners, tie them up like deer, their front legs to their back legs. (Yes, I know people don't have front legs, but they pretend.) Then the priests sacrifice them like deer which they are really. You hear them moaning, 'Oh, deer! Oh, deer! Oh deer!' There's a lot of mess to clear up, of course. Still. It could be worse. It could be me they're sacrificing!

---

⑬ NOVEMBER This is the 'eating of the water tamales' day. They only have this once every eight years … thank the gods! The Aztecs only eat water-soaked tamales – meat and maize flour – no spices so it's like a tasteless mush. Up at the temple there are some very nice dances but the Aztecs have to go and spoil it, don't they? They end with a ceremony where they swallow water-snakes and frogs. It makes you hungry just watching them. I prefer my snake-meat roasted.

63

21 NOVEMBER – 10 DECEMBER : DAYS OF THE RAISING OF BANNERS

21 NOVEMBER The Aztecs celebrate the birthday of Huitzilopochtli, who grew up to beat Coyolxauhqui in battle. People wave paper flags from the houses and hang them from fruit trees! Everyone enjoys themselves … except the prisoners who get sacrificed at the Great Pyramid of Tenochtitlan. They don't complain for long.

---

11 DECEMBER – 30 DECEMBER: DAYS OF THE DESCENT OF WATER

14 DECEMBER It's wet. That's why they call these days the 'Days of the Descent of Water', because it usually rains about this time. Well, at least it's giving the pyramid a good wash down. But it's cold and muddy work out on the streets. At least it's a quiet time for the sacrifices. None of the nasty bits to sweep up.

---

30 DECEMBER – 19 JANUARY: DAYS OF THE STRETCHING

3 JANUARY The merchants pray for good trade. They sacrifice a few slaves, of course. And the priests dress up as gods and do some very nice dancing before a great feast with the lords. Of course, I never get invited to the feasts. Remind me never to become a merchant slave. I really don't want my heart ripped out of my chest – even if the Aztecs say it is a Great honour.

26 JANUARY Today's the day they grab the children and pull them by the neck to make them grow. Mum used to do it to me. It didn't half hurt. Still, I'm nice and tall – I've a neck like a rattlesnake, but I'm nice and tall. I held my little brother's legs while Mum pulled his head. You should have heard the neck bones creak!

---

28 JANUARY Today the children have their ears pierced. At least, the children who survived the neck stretching have their ears pierced! I held my little brother down while our mum drilled the holes. He didn't half squawk.

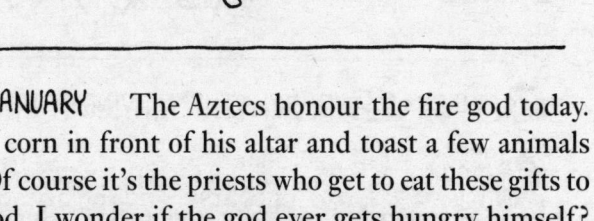

31 JANUARY The Aztecs honour the fire god today. Toast corn in front of his altar and toast a few animals too. Of course it's the priests who get to eat these gifts to the god. I wonder if the god ever gets hungry himself? Lots of sweeping up after ceremonies like this.

⑨ FEBRUARY – ⑬ FEBRUARY: THE USELESS DAYS

⑫ FEBRUARY   The Aztecs have 18 months of 20 days each in their calendar. So they have these five 'useless days' left over. Everybody says they're really unlucky. (Of course no one gets sacrificed in the useless days, so I guess slaves and prisoners think they're really useful days!) And no one does any work on these days. I decided it would be best to stay in bed so the bad luck couldn't get me. But I fell out of bed. It didn't half hurt!

---

⑭ FEBRUARY – ⑤ MARCH: THE RAISING OF THE TREES DAYS

⑱ FEBRUARY   They don't really raise trees, of course. They raise poles with banners on them, then they make sacrifices to the gods of the maize and the rain. This time they sacrifice children, but at least they take them up to the mountains to sacrifice them. Less mess for me to clean up. They say the more the children cry the happier the rain god will be. If it was me I'd squawk like a parrot.

---

⑤ MARCH – ㉕ MARCH: THE FLAYING OF MEN DAYS

⑯ MARCH   The young warriors have mock battles. Very entertaining and not too messy. But the priests make the usual sacrifices and wear the skins of the victims. I wouldn't be seen dead in a cloak of human skin myself. These Aztecs have very bad taste and they expect us slaves to clean up after them. It's a dog's life at times. (Except, of course, slaves don't get eaten like the dogs!) At least they put the skins in a holy cave in the temple. Makes a change to have priests clearing up after themselves, I can tell you. They wear those skins for 20 days. My friend cleans at the temple and says they smell dreadful!

26 MARCH – 14 APRIL : THE OFFERING OF FLOWERS DAYS

3 APRIL Spring's here so the Aztecs go into the fields to sacrifice flowers! I was sweeping between the pyramids of the Great Temple today when a priest came out. He explained that the pyramids are like life and death. 'Life needs death to exist; and death needs life,' he said. I just nodded and hoped he didn't want my life! The blood doesn't half dye the steps up to the top of the pyramids. I could scrub for days and never get those stains out. I'm glad that's not my job.

15 APRIL – 4 MAY : DAYS OF THE GREAT VIGIL

3 MAY Young Aztec girls go in procession to bless the maize in the fields. I don't get to go, of course. More children sacrificed on the mountains. It makes you wonder how there's any children left the rate these Aztecs sacrifice them!

⑤ MAY – ㉒ MAY: DAYS OF DRYNESS

⑰ MAY   It's dry. The dust in the streets is terrible and I get home filthy every night. The priests have a young man who pretends to be the god Tezcatlipoca. He has a wonderful time, him being treated like a god and all that. The trouble is gods don't get old, so they have to have a new young man every year. What happens to the old one? He gets sacrificed, of course.

㉓ MAY – ⑬ JUNE: DAYS OF EATING MAIZE AND BEANS

⑬ JUNE The end of the dry season and all that mud again. They give offerings of foods to the tools they use in the fields! I wish they'd offer some to me. They bring reeds from the lakes to make new mats, seats and decorations for the temples. There's bits of reed all over the place. Sweeping up reeds in mud isn't easy.

---

⑭ JUNE – ㉓ JULY: DAYS OF THE FEASTS OF THE LORDS

⑳ JUNE The lord of Tenochtitlan invites the common people to some great feasts. Of course the common Aztecs go but the slaves like me just get the job of clearing up after them. Still, there's always food left over so for once I can't complain.

24 JULY – 11 SEPTEMBER: DAYS OF THE FEAST OF THE DEAD

13 SEPTEMBER   Feasts, feasts, feasts. Any excuse. Now they're honouring the dead. These Aztecs have a good life. Apart from the sacrifices today they had this brilliant pole-climbing contest. My mum told my little brother to be careful not to win. It doesn't do to get yourself noticed. Not if you want to stay alive in Tenochtitlan!

---

24 SEPTEMBER – 11 OCTOBER: DAYS OF THE SWEEPING

11 OCTOBER   The Aztecs have a good old clean out. And where does their rubbish end up? On the streets. And who gets the job of clearing it? Me and the other sweepers. This is the time of the year when the gods return to the temples for the winter. At midnight last night the first god arrived and showed he was there by leaving a footprint in a bowl of flour in the temple. It's flour made out of maize and my mum says it's an a-maize-ing trick. She can be funny, my mum.

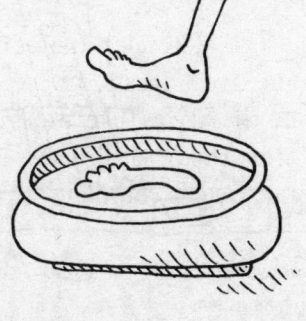

69

12 OCTOBER – 31 OCTOBER: DAYS OF THE FEAST OF THE MOUNTAINS

31 OCTOBER Those Aztecs have a plant called amaranth. Today they ground it up into a paste and baked it into models of the gods and snakes. But did they eat them? No! They offered them to the gods. I'll never understand these Aztecs if I live to be 50 years old. In fact I would be glad to reach 15 years old! I'm just grateful I've survived another year without getting myself sacrificed.

Live like an Aztec

The Aztecs were fighters. By 1500 they had conquered most of Mexico. The defeated people had to supply the Aztec homeland at Tenochtitlan with food, clothing and slaves.

But most of all the Aztecs wanted defeated warriors for their sacrifices.

Problem: How could they defeat warriors when they'd conquered Mexico and there was no one left to beat?

Answer: The Aztecs sent in spies. Aztec traders went in disguise to strange cities and looked for signs of rebellion against the Aztec rule. If they found any sign of rebel forces they encouraged it! 'Go on ... fight the Aztecs! I'll bet you could beat the loincloths off them, lads!'

As soon as the rebels went into action the Aztecs would attack and win. They would win because their trader–spies would have told them all the enemy weaknesses.

THEY ALWAYS STOP FOR TEA AT FOUR O'CLOCK

The Aztec warriors tried to capture the rebels alive so they could sacrifice them later in Tenochtitlan. That's mean and that's cheating ... but it was the Aztec way of making sure the sun kept moving in the sky.

Cruel to kids

If you wanted the gods to bring you rain or a good harvest then you had to give them gifts. You had to give them really precious gifts, of course, not just any old rubbish. What was the most precious gift they could give? A life. And what was the most precious life? The life of a child, of course. The Aztecs must have really loved children because they sacrificed dozens every year.

Of course these would usually be captured slave children. Aztecs were a bit tougher with their own children. The Aztec child was taught not to expect a happy life ... and it didn't get one! How would you like to have been an Aztec child?

THE GOOD AZTEC PARENT IS STRICT. THEN THEIR CHILD WILL GROW UP TO BE HARD-WORKING AND OBEDIENT. A USEFUL AZTEC ADULT.

FROM THE AGE OF 4 GIRLS WILL COOK AND CLEAN WHILE BOYS WILL GO FISHING OR WORKING IN THE FIELDS

THE DISOBEDIENT CHILD MAY BE PINCHED ON THE ARMS OR THE EARS

THE REALLY DISOBEDIENT CHILD MAY BE PRICKED WITH THE THORNS FROM THE MAGUEY CACTUS

Did you know…?

1 Boys were trained to be warriors. When they were baptized at a few days old they were given their warrior equipment - a miniature loincloth, a cloak, a shield and four arrows.

2 As boys grew older they were told, 'The house you were born in is not your true home - that is out there on the battlefield. Your mission is to give the sun the blood of your enemies to drink.'

3 Girls, on the other hand, were given a skirt, a blouse and weaving equipment. They were told that their place was in the home.

4 The first words a baby heard when it was born were: 'You have come to this earth which is a place of torment, a place of pain, a place of weariness, a place of illness, thirst, hunger and weeping.' Cheerful stuff. Just the sort of thing you want to hear after all the effort to get born in the first place.

AND A VERY HAPPY BIRTHDAY TO YOU TOO!

5 A child would be named after the day on which it was born. There were 20 days and 18 months but the months could have some embarrassing names. Imagine going through life as Six Dog (you'd be sick as a dog), Ten Crocodile (you'd be a bit snappy), or Eight Monkey (and if you were Aztec you would have ate monkey). Perhaps you'd prefer to be a Wind, a Vulture, a Rabbit, a Lizard, a Flower or a Death's Head?

HI, MY NAME'S 13 DEATH'S HEAD BUT YOU CAN CALL ME 'LUCKY'

6 Pottery figures of around AD 600 to 900 show Mexican native boys grinning ...with their top teeth filed to a point! It probably helped them eat their roast dog But would you like to have your teeth filed? Eeeeugh!

DO YOU HAVE ANY FILLINGS?

NOPE, BUT I'VE GOT A COUPLE OF FILINGS

7 If a family was very poor then there was a quick and easy way to make some money. Sell the kids! This was an idea copied from the Maya. Slave traders would buy healthy children and take them to market. The children would have to work hard for hours on end or be punished. A bit like school, really.

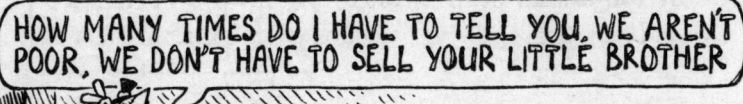

HOW MANY TIMES DO I HAVE TO TELL YOU, WE AREN'T POOR, WE DON'T HAVE TO SELL YOUR LITTLE BROTHER

8 If a child died then it wouldn't get a coffin. It would be buried in a jar. Hopefully no one would later dig up the jar and mistake it for a jar of jam.

9 The Aztecs were certainly the only people in the world of the 1500s to have schooling for all boys and girls. But they didn't start school till they were 15 years old and stopped at the age of marriage – about 20. The boys could choose between schools for priests and schools for warriors. Girls generally learned singing and dancing. Then, of course, there was…

Mexican marriage

Want to marry your loved one in a genuine Aztec ceremony? This is how boys can go about it. (Sadly, girls, you don't have a lot of say in this!)

Could you survive as an Aztec? Imagine you are an Aztec boy. Try the following test.

1 First choose your bride. Who gets you permission to marry the girl?
a) You do it yourself, boys.
b) You ask your 'Best Man' (best friend) to do it for you.
c) You ask an old woman to do it for you.

2 Who do you ask?
a) Ask the girl, of course.
b) Ask the priests if the gods agree to the marriage.
c) Ask the girl's family.

3 You also need permission to get married yourself. Who do you ask?
a) Your mum.
b) Your dad.
c) Your teacher.

4 How do you choose your wedding day?

a) You agree a day with your bride.

b) Everyone marries on the same day so you don't have to choose.

c) Read your horoscope and make sure it is a 'good' day on the Aztec calendar.

5 There is a feast before the wedding. Who arranges that?

a) You do it yourself, cooking food that you've hunted for yourself.

b) Your mother cooks your favourite meal with enough for everyone to share.

c) The bride's parents arrange the feast so you don't have to worry about a thing.

6 The wedding takes place after the feast and at night. How does the bride travel to your house for the ceremony?

a) In a taxi.

b) You carry her on your.

c) She is carried on the back of an old woman.

7 How do the guests get from the feast to the wedding at your house?

a) They ride on the backs of oxen.
b) They form a long line, join hands and dance from the bride's house to yours.
c) They have a torch-lit procession.

8 Everyone gives you a wedding present. When do you get your presents?
a) When you move into your new house.
b) Straight after the wedding.
c) Just before the wedding.

9 How are you joined together in marriage?
a) You and your bride each grip one end of a snake between your teeth – the boy takes the head and the girl takes the tail.
b) You simply join hands and swap rings.
c) The boy's cloak is tied to the girl's blouse.

10 There is a final feast with alcohol to drink. But only certain people are allowed to drink. Who can booze?
a) You and your friends.
b) Everyone except the bride and groom.
c) Any guests over the age of 30.

Answers: All c) answers are correct. All a) and b) answers are wrong.

1 Boys, choose your bride. It has to be someone of your own position in society. You must use an old woman as the messenger to carry your proposal. Your granny would do.

2 Ask the girl's family if you can marry her. Don't bother asking the girl herself because you don't need her permission.

3 Send your messenger to ask your teacher if you can marry! If the teacher says 'No!' then you won't be allowed.

HOW COME EVERYONE ELSE AROUND HERE HAS A CHANCE TO OBJECT EXCEPT ME?

4 Choose the wedding day. This needs to be a 'good' day on the Aztec calendar. Perhaps you could look up your horoscope in a book? Saturdays are good days.

5 The girl's family organizes a feast at her house which guests eat while she has her wedding dress and make-up put on.

6 After dinner you must wait until dark because marriages take place at night. The bride is carried on the back of an old woman to the boy's house. If your granny isn't worn out with all the running around maybe she can carry the bride.

7 Guests follow in a procession by the light of torches flaming torches, not electric torches, of course.

8 The couple sit on a mat spread in front of the fire and everyone gives them wedding presents. (Note: the Aztecs didn't have pop-up toasters, stainless steel butter dishes or electric kettles so don't give them.)

9 The couple are married when the boy's cloak is tied to the girl's blouse. This is still known today as tying the knot.

10 There's another feast (if you've recovered from the one at the girl's house!). This time the guests over the age of 30 can drink alcohol and it is no disgrace to get drunk. (Warning: Anyone under 30 getting drunk faces a beating for this crime. The next time they are caught they will be executed!)

How did you score?
10 Cheat
5 - 9 Lucky
1- 4 Get your brain cells cleaned
0 You would make a really good Aztec sacrifice

Now, boys, if you enjoyed that why not try it again with another girl … and again with another girl … and again with another girl. And again and again and again. How many wives can you afford?

King Nezahualpilli had 2,000 wives and 144 children. How on earth did he remember their names? And, talking about kings…

The new emperor's new clothes

In Britain the monarchs have been crowned for over a thousand years in the richest robes money can buy. Thick silks, warm velvets and fur-trimmed collars. Very cosy in London fogs and Edinburgh drizzle.

The kings and queens dressed up as if to say, 'Look how grand I am, you peasants!'

But a new Aztec emperor did the opposite. He was taken in front of the sun god and had to tell the god what a feeble little human being he really was.

The emperor spent four days fasting (or three days if he was really, really fast!).

Then he took off all his clothes and stood in front of the statue of the god and said…

> *Oh master, oh night, oh wind, I am so poor. How can I work for this city? How can I work for its people? For I am blind, I am deaf, I am brainless and I am covered in filth. Maybe you've made a mistake and you are looking for someone else to rule?*

Imagine the shock he'd get if the god said, 'All right, mate, get your kit on and push off. I'll find someone better!'

Of course all this 'humble' business didn't last long … it never does with emperors and kings. As soon as the coronation was over he went off to a feast where…

• every great lordly guest had to wear plain, simple clothes so they didn't look more grand than the emperor

• they had to bow their heads

• they were not allowed to look at emperor's face

• they were not allowed to turn their back on him so they had to walk out of his room backwards.

From then on…

• he was carried almost everywhere in a chair shaded by a canopy of precious feathers

• if he did decide to step down then nobles swept the ground in front of him and covered the ground with cloths so his feet never touched the earth

• whenever he ate he was shielded from the ordinary people by a screen of gold

• he was offered a choice of a hundred dishes of food at each meal

• he was entertained by clowns and jugglers while he ate

• he had a palace aviary with ten rooms full of birds and a palace zoo filled with animals from all over his empire – rattlesnakes were kept on a bed of feathers.

What a humble sort of life! And all he had to do was take his clothes off and admit to a stone statue he was stupid. Even you could do that!

Furious fighters

Aztec men lived to fight. When the war drum sounded every Aztec man was expected to pick up his weapons and join his group of about 800 men.

What other fantastic facts do you know about the Aztec warriors? Try this quirky quiz that Quetzalcoatl would quite quickly complete. Just answer True or False to the following...

1 Aztec warriors wore armour.

2 The Aztecs had wooden clubs, edged with stone blades that were powerful enough to cut off a horse's head.

3 Aztec leaders were easy to spot because they wore large feather and reed constructions on their shoulders.

4 Aztec warriors believed that dying in battle was a wonderful thing.

5 Rich Aztec warriors wore gold and jewels when they went into battle.

6 Warriors didn't get their hair cut till they'd killed someone in battle.

7 Aztecs believed in killing themselves rather than being captured.

8 The Aztec army needed to capture 20 enemy fighters for sacrifice and no less.

9 Young Aztec men could be made full warriors by having their faces smeared with the blood of a heart that was still beating.

10 Warriors short of food would eat their dead friends.

Answers:

1 True. But it wasn't metal armour because they didn't have steel. It was a padded cotton coat, soaked in salt water to make it hard.

2 True. At least that's what the Spanish soldiers said when they fought against them. Before the Spanish arrived the Aztecs did NOT cut off horses' heads because there were no horses in Mexico.

3 True. This was fine when they were fighting other Mexican armies. But the Spanish invaders had guns and were able to pick out the leaders easily and then pick them off.

4 True. They believed that they were immediately turned into hummingbirds and hummed off to join the sun god in his heaven. Hummmm! A likely story.

5 True. Not just because they wanted to look cute as a corpse. They believed that precious stones had magical powers to protect them.

WELL, THEY'LL PROTECT HIS EARS ANYWAY

6 True. Young men had to leave some of their hair long – a disgraceful thing which told everyone that they weren't a real man yet.

7 False. King Moquiuhix tried to rebel against his Aztec friends. When his armies were defeated he threw himself off the top of his pyramid and died. The Aztec winners were so disgusted the dead king's body was not buried but left to rot.

8 True ... but they sometimes took more. The Aztec Emperor Tizoc (ruled 1481 – 1486) ordered that every man in three defeated tribes should be executed. Not 20 – but 20,000.

I HOPE THEIR ARMS GET TOO TIRED BY THE TIME THEY GET TO US

9 True. Even the Tlaxcallan friends of the Spanish performed this ritual while the Christian Spanish soldiers looked on.

10 False. Warriors were happy to eat dead enemies but refused to eat the friends they had fought with, no matter how hungry they were. In the 1521 battle against the Spanish they boiled the bark of trees and ate that but left thousands of their dead friends untouched.

The gory games

The Maya played a ball game that was later copied by the Aztecs.

The Maya called it pok-a-tok, which sounds quite jolly - rather like ping-pong. The idea was that the better you played the 'ball game', the happier the gods would be and the better the crops would grow.

The ball game was linked with the ideas of human sacrifice and death. If you want to live like an Aztec then you may like to try this with a few friends. If you simply want to live ... then don't ever play it!

You need:

• A court 140 metres long and 36 metres wide in the shape of an 'I'. The court is surrounded by stone walls. If that's a bit too big then try a basketball or netball court.

• A ring at each side of the court about 5 metres above the ground.

• Flat stones, carved in the shape of heads, to show the score.

• A rubber ball about 15 cm across.

• Two teams of about 10 a side – allow plenty of substitutes for players killed or carried off to hospital during the game.

• A 'skull rack' to hold the heads of sacrifice victims who'll be watching the game.

• Each player needs a helmet, and arm, knee and leg protectors made from boiled leather. (But don't go killing cows or cutting up shoes for their leather – skateboard protectors will do … or simply don't play as rough as the Aztecs!)

The aim:

As in basketball the players of a team pass the ball among themselves till they are in a position to score. A score is made by putting the ball through one of the rings set in the wall.

The rules:

You can use arms and legs to pass the ball but you must not use hands or feet … and that's about it really! That's probably why players were often killed during a game – there were no rules to stop you killing an opponent, and losing often meant disgrace, which made killing the opposition a very good idea. So you might want to add a rule that makes killing an opponent a foul.

The result:

The team that scores first is the winner. Some historians say losing players were taken to a platform at the side of the pitch where their heads were cut off and stuck on wooden poles. (Although you might find that a smack in the loser's face with a stale kipper may be enough of a winning celebration.) A player who scored through the hoop could claim any jewellery or clothing from the spectators. The problem was the player would have to catch the spectator first.

Sometimes the teams can agree on prizes that the winner gets. You could gamble with gold, jade, slaves or even a house ... but ask your parents before you bet your house on the result.

The truth about the ball game

Historians don't always know the truth about ancient worlds. They guess.

Most history books will tell you that the Mayan and Aztec 'ball game' was played to the death. But other historians say that is quite silly.

The truth is there were pictures carved into the walls of the ball courts. These pictures showed a ball game in which the losers lost their heads. But the pictures didn't tell the tale of a real ball game – all they did was tell the tale of a ball game that happened in an ancient legend.

So that's the story told on the walls of the ball courts. A story made up to explain why the planet Venus disappears from our skies then comes back again.

When tourists arrived in the Mayan ball courts their guides said, 'This is what happened when they played the ball game – the losers lost their heads.'

Then historians took this story and repeated it in their books. (Check your own school books on the Maya and Aztecs.) It is probably not true!

History can be horrible … but historians can sometimes be horribler.

A game you wouldn't want to try…
Volador
You need:
• A pole – tall and solid like a Maypole with a platform on top.
• Four ropes attached to the top.
• Bird costumes.
The rules:
Four players dress up as birds, climb to the top of the pole and fasten the ropes under their arms. Each bird jumps off the top of the pole and swings round it 13 times. When four players have swung round 13 times they have created the lucky number 52 and this will make sure the Sun god continues to fly around the earth.
The result:
Nothing really. Just a sort of Aztec team-bungee-jump in honour of the Sun god, and a lot less messy than heart sacrifices.

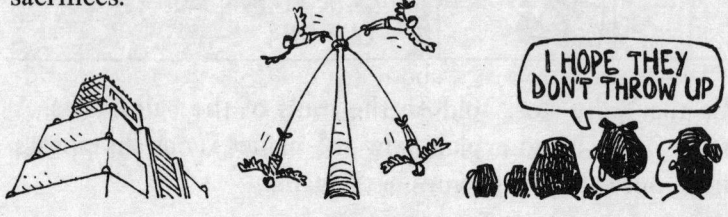

I HOPE THEY DON'T THROW UP

Foul for females

Women were not very well treated in the Aztec world. But they could do one thing that would make men respect them … they could die giving birth. That was the bravest thing a woman could do, the men said.

The unfortunate woman's ghost haunted crossroads at night. It was very unlucky to meet her. But Aztecs didn't think the dead woman's body was unlucky. Quite the opposite, they believed it had magical powers. If an Aztec warrior could just cut off a finger and some hair from her body then he could fasten it on to his shield when he went to war. The magic finger would protect him.

How did he get his hands on the fingers? Did he go to the dead woman's family and say, 'Excuse me, would you mind if I cut up her body?'

No. They were Aztecs and Aztecs never do anything so polite or simple.

When warriors heard about a suitable corpse they would get together in a gang and ambush the funeral. (Of course there couldn't be more than ten in the gang – that would make sure that everyone got a finger!)

If they missed the funeral then it still wasn't too late. They could find the grave and dig up the body!

One minute it's 'rest in peace' and the next minute it's 'rest in pieces'!

And, talking about graveyards...

Magical medicine and murderous mines

The emperor lived in his palace with some rooms large enough for 3,000 visitors. Aztec villagers lived in huts built from sun-dried bricks and whitewashed. They would have three or four rooms and enough space for 10 to 15 people to live ... and die.

Because ... when a member of the family died then they were buried under the floor of the house! This was another idea copied from the Maya. Imagine guzzling your grub over granny or sleeping over sister or drinking over Dad! Yeuch!

NOTE: This is NOT a very healthy thing to do, so don't bury your favourite goldfish under the floorboards.

If you do fall ill, then do NOT try Aztec cures. The useless ones don't work and the working ones could kill the patient. Some are still used today because the herbs worked and some seem just plain silly to us. Still, there's no harm in trying...

Curing an Aztec cold

1. FIND A CHILD WITH A COLD – THOUGH A SNEEZING TEACHER MAY DO INSTEAD

2. GET OUT OF BED AT SUNRISE AND GO TO THE NEAREST PATCH OF GRASS

3. SCOOP THE DEW OFF THE GRASS INTO A SMALL BOTTLE OR EMPTY JAM JAR

4. LIE THE PATIENT ON A BED AND TILT BACK THE HEAD

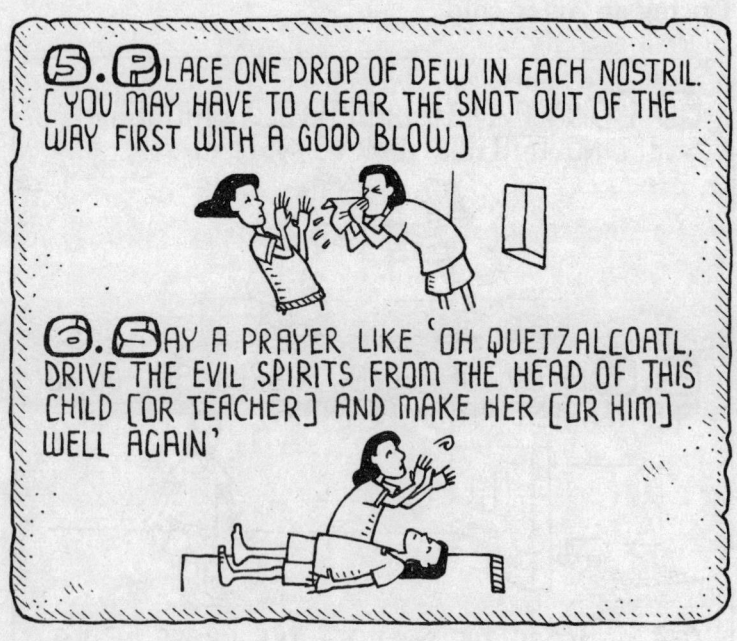

5. Place one drop of dew in each nostril. (You may have to clear the snot out of the way first with a good blow)

6. Say a prayer like 'Oh Quetzalcoatl, drive the evil spirits from the head of this child [or teacher] and make her [or him] well again'

The important bit is the prayer. Most Aztec cures were aimed at driving the evil spirits from the body of the patient. Sometimes a doctor would give a really powerful drug made from morning glory flower seeds or peyote mushrooms. They could drive the patient mad or even kill them. No evil spirit with any sense would stay in a body like that!

The dead sick Aztecs

The Aztecs had no cure for diseases like smallpox that the Spanish brought from Europe. The invaders gave the Aztecs these diseases and they spread like a plague, wiping out whole villages.

One man arrived from Spain with smallpox in 1520 and killed so many Aztecs it weakened their armies and helped the Spanish to win.

Other diseases, like measles, whooping cough, yellow fever and malaria wiped out millions more. It was worse than the Black Death in Europe! If the diseases didn't get them then the exhausting work in the silver mines and the field did.

It's a mystery where the Maya went.

Where did the Aztecs go? No mystery. This is where they went...

The cunning conquistadors

Of course all of this ripping out of living hearts made the Aztecs very unpopular with the tribes that they ruled. The only hope for the suffering Mexicans lay in an ancient legend.

In this legend the Mexican people had come from another land and their leader was a god called Quetzalcoatl. This great hero had been driven from Mexico on a raft of snakes but he said he'd return one day.

The legend said that in the First Year of the Reed Quetzalcoatl would arrive with a sword and the Mexicans would recognize him because he would be a bearded white man. Quetzalcoatl would end the reign of the Aztec bullies and bring peace to Mexico.

Well, when Hernan Cortés and the Spanish landed, the legend got most of it right!

Hernan Cortés and his 600 soldiers began their conquest. With the use of guns – and with a lot of luck – they battled their way through the Aztec empire.

Crafty Cortés

Hernan Cortés set off for Mexico with 11 ships, 508 soldiers and about a hundred sailors. He also had 16 horses. The horses were going to be very important to him in battles. The people of Mexico had never seen horses before.

Cortés didn't know that the Aztecs ruled over 20 million people, but he guessed he couldn't hope to conquer the whole empire with his little army. He had to use his brains He had to win the friendship of the natives and he had to impress them with his force.

Are you as crafty as Cortés? What would you have done in these tricky situations?

The problem of the looter

Cortes had a strict rule that said his men must not steal from the defeated tribes. That was called 'looting' and was punished by death.

Shortly after Cortés had landed he began to make friends with some of the Mexican tribes who hated the Aztecs. As

99

they marched forward some of his Mexican friends, the Zempoalans, began looting Cingapacinga villages. Cortés was angry and explained the rule against looting. 'Give back all you have taken,' he ordered.

The Zempoalans did as they were told. Cortés now had more friends – the Cingapaanga liked him too!

But then a very embarrassing thing happened. One of Cortés's own Spanish soldiers was caught looting. What could Cortés do? He was given differing advice...

They were both right! It looked as though Cortés would lose the support of his 500 conquistadors or the support of 2,000 Zempoalan warriors.

Would you follow Advice A or Advice B? Or would you accept the advice of both and lose no support at all? How could Cortés possibly do that?

Cortés still had problems with some of his soldiers who wanted to steal a ship and sail back home. How did he solve that problem?

He burned all the ships, of course. Crafty Cortés!

The power of the priests

Cortes wanted to stop the human sacrifices – about five a day in the 'friendly' towns he was marching through. He wanted to convert the Mexicans to Christianity. The problem was that the Mexican priests were awesome men.

A Spanish writer said...

They wore black cloaks and their hair down to their waists. Some even wore their hair down to their feet, and it was so clotted and matted with blood that it could not be pulled apart. Their ears were cut to pieces as a sacrifice and they smelled of rotting flesh.

These priests didn't want to give up their powerful positions. Cortés needed their support. What could he do?

Would you follow Advice A or Advice B? Or could Cortés keep both the Church and the Mexicans happy?

And it worked. The Aztec idols were thrown off the top of the pyramid and replaced with a Christian altar and cross. The bloodstains were covered with whitewash and the pyramid priests became Christian priests – after they'd had a short back and sides, of course!

The Christians came along and said to the Aztec priests, 'Eat this bread, it is the body of our Lord and drink this wine, it is his blood!' The priests could understand this! Eating humans gave you the powers of the dead human eating bread and wine at a Christian 'communion' would give you the powers of a god! No wonder they agreed.

Cortés left the friendly towns with their converted priests and marched on to Tenochtitlan and the mighty Aztec Emperor, Motecuhzoma.

Sad superstitions

The Spanish were the winners and the Spanish wrote the history books. Like most 'winners' in history they changed the story and made up the facts to make themselves look right and the enemy look wrong.

The Spanish histories make Emperor Motecuhzoma look like a weak and stupid man who threw away his empire because he believed in silly superstitions and 'signs'.

But what were these strange signs … and what would you have thought if you'd seen them or heard about them?

Motecuhzoma sent for his magicians and asked them to explain these terrifying signs. If you had been one of the magicians, how would you explain them?

If you were a clever magician, you'd have said…

Well? Would you have come up with the right answers? If you didn't … and Motecuhzoma's magicians didn't … then you would have suffered like them. A slow death by cruel torture.

The bad news is that there were some things that even a modern smart–Alec like you couldn't explain. Motecuhzoma also claimed to have experienced the following …

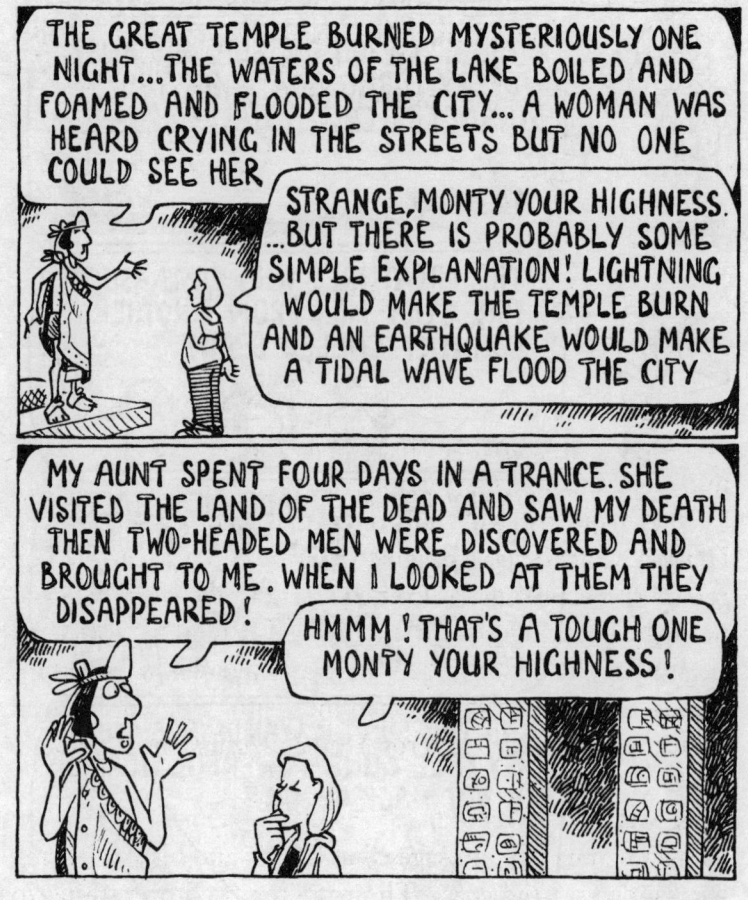

THE GREAT TEMPLE BURNED MYSTERIOUSLY ONE NIGHT…THE WATERS OF THE LAKE BOILED AND FOAMED AND FLOODED THE CITY… A WOMAN WAS HEARD CRYING IN THE STREETS BUT NO ONE COULD SEE HER

STRANGE, MONTY YOUR HIGHNESS. …BUT THERE IS PROBABLY SOME SIMPLE EXPLANATION! LIGHTNING WOULD MAKE THE TEMPLE BURN AND AN EARTHQUAKE WOULD MAKE A TIDAL WAVE FLOOD THE CITY

MY AUNT SPENT FOUR DAYS IN A TRANCE. SHE VISITED THE LAND OF THE DEAD AND SAW MY DEATH THEN TWO-HEADED MEN WERE DISCOVERED AND BROUGHT TO ME. WHEN I LOOKED AT THEM THEY DISAPPEARED!

HMMM! THAT'S A TOUGH ONE MONTY YOUR HIGHNESS!

AND, WORST OF ALL, VILLAGERS BROUGHT A BIRD TO ME. WHEN I LOOKED AT ITS FOREHEAD THERE WAS A MIRROR. AND IN THE MIRROR I SAW STARS THOUGH IT WAS DAYLIGHT! AND THE NEXT TIME I LOOKED I SAW ARMED MEN ON THE BACKS OF DEER! EXPLAIN THAT... OR DIE!

ERRRR! THERE IS REALLY ONLY ONE EXPLANATION, MONTY YOUR HIGHNESS! YOU'RE A FEW BRICKS SHORT OF A PYRAMID!

Motecuhzoma's problem was that he didn't have enough friends to help him! The people of Tlaxcallan hated the Aztecs – not surprising since the Aztecs had spent 100 years trying to enslave them and sacrifice them. The Tlaxcallan people joined the Spanish and made Cortés's little band into an army of 5,000 warriors.

The truth is Motecuhzoma probably didn't believe Hernan Cortés was the god Quetzalcoatl on earth. The reason Motecuhzoma welcomed Cortés was that he believed he was a messenger from another great king ... which he was! Naturally he welcomed this messenger as an important visitor. Imagine the shock when the visitor entered the royal palace ... and made emperor Motecuhzoma a prisoner!

The city of horrors

Motecuhzoma had messages that Cortés and his small army had landed on the coast. The emperor tried everything to keep Cortés and the conquistadors out of Tenochtitlan, the capital city. He'd tried to bribe Cortés with gold, frighten him off with threats and kill him off with an ambush that failed.

In the end he just sat back and waited for the conquistadors to arrive.

On 8 November 1519 the Spaniard marched across the causeway to the island city of Tenochtitlan and came face-to-face with the Aztec emperor.

Cortés himself wrote down Motecuhzoma's welcoming speech...

> *We have known for a long time that neither I nor the people who live here are the original inhabitants. We know it belongs to strangers who come from distant parts. We always knew that they would return one day to rule us. We will obey you and all that we own is yours.*

THAT'S JOLLY NICE OF YOU

Great news! The emperor himself was handing over power. The Spanish moved into the great palace of Motecuhzoma's father – and it was large enough to hold them all.

It gave the Spaniards a wonderful view, but they weren't too keen on what they saw. They looked out on the Great Pyramid for a start. A Spaniard called Tapia wrote...

> *At the top was a room with the greatest god of all the land.*
> *It was three metres high. He was made from seeds that were*
> *ground up into flour then mixed into a paste with the blood*
> *of boys and girls.*
>
> *There were more than 5,000 people in the service of*
> *this god. They rose promptly at midnight for their sacrifice*
> *which was letting blood from the tongue, the arms and the*
> *thighs, wetting straws with the blood and offering them to a*
> *huge oak-wood fire.*

Spaniard Bernal Diaz was most shocked by the 'skull rack' near the main gate to the temple. It was like a hat rack …but for skulls. Hundreds of skulls were set in cement into a sloping wall and seventy tall poles stood on top, each pole with dozens of pegs. Diaz went on…

> *Each peg had five skulls on. A total of 136,000 skulls were*
> *counted and this did not include the countless skulls that made*
> *up the walls.*

Still, the Spaniards managed to create their own horrors in that nightmare city. A rebel chief and his sons were brought to the city for execution. Cortés ordered that they should be burned alive at the stake.

The Mexicans were used to seeing heart sacrifices by the thousand. But the whole city turned out to watch this new type of execution. They watched in silence.

Cortés had done something even Motecuhzoma hadn't managed in the city of horrors. He had shocked the Aztecs.

The angry Aztecs

Burning Mexican chiefs did not stir the Aztecs to fight against Cortés and the little Spanish force. But the Spanish made two mistakes which made the Aztecs finally rebel.

First, Cortés went into their sacrifice temple in the capital Tenochtitlan. An Indian historian described what Cortés did next.

Cortés ordered the priests to bring water to wash the blood off the walls and he told them to take the statues of their gods away. The priests laughed and said they could not move their gods. So Cortés replied, 'It will give me great pleasure to fight for my god against your gods who are nothing.' He took up an iron bar and began to smash their statues.

The priests were horrified and the Aztec people in the city were furious. The angry Aztecs may have planned to kill the Spaniards after that. They asked the conquistadors if they could hold their great harvest festival dance at the temple and invited the soldiers to watch.

The soldiers heard a rumour that the Aztecs planned to kill them straight after the dance ... so the soldiers struck first. An Indian wrote...

> *They ran in among the dancers and attacked the man who was drumming and cut off his arms. They cut off his head and it rolled across the floor. Then they attacked the dancers, stabbing them, spearing them and striking some with their swords. They attacked some from behind and these fell instantly to the ground with their entrails hanging out. Some attempted to run away but their intestines dragged as they ran; they seemed to tangle their feet in their own entrails. Others they beheaded; they cut off their heads or split their heads to pieces. No matter how they tried to save themselves, they could find no escape.*

Now the Aztecs organized themselves and attacked the Spaniards with huge forces. The Aztec Emperor, Motecuhzoma, tried telling his people that the Spanish were their friends. The people threw rocks and fired arrows at Motecuhzoma. A rock hit the emperor on the head and he died three days later.[1]

1. Enemies of Cortés accused him of murdering Motecuhzoma since he was no more use to him. That's probably not true. The people who wrote that weren't there at the time.

Finally the ferocious Aztecs drove the Spanish out of their capital Tenochtitlan and killed two-thirds of them – many of the Spanish drowned when they slipped into the lake because of the stolen gold they had strapped to their bodies.

The Spanish conquest of Mexico was finished after just eight months ... at least, it was finished for the moment.

Quick quiz

One of Cortés's captains, Pedro Alvarado, was fighting his way across the bridge over the lake. He was on horseback and armed with a lance. His horse was killed so he battled on with just his lance. At last he reached a place where the bridge had been broken. It was just too far for a man in armour to jump across. What would you have done ... and what did Alvarado do?

> **Answer:** He pole-vaulted across using his lance! This sport is now part of the roadway out of Mexico City and it's still called Alvarado's leap.

Battling back

But Hernan Cortés wasn't going to give up the treasures of the Aztecs that easily. In 1521 he returned.

This was an important day in the Aztec world ... and the

Spanish world too. It would have made headline news if they'd had headlines. Or even if they'd had newspapers. You can just picture it...

el BINGO!

13 August 1521

el Sol

≈ PRICE ≈
Still only two pieces of eight! (or sixteen pieces of one)

EXCLUSIVE:
HAPPY HERNAN GOES FOR GOLD

Just two years after landing on the filthy-rich Aztec shores, cool Conquistador Cortés (36) has captured their capital! Today his brave little army marched into the Aztec city of Tenochtitlan and he has emperor Cuahtemoc under arrest. The battle for Tenochtitlan raged nonstop for 93 days.

The battle was fierce and the wounded Cortés was being dragged to captivity by an Aztec chief. The chief stopped dragging him when Captain Olea hacked off the Aztec's arm! It was a big Aztec mistake. They had tried to take Cortés alive so they could sacrifice him. If they'd killed him when they had the chance then the Spaniards could have lost the whole war.

A tired but happy Cortes told our reporter, 'My men did well. When we landed here we had no idea the place was so big. Otherwise we might have given up before we even started!'

The Spanish fought bravely because they saw what happened to their comrades who were captured. They watched in horror as Spanish prisoners were dragged to the top of the temple pyramid, had their beating hearts ripped out and their bodies kicked down the steps to butchers waiting below.

Footsore soldiers agreed. 'We were all for going home as soon as we got here,' Private Christofer Robino (24) agreed. 'But Captain General Cortes burned our boats so we had to go forward. Unless we wanted to sail back to Spain on a lump of charcoal!' he laughed.

Hoards of Aztec treasure are awaiting the clever conquerors but first they have to clean up the city. Our reporter says it is an amazing place, built on an island and surrounded by farms on artificial islands. There are about 200,000 people living in the city and as many as 60,000 come to the Tenochtitlan market from all over the empirc. The peasants live in wood and mud houses but the nobles and priests live in fine stone palaces.

But the real horror hovers in the centre. The city centre is dominated by the temples – huge stepped pyramids, plastered with brilliant colours. But the colours are stained by crusted dried blood and the stench of death in the midday sun has turned the stomachs of the strongest soldiers.

Captain-General Cortés has big plàns for terrible Tenochtitlan and its awful

Hernan Cortés was made Governor of the country, which was renamed New Spain. The Aztecs had been rubbed out of history; the Spaniards destroyed their great capital of Tenochtitlan utterly, the Spanish priests destroyed the Aztec statues, their libraries and their picture-writings.

Cortés then sent one of his generals, Francisco de Montejo, to conquer the tribes who remained in the old Mayan kingdom. By 1546 the northern Mayan cities had been defeated with dreadful slaughter and half a million Maya were sold into slavery. The Itza tribe hid in the dense jungles and stayed free until 1697. Then the Spanish arrived and crushed this last tribe of old Mexico.

Of course the killing didn't stop when Cortes defeated the Aztecs. The Aztec peasants became slaves and were worked to death by the Spanish conquerors. Spanish settlers took over the Aztec lands – the Spanish priests converted the Aztecs to Christianity: the great bloodstained pyramids were pulled down and the rubble from them used to build a Christian cathedral. The sacrifices stopped ... but people carried on being killed.

Conquistadors conquered

You may be pleased to hear that the Spanish conquistadors didn't have it all their own way. Stealing the treasure of the

Aztecs was easy compared to their next task … getting it back across the Atlantic to their king in Spain.

Three fat, slow transport ships set off from Mexico in 1523. Conquistador Cortés wrote:

> *I am sending you things so marvellous that they cannot be described in writing, nor can they be understood without seeing them*

These 'marvellous things' included jaguar and puma cats, sugar, emeralds, topazes, carved masks encrusted with jewels, feathered cloaks of Aztec priests, red–yellow–blue macaws, talking parrots, Aztec slaves, rings, shields, helmets, vases and polished stone mirrors. The pearls alone weighed 300 kg and there was 220 kg of gold dust, three huge cases of gold ingots and other cases of silver bars.

The gold and silver never made it to Spain … and neither did some of the Spanish conquistadors as extracts from the ship's log show…

Day 17	Sickness has killed eleven of our crew in the first two weeks. Weather bad, ship leaking and progress slow.
Day 24	Storm smashed wooden cage last night. Jaguar escaped. Beast tore arm off one sailor, ripped leg off soldier and clawed open shoulder of third before it leapt overboard. Two men died. Officers elect to

King Carlos was furious. But for the next 200 years the Spanish would have to get used to being robbed by pirates waiting, like vultures, to tear the riches from the treasure ships.

The Quetzalcoatl quiz

Now that you know everything your teacher never knew about the Aztecs, you can torture Sir or Miss even more. No, not by ripping out their heart with a stone-age knife. By testing their brain cell with these fiendishly foul questions. (If you can't torment a teacher then pester a parent – and if your parents run screaming you'll just have to test yourself!)

1 What sort of knife did the priests use to cut out a victim's heart?
a) glass
b) bronze
c) gold

2 The name Quetzalcoatl means what?
a) white man with beard
b) a coat decorated with quartz stones
c) a snake with feathers

3 Before the Aztecs came the Toltecs and before the Toltecs came the Olmecs. The Olmecs were known as what?
a) the green monkey people
b) the rubber people
c) the cactus–haired people

4 Aztec children were given the job of collecting things in the fields. What did they collect?
a) berries
b) beetles
c) bat droppings

5 Aztecs were told what to wear. Poor people wore simple clothing and lords wore rich clothing. What was the punishment for a poor person caught wearing rich clothes for a second time?

a) death

b) being stripped

c) having their house knocked down

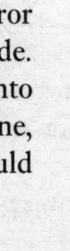

NO ONE CAN TELL HOW RICH YOU ARE WHEN YOU'RE NAKED

6 The Aztecs asked the Spanish conquerors if they could go to their temple for a harvest festival dance. The Spanish agreed. What happened when the Aztecs arrived?

a) They were preached to by Christian priests.

b) They were told that sacrifices in the temple were banned from now on.

c) They were massacred.

7 The Aztec traders became very rich and dressed in fine clothes. But the emperor would have hated this. So what did they do?

a) They had to wear a plain white cloth over the top of their fine clothes. It reached down to their ankles.

b) They wore a reversible coat. It was rich on the outside but they could turn it round quickly if the emperor appeared to show a plain side.

c) They had to creep into the city at night so no one, especially the emperor, could see them.

8 When the Spanish arrived in Mexico they noticed little wooden huts on the side of the road in both the country and the town. Aztecs popped in for a couple of minutes before coming out again looking content. What were the little wooden huts?

a) public toilets

b) Aztec national lottery shops

c) Aztec pubs for drinking maize wine

9 How did Aztecs keep their teeth clean?
a) They had toothpicks made from cactus spines.
b) They used chewing gum.
c) They made toothpaste from powdered stone in cream.

10 The Spanish discovered the Aztecs had lots of gold and they tricked them out of it by saying, 'We need your gold…'

a) '…to give to the poor and the hungry natives.'

b) '…to make you metal guns like ours which we'll give you for hunting.'

c) '…because it's the only thing that will cure you of your disease.'

Answers:

1a) The knives were made of a type of natural glass that came from hardened volcanic lava. It is called 'obsidian' and can be polished to look really sharp, shiny and attractive. It's used to make jewellery now.

SEE, IT'S A CUTE LITTLE DAGGER

2c) Quetzalcoatl was a serpent or snake with plumes or feathers. How could the Aztecs mistake a Spanish soldier for a snake with feathers? They must be a bit shortsighted. No wonder the Spanish beat them so easily!

3b) The Olmecs were NOT called the rubber people because they were like bendy toys. They got their name because they lived in the area where rubber trees grew until the Toltecs rubbed them out, of course. No one knows what name the Olmecs called themselves.

4b) The Aztec children collected female scale beetles that live on cactus plants. These beetles were crushed and used to make red dye for clothes, called cochineal.

The Spanish invaders brought the idea back to Europe and it is still used in places as food dye. The Aztecs needed 150,000 beetles to make one kilo of dye. The Aztecs dyed – the beetles simply died.

5a) A peasant trying to pose as a posh person had their house knocked down the first time they were caught. If they tried it again they would be executed. And you thought school uniforms were a rotten idea?

I'M JUST TAKING IT TO THE CLEANERS! HONEST!

6c) The Spanish killed them. And, as we've seen, this made the surviving Aztecs angrier and fight even harder to throw out the Spanish bullies.

7c) The merchants had to creep around after dark when they returned from trading. There was another way to keep them fairly poor and a little more humble. The richer they were the greater the feasts they had to give to the nobles. They were forced to give rich presents to their guests ... and buy fine slaves in the market to be sacrificed. Imagine having a birthday party where you give all the presents!

8a) The Aztecs needed human 'manure' to spread on their fields so they encouraged people to use public toilets. The toilets would be emptied on to the soil to make it richer and help the pumpkins and maize grow better. But don't worry - your cornflakes won't have been grown with human manure ... probably just lots of chemicals, weed-killers and pest-killers. Haven't things improved since Aztec times?

9b) Aztecs chewed chicle gum made from a milky fluid inside some trees and plants. It is still used for chewing gum today. Some things never change. The Aztecs didn't like people who chewed in public and especially those who made popping and snapping noises with the gum … just like some children do in their classrooms! And today's teachers don't like that either. Something else that hasn't changed!

10c) The sad Aztecs believed that the Spanish conquerors would use the gold to cure them of the diseases that had come from Europe. What was this disease supposed to be? Gold fever?

Epilogue

Some historians try to make excuses for the Aztecs. They say, 'The Aztecs lived in violent times and had to be ruthless and bloodthirsty to survive.'

That may have been true at the start of their rise to power. But they began to enjoy the cruelty. That is harder for us to forgive … and it led to their downfall in the end.

When Emperor Tizoc wanted a sacrifice he believed that he needed 20 warriors to die on the pyramid in Tenochtitlan. Instead he decided to terrify all the other tribes in Mexico with a huge massacre. He took every single man from three Mixtec tribes, 20,000 men, and sent them for sacrifice.

The victims had eagle feathers stuck to them with their own blood and were led to the Aztec capital. They were all killed on the pyramid. The Aztecs killed the first ones then the priests took over. In early sacrifices the people had eaten small parts of the victims. This time there were too many. They were simply killed and their bodies thrown into the marshes.

It terrified the other tribes in Mexico all right. But it also disgusted them. They learned to hate the Aztecs. They knew they would have to wait, but one day their chance would come to overthrow the vicious, heart-ripping people.

And that chance came when the Spaniards arrived. If the Aztecs had been popular then all the people of Mexico would have joined together to drive them back to Spain. Instead they turned against the Aztecs and destroyed them. Sadly the Spaniards just said, 'Thanks very much!' and took over from the terrors of Tenochtitlan.

An Aztec poem moaned ...

Broken spears lie in the roads;
We have torn our hair out with our sorrows.
The houses are roofless now, and their walls
Are red with blood.

Worms are swarming in the streets and in
   the squares,
And the walls are spattered with gore.
The water has turned red, as if it has been
   dyed,
And when we drink it
It has the taste of salt.

We have beaten our hands in despair
Against the walls of our houses.
For our way of life, our city is lost and dead.
The shields of our warriors were our defence
But they could not save us.

The hideously bloodstained pyramid in Tenochtitlan was blown up with 500 barrels of gunpowder. A Christian cathedral was built in its place. Things should have started to improve for the suffering Mexicans. But history is too horrible to allow 'happy ever after' endings.

Those Mexicans had slaved in the fields and died for the Aztecs. Now they slaved in the fields and died for the Spanish conquistadors – if the Mexicans were late in paying their taxes to the Aztecs they suffered the horrors of the heart sacrifice – if the Mexicans were late in paying their taxes to the Spanish then they were burned to death.

Either way they ended up dead.

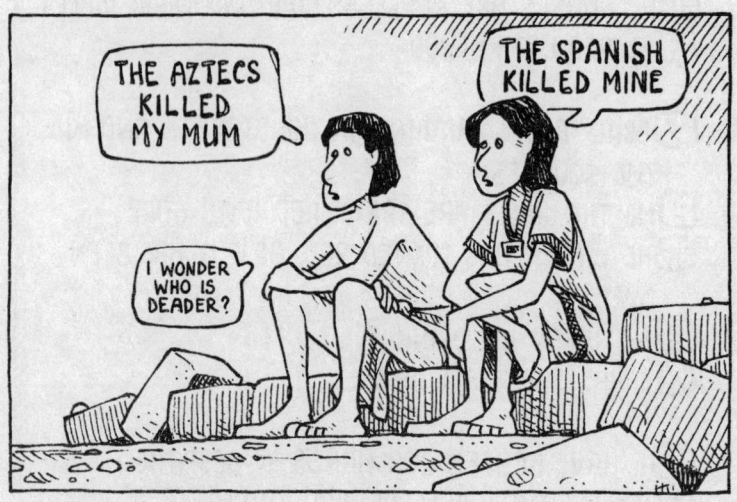

Rebels in the south of Mexico tried digging pits with sharp stakes to stop the charging Spanish horsemen ... the conquistadors threw the rebels on to their own stakes.

Rebels in other Spanish regions had their hands cut off but were allowed to live – the Spanish hung the hands around their necks and said, 'Go and show your people what happens to rebels.' And the conquistadors called the Aztecs savage!

The Mexicans had a good way of looking at death. A poem in the old Aztec language of Nahuatl puts it best. It said…

> *No one comes on this earth to stay.*
> *Our bodies are like rose trees –*
> *They grow petals then wither and die.*
> *But our hearts are like grass in the springtime,*
> *They live on and forever grow green again.*

People come and go. So do nations. The Olmecs, the Toltecs, the Aztecs. All gone.

And, if you believe the ancient Mexican legends, the earth itself comes and goes. On 22 December 2012 it will be destroyed yet again.

Or will it? History can sometimes be horribly wrong!

We'll just have to wait and see.

127

ANGRY
AZTECS

GRISLY QUIZ

Now find out if you're a
angry Aztec expert!

HORRIBLE HABITS

The people of Central America had some horrible habits. How much have you learned about their beastly beliefs?

1. What did the Mayans do to enemy peasants captured during their wars?
a) Made them slaves
b) Sacrificed them to the gods
c) Boiled them with herbs and ate them for supper

2. What did Mayan priests wear to dance in during sacrifices?
a) Grass skirts decorated with sequins
b) Nothing
c) The skin of their enemy leaders

3. Which of the following was not a method used by the Aztecs for sacrificing victims?
a) Pulling out their heart
b) Throwing them in a fire
c) Beating them over the head with the altar stone

4. The Aztecs were big dog breeders (I mean they liked to breed dogs, not that the dogs were big!). Why?
a) The dogs could keep watch for enemies
b) Dogs made tasty snacks
c) The Aztecs had a soft spot for pet pooches

5. What did the Aztecs do during the Days of Growth?
a) The pulled children by the neck to make them grow
b) They did a dance to make the crops grow
c) They built their pyramids even higher, trying to reach heaven

6. Where did the Aztecs bury their dead?
a) Under the floorboards
b) In the temples
c) They didn't – they burned them

7. What does Teotihuacan mean?
a) The place where enemies are sacrificed
b) The place where gods are born
c) The place where chocolate is eaten

8. Why did the Mayans chuck little girls into wells?
a) So they could speak to the gods
b) So they could see how deep the well was
c) The girls were thirsty

AMAZING EMPERORS

The Aztec emperors were a strange bunch. They ruled ruthlessly (you didn't make one angry if you wanted to keep you heart in your chest) but helped bring power to their people. Take this quick quiz and see how much you know about these evil emperors.

1. Who was the first Aztec emperor? (Clue: It's a capital name)
2. What did the emperor Itzcoatl order to be burned during his reign? (Clue: No more horrible history!)
3. Who did Motecuhzoma II think Hernan Cortés was when the Spaniard appeared in Tenochtitlan? (Clue: No mere mortal)
4. What did Motecuhozoma I bring to the city of Tenochtitlan during his reign? (Clue: What-a great idea!)

5. What were first created during the reign of Acamapichtli? (Clue: New rules)

6. Which industry improved during the reign of Huitzilhuitl? (Clue: It makes (fashion) sense)

7. How did Chimalpopoca die? (Clue: Come on, don't leave me hanging…)

8. What did Hernan Cortés do to the leader Cuauhtemoc? (Quite the opposite of having cold feet!)

FRIGHTENING FIGHTERS

Could you have made an awful Aztec warrior? Here are a few foul facts about the ferocious Aztec fighters – but you have to fit in the missing words.

Missing words, not in the correct order: *salt water, feather, humming, birds, precious stones, priests, arrows, enemy fighters, heart, blades, friends*

1 AZTEC BOYS WERE GIVEN A MINI LOINCLOTH, SHIELD, CLOAK AND FOUR ____ WHEN THEY WERE A FEW DAYS OLD.

2 ALL AZTEC BOYS WENT TO SCHOOL AT 15 AND COULD CHOOSE TO BE TRAINED AS WARRIORS OR AS ____.

3 YOUNG MEN COULD BE MADE FULL WARRIORS BY HAVING THEIR FACES SMEARED WITH THE BLOOD OF A ____ THAT WAS STILL BEATING.

4 AZTEC WARRIORS WORE PADDED COTTON 'ARMOUR', WHICH WAS SOAKED IN ____ TO MAKE IT HARD.

5 THE AZTECS WERE ARMED WITH POWERFUL WOODEN CLUBS, EDGED WITH STONE ____.

6 RICH AZTEC WARRIORS WORE ____ THAT THEY BELIEVED HAD MAGICAL POWERS TO PROTECT THEM IN BATTLE.

7 WARRIORS SHORT OF FOOD WOULD EAT DEAD ENEMIES BUT WOULD NEVER EAT DEAD ____.

8 THE AZTEC ARMY NEEDED TO CAPTURE AT LEAST 20 ____ FOR SACRIFICE.

9 AZTEC WARRIORS BELIEVED IF THEY DIED IN BATTLE THEY WOULD TURN INTO ____ AND GO TO HEAVEN.

10 AZTEC LEADERS WORE LARGE STRUCTURES MADE OF ____ AND REEDS ON THEIR SHOULDERS.

AZTEC FACT OR FICTION

Many mysteries surround the angry Aztecs and horrible historians still don't know the whole truth about their crazy culture. Here are a few surprising statements. Can you tell which are true and which are false?

1. The Aztec punishment for being drunk was to have your head shaved.

2. Aztec children started school at the age of five and left when they were 10.

3. When a boy was born, his umbilical cord was cut and buried on a battlefield.

4. Naughty Aztec kids were punished by being held over a fire of chilli peppers.

5. To cure earache, Aztec doctors would drop fresh dew in the patient's ears.

6. When the Europeans arrived, the Aztecs ruled over more than 20 million people.

7. Aztec men could have as many wives as they liked.

8. The Aztecs loved the game of tlachtli (pok-a-tok) so much that they used thousands of balls from the Maya.

Horrible habits
1a; 2c; 3c; 4b; 5a; 6a; 7b; 8a

Amazing emperors
1. Tencoch. He was a chief chosen to become emperor.
2. The codices (a type of Aztec book) that recorded their history and myths.
3. The god Quetzalcoatl.
4. Water – he completed an aqueduct pipe system in the capital.
5. It is believed that the first laws were introduced during his reign (1376–95).
6. Weaving – suddenly the Aztecs were comfy in cotton.
7. He hung himself by his belt after being captured by an enemy tribe.
8. Tortured him by putting his feet in a fire!

Frightening fighters
1) arrows 2) priests 3) heart 4) salt water 5) blades 6) precious stones 7) friends 8) enemy fighters 9) humming birds 10) feathers

Aztec fact or fiction

1. True. At least, that's what happened the first time you were found singing in the gutter. If it happened again you were punished by … death!

2. False. They didn't start until they were 15 (lucky Aztecs!) and they stayed until they were 20.

3. True. This was to show that his life would be devoted to war.

4. True. But you'd have to have done something reeaaally bad to have this done to you (like skiving your horrible history lesson).

5. False. That was the cure for colds. For earache they put liquid rubber in the ears, of course!

6. True. And not many of their subjects were sorry to see them squashed by the Spaniards!

7. True. In fact the more the merrier, as the wives weaved cloth that could be sold to make the families very rich.

8. True. The Aztecs stole the idea of the game from the Maya, and got them to supply more than 15,000 balls a year!

INTERESTING INDEX

Where will you find 'eating scum', 'drinking spit' and 'gut necklaces' in an index? In a Horrible Histories book, of course.

138

Terry Deary was born at a very early age, so long ago he can't remember. But his mother, who was there at the time, says he was born in Sunderland, north-east England, in 1946 – so it's not true that he writes all *Horrible Histories* from memory. At school he was a horrible child only interested in playing football and giving teachers a hard time. His history lessons were so boring and so badly taught, that he learned to loathe the subject. *Horrible Histories* is his revenge.

Martin Brown was born in Melbourne, on the proper side of the world. Ever since he can remember he's been drawing. His dad used to bring back huge sheets of paper from work and Martin would fill them with doodles and little figures. Then, quite suddenly, with food and water, he grew up, moved to the UK and found work doing what he's always wanted to do: drawing doodles and little figures.

HORRIBLE HISTORIES

STORMIN'
NORMANS

Terry Deary Illustrated by Martin Brown

■ SCHOLASTIC

To John Goddard – a true Blue.

Scholastic Children's Books,
Euston House, 24 Eversholt Street,
London NW1 1DB, UK

A division of Scholastic Ltd
London ~ New York ~ Toronto ~ Sydney ~ Auckland
Mexico City ~ New Delhi ~ Hong Kong

First published in the UK by Scholastic Ltd, 2001
This edition published by Scholastic Ltd, 2016

Text © Terry Deary, 2001
Illustration © Martin Brown, 2001, 2016

ISBN 978 1407 16568 4

Printed and bound by CPI Group (UK) Ltd, Croydon, CR0 4YY

4 6 8 10 9 7 5 3

The right of Terry Deary and Martin Brown to be identified as the author and illustrator of this work respectively has been asserted by them in accordance with the Copyright, Designs and Patents Act, 1988.

www.scholastic.co.uk

CONTENTS

Introduction

History can be horrible because *people* can be horrible. Well, *most* people can be horrible *some* of the time … even you. And *some* people can be horrible *most* of the time … school bullies, school teachers and school children who pull the wings off flies.

Then there are people who are *paid* to be horrible and torture innocent humans … tax collectors, traffic wardens and school dinner ladies…

And soldiers. Soldiers can be horrible because it's their job to kill their enemy – if they didn't the enemy would probably try to kill them. You can't go to war and behave like a gentleman, can you?

Some people in the past spent their whole lives fighting wars, so you can imagine how vicious they became. People like the Normans had to be really nasty.

The stormin' Normans were squidged into a corner of northern France and wanted to spread out – get more land. So they fought their way out. And it worked!

Some Normans, like William the Conqueror, hardly ever lost a battle. How did he do it? By being nastier than his enemies.

So you too can learn how to fight back with the help of a few lessons from the stormin' Normans. But be warned – you may become rich and successful, but you'll not be very popular. You will be remembered in history with hatred!

You have been warned!

Timeline

911 Charles the Simple, King of France, gives land in Northern France to the Viking Rollo and his people. Their nervous new neighbours call them 'North-men' … that becomes 'nor-men' … and finally Normans, geddit?

1017 The Normans set off to conquer the south of Italy. And the Italians have invited them! They've asked the Normans in to keep out some other invaders.

1047 William of Normandy, aged 19, wins his first great battle at Val-es-Dunes on the Norman border with France. Watch out for this teen terror.

1061 Normans begin their conquest of Sicily – but it will take them 30 years to complete because they are always outnumbered.

1066 William of Normandy defeats the English King Harold at the Battle of Hastings. He is crowned King of England and his Norman soldiers settle there.

1084 Germans attack Rome. Normans save the Pope and drive back the Germans – the Normans then raid Rome themselves. Well why not? They'd saved it for a rainy day.

1085 William the Conqueror orders the Domesday Book – a survey of everything everyone in England owns … so he can have a share. (Today's government still does that.) A year later he dies and Norman William II takes the throne.

1095 Pope Urban II suggests that Christian knights should capture Jerusalem from the Muslims and give it to the Christian Church. Most of Europe agrees but the Normans lead the way. Great excuse to fight with God on their side.

1099 The Crusaders finally capture Jerusalem. With God on their side they massacre the Muslim men, women and children they find there.

1100 The Normans who remain in Jerusalem carve out a new Norman kingdom in the Middle East and call it their Holy Land. Meanwhile back in England William II is killed in a hunting accident … or was it murder? Brother Henry I takes over.

1119 Henry I's only son dies in a shipwreck. There will be a long and nasty scrap to decide who gets his throne when he dies, which he does in…

1135 Henry I has chosen nephew Stephen to be the next king. Henry's

daughter, Empress Matilda, says, 'I'll fight you for the crown!' The wars bring almost 20 years of misery to England. These times are known as 'The Anarchy'.

1153 War ends when Stephen agrees that Matilda's son can have the throne when he dies. A year later Stephen keeps his promise – and dies. Peace at last.

1154 Henry II of England is from Anjou – an area in France to the south of Normandy. The Norman lords in England are no longer calling themselves Normans, but 'English'.

1199 Big Bad John becomes King of England and Duke of Normandy. But he isn't nicknamed 'Lack-land' for nothing…

1204 French King Philip II takes Normandy. The Normans in England have to choose – do they stay and become English? Or join the French to keep their Norman lands but lose their English ones? Most stay in England. The Normans become English or French but Norman no more.

9

Big bad Bill

Of all the Normans, William of Normandy (1028–1087) has to be the most famous, known to the world as William the Conqueror. Bill became Duke of Normandy at the age of 7 and had a scary childhood, always in danger of being murdered by people who wanted his land. He grew up tough enough not only to survive, but to be the first Norman to become a king when he conquered England.

Terrible teen

Bill's first major battle was in 1047, at Val-es-Dunes, at the age of just 19. Historian William of Poitiers said:

> *Young William was not scared at the sight of the enemy swords. He hurled himself at his enemies and terrified them with slaughter. Some of the enemy met their death on the field of battle, some were crushed and trampled in the rush to flee and many horsemen were drowned as they tried to cross the river Orne.*

William later marched on the town of Alençon. The defenders barred its gates and then made fun of his mother's peasant family. They cried:

Leather! Leather for the leather-worker's grandson!

William was furious. When he eventually captured the town he took 32 of the leading citizens of Alençon and paraded them in front of the townsfolk. Then he had their hands and feet cut off.

C'MON BILL! IT WAS JUST A BIT OF FUN!

Mrs Conqueror

William married Matilda in about 1052 or 1053. She was a tiny woman (about 127 cm), but tough, and proved to be a loyal and clever wife.

SHE'S MY BETTER HALF!

VERY FUNNY

You have to sort the facts from the fiction about Matilda though! French historians told the following story…

11

William was visiting Count Baldwin V when he fell in love with his daughter, Matilda. He asked if he could marry the girl but Matilda herself refused. She sneered…

I'D NEVER MARRY YOU

William secretly went to her house at night where he beat her and kicked her. As the mauled Matilda lay battered on her bed she changed her mind. She said…

I'D NEVER MARRY ANYONE ELSE BUT YOU

The story is probably not true. The Normans were trying to show that their women loved violent men – because that's what the men wanted to believe!

Bill's last battle

William was back in France, attacking the town of Mantes, when he had his last illness. He'd had the town burned to the ground and (one story says) his horse was frightened by the shower of sparks.

The horse stumbled, William slammed his stomach against the front of his saddle and burst his fat gut. He died five weeks later after suffering in agony. Before he died he handed his crown and sword to his son William Rufus. But the moment he died the Norman lords panicked. With the

Conqueror dead there could be rebellions in their lands. Orderic Vitalis, writing 50 years after the death, described what happened next...

> *As soon as William died, the richest of the Norman lords mounted their horses and hurried off to defend their castles. The servants – seeing that their masters had disappeared – laid their hands on the weapons, the gold and silver plate, the rich cloth and the royal furniture. The corpse of the king was left almost naked on the floor.*

The disappearing conqueror

William's body was eventually taken to Caen to be buried in the cathedral William had founded. The journey to the church was interrupted by a fire in the town – they dropped the body, fought the fire, then carried on.

Later the funeral service was interrupted by a local man who said...

THE GROUND WHERE YOU'RE BURYING WILLIAM BELONGS TO ME! I WANT TO BE PAID BEFORE YOU PUT HIM IN THE GRAVE!

He was paid!

Then the clumsy undertakers tried to cram the fat body into a small stone coffin and bits fell off. The smell was so disgusting the bishop rushed through the burial service and everyone ran for it.

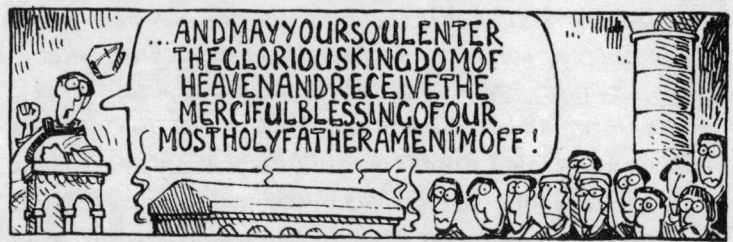

...ANDMAYYOURSOULENTER THEGLORIOUSKINGDOMOF HEAVENANDRECEIVETHE MERCIFULBLESSINGOFOUR MOSTHOLYFATHERAMENI'MOFF!

Rest in peace, William? No. Only until 1522. In that year the curious Catholic Church had the tomb opened to inspect the body.

Rest in peace, William? No. Only until 1562. In that year Protestants raided the church, broke open tombs and scattered skeletons. All that was left was Will's thigh bone. That was re-buried and a fine monument was built.

Rest in peace, William's thigh bone? No. Only until 1792 when the French Revolution mobs demolished his monument.

Rest in peace, William? For the moment. A simple stone slab now marks the spot where he was buried.

But what happened to that thigh bone? Some say the 1792 rioters threw it out – some say it's still there. Perhaps someone should open the tomb again and find out!

OVER MY DEAD BODY!

Unlikely legends

Historians have a tough time trying to sort out the truth. They may come across stories in old scripts, but those stories could be untrue.

...then in 1075 I went to the moon with the Pope.

Here are a few tale s from Norman days that may have some truth in them (one-star porkies) – or may be just legends (five-star whacking great fibs). What would you make of these tales?

✵ . . . . POSSIBLE
✵✵ . . . POSSIBLE....BUT A BIT UNLIKELY
✵✵✵ . . MAYBE A GRAIN OF TRUTH IN IT AT A PINCH
✵✵✵✵ . MORE OF A FAIRY STORY THAN CINDERELLA
✵✵✵✵✵ PULL THE OTHER ONE

Norman nonsense?

1 William the Conqueror's dad, Duke Robert, met his mum, Herleve, while she was dancing in the road. He fell in love with her. Of course this is quite possible – unlike today when dancing in a road would get you a) arrested or b) flattened by a flying Ford Fiesta.

✵✵ STARS

2 Before William the Conqueror was born his mother had a dream. She dreamed a tree was growing from her and the shade of the tree covered Normandy and England. (Just as

the son that would grow from her would cast his shadow over Normandy and England. Geddit?) Nowadays her doctor would tell her the bad dreams mean a) nothing or b) she's been eating toasted cheese sandwiches before going to bed.

✿✿✿✿✿ STARS

3 William the Conqueror was tormented by enemies who said he was just the son of a tanner's daughter – a tanner turns animal skins into leather. His grandfather, Fulbert, lived in Falaise where there were a lot of leather-makers, so it is possible. But another story says Fulbert had the charming job of preparing corpses for burial – tidying them up and dressing them.

I THINK YOU'LL LOOK FABULOUS IN THE BLUE TUNIC AND BROWN LEGGINGS

William would have liked that because a) it's a steady job and b) William could go out and kill enough people to keep Grandpa rushed off his feet! ✿ STAR

4 Rollo the Viking was offered the land of Normandy by Charles the Simple in 910. 'Let's make a deal,' Charles said (simply). 'You Vikings can simply have Normandy but I simply insist on being your king. You must simply do homage to me. To show you accept me as king you must simply kiss my foot.' Rollo didn't fancy that much … would you? So he sent one of his soldiers to kiss Charlie's foot. The soldier didn't want to grovel so he grasped the king's foot and lifted

16

it up to his lips. Of course this tipped Charles the Simple's throne back and he was simply thrown to the ground.

Big laughs for Rollo who was probably a) rolling with laughter or b) Rollo-ing with laughter. ✪✪✪ STARS

5 William the Conqueror was just a teenage duke when he was visiting the castle of one of his lords. He was tipped off that the lord planned to kill him. William escaped from the castle in darkness, rode for 16 hours through the night and came to the wide estuary of the Vire river. He was able to cross it because the tide was out (very lucky) and reached the castle of a friend before he could be caught. He was lucky that a) his horse didn't stumble on dark, uneven roads and break two necks and six legs (William's AND the horse's, if you hadn't worked it out, dummy) or b) he didn't get stopped for speeding by policemen with radar guns. ✪✪ STARS

6 In 1064 Harold Godwinson of England was the man most likely to take the English throne when Edward the Confessor died (which he did in 1066). The story goes that Harold was crossing the English Channel when his ship was caught in a storm. Harold was recognized and taken to William of Normandy (who also fancied himself as King of England when old Ed kicked the bucket). Harold had to promise he would let William become king when Ed died. William set him free … and Harold broke his promise in 1066. But is the story true? Would Harold *really* give away his kingdom?

This is a story told by Norman historians who want to show that a) Harold was a rotten cheat who broke his promises and b) William was the rightful king of England – he wasn't 'William the Conqueror' in 1066, he was 'William the I've-just-popped-over-the-Channel-to-take-what-is-rightfully-mine-old-chap'. ✦ STAR

Odd English

If the Normans had some strange beliefs, the English people had some stories that were even stranger!

1 In 1080 a man called Eadulf died in the village of Ravensworth in northern England. His relatives came to watch over the corpse but they were shocked when Eadulf sat up and said, 'Don't be afraid! I have risen from the dead. Make the sign of the cross on yourselves and on the house.' When they'd done that the house was filled with birds that flew in everyone's faces till a priest sprinkled them with holy water. Eadulf said, 'I've visited Hell, where I've seen the wicked tortured, and Heaven where I've seen a few old friends.' He also warned, 'I've seen places being prepared in Hell for some living people! One of them was Waltheof – English Earl of Northumberland.'

Shortly after this Waltheof became the only English leader to be executed by William the Conqueror. Weird? Or wacky?

✿✿✿✿✿ STARS

2 An English rebel, Edric the Wild, tried to make trouble for William the Conqueror in 1067. This Edric went out for a stroll after dinner one evening and came across a group of fairies dancing. Edric fell in love with one of these little ladies and married her. When Edric was defeated William the Conqueror ordered that this fairy wife should be brought to court so he could meet her. What on earth would big bullying Bill say to a fairy? 'Lend us your wand'?

✿✿✿✿✿ STARS

3 King Harold was slaughtered at the Battle of Hastings in 1066. But the English told a story that he survived the battle, buried under a pile of bodies. A peasant woman found him and nursed him back to health. He hid in a cellar in Winchester for two years before leading attacks on the hated Normans. In time he got religion and became Harold the hermit. Many English would love to believe their last great hero survived. Dream on. Just a little more possible than fairies. ✿✿✿✿ STARS

Painful poisoners

The Norman historians had a thing about poison! If someone died suddenly then they said, 'It could well have been poison!' Here are a few curious cases for you to judge, Sherlock…

1 William the Conqueror invited Count Conan of Brittany to join him in the conquest of England in 1066. Count Conan said:

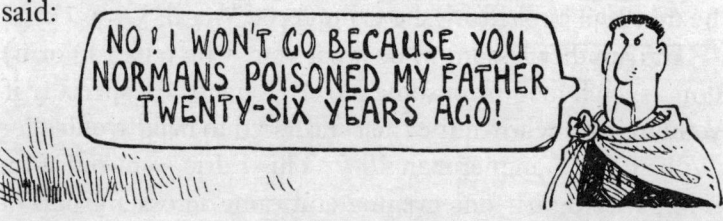

NO! I WON'T GO BECAUSE YOU NORMANS POISONED MY FATHER TWENTY-SIX YEARS AGO!

The story goes that William decided to settle Conan and got one of Conan's lords to take the count's hunting horn and gloves. These were smeared with poison. When Count Conan went hunting he wiped his mouth with the poisoned glove and died. He was really out for the count!

COUNT DOWN

Was William really guilty of this murder? Possibly, though Conan died two months after the Normans landed at Hastings.

It's a lesson to us all: **a)** don't wipe your mouth on the back of your glove or **b)** get your teacher to taste your gloves before you put them on.

2 In 1060 Robert of Gere came to a nasty and suspicious end. Norman historian Orderic wrote…

> One day Robert was sitting happily by the fire and watched his wife holding four apples in her hand. He playfully snatched two from her and didn't realize that they were poisoned. He ate them though his wife told him not to. The poison took effect and after five days he died.

Again it's possible that he *was* poisoned.

And another lesson: a) do what your wife tells you or b) don't snatch food from someone else's hand ... especially if you don't know when they last washed that hand!

3 Lady Mabel of Belleme plotted to poison her husband's enemy, Arnold of Echauffour, who was visiting them. She placed a poisoned goblet of wine on the table and waited. Unfortunately her brother-in-law, Gilbert, came in sweaty and hot from hunting. He cried...

...snatched up the poisoned cup and swallowed the lot.

He died.

Now, if you'd been Mabel, you'd have given up, wouldn't you? Not her. She bribed one of enemy Arnold's servants to put poison in his food, which he did. Arnold died. Second time lucky!

A lesson there: **a)** if at first you don't succeed, try again or **b)** don't take wine from Mabel's table (or read the label if you're able).

4 Lady Mabel then survived a poison plot against herself. The monks of Saint Evroul were fed up with her visiting them with dozens of servants to eat all their best food.

She returned, and ate ... and fell ill. She ordered that her baby be brought to her for feeding. She let the baby suck milk at her breasts. The baby died. (From poison in his mother's body?)

And Mabel? She survived.

A lesson for us all: **a)** don't go where you're not wanted and **b)** don't have a murdering meanie like Mabel for a mother!

5 William the Conqueror's dad (Robert) became Duke of Normandy only after his older brother (Richard) died suddenly. Many people believed that William's dad had poisoned his uncle in order to get his hands on Normandy.

If Robert was poisoned a few years later (and some say he was) then he must have died thinking…

The lesson seems to be: *never* trust *any* Norman who offers you food or drink!

Of course Norman cooks weren't too fussy about washing their hands after using the toilet or picking their scabs or patting a dog. They didn't know about germs and hygiene. A lot of people in those days must have died from germs in their food that gave them food poisoning.

1066 and all this

1066 was a funny old year. It saw three kings in England and three great battles. And if the year 1066 had kept its own diary[1] it would have been packed with horrible history…

---

1 January

Happy New Year, everyone in England! Edward the Confessor is King of England. But he's a poorly man. Old Ed has no children and no one's very sure about who'll get the throne when he dies. There are a lot of English people who are nervous about the coming year. Harold Godwinson for one — he is the most powerful lord in England. He practically rules the south for Edward the Confessor while his brother, Tostig Godwinson, rules the north.

Harold is a tough nut. For years the Welsh had been a problem . . . until Edward the Confessor sent Harold off to sort them out in 1063. Here's what happened. . .

1. To be honest there is a diary that was kept by monks called *The Anglo-Saxon Chronicle* but it's got lots of boring bits.

So Harold is a great warrior and the English army is in pretty good shape. I've a feeling it will need to be.

5 January
Edward the Confessor died. (I told you he was poorly, didn't I? You don't get much more poorly than that!)

6 January
Edward was buried today. That's a bit quick! His body can hardly be cold! And Harold Godwinson is crowned king. He didn't hang around did he? It will all end in tears, you mark my words.

February
That William of Normandy is upset! He's sent some of his

lords over to England with a message for King Harold. The message says...

1 Two years ago you promised that I would be King of England when Edward the Confessor died.

2 We also agreed that your sister would marry my son, while you married my sister.

Harold's reply is brief and to the point...

Dear William,

Edward the Confessor left the throne of England to me on his deathbed. We must respect the wishes of a dying man.

As for exchanging sisters I regret that I am now married to Ealdgyth. And I regret even more that my sister cannot marry your son since she has died. Perhaps you'd like me to send her corpse across to Normandy?

Harold (King of England)

I have heard that William has started building two thousand ships to invade England. There'll be trouble now!

24 April

Amazing! Fantastic and spooky! A comet has appeared in the skies over England! It's like a brilliant star with a tail. We all know it's a sign of a great disaster. The trouble is no one knows who will suffer the disaster — the English or the Normans. The English lords are telling Harold he should invade Normandy and put a stop to Wicked William's plans, but he won't do it.

> WHEN WILLIAM SETS SAIL WE'LL JUST SINK HIS SHIPS. WE'VE A STRONG NAVY. EASY.

May

Would you believe it? An invasion on the south coast and the navy was away in the north!! Were the invaders sent by that William of Normandy? No, they were led by Harold's own brother . . . treacherous Tostig. As soon as Harold marched from London to fight him, Tostig jumped in his boat and sailed away. They reckon he's doing a deal with the Viking they call Hardrada — Hard Ruler — for the two of them to attack the north of England. Poor Harold won't know if he's coming or going! But he will know who his friends are, and they don't include Wicked William, Horrible Hardrada or Terrible Tostig!

August

Still no sign of those Normans. Some say they're waiting for the right wind to carry their ships over the Channel.

8 September

Oh dear! Oh dear! Oh dear! Harold's army couldn't wait on the south coast for ever. They've had to go home to help with the harvest. But the navy's been sent to London and some terrible storms have wrecked a lot of them. I hope that Wicked William doesn't decide to come now!

They say William has lost a lot of ships in the same storms. Norman bodies were washed ashore and he had them buried secretly so the rest of the troops wouldn't be upset. Wimps. They'll never beat Heroic Harold even if they do get across the Channel!

20 September

Hardrada is here! He landed in Yorkshire and drew first blood. When I say blood I mean blood! Our Harold wasn't there so Hardrada attacked his earls. The English were driven into the marshes at Fulford near York and slaughtered. There were so many bodies the Vikings were able to cross the marsh by stepping on corpses like stepping-stones!

Now Horrible Hardrada wants food and drink from the people of York. He makes a terrible demand. . .

TO THE PEOPLE OF YORK,
   WE WANT BREAD AND WE WANT WINE.
SO THAT YOU DON'T BETRAY US I WANT
150 CHILDREN FROM YORK AS MY
PRISONERS. MY MEN WILL COLLECT THEM
FROM STAMFORD BRIDGE THIS MONDAY
25th. BE THERE OR BEWARE!

                    HARDRADA

25 September

What a day! Hardrada and Tostig turned up to collect their hostages at Stamford Bridge. But they had less than half of their army and they didn't have all their weapons! Guess who turned up to spoil their party? Our heroic Harold!

Harold made an offer to his brother Tostig.

TOSTIG, I OFFER YOU A THIRD OF THE KINGDOM IF YOU WILL GIVE IN.

WHAT ABOUT MY ALLY, HARDRADA?

I OFFER HIM JUST 7 FEET ...ENOUGH TO BURY HIM!

I DIDN'T BRING THE KING OF NORWAY TO ENGLAND TO BETRAY HIM. WE WILL FIGHT YOU, HAROLD.

And what a fight it was! A Viking hero blocked the bridge and slew 40 English before they could cross. The English sent a boat under the bridge, pushed a pike through the planks and stabbed him from below.

Harold's men swarmed over the Vikings. Hardrada, with little armour on, took an arrow in the windpipe and died. Tostig was hacked down when he refused to surrender.

Harold's English have defeated the invaders. The man is unbeatable! Now he is heading south just in case Wicked William lands there. He leaves his exhausted northern army behind. He'll have fresh men from the south if he needs them.

28 September

It's all happening this week! William the Norman has landed with his army on the south coast as Harold rides to meet him. That Wicked William was soon spreading stories about Harold. . .

DID YOU KNOW YOUR EVIL HAROLD KILLED HIS BROTHER TOSTIG AND SLICED THE HEAD OFF THE CORPSE?

14 October

Gallant Harold finally came face to face with Duke William today near Hastings. And that's where Harold will be staying. The English fought all day but in the end the Norman knights and archers destroyed them. They say Harold was wounded in the eye and cut to pieces by William's knights. There is even a story that Wicked William himself had a chop or two at the corpse. Harold's brothers died with him. So mark today in your calendars for all time. It's the end of Saxon England and the start of Norman England.

15 October

King Harold's corpse has been taken to the seashore and buried under a pile of stones. The cruel conqueror William refused to give him a Christian burial. But he did give-him a headstone reading:

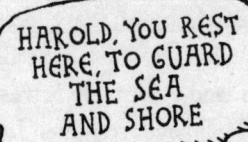

HAROLD, YOU REST HERE, TO GUARD THE SEA AND SHORE

October

William and the Normans have been taking town after town as they march to London. The English have no castles to make it harder for William. But William and his Normans were almost stopped by something they got from Canterbury . . . the disease of dysentery. William and his soldiers are starting to fall sick with vomiting, fever and diarrhoea with blood. Some die but William lives.

November

London has surrendered and begs William to take the crown.

25 December

It's 'Happy Christmas, Your Grace', as Duke William was crowned King of England. The cheers of his Normans inside Westminster Abbey made the soldiers outside think there was a riot. They started burning and looting the city. William was crowned amidst flames! Still, this is what we'll have to expect now the Normans are in charge.

31 December

Goodbye from 1066. And many happy New Years to you all. You'll forget many things in your lifetime, but you'll never forget heroic Harold, William the Conqueror or me . . . 1066.

Live like a Norman

Name that Norman

The Normans' Viking ancestors often gave their people nicknames-but they didn't always call people the nicknames to their face. Harold Bluetooth may not have minded you using his nickname too much. But you'd probably have got a clout from Olaf the Stout!

The Normans carried on this habit with some of their leaders. Duke William's mother wasn't married to his father so his enemies called him William the Bastard ... his friends (and sensible people) called him William the Conqueror.

Can you match the nicknames to these Normans?

Of course the meanest-sounding nickname went to the French king who invited the Vikings into Normandy in the first place – he was Charles the Simple. But in those days 'simple' meant 'pure' rather than stupid. Simple, isn't it?

Eat like a Norman

The Norman recipes we have are not very detailed. If you want to taste Norman-type food then you have to work a lot of it out for yourself – how much to put in each mixture and how long to cook it.

Here's a Norman dish you may like to try. It was probably eaten by the rich Normans and not their poor peasant farmers. If it doesn't work very well then have a cat or dog handy to help you eat it.

Nasty Norman pasty

You need:
Meat
Eggs
Cheese
Pastry

To make:
Boil the meat in a pan of water till it is cooked.
Make pastry and roll it out.
Chop up the cooked meat, beat the eggs and grate the cheese then stir them together.
Make the mixture into balls about the size of apples.
Wrap each ball in pastry.
Bake in a hot oven till the pastry is golden brown.

To serve:
Place on a wooden plate and eat with a knife and fingers.

Remember to get an adult to do the sharp knife bits and the boiling water stuff. It is much more fun to watch an adult chop their scalded fingers off than it is to chop your own. After all, you probably need your fingers to pick your nose, don't you?

It shouldn't kill you ... though it is best to remember: the Normans ate this and they are all dead!

Salty science

Of course your meal will taste better with salt in it. In Norman times you couldn't pop along to the local supermarket and buy a packet. To get some in your salt cellar you had to buy it from a salt seller.

Where did the salt seller get his salt?

Sometimes salt was dug from pits in the ground and you could make a lot of money if you owned a salt mine…

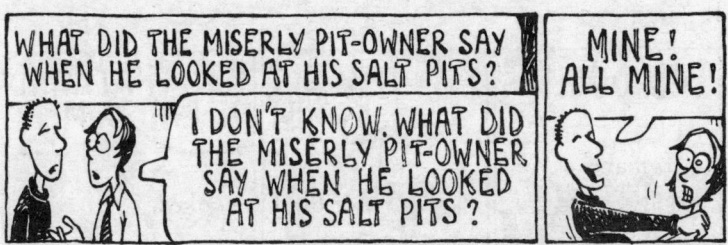

WHAT DID THE MISERLY PIT-OWNER SAY WHEN HE LOOKED AT HIS SALT PITS?

I DON'T KNOW. WHAT DID THE MISERLY PIT-OWNER SAY WHEN HE LOOKED AT HIS SALT PITS?

MINE! ALL MINE!

But if you lived close to the coast and wanted to save some money then you could make your own salt from sea water. The Normans knew enough science to be able to do it.

POOR WOMAN'S WEEKLY

Salt that supper

Want to give your family a real treat tonight? Then sprinkle their food with salt, fresh from the sea!

Simply fill a pot with sea water and set it to boil.

When the water's boiled away the salt will have formed a white crust around the pot. Wait till it cools – you don't want to burn those lovely hands, do you? Then scrape the salt from the sides of the pot and store it in a cool dry place till you need it.

Scrummy!

Horrible Histories Health Warning: Don't try this at home. Sea water in the 2000s isn't as pure as it was in the 1000s!

As well as flavouring food, salt could be used to preserve it. In the days before fridges meat could be covered in salt to stop it going bad.

This was useful in the Norman world. There wasn't usually enough grass to keep all the animals over the winter. So any spare animals were killed and the meat salted. Would you enjoy the job of deciding which of those sweet little calves and lambs and piglets should feel father's axe?

Dazzling dressers

Peacocks have the fancy feathers and the terrific tails. Peahens look boring alongside them. And it was a bit like that in Norman times. It was the rich men who were the flashy dressers.

Peculiar 'poulaines'

Norman soldiers probably invented 'poulaines' – the famous shoes that had long, pointed toes. In time the toes curled up in great loops and had to be chained to the knee to stop the flop.

But in Norman times there was a story that the shoes were invented by Fulk, Duke of Anjou. (Anjou is just a bit to the south of Normandy.) The story goes that Fulk had a lump growing on his foot and he designed the shoes to hide the fact he had an ugly foot. It's possible that Fulk did wear the shoes but he probably didn't 'invent' them – he just borrowed the idea from his knightly Norman neighbours.

WARNING: Do not read the following if you are easily shocked or need a sense of humour transplant. Two hundred and fifty years after Fulk invented (or didn't invent) 'poulaines' they were turned into something quite disgraceful by some Frenchmen. They stuffed the long toes with sawdust and shaped them to look like a man's naughty bits. The French king Charles V banned such rude shoes in 1367.

True or false

History can be horribly difficult. Even a history teacher would struggle to get ten out of ten with these quick but quirky questions. Try these on some sad teacher, get them to answer true or false, and see who will be the conqueror…

1 A Norman boy could became a monk at the age of seven and would never be able to give up the monastery.

2 The Normans ate canaries on toast.

3 The Domesday Book wasn't called the Domesday Book.

4 Some Norman women used the poisonous deadly nightshade plant to make their eyes more attractive.

5 Norman minstrels played bagpipes.

6 Norman town houses had kitchens next to the dining room so the food stayed hot.

7 A Norman knight slept better in his tent if he had a dolly over his head.

8 The Normans enjoyed Easter eggs.

9 The Normans always built their castles on waste land so no one lost fields or houses.

10 Normans on the coast had a lifeboat rescue service for ships in the English Channel.

Answers:

1 False. Before the Normans invaded England it had been true that boys took vows at the age of seven that could never be broken. If they did leave the monastery then they became outlaws. But the Normans changed this. Boys spent nine years in the monastery and, at the end of that time, they could leave – or stay for ever. But there was a catch in some monasteries. If you left before the age of 16 you might have to pay the monks for what they had taught you! Imagine that! Having to pay to leave school!

LEAVE WHEN YOU'RE *NINE* ?? I THOUGHT IT WAS NINETY!

2 False. The Normans brought canaries from the Canary Islands (believe it or not). The Canary Islanders loved to eat the little feathered foodstuff but the Normans wanted them for their singing.

3 True. A hundred years after it was written the book was nicknamed the 'Domesday Book' because it was like the Christian Day of Judgement (Doomsday) in that there could be no appeal against it. You were stuck with what the book said about your land and your wealth. The book called itself a 'descriptio' which is a Latin word meaning a 'writing down'. It was kept in the Royal Treasury at Winchester and the early Normans knew it as 'The Winchester Book'. (No prizes for guessing why.) By 1170 people were calling it 'Domesday' and as late as the 1900s it was still being used to settle arguments over who owned what. Bet your school exercise books don't last that long!

4 True. But very rarely! Norman women in Western Europe used hardly any make-up. Rich women in Eastern Europe used lip colour and drops of deadly nightshade to make the black centre of the eyes (the pupils) open wide. Gorgeous.

HOW COME HER PUPILS ARE SO WIDE?

SHE'S DEAD

5 True. The Normans enjoyed good music (which makes you wonder why they liked the bagpipes). With harps, fiddles, flutes, cymbals, bassoons, trombones and trumpets they could have tortured your eardrums till they burst.

6 False. The houses were made of wood and the roofs were thatched with reeds. If they caught fire the house could be destroyed in half an hour. Kitchens were built separately from the house so there was less chance of careless cooks setting the house on fire. Food would not be so hot when it reached the table. Better a cool dinner than a hot house, they reckoned.

AH! HERE COMES LUNCH

7 True. The tent pole went through a hole in the roof – called an 'onion'! To stop the rain coming through the gap between pole and hole a cap was put on top. This cap was called a 'dolly'.

8 True. During Lent (the weeks before Easter) the Church did not allow Christians to eat eggs. So housewives would save up all their eggs to have as a special treat on Easter Day. They would be boiled and coloured with natural dye – try boiling an egg with onion skins and see what happens! Have your boiled eggs blessed by a priest and scoff them. Sorry – no chocolate eggs, fat face.

9 False. The Normans sometimes found new sites for their castles but they often built them slap bang in the middle of a town. And what do you usually have in the middle of a town? That's right, houses. What happened to the houses? The people were thrown out and they were flattened – 160 homes in Lincoln and another hundred in Norwich, for example. Eudo Dapifer built a castle at Eaton Socon over a church and graveyard. Spooky, eh?

10 False. Quite the opposite! In 1046 a fleet from Flanders was storm-damaged in the English Channel. People from the Norman coast villages hurried to the beaches and waved lanterns to guide the ships to the shore. When the storm-bashed sailors landed the villainous villagers massacred them and stole the cargoes from the ships!

Terrific tales

People in Norman times worked hard from sunrise to sunset – then they stopped because it was too dark to carry on. They were just like you after a hard day at school – they wanted some entertainment.

You turn on the television or the computer or even pick up a book. The Normans had none of these things. What they had were 'jongleurs'. A jongleur was a musician, a juggler, and an acrobat. He was also a story-teller. He recited or sang long story-poems about great heroes like Roland and Oliver.

> YOUNG OLIVER AND ROLAND, THEY WENT OFF TO FIGHT IN SPAIN.
> THEY FOUGHT AGAINST THE SARACENS BUT GOT BATTERED IN THE BRAIN. TRA LA!
> OUR BRAVE YOUNG MEN GOT MASSACRED AND NEVER FOUGHT AGAIN.
> THEIR SAD, SAD TALE LEFT THEIR FRIENDS JUST CRYING LIKE A DRAIN. TRA LA!

IT'S SO SAD

Oliver and Roland had been Christian knights and may really have existed. They fought a gallant but hopeless battle against the Saracens (the Norman name for Muslim warriors). The two friends faced a mighty army alone but Roland was too proud to call for help. They were killed, of course. The story was told as an example to Norman crusaders who were urged to copy their bravery.

There is a legend (it may even be true) that a jongleur led William the Conqueror's troops into the Battle of Hastings.

The Norman historian, Wace, said…

A minstrel named Taillefer went in front of the Norman army, singing and juggling with his sword while the troops marched behind singing the Song of Roland.

THEY MUST BE TOUGH IF THEY CAN PUT UP WITH THAT!

Sounds a bit like a bunch of football supporters on their way to a match. We don't know what Harold's English troops sang.

WE LOVE YOU ROLAND, WE DO!
ROLAND DIED AND SO WILL YOU!

Brave Brit 1

When the Normans arrived in England they found the British had their own legends – dead and living. The dead hero was King Arthur. The Normans loved the story of Arthur and their writers and poets turned him from a British warrior into a magical king. Here's how the story grew…

- In 1135 Geoffrey of Monmouth writes about Arthur. (Though another writer at that time says, 'It is quite clear that everything Geoffrey wrote about Arthur was made up.')
- In 1155 a jongleur called Wace tells Arthur's story and added a bit about a Round Table.

- In 1160 Chretien de Troyes adds bits to the story to make Arthur a knight in armour, not just a British warrior.
- In 1190 a poet called Robert be Boron adds the bit about Arthur's knights and the Holy Grail – the cup that Jesus drank from at the last supper. People who drink from that can live for ever.
- Around 1200-ish an English priest adds that Arthur isn't dead, just sleeping. He'll wake up when England is threatened again. (So where was the sleepy old wrinkly when William the Conqueror landed?)

But there's an even stranger story about the discovery of Arthur's tomb at Glastonbury Abbey.

Arthur's grave

In 1184 there was a disaster when Glastonbury Abbey burned down. The monks were poor and were desperate for money. They needed visitors. Tourists! Pilgrims! But how could they attract them?

There was one thing that might help...

Do you know? How could they cash in on that story and make Glastonbury a tourist attraction? Someone had a brilliant idea!

And, would you believe it, when the monastery was being rebuilt Arthur's tomb *was* found there! The monks' story was a good one. They said…

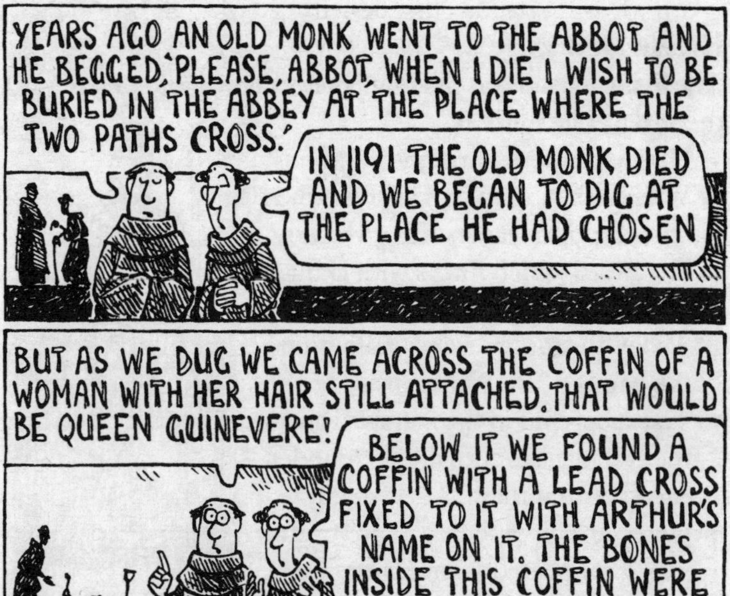

YEARS AGO AN OLD MONK WENT TO THE ABBOT AND HE BEGGED, 'PLEASE, ABBOT, WHEN I DIE I WISH TO BE BURIED IN THE ABBEY AT THE PLACE WHERE THE TWO PATHS CROSS.'

IN 1191 THE OLD MONK DIED AND WE BEGAN TO DIG AT THE PLACE HE HAD CHOSEN

BUT AS WE DUG WE CAME ACROSS THE COFFIN OF A WOMAN WITH HER HAIR STILL ATTACHED. THAT WOULD BE QUEEN GUINEVERE!

BELOW IT WE FOUND A COFFIN WITH A LEAD CROSS FIXED TO IT WITH ARTHUR'S NAME ON IT. THE BONES INSIDE THIS COFFIN WERE THOSE OF A VERY LARGE MAN. ARTHUR HIMSELF!

AND HERE'S THE LEAD CROSS TO PROVE IT!

Visitors and pilgrims flocked to the Abbey (even the King came to see the grave) and Glastonbury Abbey became the richest monastery in Britain.

But were the monks telling the truth? If you want to make a fortune then find a dead hero in your back garden. After 800 years some people still believe the story of Arthur's burial at Glastonbury! They even believe in his Round Table.

Do you believe it? Or is it just Norman nonsense?

Brave Brit 2

The living legend was the English freedom-fighter, Hereward the Wake. The truth is…

- Hereward went on fighting against William the Conqueror's forces when other English leaders had given up.
- Hereward joined forces with Danish invaders and robbed Peterborough Abbey to stop its riches falling into the hands of the Normans.
- The rebels hid in the marshes where the Normans eventually surrounded and captured them.
- Hereward escaped … and pretty well disappeared from history.

But he didn't disappear from legend. His adventures, like Arthur's, grew greater and more fantastic every time they were told by jongleurs. Maybe Hereward retired and got to hear some of the jongleur tales about himself!

Maybe Hereward's legendary deeds need a new jongleur epic for reciting around the fire at your castle hearth (or your nearest central-heating radiator will do if you don't live in a castle).

Hereward's revenge

My friends I'll sing a song to you, if you your seats will take;
I'll tell you all of our great hero, Hereward the Wake.
He was away from England when the Normans came to Hastings.
And missed the mighty battle where old Harold took a pasting.

Our hero came back home and found his younger brother dead.
'The dirty rotten Normans, they have killed our kid!' he said.
'I'll be revenged, you wait and see, with English help and Dane!'
And off he set to find some ways to bring the Normans pain.

When he arrived at his old house the great hall it was swarmin'
With knights and soldiers all around, each one a deadly Norman.
'I can't fight fifty men,' he sighed ... our hero was not thick.
'To take them on I need to think of some real clever trick!'

Our Hereward decided as a Norman he would pose,
He pinched a pointy helmet (with that straight bit down the nose).

And then he slipped inside his home where Norman soldiers feasted.
He drank pure English water while the Normans wined and eated.

The bloated Normans fell asleep but Hereward was awake,
He took his knife and slit their throats, 'Take that!' he cried,
    'That take!'
Then Hereward he cut the Norman heads off at the neck.
'I'll teach you Norman nasties to go killing us, by heck!'

Then he found some nails and a hammer (in his garden shed),
And he decorated each doorway with a nasty Norman head.
So no one would come asking him, 'Now whose dead heads are
    those?'
He left their pointy helmets on (with that straight bit down the
    nose).

Some say the Normans caught our hero Hereward the Wake,
One day when he was fast asleep, and his brave life they taked.
But I am sure he still lives on, our Hereward the Wake,
Who found that fighting Norman knights was just a piece of cake.

TRA-LA! TRA-LA! OH FOL-DE-ROL!
TRA-LA! TRA-LA! TRA-LA! TRA-LEE!
TRA-LA! TRA-LA! OH FOL-DE-ROL!
I'LL BID YOU ALL
GOOD-BYE-EE!

Did you know... ?

Hereward was given the name 'The Wake' because he was always 'watchful'. It didn't mean he was always awake.

He *did* go to sleep but he never slept in a bed! He always slept alongside it. An enemy could have sneaked in while Hereward the Wake wasn't awake. If the enemy attacked the bed then he'd miss Hereward the Wake who'd wake.

Good tip, that, for those of you who go away on school trips.

The knight visitor

Jongleurs had to be paid for their entertaining. They could choose to travel around ... then they could sing the same songs over and over again, but they weren't sure when they'd get their next pay-day. The alternative was to stay in one castle ... then they became known as minstrels and had to keep coming up with new songs all the time, but at least they were sure of food and shelter.

Generally poor people couldn't afford to hire a jongleur and they didn't have musical instruments themselves. So what could they do to entertain themselves and the kids? Tell stories, of course. Here is a story from Norman times that was told all over Europe. Are you sitting comfortably?

49

Once upon a time there was a brave young knight called Prince Hugo. There was nothing our young Hugo liked better than doing a bit of embroidery. Hugo made all his own dresses and let his hair grow down to his waist.

'He's a bit ... odd,' the courtiers in his castle whispered to one another. But Hugo had his reasons. He didn't let the gossip needle him.

Hugo could have passed for a girl ... which, as it happened, was exactly what he wanted.

You see, he'd heard about the poor princess Hilde. She was the most beautiful, clever and tragic princess in the whole of Normandy ... maybe even in the whole world. Hilde's father, Count Walgund, had locked her in a tall tower. The tower was in a forest and the forest was infested with the wildest wolves in the west.

Count Walgund was so devoted to his dear daughter that he didn't want to lose his lovely lass to some layabout lout of a lad. He didn't want her running off and getting married – unless it was to a perfect husband.

One day Hugo put on his best frock, embroidered by himself with a squillion sequins he'd sewn on, and arrived at Count Walgund's castle. 'I am a lost lady whose homeland has been conquered by a cruel king. I ask only a bed for the night, good count!'

Before the count could answer, his countess cried, 'Look at that dress! What a work of a needle-woman's wondrous art! You simply must teach our daughter how to embroider like that, mustn't she, Count?'

To say the dress was the work of a woman is, of course, sexist. Countess Walgund wouldn't get away with it today, would she lads? Boys today know their needles from their nine-pound notes, oh dear me, yes! Anyway the daft old bat was wrong because Hugo was a bloke!

Now we know that's exactly what our clever little Hugo was after all the time, don't we? Next day he was in the tower and teaching the lovely Hilde the ropes ... well the threads, if you know what I mean.

Hilde loved her new chum — loved her deep voice, her strong hands, her broad shoulders. 'Excuse me,' Hilde said after a week. 'But would I be correct in thinking that you are really a man disguised as a woman.'

Hugo clicked his long fingers. 'Curses! How did you guess?'

'I think it's probably the beard that gave you away,' Hilde confessed.

Hugo rubbed his rough chin and sighed. 'Sorry. You don't mind, do you?'

'Mind!' Hilde cried. 'I'm chuffed to fluffy fairy feathers! I think you're gorgeous!'

'You're not so bad yourself,' Hugo admitted.

Before another week was out they were married. Then Hugo declared, 'I have to leave now. I must find a way to persuade your father that I will make him a good son-in-law.'

'That's a bit sudden, my pet!' Hilde moaned, but she saw the sense in what he said. Hugo chopped his hair, and swapped his female dress for male chain-mail. Off he rode on a crusade where he fought side-by-side with Count Walgund. They were gone a long time. A long, long time ... well, a couple of years anyway ... and things had been happening in the tall tower.

'Come home with me, my brave young friend,' Count Walgund said to Hugo. Now, we know that's exactly what our clever little Hugo was after all the time, don't we?

But as they rode close to the tall tower Walgund saw a wolf cross the path and cried, 'After it! Kill it! We can't have wolves wandering my paths and putting my people in peril!'

So they chased the wolf who turned to face the fierce knights. The wolf dropped a bundle she was carrying and slipped off into the deep dark trees. But the knights saw the white linen bundle wriggling. They stopped and picked it up. It was a baby boy!

'Good grief! Wonder who you belong to, my little man!' Walgund warbled. 'What a wonderful child. Wouldn't mind one like that for my grandson! Let's visit my daughter in a nearby tower. See if she can care for it till we find the rightful mother.'

When they reached the tower and unlocked the door Hilde rushed out.

Was she going to fuss over her father?

Was she going to hug Hugo?

No!

She ran across the courtyard and snatched the baby from the two men and wailed, 'My baby! The washerwoman left the kitchen door open this morning and he crawled off into the forest! I was sure he'd be killed by wolves!'

'Your baby?' Count Walgund said in wonder. 'Who's the father?'

Hilde raised her arm and pointed at Prince Hugo. 'Why, Hugo here!'

The count was confused, you can count on that. But, when he finally understood he happily hugged his daughter, his grandson and his son-in-law.

'What a day!' Hugo sighed. 'I've gained a son I never knew I had.'

'What a day!' Walgund cried. 'I've gained a son and a grandson I never knew I had!'

'I've waited for your return before I named the child,' Hilde said. 'What should we call him?'

Walgund looked at Hugo. Hugo looked at Walgund. The two knights looked at one another. They nodded. They said it together. 'Wolf, of course'.

Hilde and Hugo lived happy hever hafter.

Norman wisdom

Are you as wise as a Norman? To understand the past you have to know how the people *thought*. Here are a few Norman beliefs…

1 *The Normans believed*… that many of their Muslim enemies were cowards. The Normans had won great victories in Europe where their charging knights smashed the enemy to the ground. But when the Norman Crusaders met the Muslim forces they had problems. The Muslims didn't line up and wait to be smashed to the ground! Instead they rode in a circle around the Crusaders and shot arrows at them from a distance.

Many Norman knights believed there was a reason for this…

Normans later learned to respect their Muslim enemies.

2 *The Normans believed*… that living too long in the Holy Land – what we call the Middle East today – was unhealthy. The hot climate and the strong wine affected the brain.

(Of course the easy answer would be not to drink the wine, but the water could be even more deadly … and Coca-Cola hadn't been invented.) As a result people back in Europe said…

THE WEATHER OUT THERE MAKES PEOPLE MAD THEN DEAD!

3 *The Normans believed*… that painful punishments were the fairest. If they locked a criminal in jail then the family might starve. That would punish the innocent family. So, instead, they thought it was better to make a public display of the criminal – parade them in the stocks so that everybody could see this was a person not to be trusted. For more serious crimes they could decide to cut a bit off a criminal – a hand or a nose, perhaps. The criminal could then go back to work and support the family!

BUT I'M A HANDY MAN!

4 *The Normans believed*… that God would help them to give justice to criminals. Like the English before them they settled some cases by having a trial by 'ordeal'. A woman accused of theft could be made to hold a red-hot iron bar. Her hand was bandaged. If it healed she was innocent. A man could be tied up and thrown into water that had been blessed – if he sank he was innocent. (A bit like witch trials of later years.)

5 *The Normans believed...* that God was on their side, especially when they were fighting against the Muslims in Sicily or the Holy Land. The head of the Catholic Church, the Pope, told them, 'Look, lads, it's OK to kill those Muslims. God will forgive you.' So the Norman knights hacked away happily, believing it wasn't murder ... even when it was. It wasn't only the Pope who said killing was all right. God sent a messenger from heaven personally! None other than Saint George! At the battle of Cerami in 1063 he turned up to help 130 Normans defeat thousands of Muslims. The soldiers reported...

> SAINT GEORGE APPEARED ON A WHITE HORSE WITH A LANCE. THERE WAS A FLAG ON THE END OF THE LANCE WITH A WONDERFUL CROSS ON IT. WE'D HAVE LOST IF HE HADN'T LED OUR CHARGES!

The Pope believed the story and sent a flag, like the one in the vision, for the Normans to carry into future battles.

Saint George turned up again 35 years later at the battle for Antioch in the Holy Land. An unknown writer said...

> *Our soldiers saw a countless army of men on white horses whose banners were all white. When our men saw this they realized this was help sent by Christ and the leader was Saint George. This is quite true for many of our men saw it.*

ALL WHITE?

YES, THANK YOU

Sadly old Georgie wasn't around at Hattin in 1187 when the Crusaders were smashed. Perhaps it was his day off! He then returned a few years later to help Richard the Lionheart win another victory in the Holy Land. Bet the Crusaders wished he'd make his mind up ... or send a letter to let them know he'd be around!

6 *The Normans believed...* that their doctors knew best. In the 1100s a knight was wounded in the leg and the wound became infected. An Arab doctor treated the wound and it started to get better.

THANKS, DOC!

عَفوًا!

it's nothing

58

An Arab soldier, Usamah Ibn Munqidh described what happened…

Yesterday a doctor arrived from Europe. A small man with a curling brown beard and rather dirty hands. 'What are you doing to this knight?' he demanded.

'I am placing a herbal plaster on the wound to help it heal,' the Arab doctor said.

'Herbal plaster! Nonsense!' the European doctor snorted. 'You Arabs are ignorant, simple people. You know as much about medicine as I do about the moon.' He turned to the knight and said, 'I have seen wounds like this many times. They fester and the leg turns green. The blood is poisoned and the poison kills the patient.'

The knight turned pale. 'Is there nothing you can do to stop this?'

'Only one thing,' the doctor from Europe told him. 'We must cut off the leg before it turns bad!'

'Cut off my leg! the knight moaned. 'I'll never ride or fight again!'

'You'll never ride or fight if you die from the poisoned blood. Make up your mind, man. Lose the leg or lose your life!'

'Then I must lose my leg,' the knight whispered.

The doctor called for a soldier to fetch an axe and he instructed the man where to strike the leg. The Arab doctor turned to me and said,'This is madness! Can you do nothing to stop him?'

I shook my head.'They are guests in our country. We must respect their customs.

The knight turned on his side and I held his arms while the doctor stretched the leg out on a board of wood. When the axe came down the scream of the kight was terrible to hear. 'Again, man! Again!' the doctor from Europe cried, 'You failed to cut through!'

The second blow removed the leg. Blood from the wound soon stopped flowing. Blood does not flow long from corpses. The horror of the operation had killed the man.

The doctor from Europe shrugged his narrow shoulders. 'Ah, well. I had to try. He would have died anyway.' Then he left to practise his brutal skills on some other unlucky patients.

The Arab doctor turned to me and said, 'Such a waste.'

If I am ever wounded in battle then I hope my God lets me be treated by an Arab doctor and not a European butcher.

Little villeins

The Normans ran their countries under a 'feudal system'. Imagine that as a pyramid…

This is the king who sits at the top and owns the lot.

These are the barons who guard the king's land, and train the men to fight for the king who sits at the top and owns the lot.

These are the knights who look after the villages, and fight for their barons who guard the king's land, and train the men to fight for the king who sits at the top and owns the lot.

These are the villeins who work on the land and work for the knights who look after the villages, who fight for their barons who guard the king's land, and train the men to fight for the king who sits at the top and owns the lot.

These are the serfs who own no land but are owned by the knights who look after the villages, who fight for their barons who guard the king's land, and train the men to fight for the king who sits at the top and owns the lot while they own nothing, not even their bodies.

And lowest of all were the village children – nothing much changes there, then.

Tasks for tots

Was it pleasant being a peasant child? You'd have no school to go to! (So you couldn't learn to read and have the joy of *Horrible Histories* books, of course.)

What would you do all day with no school to imprison and torment you – no sick-making SATs, no dreadful detentions, no rotten reports, no evil essays and hideous homework! Would you be bored without these cool classroom capers?

Of course not! Your parents would find you work as soon as you could walk. Children in Norman times didn't have newspaper rounds and they probably didn't have to keep their bedrooms tidy or help with the washing up. Instead they helped on the land.

WE HAD TO BE IN SCHOOL FOR AN EXTRA 20 MINUTES

I HAD 2 HOURS OF HOMEWORK LAST NIGHT

I'VE GOT TO REVISE DURING THE *HOLIDAYS*

I'VE BEEN WORKING 19 HOURS EVERY DAY SINCE I WAS ONE AND A HALF

You'd have to…

- **collect wood** from the forest for the family fire (but watch out for the big bad wolves and outlaws). Every November villeins (and their children) gathered baskets full of wood for their lord's winter fires. For each basket they gathered he gave them one log!

THIS IS A LOG?

- **collect acorns** and beech nuts from the forest floor in autumn to feed the family pigs. (Then kill and eat the pig in winter and get your own back!)
- **prod the oxen** in the bum with a sharp stick so they'll pull the plough. (But be careful the angry ox doesn't turn and prod you in the bum with its horns.)

I THINK YOUR SHARP STICK IS A LITTLE TOO SHARP

- **turn the grindstone** at harvest time so the men can sharpen their sickles. (Such a boring job you'll be sickle of it in no time.)
- **polish the arrow heads** of your father's arrows using sand (and an arrow strip of cloth).

The good news is the Church banned work on a Sunday. So there's just the chance you may find time to play a game or two…

Games you may want to play

Bubble beaters

Children in Norman times enjoyed blowing bubbles just as
children (and some sad grown-ups) do today. The Norman
children didn't have plastic loops – they used hollow stalks of
straw. Instead of washing-up liquid they'd use Norman bath
soap, but it worked the same. If you want to check...

You need:

- a teaspoon of washing-up liquid
  stirred in half a cup of water
- drinking straws
- a watch with a second hand

To play:

Place one end of a straw in the mixture. Blow gently at the
other end till a bubble appears. (Don't suck or you'll end up
with the cleanest tonsils in town!)

With two or more players the winner is the one whose bubble
lasts longest.

Conkering

William wasn't just a Conqueror. He was a conker-er too!
The Normans taught the English the game of conkers. People
still play it today – clever kids play conkers but so do adults
who take it quite seriously and have a world championship

every year! (They're bonkers.) If you care to try it then you will be playing a game about a thousand years old...

You need:
- at least one conker for each player
- string – cut to lengths about half a metre long
- a meat skewer

To make:
Drill a hole through the centre of the conker with the skewer. Push a piece of string through the hole. Tie a knot in the string so the conker can't slip off.

collect   drill   push   knot

To play:
Toss a coin to decide who goes first. Player 1 swings their string to smash their conker into player 2's. If you hit the conker have another go. (If you miss you don't go again till it's your turn.) Player 2 then has a go at hitting player 1's conker. The first player to shatter the other's conker is the winner.

Punching puppets
Boys dressed in chain-mail coats, carried small lances and shields and played. We don't know what the rules were but

they probably charged at one another the way the grown-ups did on horses. (A point was scored every time a knight shattered his lance on his opponent's shield.) And no doubt there were accidents where smashing shields led to broken noses and splintered lances went into eyes. In other words, nothing too serious and only the odd death here and there.

A much safer game was fighting with puppets. If the weather was bad then the children got out their string puppets. These were about 30 to 40 cm high. The children stood (or knelt) facing one another and pulled the strings to make their puppets fight.

Super skating
In the 1100s William Fitz Stephen wrote about young men skating on the ponds and rivers in winter. If you want to go to your local ice-rink and save on the cost of hiring ice-skates then here's the way to do it...

You need:
- the shin bones of a sheep or pig (from your local butcher – tell him it's for your poor pooch and he'll give them free!)
- strips of cloth (rip up your bedclothes or a teacher's shirt)
- two broom-handles
- a cushion

To make:

Boil the bones in a pot till the flesh drops off and the bones are white and clean. (Add carrots and onions to the water to make soup for when you get home chilled.)

Use strips of cloth to bind the bones to the bottom of your shoes and around your ankles.

Stuff the cushion down the back of your pants. (You'll look stupid but it will stop you getting a bruised and battered bum.)

Sharpen the bottom end of the broom handles and use them to push yourself along (like skis).

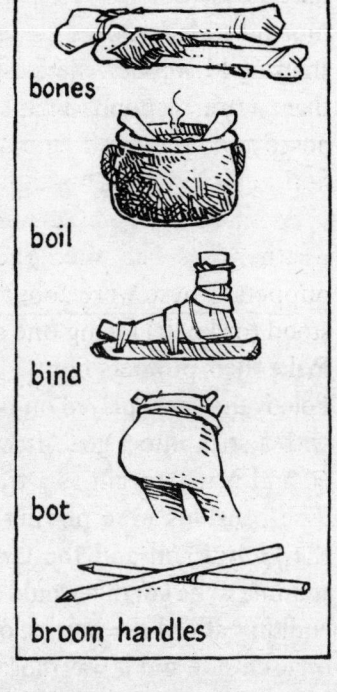

bones

boil

bind

bot

broom handles

To play:

Step on to the ice. Move one foot in front of the other and go as far as you can until you fall flat on your backside.

WHO NEEDS SKATES

Don't ask why anyone would want to do it. People do this at ice rinks all over the country and get a strange twisted pleasure out of it. Some even try it without padding in their pants! Crazy.

69

Did you know…?

Normans also enjoyed sledging down hills in snowy weather. Instead of wooden sledges they used a large chunk of ice from a nearby pond. That's an ice way to save money.

Polo

Polo is the sport played on ponies where you try to hit the ball with a stick into a goal. It was invented in Persia around 600 BC and it was meant as a training exercise for horse soldiers. The Muslims were playing it when the Normans arrived in the Holy Land and the Crusaders copied it. Norman boys training to be knights would enjoy it. (Peasants like you and me couldn't afford the horses, of course.) There could be dozens on each side and it was more like war than a ball game.

In Persia the queen and her ladies played it but the Crusaders would never have allowed women to join in. (Probably for the same reason men don't like women to play in their football teams – the men are scared of getting beaten!)

To enjoy this ancient sport today, here's an easy way to do it indoors…

You need:
- a five-a-side football pitch
- hockey sticks
- a tennis ball

To play:
Divide into two equal teams of ten- (or twelve- or fifty-) a-side. Players ride piggy-back on their team-mates. (Switch over when the 'horse' gets tired.) The hockey sticks are used to hit the ball into the opponents' goal. (The sticks must *not* be used to trip opponents' horses, smack opponents in the mouth or to annoy teacher by rattling them up and down wall bars.)

Did you know…?

In China (AD 910) one of the Emperor's favourite relatives was killed playing polo. Emperor A-pao-chi gave the order to have all of the surviving players beheaded.

Games you wouldn't want to play

Slinging scarecrows

Country children acted as killer scarecrows. They didn't just shoo the birds away – they killed the little blighters. Not only did a dead crow leave your parents' precious crops – it could also make a nice snack for dinner.

So learn the Scarecrow song from *The Wizard of Oz* ('If I Only Had a Brain') and get out there and frighten all feathered fiends. Here's how…

You need:
- a bootlace (leather is best)
- a piece of leather about 5 cm square
- a table-tennis ball

To make:

Make a hole at opposite corners of the leather and thread the lace through. Make a loop in one end of the lace and loop it over your forefinger.

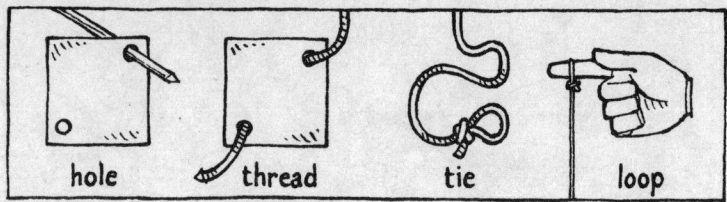

You now have a sling (similar to the one David used to kill Goliath, so be careful how you use it if you meet a giant!).

To shoot:

Place your ammunition (a table-tennis ball) in the leather pad. Hold the free end of the sling between your finger and thumb. Swing it quickly then release the free end of the lace. The ammunition will fly out.

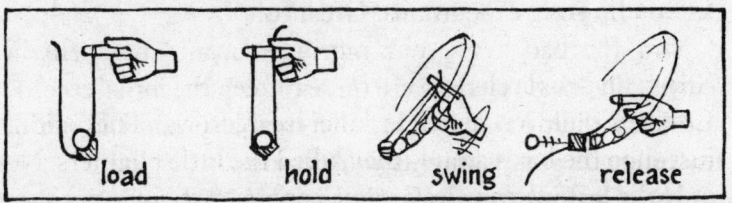

load   hold   swing   release

Note: It takes years of practice to get the action right, let alone hit a target! But don't worry, you have years sitting in freezing fields with nothing else to do. By the time you're grown up you'll be able to hit a tit at twenty paces!

Did you know... ?

Stone me, but it's true! The Norman army at the battle of Hastings is remembered for its archers. But the soldiers at the front were armed with slings. They'd have had a pocketful of stones but could always pick up more as they marched forward. Imagine getting one of those in your eye! Not a heroic way to go.

HE'S BEEN PEBBLE-DASHED!

The English fired back with stones attached to pieces of wood – a bit like a stone-age axe!

Scary school

From about the age of seven the sons of Norman lords and knights would train to be knights every afternoon. Good fun, eh? Riding and charging at targets (quintains) with your lance. Sword-fighting and murdering little rabbits and dear deer on hunting expeditions. Great fun!

Now the bad news. Your mornings would be spent in *lessons*. The castle clerks were there to keep the lords' records and keep their money right. But they also had the job of teaching you young knights your lessons.

These lessons were in lovely Latin! Yeuch!

And you don't need me to tell you what that means, do you? You do? Oh, very well. It means. 'Don't despair, have faith in God.' Write it on your next SATs paper and maybe God will give you a helping hand.

The Normans wrote their legal papers in Latin and (when you grew up) you'd have to put your seal on these so it helped if you knew what they meant.

And the really bad news ... Each clerk-teacher was armed with a stout stick. No, this wasn't to help him point at the blackboard. It was to whack you across the shoulders if you weren't trying hard enough. And, as a tough little trainee knight you must never cry ... or even show that it hurt you!

Chilling childhood

You think your life is hard, perhaps? Just be thankful you didn't grow up like one noble Norman boy. If you went through what he went through then you'd probably end up half crazed with fear. You certainly wouldn't sleep too well at night!

Here is his story...

I was just seven years old and starting to train as a knight when my father left home. He was the sixth Duke of Normandy and the only man who could keep the fighting lords from tearing it apart. The country was surrounded by our enemies. Everyone begged my father not to go but he said he wanted to go on a pilgrimage to Monte Gargano. (Some even said he went to beg God to forgive him for killing his own brother!) I never saw him alive again. He died on his way back — they say he may have been poisoned.

Before he left father got everyone to agree that I should be the next duke. I was left in the care of Count Alan but he died suddenly.

Count Gilbert took his place — he lasted a few months before he was brutally murdered while he was out riding. They told me Odo the Fat was the killer.

My tutor Turold died soon after in the same horrible way.

The head of my household was Osbern and his death was the most hideous of all. He was sleeping in my bed-chamber to protect me from my enemies. I heard the door open and saw William of Montgomery slip in. His knife glinted in the moonlight and before I could cry out he had slit Osbern's throat. Poor Osbern's blood lay in a river over my floor.

Osbern's friends avenged him – they broke into William of Montgomery's house and slew the killer and everyone else they found there. Blood for blood.

My only true friend was my mother's brother, Walter. He slept in my room and if we heard any strange noises at night he would lead me to hide in the only place we felt safe – in the cottages of the poor.

Father, Count Alan, Count Gilbert, Turold and Osbern. All died so that others could control me and so control Normandy.

Brutal and dreadful days. Maybe that's where I learned that the only way to survive was to be violent. To strike anyone who threatened me. Maybe that's where I learned that the law of the Norman duke was simple ... kill or be killed.

Who was the child that had such a grim life before his ninth birthday? William, Duke of Normandy – later called William the Conqueror. Remember that childhood when you look at the ferocious man he grew to be.

Miserable monarchs

William the Conqueror was a pretty nasty Norman at times. But the Norman kings and queen who followed him could have their nasty moments too…

Red Bill

Name: William II (nicknamed 'Rufus') 1056–1100

Claim to fame: Rufus took over the throne of England from his dad, William the Conqueror. But the Conqueror gave Normandy to one of his other sons, Robert. Rufus went back to Normandy and spent half his time helping Robert to fight the French – and the other half trying to pinch Normandy from him!

Dreadful deeds: Rufus upset everybody and especially the men of the Church. He stole Church lands and Church money and refused to make the popular Anselm the new Archbishop of Canterbury. Then Rufus fell sick. 'You're dying!' the churchmen told him. 'Give us what you want or you will burn in Hell!' Rufus panicked, gave the churchmen what they wanted – then recovered!

DO YOU THINK I SHOULD HAVE TOLD HIM HE ONLY HAD A COLD?

Dire death: Rufus went hunting in the New Forest. He fired an arrow at a stag and missed. He then called to a knight, Walter Tirel, 'Shoot!' So Walter shot him ... the king, not the stag. Rufus was so unpopular no one blamed Tirel!

YOU KILLED THE KING, YOU SAY? DEAR OH DEAR. STILL, NEVER MIND, WORSE THINGS HAPPEN AT SEA

The king's corpse was loaded on to a cart by some peasants and it's said that blood dripped all the way to Winchester Cathedral where he was buried.

Little Hen

Name: Henry I 1068–1135
Claim to fame: William the Conqueror's youngest son. The first Norman king to be born in England.
Dreadful deeds: Henry was as ruthless as his dad. In 1090 he and his brother Robert went to war against their brother, William II. They captured one of William's knights called Conan and took him up the stairs of

their castle tower. Conan begged them for mercy–but the brothers just laughed. Henry had a nasty death planned for Conan. He threw him out of the window.

Henry later had trouble with Robert, and ended up locking him away for the rest of his life ... and Robert died in his Cardiff Castle prison at the age of 80.

Dire death: Henry's doctor warned him, 'Don't eat those eels, they're bad for you.' Henry ate the eels and had a nasty pain in the gut. The doctor advised, 'What you need is a laxative. It will give you diarrhoea for a day or so but it will clear out your bowels.' Sadly the doctor wasn't a very good doctor. He gave Henry a bit of an overdose. It gave him diarrhoea all right! And it killed him. What a way to go! Pooh!

Sad Steve

Name: Stephen 1097–1154

Claim to fame: Stephen battled for the throne of England with his cousin, Matilda, and brought misery to the whole country.

Dreadful deeds: Before Henry I was dead Stephen swore Henry's daughter (Matilda) could be the next queen of England. What did he do when Henry I died? Grabbed the throne for himself. (That's a bit of a surprise because

Stephen was a good fighter but a bit of a wimp. He was badly bossed about by his mum and his wife. They probably pushed his bum on to the throne of England. This must have been painful because Stephen had a nasty condition called 'piles' which gave him a sore bum.)

Anyway, Matilda was furious and invaded and so it went on. *Dire death:* Stephen, like William the Conqueror, fell ill with a pain in the guts. It was probably a burst appendix. Today that can still kill people but, if they can get to hospital in time, doctors can operate to cut it out. Stephen didn't have any slicing surgeons so he died in agony.

Norman nastiness

The Normans could be ruthless at times. (And if they set fire to the thatch on your cottage you'd be pretty roofless yourself!)

One of William the Conqueror's cruellest acts was known as 'The Harrying of the North' when he destroyed a whole region. Usually he was merciful to his defeated enemies. What drove him to this awful act?

Evil English in darkest Durham

It would be wrong to think the cruelty was all on the part of the Normans. The English could be pretty nasty when they wanted to be.

Just 60 years before the Battle of Hastings the northerners had beaten the Scots, cut off the best-looking heads and put them on show around the walls of Durham. The message was clear to anyone who wanted to take over – 'Nothing personal, Mr Conqueror. We don't like being ruled by *anybody*!'

In January 1069 the Normans took the city of Durham … for a while. If a monk had kept a personal diary of those dire days in Durham, it might have looked something like this.

> 30th day of January, the year of our Lord one thousand and sixty-nine.
>
> Today I went to the market-place and saw our conquerors. The man Robert of Comines marched into our city at dawn with his army of seven hundred men and put soldiers at every street corner. A few brave men tried to gather and

attack them but they were hacked down by the men in chain armour. The bodies are still in the narrow streets and their blood is trickling towards the River Wear but it is freezing in the gutters before it gets there.

Comines spoke to the crowd – he spoke French so only a few of us understood. 'I am here by the right of William of Normandy, King of England,' he told us. 'Anyone who refuses to obey an order from me or one of my men will be executed on the spot.' He turned to the Bishop of Durham, Aegelwine, and said, 'Make sure these ignorant English know what I said.'

Our Bishop clutched at his cross and said boldly, 'It will end in your defeat, my lord Comines. You will be thrown out of Durham.'

The Norman sneered and said, 'Talking of being thrown out, I am throwing you out of your palace. It will become my home while I am in Durham. You can sleep in the monastery.'

It is a sad day for Durham. But as we left the market-place we heard the people muttering. A rebel army is already gathering and will attack very soon. As a man of God I hate bloodshed — but the Normans need to be taught a lesson. Let us see what God brings us tomorrow.

—

31st day of January, the year of our Lord one thousand and sixty-nine

Oh the horror and the pity and the glory of it. Early this morning the rebel army arrived and before the Normans were awake they'd broken down our city gates. The people rose to join them armed with sickles and knives. The Normans tried to attack but they were trapped as soon as they entered the narrow city streets.

The Normans were hacked to the ground. The blood of yesterday's dead English was washed away by the blood of the Norman soldiers. When the Normans saw what was happening some fled to join Robert Comines in the Bishop's palace. But the mob set fire to the house.

'You'll set fire to our church!' I tried to tell them as the flames blew towards the Minster. Then God showed his glory as the wind changed and saved our lovely building. A miracle of God!

But nothing could save Comines and his cut-throat killers. They burned to death and I still hear their screams in my mind. But it is silent out there now. A light snow is falling to cover the Norman bodies.

Every last Norman is dead. Tonight we will pray that they never return.

In fact just two Norman soldiers managed to escape and take the shocking news back to William the Conqueror.

He was not pleased. Not one bit.

The magical mist

Of course the Normans *did* return, but again they failed to take Durham. This time the people of the city believed they were saved by a miracle…

15th day of September, the year of our Lord one thousand and sixty-nine

Since those blood-soaked days of January we have been steeling ourselves for the return of Duke William's armies. Messengers arrived three days ago to say they had set off from York and probably arrive today. All of yesterday we prayed in the Minster for God to spare us and today we heard our prayers have been answered.

A rider clattered into the market-place on his sweating horse, demanding to be taken to the bishop. I was sure that the news would be bad but I led him up the steep streets to the bishop's new house. I led the man in to Bishop Aegelwine and you cannot blame me if I stayed a little while to hear the news.

'Bishop,' the man cried. 'It's a miracle! The

Norman army reached Northallerton, barely a day's march from Durham, and they've turned back!'

The bishop nodded but argued, 'That is no miracle, my son.'

'But it is! As they set off a sudden fog descended on them from heaven. The Normans could not see the road ahead of them. They were terrified. They were sure that it was a sign.'

I hurried from the room with the news for my brothers who were in the Minster. I rested my hand on the coffin of our dear Saint Cuthbert and felt it chilly and damp as if it were covered in a mist. 'Saint Cuthbert has saved us!' I told them. 'Saint Cuthbert has sent a fog to confuse our enemies! We are saved!'

And today the word has spread through Durham. We have been saved by Cuthbert's miracle.

The truth is never that simple. A Danish army had landed on the coast just as the Normans set off from York to march on Durham. That was the *real* reason the Norman army turned back. The invasion had to be dealt with first.

The miraculous path

The people and the monks of Durham may have believed the miracle of Saint Cuthbert. But they were still sure the Normans would be back – and that their first victim would be the corpse of old Saint Cuthbert in Durham Minster.

So the monks decided to move the coffin further north to the safety of the island of Lindisfarne. The island is just off the Northumberland coast and when the monks arrived they could find no boat to take them across.

Then they looked in amazement as the waters fell away and a path appeared. It let them walk all the way to the island. The monks cried...

ANOTHER ONE OF SAINT CUTHBERT'S MIRACLES!

The truth is this path appears twice a day, every day, when the tide goes out!

The monks left the coffin in safety and returned to Durham and a nasty shock – their Bishop Aegelwine had run away and taken some of Durham's richest treasures with him!

CHEEKY MONKY

Wise man, Aegelwine. He knew that this time the Normans would return and take their revenge. He didn't want to be around when they did. They were about to begin...

The Harrying of the North

Some of the stories told about the Normans show that wherever they went the message was, 'You don't mess with a Norman'.

The Norman invasion of England in 1066 didn't put William's bum safely on the throne. The English weren't going to give up just because King Harold had been hacked at Hastings.

In 1069 the English revolted in the south while the warrior-leader Edric the Wild went wild in the west. In the north the Vikings crossed the North Sea to help Saxon Prince Edgar.

The Vikings marched on York. The Norman defenders set fire to the city and left the safety of York castle to fight the enemy in open battle. They were wiped out...

The northern English towns and villages held fine fat feasts for the vicious Vikings. There were rumbles of rebellion in the rest of England.

William set off to sort out the nuisance in the north. He didn't just want to win. He wanted to destroy them so completely they would never rebel again. What he did became known as 'The Harrying of the North'.

The Vikings left York before William could catch them...

William set about destroying the northern region as he marched through it. Every English male was murdered.

The houses and the barns were burned. The farm animals were killed so there was nothing left for the people to eat.

Corpses were left to rot by the side of the roads and the desperate English survivors ate them to stay alive…

Horrible Histories Health Warning: Eating dead bodies you find in a ditch can damage your health. So don't do it.

Disease came along to add to the misery of the survivors. The northern towns and villages were still struggling to recover years later.

The North certainly didn't revolt again. The Conqueror's cruelty worked.

Twenty years after 'The Harrying of the North' William the Conqueror started to feel bad about his cruelty. It's said he was dead sorry … unlike the English who were simply dead dead.

The stuffed saint
When the Norman kingdom had settled, over 30 years later, they brought Cuthbert back to Durham to put him in the new cathedral the Normans were building there.

Before the body was moved to its new resting place the coffin was opened by ten monks. They reported that the body had not rotted and it smelled sweet!

It was 417 years old! Bet you don't look fresh and smell sweet when you're 417 years old!

A miracle? Or was the body mummified when it was first buried? Was the sweet smell the scent of the oils used?

The coffin can still be seen in Durham Cathedral today. But a) do not try to get into Cuth's coffin for a quick peek, and b) do not pour oil over your favourite granny in the hope she'll stay fresh for another 417 years!

Cuthbert appeared to have forgiven the Normans for disturbing his rest. There is a story that at the end of the 1100s the Norman Archbishop of York was seriously ill. The doctors said there was nothing they could do for him. Then he had a dream in which he was told to go to the tomb of Saint Cuthbert and sleep there. The Archbish did as he was told and ... Lo! He had a vision that old Cuth appeared and ran his hands over him. The Norman was cured immediately.

(Please note, that archbishop is now dead and has been for 800 years. Cuth's cure works once but you can't expect him to keep you going for ever.)

Whacking Walcher

The Normans gave all the top jobs in England to Norman lords. In the north the Bishop of Durham became a prince as well as a bishop. He ruled the church and the people.

The first Norman prince-bishop of Durham was William Walcher. It wasn't an easy job. English monks from a Tyneside monastery at Jarrow had to pick up the pieces of Walcher's last quarrel. If one of the young monks had written home, his letter may have described the event something like this...

16 May 1080

Dear Mum and Dad,

You never told me it was going to be so dangerous when you sent me to be a monk! Can't I come home now and work on the farm? I was in Gateshead this morning and you should see the mess! It was enough to make me sick. Far worse than slaughter-time on the farm each autumn. Let me tell you about it and then you can see why I want to come home.

You may remember Bishop Walcher was getting on quite well. He'd made a lot of friends with the great English families around here. And one of his best pals was Liulf of Lumley. Of course there were people jealous of Liulf weren't there? The ones who were most jealous were the bishop's own Norman friends. Especially that Gilbert!

That Gilbert was a monster! Worse

than William the Conqueror! You may have heard that Gilbert was so jealous of Liulf of Lumley he set off for the Lumley house and murdered him in his bed. Then he went off and tried to kill all of the rest of the Lumley family in their beds! He was wild as a fox in a chicken run.

Everybody blamed Bishop Walcher, didn't they? Gilbert was the bishop's man. There were riots up in Gateshead when the English heard about the Lumley murders. So the brave bishop said, 'Look, I'll come to a meeting with the Lumley family and make peace.'

'Yeah,' the Lumley family said. 'And make sure you bring your friend Gilbert with you!'

So off he went to Gateshead church. Naturally he had a hundred guards with him, but it didn't do him much good. You can imagine the mob that met them at the church! 'Kill the bishop! Kill the bishop!' they chanted.

Well, poor old Walcher fled into the church. But the mob forced him to send Gilbert outside to make peace. Make peace! They made pieces! Pieces of Gilbert! Bits of him in every corner of the churchyard.

And that's when they set fire to the church. The bishop staggered out, choking with the smoke. They say his eyes were so blinded by the smoke he couldn't see. Just as well, I suppose. Everybody in that English mob wanted to have a chop at him. He was a real mess.

I know this, Dad because they sent us from Jarrow this morning to tidy up and give Walcher a Christian burial. We found his body, stripped of its prince-bishop robes, and we could hardly recognize it. Like I say, a real mess. We had to pick it up, put it on a cart and take it back with us.

A few of the mob came back to the ruined church and pelted us with mud. 'Let the crows have him!' they told us. I tell you, Dad and Mum, I've never been so scared in my life!

They say the murderers have fled to Scotland. But I can't do that, can I? Please can I come home?

Your loving son, Eadulf

Cropped coast

In 1085 William the Conqueror was back in Normandy when news arrived – England was about to be invaded. King Cnut of Denmark was teaming up with his son-in-law, Robert of Flanders. Together they'd fight for the English throne that Cnut believed should be his.

William gathered a huge army and shipped it across the English Channel. Reports at the time were sensational…

READ ALL ABAHT IT! CHANNEL FILLED WITH SHIPS THAT STRETCH FROM THE ENGLISH COAST TO THE NORMANDY COAST! READ ALL ABAHT IT!

NORMAN NEWS – SHIPS SHORE TO SHORE

William wasn't sure where Cnut would land. He knew that an invading army could survive by looting the farms on the coast. So what did he do?

> *Answer:*
> William ordered that all the crops and stores of food along the English coast should be destroyed. The poor people who'd worked hard all year were moved inland for safety. The invasion never arrived so those farmers moved back to their homes by the coast … and hunger.

Caught red-handed

Bishop Odo of Bayeux was William the Conqueror's half-brother. In conquered England he acted as a judge and, with the help of a jury, decided arguments.

Being a member of a jury today means you have to be fair and honest. If you're not then you could go to prison. But prison isn't as bad as the punishment Odo saved for cheating jurymen in his day.

If there had been newspapers in Norman times then the case may have been reported like this…

English edition   Price : Half a dozen eggs

THE NORMAN NEWS

Jury Fury

Angry Odo

Bishop Odo gave the punishers some punishment today … and it didn't half hurt! Twelve members of the jury in the Islesham Manor Case have been found guilty of lying in court. Our readers will remember the case where the Bishop of Rochester and the Sheriff of Cambridge were arguing over who owned the stately home. The twelve good men and untrue of the jury decided to give it to the Sheriff.

That might have been an end to it but a Rochester monk made a sensational claim. The jury had not played fair, and, what's more, the mean monk could prove it!

Today Bishop Odo (The Basher Bishop, or Bish Bash as our readers know him) heard the evidence and decided the jury were indeed as bent as a ninegroat piece. First Bish Bash fined them till their purses were empty as Harold's eyesocket. Then he ordered that the guilty men should have their right hands plunged into boiling water.

Our ace reporter, Hugh Je Scoop, watched the sentence being carried out. 'I'd like to get my hand on the monk that fingered me,' muttered one victim (who wishes to remain nameless).

Juror in hot water

His wife Jeanne de Yorke (who also wishes to remain nameless) said, 'I told him that trying his hand at lying to Odo would get him in hot water. Once Odo takes matters in hand he always wins hands down. You have to hand it to him. Wasn't I right?'

Norman Italy

The Norman control of Italy began almost by accident, probably around the year 999. Forty Norman pilgrims were returning from Jerusalem to Normandy and rested at Salerno in Southern Italy. While they were there the town was raided by Saracens. The Normans were shocked to see that the Salerno citizens did little to stop them.

The Normans went to Prince Gaimar of Salerno and said: 'Give us horses and weapons and we'll sort out these Saracens for you!'

The Normans drove the Saracens away and the prince was delighted. Prince Gaimar begged them to stay but they refused. The prince loaded them with gifts and sent more gifts back to Normandy to persuade other Normans to return. Prince Gaimar's message was:

> Come to this land that flows with milk and honey and so many beautiful things

Normans knights returned to Italy and set about the invaders from all sides. They drove Greek invaders from Apulia in the south-west of Italy. But which were worse for the Italians? Their Greek enemies or Norman 'friends'? As William of Apulia said at the time…

All the people of Apulia feared the Normans and many perished as the victims of their cruelty

WHO ARE WE HARASSING TODAY?

DOES IT MATTER?

That's the Normans for you! Invite them in to help and they boss you about and beat you up. It's a bit like having burglars in your home and inviting bullies in to bash the burglars.

The Normans won five great victories in a row. But once the Greeks realized the power of the Normans they returned with a huge army to oppose them. The historian Amatus said…

October 1018
The Greeks swarmed over the battlefield of Ofanto like bees from an overflowing hive. Of 250 Normans only ten survived, the rest were cut to pieces.

The Normans didn't 'invade' Italy. They were just knights looking for a good fight. They'd fight for anybody who paid them. Some even joined the Greeks and fought against Normans who were on the side of Apulia. (At least they were kind to their Norman opponents when they defeated them!)

The heroic Hautevilles

And then along came the Hauteville brothers – all twelve of
them. Once these battling boys arrived then the Normans
started to take over southern Italy.

The Normans seemed to be outnumbered in every battle
they fought, yet they always won. Sometimes they avoided
fighting against huge numbers. Young William, for example,
challenged the enemy leader to 'single combat' – one against
one, a bit like a tennis match at Wimbledon only with a bit
more blood.

WILLIAM KNOCKED THE EMIR OFF HIS HORSE THEN SLEW HIM.

A KNIGHT'S GOTTA DO WHAT A KNIGHT'S GOTTA DO!

FOR THAT GREAT DEED THE KNIGHT BECAME KNOWN AS WILLIAM IRON ARM.

AND MY HEAD IS PRETTY HARD TOO!

And remember when the Normans were massacred at Ofanto by the buzzing-bee Greeks? William Iron Arm went back to the same battlefield 23 years later (1041 if you're a dummy at summies). They say William Iron Arm had a terrible fever at the time but he won this return match.

Crazy Crusaders

In 1096 the Pope asked Christians to go and capture the Holy Land from the Muslims. Of course the Normans were the first to join in. They'd had plenty of practice fighting Muslims in Italy. Now they had another excuse for a good fight.

Many knights fought in the Crusades because they were Christians or because they were serving their lord. But some knights were 'mercenary' and fought because they were paid to fight – 800 hyperperes for a knight and 400 for his squire. These mercenary knights had to work for their pay – or else. The punishment for a knight without fight could be to have his armour taken away. Still, that was better than being a cowardly ordinary soldier. He would have his hand pierced with a hot iron.

Did you know… ?

Knightly Norman William de Perci had Whitby Abbey built. He then went off on Crusade, where he died. It is said his heart was brought back for burial at Whitby Abbey. Of course Whitby is where Count Dracula was later said to have arrived in England to go in search of fresh victims. Wonder if he had a munch on de Perci's blood pump?

Powerful Prester

In 1145 a bishop of Syria wrote a startling letter to the Pope…

Your Holiness,

I have wonderful news for your brave Crusaders. There are many Muslim states between you and the Holy Land. But there is one mighty Christian state beyond Persia which may well come to the aid of the Crusaders.

This state is ruled by a priest-king called Prester John. Prester John is a descendant of the three wise men who took gifts to the baby Jesus.

Prester John has already defeated the Muslims in Persia and his armies are heading towards us. Let us pray that he arrives in time to help our brave knights.

The Bishop of Syria

When the news reached the Pope, the Crusaders became excited by the idea of having such a powerful ally – even though no one had heard of him before 1145! The excitement grew when a letter arrived from Prester John himself.

The letter was a forgery – Prester John didn't exist!

Imagine you were the Pope and you received a letter which said…

> Your Holiness
>
> I am Prester John and I rule the lands beyond Persia. I try to rule as a good Christian even though I am the most powerful king on earth. I have seventy-two lesser kings who accept me as their leader.
>
> My lands are so rich that there are no poor people in them. There is no lying, no stealing, no crime of any kind. Still, I do have a magical mirror in my palace and through it I can look into any part of my country. If there is any plotting going on then I know all about it.
>
> I have magical jewels that can control how warm or cold the weather is and a church which can grow or shrink depending on how many people are in it.
>
> I look foward to the day when you can visit my land and see these wonders and many more.
>
> Your loyal Christian friend
>
> Prester John.

Now, if you'd been the Pope you would take one look at the letter, say, 'Ho! Ho! Very funny!' and drop it into the nearest bin.

What did Pope Alexander III do? He wrote back to Prester John! This is a bit like writing to Father Christmas ... very nice for five-year-old children to believe. But the leader of the Western Christian Church? What a Popish plonker!

The seriously bad news was that an Eastern invader had indeed defeated the Muslims in Persia in the 1140s. But it wasn't a mighty Christian priest-king called Prester John. It was the ruthless Mongol warlord Kor-Khan and the coming of the Mongols was *not* good news for the Christians of Europe.

Gorgeous Saint George

Saint George was a hero to the Normans. Why? Because he was a great fighter, of course. The Normans loved fighters.

St George was also a Christian who died because of his faith. The Normans believed that anyone who died for being a Christian would go straight to heaven – that's why they were so eager to fight in the Crusades against the Muslims.

So, who was this St George and what happened to him? It's pretty gruesome, but it may be worth it to get that top spot up in heaven...

How to become a saint

In the AD 500s George had been a brilliant Roman soldier. He became a Christian and gave all his money away to the poor. When the Emperor Diocletian decided to exterminate the Christians, George was tortured.

Do you have a teacher for Religious Education? Do you

have a local vicar or priest? Do you even have someone in your class who is so good and holy they make you sick? Then this is your chance to do them a favour and make them a saint. All you have to do is copy what the Romans did to St George.

Make your own saint

For this you need a really holy person and a lot of patience.

1. First lay your saint on the ground. Cover her/him with stones then larger rocks and finally get a few little boulders and pile them on until s/he is crushed. If your saint is truly a saint then s/he will survive. So...

2. Take a wheel covered in spikes and roll it to the top of a steep hill. Tie your saint to the wheel and roll it down the hill. Just like Jack and Jill but a bit bloodier. If your saint is truly a saint then s/he will survive. So...

3. Take a pair of iron shoes and heat them till they are red hot. Put them on the feet of your saint and set her/him off to run in them. They'll set off hot foot, you can be sure. If your saint is truly a saint then s/he will survive. So...

4. Tie your saint to a cross, facing the cross. Take leather whips with knots in the end and a team of whippers. Whip the saint till their skin is hanging off their body. If your saint is truly a saint then s/he will survive. So...

5. Dig a deep pit in the ground. Throw your saint into the pit and cover her/him with quicklime (calcium oxide if you want the posh word). This will burn off their flesh till they're skinny as a skeleton key. If your saint is truly a saint then s/he will survive. So...

6. Get a bottle of poison at your local chemist shop. Slip the poison into your saint's tea and watch them drink the poison. If your saint is truly a saint then s/he will survive. So...

7. Behead your saint. That's what Diocletian did and it finally killed off Georgie.

But before he died – and in between the tortures – George…

- chatted to an angel
- raised dozens of people from the dead
- raised an ox from the dead
- converted the Emperor's wife to Christianity (she got the chop too, by the way!)
- converted 40,900 other people
- had the Emperor carried away by a whirlwind of fire

Whatever happened to the dragon?
Bet you thought Saint George was a saint because he slew a dragon? The Saint George that the Normans loved never did that. The dragon only appears in the book *Golden Legend*, written in the late 1200s. So now you know.

Horrible for horses
Life in the Norman world could be awful for horses. Especially when they went into battle…

- The charge of Norman knights was a fearsome thing, but the Muslim warriors found a way to stop it. They used their arrows and javelins to bring down the horses. Once the horse fell then the knight could be battered senseless.

One knight, de Joinville, was hit by five arrows – but his poor horse was hit by 15 and fell. Later that year de Joinville had a spear thrust through his leg. It also stuck firmly in the neck of his horse and pinned him there. This was a bit of a pain in the neck for both of them!

- An Italian historian, Amatus, described a Norman duke as follows...

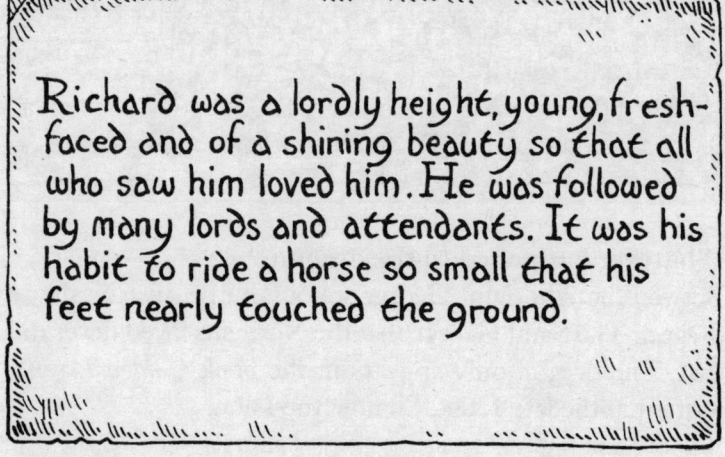

Richard was a lordly height, young, fresh-faced and of a shining beauty so that all who saw him loved him. He was followed by many lords and attendants. It was his habit to ride a horse so small that his feet nearly touched the ground.

'All who saw him loved him'? I'll bet the little horses in Italy didn't love him! 'Oh, no!' they must have whinnied when they saw him coming. 'Why can't he pick on some horse his own size?'

- Horses are reasonable swimmers. They can even swim with a rider on their back. But it's a bit much to ask a horse to swim with a heavy war saddle and a rider with chain-mail armour, iron helmet and battle sword. That's what the knights expected from their horses after the battle of Val-es-Dunes in 1047. Not only did the riders drown (which served them right) but they took the poor horses down with them. A writer who visited the battlefield said...

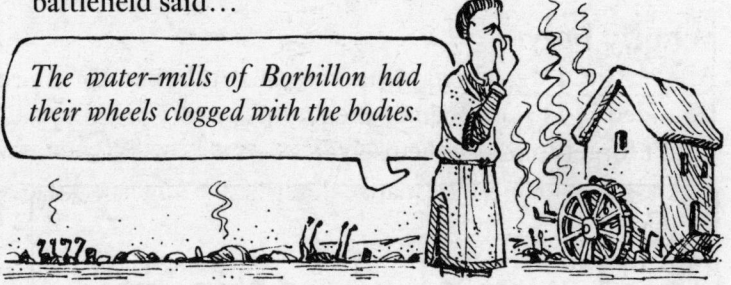

The water-mills of Borbillon had their wheels clogged with the bodies.

Crummy Crusades

By the middle of the 1200s the Crusades were not so popular. The religious writer, Humbert of Romans, said...

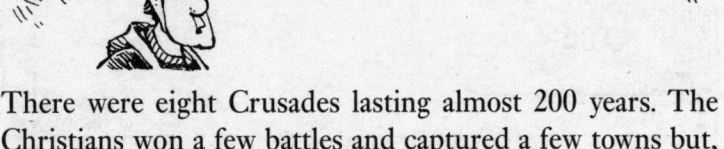

Priests who call for a Crusade are mocked these days. And the knights who sign up to go are usually drunk at the time!

There were eight Crusades lasting almost 200 years. The Christians won a few battles and captured a few towns but, in the end, they left the Holy Land in defeat.

Still, the Normans got most of what they wanted from the Crusades – an exciting punch-up, a bit of glory ... and a ticket to their Christian heaven. What more would a Norman knight need?

Mischievous monks

The Normans set up hundreds of monasteries wherever they went in Normandy, Italy, the Holy Land and England. Men and women flocked to become monks and nuns, but not every one was a saint – not every religious place was holy.

Wholly holy

Abbot Ailred was in charge of Rievaulx Abbey in Yorkshire (founded in 1131). When he died monks wrote his story and didn't forget to praise themselves!

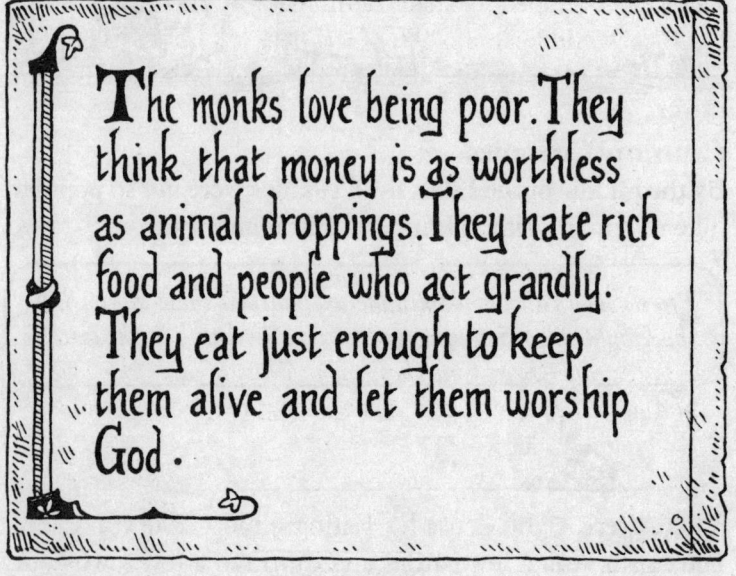

The monks love being poor. They think that money is as worthless as animal droppings. They hate rich food and people who act grandly. They eat just enough to keep them alive and let them worship God.

Sounds a pretty boring sort of life really. But of course not all monks were as goody-goody as that...

Not wholly holy

Gerald of Wales (1146–1223) said that the monasteries could be very ungodly places.

1 Wealth

They got lands by acting like saints and using 'God' as every other word.

So, the monks just *appeared* to be holy so they could get their hands on lands.

Interesting thought, using 'God' as every other word! That would mean if they read the Ruth chapter of the Bible that says 'Thy people shall be my people, and thy God my God', it would become: 'Thy God people God shall God be God my God people God and God thy God God God my God God God.'

2 Land

Once they get land they waste no time in putting it to use. The woods are cut down and levelled into a plain, bushes give way to barley and willows to wheat. They flatten villages, overthrow churches, turn villagers on to the roads and don't hesitate to cast down altars and level all under the plough.

I CAN FLATTEN ANYTHING. I'VE GOT A BULLDOZER

THAT'S NOTHING, I'VE GOT A MONASTERY

Gerald went on to say that if a man invited the monks on to part of his land, they ended up throwing him out of the rest. 'The coming of Cistercian monks is worse than the coming of a war.' Today he might have said a bit like motorway builders – except he isn't alive today and the Normans didn't have motorways.

3 Ruthlessness

The most amazing story was of a knight who refused to give up his land to the monks of Byland Abbey. Walter Map, a Welsh writer of the time, described what happened next…

> *One night they entered his house with masks over their faces, armed with swords and spears, and they murdered him and his family. When his relations arrived three days later they found the houses and barns had all disappeared and in their place was a well-ploughed field.*

BYLAND ABBEY?

THIEVELAND ABBEY, MORE LIKE!

Sort of, 'Night-night, knight!'

4 Simple food

Then there was the rule that the monks should eat simple food and be silent during meals. If they wanted to ask for salt or water then they used one of the hundred signs they had.

St Bernard of Clairvaux was horrified by what he saw at Canterbury...

> *As to the dishes and the number of them – what shall I say? I have often heard sixteen or more costly dishes were placed on the table. Many kinds of fish (roast and boiled, stuffed and fried) many dishes created with eggs and pepper by skilful cooks and so on! The meal was washed down with wine, claret, mead and all drinks that can make a man drunk. The rule of silence did not prevent monks from showing their pleasure with signs that made them look more like jesters or clowns than monks. They were all waving with fingers, hands and arms and whistling to one another instead of speaking.*

And you thought your school dining-hall was bad with mashed potato and school bags flying around? Canterbury must have looked and sounded like a meeting of football referees! If St Bernard had his way they'd all have been shown a red card. (St Bernard was a true monk and gave away everything he possessed. He even gave his name to a dog!)

5 Little food
Not all monks got away with this good living. Gerald of Wales tells of the monks of St Swithuns, Winchester...

The monks had a good excuse for having so much food. They said they gave away their left-over food to the poor. The more dishes the monks were given the more scraps there were for the poor!

Nice try, boys.

Horrible Histories Health Warning: Do not believe everything you read in history books. Gerald of Wales twice applied to become Bishop of St David's in Wales. In both cases the

116

monks persuaded the king not to give Gerald the job. In both cases the job went to a monk. Gerald had good reason to hate monks. His stories must have been written with a bit of spite.

6 Women

The Bible says, 'All wickedness is little compared to the wickedness of a woman.' (Female readers, don't write and complain to me. I didn't say it. Write to God.) Monks were expected to keep away from them.

Now if you are a monk then there is one sure way to lose interest in women. Don't let your naughty bits get over-heated. How do you keep them cool? Do not wear any underpants. And good Cistercian monks wore no underpants.

But this created other problems. One day King Henry II was riding through a town when a Cistercian monk stumbled, trying to get out of his way. The monk fell flat on his face and his robe blew over his head. The king said nothing but a priest who was riding with the king said...

Cursed be the Cistercians who show their backsides.

No doubt the monk's cheeks turned red with embarrassment ... the cheeks of his face, of course. What did you think I meant?

Did you know… ?
When a boy joined a monastery at the age of seven he was given a monk's robes and a monk's hair cut. But there was

117

one thing he didn't get until he became an adult monk at the age of 16. What was it?

Gerry's Welsh wonder

Gerald of Wales wrote a book about his travels through Wales in 1188. He tells a story that probably doesn't belong in a travel book…

nce upon a time there was a Welsh boy called Eliodorus who used to visit the kingdom of the dwarfs, deep underground. He played with a dwarf prince and their favourite game was playing with a golden ball. One day Eliodorus tried to steal the golden ball. When the dwarf king found out he was furious. From that day on the gateway to the kingdom of the dwarfs was forever closed to the boy. Eliodorus grew up to be a priest while the dwarf prince lived happily ever under.

Yes, Gerald, and there are fairies at the bottom of our garden.

Norman quiz

1   A knight who upset his leader could be punished with his own horse. How?

a) He was forced to trot along a road in full armour on his horse.

b) He was tied to the tail of the horse and had to run behind it or be dragged.

c) He was forced to eat it … raw … without salt, pepper or mustard. Not even a cup of tea to wash it down with.

2   Normans were Western Christians and during the Crusades they met Eastern Christians. Crusaders were discouraged from marrying Eastern Christian women. What happened to them if they did?

a) They were banished to the desert with just a camel for company.

b) They lost their armour which was melted down.

c) They lost the lands they owned back home.

3   The Scots did a sword dance – skipping quickly over sharp swords. What did the English dance over?

a) Smouldering coals.

b) Eggs.

c) Slithering snakes.

4   Crusaders faced a dreadful weapon in the Middle East: 'Greek Fire'. It caught alight as soon as it touched sea water

and threatened their ships. How did Norman crusaders fight Greek Fire?

a) With pee.

b) With spit.

c) They dialled 999 and let the Phrygian Fire-fighters fight it.

5 What was the Norman punishment for murder?

a) Hanging by the neck till dead.

b) Having your eyes put out.

c) Beheading (with a blunt axe).

6 Saint Godric died in 1170 at the age of 105. What did he do before he became a hermit monk and a saintly man?

a) He was a pie seller.

b) He was a pirate.

c) He was a pilot.

7 William the Conqueror knew he was dying in 1087, so he left his kingdom to…

a) His wife – but he was so ill he'd forgotten she was dead.

b) His son William Rufus (who became William II).

c) God.

8 What was the first thing William did when he jumped ashore at Hastings?

a) Fell flat on his face.

b) Fell down on his knees to pray.

c) Fell about laughing when he heard King Harold was 300 miles away.

9 Abbot Thurstan became the new Norman boss at Glastonbury but upset the monks there. The monks argued with Thurstan. What did he do?

a) He was so upset he jumped off the bell tower to his death.

b) He sent in Norman soldiers to slit a few monks' throats.

c) He prayed for a miracle and God sent angels to talk to the monks.

10 A Norman knight swore to prove his love for a lady. She told him to go off and pick up all the stones on the beaches of Brittany. What did he do?

a) Collected an army to do the job and won the heart of the lady.

b) Tried to do it himself but hurt his back and never fought again.

c) Sulked and went to bed for two years.

fig 1. a dark knight

Answers:

1 a) Trotting on a war-horse in full armour was painful. Knights walked to the battlefield and then set off at a canter into the charge. And they didn't gallop into the charge (the way you see in films). Some horses would go faster than others and the line would not be straight. The idea was to hit the enemy as a single block – a bit like the charge of pupils from the school gates at holiday time!

2 c) This didn't happen to all Norman knights but generally it was a bad idea to fall for an Eastern Christian woman, even if she was as pretty as a pot-bellied pig. Still, it could have been worse. A Greek knight who married an Eastern Christian woman could lose a hand or a foot.

3 b) The English danced over eggs. Not so brave as the Scots – unless there's a very angry hen in the room. You may like to try this in the kitchen. Place half a dozen eggs on the floor, turn on the radio and dance around. Too easy, you say? Fine! Try it blindfolded.

4 a) The recipe for Greek Fire has been lost since it was used in the Middle Ages. We can't test the fire-fighting methods to see if they'd work. But the Normans *believed* that throwing sand over the Greek Fire or pouring pee on it was the best way to kill the flames. That is not to say they stood there and risked singeing their piddling bits. If they expected an attack

of Greek Fire they'd collect barrels of the stuff. Let's hope they didn't mix them up with the wine barrels.

5 b) The Normans were cruel but they rarely gave the death sentence to criminals. Prison was only used to hold criminals until their trial. A murderer might lose his hands or his eyes. Having your eyes put out was also the punishment for killing one of William the Conqueror's deer. Does that mean a human life was worth no more than the life of a deer?

6 b) Godric was born in Norfolk the year before William the Conqueror invaded. He grew up to be a pedlar – a sort of travelling salesman. Then he became a sea pirate. When his voyages took him as a pilgrim to Compostella in Spain he saw how wicked he'd been. 'I don't want to join a monastery,' he decided. 'I want to live a holy life alone … as a hermit.' He had a fun life in a cave but was driven out by wolves. He finally settled into a specially built hermitage that the Normans built for him. See? You too can have a specially built council house if you're a good boy.

7 c) William hadn't inherited the crown of England from a father who had been king before him, so people could argue that there was no reason why his son should become the new king. Also he'd taken it in battle with a

lot of blood spilt. That wouldn't look too good when he arrived at the gates of Heaven, would it?

'What have you done on earth, William?'

'Caused a few thousand bloody deaths!'

'Then go to hell!'

So William said, 'I leave my kingdom to God … and I hope God will give it to my second son, William.'

God didn't appear to argue.

8 a) William landed and stumbled. 'Ooooh!' his followers gasped. 'That's a bad sign!' But clever Will grabbed a handful of sand and said, 'See! I've already seized Harold's land!'

9 b) Thurstan sent for soldiers so the monks locked themselves in the monastery church. The soldiers easily broke down the door. Three of the monks rushed to the altar to pray – that didn't alter their fate. They were hacked to death. Many of the other monks were wounded as the soldiers lashed out.

10 c) The knight had asked for it really. Never ask a lady, 'What can I do to win your love?' She may not want her love to be won and might set an impossible task! It's much more simple to say, 'Do you fancy going to the pictures with me?'

Epilogue

The fashion at the first millennium was for men to have hair to their shoulders and long moustaches. The Normans cut their hair short and shaved their faces (except the women who didn't cut their hair short or shave their faces). To their enemies the Normans must have looked like skinheads!

And they behaved like skinheads too. They got what they wanted by being violent and they grew to enjoy fighting. (This was before television was invented, so they had to do something to pass the time.)

Of course the Normans had the perfect excuse...

You may like to try this excuse some time...

Of course you might be punished! Most people believe we should stand up to bullies like the Normans. (So, in 1999, when Serb bullies barged into Kosovo other countries joined forces to stop them.)

The Normans, like their Viking ancestors, were fearless fighters. They charged around Europe and changed it for ever. Why did they do it?

Italian historian Geoffrey Malaterra said…

> *They are passionate about wealth and power, yet they despise it when they have it. They are always looking for more.*

Greedy, nasty Normans.

English Historian William of Malmesbury summed them up like this…

> *They are proudly dressed and delicate about their food – but not too much. They are jealous of their equals – and always want to do better than their superiors. They rob their subjects – yet they defend them against others. They are faithful to their lords – yet the slightest insult makes them wicked. They are only treacherous when they think they can get away with it.*

They probably weren't nice to know, but they were the sort of people who would survive in today's world.

But did the Normans really win?

When French King Philip II took Normandy in 1204, the Normans in England had to choose – should they stay and become English? Or join the French to keep their Norman lands but lose their English ones? They stayed in England.

Some historians say this means the English won – the English didn't become Normans – the Normans became English!

It's a horrible historical world where winners are losers and losers end up winners.

STORMIN' NORMANS

GRISLY QUIZ

Now find out if you're a Stormin' Norman expert!

QUICK QUESTIONS

1 William the Conqueror died … and then killed two of his undertakers. Explain that if you can! (Clue: a load of rot)

2 William II took his dad's throne, though his Uncle Odo fought him for it. Odo never carried a sword or sharp weapon into battle. Why not? (Clue: bishops bash)

3 William II was proud of his yellow hair, but his enemies said the colour clashed with what? (Clue: enough to make Will blush)

4 Everyone remembers that in 1066 William I invaded Hastings from Normandy. But everyone forgets that in 1094 William II invaded Normandy from … where? (Clue: tit for tat)

5 William II got the century off to a horrible historical start by getting killed in a hunting accident in 1100 – or was it murder? Huntsman Walter Tirel fired at a deer, missed and hit the king in the heart. What did he do next that looks suspicious? (Clue: channel hopper?)

6 William's corpse dripped blood all the way to Winchester Cathedral where he was buried under a tower. What happened to the tower seven years later? (Clue: t–rubble)

7 The new king was Henry I (who just happened to be hunting in the same forest when William was killed). In 1101 he met with his elder brother Robert. To show he wanted peace he gave Robert what? (Clue: 'x')

8 In 1135 King Henry I was killed by eels. How? (Clue: the eels died first)

9 Henry died and war broke out for his throne between his nephew Stephen and daughter Matilda. What horrible habit did Stephen have? (Clue: night nuisance)

10 In the war against Stephen, Matilda became trapped in the town of Devizes. They told her she'd never get out alive. Yet she escaped. How? (Clue: dead obvious really)

11 Matilda also found herself trapped in Oxford in the snow. How did she escape without being spotted? (Clue: the invisible woman)

12 Stephen was captured in battle in 1141 where he fought bravely with battle- axe and sword. But a soldier found a way to bring him down off his horse. What? (Clue: it's a knockout)

13 King Henry II's greatest enemies were his wife, Eleanor, and his sons. People said he protected his girlfriend, Rosamund, by hiding her where? (Clue: amazing)

14 Another story said Queen Eleanor found King Henry's girlfriend by attaching a thread to the heel of his boot and following him. What was Ellie

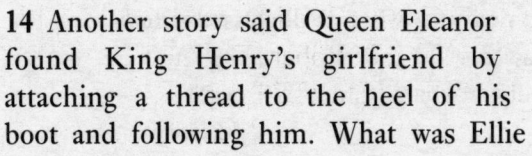

said to have done with Rosamund when she found her? (Clue: invited her for a drink)

15 Henry's best friend was Thomas à Becket, but after he made him Archbishop of Canterbury they quickly fell out. Henry said he wanted rid of Becket and four knights decided to do him a favour. What did they do? (Clue: he axed for trouble)

16 In 1173 Queen Eleanor tried to escape from her husband's prison in disguise. Disguised as what? (Clue: she wasn't)

MONK-Y BUSINESS

Could you have lived the life of a monk in the 1100s? If you think school rules are bad then could you stick to these rules? First, work out what they were by matching the right and left sides...

A MONK WILL NOT...

1. think too much of his own	a) senior monks
2. be tempted by	b) work
3. make a noise in the	c) cloister
4. argue with	d) comfort
5. be disorderly in	e) an old monk
6. be careless in his	f) world outside
7. disobey	g) brother monks
8. become as lazy as	h) way
9. want his own	i) church
10. think of the	j) rich food

CRRR

WHAT HAPPENED NEXT?

In history you can usually guess what happens next. But you may find it a little harder in Horrible History, because people don't always behave the way you would! Can you guess What Happened Next (WHN)?

1 William the Conqueror was the son of a duke but his mother was the daughter of a humble tanner – someone who made leather from animal skins. Will's enemies used this to torment him. When Will besieged the town of Alencon in 1048 the defenders stretched animal skins over the walls. William took 34 prisoners and cut off their hands and feet. WHN?

2 William slipped as he jumped ashore at the head of the invasion of England. His men were horrified because they thought this was a bad sign. William's hands scrabbled at the stones on the beach. He rose to his feet and turned to his frightened men. WHN?

3 William was crowned just two months after he landed and defeated Harold at Hastings. He was a foreign ruler with a lot of enemies who'd rather see him dead than crowned, so guards circled Westminster Abbey to keep out trouble makers. As William was crowned there was a huge cheer from the congregation. WHN?

4 William's death was caused by a fire. He set fire to an enemy town, his horse stepped on a cinder, threw him and the fall burst his bladder. He died in agony. But his funeral

was disturbed by another fire. As his coffin was carried through the streets a nearby house caught fire. WHN?

5 William II fought against his brothers Henry and Robert in 1090. The brothers captured one of Will's knights called Conan and took him up the stairs of their castle tower. Conan begged them for mercy but the brothers laughed. WHN?

6 William II's army sailed north to fight the Scots. They stopped off in Tynemouth for a break and rampaged through the town. They stole cloth from an old woman who put the curse of Saint Oswy on them. Next day the army set sail on a calm sea past the rocks off the coast of Tynemouth. WHN?

7 Robert of Rhuddlan rushed from his castle to stop Welsh raiders escaping in their ships. He was in such a hurry he went without his guards. He was easily captured and beheaded. WHN?

Quick Questions

1) Two undertakers died of a fever. They caught it from the germs on William's rotting body.

2) Odo was a bishop and religious men weren't allowed to spill human blood. Instead they carried dirty great 'maces' that would crush a man's skull and kill him just as dead – but not spill blood.

3) His red face. His nickname was 'Rufus' which is Latin for 'red'. But would they have dared to call William 'Rufus' to his face?

4) Hastings. Of course.

5) Tirel fled to France. Would an innocent man do that?

6) It collapsed! The evil spirit of dead William got the blame.

7) A kiss.

8) Henry ate the eels and died. His doctor warned him not to eat them, because they usually made him ill – but he was a stubborn king!

9) Stephen snored very loudly.

10) Matilda pretended to be dead and was carried out in a coffin.

11) Matilda used camouflage and wore a white cloak to cross the snow-covered fields.

12) The soldier threw a stone and smacked Stephen on the head.

13) In a maze. The story said only Henry knew the way to Rosamund in the centre. So how did she get fed? Or

was she fed up enough with living alone in the middle of a maze?

14) Eleanor poisoned Rosamund – it was said.

15) The knights hacked Thomas to death at the cathedral altar. The top of his head was cut off and his brains spilled on to the floor.

16) A man. But the plan failed and she was caught.

Monk-y Business
1.d) 2.j) 3.c) 4.g) 5.i) 6.b) 7.a) 8.e) 9.h) 10.f)

What Happened Next?
1) He lobbed the hands and feet over the walls and said, 'That's what'll happen if you don't surrender!' They surrendered.

2) William looked at his hands full of stones, laughed and said, 'See! How easily I grab this land!' The joke relaxed his followers who went on to victory.

3) Everyone panicked. Guards outside thought William was being attacked inside so they set fire to nearby houses in revenge. The congregation heard the noise outside and many ran for their lives.

4) The coffin-bearers put the coffin down and went to help put the fire out. William was late for his own funeral.

5) They threw him out of the tower window to his death.

6) The ships ran aground on the rocks. Waves swelled up from the calm sea and swamped the ships, killing hundreds. The revenge of Saint Oswy?

7) The raiders sailed off – with Robert's head stuck on the top of the mast.

INTERESTING INDEX

Where will you find 'burst guts', 'drunk monks'
and 'killer scarecrows' in an index?
In a Horrible Histories book, of course!

Terry Deary was born at a very early age, so long ago he can't remember. But his mother, who was there at the time, says he was born in Sunderland, north-east England, in 1946 – so it's not true that he writes all *Horrible Histories* from memory. At school he was a horrible child only interested in playing football and giving teachers a hard time. His history lessons were so boring and so badly taught, that he learned to loathe the subject. *Horrible Histories* is his revenge.

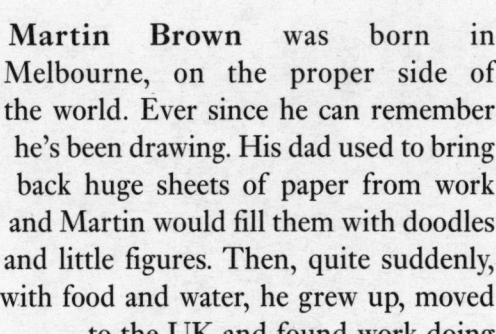

Martin Brown was born in Melbourne, on the proper side of the world. Ever since he can remember he's been drawing. His dad used to bring back huge sheets of paper from work and Martin would fill them with doodles and little figures. Then, quite suddenly, with food and water, he grew up, moved to the UK and found work doing what he's always wanted to do: drawing doodles and little figures.

HORRIBLE HISTORIES

VICIOUS
VIKINGS

Terry Deary Illustrated by Martin Brown

SCHOLASTIC

This book is for my Aunt Molly.
Simply the best.

Scholastic Children's Books,
Euston House, 24 Eversholt Street,
London NW1 1DB, UK

A division of Scholastic Ltd
London ~ New York ~ Toronto ~ Sydney ~ Auckland
Mexico City ~ New Delhi ~ Hong Kong

First published in the UK by Scholastic Ltd, 1994
This edition published by Scholastic Ltd, 2016

Text © Terry Deary, 1994, 1999
Illustration © Martin Brown, 1994, 1999, 2016

Some of the material in this book has previously been published in
Horrible Histories: The Massive Millennium Quiz Book/Horribly Huge Quiz Book

All rights reserved. Moral rights asserted.

ISBN 978 1407 16386 4

Printed and bound by CPI Group (UK) Ltd, Croydon, CR0 4YY

10 9

www.scholastic.co.uk

CONTENTS

Introduction

History is Horrible. Far too horrible for adults to learn about. You see, people change as they get older. They get "civilised" . . . that means "soft". Now young people, they enjoy a bit of horror . . .

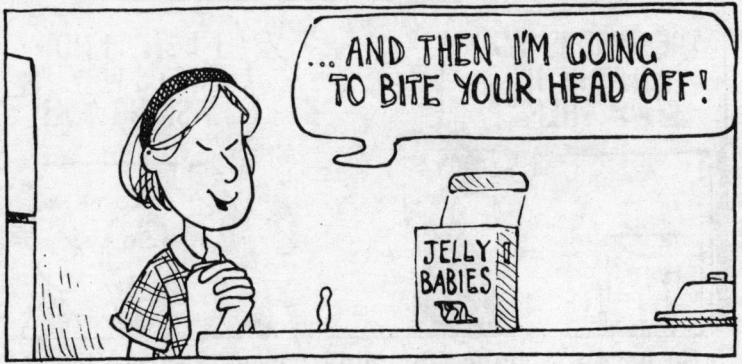

They love a bit of pain and suffering . . . as long as the sufferer is a teacher or the nasty grown-up next door who keeps your ball when it goes over the fence!

But adults try to protect poor children from horror stories. They put labels on films that say, "Not suitable for children". And they don't tell the whole truth about history.

...AND HAROLD SLEW A THOUSAND SAXONS

BUT HOW DID HE SLEW THEM SIR?

THE WORD IS *SLAY* "HOW DID HE *SLAY* THEM"?

I DON'T KNOW! THAT'S WHY I'M ASKING YOU!

So here's a chance for pupil power to strike back! Here is the *truth* about the Vikings. The things that teacher never tells you because teacher's too chicken-livered. Now you can watch Miss faint in fright as you describe some vicious Viking inventions . . . for torture! See Sir swoon as you explain how Sigurd was killed . . . by a *dead man!*

This book is not suitable for adults. They will say things like, "Yeuch!" and "How sick!" And, when they do, just look sad and say, "It's true. But that's horrible history!"

Vicious Viking invaders

The Vikings lived in Scandinavia – that's the posh word for Sweden, Denmark and Norway. The Saxons lived in England – they'd moved in when the Romans left.

All of a sudden, the Vikings started raiding Saxon England! And they weren't very nice about it. In fact they were pretty vicious! Lots of clever teachers will try to tell you why the Vikings suddenly crossed the cold North Sea and raided the suffering Saxons. But do they really know?

WANTED

Job: Pillagers. Brave, loyal men to work overseas
Qualifications: Must be ready and willing for adventure but not afraid to die
Hours: Long and hard (but a lot of excitement is to be had – would you rather stay at home and starve?)
Pay: Plunder – the more you steal the bigger your share. If you are lucky you could even end up in the Viking heaven of Valhalla!
Special note: This is an urgent vacancy – sailing tomorrow
Extra-special note: This post is not for the fainthearted
Apply within

VISIT THE SUNNY SAXON SHORES

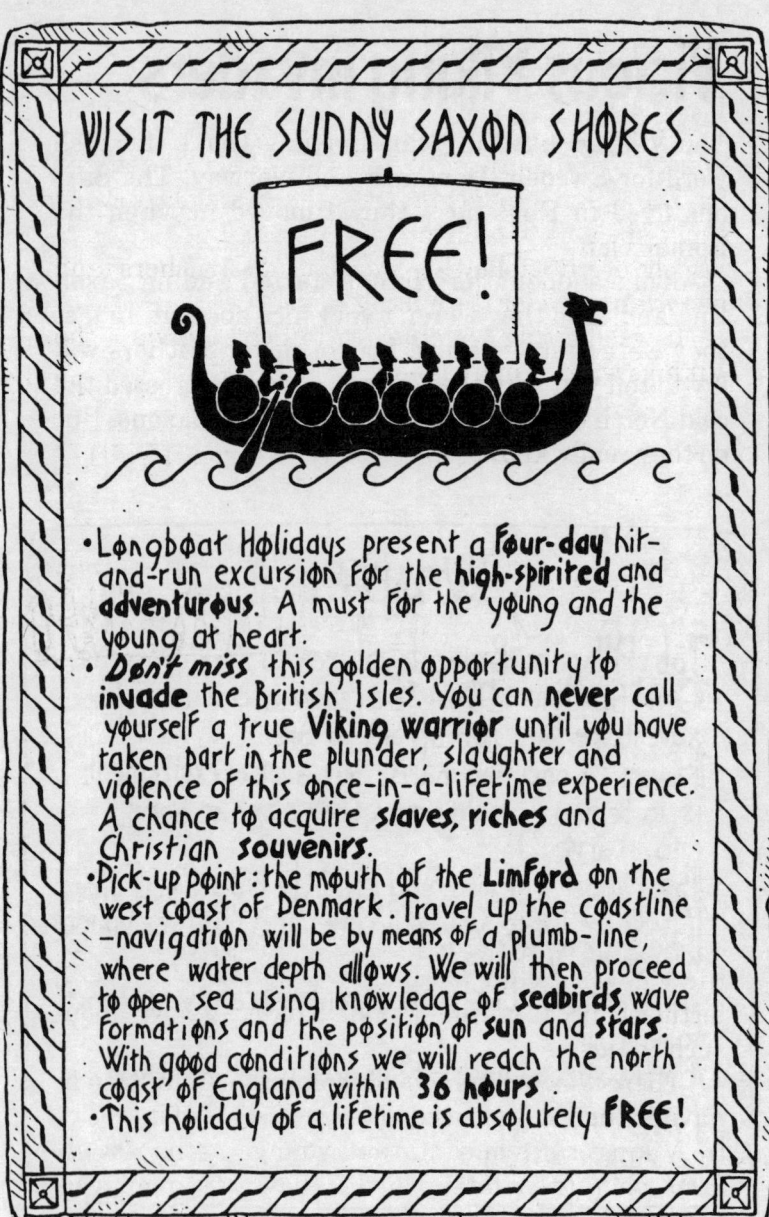

FREE!

- Longboat Holidays present a **four-day** hit-and-run excursion for the **high-spirited** and **adventurous**. A must for the young and the young at heart.
- **Don't miss** this golden opportunity to **invade** the British Isles. You can **never** call yourself a true **Viking warrior** until you have taken part in the plunder, slaughter and violence of this once-in-a-lifetime experience. A chance to acquire **slaves, riches** and Christian **souvenirs**.
- Pick-up point: the mouth of the **Limford** on the west coast of Denmark. Travel up the coastline –navigation will be by means of a plumb-line, where water depth allows. We will then proceed to open sea using knowledge of **seabirds**, wave formations and the position of **sun** and **stars**. With good conditions we will reach the north coast of England within **36 hours**.
- This holiday of a lifetime is absolutely **FREE**!

What would a Viking want in England?

Work? Or adventure? What were the real reasons for the Viking invasions? Teachers and historians *should* be able to tell you, of course . . . but can they? Which of the following reasons do teachers and historians give for the Viking raids?

1 It was getting too *crowded* in Scandinavia – the Vikings wanted more land

2 The monasteries were an easy way to *get rich quick* on treasure and slaves

3 There was *too little food* in Scandinavia because the soil was useless – it hadn't been kept fertile with fertiliser because the Vikings didn't know about such things

4 There was *too much food* being grown in Scandinavia – the Vikings needed to trade some of it

5 Viking rules meant that younger sons got *no land* when their father died – they had to go overseas and pinch someone else's land

9

6 Some pretty *vicious kings* took over in 9th-century Scandinavia – many Vikings sailed off to escape from them

7 A change in climate made Scandinavia *cold and uncomfortable* – even wild, wet England was better than that

SCANDINAVIA   ENGLAND

8 There was a sudden *shortage of herring* in the North Sea – their main food supply

9 Sea trade was growing in the north of Europe – more trade meant more chances for *piracy* . . . Viking piracy!

10 The Vikings *enjoyed sailing and fighting* better than staying home and farming

Answer: *All* of them! Historians have argued each one of these reasons at some time or another. They can't all be right. The truth is no one *really* knows why the Vikings began raiding.

(It's a bit like the dozens of reasons given for the disappearance of the dinosaurs – lots of clever ideas . . . no real proof!) In the end you have to make up your own mind.

The fact remains, the Vikings arrived. This is how it happened . . .

Vicious Viking timeline

AD

787 Three boatloads of Vikings land on Dorset coast. A Saxon tax officer orders them to appear before the Saxon king. The Vikings kill him. Perhaps they only came to trade.

793 Whirlwinds, comets and fiery dragons seen in the sky over northern England. Bad signs. Sure enough, the first Viking attack on Lindisfarne Priory follows. Monks taken as slaves or thrown in the sea. Vikings go home for the winter.

851 Vikings stay for the winter in England for the first time.

865 Vikings make first demand for Danegeld – in other words, "Pay us lots of money or we'll do nasty things to you!"

870 Vikings discover Iceland.

871 Alfred becomes King of Wessex. He batters the Vikings at Eddington. He rules the south and lets the Viking Danes rule the north of England.

878 Alfred defeats the Danish King Guthrum – they make peace.

886 Treaty of Chippenham divides England into two parts – Danelaw in the north – England in the south.

899 Alfred dies.

982 Erik the Red discovers Greenland.

986 Viking Bjarni spots America but doesn't land.

1000 Leif Erikson lands in America.

1013 Svein Forkbeard threatens to attack England. Ethelred, the English King, pays him off.

1017 Svein used the money to make an even bigger army. Svein dies and Viking Canute (Knut to his friends) becomes king of all of England.

12

1030 Christianity becomes religion for most of Norway after centuries of worshipping the gods of Norse legends.

1048 As if Viking attacks aren't enough, Derby and Worcester are hit by the worst earthquake in living memory.

1066 Viking Harald the Ruthless attacks York. English king Harold Godwinsson defeats him. But William of Normandy lands on the south coast of England. Harold Godwinsson rushes to meet him. William defeats Harold. Normans rule – end of the Viking age.

Vicious Viking legends

You may think the stories you heard as a child were vicious – *Jack and the Beanstalk*, for example, where the poor old giant bashes his brains on the ground.

Or *Red Riding Hood*, where the wolf gobbles Granny before she pops out again when the woodcutter lops its head off.

Or that poor old witch in *Hansel and Gretel* who gets pushed into her own oven – all she wanted to do was eat the grotty little boy who'd been chomping her chocolate and nibbling her nougat.

But vicious Viking legends are even more disgusting! Viking story-tellers used to recite long poems, *sagas*, that told of disgusting deeds and horrible happenings.

Gruesome gods and shocking sagas

If you believe the poets who wrote the sagas then you'll believe the following . . .

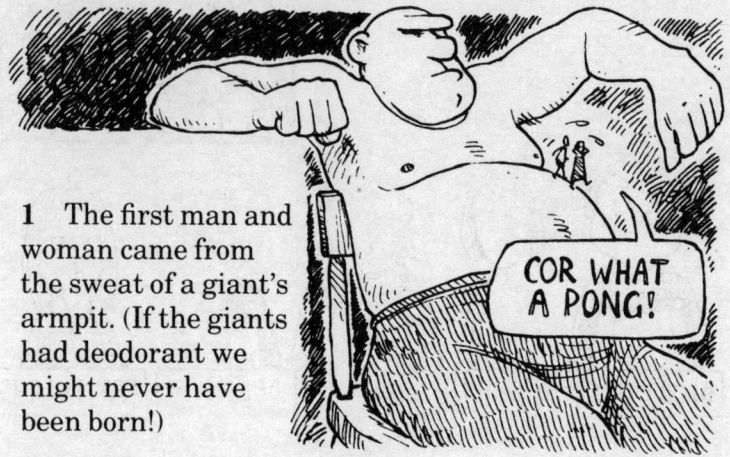

1 The first man and woman came from the sweat of a giant's armpit. (If the giants had deodorant we might never have been born!)

COR WHAT A PONG!

2 There was a huge flood in the early days of the world – just like Noah's flood in the Bible. But in the Viking story the flood was the blood of a dying Frost Giant. (Maybe that's why there's a Red Sea!)

3 Those aren't clouds
you can see in the sky –
they are the brains of
a dead giant!

HE MUST HAVE BEEN
A DIM GIANT

4 The sky is held up by four dwarves called North, South, East and West. You'd better hope their arms don't get tired!

5 If you die peacefully then you go to Hel. And Hel – unlike Hell – is very cold! If you want to go to Heaven then you'd better die in battle.

6 Some people were born to be slaves – the *thrall* class of people. They were ugly, stupid and clumsy but strong. The first thrall family had charming girls with names like Blob-nose, Oaf, Dumpy, Fat-thighs, Noisy, Servant and Bundle-of-Rags. The brothers were called Cattle-man, Hunch-backed, Ashen-face, Horse-fly, Shouter, Clott, Drott and Stinking. (And you have the nerve to complain because your parents called you Wayne or Deborah!)

BLOB - NOSE | OAF | DUMPY | DEBORAH | FAT THIGHS

15

7 *You* might not believe in giant gods who rule the world but the Vikings did. Odin was the god of magic and war, poetry and wisdom. If you wanted him on your side then you'd have to make a sacrifice to him. At one sacrifice ceremony a traveller reported seeing dead dogs, horses and humans hanging from trees. There were over 70 bodies hanging side by side.

8 Statues of the god, Frey, usually showed him with no clothes on. When a Christian bishop saw one he was so shocked he took a hammer and smashed it.

9 Heroes who died went to a heaven called Valhalla. There, they fought all day and drank all night. If they were killed in a heavenly battle they came back to life in time to fight the next day. When they feasted they drank from the skulls of their enemies.

10 The Vikings converted to Christianity around the year 960 AD after a priest called Poppo performed a miracle. He held a red-hot piece of iron in his hand without burning himself. He said this proved Jesus was greater than all the Viking gods. King Harald agreed and became a Christian there and then.

In your childhood stories, the goodies always won. Cinderella lived happily ever after because she was sweet and kind. But in vicious Viking stories the *cruellest* usually won! And the craftiest! If the Vikings had told the Cinderella story then the Ugly Sisters would have married Prince Charming ... then murdered him and lived happily ever after in his palace. Cinderella would be one dead duck.

That's the sort of story the Vikings liked as they supped their mead and listened to the poets. And poets were very, very important people, as this story shows ...

Blood, spit and tears

"Spit in this jar," the great god, Odin, ordered.

"Why should I?" the god, Thor, grumbled. He had a hammer and went around hitting people who argued with the gods.

"Don't argue, Thor, just do it," Odin sighed. It would take too long to explain to thick Thor just what he was up to. "Look," he said, holding the jar under Thor's nose. "All the other gods have had a spit."

"Cor!" Thor said thoughtfully ... or Thor-tfully. "What you going to do with that lot, Odin?"

"Make a man," the chief god said.

"Oh, well, here goes," the hammer-horror shrugged and spat into the bowl.

And, using his great and godly magic, Odin made a man. He called him Kvasir and sent him down to Midgard – Earth.

Now Kvasir was the wisest man on Earth. (So would you be if you'd been made from the spit of gods.) He solved lots of problems for the people of Midgard.

Everybody loved Kvasir. Well, nearly everybody. There were two brothers, Fjalar and Galar, who absolutely hated him! Now Fjalar and Galar were mean, nasty and jealous of Kvasir. So would you be if you were a dwarf who lived underground with hundreds of other smelly dwarves. And Fjalar and Galar were dwarves.

"It is said that the blood of Kvasir is magical," Fjalar muttered one dark day . . . underground, all the days are dark.

"Is it?" Galar asked.

"It is. And we are going to get his blood," Fjalar chuckled.

"We are?"

"We are. Now this is the plan . . ."

"The plan?"

"We invite Kvasir to a party here . . ."

"A party?"

"Yes, you know, a booze-up. And when he's good and drunk you stab him!"

"You stab him?"

"No, *you* stab him," Fjalar hissed.

"What'll *you* be doing while *I* stab him?" Galar asked.

"I'll be waiting with those jars to catch the blood. Right?"

"Right!"

So the dastardly dwarves carried out their plot and bled Kvasir drier than a smoked pork pie.

The dreadful duo mixed the blood with honey and made it into honey wine – mead. And whoever drank the mead would become a poet and a wise man.

The trouble was, no one got to drink the mead. The bloodthirsty brothers kept it to themselves.

And as the years passed they grew crueller and crueller. One day they entertained the giant Gilling and his wife.

"He eats a lot," Fjalar grumbled.

"A lot," the gruesome Galar agreed.

"Let's get rid of him!"

"Get rid of him?"

"I say, Gilling," Fjalar cried. "How about some fresh sea air. It's getting stuffy in here! How about a sail in our boat?"

"Good idea," Giant Gilling growled. "You coming, Mrs Gilling?"

"You go, dear," Mrs Gilling grumbled. "I just get sea-sick. Have fun!"

But Giant Gilling had no fun. The deadly dwarves sailed out to sea and tipped him overboard.

"I can't s . . . glug-glug-glug . . . wim . . . glug-glug . . . specially with this stone round my . . . glug . . . neck! . . . glug-glug . . . I'm going to . . . glug!"

19

"And that's the end of him!" Fjalar chuckled.

"And her?"

"We'll break the news. Perhaps she'll buzz off home," the devious dwarf muttered.

But Mrs Gilling didn't go. She just sat there and cried.

The giant tears fell on the floor and sloshed around the cave. "Me feet are sopping wet!" Fjalar fumed.

"Mine too."

"So get a large millstone and stand outside the cave," he told his brother. "When she steps out through the door just drop it on her head!"

Galar hurried to obey and Fjalar spoke to snivelling widow Gilling. "Just step outside and see the sea. I'll show you where your darling husband met his watery end . . . that's right . . . just step this way . . . no, after you. Right, Galar, drop it!"

Crunch!

"Cor! Stone the crows! It worked!" the brothers cheered. They went back to their cave and slept a happy sleep, until . . .

"Knock! Knock!"

"Who's there?"

"I'm Giant Sattung Gilling – looking for my mum and dad."

The giant boy was huge and wild and very, *very* angry.

"Your dad got drowned," wee Fjalar whimpered.

"With a great big millstone," gormless Galar grunted.

Sattung grabbed the two dwarves by the collar. "You tied a millstone around Dad's neck and threw him in the sea?"

The two dwarves tried to answer, give some explanation. But it's hard to talk when giant fingers wrap

20

themselves around your neck.

Sattung marched into the sea. He walked for miles until the water almost came up to his chin. He dumped the dwarves down on a tiny rock. "The tide is out," he roared. "And when it rises up again you'll have to swim back home!"

"It's much too far!" fat Fjalar sobbed.

"Well, then, you'll have to drown . . . and serves you right," the giant orphan said and waded back to land.

So Fjalar and his stupid brother lost the mead of poetry.

And *no one* . . . not Kvasir, Giant Gilling, Mrs Gilling, Gilling Junior or the dwarves . . . lived happily ever after. What a lovely story!

Vicious Viking myths

Myths, sagas and tales of the supernatural were common in Viking times. People believed that dwarves, giants and evil monsters were in constant battle with the gods. Stories ranged from the creation of the world, to its end, or *ragnarok*. Imagine a world in danger from demons and monsters, who at any time could create chaos and disorder!

Forget your warm and cosy houses, your televisions and computers. Gather round a blazing open fire, shut out the cold winter's night. It's story time – Nordic style.

Government Health Warning: These stories are gruesome – if you suffer from nightmares then don't read them in the dark – you'll strain your eyes for a start!

Bedtime story no. 1

Once upon a time there was a god called Loki. Loki was an evil god who caused a lot of trouble amongst the other gods. He was an absolute nuisance (just like your brother or sister); very jealous and spiteful. Such was his cheek that he once wagered his head in a bet with Brokk the dwarf.

Loki lost the bet, but to save his life he pointed out that there had been no mention of his neck in the bet. Brokk couldn't take Loki's head without harming that neck!

Knowing just how bad-tempered dwarves could be, Loki should have known better than to cheat them. But they got their revenge. How? By sewing his lips together! Moral of the tale: if you want to shut the school bully up – get the help of a dwarf.

But the story doesn't end there. This little incident did not stop the mischievous Loki. He gave blind Hod (the son of chief god, Odin) a piece of mistletoe to poison him. Hod, unable to see, took the mistletoe and died.

But the gods decided to punish Loki forever, so they tied him to a tree trunk and left him there.

Bedtime story no. 2

Thor was the god of strength and hard work. He was also the god of storms. People believed that he made thunder by riding across the skies in his chariot. Thor was also the protector of all the gods, and what did he use to protect them? A hammer.

Now Thor and his hammer were very close; so close that they never parted. He was so fond of it that he actually gave it a name: Mjolldir.

But one day (and what a day it must have been) he awoke to find his hammer GONE! It had been stolen by the arch enemies of the gods, the *GIANTS!* The only way Thor could get back his hammer was if he could persuade Freyja (the goddess of love) to marry the lord of the giants.

Freyja was desperate for a husband . . . but not *that* desperate. She refused. Now what would Thor do to get his beloved hammer back?

Well, he pretended to be Freyja to fool the giants.

He dressed himself up in a wedding gown and wore her distinctive gold necklace. Unfortunately, Thor was very manly ... he had a beard and absolutely huge muscles, but *this* didn't give him away! What did? Well, at the feast he ate rather like a *pig*. Yes, Thor put away ...

- eight whole salmon
- one whole ox
- washed down with three *barrels* of mead!

After this show, Thor's hammer was brought into the feast to bless the bride. Thor could restrain himself no longer, he jumped up to say hello to his best friend. His disguise fell off and he screamed, "I want my hammer back!" After a fight, the big soft lump got his hammer back, never to lose it again.

There are two lessons to be learned from this story. If you meet a Norse god ...

1 Don't ask him to dinner
2 Don't steal his favourite toy

25

Vicious Viking times

Some people get upset if you say the Vikings were vicious. They argue that the Vikings were a cuddly, loveable people who were really quite clever. For example, did you know that Vikings were great inventors? It's true! They liked to invent new ways for people to die! They lived in pretty vicious times. Can you match the following people to their sticky ends?

1 King Edmund didn't want to fight against the Vikings in 869 AD. He wanted to talk to the Viking leader and convert him to Christianity. The Viking leader wanted to stick to the worship of Odin, so King Edmund was . . .

2 An English woman made a wax model of her hated neighbour and stuck an iron pin through its heart. She was accused of being a witch in 900. The accused woman was . . .

3 King Edward was assassinated by the servants of his own mother. She wanted her younger son, Athelred, to become king in 978. King Edward arrived to visit his mother without a bodyguard and he was . . .

4 In 997 King Kenneth of Scotland wanted his son to be king after he died. The other Scottish nobles didn't like this idea. Kenneth was lured to a castle where he was feasted and given lots of wine, then he was . . .

5 In 1012 the Archbishop of Canterbury, Alfheah, was captured by the Danish Viking invaders. They asked for a ransom of silver. Alfheah refused to let his friends pay a ransom, so he was . . .

6 The Irish King, Brian Boru, was killed while he prayed in a wood. The killer, the Viking Brodir, was captured and he was . . .

a) Stabbed. Had one foot twisted in the stirrup of a horse's saddle. The horse was sent charging off, dragging the victim to a bumpy death

b) Taken to a room with a booby-trapped statue. When the statue was touched, several hidden crossbows were set off. The victim died in a hail of bolts

c) Beaten. Tied to a tree and shot full of arrows. Cut down and cut up! Beheaded. Had head and body thrown into a wood

d) Pelted with cattle bones and finished off with a single blow from an axe

e) Drowned in the River Thames at London Bridge

f) Cut open. The victim's intestines were attached to an oak tree and the victim led around the tree as the intestines unwound

* Be careful! The Viking sagas were written a long time after the events happened. They may not be true. And the Vikings may have made up stories about terrible tortures in order to make them sound more brave and fierce than they really were!

The Saxon historians simply said of Edmund's death, *"and they killed the king."* They don't mention horrible tortures. What do you think?

But one of the unluckiest Vikings was Sigurd the powerful. He was killed by a dead man! Sigurd killed the man in battle, cut off his head and threw it over his saddle as a trophy. But the tooth of the dead man's skull scratched Sigurd's leg. The scratch became infected . . . and Sigurd died!

(Genuine) ancient English joke

When monks weren't writing books they were writing riddles like this one:

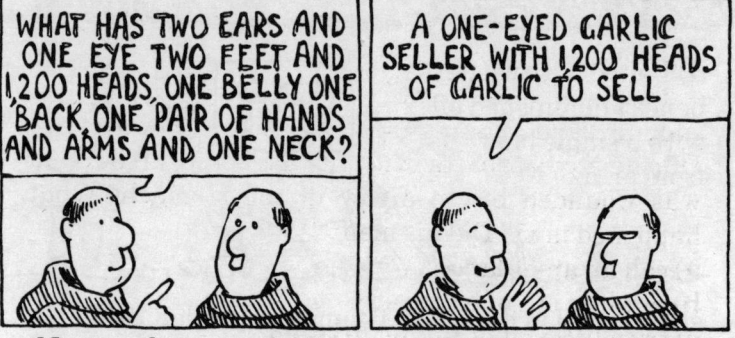

WHAT HAS TWO EARS AND ONE EYE TWO FEET AND 1,200 HEADS, ONE BELLY ONE BACK, ONE PAIR OF HANDS AND ARMS AND ONE NECK?

A ONE-EYED GARLIC SELLER WITH 1,200 HEADS OF GARLIC TO SELL

(No wonder you don't see many laughing monks with jokes like that! And no wonder the Vikings wanted to exterminate them!)

Vicious Viking medicine

Leif Erikson was probably the first European to land in America – so *there*, Columbus!

LOOK WHAT I GOT FROM THOSE FUNNY INDIANS

The Vikings called it Vinland – maybe because they found wild grapes on "vines" – Vine-land, get it? Or maybe it was because there's a Norse word, "*vin*", meaning "pasture".

Leif left and told his brother, Thorvald, of the discovery. Thorvald and a crew of 35 reached the shores of Vinland (Newfoundland) in the Spring of 1004. After making winter camp they ventured forth, first sailing east then north along the coast.

Thorvald and his crew met native American Indians. The Vikings called them the "Skraelings". During a major battle with the Skraelings, Thorvald was wounded by an arrow in the stomach. What happened next? Did his men:

a) call an ambulance?

b) put him out of his misery

c) try a little bit of Viking first-aid?

Answer: c) This is what Thorvald's men did . . .

29

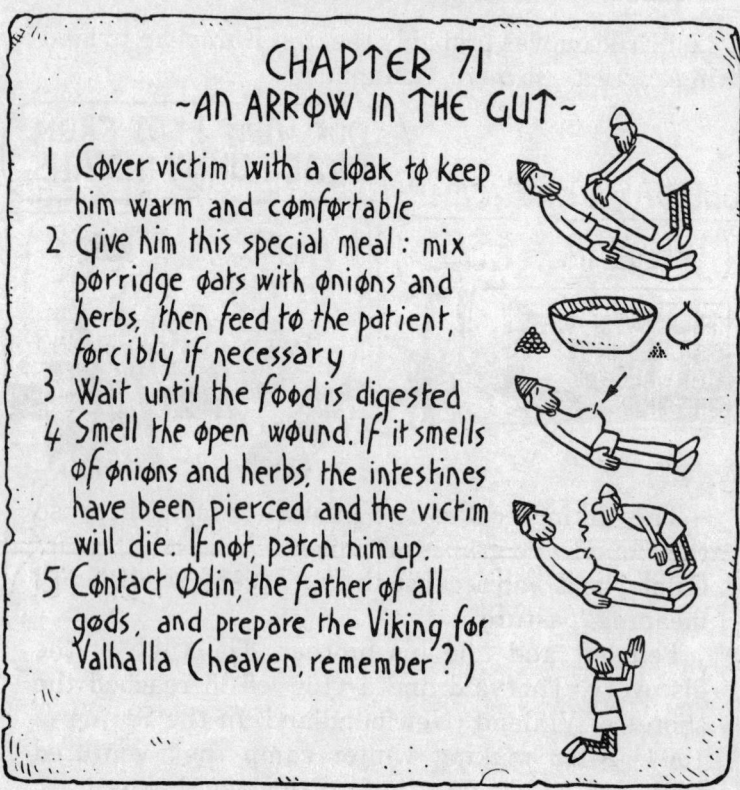

CHAPTER 71
~AN ARROW IN THE GUT~

1 Cover victim with a cloak to keep him warm and comfortable

2 Give him this special meal: mix porridge oats with onions and herbs, then feed to the patient, forcibly if necessary

3 Wait until the food is digested

4 Smell the open wound. If it smells of onions and herbs, the intestines have been pierced and the victim will die. If not, patch him up.

5 Contact Odin, the father of all gods, and prepare the Viking for Valhalla (heaven, remember?)

By the way . . . Thorvald died.

Vicious Viking vessels

The Vikings couldn't have carried out those raids on England – and Ireland – if they hadn't been great sailors and built superb boats. They went still further – to Iceland, Greenland and even North America.

The Viking ships are admired for their low, sleek look. But they weren't always like that. The story goes that one man bravely changed the shape of the Viking longboat. This is supposed to be a true story . . .

Build a Longboat

1   Choose a spot near the sea.[1]

2   Choose your trees ... watch the way they grow so you pick the ones that give the shapes you need.[2]

3   Pick straight oak trees for the keel – the backbone of the ship.[3]

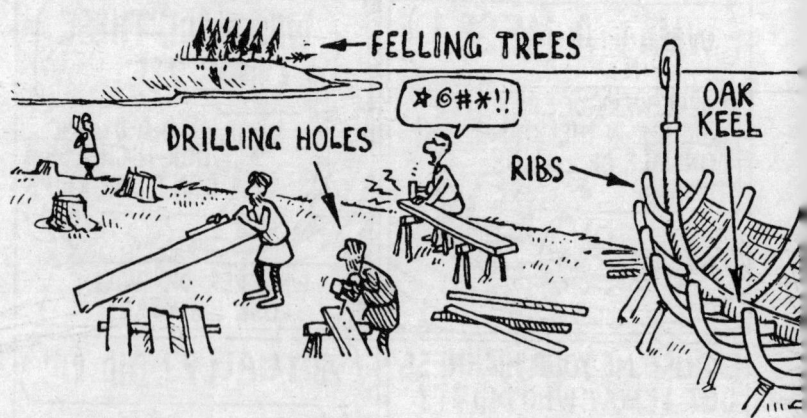

4   Cut down a few dozen pine trees for the planks – split the trunks into planks by hammering in wedges.[4]

5   Drill holes in the planks to take the nails.[5]

6   Nail the planks so they overlap.[6]

7   Build "ribs" at right angles to the keel.[7]

---

1   Well you wouldn't want to carry the boat fifty miles to the sea when it's finished, would you?

2   Trees can take hundreds of years to grow. It's better if you don't spend hundreds of years watching them.

3   Oaks are getting rare. Cut one down in modern Britain and you may end up in jail.

4   No, you can't use electric saws because they haven't been invented.

5   And no electric drills either, you wimp!

6   If you ask a teacher to hold the nails then you won't hit your thumb.

7   They're called ribs because they look like, well, ribs.

8 Find a cow (or a sheep), and make ropes from the hair, dip the ropes in tar and pack the joins with the tarry rope and leave them to dry.[1]

9 Carve a really ugly face on the front.[2]

You're ready to fit the oars, the mast, the steering oar, and the sail.

Get a crew of muscular sailors and invade somebody!

OVERLAPPING PINE PLANKS

UGLY FIGUREHEAD

TARRING JOINS

PLANKS A LOT

SPLITTING LOGS FOR PLANKS

Did you know . . .?

Ships carried tents and frames. The ends of each tent were carved with faces of fierce animals. These scared evil spirits away. The sailors could pitch the tents on the ship when they stopped for the night. But usually the sailors went ashore and snuggled into their leather sleeping bags . . . and sometimes they shared a sleeping bag to keep warm!

1 This is messy. Do NOT wear your best clothes.
2 A picture of your teacher will give you something to copy from.

The power of Viking poems

The first people to inhabit the British Isles were the battling Britons. Then along came the rotten Romans who drove the native British into the wet and western wildernesses of Wales. But the Romans went home in the fifth century AD to help defend the Roman Empire nearer home.

So the Angles, Saxons and Jutes moved in from northern Europe. You might have thought they'd be *glad* to find a deserted country to move into. But they were actually rather sad when they saw the ruined Roman towns. One of them wrote a poem called . . .

The ruin
How fearsome is this old wall,
Crushed and torn by time.
And great town buildings broken,
Work of giants dying.

Tumbling towers and fine roofs,
Broken down old gates.
Ceilings fallen, torn apart
By the hand of Fate.

Great bright inn and bath house,
Banquets in the hall
Once were filled with laughter.
Time put paid to all.

But 300 years later it was the Anglo-Saxons' turn to have their homes wrecked. By the Vikings. And those Vikings thought that poetry was pretty important too. One Viking even thought it could save his life. But did it . . . ?

The best poem of Egil's life

Eric Bloodaxe was well named. He was king because he'd killed off all his rivals – including a few half-brothers. But he still had one deadly rival . . . Egil Skallagrimsson!

Then, in 949 AD, Eric Bloodaxe had the most pleasant shock of his murderous life. The doors of the royal hall in York opened and a breathless servant scuttled in.

"King Eric, your highness, you have a visitor, sire."

Queen Gunnhild looked icicles at the humble man and her voice grated, "Who is it? Speak up!"

"Er . . . he says he's Egil Skallagrimsson, your highness!"

The pale queen turned whiter than a rat's tooth. "Impossible. He wouldn't dare come here . . . not unless he has an army with him!"

"No, your highness – just a couple of servants!" the miserable man mumbled.

"Then have him killed!" the queen hissed.

"Yes, your highness," the man said with a bow that brushed the floor.

"No, don't!" King Eric ordered.

"No, your highness," the simpering servant snivelled.

The queen glared at her husband. "You've waited ten years for this chance!" she cried.

Eric nodded. "So another hour won't make any difference. I want to see this man."

Gunnhild rose to her feet. A spot of colour glowed in her frozen face. "Have you forgotten what Egil Skallagrimsson has done? Killed your friends and family – yes, killed your own son. He has scorned you and insulted your royal person. He has to die."

"Later," the king said calmly. "First let's hear what he has to say." He looked at a guard. "Have Egil Skallagrimsson brought before me," he ordered.

Egil was unarmed and half-smiling as he was led before the royal couple.

"I thought you were hiding in Iceland," Queen Gunnhild sneered. "What are you doing in England?"

"I came to see my friend Athelstan of the English," Egil answered quietly.

"Athelstan? Athelstan's been dead for ten years," Gunnhild gasped.

The prisoner shrugged. "So I've heard. But news travels slowly in Iceland."

"So you decided to pay us a visit instead," Eric Bloodaxe said.

"No. I decided to go back home. But a storm wrecked me on the coast not far from here," Egil explained.

"The gods will it. It is a punishment for your evil deeds," the queen said smugly.

"Perhaps," the prisoner agreed. "But I escaped the wreck. Perhaps the gods wanted me to live!"

"Or perhaps drowning is too quick for you," Gunnhild grated. "Perhaps they want you to have a nice slow death at the hands of Eric!"

"Eric is a Viking. He knows that fame is not bought cheaply. He would gain no fame from killing

36

me now. If I'd tried to run from the shipwreck and hide like a common criminal, then Eric could have had me killed. But I came here freely, knowing Eric will treat me fairly. Then he will win word-fame."

Gunnhild began to speak but her husband silenced her with a wave of his hand. "Tonight I feast. Tomorrow I decide what to do with you. You may spend the night as my guest . . . in a cellar teeming with toads. Guards! Take him away."

And while Eric Bloodaxe feasted and slept, his enemy worked on his greatest art. His poetry.

HEY! THAT'S NOT HALF BAD

The next morning the proud prisoner stood before the royal couple. "Your highness," he said boldly. "Before you decide my fate, I ask you one favour."

"Kill him," Gunnhild groaned.

"No. Go on, Egil Skallagrimsson," Eric insisted.

"Allow me to recite a poem I have written to celebrate your fame. The people in this hall can hear it. My poem will bring you more than my death ever could. It will bring you word-fame."

"Kill him," Gunnhild shrilled.

"We will hear this poem," Eric said. "We can always kill him later."

And the court of King Eric gathered round the Icelander and listened. He chanted 20 verses he'd written in his head the night before. He began . . .

Listen, O king, what honour I bring;
Silence I ask while I play out my task.
Your brave deeds I'll tell, which all men know well.
Only Odin can say where the men you killed lay.

He went on to describe Eric's valour in battle . . . Then Egil changed the rhyme pattern and made his listeners wonder at his skill.

I praise this king in his own land,
I gladly sing of his just hand.
A hand so free with golden gains,
But strongly he can rule his Danes.

He finished . . .

To praise this lord, my dumb lips broke;
The words out-poured, my still tongue spoke.
From my poet's breast these words took wing,
Now all the rest may his praise sing.

There was a silence in the great royal hall when Egil had finished. At last it was broken by one harsh voice. "Kill him," Gunnhild said.

The Viking listeners muttered angrily. One spoke boldly, "King Eric, this man's poem will bring you word-fame. Your name will live forever. In return you should grant him his life."

"Kill him," Gunnhild said.

"I will decide," Eric Bloodaxe said.

But what did Eric decide? Was the Viking love of word-fame so important? Or was his wife right – the Viking love of vengeance should come first?

Answer: In return for the poem, Eric gave Egil his life.

38

Egil's poem was typical of many. The Viking poems gloried in death and destruction. One poet wrote this to the gory glory of war . . .

I have held a sword and spear
When they were slippery with blood.
Hawks were hovering at the kill,
As brave the violent Vikings stood.

Red flames swallowed up men's roofs
As we raged and cut them down;
Bodies, skewered, lay there sleepy
In the gateways of the town.

But the Vikings didn't always win . . .

Vicious Vikings vanquished

Someone with a few brains could beat the Vikings. Here are some battles the Vikings would rather forget . . .

1 The Battle of Ashdown

 ## The Wessex Star
A RIGHT RIVETING READ
April 871

YOUNG ROYAL LEADS ROUT AT READING

The Wessex Saxons washed their swords in Viking blood last night to celebrate a vital victory. And the surprise star of the battle was ex-king Athelwulf's youngest son, Alfred. Young Alfred showed big brother Athelred how to give the Danes a drubbing. The young Wessex Wonder was meant to lead half of the Saxon swordsmen, while Athelred was to lead the rest.

Imagine the popular prince's surprise when he went to King Athelred's tent and found his brother praying.

"There's a battle to be fought out there, brother!" Alf argued.

"I serve God first and men second," the crazy king replied.

So brave Alf decided to go it alone.

The Danes were favourites in the fight. They held the high ground. But Awesome Alf went at them "like a wild boar", one witness raved.

The bloody battle raged around a single stunted thorn bush. Saxons and Danes swapped places as both tried to hit that hilly height. At last the sword-swinging Saxons drove the desperate Danes back to their camp till darkness stopped the slaughter.

The Wessex Star says, "Move over, Athelred. Let's make Kid Alfred King Alfred!"

The Wessex Star's own poet wrote this ode to the great victory . . .

Ode to Alf who cuts Vikings in half

Our Alfie's the hero of
   Reading,
For he jumped like a
   flea from his bedding,
While King Athelred
   prayed
Good prince Alfred
   just slayed
Till the Danes were
   left bledding and
   dedding!

Note: Poor Athelred died soon after the Battle of Ashdown and young Alfred became King.

STILL ONLY
20 PENNIES

THE SAXON SUN

25 SEP
1066

A GOOD WIN, SON!

Heroic Harold Godwinsson has defeated the nasty Norwegians in the North of England. Yesterday, the Horrible Hardrada was stuffed at Stamford Bridge. Saxon England is free of those vile Vikings at last.

Godwinsson (known to his men as Gozza) admitted last night, "We had a bit of luck – but then, you need a bit of luck to beat the likes of Hardrada. The lads call him, Hard-as-nails Hardrada."

The "bit of luck" the great Godwinsson referred to was an incredible mistake made by hopeless Hardrada. The Norwegian ninny thought the Saxons were down in London, so he gave his men a bit of a holiday. One of the few Viking survivors described the scene to our reporter. "We was sunbathing, like. No armour – no nothing! Then we saw a cloud of dust and the sunshine on the spears. Well, we thought it was a bunch of our mates coming up from the ships, didn't we? I'd just turned over to tan the other side when they jumped on us! I couldn't find me trousers, never mind me sword. Sick as a parrot I was!"

The super Saxons tried to cross the river to get at Hardrada himself. A nutty Norwegian (a Berserker with a battle-axe) was on the bridge and battered a few of our brave lads. He also gave Hardrada time to warn his other warriors.

"Gave us a hard time," a Saxon survivor said. "Bit of a blood-bath, really. Hardrada asked Godwinsson for land but the boss just replied he'd give the Norwegian seven foot – enough for a grave . . . get it? Laugh? The lads nearly died . . . well, a lot of them did die, of course. But we won in the end."

Hardrada died in the fight. Now gutsy Godwinsson faces a new fight at the other end of the country. Our continental correspondent says that William of Normandy is planning an invasion on the south coast.

But *The Saxon Sun* says Harold will nobble the Normans in no time! That'll be one in the eye for William!

Editorial

The Saxon Sun Editor says . . .

Three cheers for brave Harold. He deserves an ode – so here's one what I wrote. We believe the people of England should sing this patriotic piece as he heads south to face William the Norman . . .

God save our gracious
   King
He done some real good
   things,
God save the King.
Send him a load of cash
As to the south he'll dash
To give old Willi-um a
   bash!
God save the king!

The Saxon Sun is offering two free tickets to the battle against the Normans, yes TWO, to the reader who comes up with the best tune for this stirring battle song.

Live like a Viking

To understand history we have to try to understand the people who lived it. Can you get inside the mind of a Viking? Can you make the same decisions a Viking would have made . . .?

Think like a Viking 1: 980 AD – Eiric's Story

Nothing is so sad as a beaten Viking. Nothing so mad. Nothing so dangerous!

Eiric was sad. To be beaten by the Norwegians in the battle of Hjorungavagr was bad enough. To be one of the 70 survivors was shameful. Eiric would rather have died in the battle. Instead he was a prisoner. Taken alive and tied with ropes to his comrades. The young man was mad . . .

"Why can't they give us a weapon and let us die fighting?" young Eiric cried.

The old warrior, Bjorn, next to him, looked at the boy wearily. "How old are you, Eiric?"

"Eighteen," Eiric answered.

"How did you live so long and be so stupid?"

Eiric's pale face turned red. "Why do you say that?"

"Because it is obvious, boy. They don't want us to die bravely. They want us to die as cowards. They want us die pleading for our lives. They want to show that the Vikings are weak. It makes the Norwegians look strong."

Eiric nodded. "But we will not die weakly. We will die as heroes."

"Better not to die at all," Bjorn sighed. "I've a wife and children who'll suffer when I'm dead. You've a mother and a father, haven't you?"

The young man turned his ice-blue eyes to the winter sky. "Yes," he said shortly.

"I don't fear death any more than the next Viking – but still it makes me sad to think of the ones we leave behind. Be brave . . . but be sad, young Eiric."

Eiric stared at the frozen ground and went silent while a flock of gulls screeched and circled overhead, sensing that death was in the Yuletide air. The young warrior struggled with the thick rope that bound him to Bjorn.

The old man shook his head. He chanted an old poem softly . . .

It is frightful now
To look around
As a blood-red cloud
Shadows the sky

The ropes were too strong. Eiric shook back his long, fair hair and said, "There is no shame in cheating death, then?"

"And how would you do that?" Bjorn asked tiredly.

Before his young friend could answer, the rope was tugged sharply and the line of captured Vikings was dragged to its feet.

Earl Hakon of Norway marched cheerfully down the line and called, "Does any man wish me to spare his life? All he has to do is ask, politely, and swear to become a slave to Norway!"

The Viking warriors stared at him with contempt. "Prepare to die," he sneered and nodded to a Norwegian soldier.

The first Viking was freed from the rope. He stepped forward, thrust his chin out and waited for the sweep of the sword. As his head was severed the Viking warriors cheered.

"Well died!" a huge warrior laughed and stepped forward to be executed. His hair was grey as the December sky. He turned to his comrades. "My friends!" he cried. "There is a better life after death!" He pulled a dagger from his belt. "When my head is off I will raise this dagger in the air."

He stretched out his arms and waited. As the sword fell . . . so did the knife in the huge Viking's hand. The cheer this time was softer. Bjorn sighed.

Another brave man stepped forward. He too turned to the waiting men and spoke. "We will show them how a Viking dies! Executioner . . . strike me in the face. You will see that I do not turn pale!"

The sword fell. His face did not turn pale . . . but the Vikings saw that the man closed his eyes at the moment of death. The cheer this time was soft as the whisper of steel on ice.

Eiric jumped to his feet. He had to gamble on his plan to save the lives of the other 67 men. "Me next!"

When the Vikings saw their youngest step forward they struggled with the ropes and argued, "No! Me! No! Me!"

Sneering Hakon cried, "Kill the boy!"

"Wait!" Eiric said. "I do not want my hair to blunt your sword. Have one of your men hold my hair up while the sword falls on my neck."

The Norwegian Earl grinned and ordered a soldier to twist Eiric's long hair round his hands.

The Vikings fell silent. The swordsman raised his sword. The sword swept through the air like a longboat through the water.

At the last instant Eiric jerked back his head sharply. He dragged down the arms of the soldier who held his hair. Dragged them down into the path of the sword.

The soldier screamed as the steel bit into his wrists.

The Vikings roared.

Earl Hakon laughed. "Young man, for that entertainment you deserve to live. Set him free!"

Eiric's life was saved.

And so the story might have ended . . . but this is a *Viking* story.

If you were a Viking, how would you want it to end?

a) Eiric goes home to his farm and lives a long and peaceful life.
b) Eiric refuses to accept the pardon unless the other Vikings are allowed to go free. Earl Hakon admires his bravery and all the remaining Vikings are spared.
c) Eiric refuses to accept the pardon unless the other Vikings are allowed to go free. Earl Hakon refuses and the boy is executed along with all the others.

47

Think like a Viking 2

An old Viking poem gives advice on how to behave if you want to be a good Viking.

> *Do not laugh at the old and grey*
> *There may be wise things they have to say!*

(This doesn't apply to *teachers*. Vikings didn't have teachers so they wouldn't know.)

> *When a guest comes to your home*
> *Give them a wash and a seat nice and warm.*

(And never insist on showing them your holiday video or you'll bore the socks off them.)

> *Beer and mead are not that good,*
> *They make your brain as thick as mud.*

(And some people are as thick as mud even without beer and mead.)

> *A coward hides – at home he'll stay*
> *But time will kill him anyway!*

(But he'll still last longer than a warrior who goes out looking for a punch-up.)

> *A man who wants to kill his foe*
> *Must get up quick and never slow.*
> *A wolf that wants to have a snack*
> *Does not lie sleeping on his back.*

(Or ... "Late to rise, late to bed, could make you healthy, wealthy and dead!" And this is why teachers get to school before their pupils.)

> *Cows and friends and parents die*
> *After some years so will I.*
> *One thing that will live the same*
> *Is a hero's famous name.*

(Not to mention the time you made a fool of yourself by being sick at your cousin's birthday party. Why do people never let you forget that?)

> *You never can tell who is out to get you;*
> *So look round a doorway before you step through.*

(And look *above* the door in case somebody's balanced a bucket of water over the top.)

> *When you go in the fields take your sword*
>   *and your spear;*
> *For some day an enemy just might appear.*

(This does not mean you have to take a weapon with you when you play football or hockey!)

49

Think like a Viking 3

That same Viking poem gave another piece of advice. It said . . .

> *Even a handless man can herd sheep,*
> *But a corpse is no good to anyone.*

So, when they faced a fight they were sure to lose, they didn't waste their lives attacking. Instead they used trickery.

Hastein and his Vikings were probably the first to sail into the Mediterranean Sea. At last they found a great fortress of gleaming white marble . . .

ROME! THE GREATEST CITY IN THE WORLD! BUT WE'LL NEVER TAKE IT ALIVE!

AND AS WE VIKINGS ALWAYS SAY, A CORPSE IS NO GOOD TO ANYBODY!

GREAT IDEA, UBBI... GET ME A COFFIN I HAVE A PLAN!

A PLAN?

SO UBBI WENT TO THE GATES OF THE CITY AND ASKED TO SEE THE BISHOP.

MY LEADER, HASTEIN, IS OLD AND SICK

51

The Luna massacre was a story told by an Italian historian, not a Viking. But modern historians think it's unlikely to have happened that way. By the time Hastein reached Luna in the ninth century, that city was in ruins anyway. And no Viking remains have ever been found there. Hastein *did* attack towns in the Mediterranean – but he never reached Rome.

Eric the Red – *This is Your Life*

54

Would *you* make a good Viking?

Answer the following questions to see how good a Viking you would be . . .

1 You come home for a meal. What would you prefer?

a) A bag of crisps

b) Bread and cheese

c) Raw polar bear meat

2 Somebody calls your sister "Reindeer-face". What do you do?

a) Agree

b) Hit them

c) Kill them

3 Your wife wears your trousers. What do you do?

a) Wear her dress to get your own back

b) Take them back

c) Divorce her

4 How would you like your bath?

a) Hot with foam

b) In cold water

c) In a steam bath until the dirt runs off with the sweat followed by a roll in deep snow.

5 What is your favourite entertainment?

a) Reading a book

b) Listening to a good story – an exciting one with lots of fighting and dying

c) Picking a fight with someone and wrestling until you're exhausted.

6 You go to a wedding. How long does it take you to enjoy your meal?

a) An hour

b) A day

c) A month

7 You go to a feast and drink strong ale and mead. When do you stop?

a) When you've had enough

b) When you're drunk

c) When you're totally unconscious

8 What is the most entertaining use for horses?

a) Pony trekking

b) Racing

c) Training them to fight one another to the death

9 What would you wear as you went into battle?

a) A bullet-proof vest under a suit of armour

b) A coat of chain mail and a helmet

c) Nothing except a small piece of animal skin to give you the strength of that animal

10 What would you use instead of toilet paper?

a) Yesterday's newspaper

b) Moss

c) Don't use anything

Answers:

Any **a)** answers: Sorry, forget it! You'll never make a Viking. Just be glad you were born in the twentieth century.

Any **b)** answers: Yes. The Vikings would do all these things. You will make a Viking . . . but not a very good one.

Any **c)** answers: You're as vicious as a Viking as Erik the Red!

More than seven **c)** answers . . . I'm only glad I'm not your teacher!

56

Viking names

Would you rather be an Orm, an Ulf or a Bjorn? Or maybe even an Ulfbjorn? If so, you'd be named after an animal.

Orm is a snake

Ulf is a wolf

Bjorn is a bear

So you can work out for yourself what an *Ulfbjorn* was!

Vikings were named after gods – Thor was very popular. Many Viking names are still in use in Britain today – Rolf, Harold and Eric for example. But the great Vikings are known in history by their nicknames. For example, one king is known to us as Harold Fine-hair . . .

Harry's Horrible Hair

The story goes that young Prince Harold fancied a beautiful princess called Gytha.

"Marry me," he begged.

But beautiful Gytha didn't fancy a poor young prince. "Ask me again when you have a proper kingdom to call your own."

Harold swore that he wouldn't cut or comb his hair until he'd made himself ruler of all of Norway. It took him ten years, but he succeeded. Imagine the state of his hair by then! But he won Gytha, so it was all worthwhile.

Then Harold went to the baths and had his hair trimmed, washed and combed. Everyone agreed that he had a fine head of hair. His name changed to Harold Fine-hair. Before, it was Harold Mop-hair!

What name would you give yourself or your friends ... or your teachers? Test your teacher. Which of the following were *really* the names of Vikings?

True or false?

1. HARALD REDBEARD

2. OLAF THE STOUT

3. KON SMELLY-FEET

4. IVAR THE BONELESS

5. SVEIN FORKBEARD

6. ODIN PUDDING-FACE

7. HAROLD BLUETOOTH

8. KEITH FLATNOSE

9. OLAF THE PEACOCK

10. RAGNAR HAIRY BREECHES

11. SIGURD SNAKE-IN-THE-EYE

12. RUDOLPH THE RED-NOSE

13. SIGTRYGG SILK-BEARD

14. SIGRID THE AMBITIOUS

15. FLOKI RAVENS

16. ASGOT THE CLUMSY

17. GLUM

18. CONAN THE LIBRARIAN

19. SIGTRYGG ONE-EYE

20. THOROLF BUTTER

Answer: All are true except 3, 6, 12 and 18

Several of these names belonged to very famous Vikings – Olaf the Stout and Ivar the Boneless, for example. Your teacher probably knows those. But, what teacher *doesn't* tell you . . . because they don't *know* . . . is that the Vikings *weren't* usually known by these nicknames when they were alive! The nicknames were usually invented by history writers in the Middle Ages to describe the different Vikings. So, it would *not* have been a good idea to go up to Viking Keith and say, "Good morning, Mr Flatnose!" The reply might have had something to do with the flattening of your own nose!

Write like a Viking

1 Viking letters were known as Runes. Vikings scratched their runes on wood or stone. It's easier to scratch straight lines than curves. So runes were made up of straight lines.

2 The runes would be used by fortune-tellers who moved from village to village giving people horoscopes.

3 Fortune-tellers were so popular they always got the best food and drink!

4 Fortune-tellers like Kon deserved it. According to a sage . . .

> *The youthful Kon knew all the runes*
> *Runes everlasting, runes life-giving;*
> *Knew also how to save men's lives,*
> *Blunt the sword blades, calm the wild waves,*
> *Could understand the cries of birds;*
> *Could put out flames and quieten sorrows.*

5 Some historians say the rune alphabet was also used for magic. Charms, spells and curses would be written in runes. But the truth is they are only guessing this because some runes couldn't be understood! Most messages were simply everyday business, rather the way someone at home might leave you a message, such as "Don't forget to feed the stick insects" or "Your dinner's in the cat".

IT SAYS "EGGS, MILK BUTTER, BACON AND A PACK OF TOILET MOSS"

6 The rune alphabet was known as the *futhark*. But the order of the letters was quite different to our own alphabet, which is based on the Latin. We learn a-b-c-d-e, the Vikings learned f-u-th-a-r-k.

7 The Viking stories, sagas, weren't written in runes – they were memorised and recited by poets. They were finally written down 200 years after the Viking attacks had finished. They were written in Latin.

8 Twentieth century writers such as J R R Tolkien have used the idea of runes as a secret language. In his book, *The Hobbit*, the runes are the writing of the dwarves.

9 Some runic inscriptions can still be found on stones by the roadside in Scandinavia. They were written on all sorts of things found in the Viking household, because quill pens, ink and parchment (used by the monks in those days) were too expensive. The sort of things that have been found include:

"*Kiss me*" on a piece of bone.

"*Odin*" on a piece of human skull! A sacrifice perhaps?

The word "*kabr*" on a comb . . . and *kabr* means comb!

10 Around the year 800 AD the runic alphabet was reduced to just 16 letters. This is very confusing for us because one letter can have several sounds – you just have to work out which! For example "u" rune can be read as u, oo, y, w, or o. No one knows why the alphabet was shortened in this way.

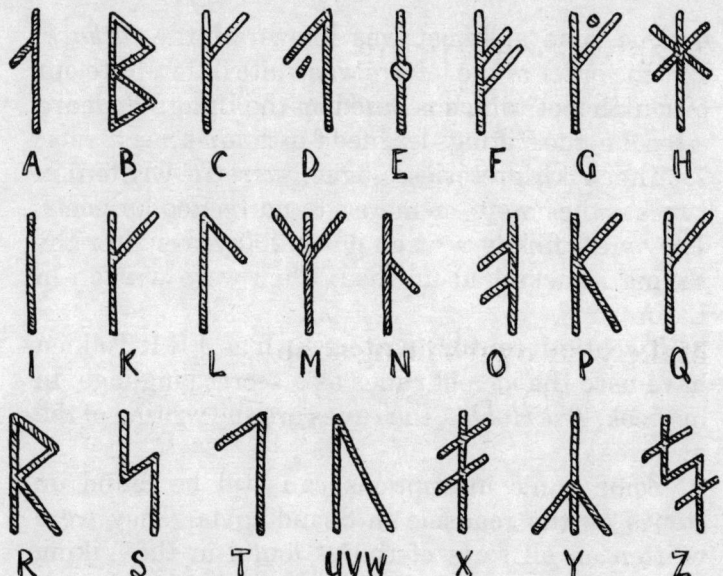

A B C D E F G H
I K L M N O P Q
R S T UVW X Y Z

And here's a rune message . . . or it could be a rude message! What would this mean if it was written by a Saxon on a Viking wall . . . ?

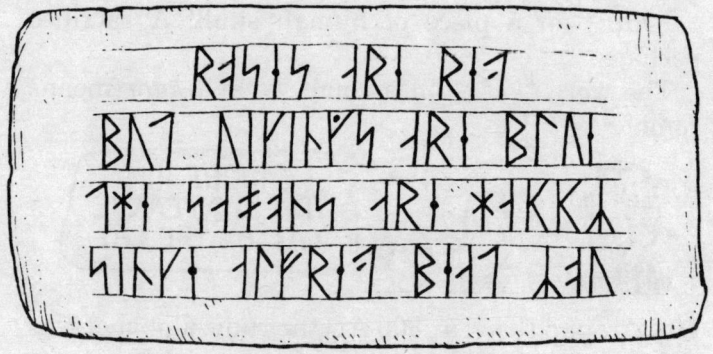

Wash like a Viking

If you decided to wash – and most Vikings did, once a week on a Saturday night – then you'd need some soap. You couldn't pop down to Boots the Chemist to buy some, though. You had to make it yourself. If you want to know what it was like then try this recipe . . .

Make your own Viking soap

1 Peel and mash up some conkers.

2 Add some water.

3 Squeeze out extra water.

4 Mould into the shape of soap.

5 Leave to dry.

6 Use as soap.

Look like a Viking

Maybe you'd like to look like a Viking. Perhaps you're off to a fancy dress party . . . perhaps you want to make a play about Vikings . . . or perhaps you just want to attack a monastery. (Take a bag of chips and then you can say, "Have a chip, monk!") Starting from the floor you'd dress like this . . .

63

Shoes: Vikings wore shoes of soft leather. But sometimes they left the fur of the animals on! Cover your own shoes with some furry material to give the same effect.

Trousers: can be narrow or baggy – the Vikings wore all sorts. Wear an old pair then wind strips of cloth up to the knee in a criss-cross pattern.

Kirtles (knee-length shirts): borrow a large, old shirt. Remove the collar or turn it inside the neck. Leave it hanging outside the trousers. Put a plain leather belt around the waist. (The Viking shirts were made of wool and could be dyed a single colour. They could be embroidered with silk or metal threads.)

Cloak: use a woollen blanket. Fasten at the neck with a brooch. (The Vikings used rough woollen cloaks and they also used animal skins. Wearing animal skins is considered cruel these days . . . so keep your hands off the neighbour's hamster – it would be too small anyway!)

Head gear: the Vikings wore long hair and long moustaches or neatly trimmed beards. (No. Not the women, stupid!) On their heads they wore hoods or fur caps. Of course, when they went into battle, they wore helmets.

Viking women

Would you like to have lived in Viking times? And, if you did, would you like to have been a woman?

Did you know?

Viking women . . .

1 managed the farms while their husbands were away – the chief would hand over his keys before he left.

2 could marry at 12 – but 15 was more usual. Something very odd for those days was that a Viking woman could divorce her husband when she wanted to. One Viking woman divorced her husband because he showed too much bare chest.

THAT'S IT! OUT!

3 would receive a bride-price (cash) from her husband which she kept. She also brought a cash present from her father – but got it back if they divorced.

4 kept their own surnames after marriage.

5 taught daughters to cook, milk cows, churn butter, make cheese, bake bread, brew beer, spin, weave, sew and skin animals – they also learned how to swim and use weapons in case they were attacked. Irish historians told stories of fighting female warriors, but they were probably untrue.

6 could claim land. If a man came to a new country then he could have as much land as he could walk around in one day carrying a flaming torch with him. But, if a woman wanted land then she could have as much as she could walk around in a day leading a two-year-old cow.

7 had names such as . . .

Sigrid	Thora	Ingrid	Gudrun
Tove	Ase	Ragnhild	Gunnhild

8 were banned from longboat raids, but when the Vikings planned to settle a land they would take the women with them on the ships. Women didn't become merchants or craft-workers, but it wasn't all bad: there is a record of a Viking woman who won

fame as travelling poet and another as a rune-carver. There is a story of the Red Maiden who was supposed to have been a warrior-princess in north-eastern Ireland for a while, but it's unlikely to be true.

9 were not treated as equal to men in death. While rich men were buried in their longboats, Viking women were often buried in a wagon instead of a coffin!

10 had work which included combing her husband's hair . . . to get rid of the nits!

The bad news for Viking women . . .

. . . the Viking tribes who settled in Russia adopted some of the strange and vicious funeral customs of the native people. The Arab traveller, Ibn Fadlan, described the funeral of a rich member of the Rus tribe.

Ibn Fadlan called this a "Viking" funeral. A lot of historians have said "this is how the Vikings treated their women". That's not true. All this bit of horrible history writing shows is how "Russian Vikings" treated *some* women. Ibn Fadlan wrote . . .

I'd heard a lot about the burial of the Rus Tribe chiefs and wanted to see one for myself. They burned the body in a ship, but that was nothing compared to what else went on! At last I was told of the death of an important man. Now was my chance to see for myself.

The man had several slave girls as wives. When he died his family asked the wives, "Who wants to go with him?"

One woman answered, "I do!"

When the day of the cremation arrived I went down to the river where his ship lay. I noticed they'd pulled it up on to the shore. Then they brought a bed and put it in the ship. They put a mattress on the bed covered with best Greek cloth.

Then along came an old woman who they called The Angel of Death! She's in charge of arranging everything and of killing the slave girl. She was a grim woman, stout and strong.

On the Friday afternoon they placed the dead man on the bed and covered it with a tent. Then they led the slave girl to a frame . . . a bit like a door frame. She placed her feet on the hands of two men who

67

*lifted her up so she could see over the top of the frame.
"What can you see?" they asked.*

"I can see my master, sitting in Paradise. He is calling for me . . . let me go to him!"

So they took her to the ship. She slipped off the two bracelets she was wearing and gave them to the Angel of Death.

The Angel of Death led the girl into the tent. The men began to beat their shields with sticks so her cries would not be heard and upset the other women.

Then as the men strangled her the Angel of Death plunged a knife into her heart.

The dead man's closest relative took a piece of lighted wood and set fire to a pile of wood beneath the ship. Flames swallowed everything – ship, tent, man and slave-girl.

A man turned to me and said, "You Arabs are stupid!"

"Why's that?" I asked.

"Because you bury your loved ones in the ground where the worms and insects eat them. But we burn them in an instant so they go straight to Paradise."

The idea of burning a body seemed to shock Ibn Fadlan more than the useless death of the slave-girl.

He also described a Rus custom of putting a favourite wife in a grave with a dead husband. The entrance to the grave is then blocked and the wife dies with him.

Today we are used to cremation but would be horrified at the idea of a woman giving up her life just because her husband died. BUT . . . this custom wasn't recorded anywhere else in Viking writings, so perhaps it was more of a rotten Russian habit than a vicious Viking one!

Trouble with the family

If you had a family then you fought to support it in Viking times. You also fought for friends, leaders and your in-laws. Everyone had so many friends and family that sooner or later they'd be involved in a "Blood Feud" – revenge taken by the shedding of blood.

The trouble was that taking revenge wasn't the end of it. The avenger would then have to be punished by his victim's family who would then be avenged by the avenger's family and . . . well, you get the idea!

Long-running feuds could only end when a referee was called in to judge what was to be done. Everyone agreed his decision would be accepted. He would then decide who had suffered the most and order the other family to pay blood-money. The payment of blood-money would even things up. There were no winners and no losers – honour was even and the feud could end.

69

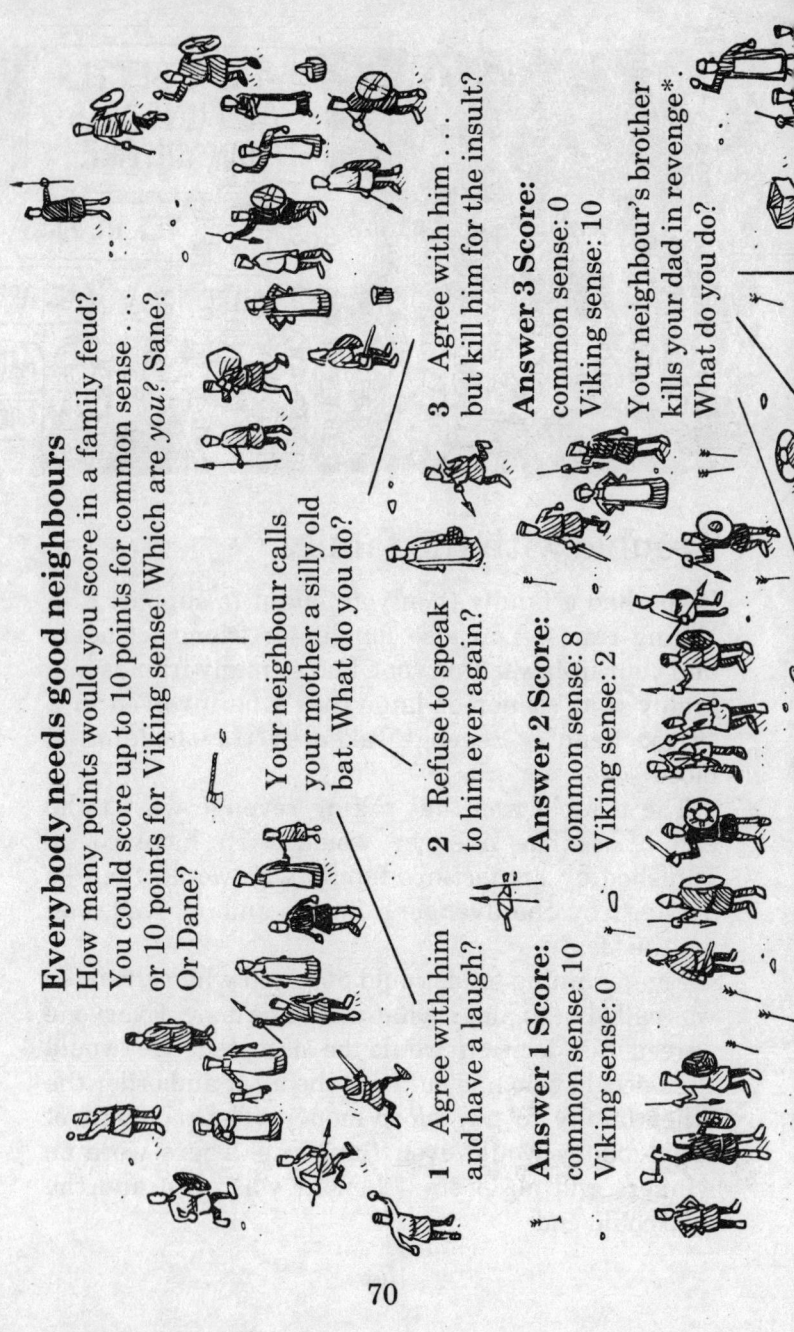

Everybody needs good neighbours

How many points would you score in a family feud? You could score up to 10 points for common sense . . . or 10 points for Viking sense! Which are *you*? Sane? Or Dane?

Your neighbour calls your mother a silly old bat. What do you do?

1 Agree with him and have a laugh?

2 Refuse to speak to him ever again?

3 Agree with him . . . but kill him for the insult?

Answer 1 Score:
common sense: 10
Viking sense: 0

Answer 2 Score:
common sense: 8
Viking sense: 2

Answer 3 Score:
common sense: 0
Viking sense: 10

Your neighbour's brother kills your dad in revenge* What do you do?

70

a) Demand "Blood Money" – cash for the life of your father?

Answer a) Score:
common sense: 2
Viking sense: 8

b) Call all of your family to fight all of the neighbour's family?

Answer b) Score:
common sense: 1
Viking sense: 9

c) Have a "Burn-in" – catch the neighbours at home, set fire to their house and give them a choice – die in the fire or come out and die by your swords?**

Answer c) Score:
common sense: 0
Viking sense: 10

*When it came to revenge the avengers didn't always pick the killer – they often picked the most important member of the family ... even if he had nothing whatever to do with the original crime or insult!!

**If you married into a feuding family you could choose whether or not you wanted to be part of the feud. A Viking woman who chose to die with her husband was Bergthora. Enemies set fire to her home in order to kill Njal, her husband, and her sons. They called to Bergthora to come outside and she would be spared. She came out and said, "When I married Njal I promised that we would share the same fate." Then she walked back inside to die with him.

71

Not all Viking women felt the same loyalty as Bergthora. Especially when their husbands had been bullies! Njal's best friend was Gunnar. And his wife had *quite* a different way of behaving when enemies came knocking on the door . . .

Hallgerd's diary

My husband Gunnar was Trouble. That's right . . . with a capital "T". Whenever there was a fight in Bergthorshvoll then you could be sure Gunnar was in the middle of it. He was a bully and a trouble-maker. Once – just once – he slapped me on the face. I couldn't hit him back. But I could wait for my revenge, couldn't I?

The day came when the council sentenced Gunnar to be exiled for three years. That meant he could leave Iceland, and live, or he could stay and the law would not stop his enemies from killing him. And believe me, Gunnar had enemies!

He decided to leave, but a strange thing happened. As he rode to the quay where his boat was moored, his horse stumbled. He fell over its head and landed on his feet . . . facing the way he had come. He took

LOOK DADDY!
AN ACROBAT

one look back at his beloved farm and said, "Right! That's it! I'm not going." And he came back home.

Word got around and by nightfall the house was surrounded. Now, not even Gunnar could fight 100 men with his sword. But he *could* stay in the house and defend himself with his bow and arrows.

That's what he did. Until suddenly his bowstring snapped. "That's done it," he sighed. "I'm a dead man."

"Shame," I said.

Then he looked at me sort of funny. He reached out a hand and stroked my hair. "Lovely hair," he muttered.

"Thanks very much," I said. "It's not like you to pay me a compliment."

"I was just thinking. That hair would make me a wonderful new bowstring!"

"Would it?" I smiled.

"It would." He raised his knife. "Can I take a piece?"

"Remember the day you slapped my face?" I asked.

"What sort of answer is that?" he asked.

"It's the sort of answer that means 'NO'!" I told him.

"You shall not be asked again," he said. And he went out to die like a Viking. I'll say that for him. He died well.

But I'll say something else – and you men take note – he'll not be slapping me on the face again!

Viking children

You may complain about Terrible Teachers and Pain-in-the-neck Parents. But life as a Viking child would have been harder than yours. For a start, childhood would have been short. The boys would begin raiding as soon as they were old enough and the girls would be farming and doing housework for most of their lives. Life was particularly horrible for the Viking slave classes – the thralls.

Children's lesson no. 1: Don't get yourself born as a thrall!

A Viking writer described thralls as . . .

Wrinkled hands and knobbled knuckles,
Fingers thick and face foul-looking,
Back bowed down, and big flat feet.

(Does that sound like anyone you know?)

Graveyard queue

A thrall's life was not a happy one.

She/he had to work on the land to make a living, but she/he also had to work for a master for no pay! And what work!

A male slave would . . .
- build walls
- cover the fields with manure
- herd pigs and goats
- dig peat (a sort of turf burned for fuel)

A female slave would . . .
- grind corn by hand
- milk cows and goats
- make cheese
- cook
- wash

Thralls had to have their master's permission to get married. They couldn't go anywhere without permission. But a thrall could work hard and buy his freedom. Apart from freedom in life he even got a better *death!* The Christian laws of south-east Norway give an order for burying people in the graveyard . . .

- the freemen, their wives and children get the best spot – near the church
- then come the thralls and their families, further from the church
- lastly come the corpses washed ashore – so long as the corpse had a Norwegian hair-style. If it didn't then it was a foreigner – and it probably didn't get into the graveyard at all.

HMM... I DON'T KNOW. I THINK HIS HAIR LOOKS A BIT THRALLISH

HE DOES STYLING ON THE WEEKEND!

Did you know . . . ?
It was against the law to call a free-born man a "thrall" (a slave). The biggest disgrace was to die in a fight with a thrall.

Icelandic houses

Children and women would spend more time at home than the men. This must have been especially hard if you lived in a Viking house in Iceland . . .

To keep out the cold the Vikings lived in houses built of turf. The walls were thick and the houses looked like little hills. The children could play on the roofs . . . and keep the animals off, because the danger was that a hungry cow would climb up and eat through your roof.

The houses were pretty air-tight. The good news was that this kept out the cold. The bad news was that it also kept out the light and kept in the smoke from your fire. As your fuel may have been cattle-droppings then you had a choice – freeze outside or choke inside!

If you wanted a bath then you'd pop down to the bath house. It was what we'd call a "sauna" today. Water was poured over hot stones and you had a steam-clean. To really freshen up you'd whip yourself with twigs . . . then run outside to roll in the snow. If you were a softie then you'd go along to one of Iceland's warm-water springs.

Viking fun

Of course, there were no schools. Children learned by working alongside their mothers and fathers. But there would be a little time for play. If you'd like to try a Viking game, then play . . .

Kingy bats

1 Take a circle of wood about 40 cm across.
2 Glue or staple a strap across the back so you can hold it like a shield. Each player needs one of these bats.
3 Make a ball out of rags bound up with string (about the size of a tennis ball).
4 Stand in a circle and pass the rag ball.
5 To make it a competition, split into pairs. The winners are the pair who can keep the ball in the air longest without letting it hit the ground.

- Other children's games included making up poems and riddles. An adult game, which children might have tried, included a type of chess.
  And just as we have the shot put in today's athletics, the Vikings threw boulders. The furthest was the winner.

HE'S STRONGER THAN HE LOOKS

- Vikings made skates for crossing frozen rivers. The skates were made from bones, and poles were used to push the skaters along, rather like skiing today. The Vikings called their skates "ice-legs"!

A Viking game you probably wouldn't want to play: P-pick up a Puffin

In Iceland today, a Viking descendant describes the national sports as gannet-egg-gathering and puffin hunting. They catch flying puffins in a net on the end of a pole then wring their necks and eat them roasted. 12,000 puffins a year die like this.

So now you know something about life for Viking warriors, women and children. Now amaze your friends, your parents and even your horrible history teachers with . . .

Ten things you didn't know about the Vikings

1 Early Vikings had no buttons – they used brooches. And their houses had no windows.

2 The Viking blacksmiths hardened their swords by cooling them quickly in water – or sometimes in blood!

3 The children's song, *London Bridge is Falling Down*, is about a Viking attack led by Olaf. English soldiers fired arrows from the bridge into Olaf's attacking longboats. So Olaf attached ropes to the bridge's wooden legs and the other ends to his ships. The Vikings rowed away as fast as they could. Result . . . London Bridge was falling down!

4 If you made a sacrifice to the gods and wanted all your neighbours to know how good you were, then you'd put it on poles outside your front door!

WE COULD ONLY AFFORD A LEMMING THIS WEEK

5 Viking warriors could make close friends into "blood brothers" by cutting themselves and letting their blood mix. They often did the mixing under a circle of turf that had been lifted from the ground. Their blood mixed with the soil to make mud!

6 The Vikings made a promise by swearing an oath on a holy ring. This was a ring that was placed on an altar and reddened with the blood of a sacrificed animal.

7 One group of Vikings were reported to have a curious funeral custom. They split the dead man's possessions up and placed them in five or six portions. They placed these within a mile of the dead man's house. Then the men took their horses and raced to the piles. The first to get there won the dead man's loot!

8 The Vikings rarely took prisoners in sea battles because there was no room for them in the longboats. They let the losers drown or killed them.

9 No one was taken on board a longboat unless they had proved they were skilled with an oar, a sword and an axe.

10 Vikings shared their treasures evenly. You agreed what your share would be when you joined the longboat crew.

Vile Viking food

Would you like to eat a "cauldron snake"? Probably. It's the Viking name for a sausage spiced with thyme and garlic.

Summers were often short, cold and wet (just like Britain really!), whilst in winter it snowed from October to February. Crops had little time to grow, and poor harvests meant no food. So Vikings either starved or . . . went hunting.

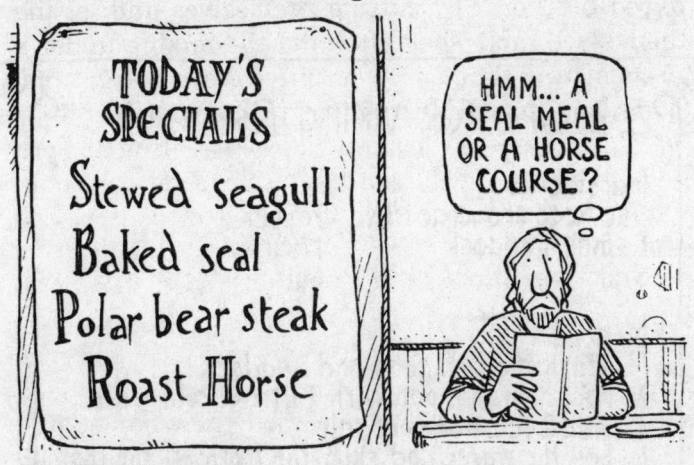

Vile Viking joke:

Viking food you might like to try . . .

Some of the food, like cheeses and smoked meats, needed no cooking. Bread was baked and meat roasted on a spit, or baked in a deep pit covered with hot stones. Sometimes it was boiled in an iron cauldron.

Food and soup was served in wooden bowls, and drink taken from cups made from the horns of animals such as reindeer. The Vikings used knives, fingers and sometimes very small spoons – but no forks.

RECIPE FOR VIKING FISH SOUP

Ingredients:
The head of a large fish   Pepper
1 small haddock   Flour
Salt   Milk

Method:
1 Wash the fish head and haddock
2 Put them in a pan with 1 litre of cold water
3 Add 2 teaspoons of salt
4 Boil the water and skim the froth off the top
5 Add pepper and leave to simmer (boil gently) for 40 minutes
6 Strain the mixture to get rid of the bones and put the liquid (fish stock) back in the pan
7 Mix 2 tablespoons of flour with a cup of milk
8 Add the flour and milk mixture to the fish stock
9 Boil until the soup thickens
10 Check if it needs more salt or pepper
11 Serve with warm bread rolls

Some Viking foods you wouldn't want to try . . .

True or False? The Vikings ate . . .

1 Easily netted and very tasty in Viking stew

2 Nothing wasted, goose feathers were also used for bedding and quilts

3 A great alternative to chicken and goose

4 Skins used for clothing

5 A wild version of today's pig

6 Meat was eaten and the fur made into clothes or used for trade with other countries

7 Waste not want not. Walrus ivory was in great demand from those in foreign countries

8 Roaming through massive forests by the fjords, even moose weren't safe from the Vikings' bows. Their antlers were used as knife handles and hair combs

9 The Vikings appear to have been the first whale hunters. It often took between 10 and 15 men to kill just one whale, all taking turns to spear the poor creature. A long and painful death for the whale, but to the Vikings the whale was the scourge of the sea, often overturning their ships, so it deserved to die

10 Even the horses didn't escape the mighty Viking sword . . . yes, once the poor family nag was past it – chop!

The Vikings also enjoyed seaweed . . . the Welsh still eat it (but they call it lava bread) and it's considered a delicacy in Japanese restaurants.

During bad winters (most winters!) the Vikings ate anything they could catch, including foxes and ravens.

A Viking you wouldn't want to have tea with . . .

Harthacnut was Viking King of England from 1040 till 1042. He *could* have had a feast set out just once a day. If guests got hungry later, they *could* have eaten the leftovers. But Harthacnut wouldn't have this. When the guests had finished a feast he had the tables cleared of leftovers. Then another feast was set out. And after that another!

Every day he had FOUR feasts set out. Surprise, surprise – Harthacnut died young from eating and drinking too much.

What did Vikings drink?

Beer and mead were drunk from the horns of cattle. This was an art in itself – a trickle could soon become a tidal wave if the horn was tipped too far!

Another major problem was the horn's shape – it couldn't be put down unless it was empty. The drink had to be drunk in one go, hence a drunken Viking was a common sight.

Viking bread . . . or, teeth don't grow on trees!

When food was scarce, Viking women made bread with flour, peas and pine-tree bark (for roughage and for vitamin C).

This, as you would imagine, would not taste very nice at all. It would be extremely heavy and filling and would most probably fall to the pit of your stomach – like a rock – AND it had rocks in it too! Experts have found small pieces of grit in samples of this bread taken from old Viking settlements in York.

Vicious Viking ancient joke:

Vicious Viking historians

We have learned a lot about the Vikings from the people who wrote histories of Britain many years ago. The trouble is that the writers often gave their opinions, which is not the same as giving us *facts*.

What they said about the Vikings . . .

For nearly 350 years we and our forebears have lived in this most lovely land. Never before has such a terror appeared in Britain as we have now suffered from this pagan race. No one thought such an attack could come from the sea.

Alcuin 735–804 AD
  – a monk and a very bad loser

The town of Hedeby (in Denmark) is poor in goods and wealth. The people's chief food is fish because there is so much of it. If a child is born there it is thrown into the sea to save bringing it up. I have never heard anything more horrible than their singing. It is more like the barking of dogs only twice as beastly.

Al-Tartushi
  – an Arab trader and a bit of a snob

... And what they didn't say!

This is what the poor English were *supposed* to have chanted as they trembled in their tiny churches. Nearly every book on the Vikings quotes this prayer of terrified people. The truth is there is no evidence that anyone ever actually said these words! It's simply something that scholars and teachers think they should have said.

What the Vikings did do ...

There is a story that King Canute (or Knut) sat at the edge of the sea and tried to tell the tide to go back, saying "I command you not to rise over my land and not to wet the clothes or feet of your lord!" The tide came in anyway and soaked him.

The story is true. Teachers used to tell it to children and say, "What a foolish man King Canute was, children!"

BUT they forgot to say that the story went on – King Knut jumped back on dry land and said, "Let it be known to all people that the power of kings is empty and weak. Only one person is fit to be called king. That is the Lord God who is obeyed by heaven, by earth and by the sea!"

Knut took his golden crown off and never wore it again. He wasn't saying, "Look how great I am." He was saying, "Look how weak we are compared to God."

. . . and what they didn't do!

Samuel Pepys wrote in his diary of 10 April 1661 that he went

> *to Rochester and saw the cathedral where the great doors of the church are, they say, covered with the skins of the Danes.*

This was said to be the fate of invaders who were caught – skinned alive in revenge and the skin nailed to the church door. But tests on a "Daneskin" at Westminster Abbey proved it to be the skin of a cow!

Rotten Riddle

True or false . . . ?

1 There was a rule to stop Vikings fighting each other on the longboats.

2 King Alfred had a beard.

3 The Viking men and women wore make-up.

YOU'RE NOT COMING ON MY BOAT LOOKING LIKE THAT!
GO AND FIX YOUR EYELINER

4 King Alfred's wife claimed that the god, Odin, was her ancestor.

5 Viking Halfdan was so wicked that God turned him mad and made him smell so rotten that no one would go near him.

6 The Viking longboats were as long as a tennis court.

7 A longboat sail could cover a tennis court.

8 The Saxon cure for losing your voice was to make the sign of the cross under your tongue.

9 Alfred the Great didn't build many monasteries because they were favourite targets of the Vikings.

10 Viking longboats had no seats.

Answers:
1 True 2 False 3 True 4 True 5 True (According to the monk, Simeon of Durham) 6 True 7 False (It would take three sails to cover a tennis court) 8 True 9 True 10 True (The oarsmen sat on the chests that carried their belongings)

91

The savage Saxons

The Vikings may have been called vicious but we have to remember they lived in harsh times. Their enemies in the British Isles, the Saxons, weren't far behind when it came to being cruel.

At least two English princes killed their brothers to win the throne of England: Harold Godwinsson did it through battle and Ethelred did it through murder. And they weren't the worst!

Six savage Saxon stories

1 King Edmund Ironside was a fierce fighter. In one battle, an enemy called Edric climbed a hill and waved a severed head in the air. "Surrender!" he called to Edmund's men. "This is the head of your leader, Edmund!"

Edmund was furious. He tore off his helmet to show his men that he was still alive. He then flung his spear at Edric. He threw it so hard that it bounced off Edric's shield and went through TWO soldiers who were standing beside him!

2 Edric's son finished Edmund off in the nastiest way you could imagine. One night Edmund went to a room with a pit that was used for a toilet. In the darkness he didn't see Edric's son hiding in the pit. As King Edmund sat down on the toilet the young man struck him twice from beneath with a dagger . . . ouch!

WHO WAS THAT BLOKE CREEPING AROUND ALL COVERED IN BLOOD?

I DON'T KNOW, BUT HE SMELLED LIKE A TOILET PIT

But the Viking King Knut was not amused by this cheating. When Edric went to tell Knut he'd got rid of the Vikings' greatest enemy he promised to reward Edric. "I will place you higher than any other English noble." He did. He cut off Edric's head and stuck it on the highest battlement of the Tower of London!

3 Earl Godwin was banished from England for disobeying the good King Edward. A year later Godwin returned. He went to dinner with the king and tried to be a bit of a creep. "People say I killed your brother," he told the king. "But, if that is true, then may God let this piece of bread choke me." A minute later Godwin was dead. He had choked on the piece of bread!

4 The Saxons were Christians and when they defeated the Vikings in battle they often made the Vikings become Christian. But Christianity at that time wasn't all sweetness and light! Early in the tenth century AD, Pope Stephen VI was elected as head of the Catholic Church in Rome. One of his first acts was to put the previous Pope, Formosus, on trial for dishonesty and evil living. Formosus was found guilty because he refused to plead when asked, "Are you guilty or not guilty?" Of course the reason he didn't plead was that he was dead at the time; Stephen VI had had him dug up and his body brought to court. The guilty corpse was thrown into the River Tiber. (You'll be pleased to hear that gruesome Stephen VI died soon after – imprisoned then strangled in his cell.) And they called the Vikings savages!

5 The Vikings attacked the north-east coast of England and its monasteries in 793 AD. Then, as your teacher and your timeline will tell you, they didn't bother much for another 40 years! Why not? The truth is too horrible for school books to tell you . . . but this *Horrible History* will tell you! After the 793 raid on Lindisfarne, the Vikings came back to attack the Jarrow monastery on the River Tyne. But this time bad weather held up their landing. By the time they reached the shore the local people were armed and ready. The Vikings landed – and were attacked fiercely. The Viking king was captured and tortured to death. The bloody remains were sent back to Denmark as a warning of what would happen if they tried to attack again! So the Vikings missed out England for 40 years . . . and went round to pillage Ireland instead!

6 The Saxons didn't like Abbot John of Athelney, even though he was King Alfred's choice. Abbot John was a German who was very harsh with the people who visited his churches. So the local people planned to kill him and dump his body outside the house of a woman. (They wanted it to look as if he was visiting her when he was killed by a jealous lover.) But the plot went wrong. The big abbot fought for his life. He was cut on the head but his cries brought help to rescue him.

Edmund's evil end

If King Edmund's serving girls could write, and if
one of them had kept a diary, then some of it might
have looked like this . . .

Ethel's Diary

27 May 946

Dear Diary,

That's it. I am packing this rotten job in. My mum
wanted me to be a servant to the King. "A great
honour," she said. "You start tomorrow!"

"That Edmund's a terrible man for chasing girls!" I
told her. "Everybody's heard the story about him
and that nun."

"Wulfhilda?" said Mum.

"That's the one. Had
her taken to a convent in
Hampshire so he could
chat her up, didn't he?" I
said.

"But he didn't," my
mum pointed out.

"Only because she
climbed down the
convent drainpipes to
escape! I don't want to go
getting chased down drainpipes," I sniffed.

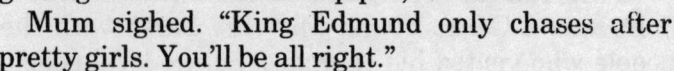

NOW WHERE'S SHE GONE?

Mum sighed. "King Edmund only chases after
pretty girls. You'll be all right."

"Thanks mum," I snapped.

And mum went on to tell me about how to serve
and clean and curtsey. She warned me not to spit or
swear.

But she didn't warn me about the mess!

I mean to say, it's bad enough normally. All that

feasting and throwing bones on the floor. And that bad-tempered King Edmund ordering you about. But last night was the end . . . the end for Edmund and for me.

Blood all over the place!

It all started all right. These parties always do. The feast of St Augustine, of course, but that was just the excuse for a booze-up.

I was rushed off me feet all night. I didn't mind too much. They were good lads, mostly, as long as I kept their mead cups full. But there was one I didn't like the look of at all. Dirty hair over a low forehead and a scowl that could kill a cat.

Suddenly the King looks at this villain. He jumps to his feet and shouts, "Leofa!"

The ugly man rose to his feet and sneered. "That's me!"

"I banished you for thieving six years ago!" the King cried and rushed forward. He grabbed this Leofa by the hair – personally, I don't know how he could bear to touch that filthy mop. But he did, and he threw the robber on to the floor.

Now everyone gathered round in a circle and started shouting. You know the kind of thing, "Get stuck in, Eddie! Put the boot in, your highness!" and so on.

So the two of them are wrestling on the floor and suddenly the King gives a great cry. He jerks up and falls back.

I knew at once there was something wrong. I could tell because there was a long dagger sticking out of the king's chest.

"Ooooh!" the crowd gasped, as they do. All I could think was that all that blood would take a lot of clearing up in the morning.

And somebody yelled, "That's cheating, that is. Using daggers isn't fighting fair!"

And someone else said, "The King's dead . . . there'll be trouble, you mark my words."

Then a man behind me growled. "That's murder, that is! Get him, lads!"

Now I saw this with my own eyes so I swear it's true. Nobody used a weapon on Leofa. But in the flutter of a butterfly's wing Leofa was torn apart. That's right, torn.

It was a nasty death . . . but a quick one.

It was also a very messy one.

Oh, yes, they took the King's body away to give him a fine funeral. A lot of weeping and moaning and sadness. Very sad, I'm sure. But who gets the nasty job of clearing up that mess?

That's right. Me.

Well, I've had enough.

It might be a great honour to serve the King. But if they're going to go tearing people apart then I'm packing it in.

LOOK WHAT THEY'VE DONE TO MY NICE CLEAN FLOOR

St Dunstan predicted the messy murder of Edmund. In a vision, he saw a devil dancing before him. It's a pity he didn't tell Edmund – the King could have worn his knife-proof vest. At least the nuns of Wessex felt a little safer after Edmund's murder! And young Wulfhilda became a saint.

The suffering Saxons

Life in the Dark Ages was tough for the Saxons. They had more problems than simply vicious Viking raids to cope with . . .

Test your friends . . .

1 Saint Dunstan was on his way to the dying King Eadred when an angel appeared and announced, "Behold! King Eadred is departed in peace." But what did Dunstan's horse do?
a) Learned to speak and said, "Nay! Do not say so!"
b) Ran off and dumped Dunstan on his head

c) Dropped dead with shock at the sight of a dirty great angel

2 The story of the Battle of Hastings is told in pictures on the Bayeux Tapestry. But what exactly is the Bayeux Tapestry?
a) A painting on cloth
b) A tapestry (that's a picture made by weaving threads)
c) An embroidery (a picture made by stitching)

3 The baby Ethelred was taken to church to be christened. The monk, St Dunstan, held the baby over the stone bowl that held the christening water – the font. Suddenly St Dunstan announced, "This is an evil sign! While this baby becomes king there will be death for many Saxons!" But what was the evil sign?

a) Lightning struck the church

b) Baby Ethelred cried all the way through the service

c) Baby Ethelred had a pee in the font

4 The Viking King Knut had a son who became king. His name was Harold Harefoot. A Saxon prince, Alfred, came to England to visit his mother. Harold Harefoot was worried that Alfred might try to take over the throne. What did horrible Harold do to Alfred's friends?

a) Locked them up in chains

b) Sold them as slaves

c) Scalped them

5 What did Harold do to Alfred himself?

a) Had his eyes put out

b) Made him promise not to lead a rebellion

c) Gave him money to go away

6 Harold Harefoot died in 1040 and his even-horribler-half-brother, Harthacnut, became king. What was his first act as king?

a) He had a statue built to honour his dear, dead brother, Harold

b) He had Harold dug up and buried in a specially-built church

c) He had Harold dug up, the head cut off and thrown into the Thames

7 King Harold Godwinsson was killed at the Battle of Hastings in 1066. But how did he die?

a) He was cut down by a knight's sword

b) He was hit in the eye with an arrow

c) He was wounded in the eye with an arrow then killed with a sword

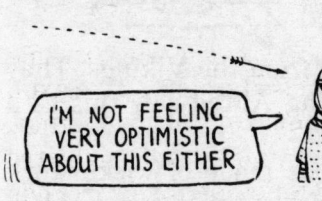 

8 King Alfred was buried in Hyde Abbey. But when Henry VIII abolished the abbeys, Alfred's bones were dug up. Eventually they ended up in Winchester Cathedral. What state are they in today?

a) Mixed up with the bones of other dead Saxons

b) Buried in their own grave

c) Cremated and the ashes scattered over the Edington battlefield

101

9 What cure would a Saxon doctor offer you for a bad stomach?

a) Drink a bowl of cat's milk mixed with a drop of dog's blood

b) Starve until noon, take a hot bath then drink treacle in warm water

c) Two indigestion tablets

10 Three Irish monks fled from the Vikings. They reached England safely. King Alfred saw this as a miracle of God because . . .

a) They had sailed in a boat made of wickerwork and stretched skins and had no food, no oars and no steering plank

b) They had walked across the Irish Sea at low tide

c) They had stolen a Viking longboat and sailed across the Irish Sea

102

Here's why!

1c) And, would you believe it, when Dunstan arrived at the palace, King Eadred was dead! He died at the moment that the angel appeared. (But he might have been able to save the king if his horse hadn't turned up its hooves and made Dunstan late!)

2c) It is a strip of embroidered linen measuring 40 metres by 50 centimetres – it tells the story a bit like a strip cartoon.

3c) Sure enough Ethelred was an unlucky king for the Saxons. Nearly as unlucky as the next baby to be christened in that font!

4a), b) and c) He also tortured and murdered some.

5a) The blinded Prince Alfred was handed over to a monastery and he spent the rest of his life with the monks.

6c) The dead Harold's head was dragged up in a fisherman's net and buried in the Danes' cemetery in London (St Clement Danes).

7c) That is the way Henry of Huntingdon described Harold's death. Some people have said the Bayeux tapestry shows Harold killed by an arrow, but it's not really clear. Harold's leg was hacked off after he was killed. William the Conqueror was so upset by this disgraceful act that he sacked the knight who did it.

The wicked woman of Wessex

In the nineteenth and twentieth centuries we've had more years when we were ruled by queens than by kings. But in the 300 years of Viking England there wasn't a single queen to be seen. Saxons reckoned this was because of one woman ruler who'd been so bad they never wanted another.

If there'd been a poet to tell her dreadful story then the poem would not have sounded like this! (Only the facts are right!)

Queen Eadburgh and Beothric

King Beothric married a woman, Eadburgh,
A bossy and vicious old crow.
He had a young pal that he liked quite a lot,
Till Eadburgh said, "He'll have to go!"

The King he refused and Eadburgh got cross,
So she poisoned poor Beothric's friend.
Alas for the King he had drunk the same stuff
And came to the same sticky end.

The Saxons they drove out the murdering fiend
And she fled with the loot from their house.
She went overseas to an Emperor's court
'Cos she wanted another rich spouse.

The Emperor said, "You may marry your choice.
Would you prefer me or my son?"
She picked the young prince and that made the dad
    mad!
He said, "Right then! You'll get neither one!"

Eadburgh was sent to a convent so quiet,
A house full of nuns good and dear.
But her parties and rave-ups became far too wild
So the nuns threw her out on her ear.

She wandered around with one servant and sank
Down to begging on streets, what a plight!
And that's how Eadburgh came to her sad end.
And the Saxons said, "Serves the bat right!"

King Alfred the cake

King Alfred the Great was a winner
A true man of God, not a sinner,
He wrote several books
But wasn't a cook
So don't ask him to look after dinner!

King Alfred is the only king in English history to be called "Great". Just when it looked as if England was going to be overrun by Vikings, he led the resistance and saved at least half of the country.

Like many of the characters who lived in those days, the truth about his life is a little bit mixed up with stories. The trouble is that most of the stories come from a monk called Asser. Asser got his facts from Alfred . . . but Alfred could have told a few fibs to make himself look a great hero. Here are . . .

Tall stories about Alfred the Great

How many of these stories do you believe?

Story 1: Alfred the clever
As a five-year-old boy, Alfie was a bit of a cheat. His mother promised her sons that the first boy who could read her book would be given it. So Alf took it to a teacher. The teacher read it. Alf learned it off by heart, went back to his mum and recited it.
Facts: This is one of Asser's stories. In another part of his book Asser says Alfred couldn't read "until the twelfth year of his age or even more".

Story 2: Alfred the spy

He was also a bit of a cheat in later years. He dressed up as a minstrel, wandered into the Viking camp and listened to the Viking plans. A few days later he wandered back to the Saxon camp, spilled the beans, and battered the Vikings.

Facts: This is a story first written down 500 years after Alfred died. Would a king really risk his life in this way? The Vikings might not have recognised him as Alf – but they could have executed him anyway as a Saxon spy!

WHO WAS THAT MINSTREL SNOOPING AROUND?

I DON'T CARE, AS LONG AS HE'S GONE.. WORST SINGING I EVER HEARD

Story 3: Alfred the friend of a ghost

Alfred seems to have had a bit of supernatural help. The Saxons claimed that the ghost of St Cuthbert appeared to Alfred and told him how to beat the Vikings! After Alfred died he was buried in the old Hyde abbey until the building of Winchester was finished. Then he was moved. But monks claimed that his ghost stayed and haunted Hyde Abbey!

Facts: Asser said it was St Neot who appeared! But perhaps Asser was trying to show how great the south-of-England Saint, Neot, was. The Cuthbert story was told by a northern monk ... trying to prove how powerful the northern St Cuthbert was!

Story 4: Alfred the inventor 1

Alfred was supposed to have invented the clock! He needed to measure time so he could spend half of each day and night praying. But sundials don't work on cloudy days . . . and they work even worse at night! So Alfred had candles marked in inches and measured the hours by the time it took to burn. But, in the draughty churches, the candles blew out. So . . .

Story 5: Alfred the inventor 2

Alfred invented the lantern! There was no glass but clever Alf had ox-horn cut so thin that you could see clean through it.

Facts: Both are stories from Asser.

Story 6: Alfred the inventor 3

Alfred invented the navy. He decided that it was a good idea to attack the Vikings at sea, before they landed. At sea the Vikings were cramped into their longboats and couldn't fight and row at the same time. Great idea . . . Alf made it work well.

Facts: The truth is his dad and his grandad both attacked the Vikings at sea as long ago as 851, off the Kent coast.

Story 7: Alfred the religious

Apart from praying day and night Alfred sent money to the Pope in Rome. In 883 Pope Marinus sent Alfred a present – a lump of wood that was supposed to be from the cross on which Jesus was crucified.

Facts: Marinus died. The next Pope, Formosus, pinched the church's money, and poisoned his brother and his wife. Alfred stopped sending money!

MAYBE IF I SENT ALFRED SOME MORE BITS OF WOOD HE'D START SENDING MONEY AGAIN

Story 8: Alfred the humble

When Alfred was having a bad time against the Viking invaders he hid out in a forest. A forester's wife gave him the job of watching her cakes to make sure they didn't burn. Alf was so busy fixing his bow that he forgot to turn the cakes over. They burned. The woman gave Alfred a piece of her mind. He could have said, "You can't talk to me like that – I'm the King!" Instead he just said, "Sorry."

Facts: This story is first found written down 400 years after it happened. Another 400 years passed and the Archbishop of Canterbury made a copy of Asser's book . . . and slipped the story of the burning cakes in! Other historians copied it, thinking it came from Asser and must be true!

Final Fact: Don't believe everything you read!!!

Judge for yourself

King Alfred took all the old laws and organised them into a new book of laws for the Saxons. Some of the laws were fair – others were pretty daft.

For example, there were four ways of finding out if a person was guilty of a crime. They were called ordeals. If you passed through the ordeal you were innocent – but if you failed you suffered from both the test and then a punishment.

Imagine you have been accused of a terrible crime – somebody has let your teacher's bicycle tyres down! The finger of suspicion is pointing at you.

"I didn't do it!" you cry.

"I think you did!" the tyreless teacher trembles. "Take a trial by ordeal! If you refuse to take the test then you are guilty – take your pick of ordeals!"

Choose your ordeal

1 **Ordeal by cake:** A special cake is baked. Swear,

"If I did this crime then may this cake choke me!"

and eat the cake.
If you're guilty
then you choke on the cake
– if you're innocent you live.

110

2 Ordeal by cold water: You are tied hand and foot. A rope is placed around you and you are lowered into a pool. If you sink then you are innocent . . . and with a bit of luck you'll be hauled out before you drown. If you float then you are guilty. You'll be dragged out and punished. (This silly test was still being used in the seventeenth century to test people accused of being witches!)

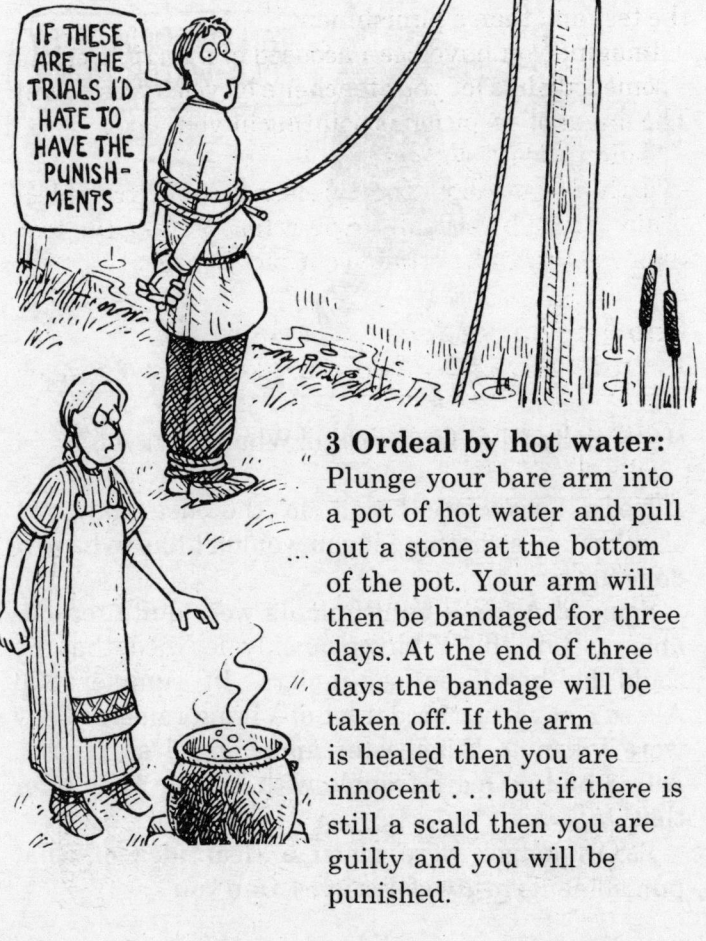

IF THESE ARE THE TRIALS I'D HATE TO HAVE THE PUNISHMENTS

3 Ordeal by hot water: Plunge your bare arm into a pot of hot water and pull out a stone at the bottom of the pot. Your arm will then be bandaged for three days. At the end of three days the bandage will be taken off. If the arm is healed then you are innocent . . . but if there is still a scald then you are guilty and you will be punished.

111

4 Ordeal by hot metal: You have to grip a rod of hot iron in your hand and walk with it for a set distance. Again the hand is bandaged for three days. If it's healed you're innocent – if there's a burn on your hand you're guilty.

CAN I DO ORDEAL BY COLD WATER NOW?

(Personally I'd go for the cake! What about you?)

Alfred's laws were based on the idea that you shouldn't do something if you wouldn't like to have it done to you.

Some of Alfred's punishments were quite reasonable . . . but the Vikings quickly learned that he could be harsh on sea-raiders. In summer 896 Alfred's navy captured a lot of Viking raiders. They were taken to Winchester and hanged as pirates. Alfred had no more trouble with Viking raids after that!

Saxon judges were given a clear idea of what punishments to give for crimes. Can you . . .

Make the punishment fit the crime?

1 The punishment for witchcraft (having dealings with the Devil) was . . .
a) Having your head shaved
b) Having to go to church every day for a year
c) Death
2 The penalty for plotting against your lord was . . .
a) Having "traitor" tattooed on your forehead
b) Death
c) Having your toes cut off

3 The penalty for stealing a hive of bees was . . .
a) A fine
b) To be covered in honey and stung to death by the bees
c) To be covered in honey and thrown into a bear's cage

4 The penalty for killing a man accidentally by letting a tree you are cutting fall on him . . .

a) You are hung from the tree

b) You are burned on a fire made from the wood of the tree

c) You must give the tree to the family of the dead man

WAIT A MINUTE, THIS CAN'T BE RIGHT

5 The penalty if your dog attacks and kills another person . . .

a) A fine of six shillings for the first killing, 12 shillings for a second killing and 30 shillings if it kills three people

b) The dog's owner is executed

c) The dog is executed

6 The penalty for telling nasty lies about a person was . . .

a) Having to walk a mile on your knees to their house and say "Sorry"

b) Having to write a letter of apology and stick it to the church door

c) Having your tongue cut out

7 The fines for beating a freeman, blinding him or cutting his hair were . . .

a) Ten shillings, twenty shillings and six shillings

b) Twenty shillings, six shillings and ten shillings

c) Six shillings, ten shillings and twenty shillings

8 The fine for accidentally stabbing a man with your spear depended on . . .

a) The *angle* the spear went into him

b) How *deep* the spear went into him

c) How much blood the victim lost

9 The penalty for murder was . . .

a) Hanging

b) Paying a fine to the relatives of the dead person

c) Going to prison for 20 years

10 The fine for offences against women varied. It depended on how important the woman was. Generally the fine for an offence against a nun was . . .

a) The same as for an offence against an ordinary woman

b) Half

c) Double

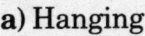

Vicious Viking law

If you didn't like Alfred's Law you could always move over the border into Danish England (Danelaw) and live by their rules. But the Viking Danes could be every bit as brutal as the English . . .

Danelaw 1: Sixty sheep to show you're sorry

Eyjolf was clumsy. Probably the clumsiest Viking in town. Tripping over sleeping dogs, dropping his sword on his toe and spilling his mead down his trousers.

"Now look what you've done! Your clumsiness will be the death of you," his wife, Thora, warned him as he crushed a cat beneath his clumsy foot.

"I'm off to the horse fight," Eyjolf muttered, and he snatched up his sword by the wrong end.

"Ouch!" he cried.

"Now look what you've done. Leave it at home,"

Thora sighed, "or else you'll kill someone."

"A Viking without a sword is like . . . is like . . ."

". . . is like a Viking with a brain. Very rare," she sniffed and stirred the stew.

Eyjolf barged through the door and there was a splintering of wood. "Now look what you've done! It helps if you lift the latch," Thora snapped.

The man walked carefully down the street and reached the horse-fighting circle without even hurting a single living thing. It was too good to last.

The horse fight was exciting. Hooves flew and men roared. "I've got my money on the black one!" Eyjolf cried as the stallion reared on its hind legs and lashed out with its front ones. "Kill!" Eyjolf shouted. He copied the lashing leg of his horse . . . and landed a punch clean in the eye of Bjarni the Brutal.

"Ooops! Sorry!" Eyjolf gasped. "Now look what I've done! It was an accident!"

Bjarni's sore eye closed. The other eye looked menacingly at Eyjolf. "You know what this means, Eyjolf!"

"Er . . . no!" Eyjolf said.

Suddenly the Viking men had lost interest in the fighting horses.

"Kill him, Bjarni!" Ragnar the Ruthless growled.

"Yeah! Chop his clumsy hand off!" someone else put in.

"I've a good mind to," the black-eyed man murmured.

"Oh, come on, Bjarni. It was an accident!" Eyjolf whined.

"It was an insult. And the only way to avenge an insult is to fight to the death! You owe me a debt of honour. I will take your life," Bjarni roared and waved his sword in the air.

117

"How about if I give you a gift instead?"

"You think you can buy my honour!" Bjarni cried.

"It was just a thought," Eyjolf shrugged.

"How much?" Bjarni demanded.

"Er . . . how about thirty sheep?"

"Sixty."

"It's a deal," Eyjolf agreed with a sigh of relief. "I'll deliver them when they're brought in from the hills this autumn."

"I'll come to your farm to pick the best," Bjarni snarled and stamped off over the muddy field.

"That Bjarni's a great fighter," Eyjolf groaned when he reached home. "He'd have killed me, Thora!"

His wife scowled at him with a look like a poisoned polar bear. "And perhaps it would be better if he had. We only have sixty-one sheep, you fool. Now look what you've done! We'll have nothing to live on this winter! Go and fetch me the bark off a tree."

"What for?"

"For your dinner. That's all you'll be eating for the next six months!"

And Eyjolf's father, Thormod, was just as bad. "Sixty sheep! Sixty sheep! You must be mad!" he raged that autumn as the sheep were being counted.

"All right, dad, no need to go on about it! Here's Bjarni now, come to collect his payment."

"Here! Bjarni! What sort of Viking do you call yourself? Taking sixty sheep from my son!" Thormod screeched. "You have the guts of a water-weed. What's the matter? Scared in case the clumsy clown beats you? Viking law says clearly that a quarrel must be settled by a fight to the death!"

The furious Bjarni said nothing. He simply turned purple with rage and drew his sword.

"Now look what you've done," Eyjolf grumbled. He drew his sword . . . and dropped it on his foot. As he bent to pick it up Bjarni's sword swept down – Eyjolf's head rolled in the mud.

"Now look what you've done," Thora said with a sad shake of the head. "Ah, well, at least honour is satisfied. I guess that means I get to keep the sheep!"

Bjarni turned and walked away without a word. Thormod was speechless. And Eyjolf wasn't saying anything . . . ever again.

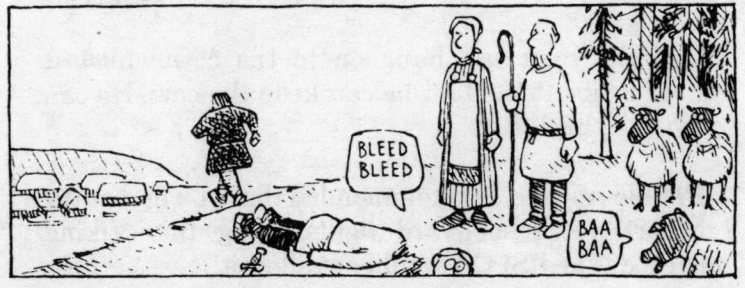

Danelaw 2: How to finish a fight

Fights were very popular in the courts of Denmark and Sweden. But if a man was beaten, and wanted to have his life spared, then he had to go through a harsh test. This is how to finish a Viking fight . . .

1 Play some music on a fiddle and a drum.

2 Bring a wild cow into the hall where the fight has taken place. (Spectators are often trampled to death at this point. Try not to be one of them or you'll miss all the fun.)

3 All the hair is shaved off the tail of the wild cow. (This is an even more dangerous job than being a spectator – don't volunteer to do it!)

4 The tail of the wild cow is covered with grease.

5 The victim puts on shoes which are also covered in grease.

6 The victim has to get hold of the wild cow's tail. (And by now it will be really wild – so would you be if someone shaved your tail!)

7 The cow is then lashed with a whip. (Just to make sure it's really, really wild!)

8 If the man can hang on to the cow whilst it charges about the hall he can keep the cow. He can also keep his life.

(**Please note:** It is recommended that you do not try to sort out school-yard fights using this Viking method. The RSPCA would not allow it!)

121

Test your teacher

After reading this book you should know a bit more about the Vikings and the Saxons. Now's your chance to shock and amaze the people who thought you were as stupid as you look . . .

Here's a quiz for anyone who thinks they know anything about Viking times . . . like a teacher. If they get more than nine out of ten they're doing pretty well.

1 Eilmer was a monk at Malmesbury Abbey and in 1030 went down in history for being the first man to cover 200 metres . . .

a) Underwater

b) Flying

c) Running in under 25 seconds wearing his habit

2 When a Viking died a long way from home what might his friends do?

a) Bury him where he died

b) Have monks boil his body till there were just bones left and carry them home in a box

c) Cut out his heart and carry that home for burial

CAN'T YOU WAIT TILL I'M DEAD?

122

3 Why did the god Odin have only one eye?

a) He lost one in a fight with a raven

b) He swapped one for a drink from the well of wisdom

c) He gave one to some starving people to eat – they mixed it with milk to make eyes-cream

4 What was a tree-smith?

a) A carpenter

b) A woodcutter

c) One of the Smith family who lived in a tree-house

5 Vikings used "kennings" or word-play. So a "horse of the waves" was a ship. What was "the sweat of the sword"?

a) Rust

b) Blood

c) The handle where the warrior placed his sweaty hand

6 One Viking called his most prized possession "Leg Biter". But what was "Leg Biter"?

a) His guard dog

b) His sword

c) His pet polar bear

7 Vikings brought a lot of their words to the English language. But what does the place-name, "Follifoot", mean?

a) Stupid place to build a castle (Folly Fort)

b) Place of the horse fight

c) Place where Earl Folli first set foot

8 Did Vikings wear horns on their helmets?
a) Sometimes . . . for important ceremonies
b) Always
c) Never

9 How did the Vikings know which direction to sail in when they were in the middle of an uncharted ocean?
a) They used a compass
b) They threw a raven into the air and saw which way it flew to land

c) They tossed a coin to decide

10 Where did the leader of a longboat crew sleep?
a) At the front of the ship to keep a lookout
b) In the middle of the ship so he was protected by men on all sides
c) At the back of the ship to be near the steersman

Here's how!

1b) Eilmer attached home-made wings to his arms and jumped off the top of the Abbey tower. After flying nearly 200 metres, the ground broke his fall. And he broke both legs and was crippled for life. He blamed his failure on the lack of a tail.

2b) A Professor Nylen believes that this explains why some graves are found with a jumble of bones rather than with them laid out correctly as if the body had been buried whole.

3b) If your teacher says the answer is c) then they're even dafter than they look!

4a) A "smith" was a craftsman. Vikings had weapon-smiths, ship-smiths, jewellery-smiths and so on.

5b) Blood was also known as the "sea of the wound".

6b) Swords were given names such as "Adder" ... because its bite could kill. Another was known as "Gleam of Battle". What would you call yours?

10c) The second-in-command slept at the front.

Epilogue

Of course, this book has looked at the vicious side of Viking life. Not all the Vikings were vicious . . . and the ones who *were*, weren't vicious *all* the time. Some people even believe they were rather nice people. Good farmers, clever craftsmen and talented artists.

And some historians even argue that the Vikings were just *misunderstood*. They never really meant to invade England anyway! An early report of a Viking landing in Wessex describes a landing by just three ships. The local tax collector thought they were trying to do a bit of smuggling so he ordered them to be taken to the castle of the local king.

AH HA! SMUGGLERS. NO ONE GETS PAST TRETHALD THE TAX COLLECTOR!

Afraid of being locked up, when all they wanted was to do a bit of trading, the Vikings killed the tax collector and his men. When they came back next time they brought their mates and decided to really teach those bossy English a lesson. That's how 300 years of misery for the English started.

But the historians who say the Vikings weren't vicious are kidding themselves. What they should say is the Vikings were no more vicious than the rest of the world at that time. Here are two final bits of horrible history. You make up your own mind.

The English king, Ethelred, wanted rid of all the Vikings in England – the farmers and traders who'd settled here, not just the warriors. On 13 November 1002 he ordered that all Danish people should be put to death. Many lost their lives, including Danish women, who were sometimes buried alive, and children. That was the vicious English for you.

Twelve years later a Viking army took hostages and demanded money and supplies for their men.

BY JOVE, THAT'S A JOLLY LONG LIST

The Viking army was driven off by Ethelred's army. As they sailed home they stopped at Sandwich in Kent to drop off those hostages. The hostages were alive . . . but the Vikings had cut off their ears, their noses and their hands. That was the vicious Vikings. Who was worse? English or Viking?

The English king, Alfred the Great, was a strong and clever ruler who did a lot for the people of this island. But so was the Viking king, Knut the Great!

At 6 p.m. on Saturday 14 October 1066, the grandson of a Viking, King Harold Godwinsson, died at the Battle of Hastings. He was cut down by the sword of a Norman knight.

The Viking age was ended and the last Viking king was gone . . . or was he? Because, in a roundabout way, the vicious Vikings won in the end. First they conquered northern France, where a Viking was known as a North Man – or "Norman". Then the "Norman" William The Conqueror invaded Britain and won. So, if Normans are Vikings, then Vikings conquered England!

Nobody has ever invaded and conquered Britain since. If your family has lived in Britain since those times, it's certain that you have some Viking blood in you! Perhaps you may find out the next time you go to the zoo. If you find yourself looking at the polar bears, and feeling a strange urge to eat one . . .

VICIOUS VIKINGS

GRISLY QUIZ

**Now find out if you're a
vicious Viking expert!**

QUICK VIKING QUESTIONS

1. The Danish Vikings had been invading England for centuries and some had settled – but they weren't popular. In 1002 the good folk of Oxford found a way to deal with the Danes who'd settled there. What way? (Clue: they liked to chop and change)

2. In 1004 the people of Norwich made a deal with the Vikings to stop the raids. What did they agree? (Clue: crime pays)

3. In 1006 King Ethelred of England was worried that his nobles were becoming too powerful. He had one noble, Aelfhelm of York, murdered. What did he do to make sure Aelfhelm's sons didn't rise up in revenge? (Clue: they didn't see the point)

4. By 1009 King Ethelred was desperate. He had paid fortunes to the Danes and they still raided and robbed England. What did he order his people to do? (Clue: oh my God!)

5. In 1010 a medical book of cures was printed, but not many people could read. They preferred old charms like 'Out little spear if you are in here.' What does that cure? (Clue: saves nine)

6. In 1014 Danish King Knut invaded Lincolnshire and took hostages. But when he was driven out by the English he didn't kill the hostages. What did he do? (Clue: a bit of this, a bit of that)

7. The Archbishop of Canterbury was captured by the Danes in 1012. He refused to pay a ransom so the drunken Danes pelted him with what? (Clue: they were feasting at the time)

8. Ethelred died in 1016 and councillors in Southampton elected Danish Knut king – while councillors in London elected English Edmund. Two kings for one kingdom? But Edmund came up with an easy solution. What? (Clue: dead easy in fact)

9. Knut became King of England in 1017. What did he do to the mother of his rival, Edmund? (Clue: knot a bad idea)

10. Eilmer the Monk broke both his legs in 1030. What was the mad man of God trying to do? (Clue: pigs might)

11. In 1040 Macbeth became King in Scotland. How did he kill the previous king, Duncan? (Clue: all's fair in love and. . .)

12. King Harthacnut accepted a drink from his half-brother and died in 1042. What sort of drink killed him? (Clue: half-brother gets the throne)

13. In 1054 King Macbeth of Scotland was beaten at the battle of Dunsinane. How long did he go on reigning after the defeat? (Clue: count Shakespeare's witches)

NAME THAT NORSEMAN

The people of the eleventh century were often named after their appearance. These nicknames were usually invented long after the person died by medieval writers. (It probably would have been a bad idea to go up to a Viking and call him 'Mr Flatnose'.)

Can you spot the real names here?

1. Viking Chief, Thorkell the ...
a) Tall
b) Thin
c) Thick–as–Two–Short Planks

2. Danish conqueror, Svein ...
a) Fork-tongue
b) Forkbeard
c) Fork-and-knife

3. Ethelred's son, Edmund ...
a) Ironheart
b) Ironside
c) Iron-me-shirt

4. Strathclyde king, Owen the ...
a) Bald
b) Hairy
c) Permed

8. King Knut's son, Harold ...
a) Flatfoot
b) Harefoot
c) Five-foot-two

9. Norse king of the Irish, Sigtrygg ...
a) Silkbeard
b) Squarebeard
c) Bottle 'o Beard

5. Earl of Orkney, Sigurd the ...
a) Stout
b) Slim
c) Stuffed

6. Archbishop of York, Wulfstan the ...
a) Wolf
b) Fox
c) Yeti

7. Duke of Normandy, Robert the ...
a) Saint
b) Devil
c) Slightly Naughty

10. Wife of King Harold, Edith ...
a) Swantail
b) Swan-neck
c) Swansbum

11. King of Norway, Magnus ...
a) Barefoot
b) Bareback
c) Bear-hug

POTTY PROVERBS

The armies that invaded England brought with them terror, destruction, fear and ... language! The Viking invaders brought many words that we still use today.

These incredibly intelligent words of wisdom would not be possible if it hadn't been for the kindly Viking conquerors. Can you spot the *three* Viking words in each of these little-known Norse proverbs?

1. A flat egg on the plate is worth two in the dirt.
2. Bulls without legs give fewer steaks to the butcher.
3. Grubby kids with freckles don't look so mucky as those with plain faces.
4. Thieves who crawl low are not seen from high windows.
5. Reindeer with scabs give rotten meat to stew at Saturday suppers.
6. Dirty fellows become dazzling when washed with soft soap.
7. A knife in the guts will get even the grandest to gasp.
8. A score of scowling scarecrows will scare scamps.
9. Those who die meekly will receive no glittering crown in heaven.
10. Walk awkwardly and cruel people will scream and call you lame.

134

Quick Viking Questions

1. The Danish men, women and children in Oxford were massacred. The English chopped them to bits or fried them alive in a church like Danish bacon!

2. The people of Norwich paid 'peace money' – a bribe. Of course the Vikings took the money and then robbed and destroyed Norwich anyway! Wouldn't you?

3. Ethelred had them blinded. Nasty.

4. Pray. King Ethelred ordered everyone to go barefoot to church and eat nothing but bread, water and herbs for three days. He also ordered them to pay taxes or be punished.

5. A stitch.

6. He cut bits off them – noses, ears, fingers, hands and so on. Nothing too serious.

7. Cattle bones. He was probably stunned and didn't feel the killer blow – with an axe. Dane leader Thorkeld was disgusted by the murder. Even Vikings have feelings.

8. Edmund died. Knut became king of all England.

9. He married her.

10. Fly. He stood on a tower with wings strapped to his arms, waited for a strong gust of wind, then he jumped and flapped. He got 200 metres before he crashed.

11. In battle. Forget William Shakespeare's play where Macbeth stabs Duncan in his bed – Macbeth won fair and square.

12. A poisoned one. This murder was never proved but no one was bothered one way or the other. No one liked Harthacnut anyway.

13. Three years. Shakespeare got it wrong again! In his play (with three witches) Macbeth is killed at the battle of Dunsinane.

Name that Norseman
1.a) 2.b) 3.b) 4.a) 5.a) 6.a) 7.b) 8.b) 9.a) 10.b) 11.a)
Please note: anyone who answered (c) for any question may need
a brain implant.

Potty Proverbs
1. Flat, Egg, Dirt
2. Bulls, Legs, Steaks
3. Kids, Freckles, Mucky
4. Crawl, Low, Windows
5. Reindeer, Scabs, Rotten
6. Dirty, Fellows, Dazzling
7. Knife, Get, Gasp
8. Score, Scowling, Scare
9. Die, Meekly,. Glittering
10. Awkwardly, Scream , Call

INTERESTING INDEX

Where will you find 'cattle-droppings', 'giants'
armpits' and 'horse-fights' in an index?
In a Horrible Histories book, of course!

137

138

Terry Deary was born at a very early age, so long ago he can't remember. But his mother, who was there at the time, says he was born in Sunderland, north-east England, in 1946 – so it's not true that he writes all *Horrible Histories* from memory. At school he was a horrible child only interested in playing football and giving teachers a hard time. His history lessons were so boring and so badly taught, that he learned to loathe the subject. *Horrible Histories* is his revenge.

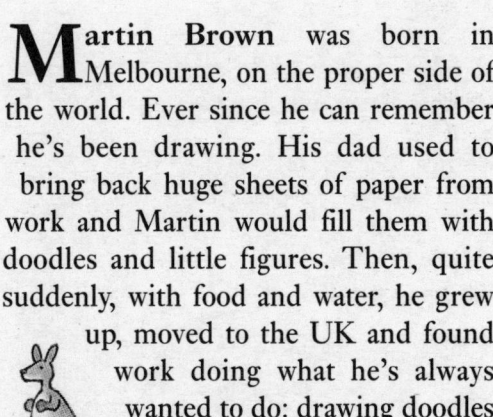

Martin Brown was born in Melbourne, on the proper side of the world. Ever since he can remember he's been drawing. His dad used to bring back huge sheets of paper from work and Martin would fill them with doodles and little figures. Then, quite suddenly, with food and water, he grew up, moved to the UK and found work doing what he's always wanted to do: drawing doodles and little figures.

HORRIBLE HISTORIES

SMASHING
SAXONS

Terry Deary Illustrated by **Martin Brown**

 SCHOLASTIC

For George Barron, with thanks.

Scholastic Children's Books,
Euston House, 24 Eversholt Street,
London NW1 1DB, UK

A division of Scholastic Ltd
London ~ New York ~ Toronto ~ Sydney ~ Auckland
Mexico City ~ New Delhi ~ Hong Kong

First published in the UK by Scholastic Ltd, 2000
This edition published by Scholastic Ltd, 2016

Text © Terry Deary, 2000
Illustration © Martin Brown, 2000, 2016

All rights reserved. Moral rights asserted.

ISBN 978 1407 16561 5

Printed and bound by CPI Group (UK) Ltd, Croydon, CR0 4YY

4 6 8 10 9 7 5

www.scholastic.co.uk

CONTENTS

Introduction

History can be horrible. Especially those history lessons where the teacher asks impossible questions. You know the sort of thing…

AFTER THE ROMANS CAME INVADERS FROM SAXONY—THE SAXONS. YOU, MYRTLE MABELWICK!

ME, SIR? WHAT, SIR?

WHY WERE THEY CALLED SAXONS?

'COS THEY SAID THEY WERE ALL SONS OF MR AND MRS SACK?

I THINK I'LL BECOME A P.E. TEACHER! OR AN UNDERTAKER! YOU GET TO MEET MORE INTELLIGENT PEOPLE IF YOU'RE AN UNDERTAKER

Forget all the confusing stuff teachers try to tell you…

ANGLES FROM ANGELN MOVED INTO THE NORTH AND MIDLANDS WHILE SAXONS FROM SAXONY MOVED INTO THE SOUTH

ANGLES? IS THIS HISTORY OR MATHS?

'Saxon' was a name the Welsh, the Scots and the Irish called all the strangers who moved into England when the Romans left. Just tell your teacher: 'It was never that simple. Let's just use the word "Saxon" the way they meant it. Saxons were the people who invaded the place we now call England.'

And don't worry ... there is an escape from the terrible tortures of teachers asking questions.

It's time for pupil power and for biting back! Now, with the help of a *Horrible Histories* book, you can turn the tables on teachers. Now *you* can ask the questions!

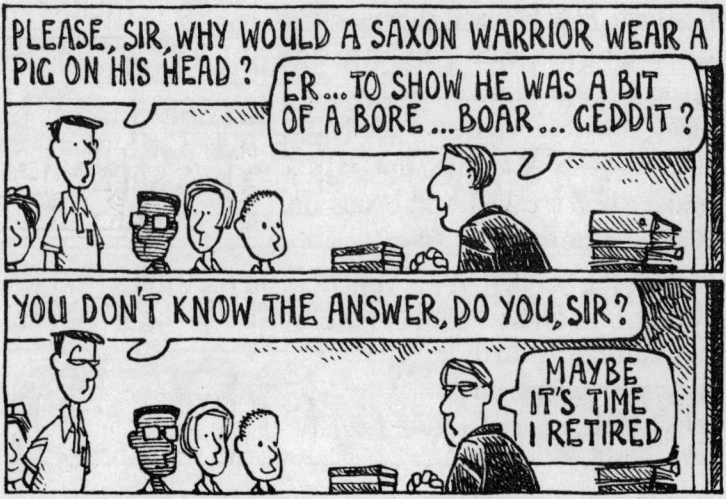

Knowledge is power, see? Now you can find out fascinating facts, like what a whip made from the skin of a dolphin would be used for, and then test your teacher.

By the time you've finished the teacher may need that whip. Why? Read on...

Timeline

410 After 300 years the Romans in Britain go back to Rome. The Brits have to fight off powerful Picts, savage Scots and invading Irish raiders.

449 The Brits hire a couple of bothersome Saxon brothers from Jutland, Hengest and Horsa, to fight for them. H & H like it so much they decided to stay, batter the Brits and settle. There's gratitude for you!

460s Horrible Hengest dies. The Brits fight back against the Saxons under a leader called Ambrosius and about twenty years later a warrior called Arthur takes over. That's not the legendary bloke with a round table. This King Arthur was probably the last great Roman British leader.

491 The Saxon leader Aelle (call him 'Ella') becomes the first ruler of a South Saxon kingdom. He attacks British defenders at the old Roman fortress in Pevensey and massacres the lot of them.

511 Brit hero King Arthur dies (probably) at the battle of Camlann. The Brits will struggle hopelessly now he's gone.

597 Christian missionaries arrive from Rome and Saxons are

converted – mostly. (Some go back to being pagans later. Maybe it's more fun.)

600s The Saxons gradually take over the land we now call England with the Northumbrian kingdom in the north, the Mercians in the middle, the Anglians in the East and the kingdom of Wessex in the south. Very neat, very cosy.

787 Mercian leader King Offa is so powerful he can organize the digging of a 20-metre-wide ditch between England and Wales, 169 miles (270 km) long to keep the wild Welsh away. His ditch is known as Offa's Dyke.

793 The Vikings are coming from Norway. Bad news for savaged Saxons and massacred monks. These are just raids – later they'll be back to stay.

871 Alfred the Great becomes king of Wessex and defeats and drives back the vicious Vikings from the south of England. But they don't go home. They stay in the north and the east. Alfie may be 'Great' but he hasn't vanquished the Vikings really.

924 Alf's grandson, Athelstan, avoids a plot to blind him and becomes king. He's a real 'great'

8

even though he's usually forgotten. He's the man to sort out the Vikings, not to mention the Welsh and the Scots. Wessex are winners! Britain is a single Saxon country for the first time. But not for long...

937 The Welsh, Scots, Irish and Vikings all gang up to rebel and destroy Athelstan. He and his Saxons beat them in a bloody battle at Brunanburh – probably in Yorkshire.

939 Athelstan dies. Guess what? The Vikings are back, led by Olaf Guthfrithsson who takes over as king in the north. He means trouble.

978 Saxon King Edward the Martyr is murdered. Ethelred the Unready (his step–brother) takes the crown. But did Eth have something to do with the death? Eth tries to pay the Vikings to go away – giving them gold weighing 10,000 kilos in 991 – so they keep coming back! Who can blame them?

1002 King Ethelred organizes a massacre of the Viking settlers – the women and children and the defenceless farmers, because they don't fight back! But the Viking warriors will avenge them.

1012 Now poor old Eth gives the greedy Vikings 20,000 kilos of gold

9

to go away. It does him (and the English) no good because…

1013 Ethelred is driven off the throne and replaced by invading Viking Sweyn. Eth runs off to Normandy till Sweyn dies. Eth tries a bit of a comeback but then Sweyn's son Cnut returns and sees him off.

1042 Edward the Confessor becomes king. He gets a bit too friendly with the Normans.

1066 … and that's that! Last Saxon king, Harold, is defeated by William the Conqueror and his Normans.

The Saxon start

Battering the Brits

Have you ever noticed how school books *tell* you things but they never seem to answer the questions you want to ask. But this is a *Horrible Histories* book, so now's your chance to quiz the author. Well? What are you waiting for?

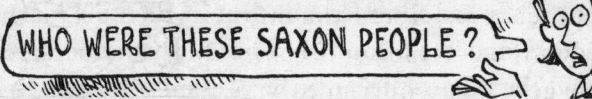

WHO WERE THESE SAXON PEOPLE?

Well they came from North Germany and invaded Britain from about AD 300 onwards. They liked it so much they stayed.

SO WHAT WAS WRONG WITH NORTH GERMANY THEN?

A lot of them lived on little islands surrounded by marsh or sea. Terrible farming land, so they went off and pinched someone else's.

DID NO ONE TRY TO STOP THEM?

Of course they did! The Romans who ran Britain stopped them. Then, when the Romans left, the Brits tried to stop them.

BUT THE SAXONS WON?

They drove the Brits west into Wales and Cornwall. Then the Vikings came across and tried to push the Saxons out.

SERVES THEM RIGHT! SO WHY ISN'T ENGLAND CALLED SAXONLAND?

11

Just one of those things. It was the Welsh and the Scots and the Irish who called them Saxons. By about 800, the Saxons were calling themselves 'Anglisc' – their spelling wasn't as good as yours.

OK, WHERE DID THE SAXONS GO?

Nowhere. They stayed in Britain. But in 1066 the Normans came across and took control. The Normans became the rulers and the Saxons became the peasants. Today's British people are a mixture of Saxon and Norman and lots of others.

SO WHAT KIND OF PEOPLE WERE THESE SAXONS?

That would take a whole book to answer.

BOOKS ARE BORING!

Horrible Histories aren't.

SO WHERE CAN I FIND A HORRIBLE HISTORY OF THE SAXONS?

You're reading it, stupid!

OOOOH! SO I AM!

Horrible Hengest

In the 420s the Brits were led by Vortigern.

HERE! I SAY, YOU CHAPS! THAT WASN'T MY *NAME* YOU KNOW! VORTIGERN WAS MY *TITLE* AND IT MEANS 'GREAT KING'. JOLLY GOOD TITLE TOO!

Vortigern led the Brits from about AD 425 till 450. He organized the Brits after the Roman armies left and his real name may have been Vitalinus – which sounds a bit like a medicine.

But Vortigern had problems, as we know from a horrible history written by a priest and historian called Gildas, who was writing almost a hundred years after Vortigern ruled.

The feathered flight of a rumour reached the ears of everyone in south Britain. Their old enemies from the north were on their way. They weren't coming to raid but to rule the country from end to end. But before they could defend themselves they rushed down that wide road that leads to death. A deadly plague killed so many and so quickly that there weren't enough left alive to bury the dead…

What did the Brits do when peppered by plague and Picts?

So what did Vortigern do? Gildas said Vortigern's council 'went blind'. What he *meant* was they couldn't see how stupid their actions were...

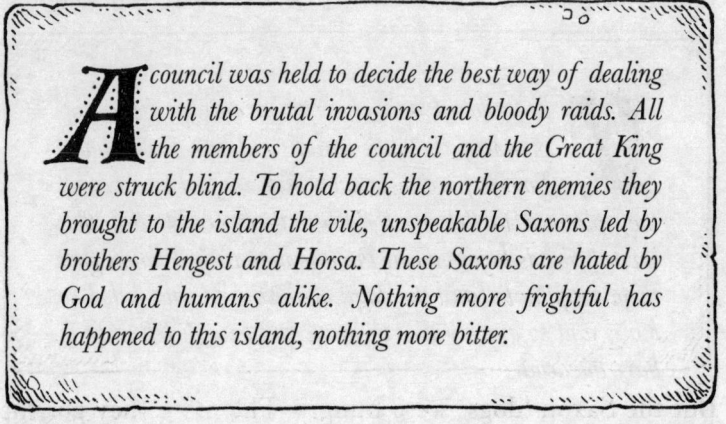

A council was held to decide the best way of dealing with the brutal invasions and bloody raids. All the members of the council and the Great King were struck blind. To hold back the northern enemies they brought to the island the vile, unspeakable Saxons led by brothers Hengest and Horsa. These Saxons are hated by God and humans alike. Nothing more frightful has happened to this island, nothing more bitter.

Do you get the feeling that Gildas didn't like the Saxons?

He went on to curse Vortigern and the council...

> *What utter blindness of their wits. What raw, hopeless stupidity!*

Sounds a bit like my teacher when he read my history homework!

Anyway, Vortigern paid the warrior-bullies Hengest and Horsa to fight for him...

... but then the Saxon visitors turned nasty and demanded a lump of Brit land for themselves. One hundred years later, Gildas was still furious at Vortigern's stupidity...

> *Vortigern's council invited an enemy under their own roof that they feared more than death. These Saxons fixed their claws on the eastern coast, as if they planned to defend it. When they were settled they invited friends to join them. For a long time the Britons gave them supplies to 'shut the dog's mouth'.*

But the Saxon 'dogs' were hungry. The more they got the more they wanted and they were ready to fight for it.

Vortigern's plan worked for a little while and the Picts and Irish were held back. The *Kentish Chronicle* history makes it sound pathetic…

> *The Saxon barbarians grew in number. They demanded the food and clothing that Vortigern promised but the Britons said, 'We cannot feed and clothe you, for your numbers are grown. Go away, for we do not need your help.'*

Imagine being in the Brits' position. You ask the school bully to help you. He turns on you and demands your school dinner money. And you say, 'Go away, for I do not need your help!' Think it would work?

Hah! No way. And it didn't work for the Britons. But then another Roman Briton called Ambrosius rebelled against Vortigern. Who did Vortigern turn to for help to fight Ambrosius?

MY BRAVE SAXON CHUMS OF COURSE. NATURALLY OLD HENGEST TOLD ME HE DIDN'T HAVE ENOUGH FIGHTING FELLOWS TO BATTLE AGAINST ALL OF AMBROSIUS' AWFUL MEN. HE WANTED TO FETCH ANOTHER TWENTY BOATLOADS OF HIS SAXON MATES ACROSS

Hengest didn't just bring more warriors. He brought a secret weapon: his daughter! The old historian describes what happened next…

In one of the ships was Hengest's daughter, a very beautiful girl. Hengest arranged a feast for Vortigern and his soldiers. They got very drunk and the Devil entered into Vortigern's heart, making him fall in love with the girl. He asked Hengest for her hand in marriage and said, 'I will give anything you want in return – even half my kingdom!'

Of course it wasn't Vortigern's kingdom to give away! The land belonged to the dukes who ruled each county. But Vortigern gave Hengest the county of Kent – without even asking the Kent lord Gwyrangon.

In around AD 442, from his new base in Kent, Hengest was ready to take over Britain and he didn't care how much blood was spilled. Gildas said…

All the great towns fell to the Saxon battering rams. Bishops, priests and people were all chopped down together while swords flashed and flames crackled. It was horrible to see the stones of towers thrown down to mix with pieces of human bodies. Broken altars were covered with a purple crust of clotted blood. There was no burial except under ruins and bodies were eaten by the birds and beasts.

Horrible history! But a bit over the top. Modern historians don't think the Saxon rebellion was all that bloody and violent.

Anyway, the Brits fought back…

I SENT MY OWN SON, VORTEMIR, OFF TO FIGHT OLD HENGEST. YOU KNOW, HE WHIPPED THE SAXONS LIKE DOGS AND KILLED OLD HENGEST'S BROTHER HORSA. I THINK THE SAVAGE SAXONS GOT MY MESSAGE: YOU DON'T MESS WITH VORTIGERN

Then young Vortemir was killed. The Saxons came back with a really 'vile, unspeakable' plot. If Vortigern had left a diary it might have looked something like this…

> 24th August, St Bartholomew's Day, AD 456
>
> Oh dear!
> Oh dear, oh dear!
> Oh dear, oh dear, oh dear!
> Those frightfully nice Saxon chappies have turned out to be simply… well, frightful. It was bad enough their killing poor little Vortemir but now they've turned nasty.

That Hengest bloke (who smells a little, to be honest) invited us over to talk about peace and one thought it was a jolly good idea, don't you know. After all, I'm married to his lovely daughter, so he wouldn't harm me. 'Bring along your top generals, no weapons though,' he said. 'We'll have a bit of a party — some ale, a few nibbles and a jolly sing song!' It sounded just like the good old days when the Saxon blokes first came over.

In fact it all sounded jolly jolly. 'When would you like us to come over?' one asked.

'Saint Bartholomew's Eve — seven thirty for eight,' he said.

'Topping!' one replied. 'See you then, old boy.' Oh dear, oh dear. The clue was there, wasn't it? Saint Bartholomew was that missionary chappie who went to Africa to convert the pagans. They skinned him alive and chopped his head off. So one ought to have guessed that it wasn't a good evening to meet the jolly old pagan enemy.

19

Sure enough I arrived with all the top chaps in Britain — my best warriors, best ministers and the best bishops. What did the savage Saxons do? Why they sat us down at the tables, waited till we were munching on the jolly old nibbles and then Hengest cried out, 'Saxons! Draw your knives!' They jolly well drew their dirty great knives that they'd hidden in their boots! Not very sporting. In fact it's cheating, don't you think?

Chop! Chop! Chop! It was over in seconds - well, actually we didn't have any seconds. They killed the chaps while they were eating their firsts! Blood all over the tables. Blood all over the rushes on the floor. Someone's going to have a sticky, messy, job cleaning that up one can jolly well tell you! The only one they left alive was me. One has to go back and tell the British chaps that 'Hengest rules OK!' Since one has lost all one's top chappies one doesn't have a lot of choice, does one?

I'm a prisoner and I had to give horrible Hengest quite a lot of land just to spare my life.
Oh dear!
Oh dear, oh dear!
Oh dear, oh dear, oh dear!

What happened to Vortigern? He survived but was hated by everyone. In the end…

Vortigern wandered from place to place till his heart broke and he died without honour.

Gildas the writer was trying to explain what a dreadful place Britain was and how it had been better in the good old Roman days. Maybe he made the Saxon rebellion sound worse than it was. Archaeologists have dug on a lot of Saxon and British sites and they can't find much proof that this violent rebellion ever happened.

But, violent or peaceful, the Saxons had arrived and they meant to stay.

Superstitious Saxons

The Dark Ages are a bit of a mystery to us – that's how they got their name. But they were also really dark! After the sun set there were no streetlights to show the way. Only moonlight, starlight and some whacking great scary shadows.

So it's no wonder the Saxons believed all sorts of weird and horrible things went on in those shadows. Devils and demons lurked there, ready to snatch your soul and carry it off to Hell!

EVEN THOUGH I SAY IT MYSELF, IF THERE'S ONE THING I DO RATHER WELL, IT'S LURK

You believed in charms and spells to protect you. You became superstitious – especially about how you buried your dead.

Dead losses

In the early days, before they became Christian, the Saxons would sometimes bury a servant with his (or her) dead master. The servant would then be able to serve the master in the afterlife. But the horrible historical fact is the servant was often buried alive! They were thrown into the open grave, a heavy stone may have been thrown on top to keep them down and then they were covered with soil.

If it wasn't a servant then it was some poor woman, buried alive to keep the man company in the afterlife – cook his dinner, wash his clothes and polish his sword. It seems that even in the afterlife men were hopeless!

Even dogs were sacrificed to go with their masters to the afterlife. What would dogs *do* there? Are there any trees for pees in heaven?

The Saxons brought a lot of their funeral habits with them from Europe. Then, in AD 597 St Augustine arrived in southern England to convert the Saxons to Christianity. When the Saxons became Christian there was a mixture of old customs and new ones ... and some customs you wouldn't want to happen to your worst enemy or even your history teacher...

A pane in the ash

Saxons were worried about the ghosts of the dead coming back to haunt them.

Would you worry about your dead Auntie Ethelburga coming back to haunt you? Then here are a few helpful early-Saxon hints...

1 Cremate her. When early Saxons cremated a dead friend they would place the ashes in a small jar or urn. Then they would leave a small window in the jar. Why? So the spirit could come and go and not make trouble if it found its ashes trapped in a sealed container.

MIND YOU, WINDOWS DO HAVE THEIR DISADVANTAGES

I CAN SEEEEE YOU!

2 Cut her head off. The living dead find it a bit hard to haunt without a head. They wouldn't even find their way out of the burial yard. So lop off their dead head and save yourself from a haunting.

3 Give her some company. Sometimes there were the ashes of more than one person in a pot. Auntie Ethelburga will be so busy gossiping to her powdered pal that she'll forget to haunt you.

4 Give her some treasure. The dead are happy if they are buried with some of their precious possessions. Women could be buried with jewellery like dress fasteners. A man might be buried with a sword or throwing spear. (He's bound to be a dead shot.)

5 Burn crops. Garlic keeps vampires away, they say, and the Saxons believed burning crops kept ghosts away. (Do *not* try this with your breakfast cornflakes. Especially after your mum's poured milk over them). This useful trick was banned by boring Archbishop Theodore in AD 672.

WHY WASTE WORTHWHILE WHEAT WHEN WE WANT WICKEDNESS WITHDRAWN?

It's just as well the Saxons had these ghost-busting ideas because there were a lot of dead people around. Half of them were dead before they reached 25 years old and not many of the rest reached 40.

Good god

When the Saxons first came to Britain they were 'pagans' – they worshipped German gods like…

GODS

Name: Tiw
Day to remember: Tuesday named after him.
Top job: God of 'Justice'.
Foul fact: He allowed himself to be used as the bait to trap a monstrous wolf. The wolf bit his hand off. Don't try this at home. (Maybe he should also be the god of stupidity.)

Name: Woden

Day to remember: Wednesday named after him.

Top job: The top god and god of poets.

Foul fact: He owned an eight-legged horse (must have cost a fortune in horse-shoes) that could fly through the air. He swapped one of his eyes for wisdom – don't try this at school.

Name: Thunor

Day to remember: Thursday named after him.

Top job: God of thunder.

Foul fact: Had a magic throwing hammer that came back to him like a boomerang. (Don't try this in the park.) Incredibly strong but has so far failed to smash the skull of the serpent of evil. He'll do it at Ragnarok – that's the end of the worlds of gods and humans.

Name: Frigg

Day to remember: Friday named after her.

Top job: Woden's wife – goddess of marriage.

Foul fact: She didn't lose an eye or a hand but she did lose her son, Balder, who was killed with the only thing that could harm him – mistletoe. (So watch what you stand under next Christmas!)

Although the Saxons later converted to being Christians they kept bits of their old religion in their religious ceremonies. They were a mixture of Christian and pagan – maybe they believed the Christian God and the pagan gods would work together for better effect!

Foul fields

Do you have a field that has been cursed? Maybe a school football field where you always seem to lose? Why not get your head teacher to try this ancient Saxon cure?

FIRST CUT FOUR SQUARES OF TURF FROM EACH CORNER OF THE FIELD. WATCH OUT FOR THOSE WORMS!

MIX OIL, HONEY, YEAST, MILK, SAWDUST AND HOLY WATER. THEN SPRINKLE THE MIXTURE ON TO THE UNDERSIDE OF THE TURF - GIVE THOSE WORMS A BATH

YUM!

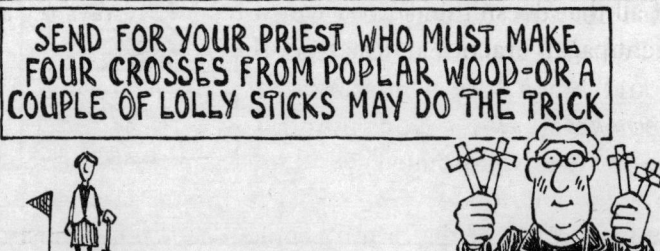

SEND FOR YOUR PRIEST WHO MUST MAKE FOUR CROSSES FROM POPLAR WOOD-OR A COUPLE OF LOLLY STICKS MAY DO THE TRICK

WRITE A NAME ON EACH: MATTHEW, MARK, LUKE AND JOHN. PLACE THE CROSSES IN THE HOLES LEFT WHERE YOU REMOVED THE TURF AND HOPE THE WORMS AREN'T TOO CROSS

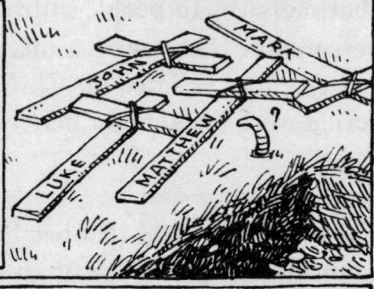

THE PRIEST MUST THEN BOW NINE TIMES TO THE EAST AND TURN NINE TIMES CLOCKWISE BEFORE PUTTING THE TURFS BACK. BET THE WORMS ARE GLAD TO BE HOME

If all that doesn't make you win you could always try an ancient pagan practice and sacrifice the referee.

Did you know…?

Even though the historian Saint Bede was a good Christian, and believed in the power of God, he also believed a lot of the superstitions of the Saxon people – and so did most of the Christians who lived at the time. He believed that God sent messages to people on earth through his miracles … and also through strange signs.

In the year 729 Bede reported that there were two comets seen in the skies. He said this was a heavenly sign that a disaster was going to happen. In fact an army from Asia attacked France and caused a lot of death and destruction to Christians there.

In 734 there were reports that the moon turned the colour of blood and blood rained down from the skies – shortly afterwards Bede died!

What other odd ideas did the Saxons have…?

Wacky weather wisdom

The Saxons watched out for signs for their weather forecasts – but signs didn't just foretell the weather! What did these signs mean?

Sign	Meaning
1. Thunder on a Sunday means...	a) ...gale-force winds will follow
2. Dolphins leaping from the water means...	b) ...calm weather will follow
3. Thunder on a Wednesday means...	c) ...the death of nuns and monks
4. Red sky at night means...	d) ...there will be a storm
5. Splashes from oars glittering on a night voyage means...	e) ...the death of lazy women

Sutton who?

In 1939 some archaeologists began digging into a Saxon burial mound. It was at a place called Sutton Hoo, not far from the town of Ipswich in East Anglia, and the site turned out to be a great discovery.

But sixty years later no one can quite agree what they uncovered. It was a 24 metre wooden ship from around the year AD 600, buried with treasure in memory of a great person. There were over 40 gold items and a great silver dish. Most historians agree on that ... but not much else. For example, there was an iron stand found in the grave. They argue it was either...

- a torch holder
- a standard (sort of a flag-pole) for soldiers to follow
- or a rack to show off the scalps of dead enemies!

HAS ANYONE SEEN MY SPEAR FRAME?

But that's not all historians disagree about…

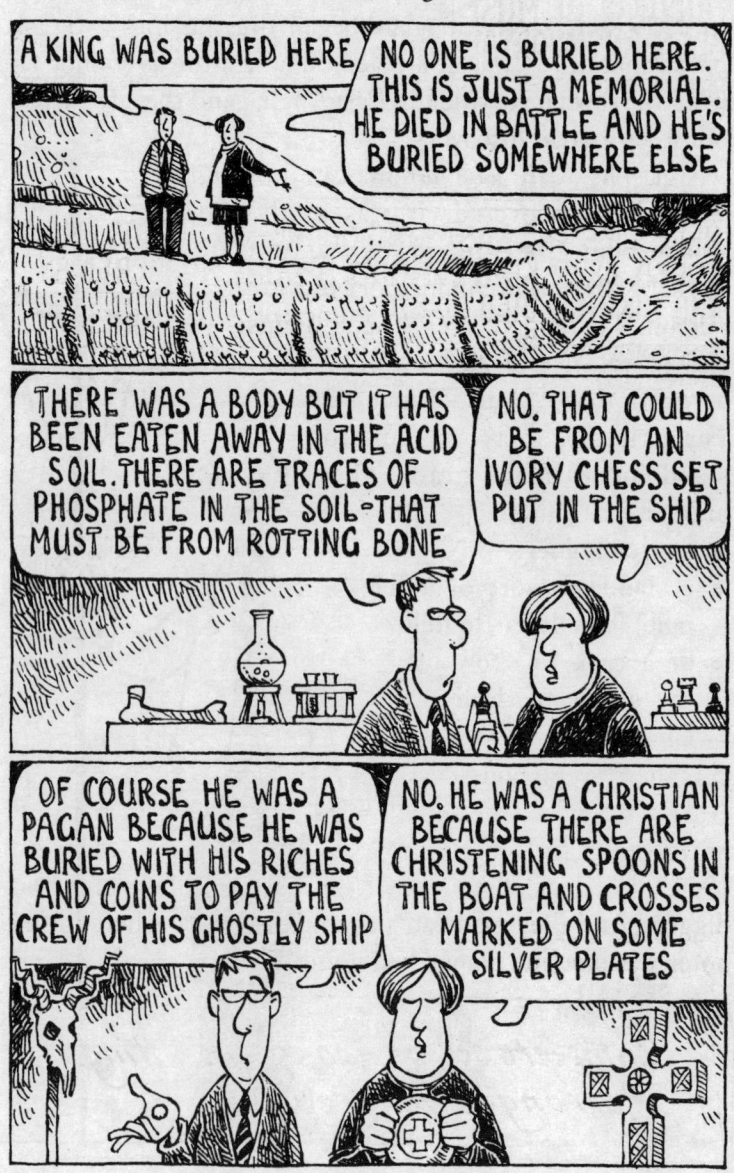

Was there ever a body in the boat?

Archaeologists and scientists looked at soil samples and grave goods for forty years and couldn't agree. Then, in 1979, they decided to look at the notes made by the first diggers. And they made an amazing discovery. There in the notes was one line no one had noticed before...

Complete set of iron coffin fittings arranged in a rectangle

There *had* been a coffin after all! So it's pretty certain there was a body in the grave! What happened to these important clues, the coffin fittings?

Hoo knows? They are missing.

Did you know…?
Some Saxon helmets had a wild pig on top. No! Not a real one, dummy. A little metal model.

WHY DID SAXON HELMETS HAVE PIGS ON?

I'm glad you asked me that.

The pig was sacred to the god of peace, Frey, and the goddess of battle and death, his sister Freyja. The pig was a good luck sign!

Next time you have a school exam or a SAT test, why not try wearing a wild pig on your head?

WILL A SLICE OF BACON BRING ME A SLICE OF LUCK?

Awesome Arthur

The years from about AD 450 till around 500 were the darkest years of the Dark Ages.

Battered Brits bite back

Luckily the priest Gildas gives us a horrible historical idea of what it was like then for the poor old Brits...

> *Some of the wretched British were caught in the hills and slaughtered in heaps. Some gave themselves up as slaves. Some hid in the thick forests and the cliffs, terrified, until the savage Saxon raiders went home again.*

The Saxons were battering the Brits, but some Brits started fighting back. They wanted a Britain the way it was in the old Roman days of eighty years before. One leader managed to win forty years of peace. He was called 'the last Roman' and his name was Arthur.

Five hundred years after Arthur died his name was remembered and storytellers came up with some great tales of Arthur's deeds. In a word they were bosh. In four words they were total and utter bosh. Any historian will tell you...

Happy History for Cute Kids

- King Arthur pulled a magical sword from a stone. *Bosh!*

- Arthur was given his war sword, Excalibur, by the Lady of the Lake. *Tosh!*

- Arthur gathered his knights at a round table at the wonderful palace of Camelot. *Piffle!*

- Arthur and his knights fought against evil in their shining armour. *Twaddle!*

- Arthur was betrayed by the wicked Mordred and beaten in battle. *Tommyrot!*

- Now Arthur is lying asleep and he will awaken and return when Britain is in danger. *Tripe!*

The truth is there are very few clues as to who Arthur was, what he did, or even where he lived and fought. A monk called Nennius wrote of twelve battles that Arthur fought in.

The twelfth battle was on Badon Hill where 960 men fell in one day from one attack by Arthur. No one killed them but he alone.

Arthur killed 960 Saxons by himself! What? His little arms must have been aching!

Nennius was writing a couple of hundred years after Arthur died. He probably copied the battle list from an old Welsh battle poem. The trouble is those poems exaggerate just a bit to make their heroes sound like Superman. The truth is (probably) that he was from a Roman family, and led the Brits so well that the Saxons were held back in the south and east of England for forty years.

What story books and history books don't tell you is that the King Arthur from the oldest legends wasn't a goody-goody leader fighting against evil. Arthur could be pretty awful!

Awful Arthur
How about hearing some of the stories about the awful side of Arthur...?

Once upon a time, in the middle of Wales, there was a tyrant who came from foreign parts and his name was Arthur. When this Arthur came to the monastery at Llanbadarn Fawr he met the bishop Paternus and he cast his eyes greedily on the bishop's fine tunic. 'Bishop!' said Arthur. 'That is a wonderful tunic and I want it for my own!'

And the bishop replied, 'This tunic is for priests! A wicked man may not wear it, and you are a wicked man.'

Then Arthur fell into a mighty rage and left the monastery, raving furiously. Later that day he returned and found bishop Paternus praying.

Arthur snatched at the bishop's tunic and tried to tear it off him. Arthur cursed and Arthur swore in the sight of God. Arthur stamped on the ground like a child.

Then bishop Paternus said, 'Let the earth swallow him up!'

The earth at once opened in a great crack and swallowed Arthur up to the chin. The wicked king was afraid and begged, 'Forgive me please, Paternus. Forgive me!'

Bishop Paternus, the saint, forgave the greedy king and at once the crack in the earth spewed King Arthur up.

And Arthur was *not* a friend to ladies in distress...

One day cruel King Arthur was riding with three of his knights when he saw a woman carried on a horse by a man. A troop of soldiers were chasing them.

'Look, Arthur! That lady is being chased by those soldiers! We should help her to escape!' the knights cried.

But when wicked Arthur saw the woman his heart was filled with desire and he wanted her for himself. 'No, my knights!' he cried. 'Take the woman and bring her to me! She's just the sort of lady that I could take for my love!'

'You can't do that!' his knights said.

'I can! I'm king!' the angry Arthur argued.

'We have to help the lady!' the knights said angrily.

Arthur scowled and Arthur fretted and then he said, 'Oh, very well. If you would rather help a lady than grab the girl for me, then go ahead.'

And so the knights rode down and saved the lady and they gave her their protection.

But Arthur, he was not a happy king.

Then there's the idea that Arthur was a 'religious' king who fought under the Christian cross against the pagan Saxons.

At the battle of Badon Arthur carried the cross of our Lord Jesus Christ on his shoulders for three days and nights and the Britons won victory.

This is the battle where he slew 960 Saxons single handed … with a cross on his back! Did he use the cross to batter the 960 to death? Whew! What a man!

But hang on … another old story says he took the altar from a church and used it to eat his dinner! Would a good Christian do that? So much for a knight of the round table – he was more like a knight of the nicked table.

And what would the noble Arthur do to a brave enemy? Spare his life and make him a friend? No chance…

In farthest Scotland was a warrior prince and this man's name was Cuill. Now Cuill was a brave warrior and a famous soldier who bowed down to no king, not even Arthur.

He would often come down from Scotland, burning and raiding and winning great victories. And Arthur, the king of all Britain, heard what this gallant young man was doing. Many people hoped Cuill would take Arthur's place one day, but Arthur sought him out and murdered him.

After the murder Arthur went home, feeling very happy to have killed such a strong enemy.

So there you have another view of Arthur. Thief and murderer with no respect for women or the Church. These story writers were writing long after Arthur's death, but it's interesting that, at the time, no one argued with the way they described him – as a wicked man. Take your pick:

THE GREAT ARTHUR DEBATE

BRAVE RESPECTED HERO	GREEDY CRUEL VILLAIN	NOBLE GOD-FEARING KNIGHT	STORY-BOOK LEGEND
BRITISH MONK AD 540	WELSH POET AD 1000	NORMAN MONK AD 1300	HISTORIAN AD 2000

We'll probably never know the whole truth now. Arthur can be whatever you want him to be.

Naughty nuns and mischievous monks

If you were a Christian Saxon peasant you could escape from the pain of the plough and the foulness of the farm by joining a monastery. The monasteries encouraged parents to send their sons at the age of seven. But it would cost them...

Making monks

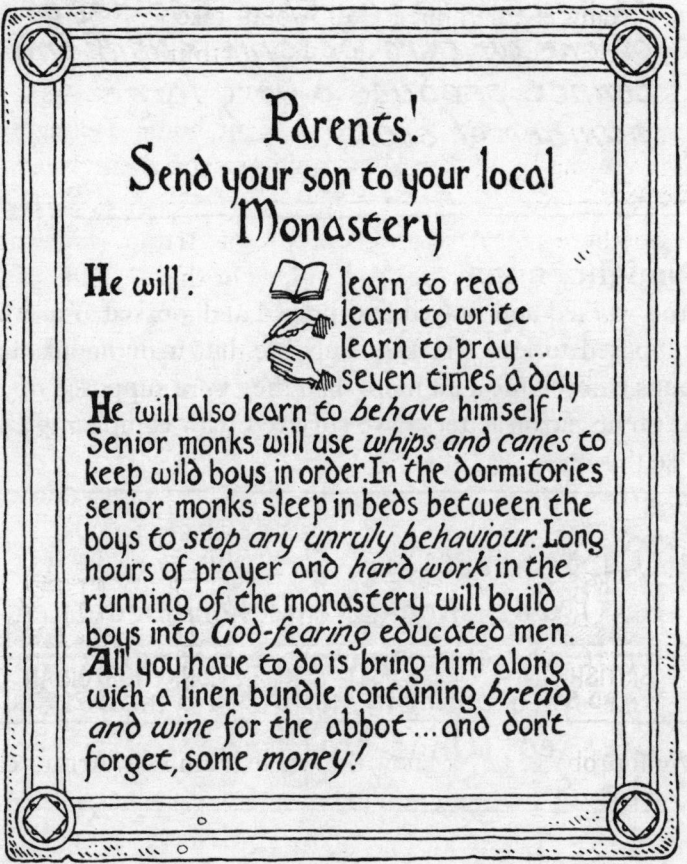

Parents!
Send your son to your local
Monastery

He will: learn to read
learn to write
learn to pray ...
seven times a day

He will also learn to *behave* himself! Senior monks will use *whips and canes* to keep wild boys in order. In the dormitories senior monks sleep in beds between the boys to *stop any unruly behaviour*. Long hours of prayer and *hard work* in the running of the monastery will build boys into *God-fearing* educated men. All you have to do is bring him along with a linen bundle containing *bread* and *wine* for the abbot ... and don't forget, some *money!*

What they didn't mention was that life could be hard. The Abbot of Monkwearmouth, a monastery in north-eastern England, wrote a letter to a friend in Germany and said:

During the past winter our island has been savagely troubled with cold and ice and with long and widespread storms of wind and rain. It is so bad that the hands of the writers become numb and cannot produce a very large number of books.

Naughty nuns

You worked and prayed and prayed and worked. You were supposed to lead a simple, holy life, but many monks and nuns enjoyed life a bit more than they were supposed to.

Some Saxon letters have survived with complaints a bit like this one...

My dear abbess,
    I was shocked and horrified on my visit to your convent. I expected to see holy women, simply and modestly dressed. What did I find?

> × Nuns who crimped their hair with curling irons.
> × Nuns wearing brightly coloured head-dresses laced with ribbons down to their ankles.
> × Nuns with sharpened fingernails like hawks' talons.
>
> I hope these disgraceful practices will cease immediately.
>
> Angry from Tunbridge Wells

And many monks were no better. The monk-historian Bede told the story of Coldingham monastery in Northumbria:

> The cells that were built for praying were turned into places of feasting and drinking.

A Celt called Adamnan warned that he had a dream in which he saw the monastery destroyed. The Coldingham monks behaved themselves for a while after Adamnan's warning.

Then they went back to their old ways and the monastery was destroyed by fire in AD 679. Bede said the fire was God's punishment.

So, be warned!

In 734 Bede himself was complaining in a letter to the Bishop of York:

Your Grace,

As you are aware, a monk vows to lead a single life, without the company of women. I was disgusted to note that monks in one of your monasteries were not only married – they were living in the monastery with their wives and children!

Bede also whinged about priests. They were guilty of 'laughter, jokes, stories, feasting and drunkenness'. Bede would not be someone you'd want to invite to your school Christmas party, then.

Even a strict monastery like Bede's own Monkwearmouth had problems with boys who preferred playing to praying. Just fifty years after Bede's death a monk was complaining that boys at Monkwearmouth monastery were having a wild time hunting foxes and hares! Monk Alcuin wrote:

How wicked to leave the service of Christ for a fox hunt

Misery for monks

Some monasteries could be very strict in their discipline. Boys were beaten with canes or whips for any misbehaviour. (Like dripping hot candle-wax on to an old monk's bald patch!)

But growing up didn't save you! Any monk could be punished by:

- beatings
- being locked in a cell alone
- being fed only bread and water.

Monks who did something really wicked (like eating meat on a Friday) would be thrown out of the monastery.

Just like schools until the 1960s really.

Nasty for nuns

Women had their own monasteries, called convents, but often shared mixed monasteries with monks. It's no surprise that the nuns got all the cooking and cleaning, sewing and serving jobs, is it?

Girls who became nuns must have liked larking about the way girls do today because there were rules to stop them. So, in the bedrooms, the nuns slept in rows – and the young nuns had old nuns sleeping between them to stop any joking, bullying or pillow fights (as girls tend to do, so they tell me).

But the naughtiest nun crime was 'vanity' – admiring your own good looks and sitting around in front of mirrors all day.

The nuns brought in one strict rule:

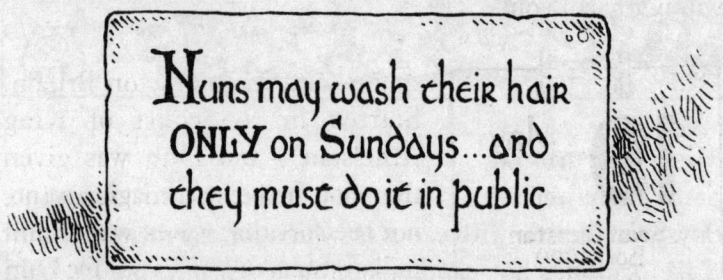

Nuns may wash their hair ONLY on Sundays...and they must do it in public

How would you like *that* rule, girls?

Suffering saints

Monks spent much of their time writing out the lives of saints. The tales of these weird and wonderful men and women were as exciting as a *Horrible Histories* book – but as believable as Enid Blyton!

Still, a saint's day was a good excuse for a holiday, so here are some excuses for a few days off from school. Just tell teacher you're a Saxon! You make up your own mind as to how true some of the curious cases on the calendar are.

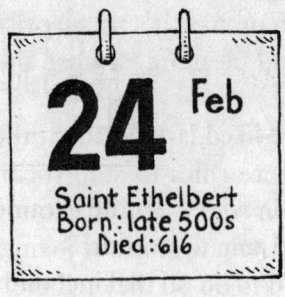

24 Feb
Saint Ethelbert
Born: late 500s
Died: 616

In 597 all England was a pagan country. Then Saint Augustine landed in King Ethelbert's kingdom and Eth said, 'I shall not harm you,' which was pretty nice, for a Saxon. King Eth not only made St Gus welcome but had himself and most of his people converted to Christianity.

This was the first ever Christian kingdom in England, so Eth became a saint. He didn't have to starve or suffer some other horrible death! Even you could be a saint if it's that easy!

Celebrate by going up to a passing monk and saying, 'I will not harm you!'

19 May
Saint Dunstan
Born: 909
Died: 988

A top saint in late Saxon Britain. Started in the court of King Athelstan – but Dun was given the boot for being a magician (no, not the sort that waves wands and pulls rabbits out of hats). Yet Dun *did* seem to have magic powers because he saw the murder of King Edmund before it happened (but never got to warn dead Ed). And an angel appeared on the road to tell Dun that King Eadred was dying – the shock of meeting the angel actually killed Dun's horse!

Dun set up a monastery and a school and for that he became a saint. Would you make your school teacher a saint?

Celebrate by waving a magic wand and making your school disappear!

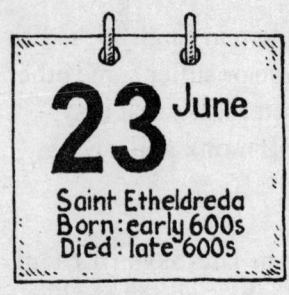

23 June

Saint Etheldreda
Born: early 600s
Died: late 600s

A Saxon princess who wanted to become a nun but had to get married. Happily her husband died … well, not so happily for him. But, would you believe it, she had to take a second husband. She was such a miserable wife he eventually divorced her and let her get on with her nunning. She gave up fine clothes and wore rough wool, only washed with cold water and caught the plague. Like most plague victims she had a dirty great lump on her neck. She said, 'This is God's punishment because I once wore a rich necklace there! Cccct!' and she died. When her coffin was opened 16 years after her death the lump on her neck was … gone! She became the saint of people with sore throats.

Celebrate by washing your wool shirt in cold water, throwing away your necklaces and marrying twice.

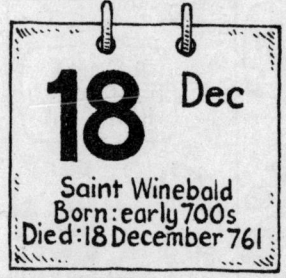

18 Dec

Saint Winebald
Born: early 700s
Died: 18 December 761

Saxon Winebald went off to Rome with his dad and his brother Willibald. (Note: I did not make up these silly names. Blame their dad, Saint Richard the Saxon.) Anyway, he set up a monastery in Germany and built a nunnery next door for his sister Walburga to run. Winebald was a poorly old man but he battled on bravely through great pain to do this Christian work. At least he got to be a saint when he died.

Celebrate by taking an aspirin – and writing a letter to your parents: 'Dear parents, thanks for not calling me Walburga, Winebald or Willibald!'

Saxon skills

Saxons had to have lots of skills to make the things they needed. Take something simple like making leather. Would you have the stomach for this lousy job?

Lousy leather
Animal skin rots and lets in water unless it is 'tanned' to turn it into leather. That's something even cave people knew and they made the animal skins into leather by pounding them with animal fat and brains! If they turned the leather into wooden-soled shoes they'd have real clever clogs! (Oh, never mind.)

Anyway, Lloyds Bank in York is on the site of a Saxon leather-making shop – a 'tannery'. Archaeologists dug there and found some interesting – but disgusting – facts about Saxon leather...

49

You can imagine a Saxon warrior running away from a battle with the Vikings and claiming it was his shoes that ran away … 'cos they were chicken!

Monk-y business

Making books was even messier than making leather. Monks used to murder kids to make books! Nah! I mean young goats – kids. What did you think I meant? They also massacred lambs and cut up calves in their thousands.

When well-behaved monks weren't praying, working in the fields, praying, helping the poor and needy, praying, sleeping in an unheated room, praying, eating some foul mush … or praying … they wrote books. Because printing hadn't been invented, they mostly copied other books by hand – the Bible and lives of saints and other people's work. Some brilliant monks, like Bede, wrote new books, including the first history of the English people.

There was also a whole horrible industry of monks providing the writing materials, because a monk couldn't pop down to the local corner shop for a pencil and paper. They hadn't been invented either! No, a lot of lambs and calves had to die to make those books.

NOTE: Vegetarians should skip this section.

Monks wrote on sheets of animal skin called 'vellum'. This is how you make vellum.

TRIM THE EDGES STRAIGHT AND KEEP THEM BETWEEN WOODEN BOARDS SO THEY DON'T CURL BACK UP INTO THE CUTE LITTLE SHAPE OF A CUTE LITTLE LAMB'S BELLY

The books from the 500s were all made on good quality skins. But by the end of the Dark Ages there were so many monks murdering so many lambs and calves and goats that they became a bit careless about the scraping and the vellum is sometimes as rough as a badger's bum.

Perfect pens and ideal ink

Next you needed a pen made from a stiff bird's feather, or quill. This was not quite as cruel as making the vellum because you didn't have to kill the birds to take their quills!

Take a seagull's or a goose's feather – it won't hurt much. (It's no more cruel than sneaking up behind a teacher and pulling a clump of their hair out with one sharp tug.) Wash the feather in hot water, then dry it. Trim off the feathery part with a sharp knife (careful!) to leave only the central shaft. Now you need to cut the end square. Finally cut away the back of the nib and make a slit half a centimetre up the shaft.

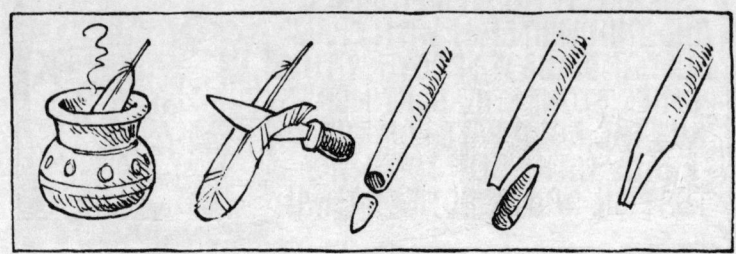

So now we've got the paper, or vellum, and pen. Of course being a big-brained *Horrible Histories* reader you'll have spotted what's missing. That's right ... ink!

Who has to suffer to make the ink? Intsy-winsy baby wasps, that's who...

Did you know…?

One book that remains from the early 700s is called *The Lindisfarne Gospels*. It took the skin of at least 129 calves so it's not suitable for reading by vegetarians.

You are only able to read this *Horrible Histories* book because monks wrote down all that history. Thousands of creatures died so you could read this book!

I hope you feel ashamed of yourself!

Games you wouldn't want to play

Life could be cruel and so sports could be crueler. Don't try these at home…

Pony clubbing

What you need:

Two stallion horses
(bad tempered ones are best)
A square of fencing
A couple of sharp sticks

How to play:
Put the two stallions in the square together. They will start to fight. (If they're in a good mood then jab them with sticks to make them wild.)

I THINK THIS ONE'S WILD NOW

Urge the stallions to attack each other with teeth and hooves. The winner is the first stallion to flatten the other.
How to win:
Bet on the horse you think will win.

Bull-baiting

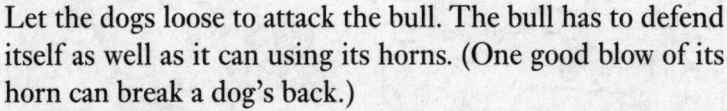

What you need:
A bull chained to a wooden stake
Dogs
How to play:
Let the dogs loose to attack the bull. The bull has to defend itself as well as it can using its horns. (One good blow of its horn can break a dog's back.)
How to win:
Bet on how many dogs the bull can kill.

Did you know...?
Christian Saxons were expected to give up drinking in the weeks leading up to Easter. The writer Aelfric told of a man who broke this rule. He got very drunk, wandered out into the street where a bull was being baited and was gored to death by the bull. Aelfric said this was God's punishment on the drinker. But then God didn't punish the bull-baiters!

Terrible truths or foul fibs?

Truth is stranger than fiction, someone very clever and very boring once said. But you have to be able to tell the difference.

First take a passing parent (or priest) and sit them in a chair. (You may have to tie them there, so have a clothes-line handy.)

Say: 'You have to help me with my homework!' Then pester your parent (or perplex your priest) with this cunning cwiz and see if they can sort out the truth from the fibs.

1 The Saxons played bagpipes.

2 The Saxons dressed in nettles.

3 The Saxons built their houses out of pig poo.

4 Saxon shepherds were paid with cattle dung.

5 Saxon gold coins were often fakes because they didn't have a test for gold.

6 The Vikings raided Saxon towns when they knew they would be deserted.

7 The wheelbarrow was invented in Saxon times.

8 If someone wanted half a penny in Saxon times then they cut a penny coin in half.

Answers:

1 True … probably! They certainly had flutes and trumpets, harps and whistles, but some archaeologists believe they had bagpipes too.

2 True. The stems of the nettles were crushed and dried. They could then be woven into a cloth to make clothes. Imagine wearing nettle knickers!

3 True. First they planted posts in the ground, then wove branches between the posts. But there were lots of gaps. The walls had to be plastered with mud, though pig droppings could be slapped on and would dry to make a nice hard wall. Don't you wonder how they trained the pigs to poo on the walls? Hey! You don't suppose the Saxons just went around picking the stuff up in their bare hands, do you?

4 True. The shepherd was given 12 days' supply of cattle droppings as a special Christmas treat. He could spread it over his fields as fertilizer. Shepherds were also allowed to keep one lamb and one fleece each year in payment. Maybe you'd like to revive this old Saxon custom and give a few buckets of manure to your best friend on Christmas Day? Then again, you may prefer to give it to your worst enemy.

5 False. The Saxons weren't great scientists but they did know how to test for gold. The king had a water butt with a fixed level of water in it. He took a certain weight of metal. If it was gold the water rose to just below the brim. If some cheap metal had been mixed in then the water overflowed. Water clever lot they were!

6 False. The Vikings raided on holy days when they knew the towns would be full of pilgrims, women and children going to church. These unarmed people would be snatched and sold as slaves as far away as north Africa. The Saxons weren't a lot better – the church objected to *Christians* like themselves being sold as slaves; they didn't object to other people being made slaves.

7 True. BUT ... not by the Saxons. It was invented by the Chinese and won't be seen in Europe till the 1200s. The Saxons hadn't even invented buttons – they had to use brooches and cords.

8 True. Don't try cutting a pound coin in half if your local sweet shop wants 50p – it's now against the law.

Awful Offa, Alf and Ath

An Offa lot of wealth

In 757 King Aethelbald (who wasn't bald), king of the Mercians, died. He was a tough old goat who chased women – and often caught them! He was also very violent. Of course some people didn't like him and he got himself murdered by the men who were supposed to protect him – his bodyguards.

But where did they get the idea to murder their boss? The finger of suspicion points at King Offa who took the throne. Offa went on to rule Mercia in the middle of England – he was the meat in a sandwich of the Northumbrians (the Saxons in the north) and the Saxons of the south. He also had a lot of trouble with the wild Welsh. That's probably why he built a wide ditch and mound to keep them out of his kingdom.

CROSS-SECTION OF OFFA'S DYKE

CROSS-SECTION OF WELSHMAN

Offa also had trouble with the kings in the tribes he took over. They weren't all happy about paying 'tribute' to Offa. Every year they had to meet him and give him payment.

This could be…

- Money, gold brooches and precious metals.
- Cattle and horses, hawks and hounds (for hunting).
- Decorated swords with magical spells on them.
- A feather bed and fine linen bed sheets.

They also had to send men to fight for Offa and almost certainly had to send the men who dug his 150 mile ditch on the Welsh border.

In return Offa's army protected them – or at least didn't destroy them!

Offa his food

Offa also demanded 'food-rent'. He travelled around his kingdom and expected his nobles to feast and entertain him with lots of grub. How would you like the bill for feeding 150 people a day? Bet you hope and pray he doesn't stay a week!

Warning people Offa

One king who grew tired of paying Offa was Aethelberht of Kent. A look at old coins gives us a clue to what happened…

The murder of Aethelberht shocked many Mercians and their other Saxon neighbours – but it kept them in line.

Mercian misery

Offa died in 795 and his son died a few months later. The kings in East Anglia and Kent revolted against the miserable Mercian rule straight away – this was the chance they'd been waiting for.

The rebels of Kent were led by a monk-king Eadberht. He was captured but the merciful Mercians *didn't* execute him, the way Offa would have done.

YEAH! WE JUST CHOPPED HIS HANDS OFF AND GOUGED HIS EYES OUT

THANKS, GUYS!

But the days of Mercian mastery were numbered once their great king hopped Offa the twig. Offa had created the idea that England could be one kingdom with one king. Yet it *wasn't* the Mercians who went on to rule that kingdom – it was the West Saxons.

When Offa died in 796 there were four great Saxon kingdoms in England – his Mercia, Wessex (West Saxons), East Anglia and Northumbria. By 878 only the kingdom of Wessex had survived.

Tough luck Offa, after you went to all that boffa...

What went wrong? The Vikings, that's what.

Silver and geld

The Saxons had come as raiders. Once they'd conquered the Brits they settled down as farmers and forgot how to fight.

So along came the Vikings from Denmark as raiders; they conquered the Saxons and settled down as farmers. If the Saxons could hang on long enough the Vikings might just forget how to fight too!

King Alfred was the first to fight back. But he wasn't quite ready to go into battle. So, at first, he just paid the

Vikings to leave him alone. This payment to the Danish Vikings has become known as 'Danegeld'.

As you'll read later, Ethelred the Unready has been called nasty names by historians because he paid fortunes in Saxon money to the Vikings so they'd go away. But those historians like to forget it was Alfred the 'Great' who did it first!

As a modern poet, Rudyard Kipling wrote, paying Danegeld was a pointless waste of money...

And that is called paying the Dane-geld;
But we've proved it again and again,
That if once you have paid him the Dane-geld
You never get rid of the Dane.

Did you know... ?

Saxon coins were made by 'moneyers' in the king's mint. They had the pattern on a stamp and hit the blank discs of silver with the stamp. The seventy mints made as many as five million coins a year this way!

A moneyer could become rich by making each coin just a little bit smaller than he was supposed to and saving all the little scraps of silver to build up a million-scrap fortune. BUT ... Athelred's Code of Laws said...

If a moneyer is found guilty of making coins too small then the hand that committed the crime shall be cut off and fastened to the mint.

Would that make a good punishment for shop assistants who give short change today?

Alf and Ath fight back

When the Danegeld ran out the Vikings squidged the Wessex king, Alfred, and his few hundred followers on to the marshes at Athelney. Alf broke out and gave the Vikings such a battering they made peace – and their king even became a Christian. Alf christened the Viking leader (Guthrum) himself.

Alf has become an English hero because the history books said he was a great leader. Who had the history books written? Alf, of course.

Alf's grandson, Athelstan, took the throne twenty-five years after Alf died and he set about snatching back all of England from the Viking settlers. He conquered England from Northumbria down to the south coast. Then he set about making the wild Welsh obey him. What a great guy. But Athelstan is forgotten in history books. Why? Because he didn't have history books written about his great victories.

History can be very unfair. It can also be full of fibs.

Hot hero

Alf, for example, is famous for the story of burning the cakes. Alf was in disguise, hiding from the Vikings (they said) when he went to a poor cottage for shelter. As the monks of St Neotts wrote over 250 years after Alf the Great died...

> THE FOLLOWING STORY IS 110% TRUE AND NOT ONE WORD OF A LIE. CROSS MY HEART AND HOPE TO DIE! HONEST! TRUTHFULLY, SINCERELY. THIS IS A LIE-FREE ZONE!

One day a peasant woman, the wife of a cowherd, was making loaves. King Alfred was sitting by the fire, looking after his bow and arrows and other weapons.

The poor woman saw that the loaves she'd put over the fire were burning. She ran up and took them off and scolded the unbeatable king. 'Look there, man! Couldn't you see the loaves were burning? Why didn't you turn them over? I'm sure you'd be the first to eat them if they were nicely done!'

The miserable woman did not realize that this was King Alfred, who had fought so many wars against the pagans and won so many victories.

The story is almost certainly a lie. But it makes Alf look like a struggling soldier, driven to hiding in the hut of a poor woman and getting nagged. What a hero he must have been to rise from that to defeat the Vikings, you'd say. Alfred is remembered for lies like this.

Athelstan didn't have historians to lie for him so he's forgotten.

But enough of these half-baked jokes.

Woeful for women

Digging up Saxon graves gives us clues about the different jobs men and women did. For example, women's graves often contained sewing boxes, so they must have been responsible for the sewing in their household, and it was probably seen as an important job.

In Saxon poetry women had a hard life and suffered it without complaining. In the real world it probably wasn't all bad. For example, unlike in many periods in history, women could be landowners ... though the only land some women got was a six foot grave.

A grave problem
One early Saxon grave was uncovered in layers. Could *you* be an archaeologist and explain what was most likely to have happened?

Explanation: The rich woman died, was put in her coffin and buried. The coffin was covered with a layer of soil and the second woman was thrown in – alive. The stone was placed on top of her to keep her there while the soil was piled on top to bury her alive.

It's harder to explain 'Why?' The second woman was possibly a slave sent to serve the rich woman in the afterlife. As if it wasn't bad enough being a slave in *this* life!

The key to success

In some women's graves there are sets of keys. This was a sign that women looked after the family's possessions and ran the house. (It makes you wonder how they got back in the house after the funeral when the keys were six foot under!)

Saxon law said that if stolen money was found in her house, the woman of the house was not to blame – unless it was found in a place she had the keys to.

And if a stolen animal was found in her house then the woman would not be blamed, so long as she swore not to eat the meat!

Wife weplacement

Divorce was rare ... but there was another way to take a second wife while the first one was still alive. If your wife was carried away by an enemy you must try to buy her back. But, if you can't afford to pay for her then you can take a new wife instead!

If a man was fed up with his first wife (and that has been known to happen) then he must have been tempted to go around making enemies. But there must have been a bit of girl-power in Saxon times. If a man was captured by an enemy then a wife could take a new husband the same way.

YOO-HOO! MR VI-KING! MY HUSBAND'S OVER THERE!

Mystic mugs

Crystal balls have been found in some Saxon graves – usually the graves of women. These wise women used them to tell the future and were called 'heahrune'.

But if a wise woman used her mystic powers to work wicked magic then she was called a 'haegtessan' ... a witch. And some still use the word 'hag' to insult a woman. (But *you* would never, ever, ever use such words about your teacher, would you?)

The witches

If you were a Saxon you probably believed that demons in the dark had the power to make a deal with you! They would give you magical powers on Earth … but as soon as you died then the Devil himself would come and take you away. If you agreed to that deal then you became a witch.

There is a story of a Saxon woman in the 800s who made such a deal with the Devil. Her story was turned into a poem a thousand years later by the Poet Laureate, Robert Southey (1774-1843)[1]. When the Devil sent his messenger raven, the old woman knew her time was up…

The Devil's Due

The raven croaked as she sat at her meal,
And the old woman knew what he said.
And she grew pale at the raven's tale,
And sickened and went to bed.

'I've anointed myself with infant's fat.
The devils have been my slaves.
From sleeping babes I have sucked the breath,
I have called the dead from their graves.

'And the Devil will fetch me now in fire,
My witchcraft to atone;
And I, who have troubled the dead man's grave
Shall have no rest in my own.'

1. The 'Poet Laureate' is supposed to be Britain's best living poet of the time. He (it's always been a 'he') is paid by the king or queen to write royal poems from time to time. Sadly being made 'Poet Laureate' doesn't mean you're always a very good poet.

They blest the old woman's winding sheet
With rites and prayers that were due.
With holy water they sprinkled her shroud,
And they sprinkled her coffin too.

And in he came with eyes of flame –
The Devil to fetch the dead.
And all the church in his presence glowed
Like a fiery furnace red.

He laid his hands on the iron chains;
And like flax they mouldered asunder.
And the coffin lid which was barred so firm
He burst with his voice of thunder.

And he called the old woman of Berkeley to rise
And come with her master away.
A cold sweat started on that cold corpse,
And the voice she was forced to obey.

The devil he flung her on a horse,
And he leapt up before.
And away like the lightning's speed she went;
And she was seen no more.

You'll notice the 'witch' was an old woman. The Saxons believed the Devil could possess a man *or* a woman, but there were many old tales such as this where women were the main suspects. Old women could not defend themselves so it was easy to accuse them of witchcraft and punish them.

Being a Saxon woman had its problems.

Did you know…?

A Saxon man could suffer an 'illness' from 'a woman's chatter'! It had its own cure like many other illnesses.

Men's Own Saxon Weekly
73

CUT THE CACKLE

Have you ever had a hard day on the farm only to come home to an earful of woman's talk? Are you needlessly nagged? Does gossip make you gag? In short, do you suffer from a woman's chatter?

Then old Doctor Bald's leechbook has the answer!

Just take a radish – yes one of those hot, red veggies-- and eat it before you go to bed. But beware, boys – eat nothing else!

Next morning the woman may still be wittering but you'll find it no longer bothers you!

Of course men today just love listening to women talk!

The cruel cave

The trouble with being a woman in Saxon times was that the world was run by men. Your life was decided by your father while you were a child, and your husband when you were married. That may have been fine for many women. But if a husband had problems then his wife would suffer too … maybe even worse!

There is an old Saxon poem called 'The Wife's Lament' preserved in *The Exeter Book* that's kept now in Exeter Cathedral. It's about a woman who came from overseas to marry a man. The man didn't tell her that he was mixed up in a feud and he soon had to escape to save his life. She was left behind, in a strange land, and had to live hidden in a cave beneath an oak tree.

The Saxon poets would go to feasts and sing her sad story...

> *I've never known such misery since I became his wife,*
> *Abandoned by a husband who sailed off to save his life.*
>
> *A victim of a vicious feud, he had to leave me here,*
> *And hide me deep within these woods where I must live in fear.*
>
> *I live beneath an ancient oak, within a deep earth cave,*
> *Alive, and yet it seems to me, I'm living in my grave.*
>
> *Each dawn I rise and leave the cave to walk through twisted trees,*
> *And moan when I remember how my lord is overseas.*
>
> *Sad grief is all there is for those who have to live apart.*
> *No friends, no parents and no love. Alone with aching heart.*

It's enough to put you off your feast, isn't it?

I suppose it's no worse than watching some miserable television programme while you're chewing your chips or slurping your soup.

We'll have none of that ear

A married woman in late Saxon times could *not* go off with another man. If she did, the church law said...

> *... her husband shall take all her property and she is to lose her nose and ears.*

Married men didn't suffer that punishment if they went off with another woman. This law didn't last long and was changed in 1035.

What would the world be like if we had that law today? Who nose?

Saxon scoffers

No baked beans, no chocolate, no chips. Would you really like to have lived in those days? Like most other ages in horrible history a lot might depend on whether you were a rich noble or a pathetic peasant. For example...

Gut grub

Take 10 jars of honey, 300 loaves of bread, 42 casks of ale, 2 oxen, 10 geese, 20 hens, 10 cheeses, 1 barrel of butter, 5 salmon and 100 eels. What have you got?

1 The food supply for one peasant family for one year?

2 The food supply for one rich farmer for one year?

3 The food eaten by a Saxon king and his friends in one *night*?

The last one, of course. There's no mention of how many indigestion tablets they needed next day.

Putrid pottage

Peasant food was plain and boring. The bread was coarse with grit from the grinding stones. Saxon skeletons found by archaeologists have teeth worn away by chewing bread like sandpaper.

Monasteries grew their own food but it could be pretty boring stuff. A vegetable stew (called 'pottage') would have been a common meal. If you'd like to know how the monks ate then try this recipe…

Monks' Mush (or Nuns' Nosh)

Here's a tasty treat for you starving sisters and brothers. Eat this three times a day to grow healthy and fit. You may not live to thirty with a potty pottage diet – but life will be so miserable you'll be happy to die!

You need:
1 leek
1 onion
half cup of peas
half cup of lentils
half litre of water
pinch of parsley
pinch of sage
salt

Cooking:
Peel and chop the onion and the leek.
Boil the water and add the parsley, sage and salt.
Add the onion, leek, peas and lentils.
Cover and boil slowly for half an hour.
Serve with thick chunks of bread.

You may enjoy this recipe. But if you try eating it three times a day, seven days a week for most of your life, you may just get a teeny-weeny bit bored with it.

Run, rabbit, run!

St Benedict made the rules that monks lived by. One rule said they should not eat flesh. But monks took this to mean they should not eat four-legged animals. They ate fish and birds – and they even ate beavers because (they said) beavers live in water, so they're fish! But, strangest of all, the Normans brought rabbits to Britain when they conquered it in 1066, and monks decided it was all right to eat them!

Test your teacher on taste

Ask your teacher these questions about Saxon food. See if they can score ten out of ten! Which of these foods did Saxons eat?

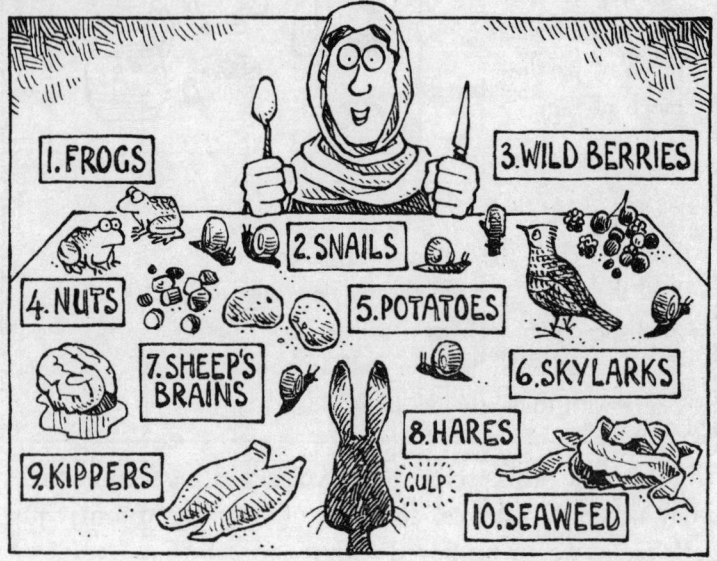

Hunger horrors

Some of the things Saxons ate may seem disgusting to you – you don't see many sheep brains on the school dinner menu, do you? But there was something worse than eating seaweed sandwiches, and that was eating nothing at all.

Food didn't keep for very long – no fridges in Saxon houses. You grew food in summer and ate it over the winter. But if you failed to grow the food in the summer then you starved over winter.

What would stop you growing food in summer? Well…

- Bad weather, heavy rain, floods or storms destroying your wheat.
- Viking invaders burning your fields and stealing your cattle.
- Plagues killing off farm workers and animal plagues destroying your flocks.

What could you do?

- Jump off a cliff.
- Eat your neighbours.
- Sell your children.
- Put your head in your lord's hands.
- Eat a tree.

Do they sound daft? Well they're horribly historically true, as the chronicles of the time tell…

OUR FAMINE FAVOURITES

Crops failed? Got a rumbling tum? Then try these top tips from the *Anglo-Saxon Chronicle* and see how you can cure those hunger pains!

1 Fall in line

In Sussex last year forty villagers cured their hunger for good. They went to the edge of a cliff, joined hands and jumped over. The ones who weren't crushed on the rocks were drowned in the sea. Fast food for fish!

2 Funeral food

It's been reported that when villagers died in a famine area they were not buried by their families (as that would be a waste of good meat). Instead they were cooked and eaten. Human hotpot saves lives.

3 Slave away

The Saxon law says: 'A father may sell a son if that child is under seven years old and if he needs to do so.' Selling children earns you money ... plus you save because you don't have to feed them! No kids is good kids – no kidding!

4 Good Lord!

It is a lord of the manor's duty to protect his people. If the worst comes to the worst visit your local lord, kneel in front of him and place your head in his hands. You then become his slave and work for him – but at least he'll feed you.

5 Tree-mendous!

When all else fails you can eat everything in sight. It's been reported that Saxon survivors ground up anything from acorns to tree-bark, nettles and wild grass to fill out the flour. Your bark can be good for your bite!

Muttering monks

It's nice to sit down at a table, eat good food and gossip with a friend. But monks were supposed to be silent while they ate their food. That's not just boring … it can also be a real nuisance. What about if you need something desperately? Don't worry – the monks had their own system of signs.

Try eating school dinners in silence (your teachers will like this historical game!) and use the monk system instead of words. Here are four to get you started.

Monastery messages

1. 'Pass the salt' – place three fingers together and shake them as if salting something

2. 'Pass the pepper' – knock two fingers together

3. 'Pour me some wine' – put chumb and forefinger together as if turning on the tap of a cask

4. 'Pass the butter' – stroke three fingers of one hand over the palm of the other hand

There are an amazing 127 different signs in the monks' guidebook that you'd have to learn. Once you've mastered the four above then make up your own … but I don't want to see the one you make up for 'I think I'll go for a pee'.

Horrible historical joke
This witty riddle was written by a monk…

QUESTION: WHAT MAKES BITTER THINGS SWEET?
ANSWER: HUNGER

It's not a very good joke, but it's survived 1200 years, which is more than you will, so don't sneer at it!

Did you know… ?
November was known as 'Blood Month'. That month was when the Saxons slaughtered cattle because (a) they wanted to eat them over the winter months, and (b) they couldn't feed many of the beasts when there was no fresh grass. So it was bye-bye to your old friend Daisy the cow and hello to scrumptious steaks. Could you eat your old friend?

Sooty bacon
Saxon houses had no chimneys – the smoke just drifted upwards and out through a hole in the roof. When a pig was killed for food it was hung from the roof and the smoke 'cured' it; that is, it stopped it going bad. So a pig killed in autumn could still be eaten in spring.

And people today still enjoy the taste of smoked bacon. But modern smoky bacon is probably not as tasty as Saxon

83

bacon which would have bits of soot from below, not to mention insects dropping down from the roof. Nothing nicer than a sprinkling of spider to add to your breakfast bacon!

The Tudors brought tobacco to Britain so maybe they invented the horrible historical joke…

Bee brave and bee have!

There was no sugar in Saxon England. The only sweetener was honey, so a family celebrated when bees set up a hive in their roof.

There was one sure way of persuading bees to come to your home. When a swarm flies past you, grab a handful of gravel and throw it over them, crying the spell:

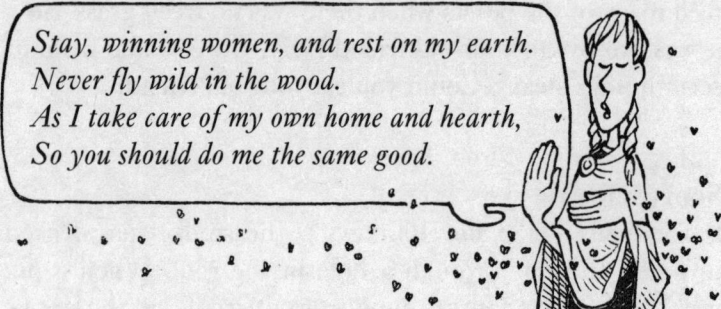

Stay, winning women, and rest on my earth.
Never fly wild in the wood.
As I take care of my own home and hearth,
So you should do me the same good.

Of course it may be dangerous to throw gravel at a swarm of bees. So get the nearest teacher to do it for you while you go inside and shut the doors and windows.

Curious cures

Luckily some marvellous medicine books have survived from the Saxon age. Books like *Bald's Leechbook* (Bald was the owner of the book) written in the late 800s. Some of the magical charms go back to Saxon days before they invaded England and are probably the oldest pieces of German writing we have.

Curl curing
The Saxons had their own treatments for baldness. You can't buy it at Boots, but you may like to offer a bald bloke you know this cure…

HORRIBLE HISTORIES® HAIR RESTORER

Is your Dad (or your history teacher) a slaphead? Is there more hair on a hen's egg than his skull's skin?

Then try Horrible Histories hair restorer! Yes, this is simply made by burning bees and rubbing the ash into the shining scalp.

This wonder cure is absolutely free – and you get your money back if it doesn't work! You'll be your parent's pet for ever more!

Helping your hair gives me a real buzz!

You're a honey!

Or you could buy a wig.

Cute cures

Pagan and Christian ideas were mixed up when Saxons tried to cure sicknesses. Could you cure these six Saxons' sicknesses? (Cure it! You couldn't even say it!)

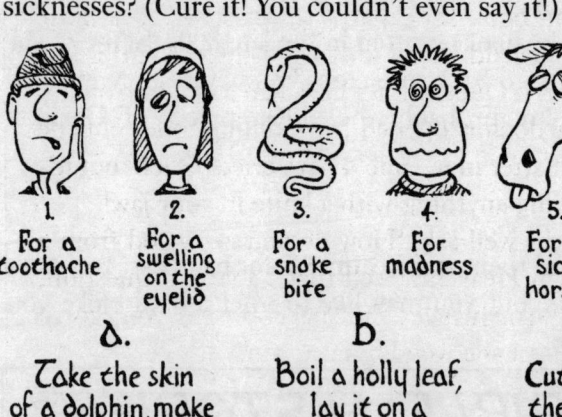

1. For a toothache

2. For a swelling on the eyelid

3. For a snake bite

4. For madness

5. For a sick horse

6. For a sick girl

a.
Take the skin of a dolphin, make it into a whip and beat yourself with it

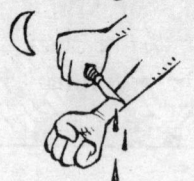

b.
Boil a holly leaf, lay it on a saucer of water, raise to the mouth and yawn

c.
Cut the sign of the cross in the forehead, back and limbs, pierce the left ear, then beat with a stick

d.
Cut a vein and let out some blood. This must be done at night

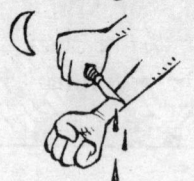

e.
Take a knife and cut out the affected part

f.
Take a piece of wood from a tree grown in Heaven and press it to the wound

Answers:

1b) You will find (a Saxon medical book promises) that 'the evil tooth-worms will tumble from the mouth'. Yeuch! Think I'd prefer the toothache!

2e) A Saxon book says that a youth survived a knife through the eyelid. Even kings and queens suffered a bit of butchery. Queen Etheldrida had a swelling on her jaw and her doctor 'opened the swelling to let out the poisonous matter in it'. She'd have cried 'Ouch' but it's difficult crying anything with a knife in your jaw!

3f) You might well ask, 'How do you get wood from a tree grown in Heaven?' Well that's a stupid question, if I may say so. Just let the snakebite kill you, go to Heaven and get the wood to cure you. Simple!

4a) You may not be mad after the whipping – but the skinless dolphin will be absolutely furious.

5c) This treatment will make your horse a little cross – or six little crosses, to be accurate. You may find that your local vet does not use this old Saxon cure.

6d) A Saxon bishop warned doctors, 'Do not do this on the fourth day of a new moon!' What sort of clock did he use to measure the timing of the moon? A lunar-tick, of course!

Don't try these cures at home because you need the right magical spells to recite with the cure. When the Saxons became Christian the magical spells became Christian prayers – they would sing 'Misere me deus'[1] three times and recite the Lord's Prayer nine times.

Some other cures you probably shouldn't try…

1 Poisonous spider bite Make three cuts into the flesh near the bite. Let the blood run into a hazel-wood spoon. Throw the spoon *and* blood over the road. Messy!

2 Dog bite Burn the jaw of a pig to ashes. Sprinkle the ashes on to the wound. Mind the pig jaw doesn't bite you too!

3 Bleeding wound To stop the bleeding take the soot from a pot, rub it into a powder and sprinkle it on the wound. If that doesn't work then take fresh horse droppings, bake them dry and rub them into a powder – put the powder on to a thick linen cloth and bind it on to the wound overnight. Yeuch! Better to bleed!

4 Thick hair To thin your hair, burn a swallow to ashes and rub the ashes into the scalp. To completely stop hair growing then rub ant eggs into the scalp. What a yolk!

1. It means 'God have mercy on me'. You can try singing that instead and just hope that God speaks English!

5 Headache Take swallow-chicks and cut them open. Look for little stones in their stomachs, sew them into a bag and place on the head. This is also a cure for people plagued by goblins.

EEK!

OH NO! HE'S GOT SWALLOW-CHICK-STOMACH-STONES ON HIS HEAD!

Cuthbert's cure

If you are ill it helps to be a saint. When St Cuthbert had a swollen knee he was advised to cook wheat flour with milk and put the hot mixture on his knee. Who told him this? His doctor? No. An angel on a horse! (Why did the angel need a horse? Weren't his wings working? And if the angel is God's messenger, then why didn't God just cure the knee without all that gooey flour? Or why did God allow Cuthbert's knee to swell in the first place? Sometimes God can be a funny woman.)

Health horrors

The good news is Saxon adults were quite tall and strong. History lessons often say that people in the past were much smaller and weedier than we are today. That may have been true for the children of Queen Victoria's smoky slums. It wasn't true of the Saxons. (Archaeologists have measured the Saxon bones in graves and proved this. Nice job, eh?)

The bad news is only half the Saxons lived to see their 25th birthday.

More bad news is that there were a lot of diseases that couldn't be cured and were quite nasty.

Four foul health horrors that Saxons lived and died with were...

1 Fleas Monks had four or five baths every year – outside the monasteries people probably had fewer – so fleas flew happily through clothes, scoffed on your skin and belched after a bellyful of your blood. One wacky cure was to take the flea-infested clothes and lock them in an air-tight box. They must have thought the fleas would starve or suffocate!

2 Lice These stubborn little friends lay their eggs in your hair and cling like a rottweiler to a burglar's bum. The Saxons used combs with very close teeth, dragged them through the hair and hoped to pull out the eggs and the lice – not to mention lumps of hair! St Cuthbert was buried with a comb made from an elephant's tusk – he must have had jumbo-sized lice!

3 Ergot Old grain went mouldy with a fungus called ergot. If you made the grain into flour and ate the fungus you got ergotism ... very nasty. If you are lucky you feel anxious, and dizzy, get noises in your ears, feel your arms and legs are on fire and can't stop them twitching. You dance out of control … but could recover. If you were unlucky you got the feeling of ants running round in your burning feet and fingers, which then turned red, then black, then dropped off. If you were really unlucky your ears and nose dropped off and you died. (But ergot was worse in France in the Dark Ages than in England, where victims usually recovered.)

POOR MAN

ERGOT?

NO. TERRIBLE SENSE OF RHYTHM

4 Worms No, not the sort of squiggly, fat things you see in the ground. These were the ones that lived inside your body. The whipworm was harmless and stayed in your gut, but the monstrous maw-worm could grow to 30 centimetres and infest your liver or lungs. It could move through your body and pop out anywhere – including the corner of your eye! Yeuch!

MUM! I THINK I'VE GOT SOMETHING IN MY EYE

AEHHHHHH HHH HHHHHHHHH

Did you know…?
The Saxons had no idea of how diseases are spread by germs. If food fell on the floor amongst the dog droppings they'd just wipe it (to take away the taste) and make a sign of the cross (to take away any evil spirits that were hanging round there) … and then pop it into their mouth. Scrummy!

Ethelred the Ready for Beddy

Kwick king kwiz

King Ethelred II was given the name Ethelred 'the Unready'. How have teachers explained this nickname?

HE WAS UNREADY BECAUSE HE WAS NEVER READY WHEN THE VIKINGS INVADED

ETHELRED COULDN'T READ – HE WAS UN-READ, AS THEY SAY

THE SAXON WORD 'RAED' MEANS ADVICE. ETHELRED REFUSED TO TAKE ADVICE, SO HE WAS 'UN-RAEDY'

'RAED' MEANS ADVICE– BUT HE WAS 'UN-RAED' BECAUSE HE WAS GIVEN BAD ADVICE

Answer: At some time or another ALL of these different explanations have been given. The nickname was first written down two hundred years after his death but it could have been used during his lifetime. It was probably meant as a joke — Ethelred was both badly advised (un-raed) AND not ready for the Viking invasions.

And that's not the only unkind thing historians have said about Eth the pathetic…

Unready, steady, go

Poor old Ethelred the Unready came to the throne in 978 and ruled until 1013. He has been remembered for a thousand years as one of the world's worst monarchs – and, as most monarchs have been pretty bad, that means Eth must have been totally useless!

Eth has been blamed for letting the Vikings return and rob the English till their purses and bellies were as empty as a traffic warden's heart. How did Eth get a thousand years of blame?

A hundred years after his death a monk, William of Malmesbury, wrote...

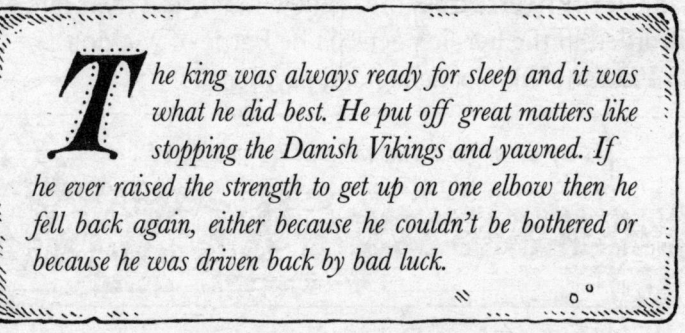

The king was always ready for sleep and it was what he did best. He put off great matters like stopping the Danish Vikings and yawned. If he ever raised the strength to get up on one elbow then he fell back again, either because he couldn't be bothered or because he was driven back by bad luck.

Of course Will of Malmesbury didn't mean Eth really spent all his time in bed. He just meant he was as dozy as someone who did. Yet Eth spent 38 years on the throne – so he must have been doing something right! And he didn't have a lot going for him:

- Bad-tempered, violent King Edward was murdered so his half-brother Ethelred could become king – church leaders made evil Edward a saint.
- Edward was murdered while he was visiting Ethelred – churchmen said killing the king brought a curse on Eth, even if he wasn't to blame for it.

- Eth was just ten years old when he took the throne – would you rule a country at that age?
- 'A cloud as red as blood' was seen after Eth was crowned – it appeared at midnight and vanished at dawn – it was a sign that God was angry.

Byrhtnoth the brave (but batty)

Eth wasn't the only one to blame for the Viking success. Byrhtnoth was an old but brave Saxon warrior. The Vikings landed on the little island of Northey in the River Blackwater near Maldon, Essex. Byrhtnoth's army faced them from the bank of the river, across the shallow water, and their fate was recorded in the heroic poem, 'The Battle of Maldon'.

First the Vikings demanded payment...

Pay us in gold and we will let you live!

Bold Byrhtnoth replied...

We will pay you with spear points and sword blades.

Tough talk!

The island was joined to the shore by a strip of mud at low tide. As the Vikings tried to cross Byrhtnoth's men cut them down.

The Vikings said…

Byrhtnoth! We cannot fight like this. Let my men cross to the shore and give you a real battle!

What a joke! A wise old warrior would say, 'No!' In fact only a bird-brained booby would say, 'Yes.'

Byrhtnoth said, 'Yes.'

Byrhtnoth was a brave and heroic man. He was soon a brave and heroic corpse as the Vikings cut him and his men to pieces.

But at least he *tried* to fight back. King Ethelred simply said…

PAY THEM!

Gruesome at Greenwich

Ethelred had a fair idea of what might happen if he didn't pay the Vikings. Look at what happened to Archbishop Aelfheah!

If one of the serving women at a Viking stronghold could have written, this is how she may have described the grisly scene…

Greenwich
Near London
20 April 1012

Dear Mum,

I am sending you a
few pieces of silver. I pinched
them from the Danish Vikings here.
Don't worry, they won't miss them—
and anyway, they owe me the money
after the way they've made me work!
'I'm not a slave!' I told them. At least
I would have told them but I was a
bit scared they'd make me one!

Anyway, last week they started
collecting that tribute Ethelred and
us Saxons have to pay. 48,000
pounds in silver! Agnes, who speaks
a bit of Viking, says they were
boasting that it would be about
twelve million silver coins!

But last night they turned really

nasty. They robbed a trade ship on the river Thames and pinched barrels and barrels of French wine. Of course, being Vikings, they had to drink it all in one feast, didn't they? I was run off my feet keeping their goblets topped up. They poured it into their hairy faces as fast as I could pour it into the cups!

And a drunk Viking is a vile Viking, I can tell you. For a bit of sport they dragged the old Archbishop of Canterbury, Aelfheah, into the hall. He's been their prisoner for seven months. They started shouting at him, 'How much are you going to pay to set yourself free, you snotty Saxon?' (At least that's what Agnes said they said.)

The old arch-bish was so calm! He just said, 'Nothing. And I will not allow the king or my church to pay you anything! The poor should not have to pay taxes to set me free.'

Well, that drove the Vikings mad as a nest of vipers. One of the Viking warriors took his sword out and raised it over the old bloke's head. 'No silver, no Saxon!' he cried.

'Wait!' the Viking leader roared. 'You cannot spill the blood of a holy man. We'll be cursed!'

So the Viking warrior looked crafty and grinned a black-and-yellow-toothed grin. He picked up an ox bone from the feast and threw it at the old arch-bish. It cracked the old guy right on the conk and he fell. 'See! No blood!' the warrior laughed.

That gave them all the idea for a bit of sport! Every Viking picked up a bone and pelted the old man – some of them even threw ox heads at him that had been picked clean. The bish took it bravely for a while – then he fell. Only one brave Viking tried to stop them but they ignored him.

At last their leader walked up to the half-dead arch-bish. Aelfheah had converted him to Christianity just the day before so I expected him to help the bish! Huh! No chance. He simply smacked him with the blunt side of his axe to finish him off.

Then they went back to their drinking till they drank themselves senseless. When they were all snoring we had to drag the old man out of the feasting hall and me and Agnes took him to the local church.

I am absolutely shattered. Working all night, dragging bodies all morning. I tell you, Mum. If you see those Vikings heading for your house then run. And pray they don't find the bones our dog buried in the garden. Your loving daughter, Hilda

Aelfheah's death was remembered and a church built on the spot where he died. It's still there in Greenwich today while his body was taken back to Canterbury.

He was made a Saxon saint … and probably deserved it!

Eth's death, then Ed's dead

Here's a totally useless bit of information for you to impress your teacher with:

In 1013 Viking king Swein arrived. (Rearrange the letters to make 'Swine' … which the Saxons must have called him!) Eth ran away to Normandy so the Vikings couldn't kill him.

Swein died in 1014. The Vikings wanted their Cnut to rule. But the Saxons welcomed back Ethelred … so long as he promised to be a better ruler. Then in 1016 he died. A really mean Victorian historian sneered…

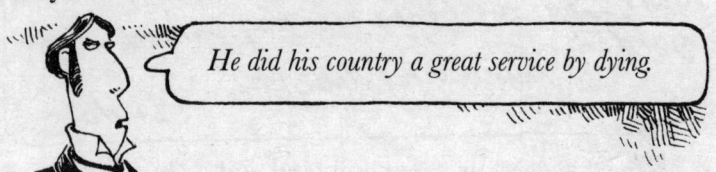

Eth's son, Edmund, gave Viking Cnut a few beatings in battle and they split the country between them, the way Alfred had – Danes in the north and east, Saxons in the south and west. It may have stayed like that but Ed did a really stupid thing – as daft as his dad Eth – he went and died! Cnut took over the whole country and Saxon rule was finished for 25 years.

How to be a Great king

Cnut may have been a Viking but a lot of historians think he was a 'good' king. He was named Cnut the Great. But we horrible historians know better. You don't get to be 'Great' without splattering blood around like water at a swimming gala.

Cnut was a Viking and he was a bad loser. He took Saxon hostages in East Anglia. When he was attacked by the Saxons he set sail into the English Channel. Cruel Cnut dropped the hostages off in Kent – but only after he'd dropped their hands and noses off into the sea.

Cnut was worried that Edmund's brothers would take over dead Ed's claim to the throne. He had Eadwig murdered.

To stop Edmund's step-bothers Edward and Alfred claiming dead Ed's throne he married their mother – if they fought him they'd have to fight their mum! Neither boy fancied that so they fled. Cnut was not bothered by the fact he already had a girlfriend and two sons (Swein and Harald) up in Northampton.

There were some English leaders that Cnut didn't trust. They had promised to obey him, but he wasn't sure. Just to be on the safe side he executed them. Earl Uhtred of Northumbria, for example, went to make peace with Cnut. Uhtred's own treacherous servant, Wighill, ran out from a hiding place and murdered him. It seems Cnut gave Wighill the order.

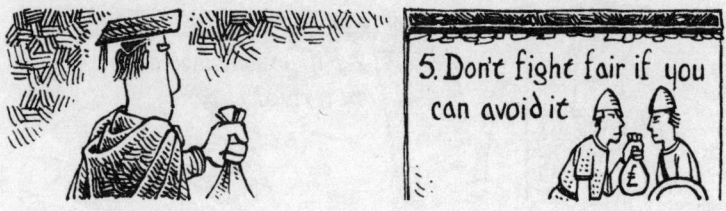

Cnut won a lot of battles. But he often cheated. When he attacked Norway in 1028 he sent large amounts of English money to princes so they would betray their king. Cnut conquered Norway with wallets for weapons.

Cnut couldn't beat Edmund in the war for the English throne, until Ed was betrayed by Mercian lord Eadric. Cnut made peace with Edmund and they swore to be 'brothers' ... and a few months later Edmund conveniently died. Surely Cnut the 'Great' wouldn't arrange to have a noble 'brother' bumped off!?! What do you think?

He was a tough nut (and a tough Cnut), but he was a 'Great' king – wasn't he?

Saxon crime and punishment

The Saxons certainly didn't mess about if you broke one of their laws.

King Edmund became an English saint – a good Christian who was captured by Viking bullies and chose to die horribly rather than give up his religion. You may be starting to feel sorry for Ed. DON'T!

Ed was not a kind and gentle king. Look at how he treated runaway slaves. (Slaves were known to the Saxons as 'thralls'.)

Grave for slaves

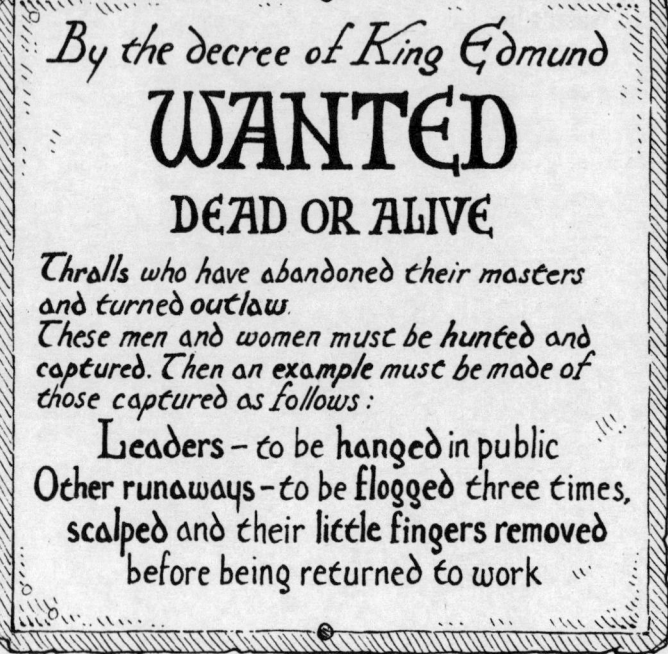

By the decree of King Edmund

WANTED

DEAD OR ALIVE

Thralls who have abandoned their masters and turned outlaw.
These men and women must be hunted and captured. Then an example must be made of those captured as follows:

Leaders – to be hanged in public
Other runaways – to be flogged three times, scalped and their little fingers removed before being returned to work

Painful punishment

In pagan Saxon times crimes were avenged by 'feuds' where people took the law into their own hands – you know, the sort of thing that still goes on in classrooms today…

The trouble is feuds could go on and on, maybe getting senseless and violent…

…and not even death stopped the feud…

So kings tried to replace revenge with payment…

Even a human life could have a price on it – a 'weregild'. If a person were killed then the killer would have to make a weregild payment to the victim's family. The richer you were the higher your weregild was. A dead lord's family would get more than a dead peasant's family would from the killer.

Even bits of your body had a price on them!

What's your nose worth compared to your toes? Can you match the body bit to the money?

Whips and lips

Traitors, outlaws, witches, wizards and frequent thieves could all receive the death penalty. But the execution method varied from place to place, time to time and crime to crime. If you were caught, how would you like to go? Which of these Saxon punishments would you choose to suffer?

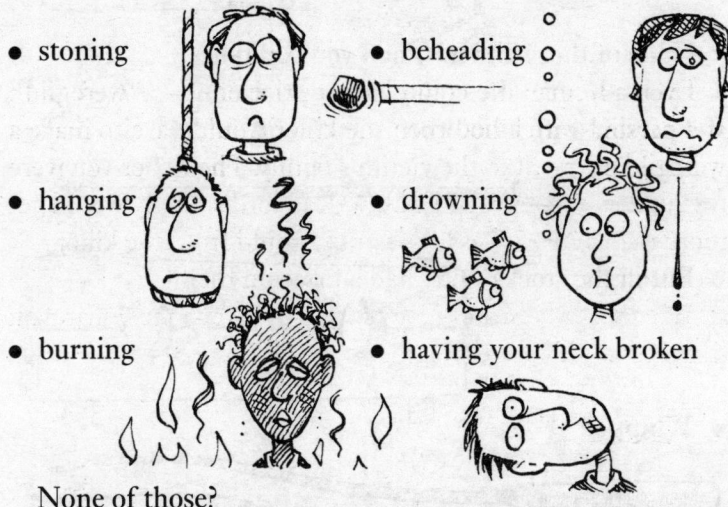

- stoning
- beheading
- hanging
- drowning
- burning
- having your neck broken

None of those?

All right. A merciful Saxon judge may teach you a lesson with a bit of mutilation – that is, he'd have bits cut off you. Which could you do without…?

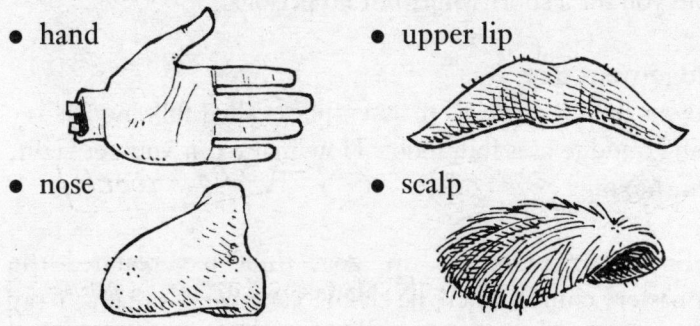

- hand
- upper lip
- nose
- scalp

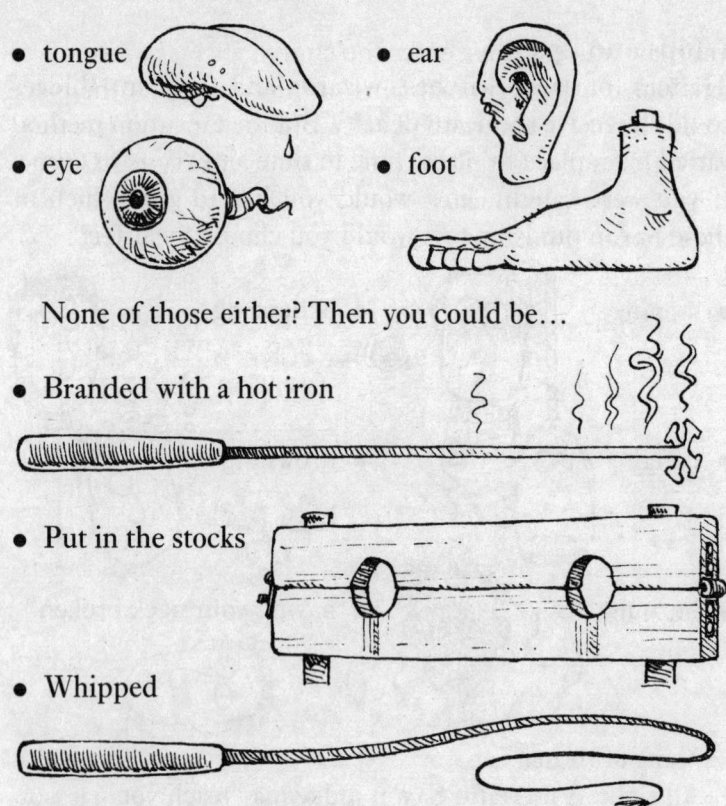

- tongue
- ear
- eye
- foot

None of those either? Then you could be...

- Branded with a hot iron

- Put in the stocks

- Whipped

You'd rather go to prison?

Sorry – there may be a cellar in the lord's manor house to hold you for a short while, but no prisons.

Judgement day

Saxons held their trials in assemblies called folk moots. Try being a judge at a folk moot. How many can you get right, your honour?

1 Sanctuary Geraint the goat thief has reached the monastery church where he claims 'sanctuary' – that is to say your law officers can't enter the church and take him off to jail. But if every criminal runs to the abbey then the place would be full of thieves and killers. So a time limit has to be put on the sanctuary. How long will you let a criminal stay in sanctuary before you send the lads in to drag him out?

a) 40 hours.

b) 40 days.

c) 40 years.

2 Thieves Some criminals like Cuthwine never learn. He has been caught stealing and you have fined him. Now he's been caught again. How are you, his Saxon judge, going to punish him this time for repeated stealing?

a) Cut off his hair.

b) Cut off his hand.

c) Cut off his head.

3 Child cruelty Some parents are accidentally cruel to their children because they try out 'cures' for illnesses without realizing the dangers. In the early 700s a law has been passed, as you know, your honour. It means you must sentence Brigit to five years of punishment if she does what to cure her daughter's fever?

a) Holds the child too close to the fire.

b) Ducks her in the village pond.

c) Puts her on the roof or puts her in the oven.

4 Foreigners Foreigners in Saxon England can't be trusted because they might be spies for an enemy. So a foreigner must stay on the main roads and tracks, and if he leaves the path he has to let everyone know by blowing a horn or shouting. Maelgwn has been arrested for breaking this law. What must you do to him, your honour?

a) Put him to death as a thief.

b) Send him back to his own country.

c) Fine him a penny for every step he took off the path.

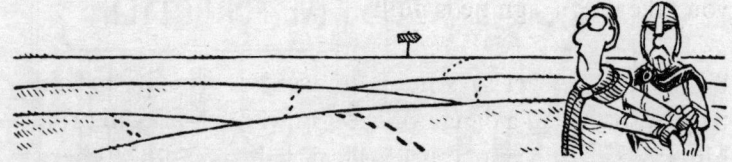

5 Fines There were no prisons in your local Saxon villages. Fines were easier to arrange. Which of these crimes must you punish with a fine, your honour?

a) Eating meat on a 'fast' or holy day.

b) Making a sacrifice to a pagan god.

c) Unlawful marriage.

IT'S MY FIRST FAST FEAST FINE!

6 Manslaughter Murder is not seen as a crime against the victim, but a crime against the victim's family. So, if a man is killed his family suffer because he is no longer there to earn a living for them. The family will demand his 'weregild' – his value in cash. But Benedict killed Alwin accidentally when a tree he was cutting fell on his neighbour. What must you order Benedict to do, your honour?

a) Pay the family the weregild money the same as for a murder.

b) Take the place of the victim in the family.

c) Kill himself.

110

7 Trials Edwin is suspected of stealing a pig. You ordered him to come to the village for a trial. (If Edwin doesn't turn up then he is 'Guilty'.) You have no police force to collect evidence – and no fingerprints to prove that a criminal was there. How can you check a suspect's story?
a) If he swears an oath on the Bible you must believe every word he says.
b) If he remains silent you must decide he is innocent.
c) If he swears an oath but stumbles over words (or stammers) you take it as a sign he is guilty.

8 Ordeals Egbert says he is innocent and wants to take a trial by 'ordeal' – a dangerous test in which God will protect him if he is innocent. What 'ordeal' will you allow Egbert to take?
a) He must grip a red–hot iron bar … and not be burned.
b) He must be tied up and thrown in the river … and float.
c) He must pull a stone from a pot of boiling water … and not be scalded.

9 Punishments Your court has found Theodoric guilty of witchcraft. You may choose to hang him. Which of these three other execution methods could you use in Saxon England, your honour?
a) Boiling.
b) Starving.
c) Guillotine.

THAT SHOULD DO THE TRICK

DO NOT FEED

10 Outlaws Cormac is a criminal who has run away from your punishment, then lived outside the law – he is declared an 'outlaw'. This means...

a) He doesn't have to pay taxes.

b) He is not allowed to go to church.

c) Anyone can kill him without having to stand trial for his murder.

Answers:

1b) Sanctuary lasted 40 days. But you only got 40 days if you handed over your weapons. If the criminal hadn't escaped in those 40 days he was taken to court and tried. Criminals could also claim sanctuary in a royal household! (They couldn't be throne out!) The trouble is someone has to sit outside the church for forty days to make sure he doesn't escape. Talk about crimewatch.

2b) A criminal could have his hand cut off, especially someone who stole from a church. Another common punishment was to 'brand' a criminal – burn a mark on his skin – so that everyone could see what he'd been up to and take extra care of their belongings when he was around.

3c) The writer of the law claimed that women put their daughters on the roof or in the oven to cure a fever! Do NOT let your mother read this book in case she gets some sad Saxon idea into her head and pops you in to bake.

4a) Very harsh, but in the days when very few people left their own village strangers were seen as dangerous. Even a great teacher and preacher like Bede never went further than a hundred miles north or south of his home monastery. Nowadays we're more trusting of strangers – even if they come from Clacton-on-Sea!

5a), b) and **c)** These were *all* fined.

6a) 'Blood money' had to be paid to the family of a victim, even if it was an accident.

7c) The accused could also call witnesses in his defence. Each witness would swear an oath that the accused was innocent. If enough witnesses took the oath *without a mistake* then that was also seen as a sign of innocence.

8 a), b) and **c)** *All* of these were Saxon tests of guilt. The hot iron bar must be carried one to three metres before being dropped. You can try this in class – you suspect Bertram Brown of pinching your pencil? See if he can carry a hot dog three metres without being burned!

9a) As well as boiling, burning was also a Saxon execution method.

10c) Outlaws did not have the protection of the law. Catch one and you could do whatever you liked with him – use him for target practice, get him to do your washing up or your homework or walk your pet rabbit. What would *you* use a captive outlaw for?

THE SCHOOL BULLY JUST HIT ME – HIT HER BACK!

Did you know… ?

Not all of the early Saxon judges had been just or honest. They did favours for friends and filled their pockets with fines. King Alfred the Great made the Saxon courts much fairer. He sorted out the cheating judges and replaced them with honest ones. What happened to the dishonest judges? Alfred had them hanged. They didn't do as much cheating after that.

Not-so-sweet sixteen

If you committed a crime you were punished, whatever your age … until King Athelstan came along. One case changed Athelstan's mind and changed the law. If there had been a Saxon newspaper in the Dark Ages then it may have broken the news like this…

BINGO

12 August 927

Saxon Times

STILL ONLY HALF A GROAT OR HALF A GOAT

KING'S KINDNESS TO KENT KID!

The people of Maidstone in Kent were cheated of their sport today by King Athelstan. The king got to hear of the case of sheep-rustling Edward Medway. We reported last week how the shepherd killed one of his own sheep and ate its leg. He said the sheep was killed by wolves but the leg had been neatly cut off and its throat slit. As the Maidstone magistrate said, 'I've never seen a wolf that carries a knife!'

The magistrate then sentenced the sheep-slasher to hang by the neck, today at noon. Crowds had gathered from around the county and a fair had been set up in the square around the gallows. Then came the sensational news! King Athelstan has changed the law so crafty criminals like evil Ed can't be killed!

The king wrote to Bishop Theodred and said, 'It is not fair that a man should die so young. Or for such a small offence when he has seen others get away with it elsewhere.' The new law says that no one can be executed if they are under sixteen years of age.

Edward Medway, of course, is twelve years old. But the *Saxon Times* says,

'If he's old enough to steal a sheep he's old enough to swing for it!' We'll soon have fourteen- and fifteen-year-olds getting away with murder!

The only killer kids who can be executed are those that try to fight their way out of being arrested or who run away. Sadly Ed Med did not try to fight or run so the Maidstone holiday crowds went home disappointed.

No hanging today!

Of course there wasn't a Saxon newspaper – there weren't enough people who could read. But the tale of the hungry shepherd is true and shows just how desperate some people could get.

Vile verse

The Saxons had no television. (Even if they had, it would have been useless because they had no electricity to switch it on.) So they entertained themselves with riddles and long stories to pass the long winter nights.

Rotten riddles

One of the most popular pastimes was creating 'riddles' for friends to solve. A riddle was usually told as if it was an object 'speaking'…

Q: I hang between sky and earth; I grow hot from fires and bubble like a whirlpool. What am I?

A: A cooking pot hanging over a fire.

Children did it, adults did it and even the monks did it. Here are some more Saxon riddles…

Q: On the way to a miracle water becomes bone.

A: Ice.

Q: I watched four fair creatures
      Travelling together; they left black tracks
      behind them. The support of the bird
      moved swiftly; it flew in the sky,
      dived under the waves.

A: Four fingers and a quill pen.

Q: I am told a certain object grows
      In the corner, rises and expands, throws up
      a crust. A proud wife carried off
      the boneless wonder, the daughter of a king
      covered that swollen thing with a cloth.

A: Bread.

Verse and worse

Since Saxons didn't have many books, and so few people could read, most of their stories had to be learned by heart. Now a storyteller can remember a story better if the tale is turned into a poem. Even bits of their history books were written in poetry when the writer got excited about it.

Monster munches

When King Athelstan defeated an army of invading Irish with their savage Scots friends, the Saxons success was recorded in the *Anglo-Saxon Chronicle*. This would be one of the good bits, like the good but gruesome bits you like to hear in your favourite fairy tales – you know the sort of thing: 'Ooooh Grandmama! What big eyes you have!' 'All the better to smell you with.'

Imagine those manic monks sitting round the fire and listening to this part…

The field grew dark with the soldiers' blood
And the corpses were left behind.
The bodies they left to be shared by the beasts
Like the ravens in dusty black coats.
And the grey-coated eagle, the greedy war hawk,
The great grey-haired beast of the forest.

You could try reciting that to someone you don't like, just as they are about to tuck into their school dinner!

As you can see, Saxon poems didn't actually rhyme though. Maybe we can ruin a couple by changing a few words around and making them rhyme…

Crime story

Today we read crime stories in books and newspapers and we watch them in films or on television. The Saxons' main entertainment was listening to story-poems, so it's not surprising there were crime stories in their poetry. But, being Saxons, the stories were so horrible they'd be given an '18' certificate in the cinema today. You would not want to read such horror, so don't read this updated Saxon poem extract below…

The Fates of Men

And now he's dead we've hung him up
Upon a roadside gibbet high.
For wicked crimes such men as this
Deserve to suffer and to die.
Such evil men should not live on,
My friends, you must not groan or cry.
See how his helpless hands cannot
Drive off the crows that peck his eyes.

Little Alfie's eyes

Then there was the murder of Prince Alfred in 1036. Poor little Alfie just wanted to be king after the Danish King Cnut died. But Earl Godwin, Saxon Earl of Wessex, had other ideas. This poem based on the *Anglo-Saxon Chronicle* report reveals all…

119

Prince Alfred was a cheerful lad, with eyes of sparkling blue,
Till Godwin had his eyes put out. Yes, both! Not one, but two!
He sent the blinded prince away to be a monk in Ely,
There the little Alfie died; did Godwin care? Not really.

Then Godwin set about the slaying of Alf's friends.
He had them caught and had them brought to really sticky ends.
Some he sold as slaves for cash and some he scalped their heads,
Others he locked up in chains and some he killed stone dead.

Some he had their hands chopped off or arms or legs or ears.
No wonder they all fled (or tried to flee) in fear.
We've never seen a crueller deed been done in all our land
Since those dread Vikings came and took peace from our hands.

The Saxons believed that God took revenge on evil doers.
'An eye for an eye', the Bible said. So they would be pleased
to know that Godwin's son, Harold, died at the battle of
Hastings 30 years later … with an arrow in his eye! And that
was the end of the gruesome Godwins.

Pester your parents

Your parents probably went to school in the days when history was planned to send them to sleep. So they won't know these fascinating facts, the odd things that make history interesting.

Find a parent – you'll probably find one stuck in front of a television – and say, 'Dearest parent, will you either give me ten pounds pocket money or help me with my history homework?' When they say, 'Homework!' then you've got them! Ask these fiendish questions...

1 In England in the 700s what were Noxgagas and Ohtgagas?
a) Instruments of torture that cut off noses and naughty bits.
b) Tribes of people.
c) The Saxon names for carrots and cabbages (or maybe cabbages and carrots).

WHY IS IT CALLED AN OHTGAGA?

'COS IT'S 'OT AN' IT MAKES 'EM GAGA!

2 The bitchy monk Alcuin complained to King Offa: 'Some idiot thinks up a new-fangled idea and the next minute the whole country is trying to copy it!' What was he talking about?
a) A new fashion for playing football.
b) A new fashion for a sort of bunjee-jumping with leather ropes.
c) A new fashion for fancy clothes.

3 In 975 King Edgar died suddenly, the harvest was poor and the Saxons starved. What was blamed?
a) A comet appearing in the skies.
b) King Ed walking under a ladder.
c) People not going to church every Sunday.

4 The Britons tried to attack Saxon Athelfrith around AD 603 but were wiped out. What nickname did they give this cunning fighter?
a) The Twister.
b) The Twirler.
c) The Twerp.

HE MIGHT *FIGHT* LIKE A TWIRLER BUT HE *LOOKS* LIKE A TWERP

WHIZZ ZZZ

LOP!

5 An assassin stabbed King Edwin of Northumbria with a long dagger. The dagger had to pass through something else first and that saved Edwin. What did the dagger pass through?
a) The wall of the tent where Edwin was sleeping.
b) A Bible that Edwin was carrying.
c) One of Edwin's soldiers.

6 Two cruel young monks discovered the historian Bede was almost blind and played a trick on him. What?
a) They took Bede out to a dangerous cliff, then ran off and left him to find his own way home – or fall off the cliff.
b) They told Bede there was a church full of monks waiting

to hear him preach and led him there. He preached, but the church was empty.

c) They pretended to read a letter to Bede that said his brother was dead, run over by a mad horse.

7 In 1006 a Scottish army was defeated at Durham. The Scots' heads were cut off and stuck on poles around the castle walls. Durham women offered to do what for the relatives of the dead heads?

a) Wash the heads' faces and comb their hair so they looked nice.

b) Act as scarecrows to stop birds pecking the heads.

c) Chase away the children who were throwing wooden balls at the heads and trying to knock them off.

8 Saxon King Ethelred was plagued by Viking raids. He came up with a way of dealing with his problems. What?

a) He had Viking leaders killed.

b) He had Viking women killed.

c) He had Saxon leaders killed.

9 There was no Saxon soap powder. They made their own detergent from ashes, animal fat and…

a) snot.

b) pee.

c) spit.

10 In 686 the villagers of Jarrow went to the local monastery and brought death to the monks. How?

a) The villagers had the plague.

b) The 'villagers' were really Viking warriors in disguise.

c) The villagers came to muck out the stables, upset a lantern in the straw and burned the monastery to the ground while the monks slept and roasted.

Answers:

1b) These people were part of the Mercian kingdom and lived south of the River Thames. Sadly their names have been forgotten in most histories, along with the Wixnas and Wigestas, the Hurstingas and the Feppingas. And you can no longer call yourself (proudly) a Hicca or a Gifla! The West Willas went with the Wigesta, the Wideringas ... and the wind.

2c) The miserable monk thought everyone should wear plain, boring clothes (like history teachers do today). But kings, queens and their courtiers liked flashy, colourful clothes with brooches and embroidery like Dark Age pop stars. Alcuin wore a habit in a delightful shade of mud brown with a smart rope belt and did not approve of painted posers.

3a) If a comet appeared in the sky it was a sure sign of disaster. One appeared in 1066 and, sure enough, the Saxon kingdom was conquered for good.

4a) Athelfrith was known as the Twister, probably because of the way he whirled his sword and not because he ran a fairground ride in his spare time. In a battle against the Welsh some British monks prayed for the Welsh to win. 'Twister' Athelfrith was upset and butchered the 1,200 unarmed monks before going on to massacre the Welsh.

5c) The assassin, Eumer, said he had a message for Edwin. He came up to the king and drew his dagger. One of Edwin's lords, Lilla, threw himself in front of the king. Eumer's powerful thrust went clean through Lilla and wounded the king. Another lord died before the assassin was finally hacked to death.

6b) Bede (so the story goes) was led to the empty church and began preaching to the empty seats while the two young monks laughed themselves sick. But Bede had the last laugh because the church filled up with angels who came down from heaven to hear the old guy.

7a) The women offered to comb the hair of the dead Scots, but they wanted to be well paid for this – a bit like hairdressers today really.

8c) Ethelred trusted no one. In 1006 he had his Saxon leader in York murdered because he was afraid the man was becoming too powerful. Just to be extra sure he took the man's sons and had their eyes put out.

9b) It's supposed to work but don't try this at home. If human pee is such a good cleaner then how come babies nappies are so disgusting when they're full of the stuff?

10a) Most people think of the plague as arriving with the Black Death in 1349, but there were deadly diseases long before that. When the sickness reached Jarrow the villagers flocked to the monastery to get the herbs and cures the monks made. The villagers died and the monks caught the plague from them. Only two monks survived. So much for helping your neighbours!

Epilogue

You can blame the Saxons for a lot.

The monk Bede practically invented English history. Other writers had written about events in the past but Bede sorted them out into some sort of order and gave them dates. As a result history teachers have something to test you on.

Bede would be delighted that we still follow his system.

You can blame him for the Millennium, by the way. Bede sorted out the calendar for you. People used to work out the year by the reign of the monarch ... so the year 2000, say, would have been 'the 47th year of Elizabeth II's reign'. Bede preferred to work time out from the date of the birth of Jesus. So he did. And we still do. Bede would be proud.

And, of course, Bede said the world was round when everyone else thought it was flat. And some sad people (like geography teachers and science teachers) still believe that round-earth nonsense when sensible people like you can see quite plainly that it isn't! But Bede would be pleased.

Then there was the Saxon King Alfred. He reckoned that the Saxons suffered Viking attacks because they had behaved badly. Viking raids were God's punishment. He said the only way for people to be better was to learn more – and people still believe it, so Alfred is partly to blame for you having to go to school and he'd be burning cakes with happiness to see you suffering there!

Athelstan was the first king to make the whole of Britain one country, and it still is – until those Scots in the north get their independence. Athelstan would be chuffed.

Of course the nasty Normans came along and the sad Saxons were defeated. But the Saxon language lived on – which is why you're reading this book in a sort of Saxon English and not Norman French.

King Offa would be pleased at that.

So, thank you Offa, Alfred, Athelstan, and Bede – but a special thanks to those ordinary Saxons whose names never went down in history books. You struggled and died, and made life better for those who came after you.

Smashing Saxons every one.

SMASHING SAXONS

GRISLY QUIZ

Now find out if you're a
Smashing Saxons expert!

SAVAGE SAXON SOCIETY

Foul food, lousy laws and putrid punishments were all part of Saxon life. And woe betide you if you got ill and had to endure a crackpot cure. How would you have coped in Saxon society? Test your knowledge by answering the following questions.

1 What did the Saxons do if their dinner fell on the floor amongst the dog-droppings?
a) They wiped it off and ate it.
b) They gave it to the dog.
c) The children had it for tea the following day.

2 What did the monks in Saxon times eat?
a) Fish and chips
b) Bread and cheese
c) Vegetable stew

3 What was the punishment for a moneyer (a coin-maker) if he made coins smaller than he was supposed to and kept the leftover silver?
a) He was forced to eat the coins.
b) His hand was cut off.

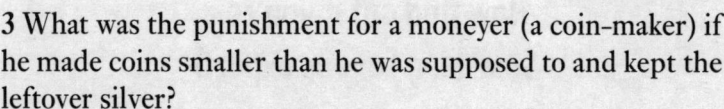

c) He had to work for free.

4 As well as using mud, the Saxon also slapped a rather more nasty substance on the walls of their houses to plaster them. What was it?
a) Chicken's blood
b) Pig's poo
c) Sheep's earwax

5 What did the Saxons write on?
a) Stone tablets
b) Animal skins
c) Early blackboards

6 According to the superstitious Saxons, which of the following was not a way of preventing the ghosts of the dead from coming back to haunt the living
a) Cremation
b) Burial at sea
c) Cutting the dead person's head off

7 What was the Saxons' gruesome cure for a headache?
a) Cut the sign off the cross in your forehead
b) Place stones from the insides of a baby bird on your head
c) Suck on the jawbone of a dog

8 What happened to a married Saxon woman in late Saxon times if she went off with another man?
a) She lost all her property.
b) She had her nose sliced off.
c) She had both ears sliced off.

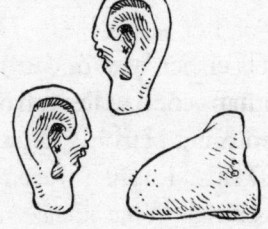

QUICK QUESTIONS

1 In the 420s the Brits were led by Vortigern, this wasn't his real name but a title given to him. What does it mean? (clue: a popular ruler)

I SENT MY OWN SON, VORTEMIR, OFF TO FIGHT OLD HENGEST. YOU KNOW, HE WHIPPED THE SAXONS LIKE DOGS AND KILLED OLD HENGEST'S BROTHER HORSA. I THINK THE SAVAGE SAXONS GOT MY MESSAGE: YOU DON'T MESS WITH VORTIGERN

2 What did the British leader Vortigern have to deal with when the Romans left Britain? (clue: boils and battles)

3 Which king built a long, 20-metre-wide ditch between England and Wales in AD 787? (clue: it was offally long)

4 William the Conqueror landed at Hastings to fight Harold for the English throne. As he jumped ashore something went wrong. What? (Clue: clowns do it all the time)

5 After King Harold Godwinsson was hacked down at Hastings his mum offered Harold's weight in gold for the return of her son's body. Did William accept? (Clue: the answer is either 'yes' or 'no')

6 What happened to the Saxons after William the Conqueror defeated King Harold? (clue: second-class citizens)

7 In 1071 the English were rebelling in Cambridgeshire led by Hereward. What sneaky trick did he use to discover the Norman plans? (Clue: Hereward Bond?)

8 The Saxons were very cruel to dolphins. What did they make from their skin? (clue: used to get animals moving)

9 Saxon monks had to eat meals in complete silence. What did they do if they desperately needed the salt? (clue: sign language)

10 What was the Saxons favourite pastime? (clue: playing with words)

VICIOUS VIKING TIMES

Why did the Vikings leave their homeland to cross the cold North Sea and raid the sunny Saxon shores of England? Which of the following reasons have experts given for the Viking raids? Answer true or false.

1 It was getting too crowded in Scandinavia – the Vikings wanted more land.

2 They ran out of iron for their swords, spear heads and battle axes and needed a new supply.

3 The Vikings set off in their longboats to see if the world was round – on the way they bumped into England.

4 Viking rules meant that younger sons got no land when their fathers died – so they had to go overseas and pinch someone else's land.

5 There was a sudden shortage of herring in the North Sea – their main food supply – England had plenty of fish to share.

6 A change in climate made Scandinavia cold and uncomfortable – even wild, wet England was better than that.

7 Some pretty vicious kings took over in 9th-century Scandinavia – many Vikings sailed off to escape from them.

8 The Vikings needed more horns for their helmets and England had lots of bulls.

WHAT HAPPENED NEXT?

In history you can usually guess what happens next. But you may find it a little harder in Horrible History, because people don't always behave the way you would! Can you guess What Happened Next (WHN)?

1 King Svein of Norway kept attacking England so King Ethelred of England paid him 36,000 pounds of silver to go away. Svein took the silver and used it wisely. WHN?

2 Earl Waltheof rebelled against the Normans and was sentenced to be executed at Winchester. He asked for time to say the Lord's prayer. He was so emotional he couldn't finish so the executioner lost his temper and knocked Waltheof's head off with one stroke. WHN?

Answers

Savage Saxon Society

1a) They'd wipe it off and make a sign of the cross to ward of evil spirits, before eating it. Makes school dinners seem tasty, doesn't it?

2c) The stew was called 'pottage'. It was very boring and if take-away restaurants had been around then, the monks would definitely have ordered in pizza!

3b) The hand that commited the crime would be cut off. Tough but fair!

4b) Pig poo - it's versatile, tough and super-smelly!

5b) They wrote on vellum - thin, stretched sheets of animal skin, usually from lambs and calves.

6b) Burial at sea was not the answer to this spooky problem, but barbequing and head-lopping were supposed to do the trick.

7b) They would take swallow-chicks, cut them open and take stones out of their stomachs. The stones were sewed into a bag and placed on the sufferer's head. A bird-brained cure indeed!

8a, b and c!) Her husband could take all her property and slice off her nose and ears – definitely a cutting-edge punishment!

Quick Questions

1) Vortigern means 'Great King'.

2) A deadly plague and an invasion by the northern Picts.

3) King Offa.

4) William slipped and fell flat on his face.

5) No. William refused to hand over King Harold's

corpse, and had him buried on the shore.

6) They became peasants under the rule of the Normans.

7) Hereward became a spy. He disguised himself and walked into the Norman camps. It did him no good and he was defeated.

8) Whips. Using the whip to beat yourself apparently cured madness!

9) They had a special system of communicating. Three fingers placed together and then shaken meant 'pass the salt'.

10) The Saxons used to enjoy creating riddles for friends to solve.

Vicious Viking Times

1) True 2) False 3) False 4) True 5) True 6) True 7) True 8) False – Vikings only had horns on their helmets for important ceremonies.

What Happened Next?

1) Svein used the money to pay an even larger army, then he returned five years later to demand even more money. King Ethelred was forced to pay him 48,000 pounds in silver the second time.

2) The head finished the prayer, saying '…deliver us from evil. Amen.'

INTERESTING INDEX

Where will you find 'horrid hags', 'jumbo-sized lice' and 'rotting skin' in an index? In a Horrible Histories book, of course!

138

Terry Deary was born at a very early age, so long ago he can't remember. But his mother, who was there at the time, says he was born in Sunderland, northeast England, in 1946 – so it's not true that he writes all *Horrible Histories* from memory. At school he was a horrible child only interested in playing football and giving teachers a hard time. His history lessons were so boring and so badly taught, that he learned to loathe the subject. *Horrible Histories* is his revenge.

Martin Brown was born in Melbourne, on the proper side of the world. Ever since he can remember he's been drawing. His dad used to bring back huge sheets of paper from work and Martin would fill them with doodles and little figures. Then, quite suddenly, with food and water, he grew up, moved to the UK and found work doing what he's always wanted to do: drawing doodles and little figures.

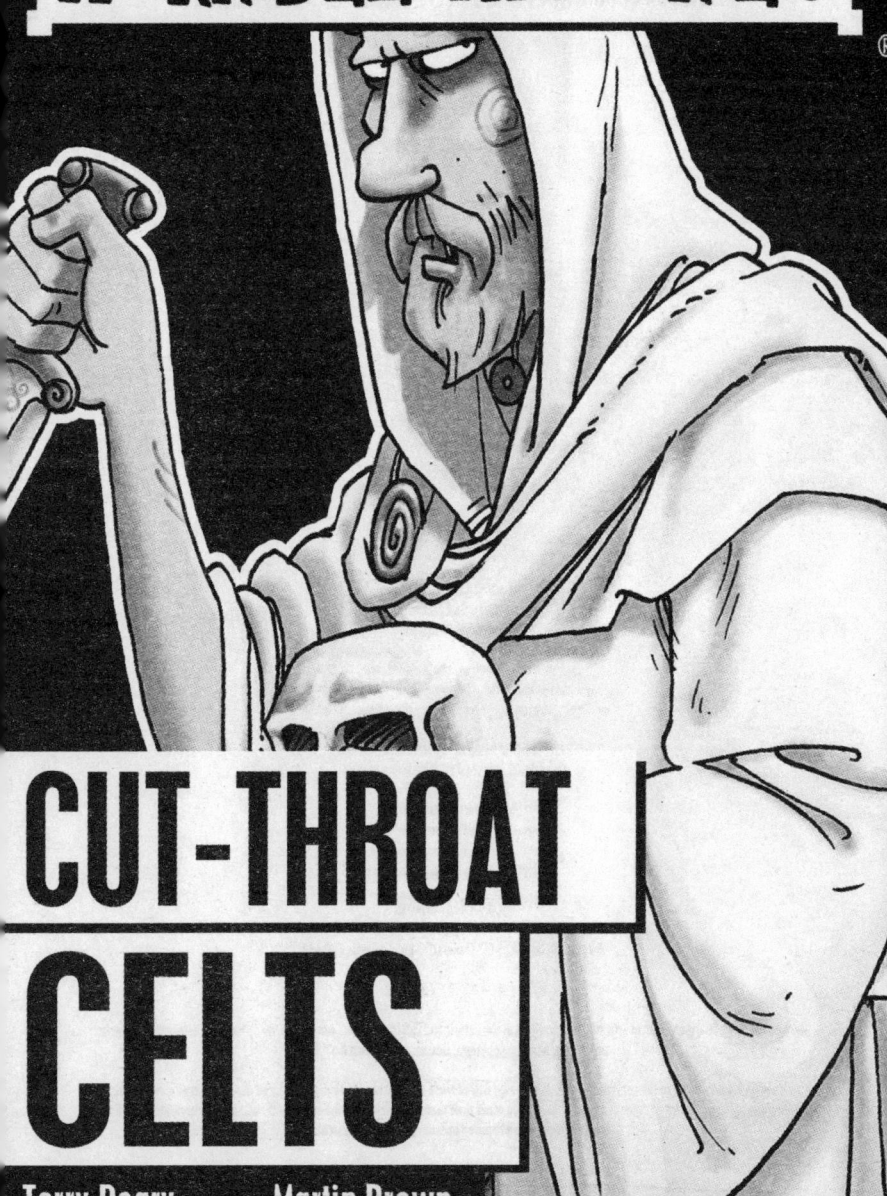

HORRIBLE HISTORIES

CUT-THROAT CELTS

Terry Deary Illustrated by Martin Brown

■SCHOLASTIC

With all good wishes and sincere thanks to Tracey Turner.

Scholastic Children's Books,
Euston House, 24 Eversholt Street,
London NW1 1DB, UK

A division of Scholastic Ltd
London ~ New York ~ Toronto ~ Sydney ~ Auckland
Mexico City ~ New Delhi ~ Hong Kong

First published in the UK by Scholastic Ltd, 1997
This edition published by Scholastic Ltd, 2016

Text © Terry Deary, 1997
Illustration © Martin Brown, 1997, 2016

All rights reserved. Moral rights asserted.

ISBN 978 1407 16540 0

Printed and bound by CPI Group (UK) Ltd, Croydon, CR0 4YY

4 6 8 10 9 7 5

The right of Terry Deary and Martin Brown to be identified as the author and illustrator of this work respectively has been asserted by them in accordance with the Copyright, Designs and Patents Act, 1988.

www.scholastic.co.uk

Contents

Introduction

History is horrible. Especially in school. Have you noticed how teachers never *tell* you anything? They *ask* you something and expect you to *know*!

They use funny new words and ask you to guess what they mean! How on earth can they expect that?

And they use posh words to describe the really horrible bits of history…

Then, just when there's a chance that history lessons may be getting interesting, the teacher stops and refuses to tell you the gory details.

Were the Celts really cut-throats? And why? And what did they do with those heads? What you need is a book that tells you the truth, the whole truth and nothing but the truth. What you need is a Horrible History of the cut-throat Celts!

Well! You lucky person! You just happen to have found one…

Timeline

750 BC The Ancient Greeks meet traders from Hallstatt (Austria). The Greeks say they call themselves Keltoi – dodgy spelling, but better than the Celts who can't write at all!

387 BC Now the Celts meet the Romans and beat them in battle. The Romans – also dodgy spellers – call them Celtae.

279 BC The Greeks drive the Celts out of Greece after the Battle of Delphi. The Greeks have the help of bad weather and landslides (which is cheating a bit).

225 BC At the Battle of Telemon in Greece the Romans beat the Celts.

218 BC The Carthaginians of North Africa attack the Romans in Italy and the Celts help them but...

202 BC The Romans beat the Carthaginians in Carthage and turn their attention to Celt lands in Spain and Northern Italy. Sweet Roman revenge.

60 BC Roman Julius Caesar decides to make a name for himself by taking over Celtic Gaul (France). Some Celts welcome him – others don't ... and are wiped out.

52 BC Vercingetorix leads a Celtic rebellion against Caesar. Romans win and rule France. Then they start looking across the English Channel...

AD 43 Emperor Claudius defeats the Celts in Britain. They're driven back to the hills of Wales and Scotland despite...

AD 61 A very bloody rebellion led by Queen Boudicca ends in another win for the Romans.

AD 84 Battle of Mons Graupius in Scotland and the last of the free Celts are now in Scotland and Ireland. The Romans rule, OK?

AD 120 Emperor Hadrian builds a wall across the North of England to keep the Pict and Scot Celts out ... or to keep them in, depending on which way you look at it!

AD 312 Emperor Constantine becomes a Christian and the Roman Empire converts to Christianity. Even the Celts are converted and their old ways die. No more sacrifices.

AD 410 The Romans leave Britain but Angles, Saxons and Jutes rush in and settle before the free Celts can get back. A bit like musical chairs!

AD 432 St Patrick goes to Ireland and converts Irish Celts to Christianity.

AD 493 The British Celts make one last effort to drive out the Saxons and win the Battle of Badon. Their leader is the Awesome King Arthur … maybe.

AD 520 Awesome Arthur loses his last battle when he fights his own nephew … maybe. But while the British Celts are squabbling the Angles and Saxons take over the south-east of Britain and create Angle-land, or England. You may have heard of it.

Getting to know the cut-throat Celts

Nobody really knows where they came from. It was far too long ago. Some historians say there were Celts in Britain about 1180 BC – others say it was earlier. They came from central Europe and spread in all directions till they came up against the Romans.

Now the Romans were a single nation – the Celts were dozens of tribes who fought against each other as often as they joined together to fight the Romans. In the end some of these tribes were wiped out, some agreed to be ruled by the Romans and some were driven to the far corners of the known world – Ireland, Scotland, Wales, Cornwall, Brittany and the small Isle of Man. These communities of Celts survive to this day.

The thing that made them Celts was that they shared a language and they shared their legends and their customs. The Romans might have ruled them ... but the Romans were still pretty scared of them!

> *The Celts are terrifying in appearance with deep-sounding and very harsh voices. They use few words and speak in riddles. They often exaggerate with the aim of making themselves look good and making others look weak. They are boasters and threateners, yet they have quick minds and a natural ability for learning.*

SAY I'M THE BEST OR I'LL BITE YOUR KNEECAPS OFF

Diodorus Siculus, 1st century BC

The largest Celt tribe that the Romans came up against were called Gauls…

> *Almost all of the Gauls are tall, fair and red-faced, terrible for the fierceness of their eyes, fond of quarrelling and of dreadful pride.*

Ammianus Marcellinus,
4th century AD

The Romans said some pretty spiteful things about the Celts, including…

> *When the Celts become drunk they fall into a deep sleep … or they fall into a terrible rage.*

Diodorus Siculus, 1st century BC

The ancient Celts were violent and loved arguing, but is it fair to call them 'cut-throat'? Maybe. Look at the evidence and decide for yourself.

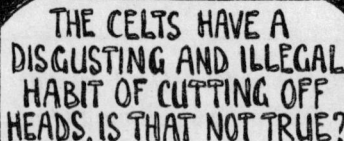

THE CELTS HAVE A DISGUSTING AND ILLEGAL HABIT OF CUTTING OFF HEADS. IS THAT NOT TRUE?

THE WHOLE POWER OF A PERSON IS IN THE HEAD. EVEN A DEAD ENEMY CAN HARM YOU UNLESS YOU CUT OFF HIS HEAD. IT'S SELF DEFENCE

IS THAT THE ONLY REASON?

THERE IS ANOTHER ADVANTAGE IN CUTTING OFF AN ENEMY'S HEAD—WE BELIEVE YOU GAIN ALL THAT ENEMY'S WISDOM AND STRENGTH

IF THAT'S TRUE THEN HAVING CHICKEN FOR SUNDAY DINNER SHOULD MAKE YOU AS WISE AS A CHICKEN!

LOTS OF PEOPLE ARE!

THERE ARE STORIES ABOUT CELT WARRIORS INVADING A COUNTRY AND MARRYING ITS WOMEN. THEY SAY THE CELTS CUT OUT THE TONGUES OF THEIR NEW WIVES SO THE PURE LANGUAGE OF THE MEN WILL NOT BE SPOILED BY THE FOREIGN LANGUAGE OF THEIR NEW WIVES

THESE STORIES ARE FOUND ONLY IN LEGENDS BUT I CAN'T HELP WONDERING IF THE STORY-TELLERS HAD SOME TRUTH TO BASE THEIR GRUESOME TALES ON...

PROVE IT

A lot of people in Britain today have Celt blood flowing through their veins. If you are one of them then be glad your blood is staying in your veins and not decorating the wall of some hill-fort hall. Be glad you'll never meet an ancient Celt!

Lousy legends

Poets were highly respected in the Celt world – like pop singers today. And, like pop singers, they were well paid. The bad news is that it was a long hard job to train as a Celtic poet. A pop singer probably trains for 12 whole minutes – a Celtic poet trained for 12 years.

Poets learned grammar and very long poems – 80 in the first six years. They learned another 95 in the next three years, and by the end of the 12 years' training they would know 350 story-poems ... if they survived, that is.

Because learning a story-poem an hour or so long took a lot of concentration. Have you ever had a teacher complain that you lack concentration? Did they nag you into concentrating? Think yourself lucky – you could have had a Celtic poetry teacher.

The poet travelled round with a metal model of a tree branch. It had bells on and they rang as he rode along or entered a feasting hall.

The branch told you what sort of poet he was – a bronze branch for a qualified poet, a silver branch for an expert and a gold branch for someone who was top of the pops.

He'd swagger around in a cloak covered in birds' feathers – the feathers of white and coloured birds were worn below the belt, the crests and necks of mallard ducks above the belt. Some say a swan's head dangled down his back (don't try making one of these – you'll just look quackers).

The poet expected to be well paid for his entertainment. If he wasn't then he was likely to compose a very sarcastic verse about the lord in charge. You know the sort of thing…

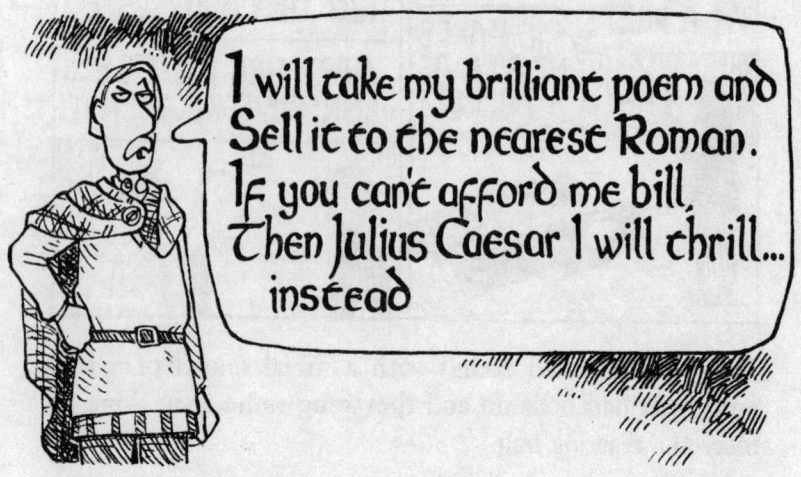

I will take my brilliant poem and
Sell it to the nearest Roman.
If you can't afford me bill,
Then Julius Caesar I will thrill…
instead

Never upset a king…
Of course some poets became too greedy and in AD 574 King Aed Mac Ainmirech banned all poets from Ireland. The King had a symbol of his power – a brooch in the shape of a wheel. Some poets got a bit cheeky and asked him for it. Lords often gave pieces of jewellery for a good story but the poets should never have asked for the wheel brooch – it

seemed like they were taking power away from the lords and the King. Saint Columba put in a good word for the poets and they were allowed to stay, but they never again asked for impossibly grand payments.

...and *never* upset a poet!

But be warned. It didn't pay to upset a poet. If he cursed you, you might...

- lose in battle
- break out in blisters
- speak only baby-talk.

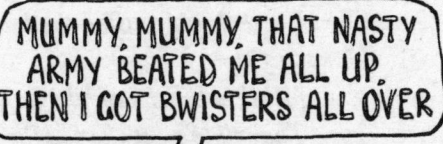

Terrible tales

Imagine the nastiest thing possible. That's the sort of thing the Celtic poets sang about. There's nothing wrong with the following story ... unless you're a member of the Pony Club and don't enjoy horse-burgers and chips.

Horses meant speed and beauty – they were linked to the Celtic Sun god. Celts believed that you could gain some of a horse's powers by eating it. (I've tried this. Does it work? Neigh!)

WARNING: Horse lovers should skip the following poem! It is loosely based on a Celtic poem ... very loosely. Well, to be honest, if it got any looser it would drop off.

17

The king was in his feasting house
Waiting to be crowned.
They killed a white horse, cut it up,
And stirred it round and round
Inside a cauldron great and deep
All filled with water, hot.
They ate the horse meat, not the bones,
Until they'd scoffed the lot.

(Well, when I say 'the lot', I mean
They didn't eat the saddle.)
The king stood up, and then he cried,
'My friends! It's time we paddled!'
The king's friends all took off their clothes
And jumped into the pot!
They splashed about in bones and soup,
And see how clean they got!

And when they all had washed and scrubbed,
They jumped back out again.
They drank the horse soup, every drop
Until the pot was drained.

Not much wrong with eating horse meat – the French do it
all the time. But would you drink bath-water after all your
smelly friends have bathed in it? Yeuch!

Batty beliefs

The Celts had gods all over the place – gods in trees, gods in streams and even gods in stones. The oak tree was especially holy and the mistletoe that grew on it was magical stuff. People today still believe this and that's why we have the Christmas custom of kissing under the mistletoe.

WARNING: Do not be tricked into kissing some snotty creep who happens to fancy you. Tell them the truth…

Ten things you need to know about Druids

1 Laws were made by the kings, but it was the Druids who advised the king. This is rather like Government Ministers advising the Queen today. They are *her* laws – but everybody knows the Government runs the country. The Druids also acted as judges to enforce those laws. It didn't pay to upset a Druid.

2 Druids were clever clogs because they spent 20 years training to become one. This is even worse than modern schools where you spend 11 to 15 years training to be an adult. You then spend another 50 years wondering if it was worth it.

3 The sacred mistletoe must not touch the ground. When the Druid with the golden sickle climbed a tree, another two Druids stood below and caught it in a white cloth as he threw it down. (This was also very handy if the Druid with the golden sickle fell out of the tree!)

4 These Druids were the village wise men (and maybe wise women) who advised the villagers on problems like the best time to plant their crops. They were like your local vicar but with an important difference. Your vicar might expect a five-pound note from each of his worshippers – a Druid expected blood. And the Druids had real power over the people. As Roman Julius Caesar said...

When a person disobeys a Druid then they ban them from attending at sacrifices. This is the cruellest punishment a Celt can suffer.

5 The Roman writer, Lucan, said Druids even sacrificed humans. Lucan claimed that, 'the trees were sprinkled with human blood.' Yeuch. Of course Lucan could have been exaggerating a bit … or a lot. The Romans didn't like the Celts and may have written a few lies about them. Of course the Celts didn't do much writing, so the Roman stories have gone down in history and the truth has been forgotten.

6 The Celts of Gaul sent their Druids over to Britain to be trained. British Celt Druids must have been the best.

7 When a Druid wanted some spirit help he slaughtered a bull and had it skinned. Then he lay down on a bed of rowan branches and wrapped the bull's hide round him, bloody side next to him. As he slept he experienced dreams that answered his questions or solved his people's problems – problems like, 'How do you get blood stains out of a Druid's best robe?'

8 Druids were also fortune-tellers who said they could see into the future. What would you do if you could see into the future? Become a fortune-teller and make your fortune? Or simply pick next Saturday's winning lottery numbers – every week for a year? It's easy. All you have to do is follow the dreadful Druid method of divining the future.

• Take the flesh of a dog.

• Chew it.
• Call upon the spirit of the dog to give you its secret.
• Have a long deep sleep OR place the palms of your hands over your eyes, crossing your hands over your face.
• A vision will reveal the wisdom that is guarded by the animal.

TREES ARE GOOD TO WEE ON

The Celtic Druids used this method to predict who the next king would be. But why would a wise dog know that? You may not be able to get the flesh of a dog – maybe next door's Rottweiler doesn't want you to bite its leg – but the Celts believed the flesh of a cat or a bull would give up that animal's secret. Could a cat's flesh reveal winning scratch cards? (Cat's – scratch … geddit? Oh, never mind.) Probably the flesh of a bull is easiest to get hold of. Chew that and soon you will either have the gift of prophecy or mad cow disease.

9 When the Christians arrived in the Celt world in the 5th century the Druids had to go. The Christians had spent a couple of hundred years being thrown to the lions and that put them off bloody sacrifices for life. You'd be surprised to learn that animal sacrifices were still being made in AD 868, wouldn't you? Then you will be astounded and gobsmacked to discover that they were still being made in AD 1868. That's right, just 130 years ago there was still a Celtic-style festival held in Cevennes in France. It involved throwing valuables and animals into a lake as offerings to the gods.

10 The Druids had some useful powers that you probably wish *you* had. They could...

• Change their shape to anything they wanted.

• Control the weather.

• Bring down mists to make themselves invisible.

• Travel through time.

Imagine that! There could be a Druid at your school. If your history teacher seems to know an awful lot about the Celts then maybe they *are* a Celt! A Druid on holiday in the 20th century. This is just one example of…

Horrible Historians
There's a dead man in the British Museum in London. Well, he's more a half-dead man because only half of his body is on show!

In 1984 a mechanical digger was cutting through turf in Lindow, Cheshire, when it came across this shrivelled body. Archaeologists and historians were excited by the discovery … they have a very sick idea of excitement, you understand. They examined the body and said it was definitely a Celt. The chemicals in the swampy land had preserved him like a pickled onion in vinegar. The one and only Celtic face to be seen in modern times!

The historians then set about discovering who he was and how he died … and it looked like a gruesome story. The man had well-shaped fingernails so he wasn't a peasant. And his death seems to have been some sort of cruel and cut-throat Celtic sacrifice. Maybe those rotten Romans were right about the Celts after all? Or maybe the victim deserved to die. We'll never know that.

What would you do with the Lindow man who was killed and dumped in a bog? Give him a nice burial and let him rest in peace? Put a headstone over his grave with a poem? Probably.

What have the horrible historians done with him? Stuck him in a glass case for people like you and me to gawp at. The least they could do was give him an epitaph – a message from the dead to the living. Maybe you could write one. This is just a suggestion…

The Lindow Lament, or The Man With No Name Who Wishes He Had One

The Celts they came and took me in the middle of the
  night,
And I knew if they meant business, I was dead.
They never asked permission, said no 'Please,' or 'By your
  leave.'
They simply went and bashed me on the head.
(Twice)

They used a choking cord until they cut off all me breath,
They used me like some sacrificial goat.
When they were really sure that I was in the arms of
*   death,*
The rotten bleeders went and cut me throat.
(Messy)

So all you living people, see the fate that I was dealt.
Captured by the cruel and wicked Druids.
Think yourself dead lucky you don't have to face those
*   Celts,*
Who would drain you dry of all your body fluids.
(Blood)

They laid me here all shrivelled up – no peace, no grave,
*   no name;*
A wrinkled mummy cut off at the pelvis.
A label calls me 'Lindow Man', and that's my lasting
*   fame.*
I'd rather be a Percy, Joe … or Elvis.
(Wouldn't you?)

Dreadful deaths

People of the Ancient world believed that all life was made up of four 'elements' – air, earth, fire and water. The Greeks were the first to put this idea down in writing around 2,500 years ago, and thinkers and doctors believed it till about 300 years ago.

The Celts believed it too. But the Ancient cut-throat Celts didn't stop at believing life could be explained by the four elements – they believed that death could too!

If there was a god of air then the Celts had to keep him or her happy by sacrificing someone using 'death by air' – suffocating, strangling or hanging. If there was a god of water then the sacrifice would be 'death by water' – drowning – and so on.

Which would you choose?

29

Obviously the Lindow man is proof that death by air was a Celtic form of execution or sacrifice.

The Roman leader Julius Caesar wrote about the Celts building huge basket-work models of men, filling them full of victims then setting fire to them. For hundreds of years historians have said that Caesar was lying. But many Celt legends include stories of victims being chained inside in an iron house which is then heated till it's red hot.

The Gaul goddess, Teutatis, was kept happy by having victims drowned in an iron cauldron, but that is only in legend. There's no proof that the Celts in Gaul actually did it. But there have been bodies found in swamps which have been covered with wooden panels. It is possible that the panels were used to hold the victim under the swamp until they drowned. No one is sure if the victims were sacrifices or criminals being executed.

No one has found a grave where a human appears to have been buried alive, but there was a nasty custom of bricking up an animal in the walls of a house to bring luck. Cats were often sacrificed in this way and in 1995 a mummified moggy was found in an old Northumberland house when it was being rebuilt. The cruel Celt custom was still being practised a hundred years ago!

I TAKE IT THE CAT REFUSED TO GO IN THE WALL

Saints alive

In time the Celts dropped their gods of streams and woods and stones and became Christian. But a lot of their beliefs were carried forward into the new religion. They still had godlike humans who performed the most incredible miracles. People like Winifride and her Uncle Beuno.

Saint Gwenfrewi (or Winifride in English)

Winifride was the niece of Saint Beuno, an abbot in 6th-century Wales. Young Prince Caradoc ap Alyn loved her but she made it clear she did not want to marry him. This upset the young Prince from Wales so he drew his sword and cut off her head, as princes sometimes do when you upset them. As her head hit the ground there wasn't so much a splatt! as a splash! Because a spring of water gushed out of the dry rock.

Along came Saint Beuno, stuck her head back on her body and she was restored to life, with just a thin white line round her neck to show where she'd had her little accident. Beuno was not so kind to Caradoc. The saint cursed the Prince till the earth opened up and swallowed him. This taught him a lesson he'd never remember because he was dead before he could forget. Even his descendants suffered from Beuno's curse. They all barked like dogs until they made a pilgrimage to the well.

31

Winifride's well waters are now said to cure illnesses and the well is still visited by tourists. So, don't go upsetting a prince of Wales ... unless your uncle is a saint.

Hope springs eternal

At one time heads must have been bouncing round Celtic lands like lottery numbers in a drum. Saint Llud, Saint Justinian, Saint Nectan and Saint Decuman all lost their heads and springs sprang as they fell. Saint Cadfan's shrine was set up in AD 516 and is said to cure rheumatism while Saint Canna's well water will soothe your stomach when you feel a gut ache coming on.

Saint Brigit was popular in all of the Celtic countries: Scotland, Wales, Cornwall, the Isle of Man and Brittany as well as her home in Ireland. She has so many wells it seems someone must have cut her head off and played football with it.

Brigit's crosses are still set up on farmland in Ireland to protect crops and animals. This is because she used to punish people who stole her cattle by drowning or scalding them. She didn't have Winifride's problem of princes chasing her because she made herself ugly by putting out one of her eyes.

Horrible historical joke:

Saints un-alive

The Celts became such great Christians that they practically invented many of the great Christian traditions. It's said that John Cassian was a Celt born in Scythia and he brought the first monasteries to Europe. (He pinched the idea from the Egyptians, though.) The main thing needed to be a saint is to have...

- a very good life
- a very messy death
- an incredible miracle happen.

Some Celt saints managed all three!

Saint Teilo

Saint Teilo, a 6th-century Welsh saint, is buried at a place called Llandeilo Fawr ... and in Penally ... and in Llandaff Cathedral. This is not very difficult if you are a saint. And, no, they didn't chop him into three and share the bits out. In one night his corpse became three bodies. Don't you wish you could do this? You could send one body to school, while one went to the seaside and the other stayed in bed and watched television.

Saint Olcan

That's Ol-can ... *not* Oil-can. Olcan's father died before he was born – the shock killed his mother who also died before he was born. She was buried and THEN Olcan was born. A passing nobleman heard baby Olcan crying, dug him up and saved his life. Don't try this in your local cemetery – body-snatching is a grave offence.

Saint Ronan

Cornish monk Saint Ronan had a pretty rough life after he was dead. His body was loaded onto a wagon and the oxen pulling it were set free. Where the wagon stopped, Ronan would be buried. But as the cart trundled along it was attacked by an angry Celt woman – people say Ronan had upset her because he took no notice when she tried to chat him up! Anyway, first she

hit one of the oxen and knocked its horn off, then she hit Ronan's corpse a mighty smack in the face. He was probably glad to get safely under the ground after that!

Saint Monessa

This beautiful Irish Princess was a non-Christian Celt, but then she heard Saint Patrick preaching. She thought old Pat was wonderful and said, 'Convert me to Christianity! I want to be baptized if it's the last thing I do!' Patrick baptized her … and it was the last thing she did. She died from the happiness. (Please note: If you die from happiness while reading this book your money will not be refunded.)

Saint Cieran

If you're a saint it is always handy if you can work miracles after you've died. Cieran managed it. It seems that all the other saints in Ireland were praying that he'd die young. Cieran didn't let them down. He was only 33 when he died of plague in AD 548 – there were plagues even before the famous 1349 Black Death and this one got him.

Dying was a very popular thing for Cieran to do and Saint Columba cheered. But Columba took a chunk of turf from Cieran's grave and carried it with him everywhere. Years later Columba was caught in a deadly whirlpool, threw the turf in the water and the whirlpool went calm.

Saint Mylor

Little Mylor was only seven when his dad was murdered. The bishops persuaded the killer not to murder Mylor too. He didn't. Instead he chopped off the boy's hand and foot. Mylor hopped along to the blacksmith and had a metal hand and foot made. Miraculously his flesh–and–blood hand grew back! But Mylor's guardian cut off his head next. The boy didn't

35

have a head-growing trick – or maybe the blacksmith didn't do heads – and he died. The murderer picked up the head happily – and dropped dead three days later.

Six dead funny facts
1 The Celts didn't mind dying too much. After all, they believed that when you left this life you woke up in the 'Otherworld'. The trouble is you could also die in the Otherworld … then you were reborn into this world. Then you die and go to the Otherworld, then you're reborn, then you die … (Once you've done this you will know how a yo-yo feels.)

IS THIS WORLD THE OTHER WORLD'S OTHERWORLD OR THE OTHERWORLD'S THIS WORLD?

2 The Celtic 'day' began at nightfall and ended with the fading light. Similarly the year began in November with the dying plants and sprang to life in the spring. It made sense to them to see Death as the start of your existence and Life as its end. (Well, it made sense to them, if not to you.)
3 This belief meant Celts would laugh at a funeral and cry at a birth. Christian Celts, even today, hold parties for the dead – called 'wakes' – and enjoy a good laugh at a funeral.

THE DOCTOR GAVE ME THREE WEEKS TO LIVE

HOW NICE!

4 The Celts buried the dead person with some of their favourite belongings from *this* life – jewellery, weapons, clothes and, of course, food. Joints of pork seem to be the corpses' favourite food though sometimes calf, sheep and cattle bones have been found. (Personally I'd take a bag of crisps. What about you?)

5 They buried the very rich with a chariot. But the crafty Celts didn't waste a good chariot on a crumbling corpse. They usually buried a clapped-out chariot. Of course, the chariot needed a horse to pull it … so the cut-throat Celts buried a clapped out horse along with it! (Archaeologists can tell the state of the horse by the condition of its teeth and bones.)

6 One wealthy Celt was buried with 40 litres of Italian wine! Just as well the Celts didn't have breath tests or he'd be banned from driving the chariot before he even got to the afterlife!

Weird war

The Celts were fierce fighters. Some of the stories about Celt warriors are reported by the Roman historians, so they are usually believed (why *is* it that people always believe horrible historians?). In fact the Romans probably exaggerated a bit to make their own soldiers look better when they defeated the Celts.

1 Cu Chulainn became temporarily insane in battle, going into warp-spasm when he was so full of blood-lust that he couldn't tell friend from foe. This strange frenzy can still be observed on soccer pitches today!

2 The early Celt warriors fought with no clothes on except perhaps a gold band around the neck called a torque. They didn't believe in wearing armour. The Celts knew their gods would decide if they were to die that day. All the armour in the world wouldn't protect them. The Romans were protected by armour … and underpants!

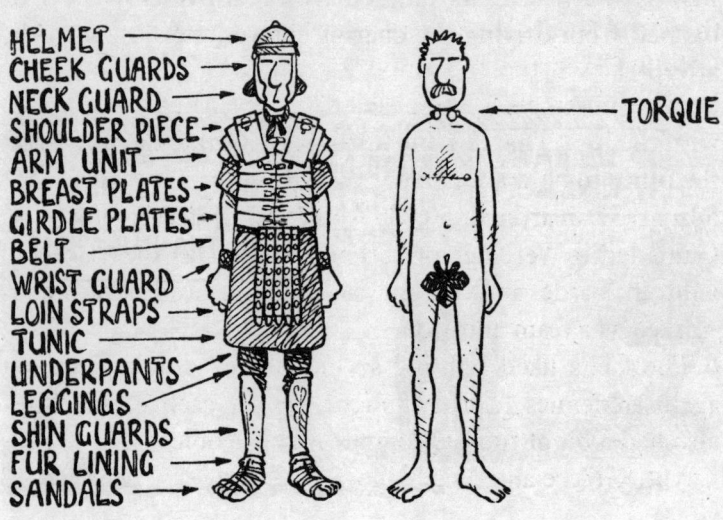

HELMET
CHEEK GUARDS
NECK GUARD
SHOULDER PIECE
ARM UNIT
BREAST PLATES
GIRDLE PLATES
BELT
WRIST GUARD
LOIN STRAPS
TUNIC
UNDERPANTS
LEGGINGS
SHIN GUARDS
FUR LINING
SANDALS

TORQUE

3 The Celts were very bad losers. If they looked like losing they killed themselves. This kind act saved their enemies the trouble. In one cheerful Roman statue a Celtic warrior is shown plunging a sword into his chest with one hand while holding his dead wife in the other. He has already killed her to save her from capture! Hope she was grateful!

I DON'T KNOW WHAT YOU'RE SMILING AT. YOU'RE NEXT!

4 The crafty Celts were great riders and invented a special saddle for fighting. They had no stirrups for their feet so there had always been a danger of the riders falling off. The Celt saddle of the 2nd and 3rd centuries BC had four high bumps (pommels is the posh word) that could be gripped with the legs. That left one hand free to guide the horse and the other to hold a weapon.

5 In AD 52 an army of 50,000 Romans defeated 250,000 Celt Gauls led by Vercingetorix. The trouble was the Celts ran wild in battle and fought as individuals. The Romans worked as a team and won.

6 The Celts liked fighting so much they didn't just fight against enemies … they fought against each other! They also had a bit of fun fighting for other people as far away as Egypt, Greece and Asia Minor.

7 The Romans were particularly shocked by rebel British leader, Boudicca. When her husband died he left his land to Emperor Nero and his daughters. The Emperor wanted it all and had Boudicca and the daughters flogged. Big Bad Boud attacked Roman towns and was especially cruel to women prisoners. They were executed and bits of their bodies were cut off and stuck in their mouths. They then had a sharp wooden stake pushed through their bodies and they were hoisted up for everyone to see. This nasty hobby became really popular 1,400 years later when a certain Count Dracula of Romania used it against his enemies...

8 And talking about Romania ... a Celt chieftain's helmet found in Ciumesti (Romania) has a large model bird perched on top. Its wings are spread and are hinged in the middle so they can flap up and down! Historians believe the chieftain would only wear it on important occasions – not in battle. It's a bit like Long John Silver having a parrot on his shoulder, only not so messy!

9 There is no doubt that the Ancient Celts believed that the greatest prize in battle was an enemy's head. They decorated both their saddles and the doors of their houses with heads. They preserved old heads in cedar oil and brought them out every now and again to boast about them. Some boasted that they refused to part with their enemy heads even though they'd been offered the head's weight in gold.

10 The Celts believed that single combat was a good way to show off your bravery and settle an argument. Two heroes would step forward and begin by insulting each other!

Then they'd start fighting while the soldiers on both sides watched to see that they fought fairly.

Awesome Arthur
The Celts usually chose the best warrior as the leader of their tribe. If two warriors both claimed to be the best then they had to fight for the honour. One didn't have to kill the other one, just beat him in single combat.

The Celts didn't usually have fine crowns for their kings. But the winner of the battle needed some sign that he was the boss. This sign would often be a fine sword.

Before the fight, the great royal sword was placed on an altar stone. The Druid presented this sword to the winner. Anyone who tried to take the new king's power from him would be cursed by the magical power of the sword.

But here's the clever bit! Some historians believe this was how a Celt called Arthur took control of the kingdom! Everybody's heard the story of Arthur and the sword IN the stone. But is the truth that Arthur fought in single combat, won, and took the sword ON the stone?

Of course, there are TWO Arthurs…

1 the warrior chief who may (or may not) have fought against the Saxon invasions of the 5th century and…

2 the King of legend who led the Knights of the Round Table into battles with dragons and giants and magic.

The trouble with Arthur 2 is that the stories always make Arthur out to be the greatest hero who ever lived. But an old saying goes, 'A man is never a hero to his personal servant.' He's probably not a hero to his wife either. Nobody ever bothers to tell Queen Guinevere's side of the story, do they? What would *she* have to say about her legendary husband?

Guinevere's grumble

A convent somewhere in Britain, 1815.

'I'll be back,' he said. I'm sure he will, but I've been waiting 1,300 years and he hasn't shown his miserable face yet. So where is he? That's what I want to know.

It was all so exciting back in AD 480. Most of the Romans had gone back to Italy but my family decided to stay. I was a noble Roman amongst all of the British peasants. I could have married anyone I wanted. But I admired those clever men who could write. And that was my downfall.

My father called me to his room one day. 'Ganhumara,' he said. 'How would you like to marry that famous Arthur?'

Well, I was so excited. I'd heard about the Saxon invaders and some British warriors fighting back. But I'd never heard of the famous Arthur.

I said, 'Oh, yes, father!' and rushed off to tell my sister.

Well, it wasn't till I got to church and saw all those nasty brutal men that I realized my mistake! He was the famous Arthur – so famous I'd never heard of him – and I thought father had said 'a famous author'! I've always been a trifle deaf.

My mistake. I had to make the most of it. First we moved into Arthur's hill fort. A filthy, draughty wooden castle he called Camelot – I always thought of it as Pong-a-lot! 'Who are you frightened of?' I asked him when I saw the place.

'I'm frightened of no one,' he said and went all huffy.

'Then why are you hiding in this castle?' I asked.

'I'm going to get a new army together to fight the Saxons,' he said.

'I'm not having hordes of sweaty soldiers tramping round

43

my clean floor, dripping blood all over those fresh rushes!'

'They're not sweaty soldiers. They're a better class. They're all knights, my lovely Guinevere,' Arthur said. He never could pronounce my Roman name. Guinevere, he called me, and the name stuck. There were a few names I'd like to have stuck on him but I decided to wait and see. And I was glad I did ... at first.

Some of those knights were really nice fellers. Galahad was always gadding about and Bedevere was a bit of a drip, but Lancelot was gorgeous. The trouble with those knights was that they were so proud. And once they'd beaten the Saxons they were bored. When knights have no one to argue with they argue with each other.

Arthur was the best fighter – ugly face, dirty fingernails and going bald – but the best fighter. Still, they weren't too happy about him being in charge.

'I sit at the top of the table with Guinevere,' Arthur demanded and there was a soft hiss of swords being drawn from belts. Arthur was as good as dead till I jumped up and

44

said, 'Why don't you have a round table!'

They looked at me as if I was gormless. 'Tables is square,' Lancelot said. He was a lovely looking feller but he didn't have two brain cells to rub together.

'Arthur has carpenters in the castle. They can make a round table. Then there's no top of the table. Everybody's equal!' I cried.

'Sounds fair enough to me,' Galahad said and the others muttered in agreement.

We had a bit of trouble with the carpenter, of course. 'My saw doesn't cut circles,' he grumbled. 'It only cuts straight lines!' But, when Arthur told him his sword could cut a straight line across the man's throat, the carpenter went off and made one.

It was a bit wobbly on its legs but it did the job. That first feast night they had just eaten a couple of pigs and a deer when a servant rushed in with the bad news. 'Oh, my lords!' he cried. 'A terrible plague has swept the country and is killing the peasants. They're dropping like flies!'

45

'Well, I'm glad I'm not a peasant!' Arthur laughed.

'Or a fly!' Lancelot nodded.

'We have to help them!' the drippy Bedevere put in.

'Help them!' Arthur squawked. 'We're not Druids! We might catch something nasty!'

But Bedevere seemed to have a lot of support around the table. 'It's better than killing dragons,' Bedevere cried.

'Why?' I asked. 'I was always told that dragons are nasty scaly creatures with bad breath!'

'If we go on killing them at this rate there'll be none left in a hundred years! Dragons are becoming an endangered species!' Bedevere argued.

'Peasants will become an endangered species if you don't help them,' I said.

'Good thing,' Lancelot said.

'Lance, dear. If there are no peasants you'll have to dig in the fields and cut the corn and grind it to make flour and feed the pigs and shoe your horse … everything,' I said.

'That's right. You'll have to do all that work yourself!' Bedevere argued.

Lancelot thought about this for a minute and his face was twisted with the effort. Finally he nodded. 'Save the peasants!' he cried and thumped the table. Of course he had to pick the spot with the wobbly leg. It took us ten minutes to pick up the wine and pig-meat off my clean rushes.

They decided that the only cure for the peasant plague was to drink from the Holy Grail – the goblet that Jesus drank from at the last supper. The trouble was nobody knew where it was.

'Why don't you have a quest?' I said quietly to Bedevere.

'Let's have a quest!' Bedevere said and his eyes went all starry. If there's one thing a knight likes it's a quest.

'It's a brilliant idea, Bedevere,' Arthur said.

'Thank you, Arthur,' Bedevere smiled.

I didn't mind. After all, it got those great clumping men out from under my feet.

Within a week they were packing their bags. 'Arthur,' I said in my sweetest voice. 'While you're away you'll need someone to run the country!'

'I've asked my nephew Mordred,' he said.

'I've never liked that shifty-eyed, weedy little cross-eyed brat,' I said. 'You should leave a trusty knight behind to keep an eye on him.'

Arthur nodded. 'I'll leave Lancelot,' he said.

'Perfect,' I said.

Now you've probably read the legends. But those stories about Lancelot and me are nothing but lies put about by that evil Mordred. Lance looked after me like a real gentleman. Maybe the odd cuddle when I got lonely but nothing more. Anyone else who says anything different is a liar. A liar like that Mordred.

The stories about his starting a rebellion were true though. Arthur dashed back from the quest and fought the devious little nephew at Camlann and beat him. Served the little traitor right.

The trouble is Arthur got a dreadful wound. The first I knew was Bedevere hammering on the gates. 'Come at once, Guinevere!' he cried. 'Arthur is close to death!'

'Close to deaf?' I said. 'I've always been a bit hard of hearing myself!' I laughed. 'Did I ever tell you that's how I came to marry him.'

'He's DYING!' Bedevere cried. 'He made me throw his sword Excalibur into the lake and a hand rose through the waters and took it below the surface. It's a sure sign death is close!'

I hurried to the scene of the battle and I got to my old feller just before he hopped the twig. That's when I heard those famous last words. 'I'll be back!' he croaked. 'Whenever Britain is threatened by the forces of dark and evil I will return and lead her to safety. I'll be back!'

BLEED
BLEED

And that was it. Lancelot went into a monastery and I went and became a nun. For 1,300 years I've waited. The Normans invaded and I thought that would bring him to Britain's rescue. Arthur slept through that and all the Middle Ages. In 1588 the Spanish Armada sailed to the attack … Arthur slept. Then in the 1800s a nasty Frenchman called Napoleon began rampaging across Europe and threatening to rule the world including poor little Britain.

Now, news is slow to reach this convent but I've just heard the news. Napoleon has been defeated by a British general at a battle in Belgium at a place called Waterloo. Our brilliant British general is known as the Duke of Wellington. He's a true British hero … just like my Arthur.

A nun brought me the news just now. 'What's the name of this British general?' I asked.

'The Duke of Wellington,' the girl replied.

'I know that. I mean the name he was christened with?'

'Oh!' the girl smiled. 'He's one of the Wellesley family, Sister Guinevere. I seem to remember his name is … Arthur. Yes, that's it. Arthur!'

I smiled and nodded. 'He said he'd be back.'

Now, Arthur Wellesley, Duke of Wellington, never claimed to be King Arthur reborn. But it's strange that our greatest general, the man who saved Britain when she was in mortal danger, should be called … Arthur.

The truth about Arthur

Over the centuries Arthur has become a British hero. Some people have built the most fantastic stories around him. They have said...

- Arthur was King of Atlantis – a kingdom that sank under the sea.

- Arthur was an alien who landed on Earth, zapped the Saxons then went off in his flying saucer.

- Arthur sailed west after his last battle and became the first European to discover America – a thousand years before Christopher Columbus.

The truth is…

1 If Arthur really existed then he lived in the 'Dark Ages' when no one was writing history. A couple of monks mentioned him. Nennius said…

> *At that time a great number of Saxons were invading Britain and increasing. Then Arthur and the British kings fought the Saxons. He was their battle leader. The pagans were put to flight that day and many of them were slaughtered. A twelfth battle took place at Mount Badon in which a single attack from Arthur killed 960 men. No other man took part in this massacre. In all these battles Arthur was the victor.*

2 The monk listed twelve battle sites and historians have argued about where they took place for a thousand years. No one really knows but it's fairly certain they were all over England, Wales and Scotland.

3 Historians argue over the line that says, 'No other man took part in this massacre' of 960 men! Most writers agree it means no other 'battle leader' took part in the massacre. If he killed 960 soldiers on his own then his little arms would be aching!

4 Arthur seems to have been the leader of some sort of travelling band of warriors. Tribal kings hired him to sort out the Saxons or pick on the Picts whenever trouble arose … but Arthur himself may not have been a king.

5 It was 600 years after his death that monks started writing histories about him and making him into the last of the Celt

super-heroes. Welsh monk, Geoffrey of Monmouth, wrote about Arthur in 1135, and added or invented or guessed at bits of Arthur's life. People believed they were 'facts' because they appeared in a history book! This is an important lesson. Never believe EVERYTHING you read in a history book! Geoffrey had the date of the last battle at Camlann as AD 542, by which time Arthur would have been 100 years old! No wonder the poor old wrinkly lost!

MY LORD, THE ENEMY ATTACKS ON OUR FLANK. WHAT ARE YOU GOING TO DO ?

HAVE A LITTLE LIE DOWN

6 Then, in the 1150s, poems were written based on Geoffrey's 'facts' – Arthur's court at Camelot was invented in an 1180s' poem and the search for the Holy Grail was added in an 1190s' poem. Other storytellers added Merlin the magician, ladies in lakes and battles with evil knights.

7 In 1344 King Edward III of England got hold of the story and decided to have his own Knights of the Round Table. Then he changed his mind and the idea became the Knights of the Garter in 1348. Other kings of England or the United Kingdom have admired Arthur too. Henry VII named his son Arthur, Prince of Wales. But Arthur died before he came to the throne and his nasty little brother, Henry VIII, took over instead. The present Prince of Wales has Arthur as one of his middle names ... and caused such a stir with

his marriage problems that some people said he should never be king. Are we doomed never to have a King Arthur? Is there a curse on the name?

8 A really large Round Table can be seen today in Winchester Castle and it is probably one of Henry III's bright ideas – it certainly isn't the real Arthur's Round Table.

9 Thomas Malory wrote a long poem called *The Death of Arthur* and it became one of the first books ever to be printed, in 1485. Arthur became a popular star and he still is today.

10 New films, books, plays, videos and magazines appear every year. There are coach trips to Arthur's sites, a King Arthur Society and you can even have a King Arthur holiday.

DORIS, WHERE'S MY KING ARTHUR SOAP?

NEAR YOUR KING ARTHUR TOOTHBRUSH, UNDER YOUR KING ARTHUR SHAVING FOAM AND THAT KING ARTHUR BATH LOTION BY YOUR KING ARTHUR FLAVOURED DENTAL FLOSS

The truth is…

- There was almost certainly a strong and successful warrior among the Celtic Britons.
- For 30 years or more he held back the flood of Saxon invaders.
- When he died the Saxons invaded the country and the Celt Britons were finished.
- We don't know the name of this last great British Celt … but we might as well call him … Arthur.

Battlefield beliefs

As well as the Roman writers there were Celt poets who told tales of daring deeds. These too became a bit exaggerated. It was many years before these stories were written down and mistakes could have been made. For example, Celt Queen Boudicca was known for many years as Boadicea because of a monk's spelling mistake!

But the stories are interesting because there could well be truth behind them. In the legend of King Ailill Olomn's spear there are three things he mustn't do – he mustn't strike a stone, he mustn't kill a woman and he mustn't straighten the tip with his tooth. In fact, he kills a woman after she bites his ear. The spear goes through her and the tip buckles against a stone. He straightens it with his tooth ... and is cursed. He goes blind, mad and (very strangely) develops bad breath. You'd think being blind and mad, having bad breath would be the least of his worries!

It's a fair guess that warriors straightened spear tips with their teeth but were warned not to. The warning became a little story – rather like Little Red Riding Hood is a warning not to talk to strange wolves in the wood.

Here are some of the other stories that Celts went into battle believing...

1 The Celts had Battle Furies to help them in war. These war-goddesses weren't actually fighters – more, frighters. The Nemhain (Frenzy), a charming goddess, had a powerful voice (like a dinner-lady telling you to line up properly). She shrieked at the Connacht army in Ulster and a hundred soldiers dropped dead with fright.

SHE'S THEIR SHRIEKRET WEAPON

2 The equally delightful Macha turned into a crow during a battle and hovered over the battlefield – she was waiting to make a meal of the heads of the dead fighters.

OOO! ANOTHER HEAD LOPPED OFF. YUM YUM!

3 If you saw the Badbh before a battle then it was serious bad news – she took the form of a crow, bleeding, with a rope around her neck. A sure sign that you are going to die. (If you see a bleeding crow before a football, hockey or netball match it is a sure sign that someone is going to lose! If the match is a draw

BLOOD STAINED ROPES ARE OK, BUT A RED TIE IS MORE COMFORTABLE

then you clearly made a mistake – you probably saw a crow that had been supping tomato sauce.)

4 On the other hand, Badbh was sometimes seen with a man. You could hardly miss him. He had one hand, one eye and one leg – he had a roast pig on his back which was still squealing. (Well, *you'd* be squealing if you'd been roasted.) If you see the bleeding hanged crow AND this feller hopping towards you it is probably time to get a tape measure and get measured for a coffin.

5 But be careful if you see the Morrigan. She will urge you to fight and promise that you will win ... trouble is, she'll be saying exactly the same thing to the other side! Will you recognize the Morrigan? Possibly. She is red, with red hair and a red cloak, riding a chariot pulled by a red horse. In case you still don't spot her then take a close look at her horse ... it only has one leg, the chariot pole passes through its body and is fastened to its head with a peg. And I forgot to mention, her mouth is on the side of her face – a useful device for people who want to lick the wax out of one ear. (If you still can't spot her then you probably need to visit your optician.)

6 The Celts were fearless fighters yet they could easily be put off a fight. They believed that there were good days for fighting and bad days. There were signs that told a warrior to fight, or to pack up and go home. If he saw a crane bird, for example, he knew that would bring him bad luck. A crane would take away your courage and your skill – three cranes would leave you with as much fight as a lettuce leaf.

Did you know … ?

Red was said by the Celts to be the colour of someone (or something) coming from the underworld. (This is not a reason to run away from pillar boxes, robins or Liverpool football players.)

How to be a hero

Celtic warriors enjoyed boasting about their victories. But they also liked to have little trophies that they could show to their friends. They were things to boast about. Here is a trophy that *you* can be proud of. To make it you will need a sharp sword, a wooden spoon and some lime (or cement).

1. Pick a fight with another hero. The more fierce he is then the greater the glory when you beat him *fig I*
2. Kill him (Please note: If he kills you then stop reading here) *see fig I*
3. Remove his head (Don't feel too bad about this. He'd do the same to you) *see fig II*
4. Remove the brain from the skull. *see fig III*
5. Mix the brain with lime to make a hard round ball
6. Show your prize at feasts and boast about your bravery

HERE'S ONE I MADE EARLIER!

57

This jolly little operation has its dangers – apart from the danger of your own brain ending up like a concrete football. The Celts believe that the brain can take its revenge, even after it's been removed.

Hero Conchobor killed Meisceadhra and made a trophy of his brain. But the brain was stolen and thrown at Conchobor. It hit him on the head ... and stuck. For ever! In the end it drove Conchobor mad and he chopped oak trees down with his sword till he dropped dead.

Did you know ... ?

The Celts did use brain power as well as muscle power sometimes. In 279 BC a Greek army broke down bridges to stop a Celt army pursuing them. The Celt land army had no boats but managed to cross the rivers by using their wooden shields as rafts. Clever Celts! Unfortunately they then went on to lose the battle, though they fought bravely – some warriors tore Greek spears out of their bodies and threw them back!

Potty prophetic hero

Place two fingers in your mouth and try speaking through them. This will not only allow you to spray your listeners with saliva, but also allow you to solve a mystery! The words you speak in this way will reveal some hidden truth.

But don't expect great things from this. The warrior

Fionn used the trick to detect the death of Lomna. He came across Lomna's body and said...

He has not been killed by a wild boar,
He has not been killed by a fall,
He has not died in his bed!

Amazing! How did he know all these things? Not really so very amazing. Lomna's body had no head on it. Even the British police could have guessed he did 'not die in his bed'!

Woe for women

Women in history are like the managers of football teams – they send their men out to battle with the weather or with the enemy. When they win the men get all the glory – when they lose the manager gets the sack ... or the woman gets the blame. Celtic women had an equally difficult life...

- Women of the Parisii Tribe (now in East Yorkshire) were around 1.58 metres in height on average and most only lived to their early twenties. Giving birth to children was very dangerous and probably killed a lot of them.

- Celt women wore make-up made from juices of berries. Eyebrows were darkened with berry juice, a herb called ruam gave a red tint to cheeks and berry juice was used to redden the lips. The women also painted their nails. But a woman had to protect her eye shadow – the men liked to use it too!

- Women were proud of their long hair and carried their combs in a special comb-bag. Hair braids have been found in Ireland that are 1.5 metres long and even a warrior like Boudicca wore her hair to her knees.

But some things never change – it seemed Celt men preferred blondes. Both men and women wore golden balls plaited into the end of their hair and the men wore earrings too, as many do today. By this time you will have realized that the Celts loved their hair. The warriors bleached it with lime and arranged it into wild spikes. When a young man left home to become a warrior he had his hair cut to show that he was no longer a child.

- Large families shared a house – children lived with aunts and uncles and grandparents. Roman Julius Caesar said that groups of 10 to 12 men often shared wives. But the fact that the men shared the house doesn't mean they shared the women! No one can be sure.

- Graves have been discovered which show that some Celt women rose to become chiefs of their tribes. They were buried with battle chariots and weapons. Famous Macha of the Red Hair was said to rule all of Ireland and some historians believe she was a real person, not just a legend.

These warrior princesses were not the only women to be involved in war...

Ten things you never knew about fighting females
1 Irish landowners were expected to fight for their lord if he went to war. And if the landowner was a woman she was expected to fight. In the 6th century AD Saint Adamnan forced the law to be changed.
2 Women warriors in Irish tribes were teachers – but they didn't teach children to read and write. They trained the boys to fight. Do you know any women teachers like that?

THE TEST TOMORROW IS ON DISEMBOWELLING, SO STUDY YOUR SWORD SLASHES TONIGHT

3 Celtic women could be tribal chiefs and there was a woman army leader who led a group of Brigantian soldiers in an attack on the Romans some time between AD 71 and 83. Teuta led a Celtic tribe in the Mediterranean that took on the Greeks then the Romans. The Romans threatened to turn the whole of their army against her and sent a message warning her to behave. She had the messenger murdered! A huge Roman fleet forced her to make peace.
4 However, the more usual role of women was to spectate from carts and platforms at the back of the fighters and shout encouragement to their own fighters and insults or curses to the opposition – a bit like cheerleaders at American Football games. When the Gergovian Celts of Gaul lost to the Romans, the Celt women took all their clothes off in the hope that the Romans would spare them. Some hope!

5 Princess Canna was forced to marry Sinorix – King of the Storms – after he had murdered her husband. But it was a stormy marriage. One evening she offered Sinorix wine.

6 Women were not restricted to staying at home, teaching children, cooking or farming while the men went off to fight. Women in Gaul followed professions including wine-seller, butcher, doctor and chemist.

7 This may make women seem strong and powerful but Roman leader Julius Caesar said that in Gaul, men had the power of life or death over the women. He was probably wrong when he went on...

> *When the head of a noble family dies and there is some suspicion about the death, then his widow is questioned under torture. If she is found guilty of his death then she is sentenced to burn and sent to the flames with the most cruel torments.*

8 It's possible that women were Druid priestesses. Tacitus described the British forces which faced Suetonius Paulinus on Anglesey...

> *On the opposite shore stood the British army with its dense crowd of armed warriors. Between the columns dashed women in black gowns like the Goddesses of war, their hair wild, waving flaming torches. All around were the Druids, terrifying our soldiers.*

These women were also involved with human sacrifices. Tacitus said the Romans found the grisly remains of blood and guts on their altars in the woods.

9 Some also had the power of seeing into the future. Diocletian was a simple soldier in the Roman Army when he was paying his bill at a tavern. A Celtic woman approached him and said...

YOU ARE MEAN AND GREEDY!

I'M A POOR SOLDIER!

I'LL BET YOU'RE NOT THAT MEAN WHEN YOU ARE EMPEROR OF ROME

ME? WHEN WILL THAT BE

WHEN YOU HAVE KILLED THE BOAR

Years later Diocletian killed the Emperor's leading bodyguard and became Emperor – just as the woman had predicted. The name of the Emperor's bodyguard was 'Aper' ... a name meaning 'Boar'!

10 You can't always trust historians, of course. A Greek geographer called Strabo lived from about 40 BC till about AD 52 and he gave a description of priestesses living on an island off the coast of France. Many historians believe this island was Britain and the people by then would have been Celts. But would you have liked to pay a visit to their church? His report goes...

Posidonius says there is an island in the ocean, not far from land. The women there honour the god Dionysus and worship him with ceremonies and sacred rituals. It is their custom, once a year, to remove the roof from their temple and cover it again the same day before sunset. Each woman must carry part of the load. But if any woman lets her load drop then she is torn to pieces by the others. They then carry the pieces of her round the temple, chanting and do not stop till the madness passes away. But it always happens that somebody pushes against a woman who is chosen to suffer this fate!

Imagine that! Being torn apart by a bunch of roofless women! Men were not allowed to land on the island. I can't imagine many men would want to!

Tall tales

And in the ancient Celtic stories naturally women are the villains. In Celt legends there are some strange women around.

1 In Irish legend Medb is cruel, jealous, unreliable and gets her power through witchcraft. In the end she was killed by the son of one of her victims. He killed her with a sling-shot like David killed Goliath ... but instead of a stone he hit her with a piece of cheese! (If it was soft cheese she'd be all right but if it was hard cheese then it was hard cheese for her.)

2 Boann made the mistake of visiting a well. Husband Nechtan was guardian of the well and told her not to go there. Nosey Boann had to have a look, didn't she? As a result the water gushed out of the well, drowned her and formed a river – now known as the Boyne in Eire. It's said she's in there somewhere. If you ever go swimming in the Boyne and find a skeleton, you'll know who it is!

3 Rhiannon was accused of murdering her baby son. In fact it was pinched by an evil spirit but Rhiannon got the blame. Her ladies-in-waiting killed a puppy and smeared Rhiannon with blood as she slept. When she woke, covered in blood with no baby, her husband believed she had got rid of the baby's body … by eating it!

4 A girl, Etain, was turned into a fly by a jealous goddess. This was quite useful because she could hum the god Midhir to sleep with her buzzing – or wake him up when danger came near. The jealous goddess was not satisfied and chased her so long and hard that Etain buzzed her way into a woman's wine glass. The woman drank the wine and swallowed Etain. (And before you ask, no, the woman did NOT swallow a spider to catch the fly, or swallow a bird to catch the spider that wriggled and wriggled and tickled inside her. That's another story altogether.) So anyway, next time you feel like swatting a fly, remember … it could be some poor cursed girl!

True tale of terror

67

Eponina's wish had been to go to the Otherworld with her husband. She got her wish and they were executed that very day. Brave Celtic woman? Or a waste of a good life? What would you have done?

Cut-throat women
Some German tribes were closely related to the Celts. The Cimbrian holy women were a tough and bloodthirsty lot…

They were grey with age, wore white tunics and, over these, cloaks of the finest linen and bronze girdles. They were barefoot. These women would enter the camp of their warriors, sword in hand, and go up to the prisoners. They would then crown them and lead them up to a large bronze vessel. One of them would mount a step and, leaning over the cauldron, cut the throat of a prisoner who was held up over the vessel's rim. Others cut the body open and, after inspecting the entrails, would foretell victory for their countrymen.

You'll notice the women do not foretell the 'result' ... they foretell the 'victory'. In other words they know what the entrails (or guts) will say before they kill their victim! Seems like a waste of a good prisoner to be honest.

This story was told by Greek geographer Strabo and may have had some truth in it. However, do NOT try this at home. It makes a terrible mess on the carpet. If you want to look into the future then read your horoscope in the daily paper.

Cut-throat corpses

Women were also the victims of cut-throat carvers. In late Roman Britain there were many examples of people being buried with their heads removed and placed between their legs. Most of these were middle-aged or elderly women.

It's hard to say if they were beheaded before or after they were dead, but they were all beheaded very cleanly at the same neck bone and from the front. But why?

Some historians think it was so the women could see their way into the next life – a pair of eyes at your feet can come in very handy sometimes!

Or it could have been a punishment for witchcraft – many of these bodies have their jaws removed. That should shut them up in the next life all right.

Some women's heads are buried in wells – one in an Oxfordshire village called Headington (honest!).

Quaint Celt calendar

The Celts are an ancient people, older than the Ancient Greeks and maybe as old as the Ancient Egyptians. They built up a lot of traditions in that time. Quaint customs and events that were held at the same time every year. (A bit like school sports days at the end of term in July … followed by National Children's Gloom Day when everyone returns to school in the first week of September.)

When the Romans brought Christianity to the Celts then the Celts had many new customs to celebrate – saints' days, Christmas and Easter, for example. But they never forgot the old customs and the old gods. The Celt calendar became a mixture of Christian and non-Christian.

If you want to remember the cut-throat Celt calendar then here are a few diary dates for you…

Deidre's Diary

> November
>
> 1st. Dear Diary. Here we go again. Another New Year's Day and the first day of winter. Old goddess Cailleach has hit the ground with her hammer and made it hard. I know it's true. I have to sleep on it. And this is my first winter married to that dear lump-head Fionn. This is also the day when the village Druid makes sacrifices to all the gods. I'll bet the Druid eats the goat himself. I think that's why he's so fat. My friend Rhiann says she saw him chewing on a goat bone. Of course we daren't say anything – we might end up on the altar instead of the goat!
>
> 9th. Time to bring the cattle in for the winter – dead or alive. Of course I get the job of killing and salting the feeble cows and sheep. I wouldn't mind but I'll get blood all over this new diary

December

18th. This is the day of the Goddess Epona, you know, the one who looks like a horse. My friend Rhiann says her sister looks like Epona but I think that's a bit cruel – horses are much better looking than Rhiann's sister! Anyway, today is the day when horses and donkeys have a day of rest. I wish I did. Work, work, work. And that lump-head husband is as much use as the icicle on the end of me nose.

21st. Longest night of the year. We light fires for the warmth and the light but the lump-head Fionne brought in damp wood and the smoke almost choked us and the pig. I said to the lump-head, "If I want smoked bacon I'll kill the pig and hang it over the fire... but I don't!"

January

25th. Dwynwen's day. This is the day when lovers give tokens to their loved ones. What did I get from that lump-head? The whole contents of his head: nothing. But my friend Rhiann says young Gildas would like to give me his heart. I'd rather have a fresh ~~piece~~ piece of pork.

31st. Feast of Oimelc. Usual over-eating and over-drinking to celebrate winter loosening its grip. Not that you'd notice. Water in the buckets still frozen. Fionn has an excuse for not washing his feet. This is the time when the old Hag of Winter, Cailleach, sends her Dragon to kill Brigit of Spring. If Brigit loses then it will be winter forever! Every year Brigit sends a lamb to fight the dragon and it always wins. Must be a tough lamb - tough as the sheep we stewed and ate last night. I wish Spring would come with its fresh meat - and fresh air.

February

1st. Ogronios - the time of ice. My friend Rhiann says that today the women of Gaul stain their bodies blue with woad and march naked through the village! At this time of year! Lump-head Fionn said I should take all my clothes off. I gave him such a smack!

14th. Rhiann's sister gave birth to a baby boy today. I was there and took part in the blessing. We passed the baby three times across the fire, then we carried it three times around the fire - sunwise, of course. Rhiann filled a bowl with water and the Druid

73

dropped a gold coin in it. The baby was washed in the golden water. The little beggar didn't like it one bit. Still, judging by the screams he has healthy enough lungs! Whining about being washed in a drop of cold water – just like a man – just like smelly Fionn.

March

21st. Alban Eiler day when the days begin to grow longer than the nights. The men go out hunting to celebrate and the women watch. My friend Rhiann's father caught a deer and even my stupid brother caught a rabbit. What did lump-head Fionn catch? A cold. Tonight we'll be eating porridge again.

April

30th. Beltain eve. At last! We can open the doors in the village wall and let the cattle out to graze. The smell has been appalling in the past few weeks. What with the cattle dung and Fionn's feet I thought I was going to choke some nights. We drove the cattle between the bonfires to purify them. Fionn got drunk and I wondered if I should purify him by pushing him onto one of the bonfires. Decided not. It'll soon be Beltain and then we'll see.

May

1st. Beltain and the first day of summer.
That's it! Went to the village druid and asked
for a divorce from Fionn. He tried to tell me that
smelly feet is not a good enough reason for
divorce... then he smelled Fionn's feet. I'm free.
Good idea this trial marriage over winter. Three
other women of the village got divorced today.
When Fionn sobers up after last night's feast I'll tell
him he's divorced then throw him out of the house.

June

20th. Midsummer's Eve. Tonight my friend
Rhiann and me went out gathering yarrow. We
chanted the old rhyme:

Good morrow, good yarrow, good morrow to thee
        Send me this night my true love to see.
The clothes he will wear and the colour of hair
        And tell me if he will wed me.

Then we put the yarrow under our pillows
and waited for our love
to appear in our dream.
Rhiann dreamed about
young Colum. I dreamed
about tucking into a leg of
fresh pork

yarrow

21st. The longest day. My friend Rhiann and me stayed up tonight for a death-watch. They do say that we see the ~~spirit~~ spirits of those who'll die before the end of the year! I thought I saw the naked body of my lump-head husband but it was only a pig in the moonlight. What a shock!

July 14th. This is the day when we make wishes at the well. Me and Rhiann dipped our strips of cloth in the magic water and hung them out to dry on a hawthorn bush. As they hang there and dry the wish starts to come true. I can't tell my wish or it will not come true. But it did have something to do with food. After all, July is called the Hungry Month — all of last year's grain is gone and this year's hasn't ripened. And I know Rhiann wished she could marry Colum.

31st. Feast of Lughnasadh. This is the time when women choose husbands — and sometimes the husbands get to choose a wife. If they want a trial marriage then they join hands through a magic stone with a hole in the middle. Colum joined hands with Mara and Rhiann was very upset. Tore her wishing cloth off the

thorn bush! I think I'll give it a miss this year.
The hay's been gathered in but there's still the
wheat and barley to gather. At least the
Lughnasadh horse fair and the horse races
give us a break.

August

6th. We had a trial in the village today. A
sheep had gone missing and Ogma was found
with a pot full of stewed mutton. First he said
it was his own sheep but then the druid counted
Ogma's sheep and found they were all there. So
the druid held a trial in the middle of the
village. He said there were three stones in his
bag; he would draw one out. Black for guilt,
white for innocence and speckled for partly
guilty. The druid pulled out the speckled stone.
Ogma admitted he was partly guilty – he didn't
steal the sheep but he did find it dead and
didn't tell the owner. The druid said the gods
would punish Ogma.

8th. The gods are right again! Ogma has
died. That sheep he found was diseased. When
he ate the meat it made him ill and killed
him. No one will ever steal a dead sheep in
this village again. I can tell you!

September

21st. Nights become longer than days again. This is the time when I'm wishing I had a man of my own. Fionn wasn't much good but at least he kept me warm in the long cold nights.

24th. A poet came to the village today and sang a ballad about a pair of lovers, Baile and Ailinn. Baile heard Ailinn was dead so he killed himself. Ailinn heard that Baile was dead so she killed herself. Even when they were dead they went and buried them in separate graves. I thought it was a waste of two lives, myself, but my friend Rhiann started blubbering. You'd never catch me crying. Well not in front of the other villagers, though my eyes were watering a little when I ~~went~~ got into my lonely bed.

October

31st. Samhain eve. Ooooh! This is the night when the spirits of the dead wander the world. Rhiann says my dad will come back and visit me. But, since he was cut to bits in a battle with the Picts I don't really want to see him in pieces! Then Rhiann told me a ghost story and scared the hair half off my head. One Samhain eve a young man called

> Nera accepted a challenge. There were two corpses hanging from a gallows on the hilltop. Nera agreed to tie a grass rope round the foot of one corpse for a bet. But as soon as the rope touched the foot Nera vanished into the Otherworld and was never seen in this world again! I wonder ~~was~~ what the new year will bring for me and Rhiann?

Did you know … ?

From the ancient laws of Hywel Dda we know that medieval Welsh kings had a servant known as a 'Foot Holder'. Believe it or not the Foot Holder held the king's feet! From the time the king sat down to eat his evening meal, the Foot Holder took the king's feet in his lap and held them till he went to bed. While the king's feet were off his kingdom he could relax – he wasn't king for a while. The Foot Holder had the power; criminals could ask the Foot Holder for a pardon and he would probably allow them to go free – the king would have had to punish them.

Crazy Celt life

The Celts were farmers – when they weren't hunting animals or fighting Romans. They kept cows and sheep and hens and so on. Sounds idyllic, doesn't it? But would you like to have lived as a Celt? Read the facts and make up your own mind...

1 The Celts dressed to keep warm but they also liked to put on a bit of a show. Women wore checked skirts and when they went to important meetings they wore make-up, bracelets, anklets, necklaces, finger-rings, earrings and hairpins. Richer women also wore the gold neck bands (torques) that were worn by hero warriors. The Celts had no buttons – they used pins or brooches and those pins would be decorated too. Imagine having decorations on your zips!

2 Irish Celts seem to have been very clean people. They washed hands and feet every morning and had a full bath every night. They scrubbed themselves with soap and a linen cloth. The good news is that the water was usually

heated. The bad news is you'd probably share that water with the rest of the family.

3 The Celt houses were made of wattle walls – thin branches 'woven' to make panels which were then plastered with mud to keep the draughts out. The roofs were thatched and the fire built in the middle of the single large room that everyone shared. The trouble is there does not seem to have been a chimney for the smoke to escape. Sparks must have caused a lot of roof fires and the smoking would definitely be bad for your health!

4 The Celts built these houses in groups – often on the top of a hill and often with a defence wall around them. You'd call it a hill fort or a village, because you are sensible. But a horrible historian show-off would call it an 'oppidum'. You do not really need to know this … but if you ever get bored on a car journey then, every time you pass a village, you can sing, 'Oppidum, oppidum, oppidum-dum-dum!' till everyone in the car is driven mad.

5 Clean fingernails were a must. If someone damaged your fingernail they had to pay you for the damage under Irish law. A great Irish insult was to call a man 'Ragged nails!'

6 They probably used iron bars as a sort of money. They'd swap the 80 cm bars for other goods. Anyone with a dirty great magnet could have made a fortune as a pick-pocket!

7 The Celts had another useful type of money. You didn't have to carry it round with you … it walked! It was called a slave. These slaves could be people captured in battle or defeated during an invasion. The Romans used slaves and made wine – the Celts enjoyed wine but lived too far north to grow grapes. So the Celts swapped slaves for wine. WARNING: Do not let your parents know this or they may take you to the local off-licence and try to trade you for a can of lager.

8 The Celts ate off plates made of pottery, but sometimes the plates were made of wood…

The Celts ate with their fingers, and a fussy Roman wrote…

They eat cleanly but like lions, raising up whole limbs with both hands and biting off the meat.

CHOMP CHOMP

9 Celts had very little furniture so they slept on the floor wrapped in animal skins – bearskin or wolfskin kept you warm. Of course, you could end up even warmer running away from the bears and wolves as you tried to nick their skins!

10 The Celts were very fond of hunting. It got rid of pests (like deer that ate their crops), provided them with food (like wild boar) and clothing (wolfskin) but above all it gave them a popular form of entertainment. They used long-handled spears, bows and metal-tipped arrows or sling shots. These weapons need a lot of practice. If you don't believe me then make one and pop off to your nearest forest. I'll bet you don't kill a single wolf or bear if you hunt all year. (No going to a zoo to win this bet! Zoos is cheating!)

Live like a Celt

If you hopped on a time machine and were dropped in a Celt settlement then would you survive? Try this quick quiz. Get all the questions right and you'll fit in well with the Celts. Get one wrong and they may suspect you are not one of them. You'll end up with something at your throat – if you're lucky it may be a slave chain – if you're unlucky it may be a Druid's sacrificial knife!

1 The Celts loved a good party. The wine or beer is passed around. As a special guest you can drink first. But how should you drink the wine?

a) Empty your goblet in one swallow.

b) Refuse the drink until the chief has drunk first. (You could say, 'Thanks but I'd rather have a Coke.')

c) Drink a small sip then pass the goblet on.

2 As the party goes on a warrior stands up and tells everyone how he bravely fought against ten Roman soldiers

84

and beat all of them. Everyone looks at you. What do you say?

a) 'Liar! Liar! Pants on fire.'

b) 'You are a brave and noble warrior. I believe you and praise your courage.'

c) 'That's nothing, mate. I beat 20 Roman soldiers; I had one hand tied behind my back, I was wearing a blindfold and the only weapon I had was a sharp fingernail.'

3 A wild boar has been roasted for the party. You are offered a trotter to chew on. What do you say?

a) 'Thank you, that is extremely kind of you.'

b) 'I hope you've checked this boar for mad pig disease! Anyway, I'm a vegetarian and I'd prefer a nut cutlet.'

c) 'I will eat nothing but the best meat. Give me the finest flesh or you will die and I'll be roasting you on the fire.'

4 The tribe explains that this is the feast of Beltain. A ceremony is about to take place. Two large bonfires are lit.

HE CAN OUTFIT US TOO...HE'S OUR TAILOR

The warriors ask if you know what happens next. What do you say?

a) 'I guess we pop Guy Fawkes on top of one fire then set off the fireworks!'

b) 'We take it in turns to plunge a hand into the fire to show our courage.'

c) 'We drive the cattle between the two fires and this will protect them from disease.'

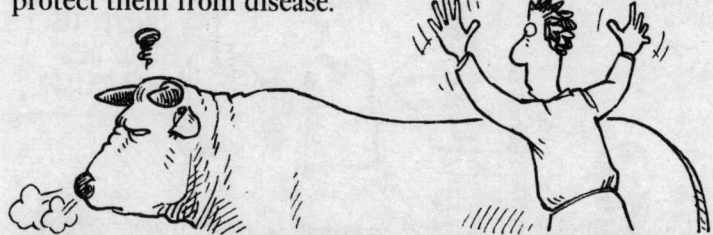

5 The Druid is a kind old bloke in a long, hooded robe. He says he has a special drink for a noble guest like you. It is made from the juice of the mistletoe. What do you do?

a) Drink it.

b) Offer to share it with the Druid.

c) Refuse to drink it. Make some excuse, like you were

always taught to 'Say NO to a stranger ...' and they don't come much stranger than the Druid!

6 The Druid suggests that it would be good to make an offering to the goddess, Sulis. She will bless the tribe in the coming battles. You go down to the river – everyone knows Sulis lives in water. You are given a fine knife with a gold pattern on the handle. What should you do with it?

a) Cut your hand and let a little blood drip into the river.

b) Throw the knife into the river as a rich gift.

c) Throw the knife into the river – but break it first so Sulis doesn't cut herself.

Answers:

All 'c)' answers are correct. If you have just one 'a)' or 'b)' you would not fit in with the Celt ways and probably not survive, either. That could be your ticket to the Otherworld! Here's why…

1 The Celts drank small sips … but drank an awful lot of those small sips until they were very drunk!

2 Warriors took part in Boasting Contests. No one ever called anyone a liar but a lot of exaggerating went on and that was all part of the enjoyment.

3 The bravest warriors expected the best meat. Only a wimp would make do with less. Being given a bone is an insult – accept it and you're a wimp. Start a fight if necessary to get the best.

4 Cattle were kept inside the village fence all winter. At the beginning of May they were driven out onto the grass meadows for summer grazing. The fires represented the warming and life-giving sun and the Druids drove the cattle between two fires to protect them from evil. Other big days included 1 February, known as Imbolc – the start of the lambing season – plenty of ewes milk for cheese. 31 July was Lughnasadh, when crops were ripening and a party for the gods would make sure they were safely gathered in.

5 A Roman historian called Pliny said, 'The Celts believe that the mistletoe, taken in a drink, is a cure for all poisons.' But the truth is that Druids must have known that mistletoe is in fact a poison – they gave it to sacrificial victims. Maybe it knocked them unconscious so they wouldn't struggle so much when the Druids cut their throats!

6 The Celts always broke or bent a knife before offering it to Sulis. They also threw their most valuable possessions into the rivers, including solid gold cups. But if Sulis lived in water, what would she want with a cup?

Did you know ... ?

The Celts grew grain and when they had spent all year growing the stuff they put most of it in a hole in the ground. This is not because they were crazy Celts, but because a hole in the ground would keep it fresh until they were ready to grind it into flour.

Flour was made by placing grain on a large flat stone called a quern – then rubbing a stone over the grain. It took 90 minutes to make a kilo of flour. After the 2nd century BC a rotary quern was invented and a kilo of flour took just 10 minutes to produce.

The grain pits were also used to dump dog or horse sacrifices. Imagine opening your flour bag from the supermarket and finding a bit of dead dog. You'd probably never eat bread again!

If you want a taste of Celtic life then try these recipes...

Pease pudding

You need:

250g dried green peas
pinch of mint herb
pinch of thyme herb
25g butter
half a teaspoonful of salt

Method:

1 Soak the dried peas for 12 hours (overnight is best).

2 Put the peas and the herbs in a saucepan and boil them in half a litre of water for half an hour. They should be soft and the skins loose.

3 Pour them into a sieve to let the water drain away, then use a spoon to force the peas through the sieve, giving a pea paste. (If you're really lazy then use a blender. Celts did not have blenders.)

4 Stir in the butter and salt then place the mixture in a greased pudding basin. Cover it with foil (which the Celts didn't have) and put the basin in a covered pan of boiling water. Boil it for an hour, but don't let it boil dry. WARNING: Puddings boiled in this way have a nasty habit of giving the cook third-degree burns. Get an adult to do this for you (so they get the burns, while you get to eat the pudding).

5 Take the foil off the basin, put a plate over the

top and turn the plate and the basin upside down. If you're lucky the pease pudding will come out in a neat, basin-shaped lump. (If you're unlucky it will come out as a slimy green mess, but eat it anyway.)

Porridge
You need:

50g oatmeal
600ml water
pinch of salt
milk

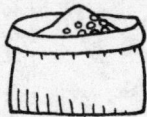 

Method:

1 Boil the water in a saucepan and add the salt.
2 Sprinkle in the oatmeal a little at a time and stir each time you add some.
3 Boil for 20 minutes.
4 Serve in bowls and stir in some milk.
5 If you prefer it sweet then stir in a spoonful of honey – the Celts didn't have sugar.

 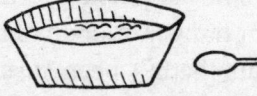

(This may taste quite pleasant, but most Celts ate it every day and you could soon become sick of it!)

Awesome animals

It was a hard life being a Celt, dodging the Druids and running from the Romans. But it was worse for the animals. The Celts were very close to nature and they told remarkable tales about animals. They also had some strange beliefs about them. Believe these stories if you want…

Deer

- Cernunnos was Lord of All the Stags and appeared as a man with antlers. It is very useful to walk around with a coat rack on your head but it's murder when you want to wash your hair in the sink.

- Irish Prince Tathan landed in Wales to set up a monastery. As his crew threw a rope to the shore a stag stepped forward and put a hoof on the rope to prevent the ship drifting away. Tathan went off to teach the wild Welsh about Christianity.
- When Tathan and his friends returned to the ship they were weak from hunger. Nobody had so much as a bag of crisps (well, they hadn't been invented, had they?). But the stag came to the rescue yet again. 'Eat me,' he said. So they did. Stag steak is very tasty they reckon, especially with mushy peas and chips.

Pigs

The Celts believed that pigs (and sows in particular) were very wise. It made sense to listen to what a pig had to say. There are lots of tales about swine-herds who turn out to be Princes in disguise. If you wanted to get a head, get a pig.

- St Brannoc set up a church where he found a sow with her piglets – a dream told him to do this.
- A boar appears on many Celtic coins (where now we have the queen's head – no comments please about bores or pigs or you could end up in the Tower of London).
- The Goddess of Hunting, Archinna, is usually pictured riding a boar with a dagger in her hand. She is clearly into pork chops.

Wrens

- The Celts told a story about a competition for the king of the birds. The eagle flew highest and claimed to be king. But a wren had hitched a ride on the eagle's back and flew still higher. The wren was king of the birds.

- Wrens had a tough time at New Year. They were killed because the Celts believed that it was a way of saying goodbye to the old year and bringing luck to the new. It was not, of course, very lucky for a wren.

- Sailors until recently still believed that the feather of a wren protected them from drowning, especially if the wren was killed on New Year's Day. This led to the mass slaughter of wrens in the old Celt kingdom, the Isle of Man, because the sailors' protection only lasted one year.

Dogs
- Dogs were respected in Celtic life. They were useful for hunting, and they also protected their owners.
- The lick of a dog was supposed to heal a wound. WARNING: Never, ever, try this even if your dog has just gargled with antiseptic!
- The God of the Underworld had a pack of white dogs with red ears. If you ever see such a dog you can tell it to go to Hell, because that's just telling it to go home!
- Druids may have respected dogs but this didn't stop them from chewing dog flesh for mystic power.

Miserable medicine
- Celt doctors bored into a patient's skull to relieve pressure on the brain. This was particularly useful if your skull had been bashed in battle.
- The Celts also believed in the healing powers of water. The Romans are famous for their healing waters at England's west-country city of Bath. But the Celts discovered it before the Romans got there and were using the waters long after the Romans had gone. The waters probably helped with some illnesses but the Celts believed it was the Goddess, Sulis, who really healed them.

- The Romans taught the Celts the trick of writing your problem on a thin piece of lead, rolling it up and dropping it into the water. (This is a bit like taking a prescription from the doctor and giving it to the chemist. The difference is we can read the lead inscriptions even today – the handwriting of doctors is impossible to read!) No one worried if they couldn't write. They simply made a little model of their poorly parts and dropped it in the water!
- While you were at the Bath waters – drinking it and bathing in it – there were doctors hanging around who offered to cure you if the waters didn't work. And, while you were there, you could also take the time to curse somebody who had upset you. A lot of curse messages have been found. They said things like...

Dear Sulis,
My best shirt was stolen last week Please make sure the thief does not eat, drink, sleep or pee until it is returned.
Sincerely,
Vespasia

Did you know ... ?
To protect yourself against illness you should take your middle two fingers, place them in your mouth and spread them. This 9th century Celtic charm against illness only works if you've washed your hands first, of course ... especially if you've just had them up your nose.

Celtic life – test your teacher

1 What did the Celts put on their ponies to protect them during races?

a) Shin guards (like footballers wear) made of whale bones.

b) Crash-helmets made of metal.

c) Leather boots cushioned with sheepskin.

2 How did Bronze-Age Scots try to strengthen their fortress walls to keep the Celts out?

a) They cemented the stones together.

b) They nailed the stones together.

c) They set huge bonfires against the wall to melt the stones together.

3 Some Celts got away with a debt in a curious way. What did they say to someone they owed money to?

a) 'I'll pay you in the next life.'

b) 'I'll toss a coin with you – double or quits.'

c) 'You can have my wife instead of the money.'

I SUPPOSE WE COULD TOSS YOUR WIFE INTO THE NEXT LIFE, DOUBLE OR QUITS

4 The Pict tribes of Scotland knew about it, but modern Brits only found it in 1933. What?

a) Celtic football team.

b) Invisible ink.

c) The Loch Ness Monster.

5 St Cybi was a brilliant child. A writer said this incredible child could do what at the age of just seven years?

a) Read a book.

b) Sacrifice a goat.

c) Learn the Bible and recite it from memory.

6 Skeletons of Celt women have been found buried with their rings. But where were they wearing them?

a) On their fingers.

b) On their toes.

c) In their noses.

7 When the Celts became Christian you could still spot the difference between their monks and the Roman monks. How?

a) They wore blue robes dyed in woad.

b) They shaved their heads from ear to ear, not in a neat circle.

c) They chanted their songs in the Gaelic language, not Latin.

8 Where did the Picts get their name from?

a) They were the chosen people of the gods – the Picked or Pict.

b) The first iron tools they made were stone-breakers called 'Picks'.

c) The Romans thought they were like 'Pictures' because they painted themselves.

9 If you killed a child under the age of seven, what would be your punishment?

a) You would be fined three cows.

b) You would be hanged.

c) You would have the hand that did the killing cut off.

10 Historians argue about exactly who King Arthur was. One thing's for certain. Arthur was not his proper name – just a nickname. What does 'Arthur' mean?

a) He who fights on two sides.

b) Great leader of 100 battles.

c) Bear.

Answers:

1 b) Pony caps, with holes for the ears, have been found at Celtic sites in the Shetlands. But what on earth were they doing to need this sort of head protector? Pony-American-Football?

2 c) The Bronze-Age Celts of Scotland created these 'vitrified forts' where the stones were heated till they were 'welded' together. One can be seen at Craig Phadrig near Inverness. Don't try this on your house – bricks don't melt.

3 a) This worked for Celts who believed they were getting a good deal if they could collect money in the Otherworld. If you really want to persuade someone that you can be trusted then take the Celtic Curse:

If I break my promise may the skies fall upon me, may the seas drown me and may the earth rise up and swallow me!

However, the bad news is that modern Celt shopkeepers don't believe this line and will not give you a bar of chocolate or a mountain bike if you promise to pay in the next life. Sorry.

99

4 c) The Picts carved pictures on stones, and one stone stands at Aberlemno village between Forfar and Brechin. It shows a long-nosed swimming creature like an elephant – except its trunk comes from between its ears. This ties in with the Celtic legend of St Columba (AD 521 – 597) who tamed such a monster in Loch Ness. Another monk was less lucky – he let the lake monster plough his field for him. When the job was finished the monster vanished … taking the monk with him!

NOW THERE'S SOMETHING YOU DON'T SEE EVERY DAY

5 a) Cybi could read. This might not amaze you as much as it amazed the monk who wrote his life story, but being able to read was very rare in the 6th century. If you can read this then you probably could read at seven. Why not go home and tell your parents, 'Did you know I could be a Saint? I really think that means you should double my pocket money.'

6 b) There wouldn't have been much point in wearing a ring under your shoes – no one would see your jewellery and it would be uncomfortable. No Celtic shoes have ever been found so the toe-rings suggest that women often wore sandals.

7 b) They shaved their heads from ear to ear but sometimes the Celt monks left a tuft of hair at the top of the head. A Saxon monk called Bede (who shaved a round bald patch) thought they looked a bit ridiculous.  Maybe he should have looked in a mirror! Some historians think the Celt monks may have copied the Druids in this hair fashion. Celt monks also amazed the Europeans by wearing black eye make-up – a fashion they kept from Celt warriors.

8 c) The Picts were nicknamed 'Picture People' by the Romans but their real name was Cruitne. The Picts lived in Scotland where they were joined by the Scots who came from Ireland. In time there were more Scots than Picts so Pictland became Scotland. Got it? It could be worse – the Britons called them Priteni. Edinburgh could now be the capital of Priteniland. Try spelling that in a geography lesson some wet Wednesday.

9 a) A child under seven was considered to be worth as much as a priest! Any child under 14 could not commit a crime – the parents had to take the blame. This hasn't changed much 2,000 years later. If you skip school then your parents end up with a fine.

10 c) 'Arthur' meant 'Bear'. The other two nicknames are from the Dark, or Middle, Ages. Celt leader Vercingetorix meant 'Great leader of 100 battles' while a leader in Gaul was named Ambigatus meaning 'He who fights on two sides' ... which is a funny thing to do. If he was fighting on both sides he'd have to try to kill himself while at the same time try to stop himself being killed by himself. He could end up in more knots than a boy scout's tent-rope.

Cheerless children

You think school is bad? You'd probably prefer it to being a Celtic child. All work and very little play. From the time you could walk you'd be given jobs like weeding the fields, combing the wool ... and watching the fleas and lice jump out onto you as you comb. (That should keep you up to scratch!)

Sets of coloured glass counters, a little like modern marbles, have been found at Celtic sites. They seem to be from some board game a bit like Ludo. Unfortunately the

102

Celts were not great writers so there's no rule book with the counters and no one knows how the game was played.

Simple games *have* survived from the period and here's one you can try...

Knife–cloth–stone
You'll need:
• two players, preferably with at least one hand each.
All you do is:
1 On the count of three each player brings a hand out from behind their back. They have made a shape with that hand.
• A pointing finger is a knife.
• A spread hand is a cloth.
• A tight fist is a stone.
2 The winner is the one whose object can destroy the other player's. So...
• A knife beats a cloth because it can cut it.
• A stone beats a knife because it can blunt it.
• A cloth beats a stone because it can wrap around it.
3 A point is scored every time a player wins. The first to score 10 is the winner.

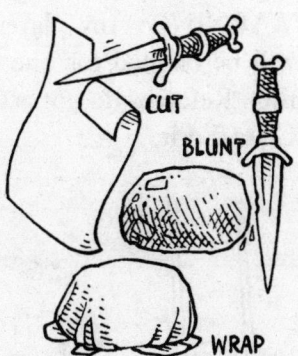

Hurley
The Irish have a rough form of hockey known to the Celts as 'hurley', and in modern Irish as 'hurling'.
You'll need:
• two teams of 15 players each with a hurling stick – like a hockey stick with a broad end

103

- two goals (like five-a-side soccer goals with extended uprights to make an 'H' shape)
- a hard ball like a rounders ball.

All you do is:

1 The aim is to score a 'Goal' – three points if it goes under the crossbar, one point over the crossbar but between the posts.

2 Play like hockey – except you can carry the ball on the hurling stick for as far as you want and you can catch the ball in the hand, but...

3 You can't pick up the ball from the ground in the hand, throw the ball or run with it in the hand more than two strides.

4 Horrible hurling: you are not allowed to use your stick to batter or trip an opponent ... but ancient warriors are said to have played this game with the head of an enemy. WARNING: Any player trying to play with a head today will be banned for one game (and probably locked up for life). Referees do not accept the excuse, 'But the cut-throat Celts did it.'

104

Baile

This game is a bit like team-golf.

You'll need:

- four or more players, each with a hockey stick and a ball
- a hole in the ground about a metre wide. (This may be difficult to dig in your school playground. A chalk circle may have to do!)

All you do is:

1 The aim is to hit the hole (or target circle) with a ball.

2 One player is the goalkeeper. He or she plays against the rest.

3 The team form a line facing the hole, at least 10 metres away. (This can be altered to more, or less, as you learn the game and want to make it more even.)

4 Team players strike a ball, one at a time, and try to hit the target. The goalkeeper tries to stop a ball hitting the target.

5 When everyone on the team has had a shot at the target then the score is counted – one point for a hit.

6 The team then defends the target while the goalkeeper takes a shot with each ball and tries to score more than the team.

A HOLE IN ONE

WHAP!

Note 1: A Celt story describes one boy playing in goal against 150 – he stopped every ball. When it was his turn to shoot he scored with every one of his 150 shots! As a modern hockey player he would be wanted by every team in the world!

Note 2: Pottery images of this game show that the players wore no clothes. You could try this if you wanted but you might be arrested by the police, who are not trained to understand Celtic laws.

Note 3: The images also appear to show the game being played with a head instead of a ball. You probably wouldn't want to use a head in your school yard because heads don't bounce as well as tennis balls. They just sort of hit the ground and go 'splatt!'

Did you know ... ?

- Boys and girls in Celt Ireland were sent away from home as soon as they were old enough – probably about seven. They went to live with a family in a neighbouring tribe. This taught them they belonged to the whole tribe and not just one father and mother. They stayed there until they were about 17 years old.
- The boys were not taught how to fight by the tribe's champion – he'd be far too busy. Instead they were often taught by women warriors.
- Girls married at the age of 12 to 14 and until then would be said to be 'beside her father's plate'.

Crime and punishment

The Celts may have seemed wild and lawless to the Romans but in fact they had their own type of law and order. The Druids took on special jobs. Some advised the people or the king, some acted as priests, some as fortune-tellers and some as judges. The judge-Druids were known as Brehons.

A Brehon settled arguments, listened to complaints and decided if there was a crime. The Brehon could also order punishments if he or she thought someone was guilty.

Trial by the gods
The Brehons could not always be sure of someone's guilt. There were no video surveillance cameras, no fingerprints, no blood tests and none of the scientific tests that today's police have. But the Brehons believed they had something better. A god who has seen everything!

All they had to do was leave the decision to chance – the god would make sure that chance pointed out the right victim. Why not try it and see if it works?

Casting the woods

This system was used by Druids in murder trials ... but we don't really want to murder someone just to test it ... no, not even the class bully deserves that.

You'll need:

● three people – one Brehon Judge, two suspects
● three pieces of wood – sticks from ice lollies would be perfect. (Yes, I know the Celts didn't have ice lollies – stop trying to be so clever and just get on with the trial, will you?) You will also need something to scratch words onto the sticks and a bag or hat to hide the sticks in.

All you do is:

1 Place a valuable object on a table – a watch, a jelly baby, the crown jewels ... anything.

2 The Brehon turns his or her back.

3 One of the suspects steals the valuable object and hides it on their person.

4 The Brehon then holds the 'casting-the-woods' trial...

I WRITE GUILTY ON ONE STICK, INNOCENT ON THE SECOND STICK AND TRINITY ON THE THIRD

YOU WILL EACH TAKE A STICK

INNOCENT!

PUT THE STICK BACK IN THE BAG, YOU ARE FREE TO GO

- If the Celt farmers discovered someone's animal had damaged a fence then who had the job of fixing the fence? The animal's owner, since cattle aren't very handy with a hammer. How will they decide whose beast did the damage? By casting the woods.

- And if a Celt accidentally hurt a bee then he had to pay the owner of the hive for the loss. Everyone had bees and hives. How did they know which hive the bee came from? No, they didn't have little rings around their bees' knees like pigeons. The Celts would cast the woods.

Why can't we just do this today? Two cars crash – who's to blame? Cast the woods! Two soccer teams are level after extra time in a cup match. Who goes on to the next round? Cast the woods! You need £5 to go to the cinema. Who should pay? Cast the woods – just make sure each wood has the letters D–A–D scratched on it!

Did you know … ?
Sometimes a Druid Judge decided that a whole family was to blame for the crime of one person. This would be a bit like your brother breaking a window … but the cost of repairing it is taken from your pocket money!

Make the punishment fit the crime
Here are five Celt crimes … if you were a judge, what would *you* do to the criminal found guilty?

CRIME

1 Deserting your tribe in battle

2 Calling a woman ugly

3 killing a woman who has run off with your husband

4 Burning a building down

5 Violent crime

Punishment

A Fined

B Exile

C Hanged from a tree

D Death by drowning

E no punishment

Answers:

1 c) Traitors and deserters were hanged from trees. Trees were particularly important to Celts because they were like a picture of life – roots in the underworld and branches in this world. Hanging sent a man straight to the Otherworld!

2 a) You were fined for insulting a woman's appearance, making up a nickname for them, making fun of some weakness they had or for telling an untrue story about them.

3 e) A woman who killed her husband's girlfriend could get her revenge in any way she wanted ... so long as she did it within three days of finding out about them. After three days she should have calmed down – any action then becomes a crime.

4 b) Celts believed that their land went as far as the ninth wave from the shore. Exiled criminals were set adrift with no oars or sail or steering paddle. They were given just a knife and some fresh water and left to the mercy of the gods. They usually died, but if they were swept back to the shore they became a slave.

In legends there were saints and heroes who survived this punishment and went on to do great deeds. In the real world it was a harsh sentence often given to women who murdered, or anyone who broke into a Christian Celt church.

5 d) Vicious criminals were sometimes drowned in swamps under a cover of wattle hurdles but this practice probably died out in the AD years. Drowning by trampling in a swamp also seems to have been a punishment for cowards and shirkers who left others to do all the work. So, next time your dad asks you to help with the washing up, make sure he's not a Celt before you refuse!

Did you know … ?

The Celts had a law against damaging trees. But your punishment depended on what sort of tree it was! You were in deep trouble if you harmed an oak, apple, ash, hazel, yew or fir tree. It was less serious if you damaged an alder, willow, birch or elm.

YOU'LL GET A FIR TRIAL!

WILLOW YEW NOT LET ME GO IF I ASH YOU NICELY?

Weird words

The Celts couldn't write because their religious leaders wouldn't let them. Those Druids believed that the written word meant power. They kept calendars (with a month counted off each time the moon appeared) and marked off what days were good for things like invading Rome or sacrificing a cow.

Eventually the Celts made an alphabet similar to the Vikings. It was made up of straight lines because these letters were carved onto stone or wood. Historians have been able to learn something of Celt life from these carvings. The Welsh alphabet had 30 letters and looked like this:

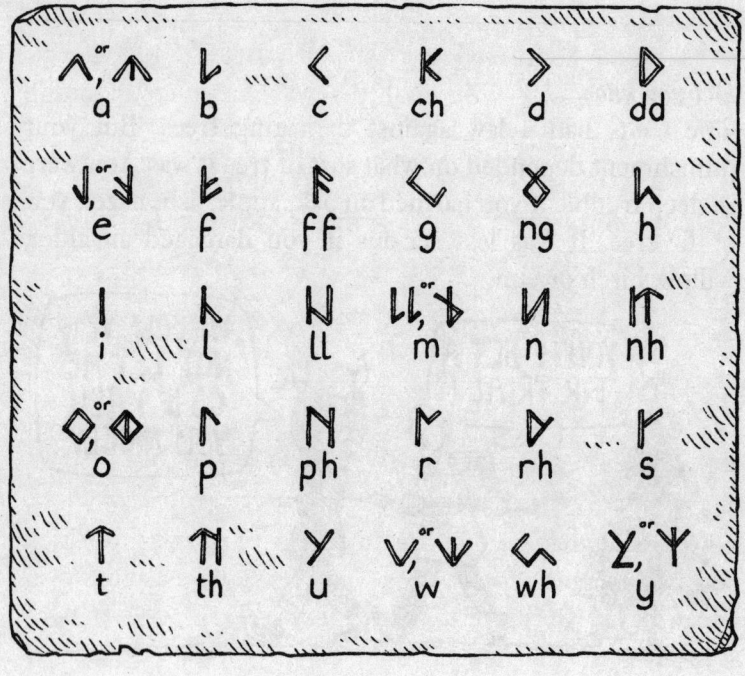

Being able to write is very useful. You can leave messages…

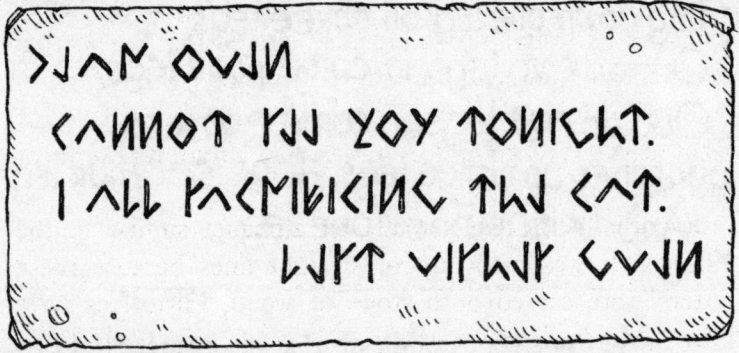

Rotten riddles

On the dark winter nights the Celts had no television to keep themselves amused. They were very fond of word games, though. In a room with just a fire it became a bit boring to do, 'I spy with my little eye something beginning with F.'

DON'T TELL ME, LET ME GUESS, COULD IT POSSIBLY BE PERHAPS, THAT YELLOWY FLICKERING HOT THINGY

So the Celts had a good line in riddles – puzzles to which you had to guess the answer. Could *you* be a Celt Clever Clogs and solve this one … ?

In come two legs carrying one leg,
Lay down one leg on three legs,
Out go two legs, in come four legs,
Out go five legs, in come two legs,
Snatches up three legs, flings it at four legs
And brings back one leg.

The awful thing about riddles is that the answer is so easy once it's explained! The longer you think about it the more satisfying it is to get the answer in the end. So, DO NOT read the answer for 24 hours! Go and read something else ... the Bible, the *Encyclopaedia Britannica*, your sister's diary – anything.

Answer:
Well? Did you guess it? If not, did you spend 24 hours trying? No? You should be ashamed of yourself. Here's the answer ... A woman (two legs) comes in carrying a leg of lamb (one leg) and puts it down on a stool (three legs). In comes a dog (four legs) and runs off with it. Now, even you can work out the ending from there!

Celtic compass

The Celts were skilful sailors and needed a good sense of direction. After all, they didn't want to sail over the edge of the world which (as we can all see) is flat. But the Celtic sailors didn't describe directions as North, South, East or West. They used colours. The sun rose in the 'purple' and by midday was in the 'white'. You too could become a geographical genius by learning this chart...

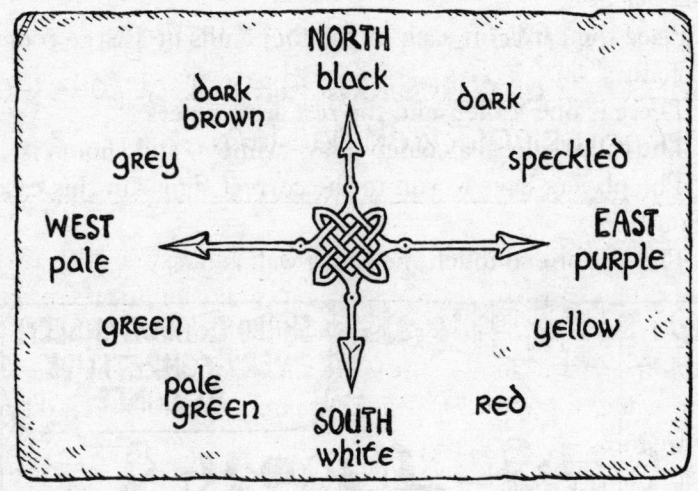

Celt compass games
Of course simply learning these directions is no fun. You have to use them. Try giving someone directions using the Celtic compass...

Game 1
You'll need:

- 10 or more players
- four signs saying North, South, East and West.

All you do is:

1 Place the cards on each of the four walls of a large room or hall.

2 There is one 'caller' and the rest are runners.

3 The caller selects a colour – say, 'white' – and shouts it.

4 The players have to run to the correct sign – in this case 'South'.

5 The last one to touch the south wall is out.

6 The game continues with one player dropping out each round. Obviously, the corners are the colours or shades between the main compass points. 'Dark' or 'Speckled' means north-east.

7 The winner is the last player in. Change callers and start again.

8 When the players are getting faster then add a new call … 'Cut-throat!' This means 'freeze'. Everyone who moves after the call is out.

Game 2

You'll need:

- at least two players
- a room full of obstructions (like chairs)
- a scarf for a blindfold.

All you do is:

1 The aim is for the leader to get the blindfolded partner safely across the room to a target without bumping, breaking or even touching an obstruction in between. (It would also be nice if the blindfolded partner does not break a leg.)

2 The leader must talk the partner through the obstacles but can only use the Celt compass to do so.

THERE'S NO SUCH COLOUR AS GREENISH PURPLE!

3 'Black' becomes straight ahead, 'White' is backwards, 'Purple' is right and 'Pale' is left. 'Dark Brown' is a little to the left and 'Grey' is more to the left and so on.

4 The leader cannot use the word 'Stop' (or left, right, ahead or back) but they can add the word 'Cut-throat!' meaning 'Stop!'

5 Score 10 for a clear run to the target; deduct a point for every obstacle touched.

6 Change the blindfold to the leader and try again. The winner is the one with the highest score as leader.

7 If there is more than one pair, then the pairs can race from one end of the room to the other. Touching any obstacle means the pair must go back to the start.

8 The winner is the pair to reach the far-wall first. In the event of a tie the winner is the blindfolded partner with the fewest broken bones.

Sadly, the Celtic compass has died out. Otherwise we'd have had cowboys riding the range in the Wild Pale and polar bears at the Black Pole.

Manchester in the Grey of England (that sounds right) would be playing soccer against Pale Ham while you'd expect to see a lot of heather on the Purple coast of Scotland or buttercups in the Yellow part of Wales.

But what would we be eating two days after Good Friday? Purple-er eggs? Yeuch!

Did you know … ?
In travelling it is considered unlucky to travel anti-clockwise? The superstitious Celts always made sure they travelled in the same direction as the sun – clockwise or 'deosil' as they called it.

Want to get good marks in that test? Then walk round the

desk deosil before you sit down. Want that horrible history teacher to fall out of bed? Walk round his car 'widdershins' (that's anti-clockwise).

Remember that the number three is lucky for Celts and nine (that's three-threes) is magical. But walking round that desk nine times would probably make you too dizzy to see the exam paper!

Epilogue

Hopeless history

The Romans were horrible historians who tried to give the Celts a bad name. But for 1500 years every other historian has repeated the same 'fact'...

The Romans never reached Ireland

(Check your school history books and you're bound to find it there somewhere.)

How do the hopeless historians know the Romans never reached Ireland? Because the Romans never said they reached Ireland. This is not the same as the Romans saying they never reached Ireland.

DID YOU SAY YOU REACHED IRELAND OR DIDN'T YOU?!

I'M NOT SAYING

And now the truth can be told at last...

THE ROMANS REACHED IRELAND

The history books are all wrong ... except this one, of course, but we don't like to boast!

THE HERALD

CELTIC MYTH DESTROYED

MYTH DESTROYED HERE!

A dull piece of land near Dublin holds the key to a Celtic mystery that has lasted for nearly 2,000 years. A team of archaeologists have announced that they've been investigating a 40-acre patch of ground about 15 miles north of Dublin. The spot, called Drumanagh, is the site of a Roman coastal fort. Earth walls and ditches show where the fort was – coins, ornaments and jewellery show that Romans lived there. Coins of emperors Titus, Trajan and Hadrian show the Romans lived in Ireland from at least AD 79 till AD 138 and historians never knew … till now.

The fort has been described as the most important find in Irish history. But here's the really strange thing. The archaeologists knew the secret of the site in the 1980s and kept it hidden for over 10 years while they worked on it! Meanwhile thousands of children in hundreds of schools have been told, 'The Romans never reached Ireland.' Huh! Historians!

Could *you* keep the 'most important find in Irish history' a secret for over 10 years? The coins and valuables went to the National Museum of Ireland where they were hidden away. The archaeologists, historians and museum staff hid the truth from us. It makes you wonder what else historians know that they won't tell us? Is Adolf Hitler still alive? Did King Arthur really exist? Did King Henry I have his brother murdered? Did Humpty Dumpty fall off the wall … or was he pushed?

STARTLING NEW EVIDENCE HAS COME TO LIGHT SUGGESTING THE BRICKS AT THE VERY TOP OF THE WALL MAY HAVE BEEN TAMPERED WITH

One day we may have answers to all of these questions…

The Celt comeback

The trouble with the Celts is they didn't bother to write much. So a lot of the things we hear about them were written by their enemies – people like the Romans. Would you trust *your* enemy to write good things about you?

Other things were written by people who did not approve of the Celts – people like the monks of the Middle Ages. The monks were Christian and the old Celts were not. You're not going to get a good school report from a teacher who doesn't approve of you!

Still the Roman writers seemed to respect these wild, strange people. Lucretius wrote…

> *And this race of people from the plains were as hard as the hard land they came from; they were built on firmer, stronger bones and given mighty muscles. They were a race unafraid of the heat or the cold, of the plague or of strange foods. For many years they led their lives among the beasts of the earth and were not tamed.*

But the people who were 'tamed' – the Romans – were able to defeat these heroic people. A Greek writer, Strabo, claimed that their fearless nature made them easy to outwit…

> *The Celt race is madly fond of war and quick to do battle. Otherwise they are honest and not evil characters. And so when they are stirred up they assemble in their bands for battle, quite openly and without careful planning. As a result they are easily handled by those who want to outwit them. For the Celts are always ready to face danger, even if they have nothing on their side but their own strength and courage.*

Strength and courage and honesty were not enough and as the years went by the Celts were driven back from the richest countries by enemies with more cunning and greed.

Of course, Strabo also pointed out that the Celts had some horrible historical habits…

> There are also other accounts of their human sacrifices; for they used to shoot men down with arrows, or making a large statue of straw and wood, throw into it cattle and all sorts of wild animals and human beings and thus make a burnt offering.

WOOF WOOF

BAAA BAAA

But at least the Celts left behind many good things they made and we know they were great artists. They also left behind their ancestors who still live in Ireland, Scotland, Brittany (France) and Cornwall (England). And though the spiky, dyed hair is gone some of the mystic powers seem to remain in some of them.

It's sad that the cunning and greedy have taken the world from the honest and courageous. Maybe one day a leader will appear who will lead the world back to the ways of courage and honesty. Maybe his name will be … Arthur! It would be nice to think so. It's something to hope for, anyway.

CUT-THROAT CELTS

GRISLY QUIZ

**Now find out if you're a
Cut-throat Celts expert!**

It's a Curious Celtic Life...

So – reckon you know all about this terrible tribe, with all their curious customs and peculiar practices? Take this quick quiz and find out.

1. England was created when the Angles and the Saxons took over the south-east of Britain in AD 520. What did they call their new land?
a) Angle-land
b) Saxonia
c) Engal-land

2. What was the name of the largest Celt tribe that fought the Romans?
a) Celtics
b) Gauls
c) Zulus

3. Why did the Celts cut off people's heads in battle?
a) They believed that they gained their enemy's wisdom and strength
b) They wanted to look down their enemy's throats
c) They wanted to eat them

4. Kissing under the mistletoe is a Celtic tradition, but the Celts only believed the mistletoe was magical when...
a) It was cut on the first day of July under a full moon
b) It was cut by a Druid using a gold sickle
c) It was plucked from a bough by a magpie

5. The Celts believed that the Druids had magical powers, but which of the following was not a Druid power?

a) Changing the weather
b) Time-travelling
c) Flying

6. The Celts believed in sacrificing people to keep their gods happy. How was the practice of 'death by air' carried out?
a) The victim was suffocated
b) The victim was strangled
c) The victim was hung

7. The first Celts lived during the Iron Age. Did this mean that...
a) They were good at getting the creases out of their favourite tunics
b) They used iron for making tools and weapons
c) They used iron bars for money

8. If you were round at a Celt's house and you smelt cedar oil coming from a chest, what would you find inside?
a) Nice-smelling blankets
b) Christmas presents
c) Heads

BONKERS BELIEFS

The Celts were a crazy bunch. If you met one on the street and they told you the following facts, would you believe them? See if you can tell the troublesome truth from the foolish fiction.

1. 'I've just thrown my favourite sheep off the cliff so the gods will bless me with more sheep.'

2. 'Can't stop. I'm off to get my nails done.'

3. 'My best friend just died, so I'm off round his place for a good cry.'

4. 'Would you mind holding my clothes while I nip off and fight a battle?'

5. 'Hang on … Just remembered. I'm not fighting today – I spotted a crane earlier.'

6. 'We've spent all year growing corn, and now that we've harvested it we're going to bury it.'

7. 'I'm off to help St Brannoc build a church because he found a cow and her calf there – and that's magic he says.'

8. 'I've just turned sixteen so I've been turfed out of me mum and dad's and made to live with another family.

COULD YOU BE A CELT?

Now you've found out all about Celts, how do you think you'd fare in the evil Iron Age? Take this quiz and find out if the Celts would welcome you as a warrior or sacrifice you by suffocation…

1. The Celts bathed every day, but would you be able to play with your rubber duck in peace? (Clue: It's a family affair)

2. You know all about Halloween, of course, but what would you do on 31 October if you were a Celt? (Clue: It's not a trick question)

3. If you were a Celtic sailor, what do you think would keep you from drowning? (Clue: A bird in the hand…)

4. If you were involved in a game of hurling with some ancient warriors, what would you use as a ball? (Clue: Use your head!)

5. You'd have to learn to fight fiercely, but who'd be teaching you? (Clue: Dress-ed to kill)

6. The Celts were good at finding their way around. They used a compass with colours to show direction. If you were off in a purple direction, which way would you be heading? (Clue: Into the sunrise)

7. Playing apple-bobbing on Halloween, you see a girl stick the apple pips on her face. What on Earth is she doing? (Clue: It's a horrible husband Halloween habit)

8. If a Celtic woman asked you to pick her up some make-up, where would you go? (Clue: It's a *berry* simple question…)

Answers

It's a Curious Celtic Life…
1a) They called it Angle-land, which eventually became England.
2b) Roman Ammianus Marcellinus noted that the Gauls were fierce, argued a lot and were proud.
3a) They believed that a person's power was all in their head – even if they were dead!
4b) They believed that the oak tree was holy and the mistletoe that grew on it had magical powers
5c) Druids could also (they said) change their shape to anything they wanted and bring down mists to make themselves invisible … but they couldn't fly.
6a,b or c) Sacrificing to the God of air was carried out by suffocation, as well as hanging and strangulation.
7b) Iron was the magnificent metal of this era and was used for all sorts of things – tools, pots, jewellery – you name it.
8c) The Celts liked to keep heads as trophies, and would preserve them in cedar oil.

Bonkers Beliefs
1. True – the Celts believed that by sacrificing animals the gods would look favourably on them.
2. True – wealthy Celts were big on manicures!

3. False – when somebody died the Celts threw a big party and had a right old laugh!

4. True – the Celts often fought naked, probably to scare their opponents. Not the wisest thing to do in the winter…

5. True – seeing a crane (the bird not the lifting machine) was unlucky, they thought, and Celtic warriors used it as an excuse to pack up and go home!

6. Totally true – it seems like a daft idea, but placing the grain in the ground it kept it fresh until it was needed.

7. Almost true – St B built a church on the site where he found a sow and her piglets, not a cow. He was told to build it in a dream.

8. False – he would have been moved out at the age of seven! This was meant to teach Celtic kids that they were part of a tribe, not just a family.

Could you be a Celt?

1. Not a chance. Better hope you were part of a small family as you'd all have to share your time in the tub.

2. You'd dress in a scary costume to ward off the spirits. No trick or treating, though.

3. A feather from a wren – especially if the feather had come from a bird that had been killed on New Year's Day.

4. Chances are you'd be throwing round the head of one of your enemies. Don't try this at school…

5. A woman – the men were too busy so the women taught fighting.

6. You'd be heading east (as long as you weren't colour blind).

7. She'd be trying to find out the name of her future husband. She'd name each of the pips and the last to fall off would be the name of the person she was going to marry.

8. No – not the local supermarket! You'd go to the woods. The juice from herbs and berries was used as make-up.

INTERESTING INDEX

Where will you find 'bad breath',
'inspecting entrails' and 'underpants' in an index?
In a Horrible Histories book, of course!

138

Terry Deary was born at a very early age, so long ago he can't remember. But his mother, who was there at the time, says he was born in Sunderland, north-east England, in 1946 – so it's not true that he writes all *Horrible Histories* from memory. At school he was a horrible child only interested in playing football and giving teachers a hard time. His history lessons were so boring and so badly taught, that he learned to loathe the subject. *Horrible Histories* is his revenge.

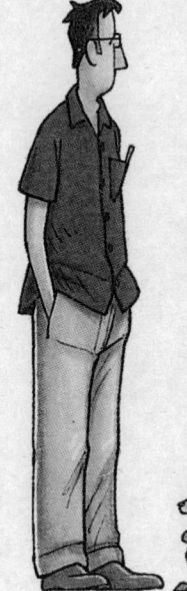

Martin Brown was born in Melbourne, on the proper side of the world. Ever since he can remember he's been drawing. His dad used to bring back huge sheets of paper from work and Martin would fill them with doodles and little figures. Then, quite suddenly, with food and water, he grew up, moved to the UK and found work doing what he's always wanted to do: drawing doodles and little figures.

HORRIBLE HISTORIES

ROTTEN
ROMANS

Terry Deary Illustrated by **Martin Brown**

■SCHOLASTIC

With thanks to Helen James for her research.
Sine qua non

Scholastic Children's Books,
Euston House, 24 Eversholt Street,
London NW1 1DB, UK

A division of Scholastic Ltd
London ~ New York ~ Toronto ~ Sydney ~ Auckland
Mexico City ~ New Delhi ~ Hong Kong

First published in the UK by Scholastic Ltd, 1994
This edition published by Scholastic Ltd, 2016

Some of the material in this book has previously been published in
Horrible Histories: The Awesome Ancient Quiz Book

Text © Terry Deary, 1994, 2001
Illustration © Martin Brown, 1994, 2001, 2016

ISBN 978 1407 16384 0

Printed and bound by CPI Group (UK) Ltd, Croydon, CR0 4YY

10

www.scholastic.co.uk

CONTENTS

Introduction

History can be horrible. Horribly hard to learn. The trouble is it keeps on *changing*. In maths, two and two is *usually* four – and in science water is *always* made up of hydrogen and oxygen.

But in history things aren't that simple. In history a "fact" is sometimes not a fact at all. Really it's just someone's "opinion". And opinions can be different for different people.

For example . . . you probably think your teacher is more horrible than the cold cabbage and custard you had for school dinner. That's *your* opinion. But teacher's mum probably thinks he's sweeter than tea with six sugars. That's *her* opinion.

You could both be right – or both be wrong . . .

See what I mean? Both right, both wrong!

Of course, honest answers like these don't get you gold stars. No! Teachers will try to tell you there are "right" and "wrong" answers even if there aren't.

There are worse things than horrible history. Want to know what? Teachers' jokes are more horrible than the Tower of London Torture Chamber . . .

So, history can be horrible. But when you find the real truth about the past you can suddenly discover it's horribly fascinating. Everyone loves a good murder story – history is full of them, like the murder of Julius Caesar. Blood all over the place.

And there are war stories, thrillers, horror stories and comedies. That's the sort of history you'll find in this book. With a bit of luck you might even horrify your teacher!

Terrible timelines

The rotten Romans' timeline

BC

753 Roman *legend* says Rome was founded by Romulus. The *truth* is that the early Romans were farmers living in a region called Latium.

509 The Romans are fed up with their cruel king, Tarquin. They throw him out and rule themselves (that's called a Republic).

264 First of the Punic Wars against the great enemy, Carthage (in North Africa). Result: Rome 1 Carthage 0.

218 Hannibal of Carthage attacks Rome with the help of elephants. He can't capture Rome but rampages round Italy terrorising people.

202 Scipio takes charge of the Roman Army and beats Hannibal. Rome 2 Carthage 0. The Roman farmers take over more and more land till they have the whole of Italy.

146 Third War to wipe Carthage out forever. Game, set and match to Rome! The Romans get to like the idea of conquering people! They start on the rest of the world.

130 By now the Romans have conquered Greece and most of Spain.

100 Julius Caesar is born.

59 Julius Caesar becomes Consul for the first time.

55 Julius Caesar invades Britain for the first time because (he says) **a)** the Belgae of south Britain are helping the Gauls of north France to rebel against the Romans, and **b)** there is a wealth of tin, copper and lead to be found in Britain.

44 Julius Caesar is elected dictator for life – then murdered!

AD

43 Claudius gives orders for the invasion of Britain . . . again!

60 One tribe, the Iceni, rebel. Queen Boudicca leads them in massacres of Romans. Roman

General Paulinus defeats her and she poisons herself.

80 Julius Agricola completes the invasion (except for the Picts in Scotland).

84 Agricola beats the Picts at Mons Graupius in Scotland.

122 Hadrian starts building a wall across northern England to keep out the Picts.

235–285 Fifty-year period with over 20 Roman emperors – mainly because they keep getting murdered.

313 Emperor Constantine allows Christian worship.

380 Christianity becomes official religion of Rome.

401 Roman troops are being withdrawn from Britain to defend Rome.

410 Barbarian tribes from Germany begin attacks on the empire and Rome itself.

476 The last Roman emperor of the western empire is forced to retire.

1453 The empire of the east falls to the Turks. End of the Roman Empire.

The battling Britons' timeline

BC

6500 The Ice Age ends, the sea level rises. The north-west corner of Europe is cut off by the sea. The British Isles are formed. The islanders are Britons.

3600 The Britons build Stonehenge.

2150 Tin is discovered in the south-west. Mixed with copper it makes the hardest metal yet known to humans – bronze.

900 Britons make human and animal sacrifices at Peterborough.

600 Iron takes over from bronze for making weapons and tools.

70 Druids are becoming powerful leaders of the Britons.

55 Julius Caesar invades but doesn't stay for long.

AD

10 Britain independent from Rome but some British leaders like to copy Roman way of life.

10

30 The rich south-east of Britain under one ruler – Cunobelinus – who gives himself the Roman name of "Rex", meaning "King".

41 Cunobelinus dies; his sons Togodumnus and Caratacus take over. They're not so keen on the Romans.

42 Verica (king of the Atribates in southern England) is thrown out by his people because he is friendly with Rome. (Caratacus was stirring them up!) Verica flees to Rome and asks for Roman help.

43 The Romans invade and Togodomnus is killed after a battle at the River Medway.

51 After years of resistance Caratacus is betrayed and handed over to the Romans in chains.

60 Queen of the Iceni in East Anglia, Boudicca, leads a rebellion against the Romans and is defeated. The Romans also destroy the Druid sanctuary in Anglesey.

122 Emperor Hadrian's wall is begun, to stop the Picts and Scots invading England.

125 Britons are encouraged to join the Roman Army – and become Roman citizens when they retire.

213 *All* free Britons become Roman citizens – but Roman citizens pay Roman taxes!

367 As the Roman Empire weakens, the attacks on Hadrian's Wall increase.

405 As the Romans leave, their way of life leaves soon after – Roman coins are replaced by the ancient custom of bartering.

410 The Emperor Honorius tells the Britons, "Defend yourselves," as the Irish, the Picts, the Scots and the Saxons (from north Germany) begin to raid Britain.

420 Saxons begin to settle in eastern Britain.

443 Plagues in the towns help drive people back to the old British ways of country living.

446 The British appeal to Rome for help against the Saxons. No help arrives. The days of Roman Britain are over. The Saxons have the rich south-east. The Britons have to make do with the poor, wild north and west.

21 Terrible Tribes

KEY
1 DAMNONII
2 VOTADINI
3 SELGOVAE
4 NOVANTAE
5 BRIGANTES
6 PARISI
7 ORDOVICES
8 CORNOVII
9 CORITANI
10 ICENI
11 DEMETAE
12 DOBUNNI
13 CATUVELLAUNI
14 TRINOVANTES
15 SILURES
16 ATREBATES
17 BELGAE
18 CANTIACI
19 REGNENSES
20 DUROTRIGES
21 DUMNONII

The rotten Roman Army

The Roman Army didn't run all of Roman Britain. Once they'd won the battles they moved on to fight somewhere else. Towns were built in the conquered territories with Roman lords in charge. Just in case the Britons felt like revolting, the Romans let retired Roman soldiers settle in the land outside the towns – a circle of trusted men to warn of danger. And, if the beaten Brits *did* give trouble then the army could get back quickly to help by marching along the new Roman roads.

Your teachers will tell you all about the legions and what they wore and how they lived. But they don't know everything.

Test your teacher . . .

Ask your teacher these questions. Can they get more than 5 out of 10? Can you?

If you were a Roman soldier . . .

1 What would you wear under your leather kilt?

a nothing

b underpants

c fig leaves

2 Where would
you drive on
the Roman roads?
a on the right
b down the centre
c on the left

3 How long would you have to stay in the army once you joined?

a 25 years

b 5 years

c the rest of your life

I'M A CENTURIAN CENTURIAN

4 Who could you marry?

a anyone

b no one

c a Roman

5 Who paid for your uniform, weapons, food and burial?

a the emperor

b they were free

c you paid for them yourself out of your wages

6 How tall did you have to be?

a over 1.8 metres

b between 1.6 and 1.8 metres

c under 1.6 metres

7 What would you use instead of toilet paper?

a a sponge on the end of a stick, dipped in cold water

b your tunic

c the daily newspaper

8 Your spear (pilum) had a 60 cm metal head that would snap off after it hit something. Why?

a so the enemy couldn't pick up the spear and throw it back

b so you could put the metal head in your pocket when you were marching

c because the Roman armourers couldn't make the heads stay on

9 Why was one Roman Centurion called "Give me another"?

a because he liked his soldiers to sing as they marched. When they'd finished one song he'd call out, "Give me another!"

b because he was greedy. After eating a pig's head he'd cry out, "Give me another!"

c because he cruelly beat his soldiers so hard he smashed his canes and had to call out, "Give me another!"

10 Why would the army doctor not notice your screams as he treated your wounds?

a because he enjoyed making you suffer

b because he was trained to carry on without paying attention to a soldier's cries

c because the Romans only employed deaf men as doctors

Answers: 1b. 2c (But they often barged straight down the middle of town streets in their chariots. They marched there too, tramp-ling anyone who got in the way with their hob-nailed boots!). 3a. 4b (But they often had wives outside of the camp). 5c. 6b (But this rule was sometimes broken when the army was desperate for men . . . and the men who were too small might still have to work for the army even if they couldn't fight). 7a (And you'd share it with everyone else in the public toilets! Some-times you'd use a lump of moss, though, and that would be flushed away). 8a. 9c. 10b.

The rottenly clever Roman Army

The Romans were the best army in the ancient world because they used something their enemies didn't. The Romans used their brains! Are you as brainy?

Here are some problems the Romans overcame. What would you have done if you'd faced these problems . . .

1 Julius Caesar had a land army in Gaul (northern France). When the Veneti tribe there rebelled, they captured two Roman messengers and sailed off with them. Caesar quickly had ships built and followed. The Veneti were excellent sailors but poor fighters. Caesar needed a weapon that would stop the Veneti ships from sailing off while Roman soldiers climbed aboard. There was no gunpowder (for cannon or bullets). What simple (but very successful) weapon did the Romans make?

2 After the British Queen Boudicca was beaten, the Romans were able to move into the fenlands of East Anglia. The grass was rich but the land was very wet. If the Romans tried to wade through the swamps, the local tribes ambushed them. Then a new general arrived from Italy's Pontine marshes. He showed the soldiers how to get through swamps without wading up to their waists in water. What did he teach them?

3 In the early days of the Roman Republic, the Romans came up against the Greek king, Pyrrhus. The Greek strategy was to go into battle led by elephants. The elephants would charge at the Romans, trample them and send them running. But the Romans learned quickly. At the battle of Beneventum they found a way to face an elephant charge . . . and win! What would *you* do?

4 Some of the young men in the conquered lands did not want to fight in the Roman Army. It meant leaving their homes, farms and families to fight (and maybe die) in some distant corner of the world. The young men cut off the thumb of their right hand so they couldn't hold a sword. If they couldn't hold a sword then they wouldn't be expected to fight in the Roman Army. The Roman generals realised that all of these thumbless young men were trying to outwit them. What was their solution?

5 One day, Emperor Hadrian went to the public baths where his skin was carefully cleaned by slaves with scrapers. He saw an old man rubbing his back against a column. The old man was one of Hadrian's old soldiers. Hadrian asked why he was rubbing himself against the marble. The old man said it was because he couldn't afford a slave with a scraper. Hadrian gave the man slaves and money. BUT . . . next day the public baths were full of old men rubbing their backs against the marble! They were obviously scrounging for a Hadrian handout! What would you do if you were Hadrian?

18

Answers:

1 The Romans attached hooked knives onto the ends of long poles. As they neared the Veneti ships, the Romans slashed the enemy ropes and sails to stop them sailing. They then climbed aboard the Veneti boats and overpowered the sailors. The leaders were executed and the sailors sold for slavery.

2 How to use stilts! They were a great success at first. Eventually the tribes of the fens learned to knock the Romans off the stilts and stab them as they fell. Ah, well, it seemed like a brilliant idea at the time!

3 The Roman front line split in two. The elephants charged harmlessly through the line. They were too clumsy for the drivers to stop and turn. The helpless riders just kept going to the back of the Roman Army, where there were special troops waiting with long, sharp spears. They jabbed the elephants until the maddened creatures turned round and charged back again. The elephants flattened the Greek army, who weren't expecting them!

4 Cut off their heads! Anyone trying to avoid army service was sentenced to death. The young men soon learned this new law and decided to fight – possible death in war was better than certain death by execution. The Romans also branded or tattooed unwilling soldiers – if the soldier deserted, then he would have trouble hiding the fact that he was supposed to be in the army.

5 Hadrian simply told the old men to rub each other!

Make the punishment fit the crime

If you think punishments at school are hard, then how would you like to have been in the Roman Army? The barbarian armies charged at the Romans like bulls at a matador – and we know who usually wins *that* contest. The Roman Army had "discipline". They did what they were told, every time. And if they didn't do as they were told – no matter how small the offence – they had to be punished. Try to guess which crime earned which punishment . . .

CRIME	PUNISHMENT
I LAZINESS	A. DECIMATION OF A UNIT – I MAN IN EVERY X IS EXECUTED
II FALLING ASLEEP ON DUTY	B. SLEEP OUTSIDE THE SAFETY OF THE CAMP
III RUNNING AWAY IN A BATTLE	C. GET THE WORST FOOD – ROUGH BARLEY INSTEAD OF GOOD CORN
IV PUTTING YOUR UNIT IN DANGER	D. DEATH BY BEATING
V RUNNING AWAY WITH YOUR UNIT	E. DEATH BY STONING

20

Let the reward fit the action

Of course there were *good* sides to being a Roman soldier too – otherwise no one would have wanted to join the army! The goodies were . . .

1 The army took two parts of every seven you earned in wages and saved it for you. When you retired they gave you all your savings and a piece of land. You could retire in comfort . . . if you lived long enough.

2 You could make extra wealth by robbing the countries you defeated. You could take money, animals or even living prisoners that you could sell for slaves.

3 For brave actions there were no medals – there were crowns:

a a crown of oak leaves – for saving the life of a fellow citizen (Caesar won one at Mytilene when he was just 20 years old)

b a crown of plaited grass – for rescuing an army under siege

c a crown of gold – for being the first soldier over the wall of an enemy town

Don't get sick!

Roman doctors knew how to . . .

BUT – Roman doctors didn't know about anaesthetics (to put you to sleep while they hacked you about!).

Roman doctors could make medicines to cure sickness.

BUT – they had to mix them with honey to try to disguise the disgusting tastes.

Did you know?

A Roman legionary always went into battle with a first-aid kit of bandages and healing herbs?

The cut-throat Celts

The Britons were part of the Celtic peoples. At one time the Celts had roamed round the world as much as the Romans did. One man put an end to all that – the Roman emperor, Julius Caesar.

The Celts used to fight fiercely for their tribal chiefs. But the tribes often fought *against* each other when they should have been fighting *together* against Julius Caesar. They needed one strong leader to bring them all together. But when that leader arrived it was too late.

Vercingetorix was a Celtic chief who was just as clever as Caesar at fighting and leading. Would you have been as clever as Vercingetorix? Here are some of the problems he faced. Could you have solved them?

Vercingetorix v Caesar

1 You meet the chiefs of the tribes every day to plan your war against Caesar. One of the chiefs argues against you. What do you do about him?

a Say to him, "Look, my friend, we must all stick together if we want to beat the rotten Romans. So, please, trust me. Remember, united we stand but divided we fall."

b Get upset. Say, "If you're going to argue with me you can find yourselves another leader. I'll fight Caesar by myself. When I've beaten him I'll beat you next. You'll be sorry!"

c Don't get upset. Simply have his ears cut off and one of his eyes gouged out. Send him back to his tribe with the message, "This is what you get if you mess with Vercingetorix!"

2 Caesar is a long way from home and a long way from fresh supplies. The Romans need food for the soldiers and their horses. They are getting it from the Celtic towns in the region of the Bituriges tribe. What can you do to stop them?

a Tell the Bituriges' chief to burn his towns to the ground and send his people to live with other tribes.
b Tell the Bituriges' chief to destroy all the food in the towns but let the people stay.
c Tell the Bituriges' chief to burn his towns to the ground but move all the people to the capital city of Avaricum.

3 Your tactics are working. Caesar is getting desperate for food. He sets off for Avaricum, which is the region's grain depot. How can you defend Avaricum against Caesar's army?
a Build a wooden wall.
b Build a stone wall with a ditch in front.
c Build a brick wall.

4 Caesar begins to build towers on wheels to push up to the walls. When these towers reach the walls the Romans will let down a drawbridge at the top and swarm over your walls. What can you do?
a Build an even taller tower behind your walls and throw down fireballs on top of them.
b Leave the town and attack Caesar's towers.
c Run away.

5 Caesar cannot get the towers near the walls because there is a ditch in front of the walls. He sends soldiers into the forest to chop down trees. He rolls the logs into the ditch and begins to fill it up.

What can you do to stop the Romans filling the ditch?

a Dig a tunnel under your walls and set fire to the logs?

b Surrender.

c Send a raiding party out to steal the Roman axes so they can't chop down any more trees.

6 The Romans manage to get towers up to the walls. You would like to set fire to them but the clever Romans have covered them with leather, which doesn't catch fire very easily. What can you throw at them instead?

a dead horses

b boiling fat and tar

c cold water.

7 Despite your efforts the Romans reach the walls. They catch hold of the top of the wall with hooks, and swarm up the ropes attached to the hooks. What's the best defence against this?

a Throw the hooks back.

b Pull the hooks up and drag them inside your fort.

c Wait for the Romans to climb them and try to kill them as they reach the top.

8 During the Roman assault it begins to rain heavily. What do your defenders do?
a Run for shelter until the rain stops and hope the Romans do the same.
b Fight on and get wet.
c Ask the Romans for a cease-fire until the weather improves.

9 The Romans reach the streets of Avaricum. They begin slaughtering every man, woman and child in sight. What should Vercingetorix do?
a Give himself up.
b Fight to the death.
c Make sure his best fighting men escape through a back entrance.

10 Vercingetorix reaches the safety of Alesia. The Romans are following. You have a large army. What should you do with it?
a Send most of the army away to gather help from other Celtic tribes and keep just a few to defend Alesia.
b Keep all the soldiers in Alesia and hope that help will arrive.
c Leave the army in Alesia and go for help yourself?

Vercingetorix's ten steps to Rome, or, Answers:

1 Vercingetorix could not afford to show any weakness or he'd be killed by the other Celtic chiefs. He could not plead (**1a**) or sulk (**1b**). He had to show he meant business and would make an example of anyone who opposed him (**1c**).

2 Vercingetorix made just one mistake. He couldn't destroy the supplies and leave the people in the towns (**2b**) – the warriors would not have fought if they knew the Romans had captured their wives and children. He should have destroyed the supplies AND the towns (**2a**). If you chose **2a** then you'd have been a crueller but better leader than Vercingetorix! But the Bituriges were proud of Avaricum. They pleaded with Vercingetorix not to destroy it. He weakened and agreed (**2c**). From then on he was pretty well doomed.

3 Vercingetorix had fought the Romans for years and knew their way of fighting. They would have simply burned a wooden wall (**3a**) and battered down a brick wall (**3c**). The best wall was a solid stone wall with a ditch in front (**3b**).

4 Caesar wasn't put out by the solid walls of Avaricum. He began building towers. Vercingetorix expected this and didn't give up (**4c**). Of course, he didn't leave the safety of the town and attack the Romans in open battle (**4b**) because that's exactly what they wanted. He just ordered bigger towers to be built behind his own walls (**4a**).

5 Caesar could defeat the ditch by filling it with

new logs. Vercingetorix couldn't stop him (5c) but didn't let it beat him (5b). The Bituriges were good iron miners and so could dig shafts. They dug one under the Roman logs and set fire to them (5a). This delayed the Roman attack ... but failed to stop it.

6 The Celtic soldiers knew that the only thing that would slow down the Roman towers wasn't anything solid (6a), but liquid, which would run through the joins in the Roman "umbrella". Cold water wasn't going to hurt them (6c) but boiling tar and oil would. This is what they did (6b).

7 The Romans were determined – and getting hungrier! They began to use grappling hooks to climb the walls. There was no point in throwing them back (7a) because the Romans would just try again at another spot. No one had been able to stop the Romans by trying to kill them at the

top (**7c**) because there were just too many of them. Clever Vercingetorix devised the plan of hauling up the hooks and taking away the Roman weapons (**7b**)!

8 When a rain-storm hit Avaricum, all of Vercingetorix's cleverness was undone by the stupidity of his men. They should have fought on (**8b**). The Romans wouldn't let some rain stop them (**8c**) and it was no use expecting them to. The defenders ran for shelter (**8a**). The Romans leapt over the walls.

HEY! WHERE DID EVERYBODY GO?

9 Vercingetorix knew that the battle for Avaricum was lost, but the war wasn't. He wasn't going to give up (**9a**). On the other hand there was no point in waiting to be killed (**9b**) when there were new Celtic armies waiting to fight. All he had to do was to escape with the soldiers and fight again (**9c**). Unfortunately, the women who were being left behind to be massacred didn't like the idea. Not surprising really! They began wailing and screaming. This gave the escape plan away to the Romans and they hurried to cut off the escape route. The Romans massacred 40,000 Avaricum people. Only Vercingetorix and 800 others escaped to fight another day.

10 Vercingetorix reached the safety of Alesia with a new large army. If he'd tried to keep the army with him (**10b**) they'd have eaten the supplies in no time and starved to death before help arrived. He couldn't get to all the dozens of tribes himself to get help (**10c**) so he sent his troops to different Celtic tribes and kept just enough to defend the town (**10a**).

It almost worked. A huge Celtic army arrived. But the Romans had built a ring of defences round the town. The soldiers in Alesia couldn't get out. The new Celtic army couldn't get in. They gave up and went away.

Vercingetorix was trapped. He gave himself up to his own people and said they could do what they needed. The Romans wanted Vercingetorix alive – that was how the Celts delivered him. In 45 BC he was paraded through the streets of Rome . . . then executed. The Celts on the continent were crushed. They survived mainly in the islands off the shores of Europe. The British Islands. If Caesar wanted to finish them off, then he had to invade Britain . . . which he did.

That's why it's thought that the defeat of Vercingetorix led to the Roman invasion of Britain! If Vercingetorix had only destroyed Avaricum (as in **2a**) then we might never have had a Roman Britain!

Heads you win, heads you lose

Heads were popular with the Celtic race to which the Britons belonged. Here are ten horrible brainless facts . . .

1 In 500 BC, the British tribespeople believed that the head had magical powers. They thought that severed heads could utter prophecies and warnings, especially if they were in groups of three.

2 Rotting human heads were stuck on poles at the entrance to a hill fort.

3 Heads could be thrown into a lake or river as a gift to the gods.

4 After a battle the Celts rode from the battlefield with the heads of enemies dangling from the necks of their horses.

5 The heads might then be nailed to the walls of their houses.

6 Sometimes they were preserved in cedar oil and taken out years later to show off to visitors. A Roman visitor said that the Britons would not part with their lucky heads for their weight in gold.

7 The Celtic Boii Tribe of the Po Valley (Northern Italy) took skulls and covered them in gold. They would then be used as cups!

8 Heads featured in many ornaments of stone, metal or wood and paintings. Severed heads could be seen staring at you from the surface of tiles, pots, sword hilts, chariot fittings and even bucket handles!

9 Because the gods were more powerful than humans, they often had more heads. An Irish goddess, Ellen, had three heads! The druids had to keep her constantly supplied with sacrifices to stop her coming out of her underworld cave and ravaging the land.

33

10 The Britons even told stories about the magical power of the head. Many legends involved severed heads.

A typical story is the Welsh legend of Bran the Blessed . . .

DAILY HEADLINE NEWS

HEADITOR : M.T. SKULL

BIG BRAN'S NOGGIN NICKED!

Some treacherous troublemaker has taken Britain's greatest treasure!

Yesterday the London burial place of Bran the Blessed was robbed. The great warrior's head was later found to be missing, along with another two skulls from the graveyard. The authorities are looking for a man with three heads!

Magical

As all our readers will know, the head of Bran the Blessed was the most magical article in the whole of Britain. Eighty years ago Bran was mortally wounded in a bloody battle with an Irish king. As he lay dying he ordered the seven surviving soldiers to cut off his head and carry it with them. This they did and they found themselves in the after-life as the guest of Bran – even though they weren't dead!

Then one warrior dis-obeyed one of Big Bran's orders. He opened a forbidden door. The warriors were heaved out of heaven. But, before they went, one of them tucked Bran's head up his tunic. And so it returned to earth. The head was buried in London, where it would guard Britain against evil for ever more.

Reward

Now it has been stolen there's no knowing what might happen. *The Daily Headline News* is offering a reward for information leading to its return. Otherwise Britain will be heading for disaster!

Did you know?

The Romans sometimes treated slaves brutally in their conquered territories and in Rome itself. In AD 157 the Roman writer Apuleius described life in a rotten Roman flour mill . . .

> *The slaves were poor, skinny things. Their skin was black and blue with bruises, their backs were covered with cuts from the whip. They wore rags, not clothes, and hardly enough to keep them decent. They had a brand mark burned into their forehead and half of their hair was shaved off. They wore chains around their ankles.*

A slave revolt was led by Spartacus at a gladiator school near Naples. The slaves formed a huge army and terrorised the area for a couple of years. At last a Roman army defeated them. Over 6000 slaves were crucified along the side of the main road from Capua to Rome.

YOU JUST CAN'T GET THE STAFF THESE DAYS

The battling Britons

If you weren't a Roman then the Romans called you "barbarian" – or stranger. This was because the Romans didn't understand the language of strange peoples. They said they sounded like sheep – "bah-bah-bah" people . . . bah-bah-rians . . . barbarians, get it?

So, when the Romans arrived in Britain they met "barbarians". But the Britons weren't "barbarous" – they weren't rough, crude, simple people. They were simply "different". Still, they *did* have one or two habits that you won't find in your school today . . .

The British way of life . . . and death

1 The Britons had priests called Druids. Druids led the worship of the gods of Nature. An important time of year was Beltane – 21 March – when night and day are exactly 12 hours each. If people wanted the days to keep getting longer, and summer to come, then they had to give the gods something they would like. The Druids thought that the gods would like nothing better than a severed head . . . so the Druids had a victim's head chopped off.

2 The Britons lived in forts with huge earth walls. They built one called Maiden Castle in the south of England. The Britons would feast there on joints of pork. They got rid of the bones by throwing them over their shoulders. When the piles of bones became too deep, they levelled them out and spread a fresh layer of earth and chalk over the top.

3 The men wore long moustaches which trapped food as they ate. A fussy Roman writer called Diodorus wrote, "Their drink passes through their moustaches like a strainer!" Yuk!

4 At a British tribal feast the guests would sit on animal skins on the floor, eat with their fingers . . . and keep on eating! When they were tired, they just rolled over onto the skin carpet and fell asleep.

5 The Britons weren't as filthy as they sound from this. They used to wash with soap long before the Romans did.

6 In battle, Celtic warriors often fought without any clothes at all. The Romans said that the Britons were painted from head to toe in a blue dye called woad . . . but maybe they were just blue with the cold!

7 The Celts believed in staying thin and fit. If a young warrior became too tubby for a normal sized belt then he was fined.

8 The Britons were related to the Celtic tribes of Gaul (northern France) who were feared by the Romans for their fierceness. And not only the men! Marcellinus said . . .

> *A whole troop of foreigners would not be able to withstand a Gaul if he called for his wife to help him. Swelling her neck, gnashing her teeth and swinging her white arms of enormous size she begins to strike blows mixed with kicks as if they were missiles sent from the string of a catapult.*

HELP

9 The Celtic men were proud of their hair. They bleached it by washing it in lime. The roots of the hair would be dark and the rest a bleached blond. The lime also made the hair stand on end. They went into battle with their hair in a crest of spikes. One writer said the spikes were so stiff and strong that you could have stuck an apple on the end of each point! And they didn't wear helmets that could save their life in a battle – it would have spoiled their hairstyle!

10 Brave British women must have looked as fearsome as their blue warrior men. They painted their fingernails, reddened their cheeks with a herb called ruan and darkened their eyebrows with the juice of berries.

But the boldest of British women – maybe the bravest ever – was Queen Boudicca.

That was what the Britons called her. Later generations changed her name to Boadicea. Some people say this change was made because Boadicea sounded nicer. Another story is that a mediaeval monk made a spelling mistake when he was copying an old history and his mistake was copied by later historians! Let's call her Boudicca . . .

Boudicca, *This is Your Life!*

1 Boudicca always looked pretty fearsome with her huge mop of bright red hair, her rough voice and her king-sized body. A Roman writer, Cassius Dio, said . . .

She was very tall. Her eyes seemed to stab you. Her voice was harsh and loud. Her thick, reddish-brown hair hung down below her waist. She always wore a great golden torc [band] around her neck and a flowing tartan cloak fastened with a brooch.

BOUDICCA

2 She married Prasutagus, King of the Iceni tribe of Britons. They had two daughters. Prasutagus, the wimp, didn't fancy fighting the Romans when they arrived. Instead he tried to make a deal with the emperor: "When I die the Iceni lands can be split between you and my daughters." Then he did a stupid and wimpy thing – he died.

3 The Roman Army simply took over. The officers ran the country while the slaves plundered the Iceni houses. Then the Romans made a BIG mistake. They had Big Boudicca whipped. Big Boud was not amused.

4 The Romans had whipped Boudicca . . . so Boudicca whipped up a rebellion. The revolting Britons captured the Roman town of Camulodunum (now called Colchester in Essex).

5 The gods appeared to be on Big Boud's side. They gave the Brits several "signs" that they were on the side of the Iceni.

- The Roman statue of Victory fell down . . . face down as if it were fleeing from the attackers.
- Women reported that ghostly, ghastly shrieks could be heard in the Roman senate house and theatre.
- At the mouth of the Thames, a phantom town was seen in ruins.
- The sea turned blood red.
- As the tide went out, the sands took on the shape of corpses.

6 Big Boud marched on to Londinium (London) and Verulamium (St Albans) where her army did a lot of murdering and pillaging. In all they killed about 70,000 people.

7 One Roman didn't run away. Paulinus had just 10,000 soldiers to fight 100,000 Brits.

8 Big Boud rode round the Brit tribes in her war chariot and gave them her famous speech . . .

> *We British are used to women commanders in war. I am the daughter of mighty men. But I am not fighting for my royal power now . . . I am fighting as an ordinary person who has lost her freedom. I am fighting for my bruised body. The gods will grant us the revenge we deserve. Think of how many of us are fighting, and why. Then you will win this battle or die. That is what I, a woman, plan to do. Let the men live as slaves if they want. I won't!*

9 The 10,000 Romans were well organised. The 100,000 Britons charged around the way they always did. The result was a great victory for the Romans.

10 Big Boud faced another flogging. The Roman historian, Tacitus, said she took poison and died. The Roman historian, Dio, said she died of a disease. Believe whichever one you like . . . or neither. Perhaps she just died of a broken heart. Boudicca, that was your life!

Did you know?

The Roman historian, Tacitus, said the Britons had 80,000 warriors killed in Boudicca's final battle. That means each of the 10,000 Roman soldiers killed (on average) *eight* Britons! He claimed that only 400 Romans died so it took 250 Britons to kill just *one* Roman! No wonder the British lost!

Of course, the fact is that Tacitus was telling *fibs*. He wanted to tell the Roman world what a great army the Romans had and how brave their leaders were . . . after all, his father-in-law was one of those fighting in that battle!

So, DON'T believe everything you read in your history books. If the Brits had been able to write then, they would have given a very different account of the battle. The Romans were very good at blaming other people for things. The truth is usually that there are good arguments on both sides . . .

45

Who's to blame for Boudicca's battles?

47

Diary of disaster

One of the great heroes of the British tribes was Caratacus of the Catuvellauni tribe (north-west of London). While many tribal leaders were making peace with the Romans, Caratacus went on fighting. In the end he was defeated, of course. But he was still a hero.

That was one big difference. The Romans loved winners. The Britons seemed to love losers. The other difference was that the Romans learned from their mistakes. The Britons didn't.

It isn't likely that Caratacus could write. But, if he could, and if he kept a diary, would it have looked like this . . .?

Summer of 43 AD Kent

Disaster! I can't believe it! After two days of battle the Romans have defeated us. All we had to do was to stop them crossing the ~~Medw~~ River Medway. There's only one bridge over the Medway. All we had to do was sit tight on the northern end, wait for the Romans to cross it, then cut them into pieces...

... We'd have killed them in their
thousands. We would! But what did
they do ??? They cheated !!! They
sent troops upstream, they crossed
where the water was shallow and
attacked us from the back. That's not
fair, is it?

Of course, we could have run them down
with our chariots. We could! But what did
they do? They cheated again!
They shot our horses. That's not fair, is it?
They even killed my brother, Togodumnus.
Poor, stupid Toggy. He should have done
what I did. Retreated. Like dad always
said, "He who fights and runs away, lives
to fight another day".
So, I'm alive and next time I'll stuff
those rotten Romans !!! !

Late Summer of 43 AD - Dorset

Disater! Again! The Romans are marching west. They're taking our hill-forts one after another. Of course, they don't fight fair. ~~Ze~~ They don't fight man to man ~~to~~ and let us kill them....

No. They shoot at our defenders with iron-tipped arrows. Hundreds at a time from some big machine. They drive us off the walls then swarm in after we've taken shelter.

They've taken 20 hill-forts that way. I never thought I'd live to see the day they'd take the mighty Maiden Castle. In fact I nearly didn't live to see today! I just managed to retreat in time. He who fights and runs away.... But I'll stay in England. They'll never drive me into Wales.. Never!!

The other leaders are all surrendering, making peace and getting fat. But they won't get a hero like me. Not like they got poor old Toggy... ~~He~~ Next time I'll get them...

Summer of 48 AD - Wales

Who is the greatest British leader??
Caratacus. Me! Alright, so I'm stuck in the
wild, wet Welsh mountains. But every now and
then I lead a raid on some Roman troops
and crack a few rotten Roman heads.

Actually it's rather hard to crack a Roman
head. They wear these metal helmets. That's not
fair, thats not. Some people might even call
it cheating!

They'd like to drive me up to North Wales
and into the Irish Sea. Well, there is absolutely
NO chance of that. My men will fight to the
the death (Not my death of course. They
need me alive to lead them)

I'll end up in North Wales over my warriors'
dead bodies!!!

North
Wales

Nth England

Welsh
Mountains

Dorset   Kent

North Wales - 51 AD

Disaster! Again!!! I never thought I'd see the day when the Romans would take a fort like Llanymynech. But they did. I still can't believe it. They couldn't attack Llanymynech from the back because that's a steep mountain face. They couldn't attack it from the front because that's the river Vrynwy and the front wall of the fort.

But they did it! They crossed the river then came to the wall. We were pouring spears and stones and ~~and~~ arrows down on their heads. We should have massacred them...

So, what did they do? They cheated, ~~us~~ usual. They put their shields over their heads and came close together. The shields formed a solid wall over them. (They copied this from a Roman animal with a shell called a "tortoise" or something)

Our weapons just bounced off their "shell" and the Romans just kept coming till everyone was captured. The rotten Romans even took my family! I was lucky to escape. He who fights and runs away...... Still, next time I'll get them. I'm going to join forces with Queen Cartimandua of the Brigantes up near York ...

..... They're the biggest tribe outside of Roman rule. With _me_ to lead them we'll chase the Romans all the way ~~x~~ back to Rome. And they can take their tortoises with them.

I even hear old Claudius brought some huge grey monsters called <u>elephants</u> with him. They can take <u>them</u> back too!!! This time next year I'll be in Rome!!!

North England - later in 51 AD

Life with Queen Cartimandua is great! I don't even miss my poor captured family. The beautiful Carti obviously fancies me. Can't blame her really Me being the grétest British hero ever seen.

Loads of food. Better than living like an outlaw in the hills. And bads of wine. Lovely stuff The very besht Roman wine. I wonder where she gets it from?

And she's even decorating me with chains Chains on my wrists. Chains on my ankles. I fink that Carti loves me ~~to~~ show mush she wantsh to keep me here forever!!! I'm very shleepy now.

Nighty night Carti dear!

53

Next day

My head hurts. And worse. Much worse I'm a prisoner. I've found out where that treacherous, ugly, vicious, lying Queen gets her Roman wine from. She gets it from the Romans!!! And what does she give the Romans in return?

Me! I've been handed over to the Romans. They're ~~too~~ taking me back to Rome. It's curtains for Caratacus! I said I'd be in Rome within a year, I never thought it would be in chains. It's a disaster! They'll execute me for sure. Me the greatest living British hero. I'm not afraid to die of course ... I just don't want to be there when it happens. ......

Next week — middle of the English Channel

I think I'm going to be sea-s...

Next month - Rome

What a place! These Romans really know how to treat a hero! Met old Claudius the emperor. Messy little weedy fellow. Dribbles and slobbers and limps about the place. But a very powerful man. Most important man in the world I reckon. And he spoke to me! (I didn't understand a word, of course, because he was blabbering away in Latin. But I could tell he was pleased to see me!)

Claudi gave an order and my chains were cut off. I thought, Aha! This is it! ~~You're~~ You're for the chop, Caratacus. But no! They treated me like a hero. They even said I was free to live in Rome. I think I might just do

that. There are huge buildings all made of stone and marble. I've never seen anything like it.

Who wants to live in cold wet Britain in a draughty wooden hut? Not me! After all, I am the greatest British hero ever. I reckon I've earned an easy life with my old mate Claudi Maybe the rotten Romans aren't so rotten after all !!!!

The diary might be imaginary but the facts are about right. Caratacus arrived in Rome and told the Romans that they could only have great victories if they had great warriors (like himself) to fight against. "If you execute me, then all your glory will be forgotten," he warned them. Claudius agreed and released him.

But Caratacus was still puzzled when he saw the wealth of Rome. "When you Romans have all this, why do you want our poor huts?" Good question.

Meanwhile, back in Britain, the treacherous Cartimandua stayed in power (with Roman help) for another 15 years. Then her husband attacked her and kicked her out. The Romans really did take the British forts with ease. The Romans made mistakes. But they didn't usually make the same mistake twice. That's what made them so successful.

Test your teacher

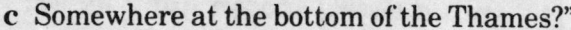

"Please sir/miss/gorilla-features! Where is Boudicca's body now? Is it . . .
a Under her statue on Westminster Bridge (opposite the Houses of Parliament),
b Under platform 8 of King's Cross Station,
c Somewhere at the bottom of the Thames?"

Answer: b Archaeologists believe they have located the grave of Big Boud under Platform 8 of King's Cross Station. However, British Rail rebuilt that platform in 1988 and aren't too keen to have it dug up again to find out if the archaeologists are right. But if you're ever standing on Platform 8 of King's Cross and a big, red-haired woman asks you, "What time's the next chariot to Camulodunum . . .?"

Did you know?

A mysterious funeral ceremony took place near London in the second century AD. A grave has been discovered in an underground room but it contains no human bodies. There are just two carvings of men who look like Roman senators. Historians think that these men must have died during fighting and were buried elsewhere. It seems that they did not have an honourable burial . . . maybe they were traitors. Whatever the reason their carved heads were walled up in this room to be forgotten. But one body was found in the tomb – the body of the family cat!

WHOSE FUNERAL IS THIS?

Rotten Roman leaders

Julius Caesar was one of the greatest Roman leaders. He was so successful he was murdered . . . by his friend! Rome had been run as a "republic" for many years. That is to say the important people in Rome decided what to do. Then Julius Caesar became so powerful there was a fear that he'd take over. The people thought he wanted to become "King of the Romans".

The last king they'd had was a disaster. His name was Tarquinius Superbus who lived in the 5th century BC. He abolished certain rights of Romans and was the rottenest Roman of the time.

Was it true that Caesar wanted to be crowned king? And would he get to be as bad as Tarquinius? If so, it would be better to kill him now! This is how it happened . . .

Caesar's sticky end

1 Caesar had himself elected "Dictator for life" . . . that was just another way of saying the dreaded word "King"!
2 Caesar started wearing red boots! Only a king wore red boots.

3 At a festival, Mark Antony, Caesar's friend, offered Caesar a diadem – a small crown. Caesar took it off – a sign that he didn't want to be king, perhaps? The crowds cheered when he took it off. But did Caesar and Mark Antony set this up to find out how the people felt? What if the people had cheered when the crown had been put *on?*

4 Caesar was due to speak to the Senate (the Roman parliament) on 15 March, 44 BC. Straight after his speech he was due to lead his troops into battle. During a war he'd be surrounded by his soldiers. No one could kill him then. If he was to die then he had to die on 15 March.

5 Caesar was a great believer in "fate" – if he was going to die then there was nothing he could do to change his fortune. A fortune-teller told Caesar not to go to the Senate on 15 March. It didn't stop him.

6 Caesar's wife asked him not to go to the Senate that day. She'd had terrible nightmares and a feeling that something bad would happen. That didn't stop him.

7 Caesar felt ill on the morning of 15 March and was almost too ill to attend the Senate . . . he was worse by the time he left!

8 The killers chose Brutus as their leader. Brutus was one of the most popular men in Rome. He was famous for being honest. If he led the killing then the people of Rome would know the murderers were "honest" – that they did it for the good of the people.

9 On the evening of 14 March someone asked Caesar, "What sort of death would you like?" Caesar answered, "A sudden one." He got his wish.

When Caesar entered the Senate the senators all stood up as a sign of respect. Some of Brutus' gang slipped behind Caesar's chair while others came to meet him. Cimber grabbed Caesar's robe with both hands and pulled it from his neck. This was the signal for the attack.

Casca struck the first blow. His knife made a wound in Caesar's neck, but not a serious one, so that Caesar could still turn around, grab the knife, and hold on.

The watchers were horrified. They didn't dare run away or help Caesar or even make a sound.

Each assassin bared his dagger now. They all closed in on Caesar in a circle. They pushed him this way and that, like a wild beast surrounded by hunters.

Brutus stabbed Caesar in the groin. Above all Caesar had trusted Brutus.

Some say Caesar defended himself against all the rest – but when he saw Brutus coming at him with a dagger, he pulled his robe over his head and sank down.

The attackers pushed Caesar against the statue of his old enemy, Pompey. The statue became drenched with blood.

Caesar received 23 wounds.

Many of the assassins wounded each other as they fought to stick so many knives into one body.

The killers made one big mistake. They didn't kill Mark Antony at the same time. "Honest" Brutus said it would be wrong. They were only out to stop wicked Caesar from becoming king. But it was Mark Antony who led a campaign of vengeance that destroyed the killers. Brutus committed suicide when he was defeated by Mark Antony at Philippi in 42 BC.

Caesar had left most of his fortune to his grand-nephew, Octavian. Young Octavian became the sort of dictator that Caesar wanted to be. The thing the Romans feared – rule by one all-powerful man – had returned. And some of the emperors that followed were a hundred times worse than Julius Caesar!

In fact, some of the Roman Emperors were pretty weird. Here are the Rottenest Romans of all . . .

Emperor Tiberius

Ruled: 14 AD–37 AD

Favourite saying: "I don't care if they hate me . . . so long as they obey me!" (Know any teachers like that?)

Nastiest habit: Breaking the legs of anyone who disobeyed him.

Rottenest act: Tiberius needed a holiday. "I think I'll take a break!" he announced. As the servants scuttled off to find their shinpads he cried, "A holiday, I mean. A short break on the island of Capri off the south coast of Italy would be very nice."

He had only been there a few days when a humble Capri fisherman caught a large crab and a huge mullet fish. The poor man decided that it would make a wonderful gift for the visiting emperor.

The cliff was steep and there was no track. The mullet was heavy. The fisherman struggled for an hour and finally reached the top.

"Take me to the emperor," he pleaded with the guard.

"The emperor wishes to be left alone today," the guard said, shaking his head.

"It's the biggest mullet I've ever caught!" the fisherman said proudly. "The gods meant it for the emperor. Tell the emperor I must see him!"

The guard shrugged. It was a boring life, standing

on the top of the cliff watching the gulls. The emperor might order him to break the fisherman's legs. "I'll see what the emperor says," he smirked.

Five minutes later he returned and said with a grin. "The emperor will see you now."

The poor little man dragged the huge fish into the emperor's room. "You'll be sorry," the guard muttered.

As the fisherman stepped through the door two huge guards grabbed his arms. "I've brought a gift for the emperor!" he squeaked.

Tiberius stepped forward. "You disturbed my rest, you smelly little man!" he snarled.

"It's the fish, your worship!" the fisherman cried.

"No!" the emperor jeered. "That fish smells sweeter than you. Guards!"

"Sir?"

"Sweeten the little man. Rub that fish over his body!"

"It was a present . . . ouch! Mullet scales are very rough!" he screamed.

The guard scrubbed the rough skin over the fisherman's face till the skin was scraped off and his face left raw and bleeding. The guard smiled as he stripped the skin off the fisherman's chest.

"Ahh! Oooh!" the man wailed.

"Enough!" the emperor snapped. The guards let the fisherman fall to the floor where he lay groaning and muttering something through his bleeding lips.

"What did you say?" Tiberius growled.

"I just said thank the gods I didn't bring you that big crab I caught this morning," the little man burbled.

The emperor's eyes lit up with evil glee. "Go to this man's house and fetch the crab," he chuckled.

The guard nodded. As he left the emperor's room he winked at the sobbing fisherman. "I told you that you'd be sorry."

And after being scrubbed with the sharp shell of a crab the little man was so sorry that he wished he'd never been born.

Sticky end: Tiberius died at the age of 78, probably suffocated by his chief helper. The Roman people went wild with joy!

Caligula

Ruled: 37 AD–41 AD

Favourite sayings: To his friends at a banquet, "It has just occurred to me that I only have to give one nod and your throats will be cut."

To the guards of a row of criminals, "Kill every man between that one with the bald head and that one over there."

To his people, "Rome is a city of necks just waiting for me to chop."

To everyone who would listen, "I am a god."

Nastiest habit: His little "jokes". At a sacrifice ceremony he was given a hammer which would knock out the beast to be sacrificed. The priest was waiting to cut the beast's throat. Caligula hit the priest over the head instead!

Rottenest act: Caligula loved to organize huge killing festivals with loads of spectators. There were fights to the death between gladiators, and fights with wild animals. But the wild animals had to be kept alive until the day of the contest. Caligula was shocked at the cost of the raw meat needed to feed the animals. So he found a cheap supply of meat . . . he fed criminals to them!

Daftest act: He made his dear friend Incitatus a consul – so Incitatus became one of the most powerful rulers in the Roman Empire. So? So, Incitatus was his favourite *horse!*

Sticky end: One of his trusted guards stabbed him to death. Others went to the palace where they killed his wife and child.

Claudius

Ruled: 41 AD–54 AD

Favourite saying: "K-k-k-k-k-k- . . . er . . . execute him!"

Nastiest habit: Watching criminals being tortured and men being executed by being flogged to death.

Rottenest act: Claudius discovered his wife was a bit of a flirt and had wild parties with her friends. Claudius not only had *her* executed but 300 party friends went too.

Sticky end: His niece, Agrippina, poisoned him with mushrooms.

Nero

Ruled: 54 AD–68 AD

Favourite sayings: He played the lyre very badly but people told him he was brilliant. The Greeks were particularly creepy about telling him he was good. "Only the Greeks are worth my genius," he would say.

When he knew he had to die all he could say was, "What a loss I shall be to the art of music!"

Nastiest habit: Murdering people. He had his half-brother, Britannicus, poisoned. (Actually, Britannicus had a food taster who ate and drank a tiny bit of every dish that the Emperor was going to eat. If the food was poisoned, the taster would die first. The taster drank some hot wine and passed it over to the emperor. The taster was fine. The wine was "safe" to drink. But Britannicus complained that the wine was too hot and ordered water to cool it. *Then* he drank it . . . and died. The cold *water* had been poisoned!)

Nero had his first wife, Octavia, murdered. Her head was sent to Nero's new girlfriend, Poppaea. But then he murdered Poppaea, too.

Nero had Christians persecuted cruelly . . .

- They would be tied to a post, covered in tar and set alight.
- They would be covered in animal skins and thrown to hungry, wild dogs.
- They were crucified in large numbers.

Rottenest act: Agrippina had poisoned Claudius and now her son, Nero, was emperor. She thought she could rule the empire through her weak and wicked son.

Nero had other ideas. His mother was always interfering – stopping his meeting with his girlfriend, Acte, because she wasn't royal. Agrippina had to go.

First he made up their row over Acte. Then he invited mum to join him at a party on the Bay of Naples. Agrippina was happy to accept, glad to be friends with her son once more.

Nero sent a boat to pick her up. A special boat with special oarsmen. For the boat was designed to fall apart at sea and the oarsmen were instructed not to let Agrippina return alive. The boat set off on a beautiful starry night.

But the boat didn't fall apart. There were heavy weights on the wooden canopy over Agrippina's seat. At the right moment they were to crash through the canopy, kill Agrippina and fall through the bottom of the boat to sink it. Everyone would say the boat hit a rock. Sad accident. Poor Nero, losing his loving mother.

That's what was *meant* to happen. But, when the weights fell through the roof they killed Agrippina's friend. Agrippina and her other friend, Aceronnia, escaped . . . and the boat didn't sink!

The oarsmen tried to rock the boat to capsize it. That's when Aceronnia did a very brave thing. She began to cry out, "Save me! I am Agrippina, the emperor's mother! I am Agrippina!"

And in the darkness the oarsmen believed her. They battered her to death with their oars while the real Agrippina slipped over the side and escaped back to her palace. She sent a message to Nero saying what a lucky escape she'd had.

Nero was furious. He decided to make sure the next time. He sent two murderers to her palace. Agrippina thought they'd come from Nero to find out if she was all right!

As the first one battered her with a club she realised her mistake. When the other drew his sword she bared her stomach and invited him to stab her where the ungrateful Nero had come from. He did.

Nero reported that she had killed herself!

Sticky end: When he knew that the Roman Army had deserted him and rebels were coming to arrest him, he placed a sword to his throat. One of his friends gave him a push. The arresting officer arrived as he bled to death.

Ten funny facts about Roman emperors

1 Emperor Caligula's real name was Gaius. Caligula was just a nickname meaning "little boot". This was because he liked dressing up and playing at being a soldier from a very early age.

2 Caligula wanted to copy Julius Caesar and invade Britain. In 40 AD he went to the Roman base in Boulogne (in northern France) where he set sail to lead the invasion. He turned back when he saw that no one wanted to follow him!

3 Augustus Caesar was one of the more human emperors. But even he had his moments – the murder of Julius Caesar really upset him. As Suetonius said, "Augustus showed no mercy to his beaten enemies. He sent Brutus' head to Rome to be thrown at the feet of Caesar's statue."

4 Julius Caesar gave us our modern calendar. The early Romans had 12 months plus a 13th month that was added every four years. In 46 BC Caesar gave us the 12-month, 365-day year with the 29-day February leap year.

5 Emperor Heliogabalus enjoyed the hobby of collecting cobwebs . . . by the ton!

OF ALL MY BELGIAN COBWEBS THIS IS MY FAVOURITE

6 Honorius loved chickens. His favourite chicken was called Rome. He was hiding in his country mansion, safe from the invading army of Goths. When the city of Rome was overrun by Alaric and his army of Goths, a messenger arrived to say, "Rome is lost!" Honorius was heart-broken . . .

until someone told him the messenger meant the capital *city* and not the *hen*.

7 Nero enjoyed the cruel "circuses" so much that he had to take part. He was dressed in the skins of wild animals and locked in a cage. The human victims were tied to stakes in the arena. Nero's cage was opened. He leapt out and attacked the victims.

8 When Emperor Pertinax was murdered there wasn't just *one* person to take his place. *Two* men claimed the throne. Both men thought it would be useful to have the support of the emperor's praetorian guard – so they tried to outbid each other for it. Julianus won. He made an offer of 25,000 sesterces (Roman money) to each man. Unfortunately he couldn't afford to pay *all* the men in *all* the Roman armies across the world. They attacked and threw him out after just 66 days on the throne. The money he spent on bribing the emperor's guards was wasted – they were easily tricked into giving up their weapons.

9 In the 50 years between 235 AD and 285 AD there were about 20 emperors. Most of them were there a short time, murdered and replaced by the murderer who was murdered and replaced by the murderer, and so on. Some of the senior Romans refused to become emperor at this time – not surprising really!

10 Septimius had particularly nasty family problems. He had two sons, Caracalla and Geta. Caracalla was allowed to become joint emperor when he was just 13. Caracalla had his father-in-law murdered, then set off with his father and brother to conquer Scotland. During the campaign, Caracalla threatened to kill his father – but didn't. Old Septimius died in York and his dying words to his sons were, "Do not disagree with each other." Fat chance. Within a year Caracalla had brother Geta murdered. Caracalla was sole emperor at last. He kept the throne for five years, then . . . no prizes for guessing what happened to him. Yes, he was murdered.

Did you know?

Julius Caesar passed burial laws for the inhabitants of new towns built in the Roman Empire:

- "No one may bring, burn or bury a dead person within the boundaries of the town."
- "No crematorium shall be established within half a mile of a town."

(Burial sites had to be either outside the city walls or just within its limits. Caesar wanted a perfect town full of grand buildings and fresh air for his faithful followers.)

Rotten Roman childhood

Children had a tough time in the age of the rotten Romans from the moment they were born. One writer, Soranus, described how each new-born child was laid on the earth and allowed to cry for a while before it was washed and clothed. Only the fit survived.

Some of the Germans in the Roman Empire gave their new-born children an even worse test. They dunked the child in cold water. If the baby came out purple with the cold or shivering then it was a weakling – it wasn't worth bringing up, so it was left to die!

Girls were named after eight days – boys on the ninth day. Girls would usually take their father's name – but change the "-us" on the end to "-a". So the daughter of Julius became Julia, the daughter of Claudius was Claudia, Flavius was the father of Flavia and so on.

Children would probably have "pet names" or nicknames. One girl was known as "Trifosa" – that means "delicious"!

The Celt names had their own meanings . . .
- Boudicca meant "Victory".
- Cartimandua meant "White Filly".
- Grata meant "Welcome".

Then, if you survived your birth and you could live with your name, you had to face the terrors of the rotten Roman schools . . .

Suffering schoolchildren – the good, the bad and the awful

Good: Schools cost parents money, so only the parents who could afford it sent their children. If you were poor you could miss going to school altogether.

Bad: Slave children didn't go to school. They were born slaves and belonged to the master.

Awful: Poor children missed school but had to work twice as hard for parents. If you didn't your parents might just decide to sell you! It was illegal to sell free children as slaves – but this didn't stop poor parents from doing it. There was not much chance of their being caught.

Good: Education was divided rather as it is today into primary, secondary and college.

Bad: Most children only went as far as primary.

Awful: For laziness in primary school you'd get the cane, or a beating if the teacher didn't have a cane handy. One poet described his bullying teacher like this . . .

His mouth's no good – but he has a hard fist. Why doesn't he become a boxer instead?

WHO ELSE FORGOT TO DO THEIR HOMEWORK?

Good: Primary schools usually had just 10–12 children.

Bad: That was not enough to pay a teacher's wage. So the poor teacher had another job – maybe in a workshop.

Awful: The Romans didn't have the figure zero. That made sums rottenly difficult to teach. Ask your teacher, "Can you add LXXXVIII and XII?" (The answer is "C")

Good: At least schoolchildren had their own goddess. Her name was Minerva. The holiday for the goddess was in March. After the holiday the school year began.

Bad: Each child had to provide their own wax tablets and stylus (sharp pen to scratch letters into the wax), their pen and ink, their paper rolls and abacus (counting frame).

Awful: For a serious offence in the secondary school – a flogging with a leather whip while other pupils held you down.

Good: Schools closed every ninth day for the market – it was probably too noisy to teach on market days.

Bad: Primary schools were pretty boring. You'd study mainly the three 'Rs' – reading, 'riting and 'rithmetic.

Awful: At secondary school you had to study mega-boring grammar and literature, with some geography and, of course, horrible history! By the time you got to college you had to study for public speaking – the Romans believed that good talkers made good leaders. (Do you agree?)

WHO WROTE THAT! ... HISTORY HORRIBILIS

A grim life for girls

Through most periods of history it's been harder being a woman than being a man. It was no different in Roman Britain . . .

1 Roman girls were lucky . . . if they lived! "If you give birth to a boy, look after it – but if it is a girl then let it die!" (Letter from Hilarion to his wife.)

2 Men weren't happy with the idea of an educated woman. "I hate a woman who reads", wrote Juvenal in the 1st century AD.

3 Roman women had to be "controlled" from an early age. They were given a lucky charm at birth. Why? Because they didn't have a man of their own to protect them. When a baby girl was eight days old she was taken to a special ceremony. A gold or leather heart was hung around her neck. She would keep it throughout her childhood.

4 When a Roman girl was 14 she was ready for marriage. Who said so? Her father. A husband would be chosen for her. Who chose? Her father. What if the girl didn't like her father's choice? Bad luck. She'd have to marry him anyway.

5 On the evening before the wedding a special event took place. The girl placed all her toys and childhood clothes on the altar of the Lares – the household gods. She also took off her lucky charm – she had a husband to protect her now.

6 The bride always wore a white woollen tunic. It was held at the waist with a woollen belt tied in a special knot. She wore a bright yellow cloak and sandals. Her head was covered with a flame-coloured veil.

7 Roman women wore make-up. They used chalk to whiten their necks because a pale skin was supposed to be a sign of beauty.

8 If a woman's lips and cheeks weren't red enough then they would use a reddish earth called ochre.

9 Women were expected to remove hair from their legs as well as from under their arms. They rubbed hair off with a stone or used a cream to dissolve it – and it's a wonder the creams didn't dissolve the skin too! One hair-remover consisted of the blood of a wild she-goat mixed with sea-palm and powdered viper. Then, if you wanted to stop the hair growing back again, you would have to rub on the blood of a hare.

10 If a girl's eyebrows weren't dark enough then she might have used a metallic stuff called antimony. No antimony? Then girls used ashes! Imagine walking around with mud on your face, chalk on your neck and ashes on your eyebrows. If you got carried away you'd look more like a scarecrow.

Rotten Roman stories

The Romans knew some pretty rotten stories. Stories of gods, graves and guts. Their own gods were a bit boring. But then they heard the stories of the Greek gods. Those gods were much more like interesting people. So the Romans pinched the Greek legends and made them their own. Stories like that of Prometheus . . .

The Eagle has landed . . . again . . . and again . . . and again . . .

The fat, feathered fiend landed on the rock and looked at the man who lay chained to it. The bird's beak was as hooked as a hairpin. His great golden eyes glinted in the harsh sun. "Cor! Stone the crows! What a tasty sight!" he croaked. If he'd had lips he would have licked them. Instead he licked his beak.

The young prisoner lifted his head wearily. He was a handsome young man with nothing on but a loin cloth. He squinted through the fierce sun and glared at the bird. "Push off," he snapped.

The bird hopped from one hot foot to the other. "Hey! That's no way to speak to me! I'll have you know I'm an eagle – king of the birds!"

"Sorry, I'm sure," the man sneered. "I should have said, 'push off, your highness'."

The eagle shrugged. "No need to be offensive. I'm only doing my job. And a bird's gotta do what a bird's gotta do!"

"And I'm tired of every sparrow on Mount Olympus stopping off here to gawp and stare," the prisoner spat.

The bird breathed in deeply and ruffled its breast feathers importantly. "I am here on a mission. Some old geezer at the top of the mountain sent me."

"The *gods* live at the top of the mountain," the man said.

"Yeah, well some old *god* sent me, then. Big guy with long white hair and a bushy great beard."

"Zeus!"

"Bless you . . . anyway, he said, 'Fly down there and you'll see young Prometheus chained to a rock,'" the eagle went on.

"That's me! You've brought me the news that the great god Zeus has forgiven me? I'm to be set free?"

"Nah! The old guy told me to fly down here, and eat your liver."

HELLO LUNCH

"Eat my liver?" the young god groaned.

"Well, I didn't argue, did I?" the eagle chuckled. "I like a nice bit of fresh liver. Specially when its fried with a few onions."

"You'll kill me!" Prometheus cried.

"Nah! You're immortal. You'll 'liver' long time yet! Heh! Heh! Heh!" the bird cackled.

The god blinked as sweat ran into his eyes. "You'll hurt me," he sniffed.

"Can't be helped," the bird croaked and took a step towards his victim. "You must have done something pretty bad to deserve this!"

79

Prometheus sighed and looked towards the sun. "Once I could move through the air, just like you. One day I flew up to the sun itself. I brought its fire back down to earth."

"Good thing too – otherwise I'd have to eat your liver raw," the eagle chuckled nastily.

The young god went on, "I gave it to the humans to use."

"Sounds fair enough to me," the eagle admitted.

"Ah, but Zeus had told me *not* to give fire to the humans. He was furious. My punishment is to be chained to this mountainside.

"And to have your liver eaten," the eagle reminded him.

"Must you?" Prometheus groaned.

"Cor, stone the crows. You're supposed to be a hero, ain't you? Well, stop whingeing and let me get me dinner."

The bird lunged forward and Prometheus screamed.

When it was over the bird gripped the dripping liver in its talons and opened its wings. The mountain air lifted it gently off the mountainside and the eagle soared upwards. "See you tomorrow, Prommy!" it cried.

"Tomorrow!" Prometheus screamed. "What bit of me are you going to eat tomorrow?"

"Same again!" the eagle cawed. "That's the worst bit of the punishment. Your liver grows back. I'll come back tomorrow and eat it again . . . and the next day . . . and the next . . . until the end of time! Bye for now!"

Prometheus twisted his head to look at his side. There wasn't a mark to show the eagle's work.

And every day the eagle returned. Day after day,

month after month and year after year. Until one day . . .

"Hello there, Prom!" the eagle called happily as it clattered down onto the sun-warmed rock.

"Hello, Eddie," Prometheus grinned.

The eagle took a step back. "Er . . . you look happy this morning, Prom!"

The young god nodded happily. There was a gleam of pure nastiness in his eyes. Suddenly his hand shot forward and he grabbed the bird around its thick neck.

"Awk!" it squawked. "Your chains!"

"A friend of mine came along and snapped them for me," Prometheus smiled and his grip on the eagle's neck tightened. A huge man stepped from behind the rock. He had muscles that rippled like waves on the sea. "Meet Hercules. The greatest hero ever to walk the earth."

"Pleased to meet you, Herc!" the eagle gasped. "Er . . . if you'll just let me go, Prom, I'll get off back to me nest."

"You're going nowhere," Prometheus promised.

"Nah! I was getting sick of liver anyway," the big bird said weakly.

"Hercules is going to kill you," Prometheus said calmly.

"Look Prommy . . . mate . . . old pal . . . there was never anything *personal*, you know! I was only doing my *job!* Stone the crows, a bird's gotta do what a bird's gotta . . ."

His words were choked off with Prometheus' tight hand. He ignored the eagle's words. "But before I let Hercules kill you, guess what I'm going to do?"

"Er . . . me liver?" the bird guessed.

Prometheus nodded.

"Aw, no, Prommy. It'll taste really nasty – yeuch! Honest! Really sour."

"Ah, but you're forgetting one thing, Eddie. There's nothing in this world that tastes so sweet as . . . revenge!"

Did you know?
The founders of Rome, Romulus and Remus, were supposed to have survived being left to die on a hillside. A she-wolf adopted them. When they grew up, Romulus killed Remus and created Rome – named after Romulus, of course. If he hadn't, then this book might have been called, *The Rotten Remans!*

Rotten Roman fun and games

Rotten Roman games

Which of the following modern games do you think the Romans had?

① HIDE-AND-SEEK

② TAG

③ COMPUTER GAMES

④ HOPSCOTCH

⑤ DOLLS WITH MOVING ARMS AND LEGS

⑥ LEAPFROG

⑦ KITES

⑧ BUILDING BLOCKS

⑨ SEE SAW

⑩ SWING

Answer: all except 3

Some Roman games you might like to try

Roman children's games were a bit like ours . . . only rottenly vicious at times!

Trigon

- Next time your parents slaughter a pig for dinner, ask them for the bladder – it's a part you won't be eating anyway.
- The bladder is cleaned out, then blown up like a balloon and tied.

- A triangle with sides about two metres long is drawn on the ground and a player stands at each corner of the triangle.
- The bladder-ball is passed from one player to another without it touching the ground.
- The aim of the game is to keep the bladder-ball in the air as long as possible.
- Easy? Then add two more balls so that each player has one. There is no set order for passing the ball. You may have to pass your ball while receiving two from the other players! (Game hint: It helps to have three hands.)
- If you drop a ball you lose a point. The winner is the one with the fewest drops in the time – say five minutes. (If you can't find a dead pig then use tennis balls.)

Knucklebones

- If your parents happen to sacrifice a sheep to the gods, ask if you can have one of its feet.
- Boil the sheep's foot until the flesh and skin fall away from the bones.
- Take the small, cubic bones and dry them. You now have five "chuck stones".
- Hold the bones in one hand. Throw them into the air. The aim is to see who can catch the most on the back of the hand.
  (Note: If your parents aren't sacrificing any sheep this week, you can use stones, dice or cubes of wood.)

Micare

- Play in pairs.
- Each player places their right hand behind their back.
- Agree on a signal – one player will nod, for example.
- On the signal, both players shoot out the right hand with a number of fingers raised.
- At the same moment each player calls out what they guess the total number of fingers will be.
- If neither guesses correctly then try again.
- The winner is the first one to guess correctly.
  (Note: This sounds easy. In fact, the more you play it, the more you learn to use clever tactics. Try it and see.)

The Jar Game

- Someone is selected to be "It".
- "It" sits on the ground – they are said to be "in the jar". The others try to prod or nip the one on the ground – rotten Roman children could be pretty vicious while playing this. (Warning! Only pinch or punch "It" if "It" happens to be a teacher.)
- The person in the jar cannot get up but they can try to grab hold of one of the touchers.
- The toucher who is grabbed goes into the jar.

Blind Man's Buff

- Someone is chosen to be blindfolded.
- The other players each have a stick and dance around tapping the "blind man" with the stick, shouting "Come and catch me!", which the blindfolded person tries to do.
- If a player is caught then the blindfolded person tries to guess who s/he is holding.
- If the blindfolded person is right then the caught player becomes the blindfolded one.

Nuts

- Each player has a supply of nuts – probably hazel nuts.
- Each player adds a nut to her/his pile to build a pyramid.
- The winner is the player who uses the most nuts before the pyramid collapses.
  (Note: This is a game for children. When you grew up the Romans would say you had "left your nuts". Perhaps you would like to ask your teacher, "When did you leave your nuts?")

Word games

If you like word-games or crosswords then you might like to make a "square" of words. They should read the same whether they are read from left to right or from top to bottom.

Here's an example from Reading in Roman Britain (now in Berkshire). It was found scratched on a tile . . .

Sator means "a sower".

Arepo is a man's name.

Tenet means "he holds".

Opera means "work" or "deeds".

Rotas means "wheels".

The square has also been translated as "The sower, Arepo, guides the wheels carefully."

BUT . . . some clever person worked out that this was not a word-game at all, but a secret, Christian prayer! Take all the letters and you can spell out the word PATERNOSTER. This is Latin for "Our Father" – the opening of the Lord's Prayer. There are two "A"s and two "O"s left over. These letters represent "the beginning and the end" to early Christians.

Clever, yes? But is it just coincidence? Or is it really a prayer? Make up your own mind.

Rotten grown-up games

The Romans enjoyed their circuses. But they weren't the sort of family day out we have at the circus today. No clowns, no jugglers, no tightrope walkers. But lots of violence, blood and death.

Augustine of Hippo wrote a book in which he told of his disgust at the bloodshed. His friend, Alypius, was taken to a Roman circus by some student friends. He set off for the circus, a real wimp. A band of trumpets played, bets were placed and the fighting began . . .

> *He shut his eyes tightly, determined to have nothing to do with these horrors. If only he had closed his ears as well! The fight drew a great roar from the crowd; this thrilled him so deeply that he could not contain his curiosity. When he saw the blood it was as though he had drunk a deep cup of savage passion. Instead of turning away he fixed his eyes upon the scene and drank in all its frenzy. He revelled in the wickedness of the fighting and was drunk with the fascination of the bloodshed.*

Julius Caesar, on the other hand, became a bit bored with the fighting and the dying. Long before the end of a contest he would begin reading reports and writing letters. This did *not* make him very popular with some of the spectators in the crowds!

SEEN ONE FIGHT TO THE DEATH, SEEN THEM ALL

BOO!

Gruesome gladiators – ten terrible truths

1 The Romans brought the gladiator fights to Britain ... battles between teams of armed men of whom half would be sure to lose their lives.

2 The idea of fighting and killing as a game probably began at funerals. The Roman Tertullian said ...

Once upon a time, people believed that the souls of the dead were kept happy with human blood, and so, at funerals, they sacrificed prisoners of war or slaves of poor quality.

DO I GET A SACRIFICE AT MY FUNERAL?

These sacrifices changed into fights to the death between two men at the funeral. They became so popular that they were taken away from the funeral and put in a huge arena. The fighters became known as gladiators.

3 In Rome there had been schools of gladiators, where a slave could train and fight for a gladiator master. If he won enough battles – and murdered enough opponents – he would win a fortune and his freedom. The greatest prize was the wooden sword – a symbol of freedom.

4 Nutty Nero even ordered a battle between a woman and a dwarf as a special spectacle.

5 When a victim fell in a battle an attendant would smack him on the head with a hammer to make sure he was dead.

6 If a fighter gave up, exhausted, he could surrender. The emperor would then decide if he deserved to live or not. The crowd would usually tell him by screaming, "*Mitte!* Let him go!" or, "*Iugula!* Kill him!" The emperor would signal his decision with his thumb. Thumb down for death – thumb up for life. And we still use that sign today.

DON'T MAKE ANY QUICK DECISIONS, MULL IT OVER A WHILE, THINK ABOUT IT, TAKE YOUR TIME

7 Some of the bloodiest battles were between criminals who were under sentence of death anyway. They fought till there was no one left – an unarmed man was put in the ring with an armed man who killed him. The armed man was then disarmed and the next man killed him. And so it went on – as soon as one victim fell, another was put in the ring.

8 There's not much evidence to show that the Romans in Britain brought the sort of wild animals to the arena that they brought to Rome itself.

9 There would be bears from Scotland which were chained to a post and tormented for the entertainment of the crowd.

10 Back in Rome they would have seen . . .

- elephants against armed men – until one day, the elephants crashed through iron railings and trampled the crowd. Caesar had a moat built round the arena to protect the spectators from the animals.
- sea battles in an arena which could be flooded to take warships.
- animals fighting each other to the death – bear against buffalo, buffalo against elephant, elephant against rhinoceros.
- crocodiles, giraffes, hippopotami and ostriches – the crocodiles were tricky because they didn't survive very well when taken out of Africa. One lot spoiled the fun by refusing to eat!

SLAVES SLAVES SLAVES, WHERE'S THE VARIETY?

- men against panthers, lions, leopards, tigers – but the men were usually heavily armed with spears, flaming torches, bows, lances and daggers. Some even took a pack of hounds into the arena to help them – they were in no more danger than the audience! One spectator made a joke about the emperor, Domitian. He was taken out of the crowd and thrown to a pack of dogs!
- men with cloaks against bulls – of the kind you can still see in Spain today.
- men fighting bears with their bare fists.
- five thousand beasts killed in one day of AD 80 in the Coliseum of Rome.

Amazing acts

But not every show in the arena was violent. Some of the acts used tame animals to perform tricks, rather as circus animals do today. The spectators were amused by . . .

- teams of tame panthers pulling chariots.
- a lion releasing a live hare from its mouth after it had caught it.
- a tiger licking the hand of its trainer.
- elephants kneeling in the sand in front of the emperor.
- elephants tracing Latin words in the sand with their trunks.

Petrifying plays

The Romans liked to visit the open-air theatres to watch plays. There were theatres in many of the bigger British towns. But if the plays were anything like the plays back in Rome, they would be banned today for being too violent!

The actors had real fights on stage. Then, Emperor Domitian allowed a real death on the stage. At the end of the play "Laureolis" the villain has to be crucified, tortured and torn apart by a bear. The actor playing the villain left the stage and his place was taken by a criminal who was under the sentence of death. The really rotten Romans enjoyed watching this horrible spectacle.

Then, of course, the Romans used the arenas as an excuse to execute people they didn't like – they put men, women and children in with wild animals, sometimes just for the simple crime of being Christians.

Strangely, it was the Christian religion that finally put an end to the massacres. When the emperors became Christian they banned the blood-thirsty events. On 1 October 326 AD, Emperor Constantine put a stop to the gladiator schools and, by the end of the century, the shows had disappeared from the empire.

Did you know?

The term "Roman Holiday" is still used to describe people enjoying themselves by watching others suffering. So, when teachers try to tell you the Romans "civilised" the Ancient Britons, you can tell them that the rotten Romans had some of the most "uncivilised" fun and games in history.

Rotten Roman food

The Romans introduced new foods to Britain, and new recipes. They'd travelled the world and weren't too keen to eat the coarse bread or drink the ale of the Britons. They could afford spices to disguise the boring taste of the smoked or salted meat and fish.

Twenty foul food facts

1 The rich had great feasts. One Roman, called Trimalchio, held a feast which included wine that was a hundred years old. It also included a wild boar that, when sliced down the belly, allowed song-thrushes to fly out.

2 During such feasts the guests could eat so much that they had to be sick; a special room was set aside for them called a vomitorium. They would then go back into the dining room to continue eating!

3 Emperor Maximian was a big eater. He was supposed to have eaten 20 kilograms of meat a day ... that's about all the meat you'd get from a small sheep!

4 Maximian also enjoyed about 34 litres of wine each day. Such gluttony killed him in the end, of course . . . but not until he'd reigned almost 20 years!

5 In the kitchen, the rich kept a special container used for fattening up their dormice. They were fed on the very best food – walnuts, acorns and chestnuts, before being killed, stuffed and served as a great delicacy. The stuffing could be made from pork sausage (or even sausage made from other dormice) and flavoured with pepper and nuts.

6 Snails fattened in milk were popular. Take your live snails out of their shells and put them in a shallow dish of milk and salt for a day. They love milk so they slurp it down, but the salt just makes the stupid creatures thirstier! Then they are placed in plain milk for a few days. They drink and drink till they become too fat to get back in their shells. Fried in oil and served covered in wine sauce – they are delicious!

7 Even fouler . . . fatten up the snails on raw flesh to add to their flavour. (Most snails would be vampire snails given the chance!)

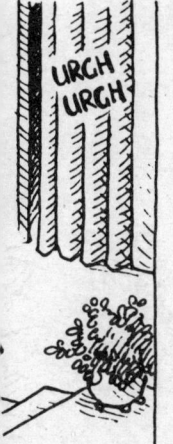

8 The Romans enjoyed stuffed thrush. No worse than your Sunday chicken, right? Wrong! They stuffed the thrush through the throat without taking the insides out! Yeuch! The Romans also ate other birds that we wouldn't usually think of eating. They enjoyed . . .

- herring-gulls
- jackdaws
- crows
- ravens
- swans
- coots
- peacocks

9 The Romans didn't waste much. One recipe by Apicius calls for the chopped-up udder of a sow. They also ate the brains of animals . . . not to mention the lungs of goats and sheep.

10 King Mithradates of Pontus in Asia was scared of being poisoned, so he ate . . . poison! In small doses, of course. That way his body built up a resistance to poison. Then he heard the Romans were coming to get him and he hadn't the guts to face them. So he swallowed poison. Of course, it didn't work! He had to fall on his sword in the end. (So, when the Romans found him he had even less guts!)

THIS JUST ISN'T MY DAY

11 The Romans had some rotten drinks, too. One was made from the guts of fish. They were salted and left to rot in the sun. After a few days the liquid was drained off and drunk or used as a sauce – the way you may sprinkle tomato ketchup on your chips. (This may sound a fishy story, but it's true!)

12 The Romans ate chicken, duck and goose, just as we still do. But the Romans probably served them at the table with the heads cut off but the feet still on!

13 In Roman times there were storks living in Britain. The Romans ate those too. (Could you tell stork from mutton?)

14 Horse bones have been found at Verulamium, which shows that the Romans ate horse-meat sausages. (Neigh! It's true!)

15 For vegetables, the Romans used some pretty odd things. Would you have eaten a salad made with dandelion leaves? How about an egg custard made with nettles? Or perhaps you'd prefer some stewed seaweed? These things are still eaten today in various parts of the world.

16 Sometimes, Roman banquet guests would drop rose petals into their wine.

17 At one meal, Heliogabalus served his guests 600 ostrich brains.

18 He also served peas mixed with grains of gold, and lentils mixed with precious stones – perhaps they liked rich food!

19 A favourite game was to disguise food so that it looked like something it wasn't! At one feast, roast piglets turned out to be made of pastry. At another, a nest seemed to be filled with eggs – but the eggs were made of pastry and inside, the "yolks" were made of spiced garden-warbler meat.

20 You might enjoy a meal while watching television. But could you eat at a Roman feast with dancers and acrobats, jugglers and clowns rushing around? Or even a pair of gladiators trying to kill each other?

The rotten Romans' daily diet

The main meals of the day for the Romans in Britain were:

MENU

BREAKFAST
BREAD AND FRUIT

LUNCH (PRANDIUM)
COLD EGGS, FISH OR VEGETABLES

DINNER (CENA)
GUSTATIO — TASTY THINGS LIKE RADISHES OR
ASPARAGUS AS A STARTER.
PRIMAE MENSALA — THE MAIN COURSE ; CHICKEN OR
HARE AND FISH AND VEGETABLE DISHES.
SECUNDAE MENSAE — SWEET COURSE , INCLUDING
FRUIT

Rotten Roman beastly banquet

Why not invite your friends to a Roman-style banquet. Or, even better, invite your enemies.

First get your slaves to lay the table with napkins for each guest, a spoon and a knife. No forks, you will notice. If you want to try a Roman banquet then you'll have to eat with your fingers and have a napkin to keep your fingers clean! For the soft food and sauces you can use a spoon, and a knife for cutting or spearing meat.

Before you start, place some of your food in a small bowl in front of the statue of the family god. (If the god doesn't eat it then the slaves will!)

Say a few prayers. The Romans would say, "*Auguste, patri patriae*" – "Good luck to the emperor, father of our country."

Have your slaves wash and dry the feet of your guests. (If you can't find any slaves at the local supermarket or corner shop then you could always use a parent or teacher.)

Warning: Do not cook this food yourself! Have it done for you by your slaves!

Starter (*Gustatio*)

If your local shop doesn't have stuffed dormice or snails fattened in milk, then you may like to try shellfish, hard-boiled eggs or a dish of olives. Serve with spiced wine – or in your case, grape juice!

SPICED WINE

INGREDIENTS:
- 1 LITRE OF GRAPE JUICE
- 3 TABLESPOONS OF HONEY
- MIXED SPICE
- CINNAMON
- NUTMEG
- BLACK PEPPER
- WATER

METHOD:
- POUR GRAPE JUICE INTO A 2 LITRE SERVING JUG
- ADD A LITRE OF WATER – LESS IF YOU LIKE YOUR WINE STRONG
- STIR IN THE HONEY TILL IT DISSOLVES
- ADD A PINCH OF MIXED SPICE, ONE OF NUTMEG, CINNAMON AND BLACK PEPPER.
- TASTE IT AND ADD MORE HONEY IF IT'S NOT SWEET ENOUGH OR SPICES IF YOU WANT IT TASTIER.

NUMIDIAN CHICKEN

INGREDIENTS:
- CHICKEN PIECES (1 FOR EACH PERSON)
- CUMIN POWDER (QUARTER TEASPOON)
- CORIANDER SEEDS (QUARTER TEASPOON)
- 4 DATES (CHOPPED INTO SMALL PIECES)
- CHOPPED NUTS (4 TABLESPOONS)
- HONEY (2 TABLESPOONS)
- WINE VINEGAR (2 TABLESPOONS)
- CHICKEN STOCK (1 CHICKEN STOCK CUBE CRUMBLED IN A CUP OF WATER)
- PEPPER (A PINCH)
- COOKING OIL (1 TABLESPOON)
- BREAD CRUMBS (1 SLICE OF DRY BREAD)

METHOD:
- PUT THE CHICKEN PIECES IN A ROASTING DISH. BRUSH THEM WITH COOKING OIL, SPRINKLE THEM WITH PEPPER AND COVER THE DISH WITH COOKING FOIL. ROAST THE PIECES AT 350°F, 180°C OR GAS MARK 4 FOR HALF AN HOUR.
- WHILE THE CHICKEN IS ROASTING, PUT THE OTHER INGREDIENTS INTO A PAN AND SIMMER FOR TWENTY MINUTES TO MAKE NUMIDIAN SAUCE.
- WHEN THE CHICKEN PIECES ARE READY, PUT THEM ON A SERVING DISH AND POUR OVER THE SAUCE
- SERVE THE CHICKEN WITH VEGETABLES – CABBAGES AND BEANS ARE VERY ROMAN.

Sweet Course (*Secundae Mensae*)

DATES COOKED IN HONEY

INGREDIENTS:
- 12 FRESH DATES*
- 12 HALF WALNUTS
- 4 TABLESPOONS HONEY
- SALT
- BLACK PEPPER
  (*IF YOU CAN'T GET FRESH DATES THEN A PACKET OF COOKING DATES WILL DO)

METHOD:
- PEEL THE DATES AND TAKE OUT THE STONES.
- REPLACE EACH STONE WITH A HALF WALNUT
- SPRINKLE EACH DATE LIGHTLY WITH SALT
- MELT THE HONEY IN A PAN AND GENTLY COOK THE DATES IN THE HONEY
- AFTER COOKING FOR FIVE MINUTES, TAKE OUT THE DATES AND ARRANGE ON A SERVING DISH
- SPOON MORE HONEY OVER THE HOT DATES
- SPRINKLE ON A LITTLE BLACK PEPPER AND SERVE

Finish off with fruit and nuts and grape-juice wine. While eating your meal, have some entertainment from jugglers, dancers, singers or musicians.

It isn't polite to talk too much at a Roman banquet. But if you must talk, then don't chatter about common things – football, fashion or the neighbour's new car – talk about important things like life, death and great teachers of our time.

Rotten Roman remedies

It didn't do to be sick in Roman times. Sometimes the cure was worse than the illness! Here's a letter from a Roman, Cassius, to his sister, Juliet. Would you like to try some of his cures . . .?

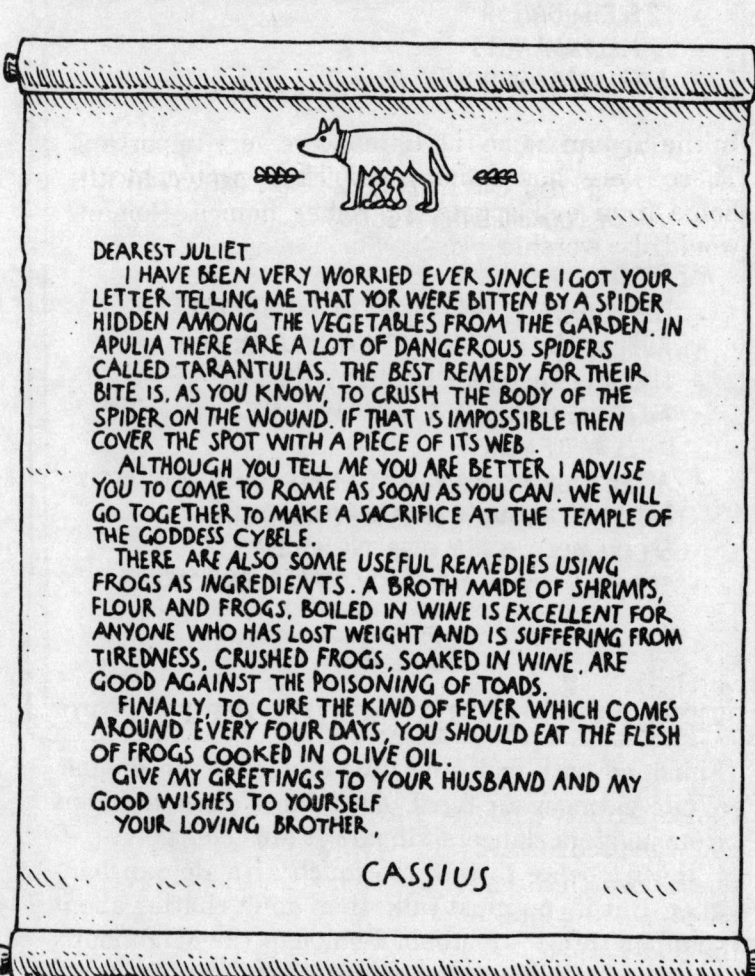

DEAREST JULIET
   I HAVE BEEN VERY WORRIED EVER SINCE I GOT YOUR LETTER TELLING ME THAT YOR WERE BITTEN BY A SPIDER HIDDEN AMONG THE VEGETABLES FROM THE GARDEN. IN APULIA THERE ARE A LOT OF DANGEROUS SPIDERS CALLED TARANTULAS. THE BEST REMEDY FOR THEIR BITE IS, AS YOU KNOW, TO CRUSH THE BODY OF THE SPIDER ON THE WOUND. IF THAT IS IMPOSSIBLE THEN COVER THE SPOT WITH A PIECE OF ITS WEB.
   ALTHOUGH YOU TELL ME YOU ARE BETTER I ADVISE YOU TO COME TO ROME AS SOON AS YOU CAN. WE WILL GO TOGETHER TO MAKE A SACRIFICE AT THE TEMPLE OF THE GODDESS CYBELE.
   THERE ARE ALSO SOME USEFUL REMEDIES USING FROGS AS INGREDIENTS. A BROTH MADE OF SHRIMPS, FLOUR AND FROGS, BOILED IN WINE IS EXCELLENT FOR ANYONE WHO HAS LOST WEIGHT AND IS SUFFERING FROM TIREDNESS. CRUSHED FROGS, SOAKED IN WINE, ARE GOOD AGAINST THE POISONING OF TOADS.
   FINALLY, TO CURE THE KIND OF FEVER WHICH COMES AROUND EVERY FOUR DAYS, YOU SHOULD EAT THE FLESH OF FROGS COOKED IN OLIVE OIL.
   GIVE MY GREETINGS TO YOUR HUSBAND AND MY GOOD WISHES TO YOURSELF
     YOUR LOVING BROTHER,

                    CASSIUS

Rotten Roman religions

The Romans brought their religion and their gods with them from Rome, though in time they became mixed with the native British religions.

Lucky charms and cruel curses

In the Roman home the Lares were very important. These were household gods. They protected the home from evil spirits. In richer homes, Romans would also worship gods like . . .

Vesta – goddess of the fire and hearth . . . and you can still buy matches called "Vestas"!

Penates – guardian of the store cupboard . . . made sure nobody sneaked any midnight feasts.

Janus – the two-faced god who used his two faces to watch the people coming into the house and those going out.

The hot spring waters in the city of Bath are used as cures for all sorts of illnesses by people today. They were used by the Romans too. The Romans were a bit superstitious and believed there was magic in the water. They threw things into the water to take advantage of its powers. They threw coins in – probably as you would into a wishing well – 12,000 Roman coins have been found there.

They also threw in written tablets, usually trying to make a deal with a god – "You do this for me, god, and I'll build an altar for you, OK?" Many of these requests were for curses – if the name of the person you wanted to curse was written backwards, then the magic would be even stronger.

One man lost his girlfriend, Vilbia, to another man. He scratched the curse on a piece of metal . . . but wrote it backwards. Then he threw it in the water where it was found hundreds of years later. It read . . .

retaw ekil diuqil otni nrut ot em morf aibliV koot ohw nosrep eht tnaw I

(Do you know anyone you'd like to turn into a real drip?)

An even nastier curse has been found in Clothall. It was nailed onto some object, perhaps a dead animal, and says . . .

Tacita is cursed by this and will be decayed like rotting blood.

The waters of Bath weren't just used for cursing. The waters were famous for healing long before the Romans came to Britain . . .

The story of Bladud

BLADUD WAS THE SON OF A KING OF THE BRITONS

THAT'S MY LAD BLAD!

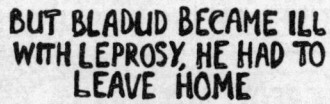

BUT BLADUD BECAME ILL WITH LEPROSY, HE HAD TO LEAVE HOME

THAT'S SAD BLAD

BYE... DAD

HIS MOTHER GAVE HIM A RING

COME BACK WHEN YOU'RE NOT SO BAD BLAD

HE LEFT AND FOUND A JOB AS A PIG KEEPER

I ONCE WORE ROBES BUT NOW I'M A POORLY CLAD BLAD

OINK

BUT TRAGEDY STRUCK! THE PIGS CAUGHT LEPROSY FROM BLAD!

WORST ITCH I'VE EVER HAD, BLAD!

THE ITCHING DROVE THE PIGS WILD, THEY RAN DOWN THE HILL AND INTO AN OOZING, BLACK BOG

I'M GOING MAD, BLAD!

Nasty native religions

1 The Celts believed that gods and spirits were present in all natural things.

2 Their priests were known as Druids. The Druids were local judges as well as priests. If they sentenced you to be kept out of the temple, then no one would want to speak to you.

3 Most of the religious ceremonies were held in woods – especially oak woods where there were magical mistletoe plants.

4 At first the Romans allowed the Celtic religion to continue alongside their own. They even allowed the Druids to build temples similar to the Roman ones.

5 After a while they began to suspect the Druids of leading the rebellions against Roman rule. Most of the Druids were put to death.

6 The Celtic heaven was like earth – only better! There was no old age or sickness and everyone was beautiful. The sun always shone, the birds always sang and there was always plenty to eat and drink. Food appeared as if by magic whenever you felt like it.

7 Death and heaven were so good that the warriors were quite keen to get there! That's why they were so fearless in battle . . . they didn't mind dying.

8 The one thing that the Celtic warrior feared was the sky falling down! That's what would happen if the gods were upset.

9 When you died, your soul went to heaven on a horse. Horses were very special to the British Celts.

10 Julius Caesar told a story of mass sacrifice carried out by the Celts. He said the priests had a huge man made out of wood and woven basket material. The giant, hollow man was then stuffed with living men, women and children . . . and set alight! Caesar could have been fibbing, of course, but the British Celts were great believers in giants . . .

107

The History of Britain . . . by a mad monk!

In the 12th century, Geoffrey of Monmouth told the story of Britain. It was not the history that you will read here and it's not the history your teachers will tell you! But we could be wrong and Geoffrey could be right. What do you think? Here's Geoffrey's history . . .

After the Trojan War – you know, the one where the siege of Troy was ended with the trick of the wooden horse – Brutus and his Trojan warriors came to Britain. Of course, the Trojan War was in the 13th century BC . . . before Rome was even thought of.

Brutus found that the British Isles were inhabited by giants. Brutus gave General Corineus the job of conquering Cornwall. Corineus killed the giants and was left with just one final giant – Gogmagog. Corineus wrestled with the four-metre man and threw him to his death in the sea. That's how Britain came to be free of giants!

Believe that, do you? Or is it just a TALL story? Old Geoffrey believed it. And so did many Britons, probably.

The Britons had their own stories and many were stories of heroes fighting giants. Some of the stories are still told today. But, because children are easily scared, most story-tellers miss out the gory bits.

Here's an old British folk-tale with the gory bits put back in. If you suffer from nightmares *don't read it* . . . or read it with your eyes shut. You have been warned!

A bloody British tale

Once upon a long-ago time in Cornwall, there lived the giant, Cormoran, with his wife, Cormelian.

Cormoran was big and Cormoran was a bully. "I want a castle and I want it built of white granite!" he told his wife.

"That'll be nice, dear," his wife nodded. "But there's no white granite round here. Only green granite. You'll have ever so far to carry it!"

"I won't carry it," Cormoran sneered. "You will!"

"Will I?" Cormelian blinked. "Why?"

"Because I'm telling you to," the cruel man cackled. "Now, get started!"

Cormelian trudged off to find the white granite and struggled to carry it back. Even though every step took her six miles it was hard and heavy work. When she returned the third time she saw that Cormoran was asleep.

"I'll just fetch a few loads of the green granite," the giant's wife sighed. "He'll never notice!"

But, as she brought the load of green stone. Cormoran woke up. "What's this?" he roared and gave her such a kick that her apron strings snapped. The stones tumbled down and sank Mount's Bay forest into the sea and drowned the people.

"Now look what you made me do!" Cormelian grumbled, rubbing her sore bum. She went off in a huff.

Cormoran piled the white granite into a castle – you can see it today in Cornwall. It's known as St Michael's Mount. The huge green stone that Cormelian dropped can be seen on the road to the mount.

Anyway, the poor people were horrified by the sinking of the forest. "Whatever shall we do?" they cried. "Mount's Bay forest has gone today – we'll be next!"

Just then, along came the local hero, Jack. Jack the giant-killer. Jack had killed giants by digging deep pits in the ground. When the giants fell in, their heads came up to the level of Jack. A quick whack with his axe would split the giants' skulls and kill them with a single blow. The pit became their gruesome, brain-spattered grave.

This time Jack had another plan.

First he collected as much food as he could find and placed it at the foot of St Michael's Mount.

Then he made a special coat with a huge pouch in the front.

Lastly he blew his horn to wake up the giant Cormoran. The angry giant glared at Jack. "What do you want, shorty?"

"I want to challenge you to an eating competition," the hero announced.

BREAKFAST?

110

"No problem," the giant shrugged and sat down to stuff himself with a pile of food. Jack pretended to eat, but really slipped the food into the pouch in the front of his coat.

The giant began to slow down. At last he stopped. Jack nibbled at a roast cow. "Give in?" he asked cheerfully.

"Certainly not!" Cormoran roared. "But I'd like to know where you're putting all that food."

Jack shrugged. "In my stomach," he said, patting the front of his pouch. "In fact, I can empty my stomach and start again. Then I'm bound to win!"

"How?" the stupid giant asked.

Jack took a dagger from his belt. He placed it at one side of his pouch and dragged it across. The pouch split open and the food tumbled out. "Easy!"

"Hah! Two can play at that game," Cormoran sniffed. He took out his knife, stuck it in his fat belly and dragged it across. "Ouch!" he cried as the food tumbled out . . . and most of his guts. "Ooooh!" he sobbed. "I think I've just killed meself!"

And he had.

A bloody end

An equally nasty story tells of the equally stupid giant, Bolster, who fell in love with the beautiful St Agnes. She asked him to prove his love by filling a hole in the ground with his blood. He agreed and opened a vein. He didn't know that the hole led to a cave that led out to the sea. Bolster bled for hours and died in the end. There's a hole at Chapel Porth in Cornwall, and red stains mark the rocks around!

The rottenest Roman religions

Chucking chickens

The Roman Army had its own religions and its own superstitions. The General of an army would look at the liver of certain animals for signs as to how a battle might go. They might also . . .

- observe the flight of birds – the ways in which crows flew, for example.
- observe the way the sacred chickens ate their food – Claudius Pulcher took chickens with him on a voyage to the Punic wars. The chickens were probably a bit seasick, because they refused to eat at all – a bad sign. So Claudius Pulcher ordered them to be thrown overboard with the words, "If they won't eat then let them drink!" He went on to lose the battle and the soldiers blamed him for drowning the sacred chickens!

I'M FEELING A LOT HUNGRIER NOW!

Stomach signals

A Roman teacher, Fronto, wrote to his pupil, Marcus, with news that he had a pain in the stomach. He believed this was a sign from the gods that there was bad luck coming to his family. (If your teacher had a pain in the stomach, she'd be more likely to blame school dinners!)

Mighty Mithras

The religion of the bull-god Mithras, was very popular with many Roman soldiers. He was probably brought to Britain by the legionaries who served in Persia, where Mithras was a popular god.

Mithras was the "judge" of the afterlife – he decided who should go to heaven and who should go to hell after they died.

The temples of Mithras were dark and gloomy places – sometimes underground – and a lot of the soldiers must have enjoyed joining this religion, because it was like joining a secret society.

I CAN ONLY LET YOU IN ONCE YOU'VE TOLD ME THE SECRET PASSWORD, SHOWN ME YOUR SECRET RING, GIVEN ME THE SECRET HANDSHAKE, AND..ER..FOUND THE KEY

You couldn't enter the temples until you'd performed certain brave deeds – like allowing yourself to be locked up for several hours in a coffin! The base of the coffin was on the stone-cold floor and the side was close to a fire – you froze and fried at the same time!

Bull's blood

Another Eastern "mystery" religion had equally gruesome rituals, as Prudentius described in the 4th century AD . . .

The worshippers dig a deep pit and the High Priest is lowered into it. Above him they put a platform of loose planks. Each plank has tiny holes drilled in it. A huge bull is stood on the platform. They take a sacred hunting spear and drive it into the bull's heart. The hot blood spurts out of the deep wound. It falls through the holes in the planks like rotten rain onto the priest below. His clothes and body are covered in the animal's gore. Afterwards he climbs out of the pit. It is a dreadful sight to see.

Christianity

From the end of the first century AD, Christianity began to enter Britain. After the exciting Roman religions some Christians seemed a bit boring. One Christian writer, Tertullian, was against fancy clothes – he didn't even like to see them dyed. He wrote . . .

If God had wanted us to wear purple and sky-blue clothes, then He would have given us purple and sky-blue sheep!

PURPLE? WITH ALL THIS GREEN GRASS AROUND? WE'D CLASH!

By 250 AD, the emperors began stamping out Christianity and killing Christians. St Alban was one of the victims in Britain. Still, Christianity continued to grow there.

Then, in 313 AD, the Act of Toleration was passed that allowed Christians to worship openly. But it was all too late for poor old Alban . . .

The legend of St Alban

The wind blew wild and wet along the wall. Two soldiers shivered behind their shields and complained.

"End of the world, this place. End of the world!" old Laganus groaned.

"Not quite the end of the world," his young partner pointed out. "There are people on the other side of the wall!"

"People!" Laganus laughed. "Them Picts aren't *people!* More what you'd call *animals.* Proper people wouldn't live out in that wild country. They're *savages*, Paul, *savages!*"

Young Paul huddled into his cloak and looked across the bleak and empty moors. "Not as savage as the Romans can be," he said carefully.

"That's no way to talk about our masters!" Laganus gasped. "That's the sort of talk that'll get you beaten!"

Paul nodded. "That's what I mean. They'll beat me. They're cruel."

The older man snorted. "You're just soft, my boy. You've got to kill your enemy. Kill or get yourself killed. That's the way it is!"

"You wouldn't say that if you were a Christian," Paul told him.

Laganus turned on him savagely. "Yeh! I've heard

115

all about your Christian God! Look at that Alban!"

"They killed him!" Paul cried. "The Romans killed him!"

"But that's nothing to what your kind and gentle God did for revenge, is it?" the old soldier sneered. He sat down in the shelter of the wall and rubbed his freezing hands. "I heard the true story from a soldier of the Seventh Legion last week."

Paul crouched down beside him. "Alban was a hero. A Christian martyr . . ."

"Alban was a soldier just like you or me. Well, more like *you*, Paul. He was soft-hearted. Soft in the head too, if you ask me. The Romans were having one of their crackdowns on the Christians. You know the sort of thing. Killing a few here and there to show them who is boss."

"Murder," Paul muttered.

"Alban was a *Roman* soldier, of course. He should have been joining in the *killing* of the Christians. Instead he gave *shelter* to a Christian priest."

"Amphibalus," the young soldier nodded.

"And worse! He let this Amphibalus talk *him* into becoming a Christian!" Laganus groaned. "They sent soldiers to arrest Alban, of course. What did he do? Disguised himself and tried to run away."

"They caught him," Paul sighed.

"Of course they caught him! But they didn't kill him for hiding the enemy – they didn't kill him for becoming a Christian . . ."

"They did!" Paul cut in.

"No, no, no! They gave him a chance. They told him to make a sacrifice to the Roman gods. Prove that he was still loyal!" the old soldier said.

"He refused."

"So it serves him right if he was sentenced to

death," Laganus snorted. "But the Romans didn't have him tortured or crucified or stoned to death. No. They were kind. They sentenced him to a quick death by beheading!"

"They murdered him," Paul repeated stubbornly.

"Ah, but that was quick and kind. What happened at the execution, eh? You Christians never tell about that!"

The young soldier shrugged. "I don't know."

Laganus grinned. "Two soldiers led Alban to the place of execution. Alban managed to convert one of them on the way. But he didn't convert the second one, did he? The second executioner cut off Alban's head! *Then* your 'kind', kind God took his cruel, cruel revenge. As Alban's head hit the ground the executioner staggered back clutching his face. When the guards reached him they found that his eyes had both dropped out! Plop! Plop!"

By the end of that century, Christianity became the religion of the Roman State. But some parts of the British Isles were converted as the result of a strange accident . . .

Pirates, pagans and Patrick – Did you know?

1 Patrick is the patron saint of Ireland, BUT he was born in Wales, lived in England and his parents were Roman.

2 When he was 16 he was kidnapped by Celtic pirates and taken as a slave to Ireland.

3 He was given a rotten job by the Irish pagans. Looking after cattle on the bleak hills.

4 A boulder crashed down the mountainside towards Patrick. Just before it flattened him it split in two. One piece went on either side of him.

5 Patrick took this as a miracle. He believed it was a sign from God that there was special work for him.

6 He escaped to Gaul, then returned home to become a farmer. He still felt that his life had been saved for some special reason.

7 He boldly went back to Ireland.

8 He performed miracles there. There is a story, for example, that there are no snakes in Ireland because Patrick got rid of them all.

9 Patrick converted the kings of many Irish kingdoms to Christianity. The kings were baptised and the people followed the kings.

10 A king of southern Ireland had a rotten baptism. Patrick carried a crook – like a shepherd. It was pointed on the bottom. During the baptism Patrick accidentally put the point clean through the king's foot. The king didn't complain; he thought it was all part of the ceremony.

Rotten Roman facts

The rottenest Roman historian

At the eastern end of the Roman Wall is a fort. In 1971 the museum at the fort proudly showed their latest find. "It is a sestertius coin, made between 135 AD and 138 AD. On the back of the coin is a large letter 'R' – standing for Roma," they said.

Then an expert, Miss Fiona Gordon, told them they were wrong. The sestertius was, in fact, a free gift given away with bottles of fruit squash. "The letter 'R' stands for the name of the makers, Robinson!"

The museum keepers discovered Miss Gordon was correct. That was embarrassing! But, most embarrassing of all, Miss Fiona Gordon was just nine years old!

True or false?

1 A favourite method of execution in ancient Rome was "stinging to death".
2 The Roman Fort at Sinodum is supposed to be the site of a money-pit full of buried treasure.
3 Druids picked their victims by going "Eeny-meeny-miney-mo . . ."

REMIND ME, WHAT COMES AFTER MO?

4 Women could be Druids.

5 Druids would stab a victim in the back, then see the future from the way he died.

6 A crash at a chariot race was called "a plane-crash".

7 The Victorians pulled down the east end of Hadrian's Wall and used the stone to mend their roads.

8 The Romans didn't have peppermint toothpaste. They preferred powdered mouse-brains.

9 The Romans stopped traffic jams in Aldborough by building a bypass.

10 In Roman horse races the losing horse was killed.

Answers:

1 True – the victim was smothered in honey then covered with angry wasps.

2 True – in the 19th century a local villager was digging at the fort one day when he came across an iron chest. A raven landed on it and said, "He is not born yet!" The villager thought this meant, "The person who can open the chest is not yet born." He filled the hole in and left. Are you the one born to open the chest?

3 True – according to Victorian experts. The shepherds of ancient Britain would count sheep with a number system that sounded very like "Eeny-meeny-miney-mo". The Druids could well have used it. Children may then have copied it as part of a gruesome game and it's been used in children's games ever since.

4 True – the Romans said that they met Druidesses. These women were good at telling fortunes.

5 True – the Roman historian, Strabo, said the way a man twisted and fell after he had been stabbed helped a Druid to read the fortunes for his tribe.

6 False – it was called a "shipwreck".

7 True. There are still large stretches of Hadrian's wall to be seen across the North of England. It's well looked after now . . . but it hasn't always been. Farmers pinched stones from the Wall to build their houses, and the Victorians were worse. They pulled the wall down, smashed up the stones into little bits and used them to repair the roads of Newcastle!

8 True – perhaps they wanted their teeth to be "squeaky" clean! They also used powdered horn, oyster-shell ash and the ashes of dogs' teeth mixed with honey.

9 True.

10 False – the *winning* horse was killed as a sacrifice to the god of war, Mars. The local people often fought fiercely to decide who would have the honour of sticking its head on their wall.

Rotten Roman towns

Everyone tells you about how marvellous the Roman baths were. But not *all* of the Romans were so keen. One Roman wrote . . .

> *I live above the public baths, and we all know what that means. Yeuch! It's sickening. Firstly there are the strong men doing exercises, swinging lead weights round with grunts and . . .*

> *. . . groans. Then there are the lazy ones having a cheap massage – I can hear them being slapped on the back. Then there are the noises of fighters and thieves being arrested. Worst is the sound of the man who likes to hear his own voice in the bath. And what about the ones who leap into the bath and make a huge splash in the water?*

Rotten Romans today

The Rotten Romans ran the world for a long time. There are still signs of their life today.

Did you know?
1 The Romans signed their "trademark" wherever they went. They wrote the letters SPQR, which stood for Senatus Populus Que Romanus – The Senate and the People of Rome. The buses and the drain covers of Rome have the letters on them today.
2 The Roman language is called Latin. It is still used in some religious ceremonies and used to be taught in many schools. But no one speaks it as an everyday language now. So it's called a "dead" language. That's why schoolchildren who still have to learn it mutter the same old school chant . . .

> LATIN IS A LANGUAGE
> AS DEAD AS DEAD CAN BE
> IT KILLED THE ANCIENT BRITONS-
> AND NOW IT'S KILLING ME!

3 Much of the Roman Wall can still be seen – and walked along – in the north of England. But the famous historian and monk, St Bede, got his facts about Hadrian's wall completely wrong! He said the Romans built it just before they abandoned Britain. It was a sort of farewell present for the Britons, planned to keep the Picts and Scots out. He wrote . . .

> *When the Wall was finished, the Romans gave clear advice to the dejected Britons, then said goodbye to their friends and never returned. The gloomy British soldiers lived in terror day and night. Beyond the Wall the enemy constantly attacked them with hooked weapons, dragging the defenders down from the Wall and dashing them to the ground. At last the Britons abandoned their cities and the Wall and fled in confusion.*

Wrong! The Wall was there 300 years before the Romans left. Don't believe everything you read in history books – even if the writer is a saint!

4 There are some rotten things in Britain today that we can blame the Romans for. They brought them here. Things like . . .

- **stinging nettles** – next time you sit on one, you can cry out in agony, "Oooh! The rotten Romans!"
- **cabbages and peas** – the sort of vegetables your parents make you eat because "they're good for you." Next time you hear that, you can say, "The Ancient Britons survived a few million years without them!"

- **cats** – yes, blame the Romans for that mangy moggy that yowls all night on the corner of your street and keeps you awake. When teacher tells you off for yawning in class, say, "Don't blame me – blame the rotten Romans!"

5 Rotten spelling – a lot of the words we use today come from Latin. They made sense to the Rotten Romans but they don't make sense to us. Take the Latin word "plumbum".... no, it doesn't mean purple bottom. It means waterworks. So we get a word for a man who fixes your leaky waterworks from that. That's right, "plumber". We say it "plummer" and any sensible Briton in their right mind would spell it "plummer". But the Romans put that useless "b" in the middle, so we have to. Next time you get two out of ten for your spelling test say, "Don't blame me – blame the rotten Romans!"

6 False teeth – the Romans generally had good teeth. They cleaned them regularly and didn't have sugar to rot them. But, if they did lose a tooth, they used false teeth. These would be made of gold or ivory. They'd be held in place with gold wire. That wire could also be used to hold loose teeth in place. The poor people just had to let them drop out.

Ancient Roman Ancient Joke:

DOCTOR DOCTOR! HAVE YOU GOT SOMETHING TO KEEP MY TEETH IN?

CERTAINLY MADAM, HERE'S A PAPER BAG!

7 Skyscrapers – the Romans made buildings with more floors than anyone else of their age. But this led to some rotten Roman tragedies. In 217 BC an ox escaped from the local market. It ran into a three-storey building and up the stairs. When it reached the top it threw itself out of a window on the top floor. By the time of Augustus the crowded cities were forcing people to build houses higher and higher – a bit like Britain in the 1960s! But many of these tower blocks began to collapse – so Augustus passed a law banning any building over 20 metres tall.

8 A family living in Hertford, England, are so keen on the Romans that they eat Roman food (like sardines stuffed with dates – yeuch!) and play Roman games after dinner. The family have organised a new Fourteenth Legion (but with only 24 legionaries so far) who go on 40-kilometre marches just as the original legion did. They also dress as Romans occasionally and go around schools to give demonstrations to children. This does not always have the desired result – sometimes younger pupils see the Roman soldier walk into the classroom and they burst into tears . . . usually the boys! Oh, and the daughter of the family isn't a fan of the Romans and is too embarrassed by her Roman family to bring her boyfriend home!

9 We have Christmas traditions today that live on from Roman times. One tradition is Roman and one British. They were . . .

- **holly** – The Romans had ceremonies for their god, Saturn, in December. The decoration they used was holly. Country people still believe that it's a protection against poison, storms, fire and "the evil eye".

- **mistletoe** – trees were sacred to the Britons. Mistletoe grew on trees and sucked the spirit from them – that's the sticky juice in the berries. The oak was the *most* sacred tree, so mistletoe from the oak was the most precious plant of all. Druids in white robes cut it with golden knives on the sixth day of a new moon. A sprig over the door protected the house from thunder, lightning and all evil.

10 Christianity put an end to the Druids' human sacrifices . . . but 2000 years later we may still have curious memories of those deadly days . . . the children's game *London Bridge is Falling Down*. Some form of this game is known all over the world.

Two children link hands and form an arch. The rest of the children have to pass under the arch while chanting the song. When a child is caught, then the bridge has fallen. That child becomes the "watchman" of the bridge.

But the legends say that, in the days of pagan beliefs, the unlucky child could only guard the bridge if he (or she) was dead! It seems the spirits of rivers hate bridges and without a sacrifice they would bring it down. The British legend says that children were sacrificed and their blood poured over the stones of the first London Bridge to keep "Old Father Thames" happy.

127

Epilogue

The Romans left to defend their homeland and Rome. The Britons were left to defend the island against enemies old and new. A historian from those times, Gildas, described how the "foul" Picts and Scots with their "lust for blood" swarmed over Hadrian's mighty Wall. They pulled the British defenders down from the Wall and killed them like "lambs are slaughtered by butchers". The men from the north with their hairy "hang-dog" faces took over.

Four hundred years before, the Britons had fought the Romans off. But in four hundred years the Britons had forgotten how to fight. Suddenly the Romans didn't seem so rotten after all. Now the Britons wrote and begged them to return . . .

> *The barbarians drive us to the sea, the sea drives us back to the barbarians. Between these two methods of death we are either massacred or drowned.*

But no help came. Rome had problems of its own. After hundreds of years of Roman rule, Britain entered "The Dark Ages".

128

ROTTEN ROMANS

GRISLY QUIZ

**Now find out if you're a
rotten Roman expert!**

EVIL EMPERORS

It's really weird but true. Some of the battiest people in history have been leaders – kings and queens, emperors and empresses, presidents and princes. It's almost as if you have to be slightly potty to be a ruler!

Rome had their fair share of rotten rulers. Here are a few foul facts about them. Only the odd word has been left out for you to complete…

Here are the missing words, in the wrong order: mother, head, chicken, horse, corpse, cobweb, cheese, wife, wrinkly, leg.

1 AUGUSTUS CAESAR (31 BC–AD 14) CAUGHT BRUTUS, THE MURDERER OF JULIUS CAESAR, AND HAD HIS _____ THROWN AT THE FEET OF CAESAR'S STATUE.

2 TIBERIUS (AD 14–37) SAID THAT HE WOULD SMASH THE _____ OF ANYONE WHO DISOBEYED HIM.

3 CALIGULA (AD 37–41) WANTED SOMEONE TO HELP HIM TO RULE SO HE GAVE THE JOB TO HIS _____.

4 CLAUDIUS (AD 41–54) HAD HIS _____ EXECUTED.

5 NERO (AD 54–68) TRIED TO DROWN HIS _____.

6 VITELLIUS (AD 69) HAD HIS _____ THROWN IN THE RIVER TIBER AT ROME.

7 HADRIAN (AD 117–138) FORCED A _____ TO COMMIT SUICIDE.

8 ANTONIUS (AD 138–161) DIED OF EATING TOO MUCH _____.

9 ELIOGABALUS (AD 218–222) HAD THE CURIOUS HOBBY OF COLLECTING EVERY _____ HE COULD FIND.

10 HONORIUS (AD 395–423) HAD A _____ CALLED 'ROME'.

STABBING JULES

Julius Caesar was a brilliant Roman leader, but he became a bit too big for his boots – his red boots, in fact. The Romans were now used to having leaders who were 'elected'. They had hated their old kings … who had worn red boots instead of a crown, but when the booted-up kings were kicked out the Romans got on much better with their elected leaders.

But Julius got himself elected for life. Just like a king. When he started wearing red boots, his number was up. There was just one way to get rid of him then – assassination.

His friend Brutus led the murderers, who struck when Caesar was entering the Roman parliament (the senate). Roman writer Plutarch told the gory story. Can you sort out the scrambled words in this version?

Some of Brutus's gang slipped behind Caesar's chair while others came to meet him. Cimber grabbed Caesar's robe and pulled it from his neck. This was the A SLING for the attack.

Casca struck the first blow. His IF KEN made a wound in ASS ACRE neck but Caesar was able to turn round, grab the knife and hold on. The HAT CREWS were horrified but didn't dare move or make a sound.

Each AS SINS AS bared his dagger now. They pushed Caesar this way and that like a wild BE SAT surrounded by hunters.

Brutus stabbed Caesar in the groin. Above all Caesar had RED TUTS Brutus. When he saw Brutus coming towards him he pulled his robe over his head and sank down.

The attackers pushed Caesar against the ASTUTE of his old enemy Pompey. The statue became drenched with DO LOB.

Caesar received 23 wounds. Many of the assassins WON DUDE each other as they fought to stick so many knives into one body.

FOUL ROMAN FOOD

Do you know what the rotten Romans ate? Have a go at this quirky quiz on cuisine (that's a posh word for 'cooking') and find out…

1 The Romans didn't have tomato ketchup but they did have sauce made from what?

a) sheep eyeballs
b) fish guts
c) elephant's tail

2 At posh Roman feasts guests ate more than their stomachs could hold. How?

a) They emptied their stomachs by vomiting every now and then.
b) They stretched their stomachs with special exercises.
c) They stuck a pin in their stomach to let out trapped air and let in more food.

3 Snails were fattened up before they were killed. They were kept in a bowl of what?

a) chopped cabbage
b) brains
c) blood

4 Emperor Eliogabalus also served a meal where the peas were mixed with what?

a) queues
b) poison
c) gold nuggets

132

5 Emperor Eliogabalus served 600 of them at one feast. What?
a) ostrich brains
b) ducks' feet
c) camel-burgers

6 A Roman called Trimalchio had a feast with a roasted boar. When it was sliced down the belly, what came out?
a) maggots
b) songbirds
c) a dancing girl

7 What could you watch as you ate at some Roman feasts?
a) television
b) two gladiators trying to murder one another
c) tap-dancing bears

8 The Romans ate cute little pets that you probably wouldn't eat. What?
a) cats
b) budgies
c) dormice

9 The Romans did *not* eat animals' what?
a) teeth
b) brains
c) lungs

10 Emperor Maximian was a strange eater. Why?
a) He was the only vegetarian emperor.
b) He ate only eggs and drank only water.
c) He ate 20 kilos of meat a day.

Evil Emperors

1 Head. Nice present for Jules!

2 Leg. Tiberius died at the age of 78, probably suffocated by his chief helper.

3 Horse. Cruel Caligula liked to feed criminals to wild animals. He was stabbed to death by one of his guards.

4 Wife. She was a bit of a flirt. But he also had 300 of her party friends chopped too! His third wife, and niece, had him poisoned with mushrooms.

5 Mother. When the plot failed he sent soldiers to give her the chop. Nero stabbed himself to death before his enemies got to him.

6 Corpse. He was murdered in the centre of Rome but not given a nice emperor's burial.

7 Wrinkly. Hadrian accused Servianus of treason and forced him to kill himself. But Servianus was 90 years old and hardly a big threat.

WHY NOT TRY *THIS* CHEESE, YOUR IMPERIAL LOFTINESS?

8 Cheese. At least that's what a Roman historian blamed his death on. Guess it was just hard cheese.

9 Cobweb. Maybe he was planning to build the world's first web-site?

10 Chicken. Trouble is he loved the chicken Rome more than he loved the city Rome, and the city was neglected.

Stabbing Jules

These are the unscrabbled words in the correct order: signal; knife; Caesar's; watchers; assassin; beast; trusted; statue; blood; wounded.

Foul Roman Food

1b) The guts were soaked in salt water and left to stew in the sun for a few days. Then the fish-gut sauce was poured over the food as a tasty treat. Oh my cod!

2a) They went to a special room called a vomitorium and threw up. They used a stick with a feather to tickle their tonsils and vomited into a bowl. When their stomach was empty they went back and ate more. Scoff-vomit, scoff-vomit, scoff-vomit all night long. Good idea for school dinners?

3c) The snails supped the blood till they were too fat to get in their shells. The blood diet made them taste nice. If they wanted creamy snails, the Romans fed them on milk before eating them.

4c) Eliogabalus mixed gold and precious stones with the peas as a sort of treat. But if one of those diamonds smashed your teeth you'd be sore. And if you swallowed a gold nugget you'd be ill! You'd have to sit on the toilet and wait for some change!

5a) Ostrich brains are quite small so he'd need 600 to keep his guests fed. But where did he get all those ostriches? Zoo knows?

6b) There were thrushes stuffed inside the roast boar. (Were they bored in there?) Trimalchio also served wine that was

100 years old at that feast.

7b) Of course, the trouble with gladiators fighting as you eat is that they could splash blood and guts all over your freshly cooked dinner. Aren't you lucky you don't suffer that while you watch telly?

8c) They fed the dormice really well on walnuts, acorns and chestnuts. They were served roasted and stuffed with pork sausage. Scrummy! Even tastier than hamster or gerbil!

9a) They ate all sorts of other things though. As well as sheep and goat lungs or brains, they ate gulls, peacocks, swans and jackdaws. They stuffed the birds just by pushing stuffing straight down their throats. They didn't clean the insides out the way you do with your Christmas turkey. Yeuch!

10c) That's about a small sheep every day. Would ewe believe it? He was also supposed to have drunk about 34 litres of wine ... but it must have been very weak. Of course, after 20 years all that eating killed him, but he was probably too drunk to notice he was dead!

INTERESTING INDEX

Where will you find 'mouse brains', 'crushed frogs', 'fish guts' and 'wild parties' in an index? In a Horrible Histories book, of course!

Juvenal (Roman writer) 76

kilts 14

Lares (gods) 76, 103
Latin (dead language) 55, 87, 92, 123, 125
leaders 58-72
legionaries 113, 126
legs, breaking 62-3
leprosy 105-6
liver, eating 79-80, 82
Llanymynech (Welsh hill fort) 52
Londinium (London) 34-5, 43, 48, 57
Lord's Prayer 87

magic
    food 107
    heads 32-6
    water 104
Maiden Castle (British hill fort) 38, 50
make-up 76
Marcellinus (Roman writer) 39
Mark Antony (Caesar's friend) 59, 61
Mars (god) 121
Maximian (Roman emperor) 94-5
Medway, battle of 11, 48
Minerva (goddess) 75
mistletoe 127
Mithradates (king of Pontus) 96
Mithras (god) 113
money 71, 74
Mons Graupius, battle of 9
mouse brains 120-1
moustaches 38
murders
    Agrippina 69
    emperors 71-2
    gladiators 89
    Julius Caesar 6, 58-61
    Nero's wife and girlfriend 67
    revolting Britons 43
    saints 116-17
mystery religions 113-14

Nature 37
necks
    chalk on 76-7
    chopping 64
Nero (Roman emperor) 66-9, 71, 89
nightmares 59, 108
North Africa 7
Nuts (game) 86

Octavia (Nero's wife) 67
Octavian (Caesar's nephew) 61
Olympus, Mount 78
Ostrich brains 97

pagans 118, 127
parties, wild 66
Patrick (patron saint) 118
Paulinus (Roman general) 9, 43
Penates (god) 103
Persia 113
Pertinax (Roman emperor) 71
Philippi, battle of 61
Picts (Scottish tribe) 9, 11-12, 115, 124, 128
pigs bladders 84
pirates 118
plagues 12
plays 93
poison 44, 67
    mushrooms 66, 68
    protection from 126
    resistance to 96
    toads 102
Pompey (Caesar's enemy) 60
Poppaea (Nero's girlfriend) 67
praetorian guard (emperors' security guards) 71
Prasutagus (Iceni wimp king) 42, 46
Prometheus (fire stealer) 78-82
prophecies 32
Prudentius (Roman writer) 113
Pulcher, Claudius (chicken drowning General) 112

Terry Deary was born at a very early age, so long ago he can't remember. But his mother, who was there at the time, says he was born in Sunderland, north-east England, in 1946 – so it's not true that he writes all *Horrible Histories* from memory. At school he was a horrible child only interested in playing football and giving teachers a hard time. His history lessons were so boring and so badly taught, that he learned to loathe the subject. *Horrible Histories* is his revenge.

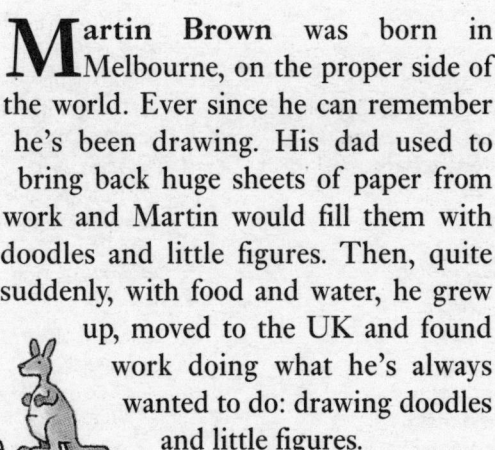

Martin Brown was born in Melbourne, on the proper side of the world. Ever since he can remember he's been drawing. His dad used to bring back huge sheets of paper from work and Martin would fill them with doodles and little figures. Then, quite suddenly, with food and water, he grew up, moved to the UK and found work doing what he's always wanted to do: drawing doodles and little figures.

HORRIBLE HISTORIES

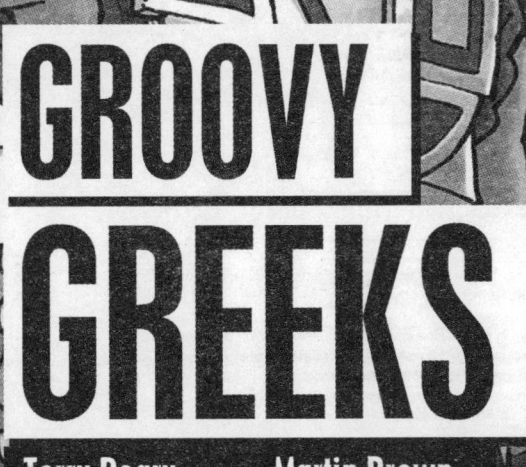

GROOVY
GREEKS

Terry Deary Illustrated by Martin Brown

For Jean Longstaff, with thanks

Scholastic Children's Books,
Euston House, 24 Eversholt Street,
London NW1 1DB, UK

A division of Scholastic Ltd
London ~ New York ~ Toronto ~ Sydney ~ Auckland
Mexico City ~ New Delhi ~ Hong Kong

First published in the UK by Scholastic Ltd, 1996
This edition published by Scholastic Ltd, 2016

Some of the material in this book has previously been published in
Horrible Histories: The Awesome Ancient Quiz Book

Text © Terry Deary, 1996, 2001
Illustration © Martin Brown, 1996, 2001, 2016

ISBN 978 1407 16383 3

Printed and bound by CPI Group (UK) Ltd, Croydon, CR0 4YY

10 9

www.scholastic.co.uk

CONTENTS

Introduction

History can be horrible. And do you know who to blame?

No, it's the Greeks!

The Greeks invented history about 2,500 years ago . . .

Inventing history is just one of the things we have to thank them for. They had the idea for plays, for the Olympic Games – even the camera . . .

Funny you should mention that. Here is a book on the groovy Greeks. A book that will tell you all the things that teacher doesn't tell you. The things you really want to know. The hilarious stories and the horror stories.

Groovy Greek timeline

BC

1600 – 1200 First Greek civilizations, ruled by the mighty Mycenaean lords of Crete.

About 1180 The siege of Troy – Troy loses to the famous wooden horse trick.

About 1100 The state of Sparta starts.

776 First recorded Olympic games.

About 750 – 550 Greeks take to the seas and become great traders.

About 730 Greeks produce the first works of written poetry in the world. Groovy Homer is the most famous.

640 World's first roof tiles manufactured at Temple of Hera at Olympia.

About 600 Thales, the Greek scientist, announces that the entire earth is actually floating in water.

585 Scientist Thales predicts an eclipse of the sun.

About 550 First plays performed. King Croesus of Lydia has gold and silver coins made; the first coins with writing on them.

About 530 Peisistratus of Athens creates a library.

About 520 Alcmaeon of Croton finds out about the human body by cutting up dead ones – groovy, eh?

490 Persians invade Greece – beaten by Greeks at The Battle of Marathon.

486 The first comedy drama at Athens.

480 Xerxes of Persia attacks the Greeks. The battle of Thermopylae. Spartan heroes die.

460 Athens v Sparta and Persia.

431 – 404 Athens tries to get too bossy so the others fight the Peloponnesian War. Sparta becomes top dog.

430 Great Plague of Athens kills Athenian leader, Pericles, not to mention a quarter of all the Athenian people.

413 A defeat at Syracuse for the army of Athens followed by . . .

404 The Fall of Athens.

About 400 Greek army engineers invent the stomach bow – the first type of crossbow.

371 Spartans lose to new top dog, the Thebans.

8

336 Alexander the Great becomes king of Macedon when his dad is assassinated. In just ten years he conquers the old enemy, Persia.

330 Aristotle invents the 'camera obscura' – a sort of pinhole camera and the idea behind today's film and television – now that really was groovy!

323 Alexander the Great dies. His generals divide up his empire.

322 The end of democracy in Athens when the Macedons take over.

215 Archimedes invents war machines like the catapult – they keep the Romans out for three years.

213 Archimedes has mirrors set along the harbour walls – they dazzle the Romans and set fire to their boats. . . Romans delayed for a while but. . .

212 Here come the Romans.

146 Greece part of the Roman Empire.

AD
393 Romans abandon Olympic Games – they don't happen again for 1500 years.

9

The gruesome gods

Before the groovy Greeks came the mighty Mycenaean people, who ruled Greece. Their greatest palace was on the island of Crete – it was so posh the queen had the world's first flushing toilet. Then the palaces were wrecked and the Mycenaean way of life went too. No more flushing toilets. What went wrong? Was it. . .

- war and attack from outside
- earthquakes
- disease and plague
- drought and famine
- change of climate?

They've all been suggested by historians. But, like the disappearance of the dinosaurs, no one really knows for sure.

The *Dorian* people moved down into Greece. They forgot how to write so we don't know a lot about those days. Historians call them the *Dark* Ages.

So, without writing, the history was preserved in stories. And, as the years passed, the stories became wilder and more unlikely. Legends, in fact.

The Greeks loved horror stories best of all. One Greek writer said that Greek children should not be told stories like this one (just as grown-ups today say you should not watch certain horror films).

But this book is a Horrible History and this story has a PG rating.

Do *not* read this story if you suffer from nightmares – or at least read it with your eyes closed so you don't suffer the most gory bits.

YOU HAVE BEEN WARNED!

Bringing up baby

Cronos was the chief god. You'd think that would make him happy, but no. Somebody told him that one of his children would take his place.

'Can't have that,' Cronos complained. 'Here, Mrs Cronos, pass me that baby!'

'What for?'

'Never mind daft questions. Just pass me that baby.'

Mrs Cronos passed across their new-born child. 'Here! What you doin' of with that baby?' she cried.

'Eatin' it.'

'Eatin' it! You great greedy lummock. You've just had your tea. You can't be hungry again already.'

NEEDS SALT

11

'I'm not hungry,' the great god growled. 'Just there's this prophecy about one of my children taking my throne. No kid, no take-over, that's the way I look at it.'

'You don't want to go takin' no notice of them horry-scopes,' Mrs Cronos sighed.

'Don't pay to take chances is what I always say,' Cronos said smugly. 'Pass them indigestion tablets.'

Time passed, as time does, and Mrs Cronos had more baby gods. . . and Cronos ate every last one. Well, not the *very* last one. Mrs Cronos was getting fed up with his gruesome guzzling. 'I'll put a stop to his little game,' she smirked as she hid the new baby, Zeus, under her bed. She picked up a big rock, wrapped it in a baby blanket and dropped it in the cot.

In walked Cronos. 'Where is it?'

'In the cot.'

'Ugly little beggar, isn't he?' the head god said, squinting at the boulder.

'Takes after his father then,' Mrs Cronos mumbled.

'Crunchy as well,' her husband said, swallowing teeth.

'Probably cos he's *bolder* than the rest,' Mrs Cronos agreed.

Cronos sat down heavily on a royal couch. 'Ooooh! I think I've eaten someone who disagrees with me.'

'It's possible,' Mrs Cronos sniffed. 'A lot of people disagree with you, sweetheart.'

'Ooooh!' The god groaned and clutched his stomach. 'I think I'm going to be sick!'

'Not on the new carpet, my love. There's a bowl over there,' Mrs Cronos warned him.

Cronos gave a heavenly heave and threw up not just his stony snack, but all the other baby gods as well. 'Just goes to show,' Mrs Cronos smiled happily. 'You can't keep a good god down!'

HI DAD

And did the young gods grow up to overthrow their dreadful dad? What do you think?

Don't feel too sorry for Cronos. He'd killed his own father, Uranus, and scattered the bits into the oceans. Cronos and the old gods were driven out by Zeus and the new gods. These new gods were much more fun. They were really one big, unhappy family. Always arguing, fighting and doing nasty things to each other.

Zeus ruled the earth and the sky from his home on the top of mount Olympus. Of all the groovy gods, Zeus was the grooviest. In a competition he got the top job. When he wasn't flirting with human women he was frying somebody with a thunderbolt.

Zeus's brother, Poseidon, ruled the sea. A job for a real drip. Old Pos wasn't too happy with this because he was a bad loser. That's why he sulked and went stomping around, whipping up the seas with a fork and creating storms. What a stirrer!

HELP!

14

A third brother, Hades, was the real loser. He won the job of ruling the underworld. That must have been hell!

Quick quiz

Prometheus, a young god, liked humans so he stole fire from the gods and gave it to men on earth. But top god, Zeus, punished men by creating something new and terrible on earth. What were these terrible things?

1 women
2 flies
3 teachers

Answer:

1 Women! The Greeks thought they were sly and lying. They attracted men so that men couldn't live without them – at the same time they were such a nuisance men couldn't live with them either. Women were a great help when it came to sharing a man's wealth but no help at all when he was poor. Of course this legend is utter nonsense – if you don't believe me then ask any woman.

15

Fight like a Greek

The wooden heads of Troy
Everybody knows the story of the wooden horse of Troy.
But can you believe it? Those Trojan twits saw a wooden
horse standing outside the gates of the city . . .

Everyone thinks it's a wonderful story. No one stops to ask, 'Would the Trojans really be that stupid?' But, if they *did* ask that question, the answer would have to be 'Yes.' If brains were gunpowder the Trojans wouldn't have had enough to blow their helmets off. Because they were tricked into letting the groovy Greeks into their city a *second* time.

That's right. Everyone knows about the wooden horse trick. Teachers forget to tell you about the *second* one over 800 years later in 360 BC. . .

Tricking a Trojan. . . again

Charidemus was fed up. He paced up and down in his tent and rubbed a strong hand through his greying hair. He complained, 'I'll never capture Troy. The walls are just too strong. . . and the Trojans don't look as if they're starving to death, do they?'

'No, sir,' his young lieutenant mumbled. 'Perhaps if we made a wooden horse and. . .'

Charidemus glared at him. 'Thank you. You are the fiftieth person to suggest that. The Trojans won't fall for that old trick again. Next time they'll just set fire to the wooden horse. Would you like to volunteer to sit inside it, eh? See if I'm right?'

The young man turned red and said, 'No, sir.'

He was relieved to hear someone approaching the tent. He jumped to the door.

'Password?'

'Ajax,' the man called.

The lieutenant opened the flap and said, 'Enter, friend.'

The guard stepped through, pulled on a short chain

18

and dragged a ragged man through after him. The guard stood to attention. 'Spy, sir. Caught him stealing food. Permission to execute him, sir?' he barked.

General Charidemus peered at the prisoner. The man's clothes were dusty but quite rich. 'Not yet, Captain. Leave us together.'

The guard saluted and strode out. Charidemus nodded to a cushion. 'Sit down,' he ordered. 'Your name?'

The prisoner grinned. 'Damon.' He was a wiry man with dark eyes that seemed to dart around and couldn't meet anyone else's gaze.

'And you've come out from Troy to steal our food? Are things that bad inside the city then?'

Damon smiled slyly. 'You Greeks eat better than the Trojans. Even before the siege the king gave us poor rations.'

19

'You don't like the king? Then why work for him?' the Greek general asked.

The prisoner shrugged. 'It's a job.'

Charidemus leaned forward. 'And if I offered you a job? A better paid and better fed job?'

Damon looked at his thumb and slowly placed it in his mouth. 'I'd be happy to work for you. I'd be loyal to you.'

The general's eyes were hard as iron as he replied, 'Oh, you'd be loyal, Damon. Men who betray me die... but they die very slowly.'

The prisoner squirmed on his cushion and gave a nervous smile. 'What do you want me to do?'

'I want you to be my wooden horse, Damon. Listen carefully and I'll tell you exactly what I want you to do . . .'.

It took a week for Charidemus to prepare the plan. His young lieutenant was nervous. As he tightened the buckle on his general's armour he asked, 'How do you know Damon won't betray us?'

The general tested the weight of his short sword. 'Damon is greedy but he's not stupid. He knows that we will take Troy sooner or later. If we have to wait too long to get inside he knows we'll be angry. We'll certainly kill the Trojan men – including him. But if he helps us he

20

lives – and doesn't have to go to bed hungry any more.'

Charidemus slid the sword into his belt. 'Pass me my cloak.'

The young man took the large, filthy cloak and slid it over his general's wide shoulders. A hood covered the man's square head. He arranged the cloak to cover the weapons, dusted his hands and gave a nod. 'You'll pass as a poor traveller, sir.' The lieutenant changed too.

The general strode out of his tent and met a dozen men dressed the same way. No one spoke. Charidemus led the way from the torch-lit camp on to the stony road to Troy. A small man sat quietly on a horse and watched them approach.

'Is everything ready, Damon?' the general asked softly.

'It is,' the small man smiled. He turned his horse and walked slowly back towards the city gates. The Greek soldiers dragged their sandals and began to limp towards the enemy city.

'Who goes there?' a guard cried from a gate tower.

'Damon!' the traitor cried.

'Ah, so it is! What have you got with you?'

'The Greeks are growing careless. I went to their camp and found some of our captured men with just a single guard. I killed him and brought them back,' Damon lied. 'But let me in quickly. They're weak and sick!'

'Aye, Damon. . . oh, you'd better give the password.'

'Castor,' Damon said quickly.

The gates creaked slowly open. The man on the horse rode in – the soldiers trudged behind him.

21

As the gates closed the men stood in the shadow of the wall and shrugged off their cloaks. They climbed the stone stairways to the gate towers and the walls.

The Trojan defenders had no chance. They were looking for Greeks outside the walls – they didn't expect the attack to come from within.

Charidemus cut the throat of the last guard and let the limp body drop into the dark and dusty ditch that ran outside the wall. The Greeks gathered in the tower above the gate.

'Now we wait for the rest of our army. . .' the general began, but his lieutenant hurried to the walls and looked over. There was a rattle of stones on the road as a body of armed men arrived and halted.

'They're here, sir, but they're too early!' the young man gasped.

'Either that or they aren't *our* men,' Charidemus said.

'How can we tell in the darkness?'

'The password, man, the password . . . you know, "Wooden Horse". Quick! Challenge them,' the general ordered.

'Who goes there?' the lieutenant called.

'Friend!' came the reply.

'Give the password.'

After a moment a voice called, 'Castor!'

The Greeks looked at General Charidemus. 'Let them in. If we don't they'll raise the alarm before our men get here. Hide behind the gates. As soon as the last man is in, you come out. Kill them. Kill every last one!'

The Greeks trotted down the stairs to their positions while the general and his lieutenant turned the winches that opened the gates. There was the sound of marching feet, cries of surprise and fear, the clash of weapons, then the silence of death.

From the darkest shadow of the Trojan street a small man gave a grim smile as he sat astride his horse. A horse that had led the enemy into Troy . . . again.

23

Petrifying plays and electrifying epics

After the stories of gods there were stories of heroes – men who were almost as powerful as gods. The only difference was they were 'mortal' – they could die.

The stories about heroes were told as poems. They were sung in the palaces of ancient Greece. Then, after the dark ages, poems were written down. The oldest written poem was by the Greek, Homer. His poem, *The Iliad*, tells the story of the siege of Troy, a story of the heroes who fought to the death to get Helen back to her hubby, King Menelaus.

It was such a great story it is still told today.

The Greeks heard the poems read on stage while a group of dancers performed. Then a clever poet called Aeschylus came along and had a great idea. He put a second reader on stage. Now you had a 'play' – the first drama in the world. Another groovy Greek invention!

Another famous playwright was Euripides – say 'you-rippa-deeze' – whose name gave lot of joy to suffering students of Greek.

Of course, like everything else in Greece, play-writing became a competition. You went to see which play was the best and would win the prize. But it wasn't like your local theatre where you can go and watch a pantomime at Christmas. Greek theatre. . .

- always had the same scenery
- was out in the open air
- had no actresses – only actors who also played the female parts
- had no action on stage – only people *talking about* the exciting bits – murders and all that happened off stage
- had the actors wearing face masks – and high platform shoes so they moved around very slowly.

OK... IN THE NEXT SCENE YOU HAVE TO PLAY SHORT PEOPLE

There were two types of play. Serious ones where lots of people died miserably – they were called 'tragedies'. Funny ones full of groovy jokes and rude bits – they were called 'comedies'.

Some of their favourite tragedies were about the Trojan War. Several writers told the same story. The skill was to tell it in an interesting way.

Playwright Aeschylus didn't write about the fighting at Troy – Homer's poem did that. Aeschylus looked at

25

the story of the women left behind. Women like Clytemnestra – wife of the Greek leader, Agamemnon. If Clytemnestra had kept a diary of those exciting years, would it have looked like this . . . ?

Diary of a murder

Dear Diary,
     You'll never believe what my sister Helen has gone and done! She's run off with that nice young man, Paris. She's a sly one that Helen. Husband Menelaus away from the palace and she chats up young Paris. <u>Disgusting</u>, I call it. You'd never catch me flirting with a guest. Of course I've got three kids to worry about. I have to set them a good example. Anyway, they reckon she's off to a place called Troy. Still, it's better than Sparta. Nasty brutal place that Sparta. I always said she'd never stick it out.

TROY

     There'll be trouble, mark my words. My husband, Agamemnon, came storming in tonight. 'Have you heard what your Helen's gone and done now?' he snaps.
     'I've heard. Can't say I blame her. Nice young chap, that Paris.' I knew that would upset him. Turned redder than blood on a sacrificial altar. I won't have him saying anything against our Helen.

She's always been flighty — I don't mind saying it. But she is my sister and I won't have anyone else saying a word against her.

'Nice young chap!' he screeches. 'He was a guest. A GUEST!! He betrayed the trust of Menelaus. Nicked his wife while he was out hunting!'

'No need to shout,' I told him. 'You'll upset Iphigenia.' I said and patted our girl on the head.

'What's he on about, Mum?' Iphigenia asked.

'Your Auntie Helen's gone off to Troy with that nice Prince Paris,' I said.

'Oh, is that all?' she said and she went back to her sewing. Lovely girl our Iphigenia. Wish our other two, Orestes and Electra, were as good. Funny couple those two.

ORESTES
AND ELECTRA

'Anyway,' Agamemnon says, 'There'll be trouble. Big trouble. They reckon we'll get a thousand ships and sail after her. Bring her back.'

'That'll take months!' I said.

'A Greek's got to do what a Greek's got to do,' he said. 'Now let me have a bit of supper, then I'll be off to organize the army.'

27

'Organize the army?' I said. 'Don't tell me you're going as well!'

'Going? Going? I'm leading the whole expedition. Menelaus is my brother, after all.'

That's Agamemnon all over. Getting into somebody else's fight. Just an excuse to go off and have a battle. Leaves me stuck here for months on end. It would serve him right if I did what Helen did and found myself a toy-boy. That would teach him. In fact I've had my eye on that Aegisthus for a while now...

AEGISTHUS

But no. Our Iphigenia would be upset. I'll just let Agamemnon get on with it. I hope he gets sea-sick

AUTUMN

I'll kill him! I will kill Agamemnon. You'll not believe what he's done. If I'd had a sword in my hand I'd have killed him there and then. But he's gone now. I'll just have to wait. If it takes six months or six years till he gets back, I'll have my revenge. I'll have his blood, I will.

I'll never forgive him. I know he had

problems. A thousand ships waiting to sail to Troy and they couldn't even get out of the harbour at Aulis. The wind kept blowing them back. Week after week.

Of course, I knew that they went to the Oracle to ask for advice. But I never did find out what the Oracle told them. Very quiet he was when he came back.

'Well? What's to do?" I asked.

'Oh, a sacrifice,' he muttered. 'Just a sacrifice and the gods will turn the wind around'.

'That's all right then. What is it? A sheep? A Deer?'

He muttered something and started to leave the room. 'What was that?' I said. I'm not going deaf. I swear he didn't want me to hear.

'Er... a maiden. We have to sacrifice a maiden,' he said, ashamed like.

'Eeh, our Agamemnon. You're never going to kill a little girl just to get that useless trollop Helen back, are you?'

'A Greek's got to do ....'

'Yeah, what a Greek's got to do. I know. I think it's a wicked shame. I just feel sorry for the lass's mother, that's all.'

'Aye,' he said, sheepish like, and slipped out.

I was so upset. I have to say, I was upset at the thought of them brutes slaughtering a young girl just to keep some god happy. So I sent for our little Iphigenia to cheer me up.

Her nurse was pale as a marble statue when I called her. 'Iphigenia's gone for the sacrifice,' she said.

'Gone to the sacrifice!' I cried. 'She's too young to go watching horrible things like that. She'll be upset. It'll put her off her dinner. She's a fussy eater at the best of times,' I said.

'No,' the nurse mumbled. 'She won't be having any dinner any more. Iphigenia's gone for the sacrifice. She _is_ the sacrifice,' the poor woman explained.

I was speechless. That double-crossing filthy rat of a husband had our little girl killed on an altar just so he could go off and play soldiers.

Of course the winds turned and he set sail before I could get my hands on him. Left me here with the 'funny couple', Orestes and Electra, to bring up.

But I can wait. Oh, I can wait. The waiting'll just make it all the nicer when I finally get him. But, believe me, I'll get him. If he doesn't get killed at Troy he'll get killed when he gets ~~home~~ back home. I can wait.

FIVE YEARS LATER

It's not as easy taking Troy as they expected. Their little game of soldiers isn't as exciting as they thought. Sitting outside the walls of Troy every day. They must be bored out of their tiny minds.

I was bored myself. But now I've got that nice, sensible Aegisthus to keep me company — sensible enough not to go to Troy.

It'll serve Agamemnon right if he gets killed. But now I've got Aegisthus to help me it's certain the old fool will be killed if he ever gets home. I've now got two reasons to get rid of him. I still haven't forgotten Iphigenia.

As for the 'funny couple', they're as strange as ever. Sometimes I think they don't love their Mother at all. That's fine, because I don't think much of them either.

ANOTHER FIVE YEARS LATER

So he's home. The conquering hero's home. Couldn't beat the Trojans in a fair fight so he beat them with a trick horse or some thing. Hid soldiers inside a wooden horse, they say.

WOODEN HORSE

Typical sneaky trick from Agamemnon. Poor Helen's back with Menelaus and everybody's happy... except me. And the Trojans of course

I pretended to welcome Agamemnon back like a loving wife, didn't I? But it was difficult when that girl stepped forward. 'This is Cassandra', he said.

'Cassandra? Isn't she the King of Troy's daughter?'

'She is – and she is my wife-to-be', he smirked.

'You've got a wife. You've got me!'

'Cassandra will be my second wife,' he said and marched into the palace. That scrawny girl trailed after him. They say she has the gift of prophecy. In that case she knows that we're going to kill her too. I could see it in her eyes. She knows. She knows

NEXT DAY

It's done. He's dead. We waited till he climbed into his bath. I walked in with the sword. I could have struck him from behind. But I wanted him to know what was going to happen — just as Iphigenia must have known ten years ago. Aegisthus finished him off. It was messy.

Cassandra was in her room. Waiting. As if she expected me. Perhaps she did. She didn't cry out or try to run away. She just closed her eyes and bowed her head.

It was harder than killing him in a way. Still, it's over now. Oh, yes, Electra and Orestes, the funny people, have had their heads together, hatching some kind of plot. They can't do anything. It's against every law of god or man to kill your own mother. I'm safe.

> Dear Diary
>
> It is against every law of god and man to kill your husband. And the gods would want us to avenge our father's death. We Killed her and her murdering lover Aegisthus. Now we await the judgement of the gods for our crime.
>
> Orestes and Electra.

The gods decided to destroy Orestes and Electra for killing their mother and sent the 'Furies' after them – sort of avenging angels. In the end the goddess, Athena, gave them a pardon.

That was the sort of story the Greeks liked to watch on the stage. People say that today's films and television programmes are too violent. But the truth is, entertainment has provided violent stories for thousands of years.

The truth about Troy
But was the story of Troy a 'history' story? Did it really happen? Homer was writing hundreds of years after the event. Of course, the story could have been passed down by word of mouth through the Dark Ages. Ask a historian . . .

WAS THERE A PLACE CALLED TROY?

YES. ARCHAEOLOGISTS HAVE FOUND THE SITE OF THE RUINS

•TROY

TURKEY

RUINS? SO WAS IT DESTROYED BY WAR?

IT WAS DESTROYED AND REBUILT SEVERAL TIMES ONCE IT WAS DESTROYED BY AN EARTHQUAKE

DID HELEN OF TROY REALLY EXIST?

DON'T KNOW. BUT IT WASN'T UNUSUAL FOR RAIDERS TO CARRY OFF QUEENS. SHE *COULD* HAVE EXISTED

AND WHAT ABOUT THE SACRIFICE OF IPHIGENIA?

POSSIBLE. THERE WERE CERTAINLY CASES OF CHILDREN BEING SACRIFICED — AND EVEN PARTLY EATEN — IN THOSE DAYS

YEUCH! WHAT ABOUT THE WOODEN HORSE?

INTERESTING, THAT ONE. IT COULD HAVE BEEN A POETIC IDEA FOR A WOODEN BATTERING-RAM

... IT WOULD HAVE HAD A COVER TO KEEP THE DEFENDERS' ARROWS OFF THE ATTACKERS. THE COVER COULD HAVE BEEN HORSE-SHAPED

Don't tell tales

As well as plays, the ancient Greeks liked a good story. And nobody told better stories than Aesop. They are still popular today. Everybody's heard of *The Tortoise and the Hare*. The moral of that story is, 'Slow and steady wins the race'. Or *The Boy who Cried Wolf*, the moral of this story being, 'No one believes a liar – even if they start telling the truth.'

He gave us wise proverbs like, 'Never count your chickens before they're hatched'. But the most terrible tale of all is about Aesop himself.

Aesop was a Greek folk hero wno is supposed to have lived in the 6th century BC. One legend says he was born in Thrace, lived for a while as a slave on Sámos Island, was set free and travelled round the other states telling his stories.

Then he arrived at Delphi where the Oracle was. In ancient Greece, a priest or priestess who passed on advice from the gods was called an Oracle. Aesop seems to have upset the priests of the Oracle. Maybe he told the story of . . .

The man and the wooden god
In the old days, men used to worship sticks and stones and idols, and prayed to them to give them luck. It happened that a man had often prayed to a wooden idol he had received from his father, but his luck never seemed to change. He prayed and he prayed, but still he remained as unlucky as ever.

One day in the greatest rage he went to the wooden god, and with one blow swept it down from its stand. The idol broke in two, and what did he see? An immense number of coins flying all over the place.

And the moral of the story is, 'Religion is just a con trick created to make money for the priests.'

Whatever Aesop said, the priests didn't like it one little bit. They took him to the top of a cliff and threw him down to his death.

The savage Spartans

The first great state to grow after the Dark Ages was Sparta. The Spartan people were a bit odd. They believed they were better than anyone else. If the Spartans wanted more land then they just moved into someone else's patch. If someone was already living there the Spartans just made them slaves. In short, they were the ungrooviest lot in the whole of Greece.

YOU HAVE A CHOICE, GIVE UP ALL YOUR LAND AND POSSESSIONS AND BECOME OUR SLAVE, OR WE KILL YOU

HMM... TRICKY ONE

Of course, a lot of people didn't enjoy being slaves. They argued with the Spartans in the only language the Spartans knew – the language of violence. They were probably the toughest of the Greek peoples because they were always having to fight to prove how good they were.

But it wasn't enough to train young men to fight. The training started from the day you were born.

Ten foul facts
1 Children were trained for fitness with running, wrestling, throwing quoits and javelins – and that was just the girls!
2 Girls also had to strip for processions, dances and temple services. That way they wouldn't learn to show off with fine clothes.

3 The marriage custom of Sparta was for a young man to pretend to carry his bride off by violence. The bride then cut off her hair and dressed like a man. The bridegroom rejoined the army and had to sneak off to visit his new wife.

4 A new-born baby was taken to be examined by the oldest Spartans. If it looked fit and strong they said, 'Let it live.' If it looked a bit sickly it was taken up a mountain and left to die.

5 A child didn't belong to its parents – it belonged to the State of Sparta. At the age of seven a child was sent off to join a 'herd' of children. The toughest child was allowed to become leader and order the others about. The old men who watched over them often set the children fighting amongst each other to see who was the toughest.

6 At the age of 12 they were allowed a cloak but no tunic. They were only allowed a bath a few times a year.

7 Children slept on rushes that they gathered from the river bank themselves. If they were cold in winter then they mixed a few thistles in with the reeds . . . the prickling gave them a feeling of warmth.

8 The Spartan children were kept hungry. They were then encouraged to steal food – sneakiness is a good skill if you're out on a battlefield. If they were caught stealing they'd be beaten. They weren't beaten for stealing, you understand – they were beaten for being careless enough to get caught. Sometimes the young men were beaten just to toughen them up. If the beating killed the youth then it was just bad luck.

9 Older boys had younger boys to serve them. If the younger boy did something wrong then a common punishment was a bite on the back of the hand.

10 If you cried out while you were fighting then not only were you punished but your best friend was punished as well.

Of course, the savage Spartans were no worse than some of their enemies, such as the Scythians. The historian, Herodotus (485 – 425 BC), described the horrors of the Scythians . . .

> *In a war, it is the custom of a Scythian soldier to drink the blood of the first man he kills. The heads of all enemies killed in battle are taken to the king; a head represents a token which allows the soldier a share in the loot – no head no loot. He strips the skin off the head by*

making a circular cut round the ears and shaking out the skull; then he scrapes the flesh off the skin with an ox's rib, and when it is clean works it supple with his fingers. He hangs these trophies on the bridle of his horse like handkerchiefs and is very proud of them. The finest warrior is the one who has the most scalps. Many Scythians sew scalps together to make cloaks and wear them like the cloak of a peasant.

The boy who didn't cry 'fox'
One Spartan story shows you how peculiar the Spartans really were. It's a story about a good little Spartan boy.

How to be a good Spartan 1: Pinch whatever you like – but don't get caught
He stole a fox cub belonging to somebody else.

How to be a good Spartan 2: Don't give up without a struggle
The boy was seen running away from the scene of the theft and arrested. But before they caught him he just had time to stuff the fox cub up his tunic.

41

How to be a good Spartan 3: Cheat, lie and trick your way out of trouble

The boy's master asked the boy where the fox cub was. The boy replied, 'Fox cub? What fox cub? I don't know anything about a fox cub!'

How to be a good Spartan 4: It's better to be a dead hero than a live whinger

The master's questioning went on . . . and on. Until suddenly the boy fell down. Dead. When the guards examined the body they found the fox cub had eaten its way into the boy's guts. The tough Spartan lad hadn't given any sign that he was suffering and he hadn't given in, even though it cost him his life.

Could you be as boldly deceitful as the Spartan boy?

Thermopylae

The story of the boy and the fox might not be true – it simply shows the sort of people the Spartans admired. But the story of the battle of Thermopylae is almost certainly true. Again it shows the Spartans dying rather than giving in.

There were just 300 Spartans led by King Leonidas defending the narrow pass of Thermopylae against tens of thousands of Persians. The Persian leader, Xerxes, sent spies to report how many soldiers were defending the pass. He couldn't believe the Spartans would be daft enough to fight and die. Xerxes didn't know the Spartans.

But the Spartans were not just unafraid. They were really cool about it. They spent the time before the battle oiling their bodies and combing their hair – now that *was* groovy.

How to be a good Spartan 5: When you're in trouble, think of something witty to say
The Spartans were warned that the Persians had so many archers that their arrows would blot out the sun. Dioneces, the Spartan general, said, 'That's good. We'll have a bit of shade to fight the battle.'

How to be a good Spartan 6: Stay cooler than an iced lolly

The Spartans held on for a week. Then a traitor guided the Persians to a secret pathway that led them behind the Spartans. The 300 Spartans were massacred. As they fought to the death some lost their swords. They battled on with their fists and their teeth.

Could you stay as cool as a Spartan in danger?

Did you know…?

One horrible historical way of proving you were a good Spartan was to be whipped at the altar of the god, Artemis. The one who suffered the most lashes was the toughest. Bleeding half to death – sometimes *all the way* to death – but *tough*. Ah yes, a *perfect* Spartan.

The spooky Spartan

Pausanius was a great Spartan general who helped to defeat the Persians in 479 BC. But the Spartans thought he was getting too big-headed and they asked him to return to Sparta to explain – or be punished.

Pausanius was not amused. He wrote to the Persian king, Xerxes, and offered to betray Sparta. Off went the messenger to Xerxes. But that messenger wondered why other messengers before him hadn't come back. So he opened the letter and read it. There on the end was a little message for Xerxes . . .

The messenger took the letter to the Spartans instead of to Xerxes – wouldn't you? The Spartans sent a force to kill Pausanius. The general fled to the temple of Athena where he sheltered in a small building. 'You can't lay a finger on me here. I'm on sacred ground,' he said.

'Right,' the leader of the assassins said. 'We won't lay a finger on you.' And they didn't. They just bricked up the door and left him to starve to death. That should have been the end of Pausanius. The trouble was his ghost started wandering round the temple making such hideous noises that the priestess was losing customers. In the end she sent for a magician – a sort of groovy Greek Ghostbuster – to get rid of him . . . finally.

The odd Athenians

Deadly Draco

The people of Athens were very different from the Spartans. One of their first rulers was a man called Draco. The Athenians thought the Spartans were pretty brutal, but the laws of Draco were nearly as cruel. He wrote the first law book for Athens, and criminals were executed for almost any crime. Under Draco's laws . . .

● you could have someone made your personal slave if they owed you money
● the theft of an apple or a cabbage was punishable by death
● people found guilty of idleness would be executed.

Draco said . . .

Yes, it's unfair. Little crimes and big crimes get the same punishment. If only I could think of a punishment worse than death for the serious ones.

Seven hundred years later a Greek writer, Plutarch, said . . .

> *Draco's laws were not written in ink but in blood.*

Other Greeks thought that Draco's laws were better than no laws. (The people who thought this were not the ones who Draco had executed, of course.)

Playful Peisistratus

Another ruler, Peisistratus, wasn't so quite so harsh. He was still a 'tyrant' – in Greece that was someone who took control of the state by force – but he stayed there only as long as the people agreed with what he was doing.

Peisistratus made the people pay heavy taxes – ten per cent of all they earned – but at least he had a sense of humour.

One day he visited a farmer. The farmer didn't recognize Peisistratus.

'WHAT DO YOU GET OUT OF THIS LAND?'

'NOTHING BUT ACHES AND PAINS. I WISH PEISISTRATUS WOULD TAKE HIS TEN PER CENT OF THOSE'

Peisistratus laughed – and ordered that the old farmer need never pay taxes again.

Plotting Peisistratus

Peisistratus became very unpopular and the people of Athens were turning against him. Then one day he drove his cart into the market place in a terrible state. He and his mules were cut and bleeding. 'I've been attacked by assassins!' he cried. 'I barely escaped with my life.'

The Athenians were worried they would lose their leader – not a popular leader, but the only leader they had. They organized the strongest and most brutal Athenian men to be his bodyguards. He then used them to seize control of the city.

The attack on Peisistratus had put him in power. Just as he meant it to. For there had been *no* attack. The crafty leader had simply made the wounds himself!

Who killed the ox?

The Athenians weren't as ruthless as the Spartans. But they had their own funny little ways. One of the strangest customs of Athens involved the sacrifice of an ox in the temple. Killing the ox wasn't strange in itself. It's what the Athenians did *afterwards* that was curious. They held a trial to decide, 'Who killed the ox?'

 I BLAME THE GIRLS WHO CARRIED THE WATER THAT SHARPENED THE AXE!

WE BLAME THE MAN WHO SHARPENED THE AXE AND THE KNIFE

 I BLAME THE MAN WHO TOOK THE KNIFE AND THE AXE

I BLAME THE MAN WHO HIT THE OX WITH THE AXE

  I BLAME THE MAN WHO STABBED THE OX WITH THE KNIFE

I BLAME THE KNIFE  WHAT HAVE YOU GOT TO SAY FOR YOURSELF, KNIFE?

 IN THAT CASE I FIND THE KNIFE GUILTY OF THE OX'S MURDER. I SENTENCE THE KNIFE TO DEATH BY DROWNING. THROW THE KNIFE IN THE SEA

TO BE BLUNT I CAN'T SEA THE POINT

49

Horrible hemlock

The Athenians didn't just have strange ways of killing knives. They also killed each other in unusual ways.

After they had lost the war with Sparta the Athenians looked for someone to blame. They blamed the old teacher, Socrates. Being a rather groovy guy, he was always hanging around with young people, telling them not to believe in the old gods. (That's a bit like your own teacher telling you not to believe in Father Christmas.) In Athens this was punishable by death.

But the Athenians didn't kill the old teacher – they told him to kill himself with poison! Plato described the gruesome scene . . .

The man who was to give the poison came in with it ready mixed in a cup. Socrates saw him and said, 'Good Sir, you understand these things. What do I have to do?'

'Just drink it and walk around until your legs begin to feel heavy, then lie down. It works very quickly.'

The man gave Socrates the cup.

The teacher took it cheerfully, without trembling, and without even turning pale. He just looked at the man and said, 'May I drink a toast?'

'You may,' the man replied.

'Then I drink to the gods and pray that we will be just as happy after death as we were in life.'

Then he drank the poison quickly and cheerfully. Until then most of us had held back our tears. But when we saw him drinking, the tears came in floods. I covered my face and wept – not for him but for myself, I had lost such a good friend.

Socrates looked at us and said sternly, 'I have heard that a person should be allowed to die in silence. So control yourselves and be quiet.' We stopped crying.

The teacher lay down. The man with the poison squeezed his foot. Socrates said he felt nothing. He said that when the poison reached the heart he would be gone.

As the numbness reached his waist Socrates called to young Crito. He said, 'Crito, we owe Asclepius a sacrifice. Be sure you pay him. Don't forget.'

[Asclepius was the god of healing.]

'Of course,' Crito replied. 'Is there anything else you want?'

But Socrates didn't reply.

This was the end of our friend. The best, wisest and most honest person I have ever known.

What a hero! Probably the only teacher in history to die so nobly. Would your teacher be as brave?

Unfortunately you'll never have the chance to find out . . . Boots the Chemist does not sell hemlock.

Dreadful democracy

Most countries today are run as *democracies* – that is to say every adult has a vote on which laws are passed and how the government spends its money.

Athens, being really groovy, had the *first* democracy. But because they still had a lot to learn, they didn't quite get it right . . .

The power of the Persians

King Darius of Persia had a large army and decided it was about time he took over Greece as well. He didn't bother going to the battle personally – he thought the Greeks would be a pushover. They *should* have been a pushover because . . .

● there was only the Athenian army to stop them – the Spartans were too busy at a religious festival and they missed the battle

● the Greek soldiers were a bit frightened by the appearance of the Persian soldiers.

The Persians were wearing *trousers* while the Greeks wore groovy *skirts*.

Still, the Athenian Greeks won the great battle at a place called Marathon.

That kept the Persians away for about ten years.

Then along came the new Persian king, Xerxes, with an absolutely *huge* army.

There were too many soldiers to transport across the Hellespont – a stretch of water almost 1200 metres wide between Greece and Persia – so Xerxes built a bridge.

A storm came and smashed the bridge. Xerxes was cross – yes, I know there are *two* crosses in Xerxes, but I don't mean that sort of cross. He was furious.

#!!*✗!

MORE LIKE *BERSERXES* IF YOU ASK ME

So, what did the potty Persian do?

1 Ordered the bridge builder to be given three hundred lashes.

2 Ordered the sea at Hellespont to receive three hundred lashes.

3 Ordered the army to swim across.

Answer: 2 Xerxes ordered that the sea should receive the lashes and have iron shackles thrown in as a punishment. One story even said he sent torturers to brand the sea with burning irons.

Paper-headed Persians

The Greeks wouldn't have feared the Persians so much if they'd known what the great historian Herodotus knew. He told a remarkable story about an earlier Persian battlefield – at Pelusium in Egypt where the Persians had fought in 525 BC.

> *On the battlefield I saw a strange thing which the natives pointed out to me. The bones of the dead lay scattered on the field in two lots — those of the Persians and those of the Egyptians. If, then, you strike a Persian skull (even with a pebble) they are so weak you will break a hole in them. But the Egyptian skulls are so strong that you may hit them with a rock and hardly crack them.*

The wooden wall

After slaughtering the Spartans, Xerxes headed south towards Athens. The Athenians retreated to the island of Salamis, just off the coast of Athens. They had to watch while Xerxes burned Athens to the ground.

But the Athenian leader was a groovy Greek called Themistocles. He went to the temple at Delphi and asked for advice from the 'Oracle' – a kind of adviser on behalf of the gods. The Oracle told him to 'put his trust in the wooden wall'. What did he do?

1 Build a navy (of wooden ships).
2 Build a wooden fence around the island of Salamis to keep the Persians out.
3 Build a wooden fence around Athens to keep the Persians in.

The spooky ship of Salamis

Herodotus also reported a strange happening at the battle of Salamis . . .

The Athenians tell this story about a captain from Corinth called Adeimantus. As the battle started he was filled with fear and dread; he hoisted his sails and hurried from the fight. When the other Corinthians saw this they turned to follow him. But just as they reached the temple of Athena on Salamis, a ship came alongside them. It was a ship of the gods for no man sent it. A voice from the strange ship called, 'Would you betray your Greek friends, Adeimantus? They are now winning the battle. Turn back and help.' The Corinthian said it was a lie. The voice replied, 'You can take this ship and destroy it if you find out I am lying. Turn back, turn back.' So Adeimantus and the Corinthians joined the battle again and helped the Greeks to win. But no one was able to tell him where the strange ship had come from . . .

Maybe it was a 'ghost ship'. Another story says the Corinthians only *pretended* to run away. It was all part of a cunning Athenian plan. The Corinthians' trick led the Persians into a trap. They then turned and attacked them when they least expected it. There never was a ship of the gods.

Which story do you believe? One fact is that lots of sailors died. Two horrible historical epitaphs read . . .

> HE WENT DOWN WITH HIS SHIP AND WHERE HIS BONES ARE ROTTING ONLY THE SEABIRD KNOWS

And . . .

> SAILORS, DON'T ASK WHOSE BODY LIES HERE. I WISH YOU BETTER LUCK THAN MINE AND A KINDER SEA

Peloponnesian wars

Xerxes the Persian went home after he lost the sea battle at Salamis. His son-in-law, Mardonius, wanted to stay and batter a few more Greeks, so Xerxes left him to get on with it. Mardonius was killed and his army defeated.

57

Of course, the Athenians were really pleased with themselves. They decided to get all the Greek states to team up in case the Persians ever came back. The trouble was the Athenians wanted to be the captain of the team.

Sparta weren't having that. They decided not to play. After that it was just a matter of time before Athens and Sparta fought each other to see who was best. And that was the start of the Peloponnesian War.

Awful armies

Alcibiades was a great Athenian general – but a terrible poser. He dressed in the grooviest clothes and would do anything to draw attention to himself. Once he cut off the tail of his favourite dog so that people would take notice.

I WONDER IF THEY'D NOTICE HIM MORE IF I BIT HIS NOSE OFF?

Half of Athens (especially the women) loved him – but the men in power hated him and wanted him dead. They sent him off to fight the Spartans while they plotted against him.

Alcibiades led the Athenian army in the attack on the Spartan allies at Syracuse (in Sicily) between 415 and 413 BC. But he was called back to Athens because he was charged with 'sacrilege' – that's being nasty to the gods. He was supposed to have gone to some statues of gods and knocked off their noses – and (because the statues didn't have any clothes on) he knocked off their 'naughty bits' as well.

Of course, clever Alcibiades knew they'd probably kill him for this. So he *didn't* go back to Athens, sensible man. He went over to the enemy – *Sparta*. He told the Spartans all the secrets of the Athenian army. The Spartans went and helped Syracuse.

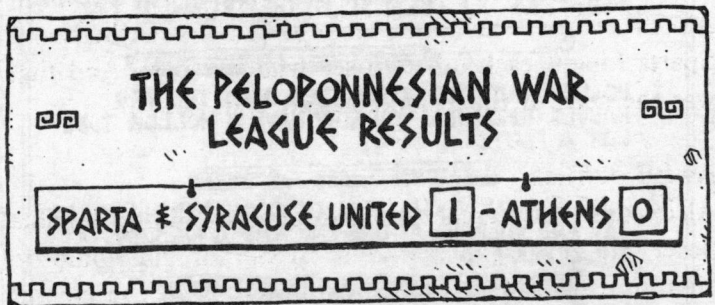

THE PELOPONNESIAN WAR
LEAGUE RESULTS

SPARTA & SYRACUSE UNITED 1 – ATHENS 0

Of course, Alcibiades came to a sticky end – just like the tail of his dog, really! The Spartans had him assassinated rather than let him switch back to fighting for Athens.

A group of men arrived at his house to kill him but hadn't the nerve to fight him face to face – even though they outnumbered him. First they set his house on fire. When Alcibiades came out into the open, carrying his sword, they shot him full of arrows from a safe distance.

Wonderful weapons
During the Peloponnesian wars, Greeks were fighting Greeks. If you know how your enemy fights, you can stop him – and at the same time he can stop you. Every battle becomes a 0–0 draw. What you need are some secret weapons to surprise and frighten the enemy.

That's what the groovy Greek army from Boetia came up with. Here's what they made . . .

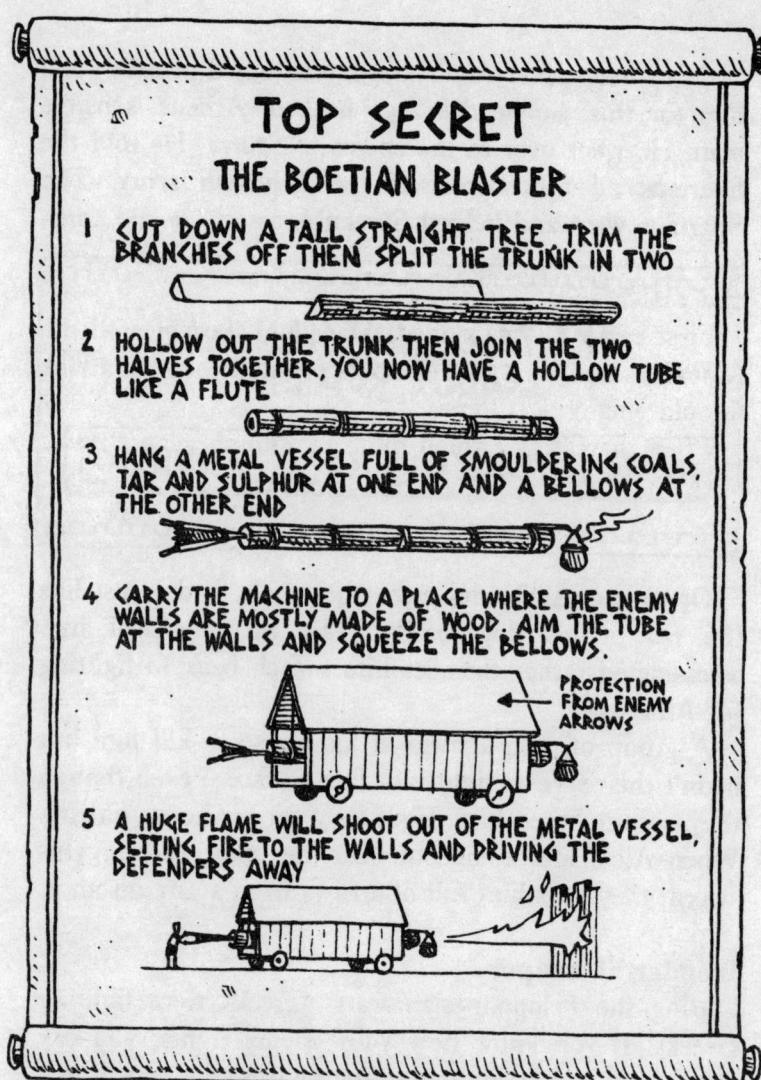

TOP SECRET

THE BOETIAN BLASTER

1 CUT DOWN A TALL STRAIGHT TREE. TRIM THE
BRANCHES OFF THEN SPLIT THE TRUNK IN TWO

2 HOLLOW OUT THE TRUNK THEN JOIN THE TWO
HALVES TOGETHER, YOU NOW HAVE A HOLLOW TUBE
LIKE A FLUTE

3 HANG A METAL VESSEL FULL OF SMOULDERING COALS,
TAR AND SULPHUR AT ONE END AND A BELLOWS AT
THE OTHER END

4 CARRY THE MACHINE TO A PLACE WHERE THE ENEMY
WALLS ARE MOSTLY MADE OF WOOD. AIM THE TUBE
AT THE WALLS AND SQUEEZE THE BELLOWS.

PROTECTION
FROM ENEMY
ARROWS

5 A HUGE FLAME WILL SHOOT OUT OF THE METAL VESSEL,
SETTING FIRE TO THE WALLS AND DRIVING THE
DEFENDERS AWAY

It worked! The Boetians captured the city of Delium
with it. They had invented the world's first *flame
thrower!*

Alexander the Great-er

Just when the Persian threat to Greece had begun to fade, a new one came from a small kingdom in the north of Greece called Macedon. Some historians have even said that Macedon wasn't Greek at all.

First came Philip, king of Macedon. He defeated the Athenians and then told them he wanted them to attack the old enemy . . . Persia.

Then there was a small hitch in Philip's plan . . . he died. But that was only a tiny complication for the plan. (A rather bigger complication for Philip, of course.) Philip's son was greater and even groovier than him. Alexander the Great-er in fact . . .

Alexander -This is Your Life

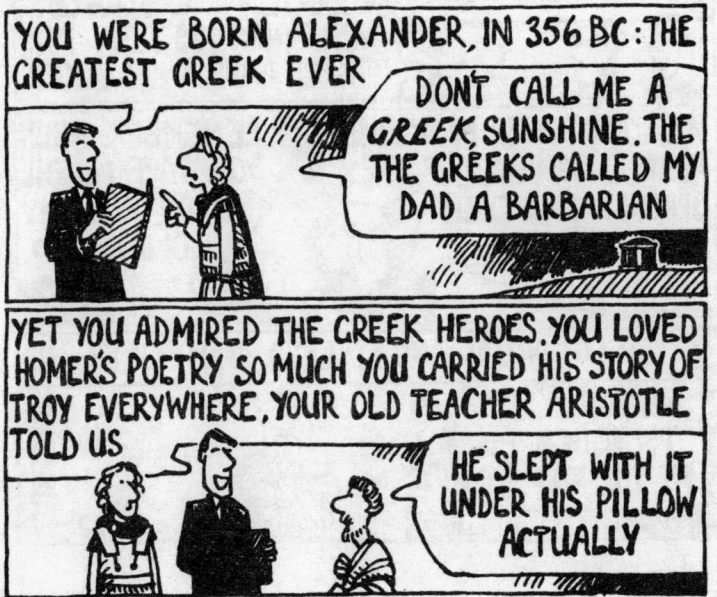

The knotty problem

Alexander entered Gordium and was told that the wagon of King Gordius was tied to its shafts with a knot that no one could untie. A legend said that the man who finally untied it would rule all Asia. How did Alexander unfasten the wagon from its shafts?

Answer: He took out his sword and cut through the knot.

Think like a Greek

The Greeks were very superstitious people. They believed in horoscopes and ghosts and the gods deciding your fate. They believed that the gods spoke through 'Oracles' and you could learn about the future . . . if you understood the Oracle.

Awesome Oracles

The Greeks liked to know what would happen in the future. They didn't have crystal balls or people reading your palm. Instead they had Oracles. You went to a holy place, made a sacrifice and asked a god to tell you what the future held.

Of course, the god didn't speak to a human directly. There were a couple of ways of getting your message. At Delphi, the god Apollo spoke through his Oracle priestess. She was a bit like a medium in a seance today. She went into a trance and spoke in a strange language. The priests then took this baffling information and told the visitor what it meant.

The priests at Delphi actually could give good advice. So many visitors came, with so much gossip, that the priests of Delphi knew more than most people about what was going on in the Greek states.

Croesus the crafty
There were several Oracles in Greece. Crafty King Croesus decided to test them to see which was the most accurate.

He sent seven messengers to seven Oracles. They all had to ask the same question at the same time . . . *What is King Croesus doing at this very moment?*

They brought their replies back to the king. The Oracle of Delphi's answer was a curious one. It said ...

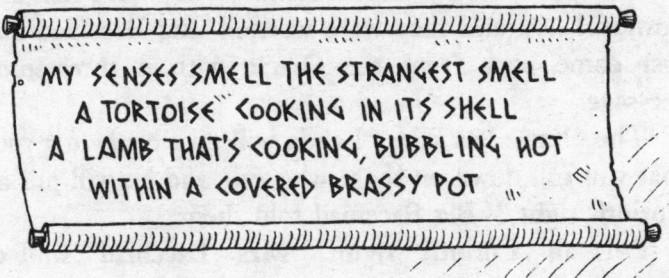

MY SENSES SMELL THE STRANGEST SMELL
A TORTOISE COOKING IN ITS SHELL
A LAMB THAT'S COOKING, BUBBLING HOT
WITHIN A COVERED BRASSY POT

Croesus was impressed. He'd deliberately chosen the daftest thing he could think of to do on that day. So he cut up a tortoise and a lamb and made a stew of them. He cooked them in a brass cauldron with a lid.

Croesus decided the Oracle of Delphi was the one to believe. Crafty Croesus. But. . .

Double-crossed Croesus
But the priests also cheated a bit. They gave curious answers that could mean more than one thing. King Croesus of Lydia spoke to the Oracle when he was about to go to war with Persia.

'What will happen if I attack Persia?' King Croesus asked.

'In the battle a great empire will be destroyed,' the Oracle said.

Croesus went off happily into battle – and lost! Lydia was destroyed. He thought the Oracle meant that *Persia* would be destroyed.

Some of the Greeks' favourite stories were about the Oracle. Many were about the ancient game of . . .

Beat the Oracle
The Bacchiad family ruled Corinth. They were rich and powerful . . . and they were worried. Big Bacchiad had just come back from the Oracle with a threatening message.

'The Oracle has said, "Labda will give birth to a rock that will roll down on those who rule and he will put all Corinth right,"' Big Bacchiad told them.

'Put all Corinth right?' Mrs Bacchiad sniffed.

'Nothing wrong with Corinth. . . at least, not while we're in charge.'

'That's not the point,' Little Bacchiad pointed out. 'If the gods say it's curtains for us, then it's curtains for us.'

'Hah! Just like a man, talking like that. Listen, if the Oracle says she's giving birth to the child who'll defeat us, we simply kill the child.'

'That's murder that is,' Big Bacchiad frowned. 'We'd never get away with it.'

'Not if the baby has an *accident*,' Mrs Bacchiad grinned an evil grin.

'Not much chance of that,' Little Bacchiad sighed.

'Oh, but there is if we *make* it have an accident,' the woman explained. 'As soon as the baby is born, we go visiting. Ask to see the new baby.'

'That's nice,' Big Bacchiad said.

'No it's not,' Mrs Bacchiad said with a slow shake of the head. 'Whoever she hands the baby to will drop it.'

'Drop it!' Little Bacchiad squeaked.

'On the stone floor,' the woman said grimly. 'On its head. End of problem.'

Of course it wasn't that simple. With the Oracle it never is. The baby was born and the Bacchiads went to visit. Mrs Bacchiad left the house ten minutes later. Her face was white with bright red spots of anger on her chubby cheeks.

'I cannot believe it. All you had to do was drop the baby. *Drop the baby!* That's what we agreed. Why did you not drop it?'

Big Bacchaid gave a faint and sheepish smile. 'It smiled at me. I couldn't drop the little feller while he was smiling at me, could I? I hadn't the heart.'

'Heart? It's not heart you're short of – it's brain,' the woman seethed. She turned to Little Bacchiad. 'Tonight you go back with a club. You creep into the house and you kill the child. Understand?'

Little Bacchiad nodded. 'I won't let you down,' he promised.

But Labda had seen Mrs Bacchiad's face when the man handed the baby back to her. She knew the woman wanted the baby dead. So that night she hid the child in a wooden chest. It slept safely and woke the next day still smiling.

Labda called the baby Cypselus – after the word meaning chest. Cypselus grew up a popular and groovy leader, while the Bacchiad family were hated in Corinth. The young man became king of Corinth – a strong king but a good-natured one. However, when it came to the Bacchiads he was quite, quite ruthless.

Cypselus was the rock that would roll down on those who ruled . . . and, like a rock, he crushed them. Just as the Oracle predicted.

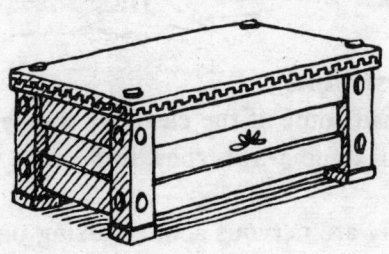

Did you know . . . ?
The Pythian Oracle at Delphi inhaled smoke from the burning leaves of certain trees to help them see into the future. The leaves gave off a drug that put them into a trance.

But at the Corinth Oracle there were cheats at work. There you could actually speak directly to a god! You spoke to the altar . . . and a voice boomed back from beneath your feet with the answer.

Was it a miracle? The visitors believed it was. But today's archaeologists know better. They found a secret tunnel that led under the altar. A priest could crawl along and lie under the feet of the visitor. He could listen to the questions and speak an answer through a funnel into a tube.

Greek superstitions

The Greeks had some of the cleverest thinkers of ancient times. Yet, in some ways, they had some very strange beliefs.

People today are nervous about walking under a ladder because they think it will bring them bad luck, or they touch wood to bring them good luck. The Greeks had their own strange superstitions. They believed. . .

1 Birds were messengers between earth and heaven, and the moon was a resting place for spirits on their way to heaven.

2 The Greeks believed that Hecate was the goddess of witchcraft and crossroads. She would appear at crossroads on clear nights, along with ghosts and howling phantom dogs. The Greeks left food at crossroads for her. (She was also asked for help with curing madness – the Greeks believed madness was caused by the spirits of the dead.)

3 The Greeks looked at the guts of dead birds and believed they could read the future from them.

4 They also thought there were spirits called 'daimons' around. Some were good and protected you; some were evil and could lead you into wickedness. Even clever people like Socrates believed in daimons. His own daimon warned him of trouble ahead . . . and it never let him down.

5 Sometimes the Greeks kept dead bodies in jars called *pithos*. But sometimes, they said, the spirits of the dead escaped from the jars and began to bother the living with illness and disease. These wicked spirits were called *keres*. The best way to stop the keres from getting into your house was to paint tar round your door frames. That way the keres would stick to the tar and not be able to get into the house.

6 The Greeks believed that if you dreamed about seeing your reflection in a mirror then you would die soon after. But don't worry, because you would soon be born again. According to some Greeks you are in three parts . . .

- body
- soul
- mind

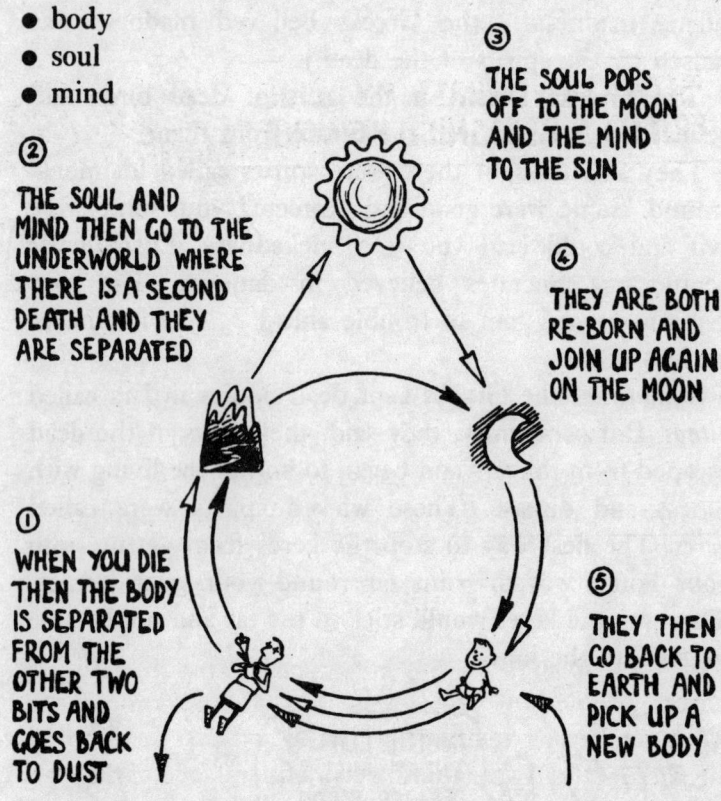

② THE SOUL AND MIND THEN GO TO THE UNDERWORLD WHERE THERE IS A SECOND DEATH AND THEY ARE SEPARATED

③ THE SOUL POPS OFF TO THE MOON AND THE MIND TO THE SUN

④ THEY ARE BOTH RE-BORN AND JOIN UP AGAIN ON THE MOON

① WHEN YOU DIE THEN THE BODY IS SEPARATED FROM THE OTHER TWO BITS AND GOES BACK TO DUST

⑤ THEY THEN GO BACK TO EARTH AND PICK UP A NEW BODY

7 They also believed that the left side is bad – the right side is good. Many people still believe that today – they try to force left-handed children to write with their right hand, for example.

Potty Pythagoras

The famous teacher, Pythagoras, set up his own religion. The Pythagoreans believed that the soul lived on after death and went into another body. One day Pythagoras saw a man beating a dog and heard it yelping. He told the man . . .

'STOP! STOP! THAT'S MY DEAR FRIEND. I RECOGNISE HIS VOICE!'

In fact it wasn't safe to have anything to do with butchers or huntsmen – when they killed that cow or that deer they may have murdered your dead mother.

They also thought that if they behaved themselves they might come back as a great person. If they were naughty in this life they'd come back as something nasty – a pig, a dog, even a tree. And if you were really, really wicked you'd come back as the worst thing of all . . . a woman!

The Pythagoreans lived apart from the rest of the Greek people and had some rather strange rules. Does your teacher have strange rules? Then ask them which of these rules Pythagoras truly had. . . and which are false.

True or False
1 Don't eat beans.
2 Don't walk along the main street.
3 Don't touch the fire with an iron poker.

4 Don't touch a white cockerel.

5 Don't eat the heart of an animal.

6 Don't stand on your fingernail clippings.

7 Don't leave the mark of your body on a bed when you get up.

8 Don't look in a mirror beside a lamp.

9 Help a man to load something – but don't help anyone to unload.

10 Don't pick your nose with the fingers of your left hand.

Answer: **10** is false. All the rest are true. Some Greeks believed that beans contained the souls of the dead and would never eat them.

ALL I DID WAS ASK HIM TO HELP ME UNLOAD THESE WHITE COCKERALS

AHHH HHHH HH HHH

The ghostly Greeks

The groovy Greeks told the first ghost stories. But it was a Roman, Pliny, who first wrote this one down.

Dear Lucias

I have just heard this strange story which I think might intrest you.

In Athens there used to be a large and beautiful house which was supposed to be badly haunted. Locals told how horrid noises were heard at the dead of night: the clanking of chains which grew louder and louder. Until there suddenly appeared the hideous phantom of an old man who was a picture of filth and misery. His beard was long and matted, his white hair wild and uncombed. His thin legs were loaded with a weight of chains that he dragged wearily along with a painful moaning; his wrists were fastened by long cruel links, while all the time he raised his arms and shook his shackles in a kind of helpless fury.

Some brave people were once bold enough to watch all night in the house. They were almost scared out of their senses at the sight of the spook. Even worse, disease and even death followed those who had braved a night in that house. The place was shunned. A 'For Sale' sign was put up but no one bought it and the house fell almost to ruin and decay.

But Athenodorus was poor. He rented it even though he knew the story of the ghost. On his first night there he sat working. He heard the rattling chain and saw the gruesome old man. The ghost beckoned him with a finger. Athenodorus said he was too busy. The ghost grew angry and rattled his chains still more. The young man stood up and followed the spook.

When they reached the garden the spirit pointed to a spot in the garden — then vanished. Athenodorus marked the spot, went to bed and had a peaceful nights sleep.

Next day he went to the law officers and told them what he had seen. They dug at the spot the young man had marked and found a skeleton... bound in chains.

When the body had been given a proper burial, peace returned to the house at night.

Pling

75

Think like a Greek

In the summer of 413 BC the army of Athens was in trouble. They were trying to beat the town of Syracuse with a siege. But one of their leaders had been killed and the other leader, Nicias, was poorly with a fever.

The Athenians decided to pack up and go home. Everyone agreed this was a good idea and they began packing to go. But that night there was an eclipse of the full moon. The soldiers said this was a sign from the gods.

A sign of disaster, some said. A sign that they should stay . . . or a sign that they should go? They couldn't agree. They asked their leader, Nicias.

'We will forget any plan to return home. We must wait for the next full moon,' Nicias said.

He waited 27 more days. What happened?

1 Nicias died and the army went home.
2 They suffered disaster anyway.
3 The Syracuse army surrendered.

Answer: 2 The extra 27 days gave the Syracuse navy time to block off the river with rows of ships chained together. The Athenian ships couldn't get out of the river to get their army back home. Their army had to march across the land instead. The enemy were waiting and the Athenian army was wiped out. The ones who weren't killed were made into slaves. This disaster was the end of Athens as a great state . . . and all because of an eclipse of the moon and the superstitious nature of a Greek general.

76

Live like a Greek

Polybius' Checkerboard

The Greeks were also very groovy with numbers. Polybius, born in 200 BC, was a Greek historian of Rome. He was one of 1,000 hostages taken to Rome in 168 BC. His main history books contained 40 volumes, but he also had time to invent this code, now known as Polybius' Checkerboard.

Each letter has a pair of numbers – the horizontal (across) number followed by the vertical (up-down). So, 'B' is 1-2, but F is 2-1. The word 'Yes' is 54 15 43. Get it?

	1	2	3	4	5
1	A	B	C	D	E
2	F	G	H	I/J	K
3	L	M	N	O	P
4	Q	R	S	T	U
5	V	W	X	Y	Z

Then work out this . . .
44 23 15   22 42 15 15 25   44 15 11 13 23 15 42   11 33
11 53 24 32 11 33 14 15 42   12 42 34 45 22 23 44   44
23 15   21 24 42 43 44   43 45 33 - 14 24 11 31   44 34
22 42 15 15 13 15.

77

Answer: The Greek teacher Anaximander brought the first sun-dial to Greece.

30, 11, 44, 15, 11, 22, 11, 24, 33, 12, 34, 54

Did you know . . . ?

Polybius' Checkerboard may have been a good way of sending secret messages. But a Greek called Histiaeus found a better one!

He was imprisoned by the Persians but was allowed to send a letter to his cousin Aristagoras. The Persians studied the message carefully. They could see no code or secret meaning. The message was a perfectly harmless letter. They let a slave take the letter to Aristagoras.

As soon as the slave arrived he said to Aristagoras, 'Shave my head.' Aristagoras shaved the slave's head. Tattooed on his scalp was the real message. 'Lead a rebellion against the Persians.' Cool, eh?

SCRAPE
SCRAPE

WE MUST BE A WHOLE BOOK!

Make a pinhole camera

The Greeks also invented other groovy devices which are still important to us today. One of the cleverest was the camera obscura – or the 'pinhole' camera. A Greek artist covered a window with a dark material, then punched a small hole through. An upside-down image of the scene was seen on the inside wall and traced by the artist.

You could have a go at making your own, slightly smaller version:

1 Make a box of black card, 20 x 10 x 10 cm.
2 Make a small pinhole in black paper at one end.
3 Place grease-proof paper across the other end.
4 Hold it up to a bright scene.
5 The scene will be 'projected' on to the grease-proof paper.

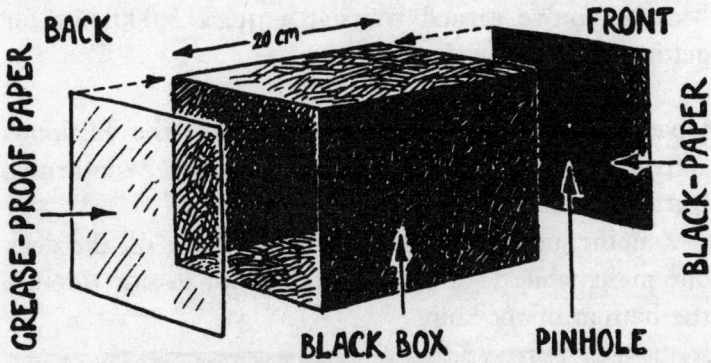

Note: this image will be upside-down – you may have to stand on your head to get the best view!

Making a dodgy drachma

The Greeks had banks. There are no records of bank robbers . . . but there were people who tried to cheat the banks out of lots of money. Here's how to do it. . .

1 Go to the bank and say, 'I want 10,000 drachmas to buy a ship. I'll fill it with corn and sell it on the other side of the Mediterranean. When the ship returns with the money for the corn I'll pay back the loan.'

2 The bank agrees. The Greek banks even agree that if the ship sinks (and you lose all their money) then you don't have to pay them a thing.

3 You buy a cheap ship and put a little bit of cheap corn in it. You spend about 5,000 drachmas and keep the other 5,000 drachmas for yourself.

4 Just as the ship reaches deep water you saw through the keel at the bottom of the boat. This will make it sink.

5 When the boat begins to sink you jump in the lifeboat, paddle back home and say to the bank, 'Sorry, you've lost your 10,000 drachmas!' and have a good laugh because you've earned yourself a quick 5,000 just for getting your feet wet.

Good idea, eh? And it nearly worked for the villainous ship owner, Hegestratos, and his partner, Zenothemis. But it all went wrong at stage 4.

Zenothemis kept the passengers chatting on the deck one night while Hegestratos crept down to saw through the bottom of the ship.

One of the passengers heard the noise and went down to investigate. Hegestratos was caught and had to escape. He fled along the deck and jumped into the waiting lifeboat. Or rather he *tried* to jump into the lifeboat. It was dark. He missed the little boat, fell in the sea . . . and drowned. Served him right.

The ship reached the shore safely and the bank got Zenothemis to pay back the money. So Hegestratos ended up dead . . . not rich.

Let the punishment fit the crime
Alexandria was a city in Egypt but ruled by the Greeks. Around 250 BC they had a set of laws which might give some idea of how the Greek law worked.
Can you match the crime to the punishment? Just remember the law wasn't completely fair. Especially if you were a slave.

Crime	Punishment
1 A free man strikes another free man or free woman.	a) A hundred lashes
2 A slave strikes a free man or free woman.	b) Fine of 100 drachmas
3 A drunk person injures somebody else.	c) A hundred lashes
4 A free man threatens another with wood, iron or bronze.	d) Fine of 100 drachmas
5 A slave threatens another with wood, iron or bronze.	e) Fine of 200 drachmas

If a master didn't want his slave to receive the 100 lashes then he had to pay 200 drachma, or 2 drachma a blow.

If you argued with a fine then you could go to court. But be careful. If you lost then you had to pay double for crime 1 or treble for crime 4.

Woe for women

Being a slave in ancient Greece wasn't much fun. Being a woman wasn't too groovy either. The Spartan women lived like men – the Athenian women lived like slaves. They were told what to do and what not to do – and they didn't have anything like the freedom that the free men enjoyed . . .

82

GREEK GOOD WIFE GUIDE

A WOMAN SHOULD	A WOMAN DOES NOT
• STAY AT HOME • BE BROUGHT UP WITH SLAVES AND LEARN HOUSEHOLD SKILLS • LEARN TO SPIN, WEAVE, COOK AND MANAGE SLAVES • HAVE A HUSBAND – CHOSEN BY HER FATHER – WHEN SHE IS 15 • WORSHIP THE GODDESS HESTIA	• VOTE • BUY OR SELL ANYTHING WORTH MORE THAN A SMALL MEASURE OF BARLEY • OWN ANYTHING OTHER THAN HER CLOTHES, JEWELLERY AND SLAVES • LEAVE THE HOUSE EXCEPT TO VISIT OTHER WOMEN OR GO TO RELIGIOUS FESTIVALS AND FUNERALS

Groovy girls

The women of Attica, the region surrounding Athens, were different from the women living in Athens. They helped their husbands in the fields. They also had a curious way of preparing their daughters for marriage.

Girls aged about 13 were sent to the Brauron temple of the goddess, Artemis. There they prepared to be mature young women, and good wives, by doing what?

1 Learning how to fire bows and arrows, to throw spears, to mend armour and sharpen swords.
2 Praying to the goddess for wisdom, and learning the secret spells to keep husbands happy and healthy.
3 Running and dancing through the woods with no clothes on pretending to be she-bears.

Answer: 3 The idea was they got their wildness 'out of their systems' before they settled down to marriage. The Brauron temple proved very popular with Greek girls around 370 - 380 BC.
However, girls, you should *not* try this at your local place of worship – you'd only get arrested, or photographed by the boys in your class, or catch pneumonia . . . or all three.

I'M BEGINNING TO REALLY ENJOY GREEK HISTORY

Dress like a Greek

Instead of running naked through the local woods, you could find out what it was like to be a groovy Greek by dressing like one. Here's a simple groovy costume to make.

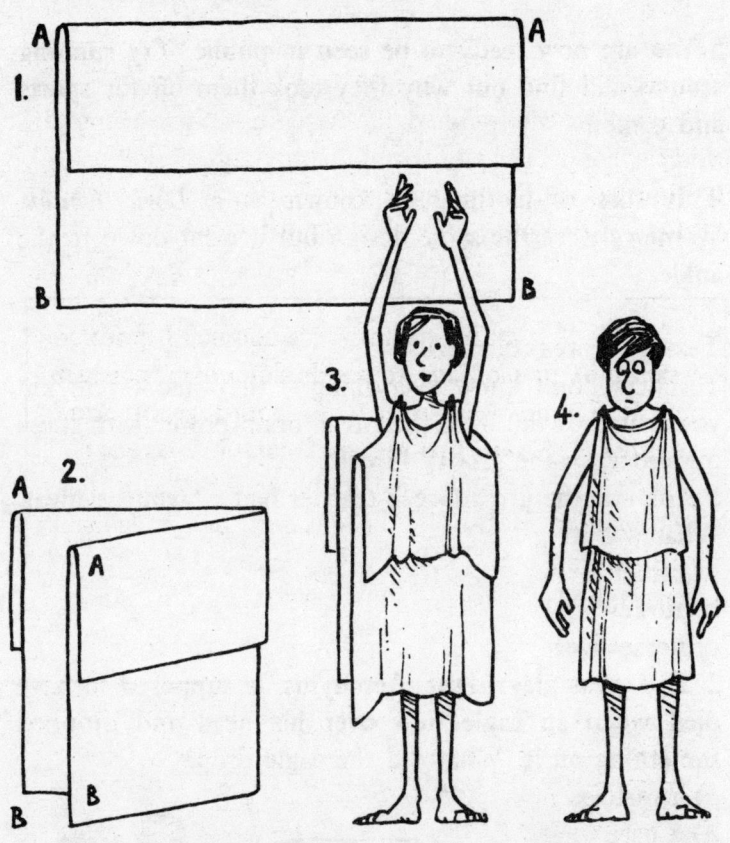

(**Warning:** Only suitable for summer weather.)

1 Fold an oblong cloth as shown – do *not* use Mum's best sheets for this – use Dad's.

2 Fold it again.

3 Wrap it round the body and pin it at each shoulder – the Greeks didn't have safety pins, but you can cheat and use a couple.

4 Fasten the open side with pins. Tie a belt around the waist. See picture 4 . . . here's one I made earlier.

5 You are now ready to be seen in public. Try running around and find out why they took them off for sports and games.

This sort of clothing is known as a *Doric Chiton.* Women's were the same design but it went down to the ankle.

Test your teacher

Teachers don't know everything – they just try to kid you that they do. Test their true brain power with these questions on the groovy Greeks . . .

1 Aristotle the great Greek teacher had a favourite meat. What was it?

a) camel

b) turkey

c) horse liver

2 The great playwright, Aeschylus, is supposed to have died when an eagle flew over his head and dropped something on it. What did the eagle drop?

a) a tortoise

b) a hare

c) a stone

A HARE ON THE HEAD

3 As well as the Olympic games there were games in Isthmia. The winners at the Isthmian games were given a crown as a prize. What was the crown made of?

a) celery
b) rhubarb
c) gold

4 Before clever Aristotle came along, the Greeks had a strange belief about elephants. What was it?

a) an elephant has no knee joints so it goes to sleep leaning against a tree
b) elephants never forget
c) eating elephant meat makes you strong

5 Which team sport did the Ancient Greeks enjoy that we still play today?

a) hockey
b) soccer
c) volleyball

6 The Greek teacher, gorgeous Gorgias, said that 'nothing exists' . . . not even himself. He nearly didn't. He had a peculiar birth. Where was he born?

a) in his dead mother's coffin
b) on a mountain in a snow storm
c) on board a sinking ship

7 The Spartan youths tried out their military training by doing what for their town?

a) becoming secret police and murdering troublemakers
b) mending roads and keeping the streets clean
c) becoming servants in old people's homes and cooking for them

8 How far did the Greek explorer, Pytheas, sail?

a) Britain and the North Sea

b) Crete in the Mediterranean

c) America and the Atlantic

9 The Greeks invented a new weapon in the 4th century BC. They set fire to inflammable liquids then threw them over enemy ships or enemy cities. What is this weapon called?

a) Greek fire

b) Zeus's revenge

c) flaming dangerous

10 A sacred plant was sprinkled on graves. But we don't consider it sacred today. What is it?

a) parsley

b) cabbage

c) garlic

Test yourself

Now test yourself. See how many answers you can remember by arranging the following into the right order . . .

A	B	C
The playwright, Aeschylus,	invented a new weapon called	hockey
A sacred plant	sailed to	a camel
Aristotle, the great Greek teacher,	died when hit on the head by	an elephant going to sleep leaning against a tree
A Greek sportsman	was born in	a tortoise
A Greek sailor	was sprinkled on graves and called	the secret police
A Spartan youth	enjoyed the team sport called	celery
The Greek explorer, Pytheas,	won a crown made from	Greek fire
The Greek teacher, Gorgias,	believed in	the North Sea
A winner at the Isthmian games	trained in	parsley
An early Greek person	enjoyed meat from	his dead mother's coffin

Die like a Greek

What's up, Doc?

The earliest Greek doctor was said to be called Aesculapius. But, since he was supposed to be the son of a god, he probably didn't exist.

But his followers, the Asculapians, did exist. They didn't work from a hospital, they worked from a temple. Most of their patients recovered with rest, sleep and good food. But Asculapians liked people to think they were gods so the patients had to say prayers and make sacrifices.

The temple was famous because no one ever died in the temple of Aesculapius and his doctor-priests! How did they manage this?

They *cheated*. If someone was dying when they arrived then they weren't allowed in. And if they started dying once they got inside they were dumped in the nearby woods.

I'M FEELING A LOT BETTER!

The doctor-priests were in it for the money. They warned patients that if they didn't pay, the gods would make them sick again. And they advertised. Carvings in the ruins show the doctor-priests made fantastic claims . . .

91

In time, the temples changed into proper medical schools. Later, the great Hippocrates (460 – 377 BC) came along and said that magical cures by the gods were nonsense. He believed in the proper study of the body, and experiments.

Hippocrates was so great that today's doctors still take the Oath of Hippocrates (though it has been modified during the 20th century) and promise, 'I will give no deadly medicine to anyone if asked . . . I will use treatment to help the sick but never to injure.'

Could you take the groovy Greek version of the oath? You would have to swear . . .

92

But Hippocrates wasn't perfect. He said there were 91 bones in the body – now we know there are 206!

He also believed in 'bleeding' as a cure. A young man with a rumbling tummy was 'bled' by Hippocrates until he hardly had any blood left in his body . . . and he recovered!

One test for a lung disease was to shake the patient – and listen for the splashing inside.

Old Doc Hippo was a bit of a whinger. He complained that, 'If a patient gets worse or dies, people always blame the doctor.'

Still, *you* would complain if you had to do what Hippo had to do. Hippo took samples of . . .

- vomit
- snot
- ear wax
- pee
- tears
- infected wounds

. . . and he tested them. But he didn't test them in a laboratory with chemicals the way modern doctors can. He tested them by what?

1 colour
2 boiling them with rhubarb juice
3 tasting them

Answer: 3 Either the doctor or the patient had to taste the sample.

93

Hippo and his followers also practised cutting into the skull to drain fluids off the brain. But he wasn't the first to do this . . . there is evidence that Stone Age people did this operation. (Would you like to be operated on by a surgeon with a flint axe?)

The superstitious Greeks kept the piece of bone as a good-luck charm. It was supposed to keep you safe from disease.

But Hippo said some things which doctors today, every day, still say to their patients. . .

Fat people die sooner than thin people.

Hippo also said how doctors should look and behave . .

A doctor must be careful not to get too fat. Someone who can't look after his own fitness shouldn't be allowed to look after other people's.

Secondly he should be clean, wear good clothes and use a sweet (but not too strong) scent. This is pleasant when visiting the sick.

He must not look too grim or too cheerful – a grim man will worry the patient while a laughing man may be seen as an idiot.

And he must have been a good doctor because he lived to the age of 99 years.

Medical monster

Not every doctor was as good and unselfish as Hippocrates. Menecrates of Syracuse was much more grasping and cruel. He was especially fond of really sick patients because he could blackmail them.

CAN YOU CURE ME DOC?

COULD IF I WANTED

THEN CURE ME!

SIGN THIS PAPER AND YOU WILL BECOME MY SLAVE IF I CURE YOU

AND IF I DON'T SIGN?

THEN YOU DIE OF COURSE

I'LL SIGN

Medical manure

Of course, if you didn't want to go to a doctor like Menecrates then you could always try curing yourself. The great thinker, Heraclitus, did this.

He fell ill with dropsy – a disease where you swell up because there's too much fluid in your body. He decided to test his doctors by asking them a riddle. 'How do you make a drought out of rainy weather?' The doctors didn't know the answer – neither do I. Do you?

So Heraclitus decided to cure himself. He reckoned

the best way to get rid of too much liquid was to apply heat. In his farmyard he had a pile of rotting animal droppings – manure. The centre of the manure pile was warm.

Heraclitus buried himself up to the neck in the manure . . . and died.

Warning: Do *not* try this at home. If the manure doesn't kill you, your mother probably will – and your friends won't speak to you till you've had a hundred and five baths.

Perilous plague
One thing Greek doctors could do nothing about was the plague. The plague which killed hundreds in Athens in 430 BC . . .

- probably came from Egypt
- came so suddenly that rumours said the enemies had put poison into the water tanks
- started with a headache and sore eyes
- made breathing difficult and turned the throat red
- made victims begin to sneeze
- caused sickness when the infection moved to the stomach
- caused the temperature to rise so a plague victim couldn't stand wearing any clothes
- made victims grow terribly thirsty so they threw themselves into wells
- covered them in spots
- usually killed the victim
- often caused survivors to lose their memory:

Birds of prey wouldn't normally go near the dead bodies as they lay waiting to be buried. The birds that did always died.

The historian, Thucydides, said. . .

People died whether they had treatment or not. What cured one person often killed another. Some caught it by nursing others and they died like sheep. In fact this was the greatest cause of death. Corpses lay where they died on top of each other and the dying lurched around the streets and wells in their crying need for water.

Some families burned their dead. Thucydides also said that passing funerals often dumped their body on somebody else's funeral fire . . . then ran off!

Deadly Docs: 1

King Pyrrhus of Greece had a deadly doctor in 278 BC. The doc wrote to the Romans and said . . .

> DEAR FABRICUS,
> I AM THE DOCTOR TO PYRRHUS, IF YOU ARE WILLING TO PAY ME I WILL POISON THE KING

But Fabricus sent the letter straight back to Pyrrhus, his enemy, and explained. . .

> UNTO KING PYRRHUS, GREETING,
> YOU HAVE MADE A BAD CHOICE OF FRIENDS AND ENEMIES, YOU ARE AT WAR WITH HONEST MEN, BUT HAVE WICKED AND UNFAITHFUL MEN ON YOUR SIDE. AS YOU WILL SEE FROM THE LETTER THERE IS SOMEONE IN YOUR CAMP WHO PLANS TO POISON YOU. WE ARE TELLING YOU THIS BECAUSE WE DO NOT WISH TO BE BLAMED FOR SUCH A TREACHEROUS ACTION. WE WISH TO END THIS WAR HONOURABLY ON THE BATTLEFIELD.
> FABRICUS

King Pyrrhus found the traitor and gave the doctor a taste of his own medicine, as it were, by having him executed. He was so grateful to the Roman enemies that he set his Roman prisoners free without a ransom.

Deadly Docs: 2

If you can't poison the enemy king then at least you can *stop* him taking medicine that would get him *better*. How? *Tell* him he's being poisoned by his doctor . . . even if he *isn't!*

THAT ASPIRIN WILL MAKE YOUR HEADACHE WORSE

That's what Darius did to his enemy, Alexander the Great. Alexander was sick and received a letter from the double-crossing Parmenio. Like Fabricus's letter, it said . . .

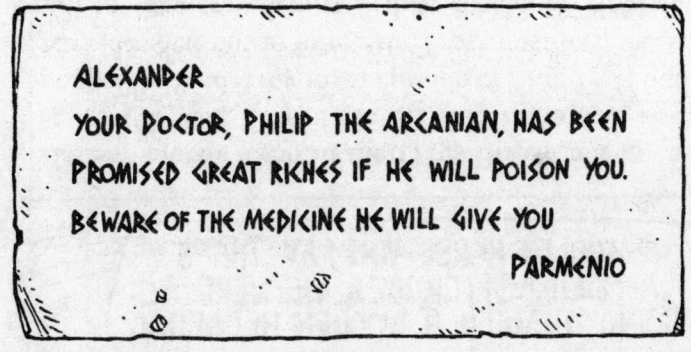

ALEXANDER

YOUR DOCTOR, PHILIP THE ARCANIAN, HAS BEEN PROMISED GREAT RICHES IF HE WILL POISON YOU.

BEWARE OF THE MEDICINE HE WILL GIVE YOU

PARMENIO

That evening, Doctor Philip arrived with a cup full of medicine. Alexander had the letter by his bedside. Was it really poison in the cup?

Alexander did a brave thing. He handed the letter to Doctor Philip. At the same time he drank the cup of medicine in one swallow.

Philip was impressed. 'But how do you know it wasn't poison?' he asked.

'I don't know about poison,' Alexander told him, 'but I do know about men. And I know you would never betray me, my friend.'

Alexander recovered. Not all doctors were cunning and treacherous.

Medical mystery

Which 'doctor' travelled through time to help the Greeks at Troy? (Clue: He gave them the idea about building a wooden horse.)

Answer: Doctor Who in the 1980s British television series. (Captain Kirk of the Starship Enterprise also popped back to Troy in an episode of *Star Trek*; but Kirk decided not to interfere. Troy must have been full of time travellers and their machines. Strange that Homer didn't mention them in his poems!)

A WOODEN HORSE YOU SAY. THAT'S A MUCH BETTER IDEA. WE WERE GOING TO BUILD A WOODEN HEDGEHOG

Odd Olympics

The groovy Greeks liked nothing better than a contest. The first Olympic contests were simple foot races. The first few Olympics had just one race on one day – a race of about 190 metres or the length of the stadium.

A second race – twice the length – was added in the 14th Olympics, and a still longer race was added to the 15th competition, four years later. But new events were added until the meeting lasted five days. There was even a Junior Olympics for kids.

● The bad news, girls . . . females were banned from the ancient Olympics.

● The bad news, boys . . . clothes were banned for the male athletes.

Choose your champion

You may wish to try an Olympic contest against the class next door. First you need to have a contest in your own class and choose your champion to represent you. Then go and cheer your champion as they compete against rival class champions.

Here's what to do. First choose your judges. They must train as judges (or referees) for ten months before the Olympics. They must also be honest. (You could have a problem finding an honest adult.) Agree the starting time and place and let the competitors battle it out.

● foot race – 200 metres
● double foot race – 400 metres
● standing long jump – with a kilo weight held in each
   hand to swing you through the air

- quoit-throwing (nearest to a fixed spot wins)
- javelin

After the contest . . .
1 Give the winners crowns made from the branches of a wild olive tree that grows in a sacred grove. (If you can't find one then make cardboard crowns from a sacred cornflakes packet.)
2 Call out the victor's name and country to the assembled crowds. (Or just phone the local newspaper.)
3 When the victor returns to their home they enter through a special gap knocked in the city wall. (Might be better if you *didn't* knock down the school wall. That's there for a purpose – to stop wild pupils escaping.)
4 The victor is treated with special favours – they either pay no taxes, or have free meals at the president's house for life. (Perhaps you could offer your victor a lifetime of free school dinners.)

5 Don't forget to cheer the loser. Losers have feelings too. (An Olympic wrestler called Timanthes lost his strength as he grew older. He was so upset he lit a big fire – then threw himself into it.)

Some groovy Olympic games you might not like to try

Mule-racing – smelly.

Relay – a bit hot. The god, Prometheus, stole fire from the gods and brought it down to earth for humans. But the humans had to escape from the other avenging gods. They ran with torches. The Olympic relay was run with flaming torches instead of batons, in memory of Prometheus. If the torch goes out your team loses. And if you grab the wrong end of the torch from the last runner . . . ouch!

IT'S NOT MY HAND I'M WORRIED ABOUT!

Four-horse chariot race – dangerous. The poet Homer described an accident. . .

Eumelos was thrown out of the chariot beside the wheel. The skin was ripped from the elbows, nose and mouth, and his forehead smashed in over the eyebrows. His eyes filled with tears and his powerful voice was silenced.

A bit rougher than your school rounders match, eh?

Hoplite racing – heavy, but not groovy. Wearing full armour and carrying weapons, this was hard work – try running with a couple of dustbins strapped to your back and that's how it might feel.

HOPLITE, NOT LIGHT HOP!

Trumpeters' competition – deafening.

Pancration . . . what? Pancration was a bit of a mixture of boxing and wrestling. The only rule was that there were no rules, apart from no biting and no gouging out the eyes. Just flatten the opponent. You could . . .

● strangle
● kick
● arm-twist
● jump up and down on your opponent.

Quite good if you're a winner. Painful for a loser.

Boxing – ordinary old boxing? Yes, harmless little fisticuffs – unless you do it the ancient Greek way, as the horrible historical story of Creugas and Damoxenos shows . . .

The Greek Guardian

still only 20 obols

Creugas the Corpse Claims Crown

In the Olympic heavyweight championship yesterday Damoxenos, the Dark Destroyer, beat challenger Creugas . . . and lost the title!

In a sensational contest the two men were both defending their unbeaten records. A crowd of two thousand sat on the grass in the afternoon sunshine to enjoy a fight to the end. They didn't know what an end it was going to be.

Boos

Big Damoxenos was booed as he stepped on to the grass and had leather wrapped around his mighty fists. The handsome Creugas was cheered as he stepped forward. The voice of the referee rang out across the grassy circle.

'Remember, slaps with the open hand, punches with the fist or blows with the back of the hand are allowed. Kicking is permitted, but no head butting. Understand?'

'Yes sir,' Creugas answered boldly. Big Damoxenos just grunted.

'The fight goes on without a break until one man has had enough,' the little ref went on. 'Show you are beaten by raising your right hand in the air. Understand?'

Damoxenos just sneered. 'I'll not need to remember that,' he boasted. 'I'll not be surrendering.'

Hammer

The crowd booed again as the referee stepped back. 'Box!' he cried and Damoxenos lunged forward. He swung his fist like a mighty hammer at Creugas's head but the young man jumped back and flicked a fist at the champion's head.

That was the pattern of the fight. Big Damoxenos lumbering round, swinging huge punches but unable to catch the slippery Creugas. Just as the crowd was growing restless, the sun sank down and the referee called a halt.

'We cannot have a draw,' he cried. 'The contest will be decided by a single blow struck by each man.'

First

The crowd seemed to like that and they closed in to get a better view.

'You go first, wimp,' Damoxenos growled. The big man held his arms by his sides – the crowd held its breath.

Creugas struck a hammer blow to the champion's head. The big man just laughed. 'My turn.'

The young man shook his head and waited for the blow that would surely knock him senseless. It didn't.

Instead the big ox hit Creugas cruelly under the ribs with straight fingers. His sharp finger nails tore through the young man's skin. He pulled back his hand and jabbed again. This time he tore out the challenger's guts.

The crowd gasped as Creugas fell lifeless to the ground.

Cheat

The ref ran forward. 'One blow is all that is allowed. You took *two* blows, Damoxenos, you cheat. I hereby disqualify you. I declare that Creugas is the champion!'

The crowd cheered with joy. The new champ was not available for comment.

His manager said, 'The boy done well. Deserved that win. We'll have a few drinks later to celebrate.'

Creugas will always be remembered as a champion who had guts.

Did you know . . .? Olympically speaking

1 There was a fine for cheating. The cheat had to pay for an expensive statue of the god Zeus. And at Olympus there were an awful lot of Zeus statues before the Greek Olympics ended. There must have been a lot of cheats.

2 The main form of cheating was to have a really good set of horses in the chariot race then have a bet that you would *lose* the race. You made sure you lost the race by pretending to whip the horses to go faster . . . while secretly tugging at the reins to slow them up. This 'pulling' of horses to win money still goes on today.

3 The Greek Olympics were banned by the rotten Romans. The Romans didn't much like sport when they conquered the Greeks. The Romans preferred their own groovy 'games' . . . like fights to the death between gladiators . . . and they built huge coliseums to stage the contests. But they let the beaten Greeks keep their Olympics until miserable Roman Emperor, Theodosius, abolished them in 394 AD.

4 The Greek Olympics had competitions in music, public speaking and theatre as well.

5 The Olympics vanished for 1500 years. They were revived in 1896 by Pierre de Coubertin, a young French nobleman, and since then they have been staged every fourth year. The ancient Greek Olympics were held in honour of Zeus, and all wars would cease during the contests. The Olympics came first. Sadly, in the modern Olympics, war came first; the games stopped during World War I and World War II (1916, 1940, 1944).

6 A cook, Coroibus of Elis, was the first recorded winner.

7 The boy athlete, Pisidorus, took his mum to the Olympics. Because women were banned, she had to be disguised as his trainer.

8 . . . and, talking about trainers. There are quite a few 'Nikes' at modern Olympics. But did you know that Nike was the goddess of victory, who watched over all athletic contests?

9 A sports arena was one 'stadion' (600 Olympian feet, 190 metres) long. That's why we have sports 'stadiums' today. The competitors raced up and down, not round and round.

10 The poet Homer described a race between Odysseus and Achilles. Odysseus was losing and said a quick prayer to the goddess, Athena. She not only made Achilles slip – she made him fall head first into cattle droppings. He stood up spitting cow dung – and lost the race, of course.

Funny food

Sacrificial snacks

A sacrifice is *supposed* to be a groovy gift to the gods. 'Here you are, gods, here's a present for you. I'm being nice to you, so you will be nice to me, won't you?'

When the Greeks sacrificed an animal to a god, they roasted it and they ate it. That's a bit like buying your mum a box of chocolates then scoffing them yourself.

- The greatest honour was to have some roasted heart, lungs, liver or kidney from the sacrificed animal.
- The best meat was shared around.
- Everything left was minced together and put into sausages or puddings – but the important people didn't bother with those.
- This didn't leave very much for the gods to eat, you understand. Just the tail, the thigh bones and the gall bladder.

The Greeks even mixed the blood and the fat together and stuffed it into the bladder of the animal. They then roasted and ate this little treat. Would you like to try this to see what the Greeks ate? (Without all the mess of sacrificing a cow, of course. That can make a terrible mess on the living-room carpet.) Then go to your local butcher's shop and ask for it. But what do you ask for?

1 haggis
2 black pudding
3 sausage

DON'T YOU THINK YOU'RE TAKING THE SACRIFICE THING A LITTLE TOO FAR?

Did you know . . .?
Vegetarians in ancient Greece wouldn't sacrifice animals to the gods. Instead they sacrificed *vegetables* – groovy, eh?

Munching Milon
Milon was a wrestler. He also thought he was pretty groovy. Before one Olympic contest he walked around the stadium with a live young bull on his shoulders.

He fancied a snack after all that effort, so he killed the bull and ate it. He finished the whole bull before the day was out.

But maybe there are some gods on Olympus with a sense of fair play. Because, in the end, Milon got what he deserved. *Exactly* what he deserved.

It started with him showing off again. He split open a tree with his bare hands . . . but his hand became stuck in the split. Try as he might he couldn't get free. When a pack of wolves came along they licked their chops and moved in on Milon.

What did they do to Milon? Just what Milon did to the young bull – except they probably didn't cook him first.

Foul food
The Greeks ate the meat of sacrifices but didn't eat a lot of meat in their normal day-to-day lives. One historian

said, 'The Greeks had meals of two courses; the first a kind of porridge – and the second a kind of porridge.'

In fact it wasn't quite that bad. The 'porridge' was more a sort of paste made up of lentils, beans and corn all ground up with oil – vegetable oil, not the sort of oil garages put in cars.

The peasants had some olives, figs, nuts or goats-milk cheese to add a bit of taste. They washed it down with water or goat's milk.

After about 500 BC the rich started to eat more meat than the peasants – goat, mutton, pork or deer – and drink wine rather than water. But what else did they eat of the following?

Spartan soup

You might not have enjoyed living in Athens and eating grasshoppers and thrushes. But you could have been worse off. You could have lived in Sparta.

The Spartans had a disgusting concoction called Black Broth. They mixed pork juices with salt and *vinegar* into a sort of soup.

The Athenians made some very cruel comments about Spartan food. Athenaeus said, 'The Spartans claim to be the bravest people in the world. To eat food like that they'd *have* to be.'

Another Athenian said, 'It isn't surprising the Spartans are ready to die on the battlefield – death has to be better than living on food like theirs.'

The groovy Greek guzzler

Archestratus wrote the first ever cookery book in Europe. It was written in *verse* and probably meant to be recited at feasts – not used as a recipe book. It contained some quirky bits of advice to eaters and to cooks. Archestratus seemed a rather grumpy man with strong views on some foods . . .

A Pontic fish, the Saperde,
Is poor and tasteless and it smells.
To those who eat this thing I say,
Both you and it can go to hell!

And Archestratus had his own favourite foods. He liked to rubbish more popular dishes . . .

> *Now some men like the taste of beef,*
> *They sing the praises of the cow.*
> *While I would rather get my teeth*
> *Into the belly of a sow.*

But Archestratus saved his nastiest comments for foreign cooks who ruined good Greek food with their recipes . .

> *If your food you want to waste,*
> *Take a Bass fish from the sea,*
> *Find a cook with awful taste*
> *Like the cooks from Italy.*
>
> *Syracuse has bad cooks too*
> *Spoiling Bass in sauce of cheese.*
> *Or in pickles, taste like glue,*
> *Keep away from cooks like these.*

Just as well he didn't live to taste our modern versions of Italian delights. He might have written a horrible verse like . . .

> *Spaghetti hoops that come in tins*
> *Belong in deep and dusty bins.*
> *As for tasteless plastic pizza*
> *Simply leave it in your frizza.*

Groovy Greek growing -up

Bother for babies
From 500 – 200 BC there was a ritual way of treating babies. Would *you* survive?

Father inspects baby. Is it fit?
Yes Go to 1.
No Go to 2.
Don't know Go to 5.

1 If you have too many boys then they'll have to split up your land when you die. Too many girls will cost you money. Do you want to keep it?
Yes Go to 6.
No Go to 2.

2 Put the baby in a pot (a pithos), then leave baby on a hillside to die. Do you care?
Yes Go to 4.
No Go to 3.

3 Baby dies before it's a week old.

4 Let a childless couple know what's going on. They will get to it before the cold or the wolves do. Baby lives with foster parents.
Go to 6.

5 Father will 'test' the baby by rubbing it with icy water, wine or urine (yeuch). Does it survive?
Yes Go to 6.
No Go to 3.

6 The baby is one of the family. Tell the world with an olive branch on the door if it's a boy, a piece of wool for a girl.
Go to 7.

7 Hold the *Amphidromia* ceremony. When baby is seven days old, sweep the house and sprinkle it with water. Father holds baby and runs round hearth with it while family sings hymns.
Go to 8.

8 When baby is ten days old have the naming ceremony. (A boy is named after his grandfather.) Congratulations – you've made it . . . unless disease or plague or war or something else gets you!

The good news: Boys didn't go to school until they were seven – girls didn't have to go to school at all.

The bad news: You didn't add up with numbers. You added up with letters – a = 1, b = 2, c = 3 and so on.

But do *you* know what number BAD + HEAD make?

Answer: 214 + 8514 = 8728

The really bad news:

Boys took a slave to school with them. No, *not* to do their work. The job of the slave was to make sure the boy behaved himself. If he didn't then the slave would give him a good beating.

Test your teacher

The Greeks loved thinking about things – the science of thinking about things became known as 'philosophy'. But it was a thinker from Italy who came up with the most curious thoughts – Zeno of Elea. The Greeks loved talking and thinking about Zeno's 'problems'. Test your teacher with this sneaky (and Greeky) question . . .

PLEASE, SIR, IMAGINE A RACE BETWEEN THE GREEK HERO, ACHILLES, AND A TORTOISE. ACHILLES RUNS TEN TIMES FASTER THAN THE TORTOISE; THE TORTOISE IS GIVEN A START OF TEN METRES. WILL ACHILLES EVER PASS THE TORTOISE?

HO HO HO. OF COURSE HE WILL!

WRONG! CLEVER MR ZENO OF ELEA SAID NO. EVERY TIME ACHILLES REACHES THE PLACE THE TORTOISE WAS, THE TORTOISE HAS MOVED FORWARD A TENTH OF THE DISTANCE THAT ACHILLES HAS RUN, SO THE TORTOISE WILL ALWAYS BE AHEAD

ERR... UM

Surviving school dinners

Have you ever been to school dinners and seen nothing you fancy? What happens? You go hungry.

The Lydians went hungry for a very long time because there was a famine. They decided to do something about the problem. They discovered that the more you think about food the hungrier you get. So they invented games to take their minds off food. They played dice and knucklebones.

The games were so interesting they didn't notice they were hungry. The next day they ate whatever they could find but didn't play games. This went on for 18 years! Games one day, food the next.

So, if you don't fancy a school dinner then play knucklebones. You need five ankle-joints from *cloven-footed* animals. (They make neat cubes of bone.) There are several cloven-footed animals – bison, pigs, goats, antelopes and sheep. If any of those appear on a school-dinner menu then you might just be in luck.

If your school cook slaughters her own wildebeest in the kitchens, then ask her for the little cube-shaped bones from the ankle joint. If she *doesn't* then you'll just have to use small cubes of wood like dice.

Knucklebones: 'Horse in the Stable'

Players: One or more players.

You need: Five knucklebones (or wooden cubes).

Rules: Put four knucklebones on the ground. Each one is a 'horse'.

Put the left hand near them with the fingers and thumb tips spread out and touching the ground. The gaps between the fingers are the 'stables'.

One knucklebone is tossed into the air with the right hand.

Before catching it the player must knock one 'horse' into a 'stable' with the right hand – that is, they must flick a knucklebone into a gap between the fingers.

With the right hand, catch the knucklebone that was thrown in the air.

Repeat until all four 'horses' are in their 'stables' – no more than one 'horse' to a 'stable'!

If all four are put in their 'stables' then move the left hand away from the 'horses'. Toss the throwing stone into the air with the right hand, pick up all four horses with the right hand, and catch the throwing stone in the right hand.

If the turn ends with a full 'stable', or if the player makes a mistake, pass the turn to the next person.

The first to 'stable' all the 'horses' ten times is the winner!

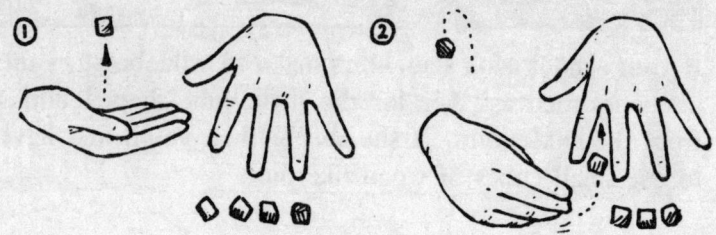

The school Olympics

Greek children invented games like knucklebones that are still played in some parts of the world today. In fact you may even have played some of the games yourself. If you haven't, and want to play like a groovy Greek, then here are the rules for six games.

Ostrakinda

This is a game for two teams that is still played in Italy, Germany and France. You need: A silver coin. Paint one side black with poster paint – this side is 'Night'. The plain side is 'Day'.

Rules: 1 Divide into two teams – the 'Nights' and the 'Days'.

2 Spin the coin in the air.

3 If it lands black side up then the Nights chase the Days – and if it lands silver side up the Days chase the Nights.

Cooking pot

Rules: 1 Choose someone to be 'It'.

2 'It' is blindfolded and sits on the ground.

3 The others try to touch or poke 'It'.

4 'It' aims to touch one of the teasers with a foot.

5 Anyone touched by a foot becomes 'It', is blindfolded and sat on the ground.

WHERE IS EVERYBODY?

ANYONE TOUCHED BY THOSE FEET WILL *NEED* TO SIT DOWN

Bronze Fly

A sort of Greek Blind-man's Buff. A Greek described it
...

> They fastened a head-band round a boy's eyes.
> He was then turned round and round and called
> out, 'I will chase the bronze fly!'
> The others called back, 'You might chase him
> but you won't catch him.'
> They then torment him with paper whips until
> he catches one of them.

ISN'T THAT A BULL WHIP?

Ephedrismos

Rules: 1 A player is blindfolded and gives a second one a piggy-back.

2 The rider then has to guide the player to a target set on the ground.

3 If the player succeeds then he becomes the rider. This could become a competition where pairs race to reach the target.

ARE YOU SURE THIS IS THE WAY TO THE TARGET?

Greecket

The Greeks also played ball games where you throw a ball at a 'wicket', rather like cricket without a batsman.

We just have pictures of these games that have been painted on Greek vases, but we don't have their written rules. Make up your own rules – maybe they played like this . . .

1 Stand on a mark a fixed distance from the wicket.

2 Take the ball and have ten attempts to hit the wicket.

3 The opponent stands behind the wicket (like a wicket-keeper) and throws the ball back to you every time.

4 Then you stand behind the wicket while your opponent has ten tries.

5 The one who has the most hits on the wicket from ten throws is the winner.

6 Try again from a different mark.

It looks (from the vase paintings) as if the loser has to give the winner a piggy-back ride.

121

Kottabos

Rules: 1 Take a wooden pole and stand it upright.

2 Balance a small metal disk on top of the pole.

3 Leave a little wine in the bottom of your two-handled drinking cup.

4 Grip the cup by one handle, flick the wine out and try to knock the disk off the top of the pole.

NOT VERY GOOD ARE YOU?

(Would you believe grown-up Greeks played this silly game at parties?)

You can try this with a cup and water and a 50p coin on the end of a broom handle . . . but *not* in your dining-room, please.

Puzzle your parents

So your parents think they're smart, do they? Give them this simple test to check their brain-power. All they have to do is answer 'Groovy Greeks', 'Terrible Tudors' or 'Vile Victorians' . . .

Who had these toys or games first? The Greeks, the Tudors or the Victorians?

1 puppets moved by strings

2 draughts

3 tug of war

4 dolls with moving parts

5 model chariots
6 yo–yos
7 babies' rattles
8 spinning-tops
9 see-saws
10 bowling hoops

Answer: All were first played by the *Greek* children. Any other answer is wrong. How did your parents score?

10 probably cheating

6–9 quite good – for an adult

3–5 go back to school – or read 'Groovy Greeks'

0–2 never *ever* let this parent offer to help with your homework. Your pet hamster could do better. In fact a *dead* hamster could do better.

123

The Romans are coming

Bodge-up at Beneventum!

As the Greek armies grew weaker, the Romans grew stronger. At first the groovy Greeks won all the battles – but lost a lot of men each time. The Romans learned from their mistakes and got better every battle, until finally, in 275 BC . . .

AND WORSE WAS TO COME. A YOUNG ELEPHANT WAS MADDENED BY THE ROMAN SPEARS. IT CHARGED AROUND THE BATTLEFIELD LOOKING FOR IT'S MUM. IT ALSO TRAMPLED ITS GREEK OWNERS

MUMMY!

RESULT: ROMAN 1 - GREEKS AND ELEPHANTS UNITED 0

Jumbo facts

1 The first Greek to come across an elephant army was Alexander the Great when he invaded India.

2 Apart from trampling and terrifying the enemy, elephants gave a good shooting platform for archers.

3 The Greeks used elephants supplied by India. The elephant trainers came with them. The elephants grew from babies with their trainer. No one else could command an elephant because it only understood the trainer's Indian language.

4 An elephant trainer was important to the Greeks and he was paid more than the average soldier.

5 A year after the bodge-up at Beneventum the Greeks arrived at Argos. In the battle an elephant lost its driver. The creature ran round the battlefield until it found him, dead on the ground. It picked him up with its trunk and rested the body across the tusks before carrying its dead master off the battlefield. And it wasn't too bothered who it trampled to death as it crossed the battlefield – Greek friends as well as Roman enemies.

Pathetic Pyrrhus

King Pyrrhus met a particularly pathetic end in his battle to defeat the Romans. In 274 BC he was fighting at the siege of Argos when a peasant with a pike hurt him. The peasant didn't hurt the King very much, you understand, but Pyrrhus was furious and turned to smash the pike man with his sword.

Poor Pyrrhus reckoned without the women of Argos. They had climbed up to the roof tops to watch the battle. They must have been like proud parents watching a school football match. You know, the sort who stand on the touchline and shout things like, 'Get stuck in, our Timothy!' And, 'Come on ref – get your eyes tested!'

Anyway, who should be watching Pyrrhus attacking the pike man peasant? The peasant's mum.

'Hey! That's my little boy you're trying to kill, you big bully!' she cried. The woman tore a tile off the roof and flung it at Pyrrhus.

Well, the woman was either an Olympic-standard discus thrower . . . or very, very lucky. The tile gave Pyrrhus a crack on the back of the neck, just below the helmet. His neck was broken and he dropped dead from his horse.

If there'd been newspapers in those days, *The Argos Chronicle* would have enjoyed that story. Imagine the headlines . . .

PROUD PIKE PEASANT'S
PARENT POTS
PATHETIC PYRRHUS

. . . perhaps?

Epilogue

After the groovy Greeks came the rotten Romans. The Romans were supposed to be an even greater people than the Greeks. After all, they eventually ruled over half the world – including Britain.

But the Romans were pretty rotten compared to the Greeks. Their games weren't great sports events like the Olympics – they were just an excuse to watch humans kill animals, animals kill humans, animals kill animals and humans kill humans. In boxing, for example, the Greeks bound their hands with leather bands like boxing gloves. The Romans bound their hands with leather bands – but put vicious spikes in them.

The Greek plays had been exciting and interesting. The Romans tried to copy them but were looking for more action and violence. Roman plays eventually killed people on stage for real.

One story about the take-over of Greece by the Romans gives a good example of what the world lost when the rotten Romans took over from the groovy Greeks . . .

Archimedes was a brilliantly clever Greek. When the Romans attacked his people in the city of Syracuse (211 BC) Archimedes used his great and groovy brain to invent wonderful new weapons.

For two years the Romans were kept out of the city as the inventor created 'death-rays' – giant mirrors that reflected the sun on to Roman ships in the harbour and set them on fire – and huge catapults that drove them off.

But at last the Romans broke through the Greek defences and brought terror to the citizens of Syracuse as they killed and stole from the houses. The Roman commander had given one strict order, however: 'Find Archimedes – but don't hurt the great man.'

At last a Roman soldier burst into Archimedes' house. The inventor was in the middle of an experiment and was too busy to bother with a small matter like an invasion at that moment.

The Roman was puzzled. Why was this old man ignoring him?

The Roman became angry. How *dare* this old man ignore him?

The Roman lost his cool. He killed the defenceless inventor. With one blow he destroyed one of the cleverest men the world has known.

The Roman soldier was punished for disobeying the commander's order not to harm Archimedes. But that didn't bring the old man back. Just as none of even the greatest Roman achievements could bring back the glory of the Greeks.

The rotten Romans ruled – the groovy Greeks went to their graves. That's horrible history for you.

GROOVY GREEKS

GRISLY QUIZ

**Now find out if you're a
groovy Greek expert!**

GRUESOME GREEK QUIZ

Simply answer 'Yea' for yes or 'Nay' for no to these facts about the grisly Greeks.

1 In the story of Troy, King Agamemnon sacrifices his daughter to the gods. Would that have really happened in ancient Greece?

2 A slave called Aesop told great stories such as 'The Tortoise and the Hare'. He was richly rewarded by the Greek priests.

3 The people who lived in the city of Sparta were super-tough kids. One Spartan boy hid a stolen fox cub under his tunic and didn't let on, even though the fox ate the boy's guts away.

4 In Draco's Athens (c. 600 BC) the laws were strict and you could be whipped for stealing a cabbage.

5 Athens' ruler Peisistratus (605–527 BC) arranged to have himself attacked so the people would feel sorry for him.

6 Teacher Socrates taught his students not to believe in the old Greek gods. Socrates was hanged.

7 General Alcibiades (450–404 BC) wanted people to notice him. Once he cut off his dog's tail to get a bit of attention.

8 The Greeks read the future using the guts of dead birds.

9 Hecate was the Greek goddess of crossroads. Greeks left food at crossroads for her.

10 The Greeks painted the doors of their houses red with blood.

SUFFERING SPARTANS

The Spartans were the toughest of all the Greek peoples – and it was extra-tough for Spartan kids.

Here's a Spartan rule book with some of the words missing. Get the answers right – or take a savage Spartan punishment!

The missing words, in the wrong order, are: no clothes, hair, herd, thistles, mountains, whipped, baths, girls, bite, beaten.

1 A bad serving-child will receive a _____ on the back of the hand.
2 A sickly baby will be taken to the _____.
3 A new bride must cut off her _____ and dress like a man.
4 Children caught stealing food will be _____.
5 A child belongs to the state of Sparta. At the age of seven children will join a _____.
6 A Spartan child may have only a few _____ a year.
7 In processions, dances and temple services girls must wear _____.
8 If a Spartan child is cold in winter, then they may sleep under _____.
9 Good Spartans are _____ at the altar of the goddess Artemis.
10 _____ are to be trained for fitness BY running, wrestling, AND throwing quoits and javelins.

TEST YOUR TEACHER QUIZ

Everyone studies the Greeks at school. Greek history lessons were even around when your teachers went to school, so they should know the answers to these ten quick questions.

1 General Alcibiades hated the Greek gods and damaged

their statues. He smashed off what part of the statues? (Clue: he only did this to the male gods)

2 The superstitious Greeks did not like dreaming of seeing your own face in a mirror. What did they think you would do soon after? (Clue: never see your face in a mirror again!)

3 Around 375 BC the girls of Attica went to the local temple and ran round the woods pretending to be bears.

What did they wear? (Clue: don't try this at the North Pole)

4 Greek teacher Aristotle had a favourite food that you will probably never eat. What? (Clue: unless you are stranded in the Sahara desert)

5 Playwright Aeschylus died (it is said) when an eagle dropped an animal on his head. What? (Clue: a slow death?)

6 Greek teacher Gorgias was born in a strange place. In his mother's what? (Clue: he was dead lucky to be alive, but Mum wasn't.)

7 Greeks invented a nasty weapon. It was a liquid that caught fire as soon as it landed and set fire to everything it touched in open air. What was it called? (Clue: not Roman water but…)

8 Aesculapius was a Greek doctor. Some of his cures worked. Some of the stories of other cures are plain daft. How did he cure (they say) water on a girl's brain? (Clue: she got it in the neck)

9 Doctor Hippocrates practised cutting out a circle of the skull to drain fluids off the brain. But why did the patient take home the circle of bone? (Clue: like a rabbit's foot?)

10 Some vegetarian Greeks refused to sacrifice animals to the gods. What did they sacrifice instead? (Clue: obvious really!)

Answers

Gruesome Greek Quiz

1) Yea. At the time of the Trojan Wars, not only were children sacrificed but bits of them were eaten too. Aren't you glad you weren't around?

2) Nay. In fact they took him to the top of a cliff and threw him off. It seems a few of his stories upset them.

3) Yea. This was a popular story told by the Spartans. Of course it may have just been Spartan boasting and a big fib. But it's a warning – don't go sticking foxes (or bears or budgies) up your jumper!

4) Nay. Draco was much tougher than that! The punishment for pinching an apple or a cabbage was death! By the way, the punishment for idleness was also death! (Think of all those dead  teachers in your school if we still had that law!)

5) Yea. Peisistratus staggered into Athens bruised and bleeding and said the city would suffer if its people didn't protect him. But he had arranged the attack on himself. The people of Athens were tricked into protecting him ... even though they hated him.

6) Nay. He was sentenced to death by poisoning. And he had to drink the poison himself. Which he did. So he carried out his own death sentence. Why not ask your teacher to demonstrate how a brave teacher behaves?

7) Yea. Alcibiades was a pretty good Athenian general but switched sides to the Spartan enemies. But the Spartans didn't trust the traitor much. In the end he was murdered, shot full of Spartan arrows, and his dog would have wagged its tail in joy – if Alcibiades hadn't cut it off, that is.

8) Yea. Don't try this at home with your pet parrot. You'll make a right mess on the carpet. Stick to reading horoscopes in the newspaper.

9) Yea. She always had a pack of howling dogs with her. (If you want to carry on this ancient Greek habit then why not leave a tin of dog food at your  nearest crossroads, eh? Seems a shame for Hecate to get all the grub.)

10) Nay. They painted them black with tar! They believed evil spirits would stick to the tar and be kept out. Messy.

Suffering Spartans

1) Bite. Younger boys had to serve older boys. If the younger boy did something wrong he could be given a nasty nip!

2) Mountains. Babies were left up a mountain to die if they failed a health check.

3) Hair. And a bridegroom had to pretend to carry his

bride off by force.

4) Beaten. Children were kept hungry and encouraged to steal food! (Spartans thought sneakiness was a handy skill in battle.) If the kids were caught stealing, they'd be beaten for being careless enough to get caught!

5) Herd. The toughest child was allowed to become leader and order the others about.

6) Baths. Stinky Spartans!

7) No clothes. So they didn't get fancy ideas about fine clothes.

8) Thistles. Children slept on beds of rushes that they gathered themselves from the river bank. In winter they could mix a few thistles in with the reeds – the prickles

were supposed to give them a feeling of warmth!

9) Whipped. A horribly historical way to prove you were a good Spartan! The one who suffered the most lashes was the toughest. Some bled to death.

10) Girls. So don't mess with a Spartan miss.

Test Your Teacher Quiz

1) Their naughty bits. Alcibiades knocked off the naughty bits on the statues of the naked gods. Ouch!

2) Die. Mind you, some people are so hideous they'd probably die if they saw themselves in a mirror awake! (Bet you know people like that!)

3) Nothing. This was supposed to prepare them for being grown women. The crazy chases were supposed to

get the last wild bits of fun out of them before they became boring adults.

4) Camel. Maybe we should start serving camel at posh tea parties. You turn to your guest and say, 'One hump or two?'

5) A tortoise. We do not know how the tortoise was after the accident. If it lived it was probably a bit shell-shocked though.

6) Coffin. Georgias's mother died and was popped in a coffin but somehow the baby was born anyway. He grew up and taught his students, 'Nothing exists – not even me!' If I'd been his student I'd have just skived off school then!

7) Greek Fire. Even today no one is sure how Greek Fire was made. But it was nasty stuff. Not the sort of thing you'd want to spray on your barbecue.

8) He cut off her head. After the water drained off he sewed the head back on. Hummmm! Believe that and you are ready for a new head yourself!

9) For luck. The superstitious Greeks kept the bone as a good-luck charm. It was supposed to keep you safe from disease.

10) Vegetables. They killed carrots, cracked corn and carved cabbages cruelly and then they probably battered some poor beans brutally. Vile vegetarians, how could they?

INTERESTING INDEX

Where will you find 'cow dung', 'ear wax', 'snot-tasting' and 'manure' in an index? In a Horrible Histories book, of course!

139

Terry Deary was born at a very early age, so long ago he can't remember. But his mother, who was there at the time, says he was born in Sunderland, north-east England, in 1946 – so it's not true that he writes all *Horrible Histories* from memory. At school he was a horrible child only interested in playing football and giving teachers a hard time. His history lessons were so boring and so badly taught, that he learned to loathe the subject. *Horrible Histories* is his revenge.

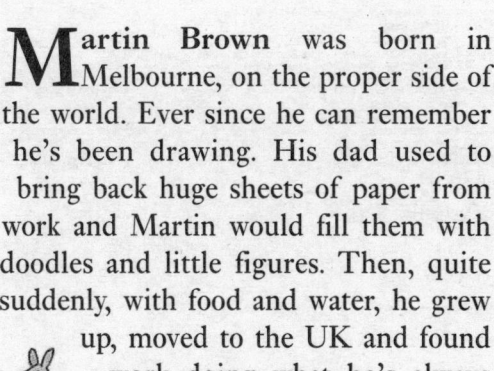

Martin Brown was born in Melbourne, on the proper side of the world. Ever since he can remember he's been drawing. His dad used to bring back huge sheets of paper from work and Martin would fill them with doodles and little figures. Then, quite suddenly, with food and water, he grew up, moved to the UK and found work doing what he's always wanted to do: drawing doodles and little figures.

HORRIBLE HISTORIES

AWESOME EGYPTIANS

Terry Deary & Peter Hepplewhite   Illustrated by Martin Brown

SCHOLASTIC

Scholastic Children's Books,
Euston House, 24 Eversholt Street,
London NW1 1DB, UK

A division of Scholastic Ltd
London ~ New York ~ Toronto ~ Sydney ~ Auckland
Mexico City ~ New Delhi ~ Hong Kong

First published in the UK by Scholastic Ltd, 1993
This edition published 2017

Some of the material in this book has previously been published in
Horrible Histories: The Awesome Ancient Quiz Book

Text © Terry Deary and Peter Hepplewhite, 1993, 2001
Illustrations © Martin Brown, 1993, 2001
All rights reserved

ISBN 978 1407 17865 3

Printed and bound by CPI Group (UK) Ltd, Croydon, CRO 4YY

4 6 8 10 9 7 5

www.scholastic.co.uk

CONTENTS

Introduction

Maths lessons are full of problems ... but English lessons are quite another story. Music lessons can break all records ... but Geography lessons have their ups and downs. Chemistry lessons can be a gas ... but Biology lessons are full of life.

P.E. lessons are one long game ... but History!

History is **horrible!** Horrible dates to remember, horrible kings fighting horrible battles against horrible people. Sometimes it all gets horribly boring!

Sometimes history can be horribly unfair!

Sometimes it can be horribly confusing!

But this book is about **really horrible** history. The sort of thing that teachers never tell you! Teachers don't always tell you the whole truth! Honestly!

Teachers think you're too young to learn about gruesome things ... like the way Egyptians took the brains out of their mummies! So they don't tell you ... then you leave school, and you may never ever learn this vital information.

And sometimes teachers don't tell you things because they don't know the facts themselves! (That's right! Teachers do *not* know everything ... just some teachers *think* they do.)

So, this book will tell you the things teachers daren't. And by the time you're finished you will be able to teach your teacher ... you'll enjoy that!

In this book, you'll find lots of other interesting things:

... stories to make your blood run colder than a crocodile's claw!

... things to do that will be more fun than eating a bag of chips under water!

... facts that are funnier than a teacher's joke, nastier than a tramp's sock or sadder than a three-legged sheep. I hope you'll find them all horrible fun!

Egypt factfile

The most awesome fact about the Egyptians was that their civilisation lasted an awfully long time – over 3000 years. They had been around so long that their monuments were ancient even in Greek and Roman times.

Time line of important events

Egyptian time is usually measured in periods called dynasties. A dynasty was the length of time that a ruling family lasted. Each dynasty could have as many as 14 kings in the family . . . or as few as one. There were 30 Egyptian dynasties altogether followed by two Greek ones, before Egypt finally fell to the Romans and then the Arabs. This is an awesomely quick race through time . . .

Awesome Egyptian events

Time: 3200 – 2300 BC
Dynasty: 1 – 6
Period: The Old Kingdom
Events: Upper and Lower Egypt joined together and Nile floods controlled by drain building.
Hieroglyphic writing in common use by scribes, and calendar invented.

The first pyramids built, including The Great Pyramid of Cheops.

Time: 2300 – 2050 BC
Dynasty: 7 – 11
Period: First Intermediate Period.
Events: Weak rule by Pepy leads to revolution and mob violence.
Starvation for many peasants.

Time:	2050 – 1775 BC
Dynasty:	11 – 12
Period:	The Middle Kingdom
Events:	Clever Pharaohs

Art, craft and writing very rich with huge temples being built and decorated.

First bakeries in the world started in Egypt.

Time:	1775 – 1575 BC
Dynasty:	13 – 17
Period:	Second Intermediate Period.

Events: 'Shepherd Kings' – invaders from Asia – rule the North.

Horses and chariots beginning to be used.

First sweets in the world made in Egypt.

Better spinning and weaving.

New musical instruments such as oboe and tambourine.

Time: 1575 – 1085 BC
Dynasty: 18 – 20
Period: The New Kingdom
Events: 'Shepherd Kings' thrown out.

The greatest period in Ancient Egypt's history.

Rock tombs in the Valley of the Kings started.

Tutankhamun lived and died.

Ramesses II fights Hittites in great battle at Kadesh.

Books of the Dead written on papyrus.

Hebrew slaves in Egypt led to freedom by Moses.

Time: 1085 – 709 BC
Dynasty: 21 – 24
Period: The Decadence Period
Events: Gradual end of the Egyptian kings.

Egypt has to use soldiers from Libya to fight its battles.

10

Time: 709–332 BC
Dynasty: 25–30
Period: The Late Period
Events: Egypt invaded by Assyrians.
Egypt ruled by Persian Kings.
Nubian rulers are first people to encourage the study of History.

Time: 332–30 BC
Dynasty: The Ptolemaic Period
Events: Egypt conquered by Alexander the Great of Greece.

Ruled by the Ptolemy family – Greeks.
Last Queen of Egypt was Cleopatra.

Time: 30 BC
Events: Egypt part of the Roman Empire.
Egypt is used to supply food to the Roman World.

Time: 641AD
Events: Egypt conquered by the Arabs.

Phascinating Pharaohs

The most awesome sight that you can see in Egypt is the pyramids. And the most awesome things that you can't see are the people who had them built – the Egyptian kings or Pharaohs. They've now turned to dust, bones, musky mummies and, of course, history. But how did they come about?

Before Egypt was a country, small villages had grown up on the banks of the River Nile. Each village had a chief. The most powerful chiefs took over other villages from neighbouring chiefs. They became kings of small kingdoms by the Nile.

Again, the most powerful would conquer neighbours and become even more powerful. In the end there were just two awesome chiefs – the King of Upper Egypt with his white crown and the King of Lower Egypt with his Red crown.

About 3200 BC, King Menes of Upper Egypt conquered Lower Egypt – he joined the two crowns as a symbol. The country we now know as ancient Egypt was born.

Villages with chiefs changed to countries with kings in a matter of only 200 years. How could this change have happened so quickly? Some historians think the new leaders were an awesomely clever group of people from outside Egypt – conquerors in fact. There is proof that these early kings were taller and had much larger heads than the peasants of Egypt!

One leading historian says they came from the East. A leading hysteric says they must have come

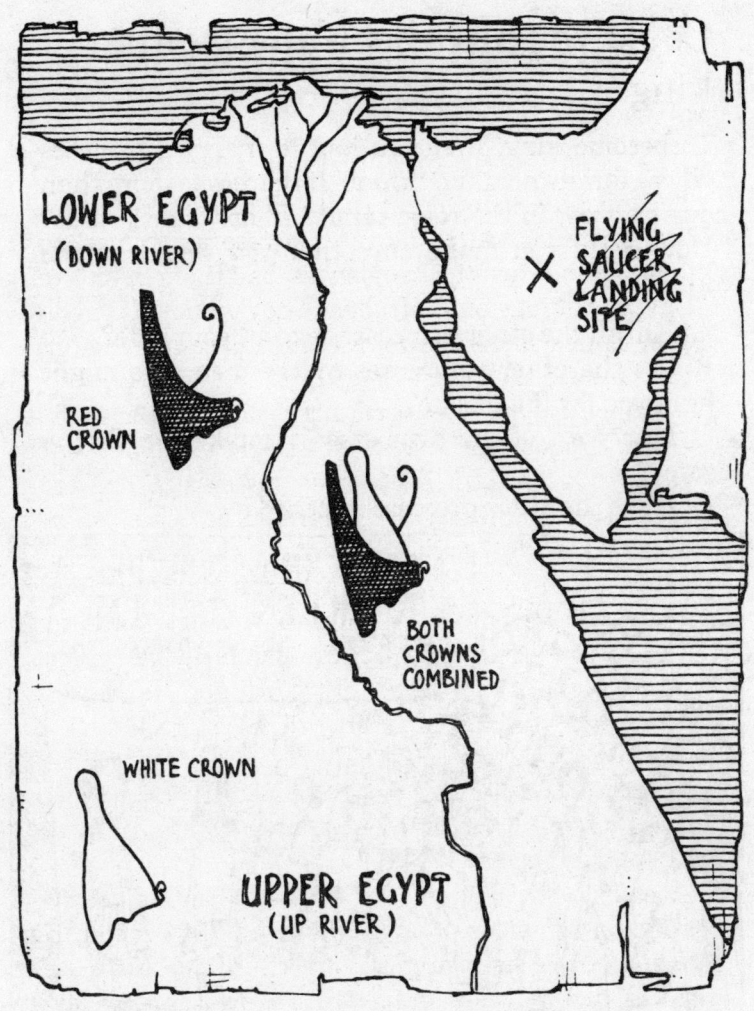

LOWER EGYPT
(DOWN RIVER)

RED
CROWN

BOTH
CROWNS
COMBINED

WHITE CROWN

UPPER EGYPT
(UP RIVER)

X FLYING
SAUCER
LANDING
SITE

from another planet! Their skeletons and their graves have been found . . . their flying saucer has not. Still, no one is certain . . . *make up your own mind.* In any case, wherever they came from, it was their even more awesome descendants who built the pyramids.

Could you have been an Egyptian king?

To become king, first you had to marry a princess whose family held the throne. If there was more than one princess in the royal family what would you do? How could you make sure that *you* would be the king?

A Kill all the other princesses except your wife?

B Let the other princesses marry men who might fight you for the throne?

C Marry *all* of the princesses to make the throne safe?

D Have the other princesses locked away?

Answer: C was the most common. There was no limit to the number of wives a king could have. The more royal princesses he could marry, the safer he would be.

Your royal role

As a king, here are some of your duties . . .

The Heb-sed festival
Are you fit? The king has to prove his fitness by running round a fixed course. This is usually held after the king has ruled for 30 years. This terrible trial is held at the Heb-sed festival.

Religious leader
Remember you are not just a king; you are also a god. Every morning the king has to make offerings to the other gods. This is to ask the sun to rise. If you don't, then the sun won't rise and the world will end! (If you are a bit lazy, don't worry. The priests usually do this job for you – the priests will also eat the offerings to the gods as part of their payment.) One of your other powers is command over the great River Nile. Each year you perform the ceremonies to make the river rise and flood the land. This keeps the land fertile for growing crops, and the people well fed.

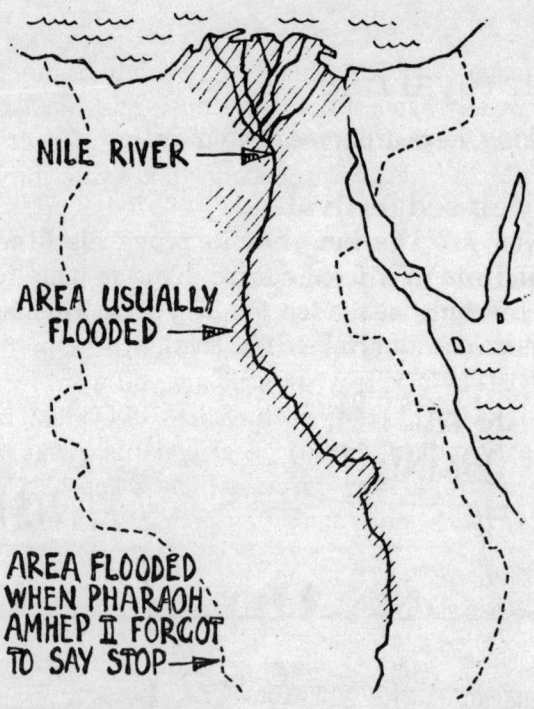

NILE RIVER →

AREA USUALLY FLOODED →

AREA FLOODED WHEN PHARAOH AMHEP II FORGOT TO SAY STOP →

Government leader

An important duty is to keep the two parts of Egypt together – Upper and Lower Egypt. Feeling a bit overwhelmed? Don't worry, you have lots of officials to help you run the country.

The royal nickname

Of course, it's very unlikely you would have been an Egyptian king, and much more likely you'd have been a commoner. As a commoner you'd have to mind your manners with the king. For a start, you'd be in big trouble if you called the king . . . well . . . "King"! If you were an ordinary Egyptian it could mean death. The Egyptians believed that their ruler was sacred. They were supposed to be in awe of him. After all, he wasn't just a king, but a god as well. So

16

it was very insulting to use his private name! Instead they used respectful nicknames. The most popular nickname was Pharaoh, which meant 'Great House' or 'Palace' – because the king's body was the human 'house' of a god.

Awesome army leader

The carvings on all Egyptian monuments show the king as a conqueror. What if you lose? Don't worry, the writers (scribes) can still say you won! Ramesses II fought the Hittites at the Battle of Qadesh in Syria – the Egyptian scribes described his great victory. The Hittite writers described the same battle – but in the Hittite story the Hittites won!

Is she a queen . . . or a king?

The king of Egypt was a man . . . but occasionally he could be a woman. Yes, a woman could be a king! If a woman was the most powerful person in Egypt then she would rule the kingdom . . . but the Egyptians would never see her as a queen.

For the king of Egypt was also the son of the chief god, Re. The son of Re had to be a man, didn't he? So, the king had to be a man even if she was a woman, see! If she didn't have the qualities of a man then the Egyptians gave them to her. She would have to have a beard . . . so they gave her a chin wig.

Hatshepsut was a woman-king, and she often dressed in men's clothes to look the part. She had her name written on monuments all over Egypt. But the kings that followed Hatshepsut were so confused, and in awe of her, they scratched her name off the monuments again. They tried to pretend that woman-king Hatshepsut had never existed.

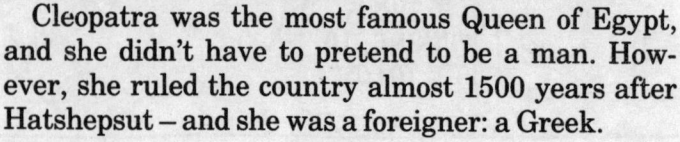

I WOULDN'T LOOK UP THERE IF I WERE YOU

Cleopatra was the most famous Queen of Egypt, and she didn't have to pretend to be a man. However, she ruled the country almost 1500 years after Hatshepsut – and she was a foreigner: a Greek.

18

The terrible tragedy of Tutankhamun . . . or Would *you* marry your grandfather?

King Akhenaten was a problem. He had a crazy idea that there was only one god in Egypt, Aten. And he spent so much time bothering about Aten that he forgot to defend Egypt against her enemies. The chief ministers must have been frantic.

King Akhenaten had to go. And he went. He died suddenly and mysteriously. His Uncle Ay, the highest minister, probably had something to do with it. He saw to it that Akhenaten's younger brother, Tutankhamun, became the new king. He was only nine when he took over the throne so he couldn't sort out Egypt's problems by himself. So his Uncle Ay helped him out . . . and helped himself to an awesome amount of power.

Uncle Ay sorted out the religion problems and the defence of the country. In fact, Uncle Ay ran the country while young Tutankhamun lived a quieter life with his wife, Ankhesenamun. They were very fond of hunting.

Then Tutankhamun died. How? He could have died of natural causes . . . but he was only 18. Or was he *murdered?* Maybe Tutankhamun had decided it was time to take over from Uncle Ay . . . and maybe Uncle Ay didn't want to let go of the power he'd enjoyed for nearly ten years.

There were only two ways that Uncle Ay could hang on to that power. He could fight for it . . . but he might lose in battle. Or he could kill Tutankhamun and marry the boy-king's widow, Ankhesenamun . . . but she was his grand-daughter.

Ankhesenamun didn't like the idea of marrying her grandfather one little bit ... would you? but what could she do? What would *you* have done if you'd been Ankhesenamun?

1. OFFER TO MARRY A FOREIGN PRINCE WHO WOULD BECOME THE NEW KING OF EGYPT?

2. POISON YOURSELF?

3. MARRY YOUR GRANDFATHER AND STAY AS QUEEN?

4. RUN AWAY?

Ankhesenamun chose number 1 – I think I would have, too. She offered to marry Prince Zennanza, the son of the Hittite king, even though the Hittites were Egypt's enemies! The Hittite king sent Prince Zennanza to marry Ankhesenamun ... but the prince never arrived! He was murdered on the way. And we can guess who arranged that!

After her plan failed Ankhesenamun agreed to marry Grandfather Ay. And the good news? Ay became king, but he only lived another four years. That probably served him right!

Kingly kuriosities . . .

1 King Pepy II ruled from the age of nine till he was over 100 – awesomely longer than any other Egyptian king.

2 King Sneferu invited 20 of his wives to row across the palace lake to entertain him. It was going well when one wife dropped her hair clip into the water. She sulked and refused to go on. The king pleaded. She refused. Finally King Sneferu had to order the court magician to find it. An ancient story says that he folded one half of the lake on top of the other and found the hair clip.

3 Many kings hired magicians. One knew how to cut off a goose's head and replace it without harming the bird. Was this a bit like the sawing a lady in half trick of modern magicians? Another one could make a wild lion as tame as a pet.

WHY COULDN'T HE PULL ME OUT OF A HAT LIKE OTHER MAGICIANS

4 King Ramesses II faced the Hittite army with no help but his pet lion . . . and lived! He prayed to the god Amun for help. At that moment an army of allies turned up and attacked the Hittites from the back. The enemy were driven into the river where many drowned. The Hittite king agreed to make peace with Ramesses . . . and the lion.

5 The kings didn't just need their mummified bodies in the afterlife. They also needed their servants. Scribes and cooks and tailors and builders and . . . every servant they ever had on earth. Most kings were buried with models of the servants they would need.

But the first few kings had a much more gruesome answer to the afterlife servant-problem . . . when they died they took their human servants with them. The servants couldn't travel to the afterlife while they were still alive, so they had to be killed!

We don't know if they died willingly or had to be brutally murdered. We do know that outside King Zer's tomb, for example, there are the graves of 338 servants who were sacrificed at his funeral. It wasn't until the eighth king, Ka'a, was buried that this 'awesome' custom died out.

Serving the king was a great honour. But would you like to have worked for him knowing that when he died, you died?

6 The Romans ruled Egypt as part of the Roman Empire. The days of the great kingdom of Egypt were ended after over 3,000 years. Ancient Egypt has been the longest-running empire in the history of humankind. Awesome!

7 The last kings of Egypt weren't Egyptian, they were all Greek. After Alexander the Great conquered the country in 332 BC, the Greek Ptolemy family ruled the country for almost 300 years. The last Ptolemy ruler was awesome Queen Cleopatra. But Cleo came to a nasty end.

Cleopatra's lover was the Roman ruler, Julius Caesar. He had protected her from a Roman invasion – but Julius was then murdered. She had to decide which of his two successors she should support . . . Augustus or Mark Antony? She decided to bet on Mark Antony . . . and became *his* lover.

She lost her bet. And when Mark Antony lost in a war against Augustus – Cleo was finished. The end would have been hilarious if it hadn't been so tragic.

Mark Antony heard that Cleopatra had killed herself. He was so upset he fell on his sword and tried to kill *himself*. He failed.

Then he heard that Cleopatra *hadn't* tried to kill herself! She was alive! He had himself carried to her . . . then he died of his wound. Cleopatra was so upset she then really did kill herself.

The power of the pyramids

12 August 1799

He was an awesome ruler – the most powerful in the
world at that time. Now this great ruler of the new
world had come to visit a great ruler of the ancient
world. He was the leader of France, the conqueror of
Europe. His name was Napoleon Bonaparte. Napoleon had come to the Pyramid of Cheops in Egypt.

His guide led him deeper and deeper into the heart of the ancient pyramid. At last they stood in the very centre of the King's chamber. The guide began to explain what he knew about its history, but Napoleon silenced the man with a wave of his hand.

"Leave me alone," he said . . . in French.

"But, sir . . ."

"Alone!"

"As you wish, sir," the guide muttered and backed out of the chamber into the dark passageway. Napoleon was alone in the warm, still, silent air. It seemed a long time before the great man came out. The guide held up the lantern. Napoleon was pale and shaking.

"Is something wrong, sir?" the guide asked.

Napoleon seemed to ignore him. Then suddenly he said in a harsh, dry voice, "Do not ever mention this matter again!"

"No, sir," the guide muttered and led the way back into the dry, white heat of the Egyptian plain.

But later in his eventful life it was Napoleon who mentioned the visit. And he hinted – just hinted – that he had experienced incredible things while he was inside that pyramid. Perhaps, he suggested, he had even seen a vision of his own future.

Then, when he lay dying on the island of St. Helena, he seemed about to tell his secret at last to a friend. "But no," he said weakly. "What is the use? You'd never believe me!"

He died shortly after. The mystery of the pyramid's power went to the grave with him.

The magic of the pyramid

One thousand years before Napoleon entered the King's Chamber, another great leader had stood in the same spot. His name was Al Mamun, the Caliph of Baghdad. Al Mamun was a young man and a very curious one. He'd heard about the magical powers of the pyramids and he wanted to find out for himself just what was inside one.

Most of the pyramids had been raided by grave robbers. They were empty. But no one had broken through the massive defences of the Pyramid of Cheops – known to this day as The Great Pyramid.

A King's Chamber had been dug deep into the
rock under the Great Pyramid – perhaps to give a
safe resting place for the king in case he died before
the pyramid was finished. Another chamber had
been designed for his queen. Finally there was a
chamber deep in the heart of the pyramid.

Once the coffin was in the chamber the passageways had been sealed with hard, granite blocks.
When Al Mamun reached the Great Pyramid he
found that no robbers had broken through the great
blocks. But the young Caliph was determined . . .
and he had an army of men to work for him.

They dug new tunnels through the rocks. At last they reached the centre. Al Mamun now entered. He'd heard the legends about the mysteries the pyramids contained. Ancient charts that showed the movement of the stars . . . maps of the world as the Egyptians knew it . . . pure metals and gold . . . and magical things like unbreakable glass.

In the centre of the King's chamber stood a stone coffin. And in the stone coffin was . . . nothing!

King Cheops had never been placed in this vast stone tomb. Why not? If it wasn't to be his burial place, then why was it built?

It's a mystery which has never been solved to this day. Maybe the answer is very simple – perhaps King Cheops was buried somewhere else because the pyramid wasn't ready in time. But for many people, that answer is too simple.

Dozens of people have put forward ideas . . . some more amazing than others.

If the Great Pyramid isn't a tomb, then why was it built? What else could a pyramid be? Which suggestion do you like best . . .?

Some awesome ideas about the pyramids

1 The Great Pyramid is a stone computer – if you take the lengths of the sides, and their heights and angles, you can calculate many different things. The pyramid will tell you how to work out the distance round the outside of a circle if you know the distance across it.

2 The Egyptians could use the Great Pyramid to work out the distance the Earth travels round the sun, and the speed of light.

3 The pyramid is a mathematical horoscope – you can calculate the future from it. The Institute of Pyramidology in London says the pyramid has already predicted the Crucifixion of Jesus and the First World War. It has also predicted that the world will end in the year 2979AD.

4 The Great Pyramid is a sign to the world how much knowledge the Egyptian priests had – and how much power. They persuaded Cheops to have it built and made him pay all the bills. Then when he died they didn't want his body inside their wonderful creation.

5 The Great Pyramid is an observatory for watching and recording the movements of the stars.

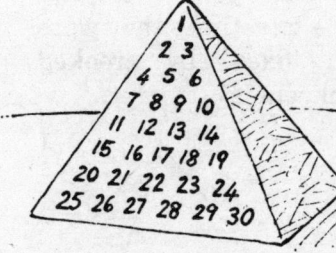

6 The Great Pyramid is a giant calendar. The Egyptians could use it to measure the length of a year to three decimal places.

7 The Great Pyramid is a sundial. The shadow fell on pavements and the pavements were marked with the day of the year and the hour of the day.

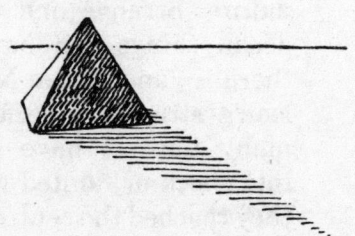

8 The Great Pyramid is a landmark. All ancient maps could use it as the starting point for drawing and measuring their charts – rather like the Greenwich Meridian is today.

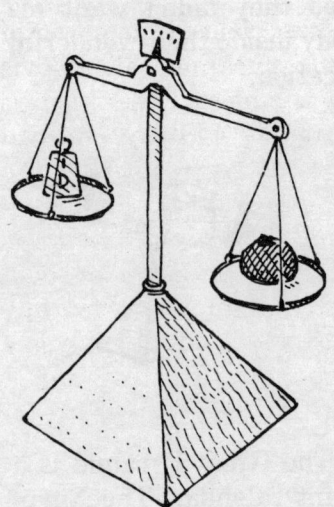

9 The Great Pyramid is a perfect store for the weights and measures of the ancient world. The government needed a master set of weights to check if traders were giving proper value when they sold goods. But weights like the *deben* were made of copper and lost weight after a few years' wear and tear – sometimes they were even 'fixed' by crooked shopkeepers.

10 The centre of the pyramid is the centre of tremendous forces of nature. Strange and wonderful things can happen there . . . apart from Napoleon's strange experience, many tourists have gone into shock or fainted when they reached the centre.

The powerful pyramid shape

Fifty years after Napoleon experienced the power of the Great Pyramid, another Frenchman called Bovis visited the great tomb. It was a mess. Other visitors had left rubbish lying around. A stray cat had wandered in and died – it was lying amongst the rubbish, forgotten. But Bovis noticed something strange about the body of the cat. It had not rotted as you'd expect. In fact it was so well preserved it could have been a mummy ... but a mummy without any wrapping or embalming. Bovis decided that only one thing could have preserved the cat in this way ... the power of the pyramid.

33

You've probably seen the way a magnifying glass can pull together the rays of the sun into one tiny, hot spot. Bovis decided that in the same way some powerful forces of nature are pulled together by the shape of the pyramid.

He went back to France and tried some experiments. He made model pyramids and placed different types of food inside them – food that usually turns bad in a very short time. He found that all the food stayed in good condition for much longer than anyone would expect!

Over a hundred years later, in 1959, an engineer from Czechoslovakia read about Bovis's experiments. His name was Karel Drbal. He wondered if the pyramid would preserve metal the way it preserved food. Razor blades were in short supply in his country in those days. So he put blunt blades under a model pyramid to see if it would stop them getting any blunter. To his astonishment, Drbal found that they actually became sharp again.

This was a great discovery. Drbal had to make sure the idea was not stolen by someone else. He needed a government patent that would allow Drbal to claim the idea was his alone. So Drbal went to the government Patent Office.

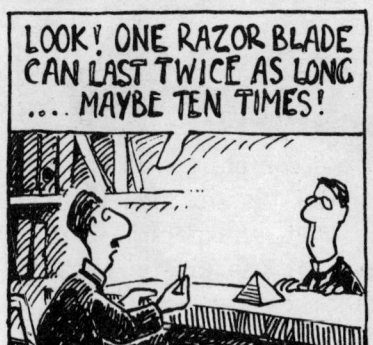

But when Drbal went back the next week the Chief Officer was a shaken man.

And Drbal sold the idea to a company who went on, very successfully, to make plastic models of pyramids and sell them as blade-sharpeners. The people of Czechoslovakia bought the plastic pyramids. They really believed that they worked.

But do you?

The Great Pyramid experiment

The best way to find out is to try your own Great Pyramid experiment.

1 Make a pyramid of cardboard – four triangles. The bottomless base of each triangle must be 15.7 centimetres (or 15.7 inches) and each side must be 14.94 centimetres (or 14.94 inches).

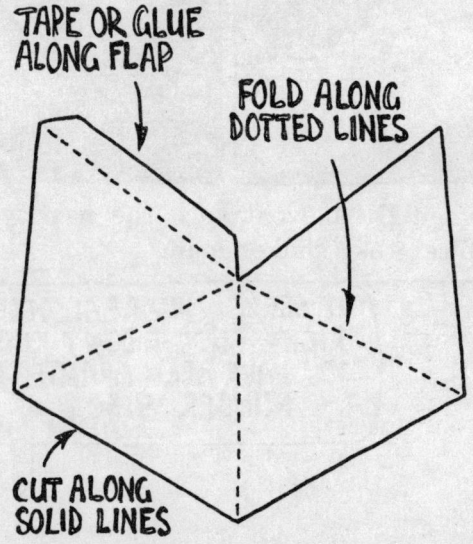

TAPE OR GLUE
ALONG FLAP

FOLD ALONG
DOTTED LINES

CUT ALONG
SOLID LINES

2 Place a piece of bread or cheese or any other food in a small block so it is raised 3.33 centimetres (or 3.33 inches) off the base.

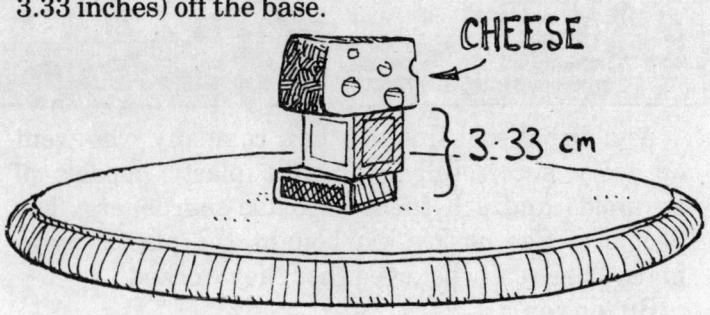

CHEESE

3.33 cm

3 Put the pyramid over the food so the food is in the centre.

4 Line up the pyramid so the sides face exactly north, south, east and west.

5 Have an identical piece of food outside the pyramid.

6 Check the food each day.

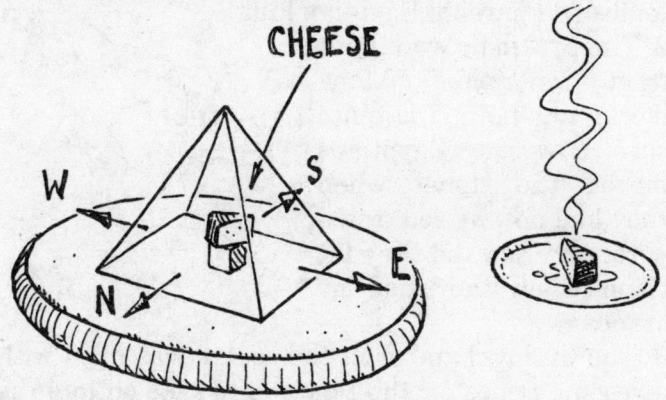

Which one goes stale or mouldy first? If you find the food inside the pyramid stays fresher, then maybe you have proved the power of the pyramid for yourself!

Did you know . . .?

There is an old soldiers' story from World War I (1914–1918). It was said that if you leave a razor blade out in the moonlight then it will go blunt. The edge of a razor is made up of tiny crystals that give a blade its sharpness. The pressure of the moonlight is enough to rub those fine crystals off. Could the forces inside a pyramid preserve the crystals in some way . . . the same way they preserve food, or the body of a dead Egyptian cat?

The pyramids

Ten awesome things you ought to know about the pyramids

1 A pyramid was supposedly built as the huge stone tomb of a Pharaoh (Egyptian king).

2 The pyramids were built from enormous stone blocks but no one is quite sure how the Egyptians moved the stones when they had no wheeled transport. And how did they lift them when they had no cranes?

3 The burial chamber in the centre was filled with awesome riches for the Pharaoh to take on into the afterlife.

4 The riches were a temptation to robbers. The pyramid builders tried to fool the thieves by making false doors, staircases and corridors.

5 The base of The Great Pyramid of Cheops is equal to the area of seven or eight football pitches (230 metres x 230 metres).

6 The burial chamber inside the Great Pyramid is as large as a small modern house (10 metres x 5 metres and 6 metres high).

7 The pyramids are close to the Nile because some of the huge stones had to be carried from the quarries by boat.

8 The pyramids are all on the West bank of the Nile – the side on which the sun sets. This is for religious reasons.

9 The Pharaohs were buried with religious writings to help them in the afterlife. The earliest ones were written on the walls of the burial chambers (they're called The Pyramid Texts). Later they were written on the coffins (The Coffin Texts). The last were written on Egyptian paper (papyrus) and rolled up and placed in the dead man's coffin. The writings described different ways to get to the afterworld and are known as the *Books Of The Dead*.

10 The Ancient Greeks visited the pyramids as tourists. They reported that each pyramid had taken 100,000 slaves ten years to build. Some modern history books still repeat these facts, yet they are almost certainly wrong in every respect. The workers were free craftsmen, not slaves, and it probably took just 70–80,000 men five years to finish a pyramid. They were paid partly in radishes and garlic which helped keep them healthy.

Test your tyrant ... er ... teacher ...

Teachers don't know everything! Awesome – but true! Try your teacher with these true-or-false questions. If they get all nine right, they're a genius!

True or false?

1 Mummies were sometimes buried with model dolls.
true/false

2 Wood was a precious material in Egypt because trees were scarce. This is one of the reasons why the Egyptians were so good at building in stone.
true/false

3 The Egyptians are thought to have dragged the stones on sledges to the early pyramids because they hadn't invented the wheel.
true/false

4 Some Pharaohs were buried with a *Book of the Dead* called *The Book of The Divine Cow*.
true/false

5 Pyramids as burial places went out of fashion for almost a thousand years between 1800 BC and 800 BC.
true/false

6 Pyramids contained everything the King would need in the afterlife . . . including a toilet.
true/false

7 The Step Pyramid at Saqqara was the first large stone building the world had ever seen.
true/false

8 The Great Pyramid is made of about 2,300,000 stone blocks.
true/false

9 There are over 90 pyramids in Egypt.
true/false

Answer: All the above statements are TRUE!

Ancient Egyptian ancient joke . . .

Ten things you'll probably never need to know about pyramids . . .

1 If you broke the Great Pyramid into slabs 30 cm thick you could build a wall 1 metre high that would stretch all the way around France. If you had a little more time you could cut the stone into rods about 6cm square – join them together and you'd have enough to reach the Moon!

2 Some people have said that the pyramids are more than simply large graves; they were granaries or treasure houses.

3 All of the pyramids were probably robbed of their treasures within a couple of hundred years of the burials. The only tombs to escape until modern times were those dug into rock, not placed in pyramids. They belonged to Tutankhamun and Queen Heterpheres.

4 The Egyptians mummified more than their Pharaohs. They mummified the Pharaohs' pets and buried them in the pyramids to keep the dead kings company.

5 If you could weigh an average pyramid it would be around 5,400,000 tons. The average stone block weighs as much as two modern cars (2.5 tons). The largest single stone block (in the Pyramid of Mycerinus) must weigh about 285 tons – that's 200 to 250 cars.

6 Pyramid-builders tried to fool thieves by placing a blocking stone at the end of a passageway and plastering it in. If the thieves broke through the plaster then they would come to the stone and give up. The real way into the tomb would then be through a hidden trapdoor in the ceiling.

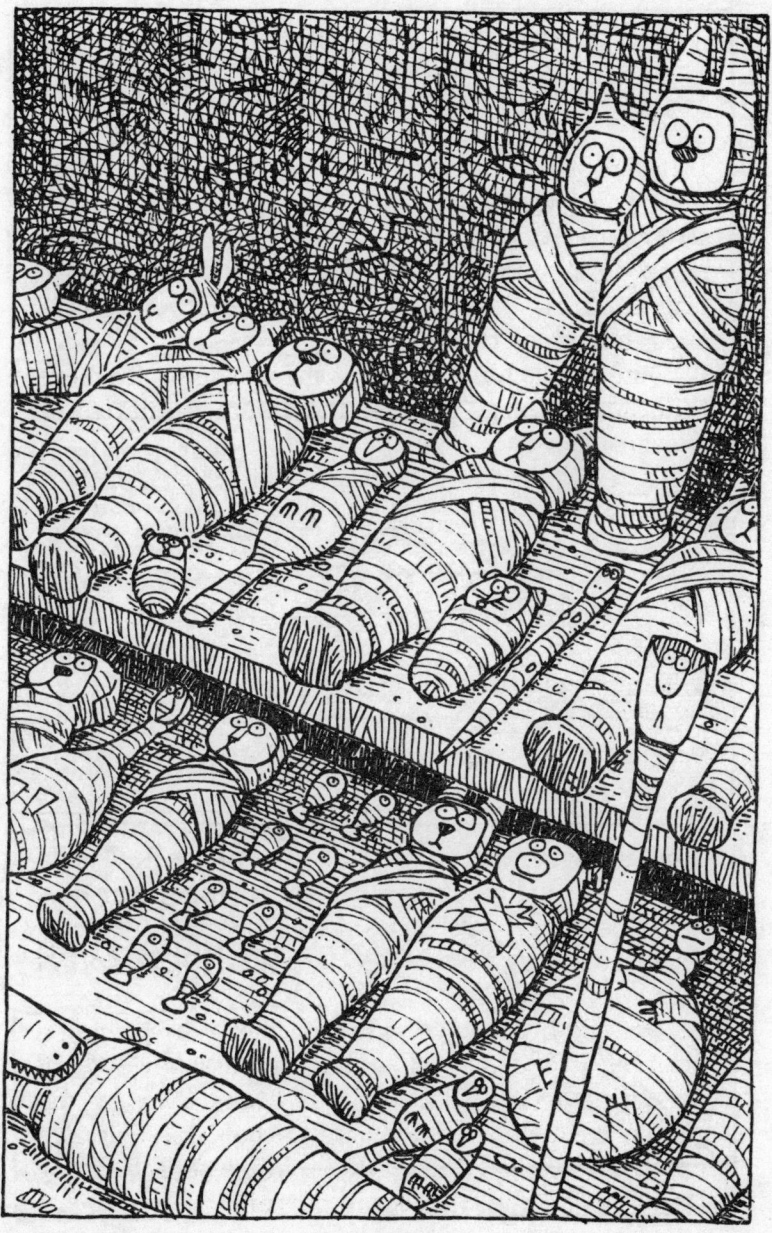

7 The Egyptians didn't have accurate metal tape measures. They used fibre cords which could shrink or stretch. Still, the greatest mistake in the Great Pyramid is just 20 centimetres on a side of 230 metres (an error of less than 0.1%). They were even more accurate in building a flat base – the south-east corner is just 1 centimetre higher than the north-west corner.

8 The pyramids are not the most awesomely large human construction. The Great Wall of China is much more awesome and the Mexican Pyramid of Quetzacoatl is an even more awesome 54 metres tall and has a volume of 3.3 million cubic metres. The Great Pyramid of Cheops is just 2.5 million cubic metres. But the pyramids of Egypt are the *oldest* stone buildings in the world.

9 Early tombs were flat-topped. These were called Mastabas because they looked like the mud-brick seat found outside Egyptian peasant homes. Mastaba tombs were easily robbed. So someone built a slightly smaller Mastaba on top of the first one . . . then another on top of that . . . and then another . . . and they ended up with a "step" pyramid.

10 It is forbidden to climb the pyramids today. There have been too many accidents, so now you have to have special permission.

STOP PRESS: *News Flash* (**7 January 1993**)
Archaeologists in Egypt have found the ruins of a small pyramid, a few metres from the Great Pyramid of Cheops at Giza. It was discovered by chance during a cleaning operation. This brings to 96 the number of known pyramids in the country.

How to build a pyramid . . . (with the help of 80,000 friends)

1 Clear the desert sand to show bare rock.

2 Level the site – perhaps allow water from the Nile to flood the base to give you a level.

3 Use the Pole Star to decide exactly where the north is.

4 Make a perfect square for the base and mark the four walls to face north, south, east and west.

5 Starting in the middle, build the first level with limestone blocks of 2 to 3 tons.

6 Add new levels, each one smaller than the one below. As the levels rise, build ramps of earth to slide the building blocks up.

SHOW OFF!

7 As you build, don't forget to leave passageways and the central burial chamber. That burial chamber must end up directly beneath the point of the pyramid.

8 Cover the finished pyramid with the best Tura limestone and smooth it off.

9 Remove the earth ramps and build a raised stone causeway from the river to the pyramid.

10 Wait for the Pharaoh to die. Mummify him. Bury him in the pyramid with his treasures. And don't forget to seal the pyramid to keep out robbers.

How to decorate a pyramid

1 Find a Pharaoh with a new pyramid – he will need some decorators.

2 Cover the inside walls in a smooth layer of gypsum, or chalk plaster. You will paint on to this.

3 Make your brushes by crushing the ends of sticks to give stumpy bristles.

4 Prepare the paints to give nine colours: black, blue, brown, green, grey, red, white and yellow – and the fashionable colour of the New Kingdom, pink.

5 Plan your work carefully by drawing a grid of squares on the walls – then you know where every figure is going to go.

6 Remember the Egyptian style. Heads are painted in profile, that is, sideways, but the eye is shown full face. Legs are more leg-like if they are shown sideways. Shoulders are more shoulder-like if they are both in view. The more important the person, the bigger they are. Pharaoh gets most space.

Use squared paper to help you copy the drawing above. If you work with some friends you could make a wall painting. DANGER – don't use the living room wall without first asking . . . or you could be history!

The magic of the mummies

Did you know . . .

1 Mummy is an Arabic word for 'bitumen' – a sort of tar that was precious as a medicine. The Arabs were the first people of modern times to discover mummies and they thought they were covered in bitumen.

2 Egyptians believed that one day the world would end. When it did they would move on to their afterlife. To make that long journey they would need their earthly body. If their body was allowed to rot then they wouldn't be able to go.

3 The men who made dead bodies into mummies were called embalmers. They took the bodies to a place they called the Beautiful House to work on them. The Beautiful House was more like a butcher's shop.

4 At first only the very rich could afford embalming. Later it became a huge industry with even the poorest hoping for it.

5 The climate of Egypt is naturally good for preserving a body. A poor peasant died 5,000 years ago and his body was covered by the dry desert sand. It is more pefectly preserved than many mummies and can be seen in the British Museum today. His nickname is Ginger.

6 The human body is made up of 75 per cent water. Anything wet or damp rots very quickly – and dead people in the fierce Egyptian heat were no exception. Something was needed to soak up all the body fluids. At first the embalmers used sand, but this left the skin very tight. Later, the embalmers discovered that natron, a salty chemical found around the sides of lakes near Cairo, did a better job. It left the person looking more like they did when they were alive.

7 Sometimes the embalmers made mistakes and a body was badly mummified. It would turn dark and brittle and bits would break off! If part of a body rotted and fell off – or was snatched by a jackal taking a quick snack when no one was looking – the embalmers replaced it with a wad of linen, or a piece of wood. If the person had a limb missing when they were alive the embalmers gave them a wooden one ready for use in the next world.

50

8 Archaeologists have found mummies wrapped in hundreds of metres of linen, up to 20 layers thick.

9 Examination of mummies showed a lot about the bodies when they were alive. Ramesses II had a lot of blackheads on his face, while Ramesses III had been a very fat man. King Sequenenre II had met a pretty horrible end. There were wounds on his scalp – one wound had pierced his skull. Blood was still clotted in his hair, and his face was twisted in agony. Some think he was murdered in his sleep – others believe he was killed in battle. If so, he may have been mummified quickly, so his hair wasn't cleaned well.

10 In Victorian England people flocked to see a mummy being unwrapped! Doctor Pettigrew at the Royal College of Surgeons provided very popular unwrappings. Even on a bitterly cold January night, tickets were sold out and many important people could not get in. Not even the Archbishop of Canterbury! Refreshments were served after the 'performance', just as if it were a theatre show. One of Pettigrew's mummies turned out to be a fake – rags and sticks wrapped up in bandages.

11 The Duke of Hamilton was very impressed by 'Mummy' Pettigrew's work. He asked to be mummified by Pettigrew after he died. After 20 years of unwrapping mummies Pettigrew finally had the chance to wrap one. This he did after the Duke died on 18 August 1852. The Duke even had an ancient Egyptian stone coffin waiting for his body. It hasn't been opened since, so we don't know if Pettigrew was as good at making mummies as the Egyptians.

12 When the Egyptians became Christians and later, Muslims, they no longer believed that you needed your earthly body to survive in the afterlife. They didn't need their mummies any more.

Making a mummy

From the evidence we have and the writing of a Greek traveller, Herodotus, this is our best guess at how bodies were mummified.

WARNING: This is very messy! Do not try this in your kitchen! Not even in your school-dinners kitchen!

1 First take a dead Pharaoh.

2 Place the body in a Beautiful House – usually a tent because it keeps the air fresher!

3 Undress the body and put it on a wooden table. This is the embalming table. The table top is not always solid. If the top is just bars of wood you can get underneath the body more easily to put the bandages on later.

4 Remove the brain by placing a chisel up the left nostril and breaking through into the skull.

They first take an iron hook and with it draw out the brain through the nostrils.

(Herodotus – visited Egypt in 455 BC.)

Sometimes embalmers would go through the head just behind the left eye. They would use a piece of stiff wire with a hook on the end. The wire would be stirred around to cut the brain up into pieces. The pieces would then be scooped out with a different rod and a cup-shaped end.

You can throw the brain away (or feed it to the cat – the Egyptians didn't think the brain was too important in the afterlife).

5 Fill the empty skull with a packing of natron and plaster – good solid stuff.

6 Cut open the front – an embalmer called a 'ripper-up' usually does this.

> They take out the whole contents of
> the stomach which they then clean,
> washing it with palm wine. After that
> they fill the hole with myrrh and
> other spices. They sew up the open-
> ing. The body is placed in natron
> for seventy days. It is washed and
> wrapped round from head to foot
> with bandages of fine linen cloth
> smeared with gum.

(The bandages can be as great as 375 square metres
– if you're not sure how much that is then cover a
basketball court with linen and you'll almost have
enough!)

7 If you want, charms and prayers may be written
on papyrus (paper) and wrapped in the bandages, or
written in ink on the bandages themselves. These
will keep away evil spirits – but not grave robbers.

8 You may wish to replace the eyes with polished
black stones. (Although when Ramesses IV was
unwrapped the king had two small onions for eyes!)

9 Stuff the body with linen rags to keep its shape,
then sew it up again. Only the heart is left inside.
This is very important. It will be weighed later when
the king reaches the afterlife.

10 Make a mask for the head. It should look like the
person when they were alive. It should also be
covered with gold . . . so it's best to make sure the
king pays you before he dies!

11 Put the mummy in a coffin (or in a coffin in a
coffin in a coffin).

I THINK WE'LL NEED A BIGGER CANOPIC JAR

12 Put the stomach, liver, intestines and lungs in their own canopic jars (see page 58), add natron and seal them.

13 Perform the ceremony of opening the mouth of the mummy – if you don't open the mouth then the mummy won't be able to eat, drink, talk or breathe in the afterlife.

14 Fasten down the coffin lid. Place the coffin in a tomb or a pyramid then seal up the tomb. This is to shut out the grave-robbers. (Don't worry about shutting the mummy *in*. The mummy has a Ba – a soul – which can come and go from the tomb as it likes. You'll know a Ba if you ever see one. It has the head of a man and the body of a bird.)

15 Sing a funeral song for the dead. An Egyptian one went like this . . .

O gods take this man into your house,
Let him hear just as you hear,
Let him see just as you see,
Let him stand just as you stand,
Let him take his seat just as you take your seats.

(You'll have to make up your own tune because we don't know how Egyptian music sounded – it was probably a chant with tambourine and drum beats to accompany it.)

16 Have a funeral party with the best wines and food, entertainers and musicians. Everyone's invited – except the mummy!

The fate of the mummy . . .

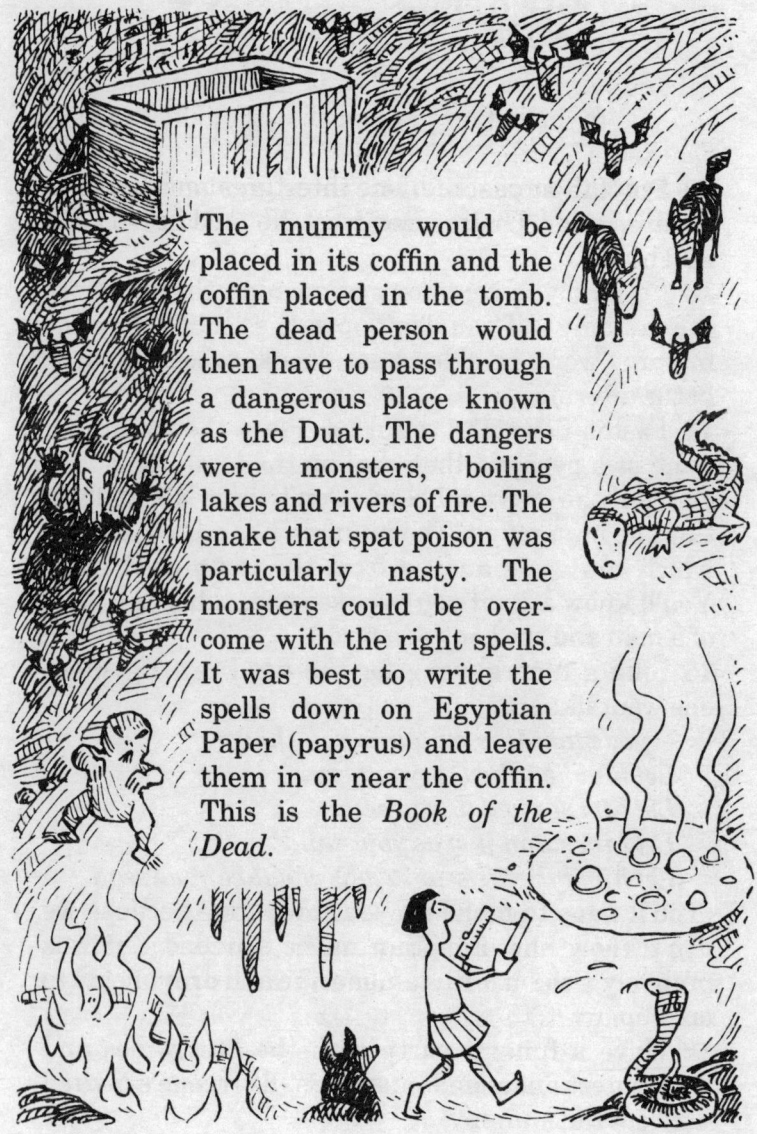

The mummy would be placed in its coffin and the coffin placed in the tomb. The dead person would then have to pass through a dangerous place known as the Duat. The dangers were monsters, boiling lakes and rivers of fire. The snake that spat poison was particularly nasty. The monsters could be overcome with the right spells. It was best to write the spells down on Egyptian Paper (papyrus) and leave them in or near the coffin. This is the *Book of the Dead*.

If they overcame the monsters then they'd reach the gates of Yaru (the Egyptian afterlife) and meet their friends again. But first they had to pass the greatest test of all in the Hall of Two Truths.

Their heart was weighed. The heart was placed in one side of the balance and in the other side was the Feather of Truth – and the Feather of Truth held all the lies of their past life. The three great gods, Osiris, Anubis and Thoth, decided the result of the weighing.

If the heart passed the test then the dead person was allowed through the gates of Yaru. But if they failed . . . their heart was eaten by a terrifying monster known as the Devourer. This Devourer was part crocodile, part hippopotamus and part lion.

Once the Devourer took your heart . . . you were lost for ever!

Make your own canopic jar . . .

Intestines can be pretty messy, so it's best to tidy them into a special container. The Egyptians made theirs out of clay. You can make one from a squeezy bottle.

You will need:
a washing-up liquid bottle
paints
modelling clay
drawing paper
sand or pebbles
glue

1 Take the nozzle off the washing-up liquid bottle and rinse it out.

2 Wrap a piece of drawing paper round the bottle and cut it to fit.

3 Decorate the paper with hieroglyphics and Egyptian pictures and symbols – look through the book for some ideas.

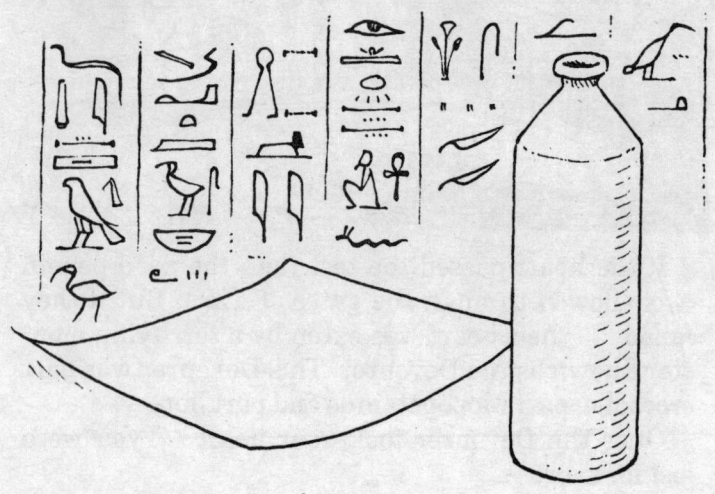

4 Glue the paper to the bottle.
5 Put some sand or pebbles in the bottle to make your canopic jar stand steadily.
6 Use the modelling clay to make a lid. Make the lid into the shape of one of the four Sons of Horus:
Imsety – an Egyptian man who guards the liver;
Duamutef – a jackal who guards the stomach;
Qebehsenuef – a falcon who guards the intestines;
Hapi – a baboon who guards the lungs.

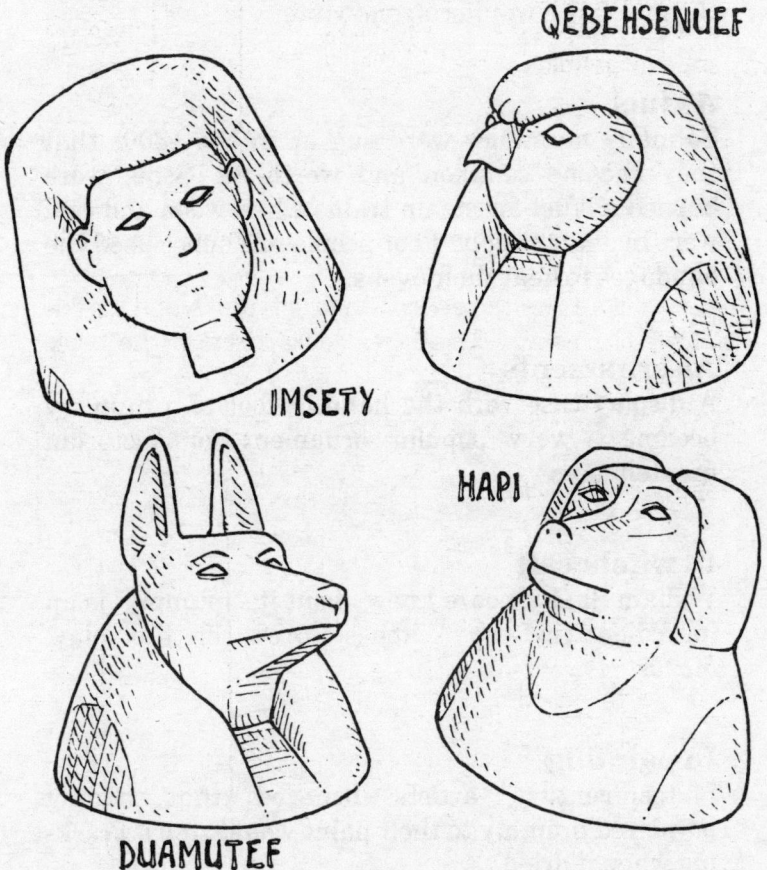

QEBEHSENUEF

IMSETY

HAPI

DUAMUTEF

Some unusual (but true) uses for mummies . . .

As magic powder
King Charles II of England (1630-1685) used to collect the dust and powder that fell from collections of mummies. He would rub this powder into his skin, all over. He believed that the "ancient greatness" of the mummies would rub on to him.

As fuel
So many mummies were dug up in the 1800s that they became common and worthless. Some were burned as fuel for steam trains when wood and coal were in short supply. Poor people in Thebes used the bandages to heat their ovens.

As ornaments
A display case with the hand or foot of a mummy became a very popular ornament for Victorian mantelpieces.

In witchcraft
William Shakespeare knew about it; "mummy" is an ingredient in the Witches' Brew in the play, *Macbeth*.

In painting
Sixteen-century artists believed that adding powdered mummy to their paint would stop it cracking when it dried.

A USER'S GUIDE TO MUMMY BITS

As medicine

From the early 13th century AD till well into the 17th century, Egyptian mummies were chopped up and fed to sick people as a cure. It was used for people with all sorts of diseases, as well as broken bones and as a cure for poisoning. So many mummies had left Egypt by the late 16th century that the Egyptian government banned their export. Egyptian mummy-sellers then made fake mummies out of any bodies lying around! A French visitor reported seeing 40 fake mummies in a mummy-factory.)

In science

The English scientist, Sir Marc Armand Ruffer, thought he could learn about the diseases of ancient Egypt by testing bits of mummies. He found the Egyptians suffered many of the diseases we do today.

In paper-making

Paper made from cloth (rag-paper) has always been valued as high-quality paper. A travelling Egyptian tribe called the Bedouin would steal mummies and sell them to paper-making factories. The American paper-manufacturer, Augustus Stanwood, was still importing mummies at the end of the 19th century to turn the bandages into paper. The stained bandages made poor writing paper but was fine for brown paper. It was sold to butchers and grocers as wrapping paper. An outbreak of the deadly disease, cholera, was traced to the mummy bandages, so the scheme was stopped. Several people died ... the mummies' revenge?

What would *you* use a mummy for? A shop-window dummy? A door-stop? A scare-crow? A scare-teacher?

MANNEQUIN

SCARECROW

SCARE TEACHER

EEK

PIT PROP

CHEST OF DRAWERS

TEDDY BEAR

Money from a mummy?

Some very unusual people became involved with the trade in mummies and relics of Egypt. They weren't archaeologists. They were people who saw the chance of making lots of easy money. People like . . .

Giovanni Belzoni

Belzoni was over two metres tall. He used to be part of a fairground strong-man act. Then he travelled to Egypt to sell machinery. He soon realised he could make a fortune selling artefacts from the tombs.

His most spectacular exploit was transporting the statue of Ramesses II across the desert, down the Nile and over the sea to England. It is now in the British Museum in London.

Before he left Egypt Belzoni was asked, "Are you so short of stones in Europe that you have to come here to take ours?"

"No," he replied. "But we prefer the Egyptian sort."

But even Belzoni wouldn't have dealt with anything as suspect as . . .

Ginger

You probably remember Ginger from page 49. Well – there's this awesome rumour about him . . .

The British Museum were collecting mummies. They already had the well-preserved ones from the tombs. They wanted one from the days before the great Pharaohs and their pyramids. They knew that ordinary Egyptians had been preserved by simple burial in the dry desert sand. Where would they find such a body?

They knew a dealer in Egyptian antiques. He soon found one with reddish-brown hair – he became known as Ginger. And Ginger can still be seen at the British Museum today.

But . . . the Egyptian dealer had a bad reputation for providing forgeries and fakes when he couldn't find the real thing a museum wanted.

Surely he wouldn't 'make' a corpse? Surely he wouldn't dry out a freshly killed victim and sell him to the British Museum as a 5000-year-old mummy?

Surely not.

And anyway, who would he kill?

It seems that about the time that Ginger appeared, the Egyptian dealer's brother disappeared!

Surely he wouldn't . . . would he?

Most gruesome mummy fact . . .

When King Louis XIV of France died in 1715 his heart was mummified as the king had instructed. A 19th century Dean of Westminster came into possession of the embalmed heart. He ate it for dinner one evening!

The curse of the mummy's tomb

A true story?

26 November 1922

The great archaeologist, Howard Carter, had searched for years for a Pharaoh's tomb that hadn't been robbed. The pyramids were empty; the treasures stolen hundreds of years before. But there was still hope that the caves in the Valley of the Kings might have kept their secrets.

At last he arrived at the entrance to an unbroken burial chamber. He called in the organiser of the expedition, Lord Carnarvon, to witness the final breakthrough. Carter described it as follows:

With trembling hands I made a tiny hole in the upper left hand corner. Darkness and empty space, as far as an iron testing-rod could reach, showed that whatever lay beyond was empty. Widening the hole a little, I put in a candle and peered in. At first I could see nothing. The hot air escaping from the chamber caused the candle to flicker a little. But as my eyes became accustomed to the light, details of the room within emerged slowly from the mist; strange animals, statues and gold – everywhere the glint of gold. I was struck dumb with amazement. Lord Carnarvon asked anxiously, "Can you see anything?" It was all I could do to get out the words, "Yes, wonderful things."

Carter spent years unearthing the most spectacular and precious find this century – he had found the grave of the young king Tutankhamun. But had he released more than hot air from the tomb? Had he also released a 3000-year-old curse that the ancient Egyptian priests had placed in the tomb to protect the king?

The curse

The stories erupted quickly. On the day the tomb was opened, the men climbed back into the evening sunshine. As the last one left a sandstorm sprang up and whirled round the mouth of the cave. When it died away a hawk was seen hovering to the west. The hawk was the symbol of the royal family of Egypt – the west was the direction of the Egyptians' land of the dead.

Lord Carnarvon died on April 6, 1923, less than a year after the discovery. He died from a mosquito bite on his left cheek which became infected. When doctors later examined the mummy of Tutankhamun they noticed a strange mark on the mummy's face . . . on his left cheek!

The night Lord Carnarvon died in the Egyptian capital, Cairo, the city lights failed and plunged the people into darkness. At the same time, back in Hampshire, England, his dog let out a howl and died. "The Revenge of Tutankhamun!" people muttered.

In the following months the deaths of several others who had visited the tomb were blamed on the curse. One was an Egyptian prince, Ali Farmy Bey, who could trace his family line back to the Pharaohs. He was murdered in a London hotel and his brother committed suicide.

In 1929 Richard Bethell, who helped Carter to catalogue Tutankhamun's treasures, was thought to have committed suicide. A few months later newspapers reported the death of his father – as the *nineteenth* victim . . .

Today Lord Westbury, aged 78, jumped from the window of his seventh-floor London flat and was instantly killed. Lord Westbury's son, who was formerly the secretary of Howard Carter, the archaeologist at the Tutankhamun diggings, was found last November dead in his apartment, though when he went to bed he appeared to be in the best of health. The exact cause of his death has never been determined . . .

Lord Westbury is supposed to have written: *I can't stand any more horrors* a few days before he died. Police searching the room from which he threw himself found a stone vase. It was a vase from the tomb of Tutankhamun.

The list of deaths grew ever longer. When Archibald Reid, another archaeologist, died as he was about to X-ray a mummy the newspaper headlines screamed: *A shudder is going through England!*

The death of the Egyptologist, Arthur Weigall, was announced as the *twenty-first* victim of the curse when he died of an 'unknown fever'. Even the unusual death of an American called Carter was laid at the tombstone of Tutankhamun.

The curse uncovered

Howard Carter called reports of the curse, "ridiculous stories", and claimed they were made up for the amusement of the public.

Howard Carter himself lived until 1939, when he died of natural causes. Surely, as the first man in the tomb, *he* should have been hunted down by any curse? Some of Carter's assistants lived a very long time. Doctor Derry, who examined the body of Tutankhamun, was 88 years old when he died.

In 1933 the German Professor, Georg Steindorff, investigated the curse. He found that neither Lord Westbury, nor his son, had the least connection with the tomb or the mummy. And Richard Bethell probably died of natural causes, not suicide. Steindorff also proved that the American called Carter had no connection at all with Howard Carter.

Mummies were not buried with a 'curse', but with a magic spell designed to frighten, not kill, the enemies of the Pharaoh, and to wish the dead king well in the next world.

WARNING
AWESOME SPELLS MAY
SERIOUSLY DAMAGE YOUR HEALTH

The story goes on

However, it's hard to keep a good story down. People love horror films, and walking mummies make ideal monsters. In 1966 the newspapers were off again. That year the Egyptian government decided to lend the Tutankhamun treasures to a Paris museum. An Egyptian museum keeper, Mohammed Ibraham, dreamed that he would face a terrible death if he allowed them to leave the country. He argued against the loan as long as he could. He left the last meeting defeated. The loan would go ahead. As Mohammed left the meeting he was knocked down by a car. He died two days later.

Do you believe in the curse of Tutankhamun?

The mummy's hand

Lots of 'true' mummy stories have been told over the past century. This is one of them: see if you believe it!

Lord Carnarvon,
In the name of God, I beg you to take care! The Ancient Egyptians had knowledge and power which we people today do not understand!
Your dear friend,
Count Louis Hamon

Lord Carnarvon read the letter and snorted with laughter and shook his head, "It'll take more than some crank letter to stop me exploring those tombs!"

Within a few days Lord Carnarvon's expedition found the fabulous tomb of Tutankhamun and four months after that Lord Carnarvon was dead! What had Louis Hamon seen that made him write to warn his friend?

It was his experience with a mummy's hand . . .

3. SO THE PRINCESS WAS BURIED... BUT HER HAND WAS NOT

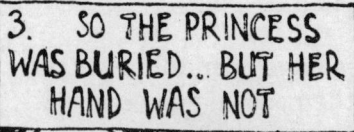

4. THE GRISLY RELIC, THE HAND, WAS PASSED DOWN THROUGH ARAB FAMILIES TILL, THIS CENTURY, IT REACHED A SHEIK

YOU HAVE CURED ME OF MALARIA. HAMON, LET ME GIVE YOU A PRECIOUS GIFT...

5. .. AND THE SHEIK GAVE HAMON THE PRINCESS'S HAND

I COULDN'T ACCEPT SUCH A... A PRECIOUS GIFT...

I INSIST!

6. HAMON'S WIFE HATED IT ON SIGHT...

CAN'T YOU GIVE IT TO A MUSEUM?

I'VE TRIED-THEY ALL REFUSE

7. THEN LOCK IT IN THE SAFE AND LET'S FORGET ABOUT IT...

8. BUT IN OCTOBER 1922 THE HAMONS OPENED THE SAFE. THEY STOOD BACK IN HORROR...

IT'S NOT MUMMIFIED. IT'S AS SOFT AND FRESH AS MINE

9. DESTROY IT!

NO... SHE DESERVES A DECENT FUNERAL

10. AND ON 31 OCTOBER, HALLOWE'EN, HAMON READ PRAYERS FROM AN ANCIENT "BOOK OF THE DEAD"

11. BUT, AS HE CLOSED THE BOOK, THE HOUSE WAS PLUNGED INTO DARKNESS.... A BLAST SHOOK THE HOUSE

12. A SUDDEN WIND TORE OPEN THE DOOR... THE HAMONS FELL TO THE FLOOR AND AN EGYPTIAN WOMAN APPEARED

13. LOOK! SHE HAS NO HAND!

14. THE FIGURE BENT OVER THE HAND AND VANISHED

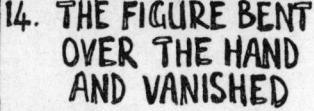

Gruesome grave robbers

What power did grave robbers have? They had the power to change the history of Egypt!

Pharaohs built pyramids to keep their mummies safe – grave-robbers broke into the pyramids and stole the wealth that was buried with the Pharaohs. So the Pharaohs built bigger and stronger and cleverer pyramids. The grave robbers didn't give in. Every pyramid was robbed.

In the end it was the Pharaohs who gave in. They realised that a pyramid was a huge stone advert saying, "Look at my grave! Look at my wealth!" The only answer was to hide the tombs. The Pharaohs switched to being buried in hidden caves in the rocks.

So the Egyptians stopped building pyramids because of the grave-robbers. But in the centuries-long battles between grave-builders and grave-robbers the thieves didn't always have things their own way . . .

The mummy's revenge

The man had reached his goal at last. The stone coffin lay before him. Perhaps it contained untold wealth — enough gold to keep a man for life?

The lid of the coffin was heavy. He struggled to heave it off. The still air of the tomb was disturbed by his struggles. Dust and pebbles fell from the roof. At last a crack appeared in the lid. He paused for a rest, pleased with his work. He set to work with fresh energy. The crack became wider. In his excitment he didn't notice the stones that fell from the limestone roof.

Another heave at the lid. A groaning "Creeee-aak!" echoed through the tomb. He reached a hand into the coffin. Another great "Creeee-aak!" But this time it wasn't the coffin lid. It was the roof of the tomb itself. His struggles to break into the tomb had weakened it. The massive roof slab was slipping down.

Too late he tried to pull his hand free from the coffin. Too late he realised that his own greed was going to kill him. The roof slab fell and crushed him. His grasping hand was still inside the coffin when he died.

And, in 1970, that was how he was found when archaeologists moved the stone to reach the coffin. A skeleton wrapped in a shred of what had once been a coat. A skeleton hand still inside the coffin lid. And in the pocket of the coat was something that shocked them. Something that told them almost exactly when the grave-robber had died.

What did they find? The remains of a newspaper. This grave-robber had been caught in the coffin in 1944 . . . AD!

A grave-robber's guide

Cast yourself back in time a few thousand years. You are travelling through ancient Egypt and you've run out of copper coins. You want to rob a pyramid or a rock-tomb (and get away with it). Here are a few hints . . .

1 Remember the penalty for being caught robbing a grave. Torture, then execution. Be careful!

2 Spend a bit of money before you set out. After all you will be fabulously wealthy when you get away with it. Make sure the local officials are on your side. Make friends with them even if it costs you money.

3 Have a gang of seven or eight. Make sure everyone has a useful skill. You may employ . . .

a couple of expert stone-masons to chisel their way in;

a smith to melt down your gold and silver;

a boatman for getting to and from the tombs as well as to act as a lookout;

water-carriers to keep your masons supplied and to act as labourers.

4 Where possible find a back way into the tomb. Then it will be a long time before the priests discover the loss. When they check the front entrances the seals will still be in one piece. They will think the mummy is safe – and as long as they think that, then *you* are safe!

5 Bribe everyone concerned with the burial:

The coffin-maker. As he makes the coffin he can turn one end into a trap-door. That way you won't have to break the seals and raise the lids to get at the mummy. You'll simply open the trap-door and slide the body out of the end.

The tomb-sealer. He has the job of sealing the

I'M IN A RUT, I SPEND ALL THE MONEY I GET FROM MY LAST TOMB ROBBERY ON BRIBING PEOPLE SO I CAN ROB A TOMB SO I CAN AFFORD TO BRIBE PEOPLE SO I CAN ROB TOMBS

three doors into the tomb. The family will watch him sealing the last door. Pay him well and he will make sure the two inside doors are not sealed. A lot less work for you later on.

The tomb guards. A boring job. A bit of tomb-robbing would liven up their lives. Of course you'll have to be sure the tomb is left the way you found it. They can still pretend to guard the tomb even after you have emptied it.

The priests. They are wealthy people. You will have to promise them a lot of money if they are going to 'look the other way' when you break in.

The court officials. If word gets around that you have robbed a tomb then the court officials will arrest you. It's best to bribe them first. They can lie for you. They can say, "We have checked and the tomb has never been touched" – and they can protect you from the law.

6 Learn some 'tricks of the trade'. Here's a quick way to get gold from a tomb: set fire to the tomb! All the wood will turn to ashes – all the gold will melt into pools. When these cool and turn hard they can simply be picked up from the ashes and carted off. Awesome!

7 Make a deal with travelling merchants. They will buy your stolen treasures from you and not ask awkward questions or betray you. (In the 20th century AD these merchants will be known as 'fences'.)

8 Do not try to spend too much of your treasure at once. Many a tomb-robber gave himself away by becoming rich suddenly. People would want to know where the wealth came from.

9 Know the tombs and their passages and rooms well, like a tomb-builder – many tomb-builders became grave-robbers. They grew hungry when their wages were late. They tried going on strike and marching on the officials' houses with chants of "We are hungry! We are hungry!" When that failed they turned to robbing the tombs they'd helped to build.

10 Best of all, try to steal the body before it is buried! Somebody, sometime, did that to the mother of a great Egyptian Pharaoh. Perhaps this is what happened . . .

I've lost my mummy!

Cheops was a vain man, it has to be said. For years the Pharaohs had been buried in pyramids. They were a wonder of his world. But Cheops' had to be the best.

"I want my pyramid to be greater than all the rest. I want the biggest pyramid Egypt has ever seen. I want it to be the biggest the world will ever see."

"Of course, your majesty." Chief Minister Yussef smiled and bowed. "The greatest pyramid for the greatest Pharaoh. I will see to it myself," the man promised. It would make Yussef the most important man in Egypt . . . apart from Cheops, of course. But Yussef could always handle Cheops.

"And I want this pyramid to be safe, Yussef, safe! I want to lie there for ever with no grave-robbers to destroy my afterlife."

"It will be the safest tomb ever built, your majesty," the Chief Minister promised.

"And the biggest!" Cheops reminded him.

"And the very biggest, your majesty!" Yussef bowed and set about the great task.

Cheops' mother, Hetepheres, sighed. "I'll never live to see it finished, my son."

"Maybe not in this life, but you will watch over it when you reach the afterlife. And one day I will join you there," Cheops promised.

"If the grave-robbers allow it, my son."

"The grave-robbers shall never enter my Great Pyramid!" Cheops boasted.

Hetepheres coughed gently. "It was *my* grave I was worried about, my son, not yours."

Cheops rose to his feet. "Mother, I swear by every god that your grave shall be as safe as mine!"

"I hope so," Hetepheres said with a sad shake of the head. "I hope so."

The Great Pyramid of Cheops grew and the years drifted by like the desert sands on the hot Sahara winds . . . and Hetepheres died.

Cheops mourned. The king gave his mother a funeral almost as great as his own was going to be. Thousands lined the dusty roads of Dashur to see Hetepheres' last journey to her resting place. Many thousand eyes saw the jewelled chests, the statues of silver and gold, the figures set in precious stones and the golden furniture follow the old queen to her grave. They watched and they longed for just one tiny part of all that treasure.

WHEN I DIE ALL I'M LIKELY TO TAKE IS MY FAVOURITE STICK AND MY COLLECTION OF INTERESTING DUNG

But the tomb was sealed with huge stones and guarded night and day. Surely no one could enter . . . Someone did.

Yussef brought the terrible news to Cheops. "Impossible!" the king cried. "I promised her! I promised that she'd be safe. Without her body she can never be there to meet me in the afterlife!" Suddenly he turned furiously on his chief minister. "I want everyone responsible killed."

"But the body is safe, your majesty," Yussef said softly. "There is no need for anyone to die."

"Safe?"

"The coffin is still there," Yussef said calmly.

"Thanks to Osiris and Isis!" the king moaned. "But this must never happen again. We must find a second resting place. A secret one ... somewhere near my own Great Pyramid. The greatest part of all her wealth is still inside that coffin."

"I know, your majesty, I know!" Yussef smiled. "And I have the perfect plan."

Yussef's plan was clever. The grave was so clever and so secret that Hetepheres' grave stayed hidden for 3000 years. Grave-robbers and archaeologists knew about the first tomb and they knew the coffin had been moved. They spent whole lifetimes searching.

They found nothing, until . . .

A photographer was recording the work of some archaeologists near the Great Pyramid of Cheops. He stood the tripod of his camera on the solid rock. One leg of the tripod sank down ... Surely nothing sinks through solid rock.

Carefully the archaeologists brushed the sand from the surface. It wasn't rock. It was plaster. It cleverly hid the opening to a shaft. The plaster was cleared but the shaft was filled with blocks of stone. One by one the stones were moved. The shaft was deep. Cut through solid rock, it had been a great feat of mining for Cheops' workers.

Thirty metres down, the archaeologists at last reached the burial chamber. The wooden furniture had crumbled to dust. But the great white stone coffin lay untouched. Just as Cheops had last seen it before the secret burial.

There was only room for eight people in that underground tomb. Only eight were there when the coffin was finally opened. They waited to gaze upon the oldest mummy ever found . . . a mummy buried 2,500 years before the birth of Christ.

But all they found were two silver bracelets – the poor remains from the once fabulous riches of Queen Hetepheres . . . and there was no mummy.

Yet that tomb had never been entered. Poor Cheops had buried an empty coffin. Perhaps he is still wandering through the afterlife looking for his mummy. And perhaps a very crafty Chief Minister is watching him . . . and still smiling.

The grave-robbers of modern times

The priests of ancient Egypt slipped silently through the moonless darkness. Their servants carried the awesome burden – 30 mummies! But the priests weren't grave-robbers, they were grave rescuers.

Robbers had been coming to the Valley of the Kings and stripping the graves of their riches. Not satisfied with just taking the gold, they had been tearing open the mummies' bandages to get at the hidden jewels. Everyone knew who was doing the thieving. No one could stop them. The robbers had friends in high places. When they were caught they were released time after time.

The loyal and caring priests could do just one last act to save their god-kings and queens. Move them. So in a secret operation, the mummies of some of the greatest kings were taken from the broken tombs and placed together in a new and hidden home, deep beneath the rocky valley.

The tattered bandages were patched, the bodies had new labels placed on them and the few treasures that were left were put with them. Then the tomb was sealed and the entrance disguised. That should keep thieves out. And it did for thousands of years.

Historians knew about the 30 great kings and queens – but archaeologists couldn't tell them where they had been buried. Then, in the 1880s, a new gang of grave-robbers solved the mystery . . .

Mohammed's story

Mohammed was fed up. His feet were almost too tender to walk on. His body was a mass of bruises. He hobbled along the street to his brother's house and almost collapsed. His oldest brother, Ahmed, led him to a chair and brought him strong coffee. "Did you tell them anything?" Ahmed asked.

Mohammed glared at him fiercely, proudly. "The police tied me up. They threw me to the floor of a cell. They beat me on the soles of my feet till I thought they were on fire!"

"But did you tell them anything?" another brother demanded.

"Not a thing!" Mohammed hissed. "They wanted to know where we got our money from. I told them we worked for it. So they beat me. They asked me what I knew about ornaments stolen from the tombs . . . I said I knew nothing. So they beat me again."

"You were brave, Mohammed," a younger brother smiled.

"I saved your miserable skins," Mohammed sneered.

"We are grateful," Abdul nodded.

Mohammed leaned forward. "How grateful?"

"Very grateful!"

85

"I mean how much money is my silence worth?" Mohammed went on as he sipped at the strong, black coffee.

The brothers shrugged. "We have always shared the money. Everything is split equally between the five of us."

"I want half in future," Mohammed said.

The brothers looked at one another. One gave a small laugh. Another joined in. Soon Mohammed's four brothers were roaring with laughter. Ahmed recovered enough to say, "You forget that I found the tomb of 30 mummies back in 1871. If anyone deserves half it is me!"

"And if you hadn't been so greedy, selling too many things, those museum people would never have put the police on to us," Mohammed argued. "I want more! I have suffered for it."

Ahmed rose to his feet, the laughter gone. "No!"

Mohammed threw the coffee cup to the floor and stumbled to the door. "So be it," he muttered as he limped into the night. Within minutes Mohammed was tapping on the door of the museum official's house.

"Mr Maspero?" he asked.

"He is away. I am his assistant, Emil Brugsch. Can I help you?"

"No. But I can help you," Mohammed said, and he told his story. Brugsch listened in silence as Mohammed explained how Ahmed had found the tomb. He had been looking for a lost goat when he came across the entrance to a steeply sloping tunnel. When he returned with a lantern he found a burial chamber with 30 mummies and their treasures.

Of course, any treasures found belonged to the Museum of Egypt. It was against the law to sell them. But he told his brothers about the find. For more than ten years they had been selling the treasures, a few at a time, secretly to collectors.

"And will you lead me to this burial chamber?" Brugsch asked.

Mohammed nodded. "The last time we were in trouble Mr Pawar, the mayor of Western Thebes, spoke up for us . . . we paid him well, of course. Will you make sure I do not go to prison, Mr Brugsch?"

Brugsch laughed. "If all you tell me is true, Mohammed, then you will not go to prison . . . you will become a hero of the Egyptian nation!"

"The stolen treasures . . ."

"Oh, they don't matter too much. It's the mummies we want to get our hands on. Shall we go?"

Brugsch found the tombs but had to fight to save his precious mummies. Men from a nearby town heard about the find and wanted to stop the archaeologist taking their dead kings from them. As they headed down the Nile to the Museum at Cairo, the local people lined the banks and wailed and ground dust into their heads, just as the ancient Egyptians did thousands of years before.

Then, on the journey, thieves attacked the boat and tried to take its treasures. This time they were too well guarded. At last they reached the safety of the Cairo Museum. And what do you think happened to Mohammed? Was he . . .

A Sent to prison?
B Given a £500 reward?
C Executed?
D Given a job in charge of the burial excavations?
E Killed by a curse on the mummy's tomb?

Answer: B & D.

87

The remarkable river

What has the River Nile to do with the pyramids?

Everything. No River Nile . . . no pyramids.

North Africa used to be rich grassland. The part that is now Egypt was all flooded. Then, about 9000 years ago, the region began to dry out and people moved in. It became drier still, so the people moved to the strip of land near the river – the Nile. But why did they start to build?

Here are four clues. Can you see how each clue might lead to making pyramids?

1 Every year the Nile flooded and gave the farmers enough rich soil for their crops. But of course they couldn't work the land when it was flooded.

2 The area outside the Nile's flood valley became desert – difficult for other people to cross. Egypt was a land cut off from the rest of the world. No troublesome neighbours.

3 The farmers had no wheeled transport. But in the floods, when their houses and villages were cut off, they learned to build boats.

4 The rains fell in the tropical forests of Africa and rushed down the Nile to make it flood. The people of Egypt never really saw much rain; the sudden, life-giving Nile floods seemed to be a magical gift.

Here are the four sides of a pyramid that might explain the link between the Nile and the pyramids.

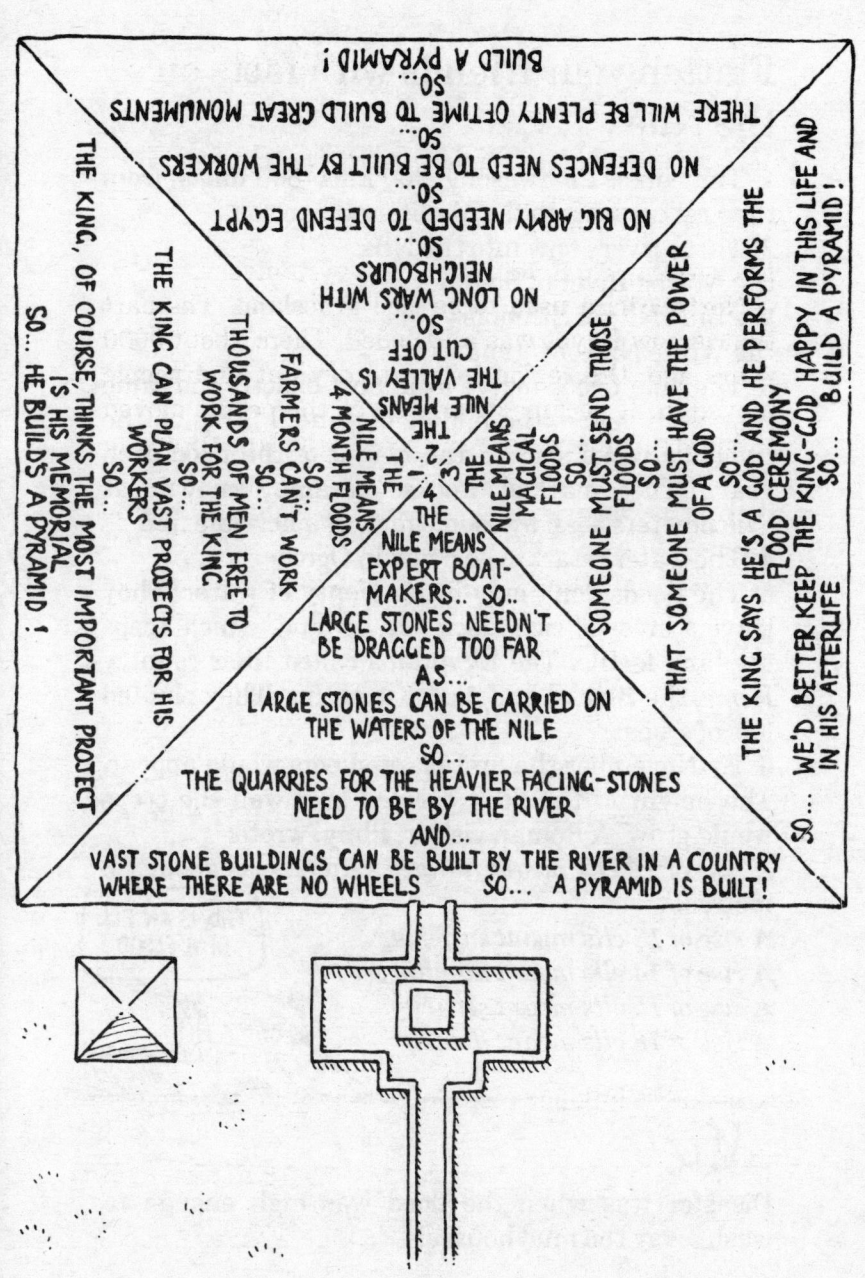

BUILD A PYRAMID !
SO...
THERE WILL BE PLENTY OF TIME TO BUILD GREAT MONUMENTS
SO...
NO DEFENCES NEED TO BE BUILT BY THE WORKERS
SO...
NO BIG ARMY NEEDED TO DEFEND EGYPT
SO...
NO LONG WARS WITH NEIGHBOURS
SO...
THE VALLEY IS CUT OFF
1 - THE NILE MEANS
2 THE NILE MEANS MAGICAL FLOODS
3 THE NILE MEANS
4 MONTH FLOODS
4 THE NILE MEANS EXPERT BOAT-MAKERS.. SO..
LARGE STONES NEEDN'T BE DRAGGED TOO FAR
AS...
LARGE STONES CAN BE CARRIED ON THE WATERS OF THE NILE
SO...
THE QUARRIES FOR THE HEAVIER FACING-STONES NEED TO BE BY THE RIVER
AND...
VAST STONE BUILDINGS CAN BE BUILT BY THE RIVER IN A COUNTRY WHERE THERE ARE NO WHEELS   SO... A PYRAMID IS BUILT!

THE KING, OF COURSE, THINKS THE MOST IMPORTANT PROJECT IS HIS MEMORIAL
SO... HE BUILDS A PYRAMID !

THE KING CAN PLAN VAST PROJECTS FOR HIS WORKERS
SO...

THOUSANDS OF MEN FREE TO WORK FOR THE KING
SO...

FARMERS CAN'T WORK
SO...

SOMEONE MUST SEND THOSE FLOODS
SO...

THAT SOMEONE MUST HAVE THE POWER OF A GOD
SO...

THE KING SAYS HE'S A GOD AND HE PERFORMS THE FLOOD CEREMONY
SO...

WE'D BETTER KEEP THE KING-GOD HAPPY IN THIS LIFE AND IN HIS AFTERLIFE
SO... BUILD A PYRAMID !

Flatten your friends with facts on the Nile . . .

1 The Nile is an awesome 960 kms (600 miles) from the first cataract to the Mediterranean sea.

2 Three rivers flow into the Nile:
the Atarba River of Sudan
the Blue Nile of Ethiopia
the White Nile of Uganda.

3 The Nile floods arrive at almost exactly the same time each year – the middle of June. Marks on the riverside rocks showed the height of the flood each year. The marked rocks became known as 'Nileometers' – an awesome fact, or a horrible fib?

4 The waters start to go down in October.

5 The floods don't only bring plenty of water. They leave a layer of rich black silt, or mud, which keeps the land fertile. The Egyptians called their country *Keme*, the Black Land, because of this. They planted lots of crops.

6 By November the first plant shoots would appear. The height of the flood decided how well the crops would grow. A Roman visitor, Pliny, wrote:

A rise of 12 ells meant hunger. (An ell was about 1.5 metres)

A rise of 13 ells meant suffering.

A rise of 14 ells meant happiness.

A rise of 15 ells meant security.

A rise of 18 ells meant disaster.

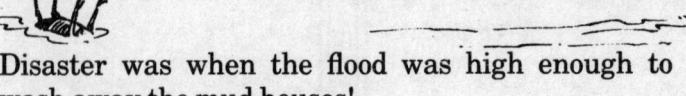

THIS IS AN ELL OF A FLOOD

Disaster was when the flood was high enough to wash away the mud houses!

7 Herodotus, a Greek visitor, wrote: . . .

When the Nile overflows the land
is converted into a vast sea, and
nothing appears but the cities, which
look like islands.

8 The Nile was the main road through Egypt. Most long journeys were made by boat.

9 The Nile no longer floods. A vast dam (opened at Aswan in 1971) now controls the flow. But the dam has brought unexpected problems. No floods – no silt. The soil becomes tired and farmers now have to pay for chemical fertilisers to replace the nutrients that the Nile brought for free every year.

10 The Nile has poems and songs written about it. A priest wrote this one:

Hail to you, O Nile . . .
You have come to feed Egypt . . .
When you flood the land rejoices . . .
Joy when you come, O Nile!
Joy when you come!
You who feed men and animals . . .
Joy when you come!

(It might not be a great pop song – but it's lasted over 3,000 years.)

11 The desert began where the floodwater ended. The difference was so clear that a person could stand with one foot in a field and the other in barren sand. The desert was known as *Dashre*, the Red Land.

POOR DEVIL, HE NEARLY MADE IT

12 The Egyptian year was divided into three seasons based on the Nile: flood season, planting season and harvesting season.

13 The peasants had to build and repair irrigation channels each year. This was part of the tax they paid to the Pharaoh. The punishment for trying to miss working on the Pharaoh's projects was a beating. It was no use trying to run away because if you weren't caught then your family would be punished instead.

14 Floodwater could be 'trapped' in reservoirs when the river sank. The fields would then have a water supply even when the river wasn't in flood. To lift the water into the fields the farmers used a shaduf. This was a trellis holding up a pole, with a counterweight on one end. On the other end was a bucket that could be lowered into the water. This invention meant that one man could lift thousands of gallons of water in a day. It was so easy to make and so successful that shadufs are still used today. You can try modelling one yourself.

Shock your friends with a shaduf

Egyptian peasants can make a shaduf out of tree branches; you can make yours look real by making one out of twigs.

1 Collect three straight twigs about 20cm (or 8 inches) long. Tie them together, but not too tightly, about 3cm (1 inch) from one end. Leave some spare string hanging loose at the knot.

2 Stand the twigs up and spread the other ends out so they make a frame or trellis (see picture 1). Push the ends into plasticine to hold the frame steady.

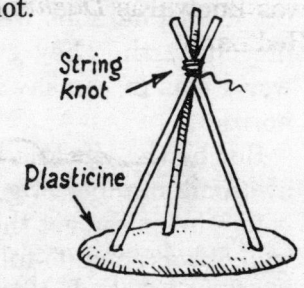

String knot

Plasticine

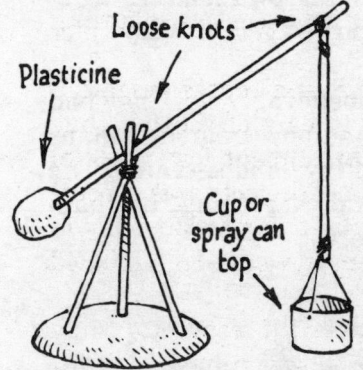

Loose knots

Plasticine

Cup or spray can top

3 Find another straight twig, about 35cms (14 inches). This will be the lever. Using the slack string, tie this to the top of the frame, where the other twigs meet. Tie the lever about 12cms (5 inches) from one end (see picture 2).

4 Weight the shorter part of the lever with plasticine. Tie another twig, about 15cm (6 inches) to the long end of the lever.

5 Now you need something for a bucket – the bottom of a plastic cup or the top of a spray-can would do. Make three holes in this and tie it to the twig hanging from the lever.

Congratulations – you have just made a simple but awesome invention!

A gallery of gods

What a life – spending half your time worrying about death! And death was an awesome problem for the Egyptians. They wanted to reach the spirit world that the priests taught about.

This wasn't as good as 'the land of the gods' that the dead Pharaohs went to, but it was better than life on earth. They even knew where their spirit world was in the sky . . . juuuust over the western horizon.

But by the left kneecap of Anubis!! There was an awesome number of gods for an Egyptian to please before he or she got there. And if they annoyed one, well, it was shadufs-full of trouble for them. (Erm . . . sorry Anubis, I think you've got a very nice kneecap.)

You see, the gods were unbelievably old. They had lived before people existed and now treated humans as if they were a mixture of toys and servants. The gods controlled the world and everything that happened. They demanded respect.

Try keeping this lot happy:

Sobek – the crocodile-headed god. He controlled water supplies.

Thoth – the ibis-headed god of wisdom who invented speaking and writing.

Set – god of the desert and storms. The enemy of Osiris.

94

Re – the Sun God. Some said he had made people. The Egyptians called themselves, 'the cattle of Re'.

Horus – the falcon-headed god who looked after the Pharaoh.

Sekhmet – the lioness goddess of war.

Hathor – the cow-horned goddess of love. She also looked after happiness, dancing and music.

Ptah – the god who spoke the names of all the things in the world. By doing this he made them exist. (Neat trick, eh? If only I could do that . . . ice-cream, Mars Bar, trip to Disney World . . .)

Isis – wife of Osiris. She took special care of women and children.

Bes – the dwarf god of happiness, and protector of the family.

Anubis – the jackal-headed god of the dead. He helped to prepare mummies.

Osiris – god of death and rebirth, the Underworld and the Earth. Long ago he had taught people to farm.

Awesome answers to powerful problems

Which god would you pray to? Fill in the missing name.

Oh great .... My land is short of water and my crops are dying.

Mighty .... My youngest son died of fever three months ago. Since then my wife is heart-broken. Please help her to enjoy life again.

Oh wise .... My son wishes to be a scribe, but is so bad at learning his hieroglyphs that his teachers are threatening to throw him out of school. Beatings don't seem to help.

Please give me strength, oh vengeful .... Raiders from the Red Land have attacked our village. Help us to defeat them.

Oh powerful .... My husband has died and I have spent most of my savings on his mummification to please you. Please help him to reach the spirit world.

Please, sweet .... I am madly in love with the most beautiful girl, but she laughs at my dancing. I am terribly clumsy and fall over my own feet.

ERRRRR

GO ON! DO YOU WANT TO DANCE WITH HER OR DON'T YOU!

Pray like an Egyptian

The story that all Egyptians believed was this one . . .

Osiris was an awesome king, everyone agreed . . . or almost everyone. He was loved by his loyal wife, Isis, and all of his people . . . well, almost all. Only Osiris's brother, Set, hated him. He was jealous. So Set plotted and Set planned. How could he kill his brother and get away with it?

What if the body of Osiris was never found? Yes, that was it! Make sure the body was never found.

It was a gruesome job, but Set had to do it. First he killed Osiris . . . and then he cut the body up into 14 parts. He scattered the pieces along the banks of the Nile and left the crocodiles to finish off the job.

But the plan failed. Isis travelled far and wide to find the 14 parts of her husband's body, and she carefully put them back together. She then wrapped Osiris's body in linen bandages to hold him in one piece. Osiris had become Egypt's first mummy.

Isis still wasn't finished. She now called on the god Anubis for help. Anubis breathed life back into Osiris. Osiris couldn't come back to earth as a man; instead he went to the afterlife as the god of the dead.

Anubis became the god of preserving the body for the afterlife. Isis became the goddess who protects the dead. And Set? Set had to deal with Horus, the son of Osiris and Isis. Set managed to pluck out Horus's eye in their long and grisly battle. But in the end, Horus won. Set was doomed to spend the rest of time in the gruesome underworld of the evil dead.

Horus went on to become the protector of the living . . . while his plucked eye became a way of allowing the dead to see.

Charm your friends

The Egyptians believed such stories and were very superstitious. They also believed in lucky charms. Here is one you could make for yourself out of card to wear around your neck.

The three symbols are Egyptian hieroglyphic signs for three words . . .

▽ 'all',   ♀ 'life'   ℞ 'protection'.

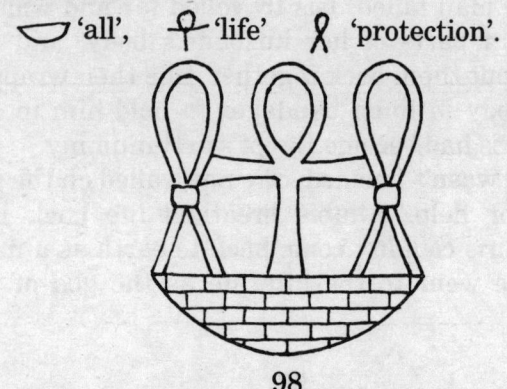

Awesomely troublesome Egyptians

Oh Pharaoh it isn't fair-o

They get the best food that there is on earth,
They're treated like gods from the day of their birth . . . the Pharaohs.

They live in a palace all graceful and tall,
While their servants slave on they do no work at all . . . the Pharaohs.

Their graves are those pyramids up to the sky,
They have a fine afterlife, they never die . . . the Pharaohs.

But who builds the pyramids? Who sweats and slaves?
Who works . . . then ends in a dusty old grave? . . . the peasants!

The horriblest thing to be in Egyptian history was a peasant in the old kingdom. They were at the bottom of a pyramid that looked like this.

1 The Pharaoh – King, chief priest and god, commander of the armies.

2 The vizier – the second most powerful man. He had to see that the country was running smoothly: everything from collecting taxes to organising the building of irrigation systems. He was also chief judge.

3 The imakhu (the honoured ones) – friends and family of the Pharaoh. They got all the best jobs: jobs like . . . General Ambassador, Governor of a district, Keeper of the Crown Jewels, Keeper of the Oils and Perfumes, Keeper of the King's clothes . . . or, Keeper of the Secret of all the Royal Sayings – that means being in control of who gets to talk to the Pharaoh.

4 The Nomarchs – local barons who control small districts. They are directly in charge of most of the people; they keep order and raise armies if Egypt is attacked.

5 The scribes – educated officials who keep the written records.

6 The priests – thousands who run the temples to the many gods.

7 The hemutiu or craftsmen – skilled workers who look after the needs of the wealthy: weavers, architects, painters, sculptors, traders, jewellers, embalmers, metal-workers . . .

8 The peasants – the remaining 90%

How to be a peasant in ten hard lessons

1 There are few slaves in Egypt – but a peasant has to work so hard he may as well be one.
2 Peasants are like property – if a Pharaoh gives land to a nobleman then the peasants are thrown in with it.
3 Peasants are counted along with the cattle to show how rich a landowner is.
4 Women aren't counted because they are not worth as much as cattle!

5 Peasants are organised into work gangs of about five.

6 Families may be broken up to work in different gangs.

7 When a peasant can't work on his land because the Nile is in flood he is ordered to work on the pyramids.

8 If a peasant doesn't work hard enough then he will be punished by whipping or by having bits chopped off his body – a finger or a toe, perhaps.

9 If you try to get really rich with a bit of tomb-robbing then the bit they chop off will be your head!

10 Before crops are harvested the Pharaoh's tax-man will come round to work out the Pharaoh's share. The good news is that the peasant's family can have what the Pharaoh leaves!

Working on the fields

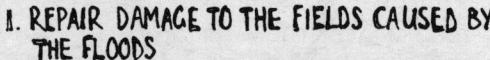

NOW.. YOU HORRIBLE PEASANT, THE FLOODS HAVE GONE DOWN. HERE'S A LITTLE LIST OF JOBS TO KEEP YOU BUSY.

1. REPAIR DAMAGE TO THE FIELDS CAUSED BY THE FLOODS
2. BREAK UP THE SOIL WITH HOES AND PLOUGH IT BEFORE THE SUN BAKES IT TOO HARD
3. SOW THE SEEDS AND USE ANIMALS (LIKE A HERD OF GOATS) TO TREAD THEM IN
4. KEEP THE FIELDS WATERED AS THE CROPS GROW
5. KEEP THE FIELDS WEEDED
6. SCARE THE BIRDS AWAY
7. HARVEST THE EARS OF WHEAT OFF THE TOP OF THE STALKS
8. THRESH THE CORN - BEAT IT WITH FLAILS TO SEPARATE THE GRAIN FROM THE HARD CHAFF ON THE OUTSIDE
9. WINNOW THE CORN - TOSS THE GRAIN IN THE AIR SO THE LIGHT CHAFF IS BLOWN AWAY
10. GO BACK TO CUT THE CORN STALKS FOR ANIMAL FEED, FOR MAKING BRICKS AND FOR BASKET MAKING

WHAT DO I DO IN MY SPARE TIME?

I'M GLAD YOU ASKED ME THAT ... YOU CAN LOOK AFTER THE PIGS AND SHEEP AND GEESE AND DUCKS - AND THEN GROW SOME GRAPES FOR WINE THEN GROW SOME FLAX TO MAKE LINEN, THEN GRIND THE CORN ....

I WISH I HADN'T ASKED. I'LL BE GLAD WHEN THE FLOOD SEASON RETURNS AND I CAN GET BACK TO WORK ON THE PYRAMIDS!

Working on the pyramids

You have dragged a huge, stone block for 60 kilometres over the burning desert. The only water you have is what you can carry with you. At last you reach the pyramid, haul the stone into place and stagger off for your pay of bread and linen and ointment. That's when the leader of the work gang gives you the dreadful news . . . no pay!

You trudge back to your barracks – rough limestone shelters with mud floors. You are tired, hungry and angry. The rooms are crowded and there's no proper water supply or toilet. The place stinks from human sewage and from the animals you share your lodgings with.

You wish you were back home with your wife and children. But you know you will die of starvation before you get there.

What will you do? You could . . .

1 Grumble and go back to work.
2 Send a begging letter to the Pharaoh.
3 Go on strike.

THESE CONDITIONS ARE NOT FIT FOR A PEASANT

Answer: Number 3. The first recorded strike in the history of the world was held on the site of a pyramid. The workers sat in the shade and refused to go back to work until they had been paid their rations. They were paid!

Ancient Egyptian ancient joke

It's no wonder there was trouble in the Old Kingdom. Around 2,300 BC the Old Kingdom began to fall apart. The power of the Pharaohs was challenged by the nomarchs. An old text explained:

THE RABBLE IS AROUSED, AND FROM EVERY CITY COMES THE CRY, "COME, LET US THROW OUT THE NOBLES". THE LAND IS FULL OF RIOTERS. WHEN THE PLOUGHMAN GOES TO WORK HE CARRIES HIS SHIELD

AND ME PLOUGHMAN'S LUNCH, OF COURSE

It wasn't until 2065 BC (and the Pharaohs of the eleventh dynasty) that control was restored again. The peasants were offered better conditions.

They were allowed to organise themselves into family groups. Each family was given enough land to feed itself. The fields were passed down from generation to generation and could not be taken away. The peasants were happier.

Wonderful women
How to be a wonderful Egyptian woman
The Egyptians had a clear idea of what made a wonderful Egyptian woman . . . the goddess Isis. To be a wonderful woman all you had to do was be like Isis, who . . .

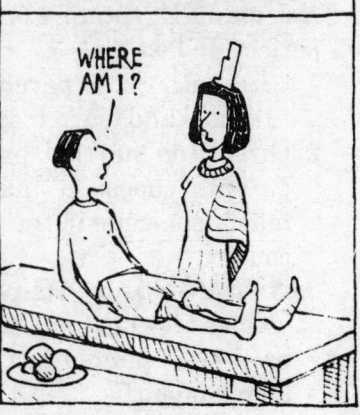

How to be a *fairly*-wonderful Egyptian woman

If being like Isis was too difficult then you could be a fairly wonderful woman by . . .

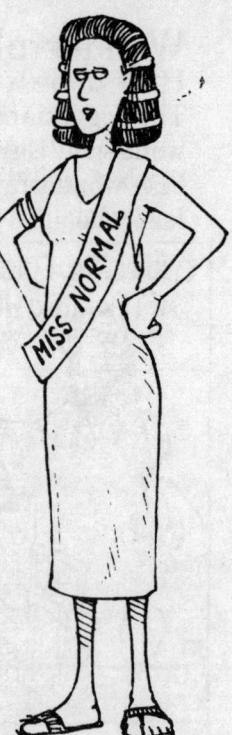

1 Staying at home and obeying your parents until you were 12 years old and old enough to marry;
2 Marrying someone suitable – someone mum and dad approved of;
3 Obeying your husband;
4 Sharing your husband with several other wives;
5 Giving your husband lots of children – six or seven were not unusual.

How to be a *normal* Egyptian woman

Not many Egyptian women managed to be quite so perfect. In fact . . .

1 Girls with richer parents would leave home and go to school and learn to read or write.
2 Girls often married for love rather than have their parents choose a husband. It was common to marry someone in the family such as an uncle or a cousin.
3 A Greek visitor, Herodotus, wrote that Egyptian women were not as obedient as he felt they should be. He complained they were much too independent!

4 An Egyptian man could have as many wives as he liked *but* he had to be able to keep them all in comfort. The chief wife was the equal of her husband and her first son would get his wealth when he died – the chief wife would get his household goods.

CHIEF WIFE   ASSISTANT CHIEF WIFE   WIFE #1   WIFE #2   TRAINEE WIFE

5 Girls often had their first baby when they were just twelve or thirteen years old. Women gave birth kneeling on special bricks. Childbirth was a dangerous time because of the high risk of infection. It was common for mother or baby to die. A woman had to hope that the goddess of childbirth, Twaret, would keep away evil spirits. Twaret should have been able to manage that – she was a ferocious, pregnant hippopotamus!

How to be a beautiful Egyptian woman

Egyptian women were proud of their appearance and loved to be fashionable. If the Egyptians had a book of beauty tips they might have told you . . .

1 Bathe often. Purify the water with natron – yes, the salt used to preserve mummies!

2 Have a massage. A servant will give you a massage – if you're lucky enough to have a servant.
3 Use eye make-up. Take the lead-ore, galena, to make a grey-black mascara and use it to give an almond shape to the eye. Pluck your eyebrows. Silver tweezers are best – if you can afford them, of course.
4 Use face make-up. Brighten your face with blusher and lipstick made out of red iron-oxides.
5 Use nail-colour. Mix up some henna to give a red tint to the nails – and it can also be used to colour the palms of your hands and the soles of your feet!

Live like an Egyptian

The Egyptians lived in houses built of mud bricks. That's not at all horrible. The mud was free and the bricks, baked by the hot summer sun, became rock hard. Mud houses could last for hundreds of years – and some Egyptians still build their homes with mud today. The more important you were, the bigger your house. Egyptians had very little furniture, but that didn't matter because they spent so much of the time outdoors. Would you like to have lived like an Egyptian?

WELL I SUPPOSE BUILDING MUD-BRICK HOUSES NAKED CUTS DOWN ON LAUNDRY BILLS

1 Egyptians wore very few clothes. Children and poor people often wore nothing. But luckily the Ancient Egyptians lived in a very warm, dry country . . . and walking round with no clothes was an obvious thing to do.

2 Egyptians ate bread. It was so rough that it wore away their teeth! There were bakeries in Egypt in 2000 BC. If you want an idea of how the bread would taste (without wearing out your teeth) try this recipe . . .

Wholemeal bread....
You need:
1. 4 cups of wholemeal flour.
2. half a teaspoon of salt.
3. 2 cups of warm water.
Method:
1. Mix the flour, salt and water
2. Knead well for five minutes
3. Shape the dough into circles or triangles
4. Place the shapes on a greased baking tray.
5. Leave overnight.
6. Decorate the edges of the shapes with finger-dents.
7. Bake in an oven at Gas mark 4 for half an hour.
(You can add a cup of chopped dates - shapes could be Egyptian animals if you like)

Your Verdict (Tick the box): Awesome □ Okay □ Horrible □

3 Egyptian food included cucumbers, celery, lettuce, onions, garlic, leeks and cress . . . but most people had to live on bread and onions. Their fruits were melons, figs, pomegranates and dates. Grapes were used for wine, and honey for sweetening. The later Egyptians grew cherries, apples and pears. Sheep, goats, cattle and geese gave them meat, but pigs were thought unclean.

4 They drank a type of beer made from barley. Bread was added to barley and water, and left to brew. The liquid had to be strained before it could be drunk, and it probably looked more like soup!

5 The Egyptians made the world's first known sweets as early as 1600 BC. The recipes were found inscribed on stone tablets. Try this one . . .

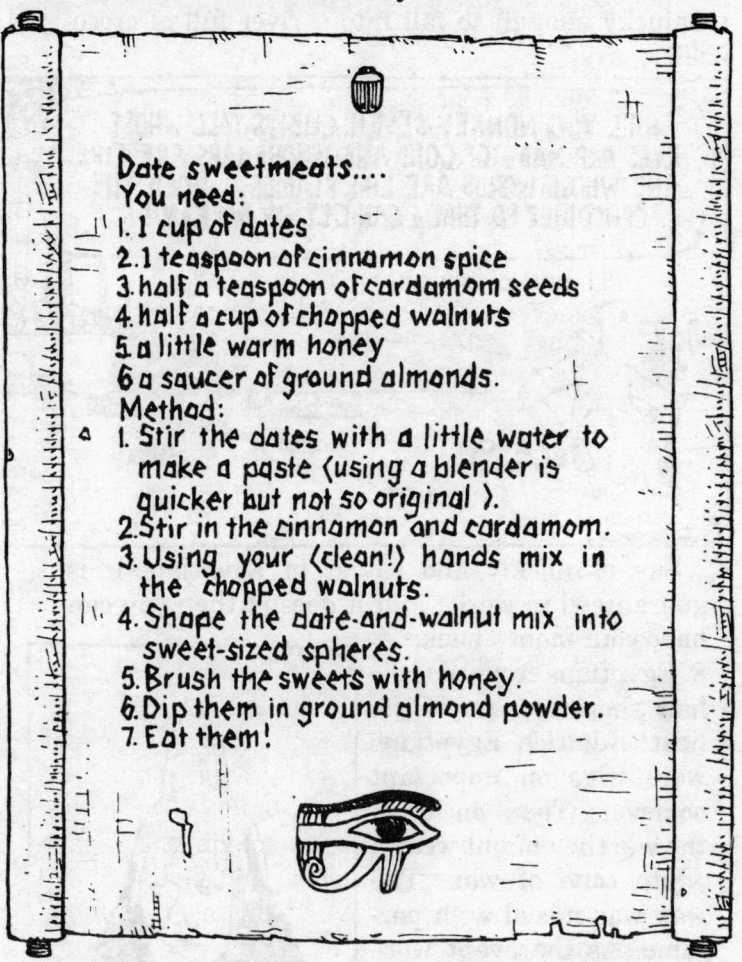

Date sweetmeats....
You need:
1. 1 cup of dates
2. 1 teaspoon of cinnamon spice
3. half a teaspoon of cardamom seeds
4. half a cup of chopped walnuts
5. a little warm honey
6. a saucer of ground almonds.
Method:
1. Stir the dates with a little water to make a paste (using a blender is quicker but not so original).
2. Stir in the cinnamon and cardamom.
3. Using your (clean!) hands mix in the chopped walnuts.
4. Shape the date-and-walnut mix into sweet-sized spheres.
5. Brush the sweets with honey.
6. Dip them in ground almond powder.
7. Eat them!

6 The Egyptians trained Ethiopian baboons to pick their dates from the trees. (If you happen to have a date tree in your back garden maybe you could train your parents to be your baboons?)

7 The Egyptians were great believers in magic. Here is the most useful hint you will ever find in a book! It might well save your life! If you are unlucky enough to fall into a river full of crocodiles, say,

HAIL YOU MONKEY SEVEN CUBITS TALL WHOSE EYES ARE MADE OF GOLD AND WHOSE LIPS ARE FIRE AND WHOSE WORDS ARE LIKE FLAMES... HOLD THE CROCODILE SO THAT I CAN GET UP SAFELY !

SCRATCH SCRATCH

Say it quickly and say it in Egyptian. It is guaranteed to work . . . if it doesn't then you can have your money back.

8 Egyptians cropped their hair short because of the heat. But rich Egyptians wore wigs on important occasions. Then, on top of the wig they might wear a white cone of wax. The wax was mixed with perfume. As the event wore on, the wax melted, the perfume was released . . . and the wax ran all over your wig!

9 Egyptian medicine was a mixture of common sense and magic. A government official, Khety, was attacked and received a serious headwound. His doctor was able to drug Khety to sleep then remove part of his damaged skull; the wound was sewn up – and Khety lived.

10 On the other hand, a cure for blindness involved mashing up the eye of a pig with honey and red ochre and pouring it in the patient's ear!

If you have a stomach-ache you can try reciting this ancient Egyptian charm as you drink your medicine, "Come, you who drive out evil things from my stomach and my limbs. He who drinks this shall be cured just as the gods above were cured."

What was it for?

Take a look at these awesome Egyptian objects, and see if you can work out how the Egyptians would have used them.

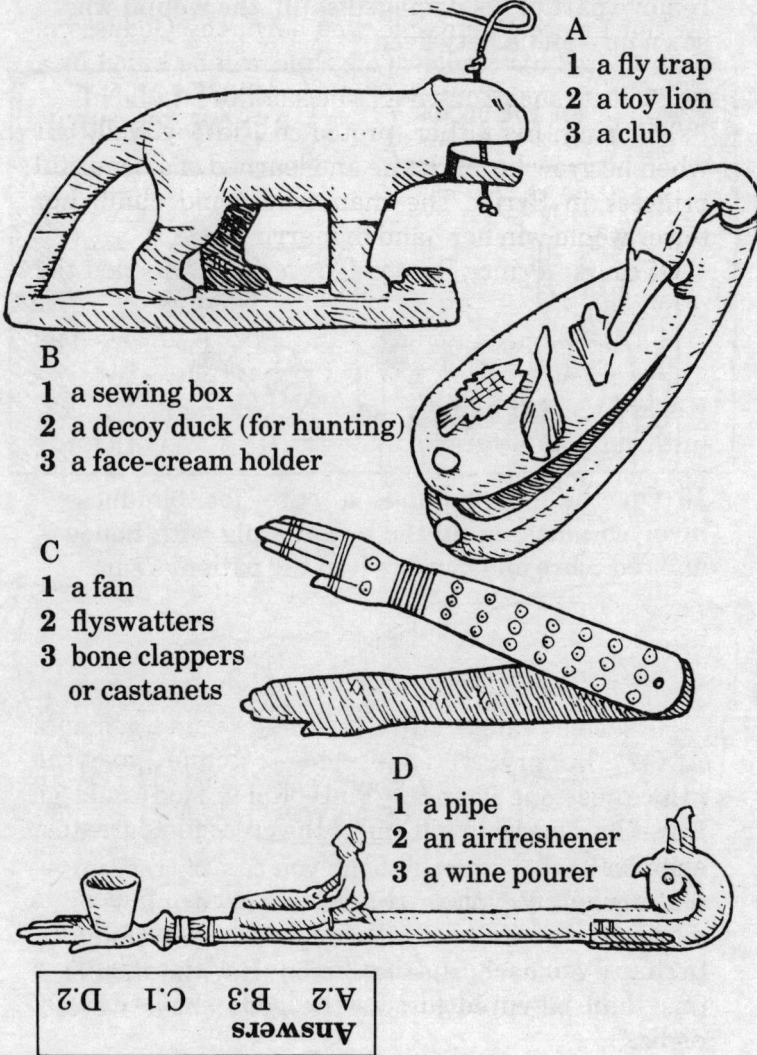

A
1 a fly trap
2 a toy lion
3 a club

B
1 a sewing box
2 a decoy duck (for hunting)
3 a face-cream holder

C
1 a fan
2 flyswatters
3 bone clappers
   or castanets

D
1 a pipe
2 an airfreshener
3 a wine pourer

Answers
A.2 B.3 C.1 D.2

116

Awesome Egyptian entertainment

Story-telling

The Ancient Egyptians were fond of stories. This one is a bit like our own fairy-stories:

"When Prince Ramesside was born, the Goddess of Fate visited his cradle. 'This child will be killed by a crocodile, a snake or a dog,' she said.

The king, his father, protected the boy well, but when he grew he left home and learned of a beautiful princess in Syria. The man who could climb her tower would win her hand in marriage.

Of course Prince Ramesside won and married the princess.

His life seemed happy . . . until he was attacked by a snake! The princess saved him that time.

His life seemed happy . . . until he was attacked by his own dog. He ran into the sea and saved himself!

He seemed safe . . . till a crocodile swam up to him. A very hungry crocodile! The crocodile gave the prince just one chance. Prince Ramesside could go free if he'd agree to kill one of the crocodile's greatest enemies . . ."

Unfortunately, the ancient papyrus paper is damaged and we've lost the end of the story. Sorry! perhaps you'd like to think of an ending. Here's a clue – the Egyptians liked a sad story with a happy ending!

Children's games

A ball would be made from leather and stuffed with grain. Catching and juggling were popular. Sometimes the catchers would ride 'piggy-back' while they threw or juggled.

Spinning-tops of polished stone were made for children – they would be spun with the fingers. The trick was to keep more than one going at a time.

Knee races could be run. All you have to do is race between two points . . . but your hands must never leave your knees!

Beautifully made toys have been found in tombs. Wooden animals had mouths that would open and close when you tugged the string.

Goat-on-the-ground game

Try playing this simple Egyptian game.
You need a group of four or more.
1 Two players are the 'Goat'
2 The two players who are the goat sit on the ground, face to face with legs outstretched.
3 The others have to jump over the Goat without being caught by the Goat's hands.
4 If a jumper is caught then the jumper becomes half of the Goat.

MY, THAT WAS A HIGH JUMP

Water sport

Okay, check your swimming certificates. You need two teams of three or four people with a boat for each team. The aim is to stand in your boats and knock the other team into the water, one by one, without being knocked in yourself. You could try it on grass with two teams standing on planks!

Hunting

Hunt the hippopotamus with harpoons, spears, ropes and nets – highly dangerous – the hippo might decide to hunt the hunter!

Do not try this sport! (You may find a hippo in your local zoo but you'll be thrown out if you try to kill it . . . and even if you succeeded you'd never get it in the microwave.)

Hunting birds – the Egyptians would use tame birds to attract the wild ones, then kill the wild birds with a 'throwing stick' – a sort of boomerang that doesn't come back – difficult.

Try hitting cardboard cut-out birds with 'throwing sticks' – the most hits out of ten throws, wins.

Alquerque

This Spanish game is thought to have come originally from ancient Egypt. It was probably introduced into Spain by the Moors – who lived in North West Africa. The Moors had conquered Egypt in the Middle Ages. You will need 12 counters each and a game-board. You can draw out a gameboard like the one below on a piece of cardboard. Only two people can play. Set the pieces out as shown below.

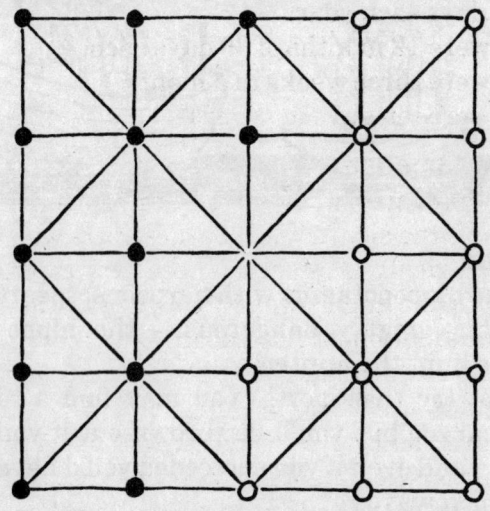

Rules

1 Only the space in the middle is left clear.

2 Throw a dice to decide who goes first and the first move has to be into that space.

3 Then any empty place next to them, pieces can be moved along the lines of the board

4 You can capture a piece and take it off the board as you would in draughts, by jumping over it. You can capture more than one piece in the same move.

5 The winner is the player who captures all the opponent's pieces.

Awesome astronomy

Marking time

The Egyptian calendar was awesomely brilliant. Some historians think it was their greatest invention. By observing the sun they calculated the length of the year at 365 days, almost the same as ours.

The year was divided into the three seasons you read about on page 92, each 120 days long with 5 'extra' days each year.

There were 12 months of 30 days each.

There were three weeks in a month.

There were ten days in a week.

Ancient records

Some time around 3000 BC an astronomer was observing the sky just before dawn. He was working in the academy at Memphis, the new capital city of united Upper and Lower Egypt. It was the first day of the Inundation, or flood-season.

On the eastern horizon the sun began to rise – but on this day at the same time, so did the star Sothis (we call it the Dog Star, or Sirius). For generations afterwards they kept watch and discovered that these three events – the start of the flood-season, the rising of the sun and the rising of Sothis happened . . . wait for it . . . once every 1,460 years. Awesome!

If we count the working life of an astronomer as about 25 years, think about how many generations searched the sky – don't be lazy, work it out – 25 into 1,460 – mumble . . . mumble . . . mumble . . . okay, okay, you can turn the page upside down to find out.

Answer: 58 generations and someone doing a ten-year shift.

121

Write like an Egyptian 1

The Egyptian writing is called hieroglyphics . . . but the Egyptians didn't call it that! The word is Greek – from *heiros* meaning sacred and *gluphe* meaning carving. The Egyptian name for it meant 'words of the gods'.

Sometimes a hieroglyphic sign meant a letter – the way it does with our alphabet. Sometimes it meant a whole word.

The 'ink' was more like our poster paints. The most common colours were red and black. The ink would be made with gum into blocks of colour, not liquid ink. (That would dry up too quickly in the Egyptian climate.)

The 'pen' would be more like a fine brush. A twig or reed would be chewed till the end was frayed like the bristles of a brush. It would then be trimmed with a knife to a very fine tip. The pen was dipped in water and then rubbed on the ink-block.

The 'paper' was called papyrus. The soft insides of reeds were taken out and laid in a criss-cross pattern. They were then hammered together to a smooth surface and dried in the sun. The longest known papyrus is an awesome 125 metres long.

Hieroglyphs were deliberately complicated so that it took a long time to read and write them. It meant that those who could read and write were more important.

Most Egyptian boys who went to school were sent there to become scribes. They had to learn to read and write before they could train for good jobs such as a civil servant, doctor or priest. Most Egyptian children stayed at home and were trained to do the same jobs as their parents.

Schools were often in temples and run by priests. Learning to be a scribe was hard. Discipline was strict and the teachers awesomely stern. Just read this text that has survived, called *Advice to a Young Scribe* . . .

O SCRIBE DO NOT BE IDLE, OR YOU SHALL BE CURSED. DO NOT GIVE YOUR HEART TO PLEASURE OR YOU SHALL FAIL. DO NOT SPEND A DAY IN IDLENESS OR YOU SHALL BE BEATEN. A BOY'S EAR IS ON HIS BACKSIDE AND HE LISTENS WHEN HE IS BEATEN...

HELP!

When the last temple was closed in the 6th century AD, the skill of reading hieroglyphs was lost. This is why people thought that the ancient Egyptians were so brilliant that they had invented a language no one else was clever enough to understand.

In 1799 the Rosetta Stone was discovered by an officer in Napoleon's army. This had the same message carved into it in both hieroglyphs and Greek lettering. In 1822 a young French scholar, Jean-Francois Champillon, used the stone and his knowledge of Greek to crack the code and translate the hieroglyphs.

Write like an Egyptian 2

Here are some of the Egyptian hieroglyphs.
Try to copy them and see how long it would take a
scribe to write his records.

A. vulture		M. owl	
B. leg		N. water	
D. hand		P. stool	
F. viper		Q. hill	
G. pot or stand		R. mouth	
CH. rope		S. cloth	
I. reed		T. loaf	
J. serpent		W. chick	
K. basket		Y. reeds	
L. lion		Z. bolt	

Now try to decipher this message – remember it is
the 'sounds' of some letters that are important, not
the spelling!

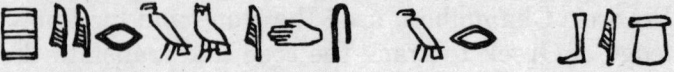

124

Awesome Egyptian arithmetic

Intoxicate your teacher with your knowledge of Egyptian arithmetic. Be cool – just drop these facts casually into the conversation.

1 The Egyptians realised that arithmetic was awesome, and encouraged their priests to develop it.

2 Teachers didn't inflict maths on everyone, it was a closely guarded secret – as much of science is today. Most of it was taught by word of mouth. If it was written down, it could have been stolen by enemies! (Who'd want it anyway?)

3 The Egyptians used maths to solve problems in their building projects. Architects made detailed plans before building began so that every tomb and temple was correctly calculated like ours (see 'How to build a pyramid' on page 46).

4 They used a decimal system like ours, except that zero didn't exist for them.

5 The important Rhind papyrus in the British Museum shows many maths problems about rectangles, circles and triangles.

6 The Egyptians used fractions but the numerator, or the top part of the fraction, was always 1. So 3/8 would be written as 1/8 1/8 1/8.

7 Have a look at the Egyptian number chart. Now see if you can work out how to write these numbers in Ancient Egyptian!

14	18	25	30
37	43	56	71
102	175	333	450

8 Test your friends with some Egyptian sums, for example: $\overset{|||}{||}$ + $\overset{|||}{||}$ $\cap$ = $\cap\cap$

Egyptian Number Chart

1	2	3	4	5	6	7	8	9	10
I	II	III	IIII	$\overset{|||}{||}$	$\overset{|||}{|||}$	$\overset{|||}{|||}$	IIII IIII	$\overset{|||}{\underset{|||}{|||}}$	$\cap$

11	15	22	39	100	1000	10,000
I$\cap$	$\overset{||||}{||}\cap$	II$\cap\cap$	$\overset{|||}{\underset{|||}{|||}}\cap\cap\cap$	੧	ଫ	↘

Dazzling dimensions

Now try out some Egyptian calculations, and see for yourself how awesome they are.

If an ancient Egyptian asked someone for a hand – they probably had some measuring to do! Egyptians used parts of their body, usually their arms and fingers, for measurements.

The width of four fingers, or digits, was called a palm. The length of an arm from finger-tip to elbow was called a cubit. Seven palms were supposed to equal one cubit. Check this with your own body. Draw out the length of your arm on a piece of paper. How many of your palms fit along it? Were they right – as far as your body is concerned?

Try measuring a few things around the house – the dog's tail, grandad's inside leg, the length of the kitchen when someone's cooking. Remember if anyone gets irritated with you, smile sweetly and say it's an educational activity.

Compare your results with those of a tame adult. Any problems? Imagine buying linen for clothes in the market. Who is the lucky one to get sent out shopping, eh? The person with the longest arm in the family, that's who. What you needed was a tall, skinny elder brother.

Well, the Egyptians noticed that they were getting into some awesome difficulties, so they had to invent a royal cubit. This was a standard measurement that was meant to be the same all over the country. It was almost 52.3cm in our metric system.

For longer lengths there was the 'rod of cord', 100 cubits, and the 'river measure', 4,000 cubits.

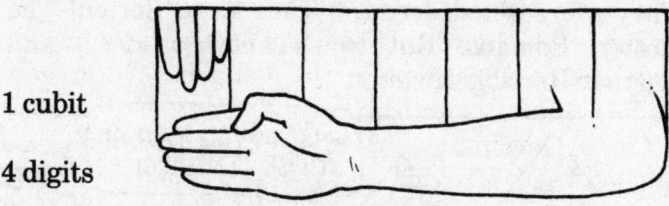

1 cubit

4 digits

4 digits = 1 palm   7 palms = 1 cubit

Epilogue

Life in Egypt could be hard and cruel. Not many people lived a peaceful life; the mummies couldn't even live a peaceful *after*life! But whatever else they were, the Egyptians were truly Awesome. After five thousand years their buildings are still unbelievable for their size.

When Tutankhamun's tomb was opened, the twentieth century world was wildly enthusiastic. The Egyptian "style" was the favourite fashion of the twenties and thirties. Everyone in the world wanted to see his fabulous treasures.

Tutankhamun and the Ancient Egyptians became far more famous after their death than they ever were when they lived. For the Ancient Egyptians never ruled much more than a corner of their ancient world.

But the people who followed them were *much* more ambitious. They wanted to take over the known world – and a few bits that were hardly known at all. They wanted to rule primitive peoples like the ones who lived in a little group of islands called Britain.

They were even more horrible than the Egyptians. They ate roasted dormice! They were Rotten! The Rotten Romans. But that's another story, and another Horrible History . . .

AWESOME EGYPTIANS

GRISLY QUIZ

Now find out if you're an awesome Egyptians expert!

GRUESOME GODS

Most awesome Egyptian myths have various versions of the same story. Here is one version of the Isis and Osiris story. Sadly our suffering scribe has scrambled the terrible tale in places! Can you unscramble the words in capitals? (It's easy – about as easy as unscrambling a scrambled egg!)

Osiris was a popular feller – for a king, that is. His people loved him! Of course someone hated him – his brother, Set, who was very up-Set. Slimy Set was jealous of popular Osiris and plotted against him. Set secretly got his brother's measurements and had a **MAGNETIC FIN** casket made to fit. This casket was in the form of a human-shaped box.

Sneaky Set then **IN DOG'S EAR** a large feast. Seedy Set invited Osiris and 72 others. At the height of the **IF IT IS STEVE** Set produced the casket and **ACNE DO NUN** that it would be given to whoever it fitted. All the guests tried the casket for size, but none fitted until finally Osiris stepped into the casket. (What a mug!)

Set (who was not a mug) immediately slammed the lid closed and sealed the casket shut (with boiling lead). The

130

SAD LEE coffin was then thrown into the Nile.

Isis was upset at the loss of her husband and **SHE CARED** for the casket all over Egypt. At last she found it where it had come to rest in the roots of a huge tree.

Isis took the coffin back for a proper **ALI RUB**. For safety she hid it in the marshes beside the Nile. Unfortunately for Isis, Set found the casket while he was out hunting and was so **ENRAGED** he chopped the body of Osiris into pieces, and **RESTED CAT** the parts throughout the land of Egypt.

Poor Isis had to then set out again looking for the bits of her husband. At last she found all the parts except one (his naughty bit) and **SMEARS BLEED** Osiris and wrapped him in bandages. The first mummy!

He was also a daddy and his son, Horus, went out to battle his savage uncle Set. After a series of battles neither was able to win. In the end Osiris was made king of the underworld, Horus king of the living, and Set ruler of the deserts as the god of evil. So they all died happy ever after!

WROTTEN WRITING

The Egyptians invented writing. They needed it to keep count of all their wealth! They invented the 'picture-writing' that we call hieroglyphics.

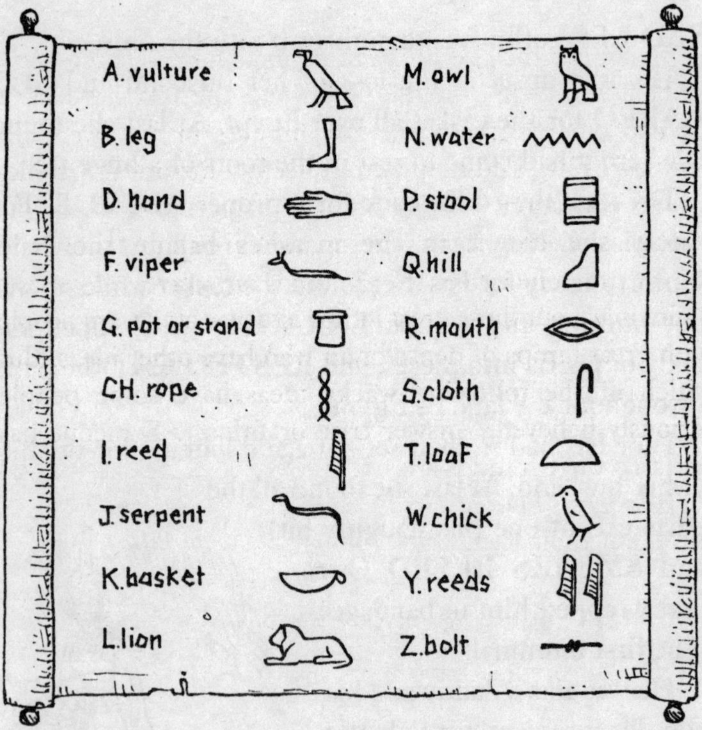

A. vulture		M. owl	
B. leg		N. water	
D. hand		P. stool	
F. viper		Q. hill	
G. pot or stand		R. mouth	
CH. rope		S. cloth	
I. reed		T. loaf	
J. serpent		W. chick	
K. basket		Y. reeds	
L. lion		Z. bolt	

Now see if you can read this message – remember, the sound of the letters is more important than the English spelling.

POTTY PYRAMIDS

They are H-U-G-E. The pyramids were built as graves for the pharaohs after they left this life. They were filled with goodies so the kings would be as rich in the next life as they were in this life.

Of course they've all been robbed now – some were robbed at the time of the burial and the rest have been cleaned out by greedy treasure hunters in the twentieth century. (They said they were collecting historical material for our education. That's a bit like a bank robber saying his hobby is collecting bank notes ... they are all just robbers!)

Not everyone agrees the pyramids are graves, of course. Thinking about those great lumps of dense stone, are people with great lumps of dense brain who have other ideas. But which of the following wacky ideas have some people seriously believed? Answer **true** or **false**... Someone has said that the pyramids are ...

1. Adverts. The priests wanted to leave something to show the world how great they were.

2. Simple landmarks. All maps would be drawn with the pyramids at the centre and distances worked out from there.

3. Chambers of horrors. Dead kings were stuck inside, then the Egyptian people were charged two onions an hour to walk around and view their kingly corpses.

4. Sundials. The shadow from the Great Pyramid would be used to work out the time.

5. Fortune-telling machines. They've been used to predict the birth of Christ, the date of World War I and the end of the world – AD 2979 if you're worried.

6. Star calculators. They help to measure the speed of light, the distances from the earth to the sun and to keep a record of the movement of the stars.

7. Calendars. They can measure the length of a year to three decimal places.

8. Star maps. The pyramids are laid out in the same pattern as a cluster of stars called Orion. Of course you could only see this pattern if you are ten miles up in the air – or a Martian in a flying saucer.

9. Centres of invisible forces of the universe. Weird things can happen there – like blunt razors turning sharp and people feeling wobbly at the knees when they enter.

10. Maths calculators. Take the distances around the edges and the angles and whatnot and you can work out the distance round a circle (its circumference) if you know the distance across (its diameter).

Quick egyptian Quiz

1. The Egyptians made houses from bricks. The bricks were made from mud mixed with straw or something else. What? (Clue: not to be sniffed at)

2. Pilgrims came to ancient Egypt like holiday-makers to Blackpool. What miniature mummies did they buy as souvenirs? (Clue: did they have to kill these creatures nine times?)

3. A weaver who took a day off work would be punished. How? (Clue: you can't beat it)

4. Priests shaved off all their hair and eyebrows. Why? (Clue: not such a lousy idea)

5. Egyptian gods were often pictured with animal heads. Hapy had a baboon's head and Qebehsenuef had a falcon's. But Pharaoh Horemheb was buried with a rare god who had what sort of head? (Clue: flipping tortoise!)

6. The god Khnum created the first Egyptian people. What did the Egyptians believe he made them from? (Clue: they were earthy people)

7. Farmers scattered corn on their fields. How did they trample the seed in so the birds couldn't eat it all? (Clue: they were seen and herd)

8. Another way to keep birds off crops was to use scarecrows. These scarecrows were better than modern ones as they could run around screaming! How? (Clue: you must be kidding)

9. After reigning 30 years a pharaoh would have to prove his strength. How? (Clue: it was a good idea in the long run)

10. How many sides has an Egyptian pyramid? (Clue: slightly sneaky)

Answers

Gruesome Gods: magnificent; organised; festivities; announced; sealed; searched; burial; angered (or enraged!); scattered; reassembled.

Wrotten Writing: My nits ar itchy

Potty Pyramids: All except 3 have been believed by someone … usually someone with more thumbnail than brain, but you can believe them if you like. Most people just admit they are huge tombs for dead kings.

Quick Egyptian Quiz:

1) Animal droppings. Poo! Imagine if your house was made of mud mixed with animal droppings! (Maybe it is!) And imagine mixing it in the days before rubber gloves had been invented. The Egyptians also burned animal droppings to make a fire.

2) Mummified cats. The cats had their necks broken, then

were wrapped like a pharaoh's mummy. Pilgrims offered the cats to the gods. Vast cemeteries have been discovered with many thousands of these cat burials. It is likely that the animals were specially bred for this purpose. By 1900 hundreds of tonnes of mummified cats had been shipped to Liverpool to be ground up and used as fertilizer.

Horrible Histories note: Some school books tell you the Egyptians turned their cats to mummies because they loved their cute little kitties so much! Nice idea – load of rubbish.

3) He was beaten. Miss a day's work, weaver, and you get fifty lashes. And weaving was a tough job – you worked all day with your knees drawn up to your chest.

4) To keep free of lice. Everyone from pharaoh to peasant suffered from lice in the hair. Priests became slapheads to keep clean.

5) A turtle. It was not a common statue in Egypt so Horemheb probably had to shell out a lot of money to buy it!

6) Mud. The early Egyptians called themselves 'black-landers' because they believed they were made from the dark, rich soil by the River Nile. Khnum, they said, breathed life into them and the mud became human beings. Muddy marvellous!

7) With a herd of sheep, goats or pigs. These herds ran around the field and trampled in the grain. Don't try this at home.

8) They used children as scarecrows. Nowadays we'd probably use traffic wardens because they are scarier than anything.

9) He had to run around his palace. Some historians believe that in the early days of Egypt, if the king failed the test he would be sacrificed. He was literally running for his life!

10) Two. An in-side and an out-side. (Oh, come on! This is a Horrible Histories book! What did you expect? A fair question?)

INTERESTING INDEX

Where will you find 'blackheads', 'Chin wigs',
'roasted dormice' and 'radishes' in an index?
In a Horrible Histories book, of course!

138

Terry Deary was born at a very early age, so long ago he can't remember. But his mother, who was there at the time, says he was born in Sunderland, north-east England, in 1946 – so it's not true that he writes all *Horrible Histories* from memory. At school he was a horrible child only interested in playing football and giving teachers a hard time. His history lessons were so boring and so badly taught, that he learned to loathe the subject. *Horrible Histories* is his revenge.

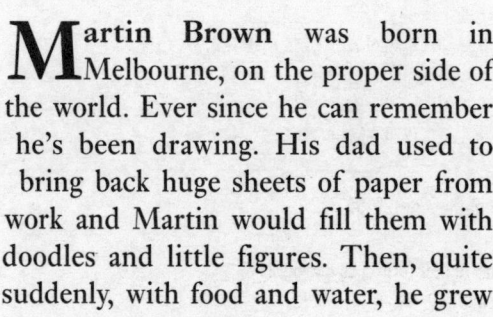

Martin Brown was born in Melbourne, on the proper side of the world. Ever since he can remember he's been drawing. His dad used to bring back huge sheets of paper from work and Martin would fill them with doodles and little figures. Then, quite suddenly, with food and water, he grew up, moved to the UK and found work doing what he's always wanted to do: drawing doodles and little figures.

HORRIBLE HISTORIES

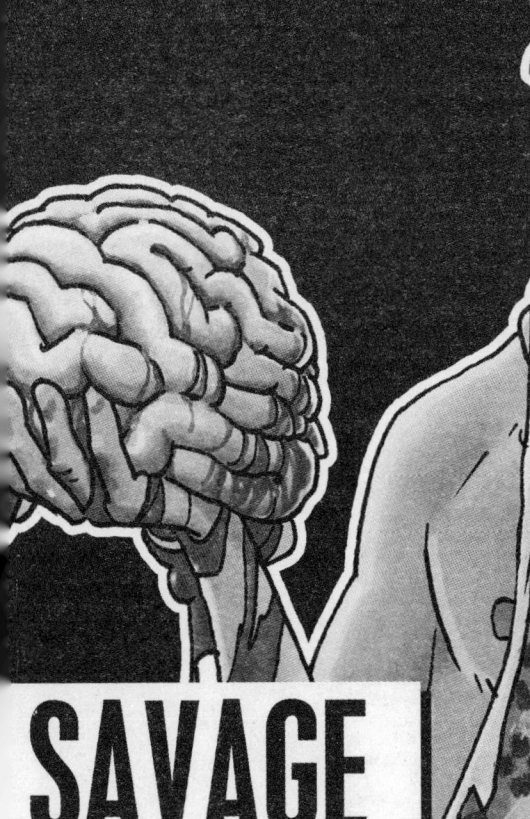

SAVAGE
STONE AGE

Terry Deary Illustrated by **Martin Brown**

SCHOLASTIC

To Erica Sheppard, with thanks.

Scholastic Children's Books,
Euston House, 24 Eversholt Street,
London NW1 1DB, UK

A division of Scholastic Ltd
London ~ New York ~ Toronto ~ Sydney ~ Auckland
Mexico City ~ New Delhi ~ Hong Kong

First published in the UK by Scholastic Ltd, 1999
This edition published by Scholastic Ltd, 2016

Text © Terry Deary, 1999
Illustration © Martin Brown, 1999, 2016

ISBN 978 1407 16559 2

Printed and bound by CPI Group (UK) Ltd, Croydon, CR0 4YY

4 6 8 10 9 7 5

www.scholastic.co.uk

CONTENTS

Introduction

History can be horrible. And the further back in time you go, the more horrible it becomes in some ways! Of course not everyone believes this! Some people would quite like the idea of time travel. They'd like to go back in time and live in another age. An age without homework, global warming and mad cow disease.

So the past isn't so attractive as it seems in the school books.

Still, some people think the past was a time when life was simple and easy. A million years ago you had no books (not even *Horrible Histories* because there was no history), no hot, soapy baths to get rid of the lice on your body and no smelly socks!

But would you like to find out what the Stone Age was really like to live in? You could go to a museum and see flint arrowheads in glass cases or poor paintings of hairy people in animal skins. But that doesn't tell you how people *lived* ... and *died*.

You may decide to climb into your time machine, set the dial to 1 million years BC, and switch on.[1]

If you can't manage a time machine then what you need is a book that will tell you the truth about the savagery of the Stone Age. What you need is a horrible history of 'prehistoric' people – people who existed in those happy times before 'history' was invented. Strange as it may seem ... stranger even than time travel ... you have the very book in your hands at this moment.

So what are you waiting for? The next Stone Age?

---

1. To get instructions on how to make a time machine you need to wait until the year AD 2346 when the first one will be invented. If you can't wait that long then you will need an alarm clock, a wire coat hanger, a banana and a copy of tomorrow's newspaper – *The Times*, of course.

Stone Age timeline

3,500,000 years ago (y.a.) Footprints have been found in east Africa that are over three-and-a-half million years old. They show that creatures we call 'hominids' can walk on two legs. Big deal, you say! Even a baby in nappies can do that! Yes, but this allows the front feet to develop into hands and to use tools.[1] These 'hominids' will take over the world, you'll see.

3,200,000 y.a. Skeleton has been found in Africa of 'Lucy', who walked on two legs. She was nicknamed after the Beatles song *Lucy in the Sky with Diamonds*! She's only four feet tall and her brain is just 400 cc big.[2] Archaeologists have found evidence that a family of nine similar hominids were killed in a sudden disaster – maybe they were too pea-brained to run away! This is the first ever horrible human history event we know about.

2,500,000 y.a. Earliest stone tools found in Ethiopia show

1. The posh name for these hominids is 'Australopithecus' which means 'southern apes' and not to be confused with 'Australians' – who are also southern apes except for Martin Brown who is wonderful.
2. Modern humans have a brain of around 1,550 cc. Take yours out and measure it. If it's as small as Lucy's then you will probably make a good teacher.

these hominids knew how to scrape the skin off their food ... but that didn't mean they had weapons to kill it. So experts think they probably stole dead meat from wild animals. (Drop some sweets on the classroom floor and see that many of today's hominids still have this dirty, thieving habit!)

2,500,000–1,500,000 y.a. Early hominids are changing into more 'modern' human beings and are using stone tools. They are called 'handy humans' (*Homo habilis* is the posh scientific name).

1,800,000 y.a. The clever humans build their first houses – in Tanzania – a half-circle of lava blocks probably covered with branches. Not too comfortable but at least there's no rent to pay, no poll tax and your neighbours don't park their BMW next door to make you jealous.

1,790,000 y.a. Another type of Australopithecine is living in Kenya. That's a bit of a mouthful to say – and as he had a bit of a mouthful of big crunching teeth he gets the name 'Nutcracker Man'. The archaeologists who found him

thought his teeth were strong enough to crack nuts. (Not to be confused with your local football hooligan who is 'Nut-caser man'.)

1,600,000 y.a. Hominids have grown larger than 'Nutcracker' and are using cleverer tools. These 'upright humans' (*Homo erectus* if you want to be posh) are spreading from Africa. But archaeologists have also found 'handy humans' who were still living at this time. The finders gave them more cheerful nick-names like 'Twiggy', 'George' and 'Cinderella'. (Not to be confused with your school goalie whose nickname is 'Cinderella' because he's always late for the ball.)

1,000,000 y.a. Possibly the first use of fire. And now there's another new type of hominid – the one that will become *you* in a million years' time: 'wise man' (or *Homo sapiens*), who has a bigger brain (1,400 cc as opposed to 840–1,066 cc of *erectus*). There are other types of hominid around at this time, but *Homo sapiens* is the only one that will become your ancestor. In June 1998 a

skull was found in Eritrea in north-east Africa belonging to the oldest *Homo sapiens* ever found – before this, most people thought *Homo sapiens* first appeared 450,000 years ago. This is the start of what historians will call the Old Stone Age – 'Palaeolithic', if you want a gold star.

800,000 y.a. Hominids arrive in Europe, probably because that's where the best food is. (No, the animals, berries and fruit – not the pizzerias, which haven't been invented yet.)

500,000 y.a. *Homo erectus* strolls into Europe.

450,000 y.a. *Homo sapiens* is spreading around the world and eating cooked food. Not that you'd want to share some of it!

200,000–130,000 y.a. Neanderthals appear in Europe. These are not *Homo sapiens* but hominids that are almost as clever. Trouble is they are not clever enough to survive and will end up extinct.

150,000 y.a. European humans in the Ice Age start to use caves to shelter from the cold. One tricky problem is that bears like them too, and there must have been a

few bedroom battles for the cosiest caves!

128,000 y.a. Sea levels rise as Ice Age ends. Britain is cut off from Europe and in the warmer weather there are hippos in the Thames. They're not there now so there's no point looking. But did some prehistoric creatures survive in deep lakes like Loch Ness?

120,000–100,000 y.a. *Homo sapiens* are becoming 'near-modern' humans – *Homo sapiens sapiens* or wise-wise human – and these clever clogs are living in Africa. You wouldn't be too shocked to see one of these in your classroom – if it had shaved and washed and dressed, of course. Those Neanderthals seem to be top hominids in Europe.

70,000–30,000 y.a. Colder again, new Ice Age and *Homo sapiens sapiens* moves into Europe. Early humans discover Australia and move in: this is bad news for kangaroos. In Europe and Asia hominids are burying their dead – men are buried with meat and tools, women with nothing.

40,000 y.a. Hominids are getting really clever at making tools. It's

becoming the first 'industry'. They are also creating art. Small sculptures and paintings. The ones that they are scratching and painting in caves will survive until today.

30,000 y.a. Neanderthals still present in Spain but about to disappear without trace, leaving just *Homo sapiens sapiens* to take over the world. Probably the first hominids arrive in America. Bad news for bison.

25,000–14,000 y.a. The Ice Age returns for the last time. Maybe the Neanderthals saw it coming and decided to become extinct rather than live through another 10,000 freezing years.

15,000 y.a. Super-humans from space built ancient monuments. Their civilization is now buried beneath Antarctic. No, that's not in your school history books, but some seriously potty people believe it. Make up your own mind. (Unless you're one of the seriously potty people in which case you haven't got a mind and can't make it up.)

12,000–10,000 BC End of last Ice Age and start of what is known as

the Middle Stone Age – Mesolithic period. Humans are making pottery and building mud-brick houses. In America, beavers the size of donkeys are hunted down till they are extinct. Just as well. Imagine one of them chewing at your telegraph poles.

8,500–7,300 BC Humans are farming cereal grasses for the first time. Dug-out canoes are being used. People settling and gathering into towns. Jericho has a population of 2,000 people.

7,000 BC Copper is being used in Turkey and Iran.

5,000 BC Bronze used widely but these times are still known as the Stone Age.

4,000 BC Start of what historians call the New Stone Age – the 'Neolithic' period.

3,200 BC Sumerian people of Mesopotamia invent writing. Now they can write horrible history, so that's the end of prehistory. Exciting things like spelling tests are now possible.

3,000 BC The earliest part of First Stonehenge is built. Archaeologists can't agree why it was built. Horrible historians

13

suspect they may be world's first football goal-posts.

2,000 BC Bronze is now being used by many humans, so this becomes known as the start of the Bronze Age. It's goodbye to the Stone Age … except in places where bronze isn't being used where it is still the Stone Age.

700–500 BC Early Iron Age, so now you can iron your clothes.

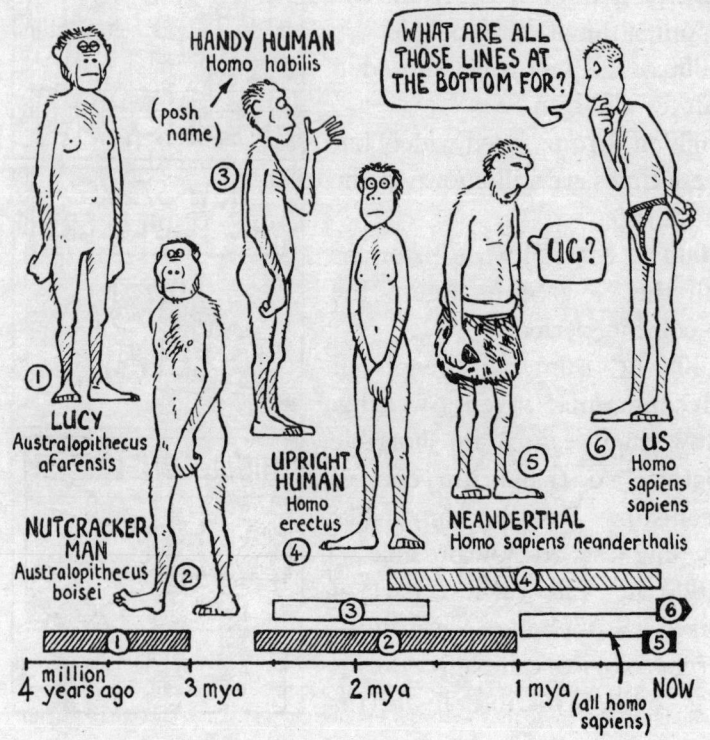

14

Awful for animals

Have you ever crunched on North American camel flavoured crisps? No.

Ever munched on mammoth mince? No.

Ever popped Kentucky Fried moa in your mouth? Noa![1]

Because they no longer exist.

All these ancient animals had lived happily on Earth for a million or more years till the hungry hominids came along. Now they're all dead, deceased, demised, defunct, defeated, discontinued, departed, dustbinned and done-for daisy-pushers.

Extinct ... or, in the case of the moa, egg-stinct.

Where have they gone? Cruelly killed by heartless hominids.

ARE WE RARE?

IT DEPENDS ON HOW THEY COOK US

1. Moas were flightless birds that lived in New Zealand – till humans arrived and had moa massacres. They could be up to three metres tall. They'd never seen humans before so they were easy to catch and kill. A few survived till about 200 years ago.

Horrible hunters

Early hominids pinched corpses from killer animals like lions and ate the scraps. They made stone tools to scrape the meat off the skin and eat it raw. (You can try this the next time your cat brings a half-eaten mouse into the house.) Then some clever hominids discovered something important…

Stone tools became stone weapons. By 700,000 years ago a new type of Stone Age tool, the hand axe, was being used. 250,000 years ago the humans had wooden spears with tips hardened in fire. By 9,000 BC the horrible humans had invented bows and arrows.

Animals used to run away to save themselves, but now the new weapons, and the human brain behind them, drove those animals to destruction.

But how *do* you kill a mighty mammoth or catch a herd of horses when you only have stone weapons? Use your 1,550 cc brain. Stone Age people did!

Hunters chase into swamp

Mammoths – feet stick in mud

Swamp – sticky mud

Mammoth – gone too far

As early as 300,000 years ago hunters in Spain stampeded elephants into swamps and butchered them. Stone Age people seem simple to us, yet an elephant hunt took a lot of organizing. (You couldn't do it if you tried! But *don't* try it because elephants are a protected species. Hunt traffic wardens instead – they are not a protected species.)

In 18,000 BC horse hunters in France used a natural cliff as a fall-trap.

I'VE JUST INVENTED THE PONY CLUB!

In America (about 10,000 years ago) they stampeded bison over cliffs. Bison were hunted because the American camels and mammoths had been wiped out.

Hunters – run and chase

Bison – break necks

Cliff – big drop

Brave warrior underneath cliff to finish off

Warning: Don't get too brave and try to catch bison as they land

American Plains Indians had a bison hunt once a year, in autumn, so they'd have meat for the winter.

The Plains Indians arranged lines of stones into a funnel that led to the cliff and stampeded the bison between the stones. One mistake could scatter the whole herd and the tribe could starve to death over the winter.

These were clever hominids and not simple, hairless apes. Can you say the same about your classmates?

Toasted tortoise
Native American Indians in Florida, 14,000 years before Disney World, hunted an extinct type of giant tortoise. (Well, it wasn't extinct when they hunted it, of course, but it's extinct now. That's what you get if you can't run away fast enough.)

Archaeologists found one of these tortoises with a sharp

18

wooden stake driven through it. This would kill the creature and then be useful for holding it over a fire to roast.

This could be proof of the world's oldest barbecue!

These Florida food-lovers also ate rattlesnakes and hairy elephants called mastodons. Slow-moving tree-loving sloths must have been easy to catch and kill.

A dog's life

Not all animals suffered at the hands of Stone-Agers. A graveyard has been found in Sweden that contains a doggy cemetery.

The dogs were buried with the same sort of grave goods that their human owners had – deer antlers, axes and flint blades (to open the tins of dog-food in the afterlife?).

If they were that respected after death then it's a fair guess they were well treated in their doggy lives – better than many dogs are today – because they were such a help in hunting.

Foul food

Stone Age humans couldn't pop down to their local supermarket and then shove food into their microwave ovens. Everything they ate had to be found or caught. If they wanted it cooked then they had to do it themselves.

By studying hunter-gatherer people who are alive today, historians have come up with a rough idea of how early Stone Age people brewed up breakfast, lapped up lunch, tucked into tea or scoffed their supper.

Dreadful dinners

Tasty tips for hungry house-husbands and weary wives

You will need:
× dead animals - enough to feed the family
× a stone knife
× a flint to strike a light and wood for a fire

Methods:
1. Catch a bird or animal. (Handy hint: hang around beasts of prey like lions. Wait till they've eaten their fill and take what's left - but make sure they don't make a snack of you!)
2. Light the fire and build it up to a good blaze. (Handy hint: once you've got a fire going it is a good idea to try and keep it going until you need it again.)

3. Throw the dead animal on to the fire and scorch it till the fur (or feathers) burns off and the skin is crisp.

4. Pull the animal off the fire, slit it open, take out the guts and throw them away.

5. Tear off flesh and share it round the family. The meat will still be raw and bloody but don't worry, that makes it all the tastier.

6. Serve with fresh water.

You may like to have a Stone Age dinner in the school canteen! Dinner ladies could prepare the food in Stone Age fashion and you can try to spot the difference.

And don't forget your manners...

Early Stone Age Table Manners

Clever cooks

Later Stone Age eaters weren't nearly as crude. They used spoons made of pottery, horn or wood and would cook stews or joints of meat in boiling water.

You may think Stone-Agers weren't as bright as you. But could you solve the problem of cooking without a metal pot?

The riddle
You have:
- straw
- plaited straw ropes
- wood
- stones
- a stone trough – slabs of stone joined to make a water-tight box
- cold water
- fire
- leg of lamb

… and a hungry family, of course.

Well? Have you worked it out? Or are you too dumb to be a Stone-Ager?

Here's what they'd do…

The Sunday Stone Age Cookery Page

Is your family tired of the same old raw eggs for Sunday lunch? Try this exciting recipe from our super chef!

1 Light the fire near the trough.
2 Put the stones in the fire.
3 Fill the trough with water.

4 Wrap the meat in a bundle of straw and tie the ends with straw ropes.

5 When the stones are red hot lift them from the fire with pieces of wood.

6 Drop the stones into the water till it begins to boil.

7 Lower the straw-wrapped meat into the boiling water using the straw ropes.

8 Keep adding hot stones to keep the water boiling.

9 Lift the meat out after a couple of hours.

10 Unwrap the meat and eat it!

The straw wrapping not only made it easy to handle the meat, it also meant the meat didn't taste of ash from the hot stones.

They could also roast the meat by starting a fire in the trough to heat the stone, dropping in the meat and covering it with hot stones. Or they might barbecue it on a wooden spit over an open fire – the trouble was the wooden spit could catch fire and dump the meat in the fire if they weren't careful. And it could end up black and charred on the outside and raw on the inside ... a bit like your dad's barbecued sausages.

Did you work out how to cook cave-style? If you did then you'd make a good Boy Scout or Girl Guide. Award yourself a Prehistoric Cookery badge!

Tasty treats

Stone-Agers had to work hard to get their food, so they didn't waste it. They'd eat things that you might not have tried...

23

- cow's udder (makes you shudder)
- blood (tastes good)
- feet (nice treat)
- brain (keeps you sane)
- lungs and tongues.

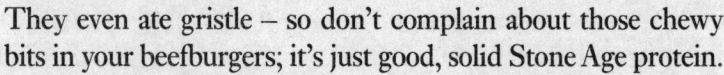

They even ate gristle – so don't complain about those chewy bits in your beefburgers; it's just good, solid Stone Age protein.

Some archaeologists think the Stone-Agers caught animals, slit open their stomachs and ate the meal that the animal had swallowed just before it was killed.

Yeuch! Remember that and you'll never complain about your mother's cooking ever again!

The bones in caves and graves tell scientists what animals Stone-Agers ate. Of course you can't cook many of them today because they're extinct (like the giant kangaroos of Australia) or they're now very rare – you don't get so many rhinos in Rotherham, elephants in Edinburgh or bears in Bournemouth as you did in the Ice Age. So you'll never know the joy of raw rhino or barbecued bear (unless you capture and cook a cute little koala).

But if you eat roast lamb or beef or chicken, then you'll be enjoying the same sort of taste as your ancient ancestors.

Shells and fish bones tell us what sort of seafood they ate – but they probably didn't invent the ancient joke …

Scientists can tell what plants humans ate by looking under the microscope at Stone Age poo. (The posh word for ancient poo is 'coprolite' – you have to soak it for three days before examining it. Just thought you might like to know that.)

Try making this Stone Age treat known today as 'frumenty'. Experimental archaeologists examined the stomach of an Iron Age body and made this porridge using the recipe. They got volunteers to sample it and, of course, they lived!

You may enjoy it. You may prefer to stick with cornflakes. If you were a Stone-Ager you wouldn't have a lot of choice.

How did Stone-Agers discover cooking methods like this? Over thousands of years a lot of Stone-Agers must have eaten a lot of horrible things before they discovered what was safe and tasty.

Your mushroom omelette is safe because thousands of Stone-Agers must have died eating deadly toadstools.

Did you know...?
Archaeologists used coprolites to study the sort of food Stone-Agers ate. But they could also use them to discover what sort of worms and parasites prehistoric people carried around in their guts! And you thought archaeology was a glamorous sort of job?

Groovy games

Human beings enjoy a good laugh. They are the only creatures that *do* laugh. So Stone-Agers must have chuckled as they chatted and guffawed over goofy games we can only guess at.

It wasn't all work and hunting. Some scientists reckon that Stone-Agers spent as little as 15 to 19 hours a week working to survive. That's even less than your teachers (though Stone-Agers didn't get the long summer holidays, of course).

What did Stone-Agers do in their leisure time?

Did they, for example, have competitions to see who could suck the brains from a skull the fastest? Did they spin a stone scraper and play Postman's Rock? Did they poke someone's eyes out with a stone spear and play Blind Man's Bluff? Who knows?

The few clues we have give us some ideas…

Follow my leader

Want to play a simple game that amused a young person three-and-a-half million years ago?

It all began in 1978 (which isn't three-and-a-half million years ago – be patient!) when a group of young scientists were working at an archaeology dig in Africa. They were having a little game of their own, which involved throwing lumps of elephant poo at one another.

One of these scientists ducked a lump of flying elephant dung, slipped and fell flat on his face.

What did he find under his nose? No, not elephant dung. Some curious dents in the rock. Dents that looked remarkably like footsteps.

When the area was cleared the scientists found two sets of footsteps, side by side. They had been printed into volcano ash that had set hard 3.7 million years ago. When they looked really closely they saw that the larger footprints (Dad's perhaps) had smaller footprints inside.

We can guess that a child had followed its parents and amused itself by stepping in father's footsteps.

Next time you're on a beach with your parents you can try it – and experience something nearly four million years old.

(You may prefer to try the game of throwing elephant poo at your friends. Of course you'll have to wait till an elephant happens to wander down your street. It has never been known to work with doggy droppings ... so don't try it.)

Wedding wisdom

For this fortune-telling game you need to go to Dundalk in Ireland. You'll find a prehistoric tomb there made of three pillars about two metres high with a 30-tonne slab of rock on top.

You'll notice that the rock slopes.

Pick up a pebble and throw it on to the roof.

If the pebble rolls off you are safe, but if the pebble stays on the roof, then you'll be married within a year!

This probably won't work if you throw stones at the roof of your house – so don't try it.

This is a modern custom but the belief in the power of the stones may go back into prehistory.

Power painting

You need:

- the bone from a fillet of lamb (ask your butcher – or use the bone from a leg of lettuce if you're a vegetarian)
- poster paint
- a cave wall (if you haven't a handy cave then use any blank wall/teacher's car/ Dad's-best-white-shirt-on-the-washing-line)
- running shoes

Method:

1 Boil the bone and scrape the marrow from the inside so you have a tube.

2 Dip the end of the tube in the paint and suck gently – but don't suck the paint into your mouth!

3 Place your hand against the cave wall/blank wall/teacher's car/Dad's-best-white-shirt-on-the-washing-line.

4 Take aim with the bone-tube at your hand and blow.

5 The paint will spray your hand and leave the outline on the cave wall.

6 If you've used a classroom wall/teacher's car/Dad's-best-shirt-on-the-washing-line, then have the running shoes handy for a fast getaway.

Sometimes the painters used reeds rather than bones to blow through. If you are really idle/boring/stupid, you can use a straw as a spray tube.

Note: Some experts don't believe that Stone-Agers spray-painted in this way.

Other methods:
Sometimes the artists picked up a lump of coloured iron mineral rock and used it as a crayon. But painting was most common. They used hair from the animals they'd killed to make brushes.

You could take a lolly stick and chew one end till it is frayed. Dip it in poster paint and use the frayed stick as a brush. This makes painting difficult but at least you'll see how clever the cave artists were to work like that.

They added delicious details to the paintings – so a bison may be shown on its back, dead, with its guts spilling out.

Some archaeologists believe this was meant to be helpful magic – if they painted a deer/mammoth/bison killed by hunters, then next day the painting, like a dream, would come true. The painting made sure the hunt would be a success.

Or maybe the cave artists simply enjoyed painting. Some people do.

You could paint a passing mammoth yourself. (If you can't find a mammoth then paint a cat.)

For light, the cave workers used dishes filled with animal fats and a reed wick. But an electric light is easier and doesn't smell half as bad.

Batty beliefs

It's impossible to know when Stone-Agers started believing in a life after death or in some sort of religion. But it's a fair guess that it happened around the time they started burying people carefully in graves with their precious objects. The oldest known grave (near Nazareth in the Middle East) is 100,000 years old.

Many Stone-Agers continued to dump their dead in the family rubbish heap where passing dogs would munch them for lunch. Historians have learned a lot from the graves where bodies were laid properly to rest and covered to protect them from becoming a sabre-toothed tiger's tea.

Grave test

Here are ten things that Stone-Agers were buried with over the centuries … can you spot which one is false?

1 Teeth that had fallen out in life
2 A hacked-off arm
3 A dead baby
4 Ropes to tie the arms and legs
5 A necklace of animal teeth
6 A live cat
7 Sea shells
8 Food
9 Flowers
10 A dead dog

Answers: All are true except **6**.

1 In Yorkshire an old woman was buried with all the teeth she'd lost during her life. Stone-Agers had no money so the tooth fairy had nothing to trade, I guess. The teeth had been tucked neatly under her chin. Did the dead woman's friends think she'd need them in the next life, perhaps?

I SPOSE IT'S TOO LATE FOR A DENTIST

2 Not far away from her a man was buried with his arm that had been cut off in some sort of fight. The chopped-off arm was placed on his shoulder with the fingertips touching his face. Weird, eh?

3 A third grave showed the cremated bones of a child, packed in clay and buried with an adult. Did the adult die first and was the child sacrificed and burned to keep the corpse company? The world's oldest burial at Nazareth also shows a six-year-old child buried at the feet of an adult. Some children have been found buried in their parent's arms. Sweet.

4 The ropes that tied up a Stone Age burial may have been an attempt to stop the corpse jumping out of the grave and haunting the family…

5 …And their 'jewellery' made sure they looked smart as they wandered around the afterlife.

SO THAT'S WHAT HAPPENED TO MY BEST LION'S TOOTH NECKLACE

OOOOOOH

7 In the Cheddar Gorge (England) a young man was found buried with a necklace of sea-shells. These must have been collected 30 miles away so his people travelled widely even though bicycles hadn't been invented! The Cheddar man had been buried after much of his flesh had rotted away. Nice job for some Stone Age undertaker.

8 In 1823 a skeleton called 'The Red Lady of Paviland' was found in Wales by a professor called William Buckland. He said it was a Roman who'd been buried along with the bones of animals that drowned in Noah's flood. In fact, the 'Roman' Red 'Lady' turned out to be a *prehistoric* 25-year-old *man* and the animal bones belonged to a mammoth. Young Mister Red Lady was buried with a handful of periwinkles (who hadn't drowned in Noah's flood).

A Polish Stone-Ager was buried with joints of wild-cat and beaver, *and* with his bow and arrows so he could catch more when he'd scoffed the cat (curried no doubt) and the beaver (boiled, perhaps). He was also buried sitting up so it was easier to hunt!

'BOUT THE ONLY THING I'M GOING TO HUNT DOWN HERE IS A MOLE

9 Flowers are placed on graves today and it seems they were used by Neanderthals too. Seven different types of flower were found in one bunch on the Turkish border. There was also a butterfly buried along with the bunch, probably by accident.

SNIFF

WILT

10 In Hungary an old man was buried with a dog. It must have been his pet when he was alive and it was killed to keep him company in the next life.

Did you know…?

Talking of grave tests, Lord Bath had some prehistoric bones taken from Cheddar Gorge (where the necklace of sea-shells was found). He had them tested to see if they were his relatives.

This sort of thing is important to aristocrats – King James I of England said he could trace his ancestors back to Noah! Lord Bath wanted to trace his ancestors back to the Stone Age.

His lordship was disappointed. The nearest living relative to the bones wasn't Lord Bath. It was his butler!

Test your teacher

Your teacher may *look* like a prehistoric Neanderthal but you can be pretty sure s/he *isn't*. Neanderthals are extinct, sadly, and teachers aren't ... sadly.

TEACHER   NEANDERTHAL

So you can test their 1,550 cc brains with this cruelly cunning cwiz and be pretty sure they aren't answering from memory.

Or test yourself. Score eight to ten and you are probably human. Four to seven and you are Neanderthal. Score one to three and you are a chimpanzee. Score nothing and you probably need to evolve for a few thousand years more.

1 Archaeologists could tell what prehistoric Egyptians were eating 11,000 years before the pyramids were built. What did they study?
a) Egyptian cookery books drawn on rocks and buried beneath the sand
b) ancient baby poo
c) ancient jawbones with food stuck between the teeth because toothbrushes hadn't been invented

2 Stone-Agers made their own paint from iron minerals coloured yellow, red, brown or black. These powder paints

had to be mixed with a liquid before they could be painted on the cave walls. What liquid?

a) mammoth's pee
b) gooseberry beer
c) blood

3 What did Stone-Agers use instead of toilet paper?
a) moss
b) deer skin
c) hedgehog skin

4 In 1915, Stonehenge monument was put up for auction. Who bought it and why?
a) a fairground owner, who planned to use it as the centre of a Stone Age theme park – 'Caveworld'

b) an American who planned to put it on display in California
c) a rich man, as a present for his wife

5 How did Bolivian Stone-Agers keep their potatoes fresh

where they lived high in the Andes mountains?
a) by burying them in a potato pit
b) by frying them in llama
fat till they had crisps and
sealing them in little
llama-leather packets
c) by freezing them

6 The fossil tooth of an ancient Chinese hominid was found where?
a) when builders were putting up the great wall of China
b) in a Chinese chemist shop
c) in a Chinese take-away restaurant

7 What did some clean Stone-Agers do that even modern humans forget?
a) cleaned their teeth
b) polished their shoes
c) washed up after dinner

8 Who had the first boomerangs?
a) Stone Age Australians
b) Stone Age North American Indians
c) modern Australians in 1822

9 How did Stone-Agers celebrate great occasions?
a) by setting off fireworks

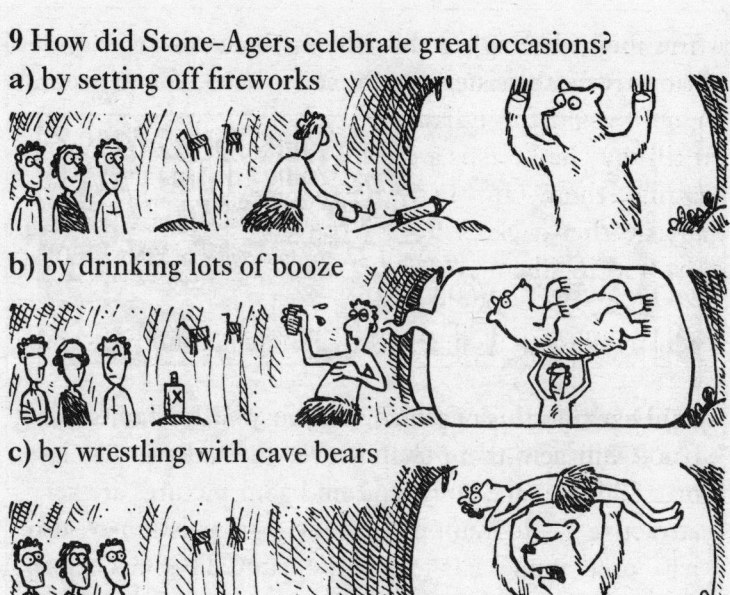

b) by drinking lots of booze

c) by wrestling with cave bears

10 How did Stone-Agers in Sweden help their dead into the afterlife?
a) scratched a map on a stone to show them the way
b) left the door to the tomb open so the spirit could get out
c) shot arrows into corpses as they lay in their graves

Answers:
1b) Most of the plants left behind by prehistoric Egyptians had rotted away. But some were preserved because they had been charred at a camp-fire. Other plants were eaten by babies and came out in their poo. The mucky little infants dropped their poo in the camp. Tidy adults swept the baby-poo into the fire where it was baked hard and preserved. All the archaeologists had to do was cut it open and examine it under a microscope.

You might like to try this in your house if you have a baby brother or sister! On the other hand, you may not.

2c) Don't try this in school. Mixing powder paints with blood will help them to flow over the walls and to last over 30,000 years. You could find your pictures are very attractive ... to vampires. Stone Age artists may also have used animal fats to mix the paint. This was before the time when they learned how to use these fats to make chips.

3a) If you said 'hedgehog skin', then you deserve to try it! A Stone Age body found preserved in ice had lumps of moss in his woven-grass handbag and this moss was his toilet paper. You don't get this sort of fascinating fact in your boring old school books, do you?

And you've always wanted to know what Stone-Agers did before toilet paper was invented, haven't you?

4c) Cecil Chubb was having breakfast with his wife and mentioned that Stonehenge was being put up for auction that day. 'Ooooh! I'd love to own it!' his wife said. 'Then I'll put in an offer,' her adoring husband told her. His offer was accepted and it became Mrs Chubb's. If it had been her birthday, they could have stuck candles on the stones to celebrate. In 1918, Cecil and his wife decided to give the monument to the British government to look after – the Brit people got Stonehenge, Cecil got a knighthood.

5c) The Tiwanaku people of Bolivia lived so high in the Andes that the temperatures dropped to minus 20°C at night. The tricky Tiwanaku divided their farm fields into long narrow strips and surrounded them with water-filled ditches. The sun warmed the water during the day and the warmth kept the fields from freezing at night – like a hot-water bottle. That allowed them to grow more potatoes than they could eat at once, so they also invented a way of freezing them to eat in the winter months. They sprinkled the potatoes with water and left them out at night to freeze and be preserved.

6b) The tooth was found in a Chinese chemist shop in 1899. For centuries chemists in China had bought fossil teeth and ground them up to use in their medicines. The chemists believed they were dragon teeth with magic powers. It was thought to be an ancient human at the time but now many scientists think it came from an ape after all.

7a) The skeleton of a Palaeolithic young man, found in

England, showed that he had almost certainly cleaned his teeth regularly. Maybe he had a mum to nag him! 'Clean those teeth or the Palaeolithic dentist will get you with his stone drill!'

8b) In 12,000 BC Stone Age Indians in Florida used a boomerang.

Archaeologists reckon that the American boomerang *didn't* come back … which, of course, spoils the joke!

9a) … if you believe an Oxford Museum professor. He reckoned Stone-Agers made pottery figures about 25,000 years ago. At a religious ceremony they'd be thrown on to a fire and explode. The figures were soaked in water so they would take a little while to dry out before they went off – that would give the firework-thrower time to get safely away, like a modern firework that tells you to light the blue touch paper and retire!

10c) Swedes fired arrows into their corpses, though we don't know why. (This is better than corpses firing arrows into swedes which would be a real turnip for the book.) They buried their dead with loving care in graves in the earth and in log canoes under water. Firing arrows into a body can't have been an insult. It must have had some special meaning – maybe it punctured the skin and let the spirit out … or maybe it was just easy target practice.

Awful archaeologists

Modern humans have been digging up ancient humans for hundreds of years and trying to work out the answer to the big question…

The diggers-up-of-the-past don't think being called 'diggers-up-of-the-past' is a posh enough name, so they call themselves *archaeologists*.

Ancient horrible historical joke 1:
The mystery writer Agatha Christie was married to an archaeologist and cracked the following joke…

An archaeologist is the best husband any woman can have: the older she gets, the more interested he is in her.

Don't blame me. I never said it was a *good* joke.

Ancient horrible historical joke 2:
An archaeologist's joke is no better…

Clearly some archaeologists have sad lives.

Battles over the birth of the Earth

The Bible says that God created the universe in six days, then had a kip on the seventh.

His last great creation was to take a lump of clay and make a man. Finally He breathed up the clay man's nostrils and brought him to life. (Yeuch! How would you like someone breathing up your nostrils?) The man was called Adam.

Early historians were interested in the actual date that God had blown up Adam's nose and risked a mouth full of snot. Perhaps every human on Earth could have a big birthday party on that day! Sadly, they couldn't agree on the year, never mind the day. The world began in…

Roman Catholics went back further. They said God made Earth in 5199 BC.

They were very annoyed when archaeologists tried to tell them they were wrong...

In 1616 the Italian thinker Lucilio Vanini said that humans evolved from apes. Church leaders went ape at the idea, decided to teach him a lesson and had him burned alive.

The archaeologists produced stones that had been shaped by prehistoric humans – arrowheads, for example. Those who believed in the Bible had different explanations...

Archaeologists showed these weapons had been found alongside creatures (like mammoths) that had been dead for hundreds of thousands of years. But until 1847 they didn't believe humans and mammoths lived on Earth at the same time. They did!

Even ancient dinosaur bones, millions of years old, could also be explained by the Bible believers...

These ancient bones were believed to have magical powers. They were set in gold rings and sold as lucky charms or ground into powder to make miraculous medicines.

When settlers from Europe saw Native American Indians using similar arrowheads they got the message. In 1699 Edward Lhwyd wrote...

These arrowheads were once used for shooting in Britain as they still are in America. Some foolish people say they have seen them drop out of the air, shot by fairies. I will believe that when I see it for myself.

In the 1600s, some scientists put together a collection of prehistoric bones and came up with this image…

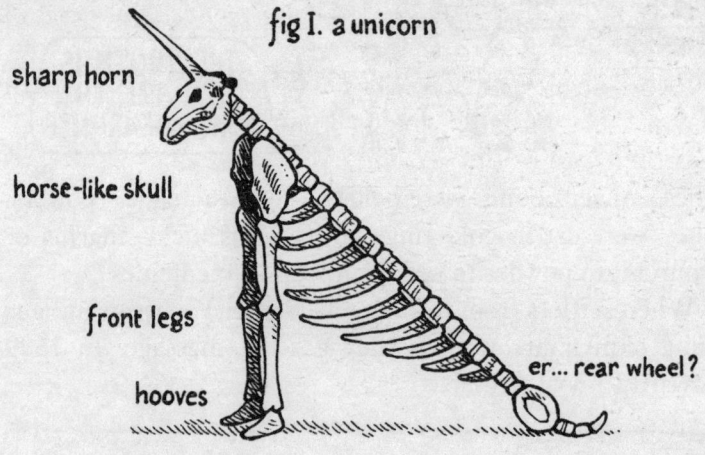

fig I. a unicorn

sharp horn

horse-like skull

front legs

hooves

er… rear wheel?

Until the late 1850s some scientists and historians still argued that the Earth was about 6,000 years old.

Not an Irish joke!

In 1857, a workman was digging in a cave in a quarry in the Neander Valley in Germany (*Neanderthal* in German). He found an old skeleton deep in the clay.

His workmates were about to throw it away when the quarry manager rescued it. He took it to a local teacher to see if he knew what it was. The skull had a low forehead and thick ridges above the eyes. The teacher said, 'I recognize this!' (No, it wasn't from

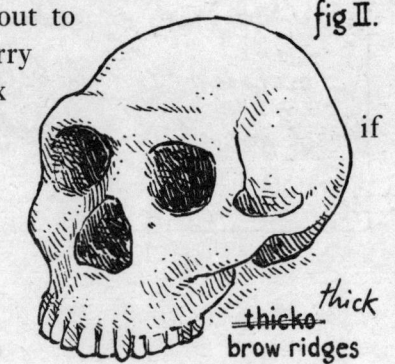

fig II.

~~thicko~~ *thick* brow ridges

looking in the mirror!) 'Look at those thick ridges over the brows – just like a gorilla. This is an ancient type of human!' He was right, of course, but not many people believed him at first.

The disbelievers said, 'This is the skull of a modern human – but it's either an idiot ... or an Irishman!'

If these people thought the Irish were Stone-Agers then *they* were the idiots, not the Irish!

Nasty Neanderthals

During the Stone Age there were two main types of hominid – *Homo sapiens* (they were your ancestors), and Neanderthals, who had flat heads, a thick bony bulge over the eyes, short legs and some very nasty habits. You'll be pleased to know that Neanderthals died out, so you needn't have nightmares about being nobbled by a Neanderthal in the night.

The nasty Neanderthals seem to have been head-hunters. Here's the evidence…

- Neanderthal skulls have been found which show they were clubbed to death.
- The base of the skulls had been opened up to get the brains out ... to eat? Or so the killer could get the strength and wisdom from the victim's brain?

- Neanderthals dug two pits in the floor of a cave and packed them with skulls. The skulls had been hacked from the

49

bodies, brought to the cave one at a time and packed in so they all faced the sunset.

- The 20 children and nine young women in these pits were buried with ornaments made of deer's teeth and snails' shells.

Just in case you think the head-hackers took the brain-boxes off bodies that had died naturally, consider this bit of evidence:

- At least five of the skulls' owners had been killed by hatchet blows to the head.

Neanderthals have been accused of being cannibals. The evidence for this is not so strong...

- Human bones have been found mixed with left-over food.
- Human bones have been smashed, perhaps to extract the tasty marrow inside.
- Human bones have been scorched by fire as if they were cooked.

Not exactly 'proof'. But if you meet someone with a flat head and short legs and they say...

I'D LIKE TO HAVE YOU OVER TO MY CAVE FOR DINNER!

… it may be wise to say, 'Thanks – but no thanks!' just to be on the safe side.

And it wasn't only humans who were sacrificed and beheaded. Twenty bears' skeletons were buried in a pit in France and in the Alps seven bears' skulls were stored in a stone chest. All of the bears' muzzles pointed towards the door. Weird, huh?

In Poland, the Neanderthals decorated their cave walls with bears' skulls while German Neanderthals kept a captive bear and filed its front teeth down to make it safer … not that it's safe trying to file a bear's teeth because it still has slashing claws. (Before you even consider doing this to a bear in your back garden … paws!)

Japanese Stone-Agers captured young bears, filed their teeth and later killed them in some sort of ceremony. 50,000 years later and humans still love their teddy bears. Nothing changes, does it?

Awesome archaeologists

In the 1800s archaeologists weren't scientists. Some were really curious about the past – like you are or you wouldn't be reading this book. But many were treasure hunters seeking lots of money and lots of glory. The money would be hidden gold and the glory would be in uncovering some great secrets of the past like...

• whatever happened to dinosaurs?
• was there really a Wooden Horse of Troy?
• who invented the wheel?

These great puzzles are still unsolved today. Though we can make some good guesses, can't we?

Victorian archaeologists were a bit like Indiana Jones ... fighting their way through dangers to uncover treasures from the past. They were also a bit like Attila the Hun – leading armies into other lands to pinch their wealth.

Sir Austen Henry Layard (1817–1894) led armies of workers into Iraq, tunnelled into ancient palaces and packed the greatest finds off to Britain. (They can still be seen in the British Museum, which refuses to give them back to the countries they were stolen from.)

It wasn't only the British who robbed ancient sites, of course. In some countries it was a full-time job!

Piecing together the past
Archaeologists who investigated the Stone Age weren't so popular. After all, they didn't bring home treasure. And it was hard work! Take this simple story from an archaeologist's notebook, for example…

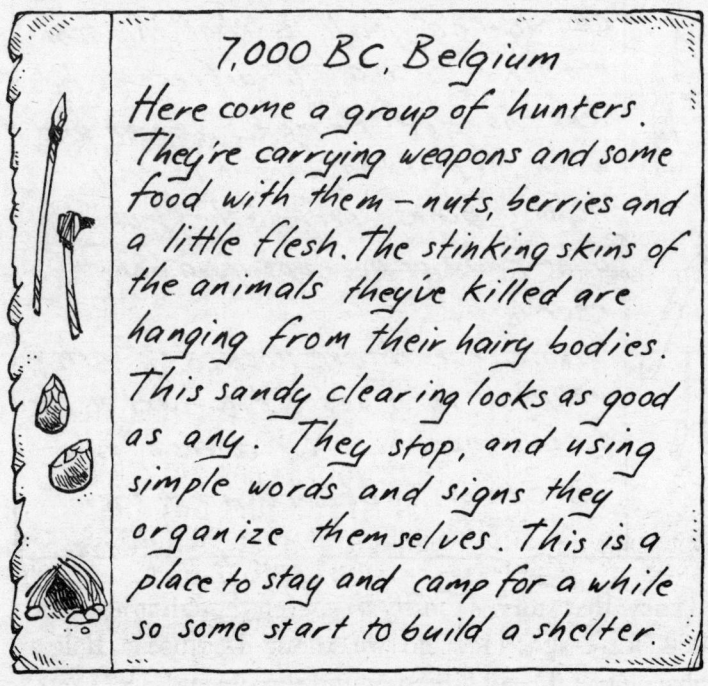

7,000 BC, Belgium

Here come a group of hunters. They're carrying weapons and some food with them – nuts, berries and a little flesh. The stinking skins of the animals they've killed are hanging from their hairy bodies. This sandy clearing looks as good as any. They stop, and using simple words and signs they organize themselves. This is a place to stay and camp for a while so some start to build a shelter.

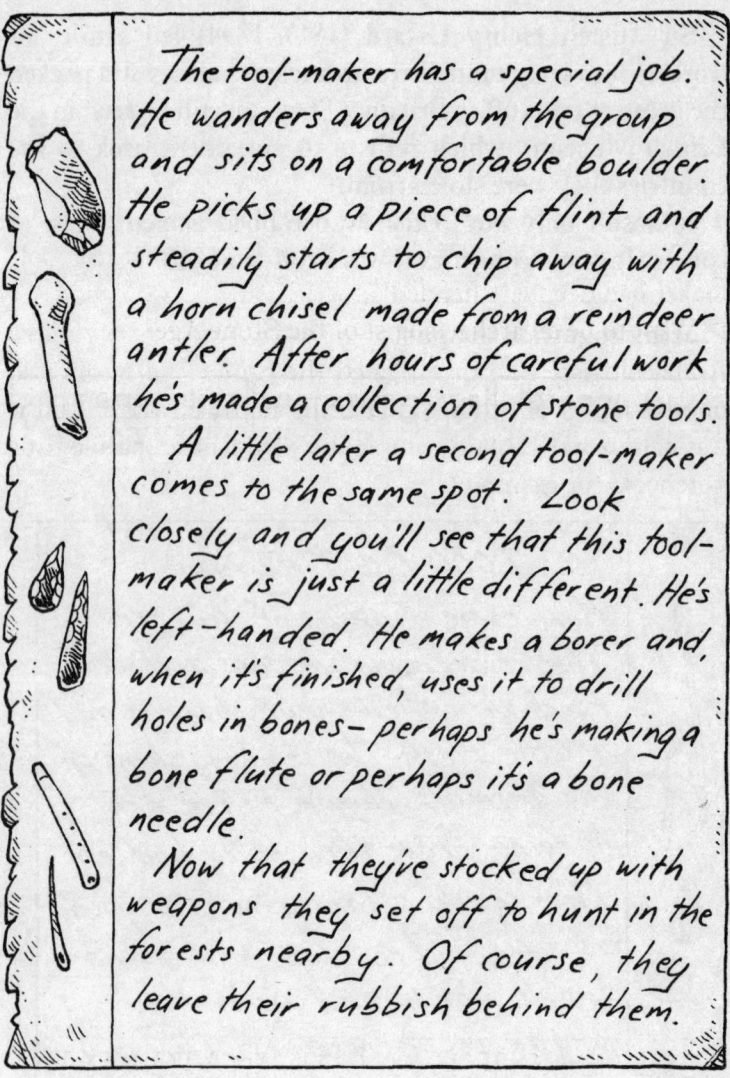

The tool-maker has a special job. He wanders away from the group and sits on a comfortable boulder. He picks up a piece of flint and steadily starts to chip away with a horn chisel made from a reindeer antler. After hours of careful work he's made a collection of stone tools.

A little later a second tool-maker comes to the same spot. Look closely and you'll see that this tool-maker is just a little different. He's left-handed. He makes a borer and, when it's finished, uses it to drill holes in bones—perhaps he's making a bone flute or perhaps it's a bone needle.

Now that they've stocked up with weapons they set off to hunt in the forests nearby. Of course, they leave their rubbish behind them.

We know that story is mostly *true*, even though it happened 9,000 years ago. How do we know? Because a Belgian archaeologist, David Cahen, found the site and…

- Marked the position of every fragment of stone.
- Put all the fragments back together again like a 3-D jigsaw puzzle.
- Examined the borer under a microscope and saw where it had been worn by the bone.

This took him *months*! He even saw that one of the borers had been used anticlockwise and worked out that the tool-maker had been left-handed!

Want to be an archaeologist of the Stone Age?

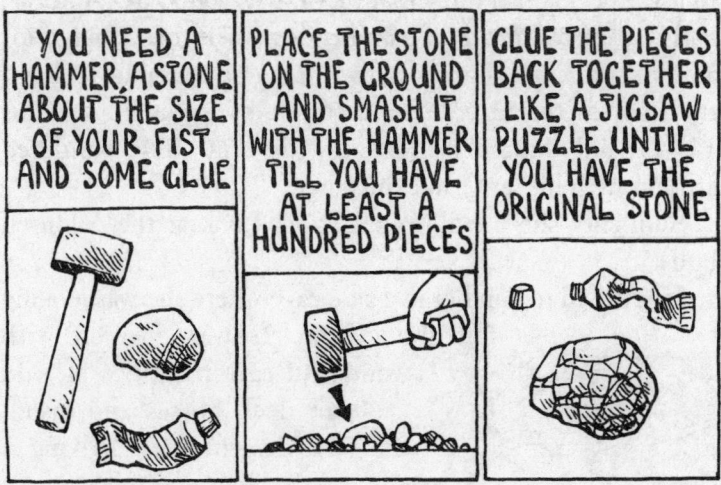

It shouldn't take you much more than a month. Do you *still* want to be an archaeologist?

Quick question:

Archaeological accidents

You may think those old archaeologists knew what they were doing when they set out to dig for ancient evidence. But some searched for years and found very little – others found amazing new things by accident.

If you want to be an archaeologist then try some of these unusual methods:

1 Take your daughter digging

In 1859, a Spanish nobleman, Don Marcelino de Sautuola, had been searching a cave on his estate. He was looking for animal bones and flint tools, so where else would he look but the floor of the cave? After a couple of weeks he took his 12-year-old daughter, Maria, with him. She wandered around with his lantern, exploring.

Suddenly she cried, 'Papa! Papa! Look at the coloured bulls!'

He rushed to join her in a side cave where she was looking at the ceiling. It was covered with wonderful cave paintings of wild boar, deer, horses and bison. He'd spent weeks looking at the floor and failed to see the art on the roof of the ceiling.

At first no one believed these were paintings done by cave-dwellers. They said they'd been done by the Don. (And, let's face it, his story

56

of failing to see the paintings is a bit odd.) It was over 30 years before more cave art was found, in France, and he was finally believed by everyone. The trouble is the Don had died by then. He died knowing everyone was calling him a liar.

The professors said 'Sorry' to Maria instead.

2 Hound hunting

During the Second World War four teenage boys were hunting in woods in France. The loutish lads were tracking a wounded bird with their dog. Suddenly the dog vanished into a hole at the foot of a cliff face. The boys crawled in to explore and discovered a hole in the ground that the dog had fallen into. They dropped stones and discovered the hole wasn't too deep. (Some stones would have fallen on the hound's head, wouldn't they?) They climbed down and rescued the dog.

The hole was the entrance to a cave and they had discovered one of the greatest cave-art displays of all time – the Lascaux caves. There were 1,500 engravings and 600 paintings, including bulls five metres long – imagine the sausages you could make from a bull like that!

The boys kept their secret for a week and returned with bicycle lamps to explore further before they told the local teacher, Leon Laval. He didn't believe their story at first!

What a distrustful teacher!

The caves were finally examined by experts who said the paintings were 17,000 years old. Well done, lads!

Visitors flocked in. They carried with them germs that formed a green mould all over the ancient artwork. Paintings that had survived 17,000 years were in danger of vanishing in 17! They were closed and sealed.

But ... there are rumours that the boys' hunting tale was a lie. One story says they were looking for a cave that an old woman had told them about. Why lie about it?

One possible explanation is that the boys didn't want to share the 'prize' with an old woman. And the prize was that the boys got comfortable jobs guiding visitors through the caves ... while the teacher got the best job of all. He was put in charge!

3 Catch butterflies
Olduvai Gorge, in west Africa, was first explored by a scientist in 1911 when a German called Doctor Kattwinkel (honest!) went looking for butterflies, not bones. He picked

up some curious fossil bones and sent them back to Germany to be examined. The Germans were excited by the discovery and sent archaeologists out to dig. Olduvai Gorge became one of the greatest areas for finding fossil hominids.

When the archaeologists started digging it's certain they didn't use caterpillar tractors. (Caterpillar – butterfly! Geddit? Oh, never mind.)

4 Walk the dog

The German investigations were interrupted by the First World War. A British family moved in, the Leakey family (Louis, Mary and their son Richard), and made some of the greatest discoveries of all time. But they still needed a lot of Kattwinkel's luck.

The Leakeys found lots of animal bones and stone tools but no human remains, though they searched for 30 years. Then one morning Mary took her Dalmatian dogs for a walk away from the camp. She saw bones sticking out from the ground where rains had washed away the soil. They were the bones of the oldest man ever found. He was nicknamed 'Nutcracker Man' because of his powerful teeth.

IT MUST HAVE RAINED KATTWINKELS AND DOGS! BOOM! BOOM!

IF THEY WERE DALMATIANS, THEY PROBABLY 'SPOTTED' THE BONES FIRST! HO! HO!

NUTCRACKER MAN LIVES ON... IN THIS VERY ROOM

5 Raft craft

In 1912 the adventurous sons of Count Begouen decided to explore an underground river called the Volp. (Warning: don't explore underground rivers like the Volp. If you get trapped you'll not get any holp.)

The boys used gas bottles as floats and wooden crates to build a raft on top. Their boat drifted into a cave. They reached a cliff and climbed it up to a gallery. They discovered some ancient cave art in the gallery and moved on.

The passage became a chimney in the rock which they struggled up – into a second gallery that hadn't been seen by humans since the last Ice Age.

The boys spotted claw marks of cave bears, old bones and even Stone Age footprints on the damp floor. They also found clay models of bison – the first ever find of Stone Age sculptures.

The case of the exploding coffin

Accidents don't *always* help archaeologists. Sometimes accidents happen to these daring diggers ... and they can be pretty gruesome, as this story from the north-east of England shows.

Dear Erica,

Don't laugh. It isn't funny. I know you've heard the story from our friends but you should hear my side of the story.

As you know we were up here investigating a medieval cemetery when we came across a wooden coffin. It took us most of the day to raise it to the side of the trench. We lowered it to the ground but a rope slipped and it had a bumpy landing. That's when we heard a hissing sound coming from the coffin. The professor cried 'Run!' and we turned our backs and scattered for cover.

I guess I was about ten metres from the coffin when it exploded. Something soft smacked into the back of my jacket. The blast blew me forward on to my hands and knees but I wasn't hurt, you'll be pleased to hear.

I stood up and took off my jacket to see what had hit me. I stared at the jacket and the jacket stared back! A medieval eyeball had been blown from the corpse and hit me. For some reason my so-called friends thought this was hilarious! But no one offered to pull the eyeball off!

That's not the end of the story. I had to give a talk to a local church society about our excavations in their graveyard. I explained, 'The gases given off by the rotting body combined with the lead lining of the coffin to make an explosive gas!'

An old lady in the second row stood up, shaking like a leaf, and moaning, 'Ooooh! Me uncle Albert's buried in a lead-lined coffin! Is he going to explode?'

She had a picture of exploding coffins popping off in every graveyard in the country!

As I say, it is NOT funny. But you have to laugh.

See you soon.

Love

Annie

But there are worse things than exploding coffins for some archaeologists. One disaster is being proved wrong, as this sad story shows...

Dead drop

Archaeologists are making new discoveries all the time. Some of these prove that the old ideas were mistaken. This is bad luck if you've spent a lifetime teaching students one thing only to discover you were wrong all along. That's what happened to one famous archaeologist in Austria in 1957...

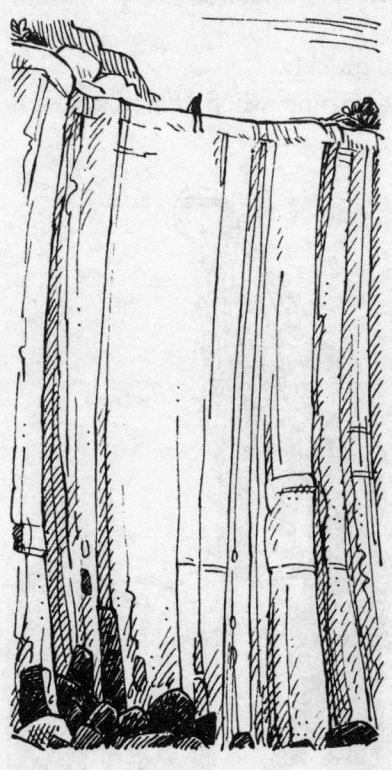

The old man lowered himself on to the ledge and looked down at the sheer drop below him. In the fading light the boulders far below him looked like pebbles. His feet hung over the edge and he shuffled forward till all that stopped him from tumbling over were his hands on the dusty trail.

He didn't see the young woman with the rucksack rounding the bend in the trail. 'Hey!' she cried. 'Be careful! You'll fall!'

The old man didn't turn or look at her. His

lank grey hair blew in the warm summer evening air and his thin body seemed to sway. The girl with the nut-brown skin knew there was something wrong. She dropped her rucksack on to the path and stepped carefully towards the man. He shifted forward till he was perched on the very edge. She stopped. She licked her dry lips and said quietly, 'No.'

For a long time they both remained still. Then the old man spoke in a firm voice. 'Good evening.'

'Good evening. Nice evening,' she replied nervously. 'I'm Ellie Griffiths.'

'And my name is Katz. Professor Gerhardt Katz. You may have heard of me?'

'No,' she said quickly. Too quickly.

He frowned. 'There was a time when that name was known around the world.'

'Really?'

'Really. For 40 years I was one of the most respected names in archaeology, you know. My books were used by colleges all over the world.'

'Wow,' Ellie said gently. 'I'll have to look out for them.'

'Don't bother,' the man said, suddenly bitter. He turned and looked at her for the first time.

She squatted on the ground and smiled. 'Tell me about them.'

He sighed. 'I looked at all the evidence and I came up with a new idea. I proved that 3,000 years ago the climate of the world became warmer and drier. There was a terrible drought across the Earth. The hunters couldn't wander across the deserts of the Middle East. All the animals would gather at a watering-hole – what they call an oasis. So human hunters began to gather at these watering-holes.'

'That makes sense,' the girl nodded.

The old man stared into the empty sky and went on eagerly: 'I could see what would happen next. Stone Age humans stopped being wandering hunters and they began to settle. They built houses and the houses gathered into villages and the villages became the world's first cities. They planted crops, they herded sheep and goats.'

'They made the world's first farms,' Ellie nodded and shifted slightly so she was closer to the man on the edge.

'That's what I told the world. I gave lectures on every continent. No one was more famous than me in archaeology. No one!' he said and sighed.

'What went wrong?' the girl asked and rested her weight on one hand. She used it to pull herself closer.

'A man called Libby had worked on the atomic bombs that could destroy the world in 1945. Then in 1949 he created the bomb that destroyed me. He invented carbon dating. Ever heard of it?'

'Yes. It's a way of telling how old things are,' the girl murmured.

'Suddenly archaeologists had a way of telling how old their finds were. A woman called Kathleen Kenyon was digging at Jericho and found an early farm village. Of course she was able to carbon-date it. Farmers worked there in 7,500 BC! Imagine that! They'd been farming thousands of years before I'd said they had. My life's work was ruined! Ruined!'

The man moaned and shifted forward so he barely sat on the ledge. If he leaned forward he would be gone. Ellie Griffiths held her breath. Then she whispered, 'No! You were right about the other things!'

'One by one my ideas were destroyed. Farming didn't start at the watering-holes – it started in Palestine. And they didn't plant crops. Not for 2,000 years.

They simply stayed in one place and learned to live off the wild grasses that grew there every year – they didn't plough and plant seeds the way I said they had. I was wrong, wrong, wrong!' he moaned.

Ellie edged closer. She couldn't think what to say. He turned suddenly and stared at her wildly, his faded eyes filled with tears. 'My whole life has been wasted! You see why I have to do this!'

'No.'

'I used to walk here when I was a young man. I know this place well. No one who goes over the edge ever comes back. No one. Wasted. Whole life.'

Ellie reached out a hand and her fingertips brushed the sleeve of his jacket. He snatched his arm away, twisted and gave a small sob as he fell. The girl grasped at the air where the old man had been.

It was a long time before she could move, before she could bring herself to look over the ledge to the pitiless rocks below.

Super science
The old archaeologist committed suicide because new methods of archaeology were making his books look out of date. Yet many of his ideas were brilliant and are still studied today.

The carbon-14 dating system that upset him so much was indeed invented by nuclear bomb scientists. They found that...

• All living plants are bombarded by radioactivity from outer space.
• Anything that eats vegetables takes on the radioactivity. (Yes! That includes *you*!)

- You have one of these carbon-14 atoms for every trillion ordinary carbon atoms.
- After death, this radioactive material (carbon-14) takes about 5,568 years for half of it to go away.
- So if an archaeologist digs up a plant or animal that has half its carbon-14 then it is 5,568 years old. Geddit?

If you want to try counting trillions of carbon atoms to find the carbon-14 then you can.

It's easier to let a machine called an *accelerator mass spectrometer* do it. All you need is a few million dollars to buy it and a few million volts of electricity to make it work!

Radiocarbon dating may be expensive ... but it could be worth it to find out if your teacher is lying about her age!

ONE, TWO, THREE, FOUR, FIVE

Silly science
On 13 May 1983 two workmen were cutting peat in a bog when they uncovered a dead body. The police were told about it and the find was reported in the newspapers.

A local man came forward and confessed that he had murdered his wife and disposed of her body in the bog back in 1960. He went to prison for the crime. But archaeologists who examined the body said that this particular corpse was almost 2,000 years old. They used radiocarbon dating.

Oooops! The man had got away with murder for 23 years and the bog body made him panic into going to the police. His wife's corpse is still missing.

Or is it...? In 1998 a row broke out over the dead head.

29 March 1998 £2·50

Archaeology Weekly

BIG BATTLE OVER BOG BODY

'MUSEUM EXPERTS ARE MUGS' SAYS TOP DOC

Archaeologists at the British Museum are furious over reports that they've made a major mistake. A head that they dated as being 2,000 years old is said to be the victim of a 38-year-old murder.

In 1960 Edmund Roberts murdered his wife Maria and hid the body in Lindow bog. Police suspected him but couldn't prove he'd anything to do with his wife's disappearance. Then, in 1983, two peat-diggers uncovered a body and Roberts owned up. 'It's my wife. I killed her and buried her there,' he said.

He was sentenced to life imprisonment even though British Museum scientists dated the corpse using the radiocarbon method and declared, 'It's been in the bog nearly 2,000 years!'

Bog Body

Now a doctor has come forward to state that they've made a major mistake. Professor Bob Conway of Manchester University says,

'I've compared pictures of the skull with pictures of the dead woman and they match. Anyway, the body in the bog was in too good a condition to belong to an ancient Briton. There was skin attached and almost a complete eyeball. You just don't get that with an old corpse – not even one preserved in a bog.'

Lindow Bog is close to Manchester Airport and is sprayed with aircraft fuel every day. Professor Conway says that could cause the radiocarbon tests to be wildly wrong. He demanded that the British Museum should hand the skull over for further tests.

A spokesperson for the British Museum says, 'There is no chance that our tests could be wrong. The skull is in the basement of the museum and there it will stay.'

The professor and eye

Radiocarbon dating has become widely used since it was invented in 1946. Much of what historians tell us about prehistory depends on radiocarbon dating being right.

What if the method can make horrible historical mistakes? It would be disastrous for archaeology.

Why won't the museum hand over the mysterious skull? Are they afraid they may be proved *wrong*?

Lousy life

You too could live like a Stone Age person – but you'd have to give up chocolate and television. Here are a few helpful hints…

Preserving pensioners 1

The first large town in the world was probably Jericho in Palestine. The people of Stone Age Jericho (around 7,300 to 6,300 BC) seemed to love their wrinklies. They didn't stick them in an old people's home or bury them in some forgotten graveyard. No, they kept them at home, even after they were dead.

And, if they had no photographs to remind them of their glamorous granny's fabulous face, they had another way of dealing with their dead.

If there had been children's television 9,000 years ago it may have looked something like this…

1. Remember, boys and girls, always have a grown-up around if a sharp knife is being used. It's much more fun to let them cut themselves.

FIRST CAREFULLY CUT OFF THE HEAD OF THE CORPSE AND PUT IT TO ONE SIDE. THEN DIG A HOLE ABOUT ONE METRE DEEP IN THE FLOOR OF YOUR HOUSE AND BURY THE BODY

NOW REMOVE THE SKIN AND BRAINS FROM THE HEAD TILL YOU ARE LEFT WITH A CLEAN SKULL. DON'T FORGET TO BURY THOSE BRAINS SO MUM DOESN'T HAVE TO TIDY THEM UP AFTER YOU!

FILL THE SKULL WITH SOME OF THE PLASTER. USE MORE PLASTER TO BUILD UP THE FACE OF THE DEAD PERSON TILL IT LOOKS JUST LIKE THEY DID IN LIFE

USE TWO SHELLS FOR THE EYES AND PLACE THE HEAD ON A PLASTER STAND. HERE'S ONE I MADE EARLIER

And if the dead person had a moustache when he (or she) was alive, then you could paint a moustache on to the clay head.

Some archaeologists believe the whole body was buried for a few months until the flesh was rotten. Then it was dug up again and the head removed. The rotten flesh would fall off the skull and make it easier to clean. This is a nice job for someone with no sense of smell.

One group of four Palestine heads were buried together. It looks as if a couple of children were taken to the funeral and sacrificed to the dead. That's one way of keeping class sizes down, I suppose.

Preserving pensioners 2

Around 3,000 BC the Egyptians started turning their dead kings and queens into mummies. But they weren't the first people to make mummies. Three thousand years before – and on the other side of the world – one group of Stone Age people were making very different types of mummies.

Between 6,000 and 1,500 BC the Chinchorro people of northern Chile were mummifying their dead. The special skills must have been passed down from parents to children. It would have been easier if they'd had schools, exercise books and teachers, of course...

Making a mummy just like Mummy used to make

1. First cut off the head, arms and legs. (Handy hint: make sure the person is dead first.)

2. Skin the body parts and put the skin ~~too~~ to one side to be used later on. (Handy hint: skin on legs can be rolled down like stockings.)

3. Empty the body of all the soft parts and fill it with hot coals or sand to dry it out. (Handy hint: don't make the coals too hot or you'll have cooked corpse.)

4. Slice open the arms and legs, take out the bones, scrape and clean them. (Handy hint: make sure your pet dog doesn't chew on the bones.)

5. Lash sticks to the bones and replace them. Place long sticks inside the body to attach the legs, arms and head. (Handy hint: a good mummy will be so stiff it can stand as straight as you.)

6. Pack the body with grass and ashes so

it looks the same shape as it was when it was alive. (Handy hint: use cold ashes or you'll set fire to the grass and end up with a charred Chinchorro.)

7. Assemble the body and cover it with a paste made from white ash. Model it to the shape of the dead person — including the face and the naughty bits. (Handy hint: wash your hands after handling the naughty bits.)

8. Put the skin back over the body. Don't forget the hair on the head. (Handy ~~boo~~ hint: check for nits.)

9. Paint the whole body in black using special paint. Use different colours for the eyes, lips and eyebrows. (Handy hint: use your mother's make-up... or your father's.)

10. Dress the mummy in the clothes it wore in life.

—Homework—practise on a rat.

Some Chinchorro mummies were painted red. Others were made without removing the arms and legs. Simple mummies were preserved by smoking them (like bacon) and then covering the corpse in mud.

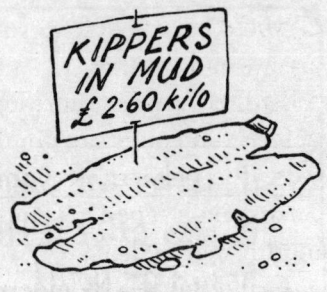

We'll probably never know why the Chinchorro people mummified their dead, but there are two interesting clues...
• The sticks inside allowed the mummies to be stood up.
• Many were repainted several times.
One idea is that the mummies were taken out for special occasions so the dead Chinchorro ancestors could watch over important ceremonies. If your grandparents had thought of mummifying your Victorian ancestors, then they could be taken along to your wedding ... or your school sports day ... to give their blessing and support!

Doctor, doctor!

The Stone Age was a dangerous age. No chance of being run down by a Range Rover on the road to school ... but there were things nearly as dangerous in those days. If the mammoths didn't mash you then a bear might bash you, and all you'd have to defend yourself with would be flint-headed arrows and spears.

Animal attacks, accidents and illnesses could kill you before you could say, 'Is there a doctor in the cave?' What were the chances of finding a doctor in the Stone Age? Surprisingly good … and they probably didn't have six-month waiting lists!

Could you be a Neanderthal nurse or a Stone Age surgeon? Try matching the sickness to the cure…

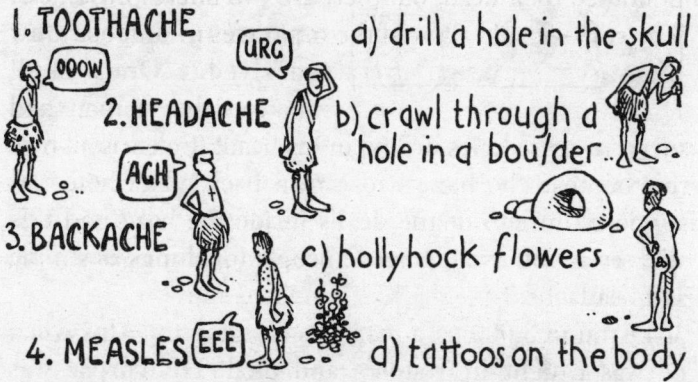

1. TOOTHACHE (OOOW) (URG)   a) drill a hole in the *skull*

2. HEADACHE   b) crawl through a hole in a boulder

(AGH)

3. BACKACHE   c) hollyhock flowers

4. MEASLES (EEE)   d) tattoos on the body

Answers:

1c) All the types of flowers found in a Neanderthal grave in Iraq have been used to make medicines in modern times. So they probably weren't just put there for decoration – they were put there to help the corpse in the next life. Hollyhocks were used to cure toothache. Obviously there are no dentists in the afterlife so we have that to look forward to!

2a) The first brain surgeons lived in the New Stone Age. They were able to peel back the scalp with stone knives

then drill holes in the skull with a sharp flint drill. This would be used to release the pressure of swollen brain or to fix a caved-in skull. Most of the victims would die after this sort of operation, but a few survived. One skull showed that a man had survived *seven* holes drilled in his head! (Scientists know this because the bone had grown back.) The hole was supposed to let out the devils inside the head and this surgery is still used by some people for things as simple as a headache.

3d) Around 3,000 BC a man was crossing the Alps when he was caught in a storm and died. His corpse was preserved in ice and discovered by hikers in 1991. It's the oldest fully preserved human body ever found. It would have been in perfect condition if the workmen sent to collect him hadn't used a pneumatic drill to break him from the ice and shattered his hip. They also managed to break his arm by forcing him into a coffin. X-rays show he had arthritis that would have made his neck and back ache. There are tattoos on his leathery skin – parallel, vertical blue lines on both sides of his spine where he must have felt pain. It seems likely that the tattoos were meant to cure the back pain. There is no cure for pains in the neck who attack you with pneumatic drills!

4b) Some stones have natural holes in them and children are still sent to crawl through the holes as a cure for things like measles, whooping cough and other diseases. We can guess that this custom goes back to the Stone Age when the stones were set up inside a stone circle. At Dingwall in the Scottish Highlands the child's clothes are passed through the hole first and then the child. Imagine how embarrassed you'd be!

Terrible trepanning

Drilling a hole in the skull to cure a brain problem is called 'trepanning'. It seems crazy and cruel to us. You may think it's the sort of thing only a Stone-Ager could do. You'd be wrong!

In 1962, the Dutch doctor Bart Hughes put forward the idea that a hole in the skull keeps you young. He used an electric drill to make a hole in his own head. He survived the drilling but was locked away in a Dutch mental hospital.

But three years later a British student, Joe Mallam, met the daft Dutch doctor and decided to try trepanning for himself. He had a painkilling injection in the scalp (which Stone-Agers didn't have) but he had no help – the Dutch doc was refused entry into Britain … probably because Britain already has enough mad doctors.

At his first attempt, Joe collapsed and ended up in hospital. But the next time he succeeded. You don't want to know what happened next. Skip the rest of this section and go on to the next ... or have a sick-bucket handy. Joe described his scientific breakthrough – or his skull-entific breakthrough.

> *After some time there was a grim sounding schlurp and the sound of bubbling. I drew the drill out and the gurgling continued. It sounded like air bubbles rising under the skull as they were pressed out. I looked at the drill and there was a bit of bone in it.*
> *At last! If only I had an electric drill it would have been much simpler. I bandaged up my head and cleared away the mess.*

Don't try this at home ... even if your dad's bald spot *does* look in need of a hole.

Fighting farmers

By 5,000 BC Stone-Agers had begun to settle in Europe to farm the land. The wandering hunters stopped wandering, stayed in one place and built villages, herded cattle, planted crops and made pottery.

Peaceful. Right?

Wrong.

Many of the villages were protected by ditches and wooden walls. Historians guessed that the farmers had to protect themselves against the Stone-Agers who hadn't settled – the ones who still wandered the land, hunting animals and gathering plants.

But the historians were just *guessing*. The truth was finally discovered in 1983. A man in Talheim, Germany, was digging in his garden when he uncovered some bones ... human bones!

The man told the police, who realized the bones were ancient. They called in the archaeologists, who made some gruesome discoveries.

• there were 34 skeletons in a pit
• they had all died violently
• most of them had their skulls smashed by clubs – some had a hole smashed through
• there were signs of some being hit by flint arrows
• almost half of the victims were children and one was over 60 – very old for a Stone-Ager
• seven of the adults were female

This *wasn't* a funeral site – these farming people had been massacred, then dumped there in a mass grave.

The skulls had been smashed with stone axes that the farmers used. So this *wasn't* an attack by a wandering band of hunters.

This was one farming group wiped out by another.

We'll never know what they argued about. Land? Animals? Mates?

But it does look as if Stone Age farmers didn't always have the peaceful life prehistorians had once imagined.

The Talheim pit shows that 7,000 years ago humans weren't just learning the special human arts of farming and making pottery. They were learning that other quaint human custom that we know so well in the 20th century – the nasty little habit of mass murder.

> *When you're fighting a war being right doesn't matter. It is winning!*[1]

Dead unlucky

In prehistoric USA there was a massacre of a tribe in what is now known as South Dakota. There were few women and children found by archaeologists amongst the skeletons, so they may have been taken prisoner.

Many of the bodies had been chopped up after death – the hands and feet cut off and the heads scalped so the winners could take the hair as a prize.

But the unluckiest man was one who had been scalped a few years before the attack. His head had healed and he'd survived that first scalping. He must have thought his luck was in until the sad slap-head was attacked and scalped again.

He didn't survive the second time.

1. Actual words spoken by a mass murderer 7,000 years after the Talheim massacre. Imagine that! The mind of a Stone-Ager in the body of a 20th century national leader. There aren't any of those around today … are there?

Rotten rituals

If you lived in the Stone Age, then you worried about the weather. A bad harvest meant starvation. There were no Stone Age supermarkets to stock up your larder.

The weather is a matter of luck. But the Stone-Agers believed there were ways you could bring yourself good luck in this life and the next life.

The ancient Greeks and Egyptians had their 'gods'. But Stone-Agers seemed to worship their dead ancestors whose spirits had travelled to an afterlife.

It was important to keep your dead ancestors happy. Look after their spirits and the spirits will look after you.

First you had to release the spirit from the dead body it is trapped in. The spirit could only leave when the flesh is falling off the bones. So, you can wait till your friend's/Dad's/teacher's corpse has gone mouldy and then bury it. If you want to speed things up you can help him or her by hacking the flesh off the body with a stone knife or leaving it outside for animals and birds to pick clean.

BUT I'M NOT DEAD!

PERHAPS... BUT YOU'RE NOT VERY WELL

In Denmark, there are marks on one corpse that show it was scalped before death. This could have been to let the spirit out – or it could have been an attempt by a hungry

Stone-Ager to get *in* and steal the brain to eat it. (Minced up with a small onion and fried, you'd have a tasty Stone-Age brain-burger! Yummy!)

Of course, keeping the spirits happy needed some revolting rituals...

Funeral stew

On Anglesey, in Wales, there's a stone burial chamber called Barclodiad y Gawres. Archaeologists have worked out the revolting ritual that went on at the funeral of two boys...

• The bodies were cremated till the flesh burned off.

• The bones were scraped, mixed with sheep bones and buried under a layer of earth.

• Inside the chamber, a fire was lit under a water pot.

• A stew was stirred into the water…

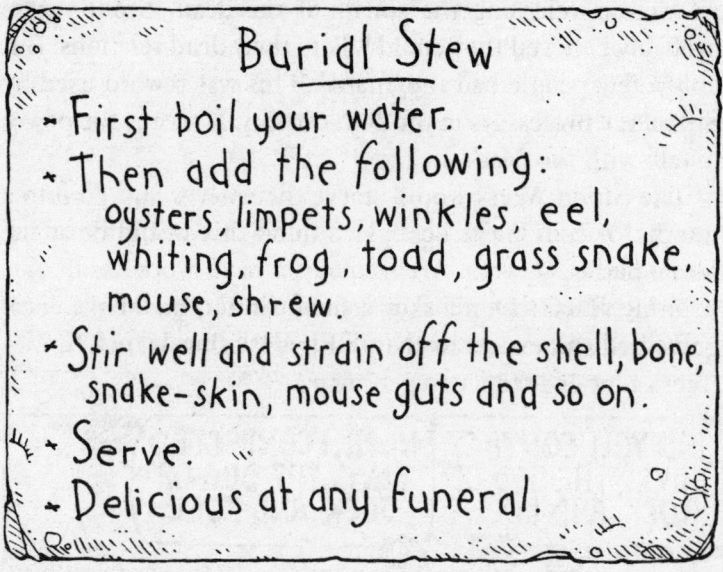

Burial Stew

- First boil your water.
- Then add the following:
  oysters, limpets, winkles, eel,
  whiting, frog, toad, grass snake,
  mouse, shrew.
- Stir well and strain off the shell, bone,
  snake-skin, mouse guts and so on.
- Serve.
- Delicious at any funeral.

The rubbish left from the tasty soup was poured on to the dying fire and trampled down to put it out.

Did you know…?
A curious custom among Australian Stone-Agers was for men to have their front two teeth knocked out. This was done when they grew up and seems to have been a sign of becoming a man.

Good manas

As well as releasing the spirits of the dead, Stone-Agers probably believed they could talk to their dead relations. But only a few people had the 'mana'. This was a word used by Stone Age professors in the 20th century. It means the power to talk with the dead.

The Stone-Agers would starve themselves and go into a trance. Of course the best place to do this would be at the burial places.

WARNING: Don't skip school dinner, go to the local graveyard and expect to chat to Elvis Presley. It took Stone-Agers a lot of practice to get 'mana'.

DID YOU CONTACT ELVIS, THE GOD OF ROCK AND ROLL?

NOPE. I CONTACTED ELVIS, THE DOG OF JOCK AND JOEL

THANGYOUVRYMUCH

Christians who worship in a church today have their dead buried all around them in the churchyard. But Stone-Agers often buried the bones of their dead in one place and worshipped in another. In western Europe you would walk up a long straight path edged with stones until you reached your temple – a stone circle like the mighty Stonehenge...

Horrible henges

Archaeologists can explain how Stonehenge was built in the days before cranes and bulldozers. They've experimented with raising stones using ropes and wood. They can tell you when it was built and show how it used to look. But they *can't* agree on what happened inside the stone circle. There have been some strange ideas:

But no Egyptian remains have ever been found there. So let's forget *that* idea.

But Stonehenge is much older than 1,600 BC. Forget *that* idea too.

Would you Adam-and-Eve it? (That's Cockney rhyming slang for 'believe it', okey dokey?) That charming idea was put forward in 1943 by a Scotsman who maybe had porridge instead of brains.

Errr … *you* may like to believe that. People with half a brain read on and see some more likely ideas.

True history of the henge

It became a deserted holy place. Huge stone graves (long barrows) were scattered over the plain and were filled with skeletons. But the heads were removed and buried in a sacred enclosure on Windmill Hill where rituals took place.

After hundreds of years the heads in the ditches were abandoned and the Stone-Agers went back to the old site of the three poles, where they built a circular ditch – a 'henge' – with earth banks.

The moon was special to these henge people. Maybe they thought it was a place where the spirits of the dead went, or where spirits came from. The stone circle seems to have been used to measure the movement of the moon in the sky. Posts marked the spot where the moon rose at its most southerly point.

Every month the full moon disappears to nothing then grows again. It dies and comes back to life. Maybe the Stone-Agers thought humans were like that! They die then they are born again … then die and are born again … and so on!

And maybe, they thought, the living humans can use the power of the moon to help the dead of the tribe to be reborn. Of course when *you* die then the tribe will do the same for *you*. That seems like a fair deal, doesn't it? Worship your ancestors, worship the moon and your spirit will never die.

AROUND 2500BC THE WOODEN TEMPLE WAS REPLACED BY THE STONE CIRCLE – THE ONE THAT IS STILL LARGELY THERE TODAY. TWO MORE CIRCLES OF HOLES WERE DUG OUTSIDE STONEHENGE READY TO TAKE NEW STONES. THEY WERE NEVER FILLED. STONEHENGE WAS NEVER EVER FINISHED!

JUST LIKE YOUR HOMEWORK, DARREN GRINT!

Later the sun became as important as the moon and its positions at the solstices were marked by a stone called a 'heel' stone. A straight avenue leads up to Stonehenge and if you walk up it on the shortest day of the year you can see the sun set exactly ahead of you.

Picture the scene in Stone Age times. The days have been getting shorter for six months – if they keep on getting shorter then the sun will vanish for good and everyone will die! But after that important day (21 December) the dying days grow longer again. Phew!

There you have it again. Death followed by birth.

21 December is the edge of time. This was the time of the year when the walls between life and death were weak. This

was the time that the people with the 'mana' could talk to the ancestors.

The people who came after the Stone-Agers stopped believing in ancestor spirits. They believed in spirits in water and sacred groves of trees instead. Around 1,500 BC Stonehenge was abandoned after being used for 1,500 years – longer than any of today's churches and cathedrals.

Henge head-scratchers

A modern archaeologist has said…

Most of what has been written about Stonehenge is nonsense!

Here is some of that nonsense in a simple quiz for simple stone brains. Stonehenge has seen a lot of curious things in 5,000 years – and they're not all nonsense. But can you tell which facts are false and which are true?

1 Stonehenge was close to being destroyed in an air crash.

2 The 'Altar Stone' was given its name by the Stone-Agers who used it for sacrifices.

3 Stonehenge was built in a circle to make the music played inside sound better.

4 Stonehenge was built by the high priests of the Celtic people – the Druids.

5 Some of the Stonehenge stones are set in concrete.

6 In 1920 an archaeologist excavated under the Slaughter Stone. He found a bottle of port wine.

7 The Romans came to Stonehenge and knocked some of the stones down.

8 Stonehenge is a giant computer that can be used to calculate when there will be an eclipse of the sun.

Answers:

1 True. Accidents have helped to uncover some of the greatest archaeology finds. But they have also come close to destroying them! In 1910 Horatio Barber designed a new aeroplane. He chose his chauffeur as the test pilot.

The chauffeur had never flown an aeroplane before, but the brilliant Barber said...

You can drive my cars, you can drive my aeroplane.

Flying a plane is just a bit more difficult than driving a car ... as the poor chauffeur found out. The ASL Monoplane took off from Larkhill near Stonehenge ... narrowly missed demolishing it, and was wrecked close by.

There was a story that the army wanted Stonehenge torn down because it was a danger to their airmen.

When the First World War started four years later in 1914, part of Stonehenge *was* destroyed, but not by enemy action or by low-flying loonies. The British Army set up a huge camp on Salisbury Plain that spread over the ditch around the stone circle and ruined any chance of archaeologists finding anything there.

YOU WOULDN'T BELIEVE IT SARGE. I SITS DOWN TO 'AVE ME TEA, AN' I GETS AN ARROW 'EAD IN ME BUM!

2 False. 'Altar Stone' was a name invented by people who liked to imagine there'd been bloodthirsty rituals at Stonehenge. But the 'Altar Stone' was set upright in the

ground when the Stone-Agers built Stonehenge. Anyone wanting to make a sacrifice on the 'Altar Stone' would have had to get the victim up a long pair of ladders!

Stonehenge also has a 'Slaughter Stone' where people weren't slaughtered, a 'Heel Stone' with a mark like a heel-print that isn't a heel-print. It even has two 'Station Stones' ... and no train has ever stopped there!

3 True ... if you believe scientists at Southampton University. They say sounds would bounce off the stones and they could act like giant amplifiers. Drums played in a Stone Age ceremony would boom around and sound as exciting as a modern pop concert.

4 False. Everyone confuses the Druids with Stonehenge. That's because Druids, with their long white beards and longer white robes, have used the stone circle for over 2,000 years and they still use it today. But Stonehenge was there 2,000 years before them!

The 'Ancient order of Druids' isn't all that ancient. It

was founded in 1781 as a sort of secret society for overgrown boys. Apart from the magical meetings and secret ceremonies they helped each other out with much more simple, day-to-day problems. Their secret newspaper made special offers like…

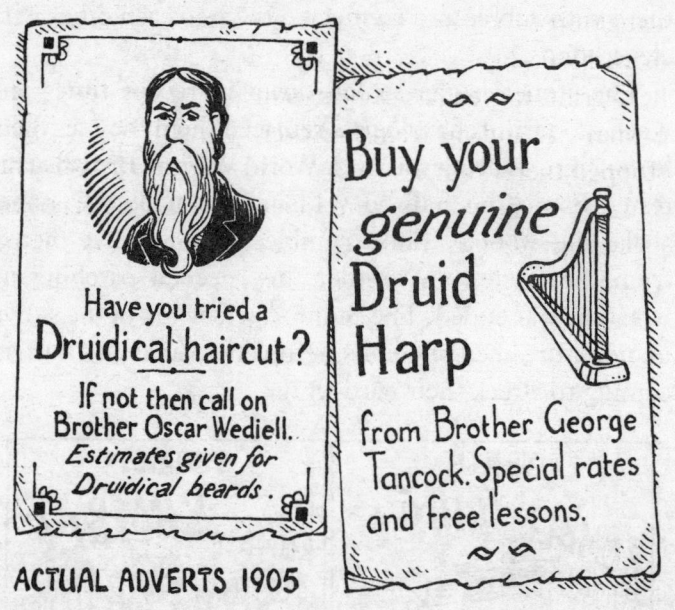

Have you tried a
Druidical haircut?
If not then call on
Brother Oscar Wediell.
*Estimates given for
Druidical beards.*

Buy your *genuine* Druid Harp

from Brother George Tancock. Special rates and free lessons.

ACTUAL ADVERTS 1905

The modern Druids held their first great feast at Stonehenge in 1905 when about 700 turned up. A rival group of Druids also turned up in 1905 but were in trouble when they refused to pay the entrance fee to get in and tried to bury the ashes of dead members in the middle of the circle.

The Druids were banned in 1926 and cursed the caretaker who kept them out. The man died soon after and the Druids said, 'See what you get!' But they gave up; some Druids planned to build a full-size copy of

Stonehenge about a mile away, some went to worship at the Tower of London, but most simply agreed to pay to get in.

5 True. But it isn't Stone Age concrete – the Stone-Agers hadn't invented it. They placed the stones in pits, packed them with rubble and connected them to each other with clever joints.

The stones began to fall down in recent times and when modern archaeologists replaced them they set them in concrete. During the First World War the British army tested bombs on Salisbury Plain that made the stones shake and wobble. Tanks rumbled past just five metres from the circle. No wonder they needed patching up when the war ended. The Stone-Agers who put the stones up never dreamed of bombs, aeroplanes, tanks and tourists coming to wreck their hard work.

In 1963 one of the stones was so wobbly it blew down in a gale. But a lot of modern houses blew down in the same gale and they hadn't been around for 5,000 years! The Stone-Agers would have been proud of that.

6 True. It wasn't Stone Age port wine. The bottle had

been left there in 1810 by the last person to dig beneath the stone. Sadly the cork had rotted and most of the wine had seeped out.

But there were deadlier things left beneath the stones than a bottle of port wine. In 1723 the owner was Thomas Hayward and he brought rabbits to Stonehenge. They would make nice pies, he thought. Unfortunately, the rotten rabbits didn't want to be made into pies so they dug themselves long burrows into the soil beneath the stones. The burrows collapsed and the stones began to fall. Some of the falling stones may have crushed the wrecking rabbits and their burrows – but maybe they should have hit the hopeless Hayward!

7 **False.** The Romans are often blamed for ruining Stonehenge. Even in the 1950s *The Times* newspaper was pointing a finger of blame at Roman wreckers. It's just not true. The Romans *did* come to Stonehenge – but stones like the one known as number 55 had already fallen *before* they arrived. 'How on earth do the archaeologists know *that*?' you ask in amazement. (Go on. Ask, and I'll tell you.)

The Romans probably camped there while they built their road over Salisbury Plain. They dropped coins and tools and bits of uniform and pottery, the way Romans do. Archaeologists found Roman bits and bobs all *around* fallen stone 55 but none *underneath* it. Why? Because the stone was already flattened before they got there.

Archaeologists are sometimes like detectives. If Sherlock Holmes finds a corpse lying on dry ground on a rainy day then he says, 'Aha! This corpse was deaded *before* it started to rain! Elementary, my dear Watson!' And that's how sensible archaeologists know about the flattening of 55. Dumb archaeologists have argued the Romans ruined Stonehenge – some have even said Stonehenge was *built* by the Romans. But you know better. (In any case, carbon-dating has proved it's Stone Age.)

> My discovery of the Roman origins
> of Stonehenge is one of the triumphs
> of modern ~~arki archeagogy archy~~
> ~~archeeolelie~~ ~~eolel~~ digging up of
> old stuff!

8 Errrr … probably false. A very clever professor wrote a book in which he tried to prove that Stone-Agers placed the stones so the shadows acted like a calendar. But the very clever professor had books and calculators to help him. The Stonehenge Stone-Agers didn't even have writing. All that knowledge would have to be kept in their heads and passed down by word of mouth. The builders were clever, but not that clever.

The day of the Druid
For ten years British police banned all visitors from Stonehenge on the longest and shortest days of the year. This followed the 'Battle of the Bean Field' in 1985 when police battled with travellers arriving for a mid-summer festival.

Then in December 1997 and June 1998 just a hundred people were allowed back to worship the sun on those days. They were guarded by a ring of 500 policemen who tried to keep out troublemakers. The police had missed a small group who had crawled four miles in darkness to sneak into the circle before the sunrise. Troublemakers in Salisbury, led by a man who called himself 'King Arthur', had been arrested the night before.

The worshippers followed the beliefs of the Celtic Druids, and there were black witches there too. At 4:52 a.m. the worshippers turned to the Heel Stone to see the sunlight flood over the ancient site. 'Hail ye, O Sun!' the chief Druid called.

But it was a cloudy morning and the sun didn't appear. Everyone wished one another 'Happy solstice' anyway.

A young couple held a pagan wedding. Their wrists were joined with a loop of red wool while they jumped over a crystal and a bunch of flowers. They kissed and that meant they were married for a year and a day.

After a few hours of chanting, dancing and hugging stones the group started to leave. *Then* the sun came out! 'Hail ye, O Sun!' everyone cried and went home.

Harmless amusement. But what would the ancient Stone Age worshippers at Stonehenge have made of it all? They had abandoned the site hundreds of years before Celtic Druids were even thought of.

They might have smiled at the curious Druids, but they would have been amazed to see the chief Druid climb into his chariot and drive off. Because his chariot was a battered and rusty Austin Montego car!

White cow, black witch

Stonehenge is one of the most famous stone circles in the world. But it isn't the only one and it certainly isn't the largest one.

Many of the other stone circles have stories to explain their existence. They are believed to be lucky places where the goodness of nature is concentrated.

(Note to readers: The following story is to be read aloud in one of those strong country yokel accents with plenty of your own 'Ooooh-arrrrhhhhs!' sprinkled around. Try and find some snotty little infant to tell it to. They may sneer, but just remember – seriously grown-up adults invented this story in the dim and distant past to explain a stone circle on the Welsh–English border!)

Never go to Mitchell's Fold in Shropshire, me dears, not if you values your life! Ye will see an old stone circle there, me dears. Beware! Don't you not be going near it! For there be a witch there, me dears, and she be trapped inside the biggest stone in the circle!

Ye see, it all starts with a strange white cow – you know the sort? It's just like a black cow only white. Anyway, there's this terrible famine throughout the land and everybody they be starving and dying of hunger, they be. When along comes this white cow and plonks herself in the middle of the old stone circle. This there white cow lets everyone take a bucket of milk and she never runs dry. Them there buckets of milk saves the lives of the villagers.

But the cow warns them (she's a talking cow, see?), she warns them, 'If any of you greedy beggars takes more than a bucketful, I'll go away and never come back!' She's a huffy cow you see, me dears?

Then one dark night a spiteful witch comes along. The white cow can't see what's going on 'cos it's dark, it being night an' all. And the witch is milking the white cow into a sieve! Well! The milk runs out, doesn't it?

Suddenly there's a flash of lightning (did I mention there were a thunderstorm brewing? No? Well there were). Anyway, the cow sees the sieve in the light of the flash and gets fair mad as a bull with a red rag ('cos cows is a bit like bulls).

The mad cow kicks the witch who turns into a stone and there she stands to this very day. Then the cow vanishes and never comes back – and there she *doesn't* stand to this very day.

The thunderstorm brought an end to the drought that caused the famine and the people had food and didn't need no never-ending milk no more and they all lives happy ever after, don't they? (Oooohaaaarrrrhhhh!)

But they still remember that there white cow in Mitchell's Fold.

Which just goes to show.

Something.

Many stone circle legends say the stones were once people or animals. Others say stones were…

A complete wedding party, turned to stone for dancing on a Sunday (Stanton Drew, Avon, England)

Three women who sinned by working on a Sunday (Moelfre Hill, Wales)

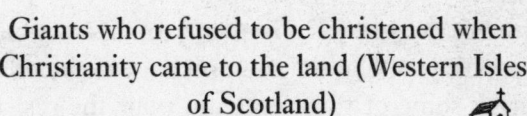

A robber caught stealing from a church (various places)

Giants who refused to be christened when Christianity came to the land (Western Isles of Scotland)

Women who gave false evidence that led to a man being hanged (Cottrell, South Wales)

A girl running away from a wizard who wanted to marry her (Aberdeen, Scotland)

A cow, a witch and a fisherman (Inisbofin, Ireland)

A giant and his seven sons who went to war with a wizard (Kerry, Ireland)

A mermaid's children (Cruckancornia, Ireland)

A history teacher who gave impossibly hard homework and was turned to stone by a pupil with witch powers … you wish!

Cwaint henge customs

Many henges and Stone Age sites still have odd beliefs attached to them. Here are a few you may like to try ... if you are a seriously sad person.

1 Want to know if a sick friend will live? Go to Brahan Woods near Dingwall in Scotland and find the stone circle. Bring some cakes to the circle and leave them overnight. If the cakes are gone the next morning your friend will survive. But if the cakes are still there ... call the undertaker (or the under-caker!).

2 Want to win the lottery? Go to any Irish stone circle and take a cow with you. Cut the cow and let some blood out into a cup. Drink some of the blood and pour the rest into the soil. This will bring you luck – unless the cow is upset by the bleeding and sends you flying when you bend over to pour its blood away! This bloody custom was still being carried out in Queen Victoria's day.

3 Want to know who you'll marry? If you are a girl you can go to Arthur's Stone at Gower near Swansea, Wales. Wait till midnight when the moon is full and put cakes, milk and honey on the ancient stone. Crawl round the stone three times on your hands and knees. If the vision of your lover appears then you will marry him. If not, then he's probably too busy watching the telly. Of course this only works for

girls. Boys can simply follow the girls with a video camera and catch them crawling round in circles (which is much more fun and less painful).

4 Want your own private jet/yacht/bicycle? Go to Ben Loyal in Scotland and find the 'Stone of the Little Men'. Place a silver coin with a model or a drawing of any metal object you want. In a week's time you'll find a perfect one made by the little men who live under the stone.

5 Can you count the stones in a circle? Many stone circles are said to be so magical you can't actually count the number of stones there. (Mind you, some people have trouble counting the fingers on one hand!) Several stone circles have legends about bakers laying a loaf of bread on each stone to help them count them. A loaf always seemed to go missing and spoil the plan. In one story a baker stood up and said, 'The number of stones in the circle is … cccct!' and he dropped down dead before he could announce it.

Hanging around the henge

Stonehenge was the only Stone Age circle known by early historians. Other circles were buried or destroyed or not seen.

'Not seen?' I hear you gasp. 'How can a dirty great ring of blooming big stone slabs not be *seen?*' you cry.

Well stop crying and I'll tell you.

Historians in the Middle Ages looked at them and said...

These circles are natural objects. God stood them on end and put them in some sort of order. We know not why he did this.

If God stood these stones on end then he (or she) must have been pretty strong. And it must have been done on a quiet day when he wasn't creating suns, moons and stars or sending plagues of locusts to sad Stone-Agers.

Some of the stone circles like Avebury in Wiltshire, England, were so large a village was built inside the circle and the stones used to make the houses.[1] That sort of destruction made many circles hard to spot. But there was never any confusion about Stonehenge – only arguments about *who* had built it and *why* it had been built.

'Stonehenge' was given its name in the Old English language. The 'Stone' half of the name meant 'stone'. (I'll bet you'd never have guessed that!) But what did some people say the 'henge' part of the word meant?

It was Old English for...

a) circle

b) stool

c) gallows

1. Avebury is 425 metres across – the ditch round 'little' Stonehenge is just 100 metres across.

WOOD? COULDN'T
I HAVE ONE OF
THOSE NICE
STONE ONES?

The counting king

Stonehenge was visited by King James I in 1620 when he was touring the country to meet his people. James I's best friend tried to buy Stonehenge from its owner.

This was the start of the Stonehenge tourist industry. During the rest of the 17th century stones were stolen – one was used to make a bridge – or chipped to bits by visitors who wanted a souvenir lump of rock to take home. (Which is where the idea of Blackpool Rock came from. Only joking.)

In the middle of the 1600s it would cost you six pence to hire horses and a further four pence for a woman to guide you from the nearest town.

But the most famous visitor was in fear of his life when he took a day-trip to Stonehenge. He was James I's grandson, Charles – the man who would later become King Charles II. In September 1651 he was on the run from the Roundheads with a few faithful guards. If a guard had told his story then it might have gone something like this…

3 September 1650

Battle at Worcester against the Roundheads. Good name, Worcester — 'cos we came off worst-er! Me and Prince Charles had to flee before they done us like they done his dad, King Charles the first. Head on the block — chop — splatt.

Not that I'm scared of no Roundheads. It's just I'm very attached to me head. We are heading south to another country that must remain a deadly secret. We should get to France next week, Prince Charles reckons.

5 September 1651

Flitting from safe house to safe house. I'm worn out. And me boots are worn out and me bum is saddle sore. So we are resting here at Heale House in some God-forsaken place called Woodford. We're stuck in a secret room and it's doing my head in. You see we can't trust the servants. 'They'll rat on us for a sovereign!' Prince Charles reckons.

'So let's go for a ride tomorrow,' the lord of the house says. 'The servants are all at Salisbury Fair!'

A ride! What about my sore bum! Oh, well. A loyal servant (like what I am) never complains.

6 September 1651

What a strange sort of day. When all the

servants had gone me and the prince and Sir
Robert Philips saddled up and rode over the hills.
I never complained once about me sore bits. But I
forgot about them, to be honest, when we got to
this place called Stonehenge. A great circle of
huge stones. Prince Charles jumps off his horse
and says, 'This was the meeting place of my
ancestors! The great King Brutus of the Britons!
He came from Troy, you know.'

'So what was this place?' I ask.

'His palace,' Prince Charles says.

A bit draughty, I thought, what with no roof or
nothing. Not the sort of palace I'd want to live
in. But then Sir Robert Philips (a man with a
very high opinion of himself and very smarmy to
my Prince Charles if you ask me) says, 'It is said,
sire, that no one can count the stones! Whenever
they try they come up with a different answer
every time. It is the magic of King Brutus.'

Now Prince Charles likes a bit of a challenge
so he says, 'I'll bet a silver penny I can do it.' Then
he turns to me and says, 'Help me, George.'

After an age Prince Charles turns to me and
says, 'Well? I make it 93, George. How many did
you count to?'

'Ten,' I tells him.

'Ten! There's more than ten! Why did you stop at
ten?'

'Ran out of fingers,' I tells him.

Anyway he counts them again. He cries out, 'Ninety-three!' Again!'

Sir Robert Philips (did I mention he's a smarmy creep?) drops to one knee and says, 'That proves Your Majesty is the rightful heir to the throne. Only a man of Brutus's blood could count the magic stones.'

Prince Charles is pleased with that. 'The rightful king,' he says, nodding like a horse at a nose-bag. 'I'll be back!'

We rode back and hid at Heale before the servants got home. It's been a funny sort of day. But them stones is creepy – nearly as creepy as Sir Robert Philips. Definitely something magic about them. If they told my Charlie he's the rightful king then I just might believe it. He'll be back, will young Charlie. He'll be back.

And, of course, Charles returned as king within ten years. His friends were right about that – but they were wrong when they believed the circle was built by Ancient Briton King Brutus.

Stone sorcery
Many people have visited stone circles and said they 'feel' the strange power of the stones. It's not only Druids who worshipped at stone circles. Witches were said to use them as meeting places.

Of course the Christian church was worried. In AD 452 the church ordered…

You shall not worship stones!

If they were passing rules *against* it then someone must have been *doing* it!

In the village of Avebury in 1326 the Church leaders didn't just warn the villagers. They decided to do something about it – they decided to attack the stones. The question is, did the stones fight back?

'Where have all the stones gone?' the traveller asked. He wiped the drizzling rain from his eyes and peered across the muddy ditch.

A grey-haired freeman stuck his narrow, iron spade into a pile of soil, took off his wide-brimmed hat and shook the water off. He looked at the stranger through narrow eyes. 'Who're you then?'

'I'm Henry Barber the travelling surgeon. I've got leeches to suck out your bad blood and I've razors to trim your hair and beard. You must know me! I come this way every year at this time. But there's always been a great ring of stones here. Half of them have gone!' he looked around and lowered his voice. 'They say the Devil put them there. Has he taken them back again?'

The freeman rested on his spade, glad of an excuse to stop the back-breaking work but looking nervously at the priests who wandered round the great stone with prayers and flasks of holy water. 'Don't speak of the Devil. You may raise him up,' he warned.

The travelling barber–surgeon nodded wisely and tapped the side of his nose. 'You're right, friend. So what has happened to the stones?'

'The church has told us to bury them. That's what we've been doing for the past year. It's hard work in this cursed rain, though.'

'It can't have rained all year,' the traveller laughed.

The freeman didn't even smile. 'Seems like it. Seems every time we come near the stones a storm cloud can appear out of the clearest sky. I wish they were gone.'

The traveller shrugged. 'You have to do what the Church tells you. But tell me, friend, can I interest you in a pair of fine fat slimy leeches. Just three silver pennies?'

'I'd pay that much for you to take my place on this digging. I'm heart-sick of it.'

The traveller was a strong man and the work looked a simple way to make enough for a good meal and a few drinks at the tavern. The two men agreed and the freeman passed the spade to the traveller. 'What do I do?' the man asked, spitting on the palms of his hands.

'We dig a deep pit alongside each stone. When the pit's long enough we tunnel under the stone till it topples into the pit. Then we cover it over. We bury it.'

'It looks long enough now!' the traveller said.

'Aye. We're about to start digging away under the stone. Get yourself down there next to Peter the Ploughboy,' the freeman ordered.

The stranger slipped on the wet grass and slid quickly into the pit, splashing the workers with mud. They glared at him. He grinned back. 'The Devil's sent you lovely weather for this work!' he laughed.

The workers looked afraid and turned their backs on him. They began to dig the soil from under the looming stone. What happened next happened quickly. The dim light at the bottom of the trench was lit by a sudden flash. Moments later thunder rumbled and then teeming rain began to lash at the diggers.

The rain ran down the walls of the trench into a deep pool and crept over the tops of their boots. It also washed at the soil holding the mighty stone in place.

A panic gripped the men. They scrabbled for the leather ladder. Others reached up and clawed at the helping hands. The freeman reached down and held out a hand for the stranger. As their hands touched there was a gurgling and a groaning as the stone leaned towards the greasy jaws of the pit.

The freeman looked up and leaned back a little, making the traveller's mud-slimed fingers slip from his.

The man tumbled backwards and hit the pool of water hard. His cry was smothered when his head went under the water and by the rushing noise of the falling stone.

The stone fitted the pit perfectly. Brown mud oozed up its sides with perhaps a faint trace of red. The workers stepped forward and looked at the bubbling foam around its edges. The rain stopped as suddenly as it had begun.

'What do we do?' someone asked a priest. 'We'll never get him out of there.'

The pale priest whispered. 'No need. He has a bigger gravestone than any man in Avebury. Cover it up.'

'What about the other stones?' someone asked.

The priest looked around the grim slabs of stone and at the muddy mounds of the buried ones. 'They can stay,' he said sourly. 'We'll take this as a warning.'

Awesome Avebury

It was in 1938 that a man's skeleton was found at Avebury, crushed during the attempt to bury a stone in the 1320s. The man's neck was broken. His foot was trapped by the stone so his body couldn't be taken away. He had scissors and a razor in his pockets, so he was almost certainly a travelling surgeon who'd stopped on his travels to help out.

His purse still held three silver coins. The victim of an Avebury Temple curse?

He certainly didn't rest in peace after the archaeologists found him in 1938. His skeleton went to the College of

Surgeons in London to be examined. It was destroyed by a bomb during the Second World War.

To be crushed once is unlucky. To be crushed twice sounds like a curse!

After the 1320s Avebury accident there came the Black Death in 1349. There weren't enough healthy peasants to finish the work, even if they wanted to. The stones were safe ... for a while.

- In the 1600s and 1700s stones were broken up to make houses.
- Some were removed because the local council said they scared horses as it grew dark. (Maybe the horses could sense something their drivers couldn't!)

- In the 1800s some were moved to make farming easier.
- Even in 1976 the road ran so close to the ring that cars bumped it and a lorry knocked stone number 46 out of line.

Stone Age spooks

People are finding Stone Age objects all the time. It's not just professional archaeologists who dig them up but people on picnics, walkers in woods and maniacs with metal detectors.

Of course a lot of the people who go out looking for ancient relics aren't interested in history at all – they are interested in finding valuable things that they can sell. Buried treasure, in fact!

LOOK! IT'S AN EARLY TECHNOLOGY AGE BARTERING POUCH!

HE'S FOUND SOMEONE'S WALLET

But before you go ferreting in Farmer Fowl's fields for your fortune it is only fair to warn you ... there are *dangers*.

1 You need a landowner's permission to dig in a field or to walk on it looking for objects. If you don't have that, the landowner may simply shoot you with a shotgun. And shotgun pellets take a long, painful time to pick out from under the skin of your backside.

2 Amateurs without training can destroy more than they uncover. Best to join your local Young Archaeologists group – your local library should give you their address.

3 The ghosts of the Stone-Agers you disturb may come and get you.

Now you may think the third one there, the idea of Stone Age spooks, is just plain silly. But some people take them very seriously. And some people take them very, very, very, seriously...

Blood-chilling barrows

Stone-Agers were often buried in barrows. (No, dummy, that *doesn't* mean they were stuck in a *wheel*barrow instead of a coffin. 'Barrows' or 'cairns' are what archaeologists call the mounds where humans were buried.)

Barrows were built of earth, cairns of stone. The materials could be heaped over the corpses or there could be a stone or wooden room built and then covered over.

A barrow was just a little house for your putrefying pals. Some archaeologists reckon they were made to look like the Stone Age houses of the living – a sort of retirement hostel for the dead where they would feel at home.

Very cosy. There were different types of barrow and some have been given cute names by archaeologists…

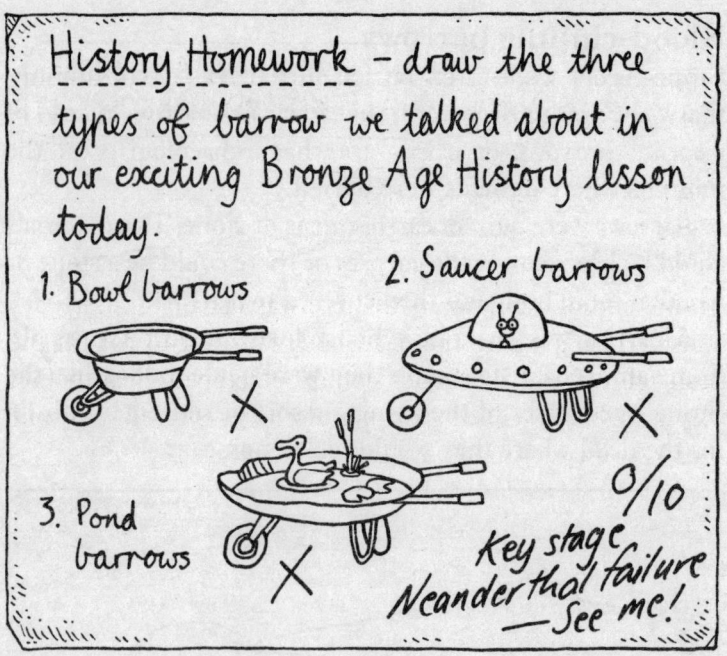

History Homework – draw the three types of barrow we talked about in our exciting Bronze Age History lesson today.

1. Bowl barrows ✗

2. Saucer barrows ✗

3. Pond barrows ✗

0/10

Key stage Neanderthal failure —See me!

These barrows are found all over the world and were still being used by people like the Vikings up until the Middle Ages. The most common type of barrows built during the earlier Neolithic Age are 'Long' Barrows. They are called that because, believe it or not, they are *long*!

A good example is the Fussell's Lodge Barrow – an early English barrow. Archaeologists reckon it took at least ten people to build it. Fussell's Lodge is a log house over 100 metres long. The low wooden house was then buried under a *thousand* tonnes of chalk and soil.

The chalk was dug out of trenches at the side of the Lodge using only picks made of deer antlers. Digging must have been back-breaking work and carrying it over to the barrow must have been exhausting…

I DON'T EVEN HAVE A BARROW TO HELP WITH MY BARROW!

At one end of a long barrow there was usually a 'mortuary house'. That's where the dead body was left to rot till the flesh fell off and the bones could be scraped clean before they were buried. The barrows could be re-entered so people could perform rituals with the bones. Fussell's Lodge was used for hundreds of years then abandoned.

Then, in the later Neolithic and Bronze Age, the barrows changed to 'round' barrows. Bet you'll never guess what shape they were! Yes! They were triangular ... no, only joking. They were shaped as a round dome – like a giant Christmas pudding that's trying to get in the *Guinness Book of Records*.

ROUND IS THE FASHIONABLE SHAPE FOR A MODERN CORPSE

Silly Hill 1

The strangest of these prehistoric monuments has to be Silbury Hill which was built around 2,700 BC. It's 40 metres high and is 160 metres across – so it's as wide as St Paul's Cathedral and a third of its height. It would have taken 700 men 10 years to build it. It needed more effort than Stonehenge and it's the greatest piece of prehistoric building in England.

In 1776 a group of miners dug a hole from the top to the bottom to find the secret of the hill. In 1849 a tunnel was dug through the side of the hill. In 1969 a television expedition recorded the digging of another tunnel.

What did they find?

a) the grave of a Stone Age chief – probably the first chief of Wiltshire

b) the treasure of the first Stone Age royal family – gold, silver and coins

c) the grave of a warrior, seated on his horse and covered in stone armour

d) a store of corn that was buried and never unearthed by the farmers

Answer: You are wrong! That's right! *Whatever* answer you chose is *wrong*. Because the answer is that the diggers found *nothing*. A big fat zippo, zilch and zippety plonk. Nil, naught and nix.

Modern humans like to think they're cleverer than Stone-Agers ... but they can't work out why Silbury Hill was built. But we know, don't we ...

WORLD'S FIRST ARTIFICIAL SKI SLOPE! MORE FUN THAN THE PYRAMIDS OF EGYPT – AND MORE SNOW!

Silly Hill 2

There have been lots of legends that try to explain how Silbury hill got there. Many involve the Devil. One story says the Devil was planning to drop a vast shovel of earth on the town of Devizes. The townsfolk sent out a cobbler with a sack of old boots. He met the Devil, who was having a rest.

'How far is it to Devizes?' the Devil asked.

The cobbler tipped out the boots on to the ground. 'Well, I left Devizes three years ago and these are the boots I've worn out,' the cobbler explained.

The Devil groaned and said, 'Aw, Hell![1] I'm not walking all that way!' and he dumped the soil on the spot. That pile of soil is Silbury Hill.

It's good to know that someone as evil as the Devil is so thick! Anyone with any sense would have checked the map before he set out and seen that Devizes is just 8 miles away along the A361!

If you want to visit this useless lump of soil be warned! It is said to be haunted by the ghost of King Sil, who is buried there, in gold armour, astride his horse. (Except he *isn't* because archaeologists didn't find him when they dug through the soil. Of course, he may have just popped out for a ride.)

Golden ghosts

Many of the ancient tales about barrows seem to be about hidden treasures. *You* know that Stone-Agers didn't have gold (though some of the later barrow-builders did). *You* know that it's stupid to wreck an ancient barrow grave in a greedy search for golden gain. But that hasn't stopped

1. Don't worry ... this is *not* swearing. Hell is where the devil lives. So, when he says, 'Oh, Hell!' it's a bit like you saying, 'Oh! Home!' or, 'Oh, 25 Duckpool Terrace!'

devilish diggers delving down to the depths to find ... what?

In Cornwall a barrow was supposed to hold the ancient king of Cornwall in a golden boat with silver oars – grave plunderers found only a chest full of ashes. Other sites are said to hold cauldrons of gold, a golden calf (that's a popular one), a silver coffin, a man in golden armour on horseback, a golden chest, a golden table and even a golden wheelbarrow!

DO I GET A COFFIN OR A CAULDRON OR A CALF? NO. I GET A PIECE OF HANDY GARDENING EQUIPMENT!

It's true that there was an old legend of gold in Bryn yr Ellyhon (Goblin Hill) in Wales and in 1833 a golden cape *was* dug up. (The cape is now in the British Museum, so it's true.)

The horrible historical legend was that a ghost haunted the barrow at Goblin Hill and the ghost was dressed in gold; when the barrow was broken into, the gold cape was found. Does that prove the ghost story was true?

Strange, huh?

Almost as strange as the tale of a potty priest with a potion...

The huntsman's horror

Seriously spooky

The ghost stories that surround Stone Age sites may sound daft and doubtful to us. But the spirits of the dead Stone-Agers are causing *serious* problems for archaeologists today.

For hundreds of years people have been digging up these ancient bones and forgetting something very important: these bones once belonged to a living person.

Imagine your grave being dug up 5,000 years from now and your bones tested with radiocarbon dating. *You* would be upset at the thought.

Since the late 1970s some people have become just as upset. In Australia, the Aborigines are demanding that all the archaeological finds are returned to their holy grounds. In the USA, the Native Americans went even further, as a 1998 case shows…

The case of the missing bones

124

So? What would you say if you were the judge? Would you agree with the archaeologists that old bones can be dug up, examined and kept in a museum? If you say *that*, then how many unhappy spirits will be stirred up?

Or would you support the Native Americans and insist that they be given a proper burial? If you do, then the science of archaeology could end in 1998!

Not a very easy choice, is it?

Verdict: The judge declared the bones must be 'made available to science'. The archaeologists won the right to dig up and examine all the bones they want. When a ghost of the Ancient One appears at the foot of his bed the judge may regret that!

Nowadays, good archaeologists rebury the bones whenever it is possible.

Epilogue

People can't agree about what happened yesterday. When it comes to the truth about hominids who lived before writing was invented we have even less chance of agreeing.

Our understanding of prehistoric people changes with every new discovery; it changes every year ... every week! Ideas that were 'right' ten years ago are shown to be totally 'wrong' today ... and today's ideas will probably be proved wrong in another ten years.

So what is the very latest news on Stone-Agers? What is the hottest horrible history? It is this...

STONE AGERS WEREN'T AS HORRIBLE AS WE ONCE THOUGHT!

Stories of hideous hunters sucking brains out of fresh skulls may be wrong. And more. People may actually have been kind and thoughtful.

Here's a story about a Neanderthal with some clues about his life. You make up your own mind about the truth...

The man was quite old for a Neanderthal – around 40 years old in fact. He'd had a lot of bad luck and hardship in his life and, finally, he found himself in a cave when an earthquake shook the region. The cave roof cracked and collapsed on him. He was dead.

As a child he'd had a withered right arm that had never grown to full length or strength. The man had swollen joints (arthritis) and was blind in one eye. He'd been wounded on the skull but that had healed. Most gruesome of all he seems to have come off worst in a fight with a wild animal and damaged the end of his arm. One hand had been amputated by a sharp but crude stone knife.

His Neanderthal tribe would have been hunters who wandered the forests trapping and shooting animals or gathering fruits and nuts. This half-blind, limping, damaged man couldn't hold a bow and couldn't have been a lot of use to the others.

In Victorian times they might have shut him away in a hospital; in the Middle Ages they might have put him on display in a travelling fair; in Ancient Greece they may have left him in the hills to die in the jaws of a wolf.

But, in the Stone Age, this man *lived*.

Someone helped him, someone shared their hard-earned food, someone tended his wounds.

Someone *cared*.

The savage Stone Age?

SAVAGE
STONE AGE

GRISLY QUIZ

**Now find out if you're a
Savage Stone Age expert!**

HORRIBLE HOMINID HABITS

Human ancestors were a strange bunch and no mistake, but then, life was hard for hominids – they had no TV, no microwaves, no MP3 players (no school either, though, so maybe it wasn't so bad). They had to fight daily dangers just to survive. How would you get on in prehistoric times? Take this quick quiz and find out.

1. How did early Stone Age hunters trap a delicious woolly mammoth for their tea?
a) By cornering it in a cave
b) By stampeding it into a swamp
c) By tempting it with a teacake

2. How did Stone Age people go into a trance to talk with their dead ancestors?
a) By starving themselves
b) By eating a type of fungus
c) By holding their breath until they turned blue

3. What was trepanning?
a) Drilling a hole in someone's skull while they were alive
b) Dancing in a circle around a fire
c) Skinning a bison with a flint

4. What did Stone Age people wear?
a) Thermal knickers (it was cold in the Ice Age)
b) Animal skins
c) Woven leaves

5. What is a barrow?
a) A Stone Age device with one wheel, used for carrying dead animals
b) A Stone Age farming tribe
c) A Stone Age burial place

6. What weapons did Stone Age hunters use?
a) Flint axes
b) Machine guns
c) Wooden swords

7. What did prehistoric people use to draw on cave walls?
a) Brushes made of animal hair and juice from different fruit
b) Their fingers, flint and soft clay
c) Paint and a padded roller

8. How did Stone Age chefs cook up a feast?
a) Throw an animal in the fire – fur, feathers and all
b) Order takeaway from the pizza cave around the corner
c) Skin an animal then cook it in a clay pot over a fire

EXTRAORDINARY EVIDENCE

Archaeologists have learned all sorts of fascinating facts about life in the Stone Age just from studying the bones and stones they have discovered. Some things are strange but true, others are prehistoric porky-pies. Can you tell which is which?

1. There were dentists around in Stone Age times.

I SPOSE IT'S TOO LATE FOR A DENTIST

2. Stone Age people lived alone, hunting and gathering for themselves.

3. Neanderthals – relations of early humans – were known to track and kill small dinosaurs.

4. Even cavemen liked to look good, and shaved or plucked their body hair.

5. Some Stone Age people may have slit open the stomachs of animals and helped themselves to the creature's last meal.

6. Stone Age people believed in a god they called Homo Sapiens Rulus.

7. Some of the stones used to make Stonehenge were carried from a site in Wales nearly 400 kilometres away.

8. Nasty Neanderthals collected human heads, which they'd smash open to remove the brains.

AWFUL ANCESTORS AND ROTTEN RELATIONS

Archaeologists have given some tongue-twisterish names to our early relations. See if you can figure out what each of these lunatic Latin names actually means. The pictures below should help you out…

1. *Homo sapiens sapiens*
2. *Homo ergaster*
3. *Homo erectus*
4. *Homo habilis*
5. *Homo neanderthalensis*
6. *Homo rhodesiensis*
7. *Homo sapiens*
8. *Homo rudolfensis*

a) Handy human
b) Lake Turkana man
c) Wise human
d) Working human
e) Rhodesian human
f) Wise wise human
g) Neander Valley human
h) Upright human

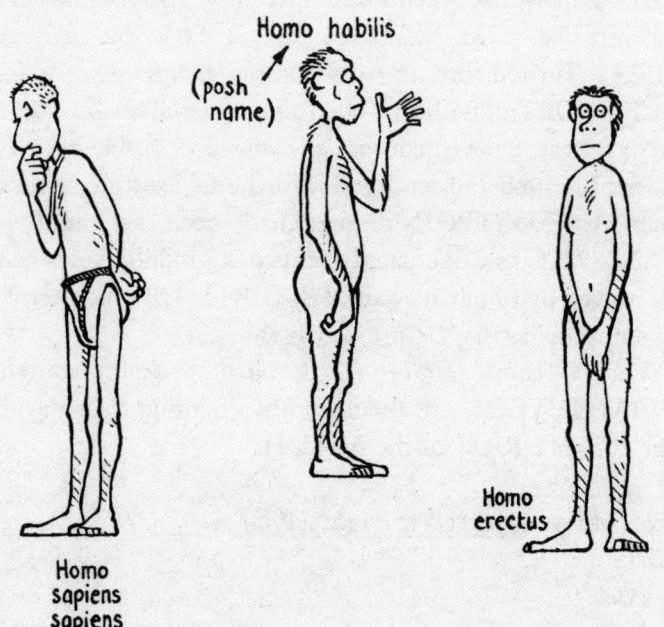

Homo habilis

(posh name)

Homo sapiens sapiens

Homo erectus

THE LOOPY LEAKEYS

Louis Leakey and his wife Mary were two of the most famous anthropologists (that's the posh name for someone who studies ancient humans) that ever lived. Mary in particular made some amazing discoveries. Here is what she might have written in her diary, looking back at a lifetime spent sweating in the sun to uncover the secrets of strange Stone Agers. See if you can unscramble the words in capitals.

Dear Diary,

Well, I have certainly proved that I am the most awesome anthropologist *ever* – loads better than my hominid-hunting 1) SAND HUB. There was my first great discovery, back in 1948. Imagine my surprise when I dug up a 2) SULLK. It looked a little bit like a 3) MANUH and a little bit like an 4) PEA. Turned out it was *Proconsul africanus* – an 5) ACE SNORT of both that lived about 25 million years ago!

My greatest achievement though came in 1978. There I was, wandering around Tanzania, and what should I stumble across? Some 6) FROSTPOINT that had been set hard in 7) VANCOLIC ash. We dated them to 3.5 million years ago! This proved that humans walked 8) GIRTH UP much earlier than stupid scientists had previously thought.

When I think about it, I have probably taught 9) SCOREDIVED more about human evolution than anyone in the 10) SHY RIOT of the world. Ha!

Lots of love to myself from myself.
Mary
    xxxx

Answers

Horrible Hominid Habits
1b) 2a) 3a) 4b) 5c) 6a) 7b) 8a)

Extraordinary Evidence
1. True – tooth drills made of flint have been found in Pakistan that date from 9,000 years ago!
2. False – they lived and moved about in groups.
3. False – dinosaurs had died out long before early humans walked the Earth.
4. True – stone razors have been discovered that date from 30,000 BC.
5. True
6. False – they worshipped the spirits of their dead ancestors.
7. True
8. True – some sick scientists believe they ate the brains!

Awful Ancestors and Rotten Relations
1f) 2d) 3h) 4a) 5g) 6e) 7c) 8b) (actually, that's a bit of a swizz – the rudolfensis part comes from Lake Rudolf, which is where this horrible hominid was discovered and what Lake Turkana used to be called)

The Loopy Leakeys
1) SAND HUB = HUSBAND
2) SULLK = SKULL
3) MANUH = HUMAN
4) PEA = APE
5) ACE SNORT = ANCESTOR

6) FROSTPOINT = FOOTPRINTS
7) VANCOLIC = VOLCANIC
8) GIRTH UP = UPRIGHT
9) SCOREDIVED = DISCOVERED
10) SHY RIOT = HISTORY

INTERESTING INDEX

Where will you find 'ancient poo', 'exploding coffins' and 'twisted tortoises' in an index? In a Horrible Histories book, of course!

139

Terry Deary was born at a very early age, so long ago he can't remember. But his mother, who was there at the time, says he was born in Sunderland, north-east England, in 1946 – so it's not true that he writes all *Horrible Histories* from memory. At school he was a horrible child only interested in playing football and giving teachers a hard time. His history lessons were so boring and so badly taught, that he learned to loathe the subject. *Horrible Histories* is his revenge.

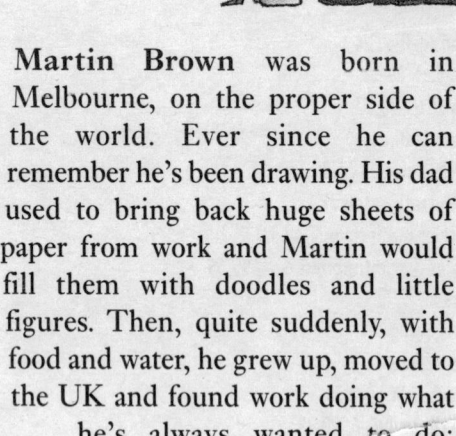

Martin Brown was born in Melbourne, on the proper side of the world. Ever since he can remember he's been drawing. His dad used to bring back huge sheets of paper from work and Martin would fill them with doodles and little figures. Then, quite suddenly, with food and water, he grew up, moved to the UK and found work doing what he's always wanted to do: drawing doodles and little figures.